PLACES
RATED
a·l·m·a·n·a·c

....

Your Guide to Finding the Best Places to Live in America

RICHARD BOYER & DAVID SAVAGEAU

Prentice Hall
New York

Acknowledgements

This revision of *Places Rated Almanac* could not have been written but for the help we've gotten from scores of people in government and with private organizations, many of whom we've come to know personally over the years. Many of the improvements in this thoroughly updated and revised edition were originally suggested by them.

We are especially indebted to Karen Katz, our editor at Prentice Hall, for her energy and enthusiasm every step of the way. Not only did she endure everything the authors endured, she also endured the authors.

For their insights and criticisms, for generous use of their data, or for their help in completing the manuscript, we specifically thank Rick Becker, Joe Beditz, Tom Bowman, Cindy Carson, Lisa Clyde, Jack DuSatko, Dick Forstall, Bob Garrett, Rory Gillespie, George Giuliani, Martin Holdrich, John Hood, Clair Jensen, Geoff Loftus, Susan Messer, M. Ronald Minge, Ian Nielsen, David Sawicki, Howard Stambler, Tim Sullivan, Henry Tom, and Allan Wilks.

Finally, special thanks are due Woods & Poole Economics, Inc., of Washington, DC, for their population, income, and employment forecasts for each of the metro areas. The use of this information, and the conclusions drawn from it, are solely the responsibility of the authors.

Publisher's Note

This book contains information gathered from many sources. It is published for general reference and not as a substitute for independent verification by users when circumstances warrant. Although care and diligence have been used in its preparation, the Publisher does not guarantee the accuracy of the information. The interpretation of the data and the views expressed are the authors' and not necessarily those of Prentice Hall.

Published by Prentice Hall Travel
A division of Simon & Schuster, Inc.
15 Columbus Circle
New York, NY 10023

Printed in the United States of America
Library of Congress Catalog Card No.: 89-22971

Contents

Introduction

If you could snap your fingers and suddenly find yourself living in another city, would you?

Forget for a moment the usual constraints. True enough, family obligations, friendships, a job, and sentimental attachment to familiar turf will quickly jar anyone out of such fantasies. Let's put the question another way: What if there were a city somewhere in this country that suited you better than the one in which you're living now, and you didn't know of it?

From time to time a majority of persons polled by the Gallup Organization say they would prefer living somewhere else. Most persons indeed change their address 11 times during their lives, but they do it by simply moving from one house to another within the same city. Each year, however, seven million Americans move to another state. They may count seven million different reasons among them for relocating a long distance, but they do have one thing in common—the need for information.

Like its 1981 and 1985 predecessors, this edition of *Places Rated Almanac* is meant for people who are mulling over a relocation as well as for anyone who enjoys finding out about American cities and towns and what they have to offer. As an almanac, it provides thousands of facts—found neither in standard guidebooks nor in chamber of commerce blandishments—about all 333 officially defined metropolitan areas where 75 percent of us live.

But *Places Rated Almanac* is more than a collection of interesting, odd, and useful information about metropolitan areas. It also rates and ranks these metro areas on nine factors that greatly influence the quality of place: costs of living, job outlook, crime, health care, transportation, education, the arts, recreation, and climate.

Places Rated Almanac might be considered a self-help book with one difference: instead of pointing the way toward inner peace or upward mobility as most such books do, it helps you decide whether geographical mobility might be the route to a more satisfying life. Where you live can affect your happiness and personal success; it just may be that your present location doesn't fit your needs and preferences. After all, given the extraordinary variety American cities offer, what are the odds that the place where you happen to live is the right one for you?

After using *Places Rated Almanac*, your hunch that you've never had it so good might well be confirmed. On the other hand, you may be in for a surprise. And if you're part of the discontented majority identified by pollsters, you may find yourself asking: What am I waiting for?

RATING PLACES: AN AMERICAN TRADITION

"The tradition of hating New York started long before it began asking the rest of us to pay its bills while condescendingly viewing us as amusing rustics," Mike Royko wrote in a Chicago *Sun-Times* column a decade ago. "Actually, I like New York," he continued. "There are better reasons to hate cities like Cleveland or Indian-

Young and Old Metro Areas

YOUNGEST METRO AREAS	Median Age
Provo–Orem, UT	22.90 years
Jacksonville, NC	24.18
Bryan–College Station, TX	24.34
State College, PA	26.46
Grand Forks, ND	26.50
Bloomington, IN	26.56
Champaign–Urbana–Rantoul, IL	26.67
Salt Lake City–Ogden, UT	26.71
Iowa City, IA	26.77
Laredo, TX	26.90
Lawrence, KS	26.98
Columbia, MO	27.12
McAllen–Edinburg–Mission, TX	27.19
Fayetteville, NC	27.20
Lafayette–West Lafayette, IN	27.23

OLDEST METRO AREAS	Median Age
Sarasota, FL	51.86 years
Bradenton, FL	44.94
Fort Myers–Cape Coral, FL	43.10
West Palm Beach–Boca Raton–Delray Beach, FL	42.40
Daytona Beach, FL	41.95
Naples, FL	41.50
Tampa–St. Petersburg–Clearwater, FL	40.62
Fort Pierce, FL	40.35
Fort Lauderdale–Hollywood–Pompano Beach, FL	40.13
Ocala, FL	40.05
Stamford, CT	39.08
Melbourne–Titusville–Palm Bay, FL	37.82
Scranton–Wilkes-Barre, PA	37.51
Cumberland, MD–WV	37.33
Monmouth–Ocean, NJ	36.83

Source: Woods & Poole Economics, Inc., population forecasts.

The median age of the United States is 32.68 years.

Population Size

LARGEST METRO AREAS	1989 Population
Los Angeles–Long Beach, CA	8,707,470
New York, NY	8,562,900
Chicago, IL	6,251,360
Philadelphia, PA–NJ	4,901,690
Detroit, MI	4,347,160
Washington, DC–MD–VA	3,739,240
Houston, TX	3,262,530
Boston, MA	2,839,030
Atlanta, GA	2,781,410
Nassau–Suffolk, NY	2,710,460
Dallas, TX	2,608,660
St. Louis, MO–IL	2,471,380
Minneapolis–St. Paul, MN–WI	2,378,700
San Diego, CA	2,347,360
Anaheim–Santa Ana, CA	2,343,640

SMALLEST METRO AREAS	1989 Population
Enid, OK	61,880
Grand Forks, ND	70,030
Casper, WY	73,210
Lawrence, KS	74,560
Cheyenne, WY	75,830
Bristol, CT	77,630
Victoria, TX	77,760
Rapid City, SD	78,300
Great Falls, MT	79,230
Jackson, TN	80,150
Pittsfield, MA	81,200
Bangor, ME	84,030
Lewiston–Auburn, ME	85,780
St. Joseph, MO	86,680
Iowa City, IA	87,130
Middletown, CT	87,360

Source: Woods & Poole Economics, Inc., population forecasts.

apolis or Detroit or Dallas. But I do dislike New Yorkers. . . ."

It may seem the utmost of brass, this business of judging places. Yet everyone does it, privately. Some suspect that culture in Omaha or Des Moines is a contradiction. Others surmise that daily life in Miami consists of surviving drug-trade shoot-outs, that wet and cloudy Seattle is no place for the seasonally depressed, and that residents of Los Angeles spend most of their waking hours gripping a steering wheel.

Judging places from best to worst with numbers may seem the highest effrontery of all. Ultimately, how can intangible things like friendliness and optimism be measured with statistics? Yet *numeracy* is almost as strong a national character trait as *literacy*. When it comes to choosing where to live, Americans have been digesting statistics for a long, long time.

To sell colonists on settling in Maryland, 17th-century promoters assembled figures showing heavier livestock, more plentiful game, and lower mortality from summer diseases and Indian attacks than in neighboring Virginia.

California for Health, Wealth, and Residence, just one volume in a library of post-Civil War guides touting the West's superior quality of life, compiled data to show the climate along the southern Pacific coast to be the world's best. Not so, countered the Union Pacific Railroad's land

office in 1871; settlers will find the most "genial and healthy" seasons in western Kansas.

In this century, the statistical nets were flung even wider. "There are plenty of Americans who regard Kansas as almost barbaric," noted H. L. Mencken in 1931, "just as there are other Americans who shudder whenever they think of Arkansas, Ohio, Indiana, Oklahoma, Texas, or California." Mencken wrote these words in his *American Mercury* magazine to introduce his formula for statistically measuring the progress of civilization in each of the states. He mixed the numbers of Boy Scouts and *Atlantic Monthly* subscribers with lynchings and pellagra cases, added a dash of *Who's Who* listings along with rates for divorce and murder, threw in figures for rainfall and gasoline consumption, and found that, hands down, Mississippi was the worst American state.

METROPOLITAN AREAS

Places Rated Almanac, we believe, is more useful than any system that considers only states, because statewide averages hide local realities. For persons who can live anywhere they wish, there may be more differences between the Texas metro areas of San Antonio and San Angelo than there are between the Lone Star State and Florida.

Places Rated Almanac focuses instead on metropoli-

Population Growth

FASTEST GROWING METRO AREAS	Population Growth, 1980–1989
Naples, FL	60.5%
Ocala, FL	56.9
Fort Myers–Cape Coral, FL	55.8
Fort Pierce, FL	54.9
West Palm Beach–Boca Raton–Delray Beach, FL	49.0
Austin, TX	45.4
Orlando, FL	44.9
Midland, TX	44.1
Fort Walton Beach, FL	42.6
Riverside–San Bernardino, CA	42.4

NO GROWTH METRO AREAS	Population Loss, 1980–1989
Duluth, MN–WI	−8.3%
Elmira, NY	−8.3
Peoria, IL	−8.1
Waterloo–Cedar Falls, IA	−7.5
Muncie, IN	−6.1
Steubenville–Weirton, OH–WV	−5.9
Gary–Hammond, IN	−5.7
Kankakee, IL	−5.7
Beaver County, PA	−5.4
Eugene–Springfield, OR	−4.8

Source: Woods & Poole Economics, Inc., population forecasts

Finding Your Way in the Chapters

Places Rated Almanac contains thousands of useful facts and many descriptive sections. It is organized so that readers can find specific items that interest them. Most of the chapters have five parts:

- The **introductory** section gives basic information on the chapter's topic, interspersed with facts and figures to help you evaluate metro areas.
- **Scoring:** Here the system used to rate and rank the 333 metro areas for the chapter's topic is fully described, and several metro areas are selected as "scoring examples" to show why one place performs better than another in the ratings.
- **Rankings:** Here the 333 metro areas are listed in their rank order, from best to worst, along with their score. (Metro areas that receive the same score are assigned the same rank and are listed in alphabetical order.)
- **Place Profiles:** Arranged alphabetically by metro area, these capsule comparisons cover all the elements used to rate the metro areas. These Place Profiles can be columns of information (like the recreation profiles) or page-wide charts (like the transportation profiles); the climate profiles have their own special format. All are designed to help you see differences among metro areas at a glance.
- **Et Cetera:** This section expands on the quality-of-place features mentioned in the introductory section. Moreover, it contains information on other topics ranging all the way from lists of metro area professional sports championships, state-by-state high school graduation requirements, and metro area Fortune 500 headquarters, to essays on water shortages and contradictory traffic laws.

The final chapter, "Putting It All Together," adds up the rankings to identify America's best all-around metro areas. Here, too, examples of using personal preferences to devise your own scoring system are given.

tan areas, the smallest units of urban geography for which there is the largest amount of comparable data. From Abilene to Yuba City; from huge Los Angeles–Long Beach (pop. 8,707,470) to tiny Enid (pop. 61,880); from Anchorage to Miami–Hialeah; these 333 metro areas cover a wide spectrum, indeed. Here, you'll find agricultural centers and fashion markets, mill towns and bedroom communities, financial centers and college towns, resorts and retirement colonies, and cultural havens right next to ports of entry and industrial giants.

Metropolitan areas are defined according to detailed federal standards. Broadly speaking, an area qualifies as "metropolitan" in one of two ways: if there is a city with a population of at least 50,000, or an urbanized area (embracing one or more towns) of at least 50,000 located in a county or counties with a total population of at least 100,000 (75,000 in New England). In either case, the metropolitan area's boundaries coincide with those of the surrounding county or counties (in New England, metropolitan areas are defined by towns and cities instead). Most metro areas are within single states; 35 of them, however, cross state lines. Metropolitan Cincinnati, for example, includes three counties in Ohio, three in Kentucky, and one in Indiana; Memphis takes in two counties in Tennessee, plus one in Arkansas and one in Mississippi.

There are ample reasons for focusing on metro areas rather than on cities, counties, or states. Thanks to the four-lane highway, cities, counties, and states are less relevant to our daily personal geography. Commonly, we live in one community, such as the suburb of a large city; commute to work in another; eat at the restaurants, shop at the stores, and take advantage of the recreation assets of all the towns around. Every two years, we approve or disapprove of our district's congressional representative. We pay taxes or fees to water, sewer, park, and school districts that often cross city lines. The perimeters of metro areas supersede the anachronistic political boundaries of incorporated areas and include not just the troubled and depressed older city cores but also the newer parts of suburbia with their sleek new malls, office parks, factories, and choice neighborhoods. For example, metropolitan Newark includes affluent Morris County; Niagara Falls includes quaint and tony Lewiston; Cleveland embraces Shaker Heights; and Boston, with its 106 cities and towns, takes in a wealthy fringe of high-tech industries.

The list on the next page provides the county definitions of the metropolitan areas rated in this edition of *Places Rated Almanac*. The chances are good that you, like three of every four Americans, live in one of the official metropolitan areas surveyed here.

Places Rated:
333 Metropolitan Areas

Metro Areas and Component Counties	Population 1980	Population 1989	%Population Change, 1980–1989	Metro Areas and Component Counties	Population 1980	Population 1989	%Population Change, 1980–1989
Abilene, TX Taylor County	110,932	127,020	+14.5%	**Aurora–Elgin, IL*** Kane and Kendall Counties	315,607	357,580	+13.3
Akron, OH* Portage and Summit Counties	660,328	656,680	– 0.6	**Austin, TX** Hays, Travis, and Williamson Counties	536,688	780,510	+45.4
Albany, GA Dougherty and Lee Counties	112,402	119,980	+ 6.7	**Bakersfield, CA** Kern County	403,089	514,120	+27.5
Albany–Schenectady–Troy, NY Albany, Greene, Montgomery, Rensselaer, Saratoga, and Schenectady Counties	835,880	854,120	+ 2.2	**Baltimore, MD** Baltimore City; Anne Arundel, Baltimore, Carroll, Harford, Howard, and Queen Annes Counties	2,199,531	2,331,900	+ 6.0
Albuquerque, NM Bernalillo County	419,700	494,690	+17.9	**Bangor, ME** Parts of Penobscot and Waldo Counties	83,919	84,030	+ 0.1
Alexandria, LA Rapides Parish	135,282	139,630	+ 3.2	**Baton Rouge, LA** Ascension, East Baton Rouge, Livingston, and West Baton Rouge Parishes	494,151	571,470	+15.6
Allentown–Bethlehem, PA–NJ Carbon, Lehigh, and Northampton Counties, PA; Warren County, NJ	635,481	667,190	+ 5.0	**Battle Creek, MI** Calhoun County	141,557	134,850	– 4.7
Altoona, PA Blair County	136,621	133,850	– 2.0	**Beaumont–Port Arthur, TX** Hardin, Jefferson, and Orange Counties	375,497	376,250	+ 0.2
Amarillo, TX Potter and Randall Counties	173,699	201,320	+15.9	**Beaver County, PA*** Beaver County	204,441	193,490	– 5.4
Anaheim–Santa Ana, CA* Orange County	1,932,709	2,343,640	+21.3	**Bellingham, WA** Whatcom County	106,701	116,980	+ 9.6
Anchorage, AK Anchorage Borough	174,431	243,990	+39.9	**Benton Harbor, MI** Berrien County	171,276	166,540	– 2.8
Anderson, IN Madison County	139,336	132,750	– 4.7	**Bergen–Passaic, NJ*** Bergen and Passaic Counties	1,292,970	1,310,140	+ 1.3
Anderson, SC Anderson County	133,235	144,610	+ 8.5	**Billings, MT** Yellowstone County	108,035	119,380	+10.5
Ann Arbor, MI* Washtenaw County	264,748	270,010	+ 2.0	**Biloxi–Gulfport, MS** Hancock and Harrison Counties	182,202	212,610	+16.7
Anniston, AL Calhoun County	119,761	123,850	+ 3.4	**Binghamton, NY** Broome and Tioga Counties	263,460	262,310	– 0.4
Appleton–Oshkosh–Neenah, WI Calumet, Outagamie, and Winnebago Counties	291,369	313,870	+ 7.7	**Birmingham, AL** Blount, Jefferson, St. Clair, Shelby, and Walker Counties	883,946	923,340	+ 4.5
Asheville, NC Buncombe County	160,934	174,490	+ 8.4	**Bismarck, ND** Burleigh and Morton Counties	79,988	88,510	+10.7
Athens, GA Clarke, Jackson, Madison, and Oconee Counties	130,015	143,730	+10.5	**Bloomington, IN** Monroe County	98,785	104,260	+ 5.5
Atlanta, GA Barrow, Butts, Cherokee, Clayton, Cobb, Coweta, De Kalb, Douglas, Fayette, Forsyth, Fulton, Gwinnett, Henry, Newton, Paulding, Rockdale, Spalding, and Walton Counties	2,138,231	2,781,410	+30.1	**Bloomington–Normal, IL** McLean County	119,149	122,890	+ 3.1
				Boise City, ID Ada County	173,036	200,110	+15.6
Atlantic City, NJ Atlantic and Cape May Counties	276,385	314,670	+13.9	**Boston, MA*** Parts of Bristol, Essex, Middlesex, Norfolk, Plymouth, and Worcester Counties; Suffolk County	2,805,911	2,839,030	+ 1.2
Augusta, GA–SC Columbia, McDuffie, and Richmond Counties, GA; Aiken County, SC	345,918	410,510	+18.7	**Boulder–Longmont, CO*** Boulder County	189,625	223,440	+17.8

Metro Areas and Component Counties	Population 1980	Population 1989	%Population Change, 1980–1989	Metro Areas and Component Counties	Population 1980	Population 1989	%Population Change, 1980–1989
Bradenton, FL Manatee County	148,442	193,120	+30.1	**Cincinnati, OH–KY–IN*** Clermont, Hamilton, and Warren Counties, OH; Boone, Campbell, and Kenton Counties, KY; Dearborn County, IN	1,401,491	1,440,170	+ 2.8
Brazoria, TX* Brazoria County	169,587	192,310	+13.4				
Bremerton, WA Kitsap County	147,152	178,190	+21.1				
Bridgeport–Milford, CT* Parts of Fairfield and New Haven Counties	438,557	453,770	+ 3.5	**Clarksville–Hopkinsville, TN–KY** Montgomery County, TN; Christian County, KY	150,220	158,960	+ 5.8
Bristol, CT* Parts of Hartford and Litchfield Counties	73,762	77,630	+ 5.2	**Cleveland, OH*** Cuyahoga, Geauga, Lake, and Medina Counties	1,898,825	1,851,300	− 2.5
Brockton, MA* Parts of Bristol, Norfolk, and Plymouth Counties	182,891	199,430	+ 9.0	**Colorado Springs, CO** El Paso County	309,424	401,140	+29.6
Brownsville–Harlingen, TX Cameron County	209,727	273,580	+30.4	**Columbia, MO** Boone County	100,376	109,410	+ 9.0
Bryan–College Station, TX Brazos County	93,588	132,070	+41.1	**Columbia, SC** Lexington and Richland Counties	410,088	467,250	+13.9
Buffalo, NY* Erie County	1,015,472	967,990	− 4.7	**Columbus, GA–AL** Chattahoochee and Muscogee Counties, GA; Russell County, AL	239,196	254,590	+ 6.4
Burlington, NC Alamance County	99,319	104,770	+ 5.5	**Columbus, OH** Delaware, Fairfield, Franklin, Licking, Madison, Pickaway, and Union Counties	1,243,833	1,332,910	+ 7.2
Burlington, VT Parts of Chittenden, Franklin, and Grand Isle Counties	115,308	132,680	+15.1				
Canton, OH Carroll and Stark Counties	404,421	410,340	+ 1.5	**Corpus Christi, TX** Nueces and San Patricio Counties	326,228	369,010	+13.1
Casper, WY Natrona County	71,856	73,210	+ 1.9	**Cumberland, MD–WV** Allegany County, MD; Mineral County, WV	107,782	104,520	− 3.0
Cedar Rapids, IA Linn County	169,775	169,600	− 0.1	**Dallas, TX*** Collin, Dallas, Denton, Ellis, Kaufman, and Rockwall Counties	1,957,378	2,608,660	+33.3
Champaign–Urbana–Rantoul, IL Champaign County	168,392	178,760	+ 6.2				
Charleston, SC Berkeley, Charleston, and Dorchester Counties	430,462	510,220	+18.5	**Danbury, CT*** Parts of Fairfield and Litchfield Counties	170,369	191,080	+12.2
Charleston, WV Kanawha and Putnam Counties	269,595	270,230	+ 0.2	**Danville, VA** Danville City and Pittsylvania County	111,789	110,560	− 1.1
Charlotte–Gastonia–Rock Hill, NC–SC Cabarrus, Gaston, Lincoln, Mecklenburg, Rowan, and Union Counties, NC; York County, SC	971,391	1,120,350	+15.3	**Davenport–Rock Island–Moline, IA–IL** Scott County, IA; Henry and Rock Island Counties, IL	383,958	373,430	− 2.7
Charlottesville, VA Charlottesville City; Albemarle, Fluvanna, and Greene Counties	113,568	125,020	+10.1	**Dayton–Springfield, OH** Clark, Greene, Miami, and Montgomery Counties	942,083	935,920	− 0.7
Chattanooga, TN–GA Hamilton, Marion, and Sequatchie Counties, TN; Catoosa, Dade, and Walker Counties, GA	426,540	428,950	+ 0.6	**Daytona Beach, FL** Volusia County	258,762	344,170	+33.0
Cheyenne, WY Laramie County	68,649	75,830	+10.5	**Decatur, AL** Lawrence and Morgan Counties	120,401	130,790	+ 8.6
Chicago, IL* Cook, Du Page, and McHenry Counties	6,060,387	6,251,360	+ 3.2	**Decatur, IL** Macon County	131,375	126,480	− 3.7
Chico, CA Butte County	143,851	177,810	+23.6	**Denver, CO*** Adams, Arapahoe, Denver, Douglas, and Jefferson Counties	1,428,836	1,711,910	+19.8
				Des Moines, IA Dallas, Polk, and Warren Counties	367,561	388,390	+ 5.7

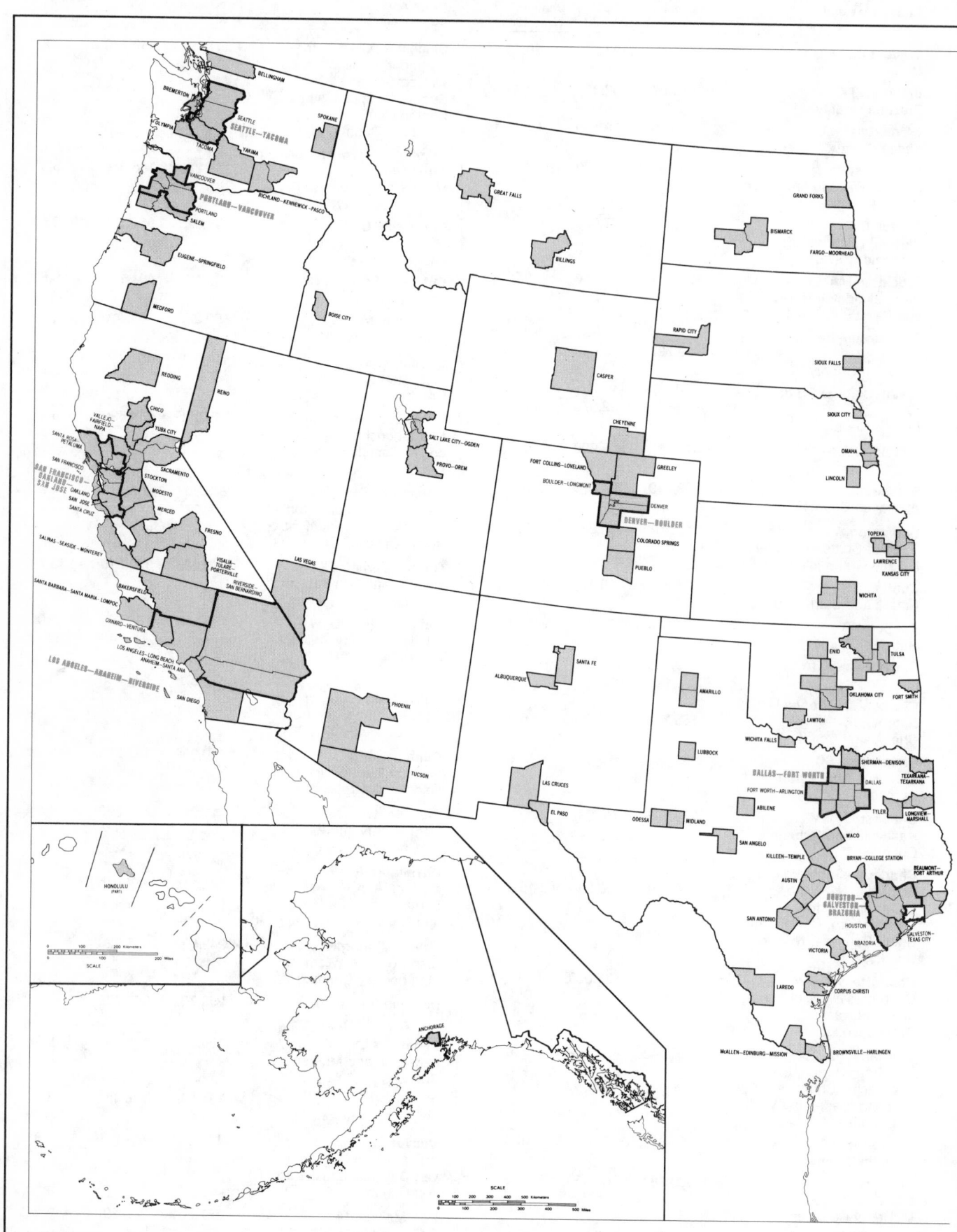

Places Rated Almanac
333 Metropolitan Areas

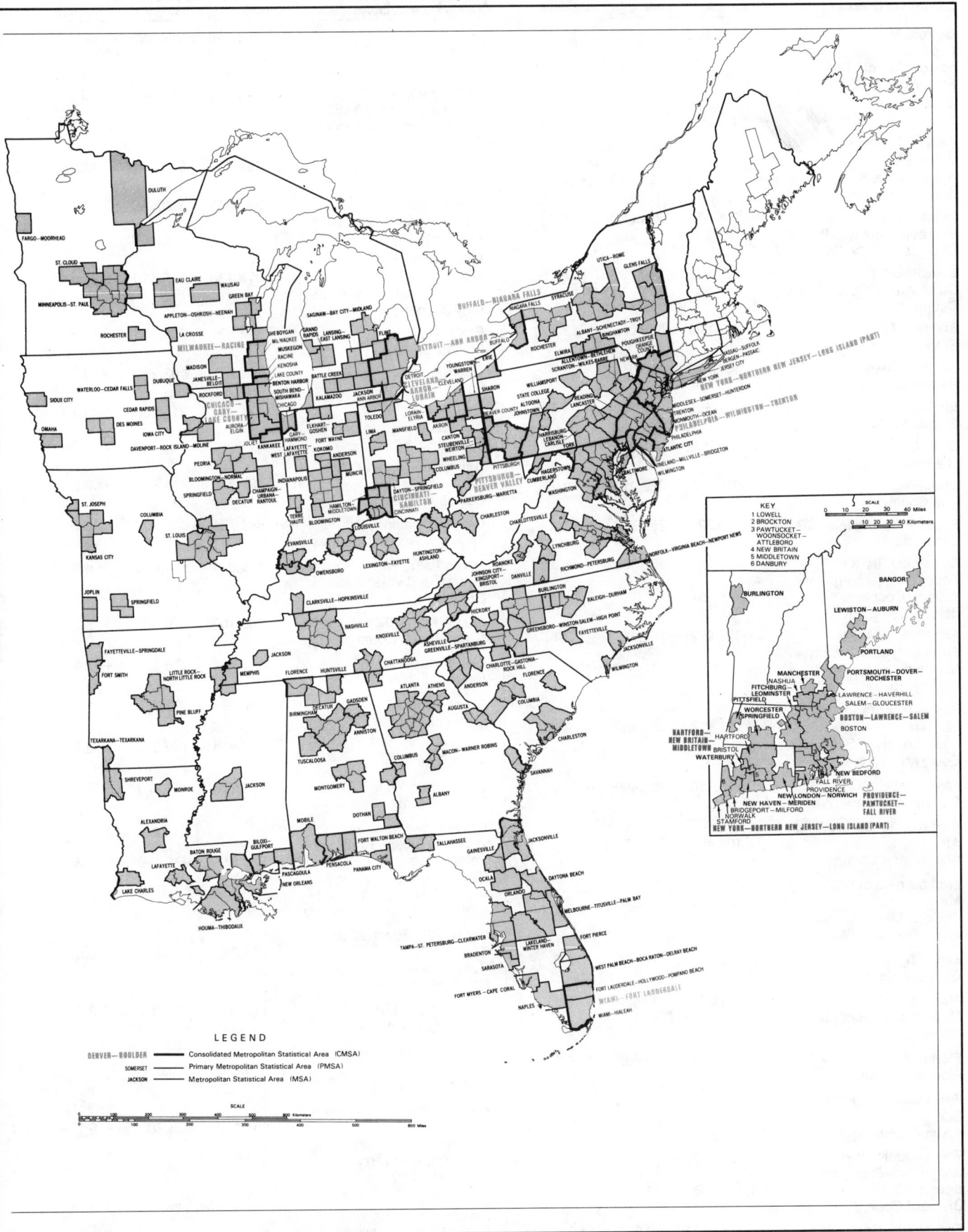

LEGEND

DENVER—BOULDER ━━━━ Consolidated Metropolitan Statistical Area (CMSA)

SOMERSET ──── Primary Metropolitan Statistical Area (PMSA)

JACKSON ──── Metropolitan Statistical Area (MSA)

KEY
1 LOWELL
2 BROCKTON
3 PAWTUCKET—WOONSOCKET—ATTLEBORO
4 NEW BRITAIN
5 MIDDLETOWN
6 DANBURY

Metro Areas and Component Counties	Population 1980	Population 1989	%Population Change, 1980–1989
Detroit, MI* Lapeer, Livingston, Macomb, Monroe, Oakland, St. Clair, and Wayne Counties	4,488,072	4,347,160	− 3.1
Dothan, AL Dale and Houston Counties	122,453	134,020	+ 9.4
Dubuque, IA Dubuque County	93,745	91,440	− 2.5
Duluth, MN–WI St. Louis County, MN; Douglas County, WI	266,650	244,620	− 8.3
Eau Claire, WI Chippewa and Eau Claire Counties	130,932	140,220	+ 7.1
El Paso, TX El Paso County	479,899	589,020	+22.7
Elkhart–Goshen, IN Elkhart County	137,330	150,610	+ 9.7
Elmira, NY Chemung County	97,656	89,830	− 8.3
Enid, OK Garfield County	62,820	61,880	− 1.5
Erie, PA Erie County	279,780	280,220	+ 0.2
Eugene–Springfield, OR Lane County	275,226	261,910	− 4.8
Evansville, IN–KY Posey, Vanderburgh, and Warrick Counties, IN; Henderson County, KY	276,252	281,330	+ 1.8
Fall River, MA–RI* Parts of Bristol County, MA; parts of Newport County, RI	157,222	162,110	+ 3.1
Fargo–Moorhead, ND–MN Cass County, ND; Clay County, MN	137,574	148,830	+ 8.2
Fayetteville, NC Cumberland County	247,160	264,490	+ 7.0
Fayetteville–Springdale, AR Washington County	100,494	109,370	+ 8.8
Fitchburg–Leominster, MA Parts of Middlesex and Worcester Counties	94,018	100,690	+ 7.1
Flint, MI Genesee County	450,449	446,620	− 0.9
Florence, AL Colbert and Lauderdale Counties	135,065	139,520	+ 3.3
Florence, SC Florence County	110,163	119,090	+ 8.1
Fort Collins–Loveland, CO Larimer County	149,184	183,990	+23.3
Fort Lauderdale–Hollywood–Pompano Beach, FL* Broward County	1,018,200	1,231,250	+20.9
Fort Myers–Cape Coral, FL Lee County	205,266	319,880	+55.8

Metro Areas and Component Counties	Population 1980	Population 1989	%Population Change, 1980–1989
Fort Pierce, FL Martin and St. Lucie Counties	151,196	234,150	+54.9
Fort Smith, AR–OK Crawford and Sebastian Counties, AR; Sequoyah County, OK	162,813	184,430	+13.3
Fort Walton Beach, FL Okaloosa County	109,920	156,770	+42.6
Fort Wayne, IN Allen, De Kalb, and Whitley Counties	354,156	359,480	+ 1.5
Fort Worth–Arlington, TX* Johnson, Parker, and Tarrant Counties	973,138	1,315,510	+35.2
Fresno, CA Fresno County	514,621	605,980	+17.8
Gadsden, AL Etowah County	103,057	103,250	+ 0.2
Gainesville, FL Alachua and Bradford Counties	171,371	211,200	+23.2
Galveston–Texas City, TX* Galveston County	195,940	214,830	+ 9.6
Gary–Hammond, IN* Lake and Porter Counties	642,781	606,000	− 5.7
Glens Falls, NY Warren and Washington Counties	109,649	114,020	+ 4.0
Grand Forks, ND Grand Forks County	66,100	70,030	+ 5.9
Grand Rapids, MI Kent and Ottawa Counties	601,680	676,130	+12.4
Great Falls, MT Cascade County	80,696	79,230	− 1.8
Greeley, CO Weld County	123,438	139,290	+12.8
Green Bay, WI Brown County	175,280	194,120	+10.7
Greensboro–Winston-Salem–High Point, NC Davidson, Davie, Forsyth, Guilford, Randolph, Stokes, and Yadkin Counties	851,851	931,090	+ 9.3
Greenville–Spartanburg, SC Greenville, Pickens, and Spartanburg Counties	569,066	630,490	+10.8
Hagerstown, MD Washington County	113,086	116,280	+ 2.8
Hamilton–Middletown, OH* Butler County	258,787	273,000	+ 5.5
Harrisburg–Lebanon–Carlisle, PA Cumberland, Dauphin, Lebanon, and Perry Counties	555,158	588,880	+ 6.1
Hartford, CT* Parts of Hartford, Litchfield, Middlesex, New London, and Tolland Counties	715,923	752,560	+ 5.1

Metro Areas and Component Counties	Population 1980	Population 1989	%Population Change, 1980–1989	Metro Areas and Component Counties	Population 1980	Population 1989	%Population Change, 1980–1989
Hickory, NC Alexander, Burke, and Catawba Counties	202,711	227,530	+12.2	Johnson, Leavenworth, Miami, and Wyandotte Counties, KS			
Honolulu, HI Honolulu County	762,565	839,100	+10.0	**Kenosha, WI*** Kenosha County	123,137	120,370	− 2.2
Houma–Thibodaux, LA Lafourche and Terrebonne Parishes	176,876	192,700	+ 8.9	**Killeen–Temple, TX** Bell and Coryell Counties	214,656	242,160	+12.8
Houston, TX* Fort Bend, Harris, Liberty, Montgomery, and Waller Counties	2,735,766	3,262,530	+19.3	**Knoxville, TN** Anderson, Blount, Grainger, Jefferson, Knox, Sevier, and Union Counties	565,970	605,870	+ 7.0
Huntington–Ashland, WV–KY–OH Cabell and Wayne Counties, WV; Boyd, Carter, and Greenup Counties, KY; Lawrence County, OH	336,410	332,560	− 1.1	**Kokomo, IN** Howard and Tipton Counties	103,715	103,140	− 0.6
Huntsville, AL Madison County	196,966	245,450	+24.6	**La Crosse, WI** La Crosse County	91,056	96,070	+ 5.5
Indianapolis, IN Boone, Hamilton, Hancock, Hendricks, Johnson, Marion, Morgan, and Shelby Counties	1,166,575	1,240,050	+ 6.3	**Lafayette, LA** Lafayette and St. Martin Parishes	190,231	217,790	+14.5
Iowa City, IA Johnson County	81,717	87,130	+ 6.6	**Lafayette– West Lafayette, IN** Tippecanoe County	121,702	125,520	+ 3.1
Jackson, MI Jackson County	151,495	144,420	− 4.7	**Lake Charles, LA** Calcasieu Parish	167,223	175,040	+ 4.7
Jackson, MS Hinds, Madison, and Rankin Counties	362,038	404,180	+11.6	**Lake County, IL*** Lake County	440,372	501,330	+13.8
Jackson, TN Madison County	74,546	80,150	+ 7.5	**Lakeland–Winter Haven, FL** Polk County	321,652	397,200	+23.5
Jacksonville, FL Clay, Duval, Nassau, and St. Johns Counties	722,252	907,850	+25.7	**Lancaster, PA** Lancaster County	362,346	409,420	+13.0
Jacksonville, NC Onslow County	112,784	131,010	+16.2	**Lansing–East Lansing, MI** Clinton, Eaton, and Ingham Counties	419,750	431,040	+ 2.7
Janesville–Beloit, WI Rock County	139,420	138,070	− 1.0	**Laredo, TX** Webb County	99,258	128,020	+29.0
Jersey City, NJ* Hudson County	556,972	555,910	− 0.2	**Las Cruces, NM** Dona Ana County	96,340	132,560	+37.6
Johnson City–Kingsport– Bristol, TN–VA Carter, Hawkins, Sullivan, Unicoi, and Washington Counties, TN; Bristol City and Scott and Washington Counties, VA	433,638	448,540	+ 3.4	**Las Vegas, NV** Clark County	463,087	631,590	+36.4
				Lawrence, KS Douglas County	67,640	74,560	+10.2
Johnstown, PA Cambria and Somerset Counties	264,506	252,130	− 4.7	**Lawrence–Haverhill, MA–NH*** Parts of Essex County, MA; parts of Rockingham County, NH	339,090	385,920	+13.8
Joliet, IL* Grundy and Will Counties	355,042	380,670	+ 7.2	**Lawton, OK** Comanche County	112,456	122,630	+ 9.0
Joplin, MO Jasper and Newton Counties	127,513	136,380	+ 7.0	**Lewiston–Auburn, ME** Parts of Androscoggin County	84,690	85,780	+ 1.3
Kalamazoo, MI Kalamazoo County	212,378	219,680	+ 3.4	**Lexington–Fayette, KY** Bourbon, Clark, Fayette, Jessamine, Scott, and Woodford Counties	317,629	337,510	+ 6.3
Kankakee, IL Kankakee County	102,926	97,090	− 5.7	**Lima, OH** Allen and Auglaize Counties	154,795	157,230	+ 1.6
Kansas City, MO–KS Cass, Clay, Jackson, Lafayette, Platte, and Ray Counties, MO;	1,433,458	1,550,590	+ 8.2	**Lincoln, NE** Lancaster County	192,884	210,490	+ 9.1
				Little Rock–North Little Rock, AR Faulkner, Lonoke, Pulaski, and Saline Counties	474,484	519,810	+ 9.6

Metro Areas and Component Counties	Population 1980	Population 1989	%Population Change, 1980–1989
Longview–Marshall, TX Gregg and Harrison Counties	151,752	170,790	+12.5
Lorain–Elyria, OH* Lorain County	274,909	268,330	– 2.4
Los Angeles–Long Beach, CA* Los Angeles County	7,477,503	8,707,470	+16.4
Louisville, KY–IN Bullitt, Jefferson, Oldham, and Shelby Counties, KY; Clark, Floyd, and Harrison Counties, IN	956,756	969,210	+ 1.3
Lowell, MA–NH* Parts of Middlesex County, MA; parts of Hillsborough County, NH	243,142	254,580	+ 4.7
Lubbock, TX Lubbock County	211,651	230,760	+ 9.0
Lynchburg, VA Lynchburg City; Amherst and Campbell Counties	141,289	145,450	+ 2.9
Macon–Warner Robins, GA Bibb, Houston, Jones, and Peach Counties	263,591	288,150	+ 9.3
Madison, WI Dane County	323,545	355,590	+ 9.9
Manchester, NH Parts of Hillsborough, Merrimack, and Rockingham Counties	129,305	155,120	+20.0
Mansfield, OH Richland County	131,205	128,180	– 2.3
McAllen–Edinburg–Mission, TX Hidalgo County	283,229	388,910	+37.3
Medford, OR Jackson County	132,456	144,080	+ 8.8
Melbourne–Titusville–Palm Bay, FL Brevard County	272,959	380,460	+39.4
Memphis, TN–AR–MS Shelby and Tipton Counties, TN; Crittenden County, AR; De Soto County, MS	913,472	981,780	+ 7.5
Merced, CA Merced County	134,560	171,240	+27.3
Miami–Hialeah, FL* Dade County	1,625,781	1,853,900	+14.0
Middlesex–Somerset–Hunterdon, NJ* Hunterdon, Middlesex, and Somerset Counties	886,383	1,003,320	+13.2
Middletown, CT* Parts of Middlesex County	81,582	87,360	+ 7.1
Midland, TX Midland County	82,636	119,100	+44.1
Milwaukee, WI* Milwaukee, Ozaukee, Washington, and Waukesha Counties	1,397,143	1,387,740	– 0.7
Minneapolis–St. Paul, MN–WI Anoka, Carver, Chisago, Dakota, Hennepin, Isanti,	2,137,133	2,378,700	+11.3

Metro Areas and Component Counties	Population 1980	Population 1989	%Population Change, 1980–1989
Ramsey, Scott, Washington, and Wright Counties, MN; St. Croix County, WI			
Mobile, AL Baldwin and Mobile Counties	443,536	480,790	+ 8.4
Modesto, CA Stanislaus County	265,900	327,950	+23.3
Monmouth–Ocean, NJ* Monmouth and Ocean Counties	849,211	992,630	+16.9
Monroe, LA Ouachita Parish	139,241	149,360	+ 7.3
Montgomery, AL Autauga, Elmore, and Montgomery Counties	272,687	308,300	+13.1
Muncie, IN Delaware County	128,587	120,750	– 6.1
Muskegon, MI Muskegon County	157,589	159,120	+ 1.0
Naples, FL Collier County	85,971	137,950	+60.5
Nashua, NH* Parts of Hillsborough and Rockingham Counties	142,527	176,440	+23.8
Nashville, TN Cheatham, Davidson, Dickson, Robertson, Rutherford, Sumner, Williamson, and Wilson Counties	850,505	974,960	+14.6
Nassau–Suffolk, NY* Nassau and Suffolk Counties	2,605,813	2,710,460	+ 4.0
New Bedford, MA Parts of Bristol and Plymouth Counties	166,699	175,760	+ 5.4
New Britain, CT* Parts of Hartford County	142,241	146,180	+ 2.8
New Haven–Meriden, CT Parts of Middlesex and New Haven Counties	500,474	521,750	+ 4.3
New London–Norwich, CT–RI Parts of New London and Windham Counties, CT; parts of Washington County, RI	250,839	261,970	+ 4.4
New Orleans, LA Jefferson, Orleans, St. Bernard, St. Charles, St. John The Baptist, and St. Tammany Parishes	1,256,256	1,376,050	+ 9.5
New York, NY* Bronx, Kings, New York, Putnam, Queens, Richmond, Rockland, and Westchester Counties	8,274,961	8,562,900	+ 3.5
Newark, NJ* Essex, Morris, Sussex, and Union Counties	1,878,959	1,911,920	+ 1.8
Niagara Falls, NY* Niagara County	227,354	218,080	– 4.1
Norfolk–Virginia Beach–Newport News, VA Chesapeake, Hampton, Newport News, Norfolk,	1,160,311	1,371,280	+18.2

Metro Areas and Component Counties	Population 1980	Population 1989	%Population Change, 1980–1989	Metro Areas and Component Counties	Population 1980	Population 1989	%Population Change, 1980–1989
Poquoson, Portsmouth, Suffolk, Virginia Beach, and Williamsburg Cities; Gloucester, James City, and York Counties				ington, and Westmoreland Counties			
Norwalk, CT* Parts of Fairfield County	126,692	131,110	+ 3.5	**Pittsfield, MA** Parts of Berkshire County	83,490	81,200	− 2.7
Oakland, CA* Alameda and Contra Costa Counties	1,761,759	2,029,090	+15.2	**Portland, ME** Parts of Cumberland and York Counties	193,831	212,760	+ 9.8
Ocala, FL Marion County	122,488	192,130	+56.9	**Portland, OR*** Clackamas, Multnomah, Washington, and Yamhill Counties	1,105,699	1,178,960	+ 6.6
Odessa, TX Ector County	115,374	134,090	+16.2	**Portsmouth–Dover– Rochester, NH–ME** Parts of Rockingham and Strafford Counties, NH; part of York County, ME	190,938	236,430	+23.8
Oklahoma City, OK Canadian, Cleveland, Logan, McClain, Oklahoma, and Pottawatomie Counties	860,969	1,002,290	+16.4	**Poughkeepsie, NY** Dutchess County	245,055	266,360	+ 8.7
Olympia, WA Thurston County	124,264	157,250	+26.5	**Providence, RI*** Parts of Bristol, Kent, Newport, Providence, and Washington Counties	618,514	651,190	+ 5.3
Omaha, NE–IA Douglas, Sarpy, and Washington Counties, NE; Pottawattamie County, IA	585,122	624,600	+ 6.7	**Provo–Orem, UT** Utah County	218,106	253,670	+16.3
Orange County, NY* Orange County	259,603	294,890	+13.6	**Pueblo, CO** Pueblo County	125,972	129,950	+ 3.2
Orlando, FL Orange, Osceola, and Seminole Counties	700,055	1,014,440	+44.9	**Racine, WI*** Racine County	173,132	172,050	− 0.6
Owensboro, KY Daviess County	85,949	87,920	+ 2.3	**Raleigh–Durham, NC** Durham, Franklin, Orange, and Wake Counties	561,222	703,170	+25.3
Oxnard–Ventura, CA* Ventura County	529,174	661,970	+25.1	**Rapid City, SD** Pennington County	70,361	78,300	+11.3
Panama City, FL Bay County	97,740	131,220	+34.3	**Reading, PA** Berks County	312,509	322,760	+ 3.3
Parkersburg–Marietta, WV–OH Wood County, WV; Washington County, OH	157,914	156,950	− 0.6	**Redding, CA** Shasta County	115,715	140,730	+21.6
Pascagoula, MS Jackson County	118,015	131,710	+11.6	**Reno, NV** Washoe County	193,623	238,730	+23.3
Pawtucket–Woonsocket– Attleboro, RI–MA* Parts of Providence County, RI; parts of Bristol, Norfolk, and Worcester Counties, MA	307,403	324,250	+ 5.5	**Richland–Kennewick– Pasco, WA** Benton and Franklin Counties	144,469	151,550	+ 4.9
Pensacola, FL Escambia and Santa Rosa Counties	289,782	356,620	+23.1	**Richmond–Petersburg, VA** Colonial Heights, Hopewell, Petersburg, and Richmond Cities; Charles City, Chesterfield, Dinwiddie, Goochland, Hanover, Henrico, New Kent, Powhatan, and Prince George Counties	761,311	841,110	+10.5
Peoria, IL Peoria, Tazewell, and Woodford Counties	365,864	336,060	− 8.1				
Philadelphia, PA–NJ* Bucks, Chester, Delaware, Montgomery, and Philadelphia Counties, PA; Burlington, Camden, and Gloucester Counties, NJ	4,716,818	4,901,690	+ 3.9	**Riverside–San Bernardino, CA*** Riverside and San Bernardino Counties	1,558,182	2,219,580	+42.4
Phoenix, AZ Maricopa County	1,509,052	2,079,570	+37.8	**Roanoke, VA** Roanoke and Salem Cities; Botetourt and Roanoke Counties	220,393	226,720	+ 2.9
Pine Bluff, AR Jefferson County	90,718	90,330	− 0.4	**Rochester, MN** Olmsted County	92,006	102,000	+10.9
Pittsburgh, PA* Allegheny, Fayette, Wash-	2,218,870	2,132,290	− 3.9	**Rochester, NY** Livingston, Monroe, Ontario, Orleans, and Wayne Counties	971,230	992,850	+ 2.2

Metro Areas and Component Counties	Population 1980	Population 1989	%Population Change, 1980–1989	Metro Areas and Component Counties	Population 1980	Population 1989	%Population Change, 1980–1989
Rockford, IL Boone and Winnebago Counties	279,514	282,970	+ 1.2	Seattle, WA* King and Snohomish Counties	1,607,469	1,817,900	+13.1
Sacramento, CA El Dorado, Placer, Sacramento, and Yolo Counties	1,099,814	1,376,010	+25.1	Sharon, PA Mercer County	128,299	123,480	− 3.8
Saginaw–Bay City–Midland, MI Bay, Midland, and Saginaw Counties	421,518	404,030	− 4.1	Sheboygan, WI Sheboygan County	100,935	102,230	+ 1.3
St. Cloud, MN Benton, Sherburne, and Stearns Counties	163,256	183,380	+12.3	Sherman–Denison, TX Grayson County	89,796	98,450	+ 9.6
St. Joseph, MO Buchanan County	87,888	86,680	− 1.4	Shreveport, LA Bossier and Caddo Parishes	333,079	369,320	+10.9
St. Louis, MO–IL St. Louis City and Franklin, Jefferson, St. Charles, and St. Louis Counties, MO; Clinton, Jersey, Madison, Monroe, and St. Clair Counties, IL	2,376,998	2,471,380	+ 4.0	Sioux City, IA–NE Woodbury County, IA; Dakota County, NE	117,457	115,610	− 1.6
				Sioux Falls, SD Minnehaha County	109,435	128,140	+17.1
Salem, OR Marion and Polk Counties	249,895	265,180	+ 6.1	South Bend–Mishawaka, IN St. Joseph County	241,617	239,790	− 0.8
Salem–Gloucester, MA* Parts of Essex County	258,175	265,550	+ 2.9	Spokane, WA Spokane County	341,835	361,480	+ 5.7
Salinas–Seaside–Monterey, CA Monterey County	290,444	366,030	+26.0	Springfield, IL Menard and Sangamon Counties	187,789	192,310	+ 2.4
Salt Lake City–Ogden, UT Davis, Salt Lake, and Weber Counties	910,222	1,095,280	+20.3	Springfield, MA Parts of Hampden and Hampshire Counties	515,259	520,380	+ 1.0
San Angelo, TX Tom Green County	84,784	99,410	+17.3	Springfield, MO Christian and Greene Counties	207,704	235,120	+13.2
San Antonio, TX Bexar, Comal, and Guadalupe Counties	1,071,954	1,360,150	+26.9	Stamford, CT* Parts of Fairfield County	198,854	200,190	+ 0.7
San Diego, CA San Diego County	1,861,846	2,347,360	+26.1	State College, PA Centre County	112,760	116,260	+ 3.1
San Francisco, CA* Marin, San Francisco, and San Mateo Counties	1,488,871	1,659,760	+11.5	Steubenville–Weirton, OH–WV Jefferson County, OH; Brooke and Hancock Counties, WV	163,099	153,480	− 5.9
San Jose, CA* Santa Clara County	1,295,071	1,460,040	+12.7	Stockton, CA San Joaquin County	347,342	447,750	+28.9
Santa Barbara–Santa Maria–Lompoc, CA Santa Barbara County	298,694	362,320	+21.3	Syracuse, NY Madison, Onondaga, and Oswego Counties	642,971	658,040	+ 2.3
Santa Cruz, CA* Santa Cruz County	188,141	237,940	+26.5	Tacoma, WA* Pierce County	485,643	549,250	+13.1
Santa Fe, NM Los Alamos and Santa Fe Counties	92,959	113,140	+21.7	Tallahassee, FL Gadsden and Leon Counties	190,220	232,850	+22.4
Santa Rosa–Petaluma, CA* Sonoma County	299,681	374,560	+25.0	Tampa–St. Petersburg–Clearwater, FL Hernando, Hillsborough, Pasco, and Pinellas Counties	1,613,603	2,092,990	+29.7
Sarasota, FL Sarasota County	202,251	270,360	+33.7	Terre Haute, IN Clay and Vigo Counties	137,247	133,500	− 2.7
Savannah, GA Chatham and Effingham Counties	220,553	244,190	+10.7	Texarkana, TX–Texarkana, AR Bowie County, TX; Miller County, AR	113,067	119,880	+ 6.0
Scranton–Wilkes-Barre, PA Columbia, Lackawanna, Luzerne, Monroe, and Wyoming Counties	728,796	730,960	+ 0.3	Toledo, OH Fulton, Lucas, and Wood Counties	616,864	613,630	− 0.5
				Topeka, KS Shawnee County	154,916	162,120	+ 4.7

Metro Areas and Component Counties	Population 1980	Population 1989	%Population Change, 1980–1989	Metro Areas and Component Counties	Population 1980	Population 1989	%Population Change, 1980–1989
Trenton, NJ* Mercer County	307,863	327,320	+ 6.3	**Waterbury, CT** Parts of Litchfield and New Haven Counties	204,968	215,930	+ 5.3
Tucson, AZ Pima County	531,443	629,830	+18.5	**Waterloo–Cedar Falls, IA** Black Hawk and Bremer Counties	162,781	150,560	− 7.5
Tulsa, OK Creek, Osage, Rogers, Tulsa, and Wagoner Counties	657,173	750,000	+14.1	**Wausau, WI** Marathon County	111,270	113,550	+ 2.0
Tuscaloosa, AL Tuscaloosa County	137,541	143,700	+ 4.5	**West Palm Beach–Boca Raton–Delray Beach, FL** Palm Beach County	576,863	859,800	+49.0
Tyler, TX Smith County	128,366	156,630	+22.0	**Wheeling, WV–OH** Marshall and Ohio Counties, WV; Belmont County, OH	185,566	176,740	− 4.8
Utica–Rome, NY Herkimer and Oneida Counties	320,180	315,320	− 1.5	**Wichita, KS** Butler, Harvey, and Sedgwick Counties	441,844	482,570	+ 9.2
Vallejo–Fairfield–Napa, CA* Napa and Solano Counties	334,402	429,650	+28.5				
Vancouver, WA* Clark County	192,227	221,480	+15.2	**Wichita Falls, TX** Wichita County	121,082	128,700	+ 6.3
Victoria, TX Victoria County	68,807	77,760	+13.0	**Williamsport, PA** Lycoming County	118,416	116,650	− 1.5
Vineland–Millville–Bridgeton, NJ* Cumberland County	132,866	137,270	+ 3.3	**Wilmington, DE–NJ–MD*** New Castle County, DE; Salem County, NJ; Cecil County, MD	523,221	564,130	+ 7.8
Visalia–Tulare–Porterville, CA Tulare County	245,738	296,530	+20.7	**Wilmington, NC** New Hanover County	103,471	120,040	+16.0
Waco, TX McLennan County	170,755	192,500	+12.7	**Worcester, MA** Parts of Worcester County	402,918	423,740	+ 5.2
Washington, DC–MD–VA District of Columbia; Calvert, Charles, Frederick, Montgomery, and Prince Georges Counties, MD; Alexandria, Fairfax, Falls Church, Manassas, and Manassas Park Cities, VA; Arlington, Fairfax, Loudoun, Prince William, and Stafford Counties, VA	3,250,822	3,739,240	+15.0	**Yakima, WA** Yakima County	172,508	184,780	+ 7.1
				York, PA Adams and York Counties	381,255	407,240	+ 6.8
				Youngstown–Warren, OH Mahoning and Trumbull Counties	531,350	509,300	− 4.1
				Yuba City, CA Sutter and Yuba Counties	101,979	116,560	+14.3

Source: U.S. Bureau of the Census; Woods & Poole Economics, Inc., population forecasts.

*An asterisk identifies a Primary Metropolitan Statistical Area.

The list above includes Metropolitan Statistical Areas and Primary Metropolitan Statistical Areas as defined by the Office of Management and Budget as of January 1989.

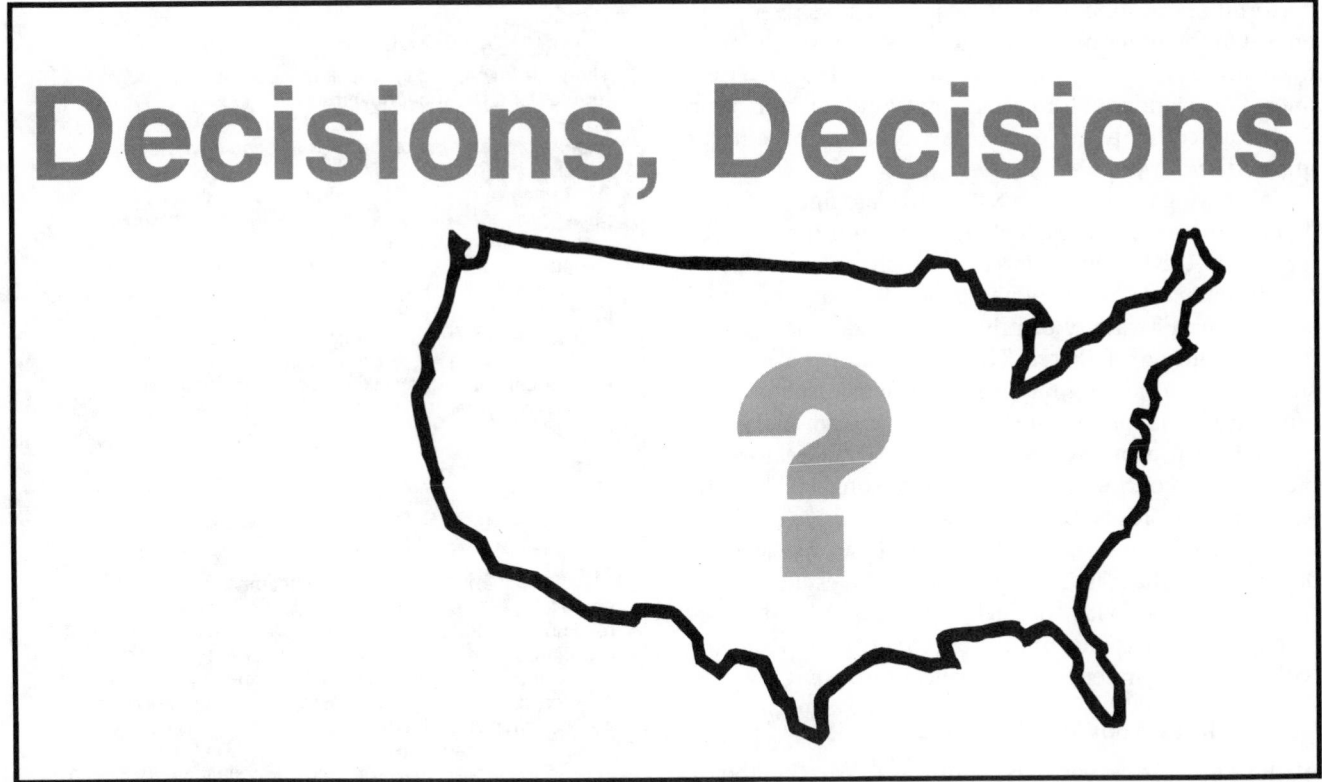

Decisions, Decisions

Seventeen years ago a group of futurists, academics, and government scientists came together at a hotel in northern Virginia for a conference sponsored by the U.S. Environmental Protection Agency. Their purpose was to discover just what should be meant by "Quality of Life."

The players quickly split into three distinct groups over the issue. The first held that defining quality of life for all people at all times wasn't just unfair, it was impossible and shouldn't be tried at all. The second held that it could be done–but shouldn't–because measuring a touchy thing like quality of life makes places unwilling competitors of one another and often leads to wrong conclusions. The third group held that judging local liveability could be done as long as you make clear what your statistical yardsticks are and go on to use them consistently.

Although the first and second positions may indeed be valid, *Places Rated Almanac* sides with the third.

Rating Places: One Way

This is a book of current statistics about metropolitan America. Certainly, it is a more objective source of information about metropolitan life than the hearsay opinions that people share at a dinner party, a rest stop on the interstate, or an airport bar. Each of the 333 metro areas is rated by nine factors that anyone contemplating a geographic move would think were highly important.

- The **Costs of Living** chapter looks at household incomes and taxes, and it also measures the costs of important items such as housing, food, health care, and college tuition.
- **Jobs** evaluates prospects for local employment growth in nine basic areas, including manufacturing, trade, services, finance, and government.
- A metro area's **Crime** rating is measured by the average annual number of violent and property crimes per 100,000 people over the past five years.
- The supply of general health care facilities and practitioners, plus available special options, forms the basis for a metro area's **Health Care** rating.
- **Transportation** is rated by local commuting time, public transit, and the diverse inter-city travel options by air, rail, and interstate highway.
- Each metro area's public school systems and private school alternatives, as well as their local colleges and universities, produce an **Education** rating.
- The chapter on **The Arts** compares cultural assets, among them museums and public libraries, opera companies and symphony orchestras.
- **Recreation** also rates assets, from good restaurants to public golf courses, zoos, professional sports, inland lakes, and national parks acreage.
- **Climate** is rated on mildness; that is, how close temperatures remain to 65 degrees Fahrenheit throughout the year.

Some readers may fault *Places Rated's* choice of criteria. Admittedly, our yardsticks for health care, public transportation, options for higher education, and performing arts amenities all favor big places over small ones. On the other hand, our methods for scoring safety from crime and living costs favor smaller places over big ones. Our standards for climate and outdoor recreation assets are certainly not everyone's. But they have nothing to do with population size.

We have gathered the most up-to-date figures for all 333 metro areas. In most instances, the information is as fresh as 1989. Our sources, which we document throughout this book, come from federal and state agencies and a variety of private organizations.

This edition of *Places Rated Almanac* is as much a snapshot of a moving target as its predecessors. Metro areas are dynamic and just don't sit still for statistical portraits. An economic rebound in many Great Lakes metro areas continues to draw native sons and daughters back from Texas. Likewise, the costs of living in New Jersey may become as moderate as they once were a decade ago if the state's hyper-inflated real estate market should collapse. With so much in life that is unpredictable, you'd be wise to supplement *Places Rated Almanac* with your own independent verification.

Rating Places: Your Way

At the end of this book, in "Putting It All Together," costs of living, climate, crime, health care, transportation, education, the arts, recreation, and jobs get equal weight when identifying metro areas with across-the-board strengths.

You may not agree with this scoring system. You may give more weight to forecasted job growth than to a relative lack of crime or air pollution. For you, a place where living costs are least may be much more important than an ocean coastline, an abundance of medical specialists, or a busy performing arts calendar. To identify which factors are more important and which factors are less, you may want to take stock of your preferences.

YOUR PREFERENCE INVENTORY

The following Preference Inventory has 72 pairs of statements. For each pair, decide which statement is more important to you when judging a liveable place.

> ### RELOCATION RESOURCES
> There are two basic impressions about places you can form at long distance; how they slick themselves up for presentation to the outside world, and what's really important every day of the year to people who actually live there.
>
> Writing to chambers of commerce for their "newcomer's pack" produces a collection of promotional brochures, maps, business statistics, cost-of-living data, and events calendars (it may also trigger mail and telephone calls from real-estate brokers). The annual *World Wide Chamber of Commerce Directory* lists the chamber of commerce name, address, and telephone number, as well as the name of the chamber's executive or other contact person, for over 4,000 locations in the United States. It is available in libraries, or order it for $24.00 (price includes handling and shipping) from
>
> *World Wide Chamber of Commerce Directory*
> P.O. Box 1029
> Loveland, CO 80539
> (303) 663-3231
>
> An invaluable addition to the chamber's picture is a short-term subscription to the local newspaper. After reading a month's worth, you can get an excellent idea of consumer prices, political issues, and other matters on the minds of residents. For the name, address, telephone number, monthly subscription cost, special features, and politics (typically independent) of each of the country's 1,645 daily newspapers, the best source is Editor & Publisher's *International Yearbook*. For similar information on 6,798 weekly newspapers (often the only publication covering suburban areas), the *IMS Directory of Publications* is an alternative source.

Even if both statements are equally important or neither is important, select one anyway. If you can't decide quickly, pass up the item but return to it after you complete the rest of the inventory.

Don't worry about being consistent. The paired statements aren't repeated. There aren't any right or wrong answers, only those that are best for you. Although the inventory takes about 20 minutes to finish, there is no time limit. Before you start, you might want to photocopy the inventory and ask your spouse or a friend to take it independently. Comparing your preference inventory with another person's can be an interesting exercise.

Directions

For each numbered item, decide which of two statements is more important to you when choosing a place to live. Mark the box next to that statement. Be sure to make a choice for all items.

1. I. ☐ The number of days over 90 degrees,
   or
   A. ☐ Average property taxes.

2. C. ☐ The number of murders,
   or
   F. ☐ The size of public school districts.

3. D. ☐ The supply of medical specialists,
   or
   E. ☐ Supply of local public transit.

4. G. ☐ New books added in local libraries,
   or
   I. ☐ Local elevation, wind speed, and humidity.

5. A. ☐ The cost of food and clothing,
    or
    E. ☐ How long it takes to commute to work.

6. G. ☐ Libraries and museums,
    or
    H. ☐ Local college sports.

7. D. ☐ Air pollution throughout the year,
    or
    I. ☐ Annual amount of rain and snow.

8. A. ☐ The price of houses,
    or
    C. ☐ Local property crime rates.

9. B. ☐ Forecasted job growth,
    or
    F. ☐ The pupil/teacher ratio in public schools.

10. G. ☐ Museums and repertory theatres,
    or
    C. ☐ The number of auto thefts in a year.

11. H. ☐ The number of public golf courses,
    or
    E. ☐ Freeway traffic congestion.

12. D. ☐ Local specialized medical care,
    or
    G. ☐ Fine-arts broadcasting.

13. G. ☐ Libraries and museums,
    or
    A. ☐ The cost of living.

14. A. ☐ The cost of food and clothing,
    or
    B. ☐ The outlook for employment growth.

15. D. ☐ Air pollution levels,
    or
    F. ☐ The size of public school districts.

16. G. ☐ Fine-arts radio and TV broadcasting,
    or
    B. ☐ Job opportunities in the service sector.

17. B. ☐ Local threat of unemployment,
    or
    I. ☐ Annual number of clear and cloudy days.

18. H. ☐ Movie theatres and good restaurants,
    or
    F. ☐ Variety of public and private colleges.

19. E. ☐ The supply of public transit,
    or
    A. ☐ Median prices of homes.

20. A. ☐ State income tax and sales tax bite,
    or
    D. ☐ Medical schools and teaching hospitals.

21. A. ☐ The cost of health care,
    or
    H. ☐ The supply of public golf courses.

22. G. ☐ Fine-arts radio and TV broadcasting,
    or
    E. ☐ Airlines and interstate highways.

23. D. ☐ Supply of family medical practitioners,
    or
    H. ☐ Good restaurants and movie theatres.

24. C. ☐ The violent crime rate,
    or
    I. ☐ Annual amounts of rain and snow.

25. F. ☐ Pupil/teacher ratio in public schools,
    or
    I. ☐ Annual number of clear and cloudy days.

26. H. ☐ Local professional sports teams,
    or
    C. ☐ Number of robberies and assaults.

27. D. ☐ Air pollution,
    or
    C. ☐ Number of burglaries during the year.

28. F. ☐ Local support of public schools,
    or
    G. ☐ Dance companies and repertory theatres.

29. H. ☐ Nearby water recreation,
    or
    B. ☐ Number of new manufacturing jobs by 1995.

30. H. ☐ Nearby national parks and forests,
    or
    I. ☐ Number of stormy days during the year.

31. B. ☐ The mix of white- and blue-collar jobs,
    or
    C. ☐ Number of robberies in a year.

32. E. ☐ Airlines serving the local airport,
    or
    C. ☐ Number of auto thefts in a year.

33. E. ☐ Buses, subways, and commuter railroads,
    or
    F. ☐ Local colleges and universities.

34. A. ☐ State income and sales tax bite,
    or
    D. ☐ General hospitals and family doctors.

35. F. ☐ Dollars/student in the public schools,
    or
    A. ☐ Costs for utilities and property taxes.

36. E. ☐ Interstate highways and airline service,
    or
    I. ☐ How cold the winters are.

37. D. ☐ Supply of specialized doctors,
    or
    I. ☐ Number of annual rainy and snowy days.

38. C. ☐ Local auto thefts and burglaries,
    or
    A. ☐ Local household income and taxes.

39. G. ☐ Fine-arts radio and TV broadcasting,
    or
    H. ☐ Zoos and family amusement parks.

40. C. ☐ Annual muggings per capita,
    or
    F. ☐ Pupil/teacher ratio in public schools.

41. B. ☐ Outlook for job growth,
    or
    E. ☐ Average daily commuting time.

42. I. ☐ Seasonal temperature variation,
    or
    A. ☐ Typical property taxes.

43. D. ☐ Medical schools and teaching hospitals,
    or
    G. ☐ Operas and symphony orchestras.

44. H. ☐ Opportunities for pari-mutuel wagering,
    or
    E. ☐ Freeway traffic congestion.

45. B. ☐ Mix of white- and blue-collar jobs,
    or
    F. ☐ Alternatives to public schools.

46. I. ☐ Seasonal temperature variation,
    or
    B. ☐ Forecasted growth of employment.

47. C. ☐ Auto thefts, muggings, and shootings,
    or
    I. ☐ Annual number of freezing days.

48. A. ☐ Cost of heating a home,
    or
    F. ☐ Variety of private K–12 schools.

49. B. ☐ Expected white-collar job growth,
    or
    C. ☐ Annual property crime rate.

50. B. ☐ The number of new jobs created by 1995,
    or
    A. ☐ Annual state income and sales tax bite.

51. G. ☐ Classical music broadcasting,
    or
    E. ☐ Freeway traffic congestion.

52. D. ☐ Specialized medical care,
    or
    H. ☐ Nearby state parks and forests.

53. F. ☐ Variety of private K–12 schools,
    or
    I. ☐ Local wind speed and humidity.

54. A. ☐ The cost of food and clothing,
    or
    B. ☐ Employment in the service industries.

55. I. ☐ Number of days over 90 degrees,
    or
    E. ☐ Supply of public transit.

56. H. ☐ Golf, bowling, movies, and eating out,
    or
    F. ☐ Variety of public and private colleges.

57. G. ☐ The number of books in public libraries,
    or
    B. ☐ The threat of unemployment.

58. H. ☐ Professional sports home teams,
    or
    I. ☐ Annual amounts of rain and snow.

59. G. ☐ Operas and symphonies,
    or
    I. ☐ How cold the winters are.

60. A. ☐ Median price of homes,
    or
    G. ☐ Local performing arts bookings.

61. C. ☐ The violent crime rate,
    or
    G. ☐ Variety of performing arts.

62. C. ☐ Burglaries and auto thefts,
    or
    D. ☐ Specialized medical care.

63. B. ☐ Job outlook from now to the year 1995,
    or
    E. ☐ Freeway traffic congestion.

64. C. ☐ The property crime rate,
    or
    H. ☐ Nearby national parks and forests.

65. D. ☐ Supply of medical specialists,
    or
    B. ☐ Forecast for white-collar job growth.

66. F. ☐ Higher education opportunities,
    or
    G. ☐ Number of public libraries.

67. E. ☐ Access to interstate highways,
    or
    F. ☐ Private alternatives to public schools.

68. H. ☐ Movie theatres and good restaurants,
    or
    A. ☐ The cost of food and clothing.

69. D. ☐ Local air pollution levels,
    or
    F. ☐ Variety of public school districts.

70. E. ☐ Airlines serving the area,
    or
    C. ☐ Burglaries and auto thefts there.

71. D. ☐ Supply of doctors and hospitals,
    or
    E. ☐ Supply of public transit.

72. D. ☐ Variety of specialized medical care,
    or
    B. ☐ Prospects for white-collar job growth.

Source: Adapted from ''The Prospering Test,'' courtesy Thomas F. Bowman, Ph.D; George Giuliani, Ph. D; and M. Ronald Minge, Ph.D.

Plotting Your Preference Profile

It is important that you make a choice for each of the 72 items. Have you left any unchecked? If not, you're ready to draw your Preference Profile.

First Step. Count all the marks you've made in the boxes next to the letter A. Then enter the number of "A" statements at the top of your Preference Profile. In the same way, count the number of statements for each of the other letters. Enter their totals in their respective places at the top of your Preference Profile.

Second Step. Now plot your totals on the blank chart. Place a dot on the appropriate line for each of the numbers and connect the dots to form a line graph of your results (see the sample Preference Profile).

Analyzing Your Preference Profile

Each of the factors in your Preference Profile—the costs of living, climate, crime, health care, transportation, education, the arts, recreation, and jobs—is not only a big concern when choosing a place to live; it also has a complete chapter in this book. The purpose of the Preference Inventory is to help you decide the relative importance of each of the chapters to you personally.

If your scores are high for one or two of these factors, you may want to give extra attention to the chapters devoted to them. Likewise, if your scores are low for any of the nine, you may not need to give as much consideration to them as you would the ones with high scores. Bear in mind that the inventory *orders* your preferences in a hierarchy, that each of the factors has some importance to you, and that none should be completely ignored.

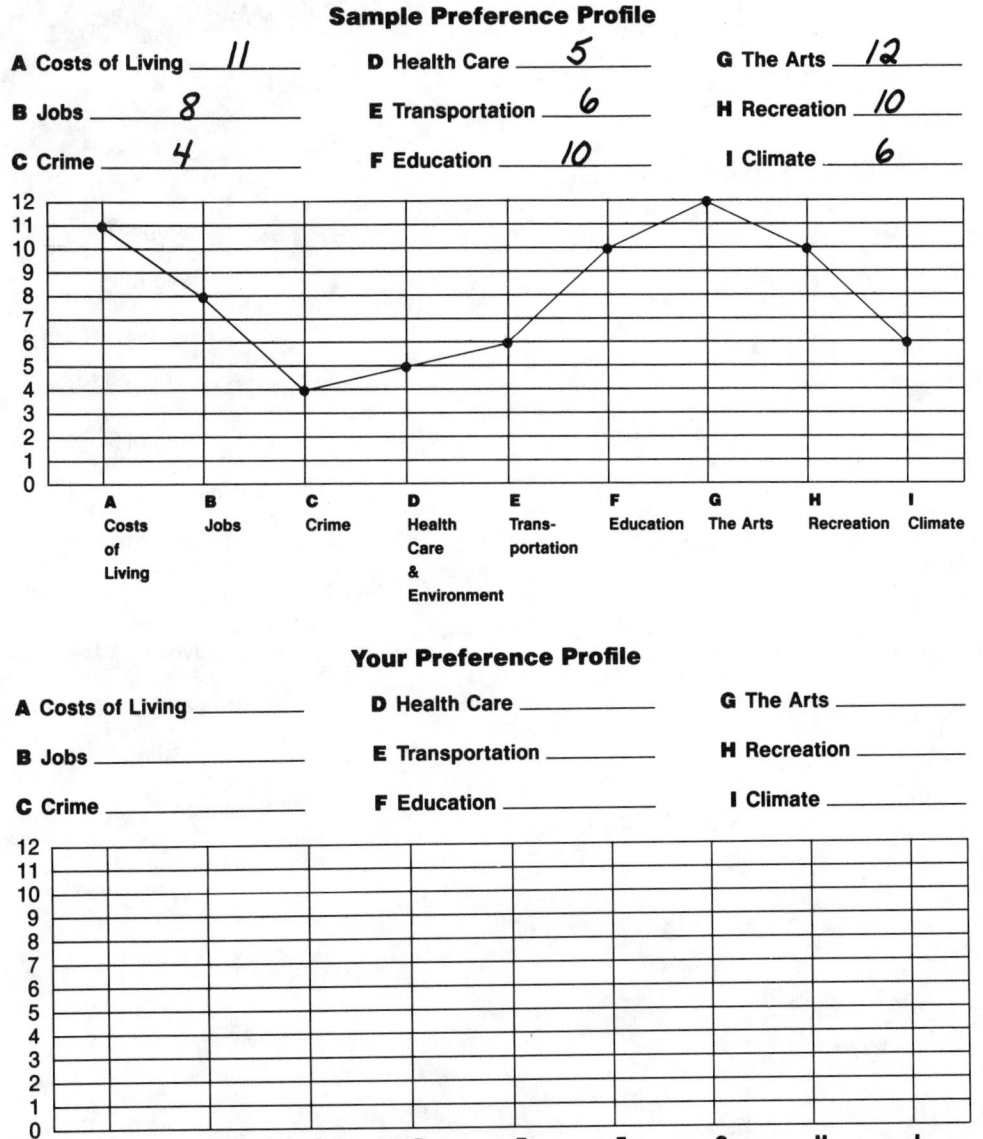

Sample Preference Profile

A Costs of Living __11__   D Health Care __5__   G The Arts __12__

B Jobs __8__   E Transportation __6__   H Recreation __10__

C Crime __4__   F Education __10__   I Climate __6__

Your Preference Profile

A Costs of Living _____   D Health Care _____   G The Arts _____

B Jobs _____   E Transportation _____   H Recreation _____

C Crime _____   F Education _____   I Climate _____

Costs of Living

In the detached view of some economists, we're all living resources, continually searching for our highest valued use. We will switch jobs readily if the money is right. We'll change careers, too, if the prospects are promising. And we may risk these changes even if it means packing up and moving far away.

We'll also flee living costs that have risen so high we can no longer afford them. Metro areas may attract people because of expanding job opportunities, but they also draw people because local costs of living are low enough to seem like bargains to many migrating people.

This is nothing new. For centuries, Americans have moved from rich places, where the benefits of high incomes are made empty by even higher costs of living, to low-income places, where cheap land and no taxes more than made up for the liabilities of paltry incomes.

"Money's no problem," an accountant will tell you. "Lack of money . . . now *that's* a problem." As is the case for most people, your own short-term economic frets probably center on the price of hamburger, jeans, gasoline, or haircuts. Over the long run, your concerns may focus on tax bites and boosting your household's income at least to the level where it can provide basic day-to-day necessities.

SCRAPING BY ON $45,144 A YEAR

Do average household incomes in different parts of the country indicate local living costs? For the most part, they do. According to a recent U.S. Labor Department report, two-thirds of the difference in personal incomes between, say, Baltimore and San Francisco reflects their different costs of living; the other third reflects their different employers, worker skills, and prevailing wages.

Households aren't always made up of families. According to the latest Census Bureau survey on living arrangements, one-quarter of all households are composed either of one person or of several people unrelated to one another (including two million POSSLQs—Persons of Opposite Sex Sharing Living Quarters). There are 12 million single-parent households with at least one child present, and two million of them are headed by men. The rest of the households comprise married couples, some with children, some childless, and some whose children have scattered from the nest.

The average household income for all U.S. metro areas is $45,144 a year, according to forecasts by the Washington, DC-based firm of Woods & Poole Economics, Inc. These incomes range from $99,171 in Stamford,

CT, to $16,317 in Laredo, in historically poor southmost Texas.

TAXES: ONE OF LIFE'S CERTAINTIES

In a calendar year, May 5 marks the mythical Tax Freedom Day on which we stop handing over all of our earnings to federal, state, and local tax collectors and start pocketing that money for ourselves. Looking at it another way, we spend two hours and 48 minutes of every eight-hour working day earning enough money to pay taxes, according to the District of Columbia-based Tax Foundation. That amounts to $28 a day for each employed person.

No matter where you live, Social Security taxes hit you with the same impact. So can federal personal income taxes. But state and local taxes differ tremendously. To determine the relative tax bite among metro areas, *Places Rated* focuses on the two most common levies: state personal income taxes and state sales taxes. Based on a metro area's average household income, state incomes are estimated for a two-paycheck couple with two children, filing either a joint or a combined separate return (whichever would result in the smaller amount of taxes owed in each state), after taking typical exemptions and deductions. The taxes that a family pays throughout the year on retail purchases are also based on the household's average income, using Internal Revenue Service estimates.

As a percentage of average household incomes, state income and sales taxes take some of the biggest bites from household incomes in the District of Columbia, Michigan, Minnesota, New York, Oregon, Utah, and Wisconsin. In New Mexico, Texas, and Wyoming, the bite is smallest. And in Alaska and New Hampshire, there is no bite at all. (See the tables on page 23.)

SINGLE-FAMILY HOMES: AFFORDING THE AMERICAN DREAM

The United States is tilting southwest in population growth, and one might think that the shift would be accompanied by dramatically inflated home prices in that direction. In fact, some of the highest average prices estimated for 1989 are found in places where houses have always been expensive—Honolulu, New York City (and its suburbs in Connecticut and New Jersey), and the District of Columbia and its environs. They are also found in many of California's metro areas, where construction had managed to keep up with demand—at least until land prices began skyrocketing in Orange County 15 years ago, a phenomenon that has spread as far north as Sacramento. (See the tables on this page.)

Stories of panic home buying in southern California received national attention in 1988. A man in Redondo Beach bought a stucco box on a small lot for $200,000 and sold it five years later for $350,000; a blueprinted house in one of the many new developments in River-

Home Ownership Costs in the Metro Areas
Highest Costs

Metro Area	Costs (U.S. Average=100)
Stamford, CT	407
Norwalk, CT	343
San Francisco, CA	266
Honolulu, HI	258
Anaheim–Santa Ana, CA	255
San Jose, CA	246
Danbury, CT	237
Bergen–Passaic, NJ	225
Los Angeles–Long Beach, CA	219
Newark, NJ	219
Oakland, CA	218

Source: Places Rated Partnership estimates, 1989.

Home ownership costs include mortgage payments, property taxes, and utilities.

Home Ownership Costs in the Metro Areas
Lowest Costs

Metro Area	Costs (U.S. Average =100)
McAllen–Edinburg–Mission, TX	43
Peoria, IL	46
Dothan, AL	48
Florence, AL	51
Sherman–Denison, TX	51
Waco, TX	51
Danville, VA	52
Laredo, TX	52
Pine Bluff, AR	52
Brownsville–Harlingen, TX	53

Source: Places Rated Partnership estimates, 1989.

side County sold out of a builder's trailer for $245,000 and four months later, still unbuilt, went for $285,000.

House price inflation stories are still being traded, but now the stories come from northern New Jersey, southern Connecticut, the Baltimore–Washington beltway, and even rural Vermont and New Hampshire. In 1989, according to the National Association of Realtors, an existing single-family house in the United States carried a median price tag of $91,600, but any family looking for a decent detached single-family home within a large metro area had better think in terms of six figures, 20 percent down, and two paychecks to make the American Dream happen. This isn't to say that a $200,000 house can't be bought for $75,000. It can, in the smaller metro areas of Illinois, Arkansas, Texas, and Alabama. Location, location, and location are still the three major factors that influence house prices, as the shopworn real estate broker's rule goes.

PROPERTY TAXES: BUYING BACK YOUR OWN HOME

Critics of high property taxes during the late 1970s likened them to a ransom that homeowners were forced to pay to keep their homes off the local tax assessor's auction block. Using this analogy, homeowners in Islip, NY, buy their homes back from the town every 22 years, since the effective tax rate (a tax on the home's full value) is 4.63 percent. Down in Mobile County, AL, on the other hand, the "ransom period" is 526 years bcause of

House Property Tax Bills
Lowest

Metro Area	Tax Bill
Monroe, LA	$128
Alexandria, LA	129
Baton Rouge, LA	134
Shreveport, LA	138
Lake Charles, LA	139
Houma–Thibodaux, LA	142
New Orleans, LA	157
Lafayette, LA	158
Dothan, AL	170
Florence, AL	181
Gadsden, AL	199
Mobile, AL	199

House Property Tax Bills
Highest

Metro Area	Tax Bill
Stamford, CT	$5,443
Bergen–Passaic, NJ	4,915
Newark, NJ	4,770
Norwalk, CT	4,581
Middlesex–Somerset–Hunterdon, NJ	3,984
Monmouth–Ocean, NJ	3,984
New York, NY	3,761
Trenton, NJ	3,418
Danbury, CT	3,165
Nassau–Suffolk, NY	3,117
Orange County, NY	2,964

Source: Places Rated estimates based on average market values multiplied by each state's average effective property tax rate as reported by the Advisory Commission on Intergovernmental Relations, Significant Features of Fiscal Federalism, 1989.

Smallest Bite

Metro Area	Tax Percentage
Las Cruces, NM	0.62%
Midland, TX	0.63
Houston, TX	0.67
Dallas, TX	0.68
Wichita Falls, TX	0.69
Beaumont–Port Arthur, TX	0.70
Casper, WY	0.70
Cheyenne, WY	0.70
Fort Worth–Arlington, TX	0.70
Lafayette, LA	0.70

Biggest Bite

Metro Area	Tax Percentage
Washington, DC–MD–VA	5.66%
Honolulu, HI	5.38
Nassau–Suffolk, NY	5.18
Minneapolis–St. Paul, MN–WI	5.08
Rochester, MN	5.04
Provo–Orem, UT	4.85
Milwaukee, WI	4.83
Salt Lake City–Ogden, UT	4.82
Ann Arbor, MI	4.70
Portland, OR	4.70

Source: Derived from Advisory Commission on Intergovernmental Relations, "Tax Burdens for Families Residing in the Largest Cities in Each State," 1989.

an extremely low effective rate of 0.19 percent. The difference in these figures illustrates the wide variation in property taxes around the country. (See the tables above.)

Locally, too, property taxes can vary enormously and can be madly confusing to homeowners. In California, two houses on the same block with identical prices and physical characteristics can have substantially different, yet legally impeccable, tax bills if one of them was sold before the approval of Proposition 13 and the other after. In Texas, a home's value can be assessed at different levels at different times of the year by different assessors.

Although residential property taxes aren't collected by metro areas (that is done by more than 13,500 cities, townships, counties, school districts, sanitary districts, hospital districts, and other special districts), statewide average property tax rates are useful in estimating local property tax bills. Clearly, homeowners in Connecticut, New Jersey, and New York have good reason for envying their counterparts in Alabama and Louisiana.

PAYING FOR POWER

Household electric bills around the country vary widely in dollar amounts, for several reasons. Customer density, distance from oil and coal fuel sources, age of the power plant, and the type and size of equipment used in generating electricity all play a part in the charges to consumers. Who owns the company, however, may be the biggest factor in determining the amount of your bill.

The Energy Department's latest nationwide price comparison of electricity shows that, in general, publicly owned (municipal) electric power companies charge much lower rates than their larger, privately owned counterparts.

In communities of 2,500 or more, the ten lowest bills for 750 kilowatt-hours of monthly service range from $160 (Cowlitz [WA] County Public Utilities) to $249 (City of Ilion [NY]). In contrast, the ten highest bills for the same service are mailed out by such privately owned giants as San Diego Gas & Electric ($1,144) and Consolidated Edison of New York ($926). See the tables below for specifics.

Highest Annual Electric Bills

Electric Company	Average Annual Bill
1. San Diego Gas & Electric (California)	$1,144
2. Kauai (Hawaii) Citizens Utilities	1,101
3. Hawaii Electric Light Company	1,025
4. Fitchburg (Massachusetts) Gas & Electric	1,003
5. Long Island (New York) Lighting Company	992
6. Michigan Power	979
7. Maui (Hawaii) Electric Company, Ltd.	955
8. Bethel (Alaska) Utilities Corporation	939
9. CP (California) National Corporation	928
10. Consolidated Edison of New York	926

Lowest Annual Electric Bills

Electric Company	Average Annual Bill
1. Cowlitz (Washington) County Utilities	$160
2. Douglas (Washington) County Utilities	165
3. Chelan (Washington) County Utilities	172
4. Grant (Washington) County Utilities	204
5. City of Spencerport (New York)	205
6. City of Plattsburgh (New York)	206
7. Village of Akron (New York)	232
8. City of Wellsville (New York)	233
9. City of Westfield (New York)	248
10. City of Ilion (New York)	249

Source: Department of Energy, Typical Electric Bills, 1989.

THE HIGH COST OF COLLEGE

Some say that in the future white-collar workplace, only those who have college degrees will get the nod for new slots in management training, or even entry-level jobs behind the counter or in the mail room. But coming up with four years of tuition and fees to help their children launch a career is breaking a lot of middle-income families. To go away to college and make it through in standard time, most students need at least two out of these three sources of money (aside from parental largesse): a scholarship, a student loan, and a part-time job. (See the adjacent table for basic charges at public colleges.)

The best way to cut costs at the very start is to do some sharp thinking when choosing a college. If you are planning on college, consider your options. You can:

- Live at home, enroll in a low-cost two-year college that offers courses good toward a bachelor's degree, and then transfer to a local four-year state college for your junior and senior years. This is the least expensive way to get a college education.
- Enroll in a public four-year college or university in your home state. The tuition will definitely be higher than that of a two-year college. And if you decide to live on campus, it will cost you $3,000 more per year than attending college while living at home.
- Enroll in a public college or university outside your home state. This will mean paying stiff tuition charges. But establishing legal residency could save you a significant amount. Tuitions in California public colleges, for example, are one-fifth what you'd pay in several northeastern states. See the table "Basic Yearly Student Charges in Public Colleges by State."
- Register at a private college or university. This is the most expensive option, even if you live at home.

Basic Yearly Student Charges in Public Colleges by State

	Tuition	Room	Board	Total
U.S. Average	$1,414	$1,373	$1,471	$4,208
1. Arkansas	931	784	1,132	2,847
2. Oklahoma	757	944	1,285	2,986
3. North Carolina	818	1,131	1,163	3,112
4. North Dakota	1,198	682	1,312	3,192
5. Kentucky	1,152	889	1,294	3,335
6. Wyoming	778	1,088	1,471	3,337
7. Nebraska	1,292	870	1,239	3,401
8. Tennessee	1,133	1,029	1,274	3,436
9. Missouri	1,277	1,162	1,015	3,454
10. Alabama	1,275	1,043	1,142	3,460
11. South Dakota	1,409	798	1,261	3,468
12. Delaware	906	1,120	1,471	3,497
13. Iowa	1,385	1,008	1,117	3,510
14. Kansas	1,271	1,143	1,171	3,585
15. Nevada	988	1,302	1,299	3,589
16. Louisiana	1,341	1,051	1,242	3,634
17. Wisconsin	1,271	1,126	1,260	3,657
18. Georgia	1,369	959	1,360	3,688
19. New Mexico	915	1,121	1,661	3,697
20. Idaho	1,036	846	1,955	3,837
21. Arizona	1,136	1,361	1,402	3,899
22. Mississippi	1,603	1,050	1,273	3,926
23. Texas	885	1,443	1,601	3,929
24. Florida	1,055	1,254	1,639	3,948
25. Utah	1,159	1,638	1,210	4,007
26. Washington	1,339	1,268	1,400	4,007
27. Oregon	1,296	1,052	1,669	4,017
28. Minnesota	1,814	1,113	1,132	4,059
29. Alaska	975	1,429	1,658	4,062
30. West Virginia	1,003	1,627	1,550	4,180
31. Montana	1,205	1,205	1,793	4,203
32. South Carolina	1,733	1,105	1,455	4,293
33. Massachusetts	1,388	1,294	1,615	4,297
34. Hawaii	972	1,307	2,068	4,347
35. Connecticut	1,527	1,370	1,491	4,388
36. Colorado	1,482	1,373	1,662	4,517
37. Illinois	1,708	1,339	1,473	4,520
38. New Hampshire	2,190	1,424	966	4,580
39. Maine	1,561	1,476	1,573	4,610
40. New York	1,431	1,642	1,713	4,786
41. Michigan	1,877	1,212	1,731	4,820
42. Indiana	1,627	1,890	1,370	4,887
43. Ohio	1,982	1,408	1,517	4,907
44. New Jersey	1,861	1,758	1,366	4,985
45. Virginia	2,070	1,482	1,503	5,055
46. Pennsylvania	2,496	1,408	1,305	5,209
47. California	1,031	1,986	2,281	5,298
48. Maryland	1,682	1,889	1,842	5,413
49. Rhode Island	1,845	1,803	1,838	5,486
50. Vermont	2,942	1,988	1,498	6,428

Source: National Center for Education Statistics, unpublished data, 1989.

Rankings: Costs of Living

To arrive at a score for a metro area's costs of living, four factors are indexed against the United States average of 100: (1) housing; (2) food; (3) transportation; and (4) health care.

Places that receive tie scores are given the same rank and are listed alphabetically.

Metro Areas from Best to Worst

Places Rated Rank	Places Rated Score	Places Rated Rank	Places Rated Score	Places Rated Rank	Places Rated Score
1. Pine Bluff, AR	7,351	4. Danville, VA	7,437	6. McAllen–Edinburg–Mission, TX	7,524
2. Laredo, TX	7,374	5. Fort Smith, AR–OK	7,450	7. Florence, AL	7,578
3. Canton, OH	7,434				

Places Rated Rank	Places Rated Score	Places Rated Rank	Places Rated Score	Places Rated Rank	Places Rated Score	Places Rated Rank	Places Rated Score
8. Lawton, OK	7,603	67. Jackson, MI	8,218	125. Melbourne–Titusville–Palm Bay, FL	8,601		
9. Anniston, AL	7,608	68. Terre Haute, IN	8,222				
10. Pascagoula, MS	7,641	69. Daytona Beach, FL	8,226				
		70. Provo–Orem, UT	8,240	126. Grand Forks, ND	8,625		
11. Clarksville–Hopkinsville, TN–KY	7,685			127. Lawrence, KS	8,632		
12. Dothan, AL	7,717	71. Davenport–Rock Island–Moline, IA–IL	8,244	128. Las Cruces, NM	8,648		
13. Sherman–Denison, TX	7,721	72. Medford, OR	8,249	129. Tyler, TX	8,666		
14. Salem, OR	7,758	73. South Bend–Mishawaka, IN	8,256	130. San Antonio, TX	8,667		
15. Brownsville–Harlingen, TX	7,773	74. Richland–Kennewick–Pasco, WA	8,264	131. La Crosse, WI	8,682		
16. Anderson, SC	7,787	75. Dubuque, IA	8,269	132. Casper, WY	8,686		
17. Waterloo–Cedar Falls, IA	7,794			133. Glens Falls, NY	8,697		
18. Steubenville–Weirton, OH–WV	7,807	76. Erie, PA	8,274	134. Des Moines, IA	8,698		
19. Columbus, GA–AL	7,825	77. Akron, OH	8,276	135. Fort Wayne, IN	8,703		
20. Waco, TX	7,831	78. San Angelo, TX	8,279				
		78. Macon–Warner Robins, GA	8,279	136. Gary–Hammond, IN	8,705		
21. Muncie, IN	7,835	80. Kokomo, IN	8,286	137. Fayetteville, NC	8,708		
21. Pueblo, CO	7,835			137. Lakeland–Winter Haven, FL	8,708		
23. Longview–Marshall, TX	7,836	81. Tulsa, OK	8,290	139. Toledo, OH	8,711		
24. Enid, OK	7,837	82. Niagara Falls, NY	8,297	140. Montgomery, AL	8,743		
25. Oklahoma City, OK	7,839	83. Vancouver, WA	8,320				
		84. Brazoria, TX	8,323	141. Beaumont–Port Arthur, TX	8,749		
26. Lima, OH	7,841	85. Abilene, TX	8,333	142. Hickory, NC	8,759		
27. Altoona, PA	7,851			143. Lorain–Elyria, OH	8,762		
28. Sioux City, IA–NE	7,858	86. Houma–Thibodaux, LA	8,335	144. Elkhart–Goshen, IN	8,763		
29. Youngstown–Warren, OH	7,865	87. Mobile, AL	8,337	145. New Orleans, LA	8,770		
30. Peoria, IL	7,891	88. Wichita, KS	8,341				
		89. Louisville, KY–IN	8,383	146. Grand Rapids, MI	8,771		
31. Fayetteville–Springdale, AR	7,894	90. Appleton–Oshkosh–Neenah, WI	8,386	146. Lake Charles, LA	8,771		
32. Sharon, PA	7,917			148. Janesville–Beloit, WI	8,784		
33. Gadsden, AL	7,923	91. Hamilton–Middletown, OH	8,406	149. Eau Claire, WI	8,786		
34. Beaver County, PA	7,929	92. Chattanooga, TN–GA	8,416	150. Knoxville, TN	8,789		
35. Amarillo, TX	7,960	93. Scranton–Wilkes-Barre, PA	8,424				
		94. Greenville–Spartanburg, SC	8,431	151. Fort Walton Beach, FL	8,791		
36. Decatur, IL	7,965	95. Colorado Springs, CO	8,441	152. Fargo–Moorhead, ND–MN	8,804		
37. Wheeling, WV–OH	7,967			153. Columbia, MO	8,817		
38. Greeley, CO	7,971	95. Saginaw–Bay City–Midland, MI	8,441	154. Flint, MI	8,825		
39. Spokane, WA	7,975	97. Jacksonville, NC	8,448	155. Vineland–Millville–Bridgeton, NJ	8,832		
40. Albany, GA	7,981	98. Eugene–Springfield, OR	8,452				
		98. Huntington–Ashland, WV–KY–OH	8,452	156. Evansville, IN–KY	8,850		
41. Lynchburg, VA	7,988	98. Springfield, MO	8,452	157. Pittsburgh, PA	8,874		
42. Williamsport, PA	8,011			158. Panama City, FL	8,880		
43. Decatur, AL	8,014	101. Jackson, MS	8,458	159. Salt Lake City–Ogden, UT	8,891		
44. Alexandria, LA	8,022	102. Monroe, LA	8,461	160. Charleston, WV	8,897		
44. St. Joseph, MO	8,022	103. Yakima, WA	8,464				
		104. Battle Creek, MI	8,483	161. Billings, MT	8,902		
46. Anderson, IN	8,038	105. Odessa, TX	8,487	162. Huntsville, AL	8,909		
47. Florence, SD	8,040			163. Savannah, GA	8,912		
48. Muskegon, MI	8,066	106. Augusta, GA–SC	8,488	164. Tallahassee, FL	8,913		
49. Killeen–Temple, TX	8,075	107. Cedar Rapids, IA	8,490	165. Lincoln, NE	8,916		
50. Victoria, TX	8,100	108. Baton Rouge, LA	8,491				
		109. Athens, GA	8,492	166. Charleston, SC	8,921		
51. Joplin, MO	8,107	110. Bryan–College Station, TX	8,499	167. Jacksonville, FL	8,922		
52. Mansfield, OH	8,109			168. Galveston–Texas City, TX	8,925		
53. Tuscaloosa, AL	8,118	111. Duluth, MN–WI	8,509	169. Racine, WI	8,926		
54. Utica–Rome, NY	8,120	112. Bloomington, IN	8,516	170. Topeka, KS	8,942		
55. Ocala, FL	8,123	113. Shreveport, LA	8,541				
		114. Johnson City–Kingsport–Bristol, TN–VA	8,545	171. Wilmington, NC	8,946		
56. Johnstown, PA	8,137	115. Sioux Falls, SD	8,556	172. Sheboygan, WI	8,947		
57. Jackson, TN	8,142			173. Roanoke, VA	8,961		
57. Texarkana, TX–Texarkana, AR	8,142	116. Little Rock–North Little Rock, AR	8,558	174. Champaign–Urbana–Rantoul, IL	8,971		
59. Lubbock, TX	8,155	117. Omaha, NE–IA	8,563	175. Hagerstown, MD	8,991		
60. Owensboro, KY	8,166	118. Great Falls, MT	8,564				
		119. Kankakee, IL	8,567	176. Wausau, WI	8,993		
61. Parkersburg–Marietta, WV–OH	8,181	120. Dayton–Springfield, OH	8,574	177. Cheyenne, WY	9,001		
62. Cumberland, MD–WV	8,184			178. Indianapolis, IN	9,006		
63. Elmira, NY	8,194	121. Rapid City, SD	8,576	179. Fort Collins–Loveland, CO	9,012		
64. Benton Harbor, MI	8,197	122. El Paso, TX	8,595	180. Kansas City, MO–KS	9,028		
65. Biloxi–Gulfport, MS	8,198	123. Burlington, NC	8,596				
		124. Bismarck, ND	8,599	181. Syracuse, NY	9,037		
66. Wichita Falls, TX	8,200			182. Midland, TX	9,049		
				183. Columbia, SC	9,053		
				184. Lafayette, LA	9,056		

Places Rated Rank	Places Rated Score	Places Rated Rank	Places Rated Score	Places Rated Rank	Places Rated Score
185. Harrisburg–Lebanon–Carlisle, PA	9,065	236. Charlottesville, VA	9,798	285. Fitchburg–Leominster, MA	11,696
		237. Kenosha, WI	9,800		
		238. Visalia–Tulare–Porterville, CA	9,842	286. Fall River, MA–RI	11,701
186. Lafayette–West Lafayette, IN	9,066	239. Wilmington, DE–NJ–MD	9,844	287. Providence, RI	11,796
187. Corpus Christi, TX	9,069	240. Fort Pierce, FL	9,852	288. Bakersfield, CA	11,818
188. Portland, OR	9,078			289. Anchorage, AK	11,942
189. Springfield, IL	9,081			290. Fresno, CA	11,953
190. Buffalo, NY	9,102	241. Tacoma, WA	9,871		
		242. Reading, PA	9,876	291. Lake County, IL	11,986
191. Lexington–Fayette, KY	9,108	243. Minneapolis–St. Paul, MN–WI	9,900	292. Portland, ME	12,123
192. Kalamazoo, MI	9,126	243. Rochester, MN	9,900	293. Orange County, NY	12,356
193. Asheville, NC	9,128	245. Allentown–Bethlehem, PA–NJ	9,906	294. Worcester, MA	12,388
194. Cleveland, OH	9,161			295. Portsmouth–Dover–Rochester, NH–ME	12,477
195. Olympia, WA	9,172	246. Boulder–Longmont, CO	9,918	296. Washington, DC–MD–VA	12,689
196. Pensacola, FL	9,174	247. Miami–Hialeah, FL	9,930	297. New London–Norwich, CT–RI	12,779
197. Memphis, TN–AR–MS	9,178	248. Lansing–East Lansing, MI	9,936	298. Bristol, CT	12,799
198. Gainesville, FL	9,179	249. Lancaster, PA	9,970	299. Trenton, NJ	12,804
199. Bloomington–Normal, IL	9,185	250. Albuquerque, NM	9,974	300. Waterbury, CT	12,809
199. Tampa–St. Petersburg–Clearwater, FL	9,185	251. Rochester, NY	10,093	301. Lowell, MA–NH	12,866
		252. Fort Lauderdale–Hollywood–Pompano Beach, FL	10,110	302. New Britain, CT	13,081
201. Bremerton, WA	9,259	253. Fort Myers–Cape Coral, FL	10,145	303. Manchester, NH	13,103
202. Columbus, OH	9,291	254. Redding, CA	10,155	304. Vallejo–Fairfield–Napa, CA	13,159
203. Nashville, TN	9,296	255. Las Vegas, NV	10,173	305. Lawrence–Haverhill, MA–NH	13,435
204. Bellingham, WA	9,300				
205. Lewiston–Auburn, ME	9,309	256. Aurora–Elgin, IL	10,190	306. Nassau–Suffolk, NY	13,466
		257. Modesto, CA	10,199	307. Nashua, NH	13,766
206. Houston, TX	9,324	258. Dallas, TX	10,398	308. Hartford, CT	13,787
207. Yuba City, CA	9,325	259. Sarasota, FL	10,414	309. Monmouth–Ocean, NJ	13,933
208. Birmingham, AL	9,330	260. Baltimore, MD	10,423	310. San Diego, CA	13,956
209. Tucson, AZ	9,336				
210. St. Cloud, MN	9,350	261. Seattle, WA	10,474	311. Middlesex–Somerset–Hunterdon, NJ	13,983
		262. Naples, FL	10,500	312. New Haven–Meriden, CT	14,015
211. Orlando, FL	9,351	263. Merced, CA	10,503	313. Middletown, CT	14,016
212. St. Louis, MO–IL	9,374	264. Pittsfield, MA	10,525	314. Santa Barbara–Santa Maria–Lompoc, CA	14,139
213. Green Bay, WI	9,380	265. West Palm Beach–Boca Raton–Delray Beach, FL	10,634	315. Oxnard–Ventura, CA	14,187
214. Cincinnati, OH–KY–IN	9,400				
215. Bradenton, FL	9,405	266. Burlington, VT	10,680	316. Salem–Gloucester, MA	14,526
216. Richmond–Petersburg, VA	9,408	267. Raleigh–Durham, NC	10,699	317. Santa Rosa–Petaluma, CA	14,589
217. Iowa City, IA	9,427	268. Atlantic City, NJ	10,706	318. Boston, MA	14,624
218. Charlotte–Gastonia–Rock Hill, NC–SC	9,429	269. Chicago, IL	10,780	319. New York, NY	14,878
219. Greensboro–Winston-Salem–High Point, NC	9,430	270. Albany–Schenectady–Troy, NY	10,792	320. Salinas–Seaside–Monterey, CA	14,881
220. Binghamton, NY	9,455	271. Ann Arbor, MI	10,796		
		272. New Bedford, MA	10,798	321. Santa Cruz, CA	15,131
221. York, PA	9,504	273. Santa Fe, NM	10,832	322. Newark, NJ	15,400
222. Norfolk–Virginia Beach–Newport News, VA	9,513	274. Reno, NV	10,927	323. Bridgeport–Milford, CT	15,408
223. Joliet, IL	9,516	275. Sacramento, CA	10,964	324. Los Angeles–Long Beach, CA	15,649
224. Denver, CO	9,529	276. Brockton, MA	10,971	325. Oakland, CA	15,680
225. Rockford, IL	9,563	277. Philadelphia, PA–NJ	11,017		
226. Detroit, MI	9,583	278. Pawtucket–Woonsocket–Attleboro, RI–MA	11,116	326. Bergen–Passaic, NJ	15,771
227. Atlanta, GA	9,590	279. Stockton, CA	11,285	327. Danbury, CT	16,325
228. Bangor, ME	9,595	280. Jersey City, NJ	11,333	328. San Jose, CA	16,798
229. State College, PA	9,629	281. Riverside–San Bernardino, CA	11,373	329. Anaheim–Santa Ana, CA	17,209
230. Milwaukee, WI	9,690	282. Poughkeepsie, NY	11,565	330. Honolulu, HI	17,667
231. Fort Worth–Arlington, TX	9,691	283. Chico, CA	11,679	331. San Francisco, CA	17,860
232. Madison, WI	9,701	284. Springfield, MA	11,693	332. Norwalk, CT	20,817
233. Austin, TX	9,715			333. Stamford, CT	23,582
234. Phoenix, AZ	9,716				
235. Boise City, ID	9,783				

Place Profiles: Costs of Living

The following profiles highlight selected metropolitan cost-of-living factors. These include the elements used to rank the metro areas—indexes for the costs of housing, food, health care, and transportation against the United States average of 100—as well as average household incomes and local tax bites.

The information is derived from these sources: Advisory Commission on Intergovernmental Relations, *Significant Features of Fiscal Federalism*, 1989; American Chamber of Commerce Researchers Association, "Inter-City Cost of Living Index," 4th quarter, 1988 and 1st quarter, 1989. American Gas Association, *Gas Facts*, 1989; Commerce Clearing House, *State Tax Guide*, 1989;

Equicor Group Marketing, *1987 Hospital Daily Service Charges*, 1988; National Association of Realtors, "Existing Home Sales," 1st quarter, 1989; Places Rated Partnership survey of local real estate boards; U.S. Department of Education, *Directory of Postsecondary Institutions*, 1989; U.S. Department of Energy, *Typical Electric Bills*, 1989; U. S. Department of Health and Human Services, Health Care Financing Administration, unpublished data, 1989; and Woods & Poole Economics, Inc., unpublished household income forecasts.

A star (★) preceding a metro area's name highlights it as one of the top 30 places for costs of living.

Abilene, TX
Typical Household Income: $44,260
State and Local Taxes: $1,031
Housing Cost Indexes
  Median Price: 55
  Utilities: 81
  Property Taxes: 67
Miscellaneous Living Cost Indexes
  College Tuition: 59
  Food: 104
  Health Care: 102
  Transportation: 104
Places Rated Score: 8,333
Places Rated Rank: 85

Akron, OH
Typical Household Income: $42,067
State and Local Taxes: $1,776
Housing Cost Indexes
  Median Price: 61
  Utilities: 125
  Property Taxes: 56
Miscellaneous Living Cost Indexes
  College Tuition: 149
  Food: 94
  Health Care: 90
  Transportation: 104
Places Rated Score: 8,276
Places Rated Rank: 77

Albany, GA
Typical Household Income: $34,559
State and Local Taxes: $1,786
Housing Cost Indexes
  Median Price: 60
  Utilities: 96
  Property Taxes: 54
Miscellaneous Living Cost Indexes
  College Tuition: 102
  Food: 96
  Health Care: 83
  Transportation: 94
Places Rated Score: 7,981
Places Rated Rank: 40

Albany–Schenectady–Troy, NY
Typical Household Income: $47,115
State and Local Taxes: $4,069

Housing Cost Indexes
  Median Price: 111
  Utilities: 108
  Property Taxes: 201
Miscellaneous Living Cost Indexes
  College Tuition: 124
  Food: 105
  Health Care: 87
  Transportation: 109
Places Rated Score: 10,792
Places Rated Rank: 270

Albuquerque, NM
Typical Household Income: $48,683
State and Local Taxes: $1,126
Housing Cost Indexes
  Median Price: 90
  Utilities: 113
  Property Taxes: 69
Miscellaneous Living Cost Indexes
  College Tuition: 64
  Food: 98
  Health Care: 119
  Transportation: 114
Places Rated Score: 9,974
Places Rated Rank: 250

Alexandria, LA
Typical Household Income: $36,078
State and Local Taxes: $471
Housing Cost Indexes
  Median Price: 64
  Utilities: 78
  Property Taxes: 12
Miscellaneous Living Cost Indexes
  College Tuition: 95
  Food: 103
  Health Care: 70
  Transportation: 85
Places Rated Score: 8,022
Places Rated Rank: 44

Allentown–Bethlehem, PA–NJ
Typical Household Income: $43,055
State and Local Taxes: $2,540
Housing Cost Indexes
  Median Price: 98
  Utilities: 117

Property Taxes: 119
Miscellaneous Living Cost Indexes
  College Tuition: 192
  Food: 102
  Health Care: 94
  Transportation: 99
Places Rated Score: 9,906
Places Rated Rank: 245

★ Altoona, PA
Typical Household Income: $34,534
State and Local Taxes: $1,837
Housing Cost Indexes
  Median Price: 60
  Utilities: 114
  Property Taxes: 73
Miscellaneous Living Cost Indexes
  College Tuition: 192
  Food: 100
  Health Care: 85
  Transportation: 85
Places Rated Score: 7,851
Places Rated Rank: 27

Amarillo, TX
Typical Household Income: $45,768
State and Local Taxes: $1,051
Housing Cost Indexes
  Median Price: 56
  Utilities: 80
  Property Taxes: 69
Miscellaneous Living Cost Indexes
  College Tuition: 59
  Food: 97
  Health Care: 93
  Transportation: 97
Places Rated Score: 7,960
Places Rated Rank: 35

Anaheim–Santa Ana, CA
Typical Household Income: $67,135
State and Local Taxes: $4,847
Housing Cost Indexes
  Median Price: 255
  Utilities: 101
  Property Taxes: 233
Miscellaneous Living Cost Indexes
  College Tuition: 60

Food: 101
Health Care: 158
Transportation: 115
Places Rated Score: 17,209
Places Rated Rank: 329

Anchorage, AK
Typical Household Income: $74,478
State and Local Taxes: $891
Housing Cost Indexes
  Median Price: 120
  Utilities: 104
  Property Taxes: 85
Miscellaneous Living Cost Indexes
  College Tuition: 81
  Food: 120
  Health Care: 135
  Transportation: 115
Places Rated Score: 11,942
Places Rated Rank: 289

Anderson, IN
Typical Household Income: $39,961
State and Local Taxes: $2,019
Housing Cost Indexes
  Median Price: 61
  Utilities: 97
  Property Taxes: 66
Miscellaneous Living Cost Indexes
  College Tuition: 130
  Food: 98
  Health Care: 86
  Transportation: 92
Places Rated Score: 8,038
Places Rated Rank: 46

★ Anderson, SC
Typical Household Income: $33,851
State and Local Taxes: $1,456
Housing Cost Indexes
  Median Price: 59
  Utilities: 84
  Property Taxes: 37
Miscellaneous Living Cost Indexes
  College Tuition: 117
  Food: 100
  Health Care: 85
  Transportation: 85
Places Rated Score: 7,787
Places Rated Rank: 16

Ann Arbor, MI
Typical Household Income: $66,228
State and Local Taxes: $5,146
Housing Cost Indexes
  Median Price: 106
  Utilities: 120
  Property Taxes: 193
Miscellaneous Living Cost Indexes
  College Tuition: 134
  Food: 102
  Health Care: 122
  Transportation: 115
Places Rated Score: 10,796
Places Rated Rank: 271

★ Anniston, AL
Typical Household Income: $33,288
State and Local Taxes: $1,270
Housing Cost Indexes
  Median Price: 56
  Utilities: 87
  Property Taxes: 19
Miscellaneous Living Cost Indexes
  College Tuition: 93
  Food: 92
  Health Care: 94

Transportation: 88
Places Rated Score: 7,608
Places Rated Rank: 9

Appleton-Oshkosh-Neenah, WI
Typical Household Income: $42,340
State and Local Taxes: $3,202
Housing Cost Indexes
  Median Price: 70
  Utilities: 106
  Property Taxes: 124
Miscellaneous Living Cost Indexes
  College Tuition: 100
  Food: 101
  Health Care: 77
  Transportation: 89
Places Rated Score: 8,386
Places Rated Rank: 90

Asheville, NC
Typical Household Income: $39,935
State and Local Taxes: $2,279
Housing Cost Indexes
  Median Price: 86
  Utilities: 99
  Property Taxes: 76
Miscellaneous Living Cost Indexes
  College Tuition: 52
  Food: 101
  Health.Care: 77
  Transportation: 92
Places Rated Score: 9,128
Places Rated Rank: 193

Athens, GA
Typical Household Income: $38,857
State and Local Taxes: $2,032
Housing Cost Indexes
  Median Price: 72
  Utilities: 93
  Property Taxes: 65
Miscellaneous Living Cost Indexes
  College Tuition: 102
  Food: 98
  Health Care: 100
  Transportation: 89
Places Rated Score: 8,492
Places Rated Rank: 109

Atlanta, GA
Typical Household Income: $52,502
State and Local Taxes: $2,833
Housing Cost Indexes
  Median Price: 88
  Utilities: 93
  Property Taxes: 79
Miscellaneous Living Cost Indexes
  College Tuition: 102
  Food: 99
  Health Care: 111
  Transportation: 103
Places Rated Score: 9,590
Places Rated Rank: 227

Atlantic City, NJ
Typical Household Income: $67,250
State and Local Taxes: $4,089
Housing Cost Indexes
  Median Price: 105
  Utilities: 127
  Property Taxes: 217
Miscellaneous Living Cost Indexes
  College Tuition: 128
  Food: 102
  Health Care: 112
  Transportation: 115
Places Rated Score: 10,706
Places Rated Rank: 268

Augusta, GA-SC
Typical Household Income: $37,692
State and Local Taxes: $1,988
Housing Cost Indexes
  Median Price: 69
  Utilities: 93
  Property Taxes: 62
Miscellaneous Living Cost Indexes
  College Tuition: 102
  Food: 95
  Health Care: 95
  Transportation: 98
Places Rated Score: 8,488
Places Rated Rank: 106

Aurora-Elgin, IL
Typical Household Income: $45,002
State and Local Taxes: $2,867
Housing Cost Indexes
  Median Price: 102
  Utilities: 140
  Property Taxes: 138
Miscellaneous Living Cost Indexes
  College Tuition: 123
  Food: 102
  Health Care: 90
  Transportation: 104
Places Rated Score: 10,190
Places Rated Rank: 256

Austin, TX
Typical Household Income: $52,416
State and Local Taxes: $1,571
Housing Cost Indexes
  Median Price: 93
  Utilities: 77
  Property Taxes: 114
Miscellaneous Living Cost Indexes
  College Tuition: 59
  Food: 99
  Health Care: 109
  Transportation: 100
Places Rated Score: 9,715
Places Rated Rank: 233

Bakersfield, CA
Typical Household Income: $36,696
State and Local Taxes: $2,325
Housing Cost Indexes
  Median Price: 136
  Utilities: 93
  Property Taxes: 125
Miscellaneous Living Cost Indexes
  College Tuition: 60
  Food: 104
  Health Care: 105
  Transportation: 106
Places Rated Score: 11,818
Places Rated Rank: 288

Baltimore, MD
Typical Household Income: $50,503
State and Local Taxes: $3,100
Housing Cost Indexes
  Median Price: 101
  Utilities: 94
  Property Taxes: 107
Miscellaneous Living Cost Indexes
  College Tuition: 123
  Food: 99
  Health Care: 104
  Transportation: 115
Places Rated Score: 10,423
Places Rated Rank: 260

Bangor, ME
Typical Household Income: $37,270
State and Local Taxes: $2,102

Housing Cost Indexes
  Median Price: 99
  Utilities: 100
  Property Taxes: 105
Miscellaneous Living Cost Indexes
  College Tuition: 116
  Food: 102
  Health Care: 90
  Transportation: 86
Places Rated Score: 9,595
Places Rated Rank: 228

Baton Rouge, LA
Typical Household Income: $39,878
State and Local Taxes: $545
Housing Cost Indexes
  Median Price: 67
  Utilities: 81
  Property Taxes: 13
Miscellaneous Living Cost Indexes
  College Tuition: 95
  Food: 96
  Health Care: 104
  Transportation: 99
Places Rated Score: 8,491
Places Rated Rank: 108

Battle Creek, MI
Typical Household Income: $42,725
State and Local Taxes: $3,219
Housing Cost Indexes
  Median Price: 64
  Utilities: 116
  Property Taxes: 117
Miscellaneous Living Cost Indexes
  College Tuition: 134
  Food: 101
  Health Care: 99
  Transportation: 98
Places Rated Score: 8,483
Places Rated Rank: 104

Beaumont–Port Arthur, TX
Typical Household Income: $38,293
State and Local Taxes: $1,114
Housing Cost Indexes
  Median Price: 66
  Utilities: 87
  Property Taxes: 80
Miscellaneous Living Cost Indexes
  College Tuition: 59
  Food: 104
  Health Care: 101
  Transportation: 103
Places Rated Score: 8,749
Places Rated Rank: 141

Beaver County, PA
Typical Household Income: $26,892
State and Local Taxes: $1,630
Housing Cost Indexes
  Median Price: 64
  Utilities: 126
  Property Taxes: 78
Miscellaneous Living Cost Indexes
  College Tuition: 192
  Food: 96
  Health Care: 91
  Transportation: 85
Places Rated Score: 7,929
Places Rated Rank: 34

Bellingham, WA
Typical Household Income: $37,549
State and Local Taxes: $1,503
Housing Cost Indexes
  Median Price: 88

Utilities: 82
  Property Taxes: 85
Miscellaneous Living Cost Indexes
  College Tuition: 96
  Food: 106
  Health Care: 98
  Transportation: 86
Places Rated Score: 9,300
Places Rated Rank: 204

Benton Harbor, MI
Typical Household Income: $41,276
State and Local Taxes: $3,049
Housing Cost Indexes
  Median Price: 59
  Utilities: 115
  Property Taxes: 108
Miscellaneous Living Cost Indexes
  College Tuition: 134
  Food: 103
  Health Care: 92
  Transportation: 95
Places Rated Score: 8,197
Places Rated Rank: 64

Bergen–Passaic, NJ
Typical Household Income: $68,949
State and Local Taxes: $6,831
Housing Cost Indexes
  Median Price: 225
  Utilities: 126
  Property Taxes: 467
Miscellaneous Living Cost Indexes
  College Tuition: 128
  Food: 102
  Health Care: 114
  Transportation: 115
Places Rated Score: 15,771
Places Rated Rank: 326

Billings, MT
Typical Household Income: $41,279
State and Local Taxes: $1,921
Housing Cost Indexes
  Median Price: 76
  Utilities: 87
  Property Taxes: 88
Miscellaneous Living Cost Indexes
  College Tuition: 81
  Food: 103
  Health Care: 94
  Transportation: 95
Places Rated Score: 8,902
Places Rated Rank: 161

Biloxi–Gulfport, MS
Typical Household Income: $36,649
State and Local Taxes: $1,284
Housing Cost Indexes
  Median Price: 58
  Utilities: 76
  Property Taxes: 38
Miscellaneous Living Cost Indexes
  College Tuition: 105
  Food: 101
  Health Care: 90
  Transportation: 99
Places Rated Score: 8,198
Places Rated Rank: 65

Binghamton, NY
Typical Household Income: $43,164
State and Local Taxes: $3,411
Housing Cost Indexes
  Median Price: 87
  Utilities: 118
  Property Taxes: 157

Miscellaneous Living Cost Indexes
  College Tuition: 124
  Food: 101
  Health Care: 81
  Transportation: 102
Places Rated Score: 9,455
Places Rated Rank: 220

Birmingham, AL
Typical Household Income: $41,979
State and Local Taxes: $1,624
Housing Cost Indexes
  Median Price: 84
  Utilities: 87
  Property Taxes: 29
Miscellaneous Living Cost Indexes
  College Tuition: 93
  Food: 97
  Health Care: 119
  Transportation: 99
Places Rated Score: 9,330
Places Rated Rank: 208

Bismarck, ND
Typical Household Income: $38,542
State and Local Taxes: $1,460
Housing Cost Indexes
  Median Price: 71
  Utilities: 108
  Property Taxes: 85
Miscellaneous Living Cost Indexes
  College Tuition: 102
  Food: 105
  Health Care: 97
  Transportation: 89
Places Rated Score: 8,599
Places Rated Rank: 124

Bloomington, IN
Typical Household Income: $42,006
State and Local Taxes: $2,360
Housing Cost Indexes
  Median Price: 73
  Utilities: 113
  Property Taxes: 79
Miscellaneous Living Cost Indexes
  College Tuition: 130
  Food: 105
  Health Care: 86
  Transportation: 85
Places Rated Score: 8,516
Places Rated Rank: 112

Bloomington–Normal, IL
Typical Household Income: $52,834
State and Local Taxes: $2,688
Housing Cost Indexes
  Median Price: 69
  Utilities: 141
  Property Taxes: 93
Miscellaneous Living Cost Indexes
  College Tuition: 123
  Food: 103
  Health Care: 102
  Transportation: 115
Places Rated Score: 9,185
Places Rated Rank: 199

Boise City, ID
Typical Household Income: $49,281
State and Local Taxes: $2,912
Housing Cost Indexes
  Median Price: 83
  Utilities: 77
  Property Taxes: 63
Miscellaneous Living Cost Indexes
  College Tuition: 80

Food: 104
Health Care: 107
Transportation: 113
Places Rated Score: 9,783
Places Rated Rank: 235

Boston, MA
Typical Household Income: $74,932
State and Local Taxes: $4,969
Housing Cost Indexes
  Median Price: 195
  Utilities: 136
  Property Taxes: 142
Miscellaneous Living Cost Indexes
  College Tuition: 102
  Food: 104
  Health Care: 131
  Transportation: 115
Places Rated Score: 14,624
Places Rated Rank: 318

Boulder-Longmont, CO
Typical Household Income: $52,043
State and Local Taxes: $2,106
Housing Cost Indexes
  Median Price: 98
  Utilities: 94
  Property Taxes: 79
Miscellaneous Living Cost Indexes
  College Tuition: 103
  Food: 95
  Health Care: 122
  Transportation: 101
Places Rated Score: 9,918
Places Rated Rank: 246

Bradenton, FL
Typical Household Income: $43,065
State and Local Taxes: $1,203
Housing Cost Indexes
  Median Price: 89
  Utilities: 80
  Property Taxes: 71
Miscellaneous Living Cost Indexes
  College Tuition: 78
  Food: 96
  Health Care: 105
  Transportation: 98
Places Rated Score: 9,405
Places Rated Rank: 215

Brazoria, TX
Typical Household Income: $40,247
State and Local Taxes: $1,093
Housing Cost Indexes
  Median Price: 62
  Utilities: 86
  Property Taxes: 76
Miscellaneous Living Cost Indexes
  College Tuition: 59
  Food: 106
  Health Care: 88
  Transportation: 93
Places Rated Score: 8,323
Places Rated Rank: 84

Bremerton, WA
Typical Household Income: $37,142
State and Local Taxes: $1,489
Housing Cost Indexes
  Median Price: 91
  Utilities: 83
  Property Taxes: 87
Miscellaneous Living Cost Indexes
  College Tuition: 96
  Food: 104
  Health Care: 86

Transportation: 86
Places Rated Score: 9,259
Places Rated Rank: 201

Bridgeport-Milford, CT
Typical Household Income: $49,100
State and Local Taxes: $3,487
Housing Cost Indexes
  Median Price: 218
  Utilities: 130
  Property Taxes: 277
Miscellaneous Living Cost Indexes
  College Tuition: 103
  Food: 104
  Health Care: 101
  Transportation: 113
Places Rated Score: 15,408
Places Rated Rank: 323

Bristol, CT
Typical Household Income: $57,737
State and Local Taxes: $2,763
Housing Cost Indexes
  Median Price: 152
  Utilities: 121
  Property Taxes: 193
Miscellaneous Living Cost Indexes
  College Tuition: 103
  Food: 106
  Health Care: 115
  Transportation: 115
Places Rated Score: 12,799
Places Rated Rank: 298

Brockton, MA
Typical Household Income: $41,225
State and Local Taxes: $2,883
Housing Cost Indexes
  Median Price: 127
  Utilities: 114
  Property Taxes: 93
Miscellaneous Living Cost Indexes
  College Tuition: 102
  Food: 103
  Health Care: 82
  Transportation: 95
Places Rated Score: 10,971
Places Rated Rank: 276

★ **Brownsville-Harlingen, TX**
Typical Household Income: $18,983
State and Local Taxes: $845
Housing Cost Indexes
  Median Price: 53
  Utilities: 78
  Property Taxes: 65
Miscellaneous Living Cost Indexes
  College Tuition: 59
  Food: 101
  Health Care: 53
  Transportation: 97
Places Rated Score: 7,773
Places Rated Rank: 15

Bryan-College Station, TX
Typical Household Income: $35,638
State and Local Taxes: $1,197
Housing Cost Indexes
  Median Price: 71
  Utilities: 91
  Property Taxes: 87
Miscellaneous Living Cost Indexes
  College Tuition: 59
  Food: 106
  Health Care: 92
  Transportation: 85
Places Rated Score: 8,499
Places Rated Rank: 110

Buffalo, NY
Typical Household Income: $44,019
State and Local Taxes: $3,240
Housing Cost Indexes
  Median Price: 75
  Utilities: 108
  Property Taxes: 135
Miscellaneous Living Cost Indexes
  College Tuition: 124
  Food: 104
  Health Care: 80
  Transportation: 105
Places Rated Score: 9,102
Places Rated Rank: 190

Burlington, NC
Typical Household Income: $42,040
State and Local Taxes: $2,236
Housing Cost Indexes
  Median Price: 70
  Utilities: 95
  Property Taxes: 61
Miscellaneous Living Cost Indexes
  College Tuition: 52
  Food: 100
  Health Care: 88
  Transportation: 97
Places Rated Score: 8,596
Places Rated Rank: 123

Burlington, VT
Typical Household Income: $46,817
State and Local Taxes: $3,429
Housing Cost Indexes
  Median Price: 106
  Utilities: 116
  Property Taxes: 185
Miscellaneous Living Cost Indexes
  College Tuition: 228
  Food: 106
  Health Care: 109
  Transportation: 108
Places Rated Score: 10,680
Places Rated Rank: 266

★ **Canton, OH**
Typical Household Income: $37,353
State and Local Taxes: $1,611
Housing Cost Indexes
  Median Price: 58
  Utilities: 113
  Property Taxes: 53
Miscellaneous Living Cost Indexes
  College Tuition: 149
  Food: 87
  Health Care: 77
  Transportation: 87
Places Rated Score: 7,434
Places Rated Rank: 3

Casper, WY
Typical Household Income: $46,285
State and Local Taxes: $717
Housing Cost Indexes
  Median Price: 75
  Utilities: 89
  Property Taxes: 37
Miscellaneous Living Cost Indexes
  College Tuition: 60
  Food: 98
  Health Care: 98
  Transportation: 92
Places Rated Score: 8,686
Places Rated Rank: 132

Cedar Rapids, IA
Typical Household Income: $45,654
State and Local Taxes: $2,680

Housing Cost Indexes
  Median Price: 63
  Utilities: 132
  Property Taxes: 107
Miscellaneous Living Cost Indexes
  College Tuition: 112
  Food: 102
  Health Care: 95
  Transportation: 101
Places Rated Score: 8,490
Places Rated Rank: 107

Champaign–Urbana–Rantoul, IL
Typical Household Income: $47,786
State and Local Taxes: $2,652
Housing Cost Indexes
  Median Price: 76
  Utilities: 141
  Property Taxes: 103
Miscellaneous Living Cost Indexes
  College Tuition: 123
  Food: 100
  Health Care: 97
  Transportation: 99
Places Rated Score: 8,971
Places Rated Rank: 174

Charleston, SC
Typical Household Income: $35,223
State and Local Taxes: $1,663
Housing Cost Indexes
  Median Price: 79
  Utilities: 83
  Property Taxes: 50
Miscellaneous Living Cost Indexes
  College Tuition: 117
  Food: 101
  Health Care: 86
  Transportation: 94
Places Rated Score: 8,921
Places Rated Rank: 166

Charleston, WV
Typical Household Income: $41,028
State and Local Taxes: $1,794
Housing Cost Indexes
  Median Price: 74
  Utilities: 95
  Property Taxes: 45
Miscellaneous Living Cost Indexes
  College Tuition: 73
  Food: 104
  Health Care: 101
  Transportation: 95
Places Rated Score: 8,897
Places Rated Rank: 160

Charlotte–Gastonia–Rock Hill, NC–SC
Typical Household Income: $43,486
State and Local Taxes: $2,548
Housing Cost Indexes
  Median Price: 93
  Utilities: 95
  Property Taxes: 82
Miscellaneous Living Cost Indexes
  College Tuition: 52
  Food: 100
  Health Care: 86
  Transportation: 92
Places Rated Score: 9,429
Places Rated Rank: 218

Charlottesville, VA
Typical Household Income: $45,664
State and Local Taxes: $2,463
Housing Cost Indexes
  Median Price: 92

Utilities: 103
Property Taxes: 79
Miscellaneous Living Cost Indexes
  College Tuition: 140
  Food: 100
  Health Care: 97
  Transportation: 105
Places Rated Score: 9,798
Places Rated Rank: 236

Chattanooga, TN–GA
Typical Household Income: $38,177
State and Local Taxes: $1,050
Housing Cost Indexes
  Median Price: 72
  Utilities: 76
  Property Taxes: 55
Miscellaneous Living Cost Indexes
  College Tuition: 85
  Food: 91
  Health Care: 101
  Transportation: 94
Places Rated Score: 8,416
Places Rated Rank: 92

Cheyenne, WY
Typical Household Income: $47,341
State and Local Taxes: $708
Housing Cost Indexes
  Median Price: 72
  Utilities: 89
  Property Taxes: 36
Miscellaneous Living Cost Indexes
  College Tuition: 60
  Food: 98
  Health Care: 95
  Transportation: 109
Places Rated Score: 9,001
Places Rated Rank: 177

Chicago, IL
Typical Household Income: $52,841
State and Local Taxes: $3,230
Housing Cost Indexes
  Median Price: 108
  Utilities: 134
  Property Taxes: 146
Miscellaneous Living Cost Indexes
  College Tuition: 123
  Food: 103
  Health Care: 123
  Transportation: 109
Places Rated Score: 10,780
Places Rated Rank: 269

Chico, CA
Typical Household Income: $40,947
State and Local Taxes: $2,325
Housing Cost Indexes
  Median Price: 131
  Utilities: 101
  Property Taxes: 120
Miscellaneous Living Cost Indexes
  College Tuition: 60
  Food: 96
  Health Care: 124
  Transportation: 114
Places Rated Score: 11,679
Places Rated Rank: 283

Cincinnati, OH–KY–IN
Typical Household Income: $46,738
State and Local Taxes: $2,117
Housing Cost Indexes
  Median Price: 80
  Utilities: 112
  Property Taxes: 74

Miscellaneous Living Cost Indexes
  College Tuition: 149
  Food: 103
  Health Care: 106
  Transportation: 105
Places Rated Score: 9,400
Places Rated Rank: 214

★ **Clarksville–Hopkinsville, TN–KY**
Typical Household Income: $33,172
State and Local Taxes: $906
Housing Cost Indexes
  Median Price: 58
  Utilities: 75
  Property Taxes: 45
Miscellaneous Living Cost Indexes
  College Tuition: 85
  Food: 97
  Health Care: 86
  Transportation: 85
Places Rated Score: 7,685
Places Rated Rank: 11

Cleveland, OH
Typical Household Income: $49,864
State and Local Taxes: $2,227
Housing Cost Indexes
  Median Price: 76
  Utilities: 139
  Property Taxes: 70
Miscellaneous Living Cost Indexes
  College Tuition: 149
  Food: 100
  Health Care: 109
  Transportation: 105
Places Rated Score: 9,161
Places Rated Rank: 194

Colorado Springs, CO
Typical Household Income: $42,075
State and Local Taxes: $1,542
Housing Cost Indexes
  Median Price: 70
  Utilities: 80
  Property Taxes: 57
Miscellaneous Living Cost Indexes
  College Tuition: 103
  Food: 89
  Health Care: 110
  Transportation: 98
Places Rated Score: 8,441
Places Rated Rank: 95

Columbia, MO
Typical Household Income: $44,942
State and Local Taxes: $1,671
Housing Cost Indexes
  Median Price: 76
  Utilities: 102
  Property Taxes: 55
Miscellaneous Living Cost Indexes
  College Tuition: 88
  Food: 96
  Health Care: 111
  Transportation: 96
Places Rated Score: 8,817
Places Rated Rank: 153

Columbia, SC
Typical Household Income: $44,541
State and Local Taxes: $2,028
Housing Cost Indexes
  Median Price: 78
  Utilities: 83
  Property Taxes: 49
Miscellaneous Living Cost Indexes
  College Tuition: 117
  Food: 100

Health Care: 101
Transportation: 98
Places Rated Score: 9,053
Places Rated Rank: 183

★ Columbus, GA–AL
Typical Household Income: $36,074
State and Local Taxes: $1,841
Housing Cost Indexes
   Median Price: 60
   Utilities: 93
   Property Taxes: 54
Miscellaneous Living Cost Indexes
   College Tuition: 102
   Food: 98
   Health Care: 89
   Transportation: 85
Places Rated Score: 7,825
Places Rated Rank: 19

Columbus, OH
Typical Household Income: $47,098
State and Local Taxes: $2,112
Housing Cost Indexes
   Median Price: 81
   Utilities: 117
   Property Taxes: 74
Miscellaneous Living Cost Indexes
   College Tuition: 149
   Food: 96
   Health Care: 104
   Transportation: 107
Places Rated Score: 9,291
Places Rated Rank: 202

Corpus Christi, TX
Typical Household Income: $34,053
State and Local Taxes: $1,140
Housing Cost Indexes
   Median Price: 69
   Utilities: 77
   Property Taxes: 85
Miscellaneous Living Cost Indexes
   College Tuition: 59
   Food: 102
   Health Care: 109
   Transportation: 110
Places Rated Score: 9,069
Places Rated Rank: 187

Cumberland, MD–WV
Typical Household Income: $35,970
State and Local Taxes: $2,121
Housing Cost Indexes
   Median Price: 70
   Utilities: 86
   Property Taxes: 74
Miscellaneous Living Cost Indexes
   College Tuition: 123
   Food: 99
   Health Care: 71
   Transportation: 85
Places Rated Score: 8,184
Places Rated Rank: 62

Dallas, TX
Typical Household Income: $60,846
State and Local Taxes: $1,660
Housing Cost Indexes
   Median Price: 97
   Utilities: 85
   Property Taxes: 118
Miscellaneous Living Cost Indexes
   College Tuition: 59
   Food: 104
   Health Care: 124
   Transportation: 112
Places Rated Score: 10,398
Places Rated Rank: 258

Danbury, CT
Typical Household Income: $65,431
State and Local Taxes: $3,924
Housing Cost Indexes
   Median Price: 237
   Utilities: 127
   Property Taxes: 301
Miscellaneous Living Cost Indexes
   College Tuition: 103
   Food: 104
   Health Care: 120
   Transportation: 115
Places Rated Score: 16,325
Places Rated Rank: 327

★ Danville, VA
Typical Household Income: $33,570
State and Local Taxes: $1,615
Housing Cost Indexes
   Median Price: 52
   Utilities: 86
   Property Taxes: 45
Miscellaneous Living Cost Indexes
   College Tuition: 140
   Food: 100
   Health Care: 64
   Transportation: 85
Places Rated Score: 7,437
Places Rated Rank: 4

Davenport–Rock Island–Moline, IA–IL
Typical Household Income: $40,747
State and Local Taxes: $2,631
Housing Cost Indexes
   Median Price: 65
   Utilities: 118
   Property Taxes: 111
Miscellaneous Living Cost Indexes
   College Tuition: 112
   Food: 96
   Health Care: 91
   Transportation: 95
Places Rated Score: 8,244
Places Rated Rank: 71

Dayton–Springfield, OH
Typical Household Income: $45,958
State and Local Taxes: $1,997
Housing Cost Indexes
   Median Price: 70
   Utilities: 121
   Property Taxes: 65
Miscellaneous Living Cost Indexes
   College Tuition: 149
   Food: 94
   Health Care: 101
   Transportation: 99
Places Rated Score: 8,574
Places Rated Rank: 120

Daytona Beach, FL
Typical Household Income: $39,014
State and Local Taxes: $969
Housing Cost Indexes
   Median Price: 65
   Utilities: 80
   Property Taxes: 52
Miscellaneous Living Cost Indexes
   College Tuition: 78
   Food: 100
   Health Care: 93
   Transportation: 90
Places Rated Score: 8,226
Places Rated Rank: 69

Decatur, AL
Typical Household Income: $33,751
State and Local Taxes: $1,286

Housing Cost Indexes
   Median Price: 57
   Utilities: 74
   Property Taxes: 19
Miscellaneous Living Cost Indexes
   College Tuition: 93
   Food: 95
   Health Care: 103
   Transportation: 98
Places Rated Score: 8,014
Places Rated Rank: 43

Decatur, IL
Typical Household Income: $42,444
State and Local Taxes: $2,197
Housing Cost Indexes
   Median Price: 58
   Utilities: 141
   Property Taxes: 78
Miscellaneous Living Cost Indexes
   College Tuition: 123
   Food: 95
   Health Care: 83
   Transportation: 98
Places Rated Score: 7,965
Places Rated Rank: 36

Denver, CO
Typical Household Income: $51,533
State and Local Taxes: $2,071
Housing Cost Indexes
   Median Price: 88
   Utilities: 94
   Property Taxes: 71
Miscellaneous Living Cost Indexes
   College Tuition: 103
   Food: 91
   Health Care: 121
   Transportation: 106
Places Rated Score: 9,529
Places Rated Rank: 224

Des Moines, IA
Typical Household Income: $49,447
State and Local Taxes: $2,844
Housing Cost Indexes
   Median Price: 63
   Utilities: 111
   Property Taxes: 107
Miscellaneous Living Cost Indexes
   College Tuition: 112
   Food: 96
   Health Care: 99
   Transportation: 114
Places Rated Score: 8,698
Places Rated Rank: 134

Detroit, MI
Typical Household Income: $51,621
State and Local Taxes: $3,931
Housing Cost Indexes
   Median Price: 78
   Utilities: 120
   Property Taxes: 143
Miscellaneous Living Cost Indexes
   College Tuition: 134
   Food: 100
   Health Care: 117
   Transportation: 115
Places Rated Score: 9,583
Places Rated Rank: 226

★ Dothan, AL
Typical Household Income: $35,808
State and Local Taxes: $1,316
Housing Cost Indexes
   Median Price: 48
   Utilities: 84

Property Taxes: 16
Miscellaneous Living Cost Indexes
  College Tuition: 93
  Food: 98
  Health Care: 97
  Transportation: 99
Places Rated Score: 7,717
Places Rated Rank: 12

Dubuque, IA
Typical Household Income: $32,954
State and Local Taxes: $2,236
Housing Cost Indexes
  Median Price: 65
  Utilities: 92
  Property Taxes: 111
Miscellaneous Living Cost Indexes
  College Tuition: 112
  Food: 94
  Health Care: 80
  Transportation: 99
Places Rated Score: 8,269
Places Rated Rank: 75

Duluth, MN–WI
Typical Household Income: $38,629
State and Local Taxes: $2,278
Housing Cost Indexes
  Median Price: 71
  Utilities: 101
  Property Taxes: 62
Miscellaneous Living Cost Indexes
  College Tuition: 141
  Food: 102
  Health Care: 91
  Transportation: 89
Places Rated Score: 8,509
Places Rated Rank: 111

Eau Claire, WI
Typical Household Income: $36,879
State and Local Taxes: $3,016
Housing Cost Indexes
  Median Price: 82
  Utilities: 105
  Property Taxes: 145
Miscellaneous Living Cost Indexes
  College Tuition: 100
  Food: 102
  Health Care: 78
  Transportation: 85
Places Rated Score: 8,786
Places Rated Rank: 149

El Paso, TX
Typical Household Income: $25,054
State and Local Taxes: $1,002
Housing Cost Indexes
  Median Price: 62
  Utilities: 85
  Property Taxes: 77
Miscellaneous Living Cost Indexes
  College Tuition: 59
  Food: 103
  Health Care: 84
  Transportation: 106
Places Rated Score: 8,595
Places Rated Rank: 122

Elkhart–Goshen, IN
Typical Household Income: $45,649
State and Local Taxes: $2,264
Housing Cost Indexes
  Median Price: 68
  Utilities: 104
  Property Taxes: 74
Miscellaneous Living Cost Indexes
  College Tuition: 130

Food: 99
  Health Care: 100
  Transportation: 105
Places Rated Score: 8,763
Places Rated Rank: 144

Elmira, NY
Typical Household Income: $35,898
State and Local Taxes: $2,734
Housing Cost Indexes
  Median Price: 72
  Utilities: 118
  Property Taxes: 130
Miscellaneous Living Cost Indexes
  College Tuition: 124
  Food: 95
  Health Care: 79
  Transportation: 85
Places Rated Score: 8,194
Places Rated Rank: 63

★ Enid, OK
Typical Household Income: $40,900
State and Local Taxes: $1,419
Housing Cost Indexes
  Median Price: 55
  Utilities: 90
  Property Taxes: 36
Miscellaneous Living Cost Indexes
  College Tuition: 57
  Food: 97
  Health Care: 95
  Transportation: 94
Places Rated Score: 7,837
Places Rated Rank: 24

Erie, PA
Typical Household Income: $37,042
State and Local Taxes: $1,933
Housing Cost Indexes
  Median Price: 62
  Utilities: 114
  Property Taxes: 76
Miscellaneous Living Cost Indexes
  College Tuition: 192
  Food: 101
  Health Care: 85
  Transportation: 96
Places Rated Score: 8,274
Places Rated Rank: 76

Eugene–Springfield, OR
Typical Household Income: $38,107
State and Local Taxes: $2,991
Housing Cost Indexes
  Median Price: 66
  Utilities: 71
  Property Taxes: 129
Miscellaneous Living Cost Indexes
  College Tuition: 88
  Food: 93
  Health Care: 94
  Transportation: 104
Places Rated Score: 8,452
Places Rated Rank: 98

Evansville, IN–KY
Typical Household Income: $44,717
State and Local Taxes: $2,263
Housing Cost Indexes
  Median Price: 70
  Utilities: 107
  Property Taxes: 76
Miscellaneous Living Cost Indexes
  College Tuition: 130
  Food: 111
  Health Care: 93

Transportation: 95
Places Rated Score: 8,850
Places Rated Rank: 156

Fall River, MA–RI
Typical Household Income: $40,441
State and Local Taxes: $2,884
Housing Cost Indexes
  Median Price: 147
  Utilities: 114
  Property Taxes: 107
Miscellaneous Living Cost Indexes
  College Tuition: 102
  Food: 99
  Health Care: 91
  Transportation: 93
Places Rated Score: 11,701
Places Rated Rank: 286

Fargo–Moorhead, ND–MN
Typical Household Income: $45,140
State and Local Taxes: $1,506
Housing Cost Indexes
  Median Price: 69
  Utilities: 99
  Property Taxes: 83
Miscellaneous Living Cost Indexes
  College Tuition: 102
  Food: 102
  Health Care: 90
  Transportation: 104
Places Rated Score: 8,804
Places Rated Rank: 152

Fayetteville, NC
Typical Household Income: $30,688
State and Local Taxes: $1,809
Housing Cost Indexes
  Median Price: 76
  Utilities: 95
  Property Taxes: 67
Miscellaneous Living Cost Indexes
  College Tuition: 52
  Food: 99
  Health Care: 87
  Transportation: 92
Places Rated Score: 8,708
Places Rated Rank: 137

Fayetteville–Springdale, AR
Typical Household Income: $37,667
State and Local Taxes: $1,287
Housing Cost Indexes
  Median Price: 64
  Utilities: 77
  Property Taxes: 36
Miscellaneous Living Cost Indexes
  College Tuition: 67
  Food: 93
  Health Care: 80
  Transportation: 88
Places Rated Score: 7,894
Places Rated Rank: 31

Fitchburg–Leominster, MA
Typical Household Income: $43,729
State and Local Taxes: $2,998
Housing Cost Indexes
  Median Price: 140
  Utilities: 136
  Property Taxes: 102
Miscellaneous Living Cost Indexes
  College Tuition: 102
  Food: 100
  Health Care: 105
  Transportation: 101
Places Rated Score: 11,696
Places Rated Rank: 285

Flint, MI
Typical Household Income: $46,035
State and Local Taxes: $3,463
Housing Cost Indexes
  Median Price: 68
  Utilities: 116
  Property Taxes: 124
Miscellaneous Living Cost Indexes
  College Tuition: 134
  Food: 100
  Health Care: 101
  Transportation: 106
Places Rated Score: 8,825
Places Rated Rank: 154

★ Florence, AL
Typical Household Income: $32,384
State and Local Taxes: $1,211
Housing Cost Indexes
  Median Price: 51
  Utilities: 80
  Property Taxes: 17
Miscellaneous Living Cost Indexes
  College Tuition: 93
  Food: 95
  Health Care: 92
  Transportation: 93
Places Rated Score: 7,578
Places Rated Rank: 7

Florence, SC
Typical Household Income: $31,740
State and Local Taxes: $1,434
Housing Cost Indexes
  Median Price: 66
  Utilities: 87
  Property Taxes: 42
Miscellaneous Living Cost Indexes
  College Tuition: 117
  Food: 100
  Health Care: 69
  Transportation: 85
Places Rated Score: 8,040
Places Rated Rank: 47

Fort Collins–Loveland, CO
Typical Household Income: $40,552
State and Local Taxes: $1,600
Housing Cost Indexes
  Median Price: 81
  Utilities: 84
  Property Taxes: 65
Miscellaneous Living Cost Indexes
  College Tuition: 103
  Food: 95
  Health Care: 113
  Transportation: 96
Places Rated Score: 9,012
Places Rated Rank: 179

**Fort Lauderdale–Hollywood–
Pompano Beach, FL**
Typical Household Income: $57,596
State and Local Taxes: $1,329
Housing Cost Indexes
  Median Price: 89
  Utilities: 80
  Property Taxes: 72
Miscellaneous Living Cost Indexes
  College Tuition: 78
  Food: 100
  Health Care: 132
  Transportation: 115
Places Rated Score: 10,110
Places Rated Rank: 252

Fort Myers–Cape Coral, FL
Typical Household Income: $41,609
State and Local Taxes: $1,298
Housing Cost Indexes
  Median Price: 102
  Utilities: 80
  Property Taxes: 82
Miscellaneous Living Cost Indexes
  College Tuition: 78
  Food: 99
  Health Care: 117
  Transportation: 100
Places Rated Score: 10,145
Places Rated Rank: 253

Fort Pierce, FL
Typical Household Income: $38,971
State and Local Taxes: $1,288
Housing Cost Indexes
  Median Price: 103
  Utilities: 72
  Property Taxes: 82
Miscellaneous Living Cost Indexes
  College Tuition: 78
  Food: 98
  Health Care: 112
  Transportation: 90
Places Rated Score: 9,852
Places Rated Rank: 240

★ Fort Smith, AR–OK
Typical Household Income: $35,515
State and Local Taxes: $1,203
Housing Cost Indexes
  Median Price: 54
  Utilities: 86
  Property Taxes: 30
Miscellaneous Living Cost Indexes
  College Tuition: 67
  Food: 95
  Health Care: 84
  Transportation: 85
Places Rated Score: 7,450
Places Rated Rank: 5

Fort Walton Beach, FL
Typical Household Income: $28,272
State and Local Taxes: $1,018
Housing Cost Indexes
  Median Price: 84
  Utilities: 71
  Property Taxes: 67
Miscellaneous Living Cost Indexes
  College Tuition: 78
  Food: 98
  Health Care: 83
  Transportation: 85
Places Rated Score: 8,791
Places Rated Rank: 151

Fort Wayne, IN
Typical Household Income: $45,325
State and Local Taxes: $2,258
Housing Cost Indexes
  Median Price: 68
  Utilities: 104
  Property Taxes: 74
Miscellaneous Living Cost Indexes
  College Tuition: 130
  Food: 103
  Health Care: 100
  Transportation: 99
Places Rated Score: 8,703
Places Rated Rank: 135

Fort Worth–Arlington, TX
Typical Household Income: $48,136
State and Local Taxes: $1,399

Housing Cost Indexes
  Median Price: 82
  Utilities: 85
  Property Taxes: 101
Miscellaneous Living Cost Indexes
  College Tuition: 59
  Food: 104
  Health Care: 108
  Transportation: 111
Places Rated Score: 9,691
Places Rated Rank: 231

Fresno, CA
Typical Household Income: $38,497
State and Local Taxes: $2,400
Housing Cost Indexes
  Median Price: 134
  Utilities: 101
  Property Taxes: 123
Miscellaneous Living Cost Indexes
  College Tuition: 60
  Food: 102
  Health Care: 113
  Transportation: 115
Places Rated Score: 11,953
Places Rated Rank: 290

Gadsden, AL
Typical Household Income: $33,255
State and Local Taxes: $1,256
Housing Cost Indexes
  Median Price: 56
  Utilities: 87
  Property Taxes: 19
Miscellaneous Living Cost Indexes
  College Tuition: 93
  Food: 99
  Health Care: 105
  Transportation: 92
Places Rated Score: 7,923
Places Rated Rank: 33

Gainesville, FL
Typical Household Income: $31,504
State and Local Taxes: $1,066
Housing Cost Indexes
  Median Price: 83
  Utilities: 69
  Property Taxes: 67
Miscellaneous Living Cost Indexes
  College Tuition: 78
  Food: 95
  Health Care: 97
  Transportation: 101
Places Rated Score: 9,179
Places Rated Rank: 198

Galveston–Texas City, TX
Typical Household Income: $46,133
State and Local Taxes: $1,204
Housing Cost Indexes
  Median Price: 67
  Utilities: 83
  Property Taxes: 83
Miscellaneous Living Cost Indexes
  College Tuition: 59
  Food: 106
  Health Care: 91
  Transportation: 106
Places Rated Score: 8,925
Places Rated Rank: 168

Gary–Hammond, IN
Typical Household Income: $32,309
State and Local Taxes: $1,954
Housing Cost Indexes
  Median Price: 79
  Utilities: 127

Property Taxes: 86
Miscellaneous Living Cost Indexes
   College Tuition: 130
   Food: 101
   Health Care: 92
   Transportation: 85
Places Rated Score: 8,705
Places Rated Rank: 136

Glens Falls, NY
Typical Household Income: $35,230
State and Local Taxes: $2,496
Housing Cost Indexes
   Median Price: 64
   Utilities: 108
   Property Taxes: 116
Miscellaneous Living Cost Indexes
   College Tuition: 124
   Food: 104
   Health Care: 68
   Transportation: 109
Places Rated Score: 8,697
Places Rated Rank: 133

Grand Forks, ND
Typical Household Income: $40,898
State and Local Taxes: $1,378
Housing Cost Indexes
   Median Price: 67
   Utilities: 99
   Property Taxes: 80
Miscellaneous Living Cost Indexes
   College Tuition: 102
   Food: 103
   Health Care: 111
   Transportation: 96
Places Rated Score: 8,625
Places Rated Rank: 126

Grand Rapids, MI
Typical Household Income: $46,718
State and Local Taxes: $3,419
Housing Cost Indexes
   Median Price: 65
   Utilities: 116
   Property Taxes: 119
Miscellaneous Living Cost Indexes
   College Tuition: 134
   Food: 101
   Health Care: 100
   Transportation: 108
Places Rated Score: 8,771
Places Rated Rank: 146

Great Falls, MT
Typical Household Income: $43,122
State and Local Taxes: $1,751
Housing Cost Indexes
   Median Price: 64
   Utilities: 87
   Property Taxes: 74
Miscellaneous Living Cost Indexes
   College Tuition: 81
   Food: 106
   Health Care: 96
   Transportation: 98
Places Rated Score: 8,564
Places Rated Rank: 118

Greeley, CO
Typical Household Income: $33,397
State and Local Taxes: $1,301
Housing Cost Indexes
   Median Price: 65
   Utilities: 91
   Property Taxes: 53
Miscellaneous Living Cost Indexes
   College Tuition: 103

Food: 94
   Health Care: 100
   Transportation: 85
Places Rated Score: 7,971
Places Rated Rank: 38

Green Bay, WI
Typical Household Income: $45,020
State and Local Taxes: $3,601
Housing Cost Indexes
   Median Price: 86
   Utilities: 102
   Property Taxes: 151
Miscellaneous Living Cost Indexes
   College Tuition: 100
   Food: 100
   Health Care: 90
   Transportation: 101
Places Rated Score: 9,380
Places Rated Rank: 213

Greensboro–Winston-Salem–High Point, NC
Typical Household Income: $45,395
State and Local Taxes: $2,617
Housing Cost Indexes
   Median Price: 92
   Utilities: 95
   Property Taxes: 81
Miscellaneous Living Cost Indexes
   College Tuition: 52
   Food: 98
   Health Care: 90
   Transportation: 95
Places Rated Score: 9,430
Places Rated Rank: 219

Greenville–Spartanburg, SC
Typical Household Income: $42,880
State and Local Taxes: $1,886
Housing Cost Indexes
   Median Price: 68
   Utilities: 85
   Property Taxes: 42
Miscellaneous Living Cost Indexes
   College Tuition: 117
   Food: 96
   Health Care: 100
   Transportation: 96
Places Rated Score: 8,431
Places Rated Rank: 94

Hagerstown, MD
Typical Household Income: $40,829
State and Local Taxes: $2,462
Housing Cost Indexes
   Median Price: 82
   Utilities: 82
   Property Taxes: 87
Miscellaneous Living Cost Indexes
   College Tuition: 123
   Food: 99
   Health Care: 87
   Transportation: 94
Places Rated Score: 8,991
Places Rated Rank: 175

Hamilton–Middletown, OH
Typical Household Income: $39,334
State and Local Taxes: $1,762
Housing Cost Indexes
   Median Price: 68
   Utilities: 119
   Property Taxes: 62
Miscellaneous Living Cost Indexes
   College Tuition: 149
   Food: 103
   Health Care: 86

Transportation: 91
Places Rated Score: 8,406
Places Rated Rank: 91

Harrisburg–Lebanon–Carlisle, PA
Typical Household Income: $43,591
State and Local Taxes: $2,194
Housing Cost Indexes
   Median Price: 69
   Utilities: 117
   Property Taxes: 84
Miscellaneous Living Cost Indexes
   College Tuition: 192
   Food: 104
   Health Care: 105
   Transportation: 109
Places Rated Score: 9,065
Places Rated Rank: 185

Hartford, CT
Typical Household Income: $61,387
State and Local Taxes: $3,196
Housing Cost Indexes
   Median Price: 181
   Utilities: 127
   Property Taxes: 229
Miscellaneous Living Cost Indexes
   College Tuition: 103
   Food: 106
   Health Care: 119
   Transportation: 106
Places Rated Score: 13,787
Places Rated Rank: 308

Hickory, NC
Typical Household Income: $37,220
State and Local Taxes: $2,127
Housing Cost Indexes
   Median Price: 81
   Utilities: 95
   Property Taxes: 72
Miscellaneous Living Cost Indexes
   College Tuition: 52
   Food: 98
   Health Care: 81
   Transportation: 88
Places Rated Score: 8,759
Places Rated Rank: 142

Honolulu, HI
Typical Household Income: $54,197
State and Local Taxes: $4,119
Housing Cost Indexes
   Median Price: 258
   Utilities: 91
   Property Taxes: 114
Miscellaneous Living Cost Indexes
   College Tuition: 63
   Food: 120
   Health Care: 129
   Transportation: 115
Places Rated Score: 17,667
Places Rated Rank: 330

Houma–Thibodaux, LA
Typical Household Income: $30,555
State and Local Taxes: $450
Housing Cost Indexes
   Median Price: 70
   Utilities: 82
   Property Taxes: 13
Miscellaneous Living Cost Indexes
   College Tuition: 95
   Food: 104
   Health Care: 74
   Transportation: 85
Places Rated Score: 8,335
Places Rated Rank: 86

Houston, TX
Typical Household Income: $50,411
State and Local Taxes: $1,225
Housing Cost Indexes
  Median Price: 69
  Utilities: 87
  Property Taxes: 84
Miscellaneous Living Cost Indexes
  College Tuition: 59
  Food: 106
  Health Care: 115
  Transportation: 115
Places Rated Score: 9,324
Places Rated Rank: 206

Huntington–Ashland, WV–KY–OH
Typical Household Income: $30,958
State and Local Taxes: $1,382
Housing Cost Indexes
  Median Price: 69
  Utilities: 95
  Property Taxes: 41
Miscellaneous Living Cost Indexes
  College Tuition: 73
  Food: 103
  Health Care: 78
  Transportation: 92
Places Rated Score: 8,452
Places Rated Rank: 98

Huntsville, AL
Typical Household Income: $43,150
State and Local Taxes: $1,624
Housing Cost Indexes
  Median Price: 70
  Utilities: 76
  Property Taxes: 24
Miscellaneous Living Cost Indexes
  College Tuition: 93
  Food: 98
  Health Care: 114
  Transportation: 105
Places Rated Score: 8,909
Places Rated Rank: 162

Indianapolis, IN
Typical Household Income: $47,239
State and Local Taxes: $2,385
Housing Cost Indexes
  Median Price: 74
  Utilities: 103
  Property Taxes: 81
Miscellaneous Living Cost Indexes
  College Tuition: 130
  Food: 93
  Health Care: 112
  Transportation: 108
Places Rated Score: 9,006
Places Rated Rank: 178

Iowa City, IA
Typical Household Income: $52,229
State and Local Taxes: $3,098
Housing Cost Indexes
  Median Price: 79
  Utilities: 118
  Property Taxes: 134
Miscellaneous Living Cost Indexes
  College Tuition: 112
  Food: 93
  Health Care: 122
  Transportation: 115
Places Rated Score: 9,427
Places Rated Rank: 217

Jackson, MI
Typical Household Income: $39,942
State and Local Taxes: $3,063

Housing Cost Indexes
  Median Price: 63
  Utilities: 115
  Property Taxes: 115
Miscellaneous Living Cost Indexes
  College Tuition: 134
  Food: 100
  Health Care: 95
  Transportation: 92
Places Rated Score: 8,218
Places Rated Rank: 67

Jackson, MS
Typical Household Income: $40,959
State and Local Taxes: $1,482
Housing Cost Indexes
  Median Price: 67
  Utilities: 89
  Property Taxes: 44
Miscellaneous Living Cost Indexes
  College Tuition: 105
  Food: 101
  Health Care: 92
  Transportation: 94
Places Rated Score: 8,458
Places Rated Rank: 101

Jackson, TN
Typical Household Income: $35,369
State and Local Taxes: $891
Housing Cost Indexes
  Median Price: 57
  Utilities: 72
  Property Taxes: 44
Miscellaneous Living Cost Indexes
  College Tuition: 85
  Food: 100
  Health Care: 90
  Transportation: 100
Places Rated Score: 8,142
Places Rated Rank: 57

Jacksonville, FL
Typical Household Income: $37,003
State and Local Taxes: $999
Housing Cost Indexes
  Median Price: 72
  Utilities: 69
  Property Taxes: 58
Miscellaneous Living Cost Indexes
  College Tuition: 78
  Food: 101
  Health Care: 103
  Transportation: 102
Places Rated Score: 8,922
Places Rated Rank: 167

Jacksonville, NC
Typical Household Income: $31,311
State and Local Taxes: $1,823
Housing Cost Indexes
  Median Price: 76
  Utilities: 99
  Property Taxes: 66
Miscellaneous Living Cost Indexes
  College Tuition: 52
  Food: 100
  Health Care: 73
  Transportation: 85
Places Rated Score: 8,448
Places Rated Rank: 97

Janesville–Beloit, WI
Typical Household Income: $41,020
State and Local Taxes: $3,224
Housing Cost Indexes
  Median Price: 78

Utilities: 107
  Property Taxes: 138
Miscellaneous Living Cost Indexes
  College Tuition: 100
  Food: 100
  Health Care: 77
  Transportation: 93
Places Rated Score: 8,784
Places Rated Rank: 148

Jersey City, NJ
Typical Household Income: $47,933
State and Local Taxes: $4,031
Housing Cost Indexes
  Median Price: 126
  Utilities: 126
  Property Taxes: 260
Miscellaneous Living Cost Indexes
  College Tuition: 128
  Food: 102
  Health Care: 85
  Transportation: 110
Places Rated Score: 11,333
Places Rated Rank: 280

Johnson City–Kingsport–Bristol, TN–VA
Typical Household Income: $32,830
State and Local Taxes: $945
Housing Cost Indexes
  Median Price: 65
  Utilities: 72
  Property Taxes: 50
Miscellaneous Living Cost Indexes
  College Tuition: 85
  Food: 97
  Health Care: 87
  Transportation: 106
Places Rated Score: 8,545
Places Rated Rank: 114

Johnstown, PA
Typical Household Income: $31,437
State and Local Taxes: $1,797
Housing Cost Indexes
  Median Price: 66
  Utilities: 114
  Property Taxes: 80
Miscellaneous Living Cost Indexes
  College Tuition: 192
  Food: 100
  Health Care: 96
  Transportation: 85
Places Rated Score: 8,137
Places Rated Rank: 56

Joliet, IL
Typical Household Income: $39,116
State and Local Taxes: $2,624
Housing Cost Indexes
  Median Price: 96
  Utilities: 140
  Property Taxes: 129
Miscellaneous Living Cost Indexes
  College Tuition: 123
  Food: 101
  Health Care: 88
  Transportation: 90
Places Rated Score: 9,516
Places Rated Rank: 223

Joplin, MO
Typical Household Income: $36,379
State and Local Taxes: $1,323
Housing Cost Indexes
  Median Price: 59
  Utilities: 86
  Property Taxes: 42

Miscellaneous Living Cost Indexes
  College Tuition: 88
  Food: 104
  Health Care: 94
  Transportation: 91
Places Rated Score: 8,107
Places Rated Rank: 51

Kalamazoo, MI
Typical Household Income: $49,189
State and Local Taxes: $3,635
Housing Cost Indexes
  Median Price: 70
  Utilities: 116
  Property Taxes: 127
Miscellaneous Living Cost Indexes
  College Tuition: 134
  Food: 100
  Health Care: 109
  Transportation: 113
Places Rated Score: 9,126
Places Rated Rank: 192

Kankakee, IL
Typical Household Income: $36,508
State and Local Taxes: $2,267
Housing Cost Indexes
  Median Price: 76
  Utilities: 140
  Property Taxes: 102
Miscellaneous Living Cost Indexes
  College Tuition: 123
  Food: 101
  Health Care: 90
  Transportation: 85
Places Rated Score: 8,567
Places Rated Rank: 119

Kansas City, MO-KS
Typical Household Income: $48,118
State and Local Taxes: $1,931
Housing Cost Indexes
  Median Price: 81
  Utilities: 106
  Property Taxes: 58
Miscellaneous Living Cost Indexes
  College Tuition: 88
  Food: 95
  Health Care: 112
  Transportation: 97
Places Rated Score: 9,028
Places Rated Rank: 180

Kenosha, WI
Typical Household Income: $42,685
State and Local Taxes: $3,564
Housing Cost Indexes
  Median Price: 87
  Utilities: 106
  Property Taxes: 154
Miscellaneous Living Cost Indexes
  College Tuition: 100
  Food: 101
  Health Care: 89
  Transportation: 113
Places Rated Score: 9,800
Places Rated Rank: 237

Killeen-Temple, TX
Typical Household Income: $39,691
State and Local Taxes: $1,004
Housing Cost Indexes
  Median Price: 55
  Utilities: 85
  Property Taxes: 67
Miscellaneous Living Cost Indexes
  College Tuition: 59
  Food: 104

Health Care: 97
  Transportation: 95
Places Rated Score: 8,075
Places Rated Rank: 49

Knoxville, TN
Typical Household Income: $38,069
State and Local Taxes: $1,093
Housing Cost Indexes
  Median Price: 76
  Utilities: 76
  Property Taxes: 59
Miscellaneous Living Cost Indexes
  College Tuition: 85
  Food: 96
  Health Care: 94
  Transportation: 97
Places Rated Score: 8,789
Places Rated Rank: 150

Kokomo, IN
Typical Household Income: $42,843
State and Local Taxes: $2,122
Housing Cost Indexes
  Median Price: 63
  Utilities: 113
  Property Taxes: 69
Miscellaneous Living Cost Indexes
  College Tuition: 130
  Food: 95
  Health Care: 98
  Transportation: 99
Places Rated Score: 8,286
Places Rated Rank: 80

La Crosse, WI
Typical Household Income: $45,022
State and Local Taxes: $3,253
Housing Cost Indexes
  Median Price: 70
  Utilities: 105
  Property Taxes: 124
Miscellaneous Living Cost Indexes
  College Tuition: 100
  Food: 97
  Health Care: 86
  Transportation: 103
Places Rated Score: 8,682
Places Rated Rank: 131

Lafayette, LA
Typical Household Income: $40,000
State and Local Taxes: $438
Housing Cost Indexes
  Median Price: 78
  Utilities: 81
  Property Taxes: 15
Miscellaneous Living Cost Indexes
  College Tuition: 95
  Food: 106
  Health Care: 104
  Transportation: 92
Places Rated Score: 9,056
Places Rated Rank: 184

Lafayette-West Lafayette, IN
Typical Household Income: $45,459
State and Local Taxes: $2,949
Housing Cost Indexes
  Median Price: 80
  Utilities: 113
  Property Taxes: 87
Miscellaneous Living Cost Indexes
  College Tuition: 130
  Food: 100
  Health Care: 99
  Transportation: 97
Places Rated Score: 9,066
Places Rated Rank: 186

Lake Charles, LA
Typical Household Income: $33,902
State and Local Taxes: $481
Housing Cost Indexes
  Median Price: 69
  Utilities: 81
  Property Taxes: 13
Miscellaneous Living Cost Indexes
  College Tuition: 95
  Food: 102
  Health Care: 69
  Transportation: 106
Places Rated Score: 8,771
Places Rated Rank: 146

Lake County, IL
Typical Household Income: $57,357
State and Local Taxes: $3,742
Housing Cost Indexes
  Median Price: 136
  Utilities: 140
  Property Taxes: 183
Miscellaneous Living Cost Indexes
  College Tuition: 123
  Food: 101
  Health Care: 111
  Transportation: 115
Places Rated Score: 11,986
Places Rated Rank: 291

Lakeland-Winter Haven, FL
Typical Household Income: $31,189
State and Local Taxes: $930
Housing Cost Indexes
  Median Price: 70
  Utilities: 72
  Property Taxes: 56
Miscellaneous Living Cost Indexes
  College Tuition: 78
  Food: 99
  Health Care: 77
  Transportation: 103
Places Rated Score: 8,708
Places Rated Rank: 137

Lancaster, PA
Typical Household Income: $42,966
State and Local Taxes: $2,572
Housing Cost Indexes
  Median Price: 99
  Utilities: 116
  Property Taxes: 121
Miscellaneous Living Cost Indexes
  College Tuition: 192
  Food: 107
  Health Care: 97
  Transportation: 94
Places Rated Score: 9,970
Places Rated Rank: 249

Lansing-East Lansing, MI
Typical Household Income: $47,166
State and Local Taxes: $3,936
Housing Cost Indexes
  Median Price: 90
  Utilities: 111
  Property Taxes: 164
Miscellaneous Living Cost Indexes
  College Tuition: 134
  Food: 101
  Health Care: 122
  Transportation: 109
Places Rated Score: 9,936
Places Rated Rank: 248

★ Laredo, TX
Typical Household Income: $16,317
State and Local Taxes: $803

Housing Cost Indexes
  Median Price: 52
  Utilities: 77
  Property Taxes: 63
Miscellaneous Living Cost Indexes
  College Tuition: 59
  Food: 98
  Health Care: 70
  Transportation: 85
Places Rated Score: 7,374
Places Rated Rank: 2

Las Cruces, NM
Typical Household Income: $27,070
State and Local Taxes: $652
Housing Cost Indexes
  Median Price: 60
  Utilities: 103
  Property Taxes: 46
Miscellaneous Living Cost Indexes
  College Tuition: 64
  Food: 102
  Health Care: 82
  Transportation: 113
Places Rated Score: 8,648
Places Rated Rank: 128

Las Vegas, NV
Typical Household Income: $42,675
State and Local Taxes: $986
Housing Cost Indexes
  Median Price: 88
  Utilities: 79
  Property Taxes: 53
Miscellaneous Living Cost Indexes
  College Tuition: 74
  Food: 89
  Health Care: 146
  Transportation: 128
Places Rated Score: 10,173
Places Rated Rank: 255

Lawrence, KS
Typical Household Income: $38,172
State and Local Taxes: $1,641
Housing Cost Indexes
  Median Price: 73
  Utilities: 88
  Property Taxes: 70
Miscellaneous Living Cost Indexes
  College Tuition: 88
  Food: 101
  Health Care: 80
  Transportation: 94
Places Rated Score: 8,632
Places Rated Rank: 127

Lawrence–Haverhill, MA–NH
Typical Household Income: $50,026
State and Local Taxes: $3,650
Housing Cost Indexes
  Median Price: 173
  Utilities: 106
  Property Taxes: 127
Miscellaneous Living Cost Indexes
  College Tuition: 102
  Food: 100
  Health Care: 92
  Transportation: 115
Places Rated Score: 13,435
Places Rated Rank: 305

★ Lawton, OK
Typical Household Income: $31,266
State and Local Taxes: $925
Housing Cost Indexes
  Median Price: 56

Utilities: 90
  Property Taxes: 37
Miscellaneous Living Cost Indexes
  College Tuition: 57
  Food: 97
  Health Care: 88
  Transportation: 85
Places Rated Score: 7,603
Places Rated Rank: 8

Lewiston–Auburn, ME
Typical Household Income: $36,604
State and Local Taxes: $2,027
Housing Cost Indexes
  Median Price: 94
  Utilities: 88
  Property Taxes: 100
Miscellaneous Living Cost Indexes
  College Tuition: 116
  Food: 102
  Health Care: 82
  Transportation: 85
Places Rated Score: 9,309
Places Rated Rank: 205

Lexington–Fayette, KY
Typical Household Income: $48,471
State and Local Taxes: $2,115
Housing Cost Indexes
  Median Price: 82
  Utilities: 76
  Property Taxes: 62
Miscellaneous Living Cost Indexes
  College Tuition: 82
  Food: 98
  Health Care: 113
  Transportation: 95
Places Rated Score: 9,108
Places Rated Rank: 191

★ Lima, OH
Typical Household Income: $39,528
State and Local Taxes: $1,694
Housing Cost Indexes
  Median Price: 60
  Utilities: 113
  Property Taxes: 55
Miscellaneous Living Cost Indexes
  College Tuition: 149
  Food: 94
  Health Care: 82
  Transportation: 91
Places Rated Score: 7,841
Places Rated Rank: 25

Lincoln, NE
Typical Household Income: $44,393
State and Local Taxes: $2,515
Housing Cost Indexes
  Median Price: 78
  Utilities: 96
  Property Taxes: 137
Miscellaneous Living Cost Indexes
  College Tuition: 96
  Food: 89
  Health Care: 112
  Transportation: 102
Places Rated Score: 8,916
Places Rated Rank: 165

Little Rock–North Little Rock, AR
Typical Household Income: $41,893
State and Local Taxes: $1,545
Housing Cost Indexes
  Median Price: 69
  Utilities: 101
  Property Taxes: 39

Miscellaneous Living Cost Indexes
  College Tuition: 67
  Food: 98
  Health Care: 99
  Transportation: 96
Places Rated Score: 8,558
Places Rated Rank: 116

★ Longview–Marshall, TX
Typical Household Income: $38,381
State and Local Taxes: $1,025
Housing Cost Indexes
  Median Price: 57
  Utilities: 86
  Property Taxes: 70
Miscellaneous Living Cost Indexes
  College Tuition: 59
  Food: 99
  Health Care: 94
  Transportation: 88
Places Rated Score: 7,836
Places Rated Rank: 23

Lorain–Elyria, OH
Typical Household Income: $33,580
State and Local Taxes: $1,584
Housing Cost Indexes
  Median Price: 68
  Utilities: 125
  Property Taxes: 62
Miscellaneous Living Cost Indexes
  College Tuition: 149
  Food: 93
  Health Care: 112
  Transportation: 109
Places Rated Score: 8,762
Places Rated Rank: 143

Los Angeles–Long Beach, CA
Typical Household Income: $51,637
State and Local Taxes: $3,856
Housing Cost Indexes
  Median Price: 219
  Utilities: 87
  Property Taxes: 200
Miscellaneous Living Cost Indexes
  College Tuition: 60
  Food: 102
  Health Care: 141
  Transportation: 115
Places Rated Score: 15,649
Places Rated Rank: 324

Louisville, KY–IN
Typical Household Income: $43,964
State and Local Taxes: $1,799
Housing Cost Indexes
  Median Price: 62
  Utilities: 92
  Property Taxes: 47
Miscellaneous Living Cost Indexes
  College Tuition: 82
  Food: 103
  Health Care: 101
  Transportation: 96
Places Rated Score: 8,383
Places Rated Rank: 89

Lowell, MA–NH
Typical Household Income: $54,266
State and Local Taxes: $3,729
Housing Cost Indexes
  Median Price: 158
  Utilities: 106
  Property Taxes: 116
Miscellaneous Living Cost Indexes
  College Tuition: 102

Food: 100
Health Care: 107
Transportation: 115
Places Rated Score: 12,866
Places Rated Rank: 301

Lubbock, TX
Typical Household Income: $40,473
State and Local Taxes: $1,067
Housing Cost Indexes
  Median Price: 60
  Utilities: 86
  Property Taxes: 74
Miscellaneous Living Cost Indexes
  College Tuition: 59
  Food: 104
  Health Care: 98
  Transportation: 90
Places Rated Score: 8,155
Places Rated Rank: 59

Lynchburg, VA
Typical Household Income: $35,294
State and Local Taxes: $1,823
Housing Cost Indexes
  Median Price: 65
  Utilities: 90
  Property Taxes: 55
Miscellaneous Living Cost Indexes
  College Tuition: 140
  Food: 100
  Health Care: 73
  Transportation: 85
Places Rated Score: 7,988
Places Rated Rank: 41

Macon-Warner Robins, GA
Typical Household Income: $38,176
State and Local Taxes: $2,049
Housing Cost Indexes
  Median Price: 71
  Utilities: 93
  Property Taxes: 64
Miscellaneous Living Cost Indexes
  College Tuition: 102
  Food: 94
  Health Care: 95
  Transportation: 88
Places Rated Score: 8,279
Places Rated Rank: 78

Madison, WI
Typical Household Income: $54,850
State and Local Taxes: $4,089
Housing Cost Indexes
  Median Price: 82
  Utilities: 115
  Property Taxes: 144
Miscellaneous Living Cost Indexes
  College Tuition: 100
  Food: 102
  Health Care: 104
  Transportation: 115
Places Rated Score: 9,701
Places Rated Rank: 232

Manchester, NH
Typical Household Income: $49,641
State and Local Taxes: $2,303
Housing Cost Indexes
  Median Price: 162
  Utilities: 123
  Property Taxes: 219
Miscellaneous Living Cost Indexes
  College Tuition: 171
  Food: 103
  Health Care: 107

Transportation: 114
Places Rated Score: 13,103
Places Rated Rank: 303

Mansfield, OH
Typical Household Income: $40,845
State and Local Taxes: $1,742
Housing Cost Indexes
  Median Price: 63
  Utilities: 125
  Property Taxes: 58
Miscellaneous Living Cost Indexes
  College Tuition: 149
  Food: 97
  Health Care: 81
  Transportation: 93
Places Rated Score: 8,109
Places Rated Rank: 52

★ McAllen-Edinburg-Mission, TX
Typical Household Income: $17,013
State and Local Taxes: $713
Housing Cost Indexes
  Median Price: 43
  Utilities: 77
  Property Taxes: 53
Miscellaneous Living Cost Indexes
  College Tuition: 59
  Food: 105
  Health Care: 77
  Transportation: 95
Places Rated Score: 7,524
Places Rated Rank: 6

Medford, OR
Typical Household Income: $35,243
State and Local Taxes: $2,847
Housing Cost Indexes
  Median Price: 66
  Utilities: 84
  Property Taxes: 129
Miscellaneous Living Cost Indexes
  College Tuition: 88
  Food: 95
  Health Care: 103
  Transportation: 93
Places Rated Score: 8,249
Places Rated Rank: 72

Melbourne-Titusville-Palm Bay, FL
Typical Household Income: $38,082
State and Local Taxes: $1,031
Housing Cost Indexes
  Median Price: 75
  Utilities: 81
  Property Taxes: 60
Miscellaneous Living Cost Indexes
  College Tuition: 78
  Food: 100
  Health Care: 97
  Transportation: 88
Places Rated Score: 8,601
Places Rated Rank: 125

Memphis, TN-AR-MS
Typical Household Income: $40,393
State and Local Taxes: $1,162
Housing Cost Indexes
  Median Price: 84
  Utilities: 77
  Property Taxes: 65
Miscellaneous Living Cost Indexes
  College Tuition: 85
  Food: 103
  Health Care: 90
  Transportation: 93
Places Rated Score: 9,178
Places Rated Rank: 197

Merced, CA
Typical Household Income: $30,993
State and Local Taxes: $1,890
Housing Cost Indexes
  Median Price: 104
  Utilities: 101
  Property Taxes: 95
Miscellaneous Living Cost Indexes
  College Tuition: 60
  Food: 102
  Health Care: 100
  Transportation: 111
Places Rated Score: 10,503
Places Rated Rank: 263

Miami-Hialeah, FL
Typical Household Income: $40,139
State and Local Taxes: $1,173
Housing Cost Indexes
  Median Price: 90
  Utilities: 80
  Property Taxes: 72
Miscellaneous Living Cost Indexes
  College Tuition: 78
  Food: 99
  Health Care: 115
  Transportation: 111
Places Rated Score: 9,930
Places Rated Rank: 247

Middlesex-Somerset-Hunterdon, NJ
Typical Household Income: $66,383
State and Local Taxes: $5,836
Housing Cost Indexes
  Median Price: 183
  Utilities: 126
  Property Taxes: 378
Miscellaneous Living Cost Indexes
  College Tuition: 128
  Food: 103
  Health Care: 108
  Transportation: 115
Places Rated Score: 13,983
Places Rated Rank: 311

Middletown, CT
Typical Household Income: $58,867
State and Local Taxes: $3,164
Housing Cost Indexes
  Median Price: 181
  Utilities: 127
  Property Taxes: 229
Miscellaneous Living Cost Indexes
  College Tuition: 103
  Food: 106
  Health Care: 116
  Transportation: 115
Places Rated Score: 14,016
Places Rated Rank: 313

Midland, TX
Typical Household Income: $45,277
State and Local Taxes: $1,135
Housing Cost Indexes
  Median Price: 66
  Utilities: 85
  Property Taxes: 81
Miscellaneous Living Cost Indexes
  College Tuition: 59
  Food: 113
  Health Care: 111
  Transportation: 103
Places Rated Score: 9,049
Places Rated Rank: 182

Milwaukee, WI
Typical Household Income: $49,768
State and Local Taxes: $3,916

Housing Cost Indexes
  Median Price: 81
  Utilities: 106
  Property Taxes: 144
Miscellaneous Living Cost Indexes
  College Tuition: 100
  Food: 102
  Health Care: 105
  Transportation: 115
Places Rated Score: 9,690
Places Rated Rank: 230

Minneapolis–St. Paul, MN–WI
Typical Household Income: $54,262
State and Local Taxes: $3,616
Housing Cost Indexes
  Median Price: 94
  Utilities: 108
  Property Taxes: 82
Miscellaneous Living Cost Indexes
  College Tuition: 141
  Food: 98
  Health Care: 122
  Transportation: 104
Places Rated Score: 9,900
Places Rated Rank: 243

Mobile, AL
Typical Household Income: $34,140
State and Local Taxes: $1,284
Housing Cost Indexes
  Median Price: 56
  Utilities: 87
  Property Taxes: 19
Miscellaneous Living Cost Indexes
  College Tuition: 93
  Food: 100
  Health Care: 102
  Transportation: 107
Places Rated Score: 8,337
Places Rated Rank: 87

Modesto, CA
Typical Household Income: $38,602
State and Local Taxes: $2,131
Housing Cost Indexes
  Median Price: 109
  Utilities: 77
  Property Taxes: 100
Miscellaneous Living Cost Indexes
  College Tuition: 60
  Food: 102
  Health Care: 113
  Transportation: 89
Places Rated Score: 10,199
Places Rated Rank: 257

Monmouth–Ocean, NJ
Typical Household Income: $59,591
State and Local Taxes: $5,599
Housing Cost Indexes
  Median Price: 183
  Utilities: 110
  Property Taxes: 378
Miscellaneous Living Cost Indexes
  College Tuition: 128
  Food: 103
  Health Care: 97
  Transportation: 115
Places Rated Score: 13,933
Places Rated Rank: 309

Monroe, LA
Typical Household Income: $37,293
State and Local Taxes: $493
Housing Cost Indexes
  Median Price: 63
  Utilities: 78
  Property Taxes: 12

Miscellaneous Living Cost Indexes
  College Tuition: 95
  Food: 95
  Health Care: 82
  Transportation: 108
Places Rated Score: 8,461
Places Rated Rank: 102

Montgomery, AL
Typical Household Income: $37,943
State and Local Taxes: $1,460
Housing Cost Indexes
  Median Price: 72
  Utilities: 87
  Property Taxes: 24
Miscellaneous Living Cost Indexes
  College Tuition: 93
  Food: 101
  Health Care: 94
  Transportation: 97
Places Rated Score: 8,743
Places Rated Rank: 140

★ **Muncie, IN**
Typical Household Income: $39,898
State and Local Taxes: $1,971
Housing Cost Indexes
  Median Price: 57
  Utilities: 104
  Property Taxes: 62
Miscellaneous Living Cost Indexes
  College Tuition: 130
  Food: 96
  Health Care: 93
  Transportation: 92
Places Rated Score: 7,835
Places Rated Rank: 21

Muskegon, MI
Typical Household Income: $38,217
State and Local Taxes: $2,958
Housing Cost Indexes
  Median Price: 62
  Utilities: 112
  Property Taxes: 112
Miscellaneous Living Cost Indexes
  College Tuition: 134
  Food: 100
  Health Care: 100
  Transportation: 88
Places Rated Score: 8,066
Places Rated Rank: 48

Naples, FL
Typical Household Income: $50,759
State and Local Taxes: $1,352
Housing Cost Indexes
  Median Price: 100
  Utilities: 80
  Property Taxes: 80
Miscellaneous Living Cost Indexes
  College Tuition: 78
  Food: 101
  Health Care: 119
  Transportation: 115
Places Rated Score: 10,500
Places Rated Rank: 262

Nashua, NH
Typical Household Income: $55,570
State and Local Taxes: $2,511
Housing Cost Indexes
  Median Price: 177
  Utilities: 123
  Property Taxes: 238
Miscellaneous Living Cost Indexes
  College Tuition: 171
  Food: 103

Health Care: 114
  Transportation: 115
Places Rated Score: 13,766
Places Rated Rank: 307

Nashville, TN
Typical Household Income: $45,074
State and Local Taxes: $1,249
Housing Cost Indexes
  Median Price: 87
  Utilities: 75
  Property Taxes: 67
Miscellaneous Living Cost Indexes
  College Tuition: 85
  Food: 95
  Health Care: 101
  Transportation: 99
Places Rated Score: 9,296
Places Rated Rank: 203

Nassau–Suffolk, NY
Typical Household Income: $58,142
State and Local Taxes: $6,129
Housing Cost Indexes
  Median Price: 164
  Utilities: 133
  Property Taxes: 296
Miscellaneous Living Cost Indexes
  College Tuition: 124
  Food: 113
  Health Care: 105
  Transportation: 115
Places Rated Score: 13,466
Places Rated Rank: 306

New Bedford, MA
Typical Household Income: $39,519
State and Local Taxes: $2,690
Housing Cost Indexes
  Median Price: 127
  Utilities: 112
  Property Taxes: 93
Miscellaneous Living Cost Indexes
  College Tuition: 102
  Food: 99
  Health Care: 90
  Transportation: 91
Places Rated Score: 10,798
Places Rated Rank: 272

New Britain, CT
Typical Household Income: $56,606
State and Local Taxes: $2,840
Housing Cost Indexes
  Median Price: 159
  Utilities: 127
  Property Taxes: 201
Miscellaneous Living Cost Indexes
  College Tuition: 103
  Food: 106
  Health Care: 114
  Transportation: 115
Places Rated Score: 13,081
Places Rated Rank: 302

New Haven–Meriden, CT
Typical Household Income: $53,482
State and Local Taxes: $3,145
Housing Cost Indexes
  Median Price: 182
  Utilities: 130
  Property Taxes: 231
Miscellaneous Living Cost Indexes
  College Tuition: 103
  Food: 105
  Health Care: 110
  Transportation: 115
Places Rated Score: 14,015
Places Rated Rank: 312

New London–Norwich, CT–RI
Typical Household Income: $48,025
State and Local Taxes: $2,745
Housing Cost Indexes
  Median Price: 159
  Utilities: 127
  Property Taxes: 202
Miscellaneous Living Cost Indexes
  College Tuition: 103
  Food: 101
  Health Care: 100
  Transportation: 111
Places Rated Score: 12,779
Places Rated Rank: 297

New Orleans, LA
Typical Household Income: $42,309
State and Local Taxes: $605
Housing Cost Indexes
  Median Price: 78
  Utilities: 94
  Property Taxes: 15
Miscellaneous Living Cost Indexes
  College Tuition: 95
  Food: 96
  Health Care: 116
  Transportation: 90
Places Rated Score: 8,770
Places Rated Rank: 145

New York, NY
Typical Household Income: $57,095
State and Local Taxes: $6,353
Housing Cost Indexes
  Median Price: 198
  Utilities: 135
  Property Taxes: 357
Miscellaneous Living Cost Indexes
  College Tuition: 124
  Food: 112
  Health Care: 108
  Transportation: 115
Places Rated Score: 14,878
Places Rated Rank: 319

Newark, NJ
Typical Household Income: $59,277
State and Local Taxes: $6,406
Housing Cost Indexes
  Median Price: 219
  Utilities: 126
  Property Taxes: 453
Miscellaneous Living Cost Indexes
  College Tuition: 128
  Food: 100
  Health Care: 105
  Transportation: 115
Places Rated Score: 15,400
Places Rated Rank: 322

Niagara Falls, NY
Typical Household Income: $38,727
State and Local Taxes: $2,797
Housing Cost Indexes
  Median Price: 67
  Utilities: 107
  Property Taxes: 120
Miscellaneous Living Cost Indexes
  College Tuition: 124
  Food: 104
  Health Care: 73
  Transportation: 89
Places Rated Score: 8,297
Places Rated Rank: 82

Norfolk–Virginia Beach–Newport News, VA
Typical Household Income: $40,827
State and Local Taxes: $2,197

Housing Cost Indexes
  Median Price: 81
  Utilities: 103
  Property Taxes: 69
Miscellaneous Living Cost Indexes
  College Tuition: 140
  Food: 102
  Health Care: 93
  Transportation: 110
Places Rated Score: 9,513
Places Rated Rank: 222

Norwalk, CT
Typical Household Income: $86,484
State and Local Taxes: $5,585
Housing Cost Indexes
  Median Price: 343
  Utilities: 127
  Property Taxes: 435
Miscellaneous Living Cost Indexes
  College Tuition: 103
  Food: 102
  Health Care: 144
  Transportation: 115
Places Rated Score: 20,817
Places Rated Rank: 332

Oakland, CA
Typical Household Income: $63,499
State and Local Taxes: $4,329
Housing Cost Indexes
  Median Price: 218
  Utilities: 107
  Property Taxes: 199
Miscellaneous Living Cost Indexes
  College Tuition: 60
  Food: 102
  Health Care: 158
  Transportation: 115
Places Rated Score: 15,680
Places Rated Rank: 325

Ocala, FL
Typical Household Income: $30,337
State and Local Taxes: $900
Housing Cost Indexes
  Median Price: 67
  Utilities: 79
  Property Taxes: 53
Miscellaneous Living Cost Indexes
  College Tuition: 78
  Food: 99
  Health Care: 88
  Transportation: 85
Places Rated Score: 8,123
Places Rated Rank: 55

Odessa, TX
Typical Household Income: $36,093
State and Local Taxes: $1,047
Housing Cost Indexes
  Median Price: 61
  Utilities: 85
  Property Taxes: 75
Miscellaneous Living Cost Indexes
  College Tuition: 59
  Food: 104
  Health Care: 89
  Transportation: 102
Places Rated Score: 8,487
Places Rated Rank: 105

★ Oklahoma City, OK
Typical Household Income: $40,794
State and Local Taxes: $1,417
Housing Cost Indexes
  Median Price: 57
  Utilities: 90
  Property Taxes: 38

Miscellaneous Living Cost Indexes
  College Tuition: 57
  Food: 98
  Health Care: 102
  Transportation: 88
Places Rated Score: 7,839
Places Rated Rank: 25

Olympia, WA
Typical Household Income: $39,458
State and Local Taxes: $1,519
Housing Cost Indexes
  Median Price: 89
  Utilities: 83
  Property Taxes: 85
Miscellaneous Living Cost Indexes
  College Tuition: 96
  Food: 96
  Health Care: 100
  Transportation: 91
Places Rated Score: 9,172
Places Rated Rank: 195

Omaha, NE–IA
Typical Household Income: $43,863
State and Local Taxes: $2,303
Housing Cost Indexes
  Median Price: 66
  Utilities: 96
  Property Taxes: 116
Miscellaneous Living Cost Indexes
  College Tuition: 96
  Food: 92
  Health Care: 115
  Transportation: 104
Places Rated Score: 8,563
Places Rated Rank: 117

Orange County, NY
Typical Household Income: $41,132
State and Local Taxes: $4,634
Housing Cost Indexes
  Median Price: 156
  Utilities: 133
  Property Taxes: 282
Miscellaneous Living Cost Indexes
  College Tuition: 124
  Food: 108
  Health Care: 85
  Transportation: 95
Places Rated Score: 12,356
Places Rated Rank: 293

Orlando, FL
Typical Household Income: $40,668
State and Local Taxes: $1,151
Housing Cost Indexes
  Median Price: 86
  Utilities: 75
  Property Taxes: 69
Miscellaneous Living Cost Indexes
  College Tuition: 78
  Food: 99
  Health Care: 106
  Transportation: 97
Places Rated Score: 9,351
Places Rated Rank: 211

Owensboro, KY
Typical Household Income: $39,309
State and Local Taxes: $1,662
Housing Cost Indexes
  Median Price: 62
  Utilities: 77
  Property Taxes: 47
Miscellaneous Living Cost Indexes
  College Tuition: 82
  Food: 103

Health Care: 88
Transporation: 90
Places Rated Score: 8,166
Places Rated Rank: 60

Oxnard–Ventura, CA
Typical Household Income: $46,817
State and Local Taxes: $3,276
Housing Cost Indexes
  Median Price: 192
  Utilities: 100
  Property Taxes: 175
Miscellaneous Living Cost Indexes
  College Tuition: 60
  Food: 101
  Health Care: 120
  Transportation: 108
Places Rated Score: 14,187
Places Rated Rank: 315

Panama City, FL
Typical Household Income: $30,533
State and Local Taxes: $1,061
Housing Cost Indexes
  Median Price: 85
  Utilities: 71
  Property Taxes: 68
Miscellaneous Living Cost Indexes
  College Tuition: 78
  Food: 99
  Health Care: 90
  Transportation: 85
Places Rated Score: 8,880
Places Rated Rank: 158

Parkersburg–Marietta, WV–OH
Typical Household Income: $35,929
State and Local Taxes: $1,545
Housing Cost Indexes
  Median Price: 68
  Utilities: 99
  Property Taxes: 41
Miscellaneous Living Cost Indexes
  College Tuition: 73
  Food: 100
  Health Care: 87
  Transportation: 85
Places Rated Score: 8,181
Places Rated Rank: 61

★ Pascagoula, MS
Typical Household Income: $31,333
State and Local Taxes: $1,153
Housing Cost Indexes
  Median Price: 56
  Utilities: 77
  Property Taxes: 37
Miscellaneous Living Cost Indexes
  College Tuition: 105
  Food: 100
  Health Care: 78
  Transportation: 85
Places Rated Score: 7,641
Places Rated Rank: 10

Pawtucket–Woonsocket–Attleboro, RI–MA
Typical Household Income: $42,444
State and Local Taxes: $3,201
Housing Cost Indexes
  Median Price: 131
  Utilities: 121
  Property Taxes: 170
Miscellaneous Living Cost Indexes
  College Tuition: 130
  Food: 99
  Health Care: 80

Transportation: 98
Places Rated Score: 11,116
Places Rated Rank: 278

Pensacola, FL
Typical Household Income: $28,823
State and Local Taxes: $1,044
Housing Cost Indexes
  Median Price: 86
  Utilities: 72
  Property Taxes: 68
Miscellaneous Living Cost Indexes
  College Tuition: 78
  Food: 94
  Health Care: 92
  Transportation: 99
Places Rated Score: 9,174
Places Rated Rank: 196

★ Peoria, IL
Typical Household Income: $43,815
State and Local Taxes: $2,053
Housing Cost Indexes
  Median Price: 46
  Utilities: 127
  Property Taxes: 62
Miscellaneous Living Cost Indexes
  College Tuition: 123
  Food: 107
  Health Care: 105
  Transportation: 98
Places Rated Score: 7,891
Places Rated Rank: 30

Philadelphia, PA–NJ
Typical Household Income: $48,647
State and Local Taxes: $2,860
Housing Cost Indexes
  Median Price: 110
  Utilities: 123
  Property Taxes: 133
Miscellaneous Living Cost Indexes
  College Tuition: 192
  Food: 109
  Health Care: 129
  Transportation: 109
Places Rated Score: 11,017
Places Rated Rank: 277

Phoenix, AZ
Typical Household Income: $48,025
State and Local Taxes: $2,093
Housing Cost Indexes
  Median Price: 86
  Utilities: 98
  Property Taxes: 49
Miscellaneous Living Cost Indexes
  College Tuition: 75
  Food: 104
  Health Care: 121
  Transportation: 104
Places Rated Score: 9,716
Places Rated Rank: 234

★ Pine Bluff, AR
Typical Household Income: $31,606
State and Local Taxes: $1,065
Housing Cost Indexes
  Median Price: 52
  Utilities: 99
  Property Taxes: 29
Miscellaneous Living Cost Indexes
  College Tuition: 67
  Food: 95
  Health Care: 80
  Transportation: 85
Places Rated Score: 7,351
Places Rated Rank: 1

Pittsburgh, PA
Typical Household Income: $44,675
State and Local Taxes: $2,218
Housing Cost Indexes
  Median Price: 74
  Utilities: 127
  Property Taxes: 91
Miscellaneous Living Cost Indexes
  College Tuition: 192
  Food: 96
  Health Care: 115
  Transportation: 100
Places Rated Score: 8,874
Places Rated Rank: 157

Pittsfield, MA
Typical Household Income: $47,370
State and Local Taxes: $2,925
Housing Cost Indexes
  Median Price: 106
  Utilities: 117
  Property Taxes: 78
Miscellaneous Living Cost Indexes
  College Tuition: 102
  Food: 101
  Health Care: 99
  Transportation: 109
Places Rated Score: 10,525
Places Rated Rank: 264

Portland, ME
Typical Household Income: $51,578
State and Local Taxes: $3,247
Housing Cost Indexes
  Median Price: 141
  Utilities: 88
  Property Taxes: 150
Miscellaneous Living Cost Indexes
  College Tuition: 116
  Food: 100
  Health Care: 100
  Transportation: 115
Places Rated Score: 12,123
Places Rated Rank: 292

Portland, OR
Typical Household Income: $46,182
State and Local Taxes: $3,687
Housing Cost Indexes
  Median Price: 73
  Utilities: 81
  Property Taxes: 144
Miscellaneous Living Cost Indexes
  College Tuition: 88
  Food: 97
  Health Care: 119
  Transportation: 107
Places Rated Score: 9,078
Places Rated Rank: 188

Portsmouth–Dover–Rochester, NH–ME
Typical Household Income: $40,736
State and Local Taxes: $2,314
Housing Cost Indexes
  Median Price: 163
  Utilities: 123
  Property Taxes: 220
Miscellaneous Living Cost Indexes
  College Tuition: 171
  Food: 101
  Health Care: 96
  Transportation: 94
Places Rated Score: 12,477
Places Rated Rank: 295

Poughkeepsie, NY
Typical Household Income: $48,912

State and Local Taxes: $4,573
Housing Cost Indexes
    Median Price: 127
    Utilities: 125
    Property Taxes: 228
Miscellaneous Living Cost Indexes
    College Tuition: 124
    Food: 106
    Health Care: 90
    Transportation: 113
Places Rated Score: 11,565
Places Rated Rank: 282

Providence, RI
Typical Household Income: $46,171
State and Local Taxes: $3,457
Housing Cost Indexes
    Median Price: 141
    Utilities: 111
    Property Taxes: 182
Miscellaneous Living Cost Indexes
    College Tuition: 130
    Food: 100
    Health Care: 84
    Transportation: 106
Places Rated Score: 11,796
Places Rated Rank: 287

Provo–Orem, UT
Typical Household Income: $30,102
State and Local Taxes: $2,092
Housing Cost Indexes
    Median Price: 71
    Utilities: 84
    Property Taxes: 60
Miscellaneous Living Cost Indexes
    College Tuition: 93
    Food: 96
    Health Care: 91
    Transportation: 85
Places Rated Score: 8,240
Places Rated Rank: 70

★ Pueblo, CO
Typical Household Income: $30,579
State and Local Taxes: $1,141
Housing Cost Indexes
    Median Price: 55
    Utilities: 90
    Property Taxes: 45
Miscellaneous Living Cost Indexes
    College Tuition: 103
    Food: 92
    Health Care: 105
    Transportation: 96
Places Rated Score: 7,835
Places Rated Rank: 21

Racine, WI
Typical Household Income: $43,379
State and Local Taxes: $3,345
Housing Cost Indexes
    Median Price: 74
    Utilities: 105
    Property Taxes: 131
Miscellaneous Living Cost Indexes
    College Tuition: 100
    Food: 102
    Health Care: 90
    Transportation: 100
Places Rated Score: 8,926
Places Rated Rank: 169

Raleigh–Durham, NC
Typical Household Income: $49,990
State and Local Taxes: $3,015
Housing Cost Indexes
    Median Price: 111

Utilities: 99
Property Taxes: 98
Miscellaneous Living Cost Indexes
    College Tuition: 52
    Food: 100
    Health Care: 96
    Transportation: 109
Places Rated Score: 10,699
Places Rated Rank: 267

Rapid City, SD
Typical Household Income: $41,833
State and Local Taxes: $1,742
Housing Cost Indexes
    Median Price: 64
    Utilities: 105
    Property Taxes: 121
Miscellaneous Living Cost Indexes
    College Tuition: 78
    Food: 107
    Health Care: 94
    Transportation: 97
Places Rated Score: 8,576
Places Rated Rank: 121

Reading, PA
Typical Household Income: $48,398
State and Local Taxes: $2,584
Housing Cost Indexes
    Median Price: 88
    Utilities: 118
    Property Taxes: 107
Miscellaneous Living Cost Indexes
    College Tuition: 192
    Food: 105
    Health Care: 91
    Transportation: 111
Places Rated Score: 9,876
Places Rated Rank: 242

Redding, CA
Typical Household Income: $39,761
State and Local Taxes: $2,076
Housing Cost Indexes
    Median Price: 109
    Utilities: 73
    Property Taxes: 100
Miscellaneous Living Cost Indexes
    College Tuition: 60
    Food: 99
    Health Care: 105
    Transportation: 92
Places Rated Score: 10,155
Places Rated Rank: 254

Reno, NV
Typical Household Income: $51,489
State and Local Taxes: $1,258
Housing Cost Indexes
    Median Price: 120
    Utilities: 99
    Property Taxes: 72
Miscellaneous Living Cost Indexes
    College Tuition: 74
    Food: 95
    Health Care: 141
    Transportation: 101
Places Rated Score: 10,927
Places Rated Rank: 274

Richland–Kennewick–Pasco, WA
Typical Household Income: $36,643
State and Local Taxes: $1,159
Housing Cost Indexes
    Median Price: 58
    Utilities: 83
    Property Taxes: 56

Miscellaneous Living Cost Indexes
    College Tuition: 96
    Food: 98
    Health Care: 102
    Transportation: 102
Places Rated Score: 8,264
Places Rated Rank: 74

Richmond–Petersburg, VA
Typical Household Income: $49,997
State and Local Taxes: $2,568
Housing Cost Indexes
    Median Price: 79
    Utilities: 103
    Property Taxes: 67
Miscellaneous Living Cost Indexes
    College Tuition: 140
    Food: 104
    Health Care: 110
    Transportation: 105
Places Rated Score: 9,408
Places Rated Rank: 216

Riverside–San Bernardino, CA
Typical Household Income: $40,634
State and Local Taxes: $2,328
Housing Cost Indexes
    Median Price: 127
    Utilities: 103
    Property Taxes: 116
Miscellaneous Living Cost Indexes
    College Tuition: 60
    Food: 99
    Health Care: 131
    Transportation: 105
Places Rated Score: 11,373
Places Rated Rank: 281

Roanoke, VA
Typical Household Income: $48,665
State and Local Taxes: $2,395
Housing Cost Indexes
    Median Price: 71
    Utilities: 90
    Property Taxes: 60
Miscellaneous Living Cost Indexes
    College Tuition: 140
    Food: 101
    Health Care: 101
    Transportation: 106
Places Rated Score: 8,961
Places Rated Rank: 173

Rochester, MN
Typical Household Income: $55,845
State and Local Taxes: $3,651
Housing Cost Indexes
    Median Price: 91
    Utilities: 107
    Property Taxes: 79
Miscellaneous Living Cost Indexes
    College Tuition: 141
    Food: 100
    Health Care: 99
    Transportation: 110
Places Rated Score: 9,900
Places Rated Rank: 243

Rochester, NY
Typical Household Income: $49,125
State and Local Taxes: $3,934
Housing Cost Indexes
    Median Price: 92
    Utilities: 116
    Property Taxes: 166
Miscellaneous Living Cost Indexes
    College Tuition: 124

Food: 104
Health Care: 94
Transportation: 113
Places Rated Score: 10,093
Places Rated Rank: 251

Rockford, IL
Typical Household Income: $46,474
State and Local Taxes: $2,678
Housing Cost Indexes
  Median Price: 84
  Utilities: 140
  Property Taxes: 113
Miscellaneous Living Cost Indexes
  College Tuition: 123
  Food: 100
  Health Care: 114
  Transportation: 107
Places Rated Score: 9,563
Places Rated Rank: 225

Sacramento, CA
Typical Household Income: $50,048
State and Local Taxes: $2,525
Housing Cost Indexes
  Median Price: 109
  Utilities: 94
  Property Taxes: 100
Miscellaneous Living Cost Indexes
  College Tuition: 60
  Food: 102
  Health Care: 123
  Transportation: 115
Places Rated Score: 10,964
Places Rated Rank: 275

Saginaw–Bay City–Midland, MI
Typical Household Income: $40,962
State and Local Taxes: $3,205
Housing Cost Indexes
  Median Price: 68
  Utilities: 116
  Property Taxes: 123
Miscellaneous Living Cost Indexes
  College Tuition: 134
  Food: 99
  Health Care: 95
  Transportation: 94
Places Rated Score: 8,441
Places Rated Rank: 95

St. Cloud, MN
Typical Household Income: $32,892
State and Local Taxes: $2,016
Housing Cost Indexes
  Median Price: 81
  Utilities: 115
  Property Taxes: 70
Miscellaneous Living Cost Indexes
  College Tuition: 141
  Food: 101
  Health Care: 81
  Transportation: 108
Places Rated Score: 9,350
Places Rated Rank: 210

St. Joseph, MO
Typical Household Income: $39,153
State and Local Taxes: $1,455
Housing Cost Indexes
  Median Price: 61
  Utilities: 93
  Property Taxes: 44
Miscellaneous Living Cost Indexes
  College Tuition: 88
  Food: 97
  Health Care: 99

Transportation: 90
Places Rated Score: 8,022
Places Rated Rank: 44

St. Louis, MO–IL
Typical Household Income: $47,166
State and Local Taxes: $1,926
Housing Cost Indexes
  Median Price: 89
  Utilities: 118
  Property Taxes: 64
Miscellaneous Living Cost Indexes
  College Tuition: 88
  Food: 97
  Health Care: 106
  Transportation: 96
Places Rated Score: 9,374
Places Rated Rank: 212

★ Salem, OR
Typical Household Income: $34,992
State and Local Taxes: $2,732
Housing Cost Indexes
  Median Price: 59
  Utilities: 81
  Property Taxes: 116
Miscellaneous Living Cost Indexes
  College Tuition: 88
  Food: 95
  Health Care: 103
  Transportation: 85
Places Rated Score: 7,758
Places Rated Rank: 14

Salem–Gloucester, MA
Typical Household Income: $58,818
State and Local Taxes: $4,235
Housing Cost Indexes
  Median Price: 197
  Utilities: 106
  Property Taxes: 144
Miscellaneous Living Cost Indexes
  College Tuition: 102
  Food: 101
  Health Care: 112
  Transportation: 115
Places Rated Score: 14,526
Places Rated Rank: 316

Salinas–Seaside–Monterey, CA
Typical Household Income: $43,583
State and Local Taxes: $3,512
Housing Cost Indexes
  Median Price: 213
  Utilities: 106
  Property Taxes: 194
Miscellaneous Living Cost Indexes
  College Tuition: 60
  Food: 100
  Health Care: 131
  Transportation: 100
Places Rated Score: 14,881
Places Rated Rank: 320

Salt Lake City–Ogden, UT
Typical Household Income: $47,516
State and Local Taxes: $2,935
Housing Cost Indexes
  Median Price: 73
  Utilities: 84
  Property Taxes: 61
Miscellaneous Living Cost Indexes
  College Tuition: 93
  Food: 94
  Health Care: 113
  Transportation: 105
Places Rated Score: 8,891
Places Rated Rank: 159

San Angelo, TX
Typical Household Income: $43,489
State and Local Taxes: $1,075
Housing Cost Indexes
  Median Price: 59
  Utilities: 87
  Property Taxes: 72
Miscellaneous Living Cost Indexes
  College Tuition: 59
  Food: 100
  Health Care: 101
  Transportation: 100
Places Rated Score: 8,279
Places Rated Rank: 78

San Antonio, TX
Typical Household Income: $38,472
State and Local Taxes: $1,146
Housing Cost Indexes
  Median Price: 66
  Utilities: 80
  Property Taxes: 81
Miscellaneous Living Cost Indexes
  College Tuition: 59
  Food: 100
  Health Care: 93
  Transportation: 104
Places Rated Score: 8,667
Places Rated Rank: 130

San Diego, CA
Typical Household Income: $52,229
State and Local Taxes: $3,319
Housing Cost Indexes
  Median Price: 179
  Utilities: 124
  Property Taxes: 163
Miscellaneous Living Cost Indexes
  College Tuition: 60
  Food: 103
  Health Care: 136
  Transportation: 115
Places Rated Score: 13,956
Places Rated Rank: 310

San Francisco, CA
Typical Household Income: $84,293
State and Local Taxes: $6,127
Housing Cost Indexes
  Median Price: 266
  Utilities: 107
  Property Taxes: 243
Miscellaneous Living Cost Indexes
  College Tuition: 60
  Food: 103
  Health Care: 189
  Transportation: 115
Places Rated Score: 17,860
Places Rated Rank: 331

San Jose, CA
Typical Household Income: $67,463
State and Local Taxes: $4,926
Housing Cost Indexes
  Median Price: 246
  Utilities: 102
  Property Taxes: 224
Miscellaneous Living Cost Indexes
  College Tuition: 60
  Food: 98
  Health Care: 186
  Transportation: 113
Places Rated Score: 16,798
Places Rated Rank: 328

Santa Barbara–Santa Maria–Lompoc, CA
Typical Household Income: $58,424
State and Local Taxes: $3,743

Housing Cost Indexes
  Median Price: 184
  Utilities: 100
  Property Taxes: 169
Miscellaneous Living Cost Indexes
  College Tuition: 60
  Food: 102
  Health Care: 131
  Transportation: 115
Places Rated Score: 14,139
Places Rated Rank: 314

Santa Cruz, CA
Typical Household Income: $54,132
State and Local Taxes: $3,646
Housing Cost Indexes
  Median Price: 207
  Utilities: 106
  Property Taxes: 189
Miscellaneous Living Cost Indexes
  College Tuition: 60
  Food: 102
  Health Care: 143
  Transportation: 115
Places Rated Score: 15,131
Places Rated Rank: 321

Santa Fe, NM
Typical Household Income: $51,476
State and Local Taxes: $1,267
Housing Cost Indexes
  Median Price: 105
  Utilities: 113
  Property Taxes: 80
Miscellaneous Living Cost Indexes
  College Tuition: 64
  Food: 106
  Health Care: 114
  Transportation: 115
Places Rated Score: 10,832
Places Rated Rank: 273

Santa Rosa–Petaluma, CA
Typical Household Income: $59,557
State and Local Taxes: $3,616
Housing Cost Indexes
  Median Price: 193
  Utilities: 102
  Property Taxes: 176
Miscellaneous Living Cost Indexes
  College Tuition: 60
  Food: 102
  Health Care: 154
  Transportation: 115
Places Rated Score: 14,589
Places Rated Rank: 317

Sarasota, FL
Typical Household Income: $58,735
State and Local Taxes: $1,401
Housing Cost Indexes
  Median Price: 99
  Utilities: 80
  Property Taxes: 80
Miscellaneous Living Cost Indexes
  College Tuition: 78
  Food: 98
  Health Care: 119
  Transportation: 115
Places Rated Score: 10,414
Places Rated Rank: 259

Savannah, GA
Typical Household Income: $42,398
State and Local Taxes: $2,240
Housing Cost Indexes
  Median Price: 75
  Utilities: 100

Property Taxes: 67
Miscellaneous Living Cost Indexes
  College Tuition: 102
  Food: 99
  Health Care: 108
  Transportation: 98
Places Rated Score: 8,912
Places Rated Rank: 163

Scranton–Wilkes-Barre, PA
Typical Household Income: $39,200
State and Local Taxes: $2,054
Housing Cost Indexes
  Median Price: 67
  Utilities: 117
  Property Taxes: 81
Miscellaneous Living Cost Indexes
  College Tuition: 192
  Food: 103
  Health Care: 97
  Transportation: 91
Places Rated Score: 8,424
Places Rated Rank: 93

Seattle, WA
Typical Household Income: $55,441
State and Local Taxes: $1,912
Housing Cost Indexes
  Median Price: 102
  Utilities: 74
  Property Taxes: 98
Miscellaneous Living Cost Indexes
  College Tuition: 96
  Food: 106
  Health Care: 117
  Transportation: 105
Places Rated Score: 10,474
Places Rated Rank: 261

Sharon, PA
Typical Household Income: $31,674
State and Local Taxes: $1,786
Housing Cost Indexes
  Median Price: 63
  Utilities: 112
  Property Taxes: 77
Miscellaneous Living Cost Indexes
  College Tuition: 192
  Food: 97
  Health Care: 74
  Transportation: 87
Places Rated Score: 7,917
Places Rated Rank: 32

Sheboygan, WI
Typical Household Income: $45,670
State and Local Taxes: $3,365
Housing Cost Indexes
  Median Price: 70
  Utilities: 107
  Property Taxes: 124
Miscellaneous Living Cost Indexes
  College Tuition: 100
  Food: 103
  Health Care: 93
  Transportation: 105
Places Rated Score: 8,947
Places Rated Rank: 172

★ Sherman–Denison, TX
Typical Household Income: $45,584
State and Local Taxes: $986
Housing Cost Indexes
  Median Price: 51
  Utilities: 85
  Property Taxes: 62
Miscellaneous Living Cost Indexes
  College Tuition: 59

Food: 103
  Health Care: 107
  Transportation: 88
Places Rated Score: 7,721
Places Rated Rank: 13

Shreveport, LA
Typical Household Income: $41,379
State and Local Taxes: $568
Housing Cost Indexes
  Median Price: 68
  Utilities: 78
  Property Taxes: 13
Miscellaneous Living Cost Indexes
  College Tuition: 95
  Food: 98
  Health Care: 110
  Transportation: 95
Places Rated Score: 8,541
Places Rated Rank: 113

★ Sioux City, IA–NE
Typical Household Income: $39,694
State and Local Taxes: $2,333
Housing Cost Indexes
  Median Price: 58
  Utilities: 106
  Property Taxes: 99
Miscellaneous Living Cost Indexes
  College Tuition: 112
  Food: 97
  Health Care: 84
  Transportation: 91
Places Rated Score: 7,858
Places Rated Rank: 28

Sioux Falls, SD
Typical Household Income: $46,105
State and Local Taxes: $1,723
Housing Cost Indexes
  Median Price: 61
  Utilities: 100
  Property Taxes: 115
Miscellaneous Living Cost Indexes
  College Tuition: 78
  Food: 102
  Health Care: 96
  Transportation: 106
Places Rated Score: 8,556
Places Rated Rank: 115

South Bend–Mishawaka, IN
Typical Household Income: $45,228
State and Local Taxes: $2,195
Housing Cost Indexes
  Median Price: 63
  Utilities: 104
  Property Taxes: 69
Miscellaneous Living Cost Indexes
  College Tuition: 130
  Food: 99
  Health Care: 96
  Transportation: 94
Places Rated Score: 8,256
Places Rated Rank: 73

Spokane, WA
Typical Household Income: $39,184
State and Local Taxes: $1,183
Housing Cost Indexes
  Median Price: 55
  Utilities: 79
  Property Taxes: 52
Miscellaneous Living Cost Indexes
  College Tuition: 96
  Food: 100
  Health Care: 100

Transportation: 95
Places Rated Score: 7,975
Places Rated Rank: 39

Springfield, IL
Typical Household Income: $52,773
State and Local Taxes: $2,877
Housing Cost Indexes
  Median Price: 83
  Utilities: 106
  Property Taxes: 112
Miscellaneous Living Cost Indexes
  College Tuition: 123
  Food: 95
  Health Care: 102
  Transportation: 97
Places Rated Score: 9,081
Places Rated Rank: 189

Springfield, MA
Typical Household Income: $44,151
State and Local Taxes: $2,988
Housing Cost Indexes
  Median Price: 136
  Utilities: 117
  Property Taxes: 99
Miscellaneous Living Cost Indexes
  College Tuition: 102
  Food: 105
  Health Care: 84
  Transportation: 105
Places Rated Score: 11,693
Places Rated Rank: 284

Springfield, MO
Typical Household Income: $42,809
State and Local Taxes: $1,585
Housing Cost Indexes
  Median Price: 69
  Utilities: 87
  Property Taxes: 50
Miscellaneous Living Cost Indexes
  College Tuition: 88
  Food: 101
  Health Care: 89
  Transportation: 92
Places Rated Score: 8,452
Places Rated Rank: 98

Stamford, CT
Typical Household Income: $99,171
State and Local Taxes: $6,593
Housing Cost Indexes
  Median Price: 407
  Utilities: 127
  Property Taxes: 517
Miscellaneous Living Cost Indexes
  College Tuition: 103
  Food: 102
  Health Care: 159
  Transportation: 115
Places Rated Score: 23,582
Places Rated Rank: 333

State College, PA
Typical Household Income: $39,098
State and Local Taxes: $2,508
Housing Cost Indexes
  Median Price: 102
  Utilities: 102
  Property Taxes: 124
Miscellaneous Living Cost Indexes
  College Tuition: 192
  Food: 100
  Health Care: 61
  Transportation: 90
Places Rated Score: 9,629
Places Rated Rank: 229

★ Steubenville–Weirton, OH–WV
Typical Household Income: $32,424
State and Local Taxes: $1,489
Housing Cost Indexes
  Median Price: 61
  Utilities: 113
  Property Taxes: 56
Miscellaneous Living Cost Indexes
  College Tuition: 149
  Food: 98
  Health Care: 77
  Transportation: 85
Places Rated Score: 7,807
Places Rated Rank: 18

Stockton, CA
Typical Household Income: $39,163
State and Local Taxes: $2,452
Housing Cost Indexes
  Median Price: 136
  Utilities: 101
  Property Taxes: 125
Miscellaneous Living Cost Indexes
  College Tuition: 60
  Food: 99
  Health Care: 111
  Transportation: 90
Places Rated Score: 11,285
Places Rated Rank: 279

Syracuse, NY
Typical Household Income: $44,269
State and Local Taxes: $3,385
Housing Cost Indexes
  Median Price: 84
  Utilities: 108
  Property Taxes: 151
Miscellaneous Living Cost Indexes
  College Tuition: 124
  Food: 94
  Health Care: 83
  Transportation: 98
Places Rated Score: 9,037
Places Rated Rank: 181

Tacoma, WA
Typical Household Income: $39,593
State and Local Taxes: $1,580
Housing Cost Indexes
  Median Price: 93
  Utilities: 74
  Property Taxes: 89
Miscellaneous Living Cost Indexes
  College Tuition: 96
  Food: 101
  Health Care: 117
  Transportation: 102
Places Rated Score: 9,871
Places Rated Rank: 241

Tallahassee, FL
Typical Household Income: $32,088
State and Local Taxes: $1,095
Housing Cost Indexes
  Median Price: 86
  Utilities: 78
  Property Taxes: 69
Miscellaneous Living Cost Indexes
  College Tuition: 78
  Food: 98
  Health Care: 92
  Transportation: 85
Places Rated Score: 8,913
Places Rated Rank: 164

Tampa–St. Petersburg–Clearwater, FL
Typical Household Income: $43,843
State and Local Taxes: $1,116

Housing Cost Indexes
  Median Price: 78
  Utilities: 81
  Property Taxes: 63
Miscellaneous Living Cost Indexes
  College Tuition: 78
  Food: 100
  Health Care: 115
  Transportation: 101
Places Rated Score: 9,185
Places Rated Rank: 199

Terre Haute, IN
Typical Household Income: $36,983
State and Local Taxes: $1,853
Housing Cost Indexes
  Median Price: 55
  Utilities: 113
  Property Taxes: 59
Miscellaneous Living Cost Indexes
  College Tuition: 130
  Food: 105
  Health Care: 86
  Transportation: 102
Places Rated Score: 8,222
Places Rated Rank: 68

Texarkana, TX–Texarkana, AR
Typical Household Income: $38,620
State and Local Taxes: $1,049
Housing Cost Indexes
  Median Price: 59
  Utilities: 79
  Property Taxes: 72
Miscellaneous Living Cost Indexes
  College Tuition: 59
  Food: 102
  Health Care: 87
  Transportation: 95
Places Rated Score: 8,142
Places Rated Rank: 57

Toledo, OH
Typical Household Income: $46,134
State and Local Taxes: $1,931
Housing Cost Indexes
  Median Price: 63
  Utilities: 139
  Property Taxes: 58
Miscellaneous Living Cost Indexes
  College Tuition: 149
  Food: 110
  Health Care: 110
  Transportation: 98
Places Rated Score: 8,711
Places Rated Rank: 139

Topeka, KS
Typical Household Income: $47,962
State and Local Taxes: $1,927
Housing Cost Indexes
  Median Price: 67
  Utilities: 88
  Property Taxes: 65
Miscellaneous Living Cost Indexes
  College Tuition: 88
  Food: 101
  Health Care: 104
  Transportation: 110
Places Rated Score: 8,942
Places Rated Rank: 170

Trenton, NJ
Typical Household Income: $62,091
State and Local Taxes: $5,119
Housing Cost Indexes
  Median Price: 157
  Utilities: 126

Property Taxes: 325
Miscellaneous Living Cost Indexes
  College Tuition: 128
  Food: 100
  Health Care: 105
  Transportation: 115
Places Rated Score: 12,804
Places Rated Rank: 299

Tucson, AZ
Typical Household Income: $46,139
State and Local Taxes: $1,881
Housing Cost Indexes
  Median Price: 83
  Utilities: 83
  Property Taxes: 48
Miscellaneous Living Cost Indexes
  College Tuition: 75
  Food: 99
  Health Care: 116
  Transportation: 100
Places Rated Score: 9,336
Places Rated Rank: 209

Tulsa, OK
Typical Household Income: $41,890
State and Local Taxes: $1,507
Housing Cost Indexes
  Median Price: 66
  Utilities: 90
  Property Taxes: 44
Miscellaneous Living Cost Indexes
  College Tuition: 57
  Food: 100
  Health Care: 102
  Transportation: 89
Places Rated Score: 8,290
Places Rated Rank: 81

Tuscaloosa, AL
Typical Household Income: $35,199
State and Local Taxes: $1,360
Housing Cost Indexes
  Median Price: 68
  Utilities: 87
  Property Taxes: 23
Miscellaneous Living Cost Indexes
  College Tuition: 93
  Food: 95
  Health Care: 96
  Transportation: 85
Places Rated Score: 8,118
Places Rated Rank: 53

Tyler, TX
Typical Household Income: $46,061
State and Local Taxes: $1,146
Housing Cost Indexes
  Median Price: 63
  Utilities: 85
  Property Taxes: 78
Miscellaneous Living Cost Indexes
  College Tuition: 59
  Food: 104
  Health Care: 108
  Transportation: 102
Places Rated Score: 8,666
Places Rated Rank: 129

Utica–Rome, NY
Typical Household Income: $37,612
State and Local Taxes: $2,667
Housing Cost Indexes
  Median Price: 66
  Utilities: 108
  Property Taxes: 118
Miscellaneous Living Cost Indexes
  College Tuition: 124

RELOCATION RESOURCES

For many people, money matters are a major consideration when choosing where to live. The following resource provides information on what it costs to live in various locations throughout the country

General living costs. Every three months, the American Chamber of Commerce Researchers Association (ACCRA) surveys the costs of housing, food, services, transportation, and health care in 250 locations around the United States. While the ACCRA survey is modeled on the consumption patterns of a young family of four and hence isn't meant for all kinds of households, it is still enormously useful for making comparisons.

You can order a four-quarter subscription for $75, or the latest quarter's survey for $40, from:
  ACCRA
  1 Riverfront Plaza
  Louisville, KY 40202

Better yet, save your money. If you're thinking of only one or two destinations, call your local chamber of commerce. If it belongs to ACCRA, it can readily give you cost comparisons over the telephone.

  Food: 102
  Health Care: 73
  Transportation: 87
Places Rated Score: 8,120
Places Rated Rank: 54

Vallejo–Fairfield–Napa, CA
Typical Household Income: $43,007
State and Local Taxes: $2,909
Housing Cost Indexes
  Median Price: 171
  Utilities: 102
  Property Taxes: 156
Miscellaneous Living Cost Indexes
  College Tuition: 60
  Food: 101
  Health Care: 144
  Transportation: 99
Places Rated Score: 13,159
Places Rated Rank: 304

Vancouver, WA
Typical Household Income: $36,751
State and Local Taxes: $1,310
Housing Cost Indexes
  Median Price: 71
  Utilities: 81
  Property Taxes: 68
Miscellaneous Living Cost Indexes
  College Tuition: 96
  Food: 98
  Health Care: 98
  Transportation: 85
Places Rated Score: 8,320
Places Rated Rank: 83

Victoria, TX
Typical Household Income: $39,087
State and Local Taxes: $1,075
Housing Cost Indexes
  Median Price: 61
  Utilities: 77
  Property Taxes: 75
Miscellaneous Living Cost Indexes
  College Tuition: 59
  Food: 100
  Health Care: 96
  Transportation: 90
Places Rated Score: 8,100
Places Rated Rank: 50

Vineland–Millville–Bridgeton, NJ
Typical Household Income: $36,773
State and Local Taxes: $2,838
Housing Cost Indexes
  Median Price: 85
  Utilities: 128
  Property Taxes: 176
Miscellaneous Living Cost Indexes
  College Tuition: 128
  Food: 99
  Health Care: 77
  Transportation: 85
Places Rated Score: 8,832
Places Rated Rank: 155

Visalia–Tulare–Porterville, CA
Typical Household Income: $31,484
State and Local Taxes: $1,810
Housing Cost Indexes
  Median Price: 96
  Utilities: 88
  Property Taxes: 87
Miscellaneous Living Cost Indexes
  College Tuition: 60
  Food: 96
  Health Care: 100
  Transportation: 105
Places Rated Score: 9,842
Places Rated Rank: 238

★ Waco, TX
Typical Household Income: $42,074
State and Local Taxes: $964
Housing Cost Indexes
  Median Price: 51
  Utilities: 85
  Property Taxes: 62
Miscellaneous Living Cost Indexes
  College Tuition: 59
  Food: 101
  Health Care: 85
  Transportation: 98
Places Rated Score: 7,831
Places Rated Rank: 20

Washington, DC–MD–VA
Typical Household Income: $62,053
State and Local Taxes: $5,193
Housing Cost Indexes
  Median Price: 157

Utilities: 94
Property Taxes: 160
Miscellaneous Living Cost Indexes
    College Tuition: 35
    Food: 103
    Health Care: 120
    Transportation: 105
Places Rated Score: 12,689
Places Rated Rank: 296

Waterbury, CT
Typical Household Income: $50,491
State and Local Taxes: $2,751
Housing Cost Indexes
    Median Price: 155
    Utilities: 127
    Property Taxes: 197
Miscellaneous Living Cost Indexes
    College Tuition: 103
    Food: 102
    Health Care: 107
    Transportation: 115
Places Rated Score: 12,809
Places Rated Rank: 300

★ **Waterloo–Cedar Falls, IA**
Typical Household Income: $32,481
State and Local Taxes: $2,196
Housing Cost Indexes
    Median Price: 62
    Utilities: 105
    Property Taxes: 106
Miscellaneous Living Cost Indexes
    College Tuition: 112
    Food: 97
    Health Care: 70
    Transportation: 85
Places Rated Score: 7,794
Places Rated Rank: 17

Wausau, WI
Typical Household Income: $36,753
State and Local Taxes: $2,987
Housing Cost Indexes
    Median Price: 79
    Utilities: 102
    Property Taxes: 139
Miscellaneous Living Cost Indexes
    College Tuition: 100
    Food: 95
    Health Care: 82
    Transportation: 104
Places Rated Score: 8,993
Places Rated Rank: 176

West Palm Beach–Boca Raton–Delray Beach, FL
Typical Household Income: $57,222
State and Local Taxes: $1,412
Housing Cost Indexes
    Median Price: 103
    Utilities: 80
    Property Taxes: 82
Miscellaneous Living Cost Indexes
    College Tuition: 78
    Food: 100
    Health Care: 122
    Transportation: 115
Places Rated Score: 10,634
Places Rated Rank: 265

Wheeling, WV–OH
Typical Household Income: $34,529
State and Local Taxes: $1,474
Housing Cost Indexes
    Median Price: 63
    Utilities: 101
    Property Taxes: 38

Miscellaneous Living Cost Indexes
    College Tuition: 73
    Food: 100
    Health Care: 80
    Transportation: 85
Places Rated Score: 7,967
Places Rated Rank: 37

Wichita Falls, TX
Typical Household Income: $47,964
State and Local Taxes: $1,029
Housing Cost Indexes
    Median Price: 54
    Utilities: 85
    Property Taxes: 66
Miscellaneous Living Cost Indexes
    College Tuition: 59
    Food: 102
    Health Care: 98
    Transportation: 103
Places Rated Score: 8,200
Places Rated Rank: 66

Wichita, KS
Typical Household Income: $45,320
State and Local Taxes: $1,862
Housing Cost Indexes
    Median Price: 66
    Utilities: 110
    Property Taxes: 64
Miscellaneous Living Cost Indexes
    College Tuition: 88
    Food: 93
    Health Care: 107
    Transportation: 97
Places Rated Score: 8,341
Places Rated Rank: 88

Williamsport, PA
Typical Household Income: $36,652
State and Local Taxes: $1,934
Housing Cost Indexes
    Median Price: 63
    Utilities: 116
    Property Taxes: 77
Miscellaneous Living Cost Indexes
    College Tuition: 192
    Food: 99
    Health Care: 97
    Transportation: 85
Places Rated Score: 8,011
Places Rated Rank: 42

Wilmington, DE–NJ–MD
Typical Household Income: $49,771
State and Local Taxes: $2,544
Housing Cost Indexes
    Median Price: 89
    Utilities: 108
    Property Taxes: 53
Miscellaneous Living Cost Indexes
    College Tuition: 81
    Food: 106
    Health Care: 92
    Transportation: 107
Places Rated Score: 9,844
Places Rated Rank: 239

Wilmington, NC
Typical Household Income: $39,543
State and Local Taxes: $2,248
Housing Cost Indexes
    Median Price: 82
    Utilities: 99
    Property Taxes: 72
Miscellaneous Living Cost Indexes
    College Tuition: 52
    Food: 100
    Health Care: 83

Transportation: 92
Places Rated Score: 8,946
Places Rated Rank: 171

Worcester, MA
Typical Household Income: $46,285
State and Local Taxes: $3,205
Housing Cost Indexes
    Median Price: 152
    Utilities: 106
    Property Taxes: 111
Miscellaneous Living Cost Indexes
    College Tuition: 102
    Food: 100
    Health Care: 109
    Transportation: 107
Places Rated Score: 12,388
Places Rated Rank: 294

Yakima, WA
Typical Household Income: $32,400
State and Local Taxes: $1,150
Housing Cost Indexes
    Median Price: 61
    Utilities: 82
    Property Taxes: 59
Miscellaneous Living Cost Indexes
    College Tuition: 96
    Food: 108
    Health Care: 84
    Transportation: 98
Places Rated Score: 8,464
Places Rated Rank: 103

York, PA
Typical Household Income: $43,635
State and Local Taxes: $2,442
Housing Cost Indexes
    Median Price: 87
    Utilities: 117
    Property Taxes: 106
Miscellaneous Living Cost Indexes
    College Tuition: 192
    Food: 103
    Health Care: 88
    Transportation: 100
Places Rated Score: 9,504
Places Rated Rank: 221

★ **Youngstown–Warren, OH**
Typical Household Income: $36,416
State and Local Taxes: $1,617
Housing Cost Indexes
    Median Price: 61
    Utilities: 125
    Property Taxes: 56
Miscellaneous Living Cost Indexes
    College Tuition: 149
    Food: 96
    Health Care: 95
    Transportation: 86
Places Rated Score: 7,865
Places Rated Rank: 29

Yuba City, CA
Typical Household Income: $34,034
State and Local Taxes: $1,832
Housing Cost Indexes
    Median Price: 97
    Utilities: 101
    Property Taxes: 89
Miscellaneous Living Cost Indexes
    College Tuition: 60
    Food: 97
    Health Care: 83
    Transportation: 85
Places Rated Score: 9,325
Places Rated Rank: 207

Et Cetera

EXPENSIVE NEIGHBORHOODS: WHERE MONEY INCOME IS HIGHEST

Just as incomes are higher in metro areas than in the rural countryside, so are they higher in certain suburbs within a metro area. Among all the 41,000 incorporated cities, towns, boroughs, villages, and minor civil divisions in the United States, per capita money incomes in 260 metro area suburbs are at least $30,000, or about two and a half times the national average.

Where is the highest figure found? Not in tony Beverly Hills, CA; Lake Forest, IL; nor Chevy Chase, MD. It's in the tiny village of Golf, off I-95 between Boca Raton and Palm Beach, on the east coast of Florida. In Golf, the average per capita income is a very comfortable $111,815 a year. The accompanying list gives the 46 metro areas that have the most affluent suburbs.

The 46 Metro Areas with the Most Affluent Suburbs

Ann Arbor, MI
Barton Hills
Austin, TX
Lakeway
Bergen–Passaic, NJ
Alpine
Franklin Lakes
Saddle River
Boston, MA
Weston
Canton, OH
Hills and Dales
Chicago, IL
Barrington Hills
Glencoe
Kenilworth
New Trier Township
Oak Brook
Olympia Fields
Winnetka
Cincinnati, OH–KY–IN
Village of Indian Hills
Cleveland, OH
Bratenahl
Hunting Valley
Pepper Pike
Waite Hill
Dallas, TX
Highland Park
Denver, CO
Cherry Hills Village
Detroit, MI
Bingham Farms
Bloomfield Hills
Bloomfield Township
Franklin
Grosse Pointe Farms
Grosse Pointe Shores
Grosse Pointe Township
Lake Township
Southfield Township
Fort Pierce, FL
Jupiter Island
Fort Worth–Arlington, TX
Westover Hills
Gary–Hammond, IN
Dune Acres

Houston, TX
Bunker Hill Village
Hunters Creek Village
Piney Point Village
Indianapolis, IN
Crows Nest
Kansas City, MO–KS
Mission Hills
Mission Woods
Lake County, IL
Lake Forest
Lincolnshire
Riverwoods
Los Angeles–Long Beach, CA
Beverly Hills
Hidden Hills
Rolling Hills
San Marino
Louisville, KY–IN
Anchorage
Glenview Hills
Hills and Dales
Indian Hills
Maryhill Estates
Mockingbird Valley
Riverwood
Robinswood
Rolling Fields
Sycamore
Madison, WI
Maple Bluff
Miami–Hialeah, FL
Bal Harbour
Middlesex–Somerset–Hunterdon, NJ
Bedminster Township
Far Hills
Tewksbury Township
Milwaukee, WI
River Hills
Minneapolis–St. Paul, MN–WI
Dellwood
Lilydale
Woodland
Monmouth–Ocean, NJ
Mantoloking

Nashville, TN
Belle Meade
Forest Hills
Nassau–Suffolk, NY
Asharoken
Centre Island
Cove Neck

East Hills
Flower Hill
Great Neck Estates
Hewlett Bay Park
Hewlett Harbor
Hewlett Neck
Huntington Bay

The 15 Highest Average Household Incomes in the Metro Areas

Metro Area	Average Income
1. Stamford, CT	$99,171
2. Norwalk, CT	$86,484
3. San Francisco, CA	$84,293
4. Boston, MA	$74,932
5. Anchorage, AK	$74,478
6. Bergen–Passaic, NJ	$68,949
7. San Jose, CA	$67,463
8. Atlantic City, NJ	$67,250
9. Anaheim–Santa Anna, CA	$67,135
10. Middlesex–Somerset–Hunterdon, NJ	$66,383
11. Ann Arbor, MI	$66,228
12. Danbury, CT	$65,431
13. Oakland, CA	$63,499
14. Trenton, NJ	$62,091
15. Washington,CD–MD–VA	$62,053

Source: Woods & Poole Economics, Inc., household income forecasts, 1989.

The 15 Lowest Average Household Incomes in the Metro Areas

Metro Area	Average Income
1. Laredo, TX	$16,317
2. McAllen–Edinburg–Mission, TX	$17,013
3. Brownsville–Harlingen, TX	$18,983
4. El Paso, TX	$25,054
5. Beaver County, PA	$26,892
6. Las Cruces, NM	$27,070
7. Fort Walton Beach, FL	$28,272
8. Pensacola, FL	$28,823
9. Provo–Orem, UT	$30,102
10. Ocala, FL	$30,337
11. Panama City, FL	$30,533
12. Houma–Thibodaux, LA	$30,555
13. Pueblo, CO	$30,579
14. Fayetteville, NC	$30,688
15. Huntington–Ashland, WV–KY–OH	$30,958

Source: Woods & Poole Economics, Inc., household income forecasts, 1989.

Kensington
Kings Point
Lake Success
Lattingtown
Laurel Hollow
Lloyd Harbor
Matinecock
Mill Neck
Muttontown
North Hills
Old Brookville
Old Field
Old Westbury
Oyster Bay Cove
Plandome
Plandome Manor
Roslyn Estates
Roslyn Harbor
Russell Gardens
Saddle Rock
Sands Point
Upper Brookville
Woodsburgh

New York, NY
Bronxville
New Castle Town
Scarsdale

Newark, NJ
Harding Township
Millburn Township

Norwalk, CT
Weston
Westport

Oaklahoma City, OK
Nichols Hills

Orange County, NY
Tuxedo Park

Phoenix, AZ
Carefree

Pittsburgh, PA
Edgeworth
Fox Chapel
Sewickley Heights

Racine, WI
North Bay

Riverside–San Bernardino, CA
Indian Wells
Rancho Mirage

St. Louis, MO–IL
Clarkson Valley
Frontenac
Grantwood
Huntleigh
Ladue
Town and Country
Westwood

San Antonio, TX
Hill Country Village
Olmos Park

San Francisco, CA
Atherton
Belvedere
Hillsborough
Portola Valley
Ross
Sausalito
Woodside

San Jose, CA
Los Altos Hills

Seattle, WA
Hunts Point

Stamford, CT
Darien
New Canaan

Washington, DC–MD–VA
Chevy Chase
Chevy Chase Village
Somerset

West Palm Beach–Boca Raton–Delray Beach, FL
Atlantis
Gulf Stream
Highland Beach
Manalapan
Ocean Ridge
Palm Beach
South Palm Beach

Wichita, KS
Eastborough

Source: Bureau of the Census, *Population and Per Capita Income Estimates: Governmental Units,* 1987.

Jobs

Economists who follow employment trends have an old joke: If you take each local planner's forecast for job growth in his or her area and add them all together, the total number of jobs forecasted would require that every man, woman, and child hold down one day job and moonlight two others. Fortunately, it doesn't quite work out that way, and job forecasters at the national level try to adopt a more balanced perspective. Although no one can predict the future with certainty, predicting where jobs will be plentiful over the next few years isn't merely a matter of gazing into a crystal ball. Forecasters use reliable indicators.

To start with, do people move to where the jobs are, or do jobs come to where the people are? Economists argue about this quite a bit, but most believe that jobs come to where the people are. In other words, any place that has a concentration of people and is also growing is by definition a jobs mecca.

How, then, do you explain the fact that Pittsburgh or Buffalo or Cleveland—metro areas *losing* population since the 1960s—have forecasted job expansion over the next five years? The answer is that employers facing labor shortages (in the Northeast, for example) are looking for new locations with a higher percentage of unemployed people and lower costs of both living and doing business. In such places the workforce has seen jobs disappear in the past and is grateful and ready to work. Employers can do very well with such a work-force. Thus metro areas that are growing produce jobs, as do some shrinking ones.

LIFE IN A BOOM TOWN, AND OTHER QUALITY CONCERNS

If you could live anywhere you choose, would you select a boom town? The advantages include rising personal incomes, which ensure real estate appreciation; expanding personal employment opportunities; improved infrastructures; somewhat lower violent crime; increasing amenities; and high-quality health care and education. On the other hand, the disadvantages of living in a boom town include rising costs of living; increased property crime rates; environmental pollution; and, maybe worst of all, noticeable loss of personal discretionary time.

But if you stay in a no-growth area, you face possible job loss, depreciating value of real estate, boarded-up businesses, and backwater schools and health care. Any advantages? Try declining living costs, increased personal time, and lower crime rates.

Employment opportunities are the single most important factor behind geographic mobility. Joblessness or underemployment can push a settled person to become a mobile one. Consider, for example, that in 1980 you moved from withering Detroit to booming Houston. Now it's 1989 and you're thinking about your

The Work Force Keeps Growing

In 1948, 48 million people had jobs. In 1977, 80 million people were working. Today, the number exceeds 100 million. In each year over the past three decades, there have been more people working than the year before.

Paradoxically, there have also been more people out of work each successive year during the same period. The number includes not only people who left their jobs to look for better ones, but also housewives searching for part-time jobs, youngsters looking for work as caddies or delivery boys, physically or mentally handicapped persons who were unemployable, and workers whose trade lost out to technological change. This last group embraced millions of farmers, hundreds of thousands of self-employed grocers, and thousands of blacksmiths, furriers, railroad conductors and locomotive engineers, sailors and deckhands, and loom fixers.

The jobless rate isn't a matter to be treated lightly. Yet we tend to forget that the number of men and women who are working has increased at a faster rate than the population since the end of World War II.

next move. Who would have guessed during the 1980 job boom that the mighty oil patch would now be on the ropes, or that the Rust Belt and the Great Lakes states would be making a comeback?

The last decade has seen some surprising shifts in regional economic growth. So the big question remains: Will a move to Anaheim or San Jose or Raleigh really solve your jobless or underemployment problem? The forecasts that follow may be able to help you make a more educated guess.

VITAL SIGNS: REGIONAL ECONOMIC CLIMATES

Just knowing the business climate of a region won't necessarily tell you whether you will find a career waiting there for you. For example, employment in the Midwest's auto industry is expected to fall below the 1986 level—even with more domestic-based production of foreign automobiles. Other forces, such as tapering demand and greater production efficiency, mean gains for the industry and the region's economy but losses for auto workers. On the other hand, knowing that one of the fastest-growing industries is the drug or pharmaceutical industry *and* that the number of jobs in that field is expected to rise by 17,000 to 224,000 in the next decade might give you a comfortable feeling if you've got the right skills and you're considering a move to a geographic area with a rich pharmaceutical industry.

So, in considering your move, you need to know at least three things. First, is the regional climate warm to business? Second, are the jobs in your field or industry concentrated there? And, third, how is that industry doing—not just in terms of output, but in terms of employment growth? Let's look at the business climate and the industry concentration in the nation's major regions.

New England—It's Even Getting Warmer in the Winter

New England attracts many people because it has history. But the region also has a strong present and an extremely promising future as far as business and jobs are concerned. Rated the climate warmest to business in 1988 by the Corporation for Enterprise Development, it is way ahead of the rest of the country and has a remarkably low unemployment rate. A strong service sector, a growing high-tech base, and a solid manufacturing strata make the difference here. In fact, a growing problem in the Northeast is labor shortages, especially in small firms. Job seekers in the Northeast may soon encounter vigorous recruiting efforts to attract them and competitive employee benefit packages to inspire their loyalty once they are hired.

The South Atlantic—Plenty of Action

Moving down the Atlantic coast, Delaware, the District of Columbia, Florida, Georgia, Maryland, North and South Carolina, Virginia, and West Virginia form an economic region that is expected to remain very strong. With chemical firms, government-related services, a blossoming research triangle area, and Florida's tourist-oriented, service-based economy, steady growth is expected. The Raleigh–Durham area, a hotbed for high-tech industries, is considered one of the best places in the country to work, based on economic and lifestyle factors. And although some analysts see danger signs for Florida—a lower cost of living and lower crime rates in neighboring states, rising wages taking away its advantages over northern states—it's moving in the fast track now. Indeed, seven Florida metro areas are ranked among *Places Rated Almanac's* top 30 for future job growth.

East South Central—You Win Some, You Lose Some

This area, including Alabama, Kentucky, Mississippi, and Tennessee, has been showing a downturn in its unemployment rate in the last few years: an encouraging trend that is expected to continue. Population, on the other hand, has been growing in these states, along with per capita income—encouraging signs as well. Continued growth of manufacturing in small towns and the expanding number of companies that serve the Japanese are contributing to the health of this region. Nashville, however, booming with jobs and construction just a few years ago, has seen some hard times. The uncontrolled growth and speculative overbuilding went too far too quickly. A glutted real estate market brought construction to a halt, and the city actually saw a loss of jobs throughout 1988 and into 1989.

The Rust Belt—Less Rusty Every Day

In the so-called Rust Belt and the Great Lakes states, you'll find a refreshing and unpredicted comeback. Factories that were closed for restructuring are now open, and in their new, sleek incarnations they are benefiting from the trade turnaround and the falling value of the dollar. The big news in the auto industry—in this region as well as in Kentucky and Tennessee—is the entry of Japanese manufacturers, who build their cars here and then ship them to Japan. The news is good for the economy of the region, but not necessarily for the unemployment rate.

In the country's midsection, an important economic determinant will be the weather, so the farmers are keeping an anxious eye on the rain clouds. If the drought of 1988 repeats itself, many areas dependent on farming could be devastated.

The Oil Patch—A Slippery Slope

The southwestern oil patch is doing a little better now than it did in the early years of the 1980s, to the extent that it has gotten away from the energy industry. In Texas, new manufacturing and factory jobs are giving things a rosier look, but the state faces a big challenge in the rescue of the troubled savings-and-loan industry, which experienced the highest percentage of failures in Texas. Texans are still adjusting to the era of the "half-gallon hat," as one editorial cartoon depicted it—not a pleasant experience for this once-thriving region.

The Mountain and Pacific States—It's Up and Down

Arizona, Colorado, Idaho, Montana, New Mexico, Nevada, Utah, and Wyoming, the mountain states, show varied patterns. Lumber, mining, tourism, and manufacturing are important pieces of the economic pie here, and all are expected to show some growth. In the Pacific states of Alaska, California, Hawaii, Oregon, and Washington, it is California that dominates the region with its thriving service sector. And California's Central Valley (e.g., Merced, Stockton, Fresno) is hot, drawing a growing stream of firms fleeing the high costs and hassles of the big cities. Washington and Oregon will continue to benefit from the demand for lumber, though an important conflict is growing between environmentalists, who wish to see conservation in the forest areas, and the lumber companies, whose business is based there. The oil-price recession has had its impact here as well. Not concentrated in the South alone, it hit hard in Alaska and Colorado.

JOBS, JOBS, JOBS: PROJECTIONS TO THE YEAR 2000

The great American job machine has been churning out record numbers of jobs for the past six years and, apparently, the machine is not showing any significant wear and tear. By the year 2000, which is no longer just a year in which science-fiction stories are set, more than 21 million new jobs could be added to the U.S. econo-

Business Climates: How States Stack Up

Does it make a difference where in the country a company makes its products? According to Grant Thornton, an international accounting firm, it may matter a great deal.

Each year, the Chicago-based firm surveys state manufacturing associations for their views on local economic factors they deem necessary for business success. These factors include labor costs, productivity, unionization, and energy costs, plus such considerations under local government control as taxes, debts, welfare expenditures, and environmental regulations.

States that had flexible environmental controls, laws that kept organized labor in check, and the lowest taxes, welfare aid, and debts received the highest scores and were judged the most favorable places to do business. Depending on the value of manufacturing shipments and the percent of workers employed in manufacturing, states are classified as industrial or non-industrial in the rankings.

Industrial States

1. New Hampshire	15. Rhode Island
2. Missouri	16. Connecticut
3. North Carolina	17. New York
4. Delaware	18. Illinois
5. Florida	19. California
6. Massachusetts	20. Indiana
7. Mississippi	21. Pennsylvania
8. New Jersey	22. Maine
9. Arkansas	23. Alabama
10. South Carolina	24. Texas
11. Georgia	25. Ohio
12. Vermont	26. Michigan
13. Tennessee	27. Louisiana
14. Wisconsin	

Non-Industrial States

1. South Dakota	12. Iowa
2. North Dakota	13. Idaho
3. Nebraska	14. Washington
4. Nevada	15. Minnesota
5. Kansas	16. Kentucky
6. Virginia	17. Oregon
7. Arizona	18. Oklahoma
8. Colorado	19. Wyoming
9. Maryland	20. Montana
10. Utah	21. West Virginia
11. New Mexico	

Source: Grant Thornton, *Manufacturing Climates Study,* 1988.

my. Although projected employment increases are expected to occur at a slower pace than in the past, the growth in certain occupations will be quite healthy.

The biggest continuing trend is massive growth in service-oriented sectors and marked decline in goods-producing industries. In other words, opportunities for highly trained white-collar workers are growing rapidly, with the blue-collar shade of many metro areas fading to white. The following projections give more detailed scenarios for the next decade.

Blue-Collar Blues

Shortly after the end of World War II, white-collar jobs outnumbered blue-collar jobs for the first time in the history of the country. White-collar workers as a group earn somewhat less than blue-collar workers because so many white-collar jobs are low-pay clerical and retail positions and so many blue-collar jobs are skilled occupations protected by union contracts. But white-collar jobs, though paying less, provide a ladder of opportunity that blue-collar jobs don't. And the work is steadier. It's ironic that some of the biggest union issues now are security against layoffs and plant closings rather than higher wages. Blue-collar workers are beginning to want what's best in the white-collar world, and they are willing to sacrifice exorbitant wage demands.

The shrinking world of blue-collar jobs is divided into four basic industries. For the most part, employment opportunities in these fields are expected to decline or merely hold steady up to the year 2000.

Farming and Mining. It's axiomatic that the family farm is disappearing as mechanized agribusiness rounds up more acreage and concentrates on many crops. Despite some modest recovery from the agricultural production slump in the mid-1980s, U.S. exports will probably not regain the world dominance they once enjoyed. Thus this group as a whole is projected to have an employment decline over the next decade. Still, some metro areas—for example, those in California's Central Valley (Stockton, Merced, Bakersfield, Fresno)—have large numbers of farming jobs. One portion of the agricultural sector—the agricultural services (such as landscaping and lawn services)—has been growing rapidly, and the growth is expected to continue. Here is yet another indication of the shift toward a service economy.

Jobs in mining, once the stable employer in the West, are in a deep hole and likely to remain there. This includes oil and natural gas production, two disaster industries in the Southwest and Rockies (Texas, Oklahoma, Louisiana, Colorado, Arizona, and Wyoming). Employment in crude oil production is projected to fall even further below its depressed 1986 level, and metal mining is not projected to recover any of the deep cuts experienced in both output and employment since 1979. And while coal is expected to increase in importance as an alternative energy source, the jobs in coal production are not expected to increase. Instead, new production methods will mean continued shrinking of employment.

Construction. Here's a footloose industry if there ever was one. Building contracts run out? Move on to another boom town. Why do you think so many Texas and Louisiana residential contractors moved to Tennessee and Georgia? This industry, which likes to think that half of America should be rebuilt before the end of the century, is predicted to provide most of the blue-collar jobs to 1995 and beyond. Whenever you see a place that is forecasted to have a large number of blue-collar jobs, you'll be seeing hard-hat construction jobs with hammers, bulldozers, bricks, and lumber.

Residential construction is expected to slow dramatically in the 1990s. A little growth is likely for new single-family homes and for residential alterations and additions, but this trend will be just about offset by declines in new apartment and condominium construction. In the meantime, though, nonresidential construction is projected to recover from the recent oversupply of office and commercial space. Thus, as a whole, construction employment is projected to rise each year until the year 2000. The rate of increase should amount to 890,000 jobs.

Manufacturing. Here is another employment sector that's predicted to grow glacially or not at all. Smoke stacks, low-rise buildings near rail tracks, even high-tech assembly work—we can tell it all goodbye over time. Much of it is moving offshore or to third-world countries.

Although manufacturing is expected to lose 834,000 jobs by the year 2000, manufacturing output is expected to almost keep pace with total GNP growth. At the same time, the occupational composition of the remaining manufacturing jobs is expected to change. In general, following the trend of the disappearing blue-collar job, manufacturing employment is expected to shift away from production and assembly-line jobs toward professional, managerial, and technical occupations. The shift is more pronounced in industries where imports play a significant role. In some of those cases, design and engineering are done domestically, but much of the actual assembly is performed overseas.

The computer manufacturing industry, as we all might have guessed, has been one of the fastest-growing U.S. industries during the last 25 years. The nature of work in this industry, however, is uncharacteristic of manufacturing industries as a whole. It employs a high concentration of scientific personnel and a relatively low concentration of production workers. Employment in computer manufacturing is expected to expand to 503,000 jobs in 2000, with even more of a shift at that time from production to research and development occupations.

The printing and publishing business is one of the few manufacturing sectors to have registered consistent job gains in the last few years. Even during the recession, both output and employment increased steadily. And the introduction of electronic composition systems and other new technologies has not put a damper on this trend. As elsewhere, however, occupational shifts are occurring within the printing trades, from fewer typesetters and other craftsworkers to more front-office personnel such as writers, editors, managers, and salesworkers. Growth is expected to continue with vigor through the 1990s.

Transportation, Communications, and Public Utilities. This catch-all industry classification embraces electric power generation, 18-wheel trucking of goods, line workers, food and baggage handlers working for airlines, and much more. In recent years, deregulation has boosted employment in the air transportation industry,

An Occupational Directory

Using "white collar" or "blue collar" to differentiate between a job that deals either with information or things, is physical or mental, clean or messy, salaried or nonsalaried, high-paying or low-paying, seasonal or year-round, skilled or unskilled, unionized or professional, is somewhat imprecise.

According to U.S. Standard Occupational Classification (SOC) definitions, white-collar jobs include professional and technical workers, managers and administrators, sales workers, and clerical workers. Blue-collar occupations include craftsworkers, operatives, drivers, and nonfarm laborers.

But a quick look at some of the white-collar clerical job titles shows that many of them can be as unskilled, nonsalaried, and seasonal as jobs in the laboring category, while many blue-collar craftsworker jobs can be as skilled, salaried, and highly paid as those in the professional and technical category.

The SOC also identifies two other categories of occupations: service workers and farm workers. Service jobs include police and health-service, food-service, and child-care workers; farmers, farm laborers, and farm managers compose the farm workers category.

White Collar

Professional and Technical
Accountants
Computer specialists
Engineers
Health technologists and technicians
Lawyers and judges
Librarians, archivists, and curators
Life and physical scientists
Personnel and labor relations workers
Physicians, dentists, and related practitioners
Registered nurses, dietitians, and therapists
Religious workers
Research workers
Social scientists
Social and recreation workers
Teachers
Technicians (except health)
Vocational and educational counselors
Writers, artists, and entertainers

Managers and Administrators (Except Farm)
Bank officers and financial managers
Building managers and superintendents
Buyers, wholesale and retail trade
Health administrators
Office managers
Officials and administrators
Restaurant, cafeteria, and bar managers
Sales managers
School administrators

Sales Workers
Hucksters and peddlers
Insurance agents, brokers, and underwriters
Real estate agents and brokers
Retail store sales clerks
Stock and bond sales agents
Sales representatives
Salespeople

Clerical Workers
Bank tellers
Billing clerks
Bookkeepers
Cashiers
Clerical supervisors
Counter clerks, except food
Estimators and investigators
File clerks
Insurance adjusters, examiners, and investigators
Postal clerks and mail carriers
Receptionists
Secretaries
Shipping and receiving clerks
Statistical clerks
Stenographers
Stock clerks and storekeepers
Telephone operators
Typists and office-machine operators

Blue Collar

Craftsworkers
Carpenters
Construction craftsworkers
Machinists and job-setters
Metalcraft workers
Mechanics
Other craftsworkers
Print craftsworkers

Operatives (Except Transport)
Assemblers
Checkers, examiners, and inspectors of manufactured goods
Cutters

Dressmakers and seamstresses, except factory
Garage workers and gas station attendants
Laundry and dry-cleaning operatives
Machine operatives
Meat cutters and butchers
Miners
Packers and wrappers
Painters of manufactured goods
Precision machine operatives
Punch and stamping press operatives
Sewers and stitchers

Textile operatives
Welders and flame cutters

Transport Equipment Operatives
Bus drivers
Delivery and route workers
Forklift and tow motor operators
Taxi drivers and chauffeurs
Truck drivers

Laborers (Except Farm)
Construction laborers
Freight, material, and stock handlers
Gardeners and groundskeepers

Source: U.S. Standard Occupational Classification.

as many smaller firms entered the market and price competition stimulated demand. But, in the long run, consolidation and takeovers are expected to dampen the rate of job growth.

Overall, employment in this group is expected to decrease in the next decade due to declining industry employment and technological changes. The railroad industry, for example, is expected to lose about 190,000 jobs. The number of water transportation workers is expected to decline by 8 percent. Greater efficiency in

scheduling, marketing, and cost control in the trucking industry is expected to produce greater gains in output than in employment. The same goes for telephone workers: competition in the 1990s in that industry is expected to lead to an employment decline of about 121,000.

. . . And a White-Collar Chorus

White-collar jobs, which correspond roughly with service-oriented occupations, are also divided into four

Winners and Losers: Jobs

As indicated on the Job Winners table below, nine of the 20 metro areas with forecasted job losses from 1989 to 1995 are located in the Sun Belt. Most are stricken by the continuing slump in oil and natural gas production.

On the other hand, as the Job Losers table shows, six metro areas forecasted to gain more than 100,000 jobs apiece by 1995 are either in the Great Lakes states or in the Northeast—regions most pundits predicted would decline throughout the rest of this century.

Job Winners, 1989–1995

Metro Area	Total New Jobs
Los Angeles–Long Beach, CA	407,770
Anaheim–Santa Ana, CA	367,420
Washington, DC–MD–VA	312,040
Atlanta, GA	262,240
Dallas, TX	235,360
Chicago, IL	218,230
Tampa–St. Petersburg–Clearwater, FL	198,920
Nassau–Suffolk, NY	192,360
Phoenix, AZ	189,830
San Diego, CA	160,550
Philadelphia, PA–NJ	157,660
San Jose, CA	151,240
Orlando, FL	143,760
Oakland, CA	140,830
Boston, MA	136,850
San Francisco, CA	135,940
Fort Lauderdale–Hollywood–Pompano Beach, FL	134,550
Riverside–San Bernardino, CA	133,900
West Palm Beach–Boca Raton–Delray Beach, FL	118,610
Middlesex–Somerset–Hunterdon, NJ	118,210

Job Losers, 1989–1995

Metro Area	Employment Decline
Casper, WY	−4.27%
Lake Charles, LA	−3.15
St. Joseph, MO	−2.87
Terre Haute, IN	−2.27
Jackson, MI	−1.99
Tuscaloosa, AL	−1.53
Benton Harbor, MI	−1.41
Houma–Thibodaux, LA	−1.00
Danville, VA	−1.00
Owensboro, KY	−0.91
Battle Creek, MI	−0.85
Dubuque, IA	−0.62
Pine Bluff, AR	−0.42
Decatur, IL	−0.39
Williamsport, PA	−0.28
Flint, MI	−0.27
Odessa, TX	−0.25
Enid, OK	−0.21
Gadsden, AL	−0.14
Billings, MT	−0.04

Source: Woods & Poole Economics, Inc., employment forecasts, 1989.

(hamburger flipping, counter help, damage estimating, aisle sweeping, cashiering) are not worth having if your cash needs are immediate and above average. These jobs do, however, provide rapid advancement to managerial slots, which are still lower-paid despite the title. Retail trade stores are the most ubiquitous business establishments in the United States, and heavy opportunity in this sector goes hand in hand with a local area that is swelling with people.

A crisis is looming here, however. Traditionally, a large portion of those in retail trade work part time, and these workers are traditionally teenagers and women. The supply of part timers, however, is projected to decline enough in the future to trouble the retail trade. For one thing, the teenage labor force will be shrinking, and for another, women have been showing a declining preference for part-time work. Retailers in some areas have already found it difficult to staff their part-time positions and are considering older workers, for example, to fill these jobs. So, if you're interested in a part-time job in retail, the future may be smiling at you.

Eating and drinking establishments should have jobs to offer—about 2.5 million of them by 2000—even though the rate of increase will be slower than the rate in the past. And grocery stores, too, with their longer hours and expanded services (carry-out prepared foods, deli counters) are expected to add nearly 600,000 jobs by the year 2000.

Finance, Insurance, and Real Estate. Referred to in regional developers' shorthand as FIRE, this is the purest of the white-collar industrial classifications. Here the compensation is greater than in the retail trade, and potentially greater by far than in any other industry. It is a briefcase and tie industry—an office-with-a-capital-O environment. It has both heavier government regulation than other industries and more unreported crime.

Banking, credit agencies, and investment offices—a big part of the FIRE industries—should enjoy substantial rates of business growth in the next decade, but not necessarily such growth in numbers of jobs. Consolidation and technological advances in automatic banking and other financial transactions will actually slow rates of employment gain. This doesn't mean *no* new jobs in these fields; there will be some growth—for example, 495,000 more in credit agencies and investment offices by the year 2000. But the rate of employment growth will be slower than in the past and will not match the growth in business output.

Similarly, greater efficiency in the insurance industry—computerized underwriting, for example—will mean that job gains will be limited for insurance carriers and for independent agents and brokers. Not *no* growth, but slower growth. Rapid projected growth in the real estate industry is expected to have a favorable impact on employment for brokers (increasing by 44 percent) and appraisers (increasing by 41 percent).

Service. Think of high-rise copper-glass office buildings and medical centers with piped-in music. Think of

basic industry categories. With some variations within categories, this is where the real action is expected to occur in the remaining years of the 20th century.

Trade. Retail jobs outnumber wholesale positions by five to one and are expected to gain by some 4.9 million over the next decade. Unfortunately, retail trade jobs

white smocks and clipboards and shaded college campuses. These are the most desirable kinds of developments—the kinds city fathers and mothers dream of. If the landscape is full of these buildings, you've got a well-educated work force, higher incomes, and a stable, service-oriented economy.

The service division includes careers in business, health, recreation, the professions, and education—an increasing proportion of which will require formal education and certification. Health and education, typically underwritten by government or third-party payors, lead the way in this division. It makes sense if you think about it: The numbers of educational staff are rising with the numbers of children of the baby-boom generation, and the health care industry is growing as the population ages and needs more medical attention. Overall, this category has been and is projected to be the fastest-growing for new jobs, adding 10 million by the year 2000, for a total awesome growth of more than 32 million payroll jobs.

The big story in services is, as expected, computer and data processing—systems design, programming, and software development. Another big story in business services, with a very large projected increase in employment, is the personnel supply business, especially the temporary help industry. No longer limited to placing office workers, temporary personnel service businesses are beginning to place workers from industrial, medical, managerial, engineering, and technical occupations as well. The employers like the lower fringe benefits and the access to added help during peak times, and the temporary workers like the flexibility, variety, and experience.

With the trend toward development of new service businesses, the demand for research, management, and consulting services grows. Independent laboratories for research and development, market researchers, personnel training or management consultants, economic researchers, efficiency experts, lobbyists, and other business consultants will be in increasing demand.

In the professions, the legal services industry has been booming (and is expected to continue doing so), taking a place among the top ten fastest-growing employment industries. If you thought the legal profession was filled to capacity, think again. Increasing liability litigation, corporate mergers and acquisitions, high divorce levels, geographic expansion of law firms, a greater degree of legal specialization within firms, and an increase in litigation in general are keeping things moving in this industry. Interestingly, a rising proportion of the 519,000 payroll jobs projected for legal services by the year 2000 are expected to be filled by paralegals, who will find themselves on an extremely hot career path—by some predictions, the hottest of the future.

In health care, too, important shifts are taking place. Cost containment policies have halted the expansion of hospitals and hospital employment, with health care

The 20 Fastest Growing Jobs, 1986–2000
(numbers in thousands)

Occupation	New Jobs, 1986–2000	
	Number	Percent
Legal assistants	64	103.7%
Medical assistants	119	90.4
Physical therapists	53	87.5
Physical and corrective therapy assistants and aides	29	81.6
Data processing equipment repairers	56	80.4
Homemaker–home health aides	111	80.1
Podiatrists	10	77.2
Computer systems analysts	251	75.6
Medical record technicians	30	75.0
Employment interviewers	54	71.2
Computer programmers	335	69.9
Radiologic technologists and technicians	75	64.7
Dental hygienists	54	62.6
Dental assistants	88	57.0
Physician assistants	15	56.7
Operations research analysts	21	54.1
Occupational therapists	15	52.2
Peripheral electronic data processing equipment operators	24	50.8
Data entry keyers, composing	15	50.8
Optometrists	18	49.2

Source: Bureau of Labor Statistics, Occupational Outlook Quarterly, Spring 1988.

The Top 25 Job Gainers, 1986–2000
(numbers in thousands)

Occupation	New Jobs, 1986–2000	
	Number	Percent
Salespersons, retail	1,201	33.5%
Waiters and waitresses	752	44.2
Registered nurses	612	43.6
Janitors and cleaners	604	22.6
General managers and top executives	582	24.2
Cashiers	575	26.5
Truckdrivers	525	23.8
General office clerks	462	19.6
Food counter and related workers	449	29.9
Nursing aides, orderlies, and attendants	433	35.4
Secretaries	424	13.1
Guards	383	48.3
Accountants and auditors	376	39.8
Computer programmers	335	69.9
Food preparation workers	324	34.2
Teachers, kindergarten and elementary	299	19.6
Receptionists and information clerks	282	41.4
Computer systems analysts	251	75.6
Cooks, restaurant	240	46.2
Licensed practical nurses	238	37.7
Gardeners and groundskeepers	238	31.1
Maintenance repairers	232	22.3
Stock clerks	225	20.7
First-line clerical supervisors and managers	205	21.4
Dining room and cafeteria attendants	197	45.6

Source: Bureau of Labor Statistics, Occupational Outlook Quarterly, Spring 1988.

delivery moving from the hospital to outpatient care centers. Look for employment growth in the emergency care clinics, surgicenters, and walk-in treatment centers that are popping up all around us. The medical assistant occupation, with a growth rate of 90 percent, is projected to be one of the fastest-growing fields during the next decade. Medical assistants are extremely cost-effective

The 20 Fastest Disappearing Jobs, 1986–2000
(numbers in thousands)

Occupation	Decline in Employment, 1986–2000	
	Number	Percent
Electrical and electronics assemblers	-133	-53.7%
Electronic semiconductor processors	15	51.1
Railroad conductors and yardmasters	12	40.9
Railroad brake, signal, and switch operators	17	39.9
Gas and petroleum plant and system occupations	11	34.3
Industrial truck and tractor operators	143	33.6
Shoe sewing-machine operators and tenders	9	32.1
Station installers and repairers, telephone	18	31.8
Chemical equipment controllers, operators, and tenders	21	29.7
Chemical plant and system operators	10	29.6
Stenographers	50	28.2
Farmers	332	28.1
Statistical clerks	19	26.4
Textile draw-out and winding machine operators and tenders	55	25.2
Central office and PBX installers and repairers	17	23.1
Farm workers	190	20.3
Coil winders, tapers, and finishers	6	18.5
Central office operators	8	17.9
Directory assistance operators	5	17.7
Compositors, typesetters, and arrangers, precision	5	17.1

Source: Bureau of Labor Statistics, *Occupational Outlook Quarterly,* Spring 1988.

and provide both clinical and clerical support to physicians and other health professionals.

Government. If you're considering a job in government, especially the federal government, you might reconsider. The federal government will definitely be shrinking because of extensive military base closings and budgetary reductions. Total public employment is, however, projected to rise by 1.6 million in the next decade, with almost all of the increase occurring among state and local government service workers, such as police and firefighters. On the other hand, a loss of 45,000 jobs among administrative support workers, including clerical staff, is projected.

For government jobs, though, some places—Columbus, OH; Austin, TX; Atlanta, GA; and Boston, MA—are in enviable situations. They are state capitals with large bureaucracies that face no unemployment threat, and the fact that they are all higher education centers doesn't hurt their general economic outlook.

HOT (AND COLD) CAREERS TO THE YEAR 2000

Tomorrow's jobs will call for higher and higher levels of skills, and there appears to be a growing mismatch between the emerging jobs and the people available to fill them. Generally, occupations that require the most education are projected to have the most rapid growth rates. Persons with less than a high-school education will have more difficulty finding a job—particularly a job with good pay and chances for advancement.

Five occupational groups are projected to grow fastest during the next decade: technicians, service workers, professional workers, sales workers, and executive and managerial employees. As the table on the previous page shows, if you're interested in becoming a legal or medical assistant (two extremely cost-effective occupations), you're interested in two of the fastest-growing job categories.

Half of all new jobs for the next decade will be found in only 25 occupations and, as indicated in the table on the previous page, most of these top 25 gainers are white-collar, service-oriented jobs. Computer analysts and programmers show the top percentage gains, while retail salespersons will gain the most new jobs in sheer numbers.

Only two groups—agricultural workers and private household workers—are projected to decline in the next decade. And, in fact, as you can see in the adjacent table, most of the 20 rapidly disappearing occupations are in the blue-collar realm, with jobs for electrical and electronics assemblers disappearing the most rapidly in both numbers and percentages.

SCORING: JOBS

If you're out of work or looking for better employment, would the raw odds of tracking down a job be better in Dallas, Denver, or Detroit? What about Honolulu, Houston, or Huntsville?

To help you answer these questions, *Places Rated* compares two factors in each metro area: the total number of new blue- and white-collar jobs forecasted between now and 1995, and the percentage rate of job growth during this period. These two factors, multiplied together, produce the *Places Rated* score.

SCORING EXAMPLES

The metro area with the largest labor force in the country, a small metro area dominated by mining occupations, and a large metro area symbolic in the American mind with industrial decline illustrate the scoring method for jobs.

Los Angeles–Long Beach, CA (#6)

Why does a sprawling, congested metro area at the edge of a desert, smack in the middle of a major earthquake hazard, far from adequate water supplies, and far from basic raw materials continue to thrive? The only answer is that its residents want it to.

Los Angeles–Long Beach, now the nation's largest metro area, may be a kind of blue-collar paradise. The low-paying clothing, furniture, and food-processing industries are not the only employers in town. Manufacturing workers make good money in the area's many technology-based aerospace and electronics industries. Moreover, this is one of a few metro areas with a significant increase (32,000) in blue-collar employment forecasted by 1995.

The metro area's real strength, however, lies in its emergence as a national and international banking and financial center. Many of the projected 375,000 new jobs in predominantly white-collar industries by 1995 will be created in the finance, insurance, and real estate fields.

When Los Angeles–Long Beach's projected rate of employment growth (7.92 percent) is multiplied by its number of new jobs (407,000), the result is a score of 32,395, sixth highest among all metro areas.

Casper, WY (#333)

Originally a small town along the Oregon–Mormon trail, Casper experienced its first boom when oil was discovered in the Salt Creek area a century ago, in 1889. But it was during the latter half of the 1970s that Wyoming's largest city saw its biggest boom, a period during which Casper was among the top ten fastest-growing metro areas in the United States.

Unfortunately, this phenomenal growth came to an abrupt end in the early 1980s with the collapse of world prices for uranium, oil, and coal. Employment prospects in Casper to the year 1995 look unpromising. With a forecasted loss of 1,660 jobs, and a resulting growth rate of minus 4.27 percent, Casper's score for jobs is the lowest among all 333 metro areas.

Pittsburgh, PA (#76)

Pittsburgh's boom years are behind it. For most of its history, nearby anthracite coal and an industrial base dominated by primary metals established the metro area as the country's Steel City, but because of the sharp decline in domestic steel production, the nickname no longer applies.

For all of its past troubles, Pittsburgh still has more promising job prospects than other metro areas such as Albuquerque, NM, El Paso, TX, and Portland, OR. How so?

Pittsburgh is still among the 20 largest metro areas in the country, and while it is forecasted to lose another 35,000 blue-collar jobs by 1995, it is also forecasted to gain more than 86,000 white-collar jobs. Multiplying its projected growth rate (4.70 percent) by its total number of new jobs (50,950) produces a score of 2,493, or 76th among America's 333 metro areas.

Rankings: Jobs

In ranking the 333 metro areas for near-term job growth, *Places Rated Almanac* uses two criteria: (1) the percent increase in new jobs, and (2) the number of new jobs created between now and 1995. The product of these two criteria, rounded off, is the metro area's score. The higher the score, the more promising the metro area's job outlook. Places that receive tie scores get the same rank and are listed in alphabetical order.

Metro Areas from Best to Worst

Places Rated Rank	Places Rated Score	Places Rated Rank	Places Rated Score	Places Rated Rank	Places Rated Score
1. Anaheim–Santa Ana, CA	88,669	16. Oakland, CA	17,895	35. Fort Worth–Arlington, TX	7,629
2. Atlanta, GA	38,554	17. San Francisco, CA	14,662		
3. Tampa–St. Petersburg–Clearwater, FL	36,806	18. Chicago, IL	13,349	36. Seattle, WA	7,242
4. Washington, DC–MD–VA	36,456	19. Raleigh–Durham, NC	13,000	37. Baltimore, MD	7,241
5. Orlando, FL	33,346	20. Las Vegas, NV	12,284	38. Santa Rosa–Petaluma, CA	7,183
				39. Houston, TX	7,001
		21. Miami–Hialeah, FL	11,893	40. Newark, NJ	6,627
6. Los Angeles–Long Beach, CA	32,395	22. Sacramento, CA	11,782		
7. Dallas, TX	31,408	23. Oxnard–Ventura, CA	11,263	41. Salt Lake City–Ogden, UT	6,553
8. Phoenix, AZ	30,087	24. Austin, TX	11,180	42. Nashville, TN	6,137
9. West Palm Beach–Boca Raton–Delray Beach, FL	29,791	25. Atlantic City, NJ	10,438	43. Vallejo–Fairfield–Napa, CA	5,283
10. Fort Lauderdale–Hollywood–Pompano Beach, FL	27,744	26. Philadelphia, PA–NJ	9,637	44. Norfolk–Virginia Beach–Newport News, VA	5,097
		27. Monmouth–Ocean, NJ	9,159	45. Columbus, OH	5,093
		28. Fort Myers–Cape Coral, FL	9,115		
11. Nassau–Suffolk, NY	24,534	29. Boston, MA	8,766		
12. San Jose, CA	22,401	30. Fort Pierce, FL	8,146	46. Santa Barbara–Santa Maria–Lompoc, CA	5,030
13. Middlesex–Somerset–Hunterdon, NJ	22,198	31. San Antonio, TX	8,143	47. Greensboro–Winston-Salem–High Point, NC	4,858
14. Riverside–San Bernardino, CA	20,809	32. Charlotte–Gastonia–Rock Hill, NC–SC	8,064	48. Portsmouth–Dover–Rochester, NH–ME	4,824
		33. Denver, CO	7,980	49. Lake County, IL	4,644
15. San Diego, CA	19,827	34. Minneapolis–St. Paul, MN–WI	7,776	50. Ocala, FL	4,634

Places Rated Rank	Places Rated Score	Places Rated Rank	Places Rated Score	Places Rated Rank	Places Rated Score
51. Bergen–Passaic, NJ	4,629	110. Honolulu, HI	1,486	168. Tyler, TX	671
52. New Orleans, LA	4,115			169. Sioux Falls, SD	669
53. Lawrence–Haverhill, MA–NH	4,004	111. Panama City, FL	1,460	170. Trenton, NJ	661
54. Jacksonville, FL	3,959	112. Daytona Beach, FL	1,452		
55. Greenville–Spartanburg, SC	3,866	113. Olympia, WA	1,405	171. Reno, NV	646
		114. Lancaster, PA	1,395	172. Bloomington, IN	626
56. Columbia, SC	3,806	115. Pensacola, FL	1,383	173. Allentown–Bethlehem, PA–NJ	625
57. Richmond–Petersburg, VA	3,710			174. Youngstown–Warren, OH	611
58. Bryan–College Station, TX	3,505	116. Providence, RI	1,355	175. Fitchburg–Leominster, MA	594
59. Naples, FL	3,331	117. Hickory, NC	1,338		
60. Santa Cruz, CA	3,195	118. Springfield, MO	1,274	176. Stamford, CT	589
		119. Brownsville–Harlingen, TX	1,266	177. Wheeling, WV–OH	588
61. Fort Walton Beach, FL	3,193	120. Memphis, TN–AR–MS	1,252	178. Omaha, NE–IA	586
62. Lowell, MA–NH	3,160			179. Norwalk, CT	580
63. Sarasota, FL	3,127	121. Wilmington, DE–NJ–MD	1,249	180. New London–Norwich, CT–RI	578
64. Nashua, NH	3,048	122. Bridgeport–Milford, CT	1,205		
65. Salinas–Seaside–Monterey, CA	2,961	123. Middletown, CT	1,203	181. Gary–Hammond, IN	576
		124. Little Rock–North Little Rock, AR	1,169	182. Peoria, IL	561
66. Indianapolis, IN	2,833	125. Vancouver, WA	1,168	183. New Bedford, MA	552
67. Tucson, AZ	2,792			184. Lexington–Fayette, KY	546
68. Anchorage, AK	2,753	126. Boulder–Longmont, CO	1,158	185. Richland–Kennewick–Pasco, WA	545
69. Rochester, NY	2,703	127. Madison, WI	1,137		
70. Detroit, MI	2,695	128. Knoxville, TN	1,083	186. Springfield, IL	528
		129. Springfield, MA	1,055	187. Davenport–Rock Island–Moline, IA–IL	524
71. New York, NY	2,643	130. Scranton–Wilkes-Barre, PA	1,053	188. Laredo, TX	519
72. Grand Rapids, MI	2,581			189. Waterbury, CT	513
73. Albany–Schenectady–Troy, NY	2,543	131. Harrisburg–Lebanon–Carlisle, PA	1,050	190. Biloxi–Gulfport, MS	511
74. Charleston, SC	2,526	132. Oklahoma City, OK	1,037		
75. Cincinnati, OH–KY–IN	2,517	133. Merced, CA	1,014	191. Cleveland, OH	500
		134. Killeen–Temple, TX	1,007	192. Pawtucket–Woonsocket–Attleboro, RI–MA	496
76. Pittsburgh, PA	2,493	135. Des Moines, IA	998	193. La Crosse, WI	494
77. St. Louis, MO–IL	2,433			194. Altoona, PA	491
78. Tallahassee, FL	2,417	136. Lakeland–Winter Haven, FL	988	195. Cumberland, MD–WV	485
79. Aurora–Elgin, IL	2,391	137. Dothan, AL	944		
80. Bradenton, FL	2,308	138. Green Bay, WI	940	196. Binghamton, NY	478
		139. Wilmington, NC	910	197. Joplin, MO	468
81. El Paso, TX	2,297	140. Fort Collins–Loveland, CO	909	198. Jackson, MS	465
82. Albuquerque, NM	2,238			199. Medford, OR	463
83. Syracuse, NY	2,178	141. Fort Smith, AR–OK	894	200. Burlington, NC	455
84. Manchester, NH	2,174	142. New Haven–Meriden, CT	888		
85. Buffalo, NY	2,136	143. Huntsville, AL	885	201. Johnson City–Kingsport–Bristol, TN–VA	453
		144. Redding, CA	870	202. Niagara Falls, NY	443
86. St. Cloud, MN	2,057	145. Boise City, ID	867	203. Appleton–Oshkosh–Neenah, WI	432
87. Brockton, MA	2,026			204. Kankakee, IL	417
88. Santa Fe, NM	1,949	146. Stockton, CA	863	205. Toledo, OH	416
89. Hartford, CT	1,936	147. Wichita, KS	823		
90. Kansas City, MO–KS	1,933	148. Fresno, CA	808	206. Rockford, IL	413
		149. Birmingham, AL	803	207. Amarillo, TX	399
91. Colorado Springs, CO	1,903	150. Elkhart–Goshen, IN	800	208. Pueblo, CO	398
92. Gainesville, FL	1,854			209. Iowa City, IA	384
93. McAllen–Edinburg–Mission, TX	1,796	151. Louisville, KY–IN	790	210. Eau Claire, WI	381
93. Worcester, MA	1,796	152. Modesto, CA	768		
95. Danbury, CT	1,769	153. Tulsa, OK	739	211. Fayetteville, NC	379
		154. Dayton–Springfield, OH	737	211. Lafayette, LA	379
96. Orange County, NY	1,743	154. Melbourne–Titusville–Palm Bay, FL	737	213. Columbia, MO	362
97. Ann Arbor, MI	1,714			214. State College, PA	345
98. Baton Rouge, LA	1,701	156. Champaign–Urbana–Rantoul, IL	723	215. Eugene–Springfield, OR	343
99. Provo–Orem, UT	1,672	157. Fall River, MA–RI	717		
100. Portland, OR	1,624	158. Bremerton, WA	716	216. Brazoria, TX	336
		159. Bakersfield, CA	708	217. Corpus Christi, TX	335
101. Las Cruces, NM	1,601	160. York, PA	703	218. Mobile, AL	334
101. Poughkeepsie, NY	1,601			219. Pascagoula, MS	333
103. Joliet, IL	1,585	161. Salem–Gloucester, MA	698	220. Montgomery, AL	331
104. Rochester, MN	1,558	162. Lubbock, TX	693		
105. Burlington, VT	1,542	163. Tacoma, WA	689	221. Beaumont–Port Arthur, TX	329
		164. Charlottesville, VA	687	222. Fort Wayne, IN	326
106. Chico, CA	1,504	165. Beaver County, PA	683	223. Akron, OH	316
107. Augusta, GA–SC	1,500				
108. Milwaukee, WI	1,499	166. Jersey City, NJ	682		
109. Portland, ME	1,489	166. Lansing–East Lansing, MI	682		

Places Rated Rank	Places Rated Score
224. Canton, OH	312
224. Charleston, WV	312
226. Bellingham, WA	305
226. Jacksonville, NC	305
228. Anderson, SC	283
229. Florence, SC	282
230. Glens Falls, NY	279
231. Roanoke, VA	274
232. Utica–Rome, NY	271
233. Kenosha, WI	268
234. Cedar Rapids, IA	267
235. Visalia–Tulare–Porterville, CA	262
236. Fargo–Moorhead, ND–MN	258
236. Spokane, WA	258
238. Kalamazoo, MI	244
239. Jackson, TN	238
240. Savannah, GA	235
241. Albany, GA	227
242. Bismarck, ND	225
242. Lawrence, KS	225
244. New Britain, CT	224
245. Duluth, MN–WI	223
246. Hamilton–Middletown, OH	221
247. Asheville, NC	219
248. Bristol, CT	218
249. Steubenville–Weirton, OH–WV	216
250. Pittsfield, MA	213
251. Sharon, PA	210
252. Waco, TX	209
253. South Bend–Mishawaka, IN	207
254. Janesville–Beloit, WI	206
255. Elmira, NY	201
256. Lafayette–West Lafayette, IN	199
257. Bangor, ME	194
258. Abilene, TX	192
259. Mansfield, OH	191
260. Columbus, GA–AL	177

Places Rated Rank	Places Rated Score
260. Wichita Falls, TX	177
262. San Angelo, TX	174
263. Lynchburg, VA	173
264. Chattanooga, TN–GA	170
265. Macon–Warner Robins, GA	168
266. Reading, PA	167
267. Erie, PA	163
268. Shreveport, LA	161
269. Yuba City, CA	158
270. Midland, TX	157
271. Longview–Marshall, TX	155
272. Rapid City, SD	153
273. Racine, WI	152
274. Lewiston–Auburn, ME	150
274. Wausau, WI	150
276. Hagerstown, MD	149
276. Salem, OR	149
278. Lincoln, NE	148
279. Bloomington–Normal, IL	142
280. Muncie, IN	139
281. Johnstown, PA	137
282. Lawton, OK	136
283. Greeley, CO	133
284. Huntington–Ashland, WV–KY–OH	132
285. Athens, GA	129
286. Lorain–Elyria, OH	128
287. Parkersburg–Marietta, WV–OH	127
288. Anniston, AL	126
289. Great Falls, MT	125
290. Sherman–Denison, TX	123
291. Fayetteville–Springdale, AR	122
291. Monroe, LA	122
293. Yakima, WA	121
294. Texarkana, TX–Texarkana, AR	120
295. Topeka, KS	116
296. Evansville, IN–KY	115

Places Rated Rank	Places Rated Score
297. Clarksville–Hopkinsville, TN–KY	110
298. Cheyenne, WY	109
298. Grand Forks, ND	109
300. Lima, OH	107
301. Muskegon, MI	106
302. Anderson, IN	105
302. Decatur, AL	105
302. Victoria, TX	105
305. Alexandria, LA	104
305. Kokomo, IN	104
307. Galveston–Texas City, TX	103
308. Saginaw–Bay City–Midland, MI	101
308. Sheboygan, WI	101
308. Vineland–Millville–Bridgeton, NJ	101
311. Battle Creek, MI	100
311. Billings, MT	100
311. Decatur, IL	100
311. Dubuque, IA	100
311. Enid, OK	100
311. Flint, MI	100
311. Florence, AL	100
311. Gadsden, AL	100
311. Odessa, TX	100
311. Owensboro, KY	100
311. Pine Bluff, AR	100
311. Sioux City, IA–NE	100
311. Waterloo–Cedar Falls, IA	100
311. Williamsport, PA	100
325. Danville, VA	99
325. Houma–Thibodaux, LA	99
327. Benton Harbor, MI	98
327. Jackson, MI	98
327. Tuscaloosa, AL	98
330. Terre Haute, IN	97
331. St. Joseph, MO	96
332. Lake Charles, LA	93
333. Casper, WY	92

Place Profiles: Jobs

The following charts show forecasted job growth rates in each metro area, plus the number of new jobs created in predominantly blue-collar and in predominantly white-collar industries.

All figures are derived from current employment forecasts from Woods & Poole Economics, Inc., of Washington, DC, and are used here with permission.

A star (★) in front of a metro area's name highlights it as one of the top 30 places for job growth between now and 1995.

	Growth Forecast	New Jobs Blue Collar	New Jobs White Collar	Places Rated Score	Places Rated Rank
Abilene, TX	3.46%	+1,200	+1,440	192	258
Akron, OH	2.61%	−5,540	+13,800	316	223
Albany, GA	4.45%	−50	+2,900	227	241
Albany–Schenectady–Troy, NY	7.07%	−900	+35,440	2,543	73
Albuquerque, NM	8.50%	+4,490	+20,660	2,238	82

	Growth Forecast	New Jobs Blue Collar	New Jobs White Collar	Places Rated Score	Places Rated Rank
Alexandria, LA	0.79%	−110	+600	104	305
Allentown-Bethlehem, PA-NJ	4.01%	−6,230	+19,320	625	173
Altoona, PA	7.76%	+320	+4,710	491	194
Amarillo, TX	5.28%	+760	+4,920	399	207
★ Anaheim-Santa Ana, CA	24.11%	+56,140	+311,280	88,669	1
Anchorage, AK	12.80%	+4,140	+16,580	2,753	68
Anderson, IN	0.84%	−1,530	+2,050	105	302
Anderson, SC	5.39%	−490	+3,900	283	228
Ann Arbor, MI	9.05%	−220	+18,040	1,714	97
Anniston, AL	2.07%	−150	+1,420	126	288
Appleton-Oshkosh-Neenah, WI	4.33%	+2,270	+5,410	432	203
Asheville, NC	3.48%	+160	+3,280	219	247
Athens, GA	1.91%	+540	+970	129	285
★ Atlanta, GA	14.66%	+61,360	+200,880	38,554	2
★ Atlantic City, NJ	21.94%	+660	+46,480	10,438	25
Augusta, GA-SC	8.24%	−790	+17,800	1,500	107
Aurora-Elgin, IL	11.57%	+280	+19,540	2,391	79
★ Austin, TX	14.99%	+11,920	+62,010	11,180	24
Bakersfield, CA	4.94%	+3,400	+8,910	708	159
Baltimore, MD	7.24%	−2,050	+100,720	7,241	3⁷
Bangor, ME	4.45%	−10	+2,090	194	257
Baton Rouge, LA	7.70%	−1,200	+22,000	1,701	98
Battle Creek, MI	−0.85%	−1,630	+1,080	100	311
Beaumont-Port Arthur, TX	3.75%	−3,740	+9,880	329	221
Beaver County, PA	9.84%	+1,140	+4,780	683	165
Bellingham, WA	5.85%	+180	+3,320	305	226
Benton Harbor, MI	−1.41%	−1,920	+800	98	327
Bergen-Passaic, NJ	7.40%	−3,480	+64,680	4,629	51
Billings, MT	−0.04%	−790	+760	100	311
Biloxi-Gulfport, MS	−6.23%	+2,910	+3,680	511	190
Binghamton, NY	5.12%	+540	+6,830	478	196
Birmingham, AL	3.84%	−4,860	+23,150	803	149
Bismarck, ND	5.10%	−510	+2,970	225	242
Bloomington, IN	9.25%	+390	+5,280	626	172
Bloomington-Normal, IL	2.42%	−1,010	+2,740	142	279
Boise City, ID	8.04%	+2,370	+7,160	867	145
★ Boston, MA	6.33%	+20,310	+116,550	8,766	29
Boulder-Longmont, CO	8.33%	+3,620	+9,070	1,158	126
Bradenton, FL	15.98%	+3,200	+10,630	2,308	80
Brazoria, TX	5.53%	+170	+4,070	336	216
Bremerton, WA	8.58%	+570	+6,630	716	158
Bridgeport-Milford, CT	6.27%	−1,230	+18,830	1,205	122
Bristol, CT	4.50%	+10	+2,620	218	248
Brockton, MA	14.53%	+2,200	+11,050	2,026	87
Brownsville-Harlingen, TX	11.13%	+540	+9,940	1,266	119
Bryan-College Station, TX	22.84%	+2,530	+12,380	3,505	58
Buffalo, NY	6.29%	−4,590	+36,950	2,136	85
Burlington, NC	7.49%	+440	+4,300	455	200
Burlington, VT	12.52%	+3,130	+8,390	1,542	105
Canton, OH	3.33%	−4,250	+10,600	312	224
Casper, WY	−4.27%	−1,540	−120	92	333
Cedar Rapids, IA	4.00%	−1,590	+5,770	267	234
Champaign-Urbana-Rantoul, IL	7.52%	+360	+7,930	723	156
Charleston, SC	9.50%	+2,100	+23,440	2,526	74
Charleston, WV	4.03%	−2,120	+7,390	312	224
Charlotte-Gastonia-Rock Hill, NC-SC	10.64%	+16,170	+58,680	8,064	32
Charlottesville, VA	8.48%	−130	+7,050	687	164
Chattanooga, TN-GA	1.76%	−2,490	+6,480	170	264
Cheyenne, WY	1.39%	−210	+840	109	298
★ Chicago, IL	6.07%	−25,810	+244,040	13,349	18
Chico, CA	13.56%	+1,270	+9,100	1,504	106
Cincinnati, OH-KY-IN	5.44%	−4,570	+49,000	2,517	75
Clarksville-Hopkinsville, TN-KY	1.10%	−510	+1,410	110	297
Cleveland, OH	1.95%	−17,880	+38,420	500	191
Colorado Springs, CO	8.83%	+5,780	+14,620	1,903	91
Columbia, MO	6.16%	+310	+3,960	362	213
Columbia, SC	11.28%	+4,700	+28,150	3,806	56
Columbus, GA-AL	2.35%	+670	+2,610	177	260
Columbus, OH	7.88%	−310	+63,680	5,093	45
Corpus Christi, TX	3.70%	−630	+6,990	335	217
Cumberland, MD-WV	9.33%	+330	+3,800	485	195
★ Dallas, TX	13.30%	+50,700	+184,660	31,408	7
Danbury, CT	11.41%	+1,110	+13,490	1,769	95

	Growth Forecast	New Jobs		Places Rated Score	Places Rated Rank
		Blue Collar	White Collar		
Danville, VA	−1.00%	−710	+200	99	325
Davenport-Rock Island-Moline, IA-IL	4.69%	−4,220	+13,270	524	187
Dayton-Springfield, OH	3.48%	−6,880	+25,210	737	154
Daytona Beach, FL	9.45%	+3,570	+10,760	1,452	112
Decatur, AL	0.90%	−970	+1,480	105	302
Decatur, IL	−0.39%	−1,760	+1,510	100	311
Denver, CO	8.41%	+11,690	+82,010	7,980	33
Des Moines, IA	5.91%	−1,680	+16,860	998	135
Detroit, MI	3.44%	−19,390	+94,900	2,695	70
Dothan, AL	11.01%	+600	+7,070	944	137
Dubuque, IA	−0.62%	−1,690	+1,380	100	311
Duluth, MN-WI	3.32%	−2,800	+6,520	223	245
Eau Claire, WI	6.18%	+790	+3,760	381	210
El Paso, TX	9.38%	+5,040	+18,380	2,297	81
Elkhart-Goshen, IN	7.94%	+5,940	+2,880	800	150
Elmira, NY	4.86%	−1,300	+3,390	201	255
Enid, OK	−0.21%	−470	+400	100	311
Erie, PA	2.16%	−1,980	+4,890	163	267
Eugene-Springfield, OR	4.16%	−880	+6,710	343	215
Evansville, IN-KY	0.96%	−2,230	+3,750	115	296
Fall River, MA-RI	8.44%	+490	+6,800	717	157
Fargo-Moorhead, ND-MN	4.18%	−600	+4,400	258	236
Fayetteville, NC	4.40%	+850	+5,510	379	211
Fayetteville-Springdale, AR	1.91%	+290	+880	122	291
Fitchburg-Leominster, MA	9.52%	+220	+4,970	594	175
Flint, MI	−0.27%	−4,540	+3,960	100	311
Florence, AL	0.25%	−850	+1,000	100	311
Florence, SC	5.37%	+100	+3,290	282	229
Fort Collins-Loveland, CO	9.08%	+1,270	+7,660	909	140
★ Fort Lauderdale-Hollywood-Pompano Beach, FL	20.55%	+16,980	+117,550	27,744	10
★ Fort Myers-Cape Coral, FL	23.93%	+4,200	+33,460	9,115	28
★ Fort Pierce, FL	27.76%	+5,850	+23,140	8,146	30
Fort Smith, AR-OK	9.00%	+4,190	+4,650	894	141
Fort Walton Beach, FL	19.38%	+2,870	+13,090	3,193	61
Fort Wayne, IN	3.17%	−800	+7,900	326	222
Fort Worth-Arlington, TX	10.55%	+19,670	+51,690	7,629	35
Fresno, CA	4.78%	+3,480	+11,330	808	148
Gadsden, AL	−0.14%	−610	+550	100	311
Gainesville, FL	12.36%	+700	+13,490	1,854	92
Galveston-Texas City, TX	0.60%	−1,230	+1,770	103	307
Gary-Hammond, IN	4.41%	−10,900	+21,720	576	181
Glens Falls, NY	5.46%	+360	+2,920	279	230
Grand Forks, ND	1.50%	−190	+810	109	298
Grand Rapids, MI	7.88%	+4,670	+26,830	2,581	72
Great Falls, MT	2.39%	−460	+1,490	125	289
Greeley, CO	2.31%	+780	+670	133	283
Green Bay, WI	8.51%	2,810	+7,070	940	138
Greensboro-Winston-Salem-High Point, NC	9.02%	+10,920	+41,780	4,858	47
Greenville-Spartanburg, SC	10.03%	+4,640	+32,890	3,866	55
Hagerstown, MD	2.85%	−2,210	+3,940	149	276
Hamilton-Middletown, OH	3.27%	−1,730	+5,410	221	246
Harrisburg-Lebanon-Carlisle, PA	5.20%	−610	+18,880	1,050	131
Hartford, CT	5.94%	+1,400	+29,500	1,936	89
Hickory, NC	9.24%	+6,700	+6,700	1,338	117
Honolulu, HI	5.22%	+20	+26,560	1,486	110
Houma-Thibodaux, LA	−1.00%	−1,980	+1,240	99	325
Houston, TX	6.18%	−4,680	+116,410	7,001	39
Huntington-Ashland, WV-KY-OH	1.57%	−3,010	+5,040	132	284
Huntsville, AL	7.25%	+6,210	+4,630	885	143
Indianapolis, IN	6.07%	−1,310	+46,300	2,833	66
Iowa City, IA	6.88%	+430	+3,680	384	209
Jackson, MI	−1.99%	−1,710	+490	98	327
Jackson, MS	4.09%	+80	+8,840	465	198
Jackson, TN	5.47%	+270	+2,260	238	239
Jacksonville, FL	8.65%	+11,070	+33,560	3,959	54
Jacksonville, NC	5.17%	+710	+3,260	305	226
Janesville-Beloit, WI	3.95%	−1,220	+3,930	206	254
Jersey City, NJ	4.50%	−8,460	+21,420	682	166
Johnson City-Kingsport-Bristol, TN-VA	4.09%	+50	+8,590	453	201
Johnstown, PA	1.99%	−1,620	+3,460	137	281
Joliet, IL	10.60%	−1,700	+15,710	1,585	103
Joplin, MO	6.97%	+1,930	+3,340	468	197
Kalamazoo, MI	3.45%	+270	+3,900	244	238

	Growth Forecast	New Jobs Blue Collar	New Jobs White Collar	Places Rated Score	Places Rated Rank
Kankakee, IL	8.58%	−1,520	+5,210	417	204
Kansas City, MO-KS	4.39%	+140	+41,570	1,933	90
Kenosha, WI	5.89%	−1,690	+4,520	268	233
Killeen-Temple, TX	8.19%	+1,140	+9,930	1,007	134
Knoxville, TN	5.57%	+1,560	+16,100	1,083	128
Kokomo, IN	0.86%	−800	+1,270	104	305
La Crosse, WI	7.89%	+100	+4,890	494	193
Lafayette, LA	4.87%	+700	+5,040	379	211
Lafayette-West Lafayette, IN	3.68%	−80	+2,760	199	256
Lake Charles, LA	−3.15%	−2,480	+250	93	332
Lake County, IL	12.97%	+3,030	+32,010	4,644	49
Lakeland-Winter Haven, FL	6.97%	−1,290	+14,040	988	136
Lancaster, PA	7.50%	+3,170	+14,070	1,395	114
Lansing-East Lansing, MI	5.05%	−310	+11,840	682	166
Laredo, TX	9.64%	+1,280	+3,090	519	188
Las Cruces, NM	16.66%	+1,490	+7,500	1,601	101
★ Las Vegas, NV	18.38%	+6,800	+59,490	12,284	20
Lawrence, KS	5.67%	−20	+2,240	225	242
Lawrence-Haverhill, MA-NH	13.42%	+5,950	+23,130	4,004	53
Lawton, OK	2.34%	+560	+950	136	282
Lewiston-Auburn, ME	3.41%	−630	+2,110	150	274
Lexington-Fayette, KY	4.48%	+1,740	+8,240	546	184
Lima, OH	0.89%	−590	+1,360	107	300
Lincoln, NE	1.91%	−650	+3,170	148	278
Little Rock-North Little Rock, AR	5.98%	−800	+18,660	1,169	124
Longview-Marshall, TX	2.50%	+290	+1,920	155	271
Lorain-Elyria, OH	1.67%	−2,430	+4,150	128	286
★ Los Angeles-Long Beach, CA	7.92%	+32,070	+375,700	32,395	6
Louisville, KY-IN	3.59%	−6,420	+25,640	790	151
Lowell, MA-NH	12.69%	+5,780	+18,340	3,160	62
Lubbock, TX	6.87%	+270	+8,340	693	162
Lynchburg, VA	2.95%	−160	+2,650	173	263
Macon-Warner Robins, GA	2.12%	+160	+3,040	168	265
Madison, WI	6.52%	+2,180	+13,720	1,137	127
Manchester, NH	14.06%	+3,320	+11,420	2,174	84
Mansfield, OH	3.57%	−150	+2,700	191	259
McAllen-Edinburg-Mission, TX	11.63%	+1,860	+12,710	1,796	93
Medford, OR	7.34%	+1,220	+3,740	463	199
Melbourne-Titusville-Palm Bay, FL	5.89%	+2,090	+8,720	737	154
Memphis, TN-AR-MS	4.59%	+4,410	+20,720	1,252	120
Merced, CA	11.14%	+4,400	+3,840	1,014	133
★ Miami-Hialeah, FL	10.37%	+6,960	+106,760	11,893	21
★ Middlesex-Somerset-Hunterdon, NJ	18.69%	+11,120	+107,070	22,198	13
Middletown, CT	14.59%	+640	+6,900	1,203	123
Midland, TX	2.94%	+1,800	+140	157	270
Milwaukee, WI	4.11%	−8,910	+42,990	1,499	108
Minneapolis-St. Paul, MN-WI	7.03%	+14,280	+94,960	7,776	34
Mobile, AL	3.30%	−1,050	+8,130	334	218
Modesto, CA	6.77%	+2,930	+6,930	768	152
★ Monmouth-Ocean, NJ	14.41%	+8,260	+54,600	9,159	27
Monroe, LA	1.77%	−660	+1,900	122	291
Montgomery, AL	3.79%	+2,430	+3,650	331	220
Muncie, IN	2.54%	−1,280	+2,800	139	280
Muskegon, MI	0.93%	−1,970	+2,620	106	301
Naples, FL	20.86%	+2,520	+12,970	3,331	59
Nashua, NH	15.71%	+4,450	+14,290	3,048	64
Nashville, TN	9.96%	+14,080	+46,530	6,137	42
★ Nassau-Suffolk, NY	12.70%	+24,740	+167,620	24,534	11
New Bedford, MA	7.13%	+160	+6,200	552	183
New Britain, CT	3.36%	−330	+4,020	224	244
New Haven-Meriden, CT	5.18%	−1,590	+16,810	888	142
New London-Norwich, CT-RI	5.56%	+2,260	+6,340	578	180
New Orleans, LA	7.74%	−3,900	+55,750	4,115	52
New York, NY	2.26%	−71,280	+183,610	2,643	71
Newark, NJ	7.50%	−4,450	+91,500	6,627	40
Niagara Falls, NY	5.92%	−700	+6,520	443	202
Norfolk-Virginia Beach-Newport News, VA	7.86%	+16,250	+47,360	5,097	44
Norwalk, CT	7.39%	−250	+6,740	580	179
★ Oakland, CA	12.64%	+14,730	+126,100	17,895	16
Ocala, FL	23.60%	+7,250	+11,970	4,634	50
Odessa, TX	−0.25%	−850	+700	100	311
Oklahoma City, OK	4.09%	+9,470	+13,430	1,037	132
Olympia, WA	13.24%	+850	+9,000	1,405	113

	Growth Forecast	New Jobs Blue Collar	White Collar	Places Rated Score	Places Rated Rank
Omaha, NE-IA	3.56%	−1,480	+15,160	586	178
Orange County, NY	11.01%	+630	+14,320	1,743	96
★ Orlando, FL	23.13%	+20,820	+122,930	33,346	5
Owensboro, KY	−0.91%	−1,120	+710	100	311
★ Oxnard-Ventura, CA	19.26%	+9,130	+48,850	11,263	23
Panama City, FL	14.05%	+1,680	+8,000	1,460	111
Parkersburg-Marietta, WV-OH	1.92%	−1,370	+2,800	127	287
Pascagoula, MS	6.47%	−360	+3,950	333	219
Pawtucket-Woonsocket-Attleboro, RI-MA	4.70%	−490	+8,940	496	192
Pensacola, FL	8.74%	+960	+13,710	1,383	115
Peoria, IL	5.21%	−2,270	+11,120	561	182
★ Philadelphia, PA-NJ	6.05%	−17,990	+175,650	9,637	26
★ Phoenix, AZ	15.80%	+36,410	+153,430	30,087	8
Pine Bluff, AR	−0.42%	−440	+260	100	311
Pittsburgh, PA	4.70%	−35,150	+86,110	2,493	76
Pittsfield, MA	5.01%	+50	+2,230	213	250
Portland, ME	9.44%	+1,730	+12,990	1,489	109
Portland, OR	4.62%	+2,400	+30,610	1,624	100
Portsmouth-Dover-Rochester, NH-ME	19.35%	+4,800	+19,590	4,824	48
Poughkeepsie, NY	10.14%	+2,820	+11,990	1,601	101
Providence, RI	5.87%	−90	+21,490	1,355	116
Provo-Orem, UT	12.37%	+1,010	+11,700	1,672	99
Pueblo, CO	7.48%	−1,020	+5,020	398	208
Racine, WI	2.48%	−1,450	+3,530	152	273
★ Raleigh-Durham, NC	16.47%	+21,080	+57,250	13,000	19
Rapid City, SD	3.24%	+340	+1,320	153	272
Reading, PA	1.93%	−1,980	+5,450	167	266
Redding, CA	11.14%	+800	+6,130	870	144
Reno, NV	5.82%	+270	+9,130	646	171
Richland-Kennewick-Pasco, WA	7.67%	+1,520	+4,320	545	185
Richmond-Petersburg, VA	8.14%	+6,420	+37,950	3,710	57
★ Riverside-San Bernardino, CA	15.47%	+28,650	+105,250	20,809	14
Roanoke, VA	3.42%	−320	+5,420	274	231
Rochester, MN	13.90%	+1,250	+9,260	1,558	104
Rochester, NY	6.79%	+1,440	+36,880	2,703	69
Rockford, IL	4.44%	−1,890	+8,940	413	206
★ Sacramento, CA	12.57%	+12,540	+80,370	11,782	22
Saginaw-Bay City-Midland, MI	0.17%	−4,990	+5,300	101	308
St. Cloud, MN	14.31%	+1,910	+11,770	2,057	86
St. Joseph, MO	−2.87%	−360	−950	96	331
St. Louis, MO-IL	4.07%	−4,370	+61,690	2,433	77
Salem, OR	1.94%	+510	+2,020	149	276
Salem-Gloucester, MA	6.36%	+900	+8,500	698	161
Salinas-Seaside-Monterey, CA	12.06%	+4,390	+19,340	2,961	65
Salt Lake City-Ogden, UT	10.52%	+11,250	+50,090	6,553	41
San Angelo, TX	3.69%	+780	+1,200	174	262
San Antonio, TX	10.75%	+13,140	+61,690	8,143	31
★ San Diego, CA	12.29%	+29,060	+131,500	19,827	15
★ San Francisco, CA	10.71%	−3,360	+139,300	14,662	17
★ San Jose, CA	14.75%	+46,050	+105,190	22,401	12
Santa Barbara-Santa Maria-Lompoc, CA	14.97%	+8,810	+24,150	5,030	46
Santa Cruz, CA	16.36%	+2,750	+16,170	3,195	60
Santa Fe, NM	16.07%	+1,340	+10,190	1,949	88
Santa Rosa-Petaluma, CA	19.29%	+8,190	+28,510	7,183	38
Sarasota, FL	14.29%	+2,870	+18,350	3,127	63
Savannah, GA	3.19%	−210	+4,470	235	240
Scranton-Wilkes-Barre, PA	5.17%	−4,520	+22,980	1,053	130
Seattle, WA	7.85%	+21,580	+69,440	7,242	36
Sharon, PA	4.64%	−1,400	+3,790	210	251
Sheboygan, WI	0.49%	+60	+220	101	308
Sherman-Denison, TX	2.18%	−150	+1,210	123	290
Shreveport, LA	1.83%	−1,070	+4,440	161	268
Sioux City, IA-NE	0.27%	+310	−130	100	311
Sioux Falls, SD	8.29%	+490	+6,350	669	169
South Bend-Mishawaka, IN	2.85%	−2,130	+5,910	207	253
Spokane, WA	2.91%	−230	+5,670	258	236
Springfield, IL	5.90%	−1,590	+8,850	528	186
Springfield, MA	5.82%	−1,680	+18,080	1,055	129
Springfield, MO	8.93%	+1,110	+12,050	1,274	118
Stamford, CT	6.03%	−920	+9,010	589	176
State College, PA	6.14%	+80	+3,920	345	214
Steubenville-Weirton, OH-WV	4.31%	−970	+3,640	216	249
Stockton, CA	6.20%	+2,620	+9,720	863	146

	Growth Forecast	New Jobs		Places Rated Score	Places Rated Rank
		Blue Collar	White Collar		
Syracuse, NY	7.54%	+2,340	+25,210	2,178	83
Tacoma, WA	4.79%	+1,160	+11,110	689	163
Tallahassee, FL	13.18%	+1,720	+15,850	2,417	78
★ Tampa-St. Petersburg-Clearwater, FL	18.45%	+35,050	+163,860	36,806	3
Terre Haute, IN	−2.27%	−1,890	+420	97	330
Texarkana, TX-Texarkana, AR	1.85%	−520	+1,620	120	294
Toledo, OH	3.08%	−5,590	+15,870	416	205
Topeka, KS	1.26%	−1,110	+2,420	116	295
Trenton, NJ	5.09%	−1,140	+12,170	661	170
Tucson, AZ	9.07%	+6,380	+23,290	2,792	67
Tulsa, OK	3.98%	−1,010	+17,050	739	153
Tuscaloosa, AL	−1.53%	−50	−940	98	327
Tyler, TX	8.07%	+840	+6,250	671	168
Utica-Rome, NY	3.33%	−1,860	+6,980	271	232
Vallejo-Fairfield-Napa, CA	16.79%	+6,460	+24,400	5,283	43
Vancouver, WA	10.90%	+3,040	+6,760	1,168	125
Victoria, TX	1.15%	−100	+540	105	302
Vineland-Millville-Bridgeton, NJ	0.47%	−1,850	+2,150	101	308
Visalia-Tulare-Porterville, CA	3.46%	+1,690	+3,020	262	235
Waco, TX	3.31%	+300	+2,970	209	252
★ Washington, DC-MD-VA	11.65%	+35,360	+276,680	36,456	4
Waterbury, CT	5.89%	−70	+7,100	513	189
Waterloo-Cedar Falls, IA	0.12%	−3,170	+3,260	100	311
Wausau, WI	2.85%	−120	+1,860	150	274
★ West Palm Beach-Boca Raton-Delray Beach, FL	25.03%	+20,450	+98,150	29,791	9
Wheeling, WV-OH	8.31%	−1,980	+7,850	588	177
Wichita, KS	4.95%	+600	+14,000	823	147
Wichita Falls, TX	3.12%	+880	+1,600	177	260
Williamsport, PA	−0.28%	−1,210	+1,050	100	311
Wilmington, DE-NJ-MD	5.96%	−450	+19,720	1,249	121
Wilmington, NC	10.59%	−470	+8,110	910	139
Worcester, MA	8.60%	+260	+19,470	1,796	93
Yakima, WA	1.55%	+170	+1,220	121	293
York, PA	5.37%	−460	+11,700	703	160
Youngstown-Warren, OH	4.69%	−2,660	+13,530	611	174
Yuba City, CA	3.44%	−570	+2,250	158	269

Et Cetera

MINIMUM WAGE LAWS

The federal government is considering an increase in the federal minimum wage from $3.35 to $5.05. Although at least 16 states have a minimum wage above the current federal level, not one has a minimum at or above $5.05—the new proposed federal amount. Thirteen states have minima below the current federal level, and nine have no minimum wage at all. Twelve states and the District of Columbia either recently raised or are considering raising their minimum wage above the current federal level.

The District of Columbia, California, and Connecticut have the highest minimum wages in the country. Alabama, Arizona, Florida, Iowa, Louisiana, Mississippi, Missouri, South Carolina, and Tennessee have no minimum wage requirement. Typically, states with high minimum wages have low levels of unemployment and/or high costs of living. Those who argue against a higher federal minimum wage believe that the different minimum-wage levels reflect important regional differences. A minimum wage that is appropriate in Connecticut, for example, could prove devastating to employers in, say, Mississippi.

COLLECTING UNEMPLOYMENT

If you are laid off or fired (for a reason other than your misconduct), or if you leave your job for a category of reasons called "good cause attributable to the employer," you are eligible for weekly cash benefits under local unemployment insurance programs. Examples of "good cause" for quitting a job are sexual harassment on the

Drug Testing on the Job

If your employer suspects you of using drugs on the job, can he require you to take a drug test? Can an employer require random drug testing—without a good reason to suspect that you use drugs? Employee drug testing first hit the papers in 1987, and in some states it hit the courts and the legislatures as well. Civil libertarians filed at least 20 lawsuits, arguing that random drug testing is an invasion of privacy if the employer does not have probable cause to suspect illegal activity. Those in favor of testing, of course, argue that they are concerned with safety, not with invading anyone's privacy, and that only those who have something to hide will fear and resist the testing.

The federal government led the way in this controversial policy with its drug testing of soldiers, law enforcement agents, and other department employees. Thirteen states passed drug-testing laws as of 1988. Some states, such as Vermont, Rhode Island, Iowa, and Montana, prohibit random testing. At the other extreme, Louisiana's law says that an employee who refuses testing is presumed to be in violation of drug policy, and Nebraska's law allows employers to discipline workers who refuse to take a test. Other laws, such as those of New York, Maryland, Illinois, and Oregon, deal primarily with issues of licensing of testing laboratories. Drug-testing bills have failed in Maine, Wisconsin, and Washington and have been considered in New Jersey, Pennsylvania, Michigan, Wisconsin, and North Carolina.

Unemployment Insurance Benefits by State

State	Average Weekly Check	Average Duration (weeks)
Alabama	$101.09	10
Alaska	156.57	16
Arizona	113.91	14
California	122.29	15
Colorado	158.32	15
Connecticut	179.25	19
Delaware	169.66	11
Florida	139.50	19
Georgia	128.63	13
Hawaii	168.41	9
Idaho	136.48	18
Illinois	152.17	12
Indiana	104.15	16
Iowa	149.50	11
Kansas	162.43	12
Kentucky	115.13	16
Louisiana	125.86	13
Maine	139.84	19
Maryland	158.33	11
Massachusetts	197.93	13
Michigan	183.82	15
Minnesota	181.31	16
Mississippi	101.28	18
Missouri	119.59	12
Montana	130.50	13
Nebraska	117.30	14
Nevada	146.37	12
New Hampshire	125.06	12
New Jersey	179.84	6
New Mexico	122.49	15
New York	143.48	16
North Carolina	133.45	17
North Dakota	132.28	8
Ohio	151.33	13
Oklahoma	142.68	18
Oregon	146.75	13
Pennsylvania	164.47	14
Rhode Island	166.91	15
South Carolina	110.94	12
South Dakota	121.08	10
Tennessee	105.34	13
Texas	158.55	11
Utah	157.04	15
Vermont	132.61	13
Virginia	134.71	13
Washington	151.51	9
West Virginia	141.42	15
Wisconsin	148.59	14
Wyoming	158.79	13

Source: U.S. Department of Labor Employment and Training Administration, unpublished data, 1989.

job or a conflict between a work policy (such as working on Sunday) and a sincerely held religious belief.

The unemployment insurance program is not a welfare program, so unlike an applicant for food stamps or Medicaid, when you apply for unemployment compensation you do not have to prove financial need. You must only show that you are involuntarily out of work, that you are able and available to work, and that you are looking for a new job. Of course, you must also have worked for a covered employer (if you are a consultant or independent contractor, you probably won't be able to collect benefits), and you must have worked a certain number of weeks (this varies by state).

The unemployment insurance program, established in 1935 as part of the Social Security Act, is run jointly by the federal and state governments and covers nearly all salaried non-farm workers. In southern California, actors and aerospace workers queue up for weekly checks; in New York, so do longshoremen and advertising executives. The program was designed to provide both people and the local economy with partial replacement of wages and purchasing power during short periods of joblessness.

The amount of your unemployment check is related to what you were earning before you became unem-

ployed, subject to a ceiling. In Massachusetts, for example—the location with the highest weekly benefits—the average weekly benefit amount for 1988 was $198. In Mississippi and Alabama, on the other hand—the two states paying the lowest benefits—the average weekly benefit amount was $101. The 1988 average weekly benefit for each state is listed on the table above.

Most states limit eligibility to 26 weeks, although as you can see on the above table, the average unemployed worker actually received only about 15 weeks of benefits in 1988. The figures on average actual duration of benefits give some insight into the employment picture in each state, and also into the rigorousness of its eligibility requirements. For example, workers in New

Hampshire are eligible to collect a maximum of 26 weeks of benefits. The average unemployed worker, however, only collected five weeks' worth in 1988. What gives? Well, that average worker either found new employment pretty quickly or had a hard time establishing ongoing eligibility for benefits, or some combination of the two. The second trend—toward more stringent eligibility requirements—is growing.

Most state legislatures, reacting to declining reserve funds and a GAO warning that a recession would force them to borrow heavily from the federal government to pay benefits, have tightened eligibility requirements and cut the number of weeks a claimant can receive benefits. Even in this time of high employment, the number of long-term unemployed remains high, and these people have, for the most part, been unable to receive unemployment benefits. In 1987, only one out of every three unemployed workers qualified to receive unemployment benefits.

METROPOLITAN HEADQUARTERS: *FORTUNE'S* INDUSTRIAL 500

Imagine how long it would take to squander an inheritance of $2 trillion. If you were to spend or give away $1 million of your endowment every hour, it would take you more than 228 years to come up with empty pockets. In 1988, the combined sales of the 500 industrial companies rated the nation's largest by *Fortune* magazine reached that figure, the largest annual total since *Fortune* compiled its first list in 1955.

To be counted among the top 500, a corporation must not only ring up sufficient annual sales, it must also derive more than half its sales from manufacturing or mining or both, and its stock must be publicly traded rather than privately held so that its financial records can be examined by anyone.

Since 1970, there have been remarkable southerly and westerly shifts in the locations of corporate headquarters of these top 500 industrial firms. Atlanta, the home of Coca-Cola since the turn of the century, is now on the home office letterhead of nine other firms on *Fortune's* list. The number of high-tech members based in California's Silicon Valley (otherwise known as San Jose) has jumped from two to 12. Only 59 of the 500 industrials had their headquarters in the Sun Belt in 1970; today, the number has more than doubled to 140.

Following are the 115 metro areas that were headquarters of one or more Fortune 500 industrial firms as of 1988, along with the companies located there. The firms are listed in order of their sales rank in the industrial 500, and each firm's primary industry is given in parentheses. Detroit's General Motors (Motor Vehicles and Parts) is ranked first; Cincinnati's Chemed (Chemicals) is number 500.

Fortune's Top 500 Industrial Firms

Akron, OH
32. Goodyear Tire (Rubber Products)
169. B.F. Goodrich (Chemicals)
204. Gencorp (Aerospace)
449. A. Schulman (Chemicals)

Allentown–Bethlehem, PA–NJ
82. Bethlehem Steel (Metals)
176. Air Products (Chemicals)
199. Mack Trucks (Motor Vehicles and Parts)

Anaheim–Santa Ana, CA
380. Western Digital (Electronics)

Ann Arbor, MI
475. J.P. Industries (Industrial and Farm Equipment)

Appleton–Oshkosh–Neenah, WI
482. George Banta (Publishing, Printing)

Atlanta, GA
20. RJR Nabisco (Food)
43. Georgia–Pacific (Forest Products)
49. Coca-Cola (Beverages)
121. Coca-Cola Enterprises (Beverages)
260. National Service industries (Electronics)
324. Georgia Gulf (Chemicals)
328. Gold Kist (Food)
336. Fuqua Industries (Industrial and Farm Equipment)
456. Oxford Industries (Apparel)
492. Scientific–Atlanta (Electronics)

Baltimore, MD
187. Black & Decker (Industrial and Farm Equipment)
300. McCormick (Food)
308. Crown Central (Petroleum Refining)
484. Noxell (Soaps, Cosmetics)

Baton Rouge, LA
472. Borden Chemicals (Chemicals)

Battle Creek, MI
106. Kellogg (Food)

Benton Harbor, MI
104. Whirlpool (Electronics)

Bergen–Passaic, NJ
100. CPC International (Food)
101. American Cyanamid (Chemicals)
146. Ingersoll–Rand (Industrial and Farm Equipment)
163. Union Camp (Forest Products)
220. Becton Dickinson (Scientific and Photographic Equipment)
313. Federal Paper Board (Forest Products)

342. GAF (Chemicals)

Birmingham, AL
326. Vulcan Materials (Mining, Crude-Oil Production)

Boise City, ID
112. Boise Cascade (Forest Products)

Boston, MA
30. Digital Equipment (Computers and Office Equipment)
53. Raytheon (Electronics)
128. Gillette (Metal Products)
218. Polaroid (Scientific and Photographic Equipment)
232. Cabot (Chemicals)
241. Prime Computer (Computers and Office Equipment)
265. EG&G (Scientific and Photographic Equipment)
394. Dennison Manufacturing (Forest Products)
433. Millipore (Rubber Products)
476. Foxboro (Scientific and Photographic Equipment)
477. Affiliated Publications (Publishing, Printing)

Boulder–Longmont, CO
362. Storage Technology (Computers and Office Equipment)

444. Miniscribe (Computers and Office Equipment)

Bridgeport–Milford, CT
5. General Electric (Electronics)
414. SSMC (Electronics)

Brockton, MA
382. Ocean Spray (Food)

Buffalo, NY
301. Armtek (Rubber Products)

Canton, OH
245. Timken (Industrial and Farm Equipment)

Charlotte–Gastonia–Rock Hill, NC–SC
222. Springs Industries (Textiles)
323. Nucor (Metals)

Chattanooga, TN–GA
441. Dixie Yarns (Textiles)
464. Constar International (Rubber Products)

Chicago, IL
12. Amoco (Petroleum Refining)
36. Sara Lee (Food)
52. Motorola (Electronics)
57. Beatrice (Food)
88. Quaker Oats (Food)
113. Navistar International (Motor Vehicles and Parts)

116. Inland Steel Industries (Metals)
119. Whitman (Food)
122. Stone Container (Forest Products)
136. FMC (Chemicals)
137. Brunswick (Transportation Equipment)
142. Borg–Warner (Motor Vehicles and Parts)
149. R.R. Donnelly (Publishing, Printing)
152. USG (Building Materials)
159. Zenith Electronics (Computers and Office Equipment)
181. Tribune (Publishing, Printing)
183. Morton Thiokol (Chemicals)
213. Illinois Tool Works (Metal Products)
233. Square D (Electronics)
247. Dean Foods (Food)
250. Chicago Pacific (Electronics)
254. International Minerals & Chemical (Chemicals)
280. AM International (Industrial and Farm Equipment)
304. Hartmarx (Apparel)
333. Fruit of the Loom (Apparel)
335. Nalco Chemical (Chemicals)
343. Amsted Industries (Metals)
356. Interlake (Industrial and Farm Equipment)
357. William Wrigley, Jr. (Food)
377. Pittway (Electronics)
443. Alberto Culver (Soaps, Cosmetics)
447. Bell & Howell (Scientific and Photographic Equipment)
458. Allied Products (Industrial and Farm Equipment)
467. Jepson (Industrial and Farm Equipment)
497. Molex (Electronics)

Cincinnati, OH–KY–IN
15. Procter & Gamble (Soaps, Cosmetics)
130. United Brands (Food)
248. Penn Central (Metals)
364. Cincinnati Milacron (Industrial and Farm Equipment)
379. Eagle–Picher Industries (Motor Vehicles and Parts)
462. Carlisle (Rubber Products)
500. Chemed (Chemicals)

Cleveland, OH
62. TRW (Electronics)
108. Eaton (Motor Vehicles and Parts)
189. Parker Hannifin (Industrial and Farm Equipment)
209. Sherwin–Williams (Chemicals)
246. Reliance Electric (Electronics)
295. Figgie International (Industrial and Farm Equipment)

303. American Greetings (Publishing, Printing)
330. M.A. Hanna (Chemicals)
332. Ferro (Rubber Products)
434. Nacco Industries (Industrial and Farm Equipment)
473. Banner Industries (Metal Products)
478. Sudbury (Motor Vehicles and Parts)
493. Standard Products (Rubber Products)

Columbus, OH
354. Worthington Industries (Metals)

Dallas, TX
56. LTV (Metals)
68. Texas Instruments (Electronics)
85. Kimberly-Clark (Forest Products)
118. Dresser Industries (Industrial and Farm Equipment)
164. American Petrofina (Petroleum Refining)
188. Valhi (Chemicals)
257. E-Systems (Electronics)
292. National Gypsum (Building Materials)
334. Tyler (Metal Products)
397. Rexene (Petroleum Refining)
405. Philips Industries (Industrial and Farm Equipment)
428. Texas Industries (Metals)
431. Trinity Industries (Transportation Equipment)
460. Maxus Energy (Mining, Crude-Oil Production)
491. Dr. Pepper/Seven-Up (Beverages)
499. NCH (Chemicals)

Danbury, CT
50. Union Carbide (Chemicals)

Danville, VA
470. Dibrell Brothers (Tobacco)

Davenport–Rock Island–Moline, IA–IL
87. Deere (Industrial and Farm Equipment)

Dayton–Springfield, OH
72. NCR (Computers and Office Equipment)
103. Mead (Forest Products)
409. Leslie Fay (Apparel)
413. Standard Register (Publishing, Printing)
446. Reynolds & Reynolds (Publishing, Printing)

Decatur, IL
65. Archer Daniels (Food)

Denver, CO
190. Manville (Building Materials)
249. Coors (Beverages)
275. Cyprus Minerals (Mining, Crude-Oil Production)

Des Moines, IA
411. Meredith (Publishing, Printing)

Detroit, MI
1. General Motors (Motor Vehicles and Parts)

2. Ford Motors (Motor Vehicles and Parts)
7. Chrysler (Motor Vehicles and Parts)
175. Masco (Furniture)
196. Fruehauf (Motor Vehicles and Parts)
236. Masco Industries (Motor Vehicles and Parts)
302. Federal–Mogul (Motor Vehicles and Parts)
452. Thorn Apple Valley (Food)

Fayetteville–Springdale, AR
212. Tyson Foods (Food)

Fort Wayne, IN
193. Central Soya (Food)

Grand Rapids, MI
398. Herman Miller (Furniture)

Greeley, CO
141. Sipco (Food)

Green Bay, WI
219. Fort Howard (Forest Products)

Greensboro–Winston-Salem–High Point, NC
457. Guilford Mills (Textiles)

Harrisburg–Lebanon–Carlisle, PA
161. AMP (Electronics)
167. Hershey Foods (Food)
282. Harsco (Metal Products)

Hartford, CT
16. United Technologies (Aerospace)
155. Emhart (Metal Products)
369. Dexter (Chemicals)
381. Kaman (Aerospace)

Honolulu, HI
361. Pacific Resources (Petroleum Refining)

Houston, TX
13. Shell Oil (Petroleum Refining)
24. Tenneco (Industrial and Farm Equipment)
54. Coastal (Petroleum Refining)
107. Cooper Industries (Electronics)
184. Baker Hughes (Industrial and Farm Equipment)
201. Pennzoil (Petroleum Refining)
202. Compaq Computer (Computers and Office Equipment)
310. Union Texas (Mining, Crude-Oil Production)
375. Vista Chemical (Chemicals)
403. Sterling Chemicals (Chemicals)
445. Southdown (Building Materials)
466. Mitchell Energy (Mining, Crude-Oil Production)
483. Big Three Industries (Chemicals)
498. Cameron Iron Works (Industrial and Farm Equipment)

Huntington–Ashland, WV–KY–OH
55. Ashland Oil (Petroleum Refining)

Huntsville, AL
372. Intergraph (Computers and Office Equipment)
376. SCI Systems (Computers and Office Equipment)

Indianapolis, IN
115. Eli Lilly (Pharmaceuticals)

Joplin, MO
371. Leggett & Platt (Furniture)

Kalamazoo, MI
156. Upjohn (Pharmaceuticals)
401. International Controls (Motor Vehicles and Parts)

Kansas City, MO–KS
153. Farmland Industries (Petroleum Refining)
365. IBC Holdings (Food)
389. Marion Laboratories (Pharmaceuticals)
426. Butler Manufacturing (Metal Products)

Kenosha, WI
366. Snap-on Tools (Metal Products)

Lafayette–West Lafayette, IN
435. Great Lakes Chemical (Chemicals)

Lake County, IL
64. Baxter International (Scientific and Photographic Equipment)
94. Abbott Laboratories (Pharmaceuticals)
178. Premark International (Rubber Products)
237. Outboard Marine (Transportation Equipment)
345. CF Industries (Chemicals)
412. Gaylord Container (Forest Products)
437. Commerce Clearing House (Publishing, Printing)

Lancaster, PA
160. Armstrong World Industries (Textiles)

Los Angeles–Long Beach, CA
14. Occidental Petroleum (Food)
17. Atlantic Richfield (Petroleum Refining)
28. Rockwell International (Aerospace)
33. Lockheed (Aerospace)
47. Unocal (Petroleum Refining)
75. Northrop (Aerospace)
96. Litton Industries (Scientific and Photographic Equipment)
105. Teledyne (Electronics)
138. Times Mirror (Publishing, Printing)
244. Avery International (Forest Products)
309. Tosco (Petroleum Refining)
337. Mattel (Toys, Sporting Goods)
352. Magnetek (Electronics)
420. Warnaco (Apparel)
422. Calmat (Building Materials)
485. Maxxam (Metals)

Louisville, KY–IN
320. Brown–Forman (Beverages)

Lowell, MA
145. Wang Laboratories (Computers and Office Equipment)
423. Apollo Computer (Computers and Office Equipment)

Melbourne–Titusville–Palm Bay, FL
203. Harris (Electronics)

Memphis, TN–AR–MS
243. Holly Farms (Food)

Miami–Hialeah, FL
192. Knight–Ridder (Publishing, Printing)
306. DWG (Textiles)

Middlesex–Somerset–Hunterdon, NJ
45. Johnson & Johnson (Pharmaceuticals)
67. Hanson Ind. NA (Chemicals)
78. Hoechst Celanese (Chemicals)
180. Engelhard (Chemicals)
489. Thomas & Betts (Electonics)

Milwaukee, WI
144. Johnson Controls (Rubber Products)
298. Harnischfeger Industries (Industrial and Farm Equipment)
322. A.O. Smith (Motor Vehicles and Parts)
350. Briggs & Stratton (Industrial and Farm Equipment)
384. Harley–Davidson (Motor Vehicles and Parts)
396. Universal Foods (Food)

Minneapolis–St. Paul, MN–WI
34. Minnesota Mining (Scientific and Photographic Equipment)
60. Honeywell (Electronics)
70. Pillsbury (Food)
76. General Mills (Food)
125. Control Data (Computers and Office Equipment)
179. Land O'Lakes (Food)
231. International Multifoods (Food)
287. Farmers Union (Petroleum Refining)
296. Deluxe (Publishing, Printing)
319. Bemis (Forest Products)
370. Pentair (Industrial and Farm Equipment)
385. Cray Research (Computers and Office Equipment)
407. IMO Industries (Industrial and Farm Equipment)
424. Medtronic (Scientific and Photographic Equipment)
438. Toro (Industrial and Farm Equipment)
450. Jostens (Jewelry, Silverware)
486. Minstar (Transportation Equipment)

Monmouth–Ocean, NJ
410. Harvard Industries (Motor Vehicles and Parts)

Muncie, IN
318. Ball (Metal Products)

Muskegon, MI
360. SPX (Motor Vehicles and Parts)

Nassau–Suffolk, NY
126. Grumman (Aerospace)
267. Esselte Business Systems (Forest Products)
465. Tambrands (Forest Products)

New Britain, CT
215. Stanley Works (Metal Products)

New Haven–Meriden, CT
281. Echlin (Motor Vehicles and Parts)
387. Insilco (Chemicals)
425. LPL Investment Group (Electronics)
436. Hubbell (Electronics)

New Orleans, LA
206. McDermott (Electronics)
211. Freeport–McMoran (Chemicals)
395. Louisiana Land & Exploration (Mining, Crude-Oil Production)
454. Avondale Industries (Transportation Equipment)

New York, NY
3. Exxon (Petroleum Refining)
4. IBM (Computers and Office Equipment)
6. Mobil (Petroleum Refining)
8. Texaco (Petroleum Refining)
10. Philip Morris (Tobacco)
26. Pepsico (Beverages)
42. International Paper (Forest Products)
59. Borden (Food)
63. Unilever U.S. (Soaps, Cosmetics)
69. W.R. Grace (Chemicals)
73. Bristol–Myers (Pharmaceuticals)
81. American Home Products (Pharmaceuticals)
83. Colgate–Palmolive (Soaps, Cosmetics)
84. North American Philips (Electronics)
86. Pfizer (Pharmaceuticals)
102. Time, Inc. (Publishing, Printing)
109. Warner Communication (Electronics)
110. Amerada Hess (Petroleum Refining)
111. Triangle Industries (Metal Products)
117. Amax (Metals)
123. American Standard (Building Materials)
132. Avon Products (Soaps, Cosmetics)
139. Quantum Chemical (Chemicals)
172. Revlon Group (Soaps, Cosmetics)
174. Burlington Holdings (Textiles)
191. Joseph E. Seagram (Beverages)
197. Westvaco (Forest Products)
207. Asarco (Metals)
208. Dover (Industrial and Farm Equipment)
210. Sequa (Aerospace)
223. McGraw–Hill (Publishing, Printing)
228. New York Times (Publishing, Printing)
234. Colt Industries (Aerospace)
238. Dow Jones (Publishing, Printing)
242. Witco (Chemicals)
255. Crane (Industrial and Farm Equipment)
256. Loral (Electronics)
263. Lorillard (Tobacco)
270. Inspiration Resources (Chemicals)
277. General Instrument (Electronics)
299. Liz Claiborne (Apparel)
331. Macmillan (Publishing, Printing)
367. International Flavors (Soaps, Cosmetics)
393. United Merchants (Textiles)
402. Ametek (Electronics)
408. Fuller (Chemicals)
418. Handy & Harman (Metals)
453. Faberge (Soaps, Cosmetics)
463. Phillips–Van Heusen (Apparel)
468. UIS (Motor Vehicles and Parts)
479. Avery (Chemicals)
495. Grow Group (Chemicals)

Newark, NJ
29. Allied–Signal (Aerospace)
74. Merck (Pharmaceuticals)
93. BASF (Chemicals)
120. Warner–Lambert (Pharmaceuticals)
140. Armco (Metals)
147. Schering–Plough (Pharmaceuticals)
383. C.R. Bard (Scientific and Photographic Equipment)

Norwalk, CT
127. Great Northern Nekoosa (Forest Products)
258. Perkin–Elmer (Scientific and Photographic Equipment)

Oakland, CA
286. Clorox (Soaps, Cosmetics)
471. Sun–Diamond Growers (Food)

Oklahoma City, OK
157. Kerr–McGee (Petroleum Refining)
276. Wilson Foods (Food)

Omaha, NE–IA
44. Conagra (Food)
205. Berkshire Hathaway (Publishing, Printing)
351. AG Processing (Food)
415. Valmont Industries (Electronics)

Pawtucket–Woonsocket–Attleboro, RI–MA
273. Hasbro (Toys, Sporting Goods)

Peoria, IL
35. Caterpillar (Industrial and Farm Equipment)

Philadelphia, PA–NJ
38. Unisys (Computers and Office Equipment)
48. Sun (Petroleum Refining)
95. Campbell Soup (Food)
97. Smithline Beckman (Pharmaceuticals)
·98. Scott Paper (Forest Products)
168. Rohm & Haas (Chemicals)
221. Crown Cork & Seal (Metal Products)
284. Certainteed (Building Materials)
291. Pennwalt (Chemicals)
329. Rorer Group (Pharmaceuticals)
442. Lukens (Metals)
451. Westmoreland Coal (Mining, Crude-Oil Production)

Phoenix, AZ
182. Phelps Dodge (Metals)

Pittsburgh, PA
23. USX (Petroleum Refining)
27. Westinghouse Electric (Electronics)
40. Aluminum Company of American (Metals)
79. PPG Industries (Chemicals)
89. H.J. Heinz (Food)
99. Bayer USA (Chemicals)
165. National Steel (Metals)
289. Cyclops Industries (Metals)
294. Allegheny Ludlum (Metals)
321. Aristech Chemical (Chemicals)
341. Allegheny International (Electronics)
494. H.H. Robertson (Metal Products)

Portland, OR
217. Louisiana–Pacific (Forest Products)
229. Willamette Industries (Forest Products)
261. Tektronix (Scientific and Photographic Equipment)
416. Nerco (Mining, Crude-Oil Production)
488. Pope & Talbot (Forest Products)

Portsmouth–Dover–Rochester, NH–ME
148. Henley Group (Scientific and Photographic Equipment)
239. Tyco Laboratories (Metals)

Providence, RI
61. Textron (Aerospace)
259. Nortek (Building Materials)

Reading, PA
170. VF (Apparel)
469. Carpenter Technology (Metals)

Richmond–Petersburg, VA
80. Reynolds Metals (Metals)
92. James River (Forest Products)
158. Ethyl (Chemicals)
177. Universal (Tobacco)
346. A.H. Robins (Pharmaceuticals)
386. Media General (Publishing, Printing)
399. Chesapeake (Forest Products)

Riverside–San Bernardino, CA
266. Fleetwood Enterprises (Transportation Equipment)

Rochester, NY
18. Eastman Kodak (Scientific and Photographic Equipment)
339. Bausch & Lomb (Scientific and Photographic Equipment)

Rockford, IL
251. Sundstrand (Aerospace)

Saginaw–Bay City–Midland, MI
21. Dow Chemical (Chemicals)
252. Dow Corning (Chemicals)

St. Louis, MO–IL
25. McDonnell Douglas (Aerospace)
41. General Dynamics (Aerospace)
46. Anheuser–Busch (Beverages)
51. Monsanto (Chemicals)
66. Emerson Electric (Electronics)
71. Ralston Purina (Food)
133. Interco (Furniture)
288. Jefferson Smurfit (Forest Products)
404. Kellwood (Apparel)

San Antonio, TX
224. Diamond Shamrock R&M (Petroleum Refining)
378. Valero Energy (Petroleum Refining)

San Diego, CA
353. Rohr Industries (Aerospace)

San Francisco, CA
11. Chevron (Petroleum Refining)
315. Raychem (Electronics)
317. Potlatch (Forest Products)
432. Shaklee (Pharmaceuticals)

San Jose, CA
39. Hewlett-Packard (Computers and Office Equipment)
114. Apple Computer (Computers and Office Equipment)
150. Intel (Electronics)
173. National Semiconductor (Electronics)
226. Amdahl (Computers and Office Equipment)
278. Tandem Computers (Computers and Office Equipment)
305. Varian Associates (Electronics)
311. Advanced Micro Devices (Electronics)
327. Sun Microsystems (Computers and Office Equipment)
349. Cooper Companies (Scientific and Photographic Equipment)
400. Atari (Computers and Office Equipment)
427. Xidex (Computers and Office Equipment)

Santa Cruz, CA
285. Seagate Technology (Computers and Office Equipment)

Savannah, Ga
347. Savannah Foods (Food)

Seattle, WA
19. Boeing (Aerospace)
143. Paccar (Motor Vehicles and Parts)
194. Burlington Resources (Mining, Crude-Oil Production)
417. Ohio Mattress (Furniture)

South Bend–Mishawaka, IN
283. Clark Equipment (Industrial and Farm Equipment)

Springfield, MO
235. Mid-America Dairymen (Food)

Stamford, CT
22. Xerox (Scientific and Photographic Equipment)
58. American Brands (Tobacco)
91. Champion International (Forest Products)
131. Combustion Engineering (Metal Products)
162. Pitney Bowes (Computers and Office Equipment)
185. Olin (Chemicals)
227. General Signal (Electronics)
262. Bowater (Forest Products)
325. Amstar (Food)
429. Finevest Foods (Food)
440. UST (Tobacco)
474. American Maize-Products (Food)
487. Sprague Technologies (Electronics)

Steubenville–Weirton, OH–WV
268. Weirton Steel (Metals)

Syracuse, NY
124. Agway (Food)

Tacoma, WA
37. Weyerhaeuser (Forest Products)

Tampa–St. Petersburg–Clearwater, FL
171. Hillsborough (Building Materials)
340. Anchor Glass (Building Materials)

Toledo, OH
90. Dana (Motor Vehicles and Parts)
129. Owens–Illinois (Building Materials)
151. Owens–Corning Fiberglass (Building Materials)
214. Trinova (Industrial and Farm Equipment)
368. Sheller–Globe (Motor Vehicles and Parts)

Trenton, NJ
166. Squibb (Pharmaceuticals)
406. Lone Star (Metal Products)

Tulsa, OK
225. Mapco (Petroleum Refining)
358. Memorex Telex (Computers and Office Equipment)

Washington, DC–MD–VA
77. Martin Marietta (Aerospace)
134. Gannett (Publishing, Printing)
269. Washington Post (Publishing, Printing)
279. Lafarge (Building Materials)
373. Mohasco (Furniture)
388. Danaher (Motor Vehicles and Parts)
455. Fairchild Industries (Electronics)

Wheeling, WV–OH
314. Wheeling- Pittsburgh (Metals)

Wichita, KS
419. Coleman (Industrial and Farm Equipment)

Wilmington, DE–NJ–MD
9. Du Pont (Chemicals)
154. Hercules (Chemicals)
230. Himont (Chemicals)
293. E.W. Scripps (Publishing, Printing)

Worcester, MA
264. Norton (Building Materials)
272. Data General (Computers and Office Equipment)

York, PA
290. York Holdings (Industrial and Farm Equipment)
461. P.H. Glatfelter (Forest Products)

Youngstown–Warren, OH
312. Lubrizol (Chemicals)

374. Champion Spark Plug (Electronics)

Source: Fortune, "The 500: The *Fortune* Directory of the Largest U.S. Industrial Corporations," May 1989, © Time, Inc.

Crime

In Duluth, MN, domestic violence out on the farm plus outside pushers developing a base for their illicit pharmaceutical trade aren't uncommon items in the local news. Down I-35 in the Twin Cities, stories of drug-related convenience-store stickups and homicides aren't uncommon either. If you were passing through either metro area and learned of these crimes, you might wonder whether you were any safer on the prairie than you'd be in East Los Angeles or the Bronx.

In reality, neither Duluth nor Minneapolis–St. Paul have crime rates anywhere near the national metro area average. The raw odds of your being a crime victim in either place are much below what they would be elsewhere. Indeed, of the 333 metro areas profiled in *Places Rated Almanac*, local police reporters in some have so few violent crime stories to write up that a casual reader of the paper may wonder whether anything interesting goes on there at all. In other metro areas, day-to-day existence seems just plain dangerous.

If you decide on living in Wheeling, WV–OH, for example, the raw odds of your meeting up with murder, armed robbery, or aggravated assault in a year's residence are 1 in 980. Should you choose Miami–Hialeah, FL, on the other hand, the chances rise to 1 in 61. One could say that living in rapidly growing southern Florida is 16 times more dangerous than it is in the lagging, post-industrial Ohio River Valley.

But quoting raw odds distorts the local crime picture. Violence isn't uniformly distributed throughout a metro area's neighborhoods; veteran cops in many metro areas will tell you that most murders and robberies occur within the same few square miles or even blocks. Moreover, if you're young, white, female, and earn enough money, your chances of meeting up with crime are much less than that of, say, an older, poor male. So why a chapter on crime if a combination of factors such as age, sex, race, income, and a wise selection of neighborhood can statistically remove you from danger?

The simple comeback is that you are a different kind of crime victim whenever you must trim back shrubbery along your home's foundation to restrict a thief's potential hiding places, or must get rid of the mailbox and install a mail slot in your front door, or must press down your car's door locks when driving down a darkened avenue, or must keep feeling for your wallet at street festivals, or must use only empty elevators, or must stay indoors evenings more than you really care to. In some metro areas such tactics are advised, in others they are merely prudent, and in still others they may not be necessary at all.

CRIME RISK: SEVEN CONNECTIONS

The question of why some metro areas are safer than others sparks disagreement among social scientists, citizens, politicians, and police. For all of the debate, criminologists recognize several factors linked to local criminal activity.

Population size is closely tied to crime rates. Metro areas with lower rates—Grand Forks, ND, or Wausau, WI, for example—are small. Metro areas with the highest rates—Los Angeles–Long Beach, CA, or New York, NY, two extreme examples—have large, overcrowded populations. There are exceptions, to be sure. Pittsburgh's crime rate looks like that of La Crosse, WI. Atlantic City's crime rate resembles that of New York.

Climate, too, has a striking connection with lawbreaking. Police and criminals are busier in warmer

Florida's Defense

In 1931, while researching his famous piece "The Worst American State," H. L. Mencken found the best source of data on causes of death was the life insurance industry and that, when it came to homicide, Florida had the highest rate.

After nearly six decades, not much has changed. Most metro areas in Florida rank near the bottom in personal safety. Of all the states, Florida has the highest rates for violent crime and for property crime. The state is the setting for Elmore Leonard's and John D. MacDonald's best-selling crime fiction, and its largest city, Miami, was the tropical backdrop for a bloody Friday night television series.

This isn't entirely fair. Local crime rates are figured per 100,000 full-time residents. But the state draws millions of four-season visitors. A truer way to measure crime rates, notes Florida's Department of Law Enforcement, would be to add a place's average daily number of tourists to its number of year-round residents, *then* determine the rate. The results would produce dramatically lower crime rates and improve the Sunshine State's national image.

U.S. Homicide Rate, 1900-1985

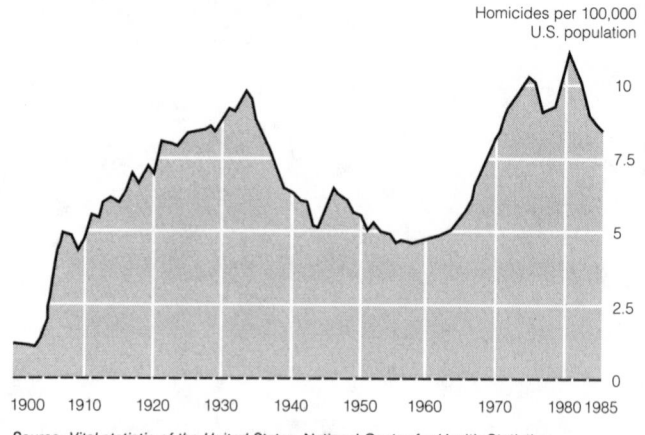

Homicides per 100,000 U.S. population

Source: *Vital statistic of the United States,* National Center for Health Statistics.

regions of the country than in colder ones. Moreover, in the Sun Belt and in the Frost Belt, these adversaries are uncommonly active during July and August when all crimes except robbery are most likely to happen. Why? Since people spend more time outdoors during these months, they are more vulnerable. Homes are vulnerable during this time of year, too, because they are more frequently left with open windows and unlocked doors. Robbery, the cold weather exception, is highest in December because pedestrians and retail stores doing brisk holiday business make tempting targets.

Time of day is another factor. After sundown is the time most cars are stolen, most persons and businesses are held up, most persons are assaulted, and most thefts are committed. Burglaries involving illegal entry or break-in, on the other hand, as well as purse-snatching and pocket-picking, happen more often during daylight hours.

Age and sex figure into the equation, too. Some 40 million persons in this country have arrest records for offenses other than traffic tickets. The proportion of suspects who are male is much higher than their proportion in the general population. Half the persons picked up by police for violent and property crimes are under 20 years of age and four-fifths are male. None of this should be taken to mean that persons knock off liquor stores, steal cars, or become involved in bar fights *because* they are young and male, but these characteristics are associated with other factors in crime.

Economics also play a role. Every time the nation's unemployment rate goes up 10 percent, the police make a half-million more arrests, according to a Johns Hopkins University study on unemployment's hidden costs.

But joblessness and loss of income won't automatically make a place unsafe. Many metro areas in the Ohio Valley and in the Northern Plains suffer job losses during business slumps but continue to experience low crime rates. More affluent areas, given similar sets of circumstances, aren't as safe as they appear: rich offenders tend to be arrested less often than poor ones, especially on suspicion. Once arrested, they are convicted with less frequency. This is especially true in juvenile cases involving thefts and break-ins.

Transience affects crime rates. A big obstacle to criminal activity is a stable neighborhood where people know one another and look out for one another's safety and property no matter how many police cruise the area. High neighborhood turnover leading to more and more strangers living next to each other is associated with high crime rates. Moreover, resort areas that draw transients—Las Vegas, NV, Orlando, FL, or Atlantic City, NJ, for instance—also have serious crime problems. When visitors are added to the year-round residents, the higher population betters the odds that victim and crook will inevitably meet.

Police strength, too, is linked to the local crime rate. Most metro areas have between 1 and 3 sworn uniformed officers for every 1,000 residents. In Manhattan, there are 1,300 police officers per square mile. It's natural to think the safety of a metro area rises or falls in direct proportion to the size of the local police force, but it just isn't so. Police definitely fight crime, but most of what they do is after the fact. They respond to complaints; they investigate; they follow up tips; they catch criminal suspects and bring them to book. A large number of police per capita is usually an indication of a high-crime area rather than an area where crime is being thwarted.

Other factors the FBI has found to be related to criminal activity include the attitudes and practices of local prosecutors, judges, juries, and parole boards; the attitudes of the community toward crime; and the willingness of typical citizens to report crime.

TRACKING CRIME

Each year, some 16,000 police departments send figures for the number of crimes reported in their jurisdictions to FBI headquarters in Washington. Eight categories of these crimes, because of their seriousness, frequency, and likelihood of being reported, make up the FBI Crime Index for measuring criminal activity across the nation. Four are classified as violent crimes; the other four are classified as property crimes:

Violent Crimes	Property Crimes
murder	burglary
forcible rape	larceny–theft
robbery	motor vehicle theft
aggravated assault	arson

Because victims often believe it futile to file complaints, many of these crimes aren't always reported and this affects the accuracy of the FBI's Crime Index. Even if a complaint is filed, the investigating officer's definition of the crime may affect the numbers. Purse-snatching, for instance, is either a robbery or a larceny depending on the jurisdiction. Likewise, a slap in the face is either an aggravated or simple assault depending on motive.

It's important to distinguish between the *incidence* of crime and the crime *rate*. Incidence is simply how many crimes are reported in a given place. The more people living in a place, the greater the crime incidence will be. In Lancaster, PA, police investigate an average of 400 aggravated assaults a year. Far to the southwest, Las Cruces, NM, police handle 300 similar crimes a year. From these figures, you might think that Lancaster is more dangerous than Las Cruces. But 395,000 people live in Lancaster, while only 125,000 live in Las Cruces.

A truer measure of safety is the crime rate—the number of crimes per 100,000 people. Lancaster's assault rate is 105.8. Las Cruces' rate is 240.6, or more than twice that of Lancaster. But neither one of these metro areas experiences assault rates near the national average—344.1.

SCORING: CRIME

One flaw in the FBI Crime Index for metro areas is that the numbers mask the seriousness of violent crime. The most common crime by far is larceny–theft (walking off

Violent vs. Property Crime

Violent crimes, which make up only 10 percent of total crime in the United States, involve bodily injury or the threat of injury.

Below are the metro areas that scored highest and lowest in overall violent crime. Six of the ten most dangerous metro areas were found in the South or the West, and eight of the safest were in the East North Central or West North Central regions.

Violent Crime in the Metro Areas

Safest Metro Areas	Violent Crime Rate	Most Dangerous Metro Areas	Violent Crime Rate
1. Grand Forks, ND	53	1. Miami–Hialeah, FL	1,633
2. Bismarck, ND	57	2. New York, NY	1,650
3. Sheboygan, WI	59	3. Los Angeles–Long Beach, CA	1,211
4. Fargo-Moorhead, ND–MN	67	4. Flint, MI	1,147
5. Rochester, MN	69	5. Baltimore, MD	1,041
6. St. Cloud, MN	70	6. Chicago, IL	1,037
7. Nashua, NH	72	7. Baton Rouge, LA	996
8. Binghamton, NY	73	8. Jacksonville, FL	973
9. Eau Claire, WI	74	9. West Palm Beach–Boca Raton–Delray Beach, FL	965
10. Kokomo, IN	78	10. Memphis, TN–AR–MS	948

Source: FBI, *Crime in the United States,* 1984, 1985, 1986, 1987, and 1988.

The violent crime rate is the sum of rates for murder, robbery, and aggravated assault.

The following metro areas were the winners and losers in property crime. Again, a preponderance of southern and western metro areas make up the Most Dangerous list; mostly Middle Atlantic or East North Central metro areas are found under the heading of Safest Metro Areas.

Property Crime in the Metro Areas

Safest Metro Areas	Property Crime Rate	Most Dangerous Metro Areas	Property Crime Rate
1. Beaver County, PA	1,426	1. Atlantic City, NJ	9,780
2. Johnstown, PA	1,461	2. Miami–Hialeah, FL	9,278
3. Wheeling, WV–OH	1,822	3. Dallas, TX	8,567
4. Steubenville–Weirton, OH–WV	1,851	4. Fort Worth–Arlington, TX	8,441
5. Danville, VA	1,961	5. Lubbock, TX	8,305
6. Cumberland, MD–WV	2,002	6. West Palm Beach–Boca Raton–Delray Beach, FL	8,224
7. Scranton–Wilkes-Barre, PA	2,141	7. San Antonio, TX	8,097
8. Sharon, PA	2,299	8. Odessa, TX	7,838
9. Utica–Rome, NY	2,363	9. Portland, OR	7,726
10. Hagerstown, MD	2,391	10. Albuquerque, NM	7,435

Source: FBI, *Crime in the United States,* 1983, 1984, 1985, 1986, and 1987.

The property crime rate is the sum of rates for burglary, larceny–theft, and motor vehicle theft.

Regional Crime Rates

Region	Violent Crime Rates				Property Crime Rates		
	Murder	Rape	Robbery	Assault	Burglary	Larceny-Theft	Motor Vehicle Theft
U.S. National Average	**8.2**	**36.4**	**210.9**	**346.1**	**1,333.1**	**3,090.8**	**529.5**
New England: Maine, New Hampshire, Vermont, Massachusetts, Rhode Island, Connecticut	3.7	27.1	145.1	247.9	1,060.9	2,404.9	635.9
Mid-Atlantic: New York, New Jersey, Pennsylvania	8.1	29.7	334.6	334.9	1,007.8	2,548.9	618.7
Great Lakes: Ohio, Indiana, Illinois, Michigan, Wisconsin	6.7	34.7	155.8	257.2	1,081.4	2,798.4	437.6
Plains: Minnesota, Iowa, Missouri, North Dakota, South Dakota, Nebraska, Kansas	4.5	26.4	98.9	222.8	1,019.8	2,898.2	291.3
South Atlantic: District of Columbia, Delaware, Maryland, Virginia, West Virginia, North Carolina, South Carolina, Georgia, Florida	9.8	38.5	215.0	397.0	1,488.5	3,238.6	437.5
East South Central: Kentucky, Tennessee, Alabama, Mississippi	9.1	34.6	144.5	307.0	1,199.4	2,284.7	358.0
West South Central: Arkansas, Louisiana, Oklahoma, Texas	10.9	44.1	197.1	350.5	1,912.4	3,880.9	639.2
Mountain: Montana, Idaho, Wyoming, Colorado, New Mexico, Arizona, Utah, Nevada	6.0	37.1	112.3	310.5	1,403.5	3,953.1	361.5
Pacific: Washington, Oregon, California, Alaska, Hawaii	9.5	45.1	268.7	494.1	1,565.1	3,471.3	738.1

Source: FBI, Crime in the United States, 1988.

with an unattended garden hose is one example; shoplifting a winter coat is another). Yet the FBI counts these heists as heavily as first-degree murder when it determines metropolitan crime rates. When it comes to comparing places, this method doesn't realistically show relative danger.

Austin, TX, for instance, has a total FBI crime rate of 7,628, roughly on par with Detroit, at 7,733. Are the two places equally dangerous? Hardly. Detroit's violent crime rate is more than twice as high as Austin's (928 versus 404). Although the Texas capital does have a high property crime rate, it nevertheless is comparatively safe for its size.

The realistic way to judge the 333 metro areas for personal safety is simple: for each place, *Places Rated* averages the rates for violent and property crimes for the latest five-year period, but since property crimes are much less serious than crimes against people, they are given one-tenth the weight of violent crimes. [Note, (1) although forcible rape is a violent crime, figures for forcible rape aren't included in the scoring because they are unavailable for the 26 metropolitan counties in Illinois, and (2) although arson has been considered a property crime since 1979, arson figures aren't included

in the scoring because they are unavailable for many metro areas.] Each place starts with a base score of zero, and points are added according to these indicators:

1. *Violent crime rate.* The rates for murder, robbery, and aggravated assault are totaled.
2. *Propety crime rate.* The rates for burglary, larceny–theft, and motor vehicle theft are added together, and the result is divided by 10.

The sum of a place's violent crime rate and one-tenth its property crime rate, rounded off, represents the score (the higher the score, the more dangerous the metro area).

SCORING EXAMPLES

A growing New England college town, a Latin-American capital on the U.S. mainland, and a struggling industrial city on the Ohio River illustrate the scoring method for crime.

Burlington, VT (#161)

This metro area—the only one in America's most rural state—embraces the city of Burlington and 15 small towns high up in Vermont's forested northwest corner.

If all places are as distinct as geographers will tell you, Burlington surely is for its criminal activity. Here the rate of violent crimes (143) is far *below* the national average, while the rate of property crimes (7,227) is far *above*. There are two explanations for the latter: owners of summer homes along the eastern shore of Lake Champlain discovering break-ins when they return for the season, and a high number of thefts year-round within the city of Burlington. For all that, this Yankee metro area's crime score (866—the violent crime rate plus one-tenth the property crime rate) puts it among the top half of all metro areas in personal safety.

Wheeling, WV–OH (#2)

Each time a West Virginia governor touts the state he seems to bundle the Mountaineer football team and John Denver's "Country Road" together with the lowest statewide crime rate in the nation to punch home his argument. He may have a point. Metropolitan Wheeling ranks second for safety from crime by the *Places Rated* formula. Adding its violent crime rate (102) to one-tenth its property crime rate (182) results in a total score of 284, second only to that of Beaver County, PA.

In fact, Wheeling is just one of a handful of very safe places found where Pennsylvania, Ohio, and West Virginia come together. Altoona, Beaver County, Johnstown, and Sharon—all in Pennsylvania; Cumberland, straddling the border of Maryland and West Virginia; and Steubenville–Weirton on the common boundary of Ohio and West Virginia, all rank in the top 95 percent of the *Places Rated* universe.

Miami–Hialeah, FL (#333)

In contrast to Wheeling, WV–OH, metropolitan Miami–Hialeah far to the south has a crime score of 2,561, the sum of its violent crime rate (1,633) and one-tenth its property crime rate (928). The idea that this area is a crime capital, not just for Florida or the southeastern states, but for the entire country, isn't drawn from television drama—it's based on fact.

Beset by rapid population growth and caught in the crosscurrents of the drug trade, criminal activity is so startlingly high in this resort metro area that the American Society of Criminology decided against holding its 1990 convention here because of the city's dubious reputation.

In a typical year some 200,000 violent and property crimes are reported to the Metro-Dade police and their fellow officers in Hialeah, Miami, Miami Beach, and Opa-locka. Most of the 100,000 arrests are for larceny, drunk driving, possession or sale of drugs, prostitution and commercial vice, and disorderly conduct.

Metro Area Crime Trends

Are the *Places Rated* crime scores improving for certain metro areas and getting worse for others? The answer to both parts of the question is yes.

METRO AREAS BECOMING SAFER	Crime Score 5-Year Trend
Danbury, CT	−18%
Great Falls, MT	−17
Johnstown, PA	−17
Glens Falls, NY	−16
Lorain–Elyria, OH	−16
Springfield, MA	−16
Lawrence–Haverhill, MA–NH	−15
Midland, TX	−15
Huntington–Ashland, WV–KY–OH	−14
Champaign–Urbana–Rantoul, IL	−13

METRO AREAS BECOMING MORE DANGEROUS	Crime Score 5-Year Trend
Tallahassee, FL	+43%
Vallejo–Fairfield–Napa, CA	+41
Fayetteville–Springdale, AR	+39
Decatur, AL	+37
Brownsville–Harlingen, TX	+33
Alexandria, LA	+32
Kankakee, IL	+31
Bradenton, FL	+31
Pine Bluff, AR	+27
Dallas, TX	+27

The above trends were derived by comparing each metro area's average crime score for the latest five years with its score for 1983.

Rankings: Crime

In ranking 333 metro areas for relative safety, *Places Rated* uses two criteria: (1) the violent crime rate and (2) the property crime rate divided by 10. The sum of these rates, rounded off, is the metro area's score. The higher the score, the more dangerous the metro area. Places with tie scores get the same rank and are listed in alphabetical order.

Metro Areas from Best to Worst

Places Rated Rank	Places Rated Score	Places Rated Rank	Places Rated Score	Places Rated Rank	Places Rated Score	Places Rated Rank	Places Rated Score
1. Beaver County, PA	251	53. Bangor, ME	552	110. Waterbury, CT	733	
2. Wheeling, WV–OH	284	54. Fitchburg–Leominster, MA	553	112. Norwalk, CT	735	
3. Johnstown, PA	295	55. Bremerton, WA	557	113. Billings, MT	736	
4. Danville, VA	307			114. Athens, GA	740	
5. Cumberland, MD–WV	313	56. Harrisburg–Lebanon–Carlisle, PA	562	115. Clarksville–Hopkinsville, TN–KY	741	
6. Scranton–Wilkes-Barre, PA	339	57. Brazoria, TX	565		
7. Binghamton, NY	342	58. Nassau–Suffolk, NY	566	115. Stamford, CT	741	
8. Nashua, NH	346	59. Green Bay, WI	567	117. Orange County, NY	750	
9. Utica–Rome, NY	360	60. Elkhart–Goshen, IN	572	118. Honolulu, HI	751	
10. Sharon, PA	365			119. Joliet, IL	753	
		61. Elmira, NY	574	120. Cedar Rapids, IA	755	
10. St. Cloud, MN	365	62. Albany–Schenectady–Troy, NY	578		
12. Altoona, PA	368	62. Burlington, NC	578	121. Richland–Kennewick–Pasco, WA	761	
12. York, PA	368	64. Fort Walton Beach, FL	588	122. Lima, OH	765	
14. Kokomo, IN	377	65. Joplin, MO	589	123. Boise City, ID	771	
14. Parkersburg–Marietta, WV–OH	377			124. Worcester, MA	774	
		66. Charleston, WV	592	125. Macon–Warner Robins, GA	775	
16. Lancaster, PA	378	67. Poughkeepsie, NY	593		
17. Williamsport, PA	383	68. Middletown, CT	597	125. Pascagoula, MS	775	
18. Steubenville–Weirton, OH–WV	396	69. Syracuse, NY	603	127. Casper, WY	781	
19. Rochester, MN	403	70. Lynchburg, VA	604	128. Gadsden, AL	783	
20. Salem–Gloucester, MA	405			129. Peoria, IL	785	
		71. Huntington–Ashland, WV–KY–OH	609	130. Davenport–Rock Island–Moline, IA–IL	787	
21. Danbury, CT	414	72. Pittsburgh, PA	613		
22. Eau Claire, WI	418	73. Knoxville, TN	614		
23. Sheboygan, WI	421	74. Olympia, WA	617	131. Augusta, GA–SC	795	
24. Grand Forks, ND	422	75. Fort Smith, AR–OK	624	131. Janesville–Beloit, WI	795	
25. Bismarck, ND	424			133. Iowa City, IA	798	
		76. Lawrence–Haverhill, MA–NH	627	134. Kenosha, WI	802	
26. State College, PA	427	77. Cheyenne, WY	628	135. Rochester, NY	804	
27. Appleton–Oshkosh–Neenah, WI	438	78. Houma–Thibodaux, LA	633		
27. Johnson City–Kingsport–Bristol, TN–VA	438	79. Lowell, MA–NH	638	136. Santa Rosa–Petaluma, CA	808	
29. Allentown–Bethlehem, PA–NJ	443	80. Waterloo–Cedar Falls, IA	639	137. Louisville, KY–IN	811	
30. Lafayette–West Lafayette, IN	447			138. Cincinnati, OH–KY–IN	815	
		81. Asheville, NC	646	139. Columbus, GA–AL	820	
31. Duluth, MN–WI	455	82. Bloomington–Normal, IL	651	140. Longview–Marshall, TX	822	
31. Fargo–Moorhead, ND–MN	455	83. Fort Wayne, IN	655		
33. Wausau, WI	465	83. Terre Haute, IN	655	141. Eugene–Springfield, OR	828	
34. Florence, AL	467	85. Lewiston–Auburn, ME	662	141. Fort Collins–Loveland, CO	828	
35. Lorain–Elyria, OH	481			143. Santa Barbara–Santa Maria–Lompoc, CA	829	
		86. Muncie, IN	664	144. New Britain, CT	831	
36. Bristol, CT	482	87. Canton, OH	669	145. Hamilton–Middletown, OH	832	
37. Sioux Falls, SD	486	87. Manchester, NH	669		
38. Decatur, AL	492	89. Monmouth–Ocean, NJ	674	146. Alexandria, LA	838	
39. Portsmouth–Dover–Rochester, NH–ME	497	90. Killeen–Temple, TX	676	146. Decatur, IL	838	
40. Provo–Orem, UT	498			148. Merced, CA	841	
		91. Bloomington, IN	681	149. McAllen–Edinburg–Mission, TX	844	
41. Hagerstown, MD	499	92. Hickory, NC	691	150. Dothan, AL	845	
42. Owensboro, KY	503	92. Montgomery, AL	691		
42. Pittsfield, MA	503	94. Madison, WI	700	151. St. Joseph, MO	846	
44. Glens Falls, NY	506	95. Medford, OR	701	152. Columbia, MO	848	
45. Reading, PA	511			153. Minneapolis–St. Paul, MN–WI	851	
		96. Charlottesville, VA	704	154. Biloxi–Gulfport, MS	852	
46. Pawtucket–Woonsocket–Attleboro, RI–MA	514	97. Vancouver, WA	706	155. Abilene, TX	853	
47. Fayetteville–Springdale, AR	541	98. Oxnard–Ventura, CA	710		
48. Dubuque, IA	543	98. Roanoke, VA	710	156. Lincoln, NE	854	
49. New London–Norwich, CT–RI	544	100. Bergen–Passaic, NJ	713	157. Enid, OK	858	
50. Erie, PA	548			158. Grand Rapids, MI	859	
		101. Lake County, IL	716	159. Chattanooga, TN–GA	860	
51. La Crosse, WI	549	102. Bellingham, WA	723	160. San Jose, CA	865	
52. Middlesex–Somerset–Hunterdon, NJ	550	103. Anderson, IN	725		
		103. Great Falls, MT	725	161. Burlington, VT	866	
		105. Aurora–Elgin, IL	729	161. Milwaukee, WI	866	
				163. Rapid City, SD	867	
		105. Springfield, MO	729	164. Anderson, SC	868	
		107. Evansville, IN–KY	730	165. Portland, ME	874	
		107. Niagara Falls, NY	730		
		107. Youngstown–Warren, OH	730		
		110. Fort Myers–Cape Coral, FL	733		

Places Rated Rank	Places Rated Score	Places Rated Rank	Places Rated Score	Places Rated Rank	Places Rated Score
166. Jacksonville, NC	876	223. Panama City, FL	1,028	279. Little Rock–North Little Rock, AR	1,277
167. Akron, OH	879	224. Corpus Christi, TX	1,033	280. Daytona Beach, FL	1,278
168. Greensboro–Winston-Salem–High Point, NC	881	224. Greeley, CO	1,033		
169. Cleveland, OH	883	226. Anchorage, AK	1,034	281. Sacramento, CA	1,283
169. Raleigh–Durham, NC	883	227. Greenville–Spartanburg, SC	1,036	282. Oklahoma City, OK	1,285
		228. Tyler, TX	1,037	283. Ocala, FL	1,293
169. Spokane, WA	883	229. Mansfield, OH	1,038	284. San Antonio, TX	1,296
172. Brockton, MA	885	229. Sarasota, FL	1,038	285. Atlanta, GA	1,304
173. Lexington–Fayette, KY	886				
174. Boulder–Longmont, CO	890	231. Albany, GA	1,047	286. Houston, TX	1,308
175. Gary–Hammond, IN	891	232. Lake Charles, LA	1,048	287. Stockton, CA	1,315
		232. Tulsa, OK	1,048	288. Tallahassee, FL	1,319
175. Salt Lake City–Ogden, UT	891	234. Victoria, TX	1,049	289. Columbia, SC	1,333
177. Chico, CA	894	235. Santa Cruz, CA	1,052	290. San Francisco, CA	1,337
178. Huntsville, AL	895				
179. Norfolk–Virginia Beach–Newport News, VA	896	236. Anniston, AL	1,053	291. Newark, NJ	1,347
		237. St. Louis, MO–IL	1,055	292. Pensacola, FL	1,348
180. Lansing–East Lansing, MI	899	238. Lafayette, LA	1,063	292. Tucson, AZ	1,348
		238. Las Cruces, NM	1,063	294. El Paso, TX	1,351
181. Buffalo, NY	905	240. Rockford, IL	1,064	295. Mobile, AL	1,359
181. Indianapolis, IN	905				
183. Providence, RI	906	241. Birmingham, AL	1,065	296. Shreveport, LA	1,364
184. Anaheim–Santa Ana, CA	907	242. Vineland–Millville–Bridgeton, NJ	1,067	297. Benton Harbor, MI	1,368
185. Sioux City, IA–NE	910	243. Salinas–Seaside–Monterey, CA	1,068	298. Kansas City, MO–KS	1,375
				299. Jackson, TN	1,379
186. Lawton, OK	911	244. Tuscaloosa, AL	1,070	300. Bakersfield, CA	1,391
187. Texarkana, TX–Texarkana, AR	918	245. Sherman–Denison, TX	1,075		
188. Salem, OR	919	245. Washington, DC–MD–VA	1,075	301. Jersey City, NJ	1,406
189. Jackson, MS	922	247. Des Moines, IA	1,085	302. Yuba City, CA	1,407
190. Omaha, NE–IA	925	247. Reno, NV	1,085	303. Las Vegas, NV	1,416
		249. Yakima, WA	1,091	304. Riverside–San Bernardino, CA	1,422
191. Philadelphia, PA–NJ	928	250. Wilmington, NC	1,102		
191. Richmond–Petersburg, VA	928			305. Fort Pierce, FL	1,428
193. Wilmington, DE–NJ–MD	938	251. Battle Creek, MI	1,104	306. Oakland, CA	1,430
194. Midland, TX	939	252. Visalia–Tulare–Porterville, CA	1,109	307. Fort Lauderdale–Hollywood–Pompano Beach, FL	1,433
195. Santa Fe, NM	944	253. San Diego, CA	1,110	308. Muskegon, MI	1,435
		254. Champaign–Urbana–Rantoul, IL	1,112	309. Fresno, CA	1,439
196. Springfield, MA	947	255. Boston, MA	1,121	310. Lakeland–Winter Haven, FL	1,443
197. Fall River, MA–RI	950				
197. Redding, CA	950	256. Trenton, NJ	1,122	311. Kalamazoo, MI	1,461
199. Beaumont–Port Arthur, TX	959	256. Vallejo–Fairfield–Napa, CA	1,122	312. Orlando, FL	1,471
200. Wichita, KS	966	258. Laredo, TX	1,125	313. Tampa–St. Petersburg–Clearwater, FL	1,514
		259. Austin, TX	1,126	314. Lubbock, TX	1,518
201. Dayton–Springfield, OH	967	260. Brownsville–Harlingen, TX	1,140	315. New Orleans, LA	1,548
201. San Angelo, TX	967				
203. Pine Bluff, AR	969	260. Jackson, MI	1,140	316. Fort Worth–Arlington, TX	1,552
204. Nashville, TN	979	262. Charleston, SC	1,144	316. Gainesville, FL	1,552
204. South Bend–Mishawaka, IN	979	263. Modesto, CA	1,145	318. Baltimore, MD	1,555
		264. Wichita Falls, TX	1,147	319. Bradenton, FL	1,560
206. New Haven–Meriden, CT	981	265. Odessa, TX	1,148	320. Memphis, TN–AR–MS	1,580
207. Lawrence, KS	994				
207. Topeka, KS	994	266. Melbourne–Titusville–Palm Bay, FL	1,155	321. Chicago, IL	1,594
209. Toledo, OH	995	267. Waco, TX	1,166	322. Portland, OR	1,608
210. Kankakee, IL	999	268. Galveston–Texas City, TX	1,169	323. Detroit, MI	1,609
		269. Florence, SC	1,178	324. Atlantic City, NJ	1,622
211. Hartford, CT	1,000	270. Seattle, WA	1,184	325. Albuquerque, NM	1,628
211. Naples, FL	1,000				
211. Racine, WI	1,000	271. Savannah, GA	1,207	326. Dallas, TX	1,662
214. Columbus, OH	1,001	272. Fayetteville, NC	1,221	327. Jacksonville, FL	1,664
215. New Bedford, MA	1,004	273. Tacoma, WA	1,255	328. Baton Rouge, LA	1,698
		274. Ann Arbor, MI	1,259	329. West Palm Beach–Boca Raton–Delray Beach, FL	1,787
216. Amarillo, TX	1,005	275. Phoenix, AZ	1,260		
216. Colorado Springs, CO	1,005			330. Los Angeles–Long Beach, CA	1,810
218. Monroe, LA	1,007	276. Denver, CO	1,261		
219. Bridgeport–Milford, CT	1,016	277. Charlotte–Gastonia–Rock Hill, NC–SC	1,262	331. Flint, MI	1,846
220. Saginaw–Bay City–Midland, MI	1,020	278. Pueblo, CO	1,264	332. New York, NY	2,280
221. Springfield, IL	1,025			333. Miami–Hialeah, FL	2,561
222. Bryan–College Station, TX	1,026				

Place Profiles: Crime

The Place Profiles show each metro area's average annual rates for seven serious crimes: murder, rape, robbery, assault, burglary, larceny–theft, and motor vehicle theft for the latest five years for which data are available. These rates are divided into violent and property categories, and a total rate for each of these categories is also given.

Note: Although figures for rape are shown for most metro areas, they are unavailable for the 13 metro areas in Illinois. Consequently, figures for rape—a violent crime—aren't included in the scoring.

Figures are mainly from the FBI's *Crime in the United States,* 1984, 1985, 1986, 1987, and 1988, or derived

from the Bureau's unpublished "Crime By County" reports for each of those years. For metro areas not included in either of these sources, figures are derived from state Uniform Crime Reporting programs.

The next-to-the-last column indicates the crime trend over the previous five years: 132 metro areas have an arrow pointing upward, meaning their *Places Rated* crime rates during this period are up; 91 metro areas have a dash, meaning their crime rates are essentially unchanged; and 110 metro areas have an arrow pointing downward, meaning their crime rates have dropped.

A star (★) next to a metro area's name highlights it as one of the top 30 places for safety from crime.

	Violent Crime Rates					Property Crime Rates						
	Murder	Rape	Robbery	Assault	Total	Burglary	Larceny-Theft	Motor Vehicle Theft	Total	SCORE	TREND	RANK
Metro Area Average	8.9	40.5	259.8	344.1	653	1,443	3,206	554	5,203	1,174	▼	
Abilene, TX	7.2	40.2	113.1	206.3	327	1,642	3,346	273	5,260	853	—	155
Akron, OH	4.3	37.0	128.8	290.8	424	1,055	3,185	309	4,549	879	▲	167
Albany, GA	13.7	65.4	193.6	380.1	587	1,775	2,621	206	4,603	1,047	▲	231
Albany-Schenectady-Troy, NY	2.4	18.9	71.2	175.3	249	975	2,166	150	3,291	578	—	62
Albuquerque, NM	10.7	59.4	266.1	607.5	884	2,408	4,561	466	7,435	1,628	▲	325
Alexandria, LA	12.8	26.6	72.4	299.7	385	1,216	3,128	185	4,530	838	▲	146
★ Allentown-Bethlehem, PA-NJ	3.0	16.3	60.3	102.3	166	713	1,928	131	2,772	443	—	29
★ Altoona, PA	1.3	16.0	34.7	88.2	124	724	1,592	128	2,443	368	▲	12
Amarillo, TX	10.8	36.5	109.4	285.4	406	1,649	4,030	313	5,992	1,005	—	216
Anaheim-Santa Ana, CA	4.8	28.7	169.5	222.7	397	1,312	3,239	553	5,104	907	—	184
Anchorage, AK	6.9	84.3	159.0	263.7	430	1,232	4,192	612	6,036	1,034	▼	226
Anderson, IN	3.7	36.6	78.5	166.5	249	1,225	3,314	219	4,757	725	▼	103
Anderson, SC	9.9	31.6	56.7	369.3	436	1,420	2,642	261	4,323	868	▼	164
Ann Arbor, MI	6.3	72.8	153.4	443.5	603	1,416	4,668	479	6,564	1,259	▲	274
Anniston, AL	8.9	24.5	93.4	596.5	699	1,013	2,345	179	3,537	1,053	▲	236
★ Appleton-Oshkosh-Neenah, WI	1.0	12.0	12.0	68.2	81	664	2,812	92	3,568	438	▼	27
Asheville, NC	5.6	21.6	67.8	197.5	271	1,080	2,455	212	3,748	646	▲	81
Athens, GA	6.4	37.5	73.3	255.2	335	1,173	2,656	225	4,054	740	▼	114
Atlanta, GA	11.5	53.2	294.7	394.7	701	1,707	3,717	607	6,031	1,304	▲	285
Atlantic City, NJ	6.8	52.9	277.0	360.6	644	2,108	7,165	508	9,780	1,622	▼	324
Augusta, GA-SC	9.7	36.3	119.2	290.4	419	1,349	2,170	237	3,756	795	—	131
Aurora-Elgin, IL	3.7	NA	88.7	199.4	292	1,290	2,888	190	4,368	729	—	105
Austin, TX	10.3	65.7	158.2	235.9	404	2,066	4,781	377	7,224	1,126	▲	259
Bakersfield, CA	10.5	48.9	234.0	497.9	742	2,095	3,924	475	6,493	1,391	—	300
Baltimore, MD	12.2	42.8	438.7	589.9	1,041	1,366	3,268	505	5,139	1,555	▼	318
Bangor, ME	1.5	14.7	38.0	72.7	112	876	3,337	185	4,397	552	—	53
Baton Rouge, LA	10.7	40.3	205.1	780.0	996	2,054	4,534	432	7,020	1,698	▲	328

	Violent Crime Rates					Property Crime Rates						
	Murder	Rape	Robbery	Assault	Total	Burglary	Larceny-Theft	Motor Vehicle Theft	Total	SCORE	TREND	RANK
Metro Area Average	**8.9**	**40.5**	**259.8**	**344.1**	**653**	**1,443**	**3,206**	**554**	**5,203**	**1,174**	▼	
Battle Creek, MI	7.8	56.3	140.6	388.1	537	1,714	3,761	191	5,665	1,104	▼	251
Beaumont–Port Arthur, TX	10.6	48.5	175.4	280.7	467	1,664	2,971	289	4,924	959	—	199
★ Beaver County, PA	1.7	10.1	25.5	80.6	108	387	901	137	1,426	251	▼	1
Bellingham, WA	2.1	37.1	32.3	145.5	180	1,354	3,817	260	5,431	723	—	102
Benton Harbor, MI	4.6	1.7	144.5	606.6	756	1,787	4,108	227	6,122	1,368	▲	297
Bergen–Passaic, NJ	3.7	12.1	173.2	152.5	329	814	2,441	589	3,844	713	▼	100
Billings, MT	4.5	24.3	49.8	73.8	128	1,374	4,413	291	6,078	736	▲	113
Biloxi–Gulfport, MS	7.9	49.6	118.6	193.6	320	1,973	3,014	336	5,323	852	▲	154
★ Binghamton, NY	1.6	13.5	16.6	54.7	73	565	2,028	101	2,693	342	—	7
Birmingham, AL	13.2	42.5	210.1	372.1	595	1,379	2,773	545	4,697	1,065	▲	241
★ Bismarck, ND	0.7	12.3	12.5	43.5	57	553	2,956	164	3,674	424	▲	25
Bloomington, IN	2.4	17.9	21.1	241.0	265	915	3,016	228	4,159	681	▲	91
Bloomington–Normal, IL	3.1	NA	42.4	174.3	220	1,073	3,102	131	4,305	651	▼	82
Boise City, ID	2.9	32.7	42.8	251.4	297	1,295	3,223	217	4,736	771	▼	123
Boston, MA	4.5	30.7	289.4	356.0	650	1,088	2,415	1,205	4,708	1,121	▼	255
Boulder–Longmont, CO	2.7	30.6	45.0	243.0	291	1,276	4,427	283	5,986	890	▼	174
Bradenton, FL	8.5	58.1	184.9	672.1	866	2,197	4,286	455	6,938	1,560	▲	319
Brazoria, TX	11.0	28.7	38.8	169.5	219	979	2,236	247	3,463	565	▲	57
Bremerton, WA	2.6	50.0	37.4	170.6	211	1,019	2,279	160	3,457	557	—	55
Bridgeport–Milford, CT	8.3	21.2	288.8	223.0	520	1,339	2,774	842	4,955	1,016	▼	219
Bristol, CT	2.6	10.4	28.5	192.5	224	810	1,598	173	2,581	482	▼	36
Brockton, MA	3.0	29.4	137.9	323.0	464	1,266	1,954	994	4,214	885	▼	172
Brownsville–Harlingen, TX	7.7	21.8	83.9	472.6	564	1,867	3,344	548	5,758	1,140	▲	260
Bryan–College Station, TX	5.9	43.3	78.3	291.7	376	1,749	4,438	311	6,497	1,026	▲	222
Buffalo, NY	4.5	34.2	169.3	323.0	497	1,151	2,501	426	4,078	905	—	181
Burlington, NC	6.4	16.9	39.4	214.5	260	904	2,118	156	3,178	578	▲	62
Burlington, VT	1.4	28.8	51.6	90.0	143	1,590	5,368	270	7,227	866	▼	161
Canton, OH	3.7	26.6	115.8	185.3	305	1,035	2,374	230	3,639	669	—	87
Casper, WY	3.2	27.8	34.3	255.5	293	1,314	3,327	236	4,876	781	▲	127
Cedar Rapids, IA	2.1	12.0	55.1	134.7	192	1,302	4,096	233	5,631	755	—	120
Champaign–Urbana–Rantoul, IL	4.7	NA	151.9	394.2	551	1,619	3,745	242	5,605	1,112	▼	254
Charleston, SC	8.7	55.2	164.4	493.4	667	1,367	3,075	327	4,769	1,144	▼	262
Charleston, WV	3.7	28.0	89.3	141.2	234	924	2,389	262	3,576	592	▼	66
Charlotte–Gastonia–Rock Hill, NC–SC	9.3	40.8	166.0	531.0	706	1,736	3,550	271	5,557	1,262	▲	277
Charlottesville, VA	7.3	29.2	67.4	186.3	261	797	3,437	198	4,432	704	—	96
Chattanooga, TN–GA	8.0	32.3	111.2	325.9	445	1,140	2,575	435	4,150	860	▲	159
Cheyenne, WY	5.8	29.2	36.9	135.3	178	638	3,721	139	4,498	628	▲	77
Chicago, IL	13.0	NA	500.8	523.6	1,037	1,322	3,304	948	5,574	1,594	▲	321
Chico, CA	4.4	41.3	59.3	303.9	368	1,692	3,270	301	5,263	894	—	177
Cincinnati, OH–KY–IN	5.1	40.1	134.2	236.2	376	999	3,167	225	4,390	815	▼	138
Clarksville–Hopkinsville, TN–KY	7.0	35.7	81.5	310.9	399	1,100	2,109	206	3,415	741	▲	115
Cleveland, OH	9.4	51.1	247.2	210.1	467	1,138	2,084	935	4,157	883	▼	169
Colorado Springs, CO	5.5	61.9	140.6	222.2	368	1,807	4,197	368	6,371	1,005	—	216
Columbia, MO	4.0	25.4	63.0	229.7	297	1,221	4,129	161	5,511	848	▼	152
Columbia, SC	9.3	49.8	173.5	607.4	790	1,468	3,584	383	5,434	1,333	▲	289

	Violent Crime Rates					Property Crime Rates						
	Murder	Rape	Robbery	Assault	Total	Burglary	Larceny-Theft	Motor Vehicle Theft	Total	SCORE	TREND	RANK
Metro Area Average	**8.9**	**40.5**	**259.8**	**344.1**	**653**	**1,443**	**3,206**	**554**	**5,203**	**1,174**	▼	
Columbus, GA–AL	11.0	40.6	148.2	254.7	414	1,066	2,728	266	4,059	820	▲	139
Columbus, OH	7.2	48.1	226.9	244.5	479	1,452	3,438	325	5,216	1,001	▲	214
Corpus Christi, TX	11.1	52.4	116.2	247.3	375	1,858	4,335	384	6,576	1,033	—	224
★ Cumberland, MD–WV	2.4	11.4	16.6	93.7	113	447	1,478	77	2,002	313	▼	5
Dallas, TX	17.5	66.7	355.1	431.9	805	2,388	5,391	788	8,567	1,662	▲	326
★ Danbury, CT	1.7	18.2	40.2	86.7	129	754	1,875	222	2,850	414	▼	21
★ Danville, VA	7.7	15.1	22.9	80.6	111	486	1,411	65	1,961	307	—	4
Davenport–Rock Island–Moline, IA–IL	2.5	NA	75.5	295.4	373	1,049	2,966	130	4,144	787	▼	130
Dayton–Springfield, OH	6.6	43.3	225.8	267.7	500	1,196	3,217	255	4,668	967	▼	201
Daytona Beach, FL	9.3	53.1	186.9	429.3	626	2,184	4,012	329	6,524	1,278	—	280
Decatur, AL	8.1	8.2	27.4	172.5	208	836	1,838	163	2,837	492	▲	38
Decatur, IL	3.1	NA	114.9	232.4	350	1,295	3,464	120	4,879	838	—	146
Denver, CO	7.8	46.7	190.8	350.3	549	1,996	4,524	600	7,121	1,261	—	276
Des Moines, IA	4.3	26.3	126.7	263.0	394	1,607	5,003	301	6,911	1,085	▲	247
Detroit, MI	17.6	64.6	501.1	408.9	928	1,877	3,518	1,411	6,805	1,609	—	323
Dothan, AL	6.8	24.3	61.5	408.3	477	974	2,582	121	3,678	845	—	150
Dubuque, IA	1.3	3.9	20.8	129.3	151	899	2,825	197	3,921	543	▲	48
Duluth, MN–WI	1.4	27.6	26.4	64.6	92	955	2,484	189	3,628	455	▲	31
★ Eau Claire, WI	1.2	7.9	14.8	58.4	74	704	2,641	92	3,437	418	▼	22
El Paso, TX	6.4	40.8	186.2	564.5	757	1,666	3,766	506	5,938	1,351	—	294
Elkhart–Goshen, IN	2.6	26.1	43.5	128.1	174	841	2,954	182	3,977	572	—	60
Elmira, NY	2.8	20.3	48.7	146.3	198	774	2,884	107	3,764	574	▲	61
Enid, OK	7.9	32.0	71.0	192.8	272	1,832	3,780	247	5,859	858	▲	157
Erie, PA	2.2	25.1	92.0	153.6	248	795	2,032	177	3,003	548	▼	50
Eugene–Springfield, OR	3.6	39.5	85.9	149.3	239	1,660	3,947	287	5,893	828	▲	141
Evansville, IN–KY	4.6	20.3	60.7	279.8	345	920	2,708	220	3,848	730	▼	107
Fall River, MA–RI	3.0	22.1	114.4	341.9	459	1,599	2,444	869	4,912	950	—	197
Fargo–Moorhead, ND–MN	0.8	18.5	14.0	52.0	67	613	3,092	176	3,882	455	▲	31
Fayetteville, NC	9.1	57.7	177.8	433.3	620	2,097	3,492	416	6,005	1,221	▲	272
Fayetteville–Springdale, AR	3.4	25.5	25.1	127.6	156	1,077	2,563	209	3,849	541	▲	47
Fitchburg–Leominster, MA	1.2	21.5	49.5	186.0	237	859	2,024	274	3,156	553	▼	54
Flint, MI	13.4	83.1	329.9	803.7	1,147	2,206	4,197	590	6,993	1,846	▲	331
Florence, AL	5.5	9.3	36.1	131.5	173	780	1,994	165	2,938	467	—	34
Florence, SC	7.5	50.1	128.3	593.0	729	1,352	2,878	259	4,489	1,178	—	269
Fort Collins–Loveland, CO	3.3	32.1	30.2	285.6	319	1,067	3,819	202	5,089	828	▼	141
Fort Lauderdale–Hollywood–Pompano Beach, FL	11.2	44.4	350.3	386.7	748	1,982	4,240	624	6,846	1,433	▲	307
Fort Myers–Cape Coral, FL	9.4	33.6	144.9	175.4	330	1,267	2,472	293	4,033	733	▲	110
Fort Pierce, FL	11.9	54.7	204.8	557.5	774	2,211	3,994	330	6,535	1,428	▲	305
Fort Smith, AR–OK	5.9	27.5	56.1	180.5	243	1,066	2,463	276	3,805	624	▲	75
Fort Walton Beach, FL	4.1	31.5	63.0	174.1	241	966	2,294	212	3,472	588	▼	64
Fort Wayne, IN	4.6	27.2	104.2	113.8	223	807	3,258	258	4,323	655	▼	83
Fort Worth–Arlington, TX	16.0	60.8	290.5	401.2	708	2,367	5,143	931	8,441	1,552	▲	316
Fresno, CA	12.9	58.4	253.1	452.5	719	2,333	4,344	525	7,203	1,439	▲	309
Gadsden, AL	10.6	22.3	68.8	369.3	449	866	2,271	204	3,341	783	▲	128
Gainesville, FL	8.0	62.3	189.7	669.4	867	2,170	4,379	304	6,854	1,552	▲	316

	Violent Crime Rates					Property Crime Rates						
	Murder	Rape	Robbery	Assault	Total	Burglary	Larceny-Theft	Motor Vehicle Theft	Total	SCORE	TREND	RANK
Metro Area Average	**8.9**	**40.5**	**259.8**	**344.1**	**653**	**1,443**	**3,206**	**554**	**5,203**	**1,174**	▼	
Galveston–Texas City, TX	12.2	42.3	182.2	376.0	570	1,834	3,686	465	5,985	1,169	—	268
Gary–Hammond, IN	12.0	33.6	171.6	272.3	456	1,071	2,485	791	4,348	891	—	175
Glens Falls, NY	1.8	11.6	28.0	157.9	188	866	2,166	152	3,183	506	▼	44
★ Grand Forks, ND	2.1	12.3	12.6	38.6	53	524	3,013	154	3,690	422	▲	24
Grand Rapids, MI	4.1	59.6	108.2	282.2	395	1,098	3,301	245	4,643	859	▼	158
Great Falls, MT	3.4	19.6	37.5	146.1	187	1,098	3,926	354	5,377	725	▼	103
Greeley, CO	5.4	45.9	44.7	366.7	417	1,448	4,466	249	6,163	1,033	▼	224
Green Bay, WI	1.5	12.8	19.7	125.6	147	643	3,411	144	4,198	567	▼	59
Greensboro–Winston-Salem–High Point, NC	7.6	24.8	88.7	402.2	499	1,136	2,489	195	3,820	881	—	168
Greenville–Spartanburg, SC	8.7	38.5	100.3	456.8	566	1,299	3,134	271	4,703	1,036	—	227
Hagerstown, MD	2.6	12.7	67.1	190.5	260	671	1,590	130	2,391	499	—	41
Hamilton–Middletown, OH	4.0	31.8	82.2	264.4	351	1,159	3,425	228	4,812	832	▼	145
Harrisburg–Lebanon–Carlisle, PA	3.1	24.8	97.5	164.2	265	712	2,118	139	2,969	562	—	56
Hartford, CT	4.2	25.6	258.2	237.3	500	1,325	3,202	475	5,003	1,000	—	211
Hickory, NC	6.2	13.4	38.5	359.0	404	885	1,829	153	2,867	691	▼	92
Honolulu, HI	4.6	32.1	131.2	81.9	218	1,177	3,770	380	5,327	751	▼	118
Houma–Thibodaux, LA	7.2	19.7	49.9	304.0	361	831	1,765	121	2,716	633	—	78
Houston, TX	18.2	57.8	365.5	271.5	655	2,005	3,283	1,242	6,530	1,308	—	286
Huntington–Ashland, WV–KY–OH	4.5	24.2	63.2	244.8	313	878	1,852	226	2,955	609	▼	71
Huntsville, AL	8.7	32.8	103.6	232.7	345	1,240	4,010	246	5,496	895	—	178
Indianapolis, IN	6.4	43.4	181.9	268.2	457	1,264	2,730	486	4,480	905	—	181
Iowa City, IA	1.7	38.3	25.7	262.4	290	956	3,943	183	5,082	798	▲	133
Jackson, MI	6.8	70.6	95.1	594.2	696	1,241	3,003	194	4,439	1,140	▲	260
Jackson, MS	14.1	43.0	146.2	274.6	435	1,679	2,919	270	4,867	922	▲	189
Jackson, TN	10.7	53.8	210.4	614.3	835	1,596	3,538	301	5,435	1,379	▲	299
Jacksonville, FL	14.9	81.4	367.9	589.7	973	2,147	4,357	405	6,908	1,664	▲	327
Jacksonville, NC	4.6	20.3	75.5	432.8	513	1,060	2,392	174	3,625	876	▼	166
Janesville–Beloit, WI	2.3	22.2	47.1	250.2	300	1,089	3,704	161	4,954	795	▲	131
Jersey City, NJ	8.6	33.6	465.7	369.1	843	1,453	2,867	1,310	5,629	1,406	—	301
★ Johnson City–Kingsport–Bristol, TN–VA	4.3	14.9	33.3	133.4	171	766	1,720	186	2,671	438	▲	27
★ Johnstown, PA	0.9	12.7	23.2	124.8	149	498	864	100	1,461	295	▼	3
Joliet, IL	5.5	NA	82.2	268.5	356	1,061	2,590	313	3,965	753	—	119
Joplin, MO	4.2	14.9	37.1	178.6	220	883	2,627	179	3,689	589	—	65
Kalamazoo, MI	2.8	75.5	140.4	739.6	883	1,466	4,103	209	5,778	1,461	—	311
Kankakee, IL	6.9	NA	153.0	376.1	536	1,337	2,977	312	4,626	999	▲	210
Kansas City, MO–KS	10.5	48.6	267.5	515.7	794	1,656	3,563	585	5,805	1,375	▲	298
Kenosha, WI	5.4	35.7	129.0	105.1	240	1,404	3,879	340	5,622	802	▼	134
Killeen–Temple, TX	8.0	53.4	85.9	152.8	247	1,293	2,787	211	4,290	676	▲	90
Knoxville, TN	6.4	25.5	94.4	181.3	282	1,212	1,713	391	3,315	614	▲	73
★ Kokomo, IN	2.4	13.9	45.8	29.6	78	724	2,111	154	2,989	377	▼	14
La Crosse, WI	3.0	15.2	14.6	83.8	101	632	3,710	135	4,477	549	▼	51
Lafayette, LA	7.8	52.8	130.5	444.3	583	1,283	3,284	231	4,799	1,063	▲	238
★ Lafayette–West Lafayette, IN	1.3	13.4	29.8	97.0	128	839	2,193	154	3,186	447	▼	30
Lake Charles, LA	7.5	30.0	82.1	395.7	485	1,506	3,918	209	5,633	1,048	▼	232

	Violent Crime Rates					Property Crime Rates						
	Murder	Rape	Robbery	Assault	Total	Burglary	Larceny-Theft	Motor Vehicle Theft	Total	SCORE	TREND	RANK
Metro Area Average	**8.9**	**40.5**	**259.8**	**344.1**	**653**	**1,443**	**3,206**	**554**	**5,203**	**1,174**	▼	
Lake County, IL	3.4	NA	88.2	225.4	317	855	2,912	223	3,990	716	▼	101
Lakeland–Winter Haven, FL	10.9	42.9	195.2	571.3	777	1,969	4,344	344	6,657	1,443	▲	310
★ Lancaster, PA	2.0	12.9	47.3	89.1	138	597	1,687	120	2,404	378	—	16
Lansing–East Lansing, MI	3.3	59.4	91.3	296.7	391	1,297	3,538	245	5,080	899	▲	180
Laredo, TX	12.8	25.5	109.4	341.3	464	1,988	4,164	454	6,606	1,125	—	258
Las Cruces, NM	6.9	47.9	80.8	294.3	382	1,697	4,764	351	6,813	1,063	▼	238
Las Vegas, NV	13.7	66.7	386.2	348.7	749	2,178	3,866	629	6,673	1,416	▼	303
Lawrence, KS	3.4	25.9	63.4	304.2	371	1,398	4,534	298	6,230	994	▼	207
Lawrence–Haverhill, MA–NH	1.3	14.9	49.5	211.9	263	955	1,862	823	3,641	627	▼	76
Lawton, OK	8.2	47.8	141.2	315.2	465	1,430	2,750	283	4,463	911	▼	186
Lewiston–Auburn, ME	2.2	13.0	44.9	171.5	219	1,164	3,087	176	4,427	662	—	85
Lexington–Fayette, KY	5.7	35.7	115.7	270.1	392	1,217	3,446	273	4,935	886	▼	173
Lima, OH	3.4	34.4	93.5	266.2	363	1,015	2,884	120	4,019	765	▼	122
Lincoln, NE	2.9	39.5	44.0	230.6	278	1,109	4,464	182	5,755	854	▲	156
Little Rock–North Little Rock, AR	10.8	60.3	201.2	494.6	707	1,656	3,717	325	5,698	1,277	▲	279
Longview–Marshall, TX	14.4	41.9	94.7	219.1	328	1,509	3,120	306	4,935	822	▼	140
Lorain–Elyria, OH	2.9	31.9	56.4	166.8	226	880	1,476	195	2,551	481	▼	35
Los Angeles–Long Beach, CA	16.6	55.2	581.4	613.4	1,211	1,773	3,068	1,144	5,985	1,810	—	330
Louisville, KY–IN	6.7	29.7	195.8	182.0	385	1,208	2,744	310	4,262	811	—	137
Lowell, MA–NH	1.7	20.5	62.5	295.9	360	732	1,507	542	2,780	638	—	79
Lubbock, TX	13.0	56.8	147.2	527.2	687	2,872	5,038	396	8,305	1,518	—	314
Lynchburg, VA	8.7	23.4	49.6	257.0	315	572	2,209	109	2,890	604	—	70
Macon–Warner Robins, GA	10.9	30.0	102.4	215.1	328	1,221	2,966	284	4,470	775	▲	125
Madison, WI	1.8	27.8	65.5	107.5	175	1,058	3,981	216	5,254	700	▼	94
Manchester, NH	3.3	18.9	72.8	102.6	179	1,223	3,339	340	4,902	669	▲	87
Mansfield, OH	3.4	27.6	92.5	507.6	604	1,250	2,881	205	4,335	1,038	—	229
McAllen–Edinburg–Mission, TX	7.0	16.1	44.4	276.4	328	1,766	3,038	358	5,162	844	▲	149
Medford, OR	3.2	36.8	46.6	168.8	219	1,193	3,379	251	4,823	701	▲	95
Melbourne–Titusville–Palm Bay, FL	6.5	37.6	150.1	435.7	592	1,639	3,700	287	5,626	1,155	▲	266
Memphis, TN–AR–MS	16.4	2.2	549.5	382.4	948	2,142	2,982	1,195	6,318	1,580	▲	320
Merced, CA	6.3	30.1	96.4	279.9	383	1,271	3,093	219	4,583	841	—	148
Miami–Hialeah, FL	21.9	51.3	742.7	868.3	1,633	2,545	5,438	1,296	9,278	2,561	▲	333
Middlesex–Somerset–Hunterdon, NJ	2.1	15.1	70.7	141.9	215	759	2,241	353	3,353	550	—	52
Middletown, CT	2.0	29.5	75.7	151.7	229	921	2,447	313	3,681	597	—	68
Midland, TX	7.7	47.5	64.6	403.2	476	1,900	2,387	347	4,634	939	▼	194
Milwaukee, WI	5.5	29.4	165.5	202.2	373	964	3,492	472	4,928	866	▲	161
Minneapolis–St. Paul, MN–WI	2.7	40.1	156.1	187.3	346	1,385	3,313	355	5,053	851	▲	153
Mobile, AL	12.7	40.2	213.1	595.5	821	2,111	2,985	283	5,378	1,359	—	295
Modesto, CA	5.7	41.2	126.1	374.4	506	1,883	4,152	355	6,390	1,145	▲	263
Monmouth–Ocean, NJ	2.7	24.9	69.7	208.6	281	939	2,742	253	3,934	674	▼	89
Monroe, LA	6.7	42.3	53.8	531.4	592	1,154	2,833	160	4,146	1,007	▲	218
Montgomery, AL	11.5	20.8	84.9	177.1	274	1,114	2,859	197	4,170	691	▼	92

	Violent Crime Rates					Property Crime Rates						
	Murder	Rape	Robbery	Assault	Total	Burglary	Larceny-Theft	Motor Vehicle Theft	Total	SCORE	TREND	RANK
Metro Area Average	**8.9**	**40.5**	**259.8**	**344.1**	**653**	**1,443**	**3,206**	**554**	**5,203**	**1,174**	▼	
Muncie, IN	8.8	36.1	100.1	116.7	226	1,299	2,796	281	4,376	664	—	86
Muskegon, MI	4.2	50.4	108.9	762.0	875	1,424	3,988	193	5,604	1,435	—	308
Naples, FL	15.0	44.4	132.2	307.4	455	1,672	3,472	304	5,449	1,000	—	211
★ Nashua, NH	2.1	28.0	19.9	49.8	72	638	1,911	194	2,743	346	▼	8
Nashville, TN	11.8	53.4	224.6	268.1	505	1,485	2,892	360	4,738	979	▲	204
Nassau–Suffolk, NY	3.0	11.9	110.2	107.5	221	833	2,156	464	3,453	566	▼	58
New Bedford, MA	2.5	20.4	159.0	390.3	552	1,499	2,247	772	4,519	1,004	▲	215
New Britain, CT	3.6	29.2	186.1	172.7	362	1,315	3,028	343	4,687	831	▲	144
New Haven–Meriden, CT	4.3	33.6	261.9	210.6	477	1,366	3,109	565	5,040	981	▲	206
New London–Norwich, CT–RI	2.5	23.6	66.7	132.5	202	960	2,229	233	3,422	544	▼	49
New Orleans, LA	19.4	58.0	437.2	468.8	925	1,678	3,778	778	6,234	1,548	▲	315
New York, NY	18.9	45.8	982.2	649.3	1,650	1,662	3,532	1,107	6,301	2,280	—	332
Newark, NJ	8.5	54.4	466.4	381.5	856	1,128	2,643	1,134	4,905	1,347	—	291
Niagara Falls, NY	2.7	26.5	113.0	210.4	326	1,124	2,685	233	4,042	730	—	107
Norfolk–Virginia Beach–Newport News, VA	9.6	41.7	175.5	217.2	402	1,189	3,488	259	4,935	896	—	179
Norwalk, CT	3.4	9.8	128.7	87.7	220	1,259	3,449	439	5,147	735	▼	112
Oakland, CA	10.8	52.5	318.7	451.6	781	1,908	4,093	490	6,492	1,430	▲	306
Ocala, FL	9.4	56.7	192.7	489.9	692	2,109	3,599	298	6,006	1,293	▼	283
Odessa, TX	13.9	52.1	106.3	243.7	364	2,347	5,087	404	7,838	1,148	▼	265
Oklahoma City, OK	9.1	64.2	205.7	336.5	551	2,396	4,119	828	7,343	1,285	▲	282
Olympia, WA	2.4	37.4	30.4	122.6	155	1,247	3,180	191	4,618	617	▲	74
Omaha, NE–IA	5.6	40.2	113.7	332.1	451	1,129	3,336	279	4,744	925	▼	190
Orange County, NY	3.6	20.0	136.3	260.1	400	1,068	2,232	198	3,497	750	▼	117
Orlando, FL	7.7	51.1	252.2	585.1	845	1,961	3,909	391	6,262	1,471	▲	312
Owensboro, KY	4.1	30.5	35.3	76.5	116	1,103	2,603	162	3,869	503	▼	42
Oxnard–Ventura, CA	4.4	30.8	114.4	219.5	338	1,205	2,224	291	3,720	710	▲	98
Panama City, FL	8.2	66.5	84.6	376.7	470	1,350	3,936	295	5,582	1,028	▼	223
★ Parkersburg–Marietta, WV–OH	2.5	20.3	32.6	69.9	105	795	1,786	140	2,721	377	▼	14
Pascagoula, MS	3.0	30.7	69.4	290.3	363	1,407	2,499	216	4,123	775	▼	125
Pawtucket–Woonsocket–Attleboro, RI–MA	1.8	12.3	47.0	155.6	204	933	1,740	430	3,103	514	▼	46
Pensacola, FL	7.4	61.6	152.4	666.9	827	1,550	3,392	270	5,212	1,348	—	292
Peoria, IL	2.0	NA	71.9	327.5	401	1,051	2,678	113	3,842	785	▼	129
Philadelphia, PA–NJ	8.7	35.6	277.6	268.3	555	967	2,216	546	3,729	928	▼	191
Phoenix, AZ	8.6	46.4	173.7	387.8	570	1,924	4,523	454	6,900	1,260	▲	275
Pine Bluff, AR	9.8	44.8	100.6	433.2	544	1,293	2,791	169	4,254	969	▲	203
Pittsburgh, PA	3.6	23.9	194.7	134.3	333	774	1,441	581	2,797	613	▼	72
Pittsfield, MA	1.0	42.8	42.6	179.3	223	1,011	1,527	265	2,803	503	▼	42
Portland, ME	1.6	20.4	68.0	232.3	302	1,338	4,086	293	5,717	874	▲	165
Portland, OR	6.4	58.1	360.5	468.1	835	2,500	4,698	527	7,726	1,608	▲	322
Portsmouth–Dover–Rochester, NH–ME	1.3	20.4	19.8	112.1	133	796	2,656	190	3,643	497	—	39
Poughkeepsie, NY	2.9	14.7	97.8	211.7	312	820	1,860	133	2,813	593	▼	67
Providence, RI	4.0	25.8	145.4	245.4	395	1,447	2,818	845	5,110	906	▼	183
Provo–Orem, UT	1.7	11.7	10.8	94.2	107	553	3,226	128	3,907	498	—	40
Pueblo, CO	5.1	58.4	114.9	582.3	702	1,515	3,866	237	5,618	1,264	—	278

	Violent Crime Rates					Property Crime Rates						
	Murder	Rape	Robbery	Assault	Total	Burglary	Larceny-Theft	Motor Vehicle Theft	Total	SCORE	TREND	RANK
Metro Area Average	8.9	40.5	259.8	344.1	653	1,443	3,206	554	5,203	1,174	▼	
Racine, WI	3.3	35.8	169.9	314.3	488	1,425	3,469	226	5,119	1,000	▲	211
Raleigh–Durham, NC	9.0	30.9	119.4	243.9	372	1,454	3,382	269	5,105	883	▼	169
Rapid City, SD	3.8	56.3	62.6	260.0	326	1,153	3,999	260	5,412	867	▲	163
Reading, PA	3.0	14.9	97.4	133.6	234	817	1,774	178	2,768	511	▲	45
Redding, CA	8.1	44.8	65.0	403.0	476	1,564	2,911	268	4,742	950	▲	197
Reno, NV	7.2	75.5	208.0	270.9	486	1,643	3,929	414	5,986	1,085	▲	247
Richland–Kennewick–Pasco, WA	6.2	39.0	53.8	174.6	235	1,507	3,572	184	5,263	761	▲	121
Richmond–Petersburg, VA	13.8	43.3	204.3	238.3	456	1,286	3,166	267	4,719	928	▼	191
Riverside–San Bernardino, CA	11.3	42.9	232.1	550.1	794	2,310	3,375	598	6,283	1,422	▲	304
Roanoke, VA	8.1	22.6	89.0	138.5	236	1,043	3,529	168	4,740	710	—	98
★ Rochester, MN	1.9	18.9	17.0	49.7	69	715	2,499	126	3,340	403	▼	19
Rochester, NY	4.5	25.4	130.3	226.4	361	1,005	3,214	215	4,434	804	▼	135
Rockford, IL	4.9	NA	153.7	303.2	462	1,965	3,849	207	6,021	1,064	▲	240
Sacramento, CA	9.1	47.2	268.2	336.9	614	1,976	4,159	557	6,692	1,283	—	281
Saginaw–Bay City–Midland, MI	7.0	78.6	113.3	434.1	554	1,218	3,246	198	4,661	1,020	▼	220
★ St. Cloud, MN	1.3	16.1	13.3	55.0	70	452	2,354	143	2,948	365	▲	10
St. Joseph, MO	4.3	21.8	52.5	237.7	295	1,743	3,535	232	5,510	846	▼	151
St. Louis, MO–IL	11.4	NA	208.1	382.5	602	1,311	2,742	481	4,534	1,055	—	237
Salem, OR	4.7	43.5	103.9	203.1	312	1,636	4,147	283	6,066	919	—	188
★ Salem–Gloucester, MA	2.1	12.6	32.2	110.5	145	700	1,477	425	2,603	405	▼	20
Salinas–Seaside–Monterey, CA	6.2	40.8	146.8	419.7	573	1,354	3,356	239	4,949	1,068	▲	243
Salt Lake City–Ogden, UT	3.6	28.8	86.1	200.6	290	1,170	4,557	282	6,009	891	—	175
San Angelo, TX	9.1	32.0	57.1	372.4	439	1,336	3,711	229	5,276	967	▼	201
San Antonio, TX	15.8	69.4	248.6	221.2	486	2,547	4,783	768	8,097	1,296	▲	284
San Diego, CA	7.8	35.4	225.1	327.1	560	1,519	3,102	876	5,496	1,110	▲	253
San Francisco, CA	8.2	43.6	389.3	402.6	800	1,228	3,567	571	5,366	1,337	▼	290
San Jose, CA	4.8	46.0	128.2	252.5	386	1,105	3,332	349	4,787	865	▼	160
Santa Barbara–Santa Maria–Lompoc, CA	4.6	35.6	84.0	268.0	357	1,157	3,292	273	4,723	829	▼	143
Santa Cruz, CA	7.1	38.4	126.4	311.3	445	1,739	3,969	362	6,071	1,052	▲	235
Santa Fe, NM	5.8	22.7	46.4	475.3	528	1,304	2,622	236	4,162	944	▼	195
Santa Rosa–Petaluma, CA	5.4	35.4	81.5	247.3	334	1,464	3,011	264	4,739	808	—	136
Sarasota, FL	6.0	48.8	132.3	327.6	466	1,650	3,833	240	5,723	1,038	▲	229
Savannah, GA	16.8	55.8	278.2	269.9	565	1,882	4,232	301	6,415	1,207	▼	271
★ Scranton–Wilkes-Barre, PA	2.3	11.6	37.2	85.7	125	652	1,324	164	2,141	339	▼	6
Seattle, WA	5.6	60.2	198.6	263.7	468	2,012	4,756	388	7,156	1,184	▲	270
★ Sharon, PA	2.5	12.3	28.5	104.0	135	530	1,594	175	2,299	365	▲	10
★ Sheboygan, WI	0.8	10.3	13.6	44.6	59	705	2,810	102	3,617	421	—	23
Sherman–Denison, TX	7.7	19.4	85.0	375.2	468	1,717	4,031	326	6,074	1,075	▲	245
Shreveport, LA	14.3	49.1	178.0	486.6	679	1,875	4,647	324	6,845	1,364	—	296
Sioux City, IA–NE	2.4	22.3	58.8	254.9	316	1,800	3,885	251	5,936	910	▲	185
Sioux Falls, SD	2.2	37.3	24.5	106.3	133	718	2,673	138	3,528	486	—	37
South Bend–Mishawaka, IN	5.9	43.2	156.4	220.0	382	1,668	4,024	273	5,966	979	▲	204
Spokane, WA	4.8	30.0	114.2	188.1	307	1,754	3,740	269	5,763	883	▲	169

	Violent Crime Rates					Property Crime Rates						
	Murder	Rape	Robbery	Assault	Total	Burglary	Larceny-Theft	Motor Vehicle Theft	Total	SCORE	TREND	RANK
Metro Area Average	8.9	40.5	259.8	344.1	653	1,443	3,206	554	5,203	1,174	▼	
Springfield, IL	5.9	NA	136.1	339.7	482	1,642	3,583	200	5,425	1,025	▼	221
Springfield, MA	3.4	41.8	124.7	450.4	579	1,167	2,042	467	3,676	947	▼	196
Springfield, MO	4.1	23.8	66.2	137.8	208	1,317	3,671	221	5,210	729	▼	105
Stamford, CT	3.7	12.2	157.3	134.5	296	1,027	2,969	454	4,449	741	—	115
★ State College, PA	1.4	19.8	15.2	64.9	82	649	2,720	85	3,454	427	▼	26
★ Steubenville–Weirton, OH–WV	2.2	11.8	48.5	160.0	211	743	955	153	1,851	396	—	18
Stockton, CA	12.4	39.3	234.1	326.4	573	2,250	4,720	447	7,417	1,315	▲	287
Syracuse, NY	2.7	22.0	104.4	113.2	220	1,108	2,570	150	3,828	603	▼	69
Tacoma, WA	6.1	83.3	183.1	378.6	568	2,411	4,113	345	6,869	1,255	▲	273
Tallahassee, FL	7.1	59.9	159.0	528.5	695	1,798	4,147	299	6,243	1,319	▲	288
Tampa–St. Petersburg–Clearwater, FL	9.0	49.1	278.8	578.9	867	2,041	4,078	350	6,470	1,514	▲	313
Terre Haute, IN	3.3	21.5	42.5	198.0	244	1,333	2,421	355	4,109	655	▲	83
Texarkana, TX–Texarkana, AR	10.2	35.6	88.2	286.6	385	1,382	3,668	284	5,334	918	▲	187
Toledo, OH	6.1	51.6	208.5	215.4	430	1,419	3,773	456	5,648	995	▼	209
Topeka, KS	4.2	36.0	139.7	299.3	443	1,699	3,608	199	5,506	994	▲	207
Trenton, NJ	6.0	39.0	343.8	220.8	571	1,494	3,453	566	5,514	1,122	—	256
Tucson, AZ	7.7	58.3	174.4	434.3	616	2,054	4,845	421	7,320	1,348	▲	292
Tulsa, OK	7.8	43.5	145.0	322.2	475	1,767	3,098	867	5,732	1,048	—	232
Tuscaloosa, AL	6.4	30.7	91.2	521.8	619	1,150	3,115	246	4,512	1,070	▲	244
Tyler, TX	12.8	55.3	120.6	254.2	388	1,844	4,294	351	6,489	1,037	▲	228
★ Utica–Rome, NY	2.6	11.3	43.4	77.6	124	758	1,520	86	2,363	360	▼	9
Vallejo–Fairfield–Napa, CA	5.6	34.8	143.4	472.3	621	1,364	3,316	328	5,008	1,122	▲	256
Vancouver, WA	3.5	45.2	66.5	137.2	207	1,646	3,054	284	4,985	706	—	97
Victoria, TX	6.2	30.4	68.1	432.1	506	1,777	3,431	220	5,428	1,049	▲	234
Vineland–Millville–Bridgeton, NJ	3.8	57.7	146.5	366.5	517	1,676	3,497	326	5,498	1,067	▲	242
Visalia–Tulare–Porterville, CA	10.8	35.6	120.4	436.0	567	1,851	3,270	295	5,416	1,109	▲	252
Waco, TX	10.5	44.7	143.6	332.1	486	2,169	4,322	309	6,799	1,166	▲	267
Washington, DC–MD–VA	8.6	33.6	304.1	303.7	616	1,065	3,027	501	4,593	1,075	▼	245
Waterbury, CT	4.4	20.1	150.2	122.5	277	1,191	3,011	362	4,563	733	—	110
Waterloo–Cedar Falls, IA	1.3	14.6	55.9	175.0	232	1,061	2,897	115	4,073	639	▼	80
Wausau, WI	2.3	12.5	11.6	136.9	151	558	2,478	107	3,143	465	▼	33
West Palm Beach–Boca Raton–Delray Beach, FL	10.5	58.2	320.6	633.4	965	2,702	4,858	664	8,224	1,787	▲	329
★ Wheeling, WV–OH	3.0	11.1	48.6	50.1	102	602	1,086	134	1,822	284	▲	2
Wichita Falls, TX	11.0	56.5	195.5	295.3	502	1,910	4,168	369	6,448	1,147	—	264
Wichita, KS	6.4	58.9	140.2	230.0	377	1,438	4,140	310	5,888	966	—	200
★ Williamsport, PA	0.9	19.1	26.4	89.6	117	672	1,861	123	2,655	383	▼	17
Wilmington, DE–NJ–MD	4.3	41.8	142.0	277.4	424	1,333	3,478	322	5,144	938	—	193
Wilmington, NC	8.4	44.3	133.7	293.1	435	1,997	4,347	322	6,666	1,102	▲	250
Worcester, MA	2.8	29.4	150.0	263.5	416	1,211	1,968	403	3,582	774	—	124
Yakima, WA	8.2	47.9	113.1	249.9	371	2,077	4,845	275	7,197	1,091	▲	249
★ York, PA	3.1	16.0	47.0	56.1	106	619	1,870	128	2,617	368	—	12
Youngstown–Warren, OH	6.6	25.3	128.4	259.9	395	1,076	1,805	473	3,354	730	▼	107
Yuba City, CA	7.6	26.7	75.8	773.6	857	1,700	3,475	327	5,503	1,407	▲	302

Et Cetera

DRUNK DRIVING

Drunk driving is the most common single cause of arrest in the United States, and the penalties for the crime have been getting more serious.

More than half of the states now mandate license suspensions for first offenses, while more than 40 states require mandatory suspensions and imprisonment, counseling, terms of public service, and/or fines for repeat offenses.

Arizona has the most strict penalties for repeat offenders, with a minimum first-offense fine of $1,000 that can grow to $150,000 with a third conviction.

A dozen states have banned happy hours as a way of discouraging drunk driving. Many states have also put the burden of responsibility on restauranteurs and bar owners, creating a legal framework in which the last person to provide a drink to an intoxicated patron can be held responsible for his or her actions.

The main thrust of most state actions remains focused on efforts to remove the repeat offender from the road, as the chart entitled ''In 42 States Imprisonment is Mandatory for Driving While Intoxicated'' indicates.

In 42 States Imprisonment is Mandatory for Driving While Intoxicated

State	Is imprisonment mandatory?	After which offense does imprisonment become mandatory?	Length of imprisonment
Alabama	Yes	2nd offense	2 days
Alaska	Yes	1st	3
Arizona	Yes	1st	1
Arkansas	No		
California	Yes	2nd	2
Colorado	Yes	2nd	7
Connecticut	Yes	1st	2
Delaware	Yes	2nd	60
District of Columbia	No		
Florida	Yes	2nd	10
Georgia	Yes	2nd	2
Hawaii	Yes	1st	2
Idaho	Yes	2nd	10
Illinois	Yes	2nd	2
Indiana	Yes	2nd	5
Iowa	Yes	2nd	7
Kansas	Yes	1st	2
Kentucky	Yes	2nd	7
Louisiana	Yes	1st	2
Maine	Yes	1st	2
Maryland	Yes	2nd	2
Massachusetts	Yes	2nd	14
Michigan	No		
Minnesota	No		
Mississippi	No		
Missouri	Yes	2nd	2
Montana	Yes	1st	1
Nebraska	Yes	2nd	2
Nevada	Yes	1st	2
New Hampshire	Yes	2nd	7
New Jersey	Yes	2nd	2
New Mexico	Yes	2nd	2
New York	No		
North Carolina	Yes	2nd	7
North Dakota	Yes	2nd	4
Ohio	Yes	1st	3
Oklahoma	No		
Oregon	Yes	1st	2
Pennsylvania	Yes	2nd	30
Rhode Island	Yes	2nd	2
South Carolina	Yes	1st	2
South Dakota	No		
Tennessee	Yes	1st	2
Texas	Yes	2nd	3
Utah	Yes	1st	2
Vermont	Yes	2nd	2
Virginia	Yes	2nd	2
Washington	Yes	1st	1
West Virginia	Yes	1st	1
Wisconsin	No		
Wyoming	Yes	2nd	7

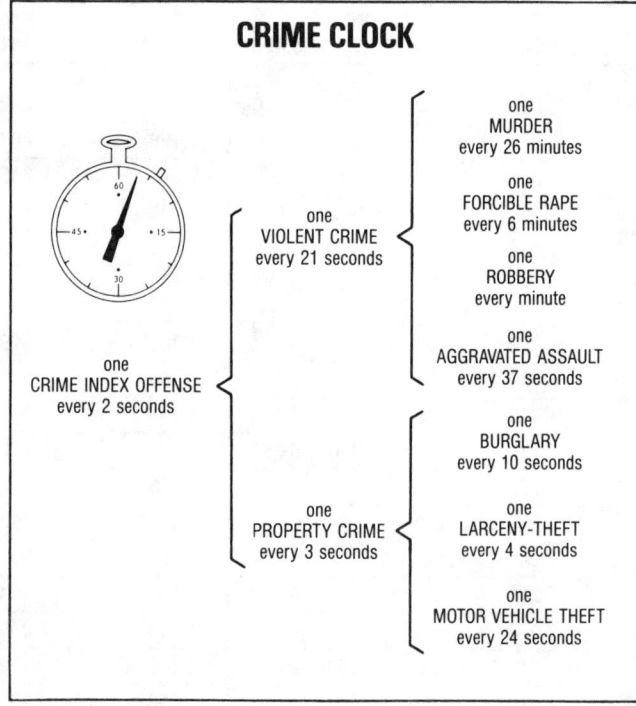

CRIME CLOCK

one CRIME INDEX OFFENSE every 2 seconds

one VIOLENT CRIME every 21 seconds

one MURDER every 26 minutes

one FORCIBLE RAPE every 6 minutes

one ROBBERY every minute

one AGGRAVATED ASSAULT every 37 seconds

one PROPERTY CRIME every 3 seconds

one BURGLARY every 10 seconds

one LARCENY-THEFT every 4 seconds

one MOTOR VEHICLE THEFT every 24 seconds

Source: FBI, *Crime in the United States*, 1988.

Figures are for 1987.

Source: National Highway Traffic Safety Administration, *A Digest of State Alcohol-Highway Safety Related Legislation, 1988.*

HANDGUNS

Handgun control is not a subject to be broached lightly in conversation unless time is of no importance and one is ready for a prolonged discussion or argument.

The controversy over handgun control has been going on for years. Changes in regulations occur frequently from state to state and even within municipalities. The gun owner or potential gun owner is well advised to pay attention to these changes, especially when moving from one jurisdiction to another.

The National Rifle Association, the fiercest defender of gun enthusiasts, attempts to keep its members abreast of regulation changes with a regular publication of state-by-state regulations, but even this comes with a disclaimer warning of the constant changes. The varia-

State Restrictions on Purchase and Carrying of Handguns

State	Apply/Wait	Registration Required	Sale Reported	Carrying Prohibited* Concealed	Open
Alabama	48 hours		•		
Alaska	None			•	
Arizona	None			•	
Arkansas	None			•	•
California	15 days		•		
Colorado	None				
Connecticut	2 weeks		•		
Delaware	None				
District of Columbia	48 hours	•		•	•
Florida	None				•
Georgia	None				
Hawaii	15 days	•	•		
Idaho	None				
Illinois	72 hours	•	•	•	•
Indiana	7 days		•		
Iowa	None		•		
Kansas	None	•			
Kentucky	None			•	
Louisiana	None				
Maine	None				
Maryland	7 days		•		
Massachusetts	None		•		
Michigan	None	•	•		
Minnesota	7 days		•		
Mississippi	None	•		•	
Missouri	7 days		•	•	
Montana	None				
Nebraska	None			•	
Nevada	None				
New Hampshire	None				
New Jersey	30-45 days		•		
New Mexico	None			•	
New York	6 months	•	•		
North Carolina	30 days		•	•	
North Dakota	None		•		•
Ohio	None		•	•	
Oklahoma	None		•	•	
Oregon	5 days		•		
Pennsylvania	48 hours		•		
Rhode Island	72 hours		•		
South Carolina	None		•		
South Dakota	48 hours		•		
Tennessee	15 days		•	•	•
Texas	None			•	•
Utah	None				•
Vermont	None				
Virginia	None				
Washington	5-60 days		•		
West Virginia	None		•		
Wisconsin	48 hours			•	
Wyoming	None				

Source: National Rifle Association, Institute for Legislative Action, 1988.

State firearms laws are subject to change. State and local statutes and ordinances, as well as local police, should be consulted for full text and meaning of statutory provisions.

*Most states that do not prohibit carrying handguns nevertheless require a license to carry them openly or concealed.

Crime Compared with Other Events in Life

The rates of some violent crimes are higher than those of other harmful life events. For example, the risk of being the victim of violent crime is higher than the risk of being affected by divorce, death from cancer, or injury or death from a fire. Anyone over 15 years old runs a greater risk of being a violent crime victim, with or without injury, than being hurt in a traffic accident. Still, a person is much more likely to die from natural causes than from being a victim of crime.

Crime Compared with Other Events in Life

Event	Annual Rate per 1,000 Adults
Accidental injury, all circumstances	290.242
Accidental injury at home	105.079
Personal theft	**82.072**
Accidental injury at work	68.058
Injury in motor-vehicle accident	23.017
Divorce	23.000
Death, all causes	11.000
Aggravated assault	**9.000**
Death of spouse	9.000
Robbery	**7.006**
Heart disease death	4.000
Cancer death	2.000
Accidental death, all circumstances	0.500
Pneumonia/influenza death	0.300
Motor-vehicle accident death	0.200
Suicide	0.200
Injury from fire	0.100
Murder	**0.100**
Death from fire	0.030

Source: Bureau of Justice Statistics, *Report to the Nation on Crime and Justice*, 1988.

Most of the states fall somewhere between these extremes, as the chart entitled "State Restrictions on Purchase and Carrying of Handguns" indicates, but the penalties for not knowing the law or for violating the law can be severe. Massachusetts, for example, has a law requiring a mandatory jail term of one year for anyone caught with an unlicensed gun.

tions in different states' restrictions can be immense, reflecting quite accurately how well those who vehemently defend their weapons and those who would take them away have done their jobs in the state legislatures.

In Georgia, Colorado, Louisiana, Maine, Nevada, and New Hampshire, there are few restrictions. One can walk into a store, buy a pistol, and walk out. There's not even a record of the sale.

On the other hand, in Illinois, a prospective gun buyer has to apply for a permit, then wait 72 hours for a check of criminal records. A gun must then be registered and the sale is reported. However, carrying a weapon, either exposed or concealed, is prohibited in the state.

In Chicago, the same rules apply, but only to old guns. No new guns may be brought into the city since a recent law change. In the suburbs of Evanston, Oak Park, and Morton Grove, there are no handguns at all; they're prohibited.

CAPITAL PUNISHMENT

While the debates over whether capital punishment is right or wrong continue in state houses and courts around the country, one thing is certain: execution does not follow quickly after conviction, regardless of the nature of the crime.

One recent execution in Florida occurred 13 years after the guilty verdict was reached. The number of inmates on Death Row in the 37 states that have death penalty laws approached 2,200 at the end of 1988; this was an increase of 600 inmates over three years, and more than 2,000 since the early 1970s.

Does it follow, then, that states such as Texas (with 284 convicts awaiting execution), Florida (with 296), or California (with 238) are getting tougher on major crime? Not necessarily, according to both sides of a debate over this issue.

States with Death Penalties and Their Methods of Execution

Lethal injection	Electrocution	Lethal gas	Hanging	Firing squad
Arkansas[a]	Alabama	Arizona	Delaware	Idaho[a]
Idaho[a]	Arkansas[a]	California	Montana[a]	Utah[a]
Illinois	Connecticut	Colorado	New Hampshire	
Mississippi[a,b]	Florida	Maryland	Washington[a]	
Montana[a]	Georgia	Mississippi[a,b]		
Nevada	Indiana	Missouri		
New Jersey	Kentucky	North Carolina[a]		
New Mexico	Louisiana	Wyoming[a]		
North Carolina[a]	Nebraska			
Oklahoma[c]	Ohio			
Oregon	Pennsylvania			
South Dakota	South Carolina			
Texas	Tennessee			
Utah[a]	Vermont			
Washington[a]	Virginia			
Wyoming[a]				

[a]Authorizes two methods of execution.
[b]Mississippi authorizes lethal injection for persons convicted after 7/1/84; executions of persons convicted before that date are to be carried out with lethal gas.
[c]Should lethal injection be found to be unconstitutional, Oklahoma authorizes use of electrocution or firing squad.

Source: Bureau of Justice Statistics, *Capital Punishment, 1988.*

Personal Safety: The States Ranked from Safest to Most Dangerous

State	Violent Crime Rate (Rank)	Property Crime Rate (Rank)	Score	State	Violent Crime Rate (Rank)	Property Crime Rate (Rank)	Score
1. West Virginia	115 (4)	2,053 (1)	320	26. Connecticut	394 (29)	4,577 (29)	852
2. North Dakota	48 (1)	2,776 (3)	325	27. North Carolina	455 (31)	4,166 (22)	871
3. South Dakota	99 (2)	2,558 (2)	355	28. Alaska	390 (28)	4,922 (33)	883
4. New Hampshire	123 (5)	3,222 (7)	445	29. Tennessee	490 (32)	4,132 (18)	903
5. Maine	136 (7)	3,380 (8)	474	30. Alabama	531 (36)	3,892 (14)	921
6. Vermont	114 (3)	4,135 (19)	527	31. Missouri	516 (35)	4,163 (21)	932
7. Mississippi	241 (14)	3,169 (6)	557	32. Oklahoma	382 (26)	5,608 (41)	943
8. Montana	131 (6)	4,448 (25)	576	33. Massachusetts	533 (37)	4,169 (23)	950
9. Idaho	197 (8)	3,942 (17)	591	34. New Jersey	508 (34)	4,721 (32)	980
10. Kentucky	317 (19)	2,932 (5)	610	35. Colorado	427 (30)	5,984 (45)	1,025
11. Iowa	219 (10)	3,909 (15)	610	36. Washington	387 (27)	6,578 (48)	1,045
12. Nebraska	230 (12)	3,880 (13)	618	37. Georgia	533 (38)	5,216 (37)	1,055
13. Wisconsin	230 (13)	3,920 (16)	622	38. South Carolina	621 (42)	4,497 (26)	071
14. Pennsylvania	343 (22)	2,794 (4)	622	39. Oregon	494 (33)	6,429 (46)	137
15. Wyoming	252 (16)	3,748 (10)	626	40. Louisiana	657 (44)	5,180 (36)	175
16. Virginia	269 (17)	3,665 (9)	635	41. New Mexico	585 (41)	5,918 (44)	177
17. Indiana	299 (18)	3,791 (11)	679	42. Maryland	728 (46)	4,710 (31)	199
18. Minnesota	251 (15)	4,330 (24)	684	43. Nevada	634 (43)	5,676 (42)	201
19. Utah	208 (9)	5,389 (38)	747	44. Illinois	758 (47)	4,620 (30)	220
20. Arkansas	379 (24)	3,833 (12)	763	45. Arizona	571 (39)	6,576 (47)	229
21. Kansas	328 (20)	4,543 (28)	782	46. Michigan	713 (45)	5,677 (43)	281
22. Hawaii	227 (11)	5,555 (39)	782	47. Texas	583 (40)	7,091 (49)	292
23. Ohio	381 (25)	4,154 (20)	797	48. California	874 (48)	5,589 (40)	433
24. Delaware	362 (23)	4,508 (27)	813	49. New York	977 (50)	4,944 (35)	471
25. Rhode Island	335 (21)	4,926 (34)	828	50. Florida	974 (49)	7,479 (50)	722

Source: FBI, *Crime in the United States,* 1988.

The score is the sum of the violent crime rate and one-tenth the property crime rate.

The debate used to center almost totally on right versus wrong and cruel versus humane questions. It began to change in 1972 when the U.S. Supreme Court took away many of the individual states' rights to decide what constituted a crime deserving the death penalty. From that point, executions all but stopped. Later court decisions restored some of the discretion to the states, prompting further challenges and the continuing build-up of Death Row's population.

Prosecutors and supporters of capital punishment express frustration with the situation, citing the huge financial burden the delays cost, and pointing to the

Neighborhood Crime Watches

It is not uncommon to see a crime in progress without recognizing it as such. Here are some situations that might be observed in any neighborhood. These are situations a trained police officer would investigate if he or she were making the observation.

Situations Involving Vehicles

Situation	Possible Significance
Moving vehicles, especially if moving slowly without lights, following an aimless or repetitive course	Casing for a place to rob or burglarize; drug pusher, sex offender, or vandal
Parked, occupied vehicle, especially at an unusual hour	Lookout for burglary in progress (sometimes two people masquerading as lovers)
Vehicle parked in neighbor's drive being loaded with valuables, even if the vehicle looks legitimate, i.e., moving van or commercial van	Burglary or larceny in progress
Abandoned vehicle with or without license plate	Stolen or abandoned after being used in a crime
Persons loitering around parked cars	Burglary of vehicle contents, theft of accessories, vandalism
Persons detaching accessories and mechanical parts	Theft or vandalism
Apparent business transactions from a vehicle near school, park, or quiet residential neighborhood	Drug sales
Persons being forced into vehicle	Kidnapping, rape, robbery
Objects thrown from a moving vehicle	Disposal of contraband

Situations Involving Property

Situation	Possible Significance
Property in homes, garages, or storage areas, especially if several items of the same kind such as TVs and bicycles	Storage of stolen property

Situations Involving Property

Situation	Possible Significance
Property in vehicles, especially meaningful at night or if property is household goods, appliances, unmounted tape decks, stereo equipment	Stolen property, burglary in progress
Property being removed from a house or building; meaningful if residents are at work, on vacation, or are known to be absent	Burglary or larceny in progress
Open doors, broken doors or windows, or other signs of a forced entry	Burglary in progress or the scene of a recent burglary

Situations Involving Persons

Situation	Possible Significance
Door-to-door solicitors— especially significant if one goes to the back of the house and one stays in front. Can be men or women, clean-cut and well-dressed	Casing for burglary, burglary in progress, soliciting violation
Waiting in front of a house	Lookout for burglary in progress
Forced entry or entry through window	Burglary, vandalism, theft
Persons short-cutting through yards	Fleeing the scene of a crime
Persons running, especially if carrying items of value	Fleeing the scene of a crime
Person carrying property, especially if property isn't boxed or wrapped	Offender leaving the scene of a burglary, robbery, or larceny
High volume of human traffic in and out of residence	Drug sales, vice activities, "fence" operation

---

demographics of Death Row: all inmates are convicted murderers; nearly 10 percent have a prior murder conviction; and 40 percent were on bail, parole, or probation at the time of their arrest.

The most compelling arguments against capital punishment are that execution is irreversible, that mistakes can be made, and that in many areas adequate legal defenses are not provided . . . and the debate goes on.

Death Penalty Differences

Thirteen states have abandoned or avoided the death penalty in the modern age, but its implementation in the 37 states which do have it are far from consistent.

Only 12 states have actually used the electric chair, lethal injection, or other approved method of execution in the past 10 years, and fewer than 100 executions have occurred among over 2,000 persons sentenced. Those executions that have taken place have occurred mainly in Florida and Texas.

Methods of execution vary. Idaho and Utah offer options of facing a firing squad or receiving a lethal injection. Lethal injections and electrocution are the most common execution methods. Delaware and New Hampshire prescribe hanging as the only acceptable method. See the chart on the previous page for more specific details.

CRIMES BY REGION

Although criminal activity varies from place to place and from year to year, regional patterns haven't changed much in decades. The murder rate in the West South Central states, where the frequency of people's killing one another has traditionally been the country's highest, is nearly three times that of the Plains states. Rape is highest in the West South Central and Pacific regions and lowest in New England and the Plains states. Armed robbery, a crime of big cities, is highest in the Mid-Atlantic states, lowest in the Plains states. The Plains states also have the lowest rates for assault, while the South Atlantic states experience the highest.

Criminologists recognize the geographic pattern of crime-ridden places immediately. Many of the country's more dangerous places are located on the East Coast from New Jersey southward. This area is rapidly growing. The resulting transience, which leads to strangers living close together, is strongly associated with crime.

There are other reasons for high crime in this area. Professional crooks migrate to where the living is easy and the pickings bountiful; they don't stay in the industrial towns of the North but head South to warm weather and popular resorts. This is one reason Miami has been plagued by high crime for decades.

Finally, most of the dangerous places are hot much of the year. Knowing what we do about climate's influence on crime, it isn't surprising that large southern cities going through a steamy summer are America's most crime-ridden. Persons bidding farewell to Cedar Rapids, Milwaukee, Pittsburgh, or Syracuse to make their new homes in West Palm Beach, Orlando, Phoenix, or Las Vegas may need time not only for acclimatizing to warm weather, but also for getting used to crime's share in the local evening news.

Health Care & Environment

You might assume that America, land of plenty, land of high technology, is the world's healthiest nation. But the fact is that we lag behind many developed nations—Canada, Sweden, and Switzerland, for example.

What is it about its health care system that keeps the U.S. behind other countries in health services? First of all, an estimated 37 million Americans are uninsured and lack access to the full range of health services they may need. Indeed, almost one-third of all American children aren't covered by any health insurance. In spite of our abundance of physicians and their advanced training and technical support, the basic problem is an unfair distribution of medical care.

WHAT THE NUMBERS SAY

Americans continue to get healthier. Judging by two universal measures of population health, infant mortality and life expectancy, the United States is healthier now than it was just a few years ago. Why are life expectancy and infant mortality such commonly accepted indicators of a nation's health? First, because these data can be found in almost every developed nation in the form of birth and death certificates.

Second, the quality of postpartum and infant care available in a nation (or state or town) generally reflects the quality of other important health services as well. As for life expectancy, it remains a very broad but meaningful indicator of a nation's ability to provide lifelong necessities for health, such as sanitary food and drinking water, proper immunization and disease screening, and professional medical attention.

In 1986, the U.S. Department of Health and Human Services reported that infant mortality in America had dropped to its lowest level ever, with data showing 10.6 deaths per 1,000 live births. At the same time, data showed that life expectancy had risen to 74.9, with girls born that year likely to live 78.3 years and boys 71.3. This represented an increase of over two years since 1978, and a gain of 30 years since 1900.

TWO SYSTEMS—INSURANCE, ACCESS, AND THE REST

Unfortunately, not all Americans share equally in these statistical gains, and the inequality contributes to the poor U.S. health ranking compared with other countries. Black/white. Rich/poor. Urban/rural. Insured/

uninsured. Profit/non-profit. Short-term/long-term care. Consumer/provider. These are the poles of a health care system that is increasingly a business enterprise. It's no surprise that one's location on the spectrum determines the kind of health care one receives—or whether he or she receives any at all.

The mortality rate for black infants is nearly twice that for white infants. And black and Hispanic children are less likely to see doctors, visit dentists, or have immunizations than are white children. In recent years, life expectancy has increased at a faster rate for blacks than for whites, but blacks still live an average of six years less than whites.

The number of hospitals in black communities has decreased by two-thirds in the last 20 years, and a study in the *Journal of the American Medical Association* presented some additional findings that show two separate health care systems emerging—one for blacks and one for whites. In the study, even black heart patients who were equally able to pay received less thorough care than whites. Blacks, too, were under-represented in the clinical testing of drugs (even when the drugs under review were meant to treat conditions suffered disproportionately by blacks). And finally, only 5 percent of medical school graduates and 3 percent of practicing doctors are black, though blacks make up 12 percent of the U.S. population.

These are only a few of the elements that shape the U.S. health care system. To get at the real essence of the system, one needs to look at the providers—the doctors and the hospitals.

PHYSICIANS AND THEIR SPECIALTIES

Not every physician is listed in the Yellow Pages. Some are hospital administrators, medical school professors, journalists, lawyers, or researchers for pharmaceutical companies. Others work for the federal government's Public Health Service, Veteran's Administration, or Department of Defense service branches. Still others are in residency training or are full-time members of hospital staffs. When it comes to the number of physicians per capita, what really counts is the number of doctors who maintain offices and see patients. It's surprising how many of them don't.

Depending on how these practitioners spend their professional hours, the American Medical Association (AMA) classifies office-based physicians into the following four groups:

General Practitioners are physicians that treat diseases and injuries, provide preventive care, give routine checkups, prescribe drugs, and perform some surgery. They also refer patients to medical specialists. General practitioners use all accepted methods of medical care.

Medical Specialists focus on specific medical disciplines, such as cardiology, allergy, gastroenterology, and dermatology. Medical specialists (and general practitioners) are likely to give attention to surgical and

---

The AMA's Physician Classifications
The American Medical Association classifies a physician as a general practitioner, medical specialist, surgeon, or other specialist by 35 specialties in which the physician reports spending the largest number of his or her professional hours.

General Practitioners
General Practice
Family Practice

Medical Specialists
Allergy
Cardiovascular Diseases
Dermatology
Gastroenterology
Internal Medicine
Pediatrics
Pediatric Allergy
Pediatric Cardiology
Pulmonary Diseases

Surgical Specialists
General Surgery
Neurological Surgery
Obstetrics and Gynecology
Ophthalmology
Orthopedic Surgery
Otolaryngology
Plastic Surgery
Colon and Rectal Surgery
Thoracic Surgery
Urology

Other Specialists
Aerospace Medicine
Anesthesiology
Child Psychiatry
Diagnostic Radiology
Forensic Pathology
Neurology
Occupational Medicine
Psychiatry
Pathology
Physical Medicine and Rehabilitation
General Preventive Medicine
Public Health
Radiology
Therapeutic Radiology

Source: American Medical Association, Physician Characteristics and Distribution, 1988.

---

non-surgical approaches to treatment. If they decide that surgery is the method of treatment, they refer their patients to surgeons.

Surgical Specialists operate on a regular basis several times a week. The letters F.A.C.S. (Fellow of the American College of Surgeons) after the surgeon's name indicate that he or she has passed an evaluation of surgical training and skills as well as ethical fitness.

Other Specialists concentrate on disciplines as familiar as psychiatry or as exotic as aerospace medicine and forensic medicine, with diagnostic radiology and neurology in between.

A complete list of the types of doctors as defined by the AMA, arranged by category, is shown in the listing entitled "The AMA's Physician Classifications."

Specialists: The Top 10 Metro Areas

Metro Area	Residents per Physician
1. Rochester, MN	405
2. Iowa City, IA	889
3. Ann Arbor, MI	890
4. Charlottesville, VA	1,012
5. Columbia, MO	1,054
6. San Francisco, CA	1,090
7. La Crosse, WI	1,494
8. Raleigh–Durham, NC	1,524
9. Gainesville, FL	1,561
9. Madison, WI	1,561
10. Lexington–Fayette, KY	1,596

Source: Derived from the American Medical Association's *Physician Characteristics and Distribution,* 1988.

General/Family Practitioners: The Top 10 Metro Areas

Metro Area	Residents per Physician
1. Santa Rosa–Petaluma, CA	2,454
2. Miami–Hialeah, FL	2,550
3. Sioux Falls, SD	2,556
4. Seattle, WA	2,653
5. Fort Collins–Loveland, CO	2,686
6. Victoria, TX	2,714
7. Lancaster, PA	2,771
8. Redding, CA	2,773
9. Eau Claire, WI	2,790
10. Spokane, WA	2,833

Source: Derived from the American Medical Association's *Physician Characteristics and Distribution,* 1988.

Where Physicians Cluster—One Measure of Health Care

Where doctors end up practicing is partly determined by sentiment, their perceptions of local quality of life, or both. But mainly it's a matter of economics. The physician has invested three to seven years in graduate medical education and frequently has to start out with a monstrous loan to repay.

Some begin work on a hospital staff, develop a practice, then open an office. Others are taken into someone else's practice as a partner or as one of a group of physicians. Still others buy practices from doctors who are preparing to retire. By whatever means they launch themselves professionally, new physicians who wish to specialize are concerned primarily with a place's population size.

Many physicians want to practice near a major hospital and also want to live in a city large enough to provide them with the amenities their incomes allow. In general, larger, more affluent places—Boston, New York, and San Francisco, for example—have a greater proportion of health care facilities, medical specialists, high-tech equipment, and exotic procedures.

As you can see from the table entitled "Specialists: The Top 10 Metro Areas," people who live in metro areas with medical schools and veterans' hospitals generally have access to a greater number of medical specialists. For example, in Rochester, MN, where the renowned Mayo Clinic is located, the ratio of people to specialists is 405 to 1. In Iowa City, IA, which has both a medical school and a veterans' hospital, the ratio of people to specialists is 889 to 1. And in Ann Arbor, MI, a metro area with the same two medical resources, the ratio is 890 persons per one specialist.

On the other hand, small metro areas tend to have more general and family practitioners than they do specialists. As the table "General/Family Practitioners: The Top 10 Metro Areas" indicates, the Santa Rosa–Petaluma, CA, metro area has the lowest proportion of residents to general practitioners in the United States. The smaller metro areas of Sioux Falls, SD, Victoria, TX, and Eau Claire, WI, also have impressive residents-to-generalists ratios. The common explanation is that the smaller metro areas don't have enough patients to

support a large number of specialists. A doctor who wants to see 30 to 40 patients a day needs to be a generalist.

Another pattern is for expensive, complex procedures to be available only in major metro areas or in areas with medical schools and veterans' hospitals. In Utica, NY, for example, no one performs open heart surgery. A patient has to go to Syracuse—about 50 miles away—for that. Surgeons, too, tend to cluster in metro areas with medical schools, veterans' hospitals, and ancillary medical centers.

A counter trend in physician-clustering is developing, however. Some newly graduated specialists are leaving the big cities, where things are so competitive that they can't find jobs and where it's simply too expensive for them to set up their own practices. They choose, instead, to go to smaller metro areas—often the towns in which they grew up—to establish a practice and to penetrate the existing referral network of doctors.

HOSPITALS

The word *health* can also mean its opposite, *illness.* A hospital is not really a health care institution; its business is to take care of sick people. The truly healthy need little health care except for an occasional shot or checkup; the unhealthy need a lot more.

Not all hospitals handle typical illnesses and emergencies. Many of them exclusively treat chronic diseases or alcohol and drug addiction, or they may be burn centers, psychiatric hospitals, or rehabilitation hospitals. When rating a metro area for its health care, *Places Rated* counts only general hospitals accredited for acute care by the Joint Commission on Accreditation of Hospitals (JCAH).

The number of JCAH-accredited acute-care hospitals and their inpatient beds varies among places. Although the number of hospital beds isn't as valuable an indicator as it was before advances in medicine and pharmacology shortened a hospital stay, it is still a valid way of gauging relative health care supply. As the "Hospital Inpatient Bed Supply" tables indicate, among the metro

Hospital Inpatient Bed Supply

Metro Area	Hospitals/Beds
Rochester, MN	3/1,757
Iowa City, IA	3/1,421
Columbia, MO	4/1,365
Jackson, TN	2/800
Sioux Falls, SD	4/1,237

For every 100,000 residents, the above metro areas have more than 1,000 inpatient hospital beds. The metro areas below have fewer than 200 hospital beds per 100,000 residents.

Metro Area	Hospitals/Beds
Boulder–Longmont, CO	3/354
Vancouver, WA	1/353
Brazoria, TX	4/340
Bryan–College Station, TX	2/232
Las Cruces, NM	1/239

Source: Derived from the American Hospital Association's *Guide to the Health Care Field*, 1988, and Woods & Poole Economics, Inc., population forecasts.

areas with the most hospital beds are the regional medical centers of Rochester, MN, and Iowa City, IA.

Hospital Services

Each year, the American Hospital Association (AHA) surveys its thousands of member hospitals, enumerating which of 54 AHA-defined services each institution provides. The number of services a hospital offers is one index of the level of care you may receive there—and certainly of the level of technology and specialization in that hospital.

Some of the AHA-defined services (a post-operative recovery room, a blood bank, an intensive care unit, for example) are basic. Others, however (a radioactive implant department, a department that provides X-ray radiation therapy, a histopathology laboratory, or a department with organ transplant capabilities) are highly specialized. Of course, it really depends upon one's situation; if a woman is of child-bearing years, access to genetic counseling services, an obstetrics unit, a neonatal intensive care unit, and a pediatric inpatient unit may be extremely important.

See the listing entitled "Hospital Services"; it provides the list of 54 hospital services from the AHA.

Quality Care—What's a Consumer To Do?

Many hospitals, pressured by public and private cost-containment efforts, have had to slash services and staff. At the same time, hospitals remain critically short of qualified nurses. No wonder the quality of care is such a concern today. Since it's just about impossible to measure quality of care in any statistical way, how do we judge the skills of a doctor or hospital? Accreditation, with certain caveats, is one way.

Hospital Accreditation

JCAH is the private non-profit body that investigates and certifies hospitals. The JCAH certification determines which hospitals are eligible for federal funds or

Hospital Services

The American Hospital Association (AHA) classifies hospital services into 54 categories.

Alcoholism/chemical dependency inpatient unit
Alcoholism/chemical dependency outpatient unit
Ambulatory surgery services
Birthing room
Blood bank
Burn care unit
Cardiac catheterization laboratory
CT scanner
Day hospital
Diagnostic radioisotope facility
Emergency department
Extracorporeal shock wave lithotripter
Family planning services
Genetic counseling
Geriatric services
Health promotion services
Hemodialysis
Histopathology laboratory
Home care program
Hospice
Hospital auxiliary
Intensive care (mixed or other)
Intensive care (cardiac only)
Magnetic resonance imaging
Megavoltage radiation therapy
Neonatal intensive care unit
Obstetrics
Occupational therapy services
Open-heart surgery facility
Organ transplant
Organized outpatient department
Patient representative services
Pediatric inpatient unit
Physical therapy services
Post-operative recovery room
Psychiatric inpatient services
Psychiatric partial hospitalization program
Psychiatric emergency services
Psychiatric education services
Psychiatric consultation-liaison services
Radioactive implants
Recreational therapy
Rehabilitation inpatient unit
Rehabilitation outpatient services
Respiratory therapy services
Self-care unit
Skilled nursing or other long-term care facility
Speech pathology services
Therapeutic radioisotope facility
Trauma center
Ultasound
Volunteer services department
Women's center
X-ray radiation therapy

Source: American Hospital Association, *Guide to the Health Care Field*, 1989.

state licensure. The commission came under question recently, however, when federal investigations found that 156 JCAH-accredited hospitals in 30 states had serious deficiencies in at least one area of operation. Texas, the state with the most hospitals on this list, had

50 hospitals that were accredited but were found to be deficient in some area by federal standards. At least two hospitals in New York continued to operate under the JCAH-accredited designation for two years after the JCAH had investigated them and found them deficient.

Since JCAH assessments have been kept confidential, consumers have no way of knowing how to interpret this discrepancy between JCAH findings and those of federal investigators. In other words, a patient could only find out whether or not a hospital was accredited—a questionable indicator of quality, considering the extent of deficiencies found over the past few years.

However, starting in 1989, the JCAH will make public the names of hospitals that provide "risky" or marginal care—400 hospitals, by some estimates. Such hospitals will in the future be given a probationary or conditional accreditation, an indication to patients or physicians that serious problems were found. Although stopping short of making actual inspection reports public, the new JCAH rating will give consumers somewhat more to go on.

A hospital has incentives to qualify for accreditation. It makes it easier to recruit doctors and operate residency programs, and it reduces malpractice liability. Now that accreditation status is becoming a more public matter, it may also become a useful tool for attracting patients—the consumers of health care.

SCORING: HEALTH CARE & ENVIRONMENT

It should be understood that what is being judged in this chapter is *health care* in each of America's metro areas, not *health* of the resident population. Moreover, *Places Rated* judges not the quality of health care *services* but health care *supply.*

Keeping these distinctions in mind will help the reader avoid assuming that a low score in this chapter means either (1) that the people in a given place are unhealthy and don't live very long, or (2) that if one were to relocate to this place, basic health care— including even such complex emergency surgery as a coronary bypass—would be unavailable or inferior. Both of these conclusions are incorrect. A low score or rank in this chapter does indicate, however, that the emphasis in that metro area is probably on basic health care and that the latest techniques and equipment, and personnel trained to implement them, are more likely to be found elsewhere.

Affluent, big-city metro areas generally score higher in the rankings than the smaller, poorer metro areas. This doesn't mean that a person cannot receive excellent medical care in a rural clinic or, conversely, experience medical care that is bad enough to be life-threatening in even the finest of big-city hospitals. The quality of medical and nursing care most people receive depends upon a number of factors, including the patient's ability to pay, blind chance, and human error.

Each metro area starts with a base score of zero, to which points are added according to the following criteria:

In the Office-Based Physicians category, metro areas are awarded points not for their number of physicians but rather how available major classifications of physicians are to patients. Access to these different physicians is given a rating of AA, A, B, or C (AA indicating the best access and C the worst), and those ratings translate into a certain number of points for the metro area: 300 for an AA rating, 200 for an A, 100 for a B, and 50 for a C.

1. *General/Family Practitioners.*

A metro area gets a rating of:	if there is one general/family practitioner for every:
AA	3,750 or fewer persons
A	3,751–4,700 persons
B	4,701–6,000 persons
C	6,001 or more persons

2. *Medical Specialists.*

A metro area gets a rating of:	if there is one medical specialist for every:
AA	2,050 or fewer persons
A	2,051–2,700 persons
B	2,701–3,500 persons
C	3,501 or more persons

3. *Surgical Specialists.*

A metro area gets a rating of:	if there is one surgeon for every:
AA	2,000 or fewer persons
A	2,001–2,400 persons
B	2,401–2,900 persons
C	2,900 or more persons

4. *Other Specialists.*

A metro area gets a rating of:	if there is one specialist for every:
AA	2,500 or fewer persons
A	2,501–3,200 persons
B	3,201–3,500 persons
C	3,501 or more persons

As stated earlier, just as not all M.D.s see patients, not all hospitals handle typical illnesses and emergencies. In the Short-Term General Hospital category, *Places Rated* counts only hospitals classified by the AHA as acute-care facilities whose patients stay less than 30 days.

1. *JCAH Accreditation.* Nationally, 91 percent of short-term general hospitals are accredited by the JCAH. While the absence of JCAH accreditation doesn't necessarily mean a facility is substandard, the presence of such accreditation means the hospital has passed rigorous and periodic reviews. Accordingly, each metro-area short-term hospital that is accredited by the JCAH earns 10 points.

2. *AMA Residency.* Nationally, one-third of short-term general hospitals have residency

training programs approved by the American Medical Association's (AMA) Accreditation Council for Graduate Medical Education. Hospitals with no residency program aren't necessarily lagging in quality, but hospitals with such programs tend to be larger urban facilities where the interaction between students and faculty encourages the development and use of the latest techniques, equipment, and therapy. Accordingly, each metro-area hospital with approved residency programs earns 20 points.

3. *Services.* Short-term hospitals annually report the number and type of inpatient and outpatient services they provide to the American Hospital Association. These services range from the typical (intensive care units) to the esoteric (extracorporeal shock wave litho-

tripter). Facilities are awarded stars according to the number of services they offer, as follows:

    1– 4 services, one star (★)
    5–14 services, two stars (★★)
    15–24 services, three stars (★★★)
    25–54 services, four stars (★★★★)

The stars are totaled, and the number of stars per 100,000 residents is added to the score.

4. *CMSA Access.* Each of the 71 metro areas that is part of a Consolidated Metropolitan Statistical Area (CMSA) is eligible for bonus points based on shared amenities: hospitals with AMA residency programs and hospitals offering more than 25 services. A place gets a bonus of 10 percent of the points accumulated by *adjacent* places in the CMSA for these shared amenities.

Rankings: Health Care & Environment

Six criteria are used in arriving at a score for the supply of health care in a metro area: (1) general/family practitioners, (2) medical specialists, (3) surgical specialists, (4) other specialists, (4) hospitals accredited by the JCAH, (5) hospitals approved for physician residency programs by the AMA, and (6) the breadth of hospital services available. Metro areas also earn bonus points for shared assets—teaching hospitals and full-service hospitals—within their CMSA.

Places that receive tie scores are given the same rank and are listed alphabetically.

Metro Areas from Best to Worst

Places Rated Rank	Places Rated Score	Places Rated Rank	Places Rated Score	Places Rated Rank	Places Rated Score
1. Los Angeles–Long Beach, CA	3,330	14. Victoria, TX	2,130	31. Galveston–Texas City, TX	1,998
2. New York, NY	3,215	17. Fargo–Moorhead, ND–MN	2,110	31. Shreveport, LA	1,998
3. Chicago, IL	2,826	18. Newark, NJ	2,104	33. Seattle, WA	1,997
4. Philadelphia, PA–NJ	2,776	19. Ann Arbor, MI	2,092	34. Little Rock–North Little Rock, AR	1,982
5. Boston, MA	2,594	20. Rochester, MN	2,088	35. Pittsburgh, PA	1,961
6. Iowa City, IA	2,290	21. Miami–Hialeah, FL	2,085	36. Albuquerque, NM	1,960
7. San Francisco, CA	2,282	22. Cleveland, OH	2,084	37. New Orleans, LA	1,952
8. Lexington–Fayette, KY	2,224	23. Columbia, MO	2,080	38. Milwaukee, WI	1,950
9. Sioux Falls, SD	2,190	24. Norwalk, CT	2,079	39. Kansas City, MO–KS	1,930
10. Anaheim–Santa Ana, CA	2,170	25. Bismarck, ND	2,070	40. Houston, TX	1,927
11. Stamford, CT	2,149	26. Portland, ME	2,067	41. Nassau–Suffolk, NY	1,922
12. Jackson, MS	2,143	27. Gainesville, FL	2,061	42. Great Falls, MT	1,920
13. Washington, DC–MD–VA	2,139	28. Nashville, TN	2,052	42. Rapid City, SD	1,920
14. Grand Forks, ND	2,130	29. Oakland, CA	2,026	44. Santa Barbara–Santa Maria–Lompoc, CA	1,919
14. Lubbock, TX	2,130	30. La Crosse, WI	2,010		

Places Rated Rank	Places Rated Score
45. Asheville, NC	1,917
46. Madison, WI	1,910
47. Baltimore, MD	1,897
48. Chico, CA	1,890
48. Worcester, MA	1,890
50. Santa Fe, NM	1,889
51. Portland, OR	1,883
52. Toledo, OH	1,871
52. Trenton, NJ	1,871
54. Medford, OR	1,869
55. Champaign–Urbana–Rantoul, IL	1,867
56. Reno, NV	1,847
57. Birmingham, AL	1,846
58. Minneapolis–St. Paul, MN–WI	1,841
59. San Diego, CA	1,833
60. St. Louis, MO–IL	1,832
61. Omaha, NE–IA	1,831
62. Danbury, CT	1,830
63. Richmond–Petersburg, VA	1,822
64. Amarillo, TX	1,820
64. Duluth, MN–WI	1,820
66. Roanoke, VA	1,812
67. Raleigh–Durham, NC	1,808
68. Tyler, TX	1,805
69. Pittsfield, MA	1,801
70. Bangor, ME	1,770
70. Fayetteville–Springdale, AR	1,770
72. Burlington, VT	1,768
73. Williamsport, PA	1,760
74. Texarkana, TX–Texarkana, AR	1,758
75. Bridgeport–Milford, CT	1,748
76. Cumberland, MD–WV	1,740
77. Detroit, MI	1,739
78. Eau Claire, WI	1,730
79. Spokane, WA	1,726
80. Charlottesville, VA	1,717
81. Wichita, KS	1,715
82. Wichita Falls, TX	1,714
83. Phoenix, AZ	1,709
84. Bergen–Passaic, NJ	1,705
85. Denver, CO	1,704
86. Salem–Gloucester, MA	1,698
86. Tucson, AZ	1,698
88. Wheeling, WV–OH	1,688
89. Jackson, TN	1,687
90. San Angelo, TX	1,680
91. Louisville, KY–IN	1,679
92. Cheyenne, WY	1,670
93. Dallas, TX	1,668
94. Enid, OK	1,660
95. Albany–Schenectady–Troy, NY	1,651
96. Florence, SC	1,650
97. Dubuque, IA	1,648
98. Sherman–Denison, TX	1,646
99. Oklahoma City, OK	1,641
100. Alexandria, LA	1,640
100. Lewiston–Auburn, ME	1,640
102. Waterloo–Cedar Falls, IA	1,630

Places Rated Rank	Places Rated Score
103. Kalamazoo, MI	1,629
104. Cincinnati, OH–KY–IN	1,620
105. Scranton–Wilkes-Barre, PA	1,618
106. Atlanta, GA	1,617
107. New Haven–Meriden, CT	1,609
108. New Britain, CT	1,606
109. Tampa–St. Petersburg–Clearwater, FL	1,605
110. San Jose, CA	1,604
111. Sacramento, CA	1,602
112. Corpus Christi, TX	1,601
113. Springfield, MO	1,597
114. Redding, CA	1,596
115. Anchorage, AK	1,590
116. Indianapolis, IN	1,587
117. Lake County, IL	1,584
118. West Palm Beach–Boca Raton–Delray Beach, FL	1,583
119. Charleston, WV	1,581
120. Santa Rosa–Petaluma, CA	1,575
121. Altoona, PA	1,570
121. Norfolk–Virginia Beach–Newport News, VA	1,570
123. Lafayette–West Lafayette, IN	1,563
124. Fort Lauderdale–Hollywood–Pompano Beach, FL	1,556
125. Sarasota, FL	1,553
126. Monroe, LA	1,551
127. Topeka, KS	1,546
128. Elmira, NY	1,543
129. Springfield, IL	1,542
130. Hartford, CT	1,537
131. Abilene, TX	1,534
132. Memphis, TN–AR–MS	1,517
133. Wilmington, NC	1,503
134. Knoxville, TN	1,502
135. Allentown–Bethlehem, PA–NJ	1,499
136. Augusta, GA–SC	1,492
136. Riverside–San Bernardino, CA	1,492
138. Dothan, AL	1,490
139. Charleston, SC	1,488
139. Manchester, NH	1,488
141. Nashua, NH	1,486
142. Jacksonville, FL	1,481
142. Kenosha, WI	1,481
144. Kokomo, IN	1,480
145. Vineland–Millville–Bridgeton, NJ	1,475
146. Billings, MT	1,470
147. Orange County, NY	1,464
147. Oxnard–Ventura, CA	1,464
149. Chattanooga, TN–GA	1,459
150. Modesto, CA	1,458
151. Lawrence–Haverhill, MA–NH	1,451
151. Lincoln, NE	1,451
153. Middletown, CT	1,439
154. Boulder–Longmont, CO	1,424
154. Johnson City–Kingsport–Bristol, TN–VA	1,424
156. Salt Lake City–Ogden, UT	1,422

Places Rated Rank	Places Rated Score
157. Pawtucket–Woonsocket–Attleboro, RI–MA	1,417
158. Rockford, IL	1,409
159. Bloomington–Normal, IL	1,408
160. Savannah, GA	1,402
161. Sioux City, IA–NE	1,400
162. Buffalo, NY	1,397
163. Columbia, SC	1,395
164. Macon–Warner Robins, GA	1,388
165. Fitchburg–Leominster, MA	1,385
166. Waterbury, CT	1,381
167. Fresno, CA	1,378
168. Lima, OH	1,373
169. Eugene–Springfield, OR	1,372
170. Pueblo, CO	1,369
170. Rochester, NY	1,369
172. San Antonio, TX	1,364
173. Lake Charles, LA	1,361
174. Biloxi–Gulfport, MS	1,360
175. Evansville, IN–KY	1,359
176. Sheboygan, WI	1,354
177. Fort Smith, AR–OK	1,352
178. Glens Falls, NY	1,342
178. Huntington–Ashland, WV–KY–OH	1,342
178. Pensacola, FL	1,342
181. Honolulu, HI	1,341
182. Santa Cruz, CA	1,338
183. Des Moines, IA	1,334
184. Killeen–Temple, TX	1,333
185. South Bend–Mishawaka, IN	1,329
186. Fort Wayne, IN	1,322
187. Jersey City, NJ	1,320
188. Anniston, AL	1,319
189. Bristol, CT	1,315
189. Providence, RI	1,315
191. Montgomery, AL	1,310
192. Anderson, IN	1,309
193. Erie, PA	1,306
193. Johnstown, PA	1,306
195. Sharon, PA	1,301
196. Monmouth–Ocean, NJ	1,298
197. Benton Harbor, MI	1,296
197. Wilmington, DE–NJ–MD	1,296
199. Longview–Marshall, TX	1,292
200. Owensboro, KY	1,291
201. Tuscaloosa, AL	1,287
202. Kankakee, IL	1,286
203. Beaumont–Port Arthur, TX	1,285
204. St. Cloud, MN	1,280
205. Peoria, IL	1,279
206. Joplin, MO	1,270
207. Richland–Kennewick–Pasco, WA	1,266
208. Daytona Beach, FL	1,257
209. Dayton–Springfield, OH	1,253
210. Syracuse, NY	1,252
211. Bellingham, WA	1,248
211. Lafayette, LA	1,248
213. Middlesex–Somerset–Hunterdon, NJ	1,247
214. Harrisburg–Lebanon–Carlisle, PA	1,242

Places Rated Rank	Places Rated Score	Places Rated Rank	Places Rated Score	Places Rated Rank	Places Rated Score
215. Vallejo–Fairfield–Napa, CA	1,241	256. Merced, CA	1,083	294. Portsmouth–Dover– Rochester, NH–ME	909
		257. New London–Norwich, CT–RI	1,075	295. Flint, MI	897
216. Battle Creek, MI	1,240	258. Steubenville–Weirton, OH–WV	1,070		
216. Lawton, OK	1,240	259. Mansfield, OH	1,069	296. Grand Rapids, MI	896
218. Hickory, NC	1,239	260. Albany, GA	1,067	297. Wausau, WI	886
219. St. Joseph, MO	1,236			298. Youngstown–Warren, OH	880
219. Tulsa, OK	1,236	261. Florence, AL	1,066	299. Clarksville–Hopkinsville, TN–KY	878
		262. Muskegon, MI	1,064	300. Brazoria, TX	876
221. Fort Collins–Loveland, CO	1,230	263. Racine, WI	1,060		
222. Orlando, FL	1,226	264. Bloomington, IN	1,053	301. Pine Bluff, AR	874
222. Parkersburg–Marietta, WV–OH	1,226	265. Visalia–Tulare–Porterville, CA	1,047	302. Elkhart–Goshen, IN	868
224. Greensboro–Winston-Salem– High Point, NC	1,223			303. Canton, OH	855
225. Columbus, OH	1,219	266. Utica–Rome, NY	1,046	304. Midland, TX	849
		267. Yuba City, CA	1,045	305. Provo–Orem, UT	837
226. Boise City, ID	1,209	268. State College, PA	1,044		
227. Tallahassee, FL	1,209	269. Naples, FL	1,039	306. Anderson, SC	814
228. Springfield, MA	1,206	270. Lorain–Elyria, OH	1,033	307. Muncie, IN	811
229. Bradenton, FL	1,202			308. Fall River, MA–RI	807
230. Casper, WY	1,194	271. Saginaw–Bay City– Midland, MI	1,030	309. Hamilton–Middletown, OH	805
		272. Columbus, GA–AL	1,028	310. Baton Rouge, LA	802
231. Yakima, WA	1,185	273. Tacoma, WA	1,024		
232. Athens, GA	1,177	274. Fort Worth–Arlington, TX	1,022	310. York, PA	802
233. Lynchburg, VA	1,176	275. Colorado Springs, CO	1,018	312. Atlantic City, NJ	796
234. Davenport–Rock Island–Moline, IA–IL	1,174			313. New Bedford, MA	792
234. Gadsden, AL	1,174	276. Melbourne–Titusville–Palm Bay, FL	1,016	314. Beaver County, PA	783
		277. Binghamton, NY	1,010	314. Fayetteville, NC	783
236. Aurora–Elgin, IL	1,171	278. Salinas–Seaside–Monterey, CA	1,000	316. Jacksonville, NC	773
237. Fort Myers–Cape Coral, FL	1,170	279. Decatur, IL	991	317. Bryan–College Station, TX	767
238. Green Bay, WI	1,168	280. Lansing–East Lansing, MI	988	318. Pascagoula, MS	766
239. Decatur, AL	1,157			319. Brownsville–Harlingen, TX	756
240. Poughkeepsie, NY	1,155	281. Huntsville, AL	973	320. Greeley, CO	750
		282. Bakersfield, CA	966		
241. Burlington, NC	1,154	283. Bremerton, WA	963	321. McAllen–Edinburg–Mission, TX	747
242. Mobile, AL	1,152	283. Reading, PA	963	322. Lawrence, KS	735
243. Austin, TX	1,151	285. El Paso, TX	962	323. Joliet, IL	718
244. Gary–Hammond, IN	1,141			324. Charlotte–Gastonia–Rock Hill, NC–SC	711
245. Greenville–Spartanburg, SC	1,139	286. Houma–Thibodaux, LA	957	324. Hagerstown, MD	711
		287. Lancaster, PA	942		
246. Olympia, WA	1,137	288. Akron, OH	938	326. Jackson, MI	666
247. Cedar Rapids, IA	1,134	289. Salem, OR	922	327. Brockton, MA	637
248. Appleton–Oshkosh–Neenah, WI	1,111	290. Fort Pierce, FL	916	328. Laredo, TX	634
249. Fort Walton Beach, FL	1,109			329. Las Cruces, NM	604
250. Lowell, MA–NH	1,105	291. Janesville–Beloit, WI	911	330. Danville, VA	602
		291. Lakeland–Winter Haven, FL	911		
251. Waco, TX	1,103	291. Las Vegas, NV	911	331. Ocala, FL	562
252. Panama City, FL	1,098			332. Vancouver, WA	546
253. Terre Haute, IN	1,096			333. Odessa, TX	505
254. Stockton, CA	1,095				
255. Niagara Falls, NY	1,093				

Place Profiles: Health Care & Environment

In the pages that follow, selected health care assets of the 333 metro areas are detailed.

Under the heading **Office-Based Physicians** are groupings by professional activity of local doctors who maintain offices and treat patients. The access rating for each group (AA, A, B, or C) is shown in the right-hand column. For 12 New England metro areas, no figures are available; in these cases, summary figures for their core counties are used in place of cities and towns.

To the right of the heading **Short-Term General**

Hospitals is the number of acute-care hospitals and their total number of beds. Under this heading are the number of facilities accredited by the JCAH, the number approved for physician residency training by the AMA, and the number grouped by range of services offered. A single star (★) indicates 1–4 services, two stars (★★) indicate 5–14 services, three (★★★) stars mean 15–24 services, and four stars (★★★★) indicate 25 or more services.

The information is derived from two sources: American Medical Association, *Physician Characteristics and Distribution in the United States*, 1988; and American Hospital Association, *Guide to the Health Care Field*, 1989.

A star (★) in front of a metro area's name highlights it as one of the top 30 places for health care.

Rating

Abilene, TX
Office-Based Physicians
General/Family Practitioners: 28	A
Medical Specialists: 51	A
Surgical Specialists: 50	B
Other Specialists: 40	A

Short-Term General Hospitals: 3 (625 beds)
JCAH Accredited: 2
AMA Residency: 1
Services: 2 ★★★, 1 ★★★★
Places Rated Score: 1,534   Places Rated Rank: 131

Akron, OH
Office-Based Physicians
General/Family Practitioners: 126	B
Medical Specialists: 206	B
Surgical Specialists: 230	B
Other Specialists: 180	B

Short-Term General Hospitals: 6 (2,133 beds)
JCAH Accredited: 5
AMA Residency: 5
Services: 2 ★★★, 4 ★★★★
CMSA Access: Cleveland–Akron–Lorain, OH (47 points)
Places Rated Score: 938   Places Rated Rank: 288

Albany, GA
Office-Based Physicians
General/Family Practitioners: 11	C
Medical Specialists: 40	B
Surgical Specialists: 53	A
Other Specialists: 33	B

Short-Term General Hospitals: 2 (586 beds)
JCAH Accredited: 2
Services: 1 ★★★, 1 ★★★★
Places Rated Score: 1,067   Places Rated Rank: 260

Albany–Schenectady–Troy, NY
Office-Based Physicians
General/Family Practitioners: 149	B
Medical Specialists: 425	AA
Surgical Specialists: 376	A
Other Specialists: 307	A

Short-Term General Hospitals: 15 (4,156 beds)
JCAH Accredited: 15
AMA Residency: 6
Services: 2 ★★, 7 ★★★, 6 ★★★★
Places Rated Score: 1,651   Places Rated Rank: 95

Albuquerque, NM
Office-Based Physicians
General/Family Practitioners: 98	B
Medical Specialists: 270	AA
Surgical Specialists: 246	AA
Other Specialists: 243	AA

Short-Term General Hospitals: 12 (2,213 beds)
JCAH Accredited: 8
AMA Residency: 5
Services: 2 ★, 5 ★★★, 5 ★★★★
Places Rated Score: 1,960   Places Rated Rank: 36

Alexandria, LA
Office-Based Physicians
General/Family Practitioners: 22	C
Medical Specialists: 44	B
Surgical Specialists: 71	AA
Other Specialists: 35	B

Short-Term General Hospitals: 6 (1,210 beds)
JCAH Accredited: 5
AMA Residency: 2
Services: 1 ★, 2 ★★, 1 ★★★, 2 ★★★★
Places Rated Score: 1,640   Places Rated Rank: 100

Allentown–Bethlehem, PA–NJ
Office-Based Physicians
General/Family Practitioners: 147	A
Medical Specialists: 248	A
Surgical Specialists: 286	A
Other Specialists: 172	B

Short-Term General Hospitals: 11 (2,723 beds)
JCAH Accredited: 10
AMA Residency: 6
Services: 1 ★, 3 ★★★, 7 ★★★★
Places Rated Score: 1,499   Places Rated Rank: 135

Altoona, PA
Office-Based Physicians
General/Family Practitioners: 40	AA
Medical Specialists: 42	B
Surgical Specialists: 41	C
Other Specialists: 31	C

Short-Term General Hospitals: 5 (802 beds)
JCAH Accredited: 5
AMA Residency: 1
Services: 1 ★★, 2 ★★★, 2 ★★★★
Places Rated Score: 1,570   Places Rated Rank: 121

Amarillo, TX
Office-Based Physicians
General/Family Practitioners: 35	B
Medical Specialists: 74	A
Surgical Specialists: 89	A
Other Specialists: 64	A

Short-Term General Hospitals: 6 (1,242 beds)
JCAH Accredited: 4
AMA Residency: 4
Services: 2 ★★, 1 ★★★, 3 ★★★★
Places Rated Score: 1,820   Places Rated Rank: 64

★ Anaheim–Santa Ana, CA
Office-Based Physicians
General/Family Practitioners: 707	AA
Medical Specialists: 1,163	AA
Surgical Specialists: 1,125	AA
Other Specialists: 1,092	AA

Short-Term General Hospitals: 35 (6,291 beds)
JCAH Accredited: 34
AMA Residency: 3
Services: 6 ★, 2 ★★, 15 ★★★, 12 ★★★★
CMSA Access: Los Angeles–Anaheim–Riverside, CA (95 points)
Places Rated Score: 2,170   Places Rated Rank: 10

Rating   Rating

Anchorage, AK
Office-Based Physicians
   General/Family Practitioners: 172   AA
   Medical Specialists: 145   C
   Surgical Specialists: 165   C
   Other Specialists: 125   C
Short-Term General Hospitals: 25 (1,679 beds)
   JCAH Accredited: 14
   Services: 4 ★, 12 ★★, 7 ★★★, 2 ★★★★
Places Rated Score: 1,590   Places Rated Rank: 115

Anderson, IN
Office-Based Physicians
   General/Family Practitioners: 41   AA
   Medical Specialists: 21   C
   Surgical Specialists: 30   C
   Other Specialists: 26   C
Short-Term General Hospitals: 3 (627 beds)
   JCAH Accredited: 3
   Services: 1 ★★★, 2 ★★★★
Places Rated Score: 1,309   Places Rated Rank: 192

Anderson, SC
Office-Based Physicians
   General/Family Practitioners: 45   AA
   Medical Specialists: 32   C
   Surgical Specialists: 39   C
   Other Specialists: 40   B
Short-Term General Hospital: 1 (430 beds)
   JCAH Accredited: 1
   AMA Residency: 1
   Services: 1 ★★★★
Places Rated Score: 814   Places Rated Rank: 306

★ Ann Arbor, MI
Office-Based Physicians
   General/Family Practitioners: 57   A
   Medical Specialists: 228   AA
   Surgical Specialists: 178   AA
   Other Specialists: 299   AA
Short-Term General Hospitals: 6 (2,222 beds)
   JCAH Accredited: 6
   AMA Residency: 4
   Services: 1 ★, 2 ★★★, 3 ★★★★
CMSA Access: Detroit–Ann Arbor, MI (138 points)
Places Rated Score: 2,092   Places Rated Rank: 19

Anniston, AL
Office-Based Physicians
   General/Family Practitioners: 21   B
   Medical Specialists: 24   C
   Surgical Specialists: 40   C
   Other Specialists: 31   B
Short-Term General Hospitals: 5 (632 beds)
   JCAH Accredited: 3
   AMA Residency: 1
   Services: 1 ★, 2 ★★, 1 ★★★, 1 ★★★★
Places Rated Score: 1,319   Places Rated Rank: 188

Appleton–Oshkosh–Neenah, WI
Office-Based Physicians
   General/Family Practitioners: 77   A
   Medical Specialists: 87   C
   Surgical Specialists: 101   C
   Other Specialists: 86   B
Short-Term General Hospitals: 6 (1,081 beds)
   JCAH Accredited: 5
   AMA Residency: 3
   Services: 1 ★★, 1 ★★★, 4 ★★★★
Places Rated Score: 1,111   Places Rated Rank: 248

Asheville, NC
Office-Based Physicians
   General/Family Practitioners: 48   AA
   Medical Specialists: 93   AA

   Surgical Specialists: 96   AA
   Other Specialists: 72   AA
Short-Term General Hospitals: 3 (1,221 beds)
   JCAH Accredited: 3
   AMA Residency: 2
   Services: 1 ★★★, 2 ★★★★
Places Rated Score: 1,917   Places Rated Rank: 45

Athens, GA
Office-Based Physicians
   General/Family Practitioners: 30   B
   Medical Specialists: 39   C
   Surgical Specialists: 61   A
   Other Specialists: 37   B
Short-Term General Hospitals: 3 (634 beds)
   JCAH Accredited: 2
   Services: 1 ★★, 2 ★★★★
Places Rated Score: 1,177   Places Rated Rank: 232

Atlanta, GA
Office-Based Physicians
   General/Family Practitioners: 329   C
   Medical Specialists: 1,203   A
   Surgical Specialists: 1,134   A
   Other Specialists: 972   A
Short-Term General Hospitals: 42 (9,636 beds)
   JCAH Accredited: 39
   AMA Residency: 7
   Services: 8 ★, 9 ★★, 14 ★★★, 11 ★★★★
Places Rated Score: 1,617   Places Rated Rank: 106

Atlantic City, NJ
Office-Based Physicians
   General/Family Practitioners: 43   C
   Medical Specialists: 114   A
   Surgical Specialists: 115   B
   Other Specialists: 69   C
Short-Term General Hospitals: 4 (1,255 beds)
   JCAH Accredited: 4
   AMA Residency: 1
   Services: 1 ★, 1 ★★, 1 ★★★, 1 ★★★★
Places Rated Score: 796   Places Rated Rank: 312

Augusta, GA–SC
Office-Based Physicians
   General/Family Practitioners: 60   C
   Medical Specialists: 178   A
   Surgical Specialists: 188   A
   Other Specialists: 136   A
Short-Term General Hospitals: 7 (3,498 beds)
   JCAH Accredited: 7
   AMA Residency: 4
   Services: 1 ★★★, 6 ★★★★
Places Rated Score: 1,492   Places Rated Rank: 136

Aurora–Elgin, IL
Office-Based Physicians
   General/Family Practitioners: 53   C
   Medical Specialists: 110   B
   Surgical Specialists: 132   B
   Other Specialists: 78   C
Short-Term General Hospitals: 5 (1,447 beds)
   JCAH Accredited: 5
   Services: 5 ★★★★
CMSA Access: Chicago–Gary–Lake County,
   IL–IN–WI (238 points)
Places Rated Score: 1,171   Places Rated Rank: 236

Austin, TX
Office-Based Physicians
   General/Family Practitioners: 157   A
   Medical Specialists: 264   B
   Surgical Specialists: 289   B
   Other Specialists: 245   A
Short-Term General Hospitals: 10 (1,719 beds)

Rating

Rating

JCAH Accredited: 9
AMA Residency: 1
Services: 1 ★★, 6 ★★★, 3 ★★★★
Places Rated Score: 1,151   Places Rated Rank: 243

Bakersfield, CA
Office-Based Physicians
  General/Family Practitioners: 89   B
  Medical Specialists: 144   B
  Surgical Specialists: 137   C
  Other Specialists: 98   C
Short-Term General Hospitals: 12 (1,315 beds)
  JCAH Accredited: 10
  AMA Residency: 1
  Services: 3 ★, 4 ★★, 4 ★★★, 1 ★★★★
Places Rated Score: 966   Places Rated Rank: 282

Baltimore, MD
Office-Based Physicians
  General/Family Practitioners: 362   C
  Medical Specialists: 1,338   AA
  Surgical Specialists: 1,191   AA
  Other Specialists: 987   AA
Short-Term General Hospitals: 27 (8,942 beds)
  JCAH Accredited: 27
  AMA Residency: 15
  Services: 4 ★, 1 ★★, 8 ★★★, 14 ★★★★
Places Rated Score: 1,897   Places Rated Rank: 47

Bangor, ME
Office-Based Physicians
  General/Family Practitioners: 43   A
  Medical Specialists: 67   A
  Surgical Specialists: 59   B
  Other Specialists: 56   A
Short-Term General Hospitals: 6 (776 beds)
  JCAH Accredited: 5
  AMA Residency: 1
  Services: 3 ★★, 1 ★★★, 2 ★★★★
Places Rated Score: 1,770   Places Rated Rank: 70

Baton Rouge, LA
Office-Based Physicians
  General/Family Practitioners: 103   B
  Medical Specialists: 186   B
  Surgical Specialists: 223   B
  Other Specialists: 149   B
Short-Term General Hospitals: 8 (1,627 beds)
  JCAH Accredited: 7
  AMA Residency: 1
  Services: 3 ★, 2 ★★, 2 ★★★, 1 ★★★★
Places Rated Score: 802   Places Rated Rank: 310

Battle Creek, MI
Office-Based Physicians
  General/Family Practitioners: 22   C
  Medical Specialists: 36   C
  Surgical Specialists: 44   C
  Other Specialists: 35   B
Short-Term General Hospitals: 4 (554 beds)
  JCAH Accredited: 4
  Services: 3 ★★★, 1 ★★★★
Places Rated Score: 1,240   Places Rated Rank: 216

Beaumont–Port Arthur, TX
Office-Based Physicians
  General/Family Practitioners: 96   A
  Medical Specialists: 106   C
  Surgical Specialists: 133   B
  Other Specialists: 97   B
Short-Term General Hospitals: 9 (2,012 beds)
  JCAH Accredited: 7
  AMA Residency: 1
  Services: 2 ★★, 4 ★★★, 3 ★★★★
Places Rated Score: 1,285   Places Rated Rank: 203

Beaver County, PA
Office-Based Physicians
  General/Family Practitioners: 37   B
  Medical Specialists: 38   C
  Surgical Specialists: 44   C
  Other Specialists: 25   C
Short-Term General Hospitals: 2 (669 beds)
  JCAH Accredited: 2
  AMA Residency: 1
  Services: 1 ★★★, 1 ★★★★
CMSA Access: Pittsburgh–Beaver County, PA (131 points)
Places Rated Score: 783   Places Rated Rank: 314

Bellingham, WA
Office-Based Physicians
  General/Family Practitioners: 35   AA
  Medical Specialists: 40   B
  Surgical Specialists: 43   B
  Other Specialists: 36   A
Short-Term General Hospitals: 2 (234 beds)
  JCAH Accredited: 2
  Services: 2 ★★★
Places Rated Score: 1,248   Places Rated Rank: 211

Benton Harbor, MI
Office-Based Physicians
  General/Family Practitioners: 37   A
  Medical Specialists: 43   C
  Surgical Specialists: 50   C
  Other Specialists: 42   B
Short-Term General Hospitals: 5 (814 beds)
  JCAH Accredited: 4
  Services: 2 ★★, 2 ★★★, 1 ★★★★
Places Rated Score: 1,296   Places Rated Rank: 197

Bergen–Passaic, NJ
Office-Based Physicians
  General/Family Practitioners: 188   C
  Medical Specialists: 913   AA
  Surgical Specialists: 677   AA
  Other Specialists: 597   AA
Short-Term General Hospitals: 13 (4,126 beds)
  JCAH Accredited: 13
  AMA Residency: 4
  Services: 1 ★, 3 ★★★, 9 ★★★★
CMSA Access: New York–Northern NJ–Long
  Island, NY–NJ–CT (191 points)
Places Rated Score: 1,705   Places Rated Rank: 84

Billings, MT
Office-Based Physicians
  General/Family Practitioners: 19   C
  Medical Specialists: 66   AA
  Surgical Specialists: 76   AA
  Other Specialists: 60   AA
Short-Term General Hospitals: 2 (562 beds)
  JCAH Accredited: 2
  Services: 2 ★★★
Places Rated Score: 1,470   Places Rated Rank: 146

Biloxi–Gulfport, MS
Office-Based Physicians
  General/Family Practitioners: 31   C
  Medical Specialists: 53   C
  Surgical Specialists: 77   B
  Other Specialists: 48   C
Short-Term General Hospitals: 7 (1,724 beds)
  JCAH Accredited: 7
  AMA Residency: 2
  Services: 1 ★★, 2 ★★★, 4 ★★★★
Places Rated Score: 1,360   Places Rated Rank: 174

Binghamton, NY
Office-Based Physicians
  General/Family Practitioners: 42   C
  Medical Specialists: 104   A

Rating

Surgical Specialists: 110 — **A**
Other Specialists: 74 — **B**
Short-Term General Hospitals: 3 (1,133 beds)
  JCAH Accredited: 2
  AMA Residency: 1
  Services: 1 ★★★, 2 ★★★★
Places Rated Score: 1,010   Places Rated Rank: 277

Birmingham, AL
Office-Based Physicians
  General/Family Practitioners: 154 — **B**
  Medical Specialists: 477 — **AA**
  Surgical Specialists: 467 — **AA**
  Other Specialists: 313 — **A**
Short-Term General Hospitals: 18 (5,383 beds)
  JCAH Accredited: 16
  AMA Residency: 8
  Services: 5 ★★, 5 ★★★, 8 ★★★★
Places Rated Score: 1,846   Places Rated Rank: 57

★ Bismarck, ND
Office-Based Physicians
  General/Family Practitioners: 18 — **B**
  Medical Specialists: 48 — **AA**
  Surgical Specialists: 51 — **AA**
  Other Specialists: 40 — **AA**
Short-Term General Hospitals: 3 (600 beds)
  JCAH Accredited: 3
  AMA Residency: 2
  Services: 1 ★★★, 2 ★★★★
Places Rated Score: 2,070   Places Rated Rank: 25

Bloomington, IN
Office-Based Physicians
  General/Family Practitioners: 29 — **AA**
  Medical Specialists: 31 — **B**
  Surgical Specialists: 33 — **C**
  Other Specialists: 39 — **A**
Short-Term General Hospital: 1 (301 beds)
  JCAH Accredited: 1
  Services: 1 ★★★★
Places Rated Score: 1,053   Places Rated Rank: 264

Bloomington–Normal, IL
Office-Based Physicians
  General/Family Practitioners: 24 — **B**
  Medical Specialists: 47 — **A**
  Surgical Specialists: 41 — **C**
  Other Specialists: 27 — **C**
Short-Term General Hospitals: 3 (602 beds)
  JCAH Accredited: 3
  Services: 3 ★★★★
Places Rated Score: 1,408   Places Rated Rank: 159

Boise City, ID
Office-Based Physicians
  General/Family Practitioners: 40 — **B**
  Medical Specialists: 70 — **B**
  Surgical Specialists: 94 — **A**
  Other Specialists: 60 — **B**
Short-Term General Hospitals: 3 (732 beds)
  JCAH Accredited: 3
  AMA Residency: 3
  Services: 3 ★★★★
Places Rated Score: 1,209   Places Rated Rank: 226

★ Boston, MA
Office-Based Physicians
  General/Family Practitioners: 422 — **C**
  Medical Specialists: 2,351 — **AA**
  Surgical Specialists: 1,717 — **AA**
  Other Specialists: 2,018 — **AA**
Short-Term General Hospitals: 58 (15,578 beds)
  JCAH Accredited: 57
  AMA Residency: 22

Rating

Services: 2 ★, 6 ★★, 10 ★★★, 40 ★★★★
CMSA Access: Boston–Lawrence–Salem, MA–NH (12 points)
Places Rated Score: 2,594   Places Rated Rank: 5

Boulder–Longmont, CO
Office-Based Physicians
  General/Family Practitioners: 71 — **AA**
  Medical Specialists: 71 — **B**
  Surgical Specialists: 74 — **B**
  Other Specialists: 94 — **AA**
Short-Term General Hospitals: 3 (354 beds)
  JCAH Accredited: 3
  Services: 1 ★★★, 2 ★★★★
CMSA Access: Denver–Boulder, CO (81 points)
Places Rated Score: 1,424   Places Rated Rank: 154

Bradenton, FL
Office-Based Physicians
  General/Family Practitioners: 52 — **AA**
  Medical Specialists: 70 — **A**
  Surgical Specialists: 74 — **A**
  Other Specialists: 57 — **A**
Short-Term General Hospitals: 2 (895 beds)
  JCAH Accredited: 2
  Services: 1 ★, 1 ★★★★
Places Rated Score: 1,202   Places Rated Rank: 229

Brazoria, TX
Office-Based Physicians
  General/Family Practitioners: 36 — **B**
  Medical Specialists: 25 — **C**
  Surgical Specialists: 19 — **C**
  Other Specialists: 19 — **C**
Short-Term General Hospitals: 4 (340 beds)
  JCAH Accredited: 3
  Services: 3 ★★, 1 ★★★
CMSA Access: Houston–Galveston–Brazoria, TX (119 points)
Places Rated Score: 876   Places Rated Rank: 300

Bremerton, WA
Office-Based Physicians
  General/Family Practitioners: 45 — **A**
  Medical Specialists: 50 — **B**
  Surgical Specialists: 44 — **C**
  Other Specialists: 42 — **B**
Short-Term General Hospitals: 2 (350 beds)
  JCAH Accredited: 2
  AMA Residency: 1
  Services: 2 ★★★★
Places Rated Score: 963   Places Rated Rank: 283

Bridgeport–Milford, CT
Office-Based Physicians
  General/Family Practitioners: 125 — **C**
  Medical Specialists: 567 — **AA**
  Surgical Specialists: 426 — **AA**
  Other Specialists: 338 — **AA**
Short-Term General Hospitals: 8 (2,578 beds)
  JCAH Accredited: 8
  AMA Residency: 7
  Services: 8 ★★★★
CMSA Access: New York–Northern NJ–Long
  Island, NY–NJ–CT (188 points)
Places Rated Score: 1,748   Places Rated Rank: 75

Bristol, CT
Office-Based Physicians
  General/Family Practitioners: 29 — **B**
  Medical Specialists: 73 — **A**
  Surgical Specialists: 51 — **C**
  Other Specialists: 49 — **B**
Short-Term General Hospitals: 4 (415 beds)
  JCAH Accredited: 4
  Services: 1 ★★, 2 ★★★, 1 ★★★★

CMSA Access: Hartford–New Britain–Middletown,
  CT (85 points)
Places Rated Score: 1,315   Places Rated Rank: 189

Brockton, MA
Office-Based Physicians
  General/Family Practitioners: 52   C
  Medical Specialists: 136   B
  Surgical Specialists: 115   C
  Other Specialists: 85   C
Short-Term General Hospitals: 2 (581 beds)
  JCAH Accredited: 2
  AMA Residency: 2
  Services: 2 ★★★★
CMSA Access: Boston–Lawrence–Salem, MA–NH (138 points)
Places Rated Score: 637   Places Rated Rank: 327

Brownsville–Harlingen, TX
Office-Based Physicians
  General/Family Practitioners: 32   C
  Medical Specialists: 77   B
  Surgical Specialists: 69   C
  Other Specialists: 38   C
Short-Term General Hospitals: 4 (669 beds)
  JCAH Accredited: 4
  Services: 1 ★★, 2 ★★★, 1 ★★★★
Places Rated Score: 756   Places Rated Rank: 319

Bryan–College Station, TX
Office-Based Physicians
  General/Family Practitioners: 22   B
  Medical Specialists: 32   C
  Surgical Specialists: 35   C
  Other Specialists: 22   C
Short-Term General Hospitals: 2 (232 beds)
  JCAH Accredited: 2
  Services: 2 ★★★
Places Rated Score: 767   Places Rated Rank: 317

Buffalo, NY
Office-Based Physicians
  General/Family Practitioners: 149   C
  Medical Specialists: 504   AA
  Surgical Specialists: 472   A
  Other Specialists: 311   A
Short-Term General Hospitals: 14 (5,297 beds)
  JCAH Accredited: 12
  AMA Residency: 6
  Services: 2 ★, 4 ★★, 3 ★★★, 5 ★★★★
CMSA Access: Buffalo–Niagara Falls, NY (3 points)
Places Rated Score: 1,397   Places Rated Rank: 162

Burlington, NC
Office-Based Physicians
  General/Family Practitioners: 26   A
  Medical Specialists: 31   B
  Surgical Specialists: 37   B
  Other Specialists: 17   C
Short-Term General Hospitals: 2 (361 beds)
  JCAH Accredited: 2
  Services: 1 ★★★, 1 ★★★★
Places Rated Score: 1,154   Places Rated Rank: 241

Burlington, VT
Office-Based Physicians
  General/Family Practitioners: 38   A
  Medical Specialists: 108   AA
  Surgical Specialists: 89   AA
  Other Specialists: 98   AA
Short-Term General Hospitals: 3 (668 beds)
  JCAH Accredited: 3
  AMA Residency: 2
  Services: 2 ★★★, 1 ★★★★
Places Rated Score: 1,768   Places Rated Rank: 72

Canton, OH
Office-Based Physicians
  General/Family Practitioners: 72   B
  Medical Specialists: 142   B
  Surgical Specialists: 123   C
  Other Specialists: 103   B
Short-Term General Hospitals: 5 (1,768 beds)
  JCAH Accredited: 4
  AMA Residency: 2
  Services: 3 ★★★, 2 ★★★★
Places Rated Score: 855   Places Rated Rank: 303

Casper, WY
Office-Based Physicians
  General/Family Practitioners: 15   B
  Medical Specialists: 27   A
  Surgical Specialists: 29   B
  Other Specialists: 23   A
Short-Term General Hospital: 1 (282 beds)
  JCAH Accredited: 1
  AMA Residency: 1
  Services: 1 ★★★★
Places Rated Score: 1,194   Places Rated Rank: 230

Cedar Rapids, IA
Office-Based Physicians
  General/Family Practitioners: 55   AA
  Medical Specialists: 43   C
  Surgical Specialists: 53   C
  Other Specialists: 53   A
Short-Term General Hospitals: 2 (890 beds)
  JCAH Accredited: 2
  AMA Residency: 2
  Services: 2 ★★★★
Places Rated Score: 1,134   Places Rated Rank: 247

Champaign–Urbana–Rantoul, IL
Office-Based Physicians
  General/Family Practitioners: 40   A
  Medical Specialists: 86   AA
  Surgical Specialists: 85   A
  Other Specialists: 65   A
Short-Term General Hospitals: 5 (995 beds)
  JCAH Accredited: 5
  AMA Residency: 2
  Services: 1 ★, 2 ★★★, 2 ★★★★
Places Rated Score: 1,867   Places Rated Rank: 55

Charleston, SC
Office-Based Physicians
  General/Family Practitioners: 96   B
  Medical Specialists: 184   A
  Surgical Specialists: 208   A
  Other Specialists: 160   A
Short-Term General Hospitals: 9 (2,223 beds)
  JCAH Accredited: 7
  AMA Residency: 5
  Services: 2 ★★, 2 ★★★, 5 ★★★★
Places Rated Score: 1,488   Places Rated Rank: 139

Charleston, WV
Office-Based Physicians
  General/Family Practitioners: 72   AA
  Medical Specialists: 103   A
  Surgical Specialists: 138   AA
  Other Specialists: 79   B
Short-Term General Hospitals: 5 (1,514 beds)
  JCAH Accredited: 4
  AMA Residency: 2
  Services: 1 ★★, 2 ★★★, 2 ★★★★
Places Rated Score: 1,581   Places Rated Rank: 119

Charlotte–Gastonia–Rock Hill, NC–SC
Office-Based Physicians
  General/Family Practitioners: 177   C

Rating   **Rating**

Medical Specialists: 353   B
Surgical Specialists: 409   B
Other Specialists: 234   C
Short-Term General Hospitals: 11 (3,434 beds)
    JCAH Accredited: 10
    AMA Residency: 1
    Services: 4 ★★, 5 ★★★, 2 ★★★★
Places Rated Score: 711   Places Rated Rank: 324

Charlottesville, VA
Office-Based Physicians
    General/Family Practitioners: 31   A
    Medical Specialists: 106   AA
    Surgical Specialists: 92   AA
    Other Specialists: 120   AA
Short-Term General Hospitals: 2 (922 beds)
    JCAH Accredited: 2
    AMA Residency: 1
    Services: 1 ★★★, 1 ★★★★
Places Rated Score: 1,717   Places Rated Rank: 80

Chattanooga, TN–GA
Office-Based Physicians
    General/Family Practitioners: 78   B
    Medical Specialists: 157   B
    Surgical Specialists: 185   A
    Other Specialists: 143   A
Short-Term General Hospitals: 13 (2,116 beds)
    JCAH Accredited: 11
    AMA Residency: 1
    Services: 2 ★, 6 ★★, 3 ★★★, 2 ★★★★
Places Rated Score: 1,459   Places Rated Rank: 149

Cheyenne, WY
Office-Based Physicians
    General/Family Practitioners: 19   A
    Medical Specialists: 26   B
    Surgical Specialists: 37   A
    Other Specialists: 20   B
Short-Term General Hospitals: 4 (481 beds)
    JCAH Accredited: 3
    AMA Residency: 2
    Services: 3 ★★★, 1 ★★★★
Places Rated Score: 1,670   Places Rated Rank: 92

★ Chicago, IL
Office-Based Physicians
    General/Family Practitioners: 1,332   A
    Medical Specialists: 3,400   AA
    Surgical Specialists: 2,559   B
    Other Specialists: 2,386   A
Short-Term General Hospitals: 85 (29,820 beds)
    JCAH Accredited: 82
    AMA Residency: 36
    Services: 1 ★, 7 ★★, 28 ★★★, 49 ★★★★
CMSA Access: Chicago–Gary–Lake County,
    IL–IN–WI (9 points)
Places Rated Score: 2,826   Places Rated Rank: 3

Chico, CA
Office-Based Physicians
    General/Family Practitioners: 57   AA
    Medical Specialists: 67   A
    Surgical Specialists: 84   AA
    Other Specialists: 63   A
Short-Term General Hospitals: 5 (603 beds)
    JCAH Accredited: 5
    Services: 2 ★★, 2 ★★★, 1 ★★★★
Places Rated Score: 1,890   Places Rated Rank: 48

Cincinnati, OH–KY–IN
Office-Based Physicians
    General/Family Practitioners: 312   A
    Medical Specialists: 675   A
    Surgical Specialists: 603   A

Other Specialists: 587   AA
Short-Term General Hospitals: 17 (6,658 beds)
    JCAH Accredited: 15
    AMA Residency: 8
    Services: 1 ★, 7 ★★★, 9 ★★★★
CMSA Access: Cincinnati–Hamilton, OH–KY–IN (1 point)
Places Rated Score: 1,620   Places Rated Rank: 104

Clarksville–Hopkinsville, TN–KY
Office-Based Physicians
    General/Family Practitioners: 16   C
    Medical Specialists: 35   C
    Surgical Specialists: 41   C
    Other Specialists: 23   C
Short-Term General Hospitals: 3 (557 beds)
    JCAH Accredited: 3
    Services: 2 ★★★, 1 ★★★★
Places Rated Score: 878   Places Rated Rank: 299

★ Cleveland, OH
Office-Based Physicians
    General/Family Practitioners: 265   C
    Medical Specialists: 1,155   AA
    Surgical Specialists: 935   AA
    Other Specialists: 837   AA
Short-Term General Hospitals: 33 (10,979 beds)
    JCAH Accredited: 30
    AMA Residency: 11
    Services: 4 ★★, 13 ★★★, 16 ★★★★
CMSA Access: Cleveland–Akron–Lorain, OH (14 points)
Places Rated Score: 2,084   Places Rated Rank: 22

Colorado Springs, CO
Office-Based Physicians
    General/Family Practitioners: 54   C
    Medical Specialists: 119   B
    Surgical Specialists: 135   B
    Other Specialists: 107   B
Short-Term General Hospitals: 7 (1,516 beds)
    JCAH Accredited: 5
    AMA Residency: 2
    Services: 2 ★, 5 ★★★★
Places Rated Score: 1,018   Places Rated Rank: 275

★ Columbia, MO
Office-Based Physicians
    General/Family Practitioners: 21   B
    Medical Specialists: 98   AA
    Surgical Specialists: 82   AA
    Other Specialists: 101   AA
Short-Term General Hospitals: 4 (1,365 beds)
    JCAH Accredited: 4
    AMA Residency: 2
    Services: 4 ★★★★
Places Rated Score: 2,080   Places Rated Rank: 23

Columbia, SC
Office-Based Physicians
    General/Family Practitioners: 99   A
    Medical Specialists: 169   A
    Surgical Specialists: 195   A
    Other Specialists: 147   A
Short-Term General Hospitals: 6 (2,201 beds)
    JCAH Accredited: 6
    AMA Residency: 2
    Services: 2 ★★★, 4 ★★★★
Places Rated Score: 1,395   Places Rated Rank: 163

Columbus, GA–AL
Office-Based Physicians
    General/Family Practitioners: 35   C
    Medical Specialists: 60   C
    Surgical Specialists: 91   B
    Other Specialists: 62   B

Rating

Short-Term General Hospitals: 5 (1,485 beds)
 JCAH Accredited: 5
 AMA Residency: 2
 Services: 4 ★★★, 1 ★★★★
Places Rated Score: 1,028   Places Rated Rank: 272

Columbus, OH
Office-Based Physicians
 General/Family Practitioners: 288   A
 Medical Specialists: 432   B
 Surgical Specialists: 463   B
 Other Specialists: 453   A
Short-Term General Hospitals: 14 (4,882 beds)
 JCAH Accredited: 13
 AMA Residency: 6
 Services: 1 ★, 5 ★★★, 8 ★★★★
Places Rated Score: 1,219   Places Rated Rank: 225

Corpus Christi, TX
Office-Based Physicians
 General/Family Practitioners: 87   A
 Medical Specialists: 124   B
 Surgical Specialists: 163   A
 Other Specialists: 103   B
Short-Term General Hospitals: 11 (1,769 beds)
 JCAH Accredited: 8
 AMA Residency: 2
 Services: 3 ★★, 6 ★★★, 2 ★★★★
Places Rated Score: 1,601   Places Rated Rank: 112

Cumberland, MD–WV
Office-Based Physicians
 General/Family Practitioners: 22   A
 Medical Specialists: 42   A
 Surgical Specialists: 41   B
 Other Specialists: 33   A
Short-Term General Hospitals: 4 (583 beds)
 JCAH Accredited: 4
 Services: 2 ★★, 2 ★★★★
Places Rated Score: 1,740   Places Rated Rank: 76

Dallas, TX
Office-Based Physicians
 General/Family Practitioners: 394   C
 Medical Specialists: 938   A
 Surgical Specialists: 1,038   A
 Other Specialists: 810   A
Short-Term General Hospitals: 45 (9,211 beds)
 JCAH Accredited: 35
 AMA Residency: 6
 Services: 2 ★, 14 ★★, 17 ★★★, 12 ★★★★
CMSA Access: Dallas–Fort Worth, TX (9 points)
Places Rated Score: 1,668   Places Rated Rank: 93

Danbury, CT
Office-Based Physicians
 General/Family Practitioners: N/A   C
 Medical Specialists: N/A   AA
 Surgical Specialists: N/A   AA
 Other Specialists: N/A   AA
Short-Term General Hospitals: 2 (543 beds)
 JCAH Accredited: 2
 AMA Residency: 1
 Services: 1 ★★★, 1 ★★★★
CMSA Access: New York–Northern NJ–Long
 Island, NY–NJ–CT (474 points)
Places Rated Score: 1,830   Places Rated Rank: 62

Danville, VA
Office-Based Physicians
 General/Family Practitioners: 11   C
 Medical Specialists: 32   B
 Surgical Specialists: 39   B
 Other Specialists: 24   C
Short-Term General Hospital: 1 (377 beds)

JCAH Accredited: 1
 AMA Residency: 1
 Services: 1 ★★★
Places Rated Score: 602   Places Rated Rank: 330

Davenport–Rock Island–Moline, IA–IL
Office-Based Physicians
 General/Family Practitioners: 74   B
 Medical Specialists: 93   C
 Surgical Specialists: 131   B
 Other Specialists: 85   C
Short-Term General Hospitals: 9 (1,641 beds)
 JCAH Accredited: 8
 AMA Residency: 2
 Services: 1 ★, 1 ★★, 3 ★★★, 4 ★★★★
Places Rated Score: 1,174   Places Rated Rank: 234

Dayton–Springfield, OH
Office-Based Physicians
 General/Family Practitioners: 236   A
 Medical Specialists: 292   B
 Surgical Specialists: 313   C
 Other Specialists: 257   B
Short-Term General Hospitals: 13 (6,004 beds)
 JCAH Accredited: 12
 AMA Residency: 9
 Services: 1 ★, 2 ★★★, 10 ★★★★
Places Rated Score: 1,253   Places Rated Rank: 209

Daytona Beach, FL
Office-Based Physicians
 General/Family Practitioners: 71   A
 Medical Specialists: 92   B
 Surgical Specialists: 107   C
 Other Specialists: 98   B
Short-Term General Hospitals: 8 (1,502 beds)
 JCAH Accredited: 7
 AMA Residency: 1
 Services: 1 ★, 1 ★★, 4 ★★★, 2 ★★★★
Places Rated Score: 1,257   Places Rated Rank: 208

Decatur, AL
Office-Based Physicians
 General/Family Practitioners: 30   A
 Medical Specialists: 26   C
 Surgical Specialists: 34   C
 Other Specialists: 21   C
Short-Term General Hospitals: 5 (625 beds)
 JCAH Accredited: 4
 Services: 1 ★, 3 ★★, 1 ★★★
Places Rated Score: 1,157   Places Rated Rank: 239

Decatur, IL
Office-Based Physicians
 General/Family Practitioners: 20   C
 Medical Specialists: 45   B
 Surgical Specialists: 41   C
 Other Specialists: 38   B
Short-Term General Hospitals: 2 (734 beds)
 JCAH Accredited: 2
 AMA Residency: 2
 Services: 2 ★★★★
Places Rated Score: 991   Places Rated Rank: 279

Denver, CO
Office-Based Physicians
 General/Family Practitioners: 329   B
 Medical Specialists: 811   AA
 Surgical Specialists: 733   A
 Other Specialists: 718   AA
Short-Term General Hospitals: 20 (5,923 beds)
 JCAH Accredited: 18
 AMA Residency: 10
 Services: 2 ★, 5 ★★★, 13 ★★★★
CMSA Access: Denver–Boulder, CO (1 point)
Places Rated Score: 1,704   Places Rated Rank: 85

Rating

Rating

Des Moines, IA
Office-Based Physicians
　General/Family Practitioners: 81　　　　B
　Medical Specialists: 124　　　　　　　　B
　Surgical Specialists: 129　　　　　　　　C
　Other Specialists: 121　　　　　　　　　A
Short-Term General Hospitals: 8 (2,528 beds)
　JCAH Accredited: 7
　AMA Residency: 4
　Services: 1 ★★, 2 ★★★, 5 ★★★★
Places Rated Score: 1,334　　　Places Rated Rank: 183

Detroit, MI
Office-Based Physicians
　General/Family Practitioners: 474　　　C
　Medical Specialists: 1,841　　　　　　　A
　Surgical Specialists: 1,541　　　　　　　B
　Other Specialists: 1,285　　　　　　　　B
Short-Term General Hospitals: 60 (17,034 beds)
　JCAH Accredited: 48
　AMA Residency: 18
　Services: 4 ★, 8 ★★, 21 ★★★, 27 ★★★★
CMSA Access: Detroit–Ann Arbor, MI (8 points)
Places Rated Score: 1,739　　　Places Rated Rank: 77

Dothan, AL
Office-Based Physicians
　General/Family Practitioners: 16　　　　C
　Medical Specialists: 45　　　　　　　　B
　Surgical Specialists: 60　　　　　　　　A
　Other Specialists: 33　　　　　　　　　B
Short-Term General Hospitals: 4 (754 beds)
　JCAH Accredited: 4
　Services: 1 ★★, 1 ★★★, 2 ★★★★
Places Rated Score: 1,490　　　Places Rated Rank: 138

Dubuque, IA
Office-Based Physicians
　General/Family Practitioners: 9　　　　　C
　Medical Specialists: 43　　　　　　　　A
　Surgical Specialists: 47　　　　　　　　AA
　Other Specialists: 30　　　　　　　　　A
Short-Term General Hospitals: 2 (558 beds)
　JCAH Accredited: 2
　Services: 2 ★★★★
Places Rated Score: 1,648　　　Places Rated Rank: 97

Duluth, MN–WI
Office-Based Physicians
　General/Family Practitioners: 78　　　　AA
　Medical Specialists: 85　　　　　　　　B
　Surgical Specialists: 95　　　　　　　　B
　Other Specialists: 81　　　　　　　　　A
Short-Term General Hospitals: 10 (1,529 beds)
　JCAH Accredited: 6
　AMA Residency: 3
　Services: 3 ★★, 3 ★★★, 4 ★★★★
Places Rated Score: 1,820　　　Places Rated Rank: 64

Eau Claire, WI
Office-Based Physicians
　General/Family Practitioners: 49　　　　AA
　Medical Specialists: 39　　　　　　　　C
　Surgical Specialists: 54　　　　　　　　B
　Other Specialists: 52　　　　　　　　　A
Short-Term General Hospitals: 5 (950 beds)
　JCAH Accredited: 4
　AMA Residency: 2
　Services: 2 ★★, 1 ★★★, 2 ★★★★
Places Rated Score: 1,730　　　Places Rated Rank: 78

El Paso, TX
Office-Based Physicians
　General/Family Practitioners: 79　　　　C
　Medical Specialists: 148　　　　　　　　C

Surgical Specialists: 175　　　　　　　　C
Other Specialists: 143　　　　　　　　　B
Short-Term General Hospitals: 11 (2,181 beds)
　JCAH Accredited: 8
　AMA Residency: 4
　Services: 1 ★, 3 ★★, 4 ★★★, 3 ★★★★
Places Rated Score: 962　　　Places Rated Rank: 285

Elkhart–Goshen, IN
Office-Based Physicians
　General/Family Practitioners: 33　　　　A
　Medical Specialists: 31　　　　　　　　C
　Surgical Specialists: 42　　　　　　　　C
　Other Specialists: 26　　　　　　　　　C
Short-Term General Hospitals: 2 (514 beds)
　JCAH Accredited: 2
　AMA Residency: 1
　Services: 1 ★★★, 1 ★★★★
Places Rated Score: 868　　　Places Rated Rank: 302

Elmira, NY
Office-Based Physicians
　General/Family Practitioners: 13　　　　C
　Medical Specialists: 46　　　　　　　　AA
　Surgical Specialists: 47　　　　　　　　AA
　Other Specialists: 26　　　　　　　　　B
Short-Term General Hospitals: 2 (573 beds)
　JCAH Accredited: 2
　Services: 1 ★★★, 1 ★★★★
Places Rated Score: 1,543　　　Places Rated Rank: 128

Enid, OK
Office-Based Physicians
　General/Family Practitioners: 16　　　　A
　Medical Specialists: 19　　　　　　　　B
　Surgical Specialists: 27　　　　　　　　A
　Other Specialists: 18　　　　　　　　　B
Short-Term General Hospitals: 3 (421 beds)
　JCAH Accredited: 2
　AMA Residency: 2
　Services: 1 ★★★, 2 ★★★★
Places Rated Score: 1,660　　　Places Rated Rank: 94

Erie, PA
Office-Based Physicians
　General/Family Practitioners: 59　　　　B
　Medical Specialists: 85　　　　　　　　B
　Surgical Specialists: 125　　　　　　　　A
　Other Specialists: 69　　　　　　　　　B
Short-Term General Hospitals: 7 (1,640 beds)
　JCAH Accredited: 5
　AMA Residency: 2
　Services: 1 ★, 1 ★★, 3 ★★★, 2 ★★★★
Places Rated Score: 1,306　　　Places Rated Rank: 193

Eugene–Springfield, OR
Office-Based Physicians
　General/Family Practitioners: 89　　　　AA
　Medical Specialists: 108　　　　　　　　A
　Surgical Specialists: 106　　　　　　　　B
　Other Specialists: 86　　　　　　　　　A
Short-Term General Hospitals: 5 (656 beds)
　JCAH Accredited: 4
　Services: 1 ★, 1 ★★, 1 ★★★, 2 ★★★★
Places Rated Score: 1,372　　　Places Rated Rank: 169

Evansville, IN–KY
Office-Based Physicians
　General/Family Practitioners: 91　　　　AA
　Medical Specialists: 102　　　　　　　　B
　Surgical Specialists: 116　　　　　　　　B
　Other Specialists: 98　　　　　　　　　A
Short-Term General Hospitals: 5 (1,755 beds)
　JCAH Accredited: 5

Rating

Rating

AMA Residency: 2
Services: 2 ★★, 3 ★★★★
Places Rated Score: 1,359   Places Rated Rank: 175

Fall River, MA–RI
Office-Based Physicians
General/Family Practitioners: 68   C
Medical Specialists: 175   B
Surgical Specialists: 167   C
Other Specialists: 93   C
Short-Term General Hospitals: 8 (1,841 beds)
JCAH Accredited: 8
Services: 1 ★, 3 ★★★, 4 ★★★★
CMSA Access: Providence–Pawtucket–Fall River,
RI–MA (21 points)
Places Rated Score: 807   Places Rated Rank: 308

★ Fargo–Moorhead, ND–MN
Office-Based Physicians
General/Family Practitioners: 25   B
Medical Specialists: 93   AA
Surgical Specialists: 82   AA
Other Specialists: 65   AA
Short-Term General Hospitals: 5 (1,107 beds)
JCAH Accredited: 5
AMA Residency: 3
Services: 1 ★★★, 4 ★★★★
Places Rated Score: 2,110   Places Rated Rank: 17

Fayetteville, NC
Office-Based Physicians
General/Family Practitioners: 23   C
Medical Specialists: 47   C
Surgical Specialists: 63   C
Other Specialists: 38   C
Short-Term General Hospitals: 4 (1,154 beds)
JCAH Accredited: 4
AMA Residency: 2
Services: 1 ★★, 1 ★★★, 2 ★★★★
Places Rated Score: 783   Places Rated Rank: 314

Fayetteville–Springdale, AR
Office-Based Physicians
General/Family Practitioners: 28   A
Medical Specialists: 31   B
Surgical Specialists: 46   A
Other Specialists: 41   A
Short-Term General Hospitals: 4 (702 beds)
JCAH Accredited: 3
AMA Residency: 2
Services: 2 ★★★, 2 ★★★★
Places Rated Score: 1,770   Places Rated Rank: 70

Fitchburg–Leominster, MA
Office-Based Physicians
General/Family Practitioners: N/A   C
Medical Specialists: N/A   AA
Surgical Specialists: N/A   B
Other Specialists: N/A   A
Short-Term General Hospitals: 2 (376 beds)
JCAH Accredited: 2
AMA Residency: 1
Services: 1 ★★★, 1 ★★★★
Places Rated Score: 1,385   Places Rated Rank: 165

Flint, MI
Office-Based Physicians
General/Family Practitioners: 92   B
Medical Specialists: 132   B
Surgical Specialists: 112   C
Other Specialists: 104   B
Short-Term General Hospitals: 6 (1,772 beds)
JCAH Accredited: 5
AMA Residency: 3
Services: 2 ★★, 1 ★★★, 3 ★★★★
Places Rated Score: 897   Places Rated Rank: 295

Florence, AL
Office-Based Physicians
General/Family Practitioners: 17   C
Medical Specialists: 45   B
Surgical Specialists: 55   B
Other Specialists: 31   C
Short-Term General Hospitals: 4 (1,004 beds)
JCAH Accredited: 4
Services: 2 ★★, 2 ★★★
Places Rated Score: 1,066   Places Rated Rank: 261

Florence, SC
Office-Based Physicians
General/Family Practitioners: 28   A
Medical Specialists: 38   B
Surgical Specialists: 56   A
Other Specialists: 29   B
Short-Term General Hospitals: 4 (685 beds)
JCAH Accredited: 3
AMA Residency: 1
Services: 1 ★★, 2 ★★★, 1 ★★★★
Places Rated Score: 1,650   Places Rated Rank: 96

Fort Collins–Loveland, CO
Office-Based Physicians
General/Family Practitioners: 65   AA
Medical Specialists: 45   C
Surgical Specialists: 68   B
Other Specialists: 42   B
Short-Term General Hospitals: 3 (386 beds)
JCAH Accredited: 3
AMA Residency: 1
Services: 1 ★★★, 2 ★★★★
Places Rated Score: 1,230   Places Rated Rank: 221

Fort Lauderdale–Hollywood–Pompano Beach, FL
Office-Based Physicians
General/Family Practitioners: 216   B
Medical Specialists: 674   AA
Surgical Specialists: 559   A
Other Specialists: 393   A
Short-Term General Hospitals: 20 (5,625 beds)
JCAH Accredited: 19
AMA Residency: 2
Services: 2 ★, 2 ★★, 12 ★★★, 4 ★★★★
CMSA Access: Miami–Fort Lauderdale, FL (18 points)
Places Rated Score: 1,556   Places Rated Rank: 124

Fort Myers–Cape Coral, FL
Office-Based Physicians
General/Family Practitioners: 58   B
Medical Specialists: 104   A
Surgical Specialists: 117   A
Other Specialists: 90   A
Short-Term General Hospitals: 4 (1,151 beds)
JCAH Accredited: 4
Services: 4 ★★★
Places Rated Score: 1,170   Places Rated Rank: 237

Fort Pierce, FL
Office-Based Physicians
General/Family Practitioners: 39   B
Medical Specialists: 74   B
Surgical Specialists: 85   B
Other Specialists: 64   B
Short-Term General Hospitals: 3 (690 beds)
JCAH Accredited: 3
Services: 2 ★★★, 1 ★★★★
Places Rated Score: 916   Places Rated Rank: 290

Fort Smith, AR–OK
Office-Based Physicians
General/Family Practitioners: 48   AA
Medical Specialists: 58   B
Surgical Specialists: 70   B
Other Specialists: 46   B

Rating

Short-Term General Hospitals: 4 (929 beds)
JCAH Accredited: 3
AMA Residency: 2
Services: 1 ★★, 2 ★★★, 1 ★★★★
Places Rated Score: 1,352   Places Rated Rank: 177

Fort Walton Beach, FL
Office-Based Physicians
General/Family Practitioners: 21   C
Medical Specialists: 37   C
Surgical Specialists: 40   C
Other Specialists: 25   C
Short-Term General Hospitals: 4 (576 beds)
JCAH Accredited: 4
AMA Residency: 1
Services: 4 ★★★
Places Rated Score: 1,109   Places Rated Rank: 249

Fort Wayne, IN
Office-Based Physicians
General/Family Practitioners: 102   AA
Medical Specialists: 88   C
Surgical Specialists: 126   B
Other Specialists: 113   A
Short-Term General Hospitals: 6 (1,776 beds)
JCAH Accredited: 5
AMA Residency: 3
Services: 1 ★★, 2 ★★★, 3 ★★★★
Places Rated Score: 1,322   Places Rated Rank: 186

Fort Worth–Arlington, TX
Office-Based Physicians
General/Family Practitioners: 232   B
Medical Specialists: 334   C
Surgical Specialists: 403   C
Other Specialists: 295   C
Short-Term General Hospitals: 21 (4,050 beds)
JCAH Accredited: 18
AMA Residency: 3
Services: 6 ★★, 8 ★★★, 7 ★★★★
CMSA Access: Dallas–Fort Worth, TX (22 points)
Places Rated Score: 1,022   Places Rated Rank: 274

Fresno, CA
Office-Based Physicians
General/Family Practitioners: 153   A
Medical Specialists: 218   A
Surgical Specialists: 210   B
Other Specialists: 193   A
Short-Term General Hospitals: 12 (1,693 beds)
JCAH Accredited: 11
AMA Residency: 2
Services: 2 ★, 5 ★★, 1 ★★★, 4 ★★★★
Places Rated Score: 1,378   Places Rated Rank: 167

Gadsden, AL
Office-Based Physicians
General/Family Practitioners: 22   A
Medical Specialists: 32   B
Surgical Specialists: 37   B
Other Specialists: 17   C
Short-Term General Hospitals: 2 (496 beds)
JCAH Accredited: 2
AMA Residency: 1
Services: 1 ★★★, 1 ★★★★
Places Rated Score: 1,174   Places Rated Rank: 234

★ Gainesville, FL
Office-Based Physicians
General/Family Practitioners: 45   A
Medical Specialists: 107   AA
Surgical Specialists: 117   AA
Other Specialists: 128   AA
Short-Term General Hospitals: 5 (1,759 beds)
JCAH Accredited: 5

AMA Residency: 3
Services: 1 ★★, 1 ★★★, 3 ★★★★
Places Rated Score: 2,061   Places Rated Rank: 27

Galveston–Texas City, TX
Office-Based Physicians
General/Family Practitioners: 56   A
Medical Specialists: 117   AA
Surgical Specialists: 98   A
Other Specialists: 125   AA
Short-Term General Hospitals: 5 (1,723 beds)
JCAH Accredited: 5
AMA Residency: 1
Services: 2 ★★★, 3 ★★★★
CMSA Access: Houston–Galveston–Brazoria, TX (90 points)
Places Rated Score: 1,998   Places Rated Rank: 31

Gary–Hammond, IN
Office-Based Physicians
General/Family Practitioners: 162   A
Medical Specialists: 160   C
Surgical Specialists: 223   B
Other Specialists: 163   B
Short-Term General Hospitals: 8 (3,157 beds)
JCAH Accredited: 8
AMA Residency: 1
Services: 1 ★, 2 ★★★, 5 ★★★★
CMSA Access: Chicago–Gary–Lake County,
IL–IN–WI (152 points)
Places Rated Score: 1,141   Places Rated Rank: 244

Glens Falls, NY
Office-Based Physicians
General/Family Practitioners: 29   A
Medical Specialists: 40   B
Surgical Specialists: 47   A
Other Specialists: 27   B
Short-Term General Hospitals: 3 (546 beds)
JCAH Accredited: 3
Services: 1 ★, 1 ★★★, 1 ★★★★
Places Rated Score: 1,342   Places Rated Rank: 178

★ Grand Forks, ND
Office-Based Physicians
General/Family Practitioners: 23   AA
Medical Specialists: 30   A
Surgical Specialists: 38   AA
Other Specialists: 32   AA
Short-Term General Hospitals: 3 (469 beds)
JCAH Accredited: 1
AMA Residency: 1
Services: 1 ★★, 1 ★★★, 1 ★★★★
Places Rated Score: 2,130   Places Rated Rank: 14

Grand Rapids, MI
Office-Based Physicians
General/Family Practitioners: 98   C
Medical Specialists: 203   B
Surgical Specialists: 269   B
Other Specialists: 197   B
Short-Term General Hospitals: 8 (2,431 beds)
JCAH Accredited: 7
AMA Residency: 3
Services: 2 ★★, 1 ★★★, 5 ★★★★
Places Rated Score: 896   Places Rated Rank: 296

Great Falls, MT
Office-Based Physicians
General/Family Practitioners: 16   B
Medical Specialists: 39   A
Surgical Specialists: 44   AA
Other Specialists: 41   AA
Short-Term General Hospitals: 3 (630 beds)
JCAH Accredited: 2
Services: 3 ★★★
Places Rated Score: 1,920   Places Rated Rank: 42

Rating

Greeley, CO
Office-Based Physicians
General/Family Practitioners: 29   A
Medical Specialists: 34   C
Surgical Specialists: 44   C
Other Specialists: 29   C
Short-Term General Hospitals: 2 (355 beds)
JCAH Accredited: 1
AMA Residency: 1
Services: 1 ★, 1 ★★★★
Places Rated Score: 750   Places Rated Rank: 320

Green Bay, WI
Office-Based Physicians
General/Family Practitioners: 30   C
Medical Specialists: 74   A
Surgical Specialists: 79   A
Other Specialists: 50   B
Short-Term General Hospitals: 3 (842 beds)
JCAH Accredited: 3
Services: 1 ★★★, 2 ★★★★
Places Rated Score: 1,168   Places Rated Rank: 238

Greensboro–Winston-Salem–High Point, NC
Office-Based Physicians
General/Family Practitioners: 162   B
Medical Specialists: 414   A
Surgical Specialists: 364   B
Other Specialists: 293   A
Short-Term General Hospitals: 14 (3,310 beds)
JCAH Accredited: 14
AMA Residency: 3
Services: 7 ★★, 4 ★★★, 3 ★★★★
Places Rated Score: 1,223   Places Rated Rank: 224

Greenville–Spartanburg, SC
Office-Based Physicians
General/Family Practitioners: 172   AA
Medical Specialists: 174   B
Surgical Specialists: 245   B
Other Specialists: 162   B
Short-Term General Hospitals: 10 (2,259 beds)
JCAH Accredited: 9
AMA Residency: 1
Services: 6 ★★, 2 ★★★, 2 ★★★★
Places Rated Score: 1,139   Places Rated Rank: 245

Hagerstown, MD
Office-Based Physicians
General/Family Practitioners: 24   B
Medical Specialists: 32   C
Surgical Specialists: 42   B
Other Specialists: 28   B
Short-Term General Hospital: 1 (277 beds)
JCAH Accredited: 1
Services: 1 ★★★★
Places Rated Score: 711   Places Rated Rank: 324

Hamilton–Middletown, OH
Office-Based Physicians
General/Family Practitioners: 43   C
Medical Specialists: 65   C
Surgical Specialists: 78   C
Other Specialists: 58   C
Short-Term General Hospitals: 4 (1,027 beds)
JCAH Accredited: 4
Services: 2 ★★★, 2 ★★★★
CMSA Access: Cincinnati–Hamilton, OH–KY–IN (49 points)
Places Rated Score: 805   Places Rated Rank: 309

Harrisburg–Lebanon–Carlisle, PA
Office-Based Physicians
General/Family Practitioners: 131   A
Medical Specialists: 217   A
Surgical Specialists: 218   B
Other Specialists: 169   B

Rating

Short-Term General Hospitals: 9 (2,428 beds)
JCAH Accredited: 8
AMA Residency: 3
Services: 1 ★, 4 ★★★, 4 ★★★★
Places Rated Score: 1,242   Places Rated Rank: 214

Hartford, CT
Office-Based Physicians
General/Family Practitioners: 157   C
Medical Specialists: 668   AA
Surgical Specialists: 511   A
Other Specialists: 444   AA
Short-Term General Hospitals: 12 (3,703 beds)
JCAH Accredited: 12
AMA Residency: 7
Services: 3 ★★★, 9 ★★★★
CMSA Access: Hartford–New Britain–Middletown,
CT (12 points)
Places Rated Score: 1,537   Places Rated Rank: 130

Hickory, NC
Office-Based Physicians
General/Family Practitioners: 61   AA
Medical Specialists: 45   C
Surgical Specialists: 79   B
Other Specialists: 45   C
Short-Term General Hospitals: 5 (819 beds)
JCAH Accredited: 5
Services: 2 ★★, 1 ★★★, 2 ★★★★
Places Rated Score: 1,239   Places Rated Rank: 218

Honolulu, HI
Office-Based Physicians
General/Family Practitioners: 138   B
Medical Specialists: 490   AA
Surgical Specialists: 390   A
Other Specialists: 318   A
Short-Term General Hospitals: 9 (2,132 beds)
JCAH Accredited: 9
AMA Residency: 6
Services: 2 ★, 3 ★★★, 4 ★★★★
Places Rated Score: 1,341   Places Rated Rank: 181

Houma–Thibodaux, LA
Office-Based Physicians
General/Family Practitioners: 28   C
Medical Specialists: 34   C
Surgical Specialists: 65   C
Other Specialists: 15   C
Short-Term General Hospitals: 5 (689 beds)
JCAH Accredited: 5
AMA Residency: 1
Services: 2 ★★, 3 ★★★
Places Rated Score: 957   Places Rated Rank: 286

Houston, TX
Office-Based Physicians
General/Family Practitioners: 690   A
Medical Specialists: 1,372   A
Surgical Specialists: 1,362   A
Other Specialists: 1,228   A
Short-Term General Hospitals: 52 (13,200 beds)
JCAH Accredited: 49
AMA Residency: 8
Services: 2 ★, 15 ★★, 19 ★★★, 16 ★★★★
CMSA Access: Houston–Galveston–Brazoria, TX (3 points)
Places Rated Score: 1,927   Places Rated Rank: 40

Huntington–Ashland, WV–KY–OH
Office-Based Physicians
General/Family Practitioners: 73   A
Medical Specialists: 102   B
Surgical Specialists: 100   C
Other Specialists: 83   B
Short-Term General Hospitals: 8 (1,682 beds)
JCAH Accredited: 7

Rating

AMA Residency: 3
Services: 1 ★, 1 ★★, 2 ★★★, 4 ★★★★
Places Rated Score: 1,342   Places Rated Rank: 178

Huntsville, AL
Office-Based Physicians
  General/Family Practitioners: 48   B
  Medical Specialists: 76   B
  Surgical Specialists: 81   B
  Other Specialists: 68   B
Short-Term General Hospitals: 4 (998 beds)
  JCAH Accredited: 4
  AMA Residency: 1
  Services: 1 ★★, 2 ★★★, 1 ★★★★
Places Rated Score: 973   Places Rated Rank: 281

Indianapolis, IN
Office-Based Physicians
  General/Family Practitioners: 339   AA
  Medical Specialists: 450   A
  Surgical Specialists: 473   B
  Other Specialists: 484   A
Short-Term General Hospitals: 18 (5,831 beds)
  JCAH Accredited: 16
  AMA Residency: 7
  Services: 4 ★★, 5 ★★★, 9 ★★★★
Places Rated Score: 1,587   Places Rated Rank: 116

★ Iowa City, IA
Office-Based Physicians
  General/Family Practitioners: 29   AA
  Medical Specialists: 79   AA
  Surgical Specialists: 79   AA
  Other Specialists: 96   AA
Short-Term General Hospitals: 3 (1,421 beds)
  JCAH Accredited: 3
  AMA Residency: 3
  Services: 1 ★★★, 2 ★★★★
Places Rated Score: 2,290   Places Rated Rank: 6

Jackson, MI
Office-Based Physicians
  General/Family Practitioners: 25   B
  Medical Specialists: 32   C
  Surgical Specialists: 40   C
  Other Specialists: 20   C
Short-Term General Hospitals: 2 (462 beds)
  Services: 1 ★★, 1 ★★★★
Places Rated Score: 666   Places Rated Rank: 326

★ Jackson, MS
Office-Based Physicians
  General/Family Practitioners: 89   A
  Medical Specialists: 203   AA
  Surgical Specialists: 214   AA
  Other Specialists: 177   AA
Short-Term General Hospitals: 11 (2,939 beds)
  JCAH Accredited: 7
  AMA Residency: 4
  Services: 2 ★★, 5 ★★★, 4 ★★★★
Places Rated Score: 2,143   Places Rated Rank: 12

Jackson, TN
Office-Based Physicians
  General/Family Practitioners: 11   C
  Medical Specialists: 47   AA
  Surgical Specialists: 64   AA
  Other Specialists: 20   B
Short-Term General Hospitals: 2 (800 beds)
  JCAH Accredited: 2
  AMA Residency: 1
  Services: 1 ★★★, 1 ★★★★
Places Rated Score: 1,687   Places Rated Rank: 89

Rating

Jacksonville, FL
Office-Based Physicians
  General/Family Practitioners: 147   B
  Medical Specialists: 318   A
  Surgical Specialists: 361   A
  Other Specialists: 274   A
Short-Term General Hospitals: 15 (3,402 beds)
  JCAH Accredited: 15
  AMA Residency: 4
  Services: 2 ★★, 9 ★★★, 4 ★★★★
Places Rated Score: 1,481   Places Rated Rank: 142

Jacksonville, NC
Office-Based Physicians
  General/Family Practitioners: 16   C
  Medical Specialists: 17   C
  Surgical Specialists: 21   C
  Other Specialists: 13   C
Short-Term General Hospitals: 2 (341 beds)
  JCAH Accredited: 2
  Services: 1 ★★★, 1 ★★★★
Places Rated Score: 773   Places Rated Rank: 316

Janesville–Beloit, WI
Office-Based Physicians
  General/Family Practitioners: 21   C
  Medical Specialists: 48   B
  Surgical Specialists: 49   B
  Other Specialists: 26   C
Short-Term General Hospitals: 3 (523 beds)
  JCAH Accredited: 3
  Services: 1 ★★, 2 ★★★
Places Rated Score: 911   Places Rated Rank: 291

Jersey City, NJ
Office-Based Physicians
  General/Family Practitioners: 79   C
  Medical Specialists: 224   A
  Surgical Specialists: 202   B
  Other Specialists: 94   C
Short-Term General Hospitals: 9 (2,427 beds)
  JCAH Accredited: 9
  AMA Residency: 2
  Services: 1 ★, 1 ★★, 2 ★★★, 5 ★★★★
CMSA Access: New York–Northern NJ–Long
  Island, NY–NJ–CT (266 points)
Places Rated Score: 1,320   Places Rated Rank: 187

Johnson City–Kingsport–Bristol, TN–VA
Office-Based Physicians
  General/Family Practitioners: 102   A
  Medical Specialists: 161   B
  Surgical Specialists: 175   B
  Other Specialists: 123   B
Short-Term General Hospitals: 11 (2,581 beds)
  JCAH Accredited: 10
  AMA Residency: 4
  Services: 4 ★★, 3 ★★★, 4 ★★★★
Places Rated Score: 1,424   Places Rated Rank: 154

Johnstown, PA
Office-Based Physicians
  General/Family Practitioners: 62   A
  Medical Specialists: 60   C
  Surgical Specialists: 85   C
  Other Specialists: 49   C
Short-Term General Hospitals: 7 (1,366 beds)
  JCAH Accredited: 7
  AMA Residency: 1
  Services: 3 ★★, 4 ★★★★
Places Rated Score: 1,306   Places Rated Rank: 193

Joliet, IL
Office-Based Physicians
  General/Family Practitioners: 43   C

Rating · Rating

Medical Specialists: 95 · C
Surgical Specialists: 77 · C
Other Specialists: 54 · C
Short-Term General Hospitals: 3 (901 beds)
JCAH Accredited: 3
Services: 1 ★★, 2 ★★★★
CMSA Access: Chicago–Gary–Lake County,
IL–IN–WI (218 points)
Places Rated Score: 718 · Places Rated Rank: 323

Joplin, MO
Office-Based Physicians
General/Family Practitioners: 28 · B
Medical Specialists: 37 · C
Surgical Specialists: 45 · C
Other Specialists: 24 · C
Short-Term General Hospitals: 5 (752 beds)
JCAH Accredited: 2
Services: 2 ★★, 1 ★★★, 2 ★★★★
Places Rated Score: 1,270 · Places Rated Rank: 206

Kalamazoo, MI
Office-Based Physicians
General/Family Practitioners: 54 · A
Medical Specialists: 126 · AA
Surgical Specialists: 110 · AA
Other Specialists: 97 · AA
Short-Term General Hospitals: 3 (953 beds)
JCAH Accredited: 3
AMA Residency: 2
Services: 1 ★★, 2 ★★★★
Places Rated Score: 1,629 · Places Rated Rank: 103

Kankakee, IL
Office-Based Physicians
General/Family Practitioners: 21 · A
Medical Specialists: 32 · B
Surgical Specialists: 28 · C
Other Specialists: 24 · B
Short-Term General Hospitals: 2 (561 beds)
JCAH Accredited: 2
Services: 2 ★★★★
Places Rated Score: 1,286 · Places Rated Rank: 202

Kansas City, MO–KS
Office-Based Physicians
General/Family Practitioners: 278 · B
Medical Specialists: 687 · A
Surgical Specialists: 617 · B
Other Specialists: 537 · A
Short-Term General Hospitals: 38 (8,318 beds)
JCAH Accredited: 30
AMA Residency: 11
Services: 3 ★, 3 ★★, 14 ★★★, 18 ★★★★
Places Rated Score: 1,930 · Places Rated Rank: 39

Kenosha, WI
Office-Based Physicians
General/Family Practitioners: 20 · B
Medical Specialists: 32 · C
Surgical Specialists: 27 · C
Other Specialists: 25 · C
Short-Term General Hospitals: 2 (425 beds)
JCAH Accredited: 2
AMA Residency: 1
Services: 2 ★★★★
CMSA Access: Chicago–Gary–Lake County,
IL–IN–WI (524 points)
Places Rated Score: 1,481 · Places Rated Rank: 142

Killeen–Temple, TX
Office-Based Physicians
General/Family Practitioners: 38 · C
Medical Specialists: 102 · A
Surgical Specialists: 72 · C
Other Specialists: 69 · B

Short-Term General Hospitals: 6 (1,561 beds)
JCAH Accredited: 6
AMA Residency: 3
Services: 2 ★★, 1 ★★★, 3 ★★★★
Places Rated Score: 1,333 · Places Rated Rank: 184

Knoxville, TN
Office-Based Physicians
General/Family Practitioners: 142 · A
Medical Specialists: 245 · A
Surgical Specialists: 273 · A
Other Specialists: 234 · A
Short-Term General Hospitals: 11 (2,901 beds)
JCAH Accredited: 9
AMA Residency: 1
Services: 3 ★★, 3 ★★★, 5 ★★★★
Places Rated Score: 1,502 · Places Rated Rank: 134

Kokomo, IN
Office-Based Physicians
General/Family Practitioners: 31 · AA
Medical Specialists: 14 · C
Surgical Specialists: 25 · C
Other Specialists: 20 · C
Short-Term General Hospitals: 3 (517 beds)
JCAH Accredited: 3
Services: 1 ★★★, 2 ★★★★
Places Rated Score: 1,480 · Places Rated Rank: 144

★ La Crosse, WI
Office-Based Physicians
General/Family Practitioners: 23 · A
Medical Specialists: 84 · AA
Surgical Specialists: 65 · AA
Other Specialists: 63 · AA
Short-Term General Hospitals: 2 (730 beds)
JCAH Accredited: 2
AMA Residency: 2
Services: 2 ★★★★
Places Rated Score: 2,010 · Places Rated Rank: 30

Lafayette, LA
Office-Based Physicians
General/Family Practitioners: 41 · B
Medical Specialists: 66 · B
Surgical Specialists: 96 · A
Other Specialists: 65 · B
Short-Term General Hospitals: 5 (799 beds)
JCAH Accredited: 4
AMA Residency: 1
Services: 2 ★★, 1 ★★★, 2 ★★★★
Places Rated Score: 1,248 · Places Rated Rank: 211

Lafayette–West Lafayette, IN
Office-Based Physicians
General/Family Practitioners: 29 · A
Medical Specialists: 48 · A
Surgical Specialists: 53 · A
Other Specialists: 50 · AA
Short-Term General Hospitals: 2 (639 beds)
JCAH Accredited: 2
Services: 2 ★★★★
Places Rated Score: 1,563 · Places Rated Rank: 123

Lake Charles, LA
Office-Based Physicians
General/Family Practitioners: 45 · A
Medical Specialists: 51 · B
Surgical Specialists: 73 · A
Other Specialists: 39 · C
Short-Term General Hospitals: 5 (803 beds)
JCAH Accredited: 4
AMA Residency: 1
Services: 3 ★★, 1 ★★★, 1 ★★★★
Places Rated Score: 1,361 · Places Rated Rank: 173

Rating   Rating

Lake County, IL
Office-Based Physicians
  General/Family Practitioners: 88   B
  Medical Specialists: 228   A
  Surgical Specialists: 191   B
  Other Specialists: 224   AA
Short-Term General Hospitals: 8 (1,760 beds)
  JCAH Accredited: 8
  AMA Residency: 1
  Services: 3 ★★★, 5 ★★★★
CMSA Access: Chicago–Gary–Lake County,
  IL–IN–WI (180 points)
Places Rated Score: 1,584   Places Rated Rank: 117

Lakeland–Winter Haven, FL
Office-Based Physicians
  General/Family Practitioners: 68   B
  Medical Specialists: 129   B
  Surgical Specialists: 147   B
  Other Specialists: 111   B
Short-Term General Hospitals: 7 (1,543 beds)
  JCAH Accredited: 6
  Services: 1 ★, 3 ★★, 2 ★★★, 1 ★★★★
Places Rated Score: 911   Places Rated Rank: 291

Lancaster, PA
Office-Based Physicians
  General/Family Practitioners: 142   AA
  Medical Specialists: 76   C
  Surgical Specialists: 94   C
  Other Specialists: 83   C
Short-Term General Hospitals: 5 (1,322 beds)
  JCAH Accredited: 4
  AMA Residency: 1
  Services: 1 ★★, 1 ★★★, 3 ★★★★
Places Rated Score: 942   Places Rated Rank: 287

Lansing–East Lansing, MI
Office-Based Physicians
  General/Family Practitioners: 82   B
  Medical Specialists: 145   B
  Surgical Specialists: 116   C
  Other Specialists: 115   B
Short-Term General Hospitals: 7 (1,596 beds)
  JCAH Accredited: 6
  AMA Residency: 3
  Services: 2 ★★, 2 ★★★, 3 ★★★★
Places Rated Score: 988   Places Rated Rank: 280

Laredo, TX
Office-Based Physicians
  General/Family Practitioners: 19   C
  Medical Specialists: 24   C
  Surgical Specialists: 22   C
  Other Specialists: 21   C
Short-Term General Hospitals: 2 (383 beds)
  JCAH Accredited: 2
  Services: 1 ★★, 1 ★★★
Places Rated Score: 634   Places Rated Rank: 328

Las Cruces, NM
Office-Based Physicians
  General/Family Practitioners: 28   A
  Medical Specialists: 30   C
  Surgical Specialists: 39   C
  Other Specialists: 27   C
Short-Term General Hospital: 1 (239 beds)
  JCAH Accredited: 1
  Services: 1 ★★★
Places Rated Score: 604   Places Rated Rank: 329

Las Vegas, NV
Office-Based Physicians
  General/Family Practitioners: 110   B
  Medical Specialists: 182   B

  Surgical Specialists: 199   B
  Other Specialists: 157   B
Short-Term General Hospitals: 8 (1,946 beds)
  JCAH Accredited: 7
  AMA Residency: 1
  Services: 1 ★, 1 ★★, 3 ★★★, 3 ★★★★
Places Rated Score: 911   Places Rated Rank: 291

Lawrence, KS
Office-Based Physicians
  General/Family Practitioners: 21   AA
  Medical Specialists: 19   C
  Surgical Specialists: 25   C
  Other Specialists: 14   C
Short-Term General Hospitals: 2 (188 beds)
  JCAH Accredited: 1
  Services: 2 ★
Places Rated Score: 735   Places Rated Rank: 322

Lawrence–Haverhill, MA–NH
Office-Based Physicians
  General/Family Practitioners: N/A   C
  Medical Specialists: N/A   A
  Surgical Specialists: N/A   B
  Other Specialists: N/A   A
Short-Term General Hospitals: 6 (1,001 beds)
  JCAH Accredited: 6
  Services: 2 ★★★, 4 ★★★★
CMSA Access: Boston–Lawrence–Salem, MA–NH (167 points)
Places Rated Score: 1,451   Places Rated Rank: 151

Lawton, OK
Office-Based Physicians
  General/Family Practitioners: 19   C
  Medical Specialists: 23   C
  Surgical Specialists: 31   C
  Other Specialists: 21   C
Short-Term General Hospitals: 4 (631 beds)
  JCAH Accredited: 4
  Services: 3 ★★★, 1 ★★★★
Places Rated Score: 1,240   Places Rated Rank: 216

Lewiston–Auburn, ME
Office-Based Physicians
  General/Family Practitioners: 19   B
  Medical Specialists: 41   A
  Surgical Specialists: 46   A
  Other Specialists: 33   A
Short-Term General Hospitals: 3 (548 beds)
  JCAH Accredited: 3
  AMA Residency: 1
  Services: 1 ★, 2 ★★★★
Places Rated Score: 1,640   Places Rated Rank: 100

★ Lexington–Fayette, KY
Office-Based Physicians
  General/Family Practitioners: 82   A
  Medical Specialists: 228   AA
  Surgical Specialists: 199   AA
  Other Specialists: 208   AA
Short-Term General Hospitals: 10 (3,031 beds)
  JCAH Accredited: 8
  AMA Residency: 4
  Services: 3 ★★, 2 ★★★, 5 ★★★★
Places Rated Score: 2,224   Places Rated Rank: 8

Lima, OH
Office-Based Physicians
  General/Family Practitioners: 50   AA
  Medical Specialists: 26   C
  Surgical Specialists: 42   C
  Other Specialists: 38   B
Short-Term General Hospitals: 4 (828 beds)
  JCAH Accredited: 3
  Services: 1 ★★, 1 ★★★, 2 ★★★★
Places Rated Score: 1,373   Places Rated Rank: 168

Rating

Rating

Lincoln, NE
Office-Based Physicians
General/Family Practitioners: 49   A
Medical Specialists: 86   A
Surgical Specialists: 88   A
Other Specialists: 61   B
Short-Term General Hospitals: 4 (957 beds)
JCAH Accredited: 4
AMA Residency: 4
Services: 3 ★★★, 1 ★★★★
Places Rated Score: 1,451   Places Rated Rank: 151

Little Rock–North Little Rock, AR
Office-Based Physicians
General/Family Practitioners: 158   AA
Medical Specialists: 205   A
Surgical Specialists: 265   AA
Other Specialists: 212   AA
Short-Term General Hospitals: 11 (3,928 beds)
JCAH Accredited: 11
AMA Residency: 3
Services: 1 ★★, 6 ★★★, 4 ★★★★
Places Rated Score: 1,982   Places Rated Rank: 34

Longview–Marshall, TX
Office-Based Physicians
General/Family Practitioners: 42   A
Medical Specialists: 46   C
Surgical Specialists: 61   B
Other Specialists: 33   C
Short-Term General Hospitals: 6 (556 beds)
JCAH Accredited: 5
AMA Residency: 1
Services: 1 ★, 2 ★★, 3 ★★★
Places Rated Score: 1,292   Places Rated Rank: 199

Lorain–Elyria, OH
Office-Based Physicians
General/Family Practitioners: 44   C
Medical Specialists: 63   C
Surgical Specialists: 67   C
Other Specialists: 60   C
Short-Term General Hospitals: 6 (1,110 beds)
JCAH Accredited: 5
Services: 2 ★★, 1 ★★★, 3 ★★★★
CMSA Access: Cleveland–Akron–Lorain, OH (81 points)
Places Rated Score: 1,033   Places Rated Rank: 270

★ Los Angeles–Long Beach, CA
Office-Based Physicians
General/Family Practitioners: 2,189   A
Medical Specialists: 4,773   AA
Surgical Specialists: 4,121   A
Other Specialists: 3,975   AA
Short-Term General Hospitals: 136 (32,677 beds)
JCAH Accredited: 130
AMA Residency: 28
Services: 33 ★, 18 ★★, 37 ★★★, 48 ★★★★
CMSA Access: Los Angeles–Anaheim–Riverside,
CA (22 points)
Places Rated Score: 3,330   Places Rated Rank: 1

Louisville, KY–IN
Office-Based Physicians
General/Family Practitioners: 248   A
Medical Specialists: 428   A
Surgical Specialists: 436   A
Other Specialists: 391   AA
Short-Term General Hospitals: 16 (4,914 beds)
JCAH Accredited: 16
AMA Residency: 5
Services: 2 ★★, 10 ★★★, 4 ★★★★
Places Rated Score: 1,679   Places Rated Rank: 91

Lowell, MA–NH
Office-Based Physicians
General/Family Practitioners: N/A   C
Medical Specialists: N/A   AA
Surgical Specialists: N/A   A
Other Specialists: N/A   AA
Short-Term General Hospitals: 3 (490 beds)
JCAH Accredited: 3
Services: 2 ★★★, 1 ★★★★
CMSA Access: Boston–Lawrence–Salem, MA–NH (225 points)
Places Rated Score: 1,105   Places Rated Rank: 250

★ Lubbock, TX
Office-Based Physicians
General/Family Practitioners: 54   A
Medical Specialists: 93   A
Surgical Specialists: 118   AA
Other Specialists: 94   AA
Short-Term General Hospitals: 8 (1,560 beds)
JCAH Accredited: 7
AMA Residency: 3
Services: 2 ★★, 4 ★★★, 2 ★★★★
Places Rated Score: 2,130   Places Rated Rank: 14

Lynchburg, VA
Office-Based Physicians
General/Family Practitioners: 36   A
Medical Specialists: 54   A
Surgical Specialists: 62   A
Other Specialists: 41   B
Short-Term General Hospitals: 2 (696 beds)
JCAH Accredited: 2
AMA Residency: 2
Services: 2 ★★★
Places Rated Score: 1,176   Places Rated Rank: 233

Macon–Warner Robins, GA
Office-Based Physicians
General/Family Practitioners: 61   A
Medical Specialists: 79   C
Surgical Specialists: 118   A
Other Specialists: 89   A
Short-Term General Hospitals: 8 (1,313 beds)
JCAH Accredited: 8
AMA Residency: 1
Services: 2 ★, 3 ★★, 2 ★★★, 1 ★★★★
Places Rated Score: 1,388   Places Rated Rank: 164

Madison, WI
Office-Based Physicians
General/Family Practitioners: 105   AA
Medical Specialists: 227   AA
Surgical Specialists: 186   AA
Other Specialists: 221   AA
Short-Term General Hospitals: 5 (1,998 beds)
JCAH Accredited: 5
AMA Residency: 4
Services: 5 ★★★★
Places Rated Score: 1,910   Places Rated Rank: 46

Manchester, NH
Office-Based Physicians
General/Family Practitioners: 78   B
Medical Specialists: 185   A
Surgical Specialists: 171   B
Other Specialists: 133   A
Short-Term General Hospitals: 9 (1,722 beds)
JCAH Accredited: 9
AMA Residency: 1
Services: 3 ★★★, 6 ★★★★
Places Rated Score: 1,488   Places Rated Rank: 139

Mansfield, OH
Office-Based Physicians
General/Family Practitioners: 22   B

Rating

Medical Specialists: 41 — **B**
Surgical Specialists: 42 — **C**
Other Specialists: 34 — **B**
Short-Term General Hospitals: 3 (562 beds)
  JCAH Accredited: 2
  Services: 1 **, 1 ***, 1 ****
Places Rated Score: 1,069   Places Rated Rank: 259

McAllen–Edinburg–Mission, TX
Office-Based Physicians
  General/Family Practitioners: 71 — **B**
  Medical Specialists: 42 — **C**
  Surgical Specialists: 62 — **C**
  Other Specialists: 46 — **C**
Short-Term General Hospitals: 5 (823 beds)
  JCAH Accredited: 4
  AMA Residency: 1
  Services: 1 **, 2 ***, 2 ****
Places Rated Score: 747   Places Rated Rank: 321

Medford, OR
Office-Based Physicians
  General/Family Practitioners: 37 — **A**
  Medical Specialists: 58 — **A**
  Surgical Specialists: 70 — **AA**
  Other Specialists: 47 — **A**
Short-Term General Hospitals: 4 (559 beds)
  JCAH Accredited: 4
  Services: 1 **, 1 ***, 2 ****
Places Rated Score: 1,869   Places Rated Rank: 54

Melbourne–Titusville–Palm Bay, FL
Office-Based Physicians
  General/Family Practitioners: 73 — **B**
  Medical Specialists: 107 — **B**
  Surgical Specialists: 118 — **C**
  Other Specialists: 119 — **A**
Short-Term General Hospitals: 5 (1,068 beds)
  JCAH Accredited: 4
  Services: 1 ***, 4 ****
Places Rated Score: 1,016   Places Rated Rank: 276

Memphis, TN–AR–MS
Office-Based Physicians
  General/Family Practitioners: 135 — **C**
  Medical Specialists: 488 — **AA**
  Surgical Specialists: 514 — **AA**
  Other Specialists: 365 — **A**
Short-Term General Hospitals: 13 (6,269 beds)
  JCAH Accredited: 13
  AMA Residency: 6
  Services: 4 **, 4 ***, 5 ****
Places Rated Score: 1,517   Places Rated Rank: 132

Merced, CA
Office-Based Physicians
  General/Family Practitioners: 40 — **A**
  Medical Specialists: 30 — **C**
  Surgical Specialists: 37 — **C**
  Other Specialists: 30 — **C**
Short-Term General Hospitals: 6 (357 beds)
  JCAH Accredited: 4
  AMA Residency: 1
  Services: 3 *, 2 **, 1 ****
Places Rated Score: 1,083   Places Rated Rank: 256

★ Miami–Hialeah, FL
Office-Based Physicians
  General/Family Practitioners: 694 — **AA**
  Medical Specialists: 1,237 — **AA**
  Surgical Specialists: 1,062 — **AA**
  Other Specialists: 942 — **AA**
Short-Term General Hospitals: 31 (9,726 beds)
  JCAH Accredited: 29
  AMA Residency: 4

Rating

Services: 5 *, 5 **, 9 ***, 12 ****
CMSA Access: Miami–Fort Lauderdale, FL (6 points)
Places Rated Score: 2,085   Places Rated Rank: 21

Middlesex–Somerset–Hunterdon, NJ
Office-Based Physicians
  General/Family Practitioners: 149 — **C**
  Medical Specialists: 509 — **AA**
  Surgical Specialists: 360 — **B**
  Other Specialists: 295 — **B**
Short-Term General Hospitals: 7 (2,400 beds)
  JCAH Accredited: 7
  AMA Residency: 6
  Services: 1 ***, 6 ****
CMSA Access: New York–Northern NJ–Long
  Island, NY–NJ–CT (223 points)
Places Rated Score: 1,247   Places Rated Rank: 213

Middletown, CT
Office-Based Physicians
  General/Family Practitioners: N/A — **A**
  Medical Specialists: N/A — **B**
  Surgical Specialists: N/A — **C**
  Other Specialists: N/A — **A**
Short-Term General Hospitals: 2 (898 beds)
  JCAH Accredited: 2
  AMA Residency: 2
  Services: 2 ***
CMSA Access: Hartford–New Britain–Middletown,
  CT (142 points)
Places Rated Score: 1,439   Places Rated Rank: 153

Midland, TX
Office-Based Physicians
  General/Family Practitioners: 13 — **C**
  Medical Specialists: 37 — **B**
  Surgical Specialists: 40 — **B**
  Other Specialists: 22 — **C**
Short-Term General Hospitals: 2 (247 beds)
  JCAH Accredited: 1
  Services: 2 ***
Places Rated Score: 849   Places Rated Rank: 304

Milwaukee, WI
Office-Based Physicians
  General/Family Practitioners: 263 — **B**
  Medical Specialists: 696 — **AA**
  Surgical Specialists: 600 — **A**
  Other Specialists: 610 — **AA**
Short-Term General Hospitals: 26 (6,848 beds)
  JCAH Accredited: 22
  AMA Residency: 11
  Services: 6 **, 8 ***, 12 ****
CMSA Access: Milwaukee–Racine, WI (1 point)
Places Rated Score: 1,950   Places Rated Rank: 38

Minneapolis–St. Paul, MN–WI
Office-Based Physicians
  General/Family Practitioners: 757 — **AA**
  Medical Specialists: 953 — **A**
  Surgical Specialists: 864 — **B**
  Other Specialists: 807 — **A**
Short-Term General Hospitals: 35 (9,146 beds)
  JCAH Accredited: 31
  AMA Residency: 13
  Services: 3 *, 6 **, 11 ***, 15 ****
Places Rated Score: 1,841   Places Rated Rank: 58

Mobile, AL
Office-Based Physicians
  General/Family Practitioners: 86 — **B**
  Medical Specialists: 174 — **B**
  Surgical Specialists: 225 — **A**
  Other Specialists: 142 — **B**

Rating

Rating

Short-Term General Hospitals: 10 (2,162 beds)
  JCAH Accredited: 10
  AMA Residency: 1
  Services: 1 ★, 5 ★★, 2 ★★★, 2 ★★★★
Places Rated Score: 1,152   Places Rated Rank: 242

Modesto, CA
Office-Based Physicians
  General/Family Practitioners: 93   **AA**
  Medical Specialists: 104   **B**
  Surgical Specialists: 121   **B**
  Other Specialists: 98   **B**
Short-Term General Hospitals: 8 (1,233 beds)
  JCAH Accredited: 8
  AMA Residency: 1
  Services: 2 ★★, 4 ★★★, 2 ★★★★
Places Rated Score: 1,458   Places Rated Rank: 150

Monmouth–Ocean, NJ
Office-Based Physicians
  General/Family Practitioners: 113   **C**
  Medical Specialists: 462   **AA**
  Surgical Specialists: 397   **A**
  Other Specialists: 221   **C**
Short-Term General Hospitals: 10 (3,286 beds)
  JCAH Accredited: 9
  AMA Residency: 2
  Services: 1 ★, 1 ★★★, 8 ★★★★
CMSA Access: New York–Northern NJ–Long
  Island, NY–NJ–CT (184 points)
Places Rated Score: 1,298   Places Rated Rank: 196

Monroe, LA
Office-Based Physicians
  General/Family Practitioners: 27   **B**
  Medical Specialists: 51   **B**
  Surgical Specialists: 62   **A**
  Other Specialists: 46   **A**
Short-Term General Hospitals: 5 (958 beds)
  JCAH Accredited: 4
  AMA Residency: 1
  Services: 1 ★, 2 ★★, 2 ★★★★
Places Rated Score: 1,551   Places Rated Rank: 126

Montgomery, AL
Office-Based Physicians
  General/Family Practitioners: 46   **C**
  Medical Specialists: 110   **B**
  Surgical Specialists: 121   **B**
  Other Specialists: 61   **C**
Short-Term General Hospitals: 9 (1,703 beds)
  JCAH Accredited: 8
  AMA Residency: 3
  Services: 3 ★★, 4 ★★★, 2 ★★★★
Places Rated Score: 1,310   Places Rated Rank: 191

Muncie, IN
Office-Based Physicians
  General/Family Practitioners: 31   **A**
  Medical Specialists: 40   **B**
  Surgical Specialists: 36   **C**
  Other Specialists: 36   **B**
Short-Term General Hospital: 1 (547 beds)
  JCAH Accredited: 1
  AMA Residency: 1
  Services: 1 ★★★★
Places Rated Score: 811   Places Rated Rank: 307

Muskegon, MI
Office-Based Physicians
  General/Family Practitioners: 35   **A**
  Medical Specialists: 39   **C**
  Surgical Specialists: 46   **C**
  Other Specialists: 35   **C**

Short-Term General Hospitals: 3 (712 beds)
  JCAH Accredited: 2
  Services: 1 ★★★, 2 ★★★★
Places Rated Score: 1,064   Places Rated Rank: 262

Naples, FL
Office-Based Physicians
  General/Family Practitioners: 34   **AA**
  Medical Specialists: 53   **A**
  Surgical Specialists: 50   **B**
  Other Specialists: 32   **B**
Short-Term General Hospital: 1 (389 beds)
  JCAH Accredited: 1
  Services: 1 ★★★★
Places Rated Score: 1,039   Places Rated Rank: 269

Nashua, NH
Office-Based Physicians
  General/Family Practitioners: N/A   **B**
  Medical Specialists: N/A   **A**
  Surgical Specialists: N/A   **B**
  Other Specialists: N/A   **A**
Short-Term General Hospitals: 3 (481 beds)
  JCAH Accredited: 2
  Services: 1 ★★, 2 ★★★★
CMSA Access: Boston–Lawrence–Salem, MA–NH (299 points)
Places Rated Score: 1,486   Places Rated Rank: 141

★ Nashville, TN
Office-Based Physicians
  General/Family Practitioners: 150   **C**
  Medical Specialists: 485   **AA**
  Surgical Specialists: 484   **AA**
  Other Specialists: 392   **AA**
Short-Term General Hospitals: 23 (5,485 beds)
  JCAH Accredited: 23
  AMA Residency: 6
  Services: 5 ★★, 12 ★★★, 6 ★★★★
Places Rated Score: 2,052   Places Rated Rank: 28

Nassau–Suffolk, NY
Office-Based Physicians
  General/Family Practitioners: 431   **C**
  Medical Specialists: 1,950   **AA**
  Surgical Specialists: 1,445   **AA**
  Other Specialists: 1,104   **AA**
Short-Term General Hospitals: 27 (9,347 beds)
  JCAH Accredited: 26
  AMA Residency: 12
  Services: 1 ★, 1 ★★, 12 ★★★, 13 ★★★★
CMSA Access: New York–Northern NJ–Long
  Island, NY–NJ–CT (127 points)
Places Rated Score: 1,922   Places Rated Rank: 41

New Bedford, MA
Office-Based Physicians
  General/Family Practitioners: N/A   **C**
  Medical Specialists: N/A   **B**
  Surgical Specialists: N/A   **C**
  Other Specialists: N/A   **C**
Short-Term General Hospitals: 3 (610 beds)
  JCAH Accredited: 3
  Services: 1 ★★, 1 ★★★, 1 ★★★★
Places Rated Score: 792   Places Rated Rank: 313

New Britain, CT
Office-Based Physicians
  General/Family Practitioners: N/A   **C**
  Medical Specialists: N/A   **AA**
  Surgical Specialists: N/A   **A**
  Other Specialists: N/A   **AA**
Short-Term General Hospitals: 3 (595 beds)

Rating   Rating

JCAH Accredited: 3
AMA Residency: 1
Services: 1 ★★, 1 ★★★, 1 ★★★★
CMSA Access: Hartford–New Britain–Middletown,
CT (90 points)
Places Rated Score: 1,606   Places Rated Rank: 108

New Haven–Meriden, CT
Office-Based Physicians
General/Family Practitioners: 94   **C**
Medical Specialists: 572   **AA**
Surgical Specialists: 436   **AA**
Other Specialists: 388   **AA**
Short-Term General Hospitals: 9 (3,265 beds)
JCAH Accredited: 9
AMA Residency: 6
Services: 1 ★★★, 8 ★★★★
Places Rated Score: 1,609   Places Rated Rank: 107

New London–Norwich, CT–RI
Office-Based Physicians
General/Family Practitioners: 71   **C**
Medical Specialists: 177   **A**
Surgical Specialists: 170   **B**
Other Specialists: 86   **C**
Short-Term General Hospitals: 7 (1,172 beds)
JCAH Accredited: 7
AMA Residency: 1
Services: 2 ★★★, 5 ★★★★
Places Rated Score: 1,075   Places Rated Rank: 257

New Orleans, LA
Office-Based Physicians
General/Family Practitioners: 172   **C**
Medical Specialists: 718   **AA**
Surgical Specialists: 753   **AA**
Other Specialists: 608   **AA**
Short-Term General Hospitals: 29 (7,065 beds)
JCAH Accredited: 24
AMA Residency: 7
Services: 4 ★, 7 ★★, 7 ★★★, 11 ★★★★
Places Rated Score: 1,952   Places Rated Rank: 37

★ New York, NY
Office-Based Physicians
General/Family Practitioners: 1,117   **C**
Medical Specialists: 6,040   **AA**
Surgical Specialists: 3,989   **A**
Other Specialists: 4,049   **AA**
Short-Term General Hospitals: 85 (41,229 beds)
JCAH Accredited: 85
AMA Residency: 53
Services: 5 ★, 115 ★★★, 55 ★★★★
CMSA Access: New York–Northern NJ–Long
Island, NY–NJ–CT (113 points)
Places Rated Score: 3,215   Places Rated Rank: 2

★ Newark, NJ
Office-Based Physicians
General/Family Practitioners: 261   **C**
Medical Specialists: 1,214   **AA**
Surgical Specialists: 952   **AA**
Other Specialists: 707   **A**
Short-Term General Hospitals: 29 (10,169 beds)
JCAH Accredited: 28
AMA Residency: 14
Services: 2 ★, 2 ★★, 7 ★★★, 18 ★★★★
CMSA Access: New York–Northern NJ–Long
Island, NY–NJ–CT (170 points)
Places Rated Score: 2,104   Places Rated Rank: 18

Niagara Falls, NY
Office-Based Physicians
General/Family Practitioners: 25   **C**
Medical Specialists: 68   **B**

Surgical Specialists: 61   **C**
Other Specialists: 30   **C**
Short-Term General Hospitals: 5 (962 beds)
JCAH Accredited: 5
AMA Residency: 1
Services: 4 ★★★, 1 ★★★★
CMSA Access: Buffalo–Niagara Falls, NY (35 points)
Places Rated Score: 1,093   Places Rated Rank: 255

Norfolk–Virginia Beach–Newport News, VA
Office-Based Physicians
General/Family Practitioners: 284   **A**
Medical Specialists: 486   **A**
Surgical Specialists: 537   **B**
Other Specialists: 436   **A**
Short-Term General Hospitals: 19 (5,220 beds)
JCAH Accredited: 19
AMA Residency: 9
Services: 2 ★★, 7 ★★★, 10 ★★★★
Places Rated Score: 1,570   Places Rated Rank: 121

★ Norwalk, CT
Office-Based Physicians
General/Family Practitioners: N/A   **C**
Medical Specialists: N/A   **AA**
Surgical Specialists: N/A   **AA**
Other Specialists: N/A   **AA**
Short-Term General Hospitals: 2 (515 beds)
JCAH Accredited: 2
AMA Residency: 1
Services: 1 ★★, 1 ★★★★
CMSA Access: New York–Northern NJ–Long
Island, NY–NJ–CT (631 points)
Places Rated Score: 2,079   Places Rated Rank: 24

★ Oakland, CA
Office-Based Physicians
General/Family Practitioners: 433   **A**
Medical Specialists: 1,183   **AA**
Surgical Specialists: 883   **A**
Other Specialists: 978   **AA**
Short-Term General Hospitals: 34 (6,023 beds)
JCAH Accredited: 32
AMA Residency: 7
Services: 6 ★, 3 ★★, 10 ★★★, 15 ★★★★
CMSA Access: San Francisco–Oakland–San Jose,
CA (39 points)
Places Rated Score: 2,026   Places Rated Rank: 29

Ocala, FL
Office-Based Physicians
General/Family Practitioners: 24   **C**
Medical Specialists: 39   **C**
Surgical Specialists: 48   **C**
Other Specialists: 42   **B**
Short-Term General Hospitals: 2 (438 beds)
JCAH Accredited: 2
Services: 1 ★★, 1 ★★★
Places Rated Score: 562   Places Rated Rank: 331

Odessa, TX
Office-Based Physicians
General/Family Practitioners: 21   **C**
Medical Specialists: 34   **C**
Surgical Specialists: 50   **B**
Other Specialists: 23   **C**
Short-Term General Hospital: 1 (361 beds)
JCAH Accredited: 1
AMA Residency: 1
Services: 1 ★★★
Places Rated Score: 505   Places Rated Rank: 333

Oklahoma City, OK
Office-Based Physicians
General/Family Practitioners: 225   **A**

Rating

Medical Specialists: 392 — A
Surgical Specialists: 392 — B
Other Specialists: 347 — A
Short-Term General Hospitals: 21 (4,456 beds)
JCAH Accredited: 18
AMA Residency: 5
Services: 1 ★, 4 ★★, 8 ★★★, 8 ★★★★
Places Rated Score: 1,641   Places Rated Rank: 99

Olympia, WA
Office-Based Physicians
General/Family Practitioners: 50 — AA
Medical Specialists: 48 — B
Surgical Specialists: 49 — C
Other Specialists: 52 — A
Short-Term General Hospitals: 2 (450 beds)
JCAH Accredited: 1
Services: 1 ★★★, 1 ★★★★
Places Rated Score: 1,137   Places Rated Rank: 246

Omaha, NE–IA
Office-Based Physicians
General/Family Practitioners: 147 — A
Medical Specialists: 294 — A
Surgical Specialists: 288 — A
Other Specialists: 241 — A
Short-Term General Hospitals: 13 (4,406 beds)
JCAH Accredited: 13
AMA Residency: 6
Services: 4 ★★★, 9 ★★★★
Places Rated Score: 1,831   Places Rated Rank: 61

Orange County, NY
Office-Based Physicians
General/Family Practitioners: 33 — C
Medical Specialists: 123 — A
Surgical Specialists: 109 — B
Other Specialists: 65 — C
Short-Term General Hospitals: 7 (1,070 beds)
JCAH Accredited: 7
Services: 3 ★★, 3 ★★★, 1 ★★★★
CMSA Access: New York–Northern NJ–Long
Island, NY–NJ–CT (320 points)
Places Rated Score: 1,464   Places Rated Rank: 147

Orlando, FL
Office-Based Physicians
General/Family Practitioners: 179 — B
Medical Specialists: 344 — A
Surgical Specialists: 407 — A
Other Specialists: 256 — B
Short-Term General Hospitals: 13 (3,718 beds)
JCAH Accredited: 13
AMA Residency: 2
Services: 1 ★★, 9 ★★★, 3 ★★★★
Places Rated Score: 1,226   Places Rated Rank: 222

Owensboro, KY
Office-Based Physicians
General/Family Practitioners: 16 — B
Medical Specialists: 37 — A
Surgical Specialists: 44 — AA
Other Specialists: 22 — B
Short-Term General Hospitals: 2 (590 beds)
JCAH Accredited: 2
Services: 1 ★★, 1 ★★★
Places Rated Score: 1,291   Places Rated Rank: 200

Oxnard–Ventura, CA
Office-Based Physicians
General/Family Practitioners: 177 — AA
Medical Specialists: 228 — A
Surgical Specialists: 234 — B
Other Specialists: 225 — A
Short-Term General Hospitals: 10 (1,477 beds)
JCAH Accredited: 10

Rating

AMA Residency: 1
Services: 3 ★, 2 ★★, 2 ★★★, 3 ★★★★
CMSA Access: Los Angeles–Anaheim–Riverside,
CA (135 points)
Places Rated Score: 1,464   Places Rated Rank: 147

Panama City, FL
Office-Based Physicians
General/Family Practitioners: 14 — C
Medical Specialists: 33 — C
Surgical Specialists: 43 — B
Other Specialists: 29 — C
Short-Term General Hospitals: 3 (505 beds)
JCAH Accredited: 3
Services: 2 ★★★, 1 ★★★★
Places Rated Score: 1,098   Places Rated Rank: 252

Parkersburg–Marietta, WV–OH
Office-Based Physicians
General/Family Practitioners: 31 — B
Medical Specialists: 34 — C
Surgical Specialists: 46 — C
Other Specialists: 38 — B
Short-Term General Hospitals: 4 (842 beds)
JCAH Accredited: 3
Services: 1 ★★, 3 ★★★★
Places Rated Score: 1,226   Places Rated Rank: 222

Pascagoula, MS
Office-Based Physicians
General/Family Practitioners: 21 — C
Medical Specialists: 25 — C
Surgical Specialists: 37 — C
Other Specialists: 22 — C
Short-Term General Hospitals: 2 (449 beds)
JCAH Accredited: 2
Services: 1 ★★★, 1 ★★★★
Places Rated Score: 776   Places Rated Rank: 318

Pawtucket–Woonsocket–Attleboro, RI–MA
Office-Based Physicians
General/Family Practitioners: N/A — C
Medical Specialists: N/A — AA
Surgical Specialists: N/A — AA
Other Specialists: N/A — A
Short-Term General Hospitals: 5 (904 beds)
JCAH Accredited: 5
AMA Residency: 1
Services: 1 ★★, 3 ★★★, 1 ★★★★
CMSA Access: Providence–Pawtucket–Fall River,
RI–MA (34 points)
Places Rated Score: 1,417   Places Rated Rank: 157

Pensacola, FL
Office-Based Physicians
General/Family Practitioners: 59 — B
Medical Specialists: 111 — B
Surgical Specialists: 132 — B
Other Specialists: 107 — A
Short-Term General Hospitals: 8 (1,869 beds)
JCAH Accredited: 7
AMA Residency: 3
Services: 1 ★, 1 ★★, 3 ★★★, 3 ★★★★
Places Rated Score: 1,342   Places Rated Rank: 178

Peoria, IL
Office-Based Physicians
General/Family Practitioners: 93 — AA
Medical Specialists: 118 — B
Surgical Specialists: 112 — C
Other Specialists: 122 — A
Short-Term General Hospitals: 6 (1,879 beds)
JCAH Accredited: 6
AMA Residency: 2
Services: 1 ★, 1 ★★, 1 ★★★, 3 ★★★★
Places Rated Score: 1,279   Places Rated Rank: 205

Rating

Rating

★ Philadelphia, PA–NJ
Office-Based Physicians
  General/Family Practitioners: 869 — **B**
  Medical Specialists: 2,647 — **AA**
  Surgical Specialists: 2,071 — **A**
  Other Specialists: 2,141 — **AA**
Short-Term General Hospitals: 75 (20,556 beds)
  JCAH Accredited: 68
  AMA Residency: 33
  Services: 4 ★, 4 ★★, 28 ★★★, 39 ★★★★
CMSA Access: Philadelphia–Wilmington–Trenton,
  PA–NJ–DE–MD (14 points)
Places Rated Score: 2,776   Places Rated Rank: 4

Phoenix, AZ
Office-Based Physicians
  General/Family Practitioners: 446 — **A**
  Medical Specialists: 785 — **A**
  Surgical Specialists: 845 — **A**
  Other Specialists: 720 — **A**
Short-Term General Hospitals: 28 (6,862 beds)
  JCAH Accredited: 26
  AMA Residency: 8
  Services: 2 ★, 3 ★★, 7 ★★★, 16 ★★★★
Places Rated Score: 1,709   Places Rated Rank: 83

Pine Bluff, AR
Office-Based Physicians
  General/Family Practitioners: 19 — **B**
  Medical Specialists: 26 — **B**
  Surgical Specialists: 35 — **B**
  Other Specialists: 23 — **B**
Short-Term General Hospital: 1 (500 beds)
  JCAH Accredited: 1
  AMA Residency: 1
  Services: 1 ★★★★
Places Rated Score: 874   Places Rated Rank: 301

Pittsburgh, PA
Office-Based Physicians
  General/Family Practitioners: 436 — **B**
  Medical Specialists: 1,012 — **A**
  Surgical Specialists: 925 — **A**
  Other Specialists: 820 — **A**
Short-Term General Hospitals: 38 (11,721 beds)
  JCAH Accredited: 35
  AMA Residency: 16
  Services: 3 ★, 2 ★★, 14 ★★★, 19 ★★★★
CMSA Access: Pittsburgh–Beaver County, PA (2 points)
Places Rated Score: 1,961   Places Rated Rank: 35

Pittsfield, MA
Office-Based Physicians
  General/Family Practitioners: 21 — **C**
  Medical Specialists: 88 — **AA**
  Surgical Specialists: 68 — **A**
  Other Specialists: 55 — **A**
Short-Term General Hospitals: 4 (722 beds)
  JCAH Accredited: 4
  AMA Residency: 1
  Services: 2 ★★★, 2 ★★★★
Places Rated Score: 1,801   Places Rated Rank: 69

★ Portland, ME
Office-Based Physicians
  General/Family Practitioners: 53 — **A**
  Medical Specialists: 137 — **AA**
  Surgical Specialists: 124 — **AA**
  Other Specialists: 100 — **AA**
Short-Term General Hospitals: 7 (1,179 beds)
  JCAH Accredited: 5
  AMA Residency: 2
  Services: 2 ★★, 4 ★★★, 1 ★★★★
Places Rated Score: 2,067   Places Rated Rank: 26

Portland, OR
Office-Based Physicians
  General/Family Practitioners: 241 — **B**
  Medical Specialists: 653 — **AA**
  Surgical Specialists: 638 — **AA**
  Other Specialists: 573 — **AA**
Short-Term General Hospitals: 21 (4,481 beds)
  JCAH Accredited: 19
  AMA Residency: 6
  Services: 2 ★, 1 ★★, 10 ★★★, 8 ★★★★
Places Rated Score: 1,883   Places Rated Rank: 51

Portsmouth–Dover–Rochester, NH–ME
Office-Based Physicians
  General/Family Practitioners: 97 — **B**
  Medical Specialists: 129 — **C**
  Surgical Specialists: 133 — **C**
  Other Specialists: 111 — **C**
Short-Term General Hospitals: 9 (997 beds)
  JCAH Accredited: 9
  Services: 2 ★★, 5 ★★★, 2 ★★★★
Places Rated Score: 909   Places Rated Rank: 294

Poughkeepsie, NY
Office-Based Physicians
  General/Family Practitioners: 32 — **C**
  Medical Specialists: 113 — **A**
  Surgical Specialists: 106 — **B**
  Other Specialists: 92 — **A**
Short-Term General Hospitals: 4 (1,232 beds)
  JCAH Accredited: 4
  AMA Residency: 1
  Services: 2 ★★★, 2 ★★★★
Places Rated Score: 1,155   Places Rated Rank: 240

Providence, RI
Office-Based Physicians
  General/Family Practitioners: 96 — **C**
  Medical Specialists: 449 — **AA**
  Surgical Specialists: 353 — **A**
  Other Specialists: 239 — **B**
Short-Term General Hospitals: 11 (3,066 beds)
  JCAH Accredited: 10
  AMA Residency: 5
  Services: 2 ★★, 5 ★★★, 4 ★★★★
CMSA Access: Providence–Pawtucket–Fall River,
  RI–MA (21 points)
Places Rated Score: 1,315   Places Rated Rank: 189

Provo–Orem, UT
Office-Based Physicians
  General/Family Practitioners: 57 — **A**
  Medical Specialists: 51 — **C**
  Surgical Specialists: 78 — **C**
  Other Specialists: 50 — **C**
Short-Term General Hospitals: 3 (516 beds)
  JCAH Accredited: 3
  Services: 1 ★★★, 2 ★★★★
Places Rated Score: 837   Places Rated Rank: 305

Pueblo, CO
Office-Based Physicians
  General/Family Practitioners: 26 — **B**
  Medical Specialists: 54 — **A**
  Surgical Specialists: 56 — **A**
  Other Specialists: 41 — **A**
Short-Term General Hospitals: 2 (561 beds)
  JCAH Accredited: 2
  AMA Residency: 1
  Services: 2 ★★★★
Places Rated Score: 1,369   Places Rated Rank: 170

Racine, WI
Office-Based Physicians
  General/Family Practitioners: 33 — **B**

Rating

Medical Specialists: 52   B
Surgical Specialists: 58   C
Other Specialists: 38   C
Short-Term General Hospitals: 3 (535 beds)
  JCAH Accredited: 3
  Services: 1 ★★★, 2 ★★★★
CMSA Access: Milwaukee–Racine, WI (92 points)
Places Rated Score: 1,060   Places Rated Rank: 263

Raleigh–Durham, NC
Office-Based Physicians
  General/Family Practitioners: 160   A
  Medical Specialists: 444   AA
  Surgical Specialists: 366   AA
  Other Specialists: 427   AA
Short-Term General Hospitals: 12 (3,638 beds)
  JCAH Accredited: 7
  AMA Residency: 5
  Services: 5 ★★, 3 ★★★, 4 ★★★★
Places Rated Score: 1,808   Places Rated Rank: 67

Rapid City, SD
Office-Based Physicians
  General/Family Practitioners: 18   A
  Medical Specialists: 29   A
  Surgical Specialists: 40   AA
  Other Specialists: 32   AA
Short-Term General Hospitals: 2 (339 beds)
  JCAH Accredited: 1
  Services: 1 ★★★, 1 ★★★★
Places Rated Score: 1,920   Places Rated Rank: 42

Reading, PA
Office-Based Physicians
  General/Family Practitioners: 106   AA
  Medical Specialists: 115   B
  Surgical Specialists: 119   B
  Other Specialists: 75   C
Short-Term General Hospitals: 3 (1,047 beds)
  JCAH Accredited: 3
  AMA Residency: 2
  Services: 1 ★★★, 2 ★★★★
Places Rated Score: 963   Places Rated Rank: 283

Redding, CA
Office-Based Physicians
  General/Family Practitioners: 48   AA
  Medical Specialists: 35   C
  Surgical Specialists: 56   A
  Other Specialists: 57   AA
Short-Term General Hospitals: 4 (458 beds)
  JCAH Accredited: 3
  AMA Residency: 2
  Services: 2 ★, 1 ★★★, 1 ★★★★
Places Rated Score: 1,596   Places Rated Rank: 114

Reno, NV
Office-Based Physicians
  General/Family Practitioners: 55   A
  Medical Specialists: 101   A
  Surgical Specialists: 146   AA
  Other Specialists: 106   AA
Short-Term General Hospitals: 5 (1,286 beds)
  JCAH Accredited: 5
  AMA Residency: 2
  Services: 1 ★★, 1 ★★★, 3 ★★★★
Places Rated Score: 1,847   Places Rated Rank: 56

Richland–Kennewick–Pasco, WA
Office-Based Physicians
  General/Family Practitioners: 43   AA
  Medical Specialists: 40   C
  Surgical Specialists: 48   C
  Other Specialists: 36   B

Rating

Short-Term General Hospitals: 4 (354 beds)
  JCAH Accredited: 3
  Services: 1 ★★, 3 ★★★
Places Rated Score: 1,266   Places Rated Rank: 207

Richmond–Petersburg, VA
Office-Based Physicians
  General/Family Practitioners: 195   A
  Medical Specialists: 451   AA
  Surgical Specialists: 373   A
  Other Specialists: 347   AA
Short-Term General Hospitals: 15 (4,881 beds)
  JCAH Accredited: 15
  AMA Residency: 4
  Services: 2 ★, 6 ★★★, 7 ★★★★
Places Rated Score: 1,822   Places Rated Rank: 63

Riverside–San Bernardino, CA
Office-Based Physicians
  General/Family Practitioners: 434   A
  Medical Specialists: 670   B
  Surgical Specialists: 679   C
  Other Specialists: 540   B
Short-Term General Hospitals: 36 (6,233 beds)
  JCAH Accredited: 34
  AMA Residency: 5
  Services: 6 ★, 7 ★★, 10 ★★★, 13 ★★★★
CMSA Access: Los Angeles–Anaheim–Riverside,
  CA (92 points)
Places Rated Score: 1,492   Places Rated Rank: 136

Roanoke, VA
Office-Based Physicians
  General/Family Practitioners: 57   A
  Medical Specialists: 109   A
  Surgical Specialists: 128   AA
  Other Specialists: 110   AA
Short-Term General Hospitals: 4 (2,190 beds)
  JCAH Accredited: 4
  AMA Residency: 3
  Services: 4 ★★★★
Places Rated Score: 1,812   Places Rated Rank: 66

★ Rochester, MN
Office-Based Physicians
  General/Family Practitioners: 21   A
  Medical Specialists: 318   AA
  Surgical Specialists: 145   AA
  Other Specialists: 242   AA
Short-Term General Hospitals: 3 (1,757 beds)
  JCAH Accredited: 3
  AMA Residency: 2
  Services: 1 ★★, 1 ★★★, 1 ★★★★
Places Rated Score: 2,088   Places Rated Rank: 20

Rochester, NY
Office-Based Physicians
  General/Family Practitioners: 128   C
  Medical Specialists: 549   AA
  Surgical Specialists: 404   B
  Other Specialists: 349   A
Short-Term General Hospitals: 15 (3,476 beds)
  JCAH Accredited: 15
  AMA Residency: 5
  Services: 5 ★★, 4 ★★★, 6 ★★★★
Places Rated Score: 1,369   Places Rated Rank: 170

Rockford, IL
Office-Based Physicians
  General/Family Practitioners: 61   A
  Medical Specialists: 133   A
  Surgical Specialists: 122   A
  Other Specialists: 96   A
Short-Term General Hospitals: 5 (1,165 beds)

Rating

Rating

JCAH Accredited: 5
AMA Residency: 3
Services: 1 ★, 1 ★★, 1 ★★★, 2 ★★★★
Places Rated Score: 1,409   Places Rated Rank: 158

Sacramento, CA
Office-Based Physicians
  General/Family Practitioners: 383   **AA**
  Medical Specialists: 588   **A**
  Surgical Specialists: 571   **A**
  Other Specialists: 561   **AA**
Short-Term General Hospitals: 17 (3,482 beds)
  JCAH Accredited: 17
  AMA Residency: 3
  Services: 2 ★, 5 ★★, 4 ★★★, 6 ★★★★
Places Rated Score: 1,602   Places Rated Rank: 111

Saginaw–Bay City–Midland, MI
Office-Based Physicians
  General/Family Practitioners: 81   **B**
  Medical Specialists: 104   **C**
  Surgical Specialists: 114   **C**
  Other Specialists: 99   **B**
Short-Term General Hospitals: 7 (1,830 beds)
  JCAH Accredited: 6
  AMA Residency: 5
  Services: 1 ★★, 3 ★★★, 3 ★★★★
Places Rated Score: 1,030   Places Rated Rank: 271

St. Cloud, MN
Office-Based Physicians
  General/Family Practitioners: 54   **AA**
  Medical Specialists: 34   **C**
  Surgical Specialists: 50   **C**
  Other Specialists: 36   **C**
Short-Term General Hospitals: 5 (698 beds)
  JCAH Accredited: 3
  Services: 2 ★★, 2 ★★★, 1 ★★★★
Places Rated Score: 1,280   Places Rated Rank: 204

St. Joseph, MO
Office-Based Physicians
  General/Family Practitioners: 19   **A**
  Medical Specialists: 29   **B**
  Surgical Specialists: 24   **C**
  Other Specialists: 15   **C**
Short-Term General Hospitals: 2 (674 beds)
  JCAH Accredited: 2
  Services: 1 ★★★, 1 ★★★★
Places Rated Score: 1,236   Places Rated Rank: 219

St. Louis, MO–IL
Office-Based Physicians
  General/Family Practitioners: 281   **C**
  Medical Specialists: 1,157   **A**
  Surgical Specialists: 1,044   **A**
  Other Specialists: 830   **A**
Short-Term General Hospitals: 42 (13,736 beds)
  JCAH Accredited: 38
  AMA Residency: 12
  Services: 1 ★, 7 ★★, 14 ★★★, 20 ★★★★
Places Rated Score: 1,832   Places Rated Rank: 60

Salem, OR
Office-Based Physicians
  General/Family Practitioners: 79   **AA**
  Medical Specialists: 69   **C**
  Surgical Specialists: 84   **C**
  Other Specialists: 75   **B**
Short-Term General Hospitals: 4 (556 beds)
  JCAH Accredited: 4
  Services: 2 ★★, 2 ★★★
Places Rated Score: 922   Places Rated Rank: 289

Salem–Gloucester, MA
Office-Based Physicians
  General/Family Practitioners: N/A   **C**

Medical Specialists: N/A   **A**
Surgical Specialists: N/A   **B**
Other Specialists: N/A   **A**
Short-Term General Hospitals: 7 (1,083 beds)
  JCAH Accredited: 7
  AMA Residency: 2
  Services: 1 ★, 3 ★★★, 3 ★★★★
CMSA Access: Boston–Lawrence–Salem, MA–NH (209 points)
Places Rated Score: 1,698   Places Rated Rank: 86

Salinas–Seaside–Monterey, CA
Office-Based Physicians
  General/Family Practitioners: 76   **A**
  Medical Specialists: 108   **B**
  Surgical Specialists: 116   **C**
  Other Specialists: 77   **C**
Short-Term General Hospitals: 6 (806 beds)
  JCAH Accredited: 6
  AMA Residency: 2
  Services: 1 ★, 1 ★★, 2 ★★★, 2 ★★★★
Places Rated Score: 1,000   Places Rated Rank: 278

Salt Lake City–Ogden, UT
Office-Based Physicians
  General/Family Practitioners: 165   **C**
  Medical Specialists: 410   **A**
  Surgical Specialists: 474   **A**
  Other Specialists: 441   **AA**
Short-Term General Hospitals: 14 (3,137 beds)
  JCAH Accredited: 13
  AMA Residency: 5
  Services: 1 ★, 1 ★★, 5 ★★★, 7 ★★★★
Places Rated Score: 1,422   Places Rated Rank: 156

San Angelo, TX
Office-Based Physicians
  General/Family Practitioners: 11   **C**
  Medical Specialists: 45   **A**
  Surgical Specialists: 49   **A**
  Other Specialists: 36   **A**
Short-Term General Hospitals: 3 (491 beds)
  JCAH Accredited: 3
  Services: 1 ★★★, 2 ★★★★
Places Rated Score: 1,680   Places Rated Rank: 90

San Antonio, TX
Office-Based Physicians
  General/Family Practitioners: 257   **B**
  Medical Specialists: 486   **A**
  Surgical Specialists: 494   **B**
  Other Specialists: 414   **A**
Short-Term General Hospitals: 18 (6,718 beds)
  JCAH Accredited: 17
  AMA Residency: 7
  Services: 1 ★, 2 ★★, 7 ★★★, 8 ★★★★
Places Rated Score: 1,364   Places Rated Rank: 172

San Diego, CA
Office-Based Physicians
  General/Family Practitioners: 596   **AA**
  Medical Specialists: 1,039   **A**
  Surgical Specialists: 1,022   **A**
  Other Specialists: 1,042   **AA**
Short-Term General Hospitals: 28 (6,881 beds)
  JCAH Accredited: 28
  AMA Residency: 7
  Services: 2 ★, 3 ★★, 9 ★★★, 14 ★★★★
Places Rated Score: 1,833   Places Rated Rank: 59

★ San Francisco, CA
Office-Based Physicians
  General/Family Practitioners: 351   **A**
  Medical Specialists: 1,519   **AA**
  Surgical Specialists: 1,129   **AA**
  Other Specialists: 1,457   **AA**

Rating   Rating

Short-Term General Hospitals: 27 (7,015 beds)
  JCAH Accredited: 27
  AMA Residency: 15
  Services: 3 ★, 2 ★★, 5 ★★★, 17 ★★★★
CMSA Access: San Francisco–Oakland–San Jose,
  CA (45 points)
Places Rated Score: 2,282   Places Rated Rank: 7

San Jose, CA
Office-Based Physicians
  General/Family Practitioners: 291   B
  Medical Specialists: 834   AA
  Surgical Specialists: 731   AA
  Other Specialists: 666   AA
Short-Term General Hospitals: 13 (4,864 beds)
  JCAH Accredited: 13
  AMA Residency: 5
  Services: 1 ★, 1 ★★, 4 ★★★, 7 ★★★★
CMSA Access: San Francisco–Oakland–San Jose,
  CA (67 points)
Places Rated Score: 1,604   Places Rated Rank: 110

Santa Barbara–Santa Maria–Lompoc, CA
Office-Based Physicians
  General/Family Practitioners: 97   AA
  Medical Specialists: 193   AA
  Surgical Specialists: 191   AA
  Other Specialists: 173   AA
Short-Term General Hospitals: 8 (967 beds)
  JCAH Accredited: 8
  AMA Residency: 1
  Services: 2 ★, 1 ★★, 3 ★★★, 2 ★★★★
Places Rated Score: 1,919   Places Rated Rank: 44

Santa Cruz, CA
Office-Based Physicians
  General/Family Practitioners: 69   AA
  Medical Specialists: 78   B
  Surgical Specialists: 91   B
  Other Specialists: 87   A
Short-Term General Hospitals: 3 (555 beds)
  JCAH Accredited: 3
  Services: 2 ★★★, 1 ★★★★
CMSA Access: San Francisco–Oakland–San Jose,
  CA (150 points)
Places Rated Score: 1,338   Places Rated Rank: 182

Santa Fe, NM
Office-Based Physicians
  General/Family Practitioners: 33   AA
  Medical Specialists: 55   AA
  Surgical Specialists: 57   AA
  Other Specialists: 59   AA
Short-Term General Hospitals: 3 (387 beds)
  JCAH Accredited: 3
  Services: 1 ★, 1 ★★, 1 ★★★★
Places Rated Score: 1,889   Places Rated Rank: 50

Santa Rosa–Petaluma, CA
Office-Based Physicians
  General/Family Practitioners: 140   AA
  Medical Specialists: 139   A
  Surgical Specialists: 149   A
  Other Specialists: 132   A
Short-Term General Hospitals: 7 (734 beds)
  JCAH Accredited: 7
  AMA Residency: 1
  Services: 2 ★, 1 ★★, 3 ★★★, 1 ★★★★
CMSA Access: San Francisco–Oakland–San Jose,
  CA (90 points)
Places Rated Score: 1,575   Places Rated Rank: 120

Sarasota, FL
Office-Based Physicians
  General/Family Practitioners: 73   AA
  Medical Specialists: 158   AA
  Surgical Specialists: 152   AA
  Other Specialists: 118   AA
Short-Term General Hospitals: 3 (1,122 beds)
  JCAH Accredited: 3
  Services: 1 ★, 1 ★★★, 1 ★★★★
Places Rated Score: 1,553   Places Rated Rank: 125

Savannah, GA
Office-Based Physicians
  General/Family Practitioners: 42   B
  Medical Specialists: 90   A
  Surgical Specialists: 121   AA
  Other Specialists: 86   A
Short-Term General Hospitals: 4 (1,225 beds)
  JCAH Accredited: 4
  AMA Residency: 1
  Services: 1 ★★, 1 ★★★, 2 ★★★★
Places Rated Score: 1,402   Places Rated Rank: 160

Scranton–Wilkes-Barre, PA
Office-Based Physicians
  General/Family Practitioners: 201   AA
  Medical Specialists: 255   B
  Surgical Specialists: 263   B
  Other Specialists: 159   C
Short-Term General Hospitals: 19 (4,204 beds)
  JCAH Accredited: 19
  AMA Residency: 6
  Services: 2 ★, 4 ★★, 7 ★★★, 6 ★★★★
Places Rated Score: 1,618   Places Rated Rank: 105

Seattle, WA
Office-Based Physicians
  General/Family Practitioners: 660   AA
  Medical Specialists: 890   AA
  Surgical Specialists: 846   A
  Other Specialists: 946   AA
Short-Term General Hospitals: 29 (5,564 beds)
  JCAH Accredited: 22
  AMA Residency: 9
  Services: 4 ★, 4 ★★, 10 ★★★, 11 ★★★★
CMSA Access: Seattle–Tacoma, WA (6 points)
Places Rated Score: 1,997   Places Rated Rank: 33

Sharon, PA
Office-Based Physicians
  General/Family Practitioners: 22   B
  Medical Specialists: 27   C
  Surgical Specialists: 43   B
  Other Specialists: 21   C
Short-Term General Hospitals: 4 (670 beds)
  JCAH Accredited: 3
  Services: 1 ★★, 2 ★★★, 1 ★★★★
Places Rated Score: 1,301   Places Rated Rank: 195

Sheboygan, WI
Office-Based Physicians
  General/Family Practitioners: 22   A
  Medical Specialists: 24   C
  Surgical Specialists: 31   C
  Other Specialists: 16   C
Short-Term General Hospitals: 3 (403 beds)
  JCAH Accredited: 3
  Services: 1 ★★, 2 ★★★★
Places Rated Score: 1,354   Places Rated Rank: 176

Sherman–Denison, TX
Office-Based Physicians
  General/Family Practitioners: 17   B
  Medical Specialists: 46   A

Rating

Surgical Specialists: 43 — **A**
Other Specialists: 32 — **A**
Short-Term General Hospitals: 3 (630 beds)
 JCAH Accredited: 3
 Services: 3 ★★★
Places Rated Score: 1,646 — Places Rated Rank: 98

Shreveport, LA
Office-Based Physicians
 General/Family Practitioners: 48 — **C**
 Medical Specialists: 186 — **AA**
 Surgical Specialists: 205 — **AA**
 Other Specialists: 148 — **AA**
Short-Term General Hospitals: 12 (2,811 beds)
 JCAH Accredited: 11
 AMA Residency: 3
 Services: 3 ★, 2 ★★, 3 ★★★, 4 ★★★★
Places Rated Score: 1,998 — Places Rated Rank: 31

Sioux City, IA–NE
Office-Based Physicians
 General/Family Practitioners: 32 — **AA**
 Medical Specialists: 30 — **C**
 Surgical Specialists: 48 — **B**
 Other Specialists: 39 — **A**
Short-Term General Hospitals: 2 (855 beds)
 JCAH Accredited: 2
 AMA Residency: 2
 Services: 2 ★★★★
Places Rated Score: 1,400 — Places Rated Rank: 161

★ Sioux Falls, SD
Office-Based Physicians
 General/Family Practitioners: 48 — **AA**
 Medical Specialists: 63 — **AA**
 Surgical Specialists: 61 — **A**
 Other Specialists: 52 — **AA**
Short-Term General Hospitals: 4 (1,237 beds)
 JCAH Accredited: 3
 AMA Residency: 3
 Services: 1 ★★, 1 ★★★, 2 ★★★★
Places Rated Score: 2,190 — Places Rated Rank: 9

South Bend–Mishawaka, IN
Office-Based Physicians
 General/Family Practitioners: 66 — **AA**
 Medical Specialists: 70 — **B**
 Surgical Specialists: 88 — **B**
 Other Specialists: 81 — **A**
Short-Term General Hospitals: 4 (1,061 beds)
 JCAH Accredited: 3
 AMA Residency: 3
 Services: 1 ★★, 1 ★★★, 2 ★★★★
Places Rated Score: 1,329 — Places Rated Rank: 185

Spokane, WA
Office-Based Physicians
 General/Family Practitioners: 126 — **AA**
 Medical Specialists: 157 — **A**
 Surgical Specialists: 177 — **A**
 Other Specialists: 146 — **AA**
Short-Term General Hospitals: 7 (1,741 beds)
 JCAH Accredited: 7
 AMA Residency: 2
 Services: 1 ★, 3 ★★★, 3 ★★★★
Places Rated Score: 1,726 — Places Rated Rank: 79

Springfield, IL
Office-Based Physicians
 General/Family Practitioners: 36 — **B**
 Medical Specialists: 112 — **AA**
 Surgical Specialists: 106 — **AA**
 Other Specialists: 78 — **AA**
Short-Term General Hospitals: 3 (1,409 beds)
 JCAH Accredited: 3

Rating

AMA Residency: 2
 Services: 1 ★, 2 ★★★★
Places Rated Score: 1,542 — Places Rated Rank: 129

Springfield, MA
Office-Based Physicians
 General/Family Practitioners: 91 — **C**
 Medical Specialists: 278 — **A**
 Surgical Specialists: 240 — **B**
 Other Specialists: 191 — **A**
Short-Term General Hospitals: 9 (2,170 beds)
 JCAH Accredited: 9
 AMA Residency: 1
 Services: 4 ★★★, 5 ★★★★
Places Rated Score: 1,206 — Places Rated Rank: 228

Springfield, MO
Office-Based Physicians
 General/Family Practitioners: 38 — **B**
 Medical Specialists: 120 — **AA**
 Surgical Specialists: 126 — **AA**
 Other Specialists: 104 — **AA**
Short-Term General Hospitals: 4 (1,814 beds)
 JCAH Accredited: 2
 Services: 1 ★★, 1 ★★★, 2 ★★★★
Places Rated Score: 1,597 — Places Rated Rank: 113

★ Stamford, CT
Office-Based Physicians
 General/Family Practitioners: N/A — **C**
 Medical Specialists: N/A — **AA**
 Surgical Specialists: N/A — **AA**
 Other Specialists: N/A — **AA**
Short-Term General Hospitals: 4 (800 beds)
 JCAH Accredited: 4
 AMA Residency: 3
 Services: 1 ★★, 1 ★★★, 2 ★★★★
CMSA Access: New York–Northern NJ–Long
 Island, NY–NJ–CT (449 points)
Places Rated Score: 2,149 — Places Rated Rank: 11

State College, PA
Office-Based Physicians
 General/Family Practitioners: 32 — **AA**
 Medical Specialists: 33 — **B**
 Surgical Specialists: 32 — **C**
 Other Specialists: 26 — **C**
Short-Term General Hospitals: 2 (330 beds)
 JCAH Accredited: 2
 Services: 1 ★★, 1 ★★★★
Places Rated Score: 1,044 — Places Rated Rank: 268

Steubenville–Weirton, OH–WV
Office-Based Physicians
 General/Family Practitioners: 24 — **C**
 Medical Specialists: 30 — **C**
 Surgical Specialists: 36 — **C**
 Other Specialists: 30 — **C**
Short-Term General Hospitals: 4 (863 beds)
 JCAH Accredited: 3
 Services: 1 ★★, 1 ★★★, 2 ★★★★
Places Rated Score: 1,070 — Places Rated Rank: 258

Stockton, CA
Office-Based Physicians
 General/Family Practitioners: 114 — **A**
 Medical Specialists: 130 — **B**
 Surgical Specialists: 151 — **B**
 Other Specialists: 97 — **C**
Short-Term General Hospitals: 8 (1,024 beds)
 JCAH Accredited: 7
 AMA Residency: 1
 Services: 1 ★, 1 ★★, 3 ★★★, 3 ★★★★
Places Rated Score: 1,095 — Places Rated Rank: 254

Rating

Syracuse, NY
Office-Based Physicians
General/Family Practitioners: 133   B
Medical Specialists: 242   A
Surgical Specialists: 282   A
Other Specialists: 198   B
Short-Term General Hospitals: 9 (2,569 beds)
JCAH Accredited: 9
AMA Residency: 5
Services: 2 ★★, 2 ★★★, 5 ★★★★
Places Rated Score: 1,252   Places Rated Rank: 210

Tacoma, WA
Office-Based Physicians
General/Family Practitioners: 155   AA
Medical Specialists: 152   C
Surgical Specialists: 168   C
Other Specialists: 165   B
Short-Term General Hospitals: 7 (1,611 beds)
JCAH Accredited: 7
AMA Residency: 2
Services: 2 ★, 2 ★★★, 3 ★★★★
CMSA Access: Seattle–Tacoma, WA (39 points)
Places Rated Score: 1,024   Places Rated Rank: 273

Tallahassee, FL
Office-Based Physicians
General/Family Practitioners: 66   AA
Medical Specialists: 76   B
Surgical Specialists: 100   A
Other Specialists: 64   B
Short-Term General Hospitals: 3 (1,002 beds)
JCAH Accredited: 3
AMA Residency: 1
Services: 1 ★★, 2 ★★★★
Places Rated Score: 1,209   Places Rated Rank: 226

Tampa–St. Petersburg–Clearwater, FL
Office-Based Physicians
General/Family Practitioners: 374   B
Medical Specialists: 827   A
Surgical Specialists: 769   B
Other Specialists: 687   A
Short-Term General Hospitals: 41 (10,329 beds)
JCAH Accredited: 34
AMA Residency: 4
Services: 7 ★, 6 ★★, 19 ★★★, 9 ★★★★
Places Rated Score: 1,605   Places Rated Rank: 109

Terre Haute, IN
Office-Based Physicians
General/Family Practitioners: 33   A
Medical Specialists: 38   C
Surgical Specialists: 48   B
Other Specialists: 39   B
Short-Term General Hospitals: 3 (649 beds)
JCAH Accredited: 3
AMA Residency: 1
Services: 1 ★, 1 ★★★, 1 ★★★★
Places Rated Score: 1,096   Places Rated Rank: 253

Texarkana, TX–Texarkana, AR
Office-Based Physicians
General/Family Practitioners: 22   B
Medical Specialists: 49   A
Surgical Specialists: 60   AA
Other Specialists: 39   A
Short-Term General Hospitals: 4 (803 beds)
JCAH Accredited: 4
Services: 2 ★★, 1 ★★★, 1 ★★★★
Places Rated Score: 1,758   Places Rated Rank: 74

Toledo, OH
Office-Based Physicians
General/Family Practitioners: 163   AA

Rating

Medical Specialists: 233   A
Surgical Specialists: 274   A
Other Specialists: 247   AA
Short-Term General Hospitals: 11 (3,774 beds)
JCAH Accredited: 10
AMA Residency: 5
Services: 3 ★★★, 8 ★★★★
Places Rated Score: 1,871   Places Rated Rank: 52

Topeka, KS
Office-Based Physicians
General/Family Practitioners: 25   C
Medical Specialists: 76   A
Surgical Specialists: 80   A
Other Specialists: 90   AA
Short-Term General Hospitals: 3 (756 beds)
JCAH Accredited: 3
AMA Residency: 1
Services: 3 ★★★★
Places Rated Score: 1,546   Places Rated Rank: 127

Trenton, NJ
Office-Based Physicians
General/Family Practitioners: 42   C
Medical Specialists: 217   AA
Surgical Specialists: 182   AA
Other Specialists: 147   AA
Short-Term General Hospitals: 5 (1,678 beds)
JCAH Accredited: 5
AMA Residency: 3
Services: 5 ★★★★
CMSA Access: Philadelphia–Wilmington–Trenton,
PA–NJ–DE–MD (188 points)
Places Rated Score: 1,871   Places Rated Rank: 52

Tucson, AZ
Office-Based Physicians
General/Family Practitioners: 105   B
Medical Specialists: 321   AA
Surgical Specialists: 284   A
Other Specialists: 290   AA
Short-Term General Hospitals: 11 (2,410 beds)
JCAH Accredited: 10
AMA Residency: 5
Services: 2 ★, 2 ★★★, 7 ★★★★
Places Rated Score: 1,698   Places Rated Rank: 86

Tulsa, OK
Office-Based Physicians
General/Family Practitioners: 121   C
Medical Specialists: 310   A
Surgical Specialists: 295   B
Other Specialists: 224   B
Short-Term General Hospitals: 16 (3,054 beds)
JCAH Accredited: 12
AMA Residency: 4
Services: 11 ★★★, 5 ★★★★
Places Rated Score: 1,236   Places Rated Rank: 219

Tuscaloosa, AL
Office-Based Physicians
General/Family Practitioners: 29   B
Medical Specialists: 53   A
Surgical Specialists: 56   B
Other Specialists: 47   A
Short-Term General Hospitals: 3 (780 beds)
JCAH Accredited: 3
AMA Residency: 1
Services: 1 ★★, 1 ★★★, 1 ★★★★
Places Rated Score: 1,287   Places Rated Rank: 201

Tyler, TX
Office-Based Physicians
General/Family Practitioners: 29   B
Medical Specialists: 75   AA

Rating　　　　　　　　　　　　　　　　　　　　　　　　　　　**Rating**

Surgical Specialists: 86　　　　　　　　　**AA**
Other Specialists: 60　　　　　　　　　　　**A**
Short-Term General Hospitals: 4 (662 beds)
　JCAH Accredited: 3
　AMA Residency: 1
　Services: 1 ★★, 1 ★★★, 2 ★★★★
Places Rated Score: 1,805　　　　Places Rated Rank: 68

Utica–Rome, NY
Office-Based Physicians
　General/Family Practitioners: 61　　　　**B**
　Medical Specialists: 86　　　　　　　　　**C**
　Surgical Specialists: 121　　　　　　　　**B**
　Other Specialists: 66　　　　　　　　　　**C**
Short-Term General Hospitals: 7 (1,228 beds)
　JCAH Accredited: 6
　AMA Residency: 1
　Services: 2 ★★, 3 ★★★, 2 ★★★★
Places Rated Score: 1,046　　　　Places Rated Rank: 266

Vallejo–Fairfield–Napa, CA
Office-Based Physicians
　General/Family Practitioners: 80　　　　**B**
　Medical Specialists: 150　　　　　　　　**A**
　Surgical Specialists: 111　　　　　　　　**C**
　Other Specialists: 121　　　　　　　　　**B**
Short-Term General Hospitals: 8 (1,964 beds)
　JCAH Accredited: 8
　AMA Residency: 1
　Services: 2 ★, 1 ★★, 2 ★★★, 3 ★★★★
CMSA Access: San Francisco–Oakland–San Jose,
　CA (130 points)
Places Rated Score: 1,241　　　　Places Rated Rank: 215

Vancouver, WA
Office-Based Physicians
　General/Family Practitioners: 43　　　　**B**
　Medical Specialists: 57　　　　　　　　　**C**
　Surgical Specialists: 69　　　　　　　　　**C**
　Other Specialists: 40　　　　　　　　　　**C**
Short-Term General Hospital: 1 (353 beds)
　JCAH Accredited: 1
　Services: 1 ★★★★
CMSA Access: Portland–Vancouver, OR (97 points)
Places Rated Score: 546　　　　Places Rated Rank: 332

★ Victoria, TX
Office-Based Physicians
　General/Family Practitioners: 28　　　　**AA**
　Medical Specialists: 32　　　　　　　　　**A**
　Surgical Specialists: 40　　　　　　　　　**AA**
　Other Specialists: 36　　　　　　　　　　**AA**
Short-Term General Hospitals: 3 (516 beds)
　JCAH Accredited: 3
　Services: 1 ★★, 1 ★★★, 1 ★★★★
Places Rated Score: 2,130　　　　Places Rated Rank: 14

Vineland–Millville–Bridgeton, NJ
Office-Based Physicians
　General/Family Practitioners: 22　　　　**C**
　Medical Specialists: 43　　　　　　　　　**B**
　Surgical Specialists: 44　　　　　　　　　**C**
　Other Specialists: 25　　　　　　　　　　**C**
Short-Term General Hospitals: 3 (595 beds)
　JCAH Accredited: 3
　Services: 1 ★★★, 2 ★★★★
CMSA Access: Philadelphia–Wilmington–Trenton,
　PA–NJ–DE–MD (382 points)
Places Rated Score: 1,475　　　　Places Rated Rank: 145

Visalia–Tulare–Porterville, CA
Office-Based Physicians
　General/Family Practitioners: 73　　　　**A**
　Medical Specialists: 81　　　　　　　　　**C**
　Surgical Specialists: 69　　　　　　　　　**C**

Other Specialists: 68　　　　　　　　　　**C**
Short-Term General Hospitals: 7 (681 beds)
　JCAH Accredited: 7
　Services: 3 ★★, 4 ★★★
Places Rated Score: 1,047　　　　Places Rated Rank: 265

Waco, TX
Office-Based Physicians
　General/Family Practitioners: 40　　　　**A**
　Medical Specialists: 56　　　　　　　　　**B**
　Surgical Specialists: 77　　　　　　　　　**B**
　Other Specialists: 52　　　　　　　　　　**B**
Short-Term General Hospitals: 3 (557 beds)
　JCAH Accredited: 3
　AMA Residency: 2
　Services: 1 ★★, 2 ★★★★
Places Rated Score: 1,103　　　　Places Rated Rank: 251

★ Washington, DC–MD–VA
Office-Based Physicians
　General/Family Practitioners: 626　　　**B**
　Medical Specialists: 2,353　　　　　　　**AA**
　Surgical Specialists: 1,860　　　　　　　**AA**
　Other Specialists: 1,927　　　　　　　　**AA**
Short-Term General Hospitals: 40 (12,918 beds)
　JCAH Accredited: 40
　AMA Residency: 18
　Services: 4 ★, 1 ★★, 11 ★★★, 24 ★★★★
Places Rated Score: 2,139　　　　Places Rated Rank: 13

Waterbury, CT
Office-Based Physicians
　General/Family Practitioners: N/A　　　**C**
　Medical Specialists: N/A　　　　　　　　**AA**
　Surgical Specialists: N/A　　　　　　　　**AA**
　Other Specialists: N/A　　　　　　　　　**AA**
Short-Term General Hospitals: 2 (618 beds)
　JCAH Accredited: 2
　AMA Residency: 2
　Services: 2 ★★★★
Places Rated Score: 1,381　　　　Places Rated Rank: 166

Waterloo–Cedar Falls, IA
Office-Based Physicians
　General/Family Practitioners: 44　　　　**AA**
　Medical Specialists: 39　　　　　　　　　**C**
　Surgical Specialists: 56　　　　　　　　　**B**
　Other Specialists: 44　　　　　　　　　　**B**
Short-Term General Hospitals: 5 (789 beds)
　JCAH Accredited: 4
　AMA Residency: 2
　Services: 1 ★★, 1 ★★★, 3 ★★★★
Places Rated Score: 1,630　　　　Places Rated Rank: 102

Wausau, WI
Office-Based Physicians
　General/Family Practitioners: 32　　　　**AA**
　Medical Specialists: 32　　　　　　　　　**C**
　Surgical Specialists: 38　　　　　　　　　**C**
　Other Specialists: 30　　　　　　　　　　**B**
Short-Term General Hospital: 1 (300 beds)
　JCAH Accredited: 1
　AMA Residency: 1
　Services: 1 ★★★★
Places Rated Score: 886　　　　Places Rated Rank: 297

West Palm Beach–Boca Raton–Delray Beach, FL
Office-Based Physicians
　General/Family Practitioners: 169　　　**A**
　Medical Specialists: 447　　　　　　　　**AA**
　Surgical Specialists: 419　　　　　　　　**AA**
　Other Specialists: 262　　　　　　　　　**A**
Short-Term General Hospitals: 13 (2,861 beds)

Rating   Rating

JCAH Accredited: 12
Services: 6 ★★, 5 ★★★, 2 ★★★★
Places Rated Score: 1,583   Places Rated Rank: 118

Wheeling, WV–OH
Office-Based Physicians
General/Family Practitioners: 56   AA
Medical Specialists: 64   B
Surgical Specialists: 82   A
Other Specialists: 59   A
Short-Term General Hospitals: 6 (1,521 beds)
JCAH Accredited: 5
AMA Residency: 2
Services: 2 ★, 1 ★★, 2 ★★★, 1 ★★★★
Places Rated Score: 1,688   Places Rated Rank: 88

Wichita, KS
Office-Based Physicians
General/Family Practitioners: 123   A
Medical Specialists: 181   A
Surgical Specialists: 198   A
Other Specialists: 157   A
Short-Term General Hospitals: 11 (2,581 beds)
JCAH Accredited: 9
AMA Residency: 4
Services: 2 ★★, 5 ★★★, 4 ★★★★
Places Rated Score: 1,715   Places Rated Rank: 81

Wichita Falls, TX
Office-Based Physicians
General/Family Practitioners: 36   AA
Medical Specialists: 47   B
Surgical Specialists: 60   A
Other Specialists: 39   B
Short-Term General Hospitals: 4 (615 beds)
JCAH Accredited: 3
AMA Residency: 2
Services: 1 ★★, 2 ★★★, 1 ★★★★
Places Rated Score: 1,714   Places Rated Rank: 82

Williamsport, PA
Office-Based Physicians
General/Family Practitioners: 35   AA
Medical Specialists: 40   B
Surgical Specialists: 45   B
Other Specialists: 37   A
Short-Term General Hospitals: 4 (751 beds)
JCAH Accredited: 4
AMA Residency: 1
Services: 1 ★, 1 ★★★, 2 ★★★★
Places Rated Score: 1,760   Places Rated Rank: 73

Wilmington, DE–NJ–MD
Office-Based Physicians
General/Family Practitioners: 101   B
Medical Specialists: 212   A
Surgical Specialists: 200   B
Other Specialists: 199   A
Short-Term General Hospitals: 7 (2,250 beds)
JCAH Accredited: 6
AMA Residency: 3
Services: 4 ★★★, 3 ★★★★
CMSA Access: Philadelphia–Wilmington–Trenton,
PA–NJ–DE–MD (140 points)
Places Rated Score: 1,296   Places Rated Rank: 197

Wilmington, NC
Office-Based Physicians
General/Family Practitioners: 13   C

Medical Specialists: 60   AA
Surgical Specialists: 82   AA
Other Specialists: 38   A
Short-Term General Hospitals: 2 (532 beds)
JCAH Accredited: 2
AMA Residency: 1
Services: 1 ★★★, 1 ★★★★
Places Rated Score: 1,503   Places Rated Rank: 133

Worcester, MA
Office-Based Physicians
General/Family Practitioners: 85   C
Medical Specialists: 301   AA
Surgical Specialists: 202   B
Other Specialists: 169   A
Short-Term General Hospitals: 14 (2,580 beds)
JCAH Accredited: 14
AMA Residency: 5
Services: 6 ★★★, 8 ★★★★
Places Rated Score: 1,890   Places Rated Rank: 48

Yakima, WA
Office-Based Physicians
General/Family Practitioners: 49   AA
Medical Specialists: 45   C
Surgical Specialists: 60   C
Other Specialists: 44   B
Short-Term General Hospitals: 5 (586 beds)
JCAH Accredited: 3
Services: 2 ★, 2 ★★★, 1 ★★★★
Places Rated Score: 1,185   Places Rated Rank: 231

York, PA
Office-Based Physicians
General/Family Practitioners: 111   AA
Medical Specialists: 77   C
Surgical Specialists: 89   C
Other Specialists: 64   C
Short-Term General Hospitals: 4 (1,022 beds)
JCAH Accredited: 3
AMA Residency: 1
Services: 1 ★★, 2 ★★★, 1 ★★★★
Places Rated Score: 802   Places Rated Rank: 310

Youngstown–Warren, OH
Office-Based Physicians
General/Family Practitioners: 59   C
Medical Specialists: 167   B
Surgical Specialists: 172   C
Other Specialists: 125   B
Short-Term General Hospitals: 7 (2,424 beds)
JCAH Accredited: 5
AMA Residency: 3
Services: 1 ★★, 2 ★★★, 4 ★★★★
Places Rated Score: 880   Places Rated Rank: 298

Yuba City, CA
Office-Based Physicians
General/Family Practitioners: 30   A
Medical Specialists: 36   B
Surgical Specialists: 44   B
Other Specialists: 28   B
Short-Term General Hospitals: 3 (282 beds)
JCAH Accredited: 2
Services: 1 ★, 1 ★★, 1 ★★★
Places Rated Score: 1,045   Places Rated Rank: 267

Et Cetera

AIR QUALITY IN THE METRO AREAS

The harm caused by air pollution has been well documented. Many people have experienced the watering eyes, shortness of breath, mild chest pain, or burning feeling in the throat or lungs that can accompany a day when air pollution is high. Air pollutants have also been known to cause mental retardation, seizures, nerve disorders, damage to heart and lung tissue, and even death. In 1948, for example, weather conditions trapped polluted air over the city of Donora, PA, for nearly a week. Of a population of 8,000, almost 6,000 people became ill, complaining of chest pains, headaches, eye irritation, coughing, and dizzy spells, and 20 people died from related causes. Four years later in London, about 4,000 people died from smog that lingered over the city for five days.

The blistering summer of 1988, with its dry, blazing hot days, saw the worst air pollution in a decade. Twenty-eight cities were added to those in which air quality did not meet Environmental Protection Agency (EPA) standards, for a total of 68 areas exceeding limits for ozone and 59 topping the EPA carbon monoxide standards. Most of the agency's 323 monitors found ozone levels averaged 5 percent higher than in 1983, which had been the decade's worst year. In 1989, the EPA calculated that a person who lived next to a very heavily polluting factory for seven years would have a one in ten chance of getting lung cancer. Although few people actually live right next door to the heaviest polluting factories, the EPA statement gives a strong warning and makes an important link between pollution and personal health.

The six major air pollutants as defined by the EPA are as follows:

- *Total Suspended Particulates* (TSP) is a name for any minute particle or group of particles—pollen, soot, asbestos, sand, or dust, for example—borne by the wind. Generally speaking, the concentration of particulates increases as one travels from west to east, because that is the direction of the wind. Like most other pollutants, particulates are found in greatest concentrations around cities and industrial centers. The exceptions are the dry regions of the Southwest, where dust storms create clouds of TSP.
- *Sulfur Dioxide* is an acrid, corrosive gas produced by burning coal that is high in sulfur. The worst polluters are the coal-burning power plants in Illinois, Indiana, Ohio, Kentucky, West Virginia, and Pennsylvania.

- *Carbon Monoxide* is especially deadly. When inhaled in great enough concentrations, it enters the bloodstream and chemically prevents the absorption of oxygen, resulting in death. Carbon monoxide is produced by the incomplete combustion of carbon fuels; about 75 percent of it is produced by automobiles, so the levels are higher around large metro areas.
- *Photochemical Oxidants* are a group of polluting chemicals that combine in the presence of strong sunlight. These chemicals are mostly nitrous oxides, hydrocarbons, and ozone. The common name for photochemical oxidants is *smog*. Because oxidant pollution involves the combination of sunshine, which can't be regulated, and automobiles, which are only partially regulated, it is the fastest-spreading and hardest to control of all pollution problems.
- *Nitrous Oxides* are produced when fossil fuels are burned at extremely high temperatures, a process that occurs most often in internal combustion engines (i.e., cars). Nitrous oxides are a primary ingredient of photochemical oxidants (smog).
- *Lead* is a poisonous element that usually occurs as a metal. However, traces can be found in living tissue, in soil and water, and even in the air we breathe. Fortunately, with the advent of unleaded gasoline, the major source of this airborne poison has been largely controlled.

Most major metropolitan areas violate the ozone requirements, and at least 75 million people live in cities with unsafe levels of ozone and carbon monoxide. As you can see from the following tables, the worst cities for ozone—based on actual ozone levels—in 1988 were Los Angeles, Houston, New York, and San Diego. The worst for actual carbon monoxide levels were New York, Steubenville, OH, Spokane, WA, and Los Angeles.

Top 10 Violators of Clean Air Standards— Ozone

1. Los Angeles, CA
2. Houston, TX
3. New York, NY
4. San Diego, CA
5. Atlanta, GA
6. Baltimore, MD
7. Chicago, IL
8. Springfield, MA
9. Fresno, CA
10. Milwaukee, WI

Source: Environmental Protection Agency, 1988.

Top 10 Violators of Clean Air Standards—Carbon Monoxide

1. New York, NY
2. Steubenville, OH
3. Spokane, WA
4. Los Angeles, CA
5. Albuquerque, NM
6. Las Vegas, NV
7. Denver, CO
8. El Paso, TX
9. Tacoma, WA
10. Fairbanks, AK

Source: Environmental Protection Agency, 1988.

The effects of some of these noxious vapors on our planet? In the Midwest, ozone pollution and acid rain are responsible for at least $5 billion in crop damage annually. Pollutants have damaged 87 percent of San Bernardino National Forest's ponderosa pines. In New York, Vermont, and New Hampshire, air pollution has killed 60 percent of high-elevation red spruce trees.

ENVIRONMENT AND HEALTH: REGIONAL TRENDS

It wasn't until the early 1970s that terms like *ecosystem, ecology,* and *environmental hazards* became part of our vocabulary. Before that, only health specialists and physicians seemed concerned about the potentially lethal effects of pollution, contaminants, and additives. More and more, experts are focusing on environmental factors to explain the distribution and concentration of various ailments and diseases.

Where you live is increasingly a determining factor in what diseases you are susceptible to. It is possible, for example, that drinking chlorinated water (chlorine is used to kill bacteria not only in swimming pools but also in most drinking water) increases the risk of gastrointestinal cancer. Many birth defects, disorders of the nervous system, and extraordinarily high rates of certain cancers have been linked directly to hazardous waste dumps, chemical spills, insecticides, industrial wastes, and other contaminants.

No part of the country is completely free of these 20th-century, self-created menaces. Some states are worse than others for certain problems—like California's smog or New Jersey's toxic wastes. At this point, then, the best we can do is consider the extent to which a given state is attempting to contain or correct its ecological problems. And that is exactly what was measured in a recent study by the non-profit environmental-information group, Renew America.

The study rated the states on their efforts to address five environmental concerns: forest management, solid waste recycling, drinking water, food safety, and growth and environment (a broad category including air and water pollution control, land-use planning, water and energy conservation, and solid waste management). The results of the study—ranking the states from 1 to 50 on their environmental efforts—are shown in the table below ("States Ranked For Environmental Effort, from Best to Worst").

The study found that only eight states encourage the use of organic farming and natural pesticides to reduce food contamination. In most states, pesticide regulation falls to the state department of agriculture, intended to help farmers, not police them—a conflict of interest that has seriously weakened pesticide-control programs. The EPA estimates that in 38 states pesticides have already fouled the ground water used by half of all Americans as their main source of drinking water. The federal agency says, too, that pesticide residues on food are even more menacing than hazardous-waste dumps or air pollution.

In addition, only eight states have implemented comprehensive recycling programs to operate when landfill space reaches capacity within the next few years. And only six states have launched water conservation plans. In ranking the states for environmental efforts, Renew America points out, a state that is considered to have an excellent environmental program is not necessarily the state with the cleanest environment. In fact, a state with a "high" ranking may have the worst problems—a fact that has forced it to take significant action.

Northeast—Toxic Dumps and Solid Waste Disposal

The Northeast is a bad area for toxic waste, containing four of the country's five most dangerous Superfund sites, areas targeted for high-priority hazardous waste cleanup efforts. The Lipari Landfill in Pitman, NJ; the Bruin Lagoon in Bruin, PA; the Helen Kramer Landfill in Mantua Township, NJ; and the Industri-Plex in Woburn, MA, although not regarded by the EPA as Love Canal equals, are among the Superfund sites considered most threatening to health and environment. The fifth is the Tybouts Corner Landfill in New Castle County, DE.

In terms of water problems, the Northeast has its share. Acid rain has damaged numerous lakes in this region. In addition, the Chesapeake Bay, the Hudson

States Ranked for Environmental Effort, from Best to Worst

1. Minnesota	18. Michigan	33. Tennessee
2. California	18. Ohio	
3. New Jersey	18. South Dakota	33. Utah
4. Massachusetts		33. West Virginia
5. Oregon	21. Delaware	33. Wyoming
	21. Iowa	39. Nebraska
6. Washington	23. Illinois	39. Nevada
7. Maryland	23. Pennsylvania	
7. Montana	23. Virginia	39. North Dakota
7. New York		39. Texas
7. Wisconsin	26. Arkansas	43. Louisiana
	27. Colorado	43. New Hampshire
11. Indiana	27. Rhode Island	45. Oklahoma
12. Hawaii	29. Georgia	
12. Kentucky	29. North Carolina	46. New Mexico
14. Connecticut		47. Idaho
14. Maine	29. South Carolina	48. Mississippi
	32. Arizona	49. Missouri
14. Vermont	33. Alaska	50. Alabama
17. Florida	33. Kansas	

Source: Conservation Foundation, 1983.

River in New York, Boston Harbor, and the Allegheny River in Pennsylvania are endangered bodies of water. And at least six New York and New Jersey beaches were closed during the summer of 1988 because of pollution (hospital wastes and raw sewage) washing ashore or contaminating the water—a case in which water pollution and problems of solid waste disposal go hand in hand. According to the Renew America study, however, Maine gets high marks for its targeting of water utilities in violation of state and federal standards—an effort that gives it the number-one ranking for its efforts to have safe drinking water.

New Jersey, long considered an ecological disaster, is becoming a leader in environmental protection, and for a good reason. The fifth-smallest state in area, it ranks among the nation's top seven producers of chemicals, pharmaceuticals, and petroleum distillates. All of its major cities periodically exceed federal smog standards, and it leads the country with 100 EPA-designated hazardous-waste cleanup sites.

Responding to this, New Jersey passed the first mandatory recycling law in the United States and began taxing chemical companies to pay for toxic cleanups—an approach that became the model for the 1980 federal Superfund law. It has passed a "right-to-know" law for chemical workers and residents, has a state-sponsored program that tests homes for radon gas free of charge, and requires plant owners to rid their sites of dangerous chemicals before they sell or close them.

South—Water, Water Everywhere, But . . .

Lake Lanier in Georgia, the Everglades in Florida, and Pamlico Sound in North Carolina are all potential victims of agricultural runoff, a serious threat to water quality. For example, in Lake Okeechobee in Florida—a 6,000-year-old body of water—a big problem is dairy farming. Phosphorous in cattle manure and fertilizer washes into the lake from dairies, cattle ranches, sod farms, and sugar cane fields.

The phosphorous acts as fertilizer in the lake and alters the balance of life there, fueling the overgrowth of plants and algae reducing the oxygen in the water, thus reducing its ability to support other life. The health of Lake Okeechobee is in turn essential to the health of the Everglades, the magnificent national park in southern Florida. The same sort of disease has already killed Lake Apopka in central Florida.

South Carolina has recently taken a giant (and highly controversial) step toward environmental protection. It has closed its borders to chemical waste. In the past, its GSX landfill near Pinewood had annually accepted 135,000 tons of hazardous waste, such as solvents, acids, and other chemicals. About 70 percent of the waste came from out of state; North Carolina, Florida, and Pennsylvania are only 3 of the 29 states affected by the ban. Opponents claim that the policy could lead to illegal dumping, but so far South Carolina is standing firm and maintaining the ban.

The Renew America study found Louisiana to be the state with the least-developed environmental program, and Tennessee leading it only by a hair. Still, Florida was ranked eighth for its environmental efforts, with North Carolina doing pretty well at number 12 in the nation, and Georgia coming in at number 18.

Midwest—Everytime It Rains, It Rains . . .

Acid rain is a mixture of precipitation and acidic air pollutants, notably sulfur dioxide and nitrogen oxide. The major source is the coal-burning power plants in the Midwest (Illinois, Indiana, and Ohio), though much of the damage is being done in the Northeast. Other prime offenders are in Kentucky, West Virginia, and Pennsylvania. The current goal of environmentalists is to see a 50-percent reduction in sulfur dioxide emissions from power plants. And they are hoping that Congress will allocate money for research and cleanup costs.

In response to serious ozone pollution, the EPA has moved to ban construction of major air-polluting plants. Among the Midwest cities from which the EPA has had enough air pollution are Chicago and its suburbs, the northwest corner of Indiana, and St. Cloud, MN.

On the more positive side, according to Renew America, Iowa leads all states in its efforts to produce harmless food. After findings that 25 percent of its drinking-water wells are at least somewhat contaminated with pesticides, the state imposed special taxes on agricultural businesses to pay for cleanups and for efforts to persuade farmers to stop using dangerous chemicals.

Facing other water problems as well, the Midwest's Mississippi River, Saginaw River in Michigan, White River in South Dakota, and Lakes Huron and Michigan are all endangered bodies of water due to problems of agricultural runoff.

Mountain and Pacific States—Smoggy But Trying

The Rio Grande in New Mexico (and Texas) and the Platte River in Colorado (a state with a pristine image) are bodies of water endangered by agricultural runoff. San Francisco Bay, Lake Tahoe in Nevada, and the Bear River in Idaho face the same problem.

California, which has the nation's worst smog, has led efforts to combat that problem and to identify and control previously ignored carcinogenic air pollutants. Plans include converting cars and trucks to clean fuels, developing stricter pollution controls for vehicles and industrial plants, and converting gas-powered lawn mowers to cleaner fuel.

Among the Pacific states are three making top-notch environmental efforts, according to the Renew America study. Oregon is doing the best job to control growth and has an outstanding waste-recycling program. Washington was considered number-one in its efforts to maintain healthy forests. And the Renew America study found California to have the best overall approach to environmental problems.

WHAT HAVE THEY DONE TO THE RAIN?

We've all heard of acid rain by now, even if we're not quite sure of the ramifications. The first noticeable effect was the wearing away of detail on stone and marble monuments around the world—the giant obelisk in St. Peter's square in Rome, the Parthenon in Athens, friezes on buildings in Washington, DC, the intricate carving on many of Northern Europe's fine Gothic cathedrals. But since the discovery of the phenomenon called acid rain in the late 1960s, increasing evidence has shown that the caustic precipitation is harmful to living creatures as well as buildings. In the United States, environmentalists warn, vast stretches of forests, important spawning grounds for fish, and even the health of a significant number of people could be in grave danger.

What Is Acid Rain?

Acid rain has been called an insidious form of air pollution, and its poisonous consequences are usually suffered a considerable distance from the source of the problem. The major cause of acid rain is the pollutant sulfur dioxide (SO_2), a principal emission of coal burning. In the United States, 48 million tons of sulfur and nitrogen fumes were spewed into the air in 1980, most of it coming from 31 states bordering on or east of the Mississippi River. Ohio, Illinois, Indiana, Michigan, Kentucky, Tennessee, and West Virginia have generally been pointed to as the most significant sources of SO_2 pollution.

In measuring acidity of water or soil, the pH scale is used (pH stands for *potential of hydrogen*). This scale has a neutral point of 7; less than 7 means acid, more than 7 means alkaline. The pH scale is logarithmic, so that pH 4.6 is ten times more acid than pH 5.6, and pH 3.6 is 100 times more acidic than pH 4.6. Ordinary rain is somewhat acidic, with a pH of 5.6, but when sulfur and nitrogen oxides react with moisture in the air, they intensify the acidity of rain.

As the list in the next column indicates, because of prevailing westerly winds and because most coal burning takes place east of the Mississippi, the effects of acid rain are seen most commonly in the Appalachian Mountains and along the eastern seaboard. The metro area of Salt Lake City–Ogden, UT, is one exception to this unfortunate rule.

Destructive Effects

The effects of acid rain on forests have long been documented in Europe but have only recently been observed in America. All along the Appalachian Mountain chain, from Georgia to Maine, the growth rate of mountain trees is slowing. The rate for red spruce, for example, is now only 74 percent of that recorded in 1965, and the decline is not from logging. In the southern half of the Appalachian chain, the new growth of loblolly pine, backbone of the southeastern timber

---

Acid Rain in the Metro Areas

Most of the country's worst areas for acid rain are in non-metropolitan locations, but according to the U.S. Geological Survey's *Water-Supply Paper 2250*, 16 metro areas have present or potential problems with acid rain:

Albany–Schenectady–Troy, NY	Monmouth–Ocean, NJ
Atlantic City, NJ	St. Cloud, MN–WI
Baltimore, MD	Salt Lake City–Ogden,
Duluth, MN–WI	UT
Eau Claire, WI	Trenton, NJ
Eugene–Springfield, OR	Vineland–Millville–
Glens Falls, NY	Bridgeton, NJ
Hagerstown, MD	Wausau, WI
Medford, OR	
Middlesex–Somerset–	
Hunterdon, NJ	

Source: U.S. Geological Survey, *Water-Supply Paper 2250*, 1984.

---

economy, is creeping to a standstill. Such trees as the beech, sugar maple, and hickory are growing deformed limbs, producing weak and brittle wood, and losing their resistance to insects and disease.

Since the pollutants are carried in clouds, the poisoning effect intensifies with altitude. In addition, hilltop trees tend to "comb" damaging particles from the air. Foresters monitoring mountaintop pH levels claim that a pH of 2 exists in some clouds, an acidity greater than that of table vinegar. Mount Mitchell, near Asheville in western North Carolina, the highest peak in the East, is fast becoming a bald mountain.

But the destructive effects of acid rain are not restricted to forests. For more than a decade, sport and commercial fishermen of the Atlantic have encountered fewer and fewer of the East's greatest saltwater sport fish, the striped bass. Initially, observers assumed that the rapid decline of this magnificent fish was the result of a natural cycle and that the bass would bounce back in a few years. This hasn't happened, and some marine biologists now fear it never will. The reason: rising acidity in the estuaries of the Chesapeake Bay, premier spawning grounds for the striper. Those spawning grounds are now practically barren, not only of the bass but also of shad, herring, perch, and alewife. Why? Biologists have measured the pH of the freshwater streams and rivers (like the Potomac, Rappahannock, James, and York Rivers) that flow into the Chesapeake and discovered that the water of these rivers is terribly acidic, with pH readings as low as 3.8. Fish eggs and larvae are sensitive to changes in the pH; the bass especially likes water that is alkaline (a pH of 8). Acid rain, falling on the coastal plain of Maryland, flows into the streams and creates acid surges that kill the eggs and larvae.

The Maryland shore, however, is not the only area with acid lakes and rivers. In the Adirondack Mountains of New York, for example, fish have disappeared from

Counting All Those Pollen Grains

The American Academy of Allergy has devised the Ragweed Pollen Index to indicate the local severity of the pollen problem. This index is derived from (1) length of the season, (2) concentration of pollen grains in the air at the season's peak, and (3) total pollen catch throughout the season. The higher the index number, the worse the problem; an index greater than 10 means lots of discomfort.

Ragweed Pollen Index for Selected Places

Alabama
Birmingham	49.0
Mobile	8.0

Alaska
All cities	0

Arizona
Phoenix	0.2
Tucson	2.0

Arkansas
Fort Smith	103.0
Little Rock	62.0

California
Alpine	3.0
Anaheim	0.5
Los Angeles	0.5
Sacramento	0.2
San Diego	11.0
San Francisco	0.2
Santa Barbara	3.0

Colorado
Colorado Springs	4.0
Denver	19.0

Connecticut
Bridgeport	23.0
Hartford	54.0
New Haven	25.0
Waterbury	27.0

Delaware
Wilmington	54.0

District of Columbia
	42.0

Florida
Bradenton	4.0
Daytona Beach	3.0
Fort Lauderdale	9.0
Fort Myers	0.2
Gainesville	20.0
Jacksonville	6.0
Melbourne	21.0
Miami	2.0
Orlando	3.0
Panama City	32.0
Pensacola	10.0
Tallahassee	6.0
Tampa	6.0
West Palm Beach	5.0

Georgia
Atlanta	24.0
Valdosta	8.0

Idaho
Boise City	5.0

Illinois
Bloomington	122.0
Champaign	76.0
Chicago	62.0
Decatur	114.0
East St. Louis	100.0
Peoria	122.0
Quincy	98.0
Rockford	96.0
Springfield	72.0

Indiana
Evansville	136.0
Fort Wayne	107.0
Gary	62.0
Indianapolis	92.0

Iowa
Cedar Rapids	122.0
Council Bluffs	148.0
Davenport	113.0
Des Moines	69.0

Kansas
Kansas City	101.0
Wichita	58.0

Kentucky
Lexington	151.0
Louisville	99.0

Louisiana
New Orleans	43.0
Tallulah	33.0

Maine
Lewiston	13.0
Portland	24.0
Presque Isle	0.4

Maryland
Baltimore	51.0

Massachusetts
Amherst	25.0
Boston	16.0
Nantucket	5.0
Springfield	20.0
Worcester	9.0

Michigan
Ann Arbor	119.0
Bay City	72.0
Charlevoix	21.0
Detroit	59.0
Escanaba	57.0
Flint	76.0
Grand Rapids	126.0
Lansing	94.0
Marquette	12.0
Saginaw	72.0

Minnesota
Duluth	44.0
Minneapolis	99.0
Moorhead	125.0
Rochester	88.0

Mississippi
Biloxi	7.0
Vicksburg	33.0

Missouri
Kansas City	109.0
St. Louis	78.0

Montana
Glacier National Park	0.1
Yellowstone National Park	0.2

Nebraska
Lincoln	63.0
North Platte	13.0
Omaha	148.0
Scottsbluff	38.0

Nevada
Reno	0.1

New Hampshire
Concord	7.0
Conway	3.0
Manchester	9.0
Nashua	29.0

New Jersey
Atlantic City	30.0
New Brunswick	60.0
Newark	18.0
Trenton	26.0

New Mexico
Albuquerque	7.0
Roswell	4.0

New York
Albany	48.0
Binghamton	31.0
Buffalo	59.0
Elmira	43.0
Manhattan	25.0
Rochester	60.0
Syracuse	25.0
Tupper Lake	8.0
Utica	26.0
Yonkers	38.0

North Carolina
Asheville	57.0
Charlotte	42.0
Raleigh	28.0

North Dakota
Fargo	125.0

Ohio
Akron	100.0
Cincinnati	122.0
Cleveland	56.0
Columbus	75.0
Dayton	90.0
Toledo	122.0
Youngstown	70.0

Oklahoma
Oklahoma City	73.0
Tulsa	65.0

Oregon
Corvallis	0
Portland	0.5

Pennsylvania
Altoona	52.0
Erie	65.0
Philadelphia	55.0
Pittsburgh	90.0

Rhode Island
Providence	26.0

South Carolina
Charleston	11.0
Columbia	40.0

South Dakota
Aberdeen	17.0
Rapid City	12.0
Sioux Falls	52.0

Tennessee
Johnson City	51.0
Knoxville	49.0
Memphis	73.0
Nashville	69.0

Texas
Amarillo	41.0
Brownsville	24.0
Dallas	115.0
El Paso	15.0
Galveston	36.0
Houston	68.0
San Antonio	16.0

Utah
Salt Lake City	8.0
Zion National Park	0.7

Vermont
Burlington	47.0

Virginia
Charlottesville	35.0
Norfolk	54.0
Richmond	42.0
Roanoke	85.0

Washington
Seattle	0
Spokane	0.1
Yakima	0.2

West Virginia
Charleston	31.0

Wisconsin
Eagle River	13.0
Madison	93.0
Milwaukee	86.0
Sheboygan	90.0
Superior	44.0

Wyoming
Lander	23.0

Source: American Academy of Allergy, 1977.

No figures are given for Hawaii because the academy has no reporting stations there.

more than 200 lakes due to acidification.

Human life may be at direct risk as well. In June 1984, the Office of Technological Assessment concluded a three-year study and reported that clouds bearing acid rain and smog from air pollution could be killing as many as 50,000 Americans and Canadians a year. Most threatened, according to the report, were persons with heart and lung ailments. Both the EPA and utilities industries contested these findings. But in a 1989 policy shift, the EPA (with presidential support) vowed to attack the problem of acid rain. The proposed Clean Air Act would require industry to reduce its sulfur dioxide emissions by 50 percent and would apply stricter emissions standards to automobiles.

Southern California has a problem of its own, acid fog, which some environmental engineers think may have a greater net impact than acid rain. The fog, which is similar to fogs that contributed to more than 12,000 deaths in London during a three-month period in 1952, is most severe in the Los Angeles Basin and San Joaquin Valley.

HAY FEVER SUFFERERS, TAKE NOTE

It doesn't come from hay, and it doesn't cause a fever, but that's not much consolation to the 18 million Americans afflicted with hay fever. Aside from the personal discomfort it causes, various government agencies estimate that it also results in more than five million workdays lost per year, at a price tag of more than $300 million.

Hay fever is any allergic reaction of the eyes, nose, or throat to certain airborne particles. These particles may be either pollen from seed-bearing trees, grasses, and weeds, or spores from certain molds. The term originated in Britain over 150 years ago, when people assumed its feverlike symptoms had something to do with the fall haying. Most individuals might think that once they're into adulthood, they already know whether they have hay fever. But if you were to relocate, would you suddenly and mysteriously develop a continual running nose and minor sore throat? Allergy problems aren't always alleviated by relocation, and sometimes a new allergen—absent where you used to live—can turn up to cause you problems with hay fever.

The incidence of hay fever varies around the world. In the Arctic, for example, it doesn't exist. Because of low temperatures and poor soil, arctic plants are small and primitive. In the tropics and subtropics, people are rarely troubled by hay fever because the plants there are generally flowered and produce pollen that is so heavy it cannot become airborne.

It is in the temperate regions that one finds the greatest amounts of irritating pollen. The worst places in America for hay fever are the middle regions, where grasses and trees without flowers predominate. Because farming continually disrupts the soil and therefore encourages the growth of weeds (especially the most troublesome of them, ragweed), America's heartland is the most hay fever ridden area. This discomfort zone extends from the Rockies to the Appalachian chain, and from the Canadian border down to the states of the mid-South.

Yet no area of the country except Alaska and the southern half of Florida is free from hay fever—it's simply a question of degree. The West Coast is almost ragweed-free, although it has other allergenic pollens.

Some places that were once havens for asthmatics and hay fever sufferers are now less free of allergens. Examples are many of the fast-growing areas of the Southwest. Thirty years ago, Tucson was virtually free of ragweed pollen. Its desert location precluded the growth of the weeds, grasses, and trees that cause hay fever. But as more and more people moved into the area, more trees were planted and lawns seeded. The result? A pollen index that's still comfortable but not quite as comfortable as it used to be.

The table on the previous page shows the ragweed pollen index for a number of places around the country.

FINDING THE RIGHT DOCTOR

Not all doctors are created equal. The doctor you select and the hospital in which you're treated may be more important in determining the outcome of your illness than the disease you have. When you're selecting a surgeon, for example, you need to know how often the surgeon has done your kind of surgery (more is better) and what the outcome has been. Compare the records of several surgeons to get a sense of what a "good" track record is. Don't forget to trust your intuitions about doctors. How comfortable do you feel with the doctor? Your gut feeling could be the deciding factor.

The American Medical Association is the national licensing body for physicians, but individual states vary in their licensing requirements. Highly populated states like New York and California have large staffs in their state licensing departments that can perform more thorough investigations of complaints against doctors. On the other hand, less densely populated states such as Idaho do not have the same investigative resources. But licensing boards alone cannot track down all the bad doctors. Medical schools, where students first enter the doctor track; licensing boards; national, state, and local professional societies; and hospitals (where most doctors have staff privileges) must work together in order to assure that patients are treated by competent, licensed professionals.

The Health Care Financing Administration, which reimburses doctors and hospitals that treat Medicare and Medicaid patients, also has plans to help consumers in their selection of doctors—a crucial decision regarding quality. It will soon begin a long-term project of rating doctors by how well their patients do—as indicated by mortality rates and speed of recovery, for example.

In the meantime, consider the following suggestions.

Chances are good that you'll have to choose a new physician at some point; even if you don't move, your doctor might. Finding a replacement for the person in whom you may have put a lot of trust isn't always easy.

Give some thought to the kind of doctor you are most comfortable with. Do you want to place complete faith in your physician? Or do you have questions about your treatment? Do you like a cooperative arrangement, in which you and your doctor work as a team? It's very important to most people that they have a doctor who will listen to their complaints, worries, and concerns, rather than one who may make patients feel that they're questioning the doctor's authority.

If you're planning to move, you might ask your present doctor if he or she knows anything about the doctors in the area to which you are going. Or you can get names from the nearest hospital at the new location, from friends you make, from medical societies, and from new neighbors.

When you have decided whom you want to contact, call that doctor's office, saying that you are a prospective patient, and ask to speak to the doctor briefly. You may have to agree to call back, but making connection with a professional voice is an important step. If you can't arrange this, if the doctor is "too busy," you probably ought to go to the next name on your list. You need a physician who is readily accessible.

When you do make contact, tell the doctor enough about yourself so that he or she has a good idea of who you are and what your problems may be. If the doctor sounds "right" to you, you could ask about fees, house calls (yes, they are again being made when necessary), and emergencies. Or you may wish to save some of these questions for a personal visit. It is important to establish through the initial phone call or visit that you and the doctor will be at ease with each other.

Evaluate the doctor's attitude. If he or she doesn't want to bother with you now, you will probably get that don't-bother-me treatment sooner or later when dealing with specific problems. Make sure that:

- You can openly discuss your feelings and personal concerns about sexual and emotional problems.
- The doctor isn't vague, impatient, or unwilling to answer all your questions about the causes and treatment of your physical problems.
- The doctor takes a thorough history on you and asks about past physical and emotional problems, family medical history, medication you are taking, and other matters affecting your health.
- The doctor doesn't automatically prescribe drugs rather than deal with real causes of your medical problems.
- The doctor has an associate to whom you can turn should your doctor retire or die.

Talk with the doctor about the transfer of your medical records. Some doctors like to have them, especially if there is any specific medical problem or chronic condition. Other doctors prefer not to see them, and to develop new records.

Even if you feel fine, arrange to have a physical or at least a quick checkup. This is more for the doctor's benefit than for yours, but it will help you, too. Should an emergency occur, the doctor will have basic information about you and some knowledge of your needs, and you will avoid the stress of trying to work with a doctor who has to learn about you in an emergency.

NUCLEAR HOT SPOTS: A NATIONWIDE LOCATOR

Would you mind living near a nuclear power plant? Given the record of the industry since new nuclear plant orders began in 1953, some feel that fears about a catastrophic meltdown or low-level environmental contamination are legitimate. Sure, things have gotten better, especially in the last three years, with automatic shutdown incidents decreasing from 487 (5.24 shutdowns per plant) in 1984 to 341 (3.25 shutdowns per plant) in 1987. The number of "potentially significant safety accidents" has also come down from the 1985 total of 3,050 to a 1987 total of 2,940. And Nuclear Regulatory Commission tests of key plant personnel show an 86 percent pass rate in 1987 as compared with a 79 percent pass rate in 1984.

After the 1979 accident at Three Mile Island, nuclear plant orders abruptly ended. Those on the anti-nuclear side are glad of that, but electric energy needs are rising, especially in the Northeast, where a legitimate electric energy crisis could occur. The issues are complicated, but some of the facts are as follows.

At the end of 1988, the United States had 110 nuclear electric plants licensed to operate, more than any other nation in the world. The map below ("Nuclear Power Plants in the United States") shows where each of these plants are located. These power plants produce 530 billion kilowatt hours, enough to meet the electricity needs of about 55 million households.

The New England region leads the nation in its use of nuclear energy, producing one-third of its electricity from the atom. In Vermont (the number-one state for reliance on nuclear energy) more than 80 percent of electricity consumed comes from nuclear power. South Carolina follows with 62 percent of its electricity coming from nuclear power, Connecticut with 61 percent, and Maine, New Jersey, and Illinois all relying on nuclear power for 50 percent of their energy needs. Illinois is the state with the most nuclear power plants—13 of them—and the greatest generating capacity.

Even though some states are relying heavily on nuclear power, there are fewer accidents, and the plant

Nuclear Power Plants in the United States

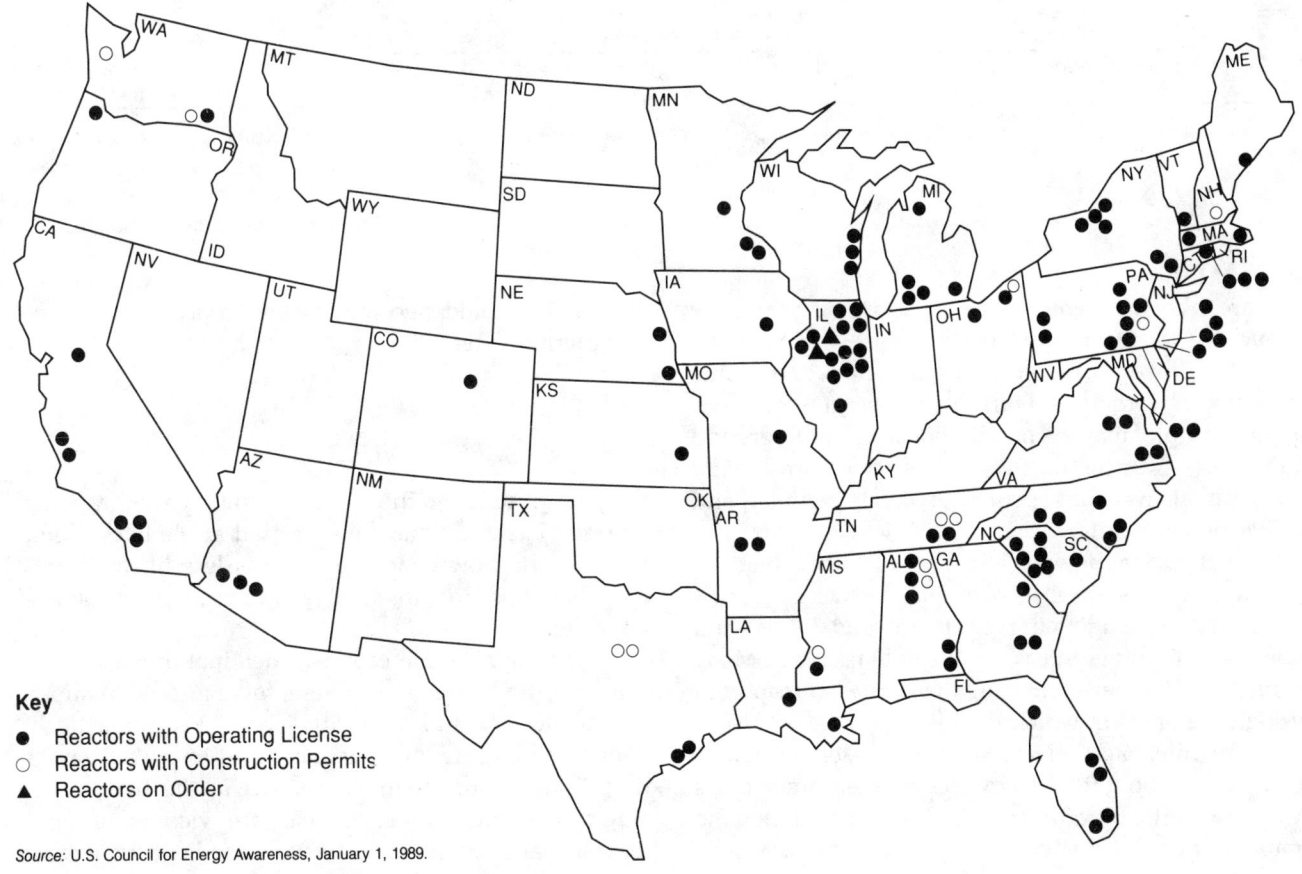

Key
- ● Reactors with Operating License
- ○ Reactors with Construction Permits
- ▲ Reactors on Order

Source: U.S. Council for Energy Awareness, January 1, 1989.

How Healthy Is Your Life-Style?

Risk Category	No Risk	Slight Risk	Substantial Risk	Heavy Risk	Dangerous Risk
Smoking	No smoking or stopped for at least 10 years	Less than 10 cigarettes, 5 pipes or cigars a day	Half pack a day	1 pack a day	2 or more packs a day
Alcohol	Nondrinker	Stopped drinker	6 drinks per week	More than 6 drinks per week	More than 2 drinks per day
Trimness	Lean	Slightly plump	Moderately obese	Considerably obese	Grossly obese
Physical activity	Walk more than 2 miles a day or climb 20 or more flights of stairs a day	Walk 1.5–2 miles a day or climb 15–20 flights of stairs a day	Walk only 0.5 to 1.5 miles a day or climb only 5–15 flights of stairs a day	Walk only 2–5 blocks a day or climb 2–4 flights of stairs a day	Walk less than 2 blocks a day or climb less than 2 flights of stairs a day
Prescription drugs	With doctor's consent, following orders carefully	Take medication daily without side effects	Take medication when needed with few side effects	Use sleeping and nerve pills regularly without doctor's supervision	Without doctor's consent, mix with other drugs or alcohol
Nonprescription drugs	Use occasionally only for short periods. Label warnings heeded				Continuing use, drinking or driving despite label warnings
Alcohol and driving —boats, cars, motorcycles, snowmobiles	Never drink. Drive only with safety aids—seat belt, helmet, life jacket	Never drive after drinking without safety aids	Drive after 2 drinks with safety aids	Drive after 2 drinks without safety aids	Drive after more than 2 drinks without safety aids
Motor vehicle safety	Always wear seat belt	Wear seat belt more than half of the time	Wear seat belt as a driver half of the time	Wear seat belt as a passenger half of the time	Wear seat belt less than half of the time
Water safety— swimming and boating	Qualified expert	Know how to swim and the safety rules	Know how to swim and may swim after 1 drink or nerve drug	Do not know how to swim but use life jacket half of the time	Do not know how to swim; never use life jacket
Blood cholesterol	Less than 180	180–220	220–280	280–320	320 and up
Blood pressure	120/80 or less	120/80–140/90	140/90–160/100	160/100–180/105	Above 180/105
Blood sugar	Less than 120 two hours after a meal of syrup and pancakes	Between 110 and 130 two hours after meals; checked each 3 months	Blood sugar more than 150 without diet control	Blood sugar more than 150 without diet control, doctor's care	Diabetes without doctor's care at less than 45 years of age
FOR WOMEN ONLY					
Breast check for lumps	Monthly self-exam and yearly check by physician	Monthly self-exam but no doctor exam	Self-exam 2–3 times a year but no doctor's exam	1 time a year by a doctor	Never
Pap smear	Every year	Every 3 years	Every 4 years	Never	Never; nonmenstrual bleeding

Source: Methodist Hospital of Indianapolis, Inc. Prepared by Pamela Hall under the supervision of Drs. Lewis C. Robbins and Jack H. Hall, developers of the Health Hazard Appraisal System. Used by permission.

staffs are more competent, none are addressing the issue of nuclear waste, a problem that has some people, especially those living in states destined to become disposal sites, tossing and turning. Southern New Mexico, for example, may eventually house an underground storage depot for the nuclear wastes which are rapidly piling up at weapons plants, research centers, and nuclear power plants.

Several nuclear power plants have already exhausted their capacity to store their own nuclear wastes, and 73 plants are expected to join them by the mid-1990s. And finding a safe storage site is not the only problem. Many people object to even having the wastes transported through the areas in which they live.

Meanwhile, back in New Mexico, unresolved technical questions about the effectiveness of the storage casks and bureaucratic procedures regarding approval dog the completion of the storage site. Nevada's Yucca Mountain Range could become the next waste site—target completion date, 2003.

HEALTHY LIFE/LONGER LIFE

Do you subscribe to the theory of when your time is up, you go? Then you may be surprised at the latest thinking. Experts now conclude that it's less likely to be a stray bullet or virus that kills you than the way you lead your life.

The most common causes of death at the turn of the century—typhoid fever, cholera, tuberculosis, smallpox, gastroenteritis, and nephritis—have been practically eliminated by scientific advances and improved sanitation. Today, more than 70 percent of the two million Americans who die each year are victims of heart disease, cancer, stroke, cirrhosis of the liver, bronchitis, asthma, and emphysema—the so-called life-style diseases that may be aggravated by such behavior as overeating, heavy drinking, smoking, and lack of exercise.

To see how your daily habits measure up, take a look at the table "How Healthy Is Your Life-Style?" The creators of this table warn that some risk factors are more important than others. Thus, an entirely accurate picture of your health may not emerge from practicing this self-analysis. However, they add, changing your habits so that you qualify for the low-risk ratings will result in a longer life.

The following are some suggestions—certainly not new ones, but still as healthful as the first time you heard them—that can help you reduce your health risks. If you haven't yet paid heed to the wisdom of these suggestions, perhaps this will nudge you into a healthier style of living.

Stop smoking and drink only in moderation. Cigarette smokers run twice the risk that nonsmokers do of death from coronary disease. Smoking also contributes to stroke, lung cancer, emphysema, and bronchitis. Likewise, an excess of alcohol can be dangerous, increasing your chances of developing cirrhosis of the liver (this condition is found six times as frequently among alcoholics as among nonalcoholics) and cardiovascular problems. Drinking, too, combined with driving multiplies the risk of dying in an automobile accident; at least half of such accidents in the United States involve drunk drivers.

Eat a balanced diet and watch your weight. Six of the ten leading causes of death have been linked to diet: heart attack, stroke, atherosclerosis, cancer, cirrhosis of the liver, and diabetes. Reducing your intake of refined flour and sugar, salt (which in excess contributes to high blood pressure), and saturated fats (which have been implicated as factors in heart disease and stroke) while choosing from a range of meat, poultry, fish, fruits, vegetables, and fiber foods (which have been shown to prevent colon cancer) is highly recommended. A balanced diet can also help you to lose extra weight, which puts added stress on the heart and organs, aggravating disease conditions.

Get regular exercise. Exercise, now seen almost as a miracle drug, can help you maintain proper weight, keep your body in good operating condition, and relieve stress (which contributes to ulcers and high blood pressure). It helps prevent premature aging and degeneration of bone (osteoporosis), muscles, and joints. The use-it-or-lose-it maxim definitely applies here.

Get regular medical care. Be sure to consult your doctor regularly and have whatever checkups or tests he or she recommends, such as a Pap smear, blood pressure, or blood cholesterol tests.

Transportation

If you travel often enough, you might take for granted the vast networks of interstate highways, airline routes, and Amtrak rails that lace up this country's different points. But a look at a national map shows certain metro areas to be hubs with many highway, rail, and air-route spokes, while others appear as lesser intersections, removed from the mainstream of intercity travel.

Population size has something to do with an area's transportation assets, and so do the hazards of geography. There are 25 metro areas larger than Denver, for example, but because the Mile High City is plunked down at the edge of the Rocky Mountains halfway between Chicago and Southern California, and midway from Houston to Seattle, only four airports are busier than Denver's Stapleton International.

Intercity travel is only one part of the picture, of course. Some metro areas have efficient and inexpensive public transit systems relied on by hundreds of thousands of commuters each working day. In other metro areas, older fleets of transit buses with optimistic schedules lurch along routes that rarely reach any neighborhoods but those close to downtown. Still other metro areas have no public transit at all; their residents must get around by car, depending on expressways, commercial arteries, and residential streets.

GETTING AROUND TOWN

If you are moving to El Paso, can your family get by without a second car? If you are being transferred to your employer's headquarters in Cleveland, will it be more convenient to carpool or to use public transportation if you settle in the suburb of Shaker Heights? How much time might you need to spend each day getting to and from work? Becoming familiar with the local transportation features of a particular metro area will help you answer some of these questions.

The Commuting Life

Every weekday morning, in cities and towns all over the country, traffic trickles out of suburban streets, flows into arterial roads, and floods freeways to capacity with people bound for work. According to most transportation experts, the morning rush hour lasts 118 minutes, between 7:01 and 8:59. Most workers travel by automobile, alone; one out of five belongs to a car pool; and one out of 15 opts for public transit.

The evening rush hour lasts longer, 150 minutes, from 4:30 to 7:00. There are more traffic delays at this time than in the morning, when people so purposefully leave home and arrive at work in the shortest possible

The Mass Transit Quarter

Public transit is available in most cities, but it is an option passed up by 93 out of every 100 persons who commute to work because the operating schedule isn't convenient, the system doesn't reach the workplace, or because they prefer the freedom of their own car. In only 17 of the 945 cities with populations over 25,000 does at least one in four workers use public transit.

Top 17 Areas in Public Transit Use

City	Commuters Using Public Transit
1. New York, NY	56%
2. San Francisco, CA	39
3. Washington, DC	38
4. Boston, MA	34
4. Jersey City, NJ	34
6. Chicago, IL	32
7. Philadelphia, PA	30
8. Cambridge, MA	28
8. Mount Vernon, NY	28
8. Oak Park, IL	28
8. Somerville, MA	28
12. Evanston, IL	27
13. Hoboken, NJ	26
13. Newark, NJ	26
15. Atlanta, GA	25
15. Baltimore, MD	25
15. Rockville Centre, NY	25

Source: U.S. Bureau of the Census, *1980 Census of Population.*

Shortest Commuting Time	Minutes per Day*	Longest Commuting Time	Minutes per Day*
4. Lawton, OK	31.5	4. Monmouth–Ocean, NJ	64.0
6. Lafayette, IN	31.7	5. Chicago, IL	63.8
6. Sheboygan, WI	31.7	6. Houston, TX	58.5
8. Appleton–Oshkosh–Neenah, WI	32.3	7. Baltimore, MD	58.3
8. Sioux Falls, SD	32.3	8. Jersey City, NJ	57.6
10. Sioux City, IA–NE	32.6	9. Philadelphia, PA–NJ	56.3
		10. New Orleans, LA	55.9
		10. Newark, NJ	55.9

Source (for journey-to-work figures): U.S. Bureau of the Census, *1980 Census of Population and Housing.*

Places Rated multiplies journey-to-work minutes by a factor of 2.2 to estimate round-trip daily commuting time.

Public Mass Transit

One reason for the long commute in big cities is the often onerous job of making linked transit trips to get to work. Nationally, the average duration of an *unlinked* transit trip—a direct route, with no transfers—is 15 minutes. But many big-city commuters have to make *linked* trips—driving to a park-and-ride lot; boarding a train, tram, or bus; and sometimes switching again before finally arriving at work.

Nevertheless, in larger cities where the tab for daily parking in a downtown garage tops ten dollars, where rush hour traffic jams approach grid-lock, where distances are long and time always seems short, public transit really counts. In three of our largest cities—Houston, Los Angeles, and Phoenix—daily driving over long distances is a way of life unrelieved by rapid public transit (see table below); taking the bus is the only alternative. In other places such as Atlanta, Washington, and San Francisco, large local bus fleets are complemented by rapid transit rail systems.

Depending on where they want to go, New York City commuters can choose from bus, heavy rail, light rail, commuter railroad, ferryboat, and even aerial tramway service. New York straphangers may not always enjoy their subway ride to work, but few among the jostled riders aboard a rocking, grimy IRT car would ever envy a Houston driver who has missed his or her exit on the Southwest Freeway at rush hour.

time. In the evening, many commuters stop for a drink, go shopping, run errands, or just dawdle. After all, one can't be fired for being late for supper. In fact, traffic experts say, even if you head straight home, the evening trip not only seems longer than the trip to work, it actually is—20 percent longer.

How much time do metro area dwellers spend going to and from work each day? To allow for the longer trip home in the evening, *Places Rated* multiplies the average journey-to-work figure by 2.2 to estimate the round-trip time in each of the metro areas. As you might suspect, daily commuting time increases with city size. Workers in Grand Forks, ND, for instance, putting in 230 working days a year, spend about 110 hours commuting. New Yorkers spend 310 hours. The contrast between Grand Forks and New York, then, is more than one between a prairie college town and the nation's largest city. Based on commuting time alone, Grand Forkers have more free time than New Yorkers, the equivalent of five 40-hour weeks (see table below).

Metro Areas with No Fixed-Route Public Transportation Systems

Anniston, AL	Jacksonville, NC
Benton Harbor, MI	Joplin, MO
Bismarck, ND	Kankakee, IL
Bryan–College Station, TX	Kokomo, IN
Burlington, NC	Las Cruces, NM
Casper, WY	Lawton, OK
Cheyenne, WY	Longview–Marshall, TX
Clarksville–Hopkinsville, TN–KY	Naples, FL
Dothan, AL	Ocala, FL
Elkhart–Goshen, IN	Odessa, TX
Enid, OK	Pascagoula, MS
Fayetteville–Springdale, AR	Rapid City, SD
Florence, AL	Richland–Kennewick–Pasco, WA
Fort Smith, AR–OK	Santa Fe, NM
Gadsden, AL	Sharon, PA
Great Falls, MT	Sherman–Denison, TX
Houma–Thibodaux, LA	Texarkana, TX–Texarkana, AR
Huntsville, AL	Victoria, TX
Jackson, TN	

Source: Places Rated Partnership survey, May 1989.

Getting to Work and Back

Shortest Commuting Time	Minutes per Day*	Longest Commuting Time	Minutes per Day*
1. Grand Forks, ND	28.6	1. New York, NY	81.0
2. Bismarck, ND	30.8	2. Nassau–Suffolk, NY	70.6
2. Rochester, MN	30.8	3. Washington, DC–MD–VA	64.5
4. Fargo–Moorhead, ND–MN	31.5		

By bus. In most cities, public transit and "the bus" are synonymous. Unlike rapid rail and trolley networks, a bus system requires no expensive construction, and routes can be easily changed to meet demand.

Each of the country's 786 urban public transit systems puts motor buses on the street, but transit systems do vary in size and type of operation. Several large systems—CTA (Chicago), Southern California RTD (Los Angeles), WMATA (Washington, DC), and NYCTA (New York), for example—operate thousands of buses, 24 hours a day, with less than one minute between buses on the heaviest routes during morning and evening rush hours. At the other extreme are the one- and two-bus "shoppers' specials" that run loops in the central business district of smaller metro areas.

On the tracks. Although buses can meet the demand for public transit nearly everywhere, rail lines are more efficient in carrying large numbers of rush hour commuters in the major cities. Several kinds of rail service are available in the big metro areas, from rapid rail to trolley car to commuter train.

Rapid rail lines. Owing to their exclusive rights-of-way, these are unaffected by traffic jams. Their trains and trams not only carry hundreds of people, they carry them quickly: The average speed of buses during peak rush hour, nationwide, is 11.8 miles per hour. Rapid rail systems average more than 20 miles per hour. There are two types of rapid rail lines in use today in 22 metro areas: heavy rail, which accounts for 2.5 billion passenger trips in a year, and light rail, which accounts for 150 million passenger trips. Both are electrically powered, and both may be found in the same city.

Heavy rail systems—known locally as subways, elevated railways, or Els—have high-level platform stations. The cars are individually powered through the third rail, and are hitched together to form longer trains during rush hours. New York City's heavy rail system, composed of two separate networks, is the world's largest, with 4,859 cars traveling more than 450 miles of track; Philadelphia also has two systems. As of January 1989, eleven U.S. metro areas have heavy rail systems:

Atlanta, GA	New York, NY
Baltimore, MD	Oakland, CA
Boston, MA	Philadelphia, PA–NJ
Chicago, IL	San Francisco, CA
Cleveland, OH	Washington, DC–MD–VA
Miami, FL	

Light rail cars. Powered by overhead electrical wires, these travel at half the speed of heavy rail cars. Because their tracks are laid above ground, they are less expensive to build and therefore are the fastest-growing form of mass transit. Fifteen metro areas now have light rail transit:

Boston, MA	Pittsburgh, PA
Buffalo, NY	Portland, OR
Cleveland, OH	Sacramento, CA
Detroit, MI	San Diego, CA
Ft. Worth, TX	San Francisco, CA
Newark, NJ	San Jose, CA
New Orleans, LA	Seattle, WA
Philadelphia, PA–NJ	

Rating the Transit Supply

Totaling up the numbers of all of the local buses, rapid rail cars, and trolley coaches will give you the size of a metro area's transportation fleet, but that isn't an accurate measure of transit supply.

A better indicator can be found if you take the number of passengers that a fleet's vehicles can carry at one time, multiply that number by the miles the fleet runs up each day in service, and then divide by the number of people living in the metro area's urban part. The result is known as seat miles per capita.

In Boulder–Longmont, there are more than eight bus seats traveling one mile of route for every person in the urbanized area, the best single-mode transit supply of any metro area. But the ultimate record for transportation supply goes to New York. If all vehicles were put in service at the same time, this metro area's multimode fleet would provide more than 17 seat miles for each resident. Not surprisingly, New York is the only city in the United States where a majority of commuters use public transit.

The Top 10 Metro Areas for Bus Transit Supply

Metro Area	Buses	Seat Miles per Capita
1. Boulder–Longmont, CO	120	8.70
2. Atlantic City, NJ	65	7.20
2. Bremerton, WA	50	5.16
4. Santa Cruz, CA	94	5.08
5. Madison, WI	145	4.52
6. Dallas, TX	1,422	4.83
7. Honolulu, HI	380	4.34
8. Duluth, MN–WI	74	3.72
9. Sheboygan, WI	31	3.53
10. Minneapolis–St. Paul, MN–WI	925	3.44

The Top 10 Metro Areas for Bus and Rapid Rail Transit Supply

Metro Area	Seat Miles per Capita
1. New York, NY	17.49
2. San Francisco, CA	11.68
3. Washington, DC–MD–VA	7.07
4. Seattle, WA	6.37
5. Oakland, CA	5.70
6. San Jose, CA	3.99
7. Atlanta, GA	3.82
8. Chicago, IL	3.68
9. Boston, MA	3.26
10. Cleveland, OH	3.23

Source: Derived from Urban Mass Transportation Administration, *Section 15 Report,* 1987, and *Directory of Urban Transportation Service,* 1988.

The average transit supply in the metro areas is 2.43 seat miles per capita.

Trolley coaches. Trolleys are street-car-type railways that travel on city streets with semiprivate or exclusive rights-of-way. They are a less efficient form of travel than rapid rail since the trams are at the mercy of automobile traffic and, in some cities, must stop for streetlights. Another disadvantage is that their routes cannot be altered. These systems have been largely replaced by bus; in fact, only five metro areas in the United States have trolley coach operations:

Boston, MA	San Francisco, CA
Dayton–Springfield, OH	Seattle, WA
Philadelphia, PA–NJ	

Commuter railroads. Railroads have been an important form of transportation from more distant suburbs to the central part of major cities since the nineteenth century. Using both locomotive-hauled and self-propelled passenger cars, this service is characterized by multitrip tickets, station-to-station fares, railroad employment practices, and usually only one or two stations in the central business district. Twelve commuter railroads in 11 metro areas ferry more than a million commuters to and from work. The largest commuter railroad network, made up of seven firms, is found in New York and uses 1,650 cars to move 525,000 riders in a typical weekday. In Chicago, the next largest commuter railroad center, nine carriers operating 850 cars transport 290,000 workers in a typical day.

Freeway Traffic

Just as most metro area commuters have a car all to themselves on the way to work, most of them drive part of the way on a functionally classified urban freeway, that is, a divided highway with fully controlled access points. The extent to which a metro area is drawn tight by ribbons of freeway is governed by its land area and population. Los Angeles is regarded as a place overburdened with concrete, partly because so many of the innovations of limited-access, high-speed arterial road construction—ramps, trumpets, and cloverleafs—were seen early in Southern California.

In U.S. cities, the length of urban freeways amounts to 3.24 percent of the total road and street mileage. If you look at freeways in this way, Los Angeles may be undeserving of its reputation as the Freeway City since limited-access divided highways there make up only 2.3 percent of the total road mileage.

Nine metro areas have no freeways, and those that have them differ in the amount of traffic their freeways must accommodate. In 21 metro areas, traffic volume averages 90 percent or more of the capacity of the freeways. Most of these congested freeways are in major metro areas or in the East: Seven of the 21 are in the New York–Northern New Jersey–Long Island consolidated area. Surprisingly, traffic volume is also very heavy in some of the less populated metropolitan areas, including Olympia, WA, and Anchorage, AK (see the following list).

Most Congested Metro Areas

Allentown–Bethlehem, PA	Los Angeles–Long Beach, CA
Anchorage, AK	Middlesex–Somerset–
Atlanta, GA	Hunterdon, NJ
Austin, TX	Monmouth–Ocean, NJ
Bergen–Passaic, NJ	New Orleans, LA
Birmingham, AL	New York, NY
Cleveland, OH	Newark, NJ
Denver, CO	Olympia, WA
Detroit, MI	Orange County, NY
Houston, TX	San Antonio, TX
Jersey City, NJ	Wilmington, DE–NJ–MD

Traffic volume on the freeways in these metro areas averages 90% or more of design capacity.

INTERCITY TRAVEL

"You can't get there from here" is the punch line of the old joke about the lost city feller who asked directions of

---

Rules of the Road Rated

If your travels take you to Massachusetts, you will find the oddest, most archaic, and most contradictory traffic laws in the United States. In Kansas, on the other hand, the most rational and up-to-date rules of the road have been on the books for years.

These judgments have been made by the National Committee on Uniform Traffic Laws, a semiofficial organization that publishes and continually revises the Uniform Vehicle Code (UVC), a complete set of motor laws designed as a model for the states. The committee—whose members are traffic court judges, state motor vehicle commissioners, and representatives of the automobile manufacturing and insurance industries—rates the states on how closely their statutes agree with the UVC. Complete agreement yields a score of 1,065.

States Ranked by Traffic Laws from Best to Worst

State	Score	State	Score
1. Kansas	932	26. Montana	586
2. Alabama	911	27. Arizona	579
3. South Carolina	862	28. Minnesota	576
4. Utah	852	29. Ohio	565
5. Idaho	837	30. Tennessee	560
6. North Dakota	833	31. Rhode Island	557
7. Georgia	827	32. Louisiana	538
8. Washington	812	33. Oregon	529
9. Pennsylvania	787	34. West Virginia	528
10. Illinois	775	35. Nevada	509
11. Colorado	747	36. South Dakota	461
12. Delaware	720	37. California	454
13. Maryland	717	38. Kentucky	448
14. Nebraska	714	39. Arkansas	434
15. Florida	711	40. Iowa	420
16. Hawaii	683	41. Connecticut	415
17. Texas	649	42. Michigan	405
18. New York	648	43. Maine	398
19. New Hampshire	630	43. Wisconsin	398
19. Vermont	630	45. North Carolina	344
21. Alaska	625	46. Mississippi	318
22. Wyoming	620	47. Virginia	315
23. Oklahoma	615	48. New Jersey	314
24. Indiana	600	49. Missouri	286
25. New Mexico	596	50. Massachusetts	253

Source: U.S. Department of Transportation, *Rules of the Road Rated,* 1981.

The District of Columbia was awarded 452 points for its traffic laws, a score that would place it 38th among the states.

a bemused farmer. The line has little meaning in today's metropolitan areas, given the networks of well-traveled highways, railroads, and airways that connect these places.

Or does it? Obviously, you can neither take to the interstate nor board a train if your destination is Anchorage or Honolulu. For that matter, you can't get to Bloomington, IN; Bremerton, WA; or Burlington, NC, by the same means. When it comes to intercity travel choices, some metro areas are better off than others.

Interstate Highways

When President Franklin Roosevelt idly penciled three east-west and five north-south lines on a U.S. map back in 1938 as part of a proposed national highway system, he probably had no idea that his drawing would be so important in determining whether many rural towns would grow and many others would decline. He envisioned a 34,000-mile network of multilane toll roads. Although the concept of collecting tolls was soon dropped by the Bureau of Public Roads, the basic routes on his map foresaw the Interstate Highway System, a river of economic life to cities and towns along the way and possibly a cause of stagnation for those that were bypassed.

The interstate system is now an almost complete 42,500-mile road network, at least four traffic lanes wide, that spans 48 states and links together nearly every city with a population of more than 50,000. Still, 60 of our metro areas are not on the interstate network. Even though interstate routes account for only 1 percent of all road and street mileage in the United States, they carry 25 percent of all the traffic. As the car is the dominant means of intercity travel, so the dominant road is the interstate.

On any given day, Americans drive nearly one billion miles on interstate highways. Three out of ten of all those miles are logged in just four states: California, Illinois, Ohio, and Texas. The heaviest traffic can be found on the stretches of the interstate system that are classified as urban. These cloverleafed freeways, spurs, and beltways in and around cities carry 55 percent of all the travel. The balance is borne by the long, often boringly straight rural routes that make up 77 percent of interstate mileage. See the lists that follow.

Busiest Stretches of Interstate Highways

I-5, I-210, I-405, I-605 in Los Angeles, CA
I-5 in Seattle, WA
I-10, I-45, I-59, I-610 in Houston, TX
I-25 in Denver, CO
I-35E, I-635 in Dallas, TX
I-75 in Atlanta, GA
I-80, I-580 in Oakland, CA
I-80, I-380 in San Francisco, CA
I-90, I-94, I-290 in Chicago, IL
I-95 in New York, NY
I-280 in San Jose, CA
I-395 in Washington, DC–MD–VA

Decoding the Interstate System

The numbers in the middle of the red-white-and-blue, shield-shaped signs along the interstate system were developed in 1957 by the American Association of State Highway Transportation officials. There are 34 odd-numbered routes, which run north and south, and 27 even-numbered routes, which run east and west. The lowest-numbered routes are in the West and the South; I-5, for example, lies along the nation's West Coast and I-10 runs along the southern border.

In cities, these one- or two-digit numbers don't change as long as they are part of the major traffic stream. Beltways around the city, on the other hand, carry three numbers: the main route number with an even-numbered prefix. For example, I-495, an 88-mile-long route around Boston, and I-287, a 94-mile-long loop skirting New York City, are the two longest beltways in the interstate system. If a main route carries an odd-numbered prefix (such as I-195 in Miami or I-780 in San Francisco), the route is a spur that connects with the main route at only one end.

Three-digit route numbers are never used twice in the same state. In New York, I-90 runs through Schenectady, Syracuse, Rochester, and Buffalo, and the beltways off this main route in those cities are numbered, respectively, I-890, I-690, I-490, and I-290. This rule isn't carried across state lines, however. Two cities on I-10 but in different states, Houston and New Orleans, have the identical beltway number of I-610.

Loneliest Stretches of Interstate Highways

I-15 between Idaho Falls, ID, and Butte, MT
I-25 between Buffalo, WY, and Casper, WY
I-29 between Grand Forks, ND, and the Canadian border
I-29 between Sioux Falls, SD, and Fargo–Moorhead, ND
I-70 between Cove Fort, Utah, and the Colorado border
I-90 between Buffalo, WY, and Gillette, WY
I-91 between Derby Line, VT, and St. Johnsbury, VT
I-94 between Billings, MT, and the North Dakota border

According to the U.S. Department of Transportation, the busiest stretches on the interstate carry 200,000 to 300,000 vehicles every 24 hours. The loneliest carry fewer than 2,500.

Boarding Pass, Please

It's said in the South that when you die and are on your way to either heaven or hell, you'll have to make connections in Atlanta. Atlanta's airport, Hartsfield International, is the world's second busiest.

Like other airports that are reached by scheduled airlines, Hartsfield is a twentieth-century urban landmark in the same way the railroad station was a sign of the times in the late nineteenth century. Most of the 595 airports served by domestic carriers in the United States are quiet, even desolate places. But some, like Hartsfield, resemble self-contained cities, and last year 42 of these airports in the nation's large hubs handled 70 percent of the nearly 400 million people who boarded domestic

The Busiest Two-Way Air Routes

Routes	Annual Passengers
1. Boston–New York City	4,220,250
2. New York City–Washington, D.C.	3,807,250
3. Los Angeles–New York City	2,453,920
4. Los Angeles–San Francisco	2,376,950
5. Chicago–New York City	2,332,640
6. Miami–New York City	1,658,080
7. New York City–San Francisco	1,458,660
8. Honolulu–Kahului, Maui	1,366,280
9. New York City–Pittsburgh	1,339,940
10. Fort Lauderdale–New York City	1,256,990
11. Las Vegas–Los Angeles	1,140,000
12. Detroit–New York City	983,010
13. Atlanta–New York City	964,580
14. Chicago–Los Angeles	936,520
15. Honolulu–Lihue, Kauai	924,830

Source: Air Transport Association of America.

The Busiest Amtrak Routes

Northeast Corridor*	Annual Passengers
1. New York–Philadelphia	2,400,000
2. Metroliners, Boston–New York–Washington	1,200,000
3. Harrisburg–Philadelphia	760,000
4. New Haven–Springfield, MA	260,000

Short Distance

	Annual Passengers
1. Los Angeles–San Diego	1,064,000
2. New York–Albany–Niagara Falls	841,000
3. Chicago–Detroit–Toledo	368,000
4. Chicago–St. Louis	274,000
5. Oakland–Bakersfield	221,000

Long Distance

	Annual Passengers
1. Chicago–Oakland–Los Angeles	725,000
2. New York–Florida	610,000
3. Los Angeles–Seattle	485,000
4. Chicago–New York–Boston	350,000
5. New York–New Orleans	250,000

Source: Amtrak, Ridership By Route.

*Another 6.1 million passengers a year travel various Amtrak routes along the Northeast Corridor not listed here.

flights. The busiest, Chicago's O'Hare International Airport, boarded more passengers than the 500 smallest U.S. airports combined. (See the following table.)

Two hundred and forty-six metro areas have one airport with scheduled service, 19 have two airports, and two—Chicago and Los Angeles–Long Beach—have three. In one day, flights from these 290 airports average one for every 8,862 residents in metro areas that have access to passenger service.

The 15 Busiest U.S. Airports

Airport	Annual Passengers
1. Chicago O'Hare International	56,280,000
2. Hartsfield International (Atlanta)	47,649,000
3. Los Angeles International	44,873,000
4. Dallas–Fort Worth Regional	41,875,000
5. Stapleton International (Denver)	32,355,000
6. John F. Kennedy International (New York)	30,192,000
7. San Francisco International	29,812,000
8. La Guardia (New York)	24,225,000
9. Miami International	24,036,000
10. Newark International	23,475,000
11. Logan International (Boston)	23,283,000
12. Honolulu International	20,380,000
13. Lambert–St. Louis International	20,362,000
14. Detroit Metropolitan–Wayne County	19,746,000
15. Minneapolis–St. Paul International	17,858,000

Source: Airport Operators Council International, 1988.

Figures are the total number, in millions, of passengers arriving and departing each airport during 1988.

You'll stand the best chance of dodging airport jams if you fly on Thursday afternoons and Saturday nights. The worst travel days used to be Fridays and Sundays. Now they are Tuesdays and Wednesdays because more people take advantage of special fares requiring midweek travel.

Riding the Rails

Sixty years ago, eight out of ten people who had to get from one city in the United States to another did it aboard a train. There were 20,000 different ones from which to choose, if you didn't care where you were going. The *Twentieth Century Limited, El Capitan, Blue Streak*—each had a unique, trademarked name. They still do—*Desert Wind, Sunset Limited, Empire Builder, Texas Eagle*—but today there are just 230 of them. Over the years, their share of the commercial passenger traffic has dwindled to 7 percent.

If passenger trains are ever to rise again, the renaissance will be due not to high gasoline prices and spot fuel shortages but to mounting congestion on intercity highways. California traffic experts, for example, foresee a four-hour automobile commute between San Jose and San Francisco by 1990. The railroads have a priceless asset: existing tracks and rights-of-way into the population centers of the nation.

The National Railroad Passenger Corporation, a profit-making body, was created by Congress to subsidize the passenger-carrying business of its member railroads. Better known as Amtrak, it began operation in 1971. Today it carries virtually all of the 25 million passengers who board intercity trains each year.

The passenger rails don't reach everywhere, however. Although Amtrak's timetable boasts stops at hundreds of cities and towns from Aberdeen, MD, to Yuma, AZ, 167 of the 333 metro areas aren't on the route system. The metro areas bypassed include such large places as Tulsa, Louisville, and Des Moines.

On the average, there is a weekday Amtrak train for every 197,497 residents among the 162 metro areas with rail passenger service. Battle Creek, MI, ought to be as renowned for passenger trains as for breakfast cereal, since there are more Amtrak departures per capita here than in any other metro area: one for every 17,695 people per weekday. By far the biggest markets for train service are in the northeast quadrant of the United States. But the fastest-growing markets are on the West Coast, particularly for the two-hour-and-forty-minute run between Los Angeles and San Diego and for the six-hour San Francisco–Bakersfield route.

SCORING: TRANSPORTATION

When it comes to evaluating the supply of travel options in a metro area, a good measure is how many people can be served by a place's transit system and by the number of intercity travel choices. Would urban dwellers in Syracuse or San Angelo have a better chance of finding a seat on a bus? Which metro area airport—Atlanta's or Denver's—has more daily departures per local population?

In rating metro areas for transit supply, *Places Rated*'s approach is similar to that taken in the previous editions of this book. As before, we examine three modes of transportation used between cities (interstate highway, airplane, and passenger train) and one used locally (mass transit). A useful new scoring element introduced in the last edition of *Places Rated Almanac* is the daily commute, the average time spent getting to and from work within a metro area. To arrive at a score for each metro area, these five criteria are compared with the national metro area averages.

In the case of judging air service, some further adjustments were made in calculating a score for metro areas that are part of a Consolidated Metropolitan Statistical Area (see the Appendix for a list of CMSAs and component metro areas). Because major airports tend to serve a very wide geographical area and are able to accommodate large numbers of travelers, *Places Rated* considers the air service assets of CMSA component metro areas to be shared equally by all members of the CMSA, no matter which metro area the airport(s) may be located in.

Each metro area starts with a base score of zero, to which points are added according to the following indicators:

1. *Daily commute.* The time spent commuting to and from work is almost entirely unproductive —and unavoidable. To rate each place for commuting time, the U.S. metro area average of 49.7 minutes is divided by the average minutes local workers spend in daily commuting. The result is then multiplied by 1,000. Consequently, the shorter the commuting time, the more points a metro area will receive. Workers in Houston, for instance, spend an average of 58.5 minutes commuting, which works out to 850 points, compared with an average time of only 28.6 minutes in Grand Forks, North Dakota. This daily commute results in a score that is more than twice Houston's.

You're Better Off in Large Hubs

The Federal Aviation Administration (FAA) rates each metro area for its share of airline service by designating it as one of the following: large hub, medium hub, small hub, or non-hub.

A metro area is a . . .	if passengers leaving its airport(s) total . . .
large hub	1% or more
medium hub	0.25% to 0.99%
small hub	0.05% to 0.24%
non-hub	less than 0.05% **of all U.S. airline passengers in a year.**

There's one big advantage to living in a large hub besides having a wider choice of carriers with more frequent nonstop flights to more destinations: Flying between large hubs is cheaper.

The cost of an airline ticket into and out of Bismarck, ND (a non-hub), or Charleston, WV (a small hub), helps subsidize the same airline's small profit from a New York vacationer's air travel to Miami or a Los Angeles conventioneer's trip to Chicago. When airlines skirmish with bargain fares between large hubs, travelers in the smaller hubs end up paying part of the tab.

---

2. *Mass transit.* Counting the number of motor buses and rapid rail cars in a metro area's transit system won't tell you enough about local transit performance. *Places Rated* instead adopts the urban mass transit industry's measure of *seat miles per capita*, which means the number of transit seats that travel one mile of transit route for each person in the urban core each day.

   Among the 288 metro areas with public transit, the average number of seat miles per capita is 1.48. To rate each metro area for transit supply, the local seat mile figure is divided by this 1.48 average and multiplied by 1,000, with a maximum total of 5,000 points per metro area. Chicago's buses and rapid rail cars provide 3.68 seat miles for each resident. The Second City therefore has a transit supply 2.486 times the metro area average, good for 2,486 points.

3. *Interstate highways.* There is an average of 1.491 main numbered routes for the 279 metro areas reached by the 42,500-mile interstate system. To rate each metro area in this category, the number of routes in the metro area is divided by the average of 1.491 and multiplied by 1,000. Dallas is reached by four routes: I–20, I–30, I–35, and I–45; the Texas metro area therefore has 2.682 times the national average of interstate routes, totaling 2,682 points.

4. *Airline flights.* For the 295 metro areas with access to airports with passenger service, the average number of residents per departing flight each day is 8,862. To rate each metro area, this average is divided by the local ratio of residents to departure, then multiplied by 1,000. (In the case of CMSA component metro areas, the ratio of residents per departure is arrived at by dividing the total number of departures in the CMSA by the total CMSA population. Each member metro area receives the same number of points.) The maximum score for each metro area is 3,000 points.

5. *Passenger train (Amtrak) departures.* The average number of residents per Amtrak departure each day for the 166 metro areas served by Amtrak is 197,497. To arrive at a score for each metro area, this average is divided by the local number of residents per daily train departure, then multiplied by 1,000, with a ceiling of 1,500 points.

Sample Comparison: New York, NY, and Houma–Thibodaux, LA

A premier world port and trade center and a pair of cities in Louisiana bayou country are the best and worst metro areas, respectively, for transportation supply according to *Places Rated*'s criteria.

In Houma–Thibodaux, which comprises Lafourche and Terrebonne parishes, workers take 52.6 minutes to get to and from their jobs each day. Dividing 49.7 minutes, the national average round-trip commuting time for the metro areas, by 52.6 and multiplying by 1,000 yields a score of 945. There is no public transportation in this metro area, nor any interstate highways linking it with other metro areas along the network.

And despite Houma–Thibodaux's population growth during the 1970s in the midst of the Louisiana oil and natural gas boom, it is served by only one airline. To board a plane for such destinations as Miami, Dallas, or Memphis means driving northeast on U.S. 90 for an hour or so to New Orleans International–Moisant Field.

Amtrak service is also lacking, meaning that the total score for this metro area is the sum of its points for commuting time—945, the lowest of all 333 metro areas.

New York, in contrast, is the core of the country's largest metro complex: the New York–Northern New Jersey–Long Island consolidated area. Workers here spend an average of 81 minutes every day commuting, good for a score of only 614. Most of New York's commuters use public transit, and it is ironic that they spend so much time—the longest daily trip of any metro area—aboard the biggest transit system in the world. New York's 3,279 buses and 4,859 rapid rail cars provide a phenomenal 17.49 seats per mile of route for each resident. When divided by the national metro area average of 2.43 and multiplied by 1,000, this figure results in a score of 7,198, which is trimmed to the maximum number of points *Places Rated* allows for this category, 5,000.

Three interstate highways reach the nation's largest city, giving it an additional 2,086 points after dividing 3 by 1.438, the national average of interstate highways per metro area, and multiplying by 1,000. As part of the New York–Northern New Jersey–Long Island consolidated area, made up of 12 metro areas, New York is served by eight passenger airports: Allaire Field, Igor I. Sikorsky Memorial, John F. Kennedy International, La Guardia, Long Island–MacArthur, Newark International, Republic, and Stewart. There are a total of 838 airline flights out of these facilities each day, or one flight for every 14,271 people. This results in a score of 621 for air travel.

Amtrak's biggest hub in the United States is at Grand Central Station, in midtown Manhattan. Twenty-seven trains leave here every day, most of which reach other metro areas in the consolidated area, which means one train for every 649,604 people. This works out to a score of 304 when divided into the national average of one daily train for every 197,497 metro area residents and then multiplied by 1,000. The sum of New York's five scores is 8,598, the highest of any metro area in the United States.

Rankings: Transportation

Determining a score for transportation means looking closely at a metro area's ability to accommodate the transportation needs of its residents, using the following criteria: (1) daily commute, (2) public transportation, (3) interstate highways, (4) air service, and (5) passenger rail service.

Places that receive tie scores are given the same rank and are listed in alphabetical order.

Metro Areas from Best to Worst

Places Rated Rank	Places Rated Score	Places Rated Rank	Places Rated Score	Places Rated Rank	Places Rated Score	Places Rated Rank	Places Rated Score
1. New York, NY	8,598	56. Gary–Hammond, IN	5,777	114. Manchester, NH	4,882		
2. Dallas, TX	8,566	57. Joliet, IL	5,727	115. Houston, TX	4,857		
3. Washington, DC–MD–VA	8,524	58. Erie, PA	5,706				
4. Atlanta, GA	8,428	59. La Crosse, WI	5,662	116. Tallahassee, FL	4,837		
5. Denver, CO	8,280	60. Louisville, KY–IN	5,634	117. Fort Worth–Arlington, TX	4,834		
				118. New London–Norwich, CT–RI	4,825		
6. Baltimore, MD	8,070	61. Lansing–East Lansing, MI	5,581	119. Stockton, CA	4,813		
7. Chicago, IL	7,996	61. Orlando, FL	5,581	120. Flint, MI	4,808		
8. San Francisco, CA	7,933	63. Cincinnati, OH–KY–IN	5,576				
9. Burlington, VT	7,722	64. Fort Wayne, IN	5,572	121. Davenport–Rock Island–Moline, IA–IL	4,803		
10. Hartford, CT	7,704	65. Tacoma, WA	5,570	122. Trenton, NJ	4,802		
				123. Wilmington, DE–NJ–MD	4,798		
11. Champaign–Urbana–Rantoul, IL	7,679	66. South Bend–Mishawaka, IN	5,566	124. Birmingham, AL	4,719		
12. Seattle, WA	7,675	67. Charleston, WV	5,564	125. Canton, OH	4,715		
13. Salt Lake City–Ogden, UT	7,571	68. New Haven–Meriden, CT	5,553				
14. Syracuse, NY	7,502	69. Las Vegas, NV	5,515	126. Detroit, MI	4,675		
15. Albany–Schenectady–Troy, NY	7,445	70. San Antonio, TX	5,495	127. Columbus, OH	4,670		
				128. Lexington–Fayette, KY	4,626		
16. Honolulu, HI	7,260	71. Philadelphia, PA–NJ	5,490	129. Jackson, MS	4,598		
17. Boulder–Longmont, CO	7,210	72. Nashville, TN	5,486	130. Tuscaloosa, AL	4,597		
18. St. Louis, MO–IL	7,172	73. Anchorage, AK	5,472				
19. Springfield, IL	7,114	74. Santa Barbara–Santa Maria–Lompoc, CA	5,430	131. Cheyenne, WY	4,581		
20. Reno, NV	7,068	75. Des Moines, IA	5,393	132. Fresno, CA	4,580		
				133. Asheville, NC	4,567		
21. Springfield, MA	7,048	76. Racine, WI	5,382	134. Bridgeport–Milford, CT	4,541		
22. Albuquerque, NM	6,716	77. Niagara Falls, NY	5,371	135. Tucson, AZ	4,535		
23. Boise City, ID	6,707	78. New Britain, CT	5,364				
24. Richland–Kennewick–Pasco, WA	6,612	78. Pittsburgh, PA	5,364	136. St. Cloud, MN	4,527		
25. Richmond–Petersburg, VA	6,586	80. Lynchburg, VA	5,346	137. Green Bay, WI	4,510		
				138. Bradenton, FL	4,500		
26. Cleveland, OH	6,560	81. Lafayette, LA	5,334	139. New Orleans, LA	4,497		
27. Billings, MT	6,503	82. Eugene–Springfield, OR	5,327	140. Oklahoma City, OK	4,456		
28. Savannah, GA	6,466	83. Dayton–Springfield, OH	5,318				
29. Memphis, TN–AR–MS	6,428	84. Omaha, NE–IA	5,281	141. Merced, CA	4,450		
30. Boston, MA	6,413	85. San Jose, CA	5,279	142. Battle Creek, MI	4,434		
				143. Kenosha, WI	4,418		
31. Charlottesville, VA	6,357	86. Kalamazoo, MI	5,278	144. Columbia, MO	4,381		
32. Fargo–Moorhead, ND–MN	6,336	87. Topeka, KS	5,271	144. Stamford, CT	4,381		
33. Bloomington–Normal, IL	6,318	88. Cedar Rapids, IA	5,267				
34. Portland, OR	6,295	89. San Deigo, CA	5,262	146. Rochester, MN	4,379		
35. Madison, WI	6,277	90. Santa Cruz, CA	5,241	147. Middlesex–Somerset–Hunterson, NJ	4,375		
				148. Midland, TX	4,362		
36. Raleigh–Durham, NC	6,273	91. Duluth, MN–WI	5,240	149. Roanoke,VA	4,352		
37. Grand Forks, ND	6,272	92. Newark, NJ	5,237	150. Amarillo, TX	4,345		
38. Spokane, WA	6,257	93. Aurora–Elgin, IL	5,229				
39. Charlotte–Gastonia–Rock Hill, NC–SC	6,246	94. Toledo, OH	5,222	150. Sheboygan, WI	4,345		
40. Oakland, CA	6,241	95. Rochester, NY	5,209	152. Muncie, IN	4,321		
				153. Salem, OR	4,316		
41. Indianapolis, IN	6,237	96. Jersey City, NJ	5,201	154. Altoona, PA	4,312		
42. Columbia, SC	6,236	97. Decatur, IL	5,188	155. Greensboro–Winston-Salem–High Point, NC	4,292		
43. Harrisburg–Lebanon–Carlisle, PA	6,224	98. Florence, SC	5,165				
44. Minneapolis–St. Paul, MN–WI	6,197	99. New Bedford, MA	5,159	156. Fort Myers–Cape Coral, FL	4,269		
45. Great Falls, MT	6,099	100. Jacksonville, FL	5,147	157. Johnstown, PA	4,263		
				158. Bismarck, ND	4,260		
46. Providence, RI	6,085	101. Olympia, WA	5,144	159. Los Angeles–Long Beach, CA	4,243		
47. Fall River, MA–RI	6,000	102. Miami–Hialeah, FL	5,060	160. Jackson, MI	4,241		
48. Lincoln, NE	5,998	103. Phoenix, AZ	5,049				
49. Atlantic City, NJ	5,950	104. Vancouver, WA	5,036	161. Rapid City, SD	4,233		
50. Redding, CA	5,916	105. Sacramento, CA	5,027	162. Charleston, SC	4,232		
				163. Poughkeepsie, NY	4,221		
51. Kansas City, MO–KS	5,899	105. Tampa–St. Petersburg–Clearwater, FL	5,027	164. Casper, WY	4,194		
52. Medford, OR	5,873	105. Utica–Rome, NY	5,027	165. Abilene, TX	4,179		
53. Bangor, ME	5,839	108. Portland, ME	4,973				
54. Buffalo, NY	5,820	109. Ann Arbor, MI	4,965	166. Sioux City, IA–NE	4,176		
55. Sioux Falls, SD	5,784	110. Milwaukee, WI	4,961	167. Parkersburg–Marietta, WV–OH	4,157		
		111. Binghamton, NY	4,948				
		112. Lafayette–West Lafayette, IN	4,903				
		113. Akron, OH	4,896				

Places Rated Rank	Places Rated Score	Places Rated Rank	Places Rated Score	Places Rated Rank	Places Rated Score
168. Austin, TX	4,155	223. Lorain–Elyria, OH	3,490	279. Williamsport, PA	2,744
169. Janesville–Beloit, WI	4,125	224. Mobile, AL	3,486	280. Riverside–San Bernardino,	
170. Shreveport, LA	4,123	225. Wichita, KS	3,483	CA	2,706
171. Lancaster, PA	4,095	226. Hamilton–Middletown, OH	3,478	281. Danbury, CT	2,690
172. Fort Lauderdale–Hollywood–		227. Lawton, OK	3,470	282. Tyler, TX	2,678
Pompano Beach, FL	4,086	228. Evansville, IN–KY	3,452	283. Albany, GA	2,676
173. Fayetteville, NC	4,085	229. Colorado Springs, CO	3,423	284. Beaumont–Port Arthur, TX	2,652
174. Little Rock–North Little		230. Laredo, TX	3,422	285. Johnson City–Kingsport–	
Rock, AR	4,079			Bristol, TN–VA	2,650
175. Elkhart–Goshen, IN	4,070	231. Kankakee, IL	3,419		
		232. Eau Claire, WI	3,407	286. Brownsville–Harlingen, TX	2,643
176. Elmira, NY	4,036	233. Iowa City, IA	3,370	286. Joplin, MO	2,643
177. Bellingham, WA	4,017	234. Rockford, IL	3,367	288. Melbourne–Titusville–	
178. Knoxville, TN	4,007	235. Norwalk, CT	3,343	Palm Bay, FL	2,557
179. Bremerton, WA	3,982			288. St. Joseph, MO	2,557
180. West Palm Beach–		236. Ocala, FL	3,340	290. Biloxi–Gulfport, MS	2,555
Boca Raton–Delray		237. Lawrence–Haverhill, MA–NH	3,326		
Beach, FL	3,969	238. Bristol, CT	3,322	291. Fitchburg–Leominster, MA	2,505
181. Pittsfield, MA	3,964	239. Macon–Warner Robins, GA	3,318	292. Waterbury, CT	2,474
182. Cumberland, MD–WV	3,961	240. Danville, VA	3,312	293. Dothan, AL	2,471
183. Scranton–Wilkes-Barre, PA	3,940			294. Lewiston–Auburn, ME	2,443
184. Appleton–Oshkosh–		241. Reading, PA	3,305	295. Fort Collins–Loveland, CO	2,414
Neenah, WI	3,934	242. Fayetteville–Springdale, AR	3,280		
184. Waco, TX	3,934	243. Vallejo–Fairfield–Napa, CA	3,263	296. Owensboro, KY	2,384
		244. Saginaw–Bay City–		297. Killeen–Temple, TX	2,366
186. Lima, OH	3,926	Midland, MI	3,239	298. Wheeling, WV–OH	2,354
187. Salinas–Seaside–		245. Lake County, IL	3,218	299. Glens Falls, NY	2,336
Monterey, CA	3,910			300. Fort Pierce, FL	2,259
188. Sarasota, FL	3,903	246. Lake Charles, LA	3,217		
189. Lubbock, TX	3,890	246. Norfolk–Virginia Beach–		301. Anderson, IN	2,250
190. Springfield, MO	3,887	Newport News, VA	3,217	302. York, PA	2,248
		248. Visalia–Tulare–		303. Longview–Marshall, TX	2,247
191. Hagerstown, MD	3,846	Porterville, CA	3,213	304. Bryan–College Station, TX	2,244
192. Greenville–Spartanburg, SC	3,842	249. San Angelo, TX	3,186	305. Pine Bluff, AR	2,239
193. Yuba City, CA	3,836	250. Huntsville, AL	3,181		
194. Wilmington, NC	3,817			306. Brazoria, TX	2,234
195. Montgomery, AL	3,812	251. Youngstown–Warren, OH	3,170	306. Clarksville–Hopkinsville,	
		252. Galveston–Texas City, TX	3,136	TN–KY	2,234
196. Worcester, MA	3,811	253. State College, PA	3,130	308. Athens, GA	2,172
197. Anaheim–Santa Ana, CA	3,807	254. Vineland–Millville–		309. Mansfield, OH	2,162
198. Chico, CA	3,754	Bridgeton, NJ	3,102	310. Portsmouth–Dover–	
199. Terre Haute, IN	3,748	255. Pueblo, CO	3,095	Rochester, NH–ME	2,152
200. Yakima, WA	3,742				
		256. Jackson, TN	3,083	311. Gadsden, AL	2,128
201. Gainesville, FL	3,741	257. Orange County, NY	3,069	312. Bloomington, IN	2,105
202. Peoria, IL	3,739	258. Fort Smith, AR–OK	3,045	313. Lawrence, KS	2,075
203. Pawtucket–Woonsocket–		259. Allentown–Bethlehem,		314. Oxnard–Ventura, CA	2,038
Attleboro, RI–MA	3,737	PA–NJ	3,041	315. Santa Fe, NM	2,029
204. Bakersfield, CA	3,734	260. Corpus Christi, TX	3,031		
205. Dubuque, IA	3,722			316. Enid, OK	2,004
		261. Beaver County, PA	3,025	317. Sharon, PA	1,992
206. Bergen–Passaic, NJ	3,721	262. Columbus, GA–AL	3,007	318. Jacksonville, NC	1,974
207. Wausau, WI	3,720	263. Salem–Gloucester, MA	3,000	319. Odessa, TX	1,919
208. Lowell, MA–NH	3,711	264. Waterloo–Cedar Falls, IA	2,980	320. Modesto, CA	1,913
209. Anniston, AL	3,695	265. Panama City, FL	2,964		
210. Huntington–Ashland,				321. Naples, FL	1,904
WV–KY–OH	3,684	266. Monmouth–Ocean, NJ	2,930	322. Sherman–Denison, TX	1,898
		267. Pensacola, FL	2,927	323. Burlington, NC	1,886
211. El Paso, TX	3,653	268. Nashua, NH	2,893	324. Greeley, CO	1,839
212. Daytona Beach, FL	3,647	269. Muskegon, MI	2,890	325. Kokomo, IN	1,798
213. Brockton, MA	3,641	270. Texarkana, TX–Texarkana,			
214. Tulsa, OK	3,620	AR	2,858	326. Victoria, TX	1,762
215. Grand Rapids, MI	3,604			327. Decatur, AL	1,730
		271. Benton Harbor, MI	2,853	328. Pascagoula, MS	1,726
216. Alexandria, LA	3,590	272. Las Cruces, NM	2,852	329. Nassau–Suffolk, NY	1,616
217. Chattanooga, TN–GA	3,586	273. Wichita Falls, TX	2,821	330. McAllen–Edinburg–	
218. Monroe, LA	3,582	274. Santa Rosa–Petaluma, CA	2,792	Mission, TX	1,493
219. Baton Rouge, LA	3,564	275. Hickory, NC	2,781		
220. Lakeland–Winter Haven, FL	3,562			331. Florence, AL	1,418
		276. Fort Walton Beach, FL	2,756	332. Steubenville–Weirton,	
221. Provo–Orem, UT	3,534	277. Anderson, SC	2,751	OH–WV	1,381
222. Middletown, CT	3,525	278. Augusta, GA–SC	2,747	333. Houma–Thibodaux, LA	1,118

Place Profiles: Transportation

The following pages provide indicators of local commuting conditions, mass public transit, and options for intercity travel in each of the 333 metro areas.

The sources for the information are the Aircraft Owners and Pilots Association, *AOPA's Airports, USA*, 1989; American Public Transit Association, *Transit Fact Book*, 1988, and its *Transit Vehicle Fleet Inventory*, 1989; Jane's Information Group, *Jane's Urban Transport Systems*, 1989; National Railroad Passenger Corporation, *Amtrak's America*, 1989, and *Amtrak Timetable*, 1989; Official Airline Guides, Inc., *Travel Planner*, Spring 1989; U.S. Department of Commerce, Bureau of the Census, *1980 Census of Population*; U.S. Department of Transportation, Federal Aviation Administration, *Air Traffic Activity*, 1989, *Statistical Handbook of Aviation*, 1988, and *Aviation Forecasts, 1989-2000*, 1989; Federal Highway Administration, unpublished Highway Performance Monitoring System data, 1989, and unpublished Interstate System Log and Finder List, 1989; and Urban Mass Transportation Administration, *Directory of Urban Public Transportation Service*, 1988.

The first entry in the profiles, Daily Commute, is the average number of minutes that workers in the metro area spend getting to and from work, regardless of the mode of transportation. These figures are the 1980 Census journey-to-work data for each metro area multiplied by 2.2 to represent a round-trip whose return half takes slightly longer than the first half.

Under the heading Public Transportation is the number of mass transit vehicles available during rush hour. Just below this figure appears the seat miles per capita, a measurement common in the transit industry, which is the number of transit seats that travel one mile of transit route daily for each person in the metro area's urban core. In metro areas with more than one mode of public transportation—such as Atlanta and San Francisco—this number is the total for all modes.

Descriptions of freeway traffic are derived from the Federal Highway Administration, which rates urban freeways for their level of service on a scale from "free-flowing," progressing through "flowout capacity," and ending at "congested." *Places Rated* adopts the following simplification, using the Federal Highway Administration's definition of a highway's full capacity as 2,000 vehicles per hour in one 12-foot-wide traffic lane: Freeway traffic is judged *very heavy* if the traffic volume is 90 percent or more of the freeway's capacity, *heavy* if the volume is 50 to 89 percent of capacity, *moderate* if the volume is 34 to 49 percent, and *light* if the volume is 33 percent or less. The entry None indicates a metro area with no freeways.

A major part of a metro area's freeway mileage comes from the beltways, spurs, and heavily traveled routes of the Interstate Highway System. But the 61 two-digit main routes are intercity travel assets, too. Accordingly, each main route in the system that reaches the metro area is listed.

The first item under the heading Air Service is the FAA's hub classification for the metro area: large hub, medium hub, small hub, or non-hub. In most CMSAs, the core metro area is designated a large hub, and other member metro areas are classified as part of that hub. Thus, the entry for Boulder–Longmont, CO, reads "Part of Denver hub." The airport's name is listed next. (Because of local boosterism, many airports have the word "international" in their title; the airport in Great Falls, MT, for example, is named International but has no international flights.) The airport's three-letter identifier, recognized internationally, is enclosed in parentheses next to its title. Every airport in the world with scheduled service has a unique identifier. All airports, including those that *Places Rated* scores as part of the air service "pool" shared by members of a consolidated area, are listed under the metro area in which they are located. In four cases, however, airports are listed under two metro areas and credited to both. Two of these exceptions involve airports that straddle the boundaries of two metro areas (Dallas–Fort Worth Regional, listed under Dallas and Fort Worth, TX, and Sarasota–Bradenton Airport, credited to both Bradenton and Sarasota, FL); the other two are cases of airports located in one metro area but roughly equidistant from two metro areas (Akron–Canton Regional, located in Akron but also close to Canton, OH, and Bradley International of Hartford, and about 20 minutes away from both downtown Hartford, CT, and Springfield, MA).

For metro areas that neither have airports nor share them, the location of the nearest airport is given along with its distance and direction from the metro area. Also listed in this category are the number of airlines that serve the airport and the total number of flights departing each day. (*Places Rated* also counts air taxis, or carriers that fly passengers on small aircraft with fewer than 30 seats and a maximum payload of less than 7,500 pounds; and commuter carriers, which are air taxis that make at least five round-trips a week between two or more points under a published flight schedule.)

Finally, figures for Amtrak service are the number of passenger trains departing from the metro area on a typical weekday. Metro areas that are part of CMSAs share in the number of Amtrak departures from the major city in the CMSA.

A star (★) preceding a metro area's name highlights it as one of the top 30 places for transportation assets.

Metro Area	Daily Commute	Public Transportation	Freeway Traffic	Interstate Highways	Air Service	Amtrak Service	Places Rated Score	Places Rated Rank
Abilene, TX	34.8 min	16 city buses Seat miles/capita: 1.07	Light	I-20	Non-hub Abilene Municipal (ABI) 2 airlines, 22 flights/day	—	4,179	165
Akron, OH	43.8 min	121 city buses Seat miles/capita: 1.56	Heavy	I-76 I-77	Part of Cleveland hub Akron–Canton Regional (CAK) 12 airlines, 32 flights/day	—	4,896	113
Albany, GA	38.9 min	8 city buses Seat miles/capita: 0.60	Light	—	Non-hub Albany–Dougherty County (ABY) 2 airlines, 15 flights/day	—	2,676	283
★ Albany– Schenectady– Troy, NY	43.3 min	192 city buses Seat miles/capita: 2.61	Light	I-87 I-88 I-90	Medium hub Albany County (ALB) 15 airlines, 126 flights/day	11 trains/day	7,445	15
★ Albuquerque, NM	41.6 min	89 city buses Seat miles/capita: 1.42	Heavy	I-25 I-40	Medium hub Albuquerque International (ABQ) 12 airlines, 161 flights/day	2 trains/day	6,716	22
Alexandria, LA	37.8 min	11 city buses Seat miles/capita: 0.79	Light	I-49	Non-hub Esler Regional (ESF) 5 airlines, 19 flights/day	—	3,590	216
Allentown– Bethlehem, PA–NJ	41.4 min	58 city buses Seat miles/capita: 1.02	Very heavy	I-78	Small hub Allentown–Bethlehem–Easton (ABE) 10 airlines, 45 flights/day	—	3,041	259
Altoona, PA	37.0 min	23 city buses Seat miles/capita: 1.94	Light	—	Non-hub Altoona–Blair County (AOO) 1 airline, 5 flights/day	4 trains/day	4,312	154
Amarillo, TX	37.8 min	20 city buses Seat miles/capita: 0.89	Moderate	I-27 I-40	Small hub Amarillo International (AMA) 4 airlines, 28 flights/day	—	4,345	150
Anaheim– Santa Ana, CA	51.9 min	327 city buses Seat miles/capita: 1.13	Heavy	I-5	Part of Los Angeles hub John Wayne–Orange County (SNA) 16 airlines, 122 flights/day	6 trains/day	3,807	197
Anchorage, AK	38.7 min	51 city buses Seat miles/capita: 1.99	Very heavy	—	Medium hub Anchorage International (ANC) 27 airlines, 207 flights/day	—	5,472	73
Anderson, IN	40.5 min	7 city buses Seat miles/capita: 0.59	Light	I-69	Nearest airport: Muncie, IN, 20 miles NE	—	2,250	301
Anderson, SC	40.9 min	6 city buses Seat miles/capita: 1.45	Light	I-85	Nearest airport: Greenville, SC, 42 miles NE	—	2,751	277
Ann Arbor, MI	41.4 min	40 city buses Seat miles/capita: 1.00	Moderate	I-94	Part of Detroit hub	5 trains/day	4,965	109
Anniston, AL	39.6 min	—	Light	I-20	Non-hub Anniston–Calhoun County (ANB) 1 airline, 4 flights/day	2 trains/day	3,695	209
Appleton–Oshkosh– Neenah, WI	32.3 min	59 city buses Seat miles/capita: 2.77	Heavy	—	Small hub Outagamie County (ATW) Wittman Field (OSH) 3 airlines, 28 flights/day	—	3,934	184
Asheville, NC	40.7 min	16 city buses Seat miles/capita: 1.04	Moderate	I-26 I-40	Small hub Asheville Regional (AVL) 4 airlines, 29 flights/day	—	4,567	133
Athens, GA	40.0 min	11 city buses Seat miles/capita: 1.17	Moderate	—	Non-hub Athens Municipal (AHN) 1 airline, 4 flights/day	—	2,172	308
★ Atlanta, GA	54.3 min	664 city buses 111 rapid rail cars Seat miles/capita: 3.82	Very heavy	I-20 I-75 I-85	Large hub William B. Hartsfield–Atlanta International (ATL) 28 airlines, 1,070 flights/day	4 trains/day	8,428	4
Atlantic City, NJ	44.2 min	65 city buses Seat miles/capita: 7.20	Moderate	—	Non-hub Bader Field (AIY) Pomona Field (ACY) 6 airlines, 20 flights/day	—	5,950	49
Augusta, GA–SC	43.6 min	27 city buses Seat miles/capita: 0.72	Moderate	I-20	Small hub Bush Field (AGS) 4 airlines, 25 flights/day	—	2,747	278
Aurora–Elgin, IL	46.0 min	47 city buses Seat miles/capita: 1.18	Heavy	I-90	Part of Chicago hub	6 trains/day	5,229	93
Austin, TX	41.8 min	112 city buses Seat miles/capita: 1.97	Very heavy	I-35	Small hub Robert Mueller Municipal (AUS) 10 airlines, 105 flights/day	—	4,155	168

Metro Area	Daily Commute	Public Transportation	Freeway Traffic	Interstate Highways	Air Service	Amtrak Service	Places Rated Score	Places Rated Rank
Bakersfield, CA	38.5 min	36 city buses Seat miles/capita: 1.08	Heavy	—	Non-hub Meadows Field (BFL) 6 airlines, 37 flights/day	4 trains/day	3,734	204
★ Baltimore, MD	58.3 min	806 city buses 42 rapid rail cars 2 commuter railroads Seat miles/capita: 3.22	Moderate	I-70 I-83 I-95 I-97	Medium hub Baltimore–Washington International (BWI) 23 airlines, 312 flights/day	31 trains/day	8,070	6
Bangor, ME	33.0 min	10 city buses Seat miles/capita: 1.11	Light	I-95	Small hub Bangor International (BGR) 6 airlines, 40 flights/day	—	5,839	53
Baton Rouge, LA	50.2 min	55 city buses Seat miles/capita: 1.04	Heavy	I-10 I-12	Small hub Baton Rouge Metropolitan–Ryan Field (BTR) 5 airlines, 42 flights/day	—	3,564	219
Battle Creek, MI	37.8 min	15 city buses Seat miles/capita: 1.28	Light	I-94	Small hub W. K. Kellogg Regional (BTL) 1 airline, 3 flights/day	8 trains/day	4,434	142
Beaumont–Port Arthur, TX	42.5 min	17 city buses Seat miles/capita: 0.47	Light	I-10	Non-hub Jefferson County (BPT) 3 airlines, 24 flights/day	—	2,652	284
Beaver County, PA	44.7 min	10 city buses Seat miles/capita: 0.32	Heavy	—	Part of Pittsburgh hub Beaver County (BFP) 1 airline, 1 daily flight	—	3,025	261
Bellingham, WA	35.9 min	18 city buses Seat miles/capita: 3.05	Heavy	I-5	Non-hub Bellingham International (BLI) 3 airlines, 2 flights/day	—	4,017	177
Benton Harbor, MI	36.5 min	—	Light	I-94 I-96	Non-hub Ross Field (BEH) 1 airline, 3 flights/day	—	2,853	271
Bergen–Passaic, NJ	54.3 min	460 city buses Seat miles/capita: 2.37	Very heavy	I-80	Part of New York hub	—	3,721	206
★ Billings, MT	35.4 min	16 city buses Seat miles/capita: 1.27	Light	I-90 I-94	Small hub Billings Logan International (BIL) 5 airlines, 49 flights/day	—	6,503	27
Biloxi–Gulfport, MS	44.9 min	12 city buses Seat miles/capita: 0.45	Moderate	I-10	Non-hub Gulfport–Biloxi Regional (GPT) 1 airline, 13 flights/day	—	2,555	290
Binghamton, NY	38.3 min	37 city buses Seat miles/capita: 1.53	Light	I-81 I-88	Non-hub Edwin A. Link Field–Broom County (BGM) 6 airlines, 44 flights/day	—	4,948	111
Birmingham, AL	51.3 min	103 city buses Seat miles/capita: 1.13	Very heavy	I-20 I-59 I-65	Medium hub Birmingham Municipal (BHM) 12 airlines, 81 flights/day	2 trains/day	4,719	124
Bismarck, ND	30.8 min	—	Light	I-94	Non-hub Bismarck Municipal (BIS) 4 airlines, 21 flights/day	—	4,260	158
Bloomington, IN	38.1 min	9 city buses Seat miles/capita: 0.94	None	—	Non-hub Monroe County (BMG) 1 airline, 3 flights/day	—	2,105	312
Bloomington–Normal, IL	33.4 min	16 city buses Seat miles/capita: 1.29	Light	I-55 I-74	Non-hub Bloomington–Normal (BMI) 3 airlines, 18 flights/day	6 trains/day	6,318	33
★ Boise City, ID	36.7 min	19 city buses Seat miles/capita: 0.94	Moderate	I-84	Small hub Boise Air Terminal (BOI) 7 airlines, 63 flights/day	2 trains/day	6,707	23
★ Boston, MA	51.7 min	765 city buses 352 rapid rail cars 26 trolley coaches 2 commuter railroads 2 ferry systems Seat miles/capita: 3.26	Heavy	I-90 I-93 I-95	Large hub General Edward Lawrence Logan International (BOS) 39 airlines, 536 flights/day	11 trains/day	6,413	30
★ Boulder–Longmont, CO	45.5 min	120 city buses Seat miles/capita: 8.70	Heavy	I-25	Part of Denver hub	—	7,210	17
Bradenton, FL	41.1 min	11 city buses Seat miles/capita: 0.49	Moderate	I-75	Small hub Sarasota–Bradenton (SRQ) 12 airlines, 54 flights/day	—	4,500	138
Brazoria, TX	50.6 min	—	Heavy	—	Part of Houston hub	—	2,234	306
Bremerton, WA	55.0 min	50 city buses Seat miles/capita: 5.16	Light	—	Nearest airport: Seattle, 52 miles SE	—	3,982	179

Metro Area	Daily Commute	Public Transportation	Freeway Traffic	Interstate Highways	Air Service	Amtrak Service	Places Rated Score	Places Rated Rank
Bridgeport–Milford, CT	44.7 min	56 city buses Seat miles/capita: 0.90	Heavy	I-95	Part of New York hub Igor I. Sikorsky Memorial (BDR) 3 airlines, 27 flights/day	9 trains/day	4,541	134
Bristol, CT	42.2 min	3 city buses Seat miles/capita: 0.24	Heavy	I-84	Part of Hartford hub	—	3,322	238
Brockton, MA	51.0 min	41 city buses Seat miles/capita: 1.53	Heavy	I-95	Part of Boston hub	—	3,641	213
Brownsville–Harlingen, TX	35.9 min	15 city buses Seat miles/capita: 1.09	Light	—	Non-hub Harlingen (HRL) Brownsville–South Padre Island International (BRO) 3 airlines, 20 flights/day	—	2,643	286
Bryan–College Station, TX	33.4 min	—	None	—	Non-hub Easterwood Field (CLL) 3 airlines, 12 flights/day	—	2,244	304
Buffalo, NY	42.9 min	400 city buses 24 rapid rail cars Seat miles/capita: 2.81	Moderate	I-90	Medium hub Greater Buffalo International (BUF) 9 airlines, 116 flights/day	11 trains/day	5,820	54
Burlington, NC	40.9 min	—	Heavy	I-85	Nearest airport: Greensboro, 32 miles W	—	1,886	323
★ Burlington, VT	38.1 min	24 city buses Seat miles/capita: 2.09	Light	I-89	Non-hub Burlington International (BTV) 8 airlines, 53 flights/day	2 trains/day	7,722	9
Canton, OH	40.9 min	42 city buses Seat miles/capita: 1.14	Heavy	I-77	Small hub Akron–Canton Regional (CAK) 12 airlines, 32 flights/day	4 trains/day	4,715	125
Casper, WY	39.8 min	—	Moderate	I-25	Non-hub Natrona County International (CPR) 5 airlines, 20 flights/day	—	4,194	164
Cedar Rapids, IA	36.3 min	23 city buses Seat miles/capita: 1.13	Light	I-80	Small hub Cedar Rapids Municipal (CID) 10 airlines, 52 flights/day	—	5,267	88
★ Champaign–Urbana–Rantoul, IL	33.7 min	42 city buses Seat miles/capita: 2.56	Moderate	I-57 I-72 I-74	Non-hub U. of Illinois–Willard (CMI) 6 airlines, 25 flights/day	2 trains/day	7,679	11
Charleston, SC	48.6 min	33 city buses Seat miles/capita: 0.67	Light	I-26	Small hub Charleston AFB International (CHS) 6 airlines, 57 flights/day	4 trains/day	4,232	162
Charleston, WV	47.5 min	54 city buses Seat miles/capita: 2.34	Moderate	I-64 I-77 I-79	Small hub Kanawha Airport (CRW) 10 airlines, 36 flights/day	—	5,564	67
Charlotte–Gastonia–Rock Hill, NC–SC	44.4 min	86 city buses Seat miles/capita: 1.25	Heavy	I-77 I-85	Medium hub Charlotte–Douglas International (CLT) 6 airlines, 372 flights/day	2 trains/day	6,246	39
Charlottesville, VA	42.0 min	10 city buses Seat miles/capita: 1.35	Light	I-64	Non-hub Charlottesville–Albemarle (CHO) 7 airlines, 33 flights/day	2 trains/day	6,357	31
Chattanooga, TN–GA	48.2 min	42 city buses 2 cable inclines Seat miles/capita: 0.96	Heavy	I-24 I-75	Small hub Lovell Field (CHA) 9 airlines, 33 flights/day	—	3,586	217
Cheyenne, WY	31.2 min	—	Moderate	I-25 I-80	Non-hub Cheyenne Municipal (CYS) 3 airlines, 14 flights/day	—	4,581	131
★ Chicago, IL	63.8 min	1,868 city buses 903 rapid rail cars 7 commuter railroads Seat miles/capita: 3.68	Heavy	I-55 I-57 I-80 I-90 I-94	Large hub Merrill C. Meigs (CGX) Chicago Midway (MDW) Chicago–O'Hare International (ORD) 46 airlines, 1,257 flights/day	21 trains/day	7,996	7
Chico, CA	35.4 min	5 city buses Seat miles/capita: 0.64	Heavy	—	Non-hub Chico Municipal (CIC) 1 airline, 10 flights/day	2 trains/day	3,754	198
Cincinnati, OH–KY–IN	49.3 min	280 city buses 1 ferry system Seat miles/capita: 1.66	Heavy	I-71 I-74 I-75	Medium hub Greater Cincinnati International (CVG) 14 airlines, 285 flights/day	2 trains/day	5,576	63

Metro Area	Daily Commute	Public Transportation	Freeway Traffic	Interstate Highways	Air Service	Amtrak Service	Places Rated Score	Places Rated Rank
Clarksville–Hopkinsville, TN–KY	36.7 min	—	None	I-24	Non-hub Outlaw Field (CKV) 2 airlines, 4 flights/day	—	2,234	306
★ Cleveland, OH	51.5 min	545 city buses 63 rapid rail cars Seat miles/capita: 3.23	Very heavy	I-71 I-77 I-90	Large hub Burke–Lakefront (BKL) Cleveland–Hopkins International (CLE) 16 airlines, 241 flights/day	3 trains/day	6,560	26
Colorado Springs, CO	38.7 min	42 city buses Seat miles/capita: 1.00	Heavy	I-25	Small hub City of Colorado Springs Municipal (COS) 4 airlines, 42 flights/day	—	3,423	229
Columbia, MO	34.8 min	15 city buses Seat miles/capita: 1.53	Light	I-70	Non-hub Columbia Regional (COU) 3 airlines, 18 flights/day	—	4,381	144
Columbia, SC	44.4 min	63 city buses Seat miles/capita: 1.35	Moderate	I-20 I-26 I-77	Small hub Columbia Metropolitan (CAE) 7 airlines, 55 flights/day	4 trains/day	6,236	42
Columbus, GA–AL	38.5 min	30 city buses Seat miles/capita: 0.93	Moderate	I-185	Small hub Columbus Metropolitan (CSG) 3 airlines, 15 flights/day	—	3,007	262
Columbus, OH	45.8 min	292 city buses Seat miles/capita: 2.20	Very heavy	I-70 I-71	Medium hub Port Columbus International (CMH) 18 airlines, 149 flights/day	—	4,670	127
Corpus Christi, TX	41.1 min	32 city buses Seat miles/capita: 0.87	Moderate	I-37	Small hub Corpus Christi International (CRP) 4 airlines, 28 flights/day	—	3,031	260
Cumberland, MD–WV	39.6 min	11 city buses Seat miles/capita: 1.22	Light	—	Non-hub Cumberland Municipal (CBE) 1 airline, 6 flights/day	2 trains/day	3,961	182
★ Dallas, TX	52.8 min	1,422 city buses Seat miles/capita: 4.83	Heavy	I-20 I-30 I-35E I-45	Large hub Dallas–Fort Worth Regional (DFW) Dallas Love Field (DAL) 26 airlines, 971 flights/day	—	8,566	2
Danbury, CT	53.9 min	9 city buses Seat miles/capita: 0.63	Heavy	I-84	Part of New York hub	—	2,690	281
Danville, VA	43.3 min	6 city buses Seat miles/capita: 0.86	Light	—	Non-hub Danville Municipal (DAN) 1 airline, 2 flights/day	2 trains/day	3,312	240
Davenport–Rock Island–Moline, IA–IL	38.1 min	67 city buses Seat miles/capita: 1.56	Moderate	I-74 I-80	Small hub Quad-City (MLI) 8 airlines, 55 flights/day	—	4,803	121
Dayton–Springfield, OH	42.2 min	137 city buses 50 trolley coaches Seat miles/capita: 1.59	Very heavy	I-70 I-75	Medium hub James M. Cox–Dayton International (DAY) 14 airlines, 208 flights/day	—	5,318	83
Daytona Beach, FL	39.4 min	25 city buses Seat miles/capita: 0.98	Moderate	I-4 I-95	Small hub Daytona Beach Regional (DAB) 7 airlines, 19 flights/day	—	3,647	212
Decatur, AL	46.9 min	6 city buses Seat miles/capita: 1.39	Moderate	I-65	Nearest airport: Huntsville, AL, 12 miles NE	—	1,730	327
Decatur, IL	34.5 min	48 city buses Seat miles/capita: 2.95	Light	I-72	Non-hub Decatur (DEC) 2 airlines, 20 flights/day	—	5,188	97
★ Denver, CO	48.6 min	651 city buses Seat miles/capita: 3.21	Very heavy	I-25 I-70 I-76	Large hub Stapleton International (DEN) 18 airlines, 663 flights/day	6 trains/day	8,280	5
Des Moines, IA	37.8 min	73 city buses Seat miles/capita: 1.82	Heavy	I-35 I-80	Small hub Des Moines Municipal (DSM) 11 airlines, 77 flights/day	—	5,393	75
Detroit, MI	51.3 min	569 city buses 2 commuter railroads Seat miles/capita: 1.00	Very heavy	I-75 I-94 I-96	Large hub Detroit City (DET) Detroit Metropolitan–Wayne County (DTW) 22 airlines, 553 flights/day	3 trains/day	4,676	126
Dothan, AL	38.5 min	—	Light	—	Non-hub Dothan (DHN) 3 airlines, 19 flights/day	—	2,471	293

Metro Area	Daily Commute	Public Transportation	Freeway Traffic	Interstate Highways	Air Service	Amtrak Service	Places Rated Score	Places Rated Rank
Dubuque, IA	33.4 min	18 city buses 1 cable incline Seat miles/capita: 1.76	Moderate	—	Non-hub Dubuque Municipal (DBQ) 5 airlines, 13 flights/day	—	3,722	205
Duluth, MN–WI	38.9 min	74 city buses Seat miles/capita: 3.72	Moderate	I-35	Small hub Duluth International (DLH) 2 airlines, 13 flights/day	1 train daily	5,240	91
Eau Claire, WI	33.2 min	15 city buses Seat miles/capita: 1.38	Heavy	I-94	Non-hub Eau Claire County (EAU) 2 airlines, 7 flights/day	—	3,407	232
El Paso, TX	42.5 min	81 city buses Seat miles/capita: 1.19	Heavy	I-10	Medium hub El Paso International (ELP) 7 airlines, 78 flights/day	—	3,653	211
Elkhart–Goshen, IN	34.1 min	—	Light	I-80	Non-hub Elkhart Municipal (EKI) 1 airline, 8 flights/day	2 trains/day	4,070	175
Elmira, NY	36.3 min	22 city buses Seat miles/capita: 2.14	Light	—	Non-hub Elmira–Corning Regional (ELM) 4 airlines, 15 flights/day	—	4,036	176
Enid, OK	33.9 min	—	Light	—	Non-hub Enid–Woodring Municipal (WDG) 1 airline, 6 flights/day	—	2,004	316
Erie, PA	37.6 min	58 city buses 1 ferry system Seat miles/capita: 2.16	Moderate	I-79 I-90	Small hub Erie International (ERI) 3 airlines, 22 flights/day	2 trains/day	5,706	58
Eugene–Springfield, OR	38.7 min	57 city buses Seat miles/capita: 2.08	Moderate	I-5	Small hub Mahlon Sweet Field (EUG) 5 airlines, 30 flights/day	2 trains/day	5,327	82
Evansville, IN–KY	40.9 min	20 city buses Seat miles/capita: 0.74	Moderate	I-64	Small hub Evansville Dress Regional (EVV) 9 airlines, 38 flights/day	—	3,452	228
Fall River, MA–RI	42.2 min	41 city buses Seat miles/capita: 1.93	Moderate	I-95	Part of Providence hub	—	6,000	47
Fargo–Moorhead, ND–MN	31.5 min	18 city buses Seat miles/capita: 1.15	Moderate	I-29	Small hub Hector Field (FAR) 4 airlines, 22 flights/day	2 trains/day	6,336	32
Fayetteville, NC	38.1 min	12 city buses Seat miles/capita: 0.37	Heavy	I-95	Small hub Fayetteville Municipal–Grannis Field (FAY) 4 airlines, 23 flights/day	2 trains/day	4,085	173
Fayetteville–Springdale, AR	36.1 min	—	None	—	Non-hub Drake Field (FYV) 5 airlines, 25 flights/day	—	3,280	242
Fitchburg–Leominster, MA	39.4 min	11 city buses Seat miles/capita: 0.96	Moderate	I-90	Nearest airport: Worcester, 29 miles S	—	2,505	291
Flint, MI	42.5 min	44 city buses Seat miles/capita: 0.88	Moderate	I-69 I-75	Small hub Bishop (FNT) 3 airlines, 21 flights/day	4 trains/day	4,808	120
Florence, AL	46.9 min	—	Light	—	Non-hub Muscle Shoals (MSL) 2 airlines, 6 flights/day	—	1,418	331
Florence, SC	41.4 min	3 city buses Seat miles/capita: 0.36	Light	I-20 I-95	Non-hub Florence City–County (FLO) 2 airlines, 13 flights/day	4 trains/day	5,165	98
Fort Collins–Loveland, CO	38.7 min	9 city buses Seat miles/capita: 0.77	Light	I-25	Nearest airport: Denver, 64 miles S	—	2,414	295
Fort Lauderdale–Hollywood–Pompano Beach, FL	49.7 min	151 city buses Seat miles/capita: 1.00	Heavy	I-95	Part of Miami hub Fort Lauderdale–Hollywood International (FLL) 23 airlines, 186 flights/day	4 trains/day	4,086	172
Fort Myers–Cape Coral, FL	45.5 min	15 city buses Seat miles/capita: 0.71	Moderate	I-75	Small hub Fort Meyers Regional (RSW) 12 airlines, 80 flights/day	—	4,269	156
Fort Pierce, FL	43.8 min	8 city buses Seat miles/capita: 0.76	Moderate	I-95	Nearest airport: West Palm Beach, 40 miles S	—	2,259	300
Fort Smith, AR–OK	41.4 min	—	Light	I-40	Non-hub Fort Smith Municipal (FSM) 4 airlines, 26 flights/day	—	3,045	258
Fort Walton Beach, FL	38.5 min	8 city buses Seat miles/capita: 0.62	Moderate	I-10	Non-hub Fort Walton Municipal (VPS) 4 airlines, 8 flights/day	—	2,756	276

Metro Area	Daily Commute	Public Transportation	Freeway Traffic	Interstate Highways	Air Service	Amtrak Service	Places Rated Score	Places Rated Rank
Fort Wayne, IN	40.3 min	52 city buses Seat miles/capita: 1.46	Light	I-69	Small hub Fort Wayne Municipal–Baer Field (FWA) 9 airlines, 56 flights/day	4 trains/day	5,572	64
Fort Worth–Arlington, TX	48.4 min	100 city buses Seat miles/capita: 0.68	Heavy	I-20 I-35W	Part of Dallas hub Dallas–Fort Worth Regional (DFW) 26 airlines, 971 flights/day	—	4,834	117
Fresno, CA	40.5 min	72 city buses Seat miles/capita: 1.45	Heavy	—	Small hub Fresno Air Terminal (FAT) 9 airlines, 107 flights/day	4 trains/day	4,580	132
Gadsden, AL	43.8 min	—	Light	I-59	Non-hub Gadsden Municipal (GAD) 1 airline, 4 flights/day	—	2,128	311
Gainesville, FL	41.1 min	30 city buses Seat miles/capita: 1.93	Moderate	I-75	Non-hub Gainesville Regional (GNV) 5 airlines, 18 flights/day	—	3,741	201
Galveston–Texas City, TX	46.2 min	7 city buses 1 ferry system Seat miles/capita: 0.23	Heavy	I-45	Part of Houston hub	—	3,136	252
Gary–Hammond, IN	49.7 min	121 city buses Seat miles/capita: 1.25	Heavy	I-65 I-80 I-90 I-94	Part of Chicago hub	4 trains/day	5,777	56
Glens Falls, NY	38.9 min	5 city buses Seat miles/capita: 0.65	Moderate	I-87	Nearest airport: Albany, 47 miles S	—	2,336	299
Grand Forks, ND	28.6 min	14 city buses Seat miles/capita: 1.77	Light	I-29	Non-hub Grand Forks International (GFK) 2 airlines, 11 flights/day	2 trains/day	6,272	37
Grand Rapids, MI	37.6 min	79 city buses Seat miles/capita: 1.40	Heavy	I-96	Small hub Kent County International (GRR) 11 airlines, 63 flights/day	—	3,604	215
Great Falls, MT	32.8 min	13 city buses Seat miles/capita: 1.53	Light	I-15	Small hub Great Falls International (GTF) 7 airlines, 30 flights/day	—	6,099	45
Greeley, CO	41.4 min	10 city buses Seat miles/capita: 1.07	Light	—	Nearest airport: Denver, 50 miles SW	—	1,839	324
Green Bay, WI	33.4 min	26 city buses Seat miles/capita: 1.21	Light	I-43	Small hub Austin–Straubel Field (GRB) 5 airlines, 38 flights/day	—	4,510	137
Greensboro–Winston-Salem–High Point, NC	40.5 min	71 city buses Seat miles/capita: 1.06	Heavy	I-40 I-85	Medium hub Greensboro Regional (GSO) Smith Reynolds (INT) 10 airlines, 85 flights/day	2 trains/day	4,292	155
Greenville–Spartanburg, SC	41.1 min	23 city buses Seat miles/capita: 0.46	Light	I-26 I-85	Small hub Greenville–Spartanburg (GSP) 8 airlines, 40 flights/day	2 trains/day	3,842	192
Hagerstown, MD	46.6 min	12 city buses Seat miles/capita: 1.21	Light	I-70 I-81	Non-hub Washington County Regional (HGR) 4 airlines, 10 flights/day	—	3,846	191
Hamilton–Middletown, OH	42.9 min	4 city buses Seat miles/capita: 0.14	Light	I-75	Part of Cincinnati hub	2 trains/day	3,478	226
Harrisburg–Lebanon–Carlisle, PA	41.1 min	60 city buses Seat miles/capita: 1.43	Moderate	I-76 I-81 I-93	Small hub Harrisburg International–Olmsted Field (MDT) 12 airlines, 78 flights/day	4 trains/day	6,224	43
★ Hartford, CT	44.4 min	224 city buses Seat miles/capita: 2.92	Heavy	I-84 I-85 I-91	Medium hub Bradley International (BDL) 17 airlines, 170 flights/day	12 trains/day	7,704	10
Hickory, NC	38.1 min	8 city buses Seat miles/capita: 0.86	Moderate	I-40	Non-hub Hickory Municipal (HKY) 2 airlines, 8 flights/day	—	2,781	275
★ Honolulu, HI	49.7 min	380 city buses Seat miles/capita: 4.34	Heavy	I-1	Large hub Honolulu International (HNL) 28 airlines, 388 flights/day	—	7,260	16
Houma–Thibodaux, LA	52.6 min	—	None	—	Nearest airport: New Orleans, 55 miles NE	—	1,118	333
Houston, TX	58.5 min	747 city buses Seat miles/capita: 2.37	Very heavy	I-10 I-45	Large hub William P. Hobby (HOU) Houston Intercontinental (IAH) 25 airlines, 552 flights/day	—	4,857	115

Metro Area	Daily Commute	Public Transportation	Freeway Traffic	Interstate Highways	Air Service	Amtrak Service	Places Rated Score	Places Rated Rank
Huntington–Ashland, WV–KY–OH	44.7 min	25 city buses Seat miles/capita: 0.92	Light	I-64	Non-hub Tri-State–Walker-Long Field (HTS) 5 airlines, 17 flights/day	2 trains/day	3,684	210
Huntsville, AL	40.7 min	—	Moderate	I-65	Small hub Huntsville–Madison County (HSV) 9 airlines, 38 flights/day	—	3,181	250
Indianapolis, IN	46.9 min	225 city buses Seat miles/capita: 1.79	Heavy	I-65 I-69 I-70 I-74	Medium hub Indianapolis International (IND) 22 airlines, 194 flights/day	1 train daily	6,237	41
Iowa City, IA	34.8 min	19 city buses Seat miles/capita: 2.13	Light	I-80	Nearest airport: Cedar Rapids, 22 miles NW	—	3,370	233
Jackson, MI	39.6 min	12 city buses Seat miles/capita: 0.98	Moderate	I-94	Non-hub Jackson County–Reynolds Field (JXN) 1 airline, 4 flights/day	5 trains/day	4,241	160
Jackson, MS	45.5 min	33 city buses Seat miles/capita: 0.83	Moderate	I-20 I-55	Small hub Allen C. Thompson Field (JAN) 6 airlines, 44 flights/day	2 trains/day	4,598	129
Jackson, TN	38.5 min	—	Light	I-40	Nearest airport: Memphis, TN, 80 miles SW	—	3,083	256
Jacksonville, FL	47.7 min	169 city buses Seat miles/capita: 1.88	Heavy	I-10 I-95	Medium hub Jacksonville International (JAX) 10 airlines, 105 flights/day	4 trains/day	5,147	100
Jacksonville, NC	33.9 min	—	Light	—	Non-hub Albert J. Ellis (OAJ) 1 airline, 4 flights/day	—	1,994	318
Janesville–Beloit, WI	34.5 min	23 city buses Seat miles/capita: 2.97	Moderate	I-90	Non-hub Rock County (JVL) 1 airline, 4 flights/day	—	4,125	169
Jersey City, NJ	57.6 min	225 city buses 1 commuter railroad Seat miles/capita: 2.69	Very heavy	I-78 I-80 I-95	Part of New York hub	—	5,201	96
Johnson City–Kingsport–Bristol, TN–VA	43.1 min	13 city buses Seat miles/capita: 0.39	Moderate	I-81	Small hub Tri-City (TRI) 7 airlines, 32 flights/day	—	2,650	285
Johnstown, PA	43.3 min	40 city buses 1 cable incline Seat miles/capita: 2.95	Light	—	Non-hub Johnstown–Cambria County (JST) 1 airline, 4 flights/day	2 trains/day	4,263	157
Joliet, IL	53.7 min	29 city buses Seat miles/capita: 1.15	Heavy	I-55 I-80	Part of Chicago hub	8 trains/day	5,727	57
Joplin, MO	36.5 min	—	Light	I-44	Non-hub Joplin Municipal (JLN) 3 airlines, 10 flights/day	—	2,643	287
Kalamazoo, MI	37.4 min	31 city buses Seat miles/capita: 1.33	Moderate	I-94	Small hub Kalamazoo Municipal (AZO) 6 airlines, 26 flights/day	7 trains/day	5,278	86
Kankakee, IL	39.8 min	—	Light	I-57	Nearest airport: Chicago, 50 miles NE	5 trains/day	3,419	231
Kansas City, MO–KS	48.0 min	241 city buses Seat miles/capita: 1.76	Heavy	I-29 I-35	Large hub Kansas City International (MCI) Kansas City Downtown (MKC) 14 airlines, 280 flights/day	3 trains/day	5,889	51
Kenosha, WI	40.5 min	27 city buses Seat miles/capita: 2.09	Heavy	I-94	Part of Chicago hub	—	4,418	143
Killeen–Temple, TX	35.0 min	—	Light	I-35	Non-hub Killeen Municipal (ILE) Draughon–Miller Municipal (TPL) 2 airlines, 8 flights/day	—	2,366	297
Knoxville, TN	49.9 min	50 city buses Seat miles/capita: 1.21	Heavy	I-40 I-75	Small hub McGhee Tyson (TYS) 12 airlines, 69 flights/day	—	4,007	178
Kokomo, IN	33.7 min	—	Light	—	Non-hub Kokomo Municipal (OKK) 1 airline, 4 flights/day	—	1,798	325
La Crosse, WI	33.9 min	11 city buses Seat miles/capita: 1.07	Light	I-90	Non-hub La Crosse Municipal (LSE) 3 airlines, 16 flights/day	2 trains/day	5,662	59

Metro Area	Daily Commute	Public Transportation	Freeway Traffic	Interstate Highways	Air Service	Amtrak Service	Places Rated Score	Places Rated Rank
Lafayette–West Lafayette, IN	31.7 min	22 city buses Seat miles/capita: 1.60	Light	I-65	Non-hub Purdue University (LAF) 3 airlines, 8 flights/day	2 trains/day	5,334	81
Lafayette, LA	47.7 min	14 city buses Seat miles/capita: 0.82	Moderate	I-10 I-49	Non-hub Lafayette Regional (LFT) 4 airlines, 56 flights/day	—	4,903	112
Lake Charles, LA	43.3	8 city buses Seat miles/capita: 0.43	Moderate	I-10	Non-hub Lake Charles Municipal (LCH) 3 airlines, 24 flights/day	—	3,217	246
Lake County, IL	53.2	38 city buses Seat miles/capita: 0.57	Heavy	I-94	Part of Chicago hub	—	3,218	245
Lakeland–Winter Haven, FL	42.9 min	11 city buses Seat miles/capita: 0.39	Moderate	I-4	Nearest airport: Tampa, 35 miles SW	6 trains/day	3,562	220
Lancaster, PA	37.4 min	30 city buses Seat miles/capita: 1.27	Moderate	—	Non-hub Lancaster (LNS) 2 airlines, 25 flights/day	12 trains/day	4,095	171
Lansing–East Lansing, MI	39.6 min	55 city buses Seat miles/capita: 1.44	Heavy	I-69 I-96	Small hub Capital City (LAN) 6 airlines, 36 flights/day	4 trains/day	5,581	61
Laredo, TX	37.2 min	21 city buses Seat miles/capita: 1.50	Light	I-35	Non-hub Laredo International (LRD) 2 airlines, 8 flights/day	—	3,422	230
Las Cruces, NM	37.6 min	—	Moderate	I-10 I-25	Non-hub Las Cruces–Crawford (LRU) 1 airline, 3 flights/day	—	2,852	272
Las Vegas, NV	41.6 min	18 city buses Seat miles/capita: 0.27	Moderate	I-15	Large hub McCarran International (LAS) 23 airlines, 375 flights/day	2 trains/day	5,515	69
Lawrence, KS	35.4 min	—	Moderate	I-70	Nearest airport: Kansas City, MO, 35 miles NE	—	2,075	313
Lawrence–Haverhill, MA-NH	44.4 min	24 city buses Seat miles/capita: 0.76	Heavy	I-93	Part of Boston hub	—	3,326	237
Lawton, OK	31.5 min	—	Light	—	Non-hub Lawton Municipal (LAW) 2 airlines, 18 flights/day	—	3,490	227
Lewiston–Auburn, ME	35.9 min	—	Light	I-95	Non-hub Auburn–Lewiston Municipal (LEW) 1 airline, 4 flights/day	—	2,443	294
Lexington–Fayette, KY	40.5 min	39 city buses Seat miles/capita: 1.34	Heavy	I-64 I-75	Small hub Blue Grass (LEX) 11 airlines, 51 flights/day	—	4,626	128
Lima, OH	37.0 min	7 city buses Seat miles/capita: 0.69	Light	I-75	Nearest airport: Dayton, OH, 60 miles S	4 trains/day	3,926	186
Lincoln, NE	34.8 min	52 city buses Seat miles/capita: 1.90	Light	I-80	Small hub Lincoln Municipal (LNK) 7 airlines, 32 flights/day	4 trains/day	5,998	48
Little Rock–North Little Rock, AR	43.8 min	50 city buses Seat miles/capita: 1.13	Heavy	I-30 I-40	Small hub Adams Field (LIT) 7 airlines, 58 flights/day	—	4,079	174
Longview–Marshall, TX	38.7 min	—	Light	I-20	Non-hub Gregg County (GGG) 3 airlines, 6 flights/day	—	2,247	303
Lorain–Elyria, OH	42.0 min	2 city buses Seat miles/capita: 0.27	Heavy	I-80 I-90	Part of Cleveland hub	2 trains/day	3,490	223
Los Angeles–Long Beach, CA	53.5 min	2,209 city buses 1 commuter railroad Seat miles/capita: 1.78	Very heavy	I-5 I-10	Large hub Burbank–Glendale–Pasadena (BUR) Long Beach–Daugherty Field (LGB) Los Angeles International (LAX) 68 airlines, 992 flights/day	13 trains/day	4,243	159
Louisville, KY-IN	48.6 min	245 city buses Seat miles/capita: 2.14	Heavy	I-64 I-65	Medium hub Standiford Field (SDF) 12 airlines, 154 flights/day	—	5,634	60
Lowell, MA-NH	47.3 min	36 city buses Seat miles/capita: 1.52	Heavy	I-95	Part of Boston hub	—	3,711	208
Lubbock, TX	35.9 min	27 city buses Seat miles/capita: 1.02	Light	I-27	Small hub Lubbock International (LBB) 4 airlines, 34 flights/day	—	3,890	189

Metro Area	Daily Commute	Public Transportation	Freeway Traffic	Interstate Highways	Air Service	Amtrak Service	Places Rated Score	Places Rated Rank
Lynchburg, VA	35.6 min	20 city buses Seat miles/capita: 1.42	Light	—	Non-hub Lynchburg Municipal–Preston Glenn Field (LYN) 8 airlines, 28 flights/day	2 trains/day	5,346	80
Macon–Warner Robins, GA	42.9 min	22 city buses Seat miles/capita: 0.79	Heavy	I-16 I-75	Non-hub Lewis B. Wilson (MCN) 2 airlines, 12 flights/day	—	3,318	239
Madison, WI	39.6 min	145 city buses Seat miles/capita: 4.52	Moderate	I-90 I-94	Small hub Dane County Regional–Truax Field (MSN) 7 airlines, 42 flights/day	—	6,277	35
Manchester, NH	42.5 min	26 city buses Seat miles/capita: 1.68	Moderate	I-93	Non-hub Manchester (MHT) 5 airlines, 38 flights/day	—	4,882	114
Mansfield, OH	36.5 min	—	Heavy	I-71	Non-hub Mansfield–Lahm Municipal (MFD) 1 airline, 2 flights/day	—	2,162	309
McAllen–Edinburg–Mission, TX	37.6 min	—	Light	—	Non-hub Miller International (MFE) 2 airlines, 8 flights/day	—	1,493	330
Medford, OR	36.7 min	22 city buses Seat miles/capita: 2.77	Moderate	I-5	Non-hub Medford–Jackson County (MFR) 5 airlines, 38 flights/day	—	5,873	52
Melbourne–Titusville–Palm Bay, FL	44.2 min	15 city buses Seat miles/capita: 0.47	Moderate	I-95	Small hub Melbourne Regional (MLB) 7 airlines, 22 flights/day	—	2,557	288
★ Memphis, TN–AR–MS	48.4 min	145 city buses Seat miles/capita: 1.25	Heavy	I-40 I-55	Medium hub Memphis International (MEM) 9 airlines, 401 flights/day	2 trains/day	6,428	29
Merced, CA	32.1 min	16 city buses Seat miles/capita: 2.35	Heavy	—	Nearest airport: Modesto, CA, 40 miles N	2 trains/day	4,450	141
Miami–Hialeah, FL	52.1 min	600 city buses 56 rapid rail cars Seat miles/capita: 2.71	Heavy	I-95	Large hub Miami International (MIA) 59 airlines, 414 flights/day	4 trains/day	5,060	102
Middlesex–Somerset–Hunterdon, NJ	53.9 min	310 city buses Seat miles/capita: 2.33	Very heavy	I-78 I-80	Part of New York hub	—	4,375	147
Middletown, CT	42.0 min	7 city buses Seat miles/capita: 0.57	Heavy	I-91	Part of Hartford hub	—	3,525	222
Midland, TX	35.9 min	—	Moderate	I-20	Small hub Midland Regional (MAF) 5 airlines, 33 flights/day	—	4,362	148
Milwaukee, WI	42.7 min	480 city buses Seat miles/capita: 2.64	Heavy	I-43 I-94	Medium hub General Mitchell Field (MKE) 13 airlines, 128 flights/day	2 trains/day	4,961	110
Minneapolis–St. Paul, MN–WI	44.2 min	925 city buses Seat miles/capita: 3.44	Moderate	I-35 I-94	Large hub Minneapolis–St. Paul International (MSP) 18 airlines, 424 flights/day	3 trains/day	6,197	44
Mobile, AL	51.7 min	39 city buses Seat miles/capita: 0.88	Light	I-10 I-65	Small hub Bates Field (MOB) 6 airlines, 38 flights/day	—	3,486	224
Modesto, CA	36.7 min	—	Heavy	I-5	Non-hub Modesto City–County (MOD) 2 airlines, 22 flights/day	—	1,913	320
Monmouth–Ocean, NJ	64.0 min	306 city buses Seat miles/capita: 2.40	Very heavy	—	Part of New York hub	—	2,930	266
Monroe, LA	39.4 min	12 city buses Seat miles/capita: 0.71	Heavy	I-20	Non-hub Monroe Regional (MLU) 4 airlines, 22 flights/day	—	3,582	218
Montgomery, AL	44.7 min	30 city buses Seat miles/capita: 1.01	Moderate	I-65 I-85	Small hub Dannelly Field (MGM) 6 airlines, 28 flights/day	—	3,812	195
Muncie, IN	36.5 min	15 city buses Seat miles/capita: 1.09	Moderate	I-69	Non-hub Delaware County–Johnson Field (MIE) 1 airline, 2 flights/day	2 trains/day	4,321	152
Muskegon, MI	38.7 min	11 city buses Seat miles/capita: 0.69	Moderate	I-96	Non-hub Muskegon County (MKG) 2 airlines, 10 flights/day	—	2,890	269

Metro Area	Daily Commute	Public Transportation	Freeway Traffic	Interstate Highways	Air Service	Amtrak Service	Places Rated Score	Places Rated Rank
Naples, FL	40.3 min	—	Moderate	I-75	Nearest airport: Fort Myers, FL, 28 miles N	—	1,904	321
Nashua, NH	43.6 min	—	Heavy	I-95	Part of Boston hub	—	2,893	268
Nashville, TN	49.3 min	81 city buses Seat miles/capita: 0.87	Heavy	I-24 I-40 I-65	Medium hub Nashville Metropolitan (BNA) 14 airlines, 228 flights/day	—	5,486	72
Nassau–Suffolk, NY	70.6 min	250 city buses 1 commuter railroad Seat miles/capita: 0.32	Heavy	—	Part of New York hub Republic (FRG) Long Island–MacArthur (ISP) 10 airlines, 52 flights/day	—	1,616	329
New Bedford, MA	39.4 min	51 city buses Seat miles/capita: 2.55	Moderate	I-95	Non-hub New Bedford Municipal (EWB) 1 airline, 36 flights/day	—	5,159	99
New Britain, CT	38.9 min	14 city buses 1 commuter railroad Seat miles/capita: 0.68	Heavy	I-84	Part of Hartford hub	11 trains/day	5,364	78
New Haven–Meriden, CT	42.9 min	100 city buses Seat miles/capita: 1.80	Heavy	I-91	Large hub Tweed–New Haven (HVN) 3 airlines, 30 flights/day	12 trains/day	5,553	68
New London–Norwich, CT–RI	40.3 min	20 city buses Seat miles/capita: 0.89	Heavy	I-95	Non-hub Groton–New London (GON) 3 airlines, 28 flights/day	11 trains/day	4,825	118
New Orleans, LA	55.9 min	400 city buses 22 rapid rail cars 1 ferry system Seat miles/capita: 2.56	Very heavy	I-10	Large hub New Orleans International– Moisant Field (MSY) 18 airlines, 196 flights/day	2 trains/day	4,499	139
★ New York, NY	81.0 min	3,279 buses 4,859 rapid rail cars 2 ferry systems Seat miles/capita: 17.49	Very heavy	I-78 I-87 I-95	Large hub John F. Kennedy International (JFK) La Guardia (LGA) 82 airlines, 862 flights/day	27 trains/day	8,598	1
Newark, NJ	55.9 min	677 city buses 26 rapid rail cars Seat miles/capita: 2.44	Very heavy	I-95	Part of New York hub Newark International (EWR) 25 airlines, 493 flights/day	27 trains/day	5,237	92
Niagara Falls, NY	37.2 min	60 city buses Seat miles/capita: 1.76	Moderate	I-90	Part of Buffalo hub	6 trains/day	5,371	77
Norfolk–Virginia Beach–Newport News, VA	47.1 min	140 city buses 2 ferry systems Seat miles/capita: 0.85	Moderate	I-64	Medium hub Norfolk International (ORF) Patrick Henry International (PHF) 14 airlines, 125 flights/day	2 trains/day	3,217	246
Norwalk, CT	54.1 min	28 city buses Seat miles/capita: 1.73	Heavy	I-95	Part of New York hub	—	3,343	235
Oakland, CA	56.3 min	690 city buses 439 rapid rail cars Seat miles/capita: 5.70	Heavy	I-80	Part of San Francisco hub Metropolitan Oakland International (OAK) 13 airlines, 169 flights/day	4 trains/day	6,241	40
Ocala, FL	42.5 min	—	Moderate	I-75	Nearest airport: Gainesville, FL, 40 miles S	2 trains/day	3,340	236
Odessa, TX	39.8 min	—	Moderate	I-20	Nearest airport: Midland, 15 miles SW	—	1,919	319
Oklahoma City, OK	44.9 min	72 city buses Seat miles/capita: 0.71	Moderate	I-35 I-40 I-44	Medium hub Will Rogers World (OKC) 9 airlines, 110 flights/day	—	4,456	140
Olympia, WA	44.0 min	32 city buses Seat miles/capita: 3.09	Very heavy	I-5	Nearest airport: Seattle, 30 miles NE	4 trains/day	5,144	101
Omaha, NE–IA	38.7 min	148 city buses Seat miles/capita: 1.91	Moderate	I-80	Medium hub Eppley Airfield (OMA) 16 airlines, 90 flights/day	4 trains/day	5,281	84
Orange County, NY	53.5 min	5 city buses Seat miles/capita: 0.13	Very heavy	I-84 I-87	Part of New York hub	—	3,069	257
Orlando, FL	45.5 min	70 city buses Seat miles/capita: 0.80	Heavy	I-4	Medium hub Orlando International (MCO) 23 airlines, 296 flights/day	6 trains/day	5,581	61
Owensboro, KY	41.1 min	6 city buses Seat miles/capita: 0.70	Light	—	Non-hub Owensboro–Daviess County (OWB) 2 airlines, 8 flights/day	—	2,384	296
Oxnard–Ventura, CA	51.0 min	26 city buses Seat miles/capita: 0.46	Heavy	—	Part of Los Angeles hub Oxnard (OXR) 3 airlines, 28 flights/day	2 trains/day	2,038	314

Metro Area	Daily Commute	Public Transportation	Freeway Traffic	Interstate Highways	Air Service	Amtrak Service	Places Rated Score	Places Rated Rank
Panama City, FL	37.8 min	—	Moderate	—	Non-hub Panama City–Bay County (PFN) 4 airlines, 26 flights/day	—	2,964	265
Parkersburg–Marietta, WV–OH	43.6 min	5 city buses Seat miles/capita: 0.53	Light	I-77	Non-hub Wood County (PKB) 1 airline, 10 flights/day	6 trains/day	4,157	167
Pascagoula, MS	47.1 min	—	Light	I-10	Nearest airport: Mobile, AL, 35 miles SW	—	1,726	328
Pawtucket–Woonsocket–Attleboro, RI–MA	40.9 min	100 city buses Seat miles/capita: 2.17	Moderate	I-95	Part of Providence hub	—	3,737	203
Pensacola, FL	43.8 min	18 city buses Seat miles/capita: 0.55	Moderate	I-10	Small hub Pensacola Municipal (PNS) 7 airlines, 34 flights/day	—	2,927	267
Peoria, IL	40.7 min	40 city buses Seat miles/capita: 1.02	Heavy	I-74	Small hub Greater Peoria (PIA) 8 airlines, 50 flights/day	—	3,739	202
Philadelphia, PA–NJ	56.3 min	1,112 city buses 458 rapid rail cars 67 trolley coaches 2 commuter railroads Seat miles/capita: 2.46	Heavy	I-76 I-95	Large hub North Philadelphia (PNE) Philadelphia International (PHL) 28 airlines, 490 flights/day	42 trains/day	5,490	71
Phoenix, AZ	47.7 min	280 city buses Seat miles/capita: 1.32	Heavy	I-10 I-17	Large hub Phoenix Sky Harbor International (PHX) Scottsdale Municipal (SCF) 25 airlines, 432 flights/day	2 trains/day	5,049	103
Pine Bluff, AR	41.8 min	6 city buses Seat miles/capita: 1.76	Light	—	Nearest airport: Little Rock, 45 miles NW	—	2,239	305
Pittsburgh, PA	50.4 min	720 city buses 40 rapid rail cars 2 cable inclines Seat miles/capita: 2.06	Heavy	I-76 I-79	Large hub Allegheny County (AGC) Greater Pittsburgh International (PIT) 14 airlines, 480 flights/day	4 trains/day	5,364	78
Pittsfield, MA	33.2 min	14 city buses Seat miles/capita: 1.62	None	—	Nearest airport: Albany, NY, 45 miles NW	2 trains/day	3,964	181
Portland, ME	37.6 min	17 city buses 1 ferry system Seat miles/capita: 1.06	Moderate	I-95	Small hub Portland International Jetport (PWM) 9 airlines, 60 flights/day	—	4,973	108
Portland, OR	45.8 min	517 city buses Seat miles/capita: 3.35	Heavy	I-5 I-80	Medium hub Portland International (PDX) 16 airlines, 222 flights/day	5 trains/day	6,295	34
Portsmouth–Dover–Rochester, NH–ME	39.6 min	6 city buses Seat miles/capita: 0.38	Moderate	I-95	Nearest airport: Manchester, 47 miles W	—	2,152	310
Poughkeepsie, NY	49.5 min	21 city buses Seat miles/capita: 1.02	Heavy	I-97	Non-hub Dutchess County (POU) 2 airlines, 14 flights/day	13 trains/day	4,221	163
Providence, RI	39.6 min	197 city buses Seat miles/capita: 2.40	Moderate	I-84 I-95	Small hub Theodore Francis Green State (PVD) 14 airlines, 76 flights/day	11 trains/day	6,085	46
Provo–Orem, UT	38.3 min	—	Moderate	I-15	Non-hub Provo Municipal (PVU) 1 airline, 2 flights/day	4 trains/day	3,534	221
Pueblo, CO	35.9 min	11 city buses Seat miles/capita: 0.67	Moderate	I-25	Non-hub Pueblo Memorial (PUB) 3 airlines, 10 flights/day	—	3,095	255
Racine, WI	37.4 min	36 city buses Seat miles/capita: 2.01	Heavy	I-94	Part of Milwaukee hub	2 trains/day	5,382	76
Raleigh–Durham, NC	42.5 min	93 city buses Seat miles/capita: 1.70	Heavy	I-40 I-85	Medium hub Raleigh–Durham (RDU) 11 airlines, 158 flights/day	4 trains/day	6,273	36
Rapid City, SD	32.6 min	—	Light	I-40	Rapid City Regional (RAP) 6 airlines, 19 flights/day	—	4,233	161
Reading, PA	39.4 min	42 city buses Seat miles/capita: 1.62	Heavy	I-76	Non-hub Reading Municipal (RDG) 2 airlines, 16 flights/day	—	3,305	241
Redding, CA	33.7 min	16 city buses Seat miles/capita: 2.02	Heavy	I-5	Non-hub Redding Municipal (RDD) 3 airlines, 18 flights/day	2 trains/day	5,916	50

Metro Area	Daily Commute	Public Transportation	Freeway Traffic	Interstate Highways	Air Service	Amtrak Service	Places Rated Score	Places Rated Rank
★ Reno, NV	36.7 min	31 city buses Seat miles/capita: 1.26	Moderate	I-80	Medium hub Reno–Cannon International (RNO) 12 airlines, 96 flights/day	2 trains/day	7,068	20
★ Richland–Kennewick–Pasco, WA	46.6 min	41 city buses Seat miles/capita: 1.79	Heavy	I-82	Non-hub Tri-Cities (PSC) 4 airlines, 42 flights/day	2 trains/day	6,612	24
★ Richmond–Petersburg, VA	48.8 min	163 city buses Seat miles/capita: 1.81	Heavy	I-64 I-85 I-95	Small hub Richard Evelyn Byrd International (RIC) 12 airlines, 102 flights/day	8 trains/day	6,586	25
Riverside–San Bernardino, CA	48.4 min	35 city buses Seat miles/capita: 0.33	Heavy	I-10	Part of Los Angeles hub Ontario International (ONT) 17 airlines, 142 flights/day	4 trains/day	2,706	280
Roanoke, VA	52.4 min	27 city buses Seat miles/capita: 1.01	Heavy	I-81	Small hub Roanoke Regional (ROA) 7 airlines, 58 flights/day	—	4,352	149
Rochester, MN	30.8 min	17 city buses Seat miles/capita: 1.87	Light	I-90	Small hub Rochester Municipal (RST) 3 airlines, 12 flights/day	—	4,379	146
Rochester, NY	42.9 min	196 city buses Seat miles/capita: 2.15	Heavy	I-90	Medium hub Rochester–Monroe County (ROC) 11 airlines, 102 flights/day	8 trains/day	5,209	95
Rockford, IL	37.2 min	20 city buses Seat miles/capita: 0.91	Light	I-39 I-90	Non-hub Greater Rockford (RFD) 1 airline, 5 flights/day	—	3,367	234
Sacramento, CA	42.7 min	199 city buses Seat miles/capita: 1.66	Heavy	I-5 I-80	Small hub Sacramento Metropolitan (SMF) 11 airlines, 142 flights/day	6 trains/day	5,027	105
Saginaw–Bay City–Midland, MI	39.4 min	93 city buses Seat miles/capita: 1.50	Moderate	I-75	Small hub Tri-City (MBS) 5 airlines, 20 flights/day	—	3,239	244
St. Cloud, MN	37.2 min	15 city buses Seat miles/capita: 1.71	Light	I-94	Nearest airport: Minneapolis, 68 miles SE	2 trains/day	4,527	136
St. Joseph, MO	37.0 min	11 city buses Seat miles/capita: 0.91	Light	I-29	Nearest airport: Kansas City, 30 miles SE	—	2,557	288
★ St. Louis, MO-IL	50.6 min	641 city buses Seat miles/capita: 2.36	Heavy	I-44 I-55 I-64 I-70	Large hub Lambert–St. Louis International (STL) 16 airlines, 512 flights/day	6 trains/day	7,172	18
Salem, OR	40.7 min	41 city buses Seat miles/capita: 2.01	Moderate	I-5	Non-hub McNary Field (SLE) 1 airline, 2 flights/day	2 trains/day	4,316	313
Salem–Gloucester, MA	52.1 min	19 city buses 1 commuter railroad Seat miles/capita: 0.49	Heavy	I-95	Part of Boston hub	—	3,000	263
Salinas–Seaside–Monterey, CA	36.1 min	39 city buses Seat miles/capita: 1.31	Heavy	—	Small hub Monterey Peninsula (MRY) 5 airlines, 40 flights/day	2 trains/day	3,910	187
★ Salt Lake City–Ogden, UT	44.2 min	320 city buses Seat miles/capita: 2.40	Heavy	I-15 I-80 I-84	Medium hub Salt Lake International (SLC) 12 airlines, 272 flights/day	4 trains/day	7,571	13
San Angelo, TX	34.5 min	6 city buses Seat miles/capita: 0.54	Moderate	—	Non-hub Mathis Field (SJT) 2 airlines, 17 flights/day	—	3,186	249
San Antonio, TX	44.9 min	385 city buses Seat miles/capita: 2.71	Very heavy	I-10 I-35 I-37	Medium hub San Antonio International (SAT) 13 airlines, 124 flights/day	—	5,495	70
San Diego, CA	43.1 min	311 city buses 30 rapid rail cars Seat miles/capita: 1.33	Heavy	I-5 I-8 I-15	Medium hub San Diego International–Lindbergh Field (SAN) 25 airlines, 238 flights/day	7 trains/day	5,262	89
★ San Francisco, CA	55.2 min	1,082 city buses 439 rapid rail cars 174 street cars 345 trolley coaches 4 ferry systems Seat miles/capita: 11.68	Heavy	I-80	Large hub San Francisco International (SFO) 39 airlines, 572 flights/day	7 trains/day	7,933	8
San Jose, CA	50.2 min	745 city buses Seat miles/capita: 3.99	Heavy	I-80	Part of San Francisco hub San Jose Municipal (SJC) 11 airlines, 142 flights/day	2 trains/day	5,279	85

Metro Area	Daily Commute	Public Transportation	Freeway Traffic	Interstate Highways	Air Service	Amtrak Service	Places Rated Score	Places Rated Rank
Santa Barbara–Santa Maria–Lompoc, CA	36.1 min	76 city buses Seat miles/capita: 2.44	Heavy	—	Non-hub Santa Barbara Municipal (SBA) 7 airlines, 76 flights/day	2 trains/day	5,430	74
Santa Cruz, CA	48.6 min	94 city buses Seat miles/capita: 5.08	Heavy	—	Part of San Francisco hub	—	5,241	90
Santa Fe, NM	36.5 min	—	Moderate	I-25	Nearest Airport: Albuquerque, NM, 65 miles SW	—	2,029	315
Santa Rosa–Petaluma, CA	49.9 min	21 city buses Seat miles/capita: 1.02	Heavy	—	Part of San Francisco hub	—	2,792	274
Sarasota, FL	38.9 min	15 city buses Seat miles/capita: 0.49	Moderate	I-75	Small hub Sarasota–Bradenton (SRQ) 12 airlines, 54 flights/day	—	3,903	188
★ Savannah, GA	47.1 min	63 city buses Seat miles/capita: 2.25	Moderate	I-16 I-95	Small hub Savannah International (SAV) 6 airlines, 36 flights/day	8 trains/day	6,466	28
Scranton–Wilkes-Barre, PA	40.9 min	102 city buses Seat miles/capita: 1.67	Moderate	I-81 I-84	Small hub Wilkes-Barre–Scranton International (AVP) 7 airlines, 34 flights/day	—	3,940	183
★ Seattle, WA	50.8 min	1,248 city buses 115 trolley coaches 1 ferry system Seat miles/capita: 6.37	Heavy	I-5 I-90	Large hub Henry M. Jackson International (SEA) 30 airlines, 368 flights/day	4 trains/day	7,675	12
Sharon, PA	37.6 min	—	Moderate	I-80	Nearest airport: Youngstown, OH, 10 miles W	—	1,992	317
Sheboygan, WI	31.7 min	31 city buses Seat miles/capita: 3.53	Light	I-43	Nearest airport: Green Bay, WI, 67 miles N	—	4,345	150
Sherman–Denison, TX	40.5 min	—	Light	I-35	Nearest airport: Dallas, 65 miles SW	—	1,898	322
Shreveport, LA	43.6 min	43 city buses Seat miles/capita: 1.09	Moderate	I-20 I-49	Small hub Shreveport Regional (SHV) 7 airlines, 44 flights/day	—	4,123	170
Sioux City, IA–NE	32.6 min	22 city buses Seat miles/capita: 1.51	Moderate	I-29	Small hub Sioux City Municipal (SUX) 6 airlines, 15 flights/day	—	4,176	166
Sioux Falls, SD	32.3 min	22 city buses Seat miles/capita: 1.71	Moderate	I-29 I-90	Small hub Joe Foss Field (FSD) 5 airlines, 29 flights/day	—	5,784	55
South Bend–Mishawaka, IN	38.1 min	48 city buses Seat miles/capita: 1.42	Light	I-80	Small hub Michiana Regional (SBN) 8 airlines, 42 flights/day	2 trains/day	5,566	66
Spokane, WA	40.5 min	99 city buses Seat miles/capita: 2.48	Heavy	I-90	Medium hub Spokane International (GEG) 9 airlines, 88 flights/day	2 trains/day	6,257	38
★ Springfield, IL	38.1 min	37 city buses Seat miles/capita: 2.00	Moderate	I-55 I-72	Non-hub Capital (SPI) 4 airlines, 41 flights/day	6 trains/day	7,114	19
★ Springfield, MA	39.8 min	25 city buses Seat miles/capita: 0.40	Moderate	I-90 I-91	Medium hub Bradley International (BDL) 18 airlines, 170 flights/day	12 trains/day	7,048	21
Springfield, MO	39.2 min	21 city buses Seat miles/capita: 1.01	Moderate	I-44	Small hub Springfield Regional (SGF) 8 airlines, 38 flights/day	—	3,887	190
Stamford, CT	53.2 min	25 city buses Seat miles/capita: 0.93	Heavy	I-95	Part of New York hub	14 trains/day	4,381	144
State College, PA	38.1 min	20 city buses Seat miles/capita: 2.34	Light	—	Non-hub University Park (SCE) 1 airline, 6 flights/day	—	3,130	253
Steubenville–Weirton, OH–WV	42.2 min	4 city buses Seat miles/capita: 0.34	Light	—	Nearest airport: Pittsburgh, PA, 33 miles NE	—	1,381	332
Stockton, CA	38.5 min	64 city buses Seat miles/capita: 2.16	Heavy	I-5	Non-hub Stockton Metropolitan (SCK) 4 airlines, 10 flights/day	4 trains/day	4,813	119
★ Syracuse, NY	41.4 min	161 city buses Seat miles/capita: 2.83	Moderate	I-81 I-90	Medium hub Syracuse Hancock International (SYR) 11 airlines, 140 flights/day	10 trains/day	7,502	14
Tacoma, WA	47.1 min	104 city buses 1 ferry system Seat miles/capita: 1.76	Heavy	I-5	Part of Seattle hub	6 trains/day	5,570	65

Metro Area	Daily Commute	Public Transportation	Freeway Traffic	Interstate Highways	Air Service	Amtrak Service	Places Rated Score	Places Rated Rank
Tallahassee, FL	40.9 min	35 city buses Seat miles/capita: 1.95	Moderate	I-10	Small hub Tallahassee Municipal (TLH) 7 airlines, 50 flights/day	—	4,837	116
Tampa–St. Petersburg–Clearwater, FL	45.1 min	279 city buses Seat miles/capita: 1.35	Heavy	I-4 I-75	Large hub Tampa International (TPA) St. Petersburg–Clearwater International (PIE) 21 airlines, 262 flights/day	10 trains/day	5,027	105
Terre Haute, IN	41.1 min	14 city buses Seat miles/capita: 1.25	Light	I-70	Non-hub Hulman Regional (HUF) 1 airline, 18 flights/day	—	3,748	199
Texarkana, TX–Texarkana, AR	40.9 min	—	Light	I-30	Non-hub Texarkana Municipal (TXK) 3 airlines, 14 flights/day	—	2,858	270
Toledo, OH	39.4 min	175 city buses Seat miles/capita: 2.40	Heavy	I-75 I-80	Small hub Toledo Express (TOL) 8 airlines, 32 flights/day	3 trains/day	5,222	94
Topeka, KS	40.5 min	22 city buses Seat miles/capita: 1.16	Moderate	I-70	Non-hub Forbes Field (FOE) 4 airlines, 23 flights/day	2 trains/day	5,271	87
Trenton, NJ	47.7 min	58 city buses Seat miles/capita: 1.48	Moderate	I-95	Part of Philadelphia hub Mercer County (TTN) 2 airlines, 8 flights/day	43 trains/day	4,802	122
Tucson, AZ	46.4 min	124 city buses Seat miles/capita: 1.83	Heavy	I-10 I-19	Medium hub Tucson International (TUS) 15 airlines, 78 flights/day	—	4,535	135
Tulsa, OK	44.7 min	80 city buses Seat miles/capita: 1.20	Moderate	I-44	Medium hub Tulsa International (TUL) 11 airlines, 101 flights/day	—	3,620	214
Tuscaloosa, AL	42.5 min	5 city buses Seat miles/capita: 0.40	Light	I-20 I-59	Non-hub Tuscaloosa Municipal (TCL) 2 airlines, 6 flights/day	2 trains/day	4,597	130
Tyler, TX	41.1 min	1 city bus Seat miles/capita: 0.09	Light	I-20	Non-hub Pounds Field (TYR) 3 airlines, 14 flights/day	—	2,678	282
Utica–Rome, NY	37.4 min	40 city buses Seat miles/capita: 1.72	Light	I-90	Non-hub Oneida County (UCA) 3 airlines, 19 flights/day	10 trains/day	5,027	105
Vallejo–Fairfield–Napa, CA	47.3 min	10 city buses Seat miles/capita: 0.51	Heavy	I-80	Part of San Francisco hub	2 trains/day	3,263	243
Vancouver, WA	48.4 min	25 city buses Seat miles/capita: 0.87	Heavy	I-5	Part of Portland hub	8 trains/day	5,036	104
Victoria, TX	44.4 min	—	Light	—	Non-hub Victoria Regional (VCT) 1 airline, 6 flights/day	—	1,762	326
Vineland–Millville–Bridgeton, NJ	37.6 min	24 city buses Seat miles/capita: 1.80	Moderate	—	Part of Philadelphia hub	—	3,102	254
Visalia–Tulare–Porterville, CA	35.4 min	3 city buses Seat miles/capita: 0.33	Moderate	—	Non-hub Visalia Municipal (VIS) 1 airline, 4 flights/day	3 trains/day	3,213	248
Waco, TX	36.7 min	12 city buses Seat miles/capita: 0.59	Heavy	I-35	Non-hub Waco–Madison Cooper (ACT) 2 airlines, 36 flights/day	—	3,934	184
★ Washington, DC–MD–VA	64.5 min	1,433 city buses 446 rapid rail cars Seat miles/capita: 7.07	Heavy	I-66 I-95	Large hub Dulles International (IAD) Washington National (DCA) 39 airlines, 578 flights/day	22 trains/day	8,524	3
Waterbury, CT	42.9 min	26 city buses Seat miles/capita: 1.08	Heavy	I-84	Nearest airport: New Haven, CT, 30 miles SE	—	2,474	292
Waterloo–Cedar Falls, IA	33.4 min	20 city buses Seat miles/capita: 1.11	Light	—	Small hub Waterloo Municipal (ALO) 7 airlines, 15 flights/day	—	2,980	264
Wausau, WI	33.2 min	14 city buses Seat miles/capita: 1.76	Light	—	Non-hub Central Wisconsin (CWA) 5 airlines, 16 flights/day	—	3,720	207
West Palm Beach–Boca Raton–Delray Beach, FL	43.6 min	46 city buses Seat miles/capita: 0.63	Heavy	I-95	Medium hub Palm Beach International (PBI) 16 airlines, 110 flights/day	4 trains/day	3,969	180
Wheeling, WV–OH	45.5 min	15 city buses Seat miles/capita: 0.99	Moderate	I-70	Nearest airport: Pittsburgh, PA, 50 miles NE	—	2,354	298

Metro Area	Daily Commute	Public Transportation	Freeway Traffic	Interstate Highways	Air Service	Amtrak Service	Places Rated Score	Places Rated Rank
Wichita, KS	39.4 min	45 city buses Seat miles/capita: 0.98	Heavy	I-35	Small hub Wichita Mid–Continent (ICT) 10 airlines, 56 flights/day	—	2,821	273
Wichita Falls, TX	34.8 min	8 city buses Seat miles/capita: 0.56	Very heavy	I-44	Non-hub Wichita Falls Municipal (SPS) 2 airlines, 6 flights/day	—	3,483	225
Williamsport, PA	38.7 min	11 city buses Seat miles/capita: 1.25	Light	—	Non-hub Williamsport–Lycoming County (IPT) 1 airline, 10 flights/day	—	2,744	279
Wilmington, DE–NJ–MD	45.5 min	85 city buses Seat miles/capita: 1.39	Very heavy	I-95	Part of Philadelphia hub Greater Wilmington–New Castle County (ILG) 1 airline, 5 flights/day	31 trains/day	4,798	123
Wilmington, NC	40.9 min	9 city buses Seat miles/capita: 0.68	Heavy	I-40	Non-hub New Hanover County (ILM) 3 airlines, 22 flights/day	—	3,817	194
Worcester, MA	41.1 min	62 city buses Seat miles/capita: 1.49	Heavy	I-90	Non-hub Worcester Municipal (ORH) 3 airlines, 16 flights/day	2 trains/day	3,811	196
Yakima, WA	37.8 min	12 city buses Seat miles/capita: 0.98	Moderate	I-82	Non-hub Yakima Air Terminal (YKM) 3 airlines, 26 flights/day	—	3,742	200
York, PA	43.3 min	14 city buses Seat miles/capita: 0.72	Moderate	I-83	Nearest airport: Harrisburg, PA, 20 miles NE	—	2,248	302
Youngstown–Warren, OH	40.9 min.	34 city buses Seat miles/capita: 0.59	Moderate	I-76 I-80	Small hub Youngstown Municipal (YNG) 4 airlines, 16 flights/day	—	3,170	251
Yuba City, CA	39.2 min	11 city buses Seat miles/capita: 1.79	Moderate	—	Nearest airport: Sacramento, CA, 35 miles SE	—	3,836	193

Et Cetera

FERRYBOATS, CABLE CARS, MONORAILS, AERIAL TRAMS, AND INCLINES

Besides the ubiquitous bus and the different rail systems in larger cities, U.S. transit systems operate other types of vehicles. Although these modes have little impact on total mass transit, they are by far the most fun to watch and ride, undeniably adding to a city's flavor.

San Francisco has the nation's only **cable car** system. In operation since the nineteenth century, the 41 cars are the only transit property in the National Register of Historic Places. New York operates the country's only public **aerial tram,** between Roosevelt Island and Manhattan. **Automated guideways,** the newest public transit mode, are electric vehicles running over fixed guideways without operators or other crewpersons. You can catch one in Detroit, MI, Miami, FL, Morgantown, WV, and Tampa, FL.

The largest transit vehicles in the United States are **ferryboats,** which range in size up to 380 feet and can carry as many as 2,500 commuters per trip. Public ferryboat systems, which provide frequent "bridge" service over a fixed route and on a published schedule between two or more points, are part of the mass-transit mix in ten metro areas:

Boston, MA	Massachusetts Bay Transit Authority
Erie, PA	Erie Metropolitan Transit Authority
Galveston, TX	Texas Department of Transportation
New Orleans, LA	Mississippi River Bridge Authority
New York, NY	City of New York—Staten Island Ferry
Norfolk, VA	Tidewater Transportation District
Portland, ME	Casco Bay Transit District
San Francisco, CA	Golden Gate Bridge Transportation
Seattle, WA	Washington State Ferries
Tacoma, WA	Pierce County Ferry

Four metro areas operate cog or cable incline cars that traverse steep hills:

Chattanooga, TN–GA: Lookout Mountain
Dubuque, IA: Fourth Street Elevator
Johnstown, PA: Johnstown-Westmont Incline
Pittsburgh, PA: Monongahela and Duquesne Heights

WHERE'S THE BUS (OR TRAM, OR STREET CAR)?

If you've got the fare and you know where your transit stops and where it's going, on a darkening and cold winter afternoon the quality of public transportation ultimately comes down to how long you have to stand around waiting for it. Basing our calculations on the assumption that all the vehicles of a transit system are in service and spaced evenly over each mile of their routes, *Places Rated* ranks the 35 largest such systems according to their waiting times (see table below).

In the second column of the table are detailed the different modes of transportation in the system. *Route miles* means the number of miles over which a system's fleet travels in service. If a bus or tram travels in only one direction within the right-of-way, each mile is counted once. If a vehicle travels in both directions, each mile is counted twice. For example, a mile of single track over which street cars operate in two directions represents two route miles.

Fleet age is simply the average number of years a transit system's collection of vehicles has been in service. The oldest fleets in the United States are the San Francisco Municipal Railway's historic cable cars (91 years old) and the charming street cars (66 years old) operated by the New Orleans Public Service Company. The transit vehicle with the shortest active life is the ever-present diesel-powered bus. By the time these roarers are finally scrapped—after an average of nine years on the street—their odometers may register more than 300,000 miles.

But just because a vehicle is old doesn't necessarily mean it's slow. The *average speed* (the average number of miles traveled per hour including frequent stops for passengers) is governed by local congestion on the roads. Seattle's METRO buses are more than twice as old as the Dallas Transit System's fleet, but they still move faster over their routes.

Headway is the distance between vehicles if they are spaced evenly over each mile of route; if you just miss a CTA bus in Chicago, for example, the next one should be only 1.18 miles behind. *Waiting time*, finally, represents the average amount of time you should have to wait for a ride given the number of vehicles in the system, their average speed, and their headway.

The transit systems are presented in order of their average waiting time for all modes of transportation, from shortest to longest. This average is a weighted average and is derived in the following way, using the NYCTA system as an example: The waiting time of 5.96 minutes for buses is multiplied by the number of buses (4,573) and then added to the product of the waiting time for rapid rail cars (0.57 minutes) and the number of cars (6,263). This sum (30,825) is then divided by the total number of transit vehicles within the system (10,836), which results in an average waiting time of 2.84 minutes, second best in this ranking.

Not all the figures for numbers of vehicles jibe with those presented in the Place Profiles. This is because the figures in the profiles are for the entire metro area—which might encompass more than one network—whereas the numbers in this table are for individual transit systems.

The 35 Largest Transit Systems Ranked by Waiting Time

System	Number of Vehicles	Route Miles	Fleet Age	Average Speed	Headway	Waiting Time
1. BART (San Francisco–Oakland)	450 rapid rail cars	142	9 yr	27.5 mph	0.63 mi	1.38 min
2. NYCTA/MTA (New York)	4,573 buses	1,841	9	8.1	0.81	5.96
	6,263 rapid rail cars	464	21	18.4	0.15	0.57
3. CTA (Chicago)	2,420 buses	1,428	10	10.1	1.18	7.01
	1,100 rapid rail cars	175	20	27.1	0.32	0.70
4. WMATA (Washington, D.C.)	2,043 buses	1,288	9	14.0	1.26	6.36
	296 rapid rail cars	78	5	17.9	0.53	1.77
5. San Francisco Municipal Railway	526 buses	445	11	9.6	1.69	10.58
	174 street cars	41	6	11.4	0.47	2.48
	345 trolley coaches	111	20	7.4	0.64	5.22
	41 cable cars	4	87	4.3	0.20	2.72
6. MBTA (Boston)	1,115 buses	1,420	9	12.7	2.55	12.03
	496 rapid rail cars	78	16	22.0	0.31	0.84
	300 street cars	59	22	15.1	0.39	1.56
	50 trolley coaches	32	14	12.8	1.28	6.00
7. Greater Cleveland RTA	1,016 buses	1,031	11	12.0	2.03	9.74
	100 rapid rail cars	38	24	31.0	0.76	1.47
	71 street cars	26	29	16.2	0.73	2.71
8. SORTA (Cincinnati)	528 buses	586	9	14.3	2.22	9.31
9. SEPTA (Philadelphia)	1,534 buses	2,006	9	10.1	2.62	15.54
	440 rapid rail cars	106	32	15.3	0.48	1.89
	368 street cars	176	27	9.3	0.96	6.24
	174 trolley coaches	42	14	8.0	0.48	3.62

System	Number of Vehicles	Route Miles	Fleet Age	Average Speed	Headway	Waiting Time
10. New Orleans Public Service	505 buses	507	8 yr	10.4 mph	2.01 mi	11.58 min
	35 street cars	13	62	8.7	0.74	5.12
11. Santa Clara County Transit (San Jose)	745 buses	1,112	7	14.1	2.99	11.94
12. Kansas City (MO) Transit Authority	350 buses	481	9	13.6	2.75	12.22
13. MTA Harris County (Houston)	860 buses	1,372	7	13.9	3.19	13.77
14. Southern California RTD (Los Angeles)	2,960 buses	4,901	10	13.5	3.31	13.89
15. Baltimore MTA	900 buses	1,274	9	11.3	2.83	14.16
16. Dallas Transit System	582 buses	1,015	5	14.6	3.49	14.33
17. Metro Dade County Transit (Miami)	865 buses	1,404	8	12.6	3.25	14.76
18. Seattle METRO	1,027 buses	1,940	11	19.1	3.78	15.96
	115 trolley coaches	108	5	18.6	1.88	8.05
19. Honolulu Department of Transportation	406 buses	796	10	14.7	3.92	15.48
20. SEMTA (Detroit)	1,346 buses	2,984	8	15.6	4.43	17.74
21. Bi-State Transit (St. Louis)	1,098 buses	2,131	8	12.8	3.88	17.78
22. Tri-County MTD (Portland, OR)	649 buses	1,367	9	16.2	4.21	18.05
23. MARTA (Atlanta)	885 buses	2,182	10	13.4	4.93	21.29
	120 rapid rail cars	31	3	19.0	0.52	1.66
24. Memphis Area Transit	313 buses	759	13	14.7	4.85	19.80
25. Milwaukee Transit System	631 buses	1,344	12	12.6	4.26	20.29
26. Alameda County Transit (Oakland)	835 buses	2,170	11	14.4	5.20	21.36
27. PAT (Pittsburgh)	903 buses	2,369	10	13.2	5.25	23.85
	92 street cars	52	37	14.9	1.13	4.55
28. MTC (Minneapolis–St. Paul)	1,012 buses	2,700	9	13.6	5.34	22.08
29. San Diego Transit Authority	341 buses	1,063	12	12.8	6.23	27.51
30. VIA MTS (San Antonio)	454 buses	1,482	8	14.0	6.53	27.98
31. River City Transit Authority (Louisville)	318 buses	995	6	13.3	6.26	28.23
32. Denver RTD	671 buses	2,850	6	16.5	8.49	35.89
33. Phoenix Transit	245 buses	1,208	10	16.6	9.86	38.17
34. Niagara Frontier Transit (Buffalo)	482 buses	1,882	12	10.9	7.81	42.99
35. Orange County Transit (Anaheim)	497 buses	2,959	6	14.4	11.91	46.70

Source: U.S. Department of Transportation, Urban Mass Transit Authority, *National Urban Mass Transportation Statistics—Section 15 Report.*

CONTRADICTORY RULES OF THE ROAD

Driving across state boundaries can mean a brush with contradictory traffic codes. Here are nine examples, with one caveat. The information comes from the National Committee on Uniform Traffic Laws, the National Highway Traffic Safety Administration, and the American Automobile Association's latest *Digest of Motor Laws*, but it may not reflect recent changes in the law.

Speed Limits. There are two kinds of speed limits—absolute and prima facie, a legal phrase meaning "at first view." If the speed limit of 55 is absolute, going 56 means breaking the law. If the speed limit of 55 is prima facie, however, going 56 or even 60 is merely apparent evidence of unreasonable and imprudent speed. Drivers may escape a fine if they can convince the traffic court that their speed was reasonable and safe in light of the

highway's condition, traffic, and visibility. All or some speed limits in 16 states are prima facie:

Alabama	Michigan
Arizona	Minnesota
Arkansas	New Hampshire
California	Ohio
Colorado	Oregon
Connecticut	Rhode Island
Idaho	Texas
Massachusetts	Utah

Right and Left Turn on Red. In 1947, California became the first state to permit drivers to turn right on a red signal after a complete stop. The last was Massachusetts, in 1980. New York City now is the only major jurisdiction that prohibits the turn. According to the

Federal Highway Administration, fewer accidents occur when drivers turn right on a red light than when they turn right on a green light. Furthermore, the rule saves each driver an average of 14 seconds at a turn, cuts gasoline consumption and exhaust emissions, and allows intersections to handle more traffic.

In the past five years, most states have enacted statutes permitting left turns on a red signal, but only after a complete stop and only from a one-way street into another one-way street. Eleven places still prohibit turning left on red:

Connecticut	North Carolina
District of Columbia	Rhode Island
Kansas	South Carolina
Mississippi	Utah
Missouri	Vermont
New Jersey	

The state of New York permits a left turn on red everywhere except New York City. Tennessee permits the turn when so marked by each city.

Studded Tires. Most states allow drivers to mount studded snow tires on their automobiles for better traction during an icy winter. Because the carbide-tipped studs damage road surfaces, nine states prohibit their use:

Alabama	Mississippi
Hawaii	Texas
Illinois	Utah
Louisiana	Wisconsin
Minnesota	

Glass Tinting. Tinted automobile window glass is a frequently chosen factory option. Over the past ten years, however, aftermarket application of black and gunmetal gray plastic sheeting to the inside of the windshield has become extremely popular. Because it interferes with night vision, it is prohibited in these states:

California	New Mexico
Delaware	North Carolina
District of Columbia	North Dakota
Idaho	Oregon
Illinois	Pennsylvania
Indiana	Rhode Island
Iowa	Utah
Minnesota	Vermont
Mississippi	West Virginia
New Hampshire	Wisconsin
New Jersey	

Audio Headsets. The issue here is whether the ears are as necessary for safe driving as the eyes. When you don't hear an ambulance siren, a ticket for failing to yield the right-of-way to an emergency vehicle is the likely consequence. But when you can't hear a train whistle or the air horn of an oncoming 18-wheeler, the result could be far more serious. Accordingly, 13 states prohibit the driver from wearing an audio headset:

Alaska	Massachusetts
California	Minnesota
Colorado	Pennsylvania
Florida	Rhode Island
Georgia	Virginia
Illinois	Washington
Maryland	

Motorcycle Helmets. The mileage fatality rate (deaths per 100 million miles) for motorcycle travel is five times that for auto travel, and the major cause is head injuries. Consequently, 42 states require motorcycle riders to wear helmets. Motorcyclists have challenged the law, but state courts have generally upheld it because it affects the biker's right to receive insurance compensation for injuries. Eight states, however, do not require protective headgear of any kind for motorcyclists and passengers:

California	Iowa
Colorado	Maine
Connecticut	Rhode Island
Illinois	Washington

Mandatory Annual Safety Inspections. Twenty-six states require regular inspection of automobiles to rid the highways of dangerous vehicles with bald tires, wobbly suspensions, smoky exhausts, and defective brakes and lights. These states are:

Arkansas	New York
California	North Carolina
Delaware	Ohio
District of Columbia	Oklahoma
Hawaii	Pennsylvania
Louisiana	Rhode Island
Maine	South Carolina
Maryland	Tennessee
Massachusetts	Texas
Michigan	Utah
Missouri	Vermont
New Hampshire	Virginia
New Jersey	West Virginia

Mandatory Seat Belt Use. Because automobile accidents are the leading cause of death among young children, all states now require the use of special vehicle restraints for children who are less than preschool age. Thirty-one of these states also require the use of seat belts by the driver and all front-seat passengers.

California	Montana
Colorado	Nevada
Connecticut	New Mexico
District of Columbia	New York
Florida	North Carolina
Georgia	Ohio
Hawaii	Oklahoma
Idaho	Oregon
Illinois	Pennsylvania
Iowa	Tennessee
Kansas	Texas
Louisiana	Utah
Maryland	Virginia
Michigan	Washington
Minnesota	Wisconsin
Missouri	

Radar Detectors. All states use radar in their speed enforcement programs, and all but two—Connecticut and Virginia—plus the District of Columbia permit drivers to install radar detectors for advance warning.

DRIVER LICENSING

When you settle in a new state, you have to surrender your out-of-state driver's license and get a new one. The time permitted to do this ranges from "immediately" in 13 states, to 30 days in 14 states, and up to 90 days in 9 other states. New Hampshire and Vermont allow you as much time as your former state gives newcomers. Hawaii lets you keep your license until it expires.

Required Tests

For a new resident with a valid driver's license from a former state, the requirement for getting a license from the new state varies considerably. In Arkansas, all you do is apply and pay the fee. In Connecticut, Massachusetts, and New Hampshire, a vision test is required, but all other tests may be waived. West Virginia requires only a test of the state's rules of the road. Six states require you to get behind the wheel with a license examiner for a road test; in 20 other states, a road test may be waived or required at the discretion of the examiner.

"Problem" Drivers

If your license has been revoked, you won't get a new one simply by moving to another state. Every license application is checked with the National Driver Register, a federal data file of persons whose license to drive has been denied or withdrawn. Moreover, 30 states belong to the National Driver License Compact, an agreement among states to share information on drivers who accumulate tickets in one jurisdiction and try to escape control in another.

Obtaining a Driver's License After Relocating: A Guide for Persons with a Current License from Their Former State

Examinations Required

State	Time Limit for Obtaining License After Establishing Residence	Rules of the Road	Signs and Signals	Vision	Vehicle Operation	Member of National Driver License Compact
Alabama	30 days	•	•	•		•
Alaska	90 days	•	•	•		
Arizona	Immediately	•	•		•	•
Arkansas	Immediately					
California	10 days	•	•	•		•
Colorado	30 days	•	•	•	X	
Connecticut	60 days	X	X	•	X	
Delaware	60 days	•	•	•	X	•
Florida	30 days	•	•	•	•	•
Georgia	30 days	•	•	•		
Hawaii	*	•	•	•	•	•
Idaho	90 days	•	•	•		•
Illinois	90 days	•	•	•		•
Indiana	60 days	•	•	•		•
Iowa	Immediately	•	•	•		•
Kansas	90 days	•	•	•		•
Kentucky	Immediately	•	•	•		
Louisiana	90 days	•	•	•		•
Maine	30 days	•		•	X	•
Maryland	30 days	•	•	•	X	
Massachusetts	Immediately	X	X	•		
Michigan	Immediately	•	•	•		
Minnesota	60 days	•	•	•	X	
Mississippi	60 days	•	•	•		•
Missouri	Immediately	•	•	•		•
Montana	90 days	•	•	•	•	•
Nebraska	30 days	•	•	•	X	•
Nevada	45 days	•	•	•	X	•
New Hampshire	Reciprocity	X	X	•		
New Jersey	60 days	•		•	X	•
New Mexico	30 days	•		•		•
New York	30 days	•	•	•		
North Carolina	30 days	•	•	•	X	
North Dakota	60 days	•	•	•	X	•
Ohio	30 days	•	•	•	X	

Examinations Required

State	Time Limit for Obtaining License After Establishing Residence	Rules of the Road	Signs and Signals	Vision	Vehicle Operation	Member of National Driver License Compact
Oklahoma	Immediately	•	•	•	•	•
Oregon	Immediately	•	•	•	X	•
Pennsylvania	60 days	•	•	•	X	
Rhode Island	30 days	•	•	•		
South Carolina	90 days	•		•	X	
South Dakota	90 days	•	•	•		•
Tennessee	90 days	•	•	•	X	•
Texas	30 days	•	•	•	X	
Utah	60 days	•	•	•		•
Vermont	Reciprocity	•	•	•	X	
Virginia	30 days	•	•	•		•
Washington	Immediately	•	•	•	•	•
West Virginia	Immediately	•				•
Wisconsin	Immediately	•	•	•	X	
Wyoming	Immediately	•	•	•	X	

Source: Federal Highway Administration, *Driver's License Administration Requirements and Fees*, 1988.

* In Hawaii, a drivers license from any state is valid until its expiration, if the driver is older than 18 years of age.

• Required.

X May be waived at the discretion of the examiner.

FINDING YOUR WAY ON THE INTERSTATE

By staying with a combination of interstate routes, it is possible to drive from one metro area in the continental United States to almost any other without having to stop for a traffic light.

Five of the principal routes are more than 2,000 miles long. The longest, I–90, stretches 3,082 miles between downtown Boston and Seattle's waterfront. The next longest routes are I–80 (2,907 miles, from San Francisco to Hackensack, New Jersey), I–10 (2,460 miles along the nation's southern border, from Los Angeles to Jacksonville, Florida), I–40 (2,461 miles, from Barstow, California, to Smithfield, North Carolina), and I–70 (2,175 miles from Cove Fort, Utah, to Baltimore). Three of these routes, I–10, I–80, and I–90, cross the country from coast to coast, and I–40 nearly makes it.

Seven interstate routes span the nation in a north–south direction, or nearly so: I–5 (1,382 miles, from San Diego to Bellingham, Washington), I–15 (1,437 miles, from San Diego to the Montana–Canada border), I–35 (1,568 miles from Laredo, Texas, to Duluth, Minnesota), I–55 (944 miles, from suburban New Orleans to Chicago), I–65 (888 miles, from Mobile, Alabama, to Gary–Hammond, Indiana), I–75 (1,787 miles, from Naples, Florida, to the Michigan–Canada border), and I–95 (1,894 miles, from the city of Miami to the Maine–Canada border).

The Interstate System: A Route Log and Finder List

Route	Total Mileage	Mileage by State		Selected Cities Served
4	132.06	Florida	132.06	Daytona Beach, Lakeland, Orlando, Tampa, Winter Haven
5	1,382.05	California	797.01	Anaheim, Los Angeles, Redding, Sacramento, San Diego, Santa Ana, Stockton
		Oregon	308.41	Eugene, Medford, Portland, Salem
		Washington	276.63	Bellingham, Olympia, Seattle, Tacoma, Vancouver
8	348.32	California	170.00	El Centro, San Diego
		Arizona	178.32	Casa Grande, Yuma
10	2,459.96	California	242.50	Los Angeles, Riverside, San Bernardino
		Arizona	391.94	Phoenix, Tucson
		New Mexico	164.28	Deming, Las Cruces
		Texas	880.60	Beaumont, El Paso, Houston, San Antonio
		Louisiana	274.42	Baton Rouge, Lafayette, Lake Charles, New Orleans
		Mississippi	77.10	Biloxi, Gulfport, Pascagoula
		Alabama	66.30	Mobile
		Florida	362.82	Jacksonville, Pensacola, Tallahassee

Route	Total Mileage	Mileage by State		Selected Cities Served
(12)	85.59	Louisiana	85.59	Baton Rouge
(15)	1,436.85	California	287.30	Riverside, San Bernardino, San Diego
		Nevada	123.77	Las Vegas
		Arizona	29.37	—
		Utah	405.49	Brigham City, Ogden, Orem, Provo, St. George, Salt Lake City
		Idaho	195.87	Blackfoot, Idaho Falls, Pocatello
		Montana	395.05	Butte, Great Falls, Helena, Sweetgrass
(16)	165.41	Georgia	165.41	Macon, Savannah
(17)	145.24	Arizona	145.24	Flagstaff, Phoenix
(19)	63.35	Arizona	63.35	Nogales, Tucson
(20)	1,538.31	Texas	635*98	Abilene, Arlington, Dallas, Fort Worth, Longview, Marshall, Midland, Odessa, Tyler
		Louisiana	189.87	Monroe, Shreveport
		Mississippi	154.50	Jackson, Meridian, Vicksburg
		Alabama	214.70	Anniston, Birmingham, Tuscaloosa
		Georgia	201.75	Atlanta, Augusta
		South Carolina	141.51	Columbia, Florence
(24)	316.52	Illinois	38.73	Metropolis
		Kentucky	93.37	Hopkinsville, Paducah
		Tennessee	180.30	Chattanooga, Clarksville, Nashville
		Georgia	4.12	—
(25)	1,062.52	New Mexico	462.68	Albuquerque, Las Cruces, Santa Fe
		Colorado	298.94	Colorado Springs, Denver, Fort Collins, Longmont, Pueblo
		Wyoming	300.90	Casper, Cheyenne
(26)	260.90	North Carolina	39.95	Asheville, Hendersonville
		South Carolina	220.95	Charleston, Columbia, Spartanburg
(27)	124.38	Texas	124.38	Amarillo, Lubbock
(29)	752.26	Missouri	130.30	Kansas City, St. Joseph
		Iowa	151.81	Council Bluffs, Sioux City
		South Dakota	252.65	Sioux Falls
		North Dakota	217.50	Fargo, Grand Forks
(30)	366.71	Texas	223.63	Dallas, Fort Worth, Texarkana
		Arkansas	143.08	Little Rock, Texarkana
(35)	1,568.27	Texas	503.83	Arlington, Austin, Dallas, Fort Worth, Laredo, San Antonio, Temple, Waco
		Oklahoma	235.96	Norman, Oklahoma City
		Kansas	235.52	Kansas City, Lawrence, Topeka, Wichita
		Missouri	114.80	Kansas City
		Iowa	218.47	Ames, Des Moines
		Minnesota	259.69	Albert Lea, Duluth, Minneapolis, St. Paul
(37)	143.06	Texas	143.06	Corpus Christi, San Antonio
(39)	64.13	Illinois	64.13	LaSalle, Rockford
(40)	2,460.68	California	154.60	Barstow, Needles
		Arizona	359.23	Flagstaff, Kingman
		New Mexico	371.37	Albuquerque, Gallup, Tucumcari
		Texas	177.00	Amarillo
		Oklahoma	331.03	Clinton, Oklahoma City
		Arkansas	284.80	Fort Smith, Little Rock
		Tennessee	455.25	Jackson, Knoxville, Memphis, Nashville
		North Carolina	327.40	Asheville, Burlington, Durham, Greensboro, Hickory, Raleigh, Winston-Salem
(43)	182.58	Wisconsin	182.58	Green Bay, Milwaukee, Sheboygan

Route	Total Mileage	Mileage by State		Selected Cities Served
44	634.03	Texas	14.70	Wichita Falls
		Oklahoma	328.53	Oklahoma City, Tulsa
		Missouri	290.80	Joplin, St. Louis, Springfield
45	284.99	Texas	284.99	Dallas, Galveston, Houston, Texas City
49	206.57	Louisiana	206.57	Alexandria, Lafayette, Nachitoches, Opelousas, Shreveport
55	943.69	Louisiana	65.81	Hammond, La Place
		Mississippi	289.70	Grenada, Jackson, McComb
		Tennessee	12.20	Memphis
		Arkansas	72.22	Blytheville, West Memphis
		Missouri	209.40	Cape Girardeau, St. Louis
		Illinois	294.36	Bloomington, Chicago, East St. Louis, Joliet, Springfield
57	380.57	Missouri	22.00	Charleston, Sikeston
		Illinois	358.57	Champaign, Chicago, Kankakee, Rantoul, Urbana
59	444.02	Louisiana	11.48	New Orleans, Slidell
		Mississippi	171.20	Hattiesburg, Laurel, Meridian
		Alabama	241.40	Birmingham, Gadsden, Tuscaloosa
		Georgia	19.94	—
64	944.19	Missouri	14.70	St. Louis
		Illinois	128.12	Belleville, East St. Louis
		Indiana	124.04	Evansville, New Albany
		Kentucky	191.55	Frankfort, Lexington, Louisville
		West Virginia	186.86	Charleston, Huntington, White Sulphur Springs
		Virginia	298.92	Charlottesville, Newport News, Norfolk, Richmond
65	888.08	Alabama	367.00	Birmingham, Decatur, Mobile, Montgomery
		Tennessee	121.40	Nashville
		Kentucky	137.60	Bowling Green, Elizabethtown, Louisville
		Indiana	262.08	Gary, Indianapolis, Lafayette
66	76.37	Virginia	75.26	Arlington, Fairfax, Falls Church, Front Royal, Vienna
		District of Columbia	1.11	Washington, D.C.
68	22.53	Maryland	22.53	Annapolis, Bowie
69	356.19	Indiana	157.79	Anderson, Fort Wayne, Indianapolis, Muncie
		Michigan	198.40	Battle Creek, Flint, Lansing
70	2,175.46	Utah	230.77	Cove Fort, Green River, Richfield
		Colorado	450.30	Denver, Grand Junction
		Kansas	424.17	Kansas City, Lawrence, Topeka
		Missouri	251.60	Columbia, Kansas City, St. Louis
		Illinois	160.25	East St. Louis, Effingham, Vandalia
		Indiana	156.27	Indianapolis, Richmond, Terre Haute
		Ohio	225.69	Columbus, Dayton, Springfield, Zanesville
		West Virginia	14.45	Wheeling
		Pennsylvania	168.73	Pittsburgh
		Maryland	93.23	Baltimore, Hagerstown
71	345.58	Kentucky	97.92	Covington, Louisville
		Ohio	247.66	Cincinnati, Cleveland, Columbus, Mansfield
72	78.66	Illinois	78.66	Champaign, Decatur, Springfield
74	416.89	Iowa	5.39	Davenport
		Illinois	220.18	Bloomington, Champaign, Moline, Peoria, Rock Island, Urbana
		Indiana	171.87	Crawfordsville, Indianapolis, Shelbyville
		Ohio	19.45	Cincinnati
75	1,786.99	Florida	472.06	Bradenton, Fort Myers, Gainesville, Lakeland, Naples, Ocala, St. Petersburg, Sarasota, Tampa
		Georgia	355.00	Atlanta, Macon, Valdosta
		Tennessee	161.60	Chattanooga, Knoxville
		Kentucky	191.60	Covington, Lexington, Richmond
		Ohio	211.53	Cincinnati, Dayton, Lima, Middletown, Toledo
		Michigan	395.20	Bay City, Detroit, Flint, Saginaw

COMPLETED OR IMPROVED AND OPEN TO TRAFFIC

Completed to full or acceptable standards, or improved to standards.

Adequate for present traffic; built with Interstate or other public funds.

MAJOR TOLL ROADS

Incorporated in the Interstate System

UNDER CONSTRUCTION

Interstate Highways

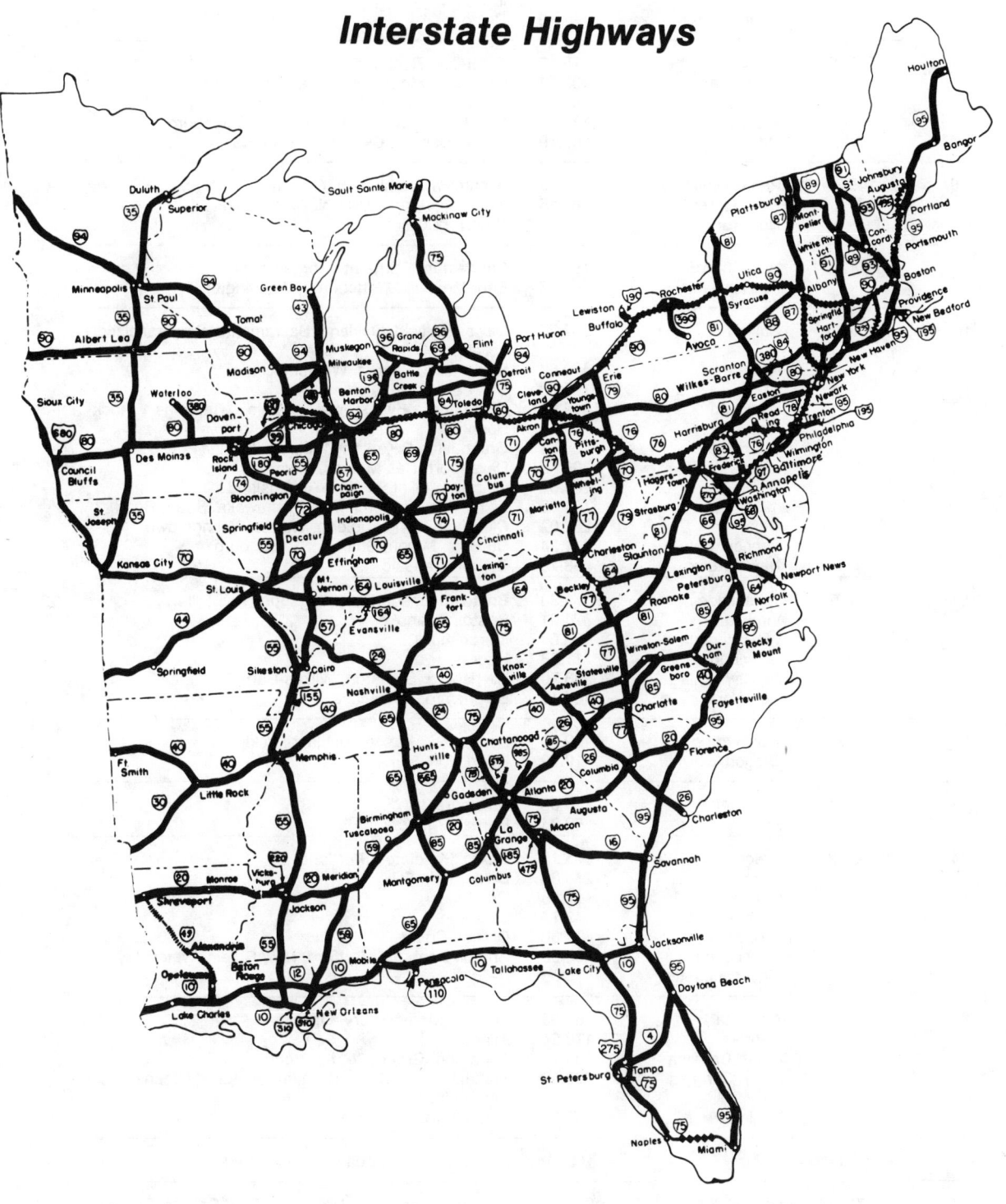

Route	Total Mileage	Mileage by State		Selected Cities Served
76	618.49	Colorado	184.14	Denver, Fort Morgan, Sterling
		Nebraska	2.48	—
		Ohio	77.82	Akron, Youngstown
		Pennsylvania	351.25	Harrisburg, Lancaster, Philadelphia, Pittsburgh, Reading
		New Jersey	2.80	Camden
77	598.25	South Carolina	75.17	Columbia, Rock Hill
		North Carolina	105.37	Charlotte, Mooresville, Statesville
		Virginia	67.40	Bluefield, Wytheville
		West Virginia	187.21	Beckley, Bluefield, Charleston, Parkersburg
		Ohio	163.10	Akron, Canton, Cleveland, Marietta
78	145.34	Pennsylvania	76.69	Allentown, Bethlehem, Easton
		New Jersey	68.15	Irvington, Jersey City, Newark, Plainfield
		New York	0.50	New York City
79	344.25	West Virginia	160.52	Charleston, Fairmont, Morgantown
		Pennsylvania	183.73	Erie, Meadville, Pittsburgh, Washington
80	2,906.75	California	202.20	Davis, Fairfield, Oakland, Sacramento, San Francisco, Vallejo,
		Nevada	410.67	Elko, Reno, Sparks, Winnemucca
		Utah	197.58	Salt Lake City
		Wyoming	402.86	Cheyenne, Evanston, Laramie, Rawlings, Rock Springs
		Nebraska	455.31	Grand Island, Kearney, Lincoln, Omaha
		Iowa	306.55	Davenport, Des Moines, Iowa City
		Illinois	163.52	Chicago, Joliet, Moline, Rock Island
		Indiana	151.65	Elkhart, Gary, Hammond, Mishawaka, South Bend
		Ohio	237.07	Cleveland, Elyria, Toledo, Warren, Youngstown
		Pennsylvania	311.24	Du Bois, Milton, Sharon, Stroudsburg
		New Jersey	68.10	Bergen–Passaic
81	855.07	Tennessee	75.30	Bristol, Johnson City, Kingsport, Knoxville
		Virginia	324.01	Bristol, Roanoke
		West Virginia	26.00	Martinsburg
		Maryland	11.96	Hagerstown
		Pennsylvania	233.70	Harrisburg, Scranton, Wilkes-Barre
		New York	184.10	Binghamton, Syracuse
82	142.99	Washington	132.20	Kennewick, Pasco, Richland, Yakima
		Oregon	10.79	Hermiston
83	84.11	Maryland	34.05	Baltimore
		Pennsylvania	50.06	Harrisburg, York
84	995.62	Oregon	375.15	Baker, Pendleton, Portland
		Idaho	275.36	Boise, Twin Falls
		Utah	117.18	Ogden
		Pennsylvania	49.75	Scranton
		New York	71.60	Orange County
		Connecticut	98.52	Bristol, Danbury, Hartford, New Britain, Waterbury
		Massachusetts	8.06	—
85	667.11	Alabama	80.00	Auburn, Montgomery, Opelika
		Georgia	178.94	Atlanta
		South Carolina	106.13	Anderson, Greenville, Spartanburg
		North Carolina	233.40	Burlington, Charlotte, Durham, Gastonia, Greensboro, High Point
		Virginia	68.64	Petersburg
86	63.18	Idaho	63.18	American Falls, Pocatello
87	333.20	New York	333.20	Albany, Glens Falls, New York City, Orange County, Poughkeepsie, Troy
88	117.77	New York	117.77	Binghamton, Oneonta, Schenectady
89	191.32	New Hampshire	60.93	Concord, Lebanon
		Vermont	130.39	Burlington, Montpelier

Route	Total Mileage	Mileage by State		Selected Cities Served
(90)	3,081.87	Washington	297.01	Seattle, Spokane
		Idaho	73.73	Coeur d'Alene, Kellogg
		Montana	549.98	Billings, Bozeman, Butte, Missoula
		Wyoming	208.79	Buffalo, Sheridan
		South Dakota	412.84	Rapid City, Sioux Falls
		Minnesota	275.70	Albert Lea, Austin, Rochester
		Wisconsin	187.17	Beloit, Janesville, La Crosse, Madison
		Illinois	108.05	Chicago, Elgin, Rockford
		Indiana	156.90	Elkhart, Gary, Hammond, Mishawaka, South Bend
		Ohio	244.13	Cleveland, Elyria, Lorain, Toledo
		Pennsylvania	46.60	Erie
		New York	386.77	Albany, Buffalo, Rochester, Rome, Schenectady, Syracuse, Troy, Utica
		Massachusetts	134.20	Boston, Pittsfield, Springfield, Worcester
(91)	290.52	Connecticut	57.98	Hartford, Meriden, New Haven
		Massachusetts	54.92	Springfield
		Vermont	177.62	Brattleboro, St. Johnsbury
(93)	188.91	Massachusetts	46.00	Boston, Lawrence, Lowell
		New Hampshire	131.85	Concord, Manchester
		Vermont	11.06	St. Johnsbury
(94)	1,606.71	Montana	247.91	Billings, Glendive, Miles City
		North Dakota	352.50	Bismarck, Fargo
		Minnesota	259.49	Minneapolis, Moorhead, St. Cloud, St. Paul
		Wisconsin	348.11	Eau Claire, Kenosha, Madison, Milwaukee, Racine
		Illinois	77.37	Chicago, Lake County
		Indiana	45.73	Gary, Hammond, Michigan City, Portage
		Michigan	275.60	Ann Arbor, Battle Creek, Benton Harbor, Detroit, Jackson, Kalamazoo
(95)	1,894.02	Florida	382.40	Boca Raton, Daytona Beach, Fort Lauderdale, Fort Pierce, Hialeah, Hollywood, Jacksonville, Melbourne, Miami, Palm Beach, Pompano Beach
		Georgia	111.69	Brunswick, Savannah
		South Carolina	198.76	Florence
		North Carolina	181.39	Fayetteville
		Virginia	174.52	Arlington, Petersburg, Richmond
		District of Columbia	0.12	Washington, D.C.
		Maryland	108.83	Baltimore
		Delaware	23.43	Wilmington
		Pennsylvania	51.95	Philadelphia
		New Jersey	79.08	Elizabeth, Newark, Trenton
		New York	23.35	New York City
		Connecticut	111.57	Bridgeport, Milford, New Haven, New London, Norwalk, Stamford
		Rhode Island	43.31	Cranston, Pawtucket, Providence, Warwick
		Massachusetts	89.60	Attleboro, Boston
		New Hampshire	16.13	Portsmouth
		Maine	297.89	Augusta, Bangor, Portland
(96)	192.70	Michigan	192.70	Detroit, Grand Rapids, Lansing, Muskegon
(97)	17.88	Maryland	17.88	Annapolis, Baltimore

Source: U.S. Department of Transportation, *Interstate System Route Log and Finder List*, undated.

Education

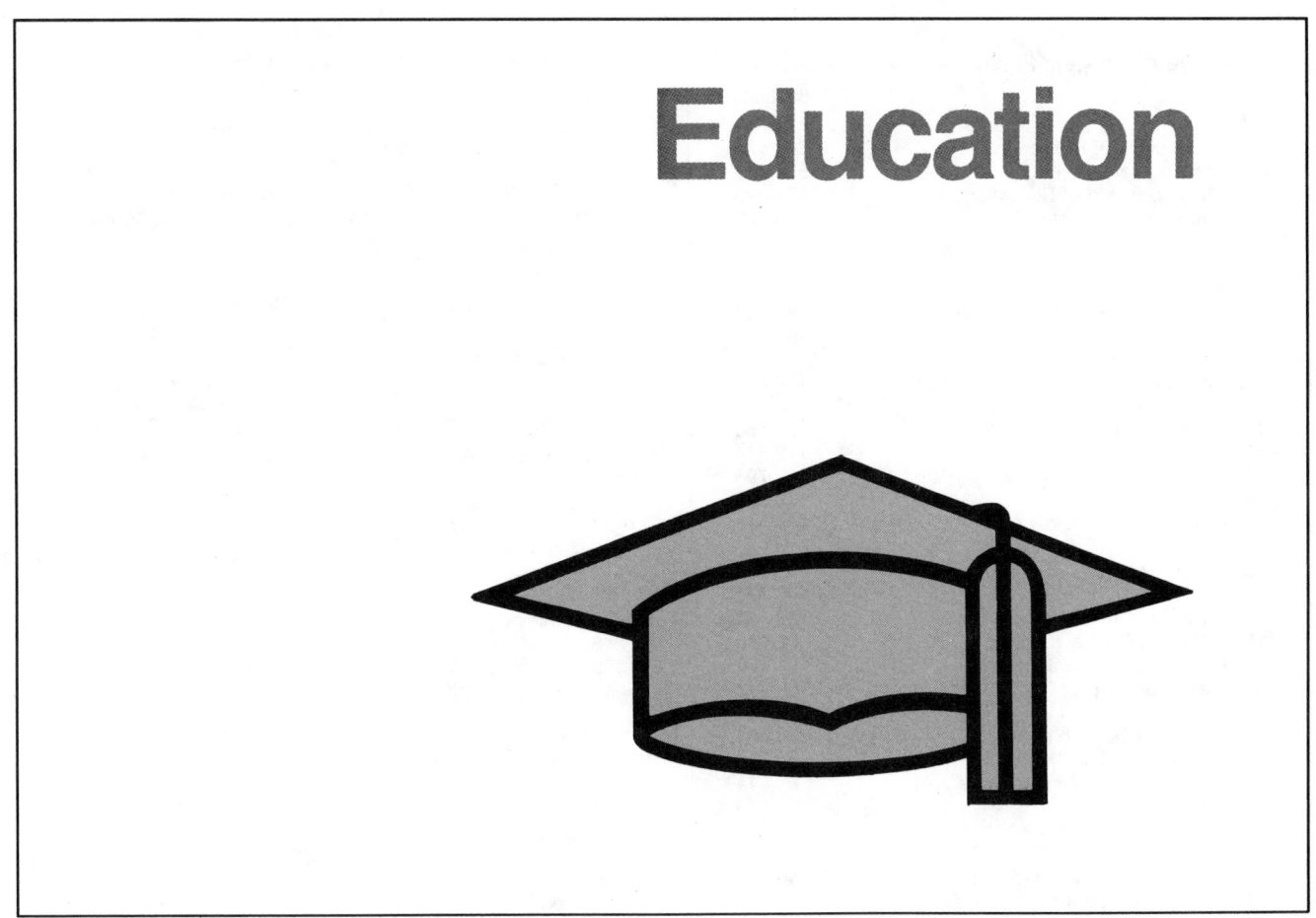

Nine months of the year, all day long, three of every ten Americans are either working for an educational institution or being taught in one. The cost of keeping this endeavor going is the biggest single item on state and municipal budgets, and perennial reviews of whether the money is well-spent are causing teachers, administrators, and taxpayers to squabble.

Education will never be the sacred cow it once was. The scores of high school students on most standardized tests are lower today than they were 30 years ago. Among high school seniors, says a report by the National Commission on Excellence in Education, nearly 40 percent can't draw inferences from written material, only one-fifth can write a persuasive essay, and only one-third can solve a math problem requiring several steps.

Privately, parents and teachers each blame the other. Although parents say they trust teachers more than politicians, journalists, or business people, they don't give teachers high marks. Only half the polled public gave teachers a grade of B or better when asked in a recent Gallup poll to choose a rating of either A, B, C, D, or F. For their part, teachers are even stingier graders—only 21 percent gave parents a grade of B or higher.

As for education and the metro areas, two things are certain: (1) if there is one public service in which shabby performance leads families to change their address, it is the education their children are getting in public schools, and (2) if schemes for improving the schools—such as merit pay and accelerated career ladders for good teachers, longer days, smaller classes, and an extra month in the academic year—are to be tried, they will all require money.

PUBLIC SCHOOLS

The quality of the public schools usually tips the balance when a relocating family weighs a neighborhood's good and bad points. Too often, the choice is influenced by a real estate agent's hearsay that the schools are great or ought to be because the town's tax rate is high. Are there ways for parents to compare districts and schools within these districts more objectively? Definitely.

Shopping for a District

The smallest political unit in the United States is the school district. In the 1930s, the country was fragmented into 128,000 of them. After decades of consolidation, there are now fewer than 16,000 that range in size from

The 40 Largest Public School Districts

Unit	Students Enrolled
1. New York City Public	930,420
2. Los Angeles Unified	553,953
3. Chicago Board of Education	431,226
4. Dade County (Miami, FL)	228,062
5. Detroit City	206,790
6. Philadelphia City	197,945
7. Houston Independent School District	187,031
8. Hawaii Public Schools	161,505
9. Dallas Independent School District	127,908
10. Broward County (Fort Lauderdale, FL)	126,852
11. Fairfax County (Fairfax, VA)	123,163
12. Baltimore City	113,574
13. Hillsborough County (Tampa, FL)	110,798
14. San Diego Unified	108,932
15. Memphis City	108,719
16. Prince Georges County (Upper Marlboro, MD)	106,377
17. Duval County (Jacksonville, FL)	99,582
18. Jefferson County (Louisville, KY)	92,440
19. Montgomery County (Rockville, MD)	91,650
20. Clark County (Las Vegas, NV)	89,742
21. District of Columbia	88,843
22. Pinellas County (Clearwater, FL)	86,814
23. Orleans Parish (New Orleans, LA)	85,411
24. Milwaukee	82,645
25. Baltimore County (Towson, MD)	81,386
26. Orange County (Orlando, FL)	80,044
27. Palm Beach County (West Palm Beach, FL)	76,185
28. Jefferson County (Lakewood, CO)	75,643
29. Cleveland	74,370
30. Albuquerque	72,994
31. Mecklenburg County–Charlotte City (Charlotte, NC)	72,361
32. DeKalb County (Decatur, GA)	72,217
33. Granite (Salt Lake City, UT)	67,898
34. Mobile City–County (Mobile, AL)	67,336
35. Atlanta City	67,278
36. Columbus (Columbus, OH)	66,897
37. Fort Worth ISD	66,085
38. Anne Arundel County (Annapolis, MD)	63,685
39. Nashville–Davidson County (Nashville, TN)	63,598
40. Long Beach Unified	60,925

Source: U.S. Department of Education, *Digest of Education Statistics,* 1988.

Private Schools in the Metro Areas

Whatever the reason for the steady enrollments in private schools—the need for religious training or a more rigorous education—private schools are a fixture on the American education scene. All of the 333 metro areas have at least one private K–12 school, and only 16 have five or fewer. The 25 areas below have the greatest proportion of private-school pupils among their school-age populations.

Metro Areas with Most Private School Pupils

Metro Area	Proportion of Children in Private Schools
1. Dubuque, IA	33.4%
2. New Orleans, LA	27.3
3. Philadelphia, PA–NJ	25.6
4. New York, NY	23.7
5. San Francisco, CA	23.0
6. Trenton, NJ	22.9
7. Jersey City, NJ	22.4
8. Grand Rapids, MI	21.5
9. Wilmington, DE–NJ–MD	21.1
10. Owensboro, KY	21.0
11. Erie, PA	20.9
11. Middletown, CT	20.9
13. Milwaukee, WI	20.7
14. Cleveland, OH	20.3
14. St. Louis, MO–IL	20.3
16. La Crosse, WI	20.2
17. Honolulu, HI	20.1
18. Bergen–Passaic, NJ	20.0
19. Chicago, IL	19.9
19. Green Bay, WI	19.9
19. Savannah, GA	19.9
22. Waterbury, CT	19.4
23. Appleton–Oshkosh–Neenah, WI	19.0
23. Baton Rouge, LA	19.0
25. Buffalo, NY	18.8

Source: Derived from Market Data Retrieval, *National School Market Index,* 1989.

the giant New York City Public and Los Angeles Unified school districts to several hundred that don't operate schools themselves, busing children instead to other districts.

Moving into a metro area often means stepping into a thicket of school districts, each with its own politics, funding, philosophy, standards, curricula—and, yes, results. Since your tax dollars will help support the district, you'll want to investigate their differences with a consumer's eye. Visit the district principal or superintendent's office and consider several factors:

- A good district can give you a written philosophy or a statement of educational objectives approved within the last five years by the state board of education. If educational philosophy and objectives are explicit and under constant examination and review, then a district takes its mission seriously.
- The classroom teachers in the district should have not only a standard certificate but also (in 50 percent of the cases or better) at least a master's degree or equivalent in the subject they teach.
- Nationally, only three-fourths of ninth-graders eventually graduate from high school. A dis-

trict's holding power—that is, the percentage of its ninth-grade pupils who stay in school and finish—should be at least 90 percent.

- If 95 percent of a district's enrollment is in average daily attendance, that's a good indication of how closely parents and schools keep tabs on children. Nationally, the average daily attendance is 90 percent; in some districts, it is a good deal less.

- Beware of the professional revolving door. A high number of eligible teachers not getting tenure might mean that the district has tough standards; but it could also be a sign that the district cuts costs by hiring beginners and then refusing them tenure at the end of their probationary period. Under this scheme, it is possible for a child to progress from kindergarten

through high school and have inexperienced, unfamiliar teachers each year.

Shopping for a School

Moving into a good school district won't necessarily mean that you'll find quality education in all of its schools. Get a district map of neighborhood boundaries for the schools as well as a list of Parent–Teacher Association (PTA) contacts. Talking with a local parent will save you time. Then visit the school's principal or the head guidance counselor to obtain specific information.

- A good high school should have one guidance counselor for every 200 students, and it should have at least one full-time career counselor.
- Classroom size in high school should average no more than 30 students.

Compulsory Education

Most state laws requiring school attendance until a specified age were passed near the beginning of the century and haven't changed much in the decades since. The span of compulsory attendance ranges from eight years in Mississippi to 12 in Hawaii, New Mexico, Ohio, South Carolina, Utah, Virginia, and Wisconsin.

State	Compulsory Attendance Age Range
Alabama	Between 7 and 16
Alaska	Between 7 and 16, or high school graduation
Arizona	Between 8 and 16
Arkansas	Between 7 and 17
California	Between 6 and 16
Colorado	Of 7 and under 16
Connecticut	Over 7 and under 16
Delaware	Between 5 and 16
District of Columbia	Between 7 and 17
Florida	Between 6 and 16
Georgia	Between 7 and 16
Hawaii	At least 6 and not 18
Idaho	Of 7 but not 16
Illinois	Between 7 and 16
Indiana	Between 7 and 16
Iowa	Over 7 and under 16
Kansas	Of 7 and under 16
Kentucky	Between 6 and 16
Louisiana	Between 7 and 16
Maine	Between 7 and 17
Maryland	Between 6 and 16
Massachusetts	Between 6 and 16
Michigan	Between 6 and 16
Minnesota	Between 7 and 16
Mississippi	From 6 to 14
Missouri	Between 7 and 16
Montana	Between 7 and 16, or completion of 8th grade

State	Compulsory Attendance Age Range
Nebraska	Not less than 7 nor more than 16
Nevada	Between 7 and 17
New Hampshire	Between 6 and 16
New Jersey	Between 6 and 16
New Mexico	Attained 6 and until attaining 18
New York	From 6 to 16
North Carolina	Between 7 and 16
North Dakota	Of 7 to 16
Ohio	Between 6 and 18
Oklahoma	Between 7 and 18
Oregon	Between 7 and 18
Pennsylvania	Not later than 8, until 17
Rhode Island	Between 7 and 16
South Carolina	Between 5 and 17
South Dakota	Of 7 and not exceeding 16
Tennessee	Between 7 and 17
Texas	Between 7 and end of academic year of 16th birthday
Utah	Between 6 and 18
Vermont	Between 7 and 16
Virginia	Between 5 and 17
Washington	Child 8 and under 18
West Virginia	Between 6 and 16
Wisconsin	Ages 6 to 18 unless excused or graduated
Wyoming	Between 7 and 16 inclusive

Source: U.S. Department of Education, *Digest of Education Statistics*, 1988.

Private Schools and Enrollments

Association	Elementary Schools	Secondary Schools	Total Schools	Total Enrollment
American Montessori Society	618	10	628	57,267
Association of Military Colleges and Schools of the U.S.	0	35	35	10,938
Christian Schools International	209	82	291	67,627
Evangelical Lutheran Church in America	465	7	472	43,794
Friends Council on Education	47	28	75	16,607
Lutheran Church–Missouri Synod	1,696	58	1,754	194,404
National Association of Epsicopal Schools	290	83	373	78,438
National Association of Independent Schools	268	655	923	376,946
National Association of Private Schools for Exceptional Children	176	10	186	18,714
National Catholic Educational Association	7,572	1,445	9,017	2,688,971
National Society for Hebrew Day Schools	214	159	373	105,368
Seventh-Day Adventist Board of Education	895	205	1,100	63,108
Solomon Schechter Day School Association	53	7	60	13,691
U.S. TOTAL	**12,419**	**2,606**	**15,025**	**3,647,030**

Source: Market Data Retrieval, *Private Schools of the United States*, 1989.

- The size of the senior class should range from 300 to 500 students. If the enrollment is much smaller than that, many worthwhile specialized courses won't be offered.
- A quality high school should offer four years of English, mathematics, and foreign languages; second-year courses in biology, astronomy, chemistry, and physics; college-preparatory courses in the humanities; at least one year of computer literacy; and Advanced Placement (AP) courses for college credit.
- A good high school averages ten National Merit Scholarship commendations a year; an excellent school averages 15 or more a year.

- Because one-fifth of all four-year public colleges must accept every high school graduate within the state, regardless of program followed or grades earned, it is no longer noteworthy that most of a high school's graduating seniors go on to college. The question to ask is: which colleges are accepting them—top schools with tough admissions standards, or open-admission institutions with no requirements but that the check be good and the diploma in hand?

Don't cross a high school off your list if it doesn't measure up on all of these points. A school can have all but one or two and still be a good one.

Many relocation experts advise their clients that the stability of a town is reflected best in its schools. If the high school is good, chances are that the schools at the lower levels will also be good. In choosing an elementary school or a junior high, again, ask questions of principals and other parents.

- In junior high schools—grades 7, 8, and 9—there should be special provision for both bright students and slow learners.
- In elementary schools, there should be a full-time librarian and a classroom-size library.
- Class size in elementary schools should average no more than 20 pupils.

FOR ONE IN TEN: PRIVATE SCHOOLS

A startling statistic about elementary and secondary education in the United States since 1930 is the nearly 100-percent growth in the number of private schools, in contrast to the 75 percent decline in the number of public schools. This isn't to say that the public schools are collapsing; most of the schools that have closed are rural, one-room buildings. But the statistic does show that private schools have become a thriving alternative.

Today, one out of nine school-age children attends a private or parochial school. In spite of the decline in school enrollments in recent years, private schools held on to more of their enrollment than did public schools, losing only 6 percent as compared with 11 percent for public schools.

Recent research from the Department of Education shows that students in private high schools take more courses than their public school counterparts and that they take these courses in smaller classes. Critics of public education point out that because private institutions forgo the smorgasbord of electives that public schools offer their students, graduates of private high schools have tougher basic courses on their transcripts and are better prepared for college study. (In fact, private school pupils score higher on average on the Scholastic Aptitude Tests than students in public schools.) There

The 15 Largest Two-Year Colleges

College (Metro Area)	Students
Miami–Dade Community College (Miami, FL)	39,980
Northern Virginia Community College (Washington, DC–MD–VA)	33,682
Macomb Community College (Detroit, MI)	31,318
Oakland Community College (Detroit, MI)	26,675
Houston Community College (Houston, TX)	26,002
El Camino College (Los Angeles–Long Beach, CA)	25,752
Tarrant County Junior College (Fort Worth, TX)	24,562
De Anza College (San Jose, CA)	24,349
Cuyahoga Community College (Cleveland, OH)	23,324
City College of San Francisco (San Francisco, CA)	23,177
College of DuPage (Chicago, IL)	23,155
Pima Community College (Phoenix, AZ)	22,959
Orange Coast College (Anaheim–Santa Ana, CA)	22,522
Rancho Santiago College (Anaheim–Santa Ana, CA)	21,514
San Antonio College (San Antonio, TX)	20,790

Source: Department of Education, *Directory of Postsecondary Institutions,* 1989.

The 15 Largest Universities

University (Metro Area)	Students
University of Minnesota (Minneapolis–St. Paul, MN–WI)	63,994
Ohio State University (Columbus, OH)	53,880
University of Texas (Austin, TX)	46,140
University of Wisconsin (Madison, WI)	44,584
Michigan State University (Lansing–East Lansing, MI)	44,088
Arizona State University (Phoenix, AZ)	42,014
University of Illinois (Champaign–Urbana–Rantoul, IL)	39,274
University of Maryland (Washington, DC–MD–VA)	38,639
Texas A & M University (Bryan–College Station, TX)	36,617
University of Cincinnati (Cincinnati, OH–KY–IN)	36,194
Pennsylvania State University (State College, PA)	35,261
University of Florida (Gainesville, FL)	35,172
San Diego State University (San Diego, CA)	35,010
University of Michigan (Ann Arbor, MI)	34,974
University of California (Los Angeles–Long Beach, CA)	34,418

Source: U.S. Department of Education, *Directory of Postsecondary Institutions,* 1989.

Educated Metro Areas

The year 1967 was a good one for education. It marked the first time in history that the majority of Americans over the age of 25 had the equivalent of a high school diploma. We won't be seeing a similar year for college, however. In spite of millions of full-time students enrolled in college, only one in five persons over 25 currently has at least 16 years of school, the equivalent of a college degree. Among the 15 largest metro areas, the educational attainment of people varies tremendously.

Educated Adults in the Largest Metro Areas

Metro Area	Percentage of adults with 4+ years of college	Percentage of adults with 4+ years of high school
Washington, DC–MD–VA	38%	88%
Boston, MA	33	84
Houston, TX	32	80
Dallas, TX	28	81
Nassau–Suffolk, NY	27	85
Atlanta, GA	27	80
Minneapolis–St. Paul, MN–WI	26	87
New York, NY	25	70
Chicago, IL	24	77
St. Louis, MO–IL	22	80
Los Angeles–Long Beach, CA	21	75
Baltimore, MD	21	73
Philadelphia, PA–NJ	20	77
Detroit, MI	18	74
Pittsburgh, PA	15	77

Source: Bureau of Census, *Educational Attainment in the United States,* 1989.

are good reasons why private schools are a preferred educational option for many families, not all of whom are Catholic or well-to-do.

Most private schools are run by some religious group, accounting for 80 percent of all private schools. The remaining institutions tend to be small schools; they enroll only 16 percent of private school pupils. Among religiously affiliated schools, Catholic schools predominate in number and enrollment, but there are also substantial numbers of pupils in Baptist, Lutheran, Christian, Jewish, Seventh-Day Adventist, and Episcopal schools.

BEYOND HIGH SCHOOL: METRO AREA COLLEGES AND UNIVERSITIES

Educators like to say that schooling leads to just three outcomes: more schooling, employment, or unemployment. When high school graduates go on to college or find jobs, the public education system is successful; if they do neither, the system is considered a flop. In fact, nearly half of metro area high school graduates eventually go to college, and six out of ten of these begin their freshman year at an institution within 50 miles of home.

More Than an Education

Everywhere from Abilene to Youngstown, chamber of commerce promotional brochures tout the diversity of local colleges and universities more frequently than other urban assets. And with good reason. Among the 12 million full-time college students in the United States, nine million are studying in metro areas. For 21 million other people, the typical location for their evening or weekend continuing education course is a local college classroom.

But colleges and universities contribute other things besides education. In smaller metro areas, a worthy theatre where a touring group of professional players can stage *Playboy of the Western World* or an auditorium where an orchestra and choir can perform *The Messiah* can often only be found at the local college campus. Colleges and universities are stable white-collar employers, too. In Iowa City, IA; Lawrence, KS; and Tuscaloosa, AL, they are the major employers.

Finally, there is the connection between research-oriented universities and healthy economies. Two historic examples are Stanford University's impetus to the growth of high-tech enterprises in San Jose and the Bay Area, and M.I.T.'s faculty and alumni who started many electronics firms along Route 128 outside of Boston.

Of the 3,587 colleges and universities now operating in the United States, more than half are located in just ten states, seven of which are in the Northeast or fronting the Great Lakes. The six states with the most colleges are also the top six in population, but such highly populated states as Florida and New Jersey do not rank among the top ten states for most colleges.

Four-year colleges outnumber two-year colleges 2,086 to 1,176. Two-year colleges are usually public institutions (992 of 1,176), created in the 1950s and 1960s by massive public aid to education. In contrast, four-year colleges are usually older, more traditional, and privately run (1,487 of 2,086), many dating back to before 1900.

SCORING: EDUCATION

To profile the academic features in the metro areas, *Places Rated* details two parts of education that have the greatest impact on the community: its public and private K–12 schools, and the local mix of public and private colleges and universities.

Places Rated's tack for scoring, however, is based only on the variety of higher education options that can meet the differing needs of a community: night and weekend continuing education courses for people who work, full-time graduate courses in the professions, courses leading to occupational certification in two-year colleges, and the traditional bachelor's degree curriculum offered in a four-year college.

Counting a metro area's number of colleges and universities will reveal which areas are enriched and which aren't, but a better picture can be produced by totaling up the number of students in the area's two-year schools and in its four-year and graduate-level institutions.

Like ratings in the arts, transportation, and health care, ratings in education increase with a place's population size. But there are many exceptions. One hundred sixty-four metro areas are larger than Ann Arbor, MI, for example, but only 27 are ranked higher in education. Likewise, San Jose, CA; Raleigh–Durham, NC; and Middlesex–Somerset–Hunterdon, NJ, are ranked much higher in education than their population size indicates.

Each metro area begins with a base score of zero, to which points are added according to the following indicators:

1. *College enrollment, two-year.* A metro area's number of students enrolled in two-year col-

leges is divided by 100, and the result is added to the score.
2. *College enrollment, four-year and beyond.* A metro area's number of students enrolled in colleges with baccalaureate and graduate programs is divided by 50, and the result is added to the score.
3. *CMSA access.* Each of the 71 metro areas that is part of a Consolidated Metropolitan Statistical Area (CMSA) is eligible for bonus points based on shared educational assets: four-year and graduate-level institutions. A place gets a bonus of 10 percent of the points accumulated by *adjacent* places in the CMSA for these amenities.

In the Denver–Boulder consolidated area, for example, Boulder–Longmont gets 102 access points based on Denver's 1,020 points for the Mile High City's five two-year colleges and ten four-year and graduate-level institutions. Likewise, Denver gets a 48-point bonus mainly because the main campus of the University of Colorado lies within metropolitan Boulder–Longmont.

SCORING EXAMPLES

One of the country's better college areas and one of its worst metro areas for higher educational options are both located in the South.

Raleigh–Durham, NC (#29)

Along with Chapel Hill, Raleigh and Durham are sometimes collectively called the Research Triangle. The metro area is fortunate, not only for being the seat of state government, but for being the home of three nationally known universities—Duke, North Carolina State, and the University of North Carolina—as well as a number of smaller colleges.

Raleigh–Durham is an example of a small metro area outperforming larger ones. There are 64 metro areas more populous than the North Carolina area, but only 28 that rank better in higher education options. With five two-year colleges enrolling 10,884 students (good for 109 points) and eight four-year and graduate-level institutions enrolling 69,245 students (good for another 1,384 points), the Research Triangle's total score is 1,494.

Pascagoula, MS (#332)

At the other end of the scale is Pascagoula, a small metro area heavily dependent on ship-building down on the Mississippi Gulf. Pascagoula is one of only four metro areas with no colleges, either two-year or four-year (the others are Bristol, CT; Naples, FL; and Racine, WI), and so receives no points for higher academic options. This is not to say that persons wanting a college education in

Pascagoula are stranded without options; many cross the Alabama border to attend classes in Mobile; others commute to a two-year college in nearby Biloxi.

Rankings: Education

The following criteria are used to rate a metro area for the higher education opportunities it affords its residents: (1) the number of students enrolled in two-year colleges, and (2) the number of students enrolled in

four-year and graduate-level institutions. Places that receive tie scores get the same rank and are listed alphabetically.

Metro Areas from Best to Worst

Places Rated Rank	Places Rated Score	Places Rated Rank	Places Rated Score	Places Rated Rank	Places Rated Score
1. New York, NY	8,216	38. Oklahoma City, OK	1,183	75. Richmond–Petersburg, VA	764
2. Los Angeles–Long Beach, CA	7,509	39. Fort Worth–Arlington, TX	1,165		
3. Chicago, IL	4,935	40. Tampa–St. Petersburg–Clearwater, FL	1,154	76. Kenosha, WI	754
4. Boston, MA	4,336			77. Baton Rouge, LA	752
5. Phildadelphia, PA–NJ	4,019	41. Lansing–East Lansing, MI	1,125	78. Brockton, MA	741
		42. Bridgeport–Milford, CT	1,124	79. Honolulu, HI	738
6. Washington, DC–MD–VA	3,866	43. Madison, WI	1,114	79. Lowell, MA–NH	738
7. Anaheim–Santa Ana, CA	2,917	44. Buffalo, NY	1,088		
8. Nassau–Suffolk, NY	2,849	45. Akron, OH	1,080	81. Greensboro–Winston-Salem–High Point, NC	734
9. Detroit, MI	2,724			82. Bryan–College Station, TX	732
10. Newark, NJ	2,412	46. Springfield, MA	1,071	83. Lake County, IL	722
		47. Denver, CO	1,069	84. State College, PA	705
11. San Diego, CA	2,381	48. Albany–Schenectady–Troy, NY	1,049	85. Salem–Gloucester, MA	701
12. Oakland, CA	2,361	49. Norfolk–Virginia Beach–Newport News, VA	1,034		
13. Minneapolis–St. Paul, MN–WI	2,197	50. Oxnard–Ventura, CA	1,028	86. Santa Rosa–Petaluma, CA	698
14. San Jose, CA	2,151			87. Indianapolis, IN	694
15. San Francisco, CA	2,063	51. Rochester, NY	1,009	88. Louisville, KY–IN	690
		52. Trenton, NJ	999	89. Aurora–Elgin, IL	686
16. Houston, TX	2,062	53. Orange County, NY	979	90. Lafayette–West Lafayette, IN	674
17. Riverside–San Bernardino, CA	1,890	54. Dayton–Springfield, OH	956		
18. Baltimore, MD	1,869	55. Portland, OR	954	91. New Haven–Meriden, CT	672
19. Middlesex–Somerset–Hunterdon, NJ	1,856	56. Hartford, CT	951	92. Provo–Orem, UT	670
20. St. Louis, MO–IL	1,832	57. New Orleans, LA	934	92. Scranton–Wilkes-Barre, PA	670
		58. Danbury, CT	918	94. Memphis, TN–AR–MS	651
21. Pittsburgh, PA	1,763	59. Wilmington, DE–NJ–MD	903	95. Bloomington, IN	648
22. Dallas, TX	1,726	60. Joliet, IL	881		
23. Atlanta, GA	1,725			96. Santa Cruz, CA	633
24. Bergen–Passaic, NJ	1,655	61. Gary–Hammond, IN	878	97. Tallahassee, FL	631
25. Phoenix, AZ	1,648	62. Toledo, OH	871	98. Lawrence–Haverhill, MA–NH	628
		63. Kansas City, MO–KS	869	98. Omaha, NE–IA	628
26. Austin, TX	1,589	64. Champaign–Urbana–Rantoul, IL	862	100. Albuquerque, NM	614
27. Columbus, OH	1,542	65. Tuscon, AZ	861		
28. Ann Arbor, MI	1,500			101. Iowa City, IA	613
29. Raleigh–Durham, NC	1,494	66. Syracuse, NY	853	102. Greenville–Spartanburg, SC	612
30. Seattle, WA	1,489	67. Norwalk, CT	850	102. Orlando, FL	612
		68. Salt Lake City–Ogden, UT	846	104. Grand Rapids, MI	610
31. Sacramento, CA	1,396	69. Providence, RI	828	105. Knoxville, TN	607
32. Monmouth–Ocean, NJ	1,384	70. Stamford, CT	810		
33. Jersey City, NJ	1,303			106. Columbia, SC	585
34. Cincinnati, OH–KY–IN	1,274	71. San Antonio, TX	799	107. Santa Barbara–Santa Maria–Lompoc, CA	583
35. Milwaukee, WI	1,245	72. Nashville, TN	793	108. Boulder–Longmont, CO	582
		73. Gainesville, FL	792	109. Fresno, CA	581
36. Cleveland, OH	1,237	74. Charlotte–Gastonia–Rock Hill, NC–SC	778	110. Lincoln, NE	571
37. Miami–Hialeah, FL	1,211			111. Vallejo–Fairfield–Napa, CA	568
				112. Kalamazoo, MI	562

Places Rated Rank	Places Rated Score	Places Rated Rank	Places Rated Score	Places Rated Rank	Places Rated Score
113. Worcester, MA	552	169. Johnson City–Kingsport–Bristol, TN–VA	281	226. Atlantic City, NJ	141
114. Birmingham, AL	547			227. Fall River, MA–RI	140
115. Lawrence, KS	540	169. Las Cruces, NM	281	227. Salinas–Seaside–Monterey, CA	140
115. Nashua, NH	540	171. Chattanooga, TN–GA	277	229. Houma–Thibodaux, LA	139
117. Columbia, MO	537	171. Montgomery, AL	277	230. Columbus, GA–AL	137
118. Lexington–Fayette, KY	523	173. Fort Wayne, IN	276		
119. Athens, GA	514	173. Reno, NV	276	230. Lakeland–Winter Haven, FL	137
120. Lubbock, TX	506	175. Bangor, ME	271	232. Cedar Rapids, IA	136
				233. Topeka, KS	132
121. Hamilton–Middletown, OH	496	176. Huntington–Ashland, WV–KY–OH	270	234. Shreveport, LA	130
122. Bloomington–Normal, IL	473			235. Bristol, CT	128
122. Charlottesville, VA	473	177. Stockton, CA	267		
124. Vineland–Millville–Bridgeton, NJ	464	178. Davenport–Rock Island–Moline, IA–IL	261	236. Fitchburg–Leominster, MA	126
125. Fort Lauderdale–Hollywood–Pompano Beach, FL	445	179. Eau Claire, WI	259	237. Racine, WI	125
		180. Beaumont–Port Arthur, TX	256	237. Wheeling, WV–OH	125
126. Tacoma, WA	419			239. Canton, OH	122
127. Springfield, MO	418	181. Saginaw–Bay City–Midland, MI	255	240. Killeen–Temple, TX	120
128. Eugene–Springfield, OR	416	182. Beaver County, PA	248		
128. Spokane, WA	416	182. Lancaster, PA	248	240. Roanoke, VA	120
130. El Paso, TX	413	184. Portland, ME	241	242. Joplin, MO	116
		185. Melbourne–Titusville–Palm Bay, FL	239	242. San Angelo, TX	116
130. Wichita, KS	413			244. Olympia, WA	113
132. Fargo–Moorhead, ND–MN	404	186. Pensacola, FL	236	245. Clarksville–Hopkinsville, TN–KY	110
133. Little Rock–North Little Rock, AR	403	187. Bakersfield, CA	235		
134. Allentown–Bethlehem, PA–NJ	400	187. La Crosse, WI	235	246. Florence, AL	109
		189. Huntsville, AL	230	247. Lawton, OK	106
135. Daytona Beach, FL	396	189. Poughkeepsie, NY	230	248. Fort Pierce, FL	105
				248. Rockford, IL	105
136. Jacksonville, FL	391	191. Lorain–Elyria, OH	229	250. Asheville, NC	104
137. Muncie, IN	390	192. Peoria, IL	228		
138. West Palm Beach–Boca Raton–Delray Beach, FL	383	192. Reading, PA	228	251. Savannah, GA	103
139. Flint, MI	378	194. Lynchburg, VA	223	252. Visalia–Tulare–Porterville, CA	102
140. Fort Collins–Loveland, CO	377	195. Anchorage, AK	222	253. Brownsville–Harlingen, TX	100
				253. Cumberland, MD–WV	100
140. Harrisburg–Lebanon–Carlisle, PA	377	196. Janesville–Beloit, WI	220	255. Johnstown, PA	99
		197. Boise City, ID	219		
142. South Bend–Mishawaka, IN	376	198. Utica–Rome, NY	216	255. New London–Norwich, CT–RI	99
143. Tuscaloosa, AL	373	199. Grand Forks, ND	215	257. Benton Harbor, MI	96
144. Las Vegas, NV	368	199. Middletown, CT	215	258. Burlington, NC	93
144. New Britain, CT	368			259. Florence, SC	92
		201. Niagara Falls, NY	214	260. Jackson, MI	91
146. Jackson, MS	365	202. Bellingham, WA	211		
147. Chico, CA	364	203. Pawtucket–Woonsocket–Attleboro, RI–MA	207	260. Medford, OR	91
148. St. Cloud, MN	362	204. Monroe, LA	205	260. Pueblo, CO	91
149. Tulsa, OK	352	205. Augusta, GA–SC	198	263. Wichita Falls, TX	89
150. Waco, TX	336			264. Billings, MT	87
		206. Modesto, CA	191	265. Sharon, PA	85
151. Duluth, MN–WI	320	207. Green Bay, WI	188		
151. Youngstown–Warren, OH	320	208. Evansville, IN–KY	186	266. Battle Creek, MI	83
153. Charleston, SC	313	209. Salem, OR	183	267. Odessa, TX	82
154. Lafayette, LA	310	210. Amarillo, TX	182	268. Hickory, NC	81
154. Portsmouth–Dover–Rochester, NH–ME	310			268. Redding, CA	81
		211. McAllen–Edinburg–Mission, TX	178	270. Yuba City, CA	79
156. Binghamton, NY	308	212. Macon–Warner Robins, GA	176		
157. Galveston–Texas City, TX	306	213. Charleston, WV	174	271. Longview–Marshall, TX	77
158. Burlington, VT	299	214. Corpus Christi, TX	166	271. St. Joseph, MO	77
159. Colorado Springs, CO	298	215. Vancouver, WA	164	273. Jackson, TN	76
160. Appleton–Oshkosh–Neenah, WI	296	215. York, PA	164	274. Kokomo, IN	75
		217. New Bedford, MA	161	274. Parkersburg–Marietta, WV–OH	75
161. Erie, PA	294	218. Abilene, TX	156		
161. Waterloo–Cedar Falls, IA	294	219. Tyler, TX	154	276. Santa Fe, NM	71
163. Des Moines, IA	292	220. Manchester, NH	151	277. Dothan, AL	70
164. Mobile, AL	291			278. Kankakee, IL	69
165. Fayetteville–Springdale, AR	289	220. Wilmington, NC	151	279. Fort Myers–Cape Coral, FL	67
		222. Springfield, IL	150	280. Decatur, IL	64
166. Brazoria, TX	288	223. Fayetteville, NC	148		
167. Greeley, CO	286	224. Lake Charles, LA	147	281. Decatur, AL	63
168. Terre Haute, IN	284	225. Anniston, AL	143	281. Merced, CA	63
				283. Bradenton, FL	62
				283. Waterbury, CT	62

Places Rated Rank	Places Rated Score		Places Rated Rank	Places Rated Score		Places Rated Rank	Places Rated Score
285. Dubuque, IA	60		300. Panama City, FL	50		315. Lewiston–Auburn, ME	36
						318. Anderson, SC	34
285. Laredo, TX	60		301. Sioux City, IA–NE	48		318. Jacksonville, NC	34
285. Muskegon, MI	60		302. Bismark, ND	46		320. Ocala, FL	32
288. Pine Bluff, AR	58		303. Victoria, TX	44			
289. Sherman–Denison, TX	57		303. Yakima, WA	44		321. Pittsfield, MA	31
289. Texarkana, TX–Texarkana, AR	57		305. Rapid City, SD	41		322. Owensboro, KY	30
						323. Glen Falls, NY	28
291. Altoona, PA	56		306. Anderson IN	40		324. Sheboygan, WI	26
291. Richland–Kennewick–Pasco, WA	56		306. Elmira, NY	40		325. Biloxi–Gulfport, MS	25
			306. Mansfield, OH	40			
293. Albany, GA	55		309. Danville, VA	39		325. Hagerstown, MD	25
293. Williamsport, PA	55		310. Cheyenne, WY	38		327. Great Falls, MT	23
295. Lima, OH	53					328. Elkhart–Goshen, IN	21
			310. Wausau, WI	38		328. Enid, OK	21
295. Sioux Falls, SD	53		312. Alexandria, LA	37		330. Casper, WY	14
297. Bremerton, WA	52		312. Fort Smith, AR–OK	37			
297. Rochester, MN	52		312. Midland, TX	37		331. Sarasota, FL	8
299. Steubenville–Weirton, OH–WV	51		315. Fort Walton Beach, FL	36		332. Naples, FL	0
						332. Pascagoula, MS	0
			315. Gadsden, AL	36			

Place Profiles: Education

The following pages detail the two sides of the education landscape in metro areas: (1) public and private elementary and secondary schools, and (2) public and private colleges and universities.

Under the heading **Elementary and Secondary** are figures for the percent of children attending public schools within the metro area, the number of public school districts, and the total number of public schools and their enrollment. Data on the percent of children attending private schools within the metro area and the number of private schools and their total enrollment are also given.

Under the heading **Colleges and Universities** are (1) the number of two-year colleges and their total enrollment, and (2) the names and enrollments of all four-year and graduate-level institutions located within the metro area.

Data on the number of school districts can be found in the Census Bureau's *Government Organization*, 1989. Data on the number of metro area public schools and their total enrollment come from the *National School Market Index*, published annually by Market Data Retrieval, Westport, CT, as do figures on metro area private schools and their total enrollment. For higher education, the source is Volume 1 of the U.S. Department of Education's *Directory of Postsecondary Institutions*, 1989.

A star (★) preceding a metro area's name highlights it as one of *Places Rated Almanac*'s top 30 places for education.

Abilene, TX
Elementary and Secondary
Public (96.6%): 5 districts, 40 schools, 21,614 pupils
Private (3.4%): 7 schools, 751 pupils
Colleges and Universities
Four-year and beyond:
Private
Abilene Christian University (4,302)
Hardin–Simmons University (1,804)
McMurry College (1,689)
Places Rated Score: 156
Places Rated Rank: 218

Akron, OH
Elementary and Secondary
Public (89.6%): 28 districts, 196 schools, 106,071 pupils
Private (10.4%): 45 schools, 12,257 pupils

Colleges and Universities
Four-year and beyond:
Public
Kent State University (20,846)
Northeastern Ohio University College of Medicine (396)
University of Akron (25,944)
Private
Hiram College (1,186)
CMSA Access: Cleveland–Akron–Lorain, OH
Places Rated Score: 1,080
Places Rated Rank: 45

Albany, GA
Elementary and Secondary
Public (91.7%): 2 districts, 35 schools, 21,844 pupils
Private (8.3%): 9 schools, 1,988 pupils

Colleges and Universities
Two-year: 1 public; 1,679 students
Four-year and beyond:
Public
Albany State College (1,902)
Places Rated Score: 55
Places Rated Rank: 293

Albany–Schenectady–Troy, NY
Elementary and Secondary
Public (86.8%): 57 districts, 231 schools, 123,568 pupils
Private (13.2%): 100 schools, 18,713 pupils
Colleges and Universities
Two-year: 3 public, 2 private; 12,834 students
Four-year and beyond:

Public
  State University of New York, Empire
    State College (5,550)
  State University of New York, Albany
    (16,112)
Private
  Albany College of Pharmacy (630)
  Albany Law School (689)
  Albany Medical College of Union
    University (601)
  College of Saint Rose (3,143)
  Rensselaer Polytechnic Institute (6,827)
  Russell Sage College (3,335)
  Siena College (3,432)
  Skidmore College (2,571)
  Union College (3,124)
Places Rated Score: 1,049
Places Rated Rank: 48

Albuquerque, NM
Elementary and Secondary
  Public (90.2%): 1 district, 114 schools,
    80,508 pupils
  Private (9.8%): 37 schools, 8,702 pupils
Colleges and Universities
  Two-year: 1 public; 13,117 students
  Four-year and beyond:
  Public
    University of New Mexico (24,124)
Places Rated Score: 614
Places Rated Rank: 100

Alexandria, LA
Elementary and Secondary
  Public (89.2%): 1 district, 52 schools,
    24,533 pupils
  Private (10.8%): 13 schools, 2,955 pupils
Colleges and Universities
  Two-year: 1 public; 1,899 students
  Four-year and beyond:
  Private
    Louisiana College (983)
Places Rated Score: 37
Places Rated Rank: 312

Allentown–Bethlehem, PA–NJ
Elementary and Secondary
  Public (86.6%): 49 districts, 192 schools,
    94,934 pupils
  Private (13.4%): 65 schools, 14,734 pupils
Colleges and Universities
  Two-year: 3 public, 1 private; 7,350
    students
  Four-year and beyond:
  Public
    Pennsylvania State University,
      Allentown (583)
  Private
    Allentown College of Saint Francis De
      Sales (1,462)
    Cedar Crest College (1,145)
    Centenary College (965)
    Lafayette College (2,330)
    Lehigh University (6,439)
    Moravian College (1,319)
    Muhlenberg College (2,087)
Places Rated Score: 400
Places Rated Rank: 134

Altoona, PA
Elementary and Secondary
  Public (87.1%): 7 districts, 41 schools,
    21,657 pupils
  Private (12.9%): 20 schools, 3,213 pupils
Colleges and Universities
  Two-year: 1 private; 869 students
  Four-year and beyond:

Public
  Pennsylvania State University, Altoona
    (2,354)
Places Rated Score: 56
Places Rated Rank: 291

Amarillo, TX
Elementary and Secondary
  Public (93.4%): 6 districts, 61 schools,
    35,748 pupils
  Private (6.6%): 15 schools, 2,526 pupils
Colleges and Universities
  Two-year: 1 public; 6,116 students
  Four-year and beyond:
  Public
    West Texas State University (6,028)
Places Rated Score: 182
Places Rated Rank: 210

★ Anaheim–Santa Ana, CA
Elementary and Secondary
  Public (87.6%): 33 districts, 467 schools,
    332,003 pupils
  Private (12.4%): 188 schools, 47,171
    pupils
Colleges and Universities
  Two-year: 8 public; 123,046 students
  Four-year and beyond:
  Public
    California State University, Fullerton
      (24,277)
    University of California, Irvine (14,532)
  Private
    Chapman College (2,071)
    Christ College, Irvine (527)
    Pacific Christian College (542)
    Southern California College (898)
    Southern California College of
      Optometry (379)
    West Coast University, Orange County
      (441)
CMSA Access: Los Angeles–
  Anaheim–Riverside, CA
Places Rated Score: 2,917
Places Rated Rank: 7

Anchorage, AK
Elementary and Secondary
  Public (94.0%): 2 districts, 78 schools,
    42,885 pupils
  Private (6.0%): 18 schools, 2,729 pupils
Colleges and Universities
  Two-year: 1 public; 8,765 students
  Four-year and beyond:
  Public
    University of Alaska, Anchorage (4,317)
  Private
    Alaska Pacific University (797)
Places Rated Score: 222
Places Rated Rank: 195

Anderson, IN
Elementary and Secondary
  Public (94.0%): 5 districts, 48 schools,
    24,466 pupils
  Private (6.0%): 9 schools, 1,563 pupils
Colleges and Universities
  Four-year and beyond:
  Private
    Anderson College (1,994)
Places Rated Score: 40
Places Rated Rank: 306

Anderson, SC
Elementary and Secondary
  Public (96.0%): 5 districts, 47 schools,
    25,536 pupils
  Private (4.0%): 7 schools, 1,061 pupils

Colleges and Universities
  Two-year: 1 public, 1 private; 3,446
    students
Places Rated Score: 34
Places Rated Rank: 318

★ Ann Arbor, MI
Elementary and Secondary
  Public (88.8%): 11 districts, 76 schools,
    37,623 pupils
  Private (11.2%): 26 schools, 4,726 pupils
Colleges and Universities
  Two-year: 1 public; 8,399 students
  Four-year and beyond:
  Public
    Eastern Michigan University (21,349)
    University of Michigan, Ann Arbor
      (34,974)
  Private
    Cleary College (1,071)
    Concordia College (424)
CMSA Access: Detroit–Ann Arbor, MI
Places Rated Score: 1,500
Places Rated Rank: 28

Anniston, AL
Elementary and Secondary
  Public (93.0%): 5 districts, 33 schools,
    21,855 pupils
  Private (7.0%): 5 schools, 1,639 pupils
Colleges and Universities
  Two-year: 1 public; 697 students
  Four-year and beyond:
  Public
    Jacksonville State University (6,814)
Places Rated Score: 143
Places Rated Rank: 225

Appleton–Oshkosh–Neenah, WI
Elementary and Secondary
  Public (81.0%): 19 districts, 106 schools,
    46,068 pupils
  Private (19.0%): 65 schools, 10,840 pupils
Colleges and Universities
  Two-year: 1 public; 3,829 students
  Four-year and beyond:
  Public
    University of Wisconsin, Oshkosh
      (11,800)
  Private
    Lawrence University (1,067)
Places Rated Score: 296
Places Rated Rank: 160

Asheville, NC
Elementary and Secondary
  Public (92.3%): 3 districts, 48 schools,
    26,256 pupils
  Private (7.7%): 15 schools, 2,204 pupils
Colleges and Universities
  Two-year: 1 public; 2,847 students
  Four-year and beyond:
  Public
    University of North Carolina, Asheville
      (2,900)
  Private
    Montreat–Anderson College (367)
    Warren Wilson College (498)
Places Rated Score: 104
Places Rated Rank: 250

Athens, GA
Elementary and Secondary
  Public (91.8%): 6 districts, 39 schools,
    21,803 pupils
  Private (8.2%): 8 schools, 1,955 pupils
Colleges and Universities
  Four-year and beyond:

Public
University of Georgia (25,698)
Places Rated Score: 514
Places Rated Rank: 119

★ **Atlanta, GA**
Elementary and Secondary
Public (91.9%): 23 districts, 659 schools,
436,868 pupils
Private (8.1%): 171 schools, 38,406 pupils
Colleges and Universities
Two-year: 6 public, 2 private; 32,388
students
Four-year and beyond:
Public
Clayton State College (3,283)
Georgia Institute of Technology
(11,494)
Georgia State University (21,835)
Kennesaw College (7,275)
Southern College of Technology (3,762)
Private
Agnes Scott College (518)
Atlanta College of Art (278)
Atlanta University (1,074)
Clark College (1,230)
Columbia Theological Seminary (526)
Emory University (8,884)
Interdenominational Theological Center
(307)
Life Chiropractic College (1,362)
Mercer University, Atlanta (1,989)
Morehouse College (2,122)
Morris Brown College (1,354)
Oglethorpe University (960)
Spelman College (1,782)
Places Rated Score: 1,725
Places Rated Rank: 23

Atlantic City, NJ
Elementary and Secondary
Public (86.1%): 46 districts, 109 schools,
45,423 pupils
Private (13.9%): 31 schools, 7,355 pupils
Colleges and Universities
Two-year: 1 public; 3,949 students
Four-year and beyond:
Public
Stockton State College (5,069)
Places Rated Score: 141
Places Rated Rank: 226

Augusta, GA–SC
Elementary and Secondary
Public (90.4%): 4 districts, 108 schools,
67,942 pupils
Private (9.6%): 35 schools, 7,250 pupils
Colleges and Universities
Two-year: 1 public; 1,235 students
Four-year and beyond:
Public
Augusta College (4,100)
Medical College of Georgia (2,312)
University of South Carolina, Aiken
(2,068)
Private
Paine College (789)
Places Rated Score: 198
Places Rated Rank: 205

Aurora–Elgin, IL
Elementary and Secondary
Public (86.2%): 17 districts, 137 schools,
76,012 pupils
Private (13.8%): 50 schools, 12,164 pupils
Colleges and Universities
Two-year: 2 public; 10,312 students
Four-year and beyond:

Private
Aurora University (1,869)
Judson College (502)
CMSA Access: Chicago–Gary–Lake
County, IL–IN–WI
Places Rated Score: 686
Places Rated Rank: 89

★ **Austin, TX**
Elementary and Secondary
Public (94.1%): 22 districts, 196 schools,
125,520 pupils
Private (5.9%): 40 schools, 7,823 pupils
Colleges and Universities
Two-year: 1 public; 18,340 students
Four-year and beyond:
Public
Southwest Texas State University
(19,375)
University of Texas, Austin (46,140)
Private
Austin Presbyterian Theological
Seminary (236)
Concordia Lutheran College (455)
Huston–Tillotson College (520)
Saint Edward's University (2,536)
Southwestern University (1,119)
Places Rated Score: 1,589
Places Rated Rank: 26

Bakersfield, CA
Elementary and Secondary
Public (95.0%): 52 districts, 179 schools,
98,192 pupils
Private (5.0%): 36 schools, 5,212 pupils
Colleges and Universities
Two-year: 3 public; 14,844 students
Four-year and beyond:
Public
California State College, Bakersfield
(4,320)
Places Rated Score: 235
Places Rated Rank: 187

★ **Baltimore, MD**
Elementary and Secondary
Public (85.5%): 15 districts, 570 schools,
341,335 pupils
Private (14.5%): 218 schools, 57,744
pupils
Colleges and Universities
Two-year: 7 public, 1 private; 45,349
students
Four-year and beyond:
Public
Coppin State College (2,315)
Morgan State University (3,752)
Towson State University (15,421)
United States Naval Academy (4,647)
University of Baltimore (5,020)
University of Maryland Professional
Schools (4,563)
University of Maryland, Baltimore
County (9,267)
Private
Baltimore Hebrew College (217)
College of Notre Dame, Maryland
(1,886)
Goucher College (826)
Johns Hopkins University (11,606)
Loyola College (5,226)
Maryland Institute College of Art
(1,257)
Ner Israel Rabbinical College (369)
Peabody Institute of Johns Hopkins
University (472)
Saint Mary's Seminary and University
(316)

Sojourner–Douglas College (380)
St. John's College (419)
Villa Julie College (1,141)
Western Maryland College (1,654)
Places Rated Score: 1,869
Places Rated Rank: 18

Bangor, ME
Elementary and Secondary
Public (91.6%): 8 districts, 29 schools,
12,724 pupils
Private (8.4%): 11 schools, 1,168 pupils
Colleges and Universities
Two-year: 1 public; 1,098 students
Four-year and beyond:
Public
University of Maine (10,954)
Private
Husson College (1,767)
Unity College (280)
Places Rated Score: 271
Places Rated Rank: 175

Baton Rouge, LA
Elementary and Secondary
Public (81.0%): 4 districts, 159 schools,
88,913 pupils
Private (19.0%): 62 schools, 20,856 pupils
Colleges and Universities
Four-year and beyond:
Public
Louisiana State University (28,421)
Southern University (9,170)
Places Rated Score: 752
Places Rated Rank: 77

Battle Creek, MI
Elementary and Secondary
Public (92.6%): 12 districts, 56 schools,
23,497 pupils
Private (7.4%): 14 schools, 1,876 pupils
Colleges and Universities
Two-year: 1 public; 5,139 students
Four-year and beyond:
Private
Albion College (1,587)
Places Rated Score: 83
Places Rated Rank: 266

Beaumont–Port Arthur, TX
Elementary and Secondary
Public (94.4%): 16 districts, 120 schools,
73,733 pupils
Private (5.6%): 24 schools, 4,415 pupils
Colleges and Universities
Two-year: 2 public; 2,388 students
Four-year and beyond:
Public
Lamar University (11,602)
Places Rated Score: 256
Places Rated Rank: 180

Beaver County, PA
Elementary and Secondary
Public (91.8%): 16 districts, 53 schools,
29,242 pupils
Private (8.2%): 19 schools, 2,609 pupils
Colleges and Universities
Two-year: 1 public; 2,511 students
Four-year and beyond:
Public
Pennsylvania State University, Beaver
(1,167)
Private
Geneva College (1,175)
CMSA Access: Pittsburgh–Beaver
County, PA
Places Rated Score: 248
Places Rated Rank: 182

Bellingham, WA
Elementary and Secondary
Public (93.1%): 7 districts, 43 schools,
18,307 pupils
Private (6.9%): 13 schools, 1,353 pupils
Colleges and Universities
Two-year: 1 public; 2,343 students
Four-year and beyond:
Public
Western Washington University (9,398)
Places Rated Score: 211
Places Rated Rank: 202

Benton Harbor, MI
Elementary and Secondary
Public (87.5%): 17 districts, 76 schools,
33,257 pupils
Private (12.5%): 30 schools, 4,761 pupils
Colleges and Universities
Two-year: 1 public; 3,504 students
Four-year and beyond:
Private
Andrews University (3,053)
Places Rated Score: 96
Places Rated Rank: 257

★ Bergen–Passaic, NJ
Elementary and Secondary
Public (80.0%): 99 districts, 400 schools,
170,618 pupils
Private (20.0%): 164 schools, 42,547
pupils
Colleges and Universities
Two-year: 2 public, 1 private; 14,951
students
Four-year and beyond:
Public
Ramapo College of New Jersey (3,858)
William Paterson College of New
Jersey (9,218)
Private
Fairleigh Dickinson University, Teaneck
(5,858)
Fairleigh Dickinson University,
Rutherford (2,576)
Felician College (548)
CMSA Access: New York–Northern
NJ–Long Island, NY–NJ–CT
Places Rated Score: 1,655
Places Rated Rank: 24

Billings, MT
Elementary and Secondary
Public (93.9%): 21 districts, 58 schools,
21,637 pupils
Private (6.1%): 9 schools, 1,407 pupils
Colleges and Universities
Four-year and beyond:
Public
Eastern Montana College (3,920)
Private
Rocky Mountain College (429)
Places Rated Score: 87
Places Rated Rank: 264

Biloxi–Gulfport, MS
Elementary and Secondary
Public (88.8%): 7 districts, 57 schools,
33,543 pupils
Private (11.2%): 18 schools, 4,211 pupils
Colleges and Universities
Two-year: 1 public; 2,500 students
Places Rated Score: 25
Places Rated Rank: 325

Binghamton, NY
Elementary and Secondary
Public (91.9%): 20 districts, 76 schools,
43,579 pupils

Private (8.1%): 28 schools, 3,857 pupils
Colleges and Universities
Two-year: 1 public; 6,178 students
Four-year and beyond:
Public
State University of New York,
Binghamton (12,306)
Places Rated Score: 308
Places Rated Rank: 156

Birmingham, AL
Elementary and Secondary
Public (92.2%): 17 districts, 282 schools,
155,036 pupils
Private (7.8%): 58 schools, 13,145 pupils
Colleges and Universities
Two-year: 4 public, 2 private; 10,568
students
Four-year and beyond:
Public
University of Alabama, Birmingham
(13,538)
University of Montevallo (2,542)
Private
Birmingham Southern College (1,725)
Miles College (461)
Samford University (3,802)
Places Rated Score: 547
Places Rated Rank: 114

Bismarck, ND
Elementary and Secondary
Public (89.5%): 23 districts, 53 schools,
16,112 pupils
Private (10.5%): 9 schools, 1,895 pupils
Colleges and Universities
Two-year: 1 public; 2,281 students
Four-year and beyond:
Private
University of Mary (1,175)
Places Rated Score: 46
Places Rated Rank: 302

Bloomington, IN
Elementary and Secondary
Public (96.4%): 2 districts, 23 schools,
13,280 pupils
Private (3.6%): 6 schools, 496 pupils
Colleges and Universities
Four-year and beyond:
Public
Indiana University, Bloomington
(32,417)
Places Rated Score: 648
Places Rated Rank: 95

Bloomington–Normal, IL
Elementary and Secondary
Public (89.5%): 11 districts, 46 schools,
18,833 pupils
Private (10.5%): 10 schools, 2,217 pupils
Colleges and Universities
Four-year and beyond:
Public
Illinois State University (21,926)
Private
Illinois Wesleyan University (1,716)
Places Rated Score: 473
Places Rated Rank: 122

Boise City, ID
Elementary and Secondary
Public (95.3%): 3 districts, 65 schools,
37,894 pupils
Private (4.7%): 11 schools, 1,869 pupils
Colleges and Universities
Four-year and beyond:

Public
Boise State University (10,933)
Places Rated Score: 219
Places Rated Rank: 197

★ Boston, MA
Elementary and Secondary
Public (84.5%): 105 districts, 771 schools,
368,319 pupils
Private (15.5%): 311 schools, 67,617
pupils
Colleges and Universities
Two-year: 6 public, 10 private; 31,855
students
Four-year and beyond:
Public
Framingham State College (5,951)
Massachusetts College of Arts (2,070)
University of Massachusetts, Boston
(12,370)
Private
Andover Newton Theological School
(417)
Babson College (3,228)
Bentley College (7,331)
Berklee College of Music (2,702)
Boston Architectural Center (692)
Boston College (13,979)
Boston Conservatory (380)
Boston University (27,055)
Brandeis University (3,668)
Cambridge College (326)
Curry College (1,254)
Eastern Nazarene College (886)
Emerson College (2,385)
Emmanuel College (944)
Harvard University (23,730)
Lesley College (4,188)
Massachusetts College of Pharmacy
(1,101)
Massachusetts Institute of Technology
(12,800)
Mount Ida College (1,710)
New England College of Optometry
(356)
New England Conservatory of Music
(737)
New England School of Law (1,089)
Northeastern University (34,093)
Pine Manor College (596)
Radcliffe College (2,799)
Regis College (1,039)
School of the Museum of Fine Arts
(1,052)
Simmons College (2,983)
Suffolk University (5,733)
Tufts University (7,428)
Wellesley College (2,257)
Wentworth Institute of Technology
(4,020)
Weston School of Theology (214)
Wheaton College (1,084)
Wheelock College (755)
CMSA Access:
Boston–Lawrence–Salem, MA–NH
Places Rated Score: 4,336
Places Rated Rank: 4

Boulder–Longmont, CO
Elementary and Secondary
Public (93.6%): 2 districts, 72 schools,
39,223 pupils
Private (6.4%): 18 schools, 2,677 pupils
Colleges and Universities
Four-year and beyond:
Public
University of Colorado (23,590)

Private
    Naropa Institute (386)
CMSA Access: Denver–Boulder, CO
Places Rated Score: 582
Places Rated Rank: 108

Bradenton, FL
Elementary and Secondary
    Public (90.1%): 2 districts, 32 schools,
        22,711 pupils
    Private (9.9%): 12 schools, 2,497 pupils
Colleges and Universities
    Two-year: 1 public; 6,211 students
Places Rated Score: 62
Places Rated Rank: 283

Brazoria, TX
Elementary and Secondary
    Public (98.2%): 10 districts, 57 schools,
        38,812 pupils
    Private (1.8%): 4 schools, 703 pupils
Colleges and Universities
    Two-year: 2 public; 7,359 students
CMSA Access:
    Houston–Galveston–Brazoria, TX
Places Rated Score: 288
Places Rated Rank: 166

Bremerton, WA
Elementary and Secondary
    Public (96.1%): 5 districts, 49 schools,
        31,575 pupils
    Private (3.9%): 15 schools, 1,277 pupils
Colleges and Universities
    Two-year: 1 public; 5,153 students
Places Rated Score: 52
Places Rated Rank: 297

Bridgeport–Milford, CT
Elementary and Secondary
    Public (82.1%): 13 districts, 123 schools,
        59,221 pupils
    Private (17.9%): 46 schools, 12,941 pupils
Colleges and Universities
    Two-year: 1 public; 2,247 students
    Four-year and beyond:
    Private
        Bridgeport Engineering Institute (713)
        Fairfield University (5,126)
        Sacred Heart University (4,831)
        University of Bridgeport (5,615)
CMSA Access: New York–Northern
    NJ–Long Island, NY–NJ–CT
Places Rated Score: 1,124
Places Rated Rank: 42

Bristol, CT
Elementary and Secondary
    Public (86.1%): 3 districts, 23 schools,
        11,789 pupils
    Private (13.9%): 6 schools, 1,908 pupils
CMSA Access: Hartford–New
    Britain–Middletown, CT
Places Rated Score: 128
Places Rated Rank: 235

Brockton, MA
Elementary and Secondary
    Public (93.6%): 9 districts, 57 schools,
        32,748 pupils
    Private (6.4%): 13 schools, 2,248 pupils
Colleges and Universities
    Two-year: 1 public; 7,805 students
    Four-year and beyond:
    Public
        Bridgewater State College (9,139)

Private
    Stonehill College (2,851)
CMSA Access:
    Boston–Lawrence–Salem, MA–NH
Places Rated Score: 741
Places Rated Rank: 78

Brownsville–Harlingen, TX
Elementary and Secondary
    Public (94.7%): 11 districts, 93 schools,
        69,140 pupils
    Private (5.3%): 19 schools, 3,868 pupils
Colleges and Universities
    Two-year: 2 public; 7,673 students
    Four-year and beyond:
    Public
        Pan American University, Brownsville
        (1,182)
Places Rated Score: 100
Places Rated Rank: 253

Bryan–College Station, TX
Elementary and Secondary
    Public (94.2%): 2 districts, 21 schools,
        15,666 pupils
    Private (5.8%): 5 schools, 956 pupils
Colleges and Universities
    Four-year and beyond:
    Public
        Texas A & M University (36,617)
Places Rated Score: 732
Places Rated Rank: 82

Buffalo, NY
Elementary and Secondary
    Public (81.2%): 30 districts, 217 schools,
        136,857 pupils
    Private (18.8%): 129 schools, 31,594
        pupils
Colleges and Universities
    Two-year: 3 public, 3 private; 13,916
        students
    Four-year and beyond:
    Public
        State University of New York College,
            Buffalo (12,011)
        State University of New York Health
            Science Center, Buffalo (2,994)
        State University of New York, Buffalo
            (23,977)
    Private
        Canisius College (4,250)
        D'Youville College (1,033)
        Daemen College (1,664)
        Medaille College (967)
CMSA Access: Buffalo–Niagara Falls, NY
Places Rated Score: 1,088
Places Rated Rank: 44

Burlington, NC
Elementary and Secondary
    Public (95.5%): 3 districts, 30 schools,
        17,101 pupils
    Private (4.5%): 6 schools, 813 pupils
Colleges and Universities
    Two-year: 1 public; 3,114 students
    Four-year and beyond:
    Private
        Elon College (3,097)
Places Rated Score: 93
Places Rated Rank: 258

Burlington, VT
Elementary and Secondary
    Public (90.9%): 15 districts, 46 schools,
        18,117 pupils
    Private (9.1%): 13 schools, 1,820 pupils

Colleges and Universities
    Two-year: 1 private; 1,697 students
    Four-year and beyond:
    Public
        University of Vermont (11,096)
    Private
        Saint Michael's College (2,040)
        Trinity College (967)
Places Rated Score: 299
Places Rated Rank: 158

Canton, OH
Elementary and Secondary
    Public (91.6%): 19 districts, 135 schools,
        71,477 pupils
    Private (8.4%): 27 schools, 6,592 pupils
Colleges and Universities
    Two-year: 2 public; 4,975 students
    Four-year and beyond:
    Private
        Malone College (1,205)
        Mount Union College (1,073)
        Walsh College (1,313)
Places Rated Score: 122
Places Rated Rank: 239

Casper, WY
Elementary and Secondary
    Public (96.5%): 2 districts, 37 schools,
        13,316 pupils
    Private (3.5%): 4 schools, 481 pupils
Colleges and Universities
    Two-year: 1 public; 1,400 students
Places Rated Score: 14
Places Rated Rank: 330

Cedar Rapids, IA
Elementary and Secondary
    Public (89.3%): 12 districts, 64 schools,
        29,377 pupils
    Private (10.7%): 16 schools, 3,509 pupils
Colleges and Universities
    Two-year: 1 public; 6,308 students
    Private
        Coe College (1,133)
        Cornell College (1,161)
        Mount Mercy College (1,334)
Places Rated Score: 136
Places Rated Rank: 232

Champaign–Urbana–Rantoul, IL
Elementary and Secondary
    Public (92.3%): 18 districts, 57 schools,
        23,172 pupils
    Private (7.7%): 13 schools, 1,927 pupils
Colleges and Universities
    Two-year: 1 public; 7,639 students
    Four-year and beyond:
    Public
        University of Illinois (39,274)
Places Rated Score: 862
Places Rated Rank: 64

Charleston, SC
Elementary and Secondary
    Public (90.2%): 5 districts, 125 schools,
        85,056 pupils
    Private (9.8%): 45 schools, 9,197 pupils
Colleges and Universities
    Two-year: 1 public, 1 private; 5,588
        students
    Four-year and beyond:
    Public
        Citadel Military College of South
            Carolina (3,339)
        College of Charleston (5,531)
        Medical University of South Carolina
            (2,066)

Private
Baptist College at Charleston (1,922)
Places Rated Score: 313
Places Rated Rank: 153

Charleston, WV
Elementary and Secondary
Public (95.0%): 2 districts, 136 schools,
46,544 pupils
Private (5.0%): 19 schools, 2,466 pupils
Colleges and Universities
Four-year and beyond:
Public
West Virginia College of Graduate
Studies (2,834)
West Virginia State College (4,383)
Private
University of Charleston (1,480)
Places Rated Score: 174
Places Rated Rank: 213

Charlotte–Gastonia–Rock Hill, NC–SC
Elementary and Secondary
Public (92.9%): 16 districts, 300 schools,
187,903 pupils
Private (7.1%): 59 schools, 14,376 pupils
Colleges and Universities
Two-year: 4 public; 25,728 students
Four-year and beyond:
Public
University of North Carolina, Charlotte
(12,109)
Winthrop College (5,323)
Private
Barber–Scotia College (383)
Belmont Abbey College (865)
Catawba College (886)
Davidson College (1,397)
East Coast Bible College (204)
Johnson C. Smith University (1,130)
Livingstone College (733)
Queens College (1,332)
Wingate College (1,697)
Places Rated Score: 778
Places Rated Rank: 74

Charlottesville, VA
Elementary and Secondary
Public (88.1%): 4 districts, 41 schools,
17,592 pupils
Private (11.9%): 14 schools, 2,365 pupils
Colleges and Universities
Two-year: 1 public; 4,104 students
Four-year and beyond:
Public
University of Virginia (21,615)
Places Rated Score: 473
Places Rated Rank: 122

Chattanooga, TN–GA
Elementary and Secondary
Public (89.3%): 9 districts, 144 schools,
75,677 pupils
Private (10.7%): 46 schools, 9,061 pupils
Colleges and Universities
Two-year: 1 public, 1 private; 5,522
students
Four-year and beyond:
Public
University of Tennessee (7,484)
Private
Covenant College (541)
Southern College of Seventh-Day
Adventist (1,328)
Tennessee Temple University (1,712)
Places Rated Score: 277
Places Rated Rank: 171

Cheyenne, WY
Elementary and Secondary
Public (96.3%): 3 districts, 39 schools,
14,315 pupils
Private (3.7%): 6 schools, 556 pupils
Colleges and Universities
Two-year: 1 public; 3,759 students
Places Rated Score: 38
Places Rated Rank: 310

★ Chicago, IL
Elementary and Secondary
Public (80.1%): 220 districts, 432 schools,
883,383 pupils
Private (19.9%): 741 schools, 219,929
pupils
Colleges and Universities
Two-year: 17 public, 4 private; 190,542
students
Four-year and beyond:
Public
Chicago State University (7,763)
Northeastern Illinois University (10,638)
University of Illinois (25,330)
Private
Catholic Theological Union (345)
Chicago College of Osteopathic
Medicine (549)
Columbia College (5,547)
Concordia College (1,203)
DePaul University (13,132)
Dr. William Scholl College of Podiatric
Medicine (555)
East–West University (277)
Elmhurst College (3,265)
Garrett Evangelical Theological
Seminary (336)
Illinois Benedictine College (2,469)
Illinois College of Optometry (575)
Illinois Institute of Technology (6,291)
John Marshall Law School (1,322)
Kendall College (359)
Loyola University of Chicago (13,906)
Lutheran School of Theology (316)
Mallinckrodt College of the North Shore
(261)
McCormick Theological Seminary (590)
Moody Bible Institute (1,398)
Mundelein College (1,144)
National College of Chiropractic (802)
North Central College (2,094)
North Park College and Theological
Seminary (1,497)
Northern Baptist Theological Seminary
(215)
Northwestern University (16,226)
Roosevelt University (5,970)
Rosary College (1,509)
Rush University (1,149)
Saint Xavier College (2,612)
School of the Art Institute of Chicago
(2,246)
Trinity Christian College (477)
University of Chicago (9,970)
Wheaton College (2,571)
CMSA Access: Chicago–Gary–Lake
County, IL–IN–WI
Places Rated Score: 4,935
Places Rated Rank: 3

Chico, CA
Elementary and Secondary
Public (94.2%): 17 districts, 59 schools,
23,871 pupils
Private (5.8%): 14 schools, 1,464 pupils
Colleges and Universities
Two-year: 1 public; 6,635 students
Four-year and beyond:

Public
California State University, Chico
(14,862)
Places Rated Score: 364
Places Rated Rank: 147

Cincinnati, OH–KY–IN
Elementary and Secondary
Public (81.4%): 56 districts, 390 schools,
222,282 pupils
Private (18.6%): 168 schools, 50,914
pupils
Colleges and Universities
Two-year: 3 public; 12,408 students
Four-year and beyond:
Public
Northern Kentucky University (8,648)
University of Cincinnati (36,194)
Private
Art Academy of Cincinnati (263)
College of Mount Saint Joseph (2,005)
God's Bible School and College (236)
Thomas More College (1,117)
Union Experimenting College and
University (903)
Xavier University (6,265)
CMSA Access: Cincinnati–Hamilton,
OH–KY–IN
Places Rated Score: 1,274
Places Rated Rank: 34

Clarksville–Hopkinsville, TN–KY
Elementary and Secondary
Public (85.6%): 2 districts, 37 schools,
25,956 pupils
Private (14.4%): 12 schools, 4,357 pupils
Colleges and Universities
Two-year: 1 public; 1,068 students
Four-year and beyond:
Public
Austin Peay State University (4,984)
Places Rated Score: 110
Places Rated Rank: 245

Cleveland, OH
Elementary and Secondary
Public (79.7%): 56 districts, 457 schools,
263,827 pupils
Private (20.3%): 202 schools, 67,169
pupils
Colleges and Universities
Two-year: 3 public; 32,094 students
Four-year and beyond:
Public
Cleveland State University (17,951)
Private
Baldwin–Wallace College (4,308)
Case Western Reserve University
(8,308)
Cleveland College of Jewish Stdies
(707)
Cleveland Institute of Art (562)
Cleveland Institute of Music (338)
Dyke College (1,300)
John Carroll University (3,488)
Lake Erie College (546)
Notre Dame College (804)
Ohio College of Podiatric Medicine
(562)
Ursuline College (1,514)
CMSA Access: Cleveland–Akron–Lorain,
OH
Places Rated Score: 1,237
Places Rated Rank: 36

Colorado Springs, CO
Elementary and Secondary
Public (94.8%): 15 districts, 131 schools,
70,823 pupils

Private (5.2%): 20 schools, 3,912 pupils
Colleges and Universities
Two-year: 1 public; 1 private; 5,435
students
Four-year and beyond:
Federal
United States Air Force Academy
(4,479)
Public
University of Colorado, Colorado
Springs (5,702)
Private
Colorado College (1,988)
Places Rated Score: 298
Places Rated Rank: 159

Columbia, MO
Elementary and Secondary
Public (95.3%): 7 districts, 33 schools,
16,116 pupils
Private (4.7%): 6 schools, 786 pupils
Colleges and Universities
Four-year and beyond:
Public
University of Missouri, Columbia
(22,727)
Private
Columbia College (3,024)
Stephens College (1,123)
Places Rated Score: 537
Places Rated Rank: 117

Columbia, SC
Elementary and Secondary
Public (91.8%): 7 districts, 111 schools,
75,891 pupils
Private (8.2%): 31 schools, 6,797 pupils
Colleges and Universities
Two-year: 1 public; 5,050 students
Four-year and beyond:
Public
University of South Carolina (22,965)
Private
Allen University (233)
Benedict College (1,469)
Columbia Bible College and Seminary
(866)
Columbia College (1,194)
Places Rated Score: 585
Places Rated Rank: 106

Columbus, GA–AL
Elementary and Secondary
Public (90.8%): 4 districts, 83 schools,
41,359 pupils
Private (9.2%): 25 schools, 4,212 pupils
Colleges and Universities
Two-year: 2 public; 5,326 students
Four-year and beyond:
Public
Columbus College (3,712)
Troy State University (458)
Places Rated Score: 137
Places Rated Rank: 230

★ Columbus, OH
Elementary and Secondary
Public (91.0%): 49 districts, 435 schools,
221,952 pupils
Private (9.0%): 89 schools, 21,891 pupils
Colleges and Universities
Two-year: 2 public; 9,085 students
Four-year and beyond:
Public
Ohio State University (53,880)
Ohio State University, Newark (1,122)
Ohio University, Lancaster (1,718)
Private
Capital University (2,752)

Columbus College of Art and Design
(1,430)
Denison University (2,134)
Franklin University (4,239)
Methodist Theological School of Ohio
(231)
Ohio Dominican College (1,182)
Ohio Wesleyan University (1,429)
Otterbein College (1,958)
Pontifical College Josephinum (208)
Trinity Lutheran Seminary (277)
Places Rated Score: 1,542
Places Rated Rank: 27

Corpus Christi, TX
Elementary and Secondary
Public (94.0%): 21 districts, 133 schools,
77,894 pupils
Private (6.0%): 28 schools, 4,978 pupils
Colleges and Universities
Two-year: 1 public; 8,927 students
Four-year and beyond:
Public
Corpus Christi State University (3,827)
Places Rated Score: 166
Places Rated Rank: 214

Cumberland, MD–WV
Elementary and Secondary
Public (92.5%): 3 districts, 39 schools,
17,499 pupils
Private (7.5%): 5 schools, 1,413 pupils
Colleges and Universities
Two-year: 2 public; 2,536 students
Four-year and beyond:
Public
Frostburg State University (3,725)
Places Rated Score: 100
Places Rated Rank: 253

★ Dallas, TX
Elementary and Secondary
Public (92.5%): 61 districts, 668 schools,
437,144 pupils
Private (7.5%): 153 schools, 35,578 pupils
Colleges and Universities
Two-year: 8 public; 49,237 students
Four-year and beyond:
Public
Texas Woman's University (7,966)
University of North Texas (21,269)
University of Texas Health Science
Center (1,519)
University of Texas (7,324)
Private
Amber University (925)
Baylor College of Dentistry (552)
Criswell Center of Bible Studies (373)
Dallas Baptist University (2,751)
Dallas Theological Seminary (1,196)
Parker College of Chiropractic (277)
Southern Methodist University (9,019)
Southwestern Assemblies of God
College (701)
Southwestern Christian College (251)
University of Dallas (2,540)
CMSA Access: Dallas–Fort Worth, TX
Places Rated Score: 1,726
Places Rated Rank: 22

Danbury, CT
Elementary and Secondary
Public (90.0%): 10 districts, 51 schools,
29,790 pupils
Private (10.0%): 14 schools, 3,300 pupils
Colleges and Universities
Four-year and beyond:

Public
Western Connecticut State University
(5,989)
CMSA Access: New York–Northern
NJ–Long Island, NY–NJ–CT
Places Rated Score: 918
Places Rated Rank: 58

Danville, VA
Elementary and Secondary
Public (93.8%): 2 districts, 40 schools,
19,000 pupils
Private (6.2%): 8 schools, 1,256 pupils
Colleges and Universities
Two-year: 1 public; 1,947 students
Four-year and beyond:
Private
Averett College (972)
Places Rated Score: 39
Places Rated Rank: 309

Davenport–Rock Island–Moline, IA–IL
Elementary and Secondary
Public (90.2%): 25 districts, 137 schools,
63,493 pupils
Private (9.8%): 32 schools, 6,935 pupils
Colleges and Universities
Two-year: 3 public; 11,065 students
Four-year and beyond:
Private
Augustana College (2,081)
Marycrest College (1,651)
Palmer College of Chiropractic (1,588)
Saint Ambrose University (2,198)
Places Rated Score: 261
Places Rated Rank: 178

Dayton–Springfield, OH
Elementary and Secondary
Public (89.7%): 40 districts, 277 schools,
162,539 pupils
Private (10.3%): 60 schools, 18,674 pupils
Colleges and Universities
Two-year: 3 public; 1 private; 21,094
students
Four-year and beyond:
Public
Central State University (2,680)
Wright State University (16,075)
Private
Antioch College (3,105)
Cedarville College (1,821)
United Theological Seminary (308)
University of Dayton (10,354)
Wilberforce University (739)
Wittenberg University (2,178)
Places Rated Score: 956
Places Rated Rank: 54

Daytona Beach, FL
Elementary and Secondary
Public (90.3%): 2 districts, 52 schools,
40,038 pupils
Private (9.7%): 28 schools, 4,292 pupils
Colleges and Universities
Two-year: 1 public; 8,169 students
Four-year and beyond:
Private
Bethune Cookman College (1,815)
Embry–Riddle Aeronautical University
(11,052)
Stetson University (2,856)
Places Rated Score: 396
Places Rated Rank: 135

Decatur, AL
Elementary and Secondary
Public (96.1%): 4 districts, 48 schools, 25,504 pupils
Private (3.9%): 7 schools, 1,026 pupils
Colleges and Universities
Two-year: 1 public; 6,341 students
Places Rated Score: 63
Places Rated Rank: 281

Decatur, IL
Elementary and Secondary
Public (90.0%): 9 districts, 54 schools, 22,658 pupils
Private (10.0%): 12 schools, 2,514 pupils
Colleges and Universities
Two-year: 1 public; 3,249 students
Four-year and beyond:
Private
    Millikin University (1,562)
Places Rated Score: 64
Places Rated Rank: 280

Denver, CO
Elementary and Secondary
Public (92.2%): 17 districts, 463 schools, 272,443 pupils
Private (7.8%): 128 schools, 23,149 pupils
Colleges and Universities
Two-year: 5 public; 22,904 students
Four-year and beyond:
Public
    Colorado School of Mines (2,561)
    Metropolitan State College (15,021)
    University of Colorado Health Sciences Center (1,404)
    University of Colorado, Denver (10,618)
Private
    Colorado Christian College (413)
    Denver Conservative Baptist Seminary (245)
    Iliff School of Theology (318)
    Loretto Heights College (715)
    Regis College (1,440)
    University of Denver (6,870)
CMSA Access: Denver–Boulder, CO
Places Rated Score: 1,069
Places Rated Rank: 47

Des Moines, IA
Elementary and Secondary
Public (90.7%): 23 districts, 152 schools, 65,328 pupils
Private (9.3%): 25 schools, 6,720 pupils
Colleges and Universities
Two-year: 1 public; 8,667 students
Four-year and beyond:
Private
    Drake University (6,207)
    Faith Baptist Bible College and Seminary (319)
    Grand View College (1,239)
    Simpson College (1,395)
    University of Osteopathic Medicine (1,090)
Places Rated Score: 292
Places Rated Rank: 163

★ Detroit, MI
Elementary and Secondary
Public (87.1%): 115 districts, 231 schools, 737,687 pupils
Private (12.9%): 405 schools, 109,390 pupils
Colleges and Universities
Two-year: 8 public, 1 private; 110,139 students

Four-year and beyond:
Public
    Oakland University (12,707)
    University of Michigan, Dearborn (7,120)
    Wayne State University (28,764)
Private
    Center for Creative Studies, College of Art (1,159)
    Detroit College of Business (1,646)
    Detroit College of Law (755)
    Lawrence Institute of Technology (6,142)
    Madonna College (3,934)
    Marygrove College (1,216)
    Mercy College of Detroit (2,329)
    Michigan Christian College (278)
    Sacred Heart Seminary College (469)
    Saint Mary's College (277)
    University of Detroit (6,165)
    William Tyndale College (379)
CMSA Access: Detroit–Ann Arbor, MI
Places Rated Score: 2,724
Places Rated Rank: 9

Dothan, AL
Elementary and Secondary
Public (88.1%): 5 districts, 41 schools, 23,570 pupils
Private (11.9%): 12 schools, 3,184 pupils
Colleges and Universities
Two-year: 2 public; 3,498 students
Four-year and beyond:
Public
    Troy State University, Dothan (1,759)
Places Rated Score: 70
Places Rated Rank: 277

Dubuque, IA
Elementary and Secondary
Public (66.6%): 2 districts, 29 schools, 13,076 pupils
Private (33.4%): 22 schools, 6,559 pupils
Colleges and Universities
Four-year and beyond:
Private
    Clarke College (803)
    Loras College (1,985)
    Wartburg Theological Seminary (231)
Places Rated Score: 60
Places Rated Rank: 285

Duluth, MN–WI
Elementary and Secondary
Public (94.7%): 21 districts, 100 schools, 42,778 pupils
Private (5.3%): 19 schools, 2,389 pupils
Colleges and Universities
Two-year: 3 public; 2,784 students
Four-year and beyond:
Public
    University of Minnesota, Duluth (10,830)
    University of Wisconsin, Superior (2,307)
Private
    College of Saint Scholastica (1,453)
Places Rated Score: 320
Places Rated Rank: 151

Eau Claire, WI
Elementary and Secondary
Public (87.0%): 11 districts, 54 schools, 21,990 pupils
Private (13.0%): 30 schools, 3,300 pupils
Colleges and Universities
Two-year: 1 public; 3,732 students

Four-year and beyond:
Public
    University of Wisconsin, Eau Claire (11,103)
Places Rated Score: 259
Places Rated Rank: 179

El Paso, TX
Elementary and Secondary
Public (95.4%): 10 districts, 149 schools, 132,731 pupils
Private (4.6%): 31 schools, 6,373 pupils
Colleges and Universities
Two-year: 1 public; 13,827 students
Four-year and beyond:
Public
    University of Texas, El Paso (13,753)
Places Rated Score: 413
Places Rated Rank: 130

Elkhart–Goshen, IN
Elementary and Secondary
Public (92.3%): 7 districts, 56 schools, 27,378 pupils
Private (7.7%): 21 schools, 2,283 pupils
Colleges and Universities
Four-year and beyond:
Private
    Goshen College (1,068)
Places Rated Score: 21
Places Rated Rank: 328

Elmira, NY
Elementary and Secondary
Public (89.0%): 3 districts, 22 schools, 13,808 pupils
Private (11.0%): 9 schools, 1,701 pupils
Colleges and Universities
Four-year and beyond:
Private
    Elmira College (1,975)
Places Rated Score: 40
Places Rated Rank: 306

Enid, OK
Elementary and Secondary
Public (95.5%): 10 districts, 33 schools, 10,733 pupils
Private (4.5%): 6 schools, 506 pupils
Colleges and Universities
Four-year and beyond:
Private
    Phillips University (1,044)
Places Rated Score: 21
Places Rated Rank: 328

Erie, PA
Elementary and Secondary
Public (79.1%): 13 districts, 79 schools, 42,251 pupils
Private (20.9%): 46 schools, 11,184 pupils
Colleges and Universities
Four-year and beyond:
Public
    Edinboro University of Pennsylvania (6,014)
    Pennsylvania State University, Behrend College (2,378)
Private
    Gannon University (3,952)
    Mercyhurst College (1,839)
    Villa Maria College (505)
Places Rated Score: 294
Places Rated Rank: 161

Eugene–Springfield, OR
Elementary and Secondary
Public (94.9%): 18 districts, 112 schools, 42,074 pupils

Private (5.1%): 18 schools, 2,247 pupils
Colleges and Universities
Two-year: 1 public; 6,800 students
Four-year and beyond:
Public
University of Oregon (17,142)
Private
Northwest Christian College (257)
Places Rated Score: 416
Places Rated Rank: 128

Evansville, IN–KY
Elementary and Secondary
Public (86.7%): 6 districts, 78 schools,
44,373 pupils
Private (13.3%): 28 schools, 6,794 pupils
Colleges and Universities
Two-year: 2 public; 2,882 students
Four-year and beyond:
Public
University of Southern Indiana (4,333)
Private
University of Evansville (3,519)
Places Rated Score: 186
Places Rated Rank: 208

Fall River, MA–RI
Elementary and Secondary
Public (86.5%): 6 districts, 59 schools,
22,918 pupils
Private (13.5%): 16 schools, 3,580 pupils
Colleges and Universities
Two-year: 1 public; 4,710 students
CMSA Access: Providence–Pawtucket–
Fall River, RI–MA
Places Rated Score: 140
Places Rated Rank: 227

Fargo–Moorhead, ND–MN
Elementary and Secondary
Public (91.7%): 19 districts, 58 schools,
24,037 pupils
Private (8.3%): 12 schools, 2,172 pupils
Colleges and Universities
Four-year and beyond:
Public
Moorhead State University (7,274)
North Dakota State University (10,422)
Private
Concordia College, Moorhead (2,525)
Places Rated Score: 404
Places Rated Rank: 132

Fayetteville, NC
Elementary and Secondary
Public (95.9%): 2 districts, 69 schools,
44,216 pupils
Private (4.1%): 10 schools, 1,879 pupils
Colleges and Universities
Two-year: 1 public; 6,284 students
Four-year and beyond:
Public
Fayetteville State University (2,921)
Private
Methodist College (1,360)
Places Rated Score: 148
Places Rated Rank: 223

Fayetteville–Springdale, AR
Elementary and Secondary
Public (96.5%): 9 districts, 39 schools,
21,147 pupils
Private (3.5%): 7 schools, 778 pupils
Colleges and Universities
Four-year and beyond:
Public
University of Arkansas, Fayetteville
(14,452)
Places Rated Score: 289
Places Rated Rank: 165

Fitchburg–Leominster, MA
Elementary and Secondary
Public (81.7%): 4 districts, 27 schools,
14,802 pupils
Private (18.3%): 12 schools, 3,315 pupils
Colleges and Universities
Four-year and beyond:
Public
Fitchburg State College (6,299)
Places Rated Score: 126
Places Rated Rank: 236

Flint, MI
Elementary and Secondary
Public (92.8%): 22 districts, 153 schools,
89,853 pupils
Private (7.2%): 29 schools, 6,967 pupils
Colleges and Universities
Two-year: 1 public; 10,364 students
Four-year and beyond:
Public
University of Michigan, Flint (6,047)
Private
Baker College (4,042)
GM Engineering and Management
Institute (3,639)
Places Rated Score: 378
Places Rated Rank: 139

Florence, AL
Elementary and Secondary
Public (93.9%): 6 districts, 51 schools,
23,824 pupils
Private (6.1%): 6 schools, 1,552 pupils
Colleges and Universities
Two-year: 1 public; 1 private; 911
students
Four-year and beyond:
Public
University of North Alabama (4,977)
Places Rated Score: 109
Places Rated Rank: 246

Florence, SC
Elementary and Secondary
Public (91.0%): 5 districts, 38 schools,
23,932 pupils
Private (9.0%): 14 schools, 2,353 pupils
Colleges and Universities
Two-year: 1 public; 1,900 students
Four-year and beyond:
Public
Francis Marion College (3,673)
Places Rated Score: 92
Places Rated Rank: 259

Fort Collins–Loveland, CO
Elementary and Secondary
Public (95.4%): 3 districts, 64 schools,
29,835 pupils
Private (4.6%): 12 schools, 1,440 pupils
Colleges and Universities
Four-year and beyond:
Public
Colorado State University (18,856)
Places Rated Score: 377
Places Rated Rank: 140

**Fort Lauderdale–Hollywood–
Pompano Beach, FL**
Elementary and Secondary
Public (83.1%): 2 districts, 161 schools,
135,984 pupils
Private (16.9%): 99 schools, 27,589 pupils
Colleges and Universities
Two-year: 1 public; 18,373 students
Four-year and beyond:

Private
Nova University (7,180)
CMSA Access: Miami–Fort Lauderdale,
FL
Places Rated Score: 445
Places Rated Rank: 125

Fort Myers–Cape Coral, FL
Elementary and Secondary
Public (91.0%): 2 districts, 53 schools,
37,680 pupils
Private (9.0%): 17 schools, 3,742 pupils
Colleges and Universities
Two-year: 1 public; 6,653 students
Places Rated Score: 67
Places Rated Rank: 279

Fort Pierce, FL
Elementary and Secondary
Public (87.3%): 3 districts, 34 schools,
27,384 pupils
Private (12.7%): 21 schools, 3,993 pupils
Colleges and Universities
Two-year: 1 public; 10,063 students
Four-year and beyond:
Private
Hobe Sound Bible College (207)
Places Rated Score: 105
Places Rated Rank: 248

Fort Smith, AR–OK
Elementary and Secondary
Public (96.3%): 24 districts, 79 schools,
32,359 pupils
Private (3.7%): 9 schools, 1,253 pupils
Colleges and Universities
Two-year: 1 public; 3,692 students
Places Rated Score: 37
Places Rated Rank: 312

Fort Walton Beach, FL
Elementary and Secondary
Public (96.6%): 2 districts, 34 schools,
24,023 pupils
Private (3.4%): 5 schools, 842 pupils
Colleges and Universities
Two-year: 1 public; 3,606 students
Places Rated Score: 36
Places Rated Rank: 315

Fort Wayne, IN
Elementary and Secondary
Public (83.5%): 16 districts, 107 schools,
61,109 pupils
Private (16.5%): 50 schools, 12,111 pupils
Colleges and Universities
Two-year: 1 public; 2,665 students
Four-year and beyond:
Public
Indiana University–Purdue University,
Fort Wayne (10,191)
Private
Concordia Theological Seminary (453)
Fort Wayne Bible College (359)
Indiana Institute of Technology (449)
Saint Francis College (1,022)
Places Rated Score: 276
Places Rated Rank: 173

Fort Worth–Arlington, TX
Elementary and Secondary
Public (93.1%): 37 districts, 325 schools,
222,134 pupils
Private (6.9%): 64 schools, 16,495 pupils
Colleges and Universities
Two-year: 2 public; 26,123 students
Four-year and beyond:

Public
    Texas College Osteopathic Medicine
    (376)
    University of Texas, Arlington (23,247)
Private
    Arlington Baptist College (224)
    Southwestern Adventist College (795)
    Southwestern Baptist Theological
    Seminary (4,001)
    Texas Christian University (6,916)
    Texas Wesleyan College (1,495)
CMSA Access: Dallas–Fort Worth, TX
Places Rated Score: 1,165
Places Rated Rank: 39

Fresno, CA
Elementary and Secondary
Public (95.8%): 48 districts, 226 schools,
    122,800 pupils
Private (4.2%): 34 schools, 5,395 pupils
Colleges and Universities
Two-year: 3 public; 1 private; 19,914
    students
Four-year and beyond:
Public
    California State University, Fresno
    (17,756)
Private
    Fresno Pacific College (1,087)
    West Coast Christian College (257)
Places Rated Score: 581
Places Rated Rank: 109

Gadsden, AL
Elementary and Secondary
Public (93.7%): 3 districts, 40 schools,
    19,025 pupils
Private (6.3%): 8 schools, 1,287 pupils
Colleges and Universities
Two-year: 1 public; 3,049 students
Four-year and beyond:
Public
    University of Alabama, Gadsden (300)
Places Rated Score: 36
Places Rated Rank: 315

Gainesville, FL
Elementary and Secondary
Public (92.6%): 3 districts, 42 schools,
    27,444 pupils
Private (7.4%): 21 schools, 2,206 pupils
Colleges and Universities
Two-year: 1 public; 8,836 students
Four-year and beyond:
Public
    University of Florida (35,172)
Places Rated Score: 792
Places Rated Rank: 73

Galveston–Texas City, TX
Elementary and Secondary
Public (96.4%): 11 districts, 71 schools,
    54,541 pupils
Private (3.6%): 12 schools, 2,021 pupils
Colleges and Universities
Two-year: 2 public; 5,166 students
Four-year and beyond:
Public
    Texas A & M University, Galveston
    (524)
    University of Texas Medical Branch,
    Galveston (1,581)
CMSA Access: Houston–
    Galveston–Brazoria, TX
Places Rated Score: 306
Places Rated Rank: 157

Gary–Hammond, IN
Elementary and Secondary
Public (89.0%): 25 districts, 193 schools,
    116,325 pupils
Private (11.0%): 56 schools, 14,322 pupils
Colleges and Universities
Two-year: 1 public; 3,126 students
Four-year and beyond:
Public
    Indiana University Northwest (4,622)
    Purdue University, Calumet (7,211)
Private
    Calumet College of Saint Joseph (935)
    Valparaiso University (3,821)
CMSA Access: Chicago–Gary–Lake
    County, IL–IN–WI
Places Rated Score: 878
Places Rated Rank: 61

Glens Falls, NY
Elementary and Secondary
Public (95.9%): 21 districts, 44 schools,
    21,231 pupils
Private (4.1%): 9 schools, 898 pupils
Colleges and Universities
Two-year: 1 public; 2,783 students
Places Rated Score: 28
Places Rated Rank: 323

Grand Forks, ND
Elementary and Secondary
Public (93.2%): 9 districts, 27 schools,
    11,053 pupils
Private (6.8%): 6 schools, 810 pupils
Colleges and Universities
Four-year and beyond:
Public
    University of North Dakota (10,764)
Places Rated Score: 215
Places Rated Rank: 199

Grand Rapids, MI
Elementary and Secondary
Public (78.5%): 28 districts, 239 schools,
    102,532 pupils
Private (21.5%): 96 schools, 28,107 pupils
Colleges and Universities
Two-year: 1 public; 10,646 students
Four-year and beyond:
Public
    Grand Valley State University (8,361)
Private
    Aquinas College (2,648)
    Calvin College (4,146)
    Calvin Theological Seminary (245)
    Davenport College (3,606)
    Grand Rapids Baptist College and
    Seminary (877)
    Hope College (2,545)
    Jordan College (2,025)
    Kendall College of Art and Design
    (738)
Places Rated Score: 610
Places Rated Rank: 104

Great Falls, MT
Elementary and Secondary
Public (94.7%): 14 districts, 30 schools,
    13,667 pupils
Private (5.3%): 8 schools, 759 pupils
Colleges and Universities
Four-year and beyond:
Private
    College of Great Falls (1,151)
Places Rated Score: 23
Places Rated Rank: 327

Greeley, CO
Elementary and Secondary
Public (98.1%): 13 districts, 53 schools,
    22,080 pupils
Private (1.9%): 6 schools, 433 pupils
Colleges and Universities
Two-year: 1 public; 7,037 students
Four-year and beyond:
Public
    University of Northern Colorado
    (10,800)
Places Rated Score: 286
Places Rated Rank: 167

Green Bay, WI
Elementary and Secondary
Public (80.1%): 9 districts, 59 schools,
    30,394 pupils
Private (19.9%): 42 schools, 7,555 pupils
Colleges and Universities
Two-year: 1 public; 5,476 students
Four-year and beyond:
Public
    University of Wisconsin, Green Bay
    (4,978)
Private
    Saint Norbert College (1,708)
Places Rated Score: 188
Places Rated Rank: 207

Greensboro–Winston-Salem–High Point, NC
Elementary and Secondary
Public (93.3%): 16 districts, 249 schools,
    149,146 pupils
Private (6.7%): 53 schools, 10,696 pupils
Colleges and Universities
Two-year: 4 public; 13,389 students
Four-year and beyond:
Public
    North Carolina A & T State University
    (5,966)
    North Carolina School of the Arts (468)
    University of North Carolina,
    Greensboro (10,696)
    Winston-Salem State University (2,590)
Private
    Bennett College (576)
    Greensboro College (553)
    Guilford College (1,702)
    High Point College (1,392)
    Piedmont Bible College (268)
    Salem College (737)
    Wake Forest University (5,054)
Places Rated Score: 734
Places Rated Rank: 81

Greenville–Spartanburg, SC
Elementary and Secondary
Public (93.1%): 9 districts, 190 schools,
    109,254 pupils
Private (6.9%): 38 schools, 8,068 pupils
Colleges and Universities
Two-year: 2 public; 2 private; 8,979
    students
Four-year and beyond:
Public
    Clemson University (13,062)
    University of South Carolina,
    Spartanburg (2,956)
Private
    Bob Jones University (4,196)
    Central Wesleyan College (450)
    Converse College (1,142)
    Furman University (2,964)
    Sherman College of Straight
    Chiropractic (262)
    Wofford College (1,095)
Places Rated Score: 612
Places Rated Rank: 102

Hagerstown, MD
Elementary and Secondary
Public (89.2%): 2 districts, 42 schools, 17,474 pupils
Private (10.8%): 12 schools, 2,115 pupils
Colleges and Universities
Two-year: 1 public; 2,512 students
Places Rated Score: 25
Places Rated Rank: 325

Hamilton–Middletown, OH
Elementary and Secondary
Public (89.6%): 9 districts, 72 schools, 47,582 pupils
Private (10.4%): 18 schools, 5,512 pupils
Colleges and Universities
Two-year: 1 public; 1,942 students
Four-year and beyond:
Public
Miami University, Middletown (1,676)
Miami University, Oxford (15,995)
CMSA Access: Cincinnati–Hamilton, OH–KY–IN
Places Rated Score: 496
Places Rated Rank: 121

Harrisburg–Lebanon–Carlisle, PA
Elementary and Secondary
Public (89.2%): 31 districts, 182 schools, 91,917 pupils
Private (10.8%): 62 schools, 11,161 pupils
Colleges and Universities
Two-year: 1 public; 1 private; 6,505 students
Four-year and beyond:
Public
Pennsylvania State University, Harrisburg (2,888)
Pennsylvania State University, Hershey Medical Center (705)
Shippensburg University of Pennsylvania (6,358)
Private
Dickinson College (1,943)
Dickinson School of Law (557)
Lebanon Valley College (1,224)
Messiah College (1,916)
Places Rated Score: 377
Places Rated Rank: 140

Hartford, CT
Elementary and Secondary
Public (88.7%): 37 districts, 225 schools, 112,916 pupils
Private (11.3%): 61 schools, 14,361 pupils
Colleges and Universities
Two-year: 5 public; 1 private; 15,396 students
Four-year and beyond:
Public
Charter Oak College (713)
University of Connecticut Health Center (504)
Private
Saint Joseph College (1,573)
The Hartford Graduate Center (2,361)
Trinity College (2,105)
University of Hartford (7,119)
CMSA Access: Hartford–New Britain–Middletown, CT
Places Rated Score: 951
Places Rated Rank: 56

Hickory, NC
Elementary and Secondary
Public (96.9%): 7 districts, 72 schools, 37,293 pupils
Private (3.1%): 9 schools, 1,180 pupils

Colleges and Universities
Two-year: 2 public; 4,975 students
Four-year and beyond:
Private
Lenoir–Rhyne College (1,539)
Places Rated Score: 81
Places Rated Rank: 268

Honolulu, HI
Elementary and Secondary
Public (79.9%): 4 districts, 161 schools, 120,333 pupils
Private (20.1%): 89 schools, 30,728 pupils
Colleges and Universities
Two-year: 4 public; 16,804 students
Four-year and beyond:
Public
University of Hawaii, Manoa (18,918)
West Oahu College (480)
Private
Brigham Young University Hawaii Campus (1,982)
Chaminade University of Honolulu (2,650)
Hawaii Loa College (400)
Hawaii Pacific College (4,071)
Places Rated Score: 738
Places Rated Rank: 79

Houma–Thibodaux, LA
Elementary and Secondary
Public (88.5%): 2 districts, 74 schools, 38,027 pupils
Private (11.5%): 15 schools, 4,932 pupils
Colleges and Universities
Four-year and beyond:
Public
Nicholls State University (6,950)
Places Rated Score: 139
Places Rated Rank: 229

★ Houston, TX
Elementary and Secondary
Public (94.1%): 45 districts, 727 schools, 599,119 pupils
Private (5.9%): 171 schools, 37,350 pupils
Colleges and Universities
Two-year: 7 public; 69,952 students
Four-year and beyond:
Public
Prairie View Agricultural and Mechanical University (4,499)
Texas Southern University (7,246)
University of Houston, Clear Lake (6,691)
University of Houston, Downtown (7,255)
University of Houston, University Park (28,164)
University of Texas Health Science Center (2,664)
Private
Baylor College of Medicine (921)
Houston Baptist University (2,621)
Rice University (3,852)
South Texas College of Law (1,337)
Texas Chiropractic College (376)
University of Saint Thomas (1,678)
CMSA Access: Houston–Galveston–Brazoria, TX
Places Rated Score: 2,062
Places Rated Rank: 16

Huntington–Ashland, WV–KY–OH
Elementary and Secondary
Public (97.4%): 16 districts, 164 schools, 63,674 pupils
Private (2.6%): 13 schools, 1,710 pupils

Colleges and Universities
Two-year: 1 public; 1,991 students
Four-year and beyond:
Public
Marshall University (11,425)
Ohio University, Ironton (650)
Private
Kentucky Christian College (415)
Places Rated Score: 270
Places Rated Rank: 176

Huntsville, AL
Elementary and Secondary
Public (91.7%): 2 districts, 58 schools, 37,570 pupils
Private (8.3%): 15 schools, 3,400 pupils
Colleges and Universities
Two-year: 1 public, 1 private; 933 students
Four-year and beyond:
Public
Alabama A & M (3,928)
University of Alabama, Huntsville (6,161)
Private
Oakwood College (947)
Places Rated Score: 230
Places Rated Rank: 189

Indianapolis, IN
Elementary and Secondary
Public (90.1%): 44 districts, 337 schools, 204,383 pupils
Private (9.9%): 97 schools, 22,488 pupils
Colleges and Universities
Two-year: 1 public; 4,155 students
Four-year and beyond:
Public
Indiana University–Purdue University, Indianapolis (23,468)
Private
Butler University (3,661)
Christian Theological Seminary (270)
Franklin College of Indiana (699)
Marian College (1,496)
University of Indianapolis (3,013)
Places Rated Score: 694
Places Rated Rank: 87

Iowa City, IA
Elementary and Secondary
Public (94.3%): 4 districts, 26 schools, 10,389 pupils
Private (5.7%): 3 schools, 624 pupils
Colleges and Universities
Four-year and beyond:
Public
University of Iowa (30,670)
Places Rated Score: 613
Places Rated Rank: 101

Jackson, MI
Elementary and Secondary
Public (88.4%): 13 districts, 52 schools, 24,617 pupils
Private (11.6%): 14 schools, 3,227 pupils
Colleges and Universities
Two-year: 1 public; 6,697 students
Four-year and beyond:
Private
Spring Arbor College (1,217)
Places Rated Score: 91
Places Rated Rank: 260

Jackson, MS
Elementary and Secondary
Public (84.2%): 10 districts, 108 schools, 66,166 pupils
Private (15.8%): 37 schools, 12,378 pupils

Colleges and Universities
Two-year: 4 public; 8,728 students
Four-year and beyond:
Public
  Jackson State University (6,319)
  University of Mississippi Medical
    Center (1,508)
Private
  Belhaven College (608)
  Millsaps College (1,358)
  Mississippi College (2,925)
  Reformed Theological Seminary (284)
  Tougaloo College (902)
Places Rated Score: 365
Places Rated Rank: 146

Jackson, TN
Elementary and Secondary
Public (91.1%): 2 districts, 27 schools,
  14,507 pupils
Private (8.9%): 8 schools, 1,411 pupils
Colleges and Universities
Two-year: 1 public; 2,239 students
Four-year and beyond:
Private
  Lambuth College (616)
  Lane College (531)
  Union University (1,546)
Places Rated Score: 76
Places Rated Rank: 273

Jacksonville, FL
Elementary and Secondary
Public (88.6%): 5 districts, 193 schools,
  141,857 pupils
Private (11.4%): 74 schools, 18,293 pupils
Colleges and Universities
Two-year: 1 public; 15,072 students
Four-year and beyond:
Public
  University of North Florida (6,645)
Private
  Edward Waters College (689)
  Flagler College (1,126)
  Jacksonville University (2,214)
  Jones College, Jacksonville (1,322)
Places Rated Score: 391
Places Rated Rank: 136

Jacksonville, NC
Elementary and Secondary
Public (95.5%): 2 districts, 24 schools,
  16,667 pupils
Private (4.5%): 4 schools, 786 pupils
Colleges and Universities
Two-year: 1 public; 3,406 students
Places Rated Score: 34
Places Rated Rank: 318

Janesville–Beloit, WI
Elementary and Secondary
Public (92.0%): 9 districts, 55 schools,
  25,168 pupils
Private (8.0%): 18 schools, 2,203 pupils
Colleges and Universities
Two-year: 1 public; 1,789 students
Four-year and beyond:
Private
  Beloit College (1,084)
Places Rated Score: 220
Places Rated Rank: 196

Jersey City, NJ
Elementary and Secondary
Public (77.6%): 14 districts, 101 schools,
  70,681 pupils
Private (22.4%): 67 schools, 20,406 pupils

Colleges and Universities
Two-year: 1 public; 3,175 students
Four-year and beyond:
Public
  Jersey City State College (7,037)
Private
  Saint Peter's College (3,575)
  Stevens Institute of Technology (3,260)
CMSA Access: New York–Northern
NJ–Long Island, NY–NJ–CT
Places Rated Score: 1,303
Places Rated Rank: 33

Johnson City–Kingsport–Bristol, TN–VA
Elementary and Secondary
Public (96.8%): 13 districts, 163 schools,
  75,646 pupils
Private (3.2%): 17 schools, 2,502 pupils
Colleges and Universities
Two-year: 2 public; 3,556 students
Four-year and beyond:
Public
  East Tennessee State University (9,969)
Private
  Emory and Henry College (769)
  King College (523)
  Milligan College (606)
  Virginia Intermont College (393)
Places Rated Score: 281
Places Rated Rank: 169

Johnstown, PA
Elementary and Secondary
Public (87.3%): 23 districts, 77 schools,
  37,807 pupils
Private (12.7%): 30 schools, 5,489 pupils
Colleges and Universities
Four-year and beyond:
Public
  University of Pittsburgh, Johnstown
    (3,215)
Private
  Saint Francis College (1,746)
Places Rated Score: 99
Places Rated Rank: 255

Joliet, IL
Elementary and Secondary
Public (87.8%): 43 districts, 133 schools,
  66,893 pupils
Private (12.2%): 41 schools, 9,294 pupils
Colleges and Universities
Two-year: 1 public; 9,303 students
Four-year and beyond:
Public
  Governors State University (5,568)
Private
  College of Saint Francis (3,988)
  Lewis University (3,262)
CMSA Access:Chicago–Gary–Lake
County, IL–IN–WI
Places Rated Score: 881
Places Rated Rank: 60

Joplin, MO
Elementary and Secondary
Public (96.1%): 13 districts, 64 schools,
  24,313 pupils
Private (3.9%): 9 schools, 987 pupils
Colleges and Universities
Two-year: 1 public; 1,351 students
Four-year and beyond:
Public
  Missouri Southern State College (4,610)
Private
  Ozark Christian College (519)
Places Rated Score: 116
Places Rated Rank: 242

Kalamazoo, MI
Elementary and Secondary
Public (88.1%): 10 districts, 71 schools,
  32,319 pupils
Private (11.9%): 20 schools, 4,370 pupils
Colleges and Universities
Two-year: 1 public; 1 private; 8,747
  students
Four-year and beyond:
Public
  Western Michigan University (21,747)
Private
  Kalamazoo College (1,103)
  Nazareth College (885)
Places Rated Score: 562
Places Rated Rank: 112

Kankakee, IL
Elementary and Secondary
Public (87.7%): 14 districts, 44 schools,
  17,608 pupils
Private (12.3%): 14 schools, 2,470 pupils
Colleges and Universities
Two-year: 1 public; 3,431 students
Four-year and beyond:
Private
  Olivet Nazarene University (1,713)
Places Rated Score: 61
Places Rated Rank: 278

Kansas City, MO–KS
Elementary and Secondary
Public (88.7%): 66 districts, 516 schools,
  258,836 pupils
Private (11.3%): 136 schools, 32,869
  pupils
Colleges and Universities
Two-year: 5 public, 2 private; 27,654
  students
Four-year and beyond:
Public
  University of Kansas Medical Center
    (2,435)
  University of Missouri, Kansas City
    (11,583)
Private
  Avila College (1,437)
  Calvary Bible College (345)
  Cleveland Chiropractic College (375)
  Kansas City Art Institute (543)
  Mid-America Nazarene College (1,008)
  Nazarene Theological Seminary (462)
  Ottawa University (474)
  Park College (4,006)
  Rockhurst College (3,198)
  Saint Mary College (867)
  Saint Paul School of Theology (315)
  University of Health Sciences (531)
  William Jewell College (2,061)
Places Rated Score: 869
Places Rated Rank: 63

Kenosha, WI
Elementary and Secondary
Public (86.4%): 13 districts, 42 schools,
  20,500 pupils
Private (13.6%): 18 schools, 3,229 pupils
Colleges and Universities
Two-year: 1 public; 12,000 students
Four-year and beyond:
Public
  University of Wisconsin, Parkside
    (5,195)
Private
  Carthage College (1,494)
CMSA Access: Chicago–Gary–Lake
 County, IL–IN–WI
Places Rated Score: 754
Places Rated Rank: 76

Killeen–Temple, TX
Elementary and Secondary
Public (97.8%): 16 districts, 79 schools, 45,881 pupils
Private (2.2%): 7 schools, 1,009 pupils
Colleges and Universities
Two-year: 2 public; 8,305 students
Four-year and beyond:
Private
American Technological University (576)
University of Mary Hardin Baylor (1,287)
Places Rated Score: 120
Places Rated Rank: 240

Knoxville, TN
Elementary and Secondary
Public (95.5%): 12 districts, 184 schools, 98,724 pupils
Private (4.5%): 29 schools, 4,617 pupils
Colleges and Universities
Two-year: 1 public; 2,658 students
Four-year and beyond:
Public
University of Tennessee, Knoxville (25,842)
Private
Carson–Newman College (1,681)
Johnson Bible College (392)
Knoxville College (436)
Maryville College (676)
Places Rated Score: 607
Places Rated Rank: 105

Kokomo, IN
Elementary and Secondary
Public (95.3%): 7 districts, 34 schools, 20,080 pupils
Private (4.7%): 11 schools, 998 pupils
Colleges and Universities
Two-year: 1 public; 1,830 students
Four-year and beyond:
Public
Indiana University, Kokomo (2,857)
Places Rated Score: 75
Places Rated Rank: 274

La Crosse, WI
Elementary and Secondary
Public (79.8%): 5 districts, 29 schools, 13,353 pupils
Private (20.2%): 24 schools, 3,371 pupils
Colleges and Universities
Two-year: 1 public; 2,200 students
Four-year and beyond:
Public
University of Wisconsin, La Crosse (9,659)
Private
Viterbo College (992)
Places Rated Score: 235
Places Rated Rank: 187

Lafayette, LA
Elementary and Secondary
Public (84.7%): 2 districts, 58 schools, 36,783 pupils
Private (15.3%): 23 schools, 6,661 pupils
Colleges and Universities
Four-year and beyond:
Public
University of Southwestern Louisiana (15,510)
Places Rated Score: 310
Places Rated Rank: 154

Lafayette–West Lafayette, IN
Elementary and Secondary
Public (91.7%): 3 districts, 30 schools, 16,520 pupils
Private (8.3%): 9 schools, 1,499 pupils
Colleges and Universities
Two-year: 1 public; 1,528 students
Four-year and beyond:
Public
Purdue University (32,912)
Places Rated Score: 674
Places Rated Rank: 90

Lake Charles, LA
Elementary and Secondary
Public (88.4%): 1 district, 58 schools, 33,245 pupils
Private (11.6%): 18 schools, 4,349 pupils
Colleges and Universities
Four-year and beyond:
Public
McNeese State University (7,340)
Places Rated Score: 147
Places Rated Rank: 224

Lake County, IL
Elementary and Secondary
Public (88.4%): 51 districts, 163 schools, 83,937 pupils
Private (11.6%): 46 schools, 10,972 pupils
Colleges and Universities
Two-year: 1 public; 11,309 students
Four-year and beyond:
Private
Lake Forest College (1,185)
Lake Forest Graduate School of Management (506)
Saint Mary of the Lake, Mundelein Seminary (229)
Trinity College (595)
Trinity Evangelical Divinity School (1,033)
University of Health Sciences, Chicago Medical School (835)
CMSA Access: Chicago–Gary–Lake County, IL–IN–WI
Places Rated Score: 722
Places Rated Rank: 83

Lakeland–Winter Haven, FL
Elementary and Secondary
Public (92.5%): 2 districts, 96 schools, 59,081 pupils
Private (7.5%): 24 schools, 4,784 pupils
Colleges and Universities
Two-year: 1 public; 4,632 students
Four-year and beyond:
Private
Florida Southern College (2,930)
Southeastern College of the Assemblies of God (1,094)
Warner Southern College (292)
Webber College (237)
Places Rated Score: 137
Places Rated Rank: 230

Lancaster, PA
Elementary and Secondary
Public (82.9%): 16 districts, 119 schools, 55,748 pupils
Private (17.1%): 103 schools, 11,507 pupils
Colleges and Universities
Two-year: 1 public; 425 students
Four-year and beyond:
Public
Millersville University of Pennsylvania (7,202)

Private
Elizabethtown College (1,679)
Franklin and Marshall College (2,684)
Lancaster Bible College (377)
Lancaster Theological Seminary (248)
Places Rated Score: 248
Places Rated Rank: 182

Lansing–East Lansing, MI
Elementary and Secondary
Public (92.7%): 27 districts, 162 schools, 75,955 pupils
Private (7.3%): 37 schools, 5,970 pupils
Colleges and Universities
Two-year: 1 public, 1 private; 21,049 students
Four-year and beyond:
Public
Michigan State University (44,088)
Private
Olivet College (731)
Thomas M. Cooley Law School (910)
Places Rated Score: 1,125
Places Rated Rank: 41

Laredo, TX
Elementary and Secondary
Public (91.6%): 5 districts, 43 schools, 31,075 pupils
Private (8.4%): 12 schools, 2,833 pupils
Colleges and Universities
Two-year: 1 public; 4,106 students
Four-year and beyond:
Public
Laredo State University (940)
Places Rated Score: 60
Places Rated Rank: 285

Las Cruces, NM
Elementary and Secondary
Public (97.3%): 3 districts, 42 schools, 26,536 pupils
Private (2.7%): 5 schools, 733 pupils
Colleges and Universities
Two-year: 1 public; 625 students
Four-year and beyond:
Public
New Mexico State University (13,718)
Places Rated Score: 281
Places Rated Rank: 169

Las Vegas, NV
Elementary and Secondary
Public (94.9%): 1 district, 126 schools, 99,913 pupils
Private (5.1%): 25 schools, 5,408 pupils
Colleges and Universities
Two-year: 1 public; 11,069 students
Four-year and beyond:
Public
University of Nevada, Las Vegas (12,847)
Places Rated Score: 368
Places Rated Rank: 144

Lawrence, KS
Elementary and Secondary
Public (96.4%): 3 districts, 27 schools, 9,577 pupils
Private (3.6%): 2 schools, 353 pupils
Colleges and Universities
Two-year: 1 public; 799 students
Four-year and beyond:
Public
University of Kansas (25,822)
Private
Baker University (776)
Places Rated Score: 540
Places Rated Rank: 115

Lawrence–Haverhill, MA–NH
Elementary and Secondary
Public (81.4%): 25 districts, 114 schools,
54,980 pupils
Private (18.6%): 44 schools, 12,544 pupils
Colleges and Universities
Two-year: 1 public, 1 private; 6,175
students
Four-year and beyond:
Private
Bradford College (392)
Merrimack College (3,612)
CMSA Access:
Boston–Lawrence–Salem, MA–NH
Places Rated Score: 628
Places Rated Rank: 98

Lawton, OK
Elementary and Secondary
Public (98.6%): 14 districts, 62 schools,
22,447 pupils
Private (1.4%): 4 schools, 330 pupils
Colleges and Universities
Four-year and beyond:
Public
Cameron University (5,304)
Places Rated Score: 106
Places Rated Rank: 247

Lewiston–Auburn, ME
Elementary and Secondary
Public (90.1%): 5 districts, 28 schools,
12,756 pupils
Private (9.9%): 8 schools, 1,394 pupils
Colleges and Universities
Two-year: 1 public, 1 private; 517
students
Four-year and beyond:
Private
Bates College (1,543)
Places Rated Score: 36
Places Rated Rank: 315

Lexington–Fayette, KY
Elementary and Secondary
Public (91.5%): 7 districts, 93 schools,
52,878 pupils
Private (8.5%): 25 schools, 4,909 pupils
Colleges and Universities
Two-year: 1 public, 1 private; 2,928
students
Four-year and beyond:
Public
University of Kentucky (20,692)
Private
Asbury College (942)
Asbury Theological Seminary (722)
Georgetown College (1,360)
Transylvania University (970)
Places Rated Score: 523
Places Rated Rank: 118

Lima, OH
Elementary and Secondary
Public (90.0%): 15 districts, 63 schools,
29,153 pupils
Private (10.0%): 10 schools, 3,243 pupils
Colleges and Universities
Two-year: 1 public; 1,795 students
Four-year and beyond:
Public
Ohio State University, Lima (1,154)
Private
Bluffton College (596)
Places Rated Score: 53
Places Rated Rank: 295

Lincoln, NE
Elementary and Secondary
Public (87.7%): 16 districts, 57 schools,
28,989 pupils
Private (12.3%): 25 schools, 4,062 pupils
Colleges and Universities
Two-year: 1 public; 5,418 students
Four-year and beyond:
Public
University of Nebraska, Lincoln (23,899)
Private
Nebraska Wesleyan University (1,311)
Union College (631)
Places Rated Score: 571
Places Rated Rank: 110

Little Rock–North Little Rock, AR
Elementary and Secondary
Public (89.6%): 21 districts, 163 schools,
87,652 pupils
Private (10.4%): 45 schools, 10,150 pupils
Colleges and Universities
Two-year: 1 private; 120 students
Four-year and beyond:
Public
University of Arkansas for Medical
Sciences (1,331)
University of Arkansas, Little Rock
(10,294)
University of Central Arkansas (6,425)
Private
Arkansas Baptist College (233)
Central Baptist College (219)
Hendrix College (1,007)
Philander Smith College (572)
Places Rated Score: 403
Places Rated Rank: 133

Longview–Marshall, TX
Elementary and Secondary
Public (97.0%): 14 districts, 73 schools,
34,620 pupils
Private (3.0%): 10 schools, 1,064 pupils
Colleges and Universities
Two-year: 1 public; 3,938 students
Four-year and beyond:
Private
East Texas Baptist University (691)
Letourneau College (763)
Wiley College (417)
Places Rated Score: 77
Places Rated Rank: 271

Lorain–Elyria, OH
Elementary and Secondary
Public (88.7%): 16 districts, 94 schools,
50,305 pupils
Private (11.3%): 21 schools, 6,388 pupils
Colleges and Universities
Two-year: 1 public; 6,013 students
Four-year and beyond:
Private
Oberlin College (2,813)
CMSA Access: Cleveland–Akron–Lorain,
OH
Places Rated Score: 229
Places Rated Rank: 191

★ Los Angeles–Long Beach, CA
Elementary and Secondary
Public (86.0%): 96 districts, 587 schools,
1,271,304 pupils
Private (14.0%): 803 schools, 206,508
pupils
Colleges and Universities
Two-year: 21 public, 4 private; 275,752
students

Four-year and beyond:
Public
California State Polytechnic University,
Pomona (17,679)
California State University, Dominguez
Hills (7,327)
California State University, Long Beach
(33,586)
California State University, Los Angeles
(20,773)
California State University, Northridge
(29,880)
University of California, Los Angeles
(34,418)
Private
Art Center College of Design (1,171)
Biola University (2,758)
California Family Study Center (230)
California Institute of Arts (820)
California Institute of Technology
(1,814)
California School of Professional
Psychology (429)
Claremont Graduate School (1,674)
Claremont McKenna College (829)
Cleveland Chiropractic College, Los
Angeles (467)
College of Osteopathic Medicine of the
Pacific (418)
Columbia College, Hollywood (274)
Fuller Theological Seminary (2,809)
Harvey Mudd College (559)
Life Bible College (459)
Los Angeles College of Chiropractic
(882)
Loyola Marymount University (6,441)
Mount Saint Mary's College (1,272)
Occidental College (1,668)
Otis Art Institute of Parsons School of
Design (746)
Pacific Coast Baptist Bible College
(239)
Pacific Oaks College (520)
Pepperdine University (6,830)
Pitzer College (789)
Pomona College (1,407)
School of Theology, Claremont (224)
Scripps College (600)
Southwestern University School of Law
(945)
The Master's College (537)
University of Laverne (4,528)
University of Southern California
(30,831)
University of West Los Angeles (627)
West Coast University (964)
Whittier College (1,538)
Woodbury University (725)
CMSA Access: Los Angeles–
Anaheim–Riverside, CA
Places Rated Score: 7,509
Places Rated Rank: 2

Louisville, KY–IN
Elementary and Secondary
Public (82.4%): 13 districts, 246 schools,
146,533 pupils
Private (17.6%): 119 schools, 31,306
pupils
Colleges and Universities
Two-year: 2 public, 1 private; 7,306
students
Four-year and beyond:
Public
Indiana University, Southeast (4,648)
University of Louisville (20,145)

Private
Bellarmine College (2,644)
Southern Baptist Theological Seminary (2,245)
Spalding University (1,154)
Places Rated Score: 690
Places Rated Rank: 88

Lowell, MA–NH
Elementary and Secondary
Public (91.1%): 8 districts, 74 schools, 42,755 pupils
Private (8.9%): 22 schools, 4,199 pupils
Colleges and Universities
Four-year and beyond:
Public
University of Lowell (14,695)
CMSA Access:
Boston–Lawrence–Salem, MA–NH
Places Rated Score: 738
Places Rated Rank: 79

Lubbock, TX
Elementary and Secondary
Public (95.8%): 8 districts, 80 schools, 41,483 pupils
Private (4.2%): 10 schools, 1,821 pupils
Colleges and Universities
Four-year and beyond:
Public
Texas Tech University (23,479)
Texas Technical University Health Science Center (775)
Private
Lubbock Christian University (1,041)
Places Rated Score: 506
Places Rated Rank: 120

Lynchburg, VA
Elementary and Secondary
Public (91.2%): 3 districts, 47 schools, 24,273 pupils
Private (8.8%): 8 schools, 2,346 pupils
Colleges and Universities
Two-year: 1 public; 3,862 students
Four-year and beyond:
Private
Liberty University (6,351)
Lynchburg College (2,188)
Sweet Briar College (663)
Places Rated Score: 223
Places Rated Rank: 194

Macon–Warner Robins, GA
Elementary and Secondary
Public (86.2%): 4 districts, 79 schools, 46,895 pupils
Private (13.8%): 29 schools, 7,504 pupils
Colleges and Universities
Two-year: 2 public; 7,227 students
Four-year and beyond:
Public
Fort Valley State College (1,811)
Private
Mercer University (2,935)
Wesleyan College (424)
Places Rated Score: 176
Places Rated Rank: 212

Madison, WI
Elementary and Secondary
Public (90.3%): 16 districts, 103 schools, 48,872 pupils
Private (9.7%): 35 schools, 5,234 pupils
Colleges and Universities
Two-year: 2 public; 20,391 students
Four-year and beyond:

Public
University of Wisconsin, Madison (44,584)
Private
Edgewood College (929)
Places Rated Score: 1,114
Places Rated Rank: 43

Manchester, NH
Elementary and Secondary
Public (84.8%): 4 districts, 35 schools, 21,027 pupils
Private (15.2%): 18 schools, 3,778 pupils
Colleges and Universities
Two-year: 2 public; 3,173 students
Four-year and beyond:
Private
Magdalen College (250)
New Hampshire College (3,016)
Notre Dame College (797)
Saint Anselm College (1,911)
Places Rated Score: 151
Places Rated Rank: 220

Mansfield, OH
Elementary and Secondary
Public (91.0%): 9 districts, 51 schools, 24,190 pupils
Private (9.0%): 9 schools, 2,397 pupils
Colleges and Universities
Two-year: 1 public; 1,729 students
Four-year and beyond:
Public
Ohio State University, Mansfield (1,141)
Places Rated Score: 40
Places Rated Rank: 306

McAllen–Edinburg–Mission, TX
Elementary and Secondary
Public (97.2%): 15 districts, 128 schools, 101,153 pupils
Private (2.8%): 19 schools, 2,915 pupils
Colleges and Universities
Four-year and beyond:
Public
Pan American University (8,887)
Places Rated Score: 178
Places Rated Rank: 211

Medford, OR
Elementary and Secondary
Public (94.2%): 11 districts, 55 schools, 23,615 pupils
Private (5.8%): 11 schools, 1,442 pupils
Colleges and Universities
Four-year and beyond:
Public
Southern Oregon State College (4,564)
Places Rated Score: 91
Places Rated Rank: 260

Melbourne–Titusville–Palm Bay, FL
Elementary and Secondary
Public (90.6%): 2 districts, 67 schools, 48,101 pupils
Private (9.4%): 27 schools, 5,018 pupils
Colleges and Universities
Two-year: 1 public; 10,864 students
Four-year and beyond:
Private
Florida Institute of Technology (6,496)
Places Rated Score: 239
Places Rated Rank: 185

Memphis, TN–AR–MS
Elementary and Secondary
Public (86.8%): 10 districts, 239 schools, 163,843 pupils

Private (13.2%): 89 schools, 24,880 pupils
Colleges and Universities
Two-year: 2 public; 11,387 students
Four-year and beyond:
Public
Memphis State University (20,043)
The University of Tennessee, Memphis (1,707)
Private
Christian Brothers College (1,645)
Crichton College (250)
Le Moyne–Owen College (906)
Memphis Academy of the Arts (278)
Mid America Baptist Seminary (420)
Rhodes College (1,226)
Southern College of Optometry (384)
Places Rated Score: 651
Places Rated Rank: 94

Merced, CA
Elementary and Secondary
Public (95.3%): 23 districts, 64 schools, 34,352 pupils
Private (4.7%): 14 schools, 1,711 pupils
Colleges and Universities
Two-year: 1 public; 6,292 students
Places Rated Score: 63
Places Rated Rank: 281

Miami–Hialeah, FL
Elementary and Secondary
Public (82.5%): 1 district, 262 schools, 253,261 pupils
Private (17.5%): 173 schools, 53,615 pupils
Colleges and Universities
Two-year: 1 public; 39,980 students
Four-year and beyond:
Public
Florida International University (16,744)
Private
Barry University (4,658)
Florida Memorial College (2,102)
Miami Christian College (209)
Saint Thomas of Villanova University (1,530)
Southeastern College of Osteopathic Medicine (330)
University of Miami (13,383)
CMSA Access: Miami–Fort Lauderdale, FL
Places Rated Score: 1,211
Places Rated Rank: 37

★ **Middlesex–Somerset–Hunterdon, NJ**
Elementary and Secondary
Public (84.8%): 77 districts, 276 schools, 133,257 pupils
Private (15.2%): 93 schools, 23,836 pupils
Colleges and Universities
Two-year: 2 public; 15,179 students
Four-year and beyond:
Public
Rutgers University, New Brunswick (33,969)
CMSA Access: New York–Northern NJ–Long Island, NY–NJ–CT
Places Rated Score: 1,856
Places Rated Rank: 19

Middletown, CT
Elementary and Secondary
Public (79.1%): 5 districts, 27 schools, 10,197 pupils
Private (20.9%): 10 schools, 2,695 pupils
Colleges and Universities
Two-year: 1 public; 2,911 students

Four-year and beyond:
Private
Wesleyan University (3,374)
CMSA Access: Hartford–New
Britain–Middletown, CT
Places Rated Score: 215
Places Rated Rank: 199

Midland, TX
Elementary and Secondary
Public (93.3%): 3 districts, 31 schools,
20,027 pupils
Private (6.7%): 5 schools, 1,437 pupils
Colleges and Universities
Two-year: 1 public; 3,659 students
Places Rated Score: 37
Places Rated Rank: 312

Milwaukee, WI
Elementary and Secondary
Public (79.3%): 54 districts, 397 schools,
212,078 pupils
Private (20.7%): 268 schools, 55,515
pupils
Colleges and Universities
Two-year: 2 public; 24,731 students
Four-year and beyond:
Public
University of Wisconsin, Milwaukee
(25,930)
Private
Alverno College (1,832)
Cardinal Stritch College (2,316)
Carroll College (1,891)
Concordia College Wisconsin (763)
Marquette University (11,778)
Medical College of Wisconsin (852)
Milwaukee Institute of Art Design (382)
Milwaukee School of Engineering
(2,834)
Mount Mary College (1,292)
CMSA Access: Milwaukee–Racine, WI
Places Rated Score: 1,245
Places Rated Rank: 35

★ Minneapolis–St. Paul, MN–WI
Elementary and Secondary
Public (87.5%): 70 districts, 529 schools,
363,703 pupils
Private (12.5%): 237 schools, 51,960
pupils
Colleges and Universities
Two-year: 8 public, 2 private; 34,314
students
Four-year and beyond:
Public
Metropolitan State University (4,396)
University of Minnesota,
Minneapolis–Saint Paul (63,994)
Private
Augsburg College (1,833)
Bethel College (1,722)
Bethel Theological Seminary (507)
College of Saint Catherine–Saint
Catherine Campus (2,425)
College of Saint Thomas (7,577)
Concordia College, Saint Paul (946)
Hamline University (1,923)
Luther Northwestern Theological
Seminary (761)
Macalester College (1,768)
Minneapolis College of Art and Design
(623)
North Central Bible College (1,031)
Northwestern College (967)
Northwestern College of Chiropractic
(548)

Saint Paul Bible College (552)
William Mitchell College of Law (1,129)
Places Rated Score: 2,197
Places Rated Rank: 13

Mobile, AL
Elementary and Secondary
Public (85.5%): 2 districts, 119 schools,
85,867 pupils
Private (14.5%): 58 schools, 14,573 pupils
Colleges and Universities
Two-year: 4 public, 1 private; 5,155
students
Four-year and beyond:
Public
University of South Alabama (9,728)
Private
Mobile College (874)
Spring Hill College (1,166)
United States Sports Academy (214)
Places Rated Score: 291
Places Rated Rank: 164

Modesto, CA
Elementary and Secondary
Public (93.2%): 31 districts, 111 schools,
62,129 pupils
Private (6.8%): 30 schools, 4,499 pupils
Colleges and Universities
Two-year: 1 public; 9,812 students
Four-year and beyond:
Public
California State University, Stanislaus
(4,621)
Places Rated Score: 191
Places Rated Rank: 206

Monmouth–Ocean, NJ
Elementary and Secondary
Public (86.4%): 87 districts, 256 schools,
148,131 pupils
Private (13.6%): 70 schools, 23,264 pupils
Colleges and Universities
Two-year: 2 public; 16,212 students
Four-year and beyond:
Private
Beth Medrash Govoha (1,017)
Georgian Court College (1,774)
Monmouth College (4,442)
CMSA Access: New York–Northern
NJ–Long Island, NY–NJ–CT
Places Rated Score: 1,384
Places Rated Rank: 32

Monroe, LA
Elementary and Secondary
Public (91.5%): 2 districts, 51 schools,
27,584 pupils
Private (8.5%): 9 schools, 2,568 pupils
Colleges and Universities
Four-year and beyond:
Public
Northeast Louisiana University (10,227)
Places Rated Score: 205
Places Rated Rank: 204

Montgomery, AL
Elementary and Secondary
Public (86.4%): 4 districts, 76 schools,
54,292 pupils
Private (13.6%): 29 schools, 8,541 pupils
Colleges and Universities
Two-year: 2 public; 1,483 students
Four-year and beyond:
Public
Alabama State University (3,540)
Auburn University, Montgomery (5,183)

Troy State University, Montgomery
(2,292)
Private
Faulkner University (1,353)
Huntingdon College (750)
Places Rated Score: 277
Places Rated Rank: 171

Muncie, IN
Elementary and Secondary
Public (95.0%): 7 districts, 41 schools,
19,781 pupils
Private (5.0%): 7 schools, 1,044 pupils
Colleges and Universities
Two-year: 1 public; 1,954 students
Four-year and beyond:
Public
Ball State University (18,531)
Places Rated Score: 390
Places Rated Rank: 137

Muskegon, MI
Elementary and Secondary
Public (92.8%): 13 districts, 66 schools,
30,948 pupils
Private (7.2%): 18 schools, 2,412 pupils
Colleges and Universities
Two-year: 1 public; 5,322 students
Four-year and beyond:
Private
Muskegon Business College (350)
Places Rated Score: 60
Places Rated Rank: 285

Naples, FL
Elementary and Secondary
Public (93.2%): 1 district, 25 schools,
16,664 pupils
Private (6.8%): 10 schools, 1,225 pupils
Places Rated Score: 0
Places Rated Rank: 332

Nashua, NH
Elementary and Secondary
Public (90.3%): 10 districts, 48 schools,
27,502 pupils
Private (9.7%): 19 schools, 2,955 pupils
Colleges and Universities
Two-year: 1 public; 1,082 students
Four-year and beyond:
Private
Daniel Webster College (860)
Rivier College (2,264)
CMSA Access: Boston–Lawrence–
Salem, MA–NH
Places Rated Score: 540
Places Rated Rank: 115

Nashville, TN
Elementary and Secondary
Public (87.8%): 11 districts, 262 schools,
152,931 pupils
Private (12.2%): 79 schools, 21,252 pupils
Colleges and Universities
Two-year: 2 public, 2 private; 8,956
students
Four-year and beyond:
Public
Middle Tennessee State University
(11,408)
Tennessee State University (6,737)
Private
Belmont College (2,364)
Cumberland University (569)
David Lipscomb College (2,248)
Fisk University (546)
Free Will Baptist Bible College (335)

Meharry Medical College (662)
Trevecca Nazarene College (1,417)
Vanderbilt University (8,883)
Places Rated Score: 793
Places Rated Rank: 72

★ Nassau–Suffolk, NY
Elementary and Secondary
Public (87.2%): 131 districts, 644 schools, 417,847 pupils
Private (12.8%): 203 schools, 61,326 pupils
Colleges and Universities
Two-year: 4 public; 43,300 students
Four-year and beyond:
Public
State University of New York College of Technology, Farmingdale (11,747)
State University of New York College, Old Westbury (3,624)
State University of New York Health Science Center, Stony Brook (1,639)
State University of New York, Stony Brook (14,527)
United States Merchant Marine Academy (936)
Private
Adelphi University (10,494)
Dowling College (3,063)
Friends World College (552)
Hofstra University (11,967)
Long Island University Southhampton College (1,268)
Long Island University, C. W. Post (9,352)
Molloy College (1,472)
New York Chiropractic College (749)
New York Institute of Technology (9,986)
Saint Josephs College, Suffolk (1,470)
CMSA Access: New York–Northern NJ–Long Island, NY–NJ–CT
Places Rated Score: 2,849
Places Rated Rank: 8

New Bedford, MA
Elementary and Secondary
Public (88.2%): 8 districts, 50 schools, 28,271 pupils
Private (11.8%): 12 schools, 3,766 pupils
Colleges and Universities
Four-year and beyond:
Public
Southeastern University of Massachusetts (8,052)
Places Rated Score: 161
Places Rated Rank: 217

New Britain, CT
Elementary and Secondary
Public (86.9%): 4 districts, 36 schools, 17,841 pupils
Private (13.1%): 11 schools, 2,698 pupils
Colleges and Universities
Four-year and beyond:
Public
Central Connecticut State University (13,348)
CMSA Access: Hartford–New Britain–Middletown, CT
Places Rated Score: 368
Places Rated Rank: 144

New Haven–Meriden, CT
Elementary and Secondary
Public (85.2%): 16 districts, 146 schools, 70,839 pupils

Private (14.8%): 58 schools, 12,337 pupils
Colleges and Universities
Two-year: 2 public; 3,367 students
Four-year and beyond:
Public
Southern Connecticut State University (11,297)
Private
Albertus Magnus College (546)
Quinnipiac College (2,769)
University of New Haven (6,481)
Yale University (10,799)
Places Rated Score: 672
Places Rated Rank: 91

New London–Norwich, CT–RI
Elementary and Secondary
Public (88.5%): 18 districts, 86 schools, 32,975 pupils
Private (11.5%): 16 schools, 4,267 pupils
Colleges and Universities
Two-year: 2 public, 1 private; 4,389 students
Four-year and beyond:
Federal
United States Coast Guard Academy (762)
Private
Connecticut College (1,999)
Places Rated Score: 99
Places Rated Rank: 255

New Orleans, LA
Elementary and Secondary
Public (72.7%): 6 districts, 303 schools, 193,439 pupils
Private (27.3%): 179 schools, 72,493 pupils
Colleges and Universities
Two-year: 2 public; 7,942 students
Four-year and beyond:
Public
Louisiana State University Medical Center (2,439)
Southern University, New Orleans (3,302)
University of New Orleans (16,083)
Private
Dillard University (1,275)
Loyola University, New Orleans (5,209)
New Orleans Baptist Theological Seminary (1,474)
Our Lady of Holy Cross College (638)
Tulane University of Louisiana (10,332)
Xavier University of Louisiana (1,991)
Places Rated Score: 934
Places Rated Rank: 57

★ New York, NY
Elementary and Secondary
Public (76.3%): 67 districts, 295 schools, 1,095,524 pupils
Private (23.7%): 494 schools, 340,026 pupils
Colleges and Universities
Two-year: 8 public, 12 private; 71,358 students
Four-year and beyond:
Public
City University of New York Bernard Baruch College (16,587)
City University of New York Brooklyn College (14,750)
City University of New York City College (12,948)
City University of New York College of Staten Island (10,285)

City University of New York Graduate School and University Center (3,670)
City University of New York Hunter College (19,657)
City University of New York John Jay College of Criminal Justice (6,844)
City University of New York Lehman College (9,260)
City University of New York Medgar Evers College (2,454)
City University of New York New York City Technical College (10,089)
City University of New York Queens College (16,613)
City University of New York School of Law, Queens College (300)
City University of New York York College (4,481)
Fashion Institute of Technology (11,774)
State University of New York College of Optometry (250)
State University of New York College, Purchase (3,989)
State University of New York Health Science Center, Brooklyn (1,404)
State University of New York Maritime College (881)
Private
Bank Street College of Education (605)
Barnard College (2,162)
Beth Hatalmud Rabbinical College (215)
Boricua College (1,140)
Brooklyn Law School (1,227)
College for Human Service (728)
College of Aeronautics (1,295)
College of Mount Saint Vincent (1,016)
College of New Rochelle (4,608)
Columbia University in the City of New York (17,574)
Concordia College (547)
Cooper Union (1,056)
Cornell University Medical Center (539)
City University of New York Mount Sinai School of Medicine (483)
Dominican College of Blauvelt (1,562)
Fordham University (12,256)
Iona College (5,904)
Jewish Theological Seminary of America (458)
Long Island University, Brooklyn (6,840)
Long Island University, Rockland (482)
Manhattan College (4,339)
Manhattan School of Music (796)
Manhattanville College (1,433)
Mannes College of Music (211)
Marymount College (1,258)
Marymount Manhattan College (1,484)
Mercy College (7,503)
Mesivta Torah Vodaath Rabbinical Seminary (455)
New School for Social Research (6,571)
New York College of Podiatric Medicine (528)
New York Institute of Technology Metro Center (3,506)
New York Law School (1,168)
New York Medical College (1,295)
New York School of Interior Design (592)
New York University (31,665)
Nyack College (766)
Pace University, New York (11,456)
Pace University, Pleasantville–Brolf Campus (4,700)
Pace University, White Plains (4,359)
Polytechnic University (5,085)

Pratt Institute (3,550)
Rabbi Isaac Elchanan Seminary (241)
Saint Francis College (2,153)
Saint John's University, New York
(19,211)
Saint Josephs College (873)
Saint Josephgs Seminary and College
(240)
Saint Thomas Aquinas College (2,149)
Sarah Lawrence College (1,083)
Teachers College at Columbia
University (3,970)
The College of Insurance (1,002)
The Juilliard School (1,102)
The King's College (574)
Touro College (4,901)
Union Theological Seminary (420)
Wagner College (1,934)
Yeshiva University (4,345)
CMSA Access: New York–Northern
NJ–Long Island, NY–NJ–CT
Places Rated Score: 8,216
Places Rated Rank: 1

★ Newark, NJ
Elementary and Secondary
Public (85.8%): 114 districts, 548 schools,
283,107 pupils
Private (14.2%): 188 schools, 46,787
pupils
Colleges and Universities
Two-year: 3 public, 2 private; 22,789
students
Four-year and beyond:
Public
Kean College of New Jersey (12,629)
Montclair State College (12,922)
New Jersey Institute of Technology
(7,589)
Rutgers University, Newark (9,611)
University of Medicine and Dentistry of
New Jersey (2,305)
Private
Bloomfield College (1,406)
Caldwell College (722)
College of Saint Elizabeth (997)
Drew University (2,341)
Northeastern Bible College (211)
Rabbinical College of America (235)
Seton Hall University (8,809)
Upsala College (1,278)
CMSA Access: New York–Northern
NJ–Long Island, NY–NJ–CT
Places Rated Score: 2,412
Places Rated Rank: 10

Niagara Falls, NY
Elementary and Secondary
Public (88.5%): 11 districts, 59 schools,
34,872 pupils
Private (11.5%): 28 schools, 4,544 pupils
Colleges and Universities
Two-year: 1 public; 4,228 students
Four-year and beyond:
Private
Niagara University (3,179)
CMSA Access: Buffalo–Niagara Falls, NY
Places Rated Score: 214
Places Rated Rank: 201

Norfolk–Virginia Beach–Newport News, VA
Elementary and Secondary
Public (92.3%): 12 districts, 302 schools,
227,613 pupils
Private (7.7%): 92 schools, 18,899 pupils

Colleges and Universities
Two-year: 2 public; 21,927 students
Four-year and beyond:
Public
Christopher Newport College (4,089)
College of William and Mary (7,008)
Norfolk State University (7,458)
Old Dominion University (15,463)
Private
CBN University (715)
Eastern Virginia Medical School (396)
Hampton University (4,482)
Virginia Wesleyan College (1,116)
Places Rated Score: 1,034
Places Rated Rank: 49

Norwalk, CT
Elementary and Secondary
Public (90.6%): 4 districts, 34 schools,
17,114 pupils
Private (9.4%): 12 schools, 1,774 pupils
Colleges and Universities
Two-year: 2 public; 4,376 students
CMSA Access: New York–Northern
NJ–Long Island, NY–NJ–CT
Places Rated Score: 850
Places Rated Rank: 67

★ Oakland, CA
Elementary and Secondary
Public (86.7%): 43 districts, 488 schools,
281,781 pupils
Private (13.3%): 226 schools, 43,293
pupils
Colleges and Universities
Two-year: 8 public, 3 private; 79,132
students
Four-year and beyond:
Public
California State University, Hayward
(12,373)
Merritt College (5,626)
University of California, Berkeley
(31,463)
Private
California College of Arts and Crafts
(1,118)
California School of Professional
Psychology (275)
Graduate Theological Union (370)
Holy Names College (542)
John F. Kennedy University (1,829)
Life Chiropractic College–West (427)
Mills College (992)
Pacific School of Religion (221)
Saint Mary's College of California
(3,658)
CMSA Access: San Francisco–
Oakland–San Jose, CA
Places Rated Score: 2,361
Places Rated Rank: 12

Ocala, FL
Elementary and Secondary
Public (91.1%): 2 districts, 33 schools,
25,372 pupils
Private (8.9%): 14 schools, 2,474 pupils
Colleges and Universities
Two-year: 1 public; 3,187 students
Places Rated Score: 32
Places Rated Rank: 320

Odessa, TX
Elementary and Secondary
Public (97.5%): 2 districts, 35 schools,
25,233 pupils
Private (2.5%): 6 schools, 639 pupils

Colleges and Universities
Two-year: 1 public; 4,312 students
Four-year and beyond:
Public
University of Texas of the Permian
Basin (1,956)
Places Rated Score: 82
Places Rated Rank: 267

Oklahoma City, OK
Elementary and Secondary
Public (94.9%): 64 districts, 344 schools,
170,035 pupils
Private (5.1%): 37 schools, 9,188 pupils
Colleges and Universities
Two-year: 4 public, 1 private; 22,858
students
Four-year and beyond:
Public
Central State University (13,806)
Langston University (1,901)
University of Oklahoma Health Science
Center (2,427)
University of Oklahoma, Norman
(22,313)
Private
Mid America Bible College (272)
Oklahoma Baptist University (1,653)
Oklahoma Christian College (1,457)
Oklahoma City University (2,794)
Southern Nazarene University (1,108)
Places Rated Score: 1,183
Places Rated Rank: 38

Olympia, WA
Elementary and Secondary
Public (96.8%): 8 districts, 51 schools,
27,969 pupils
Private (3.2%): 11 schools, 936 pupils
Colleges and Universities
Two-year: 1 public; 3,601 students
Four-year and beyond:
Public
Evergreen State College (2,965)
Private
Saint Martin's College (881)
Places Rated Score: 113
Places Rated Rank: 244

Omaha, NE–IA
Elementary and Secondary
Public (84.9%): 39 districts, 213 schools,
102,394 pupils
Private (15.1%): 74 schools, 18,214 pupils
Colleges and Universities
Two-year: 2 public; 9,574 students
Four-year and beyond:
Public
University of Nebraska Medical Center
(2,188)
University of Nebraska, Omaha (13,907)
Private
Bellevue College (2,196)
Bishop Clarkson College of Nursing
(405)
College of Saint Mary (1,276)
Creighton University (5,903)
Dana College (459)
Grace College of the Bible (254)
Places Rated Score: 628
Places Rated Rank: 98

Orange County, NY
Elementary and Secondary
Public (84.9%): 18 districts, 81 schools,
50,532 pupils
Private (15.1%): 36 schools, 8,961 pupils

Colleges and Universities
Two-year: 1 public; 4,931 students
Four-year and beyond:
Federal
United States Military Academy (4,464)
Private
Mount Saint Mary College (1,114)
CMSA Access: New York–Northern
NJ–Long Island, NY–NJ–CT
Places Rated Score: 979
Places Rated Rank: 53

Orlando, FL
Elementary and Secondary
Public (90.3%): 5 districts, 167 schools,
146,125 pupils
Private (9.7%): 79 schools, 15,621 pupils
Colleges and Universities
Two-year: 2 public; 18,497 students
Four-year and beyond:
Public
University of Central Florida (16,833)
Private
Orlando College (746)
Rollins College (3,767)
Places Rated Score: 612
Places Rated Rank: 102

Owensboro, KY
Elementary and Secondary
Public (79.0%): 2 districts, 28 schools,
13,187 pupils
Private (21.0%): 16 schools, 3,515 pupils
Colleges and Universities
Four-year and beyond:
Private
Brescia College (709)
Kentucky Wesleyan College (791)
Places Rated Score: 30
Places Rated Rank: 322

Oxnard–Ventura, CA
Elementary and Secondary
Public (88.0%): 22 districts, 171 schools,
106,198 pupils
Private (12.0%): 65 schools, 14,545 pupils
Colleges and Universities
Two-year: 3 public; 26,415 students
Four-year and beyond:
Private
California Lutheran University (2,357)
CMSA Access: Los Angeles–
Anaheim–Riverside, CA
Places Rated Score: 1,028
Places Rated Rank: 50

Panama City, FL
Elementary and Secondary
Public (93.3%): 2 districts, 28 schools,
21,237 pupils
Private (6.7%): 9 schools, 1,522 pupils
Colleges and Universities
Two-year: 1 public; 5,021 students
Places Rated Score: 50
Places Rated Rank: 300

Parkersburg–Marietta, WV–OH
Elementary and Secondary
Public (95.9%): 7 districts, 76 schools,
29,752 pupils
Private (4.1%): 11 schools, 1,269 pupils
Colleges and Universities
Two-year: 2 public; 4,406 students
Four-year and beyond:
Private
Marietta College (1,312)
Ohio Valley College (221)
Places Rated Score: 75
Places Rated Rank: 274

Pascagoula, MS
Elementary and Secondary
Public (95.5%): 4 districts, 46 schools,
27,285 pupils
Private (4.5%): 7 schools, 1,287 pupils
Places Rated Score: 0
Places Rated Rank: 332

Pawtucket–Woonsocket–Attleboro, RI–MA
Elementary and Secondary
Public (87.7%): 14 districts, 104 schools,
48,142 pupils
Private (12.3%): 23 schools, 6,767 pupils
Colleges and Universities
Four-year and beyond:
Private
Bryant College of Business
Administration (6,072)
CMSA Access: Providence–
Pawtucket–Fall River, RI–MA
Places Rated Score: 207
Places Rated Rank: 203

Pensacola, FL
Elementary and Secondary
Public (91.2%): 3 districts, 84 schools,
56,744 pupils
Private (8.8%): 24 schools, 5,471 pupils
Colleges and Universities
Two-year: 1 public; 10,537 students
Four-year and beyond:
Public
University of West Florida (6,214)
Private
Liberty Christian College (325)
Places Rated Score: 236
Places Rated Rank: 186

Peoria, IL
Elementary and Secondary
Public (88.9%): 49 districts, 153 schools,
58,554 pupils
Private (11.1%): 34 schools, 7,309 pupils
Colleges and Universities
Two-year: 1 public; 12,171 students
Four-year and beyond:
Private
Bradley University (4,860)
Eureka College (455)
Places Rated Score: 228
Places Rated Rank: 192

★ Philadelphia, PA–NJ
Elementary and Secondary
Public (74.4%): 182 districts, 1,058
schools, 637,402 pupils
Private (25.6%): 641 schools, 218,832
pupils
Colleges and Universities
Two-year: 7 public, 8 private; 59,859
students
Four-year and beyond:
Public
Cheyney University of Pennsylvania
(1,507)
Glassboro State College (8,723)
Lincoln University (1,245)
Pennsylvania State University,
Delaware (1,566)
Pennsylvania State University, King of
Prussia (726)
Pennsylvania State University, Ogontz
(3,418)
Rutgers University, Camden (4,959)
Temple University (30,615)
West Chester University of
Pennsylvania (10,498)

Private
American College (1,090)
Beaver College (2,113)
Bryn Mawr College (1,794)
Cabrini College (1,033)
Chestnut Hill College (879)
Delaware Valley College of Science
and Agriculture (1,434)
Drexel University (12,494)
Eastern Baptist Theological Seminary
(385)
Eastern College (1,043)
Gratz College (229)
Gwynedd–Mercy College (1,980)
Hahnemann University (1,995)
Haverford College (1,112)
Holy Family College (1,483)
Immaculata College (1,904)
La Salle University (6,106)
Lutheran Theological Seminary,
Philadelphia (263)
Moore College of Art (659)
Neumann College (1,076)
Pennsylvania College of Optometry
(607)
Pennsylvania College of Podiatric
Medicine (458)
Philadelphia College of Osteopathic
Medicine (817)
Philadelphia College of Pharmacy and
Science (1,389)
Philadelphia College of Textiles and
Science (3,249)
Philadelphia College of the Bible (536)
Rosemont College (579)
Saint Charles Borromed Seminary (461)
Saint Joseph's University (5,714)
Spring Garden College (1,558)
Swarthmore College (1,335)
The Medical College of Pennsylvania
(559)
The University of the Arts (1,019)
Thomas Jefferson University (1,973)
University of Pennsylvania (21,742)
Ursinus College (2,293)
Valley Forge Christian College (477)
Villanova University (12,525)
Westminster Theological Seminary
(534)
Widener University (5,163)
CMSA Access: Philadelphia–
Wilmington–Trenton, PA–NJ–DE–MD
Places Rated Score: 4,019
Places Rated Rank: 5

★ Phoenix, AZ
Elementary and Secondary
Public (93.1%): 59 districts, 412 schools,
327,836 pupils
Private (6.9%): 115 schools, 24,221 pupils
Colleges and Universities
Two-year: 7 public; 70,894 students
Four-year and beyond:
Public
Arizona State University (42,014)
Private
American Graduate School of
Management (1,083)
Grand Canyon College (1,574)
Western International University (2,293)
Places Rated Score: 1,648
Places Rated Rank: 25

Pine Bluff, AR
Elementary and Secondary
Public (96.9%): 7 districts, 40 schools,
17,525 pupils
Private (3.1%): 5 schools, 569 pupils

Colleges and Universities
Four-year and beyond:
Public
    University of Arkansas, Pine Bluff
    (2,921)
Places Rated Score: 58
Places Rated Rank: 288

★ **Pittsburgh, PA**
Elementary and Secondary
    Public (83.6%): 81 districts, 535 schools,
    278,414 pupils
    Private (16.4%): 266 schools, 54,569
    pupils
Colleges and Universities
    Two-year: 5 public, 3 private; 21,792
    students
    Four-year and beyond:
    Public
        California University of Pennsylvania
        (5,542)
        Pennsylvania State University, Fayette
        (701)
        Pennsylvania State University,
        Mckeesport (1,563)
        Pennsylvania State University, New
        Kensington (1,384)
        University of Pittsburgh (28,449)
        University of Pittsburgh, Greensburg
        (1,405)
    Private
        Carlow College (1,120)
        Carnegie Mellon University (6,752)
        Chatham College (602)
        Duquesne University (6,570)
        La Roche College (1,751)
        Pittsburgh Theological Seminary (353)
        Point Park College (2,787)
        Robert Morris College (5,441)
        Saint Vincent College (1,249)
        Seton Hill College (865)
        Washington and Jefferson College
        (1,354)
CMSA Access: Pittsburgh–Beaver
    County, PA
Places Rated Score: 1,763
Places Rated Rank: 21

Pittsfield, MA
Elementary and Secondary
    Public (84.8%): 8 districts, 27 schools,
    11,199 pupils
    Private (15.2%): 12 schools, 2,015 pupils
Colleges and Universities
    Two-year: 1 public; 3,141 students
Places Rated Score: 31
Places Rated Rank: 321

Portland, ME
Elementary and Secondary
    Public (91.1%): 13 districts, 78 schools,
    28,840 pupils
    Private (8.9%): 17 schools, 2,828 pupils
Colleges and Universities
    Two-year: 1 public; 1,517 students
    Four-year and beyond:
    Public
        University of Southern Maine (9,424)
    Private
        Portland School of Art (263)
        Saint Joseph's College (584)
        Westbrook College (1,000)
Places Rated Score: 241
Places Rated Rank: 184

Portland, OR
Elementary and Secondary
    Public (91.8%): 69 districts, 374 schools,
    184,665 pupils
    Private (8.2%): 99 schools, 16,417 pupils
Colleges and Universities
    Two-year: 3 public; 31,626 students
    Four-year and beyond:
    Public
        Oregon Health Science University
        (1,200)
        Portland State University (15,640)
    Private
        Columbia Christian College (250)
        Concordia College (431)
        George Fox College (572)
        Lewis and Clark College (3,123)
        Linfield College (1,770)
        Marylhurst College (990)
        Multnomah School of Bible (662)
        Oregon Graduate Center (249)
        Pacific University (1,275)
        Reed College (1,227)
        University of Portland (2,610)
        Warner Pacific College (383)
        Western Conservative Baptist Seminary
        (732)
        Western States Chiropractic College
        (408)
CMSA Access: Portland–Vancouver, OR
Places Rated Score: 954
Places Rated Rank: 55

**Portsmouth–Dover–Rochester,
NH–ME**
Elementary and Secondary
    Public (93.7%): 23 districts, 84 schools,
    34,058 pupils
    Private (6.3%): 11 schools, 2,303 pupils
Colleges and Universities
    Two-year: 1 public; 378 students
    Four-year and beyond:
    Public
        School for Lifelong Learning (1,723)
        University of New Hampshire (12,483)
    Private
        Franklin Pierce College (360)
        Nasson College (750)
Places Rated Score: 310
Places Rated Rank: 154

Poughkeepsie, NY
Elementary and Secondary
    Public (88%): 15 districts, 71 schools,
    39,393 pupils
    Private (12.0%): 35 schools, 5,393 pupils
Colleges and Universities
    Two-year: 1 public, 1 private; 8,171
    students
    Four-year and beyond:
    Private
        Bard College (801)
        Marist College (4,315)
        Vassar College (2,319)
Places Rated Score: 230
Places Rated Rank: 189

Providence, RI
Elementary and Secondary
    Public (85.7%): 20 districts, 189 schools,
    86,144 pupils
    Private (14.3%): 69 schools, 14,429 pupils
Colleges and Universities
    Two-year: 1 public; 13,096 students
    Four-year and beyond:
    Public
        Rhode Island College (8,044)

Private
    Brown University (7,357)
    Johnson and Wales College (6,084)
    New England Institute of Technology
    (1,585)
    Providence College (5,621)
    Rhode Island School of Design (1,856)
    Roger Williams College (2,404)
    Roger Williams College (1,069)
CMSA Access: Providence–
    Pawtucket–Fall River, RI–MA
Places Rated Score: 828
Places Rated Rank: 69

Provo–Orem, UT
Elementary and Secondary
    Public (98.8%): 3 districts, 91 schools,
    62,793 pupils
    Private (1.2%): 4 schools, 765 pupils
Colleges and Universities
    Two-year: 1 public; 6,500 students
    Four-year and beyond:
    Private
        Brigham Young University (30,226)
Places Rated Score: 670
Places Rated Rank: 92

Pueblo, CO
Elementary and Secondary
    Public (96.4%): 2 districts, 46 schools,
    21,794 pupils
    Private (3.6%): 7 schools, 817 pupils
Colleges and Universities
    Two-year: 1 public; 1,756 students
    Four-year and beyond:
    Public
        University of Southern Colorado (3,696)
Places Rated Score: 91
Places Rated Rank: 260

Racine, WI
Elementary and Secondary
    Public (83.0%): 13 districts, 52 schools,
    28,202 pupils
    Private (17.0%): 33 schools, 5,779 pupils
Colleges and Universities
CMSA Access: Milwaukee–Racine, WI
Places Rated Score: 125
Places Rated Rank: 237

★ **Raleigh–Durham, NC**
Elementary and Secondary
    Public (91.6%): 9 districts, 150 schools,
    101,725 pupils
    Private (8.4%): 49 schools, 9,368 pupils
Colleges and Universities
    Two-year: 2 public, 3 private; 10,884
    students
    Four-year and beyond:
    Public
        North Carolina Central University
        (5,040)
        North Carolina State University, Raleigh
        (24,887)
        University of North Carolina, Chapel Hill
        (22,826)
    Private
        Duke University (10,552)
        Meredith College (1,903)
        Saint Augustine's College (1,655)
        Shaw University (1,402)
        Southeastern Baptist Theological
        Seminary (980)
Places Rated Score: 1,494
Places Rated Rank: 29

Rapid City, SD
Elementary and Secondary
Public (92.5%): 5 districts, 44 schools, 16,482 pupils
Private (7.5%): 12 schools, 1,338 pupils
Colleges and Universities
Four-year and beyond:
Public
South Dakota School of Mines & Technology (2,023)
Places Rated Score: 41
Places Rated Rank: 305

Reading, PA
Elementary and Secondary
Public (88.7%): 19 districts, 102 schools, 49,190 pupils
Private (11.3%): 37 schools, 6,246 pupils
Colleges and Universities
Two-year: 1 public; 1,290 students
Four-year and beyond:
Public
Kutztown University of Pennsylvania (6,647)
Pennsylvania State University, Berks (1,262)
Private
Albright College (1,961)
Alvernia College (876)
Places Rated Score: 228
Places Rated Rank: 192

Redding, CA
Elementary and Secondary
Public (92.6%): 30 districts, 65 schools, 24,187 pupils
Private (7.4%): 16 schools, 1,938 pupils
Colleges and Universities
Two-year: 1 public; 8,076 students
Places Rated Score: 81
Places Rated Rank: 268

Reno, NV
Elementary and Secondary
Public (95.1%): 1 district, 61 schools, 33,610 pupils
Private (4.9%): 11 schools, 1,748 pupils
Colleges and Universities
Two-year: 1 public; 7,688 students
Four-year and beyond:
Public
University of Nevada, Reno (9,651)
Private
Sierra Nevada College (298)
Places Rated Score: 276
Places Rated Rank: 173

Richland-Kennewick-Pasco, WA
Elementary and Secondary
Public (95.4%): 10 districts, 59 schools, 31,156 pupils
Private (4.6%): 13 schools, 1,503 pupils
Colleges and Universities
Two-year: 1 public; 5,641 students
Places Rated Score: 56
Places Rated Rank: 291

Richmond-Petersburg, VA
Elementary and Secondary
Public (94.1%): 13 districts, 232 schools, 143,015 pupils
Private (5.9%): 41 schools, 8,994 pupils
Colleges and Universities
Two-year: 3 public; 15,870 students
Four-year and beyond:

Public
Virginia Commonwealth University (19,641)
Virginia State University (3,583)
Private
Randolph-Macon College (1,013)
Union Theological Seminary in Virginia (239)
University of Richmond (4,705)
Virginia Union University (1,108)
Places Rated Score: 764
Places Rated Rank: 75

★ Riverside-San Bernardino, CA
Elementary and Secondary
Public (92.5%): 67 districts, 554 schools, 381,130 pupils
Private (7.5%): 168 schools, 31,015 pupils
Colleges and Universities
Two-year: 9 public; 54,226 students
Four-year and beyond:
Public
California State University, San Bernardino (7,423)
University of California, Riverside (5,726)
Private
California Baptist College (648)
Loma Linda University (4,569)
University of Redlands (2,658)
CMSA Access: Los Angeles-Anaheim-Riverside, CA
Places Rated Score: 1,890
Places Rated Rank: 17

Roanoke, VA
Elementary and Secondary
Public (94.3%): 4 districts, 72 schools, 36,179 pupils
Private (5.7%): 12 schools, 2,204
Colleges and Universities
Two-year: 1 public, 1 private; 7,110 students
Four-year and beyond:
Private
Hollins College (900)
Roanoke College (1,527)
Places Rated Score: 120
Places Rated Rank: 240

Rochester, MN
Elementary and Secondary
Public (88.0%): 5 districts, 32 schools, 17,388 pupils
Private (12.0%): 11 schools, 2,366 pupils
Colleges and Universities
Two-year: 1 public; 3,153 students
Four-year and beyond:
Private
Mayo Graduate School of Medicine (1,011)
Places Rated Score: 52
Places Rated Rank: 297

Rochester, NY
Elementary and Secondary
Public (86.8%): 53 districts, 237 schools, 154,923 pupils
Private (13.2%): 106 schools, 23,479 pupils
Colleges and Universities
Two-year: 2 public, 1 private; 15,106 students
Four-year and beyond:
Public
State University of New York College, Brockport (7,724)

State University of New York College, Geneseo (5,333)
Private
Colgate Rochester-Bexley-Crozer (221)
Hobart/William Smith Colleges (1,973)
Nazareth College of Rochester (2,811)
Roberts Wesleyan College (744)
Rochester Institute of Technology (12,758)
Saint John Fisher College (2,462)
University of Rochester (8,861)
Places Rated Score: 1,009
Places Rated Rank: 51

Rockford, IL
Elementary and Secondary
Public (86.7%): 14 districts, 93 schools, 47,653 pupils
Private (13.3%): 33 schools, 7,290 pupils
Colleges and Universities
Two-year: 1 public; 7,999 students
Four-year and beyond:
Private
Rockford College (1,266)
Places Rated Score: 105
Places Rated Rank: 248

Sacramento, CA
Elementary and Secondary
Public (91.0%): 62 districts, 412 schools, 217,531 pupils
Private (9.0%): 122 schools, 21,430 pupils
Colleges and Universities
Two-year: 5 public, 1 private; 52,682 students
Four-year and beyond:
Public
California State University, Sacramento (23,673)
University of California, Davis (19,809)
Places Rated Score: 1,396
Places Rated Rank: 31

Saginaw-Bay City-Midland, MI
Elementary and Secondary
Public (87.2%): 22 districts, 158 schools, 75,597 pupils
Private (12.8%): 64 schools, 11,143 pupils
Colleges and Universities
Two-year: 1 public, 1 private; 11,145 students
Four-year and beyond:
Public
Saginaw Valley State University (5,377)
Private
Northwood Institute (1,824)
Places Rated Score: 255
Places Rated Rank: 181

St. Cloud, MN
Elementary and Secondary
Public (84.3%): 17 districts, 61 schools, 32,266 pupils
Private (15.7%): 35 schools, 5,989 pupils
Colleges and Universities
Four-year and beyond:
Public
Saint Cloud State University (14,220)
Private
College of Saint Benedict (1,940)
Saint John's University (1,949)
Places Rated Score: 362
Places Rated Rank: 148

St. Joseph, MO
Elementary and Secondary
Public (92.4%): 5 districts, 34 schools, 14,953 pupils
Private (7.6%): 7 schools, 1,237 pupils
Colleges and Universities
Four-year and Beyond:
Public
Missouri Western State College (3,867)
Places Rated Score: 77
Places Rated Rank: 271

★ St. Louis, MO–IL
Elementary and Secondary
Public (79.7%): 115 districts, 707 schools, 363,778 pupils
Private (20.3%): 367 schools, 92,678 pupils
Colleges and Universities
Two-year: 8 public, 1 private; 53,047 students
Four-year and beyond:
Public
Harris–Stowe State College (1,374)
Southern Illinois University, Edwardsville (10,843)
University of Missouri, Saint Louis (12,328)
Private
Clayton University (650)
Concordia Seminary (509)
Fontbonne College (935)
Lindenwood College (1,771)
Logan College of Chiropractic (605)
Maryville College (2,675)
McKendree College (976)
Missouri Baptist College (603)
Parks College of Saint Louis University (1,068)
Principia College (691)
Saint Louis University (12,185)
St. Louis College of Pharmacy (755)
Washington University (10,481)
Webster University (6,645)
Places Rated Score: 1,832
Places Rated Rank: 20

Salem, OR
Elementary and Secondary
Public (92.9%): 42 districts, 117 schools, 42,745 pupils
Private (7.1%): 28 schools, 3,284 pupils
Colleges and Universities
Two-year: 1 public; 7,052 students
Four-year and beyond:
Public
Western Oregon State College (3,393)
Private
Western Baptist College (257)
Willamette University (1,958)
Places Rated Score: 183
Places Rated Rank: 209

Salem–Gloucester, MA
Elementary and Secondary
Public (82.4%): 15 districts, 80 schools, 33,594 pupils
Private (17.6%): 32 schools, 7,167 pupils
Colleges and Universities
Two-year: 1 public, 2 private; 4,464 students
Four-year and beyond:
Public
Salem State College (9,009)
Private
Gordon College (1,218)

Gordon–Conwell Theological Seminary (739)
CMSA Access: Boston–Lawrence–Salem, MA–NH
Places Rated Score: 701
Places Rated Rank: 85

Salinas–Seaside–Monterey, CA
Elementary and Secondary
Public (93.0%): 28 districts, 96 schools, 53,398 pupils
Private (7.0%): 18 schools, 4,030 pupils
Colleges and Universities
Two-year: 2 public; 12,930 students
Four-year and beyond:
Private
Monterey International Studies (533)
Places Rated Score: 140
Places Rated Rank: 227

Salt Lake City–Ogden, UT
Elementary and Secondary
Public (97.6%): 7 districts, 338 schools, 253,187 pupils
Private (2.4%): 31 schools, 6,326 pupils
Colleges and Universities
Two-year: 1 public, 1 private; 9,526 students
Four-year and beyond:
Public
University of Utah (24,721)
Weber State College (11,366)
Private
Westminster College of Salt Lake City (1,429)
Places Rated Score: 846
Places Rated Rank: 68

San Angelo, TX
Elementary and Secondary
Public (96.6%): 6 districts, 36 schools, 17,678 pupils
Private (3.4%): 5 schools, 625 pupils
Colleges and Universities
Four-year and beyond:
Public
Angelo State University (5,806)
Places Rated Score: 116
Places Rated Rank: 242

San Antonio, TX
Elementary and Secondary
Public (91.9%): 22 districts, 334 schools, 245,253 pupils
Private (8.1%): 91 schools, 21,489 pupils
Colleges and Universities
Two-year: 3 public; 28,894 students
Four-year and beyond:
Public
University of Texas Health Science, San Antonio (2,174)
University of Texas, San Antonio (12,413)
Private
Incarnate Word College (1,575)
Our Lady of the Lake University, San Antonio (1,780)
Saint Mary's University (3,560)
Texas Lutheran College (1,340)
Trinity University (2,674)
Places Rated Score: 799
Places Rated Rank: 71

★ San Diego, CA
Elementary and Secondary
Public (90.7%): 49 districts, 474 schools, 332,406 pupils
Private (9.3%): 180 schools, 34,102 pupils

Colleges and Universities
Two-year: 8 public; 85,772 students
Four-year and beyond:
Public
San Diego State University (35,010)
University of California, San Diego (15,912)
Private
California School of Professional Psychology (405)
California Western School of Law (505)
Christian Heritage College (435)
Coleman College (926)
National University (12,873)
Point Loma Nazarene College (2,077)
United States International University (2,582)
University of San Diego (5,445)
Places Rated Score: 2,381
Places Rated Rank: 11

★ San Francisco, CA
Elementary and Secondary
Public (77.0%): 48 districts, 327 schools, 160,957 pupils
Private (23.0%): 221 schools, 47,973 pupils
Colleges and Universities
Two-year: 5 public, 2 private; 60,924 students
Four-year and beyond:
Public
San Francisco State University (25,871)
University of California, Hastings College of Law (1,475)
University of California, San Francisco (3,608)
Private
California College of Podiatric Medicine (414)
California Institute of Integral Studies (203)
California School of Professional Psychology (250)
College of Notre Dame (1,053)
Dominican College of San Rafael (757)
Golden Gate University (9,675)
Institute of Transpersonal Psychology (217)
Menlo College (630)
New College of California (446)
San Francisco Art Institute (659)
San Francisco Theological Seminary (767)
Simpson College (266)
University of San Francisco (4,976)
CMSA Access: San Francisco–Oakland–San Jose, CA
Places Rated Score: 2,063
Places Rated Rank: 15

★ San Jose, CA
Elementary and Secondary
Public (88.9%): 38 districts, 323 schools, 214,995 pupils
Private (11.1%): 115 schools, 26,866 pupils
Colleges and Universities
Two-year: 7 public, 1 private; 81,073 students
Four-year and beyond:
Public
San Jose State University (26,507)
Private
Palmer College of Chiropractic–West (547)
Santa Clara University (7,742)

Stanford University (14,037)
CMSA Access: San Francisco–
Oakland–San Jose, CA
Places Rated Score: 2,151
Places Rated Rank: 14

Santa Barbara–Santa Maria–Lompoc, CA

Elementary and Secondary
Public (89.1%): 29 districts, 95 schools, 46,935 pupils
Private (10.9%): 35 schools, 5,739 pupils
Colleges and Universities
Two-year: 2 public; 18,710 students
Four-year and beyond:
Public
University of California, Santa Barbara (18,003)
Private
The Fielding Institute (571)
Westmont College (1,244)
Places Rated Score: 583
Places Rated Rank: 107

Santa Cruz, CA

Elementary and Secondary
Public (89.7%): 13 districts, 53 schools, 31,409 pupils
Private (10.3%): 20 schools, 3,591 pupils
Colleges and Universities
Two-year: 1 public; 10,794 students
Four-year and beyond:
Public
University of California, Santa Cruz (8,589)
Private
Bethany Bible College (549)
CMSA Access: San Francisco–
Oakland–San Jose, CA
Places Rated Score: 633
Places Rated Rank: 96

Santa Fe, NM

Elementary and Secondary
Public (86.6%): 3 districts, 34 schools, 16,998 pupils
Private (13.4%): 26 schools, 2,630 pupils
Colleges and Universities
Two-year: 3 public; 3,201 students
Four-year and beyond:
Private
College of Santa Fe (1,504)
Saint Johns College (424)
Places Rated Score: 71
Places Rated Rank: 276

Santa Rosa–Petaluma, CA

Elementary and Secondary
Public (90.7%): 43 districts, 118 schools, 52,501 pupils
Private (9.3%): 36 schools, 5,357 pupils
Colleges and Universities
Two-year: 1 public, 1 private; 20,479 students
Four-year and beyond:
Public
Sonoma State University (5,746)
CMSA Access: San Francisco–
Oakland–San Jose, CA
Places Rated Score: 698
Places Rated Rank: 86

Sarasota, FL

Elementary and Secondary
Public (88.3%): 1 district, 35 schools, 26,325 pupils
Private (11.7%): 20 schools, 3,487 pupils

Colleges and Universities
Four-year and beyond:
Private
Ringling School of Art and Design (412)
Places Rated Score: 8
Places Rated Rank: 331

Savannah, GA

Elementary and Secondary
Public (80.1%): 2 districts, 56 schools, 34,227 pupils
Private (19.9%): 31 schools, 8,510 pupils
Colleges and Universities
Four-year and beyond:
Public
Armstrong State College (2,732)
Savannah State College (1,694)
Private
Savannah College of Art and Design (705)
Places Rated Score: 103
Places Rated Rank: 251

Scranton–Wilkes-Barre, PA

Elementary and Secondary
Public (83.7%): 35 districts, 187 schools, 96,906 pupils
Private (16.3%): 99 schools, 18,856 pupils
Colleges and Universities
Two-year: 1 public, 3 private; 7,335 students
Four-year and beyond:
Public
Bloomsburg University of Pennsylvania (6,757)
East Stroudsburg University of Pennsylvania (4,320)
Pennsylvania State University, Hazleton (1,123)
Pennsylvania State University, Scranton (1,128)
Pennsylvania State University, Wilkes-Barre (1,036)
Private
Baptist Bible College of Pennsylvania (636)
College of Misericordia (1,119)
King's College (2,299)
Marywood College (3,251)
University of Scranton (4,789)
Wilkes College (3,380)
Places Rated Score: 670
Places Rated Rank: 92

★ Seattle, WA

Elementary and Secondary
Public (88.9%): 33 districts, 476 schools, 265,891 pupils
Private (11.1%): 183 schools, 33,111 pupils
Colleges and Universities
Two-year: 9 public; 56,445 students
Four-year and beyond:
Public
University of Washington (33,674)
Private
City University (2,888)
Cornish College of the Arts (429)
Northwest College of the Assemblies of God (579)
Seattle Pacific University (2,969)
Seattle University (4,348)
CMSA Access: Seattle–Tacoma, WA
Places Rated Score: 1,489
Places Rated Rank: 30

Sharon, PA

Elementary and Secondary
Public (91.2%): 12 districts, 40 schools, 19,321 pupils
Private (8.8%): 11 schools, 1,875 pupils
Colleges and Universities
Four-year and beyond:
Public
Pennsylvania State University, Shenango Valley (1,177)
Private
Grove City College (2,140)
Thiel College (927)
Places Rated Score: 85
Places Rated Rank: 265

Sheboygan, WI

Elementary and Secondary
Public (82.2%): 10 districts, 44 schools, 16,991 pupils
Private (17.8%): 25 schools, 3,679 pupils
Colleges and Universities
Four-year and beyond:
Private
Lakeland College (1,305)
Places Rated Score: 26
Places Rated Rank: 324

Sherman–Denison, TX

Elementary and Secondary
Public (97.3%): 14 districts, 45 schools, 17,596 pupils
Private (2.7%): 6 schools, 490 pupils
Colleges and Universities
Two-year: 1 public; 3,393 students
Four-year and beyond:
Private
Austin College (1,175)
Places Rated Score: 57
Places Rated Rank: 289

Shreveport, LA

Elementary and Secondary
Public (92.9%): 2 districts, 103 schools, 70,675 pupils
Private (7.1%): 28 schools, 5,433 pupils
Colleges and Universities
Two-year: 2 public; 2,699 students
Four-year and beyond:
Public
Louisiana State University–Shreveport (4,152)
Private
Centenary College of Louisiana (1,013)
Places Rated Score: 130
Places Rated Rank: 234

Sioux City, IA–NE

Elementary and Secondary
Public (84.5%): 12 districts, 53 schools, 20,223 pupils
Private (15.5%): 15 schools, 3,722 pupils
Colleges and Universities
Two-year: 1 public; 560 students
Four-year and beyond:
Private
Briar Cliff College (1,180)
Morningside College (947)
Places Rated Score: 48
Places Rated Rank: 301

Sioux Falls, SD

Elementary and Secondary
Public (85.3%): 7 districts, 46 schools, 19,678 pupils
Private (14.7%): 21 schools, 3,394 pupils

Colleges and Universities
Two-year: 1 private; 201 students
Four-year and beyond:
Private
  Augustana College (1,805)
  Sioux Falls College (767)
Places Rated Score: 53
Places Rated Rank: 295

South Bend-Mishawaka, IN
Elementary and Secondary
Public (83.4%): 5 districts, 62 schools,
  37,454 pupils
Private (16.6%): 30 schools, 7,433 pupils
Colleges and Universities
Two-year: 1 public, 1 private; 2,337
  students
Four-year and beyond:
Public
  Indiana University, South Bend (5,641)
Private
  Bethel College (472)
  Saint Mary's College (1,734)
  University of Notre Dame (9,784)
Places Rated Score: 376
Places Rated Rank: 142

Spokane, WA
Elementary and Secondary
Public (92.0%): 14 districts, 123 schools,
  61,730 pupils
Private (8.0%): 40 schools, 5,336 pupils
Colleges and Universities
Two-year: 2 public; 15,316 students
Four-year and beyond:
Public
  Eastern Washington University (8,094)
Private
  Gonzaga University (3,259)
  Whitworth College (1,764)
Places Rated Score: 416
Places Rated Rank: 128

Springfield, IL
Elementary and Secondary
Public (81.8%): 16 districts, 70 schools,
  28,279 pupils
Private (18.2%): 31 schools, 6,292 pupils
Colleges and Universities
Two-year: 1 public, 1 private; 8,000
  students
Four-year and beyond:
Public
  Sangamon State University (3,485)
Places Rated Score: 150
Places Rated Rank: 222

Springfield, MO
Elementary and Secondary
Public (95.4%): 16 districts, 86 schools,
  36,392 pupils
Private (4.6%): 11 schools, 1,741 pupils
Colleges and Universities
Four-year and beyond:
Public
  Southwest Missouri State University
    (15,233)
Private
  Assemblies of God Theological
    Seminary (310)
  Baptist Bible College (835)
  Central Bible College (757)
  Drury College (2,774)
  Evangel College (1,009)
Places Rated Score: 418
Places Rated Rank: 127

Springfield, MA
Elementary and Secondary
Public (85.1%): 20 districts, 157 schools,
  75,997 pupils
Private (14.9%): 54 schools, 13,345 pupils
Colleges and Universities
Two-year: 2 public, 1 private; 10,758
  students
Four-year and beyond:
Public
  Westfield State College (5,290)
Private
  American International College (1,738)
  College of Our Lady of Elms (911)
  Mount Holyoke College (1,954)
  Smith College (2,884)
  Springfield College (2,518)
  Western New England College (5,061)
Places Rated Score: 1,071
Places Rated Rank: 46

Stamford, CT
Elementary and Secondary
Public (83.6%): 4 districts, 41 schools,
  23,001 pupils
Private (16.4%): 14 schools, 4,498 pupils
CMSA Access: New York-Northern
  NJ-Long Island, NY-NJ-CT
Places Rated Score: 810
Places Rated Rank: 70

State College, PA
Elementary and Secondary
Public (94.0%): 4 districts, 30 schools,
  12,585 pupils
Private (6.0%): 8 schools, 808 pupils
Colleges and Universities
Four-year and beyond:
Public
  Pennsylvania State University (35,261)
Places Rated Score: 705
Places Rated Rank: 84

Steubenville-Weirton, OH-WV
Elementary and Secondary
Public (89.4%): 8 districts, 73 schools,
  26,092 pupils
Private (10.6%): 16 schools, 3,098 pupils
Colleges and Universities
Two-year: 1 public; 1,362 students
Four-year and beyond:
Private
  Bethany College (786)
  Franciscan University of Steubenville
    (1,066)
Places Rated Score: 51
Places Rated Rank: 299

Stockton, CA
Elementary and Secondary
Public (92.6%): 19 districts, 140 schools,
  85,780 pupils
Private (7.4%): 34 schools, 6,895 pupils
Colleges and Universities
Two-year: 1 public; 14,734 students
Four-year and beyond:
Private
  Humphreys College (407)
  University of the Pacific (5,599)
Places Rated Score: 267
Places Rated Rank: 177

Syracuse, NY
Elementary and Secondary
Public (92.3%): 38 districts, 189 schools,
  111,409 pupils
Private (7.7%): 54 schools, 9,331 pupils

Colleges and Universities
Two-year: 2 public, 2 private; 11,711
  students
Four-year and beyond:
Public
  State University of New York College of
    Environmental Science and Forestry
    (1,485)
  State University of New York College,
    Oswego (8,449)
  State University of New York Health
    Science Center, Syracuse (926)
Private
  Colgate University (2,696)
  Le Moyne College (2,135)
  Syracuse University (21,120)
Places Rated Score: 853
Places Rated Rank: 66

Tacoma, WA
Elementary and Secondary
Public (93.7%): 15 districts, 190 schools,
  94,360 pupils
Private (6.3%): 38 schools, 6,368 pupils
Colleges and Universities
Two-year: 2 public; 11,985 students
Four-year and beyond:
Private
  Pacific Lutheran University (3,651)
  University of Puget Sound (3,996)
CMSA Access: Seattle-Tacoma, WA
Places Rated Score: 419
Places Rated Rank: 126

Tallahassee, FL
Elementary and Secondary
Public (88.3%): 3 districts, 49 schools,
  36,158 pupils
Private (11.7%): 16 schools, 4,776 pupils
Colleges and Universities
Two-year: 1 public; 6,302 students
Four-year and beyond:
Public
  Florida A & M University (5,411)
  Florida State University (22,990)
Places Rated Score: 631
Places Rated Rank: 97

Tampa-St. Petersburg-Clearwater, FL
Elementary and Secondary
Public (88.0%): 7 districts, 305 schools,
  251,071 pupils
Private (12.0%): 172 schools, 34,112
  pupils
Colleges and Universities
Two-year: 4 public, 1 private; 34,799
  students
Four-year and beyond:
Public
  University of South Florida (29,439)
Private
  Clearwater Christian College (230)
  Eckerd College (1,179)
  Saint Leo College (5,507)
  Tampa College (1,635)
  University of Tampa (2,328)
Places Rated Score: 1,154
Places Rated Rank: 40

Terre Haute, IN
Elementary and Secondary
Public (96.2%): 2 districts, 41 schools,
  21,822 pupils
Private (3.8%): 8 schools, 852 pupils
Colleges and Universities
Two-year: 1 public; 1,780 students

Four-year and beyond:
Public
Indiana State University (11,208)
Private
Rose–Hulman Institute of Technology
(1,307)
Saint Mary-of-the-Woods College (809)
Places Rated Score: 284
Places Rated Rank: 168

Texarkana, TX–Texarkana, AR
Elementary and Secondary
Public (97.9%): 19 districts, 55 schools,
23,918 pupils
Private (2.1%): 5 schools, 506 pupils
Colleges and Universities
Two-year: 1 public; 3,380 students
Four-year and beyond:
Public
East Texas State University, Texarkana
(1,148)
Places Rated Score: 57
Places Rated Rank: 289

Toledo, OH
Elementary and Secondary
Public (83.1%): 24 districts, 184 schools,
101,936 pupils
Private (16.9%): 67 schools, 20,696 pupils
Colleges and Universities
Two-year: 2 public; 5,999 students
Four-year and beyond:
Public
Bowling Green State University
(17,799)
Medical College of Ohio, Toledo (793)
University of Toledo (21,176)
Private
Lourdes College (805)
Places Rated Score: 871
Places Rated Rank: 62

Topeka, KS
Elementary and Secondary
Public (89.0%): 6 districts, 65 schools,
26,166 pupils
Private (11.0%): 17 schools, 3,244 pupils
Colleges and Universities
Four-year and beyond:
Public
Washburn University of Topeka (6,610)
Places Rated Score: 132
Places Rated Rank: 233

Trenton, NJ
Elementary and Secondary
Public (77.1%): 12 districts, 86 schools,
46,194 pupils
Private (22.9%): 50 schools, 13,754 pupils
Colleges and Universities
Two-year: 1 public; 8,727 students
Four-year and beyond:
Public
Thomas A. Edison State College
(5,320)
Trenton State College (8,179)
Private
Princeton Theological Seminary (849)
Princeton University (6,371)
Rider College (5,010)
Westminster Choir College (340)
CMSA Access: Philadelphia–
Wilmington–Trenton, PA–NJ–DE–MD
Places Rated Score: 999
Places Rated Rank: 52

Tucson, AZ
Elementary and Secondary
Public (92.3%): 18 districts, 171 schools,
100,019 pupils
Private (7.7%): 49 schools, 8,373 pupils
Colleges and Universities
Two-year: 1 public; 22,959 students
Four-year and beyond:
Public
University of Arizona (31,563)
Places Rated Score: 861
Places Rated Rank: 65

Tulsa, OK
Elementary and Secondary
Public (94.5%): 64 districts, 271 schools,
129,252 pupils
Private (5.5%): 31 schools, 7,557 pupils
Colleges and Universities
Two-year: 2 public; 18,163 students
Four-year and beyond:
Public
The Oklahoma College of Osteopathic
Medicine (308)
Private
Oral Roberts University (4,434)
University of Tulsa (3,790)
Places Rated Score: 352
Places Rated Rank: 149

Tuscaloosa, AL
Elementary and Secondary
Public (93.0%): 2 districts, 43 schools,
24,859 pupils
Private (7.0%): 6 schools, 1,877 pupils
Colleges and Universities
Two-year: 2 public; 3,330 students
Four-year and beyond:
Public
The University of Alabama (16,210)
Private
Stillman College (791)
Places Rated Score: 373
Places Rated Rank: 143

Tyler, TX
Elementary and Secondary
Public (95.6%): 9 districts, 48 schools,
27,496 pupils
Private (4.4%): 11 schools, 1,268 pupils
Colleges and Universities
Two-year: 1 public; 7,139 students
Four-year and beyond:
Public
University of Texas, Tyler (3,642)
Private
Texas College (478)
Places Rated Score: 154
Places Rated Rank: 219

Utica–Rome, NY
Elementary and Secondary
Public (91.9%): 29 districts, 105 schools,
52,178 pupils
Private (8.1%): 30 schools, 4,613 pupils
Colleges and Universities
Two-year: 3 public, 1 private; 8,553
students
Four-year and beyond:
Public
State University of New York College of
Technology, Utica–Rome (2,471)
Private
Hamilton College (1,685)
Utica College of Syracuse (2,381)
Places Rated Score: 216
Places Rated Rank: 198

Vallejo–Fairfield–Napa, CA
Elementary and Secondary
Public (89.9%): 15 districts, 117 schools,
63,172 pupils
Private (10.1%): 39 schools, 7,092 pupils
Colleges and Universities
Two-year: 2 public; 14,001 students
Four-year and beyond:
Public
California Maritime Academy (372)
Private
Pacific Union College (1,404)
CMSA Access: San Francisco–
Oakland–San Jose, CA
Places Rated Score: 568
Places Rated Rank: 111

Vancouver, WA
Elementary and Secondary
Public (96.0%): 9 districts, 79 schools,
42,673 pupils
Private (4.0%): 13 schools, 1,770 pupils
Colleges and Universities
Two-year: 1 public; 6,904 students
CMSA Access: Portland–Vancouver, OR
Places Rated Score: 164
Places Rated Rank: 215

Victoria, TX
Elementary and Secondary
Public (90.0%): 5 districts, 29 schools,
14,969 pupils
Private (10.0%): 9 schools, 1,663 pupils
Colleges and Universities
Two-year: 1 public; 2,953 students
Four-year and beyond:
Public
University of Houston, Victoria (748)
Places Rated Score: 44
Places Rated Rank: 303

Vineland–Millville–Bridgeton, NJ
Elementary and Secondary
Public (90.1%): 17 districts, 57 schools,
25,823 pupils
Private (9.9%): 14 schools, 2,825 pupils
Colleges and Universities
Two-year: 1 public; 2,232 students
CMSA Access: Philadelphia–
Wilmington–Trenton, PA–NJ–DE–MD
Places Rated Score: 464
Places Rated Rank: 124

Visalia–Tulare–Porterville, CA
Elementary and Secondary
Public (96.7%): 51 districts, 122 schools,
61,522 pupils
Private (3.3%): 14 schools, 2,118 pupils
Colleges and Universities
Two-year: 2 public; 10,171 students
Places Rated Score: 102
Places Rated Rank: 252

Waco, TX
Elementary and Secondary
Public (94.3%): 19 districts, 69 schools,
31,089 pupils
Private (5.7%): 12 schools, 1,878 pupils
Colleges and Universities
Two-year: 2 public; 9,557 students
Four-year and beyond:
Private
Baylor University (11,556)
Paul Quinn College (464)
Places Rated Score: 336
Places Rated Rank: 150

★ Washington, DC–MD–VA
Elementary and Secondary
Public (86.5%): 21 districts, 927 schools, 566,161 pupils
Private (13.5%): 380 schools, 88,082 pupils
Colleges and Universities
Two-year: 7 public, 1 private; 73,360 students
Four-year and beyond:
Public
Bowie State College (2,867)
George Mason University (17,652)
Uniformed Services University of the Health Sciences (741)
University of Maryland University College (12,531)
University of Maryland, College Park (38,639)
University of the District of Columbia (11,098)
Private
American University (10,667)
Capitol College (1,026)
Catholic University of America (6,661)
Columbia Union College (999)
Corcoran School of Art (258)
Gallaudet University (1,983)
George Washington University (18,711)
Georgetown University (11,967)
Hood College (1,951)
Howard University (11,053)
Marymount University (2,459)
Mount Saint Marys College (1,769)
Mount Vernon College (520)
Southeastern University (1,046)
Trinity College (961)
Washington Bible College (437)
Washington Theological Union (273)
Wesley Theological Seminary (374)
Places Rated Score: 3,866
Places Rated Rank: 6

Waterbury, CT
Elementary and Secondary
Public (80.6%): 10 districts, 65 schools, 29,510 pupils
Private (19.4%): 25 schools, 7,093 pupils
Colleges and Universities
Two-year: 2 public; 5,062 students
Four-year and beyond:
Private
Post College (1,564)
Places Rated Score: 62
Places Rated Rank: 283

Waterloo–Cedar Falls, IA
Elementary and Secondary
Public (85.1%): 13 districts, 64 schools, 24,058 pupils
Private (14.9%): 15 schools, 4,226 pupils
Colleges and Universities
Two-year: 1 public; 2,106 students
Four-year and beyond:
Public
University of Northern Iowa (12,312)
Private
Wartburg College (1,329)
Places Rated Score: 294
Places Rated Rank: 161

Wausau, WI
Elementary and Secondary
Public (84.3%): 9 districts, 39 schools, 17,413 pupils
Private (15.7%): 23 schools, 3,236 pupils

Colleges and Universities
Two-year: 1 public; 3,771 students
Places Rated Score: 38
Places Rated Rank: 310

West Palm Beach–Boca Raton–Delray Beach, FL
Elementary and Secondary
Public (82.5%): 2 districts, 102 schools, 86,878 pupils
Private (17.5%): 72 schools, 18,388 pupils
Colleges and Universities
Two-year: 1 public; 12,742 students
Four-year and beyond:
Public
Florida Atlantic University (10,729)
Private
College of Boca Raton (912)
Palm Beach Atlantic College (1,133)
Places Rated Score: 383
Places Rated Rank: 138

Wheeling, WV–OH
Elementary and Secondary
Public (88.1%): 9 districts, 71 schools, 25,873 pupils
Private (11.9%): 20 schools, 3,487 pupils
Colleges and Universities
Two-year: 3 public; 5,325 students
Four-year and beyond:
Public
West Liberty State College (2,552)
Private
Wheeling College (1,030)
Places Rated Score: 125
Places Rated Rank: 237

Wichita, KS
Elementary and Secondary
Public (89.6%): 25 districts, 198 schools, 80,741 pupils
Private (10.4%): 41 schools, 9,400 pupils
Colleges and Universities
Two-year: 1 public, 1 private; 3,817 students
Four-year and beyond:
Public
Wichita State University (16,248)
Private
Bethel College (634)
Friends University (1,100)
Kansas Newman College (765)
Places Rated Score: 413
Places Rated Rank: 130

Wichita Falls, TX
Elementary and Secondary
Public (95.5%): 5 districts, 43 schools, 21,763 pupils
Private (4.5%): 7 schools, 1,027 pupils
Colleges and Universities
Four-year and beyond:
Public
Midwestern State University (4,468)
Places Rated Score: 89
Places Rated Rank: 263

Williamsport, PA
Elementary and Secondary
Public (94.8%): 9 districts, 39 schools, 19,735 pupils
Private (5.2%): 10 schools, 1,089 pupils
Colleges and Universities
Two-year: 1 public; 3,357 students

Four-year and beyond:
Private
Lycoming College (1,086)
Places Rated Score: 55
Places Rated Rank: 293

Wilmington, DE–NJ–MD
Elementary and Secondary
Public (78.9%): 23 districts, 153 schools, 82,493 pupils
Private (21.1%): 75 schools, 22,059 pupils
Colleges and Universities
Two-year: 3 public; 6,909 students
Four-year and beyond:
Public
University of Delaware (18,631)
Private
Goldey Beacom College (1,840)
Widener University, Delaware Campus (350)
Wilmington College (1,227)
CMSA Access: Philadelphia–Wilmington–Trenton, PA–NJ–DE–MD
Places Rated Score: 903
Places Rated Rank: 59

Wilmington, NC
Elementary and Secondary
Public (92.3%): 2 districts, 30 schools, 19,594 pupils
Private (7.7%): 12 schools, 1,635 pupils
Colleges and Universities
Two-year: 1 public; 2,568 students
Four-year and beyond:
Public
University of North Carolina, Wilmington (6,254)
Places Rated Score: 151
Places Rated Rank: 220

Worcester, MA
Elementary and Secondary
Public (88.8%): 27 districts, 149 schools, 62,384 pupils
Private (11.2%): 30 schools, 7,865 pupils
Colleges and Universities
Two-year: 1 public, 3 private; 7,583 students
Four-year and beyond:
Public
University of Massachusetts Medical School (507)
Worcester State College (6,867)
Private
Anna Maria College (1,233)
Assumption College (2,590)
Atlantic Union College (566)
Central New England College of Technology (620)
Clark University (3,398)
College of the Holy Cross (2,658)
Nichols College (1,345)
Worcester Polytechnic Institute (4,022)
Places Rated Score: 552
Places Rated Rank: 113

Yakima, WA
Elementary and Secondary
Public (95.8%): 15 districts, 79 schools, 36,367 pupils
Private (4.2%): 13 schools, 1,595 pupils
Colleges and Universities
Two-year: 1 public; 3,706 students

Four-year and beyond:
Private
  Heritage College (342)
Places Rated Score: 44
Places Rated Rank: 303

York, PA
Elementary and Secondary
  Public (90.2%): 21 districts, 118 schools,
    57,679 pupils
  Private (9.8%): 40 schools, 6,295 pupils
Colleges and Universities
  Four-year and beyond:
  Public
    Pennsylvania State University, York
      (1,294)

Private
  Gettysburg College (2,003)
  Lutheran Theological Seminary (256)
  York College of Pennsylvania (4,633)
Places Rated Score: 164
Places Rated Rank: 215

Youngstown–Warren, OH
Elementary and Secondary
  Public (88.7%): 35 districts, 182 schools,
    86,816 pupils
  Private (11.3%): 41 schools, 11,011 pupils
Colleges and Universities
  Two-year: 1 public, 1 private; 1,999
    students

Four-year and beyond:
Public
  Youngstown State University (15,015)
Places Rated Score: 320
Places Rated Rank: 151

Yuba City, CA
Elementary and Secondary
  Public (95.1%): 20 districts, 58 schools,
    21,325 pupils
  Private (4.9%): 9 schools, 1,105 pupils
Colleges and Universities
  Two-year: 1 public; 7,909 students
Places Rated Score: 79
Places Rated Rank: 270

Et Cetera

SOLVING THE SAT PUZZLE . . . OR TRYING

After 17 years of unbroken decline, the average scores of students on the Scholastic Aptitude Tests (SAT), given by the College Entrance Examination Board, bottomed out in 1980 and started slowly upward in 1982. At the current rate of recovery, however, math scores won't match their 1963 high until the year 2000 and verbal scores not until well into the next century.

Two researchers pointed out that SAT scores started declining 18 years after the 1945 atomic bomb tests and began rising 18 years after the United States suspended all but underground atomic testing in 1963. The steepest drops in scores occurred in states nearest the bomb detonations, especially Nevada and Utah; smaller declines occurred in the northeastern and southeastern states that were far from the proving grounds. According to these researchers, those who blame the drop in SAT scores on television viewing, the Vietnam War, the child-spacing effect, changes in the number and mix of students taking the test, and poorer performance of schools are overlooking the effects of atomic fallout on the cognitive abilities of children.

But in Texas two other scholars of SAT trends have a different theory. The states that have the records of the highest scores, they claim, are not those that spend the most money for education, nor those with a long tradition of quality public education, but those with the coldest winters: Average scores from cold-weather states are consistently higher than scores from warm-weather states. They offer two explanations for the link between cold weather and high SAT scores: (1) research on thermal conditions and human behavior suggests that cool room temperatures reduce mistakes on tests, and (2) long winters force children to remain inside after school and on weekends, thereby favoring family inter-

action, which is critical for pupil achievement.

Nonsense, another researcher points out. If one were to rank the states by their average total SATs, one would be ranking the states by the percent of college-bound seniors who actually took the test. In general, the larger the group tested, the lower the average level of performance. See the table that follows for states' average SAT scores.

CERTIFYING PUPILS . . .

In the late 1970s, parents became convinced that teachers were neglecting the primary subjects, particularly reading, writing, and mathematics. Moreover, it wasn't possible to tell from a report card just how well a child was doing in relation to other children. Students were being promoted from grade to grade regardless of accomplishment. The result: Elementary pupils and even high school graduates who couldn't read a newspaper, write an intelligent sentence, address a postcard, or balance a checkbook.

This concern about students being ill-prepared for adulthood led to a movement among taxpayers for accountability, or the holding of school districts responsible for teaching basic skills. One form of accountability is mandatory competency testing, an exam taken by each pupil to certify whether he or she can actually read, write, and solve mathematical problems.

Forty states employ competency tests mainly to identify students who need "remediation," a term that means tutoring or retaking a course. Twenty-two states, however, use the test to certify pupils for grade promotion in elementary school or for high school graduation.

Average SAT Scores: The States Ranked

State	Percent of College-Bound Seniors Tested	Average Score (Total Verbal plus Math)
1. Iowa	5%	1,090
2. South Dakota	6	1,070
3. North Dakota	5	1,053
4. Kansas	10	1,035
5. Utah	6	1,034
6. Nebraska	10	1,032
7. Tennessee	13	1,009
8. Wisconsin	14	1,007
9. Oklahoma	9	1,005
10. New Mexico	12	1,002
11. Minnesota	17	1,001
11. Mississippi	4	1,001
11. Wyoming	12	1,001
14. Alabama	9	1,000
14. Montana	20	1,000
16. Arkansas	7	995
17. Kentucky	10	990
17. Missouri	14	990
19. Louisiana	10	989
20. Illinois	18	984
21. Colorado	29	971
22. Michigan	13	970
23. Idaho	16	968
24. Arizona	22	955
25. Ohio	23	951
26. West Virginia	14	947
27. Washington	37	942
28. New Hampshire	68	933
29. Nevada	24	926
30. Oregon	50	923
31. Alaska	43	916
32. Vermont	64	909
33. California	44	908
33. Connecticut	81	908
33. Maryland	60	908
36. Massachusetts	73	906
37. Virginia	63	902
38. Rhode Island	64	900
39. Delaware	62	899
40. Maine	59	896
41. New Jersey	69	893
42. Florida	49	890
43. New York	72	889
44. Hawaii	52	888
45. Pennsylvania	63	886
46. Texas	45	879
47. Indiana	55	870
48. Georgia	63	848
49. North Carolina	58	841
50. District of Columbia	67	839
51. South Carolina	57	838

Source: College Entrance Examination Board, 1989.

Grade Promotion and High School Graduation: The 22 States That Certify Students

State	Test Required for: Grade Promotion	High School Graduation	First Graduating Class Assessed
Alabama		•	1985
Arizona		•	1976
Arkansas	•	•	
California	•	•	1979
Delaware		•	1981
Florida	•	•	1983
Georgia	•	•	1985
Hawaii		•	1983
Kentucky	•	•	
Louisiana	•		1992
Maryland		•	1982
Mississippi		•	1987
Nevada		•	1982
New Jersey		•	1985
New York		•	1979
North Carolina		•	1980
Oregon		•	1978
South Carolina	•	•	1990
Tennessee	•	•	1982
Texas		•	1986
Vermont	•		1981
Virginia		•	1981

Source: U.S. Department of Education, *Digest of Education Statistics*, 1988.

... AND TESTING THE TEACHERS

Pupils in public schools aren't the only ones encountering competency tests. To identify candidates who have neither an aptitude for teaching nor skill in an academic discipline, 20 states require new teachers to take a competency test before they get their first license. Some of these states administer the test before the candidate enters a teacher-training program, while other states test the candidate after the training sequence but before the license is awarded.

That's not the end of teacher accountability. Thirty-nine states require teachers to renew their licenses, or become recertified, by taking continuing education courses. The renewal period is usually every three to five years, though some states allow longer periods based on the candidate's successful teaching experience. Thirty-four of these states will issue no lifetime licenses. Five states—Indiana, Michigan, Rhode Island, Texas, and Washington—have periodic renewal leading to life certificates, which are increasingly being linked to advanced professional training.

CONTINUING EDUCATION: A GROWING TREND

More and more, education in the United States is seen as a lifelong experience rather than one that ends abruptly upon graduation from high school or college. There are many reasons for this: Workers in technical industries need retraining, professionals need "state of the art" courses for periodic recertification, and others pursue myriad personal and vocational interests. Today, there are more than twice as many adults enrolled in part-time education as there are full-time college students (28 million versus 13 million).

Raising Standards: The New Basics

The National Commission on Excellence in Education recommends that all college-bound high school seniors be required to take at least 16 units of the New Basics before qualifying for their diplomas. The commission defines these New Basics as one year of computer science, two years of a foreign language, four years of English, three years of mathematics, three years of science, and three years of social studies.

In ranking the states by the number of such courses their legislatures or state boards of education require of college-bound seniors, only Alabama, Texas, and Virginia come close to the recommended standard.

Eight states—Colorado, Iowa, Maine, Massachusetts, Michigan, Nebraska, Wisconsin, and Wyoming—have their own graduation requirements, determined by local boards, that do not conform to the New Basics formula.

High School Courses Required for Graduation: The States Ranked

State	New Basics Units	Computer	Foreign Language	English	Mathematics	Science	Social Studies	Physical Education	Electives
1. Alabama	16.0		2.0	4.0	3.0	3.0	4.0	1.5	4.0
1. Virginia	16.0		3.0	4.0	3.0	3.0	3.0	2.0	4.0
3. Texas	15.5	1.0	2.0	4.0	3.0	3.0	2.5	2.0	3.0
4. Tennessee	15.0		2.0	4.0	3.0	3.0	3.0	1.5	2.0
5. Louisiana	13.5	0.5		4.0	3.0	3.0	3.0	2.0	7.5
5. Rhode Island	13.5	0.5	2.0	4.0	3.0	2.0	2.0		4.0
7. Florida	13.0			4.0	3.0	3.0	3.0	1.0	9.0
7. Missouri	13.0			4.0	3.0	3.0	3.0	1.0	8.0
7. Pennsylvania	13.0			4.0	3.0	3.0	3.0	1.0	5.0
10. Oklahoma	12.5	0.5	1.0	4.0	3.0	2.0	2.0		4.0
11. Connecticut	12.0			4.0	3.0	2.0	3.0	1.0	6.0
11. Georgia	12.0	1.0		4.0	2.0	2.0	3.0	1.0	8.0
11. Hawaii	12.0			4.0	2.0	2.0	4.0	1.5	6.0
11. Maryland	12.0			4.0	3.0	2.0	3.0	1.0	5.0
11. New Mexico	12.0			4.0	3.0	2.0	3.0	1.0	9.0
11. New York	12.0			4.0	2.0	2.0	4.0	0.5	
11. South Carolina	12.0			4.0	3.0	2.0	3.0	1.0	7.0
11. Vermont	12.0			4.0	3.0	2.0	3.0	1.5	
19. Oregon	11.5		1.0	3.0	2.0	2.0	3.5	2.0	8.0
19. South Dakota	11.5	0.5		4.0	2.0	2.0	3.0		8.0
21. Alaska	11.0			4.0	2.0	2.0	3.0	1.0	9.0
21. Arkansas	11.0			4.0	2.0	2.0	3.0	1.0	6.5
21. California	11.0		1.0	3.0	2.0	2.0	3.0	2.0	
21. Delaware	11.0			4.0	2.0	2.0	3.0	1.5	6.5
21. Kansas	11.0			4.0	2.0	2.0	3.0	1.0	8.0
21. Kentucky	11.0			4.0	3.0	2.0	2.0	1.0	7.0
21. New Hampshire	11.0	0.5		4.0	2.0	2.0	2.5	1.25	4.0
21. New Jersey	11.0			4.0	3.0	2.0	2.0	4.0	4.0
21. North Dakota	11.0			4.0	2.0	2.0	3.0	1.0	5.0
21. West Virginia	11.0			4.0	2.0	2.0	3.0	2.0	7.0
31. Nevada	10.5	0.5		4.0	2.0	2.0	2.0	2.5	8.5
31. Utah	10.5	0.5		3.0	2.0	2.0	3.0	2.0	9.0
33. Arizona	10.0			4.0	2.0	2.0	2.0		9.5
33. Idaho	10.0			4.0	2.0	2.0	2.0	1.5	6.0
33. Indiana	10.0			4.0	2.0	2.0	2.0	1.0	8.0
33. Maine	10.0			4.0	2.0	2.0	2.0	1.5	3.5
33. Mississippi	10.0			4.0	2.0	2.0	2.0		8.0
33. North Carolina	10.0			4.0	2.0	2.0	2.0	1.0	9.0
39. Washington	9.5			3.0	2.0	2.0	2.5	2.0	5.5
40. Illinois	9.0		1.0	3.0	2.0	1.0	2.0	4.5	2.25
40. Minnesota	9.0			4.0	1.0	1.0	3.0	1.5	9.5
42. Montana	8.5			4.0	2.0	1.0	1.5	1.0	10.5
43. Ohio	8.0			3.0	2.0	1.0	2.0	1.0	9.0

Source: Derived from U.S. Department of Education, *Digest of Education Statistics, 1988.*

Testing the Teachers

State	Competency Test	Competency Starting	Recertification Required	Recertification Every . . .
Alabama	Yes	1981	Yes	8–12 yr*
Alaska	No		Yes	5
Arizona	Yes	1980	Yes	6
Arkansas	Yes	1983	Yes	6–10*
California	Yes	1982	Yes	5
Colorado	Yes	1983	Yes	5
Connecticut	Yes	1985	No	
Delaware	Yes	1983	No	
Florida	Yes	1980	Yes	6
Georgia	Yes	1979	Yes	5–10*
Hawaii	No		No	
Idaho	No		No	
Illinois	No		No	
Indiana	No		Yes	5–10*
Iowa	No		Yes	6–10*
Kansas	No		Yes	3–5*
Kentucky	No		Yes	10
Louisiana	Yes	1979	No	
Maine	No		Yes	5
Maryland	No		Yes	5–10*
Massachusetts	No		No	
Michigan	No		Yes	6
Minnesota	No		Yes	5
Mississippi	Yes	1977	Yes	5–10*
Missouri	No		No	
Montana	No		Yes	5
Nebraska	No		Yes	3
Nevada	No		Yes	5–6*
New Hampshire	No		Yes	3
New Jersey	No		No	
New Mexico	Yes	1983	Yes	4–10*
New York	Yes	1984	No	
North Carolina	Yes	1981	Yes	5
North Dakota	No		Yes	5
Ohio	No		Yes	4–8*
Oklahoma	Yes	1982	Yes	5
Oregon	No		Yes	3–5*
Pennsylvania	No		Yes	6
Rhode Island	No		Yes	3–5*
South Carolina	Yes	1982	Yes	5
South Dakota	No		Yes	5
Tennessee	Yes	1981	Yes	10
Texas	Yes	1985	Yes	3–5*
Utah	No		Yes	5
Vermont	No		Yes	5
Virginia	Yes	1981	Yes	5
Washington	No		Yes	4
West Virginia	Yes	1985	Yes	3–5*
Wisconsin	No		No	
Wyoming	No		Yes	5–10*

Source: Education Commission of the States, *Clearinghouse Notes,* and *Phi Delta Kappan,* October 1984.

*Certification interval depends on years of successful teaching experience.

One measure of the importance of continuing education is the way the states have responded to demands that professionals such as doctors, lawyers, accountants, and social workers be certified as competent. Mandatory continuing education is found in every state as a condition for renewing a license to practice in many professions. The most demanding states in this regard are Iowa, Florida, Kansas, Minnesota, Nevada, and New Mexico; the least are Hawaii, New York, and Wisconsin.

OUTSTANDING PUBLIC SECONDARY SCHOOLS

Since 1983, the U.S. Department of Education has periodically polled the chief education officer in each of the states and the Council For American Private Education (CAPE) for the names of the best secondary schools in the country.

Of the 2,179 schools nominated, 902 have received official recognition for excellence in education. The schools had to withstand a tough screening process, which included a careful look at curricula and academic achievement; inspection of buildings, classrooms, and facilities; informal observations of classes, lunch periods, and assemblies; and interviews with pupils, parents, teachers, and administrators. The people who did the screening, none of whom worked for the federal government, were specialists in school improvement and accreditation.

Of these outstanding secondary schools, 685 are located in metro areas. The schools include 313 junior high schools (JHS), middle schools (MS), and intermediate schools (IS), as well as 372 high schools (HS).

The Best Secondary Schools in the Metro Areas

Akron, OH
Hudson HS, Hudson
Hudson JHS, Hudson
Jennings MS, Akron
Perkins JHS, Akron
Theodore Roosevelt HS, Kent

Albany–Schenectady–Troy, NY
Koda JHS, Clifton Park
LaSalle Institute, Troy
Niskayuna HS, Schenectady
Oneida MS, Schenectady
Scotia–Glenville HS, Scotia
Shaker HS, Latham

Albuquerque, NM
Albuquerque HS, Albuquerque
Cibola HS, Albuquerque
Eisenhower MS, Albuquerque
Highland HS, Albuquerque
Hoover MS, Albuquerque
Jefferson MS, Albuquerque
John Adams MS, Albuquerque
Manzano HS, Albuquerque
Polk MS, Albuquerque
Taft MS, Albuquerque
Van Buren MS, Albuquerque
Washington MS, Albuquerque
West Mesa HS, Albuquerque

Allentown–Bethlehem, PA–NJ
Dieruff HS, Allentown, PA

Anaheim–Santa Ana, CA
Corona del Mar HS, Newport Beach
Marina HS, Huntington Beach
Parks JHS, Fullerton
University HS, Irvine
Venado MS, Irvine
Woodbridge HS, Irvine

Anchorage, AK
Romig JHS, Anchorage

Ann Arbor, MI
Huron HS, Ann Arbor
Slauson IS, Ann Arbor

Appleton–Oshkosh–Neenah, WI
Butte des Morts JHS, Menasha
Neenah HS, Neenah

Atlanta, GA
Benjamin Elijah Mays School, Atlanta
Brookwood HS, Snellville
Conyers MS, Conyers
Douglass HS, Atlanta
Garrett MS, Austell
Lakeside HS, Atlanta
Marist School, Atlanta
Newton County HS, Covington
North Fulton HS, Atlanta
Parkview HS, Lilburn
Shiloh MS, Lithonia
Tapp MS, Powder Springs
Walton HS, Marietta

Austin, TX
Austin HS, Austin

Baltimore, MD
Archbishop Keough HS, Baltimore
Centennial HS, Ellicott City
Glenelg HS, Glenelg
Loyola HS of Baltimore, Towson
Wilde Lake MS, Columbia

Baton Rouge, LA
Baton Rouge HS, Baton Rouge
Episcopal HS, Baton Rouge
McKinley MS, Baton Rouge

Bellingham, WA
Blaine HS, Blaine
Ferndale HS, Ferndale

Bergen–Passaic, NJ
Dwight–Englewood School, Englewood
Northern Highlands Regional HS, Allendale

What Teachers Earn

Parents think that teachers bail out of their profession because of burnout brought on by semester after semester of unruly and unmotivated pupils. Not entirely, say ex-teachers; it's mainly because of the money.

Their seventh- and eighth-grade pupils pull down $3.00 an hour for baby-sitting, teachers point out when they negotiate their contracts. If a teacher working five class periods were to be paid $3.00 per day for nothing more than watching over each child in an average-size classroom, he or she would earn $7,500 each month of the academic year. Yet teachers accomplish much more than keeping every five- to 17-year-old off the street. They teach them, too, throughout the long, arduous day. Therefore, the argument goes, teachers should be paid more.

Teaching requires formal preparation, certification, and a lifelong perfection of skills. Moreover, teacher earnings have suffered more from inflation than the earnings of other professionals; the average amount of money teachers earn today is about what they made in 1973, after adjustment for inflation. On the other hand, in every one of America's metro areas, teachers earn more than uniformed firemen and policemen. Some taxpayers and city managers point out that for nine months' work, classroom teachers are the best paid of municipal workers.

The $1,700 difference between the monthly paychecks of Alaska teachers and those in South Dakota may reflect the value taxpayers and city managers place on teachers as much as differences in the cost of living and average household income.

Average Teacher Salaries

State	Average Salary	Rank	State	Average Salary	Rank
Alabama	$25,190	37	Montana	24,414	41
Alaska	41,693	1	Nebraska	24,203	42
Arizona	28,684	23	Nevada	28,840	22
Arkansas	21,692	50	New Hampshire	26,703	29
California	35,285	5	New Jersey	32,923	9
Colorado	29,558	17	New Mexico	25,205	36
Connecticut	37,339	3	New York	36,500	4
Delaware	31,605	11	North Carolina	25,650	34
District of Columbia	37,504	2	North Dakota	22,249	46
Florida	26,648	30	Ohio	29,152	20
Georgia	28,038	25	Oklahoma	22,000	48
Hawaii	30,778	15	Oregon	29,500	18
Idaho	22,860	44	Pennsylvania	30,720	16
Illinois	31,195	13	Rhode Island	34,233	7
Indiana	28,664	24	South Carolina	25,060	38
Iowa	25,884	33	South Dakota	20,480	51
Kansas	27,401	27	Tennessee	25,619	35
Kentucky	24,920	40	Texas	26,513	31
Louisiana	22,470	45	Utah	23,023	43
Maine	24,933	39	Vermont	26,861	28
Maryland	33,700	8	Virginia	29,056	21
Massachusetts	31,670	10	Washington	29,176	19
Michigan	34,419	6	West Virginia	21,904	49
Minnesota	31,500	12	Wisconsin	31,046	14
Mississippi	22,036	47	Wyoming	27,685	26
Missouri	25,981	32			

Source: National Education Association, 1989.

Pompton Lakes HS, Pompton Lakes
Ridgewood HS, Ridgewood

Billings, MT
Will James JHS, Billings

Binghamton, NY
Vestal SHS, Vestal

Birmingham, AL
Bush MS, Birmingham
Homewood HS, Homewood
Homewood MS, Homewood
Mountain Brook HS, Mountain Brook
Riverchase MS, Shelby
Simmons JHS, Birmingham

Bismarck, ND
Hughes JHS, Bismarck

Boston, MA
Acton-Boxborough HS, Acton
Charles Sumner Pierce MS, Milton
Milton HS, Milton
Rockland JHS, Rockland
W. S. Parker MS, Reading
Wayland HS, Wayland
Wilson JHS, Natick

Bridgeport–Milford, CT
Fairfield College Prep School, Fairfield
Flood IS, Stratford
Wooster IS, Stratford

Buffalo, NY
School #59—Science Magnet, Buffalo

Burlington, VT
South Burlington HS, South Burlington
South Burlington MS, South Burlington

Casper, WY
Walsh HS, Casper

Cedar Rapids, IA
Franklin JHS, Cedar Rapids
Linn-Mar HS, Marion
Linn-Mar JHS, Cedar Rapids
Metro Secondary School, Cedar Rapids

Thomas Jefferson SHS, Cedar Rapids
Washington HS, Cedar Rapids

Champaign–Urbana–Rantoul, IL
Champaign MS at Columbia, Champaign
Mahomet-Seymour HS, Mahomet

Charleston, WV
Washington HS, Charleston

Charlotte–Gastonia–Rock Hill, NC-SC
Carmel JHS, Charlotte, NC
Charlotte Latin School, Charlotte, NC

States Requiring Professionals to Continue Their Education

State	Certified Public Accountants	Dentists	Lawyers	Nurses	Nursing-Home Administrators	Optometrists	Pharmacists	Physicians	Real Estate Personnel	Social Workers	Veterinarians
Alabama	•	•			•	•	•		•	•	•
Alaska	•		•			•	•	•			•
Arkansas	•				•	•	•		•	•	•
Arizona	•				•	•	•	•	•	•	•
California	•	•	•	•	•	•	•	•	•		
Colorado	•	•	•			•					•
Connecticut	•					•	•		•		
Delaware	•	•			•	•	•	•		•	
Florida	•	•	•	•	•	•	•				•
Georgia	•	•			•	•	•				
Hawaii	•					•		•			
Idaho	•	•			•	•	•				
Illinois	•				•	•	•				•
Indiana	•				•	•					
Iowa	•	•		•	•	•	•		•	•	•
Kansas	•	•	•	•	•	•	•		•		•
Kentucky	•	•	•		•	•	•				•
Louisiana	•		•		•	•		•			
Maine	•				•	•	•			•	
Maryland	•				•	•			•	•	•
Massachusetts	•	•		•	•	•	•	•		•	
Michigan	•				•	•	•		•		
Minnesota	•	•		•	•	•	•			•	
Mississippi	•		•		•	•	•				•
Missouri	•		•		•	•	•				
Montana	•		•		•	•	•				
Nebraska	•				•	•	•	•			
Nevada	•	•	•		•	•	•	•	•	•	
New Hampshire	•			•	•	•	•	•	•		•
New Jersey	•				•	•					
New Mexico	•	•	•		•	•	•	•	•		
New York	•				•				•		
North Carolina	•	•			•	•	•			•	
North Dakota	•	•	•		•	•	•		•	•	•
Ohio	•	•	•		•	•	•	•	•	•	•
Oklahoma	•	•	•		•	•	•		•		
Oregon	•		•	•	•	•			•		•
Pennsylvania	•				•						•
Rhode Island	•				•	•	•	•			
South Carolina	•	•			•					•	
South Dakota	•	•			•	•			•	•	
Tennessee	•		•		•	•				•	
Texas	•		•		•	•					
Utah	•				•	•					
Vermont	•	•			•	•					
Virginia		•			•	•				•	
Washington	•	•			•	•	•	•			•
West Virginia		•			•	•				•	
Wisconsin		•			•	•		•			
Wyoming	•	•			•	•	•		•	•	

Source: © Louis Phillips and Associates, Athens, GA, 1989.

Myers Park HS, Charlotte, NC
Providence Day School, Charlotte, NC
Rock Hill HS, Rock Hill, SC
Chattanooga, TN–GA
Brown MS, Harrison, TN
Central HS, Harrison, TN
Hixson HS, Hixson, TN
Chicago, IL
Carl Sandburg HS, Orland Park

Community HS North, Downers Grove
Glenbrook North HS, Northbrook
Glenbrook South HS, Glenview
Hoffman Estates HS, Hoffman Estates
Homewood-Flossmoor HS, Flossmoor
Leyden East Campus, Franklin Park

Leyden West Campus, Northlake
Maine Township HS East, Park Ridge
Marist HS, Chicago
Medinah ES, Roselle
Mother McAuley Liberal Arts HS, Chicago
Old Orchard JHS, Skokie
Oliver Wendell Holmes JHS, Wheeling

Rich Township HS, Richton Park
Springman JHS, Glenview
St. Louise de Marillac HS, Northfield
St. Rita HS, Chicago
Thomas JHS, Arlington Heights
University of Chicago Laboratory HS, Chicago
Wheeling HS, Wheeling

William Fremd HS, Palatine
York Community HS, Elmhurst

Cincinnati, OH–KY–IN
Harrison JHS, Harrison, OH
Highlands HS, Fort Thomas, KY
Holmes HS, Covington, KY
Indian Hill HS, Cincinnati, OH
Madeira HS, Cincinnati, OH
Mariemont HS, Cincinnati, OH
Mount Notre Dame HS, Cincinnati, OH
Ottawa MS, Cincinnati, OH
Princeton HS, Cincinnati, OH
Princeton JHS, Cincinnati, OH
School for Creative & Performing Arts, Cincinnati, OH
St. Bernard-Elmwood Place HS, St. Bernard, OH
Sycamore JHS, Cincinnati, OH
Walnut Hills HS, Cincinnati, OH
Wyoming HS, Wyoming, OH

Cleveland, OH
Berea HS, Berea
Brunswick MS, Brunswick
Mentor Shore JHS, Mentor
North Olmstead HS, North Olmstead
Shaker Heights HS, Shaker Heights
Shaker Heights MS, Shaker Heights
Villa Angela Academy, Cleveland
Woodbury JHS, Shaker Heights

Colorado Springs, CO
Cheyenne Mountain HS, Colorado Springs
Holmes JHS, Colorado Springs

Columbia, MO
Hickman HS, Columbia
Rock Bridge SHS, Columbia

Columbia, SC
Dent MS, Columbia
Irmo HS, Columbia
Richland Northeast HS, Columbia
Spring Valley HS, Columbia
Wright MS, Columbia

Columbus, GA–AL
Hardaway HS, Columbus, GA

Columbus, OH
Columbus Alternative HS, Columbus
Dublin MS, Dublin
Hastings MS, Upper Arlington
Jones MS, Columbus
Perry MS, Worthington
Upper Arlington HS, Upper Arlington
Worthingway MS, Worthington

Dallas, TX
Highland Park HS, Dallas
Plano SHS, Plano
Richardson HS, Richardson
St. Mark's School of Texas, Dallas
William H. Atwell Fundamental Academy, Dallas

Danbury, CT
New Fairfield HS, New Fairfield

Dayton–Springfield, OH
Ankeny JHS, Beavercreek
Centerville HS, Centerville

Daytona Beach, FL
Mainland HS, Daytona Beach

Denver, CO
Alameda JHS, Lakewood
Carmody JHS, Lakewood
Evergreen JHS, Evergreen
Mrachek MS, Aurora
Wheat Ridge HS, Wheat Ridge

Des Moines, IA
Indian Hills JHS, Des Moines
Valley HS, West Des Moines

Detroit, MI
Abbott MS, Orchard Lake
Andover HS, Bloomfield Hills
Berkshire MS, Birmingham
Brighton HS, Brighton
Brooks MS, Detroit
Cass Technical HS, Detroit
Cranbrook Kingswood School, Bloomfield Hills
Grosse Pointe North HS, Grosse Pointe Woods
Grosse Pointe South HS, Grosse Pointe
Lahser HS, Bloomfield Hills
Lamphere HS, Madison Heights
Larson MS, Troy
Lutheran HS North, Mount Clemens
Lutheran HS West, Detroit
Novi HS, Novi
Parcells MS, Grosse Pointe Woods
Seaholm HS, Birmingham
Southfield HS, Southfield
West Bloomfield HS, West Bloomfield
West Hills MS, West Bloomfield

Eau Claire, WI
Memorial HS, Eau Claire

El Paso, TX
Desert View MS, El Paso

Eugene–Springfield, OR
Monroe MS, Eugene
Oaklea MS, Junction City
South Eugene HS, Eugene

Evansville, IN–KY
Thompkins MS, Evansville, IN

Fargo–Moorhead, ND–MN
Franklin JHS, Fargo, ND

Florence, AL
Mars Hill Bible School, Florence

Fort Lauderdale–Hollywood–Pompano Beach, FL
Cardinal Gibbons HS, Fort Lauderdale
South Plantation HS, Plantation

Fort Myers–Cape Coral, FL
Fort Myers HS, Fort Myers

Fort Smith, AR–OK
Gans JHS, Muldrow, OK
Muldrow HS, Muldrow, OK
Southside HS, Fort Smith, AR

Fort Worth–Arlington, TX
Harwood JHS, Bedford

Fresno, CA
Clovis HS, Clovis
George W. Kastner IS, Fresno

Gary–Hammond, IN
Chesterton HS, Chesterton
Fegely MS, Portage
Valparaiso HS, Valparaiso
Westchester MS, Chesterton

Grand Rapids, MI
East Grand Rapids HS, Grand Rapids
Northview HS, Grand Rapids
West Ottawa MS, Holland

Greensboro–Winston-Salem–High Point, NC
North Davie JHS, Mocksville

Greenville–Spartanburg, SC
Hillcrest MS, Greenville
League MS, Greenville
Mauldin HS, Mauldin
Spartanburg SHS, Spartanburg

Hartford, CT
Avon MS, Avon
Conard HS, West Hartford
Granby Memorial MS, Granby
Hall HS, West Hartford
Illing JHS, Manchester
King Philip MS, West Hartford
Martin Kellogg MS, Newington
Robbins JHS, Farmington
Welles JHS, Glastonbury

Honolulu, HI
Moanalua HS, Honolulu

Houma–Thibodaux, LA
Lockport JHS, Lockport
Raceland MS, Raceland

Houston, TX
Bellaire HS, Bellaire
Bleyl JHS, Houston
Clear Lake HS, Houston
Clear Lake Intermediate School, Houston
John Foster Dulles HS, Sugar Land
Kingwood HS, Kingwood
Scarborough SHS, Houston
Stratford HS, Houston

Indianapolis, IN
Ben Davis JHS, Indianapolis
Carmel HS, Carmel
Carmel JHS, Carmel
Clay JHS, Carmel
Davis HS, Indianapolis
Eastwood MS, Indianapolis
Lawrence Central HS, Indianapolis
Lawrence North HS, Indianapolis
Marshall HS, Indianapolis
North Central HS, Indianapolis
Warren Central HS, Indianapolis
Westland MS, Indianapolis

Iowa City, IA
Northwest JHS, Coralville
South East JHS, Iowa City

Jackson, MS
Clinton HS, Clinton

Jacksonville, FL
Davis JHS, Jacksonville
Gorris JHS, Jacksonville
Kirby-Smith JHS, Jacksonville
Parker HS, Jacksonville

Ribault HS, Jacksonville
Sandalwood JSHS, Jacksonville
Southside JHS, Jacksonville
Stanton College Preparatory School, Jacksonville

Kansas City, MO–KS
Blue Springs HS, Blue Springs, MO
Blue Springs JHS, Blue Springs, MO
Blue Valley HS, Overland Park, KS
Lewis MS, Excelsior Springs, MO
Meadowbrook JHS, Shawnee Mission, KS
Oregon Trail JHS, Olathe, KS
Palmer JHS, Independence, MO
Santa Fe Trail JHS, Olathe, KS
Shawnee Mission South HS, Shawnee Mission, KS
Shawnee Mission West HS, Shawnee Mission, KS
Sumner Academy of Arts and Science, Kansas City, KS

Knoxville, TN
Farragut MS, Knoxville

Lafayette, LA
Edgar Martin MS, Lafayette
Episcopal School of Acadiana, Cade
Lafayette MS, Lafayette
Scott MS, Scott
St. Thomas More Catholic HS, Lafayette

Lafayette–West Lafayette, IN
Jefferson HS, Lafayette

Lake County, IL
Adlai E. Stevenson HS, Prairie View
Daniel Wright MS, Lake Forest
Deer Path JHS, Lake Forest
Elm Place MS, Highland Park
Shepard JHS, Deerfield
Wilmot JHS, Deerfield

Lansing–East Lansing, MI
Lansing Catholic Central HS, Lansing
Okemos HS, Okemos

Las Cruces, NM
Las Cruces HS, Las Cruces

Las Vegas, NV
Cannon JHS, Las Vegas
Guinn JHS, Las Vegas
Las Vegas HS, Las Vegas

Lewiston–Auburn, ME
Auburn MS, Auburn

Lincoln, NE
East HS, Lincoln
Lincoln HS, Lincoln
Norris MS, Firth

Los Angeles–Long Beach, CA
Artesia HS, Lakewood
Audubon JHS, Los Angeles
Claremont HS, Claremont
Gretchen Whitney HS, Cerritos
Lindero Canyon MS, Agoura Hills
Montebello MS, Montebello
Palms JHS, Los Angeles
Pioneer HS, Whittier

Rosemont JHS, La Crescenta
West HS, Torrance

Louisville, KY–IN
Ballard HS, Louisville, KY
Maryhurst School, Louisville, KY
Oldham County HS, Buckner, KY
Oldham County MS, Buckner, KY
Thomas Jefferson MS, Louisville, KY

Lynchburg, VA
Glass HS, Lynchburg

Madison, WI
Edgewood HS of the Sacred Heart, Madison
LaFollette HS, Madison
Stoughton MS, Stoughton
Van Hise MS, Madison
West SHS, Madison

Medford, OR
Crater HS, Central Point

Melbourne–Titusville–Palm Bay, FL
Jefferson JHS, Merritt Island

Memphis, TN–AR–MS
Collierville MS, Collierville, TN
Snowden MS, Memphis, TN

Miami–Hialeah, FL
American HS, Hialeah
Highland Oaks JHS, North Miami Beach
Norland MS, Miami
North Miami Beach SHS, North Miami Beach
Our Lady of Lourdes Academy, Miami
Southwood JHS, Miami

Middlesex–Somerset–Hunterdon, NJ
Ridge HS, Basking Ridge

Milwaukee, WI
Brown Deer HS, Brown Deer
Burroughs MS, Milwaukee
Franklin HS, Franklin
Hamilton HS, Milwaukee
King HS, Milwaukee
Morse MS, Milwaukee
Vincent HS, Milwaukee
Webster Transitional MS, Cedarburg
Whitman MS, Wauwatosa

Minneapolis–St. Paul, MN–WI
Cambridge MS, Cambridge, MN
Centennial SHS, Circle Pines, MN
Edina HS, Edina, MN
Hastings JHS, Hastings, MN
Hopkins HS, Minnetonka, MN
Hopkins North JHS, Minnetonka, MN
Hopkins West JHS, Minnetonka, MN
John F. Kennedy SHS, Bloomington, MN
Oak Grove JHS, Bloomington, MN
Oak-Land JHS, Elmo, MN
Richfield HS, Richfield, MN
Rosemount HS, Rosemount, MN

South St. Paul HS, South St. Paul, MN
South View JHS, Edina, MN
St. Louis Park HS, St. Louis Park, MN
Stillwater JHS, Stillwater, MN
Stillwater SHS, Stillwater, MN
Valley MS, Rosemount, MN
Valley View JHS, Edina, MN

Mobile, AL
S.S. Murphy HS, Mobile
Vigor HS, Prichard

Nashua, NH
Amherst MS, Amherst
Londonderry HS, Londonderry
Londonderry JHS, Londonderry

Nashville, TN
Hillsboro HS, Nashville

Nassau–Suffolk, NY
Garden City JHS, Garden City
Garden City SHS, Garden City
Holy Trinity Diocesan HS, Hicksville
Miller Place HS, Miller Place
Murphy JHS, Stony Brook
Northport HS, Northport
Paul D. Schreiber HS, Port Washington
Paul J. Gelinas JHS, Setauket
Shoreham-Wading River HS, Shoreham
Shoreham-Wading River MS, Shoreham
Westbury SHS, Westbury
Woodmere MS, Hewlett

New Bedford, MA
Dartmouth HS, North Dartmouth
New Bedford HS, New Bedford

New Haven–Meriden, CT
Amity Regional HS, Orange
Conte Arts MS, New Haven

New Orleans, LA
Alfred Bonnabel HS, Metairie
Archbishop Chapelle HS, Metairie
Brother Martin HS, New Orleans
Jesuit HS, New Orleans
King HS, Metairie
Lakewood JHS, Luling
Metairie Park Country Day School, Metairie
Xavier Prep School, New Orleans

New York, NY
A. Phillip Randolph Campus HS, New York
Academy of Mount St. Ursula, Bronx
Academy of Our Lady of Good Counsel, White Plains
Archbishop Molloy HS, Briarwood
Blind Brook HS, Rye Brook
Blue Mountain MS, Peekskill
Bronx HS of Science, Bronx
Brooklyn Technical HS, Brooklyn
Cardozo HS, Bayside
Dr. Roland N. Patterson IS 229, Bronx

Edgemont HS, Scarsdale
Fox Lane MS, Bedford
Irvington MS, Irvington
Jamaica HS, Jamaica
Midwood HS at Brooklyn College, Brooklyn
Mother Cabrini, New York
Mount Vernon HS, Mount Vernon
New Rochelle HS, New Rochelle
North Salem MS, North Salem
Pierre Van Cortlandt MS, Croton-on-Hudson
Port Jefferson JHS, New York
Scarsdale HS, Scarsdale
Seth Low Intermediate School 96, Brooklyn
Shulamith HS for Girls, Brooklyn
Stuyvesant HS, New York
Tottenville HS, Staten Island
White Plains HS, White Plains
White Plains MS, White Plains

Norfolk–Virginia Beach–Newport News, VA
Denbigh HS, Newport News
Dunbar-Erwin MS, Newport News
Hampton HS, Hampton
Hines MS, Newport News
Huntington MS, Newport News
Lynnhaven JHS, Virginia Beach
Menchville HS, Newport News

Norwalk, CT
Middlebrook MS, Wilton
Wilton HS, Wilton

Oakland, CA
Alvarado MS, Union City
Castro Valley HS, Castro Valley
James Logan HS, Union City
Logan HS, Union City
Miramonte HS, Orinda
Mission San Jose HS, Fremont
Piedmont HS, Piedmont

Oklahoma City, OK
Marshall HS, Oklahoma City
Millwood HS, Oklahoma City
Northeast HS, Oklahoma City

Olympia, WA
Capital HS, Olympia
Jefferson MS, Olympia

Omaha, NE–IA
Arbor Heights JHS, Omaha, NE
Bellevue East HS, Bellevue, NE
Burke HS, Omaha, NE
Creighton Prep School, Omaha, NE
Kirn JHS, Council Bluffs, IA
McMillian JHS, Omaha, NE
Millard North HS, Omaha, NE
Millard North JHS, Omaha, NE
Millard South HS, Omaha, NE
Valley View JHS, Omaha, NE
Westbrook JHS, Omaha, NE
Westside HS, Omaha, NE

Orange County, NY
Newburgh Free Academy, Newburgh

Orlando, FL
Lyman HS, Longwood

Oxnard–Ventura, CA
Los Altos IS, Camarillo
Mesa Union School, Somis

Pawtucket–Woonsocket–Attleboro, RI–MA
Lincoln HS, Lincoln, RI

Philadelphia, PA–NJ
Academy of Notre Dame de Namur, Villanova, PA
Bala-Cynwyd MS, Bala-Cynwyd, PA
Central HS, Philadelphia, PA
Conestoga HS, Berwyn, PA
Downingtown Area HS, Downingtown, PA
E. T. Richardson MS, Springfield, PA
East HS, West Chester, PA
General Wayne MS, Malvern, PA
Great Valley HS, Malvern, PA
Harriton HS, Rosemont, PA
Haverford SHS, Havertown, PA
Henderson HS, West Chester, PA
Nether Providence MS, Wallingford, PA
Pennsbury HS, Fairless Hills, PA
Philadelphia HS for Girls, Philadelphia, PA
Radnor HS, Radnor, PA
Strath Haven HS, Wallingford, PA
Tredyffrin/Easttown JHS, Berwyn, PA
Welsh Valley MS, Narberth, PA
Wissahickon MS, Ambler, PA

Phoenix, AZ
Agua Fria Union HS, Avondale
Chandler HS, Chandler
Desert Shadows MS, Scottsdale
Dobson HS, Mesa
Foston JHS, Mesa
Greenway MS, Phoenix
Harvey L. Taylor JHS, Mesa
Kino JHS, Mesa
Mesa HS, Mesa
Mountain View HS, Mesa
Rhodes JHS, Mesa
Shea MS, Phoenix
Westwood HS, Mesa
Willis JHS, Chandler

Pine Bluff, AR
White Hall HS, Pine Bluff

Pittsburgh, PA
Central Catholic HS, Pittsburgh
Fort Couch MS, Upper St. Clair
Mount Lebanon HS, Pittsburgh
Schenley HS Teacher Center, Pittsburgh
Upper St. Clair HS, Pittsburgh

Pittsfield, MA
Nessacus MS, Dalton

Portland, ME
Deering HS, Portland
Gray-New Gloucester JHS, Gray

Greely HS, Cumberland
Greely JHS, Cumberland
King MS, Portland
Portland HS, Portland
Yarmouth JH/SHS, Yarmouth

Portland, OR
Beaumont MS, Portland
Beaverton HS, Beaverton
Cedar Park IS, Beaverton
Clackamas HS, Milwaukie
Gladstone HS, Gladstone
Lake Oswego HS, Lake
  Oswego
Lake Oswego JHS, Lake
  Oswego
Lakeridge HS, Lake Oswego
Light MS, Portland
McLoughlin JHS, Milwaukie
Ogden JHS, Oregon City
Oregon City HS, Oregon City
Renne IS, Newburg
Rex Putman HS, Milwaukie
Sunset HS, Beaverton
West Linn HS, West Linn
Wilbur Rowe JHS, Milwaukie

Portsmouth–Dover–Rochester, NH–ME
Exeter JHS, Exeter, NH

Providence, RI
Bain JHS, Cranston
East Greenwich HS, East
  Greenwich
Narragansett HS,
  Narragansett
Western Hills JHS, Cranston

Provo–Orem, UT
Timpview HS, Provo

Raleigh–Durham, NC
Broughton HS, Raleigh
Enloe HS, Raleigh

Reno, NV
Edward C. Reed HS, Sparks
Procter Hug HS, Reno
Reno HS, Reno
Swope MS, Reno

Richland–Kennewick–Pasco, WA
Hanford HS, Richland
Pasco HS, Pasco

Richmond–Petersburg, VA
Brookland MS, Richmond
Dooley School, Richmond
Hermitage HS, Richmond

Riverside–San Bernardino, CA
Mission JHS, Riverside
Terrace Hills JHS, Grand
  Terrace

Roanoke, VA
Breckinridge JHS, Roanoke
Cave Spring HS, Roanoke
Hidden Valley JHS, Roanoke
James Madison JHS, Roanoke

Rochester, MN
Adams JHS, Rochester

Rochester, NY
Greece Athena HS, Rochester
McQuaid Jesuit HS, Rochester
Pittsford MS, Pittsford

Rockford, IL
Boylan Central Catholic HS,
  Rockford

Sacramento, CA
Valley HS, Sacramento

Saginaw–Bay City–Midland, MI
Garber HS, Essexville

St. Louis, MO–IL
Brentwood JHS, Brentwood,
  MO
Clayton HS, Clayton, MO
Holman MS, St. Ann, MO
Jennings JHS, Jennings, MO
Ladue JHS, Ladue, MO
McCluer North HS, Florissant,
  MO
O'Fallon Township HS,
  O'Fallon, IL
Parkway Central HS, Chester-
  field, MO
Parkway East JHS, Creve
  Coeur, MO
Parkway North HS, Creve
  Couer, MO
Parkway South HS, Manches-
  ter, MO
Parkway West SHS, Ballwin,
  MO
Patonville Heights MS, Mary-
  land Heights, MO
Watkins HS, St. Louis, MO
Wydown JHS, Warson Woods,
  MO

Salem, OR
South Salem HS, Salem

Salinas–Seaside–Monterey, CA
North Monterey County HS,
  Castroville

Salt Lake City–Ogden, UT
Bountiful HS, Bountiful
Brighton HS, Salt Lake City
Butler MS, Salt Lake City
Eastmont MS, Salt Lake City
Highland HS, Salt Lake City
Mound Fort MS, Ogden
Olympus HS, Salt Lake City
Olympus JHS, Salt Lake City
South HS, Salt Lake City

San Antonio, TX
Bradley MS, San Antonio
Churchill HS, San Antonio
Robert G. Cole JH/SHS, San
  Antonio

San Diego, CA
Borrego Springs HS, Borrego
  Springs
Chula Vista HS, Chula Vista
Fallbrook Union HS, Fallbrook
Meadowbrook MS, Poway
Orange Glen HS, Escondido
Santana HS, Santee
Southwest HS, San Diego
Torrey Pines HS, Leucadia
Twin Peaks MS, Poway

San Francisco, CA
Borel MS, San Mateo
Crocker JHS, Hillsborough
Davidson MS, San Rafael
Horace Mann Academic MS,
  San Francisco
Lowell HS, San Francisco
Menlo-Atherton HS, Atherton

San Jose, CA
Homestead HS, Cupertino
Leyva JHS, San Jose

School Spankings and Paddlings

During a given school year, one of every 36 pupils is spanked or paddled at least once, and one in 19 is suspended for breaking school rules. According to the U.S. Department of Education, the states in which suspensions exceed the national average are, with the exception of California, all located east of the Mississippi River.

Paddling and spanking, typical forms of discipline in elementary school, are concentrated in the Southeast and adjacent southwestern states. In spite of a large number of teachers who approve of corporal punishment, however, it is outlawed in California, Hawaii, Maine, Massachusetts, Nebraska, New Hampshire, New Jersey, New York, Rhode Island, Vermont, and Wisconsin.

States Reporting Corporal Punishment Exceeding National Average

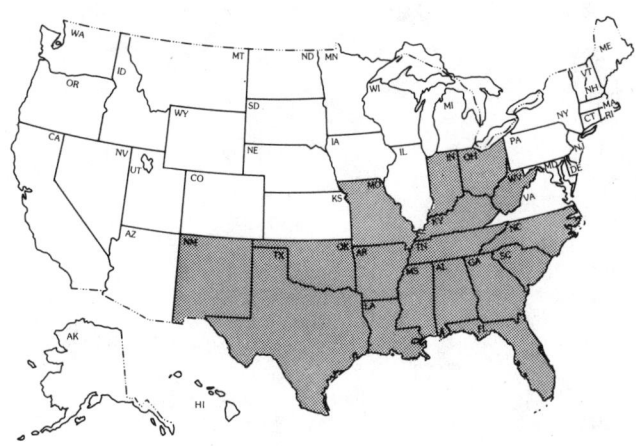

Source: National Center for Education Statistics, *Condition of Education*, 1984.

The national average for corporal punishment is 3.5% of public elementary and secondary school enrollment. The shaded area of the map shows states exceeding this level.

Los Gatos HS, Los Gatos
Miller JHS, San Jose
Palo Alto HS, Palo Alto

Santa Barbara–Santa Maria–Lompoc, CA
Cate School, Carpinteria

Scranton–Wilkes-Barre, PA
Scranton Prep School,
  Scranton

Seattle, WA
John H. McKnight MS, Renton
Kentridge HS, Kent
Lake Washington HS, Kirkland
Lindbergh HS, Renton
Meany MS, Seattle
Meridian JHS, Kent
Mount Rainier HS, Seattle
Redmond HS, Redmond
Ringdall MS, Bellevue
Shorewood HS, Seattle

Sheboygan, WI
Sheboygan South HS,
  Sheboygan

Shreveport, LA
Broadmoor Middle Laboratory
  School, Shreveport
Caddo Middle Magnet School,
  Shreveport
Captain Shreve HS,
  Shreveport
Parkway HS, Bossier City
Youree Drive MS, Shreveport

Spokane, WA
Sacajawea JHS, Spokane

Springfield, MO
Kickapoo HS, Springfield

Springfield, MA
Glenbrook MS, Longmeadow

Stamford, CT
Darien HS, Darien
Middlesex MS, Darien

Syracuse, NY
Liverpool HS, Liverpool

Tacoma, WA
Curtis HS, Tacoma
Curtis JHS, Tacoma

Tampa–St. Petersburg–Clearwater, FL
Brandon HS, Brandon
Hollins HS, St. Petersburg
Jesuit HS, Tampa
Largo MS, Largo

Toledo, OH
Arbor Hills JHS, Sylvania

Topeka, KS
Robinson MS, Topeka
Seaman HS, Topeka
Topeka West HS, Topeka

Tucson, AZ
Amphitheatre HS, Tucson
Baboquivari JHS, Sells
Flowing Wells HS, Tucson
Flowing Wells JHS, Tucson
Santa Rita HS, Tucson
Utterback JHS, Tucson

Tulsa, OK
Washington HS, Tulsa

Vallejo–Fairfield–Napa, CA
Vacaville HS, Vacaville

Vancouver, WA
Battle Ground HS, Battle
  Ground, WA
Pleasant Valley IS, Vancouver,
  WA

Washington, DC–MD–VA
Alice Deal JHS, Washington,
  DC
Brookland JHS, Washington,
  DC
Browne JHS, Washington, DC
Farquhar MS, Olney, MD
George Mason HS, Falls
  Church, VA
Georgetown Visitation Prep
  School, Washington, DC

Hobson MS, Washington, DC
Jefferson JHS, Washington,
  DC
Jefferson JHS, Washington,
  DC
Middletown HS, Middletown,
  MD
Milton M. Somers MS, La
  Plata, MD
Parkland JHS, Rockville, MD
Poolesville JH/SHS,
  Poolesville, MD
Redland MS, Rockville, MD
Stone Ridge Country Day
  School, Bethesda, MD
The Madeira School, Green-
  way, MD
Thomas S. Wootton HS,
  Rockville, MD
Washington-Lee HS, Arlington,
  VA

Williams HS, Alexandria, VA

Wheeling, WV–OH
Bridge Street JHS, Wheeling,
  WV
Triadelphia JHS, Wheeling,
  WV
Wheeling JHS, Wheeling, WV
Wheeling Park HS, Wheeling,
  WV

Wichita, KS
Horace Mann MS, Wichita

Wilmington, DE–NJ–MD
Brandywine HS, Wilmington,
  DE
Skyline MS, Wilmington, DE

Yakima, WA
West Valley JHS, Yakima

Source: U.S. Department of Education, Secondary School Recognition Program, 1989.

The Arts

Most people would want to trade any city that is wearing them and itself out for a serene spot that's less crowded, safer, and cheaper. This great escape is a sustaining dream for a majority of big-city residents, according to current opinion polls.

Picture this, then. When the chance arrives in the form of a job transfer, a mid-life change, or retirement, you pack up and make your break. You're delighted to find that a scaled-down environment is all it's cracked up to be. There is a sense of cohesion, of continuity and tradition, of community spirit and neighborliness that you thought no longer existed in America. You're happier than you've been in years.

For about four months.

Because in your headlong rush to abandon the aggravations of big-city life, you abandoned the art museum done in classical marble that you barely glanced at in passing twice each day in the crush of commuter traffic. You left behind a library system with a generous budget not only for books but for software, videos, compact-disc recordings, and interesting lectures and exhibits. You also turned your back on the local newspaper's discerning arts section, the local public television station's earnest fundraising auctions, and your subscription to the repertory theatre's season.

You trot down to the public library in your new location, only to discover a well-worn selection of fiction, mainly published in the last decade, and back issues of *Family Circle, Motor Trend,* and *Field & Stream.*

You search for a theatre or musical event and find your only choices are an amateur production of "Dancing Down to Rio" in a local church basement or a concert stop by AirHead, a touring heavy-metal group.

Of all the factors that coalesce into quality of life, the one called the arts singularly and inevitably improves with the size of the city. True, the supply of recreation amenities such as professional sports teams, zoological gardens, and amusement parks expands with population. Even so, many of the most valuable recreation assets—lakes, hiking trails, forests, campgrounds—are found far from cities; indeed, they *must* be far from cities. The arts alone are big-city phenomena.

It should surprise no one, then, that *Places Rated Almanac's* top two metro areas for the arts are New York and Los Angeles. This isn't to say that culture cannot be found in smaller metro areas. Although it is safe to assume that the larger a metro area is, the more artistic and cultural amenities it will possess, there are interesting exceptions to this rule.

WHAT *ARE* THE ARTS, ANYWAY?

Although people can't get together on a single definition, or even on one element that all art shares, it's possible to name certain things that seem to ring true. For example, the following two lists draw a distinction that most of us would recognize:

Definitely Art	Possibly Art
paintings	subway graffiti
ballet	tap dancing
stained glass	rap music
Placido Domingo	monogrammed cuff-links
anything by Shakespeare	comic books
poet Dylan Thomas	pop star Bon Jovi
Chicago Symphony Orchestra	folk music, blues, jazz
Greek sculpture	Woody Allen

Places Rated Almanac doesn't make definitive choices from the right-hand list on what precisely constitutes art. Instead, it focuses on the easily identifiable categories of cultural merit implied in the first list, those which most people agree have artistic or cultural merit. Whether any or all of the items in the second list are art is a moot question; most are controversial or dubious simply because they haven't yet withstood the test of time.

The broad categories of cultural wealth that *Places Rated Almanac* identifies include fine-arts museums, concert radio stations and public television stations, symphony orchestras, professional theatres, opera companies, dance troupes, and public libraries. Together, they reflect the cultural and intellectual tone of an area. Their presence also indicates a second layer of cultural life: commercial art galleries, music stores, amateur music ensembles; the ethnic restaurants, literary clubs, and lecture groups that flourish in the atmosphere produced by artists, musicians, and professors; perhaps even the kind of conversation made at a bridge party, cookout, or day at the beach.

TUNING IN TO THE ARTS: CONCERT RADIO AND PUBLIC TELEVISION

When television channels were first allocated, some were set aside by the Federal Communications Commission for non-profit "educational" television stations intended to be electronic extensions of the classroom. The first such station to go on the air was Houston's KUHT in 1953. Two years later, Alabama established the first state education TV network.

Gradually the concept expanded. "Educational television" became "public television," which included all kinds of artistic and intellectual fare not readily available on commercial television: discussion programs, opera, symphony, Shakespeare, engrossing explanations of science and the universe, and creative children's shows. The finest programs of the various stations were shared through a national network—the Public Broadcasting Service (PBS).

Viewers in every metro area can tune in to PBS programming by way of cable, and 172 have at least one station broadcasting within their boundaries. Washington, DC–MD–VA, counts four stations in the district and in suburban Maryland. Twenty other metro areas have two outlets, and two—Charlotte–Gastonia–Rock Hill, NC–SC, and San Francisco, CA—have three.

In addition to non-commercial television, metropolitan audiences can tune in to music aired around the clock by 303 concert- or classical-format radio stations.

A handful of these stations with the biggest share of the fine-arts audience are commercial operations, but most belong to the National Public Radio network. The city of license for nearly all are within 178 metro areas; 34 metro areas have two stations, and 11 have three or more. The top markets for classical-format radio are shown in the list below.

Classical-Format Radio: The Top Markets

Atlanta, GA (3)	New York, NY (4)
Boston, MA (3)	Omaha, NE–IA (3)
Chicago, IL (3)	Philadelphia, PA–NJ (3)
Denver, CO (3)	Portland, OR (3)
Indianapolis, IN (3)	San Francisco, CA (4)
Los Angeles–Long Beach, CA (3)	

Source: Broadcasting Publications, Inc., *Broadcast–Cablecast Yearbook*, 1989; Concert Music Broadcasters Association, *Directory of Concert Music Stations*, 1988.

ART MUSEUMS AND GALLERIES

In ancient Greece, it wasn't just the devoutly religious who visited temples; uninvited tourists also stole in to admire the statues and paintings. In Revolutionary France, artists had their daily exclusive run of the Louvre in order to copy the great works of the past. But on infrequent public days, the peasants, prostitutes, soldiers, and common laborers came in great numbers. To this day, going to an art museum has something of the democratic, the sacred, and the carnival to it.

The first great American art museums were founded in Boston and New York, both in the year 1870. New York now has more art museums than any other American city, and The Metropolitan Museum, with some four million visitors a year, is its most popular tourist attraction.

To qualify for inclusion in *Places Rated Almanac*, an art museum must fit the American Association of Museums' definition of "an organized and permanent non-profit institution, essentially educational or aesthetic in purpose, with professional staff, which owns and utilizes tangible objects, cares for them, and exhibits them to the public on some regular schedule." In all, 274 metro areas have at least one such institution, and 16 have nine or more. These 16 areas are listed in the following chart.

Art Museums: The Top 16 Metro Areas

Metro Area	Art Museums
New York, NY	49
Los Angeles, CA	33
Washington, DC–MD–VA	31
Boston, MA	22
Philadelphia, PA–NJ	22
Chicago, IL	19
San Francisco, CA	14
Pittsburgh, PA	12
Oakland, CA	11
Minneapolis–St. Paul, MN–WI	10
Nassau–Suffolk, NY	10
Baltimore, MD	9
Detroit, MI	9
Norfolk–Virginia Beach–Newport News, VA	9
San Jose, CA	9
Tampa–St. Petersburg, FL	9

Source: American Association of Museums, *Official Museum Directory*, 1989.

THE LIVELY ARTS CALENDAR

The cultural side of urban life might be divided into two categories: possessions and performances. Collected art on museum walls and books on a public library's shelves belong in the first group. The lively arts—symphony, opera, dance, and theatre—belong in the second.

Despite the competition, the audience's increasingly precious leisure time, and the drop in government arts funding during the Reagan years, the lively arts continue to endure. This isn't the case everywhere, however.

Last year, the Nashville Symphony filed for bankruptcy, the Oklahoma Symphony's board voted to close for good, and the New Orleans Symphony cancelled its season. Most professional theatres are operating in the red, and major ballet companies are merging—Cleveland's with San Jose's, Milwaukee's with Philadelphia's, and Denver's with Tampa's—to cut costs and, ultimately, to survive.

For all their troubles, the lively arts still outdraw professional sports. Unlike professional football or major-league baseball, however, resident symphony orchestras, opera companies, professional theatre, and dance companies are urban amenities that are all the more exceptional in a metro area because they are endangered.

Opera

Opera fans boast that their passion embraces the greatest of the performing arts, since it combines a love for orchestral and vocal music, theatre, and dance. The first grand opera performed in this country was Rossini's *The Barber of Seville*, at New York's Park Theatre in 1825. To this day, New York remains America's operatic capital, though the art form has been diffused throughout the nation. From 650 performing groups 15 years ago, opera has expanded to nearly 1,000 professional and amateur groups, reaching an audience of 17 million during the 1987–1988 season.

Some of these performing groups are college and university workshops, whereas others are local clubs and choruses. But 148 are companies with annual budgets exceeding $250,000. Full-scale opera productions using professional orchestras and bringing the world's leading singers to the stage are a costly business, and most metro areas haven't the resources or the audiences to support this singular form of the lively arts. The list below shows the ten operas that accounted for almost one-third of all 1987-1988 performances.

Operatic Chestnuts

According to Opera America, ten operas accounted for nearly one-third of all performances during the 1987–1988 season. These works, by number of their productions, were:

Tosca, 18	Madame Butterfly, 13
The Barber of Seville, 16	Rigoletto, 12
La Bohéme, 15	La Traviata, 10
Porgy and Bess, 15	The Marriage of Figaro, 9
Carmen, 13	Romeo and Juliet, 8

Source: Opera America, *Profile*, 1988.

New York, New York

"New York, New York, it's a wonderful town!" says the song from *On the Town*. Certainly the Big Apple is less wonderful for its violent crime, gridlock traffic, and appalling living costs. Yet the lyrics hold true as applied to the arts. The city's government may be unresponsive to certain interest groups, but it does maintain a revolving loan fund to help performing arts groups end their "space chase," a constant quest for affordable, long-term work and performance rental property.

For many reasons, New York is beyond a doubt the culture capital of America. Consider these assets:

Museums: Metropolitan New York has no fewer than 49 art museums, including 10 of world renown.

Concert radio: Four FM radio stations, airing a total of 500 hours per week, compete fiercely for a share of the limited classical-music market.

Public television: One of the metro area's two public television stations, WNET, produces more fine arts programming than any other of Public Broadcasting's 300 stations.

Symphony orchestras: Metropolitan New York has 26 orchestras, including one major orchestra (the New York Philharmonic), 3 regional orchestras, and 4 metropolitan orchestras.

Professional theatres: The actual number of theatres is unknown, when one considers not only Broadway, but also off-Broadway, and Off-Off-Broadway, as well. The Big Apple has 34 professional theatres with budgets over $300,000, thus qualifying them for inclusion in *Places Rated Almanac*.

Opera companies: Fourteen professional companies, including two Grand Operas (The Met and the New York City Opera) make New York the opera capital of America.

Dance companies: Among all companies in the United States with annual budgets over $200,000, one in six is headquartered in metropolitan New York.

Dance

New York is the center for great dance, as it is a center for so much more in the performing arts. America's top companies are here, including the New York City Ballet, the American Ballet Theatre, the Joffrey Ballet, the Alvin Ailey American Dance Theatre, the Martha Graham Company, the Merce Cunningham Dance Company, the Paul Tayler Dance Company, and the Dance Theatre of Harlem.

In the 1960s, Rudolf Nureyev heralded a boom in dance when he jumped the fence from Russia to the West. He showed Americans how athletic dance could be, and suddenly it was socially acceptable for teenage boys to join dance classes. The growth decade for dance was the 1970s, when touring New York dance troupes spread the gospel to new audiences. The charisma of another Russian emigré, Mikhail Baryshnikov, now the artistic director of the American Ballet Theatre, helped consolidate the popularity of dance.

America has a number of well-established dance companies. The New York City Ballet is 40 years old, and the Pennsylvania Ballet is 25. Unlikely as it may seem, the ballet company of Dayton, OH, is older than both, at half a century. There are some 700 dance companies performing throughout America; they vary in stability, continuity, and quality.

Symphonies

The original definition—"to sound together," from the Greek—is just vague enough to embrace all the ensembles playing some type of symphonic music today in America. In all, according to the American Symphony Orchestra League, there are some 1,500 groups, ranging in size and experience from youths playing before captive audiences of parents to accomplished and well-paid professionals working under the baton of Leonard Bernstein at the New York Philharmonic. Thirty-three orchestras are classified by the league as "major"; that is, each has an annual operating budget of more than $5 million. (See the table below for the 33 major symphonies.) Just one metropolitan area supports more than one major orchestra, and it's not New York, Chicago, or Los Angeles. Up on the northern Great Plains, Minneapolis–St. Paul is home to both the St. Paul Chamber Orchestra and the Minnesota Orchestra.

The 33 Major Symphonies and Their Annual Performances

Symphony	Performances
Atlanta Symphony Orchestra	267
Baltimore Symphony Orchestra	200
Boston Symphony Orchestra	70
Buffalo Philharmonic Orchestra	160
Chicago Symphony Orchestra	185
Cincinnati Symphony Orchestra	300
Cleveland Orchestra	185
Columbus Symphony Orchestra	100
Dallas Symphony Orchestra	263
Denver Symphony Orchestra	164
Detroit Symphony Orchestra	200
Houston Symphony Orchestra	175
Indianapolis Symphony Orchestra	180
Los Angeles Philharmonic	200
Milwaukee Symphony Orchestra	200
Minnesota Orchestra, Minneapolis	215
National Symphony Orchestra, Washington	180
New Jersey Symphony Orchestra	105
New Orleans Symphony Orchestra	150
New York Philharmonic	190
Oregon Symphony Orchestra, Portland	135
Philadelphia Orchestra	175
Phoenix Symphony Orchestra	157
Pittsburgh Symphony Orchestra	115
Rochester Philharmonic Orchestra	180
St. Louis Symphony Orchestra	230
St. Paul Chamber Orchestra	160
San Antonio Symphony Orchestra	180
San Diego Symphony Orchestra	120
San Francisco Symphony	216
Seattle Symphony Orchestra	84
Syracuse Symphony Orchestra	325
Utah Symphony Orchestra, Salt Lake City	250

Source: American Symphony Orchestra League, *Orchestra and Business Directory*, 1989; ABC Leisure Magazines, *Musical America: International Directory of the Performing Arts*, 1989.

Orchestras are far from uncommon in metro areas; 275 metro areas claim at least one. Forty-six of these places support four or more orchestras, and 12 metro areas support eight or more. The table below, "Symphony Orchestras: The Top 12 Metro Areas," details the numbers of orchestras and annual concerts in these top 12 areas.

Symphony Orchestras: The Top 12 Metro Areas

Metro Area	Orchestras	Annual Concerts
New York, NY	26	668
Boston, MA	20	218
Los Angeles, CA	20	419
Washington, DC–MD–VA	20	432
Philadelphia, PA–NJ	14	381
Chicago, IL	13	318
San Francisco, CA	10	276
Baltimore, MD	9	248
Newark, NJ	9	165
Atlanta, GA	8	313
Detroit, MI	8	260
Minneapolis–St. Paul, MN–WI	8	484

Source: American Symphony Orchestra League, *Orchestra and Business Directory*, 1989; ABC Leisure Magazines, *Musical America: International Directory of the Performing Arts*, 1989.

Repertory Theatre

Long known as the "fabulous invalid," theatre continues to hold its own, despite perennial predictions of its demise. In *Huckleberry Finn*, Mark Twain described two hucksters who arrive in a small Arkansas town and tout a theatrical production pompously titled the "Royal Nonesuch." The performance consisted of an actor, wearing bright body paint but nothing else, streaking across the stage to the delight and outrage of the audience.

The history of American theatre is a blend of the grand and comic. Its many forms have encompassed Shakespeare, vaudeville, and Broadway musicals, and its first challenge came with silent movies at the century's turn, when the number of legitimate theatres fell from 1,500 to 500. In the 1920s, a resurgence took place on Broadway, which opened more than 400 new theatres in less than a decade. In the 1950s, Off-Broadway grew in response to the over-commercialized mainstream theatre.

Broadway once was the center of American theatre. It alone established what was successful and sent these hits on the road to the provinces. New York still has the greatest concentration of theatres. Yet a number of regional theatres are now recognized for their vigor and innovation, including the Washington, DC, Arena Stage, the Guthrie in Minneapolis, MN, and the Trinity Rep in Providence, RI.

On another level are the small theatre groups all across America, surviving on a shoestring, or disappearing only to be replaced by another. Some of the productions undoubtedly make Twain's "Royal Nonesuch" seem like great theatre. Yet the appeal of small theatre is that you may be happily surprised by its spunk and sense of craft. It's worth quoting the self-description of Germinal Stage Denver, a group that calls itself "the runt stepchild of regional theatres, a mom-and-pop store of Thespis, a vestige of the little theatre movement masquerading as an institution. In 13 years, we've gone through several periods of artistic coherence, but these days we're just trying to do the best plays we can, as well as we can, without talking too much about it."

Theatre Profiles, a publication of New York's Theatre Communications Group, lists all the country's repertory theatres. Repertory theatres have a professional company of actors in residence whose full-time job is performing. This differs from community theatres, whose actors are part-time, usually unpaid amateurs. In its survey of metropolitan theatre, *Places Rated Almanac* includes only those theatres with annual budgets of $300,000 or more.

There are 168 companies—found in just 74 metro areas—with such large budgets. Twenty-eight metro areas have two or more qualifying theatres; seven support six or more (see the following table for the seven top areas).

Professional Theatre: The Top 7 Metro Areas

Metro Area	Theatres
New York, NY	34
Chicago, IL	9
Minneapolis–St. Paul, MN–WI	7
Philadelphia, PA–NJ	7
Seattle, WA	7
Washington, DC–MD–VA	7
San Francisco, CA	6

Source: *Theatre Communications Group, Theatre Profiles/8*, 1988.

SCORING: THE ARTS

The nine kinds of amenities most people usually associate with the arts embrace not hundreds but thousands of institutions throughout the country. To list them all would require a book several times the size of this one. The Amerian Association of Museums' *Official Museum Directory*, for example, catalogues more than 6,000 American museums, many very specialized, many others small and existing only to make money or to serve as a tax shelter for their proprietors.

How can the amenities that really count be filtered out from the dross and used to measure the relative artistic climates of places? We start by excluding institutions run for profit. This means commercial television, commercial theatres and supper clubs, and libraries and museums that either are appendages of corporations or otherwise closed to the public. Then we rely on ratings and classifications devised by appropriate associations or accrediting bodies such as the Concert Music Broadcasters Association and the American Association of Museums.

It can still be argued that it is impossible to rank metro areas by their artistic climates with total fairness. Nevertheless, one can focus on certain amenities and illustrate their *supply* among metro areas. Accordingly, each metro area starts with a base score of zero, to which points are added according to the following indicators:

1. *Fine Arts Broadcasting*. Local radio stations, whether they are commercial or non-commercial, contribute one point for each weekly hour of air time they dedicate to classical- or concert-music format. Local non-commercial television stations, on the other hand, contribute a constant 100 points each.

   San Francisco, for example, has four FM stations broadcasting a total of 468 hours of classical music per week, plus three non-commercial TV outlets. These seven facilities, then, furnish 768 points toward San Francisco's score for The Arts.

2. *Public Libraries*. The points awarded for libraries are the number of new books all public libraries within the metro area add each year per 10,000 residents.

   The 277 public libraries within metropolitan New York, for example, cumulatively acquire 1,734,370 new books according to the New York State Library's latest annual report. That works out to 203 new books per 10,000 people, good for 203 points.

3. *Art Museums and Galleries*. Among America's more than 6,000 museums, 827 are classified by the American Association of Museums as non-profit "Art Museums and Galleries," or "Civic Art and Cultural Centers," and are located in metro areas. Each of these museums contributes 50 points toward a metro area's score.

   Metropolitan Los Angeles's 7 university, 24 private, and 2 civic art museums and galleries, for example, account for 1,650 points of the metro area's total 5,115 points.

4. *The Lively Arts Calendar*. Throughout the year, for each performance of a touring fine arts musical group booked at local campus and civic auditoriums, as well as each performance of a local resident ensemble—whether a symphony orchestra, an opera company, a dance company, or a professional theatre—the metro area receives one point.

   Touring artists bookings are defined as the number of dates at metropolitan campus and civic auditoriums with performing arts series as reported in *Musical America*'s latest survey. Symphony orchestras are institutions recognized by the American Symphony Orchestra League. Opera companies are defined as those having paid professional singers and actors, orchestral accompaniment, and recognized by either Opera America in Washington or the Central Opera Service in New York. Professional theatres are non-profit theatres with established seasons, paid actors, and annual budgets greater than $300,000.

5. *CMSA Access.* Each of the 71 metro areas that is part of a Consolidated Metropolitan Statistical Area is eligible for bonus points based on shared amenities: fine arts broadcasting, art museums and galleries, and the lively arts calendar. A place gets a bonus of 10 percent of the points accumulated by *adjacent* places in the CMSA for these amenities.

In the Denver–Boulder consolidated area, for example, Boulder–Longmont gets 84 access points based on Dever's 840 points for the Mile High City's fine arts broadcasting, art museums and galleries, and lively arts calendar. Likewise, Denver gets a 34 point bonus thanks to the Boulder–Longmont area's similar amenities.

Touring Artists Bookings: The Top 20 Markets

Metro Area	Dates	Metro Area	Dates
New York, NY	2,257	Oakland, CA	344
Los Angeles–Long Beach, CA	1,259	Milwaukee, WI	343
Boston, MA	733	Cleveland, OH	338
Washington, DC–MD–VA	622	Salt Lake City–Ogden, UT	335
Chicago, IL	580	Phoenix, AZ	329
San Francisco, CA	555	Dallas, TX	319
Tampa–St. Petersburg–Clearwater, FL	547	Baltimore, MD	319
Minneapolis–St. Paul, MN–WI	416	Huntsville, AL	311
Philadelphia, PA–NJ	375	Anaheim–Santa Ana, CA	308
Nassau–Suffolk, NY	368		
Ann Arbor, MI	347		

Source: Derived from ABC Leisure Magazines, *Musical America: International Directory of the Performing Arts*, 1989.

Public Library Acquisitions

Best Metro Areas	Libraries	Volumes	New books per 10,000 readers	Worst Metro Areas	Libraries	Volumes	New books per 10,000 readers
Stamford, CT	10	73,334	336	Tyler, TX	2	2,731	17
Flint, MT	8	158,218	354	Fort Walton Beach, FL	5	3,169	20
Cleveland, OH	89	576,367	311	Tuscaloosa, AL	3	3,474	24
Utica–Rome, NY	34	92,987	295	Lakeland–Winter Haven, FL	10	11,401	29
Nassau–Suffolk, NY	121	753,031	278	Killeen–Temple, TX	8	7,239	30
South Bend–Mishawaka, IN	11	65,092	271	Odessa, TX	1	4,333	32
Fort Wayne, IN	19	93,441	260	Beaumont–Port Arthur, TX	14	13,286	35
Raleigh–Durham, NC	32	180,005	256	Jackson, TN	1	3,009	38
Norwalk, CT	7	32,283	246	Longview–Marshall, TX	6	6,546	38
Baltimore, MD	66	559,471	240	McAllen–Edinburg–Mission, TX	10	15,399	40
Middletown, CT	8	20,888	239	Laredo, TX	1	5,246	41
Canton, OH	17	97,830	238	St. Joseph, MO	2	3,594	41
Salinas–Seaside–Monterey, CA	23	86,930	237	Wichita Falls, TX	4	5,246	41
Columbus, OH	46	308,720	232	Waco, TX	6	8,227	43
Toledo, OH	35	140,766	229	Fort Smith, AR–OK	21	8,101	44

Source: Places Rated Partnership survey of state library associations, 1988–1989.

Rankings: The Arts

Nine amenities are used to arrive at a metro area's score for the arts: (1) concert or classical-format radio stations; (2) public television stations; (3) public libraries; (4) non-profit art museums and galleries; (5) touring-artist bookings at local campus and civic auditoriums; (6) resident symphony orchestras; (7) resident opera companies; (8) resident professional theatres; and (9) resident dance companies. Metro areas also earn bonus points for shared amenities if they are part of Consolidated Metropolitan Statistical Areas (CMSAs).

Metro Areas from Best to Worst

Places Rated Rank	Places Rated Score	Places Rated Rank	Places Rated Score	Places Rated Rank	Places Rated Score	Places Rated Rank	Places Rated Score
1. New York, NY	15,487	58. Ann Arbor, MI	1,026	114. Wichita, KS	609		
2. Los Angeles–Long Beach, CA	5,115	59. Portland, OR	1,015	115. Nashville, TN	607		
3. Chicago, IL	4,452	60. San Antonio, TX	1,002				
4. Washington, DC–MD–VA	4,178			116. Harrisburg–Lebanon–Carlisle, PA	600		
5. San Francisco, CA	4,006	61. Tucson, AZ	973	117. Spokane, WA	598		
		62. Honolulu, HI	947	118. Gainesville, FL	594		
6. Philadelphia, PA–NJ	3,784	63. Tulsa, OK	944	119. Lincoln, NE	592		
7. Boston, MA	3,215	64. Omaha, NE–IA	943	120. Sarasota, FL	589		
8. Minneapolis–St. Paul, MN–WI	3,110	65. Orlando, FL	937				
9. Nassau–Suffolk, NY	2,981			121. Boulder–Longmont, CO	588		
10. Newark, NJ	2,972	66. Tacoma, WA	910	122. Grand Rapids, MI	583		
		67. Albuquerque, NM	904	123. Youngstown–Warren, OH	578		
11. Seattle, WA	2,714	68. Akron, OH	903	124. Peoria, IL	575		
12. Baltimore, MD	2,599	69. Salem–Gloucester, MA	852	125. Pensacola, FL	570		
13. Stamford, CT	2,415	70. Wilmington, DE–NJ–MD	851				
14. Atlanta, GA	2,382			126. Columbia, SC	565		
15. Middlesex–Somerset–Hunterdon, NJ	2,363	71. Santa Cruz, CA	850	126. Santa Barbara–Santa Maria–Lompoc, CA	565		
		72. Greensboro–Winston-Salem–High Point, NC	836	128. Binghamton, NY	559		
16. Bridgeport–Milford, CT	2,188	73. Oklahoma City, OK	833	129. Lexington–Fayette, KY	552		
17. San Diego, CA	2,153	74. Fort Worth–Arlington, TX	825	130. Pittsfield, MA	550		
18. San Jose, CA	2,129	74. Lake County, IL	825				
19. Anaheim–Santa Ana, CA	2,082			131. Little Rock–North Little Rock, AR	547		
20. Oakland, CA	2,069	76. Springfield, MA	823	132. Bangor, ME	544		
		77. Medford, OR	799	132. Boise City, ID	544		
21. Cleveland, OH	2,051	78. West Palm Beach–Boca Raton–Delray Beach, FL	785	132. Eugene–Springfield, OR	544		
22. Bergen–Passaic, NJ	2,049	79. Toledo, OH	782	135. Davenport–Rock Island–Moline, IA–IL	536		
23. Milwaukee, WI	1,950	80. Aurora–Elgin, IL	777				
24. Norwalk, CT	1,938			135. Knoxville, TN	536		
25. Jersey City, NJ	1,932	81. Fort Lauderdale–Hollywood–Pompano Beach, FL	765	137. Anchorage, AK	535		
		82. New Orleans, LA	758	138. Fort Wayne, IN	516		
26. Danbury, CT	1,855	83. Providence, RI	746	138. Shreveport, LA	516		
27. Orange County, NY	1,839	84. Memphis, TN–AR–MS	744	140. Saginaw–Bay City–Midland, MI	507		
28. Tampa–St. Petersburg–Clearwater, FL	1,835	85. Flint, MI	742				
29. St. Louis, MO–IL	1,828	86. Oxnard–Ventura, CA	724	141. Canton, OH	499		
30. Monmouth–Ocean, NJ	1,800	87. Greenville–Spartanburg, SC	721	142. South Bend–Mishawaka, IN	493		
		88. Jacksonville, FL	717	143. New London–Norwich, CT–RI	488		
31. Houston, TX	1,668	89. Lansing–East Lansing, MI	715	144. Las Vegas, NV	482		
32. Detroit, MI	1,615	90. Salinas–Seaside–Monterey, CA	710	145. Charleston, SC	472		
33. Pittsburgh, PA	1,596						
34. Salt Lake City–Ogden, UT	1,574	91. Vallejo–Fairfield–Napa, CA	704	145. Vineland–Millville–Bridgeton, NJ	472		
35. Denver, CO	1,559	92. Santa Rosa–Petaluma, CA	697	147. Fargo–Moorhead, ND–MN	471		
		93. Kenosha, WI	695	148. Lorain–Elyria, OH	469		
36. Louisville, KY–IN	1,556	94. Gary–Hammond, IN	691	149. Evansville, IN–KY	468		
37. Raleigh–Durham, NC	1,545	95. Huntsville, AL	685	150. Springfield, MO	467		
38. Riverside–San Bernardino, CA	1,505						
39. Dallas, TX	1,481	96. Jackson, MS	684	151. Brockton, MA	465		
40. Albany–Schenectady–Troy, NY	1,431	97. Portland, ME	678	151. Corpus Christi, TX	465		
		98. Johnson City–Kingsport–Bristol, TN–VA	667	153. Montgomery, AL	462		
41. Cincinnati, OH–KY–IN	1,366	98. Utica–Rome, NY	667	153. Waterloo–Cedar Falls, IA	462		
42. Richmond–Petersburg, VA	1,365	100. Austin, TX	657	155. Provo–Orem, UT	461		
43. Phoenix, AZ	1,362						
44. Miami–Hialeah, FL	1,357	100. Madison, WI	657	156. Champaign–Urbana–Rantoul, IL	459		
45. Charlotte–Gastonia–Rock Hill, NC–SC	1,235	102. Joliet, IL	650	157. Bloomington, IN	456		
		103. Santa Fe, NM	640	158. Erie, PA	451		
45. New Haven–Meriden, CT	1,235	104. Duluth, MN–WI	639	159. Chattanooga, TN–GA	449		
47. Rochester, NY	1,219	105. Portsmouth–Dover–Rochester, NH–ME	631	160. Glens Falls, NY	448		
48. Norfolk–Virginia Beach–Newport News, VA	1,217						
49. Indianapolis, IN	1,180	106. Birmingham, AL	629	161. Burlington, VT	445		
50. Columbus, OH	1,174	107. Allentown–Bethlehem, PA–NJ	627	162. Des Moines, IA	443		
		108. Scranton–Wilkes-Barre, PA	626	163. Hamilton–Middletown, OH	440		
51. Trenton, NJ	1,125	109. Lowell, MA–NH	624	164. Columbia, MO	439		
52. Sacramento, CA	1,078	110. Colorado Springs, CO	616	165. Joplin, MO	437		
53. Dayton–Springfield, OH	1,076						
54. Kansas City, MO–KS	1,071	110. Nashua, NH	616	166. Middletown, CT	436		
55. Hartford, CT	1,056	112. Fort Myers–Cape Coral, FL	614	167. Huntington–Ashland, WV–KY–OH	431		
		113. Lawrence–Haverhill, MA–NH	611				
56. Buffalo, NY	1,052						
57. Syracuse, NY	1,045						

Places Rated Rank	Places Rated Score	Places Rated Rank	Places Rated Score	Places Rated Rank	Places Rated Score
168. Kalamazoo, MI	427	222. Wausau, WI	300	276. Pawtucket–Woonsocket– Attleboro, RI–MA	176
169. Baton Rouge, LA	425	225. St. Cloud, MN	296	279. Amarillo, TX	175
170. Savannah, GA	419			280. Fort Pierce, FL	174
		226. Wheeling, WV–OH	294		
171. Elkhart–Goshen, IN	418	227. Bismarck, ND	289	280. Waterbury, CT	174
172. Augusta, GA–SC	417	228. Bloomington–Normal, IL	286	282. Altoona, PA	172
172. Macon–Warner Robins, GA	417	229. Melbourne–Titusville– Palm Bay, FL	284	283. Fall River, MA–RI	164
174. Springfield, IL	412	230. Bryan–College Station, TX	282	284. Richland–Kennewick–Pasco, WA	159
175. Worcester, MA	407			285. Gadsden, AL	158
176. Iowa City, IA	399	230. Daytona Beach, FL	282	286. Midland, TX	157
176. Tallahassee, FL	399	232. Galveston–Texas City, TX	281	287. Abilene, TX	156
178. Fresno, CA	393	233. Modesto, CA	280	288. Danville, VA	152
178. Roanoke, VA	393	234. Fayetteville–Springdale, AR	279	288. Decatur, AL	152
180. Poughkeepsie, NY	387	235. Sheboygan, WI	274	288. Hickory, NC	152
181. Lubbock, TX	386	236. Lawrence, KS	271	291. Casper, WY	147
182. Wilmington, NC	386	237. Beaumont–Port Arthur, TX	269	291. Jacksonville, NC	147
183. Muncie, IN	381	238. Sioux Falls, SD	264	293. Panama City, FL	146
184. Rockford, IL	378	239. Parkersburg–Marietta, WV–OH	262	293. Pine Bluff, AR	146
185. La Crosse, WI	376	240. Cedar Rapids, IA	261	295. Jackson, MI	145
186. Racine, WI	376	240. Green Bay, WI	261	296. Steubenville–Weirton, OH–WV	143
187. Bellingham, WA	375	242. Terre Haute, IN	255	297. Merced, CA	141
188. Lafayette–West Lafayette, IN	375	243. Charleston, WV	253	297. Tuscaloosa, AL	141
189. Bakersfield, CA	366	244. Brazoria, TX	252	299. Waco, TX	139
190. Hagerstown, MD	366	244. Janesville–Beloit, WI	252	300. Bradenton, FL	137
191. Albany, GA	365	246. Lancaster, PA	251	301. Johnstown, PA	136
192. Sioux City, IA–NE	362	247. Olympia, WA	250	302. Texarkana, TX–Texarkana, AR	135
193. Alexandria, LA	361	248. Florence, SC	249	303. York, PA	130
194. Asheville, NC	355	248. Muskegon, MI	249	304. Chico, CA	126
195. Benton Harbor, MI	353	250. Elmira, NY	248	305. San Angelo, TX	124
196. Lima, OH	346	251. Athens, GA	240	306. St. Joseph, MO	123
197. Grand Forks, ND	344	251. Mansfield, OH	240	307. Anderson, SC	122
198. Billings, MT	342	253. Decatur, IL	238	308. Bremerton, WA	121
199. State College, PA	338	254. Redding, CA	231	309. Anderson, IN	114
200. Rapid City, SD	335	255. Kokomo, IN	227	310. Lakeland–Winter Haven, FL	108
201. Atlantic City, NJ	333	256. Lynchburg, VA	224	311. Laredo, TX	107
202. Vancouver, WA	331	257. Salem, OR	222	312. Clarksville–Hopkinsville, TN–KY	106
203. Reno, NV	330	258. Bristol, CT	220	312. Fort Smith, AR–OK	106
204. Lafayette, LA	329	258. Lake Charles, LA	220	312. Kankakee, IL	106
205. Appleton–Oshkosh–Neenah, WI	325	260. Fitchburg–Leominster, MA	213	315. Dothan, AL	101
206. Charlottesville, VA	324	261. Monroe, LA	212	315. Longview–Marshall, TX	101
207. Las Cruces, NM	323	261. New Bedford, MA	212	317. McAllen–Edinburg–Mission, TX	98
208. Eau Claire, WI	322	263. Greeley, CO	209	317. Victoria, TX	98
209. Topeka, KS	320	264. Florence, AL	208	319. Houma–Thibodaux, LA	95
210. Biloxi–Gulfport, MS	319	265. New Britain, CT	206	319. Sherman–Denison, TX	95
210. Rochester, MN	319	266. Wichita Falls, TX	204	319. Yuba City, CA	95
212. Niagara Falls, NY	318	267. Great Falls, MT	201	322. Williamsport, PA	89
213. Columbus, GA–AL	316	268. Fayetteville, NC	200	323. Naples, FL	88
214. Pueblo, CO	314	268. Ocala, FL	200	324. Tyler, TX	87
215. El Paso, TX	313	270. Brownsville–Harlingen, TX	197	325. Cumberland, MD–WV	79
216. Battle Creek, MI	312	271. Enid, OK	195	326. Pascagoula, MS	75
217. Manchester, NH	309	272. Reading, PA	194	327. Lawton, OK	74
217. Yakima, WA	309	273. Odessa, TX	193	328. Burlington, NC	69
219. Lewiston–Auburn, ME	306	274. Dubuque, IA	191	329. Anniston, AL	67
220. Beaver County, PA	304	275. Killeen–Temple, TX	182	330. Sharon, PA	62
221. Owensboro, KY	301			331. Fort Walton Beach, FL	54
222. Mobile, AL	300	276. Cheyenne, WY	176	332. Visalia–Tulare–Porterville, CA	52
222. Stockton, CA	300	276. Fort Collins–Loveland, CO	176	333. Jackson, TN	50

Place Profiles: The Arts

The following metro area profiles are a selective listing of local amenities related to the arts.

Under the heading of **Fine Arts Broadcasting** are concert radio stations and all non-commercial television stations whose city of license is within the metro area. Concert radio stations—non-commercial or commercial—are defined here as stations with part or all of their programming dedicated to a classical-music format. Included in these radio listings are broadcast frequencies and hours per week of concert programming. For powerful radio and television stations, programming may also be received in nearby metro areas.

Under **Public Libraries** is the total number of public library buildings within the metro area, including central city, suburban, and rural branches, along with figures on their total number of volumes and the total number of new books acquired during their latest fiscal year. For more data on public libraries, see the table entitled "Public Library Acquisitions."

Under the heading **Art Museums/Galleries** is the number of local non-profit institutions which are categorized by the American Association of Museums as "Art Museums and Galleries" and are open to the public. Each institution is further identified by its governing control, whether private (typically society or foundation), civic (usually municipal, county, or state), or university. The name of each museum accredited by the American Association of Museums is also given.

Finally, **The Lively Arts Calendar** heading encompasses the total number of touring artists bookings at local campus and civic auditoriums, and the names of resident symphony orchestras, opera companies, professional theatres, and dance companies. Next to each named ensemble, in parentheses, is the ensemble's number of annual performances. (Also, see the table on the top 20 markets for touring artists bookings.)

The information is derived from these sources: ABC Leisure Magazines, *Musical America: 1989 International Directory of the Performing Arts,* 1989; The American Association of Museums, *Official Museum Directory,* 1989, and its unpublished "AAM Accredited Museums" listing, 1989; American Library Association, *American Library Directory, 1988–1989,* 1988, and its *Output Measures for Public Libraries,* no date; American Symphony Orchestra League, *Symphony Magazine,* January–February, 1989, and its *Orchestra and Business Directory,* 1989; Arbitron Ratings Company, *1988 Radio County Directory,* and its *1988–89 Television Universe Estimates Summary;* Broadcasting Publications, Inc., *Broadcast-Cablecast Yearbook,* 1989; Central Opera Service, *1988–1989 Directory;* Concert Music Broadcasters Association, *Directory of Concert Music Stations,* 1988; Corporation for Public Broadcasting, *Public Broadcasting Directory,* 1988, and its *Public Broadcasting Statistics in Brief;* Dance Magazine, *Stern's Performing Arts Directory,* 1989; Opera America, *Season Performance Schedule,* 1989, and its *Profile: 1989;* and Places Rated Partnership, Survey of State Library Association Annual Reports, 1988–1989.

A metro area's score is the sum of the points in parentheses to the right of the **Fine Arts Broadcasting, Public Libraries, Art Museums/Galleries,** and **The Lively Arts Calendar** headings. In addition, if the metro area is part of a Consolidated Metropolitan Statistical Area (CMSA) complex and receives bonus points for shared amenities, the number of points is shown in parentheses after the name of the consolidated area.

A star (★) in front of a metro area's name highlights it as one of the top 30 places for the arts.

Abilene, TX
Public Libraries (61 points):
  2 branches, 257,782 volumes
  Books added per year: 7,710
Art Museum/Gallery (50 points):
  1 private
The Lively Arts Calendar (45 points):
  Touring Artists Bookings (28)
  Symphony Orchestra:
    Abilene Philharmonic, 17
Places Rated Score: 156
Places Rated Rank: 287

Akron, OH
Fine Arts Broadcasting (172 points):
  Concert Radio: WKSU-FM 89.7, 72 hours
  Non-Commercial TV: WEAO Channel 49

Public Libraries (214 points):
  24 branches, 1,873,194 volumes
  Books added per year: 140,436
Art Museums/Galleries (150 points):
  1 private, 2 university
  Akron Art Museum
The Lively Arts Calendar (200 points):
  Touring Artists Bookings (80)
  Symphony Orchestras:
    Akron Symphony Orchestra, 37
    Akron Youth Symphony, 3
  Dance Company:
    Ohio Ballet, 80
CMSA Access: Cleveland–Akron–
  Lorain, OH (167 points)
Places Rated Score: 903
Places Rated Rank: 68

Albany, GA
Fine Arts Broadcasting (100 points):
  Non-Commercial TV: WABW Channel 14
Public Libraries (206 points):
  5 branches, 203,828 volumes
  Books added per year: 24,756
Art Museum/Gallery (50 points):
  1 private
The Lively Arts Calendar (9 points):
  Touring Artists Bookings (4)
  Symphony Orchestra:
    Albany Symphony Orchestra, 5
Places Rated Score: 365
Places Rated Rank: 191

Albany–Schenectady–Troy, NY
Fine Arts Broadcasting (428 points):
Concert Radio: WAMC-FM 90.3, 60 hours
WMHT-FM 89.1, 168 hours
Non-Commercial TV: WMHT Channel 17
WMHX Channel 45
Public Libraries (156 points):
60 branches, 1,851,503 volumes
Books added per year: 132,956
Art Museums/Galleries (300 points):
4 private, 2 university
Albany Institute of History and Art
The Lively Arts Calendar (547 points):
Touring Artists Bookings (173)
Symphony Orchestras:
Albany Symphony Orchestra, 30
Empire State Youth Orchestra, 8
Music Company Orchestra, 12
Schenectady Symphony Orchestra, 4
Professional Theatres:
Capital Repertory Company, 120
Empire State Institute for the
Performing Arts, 100
Heritage Artists, Ltd., 100
Places Rated Score: 1,431
Places Rated Rank: 40

Albuquerque, NM
Fine Arts Broadcasting (228 points):
Concert Radio: KHFM-FM 96.3, 128 hours
Non-Commercial TV: KNME Channel 5
Public Libraries (173 points):
12 branches, 535,830 volumes
Books added per year: 85,745
Art Museums/Galleries (150 points):
1 civic, 2 university
The Lively Arts Calendar (353 points):
Touring Artists Bookings (57)
Symphony Orchestras:
Albuquerque Youth Symphony, 8
Chamber Orchestra of Albuquerque, 18
New Mexico Symphony Orchestra, 60
Opera Company:
Albuquerque Civic Light Opera, 40
Professional Theatre:
New Mexico Repertory Theatre, 120
Dance Company:
Southwest Ballet Company, 50
Places Rated Score: 904
Places Rated Rank: 67

Alexandria, LA
Fine Arts Broadcasting (100 points):
Non-Commercial TV: KLPA Channel 25
Public Libraries (206 points):
11 branches, 274,835 volumes
Books added per year: 28,763
Art Museum/Gallery (50 points):
1 private
Alexandria Museum, Visual Art Center
The Lively Arts Calendar (5 points):
Symphony Orchestra:
Rapides Symphony Orchestra, 5
Places Rated Score: 361
Places Rated Rank: 193

Allentown–Bethlehem, PA–NJ
Fine Arts Broadcasting (100 points):
Non-Commercial TV: WLVT Channel 39
Public Libraries (110 points):
28 branches, 1,565,424 volumes
Books added per year: 73,233
Art Museums/Galleries (100 points):
1 private, 1 university
Allentown Art Museum

The Lively Arts Calendar (317 points):
Touring Artists Bookings (77)
Symphony Orchestras:
Allentown Symphony, 17
Greater Lehigh Valley Youth
Symphony, 2
Lehigh Valley Chamber Orchestra, 66
Pennsylvania Sinfonia Orchestra, 15
Professional Theatre:
Pennsylvania Stage Company, 140
Places Rated Score: 627
Places Rated Rank: 107

Altoona, PA
Public Libraries (166 points):
8 branches, 368,860 volumes
Books added per year: 22,177
The Lively Arts Calendar (6 points):
Symphony Orchestra:
Altoona Symphony Orchestra, 6
Places Rated Score: 172
Places Rated Rank: 282

Amarillo, TX
Public Libraries (62 points):
5 branches, 426,094 volumes
Books added per year: 12,546
Art Museum/Gallery (50 points):
1 private
Amarillo Art Center
The Lively Arts Calendar (63 points):
Symphony Orchestra:
Amarillo Symphony, 63
Places Rated Score: 175
Places Rated Rank: 279

★ Anaheim–Santa Ana, CA
Fine Arts Broadcasting (100 points):
Non-Commercial TV: KOCE Channel 50
Public Libraries (105 points):
52 branches, 3,812,732 volumes
Books added per year: 245,157
Art Museums/Galleries (350 points):
1 civic, 5 private, 1 university
Newport Harbor Art Museum
The Lively Arts Calendar (966 points):
Touring Artists Bookings (308)
Symphony Orchestras:
Chapman Symphony & Chamber
Orchestra, 10
Garden Grove Symphony, 11
Orange County Youth Symphony, 12
Pacific Symphony Orchestra, 60
South Coast Symphony, 5
Opera Companies:
Fullerton Civic Light Opera, 36
Opera Pacific, 34
Professional Theatres:
Grove Theatre Company, 180
South Coast Repertory, 240
Dance Company:
Ballet Pacifica, 70
CMSA Access: Los Angeles–Anaheim–
Riverside, CA (561 points)
Places Rated Score: 2,082
Places Rated Rank: 19

Anchorage, AK
Fine Arts Broadcasting (161 points):
Concert Radio: KSKA-FM 91.1, 61 hours
Non-Commercial TV: KAKM Channel 7
Public Libraries (129 points):
9 branches, 446,907 volumes
Books added per year: 31,415
Art Museums/Galleries (100 points):
1 civic, 1 private
Anchorage Museum of History and Art

The Lively Arts Calendar (145 points):
Touring Artists Bookings (15)
Symphony Orchestras:
Anchorage Symphony, 19
Anchorage Youth Symphony, 3
Opera Company:
Anchorage Opera, 8
Professional Theatre:
Alaska Repertory Theatre, 100
Places Rated Score: 535
Places Rated Rank: 137

Anderson, IN
Public Libraries (51 points):
5 branches, 101,076 volumes
Books added per year: 6,712
Art Museum/Gallery (50 points):
1 civic
The Lively Arts Calendar (13 points):
Touring Artists Bookings (7)
Symphony Orchestra:
Anderson Symphony Orchestra, 6
Places Rated Score: 114
Places Rated Rank: 309

Anderson, SC
Public Libraries (56 points):
8 branches, 204,277 volumes
Books added per year: 8,145
Art Museum/Gallery (50 points):
1 private
The Lively Arts Calendar (16 points):
Touring Artists Bookings (12)
Symphony Orchestra:
Anderson Symphony, 4
Places Rated Score: 122
Places Rated Rank: 307

Ann Arbor, MI
Fine Arts Broadcasting (112 points):
Concert Radio: WUOM-FM 91.7, 112
hours
Public Libraries (176 points):
11 branches, 681,100 volumes
Books added per year: 47,531
Art Museums/Galleries (200 points):
2 private, 2 university
University of Michigan Museum of Art
The Lively Arts Calendar (394 points):
Touring Artists Bookings (347)
Symphony Orchestras:
Ann Arbor Chamber Orchestra, 45
Michigan Youth Symphony, 2
CMSA Access: Detroit–Ann Arbor, MI
(144 points)
Places Rated Score: 1,026
Places Rated Rank: 58

Anniston, AL
Public Libraries (62 points):
6 branches, 237,389 volumes
Books added per year: 7,689
The Lively Arts Calendar (5 points):
Touring Artists Bookings (5)
Places Rated Score: 67
Places Rated Rank: 329

Appleton–Oshkosh–Neenah, WI
Public Libraries (193 points):
16 branches, 941,087 volumes
Books added per year: 60,717
Art Museums/Galleries (100 points):
2 private
Bergstrom-Mahler Museum
Paine Art Center

The Lively Arts Calendar (32 points):
  Touring Artists Bookings (27)
  Symphony Orchestra:
    Oshkosh Symphony Orchestra, 5
Places Rated Score: 325
Places Rated Rank: 205

Asheville, NC
Fine Arts Broadcasting (185 points):
  Concert Radio: WCQS-FM 88.1, 85 hours
  Non-Commercial TV: WUNF Channel 33
Public Libraries (90 points):
  9 branches, 239,704 volumes
  Books added per year: 15,711
Art Museum/Gallery (50 points):
  1 private
  Asheville Art Museum
The Lively Arts Calendar (30 points):
  Touring Artists Bookings (15)
  Symphony Orchestra:
    Asheville Symphony Orchestra, 15
Places Rated Score: 355
Places Rated Rank: 194

Athens, GA
Fine Arts Broadcasting (55 points):
  Concert Radio: WUGA-FM 91.7, 55 hours
Public Libraries (76 points):
  10 branches, 292,842 volumes
  Books added per year: 10,984
Art Museums/Galleries (100 points):
  1 civic, 1 university
  Georgia Museum of Art, University of
    Georgia
The Lively Arts Calendar (9 points):
  Touring Artists Bookings (9)
Places Rated Score: 240
Places Rated Rank: 251

★ Atlanta, GA
Fine Arts Broadcasting (510 points):
  Concert Radio: WABE-FM 90.1, 140 hours
    WGKA-AM 1190, 82 hours
    WJSP-FM 88.1, 88 hours
  Non-Commercial TV: WGTV Channel 8
    WPBA Channel 30
Public Libraries (157 points):
  91 branches, 3,890,730 volumes
  Books added per year: 437,576
Art Museums/Galleries (400 points):
  1 civic, 4 private, 3 university
  High Museum of Art
The Lively Arts Calendar (1,315 points):
  Touring Artists Bookings (252)
  Symphony Orchestras:
    Atlanta Community Orchestra, 5
    Atlanta Symphony Orchestra, 267
    Atlanta Symphony Youth Orchestra, 6
    Atlanta-Emory Orchestra, 6
    Cobb Symphony Orchestra, 7
    DeKalb Symphony Orchestra, 10
    Georgia State University Orchestra, 6
    Sandy Springs Chamber Orchestra, 6
  Opera Company:
    Atlanta Opera, 15
  Professional Theatres:
    Academy Theatre, 280
    Alliance Theatre Company, 240
    Center for Puppetry Arts, 140
  Dance Company:
    Atlanta Ballet Company, 75
Places Rated Score: 2,382
Places Rated Rank: 14

Atlantic City, NJ
Public Libraries (199 points):
  12 branches, 937, 381 volumes
  Books added per year: 62,515

Art Museum/Gallery (50 points):
  1 private
The Lively Arts Calendar (84 points):
  Touring Artists Bookings (54)
  Dance Company:
    Atlantic Contemporary Ballet
      Theatre, 30
Places Rated Score: 333
Places Rated Rank: 201

Augusta, GA–SC
Fine Arts Broadcasting (188 points):
  Concert Radio: WACG-FM 90.7, 88 hours
  Non-Commercial TV: WCES Channel 20
Public Libraries (84 points):
  12 branches, 573,600 volumes
  Books added per year: 34,405
Art Museums/Galleries (100 points):
  2 private
The Lively Arts Calendar (45 points):
  Symphony Orchestra:
    Augusta Symphony Orchestra, 8
  Opera Company:
    Augusta Opera Association, 12
  Dance Company:
    Augusta Ballet Company, 25
Places Rated Score: 417
Places Rated Rank: 172

Aurora–Elgin, IL
Public Libraries (181 points):
  15 branches, 989,911 volumes
  Books added per year: 64,766
Art Museum/Gallery (50 points):
  1 private
The Lively Arts Calendar (101 points):
  Touring Artists Bookings (61)
  Symphony Orchestras:
    Elgin Area Youth Orchestra, 5
    Elgin Symphonette, 5
    Elgin Symphony Orchestra, 25
    Fox River Valley Symphony
      Orchestra, 5
CMSA Access: Chicago–Gary–Lake
  County, IL–IN–WI (445 points)
Places Rated Score: 777
Places Rated Rank: 80

Austin, TX
Fine Arts Broadcasting (233 points):
  Concert Radio: KMFA-FM 89.5, 133 hours
  Non-Commercial TV: KLRU Channel 18
Public Libraries (74 points):
  31 branches, 1,115,710 volumes
  Books added per year: 58,041
Art Museums/Galleries (200 points):
  3 private, 1 university
  Huntington Art Gallery, University of
    Texas
The Lively Arts Calendar (150 points):
  Touring Artists Bookings (62)
  Symphony Orchestra:
    Austin Symphony Orchestra, 63
  Opera Company:
    Austin Lyric Opera, 5
  Dance Company:
    Ballet Austin, 20
Places Rated Score: 657
Places Rated Rank: 100

Bakersfield, CA
Fine Arts Broadcasting (168 points):
  Concert Radio: KIWI-FM 92.1, 168 hours
Public Libraries (113 points):
  28 branches, 941,950 volumes
  Books added per year: 58,214
Art Museum/Gallery (50 points):
  1 private

The Lively Arts Calendar (35 points):
  Touring Artists Bookings (11)
  Symphony Orchestra:
    Bakersfield Symphony, 24
Places Rated Score: 366
Places Rated Rank: 189

★ Baltimore, MD
Fine Arts Broadcasting (493 points):
  Concert Radio: WBJC-FM 91.5, 153 hours
    WJHU-FM 88.1, 140 hours
  Non-Commercial TV: WMPB Channel 67
    WMPT Channel 22
Public Libraries (240 points):
  66 branches, 7,121,338 volumes
  Books added per year: 559,471
Art Museums/Galleries (450 points):
  6 private, 3 university
  Walters Art Gallery
  Baltimore Museum of Art
The Lively Arts Calendar (1,416 points):
  Touring Artists Bookings (319)
  Symphony Orchestras:
    Annapolis Symphony Orchestra, 8
    Baltimore Chamber Players, 4
    Baltimore Symphony Orchestra, 200
    Greater Baltimore Youth Orchestra, 4
    Hopkins Symphony Orchestra, 4
    Maryland Youth Symphony
      Orchestra, 5
    Peabody Symphony Orchestra, 11
    Susquehanna Symphony Orchestra, 5
    UMBC Symphony, 7
  Opera Company:
    Baltimore Opera Company, 16
  Professional Theatres:
    Center Stage, 120
    Theatre Project, 680
  Dance Companies:
    Ballet Theatre of Annapolis, 15
    Washington Ballet, 18
Places Rated Score: 2,599
Places Rated Rank: 12

Bangor, ME
Fine Arts Broadcasting (208 points):
  Concert Radio: WMEH-FM 90.9, 108
    hours
  Non-Commercial TV: WMEB Channel 12
Public Libraries (176 points):
  9 branches, 691,405 volumes
  Books added per year: 14,822
Art Museums/Galleries (100 points):
  1 private, 1 university
The Lively Arts Calendar (60 points):
  Touring Artists Bookings (40)
  Symphony Orchestra:
    Bangor Symphony Orchestra, 20
Places Rated Score: 544
Places Rated Rank: 132

Baton Rouge, LA
Fine Arts Broadcasting (219 points):
  Concert Radio: WRKF-FM 89.3, 119 hours
  Non-Commercial TV: WLPB Channel 27
Public Libraries (51 points):
  24 branches, 701,615 volumes
  Books added per year: 29,306
Art Museums/Galleries (100 points):
  2 private
  Louisiana Arts and Science Center
The Lively Arts Calendar (55 points):
  Touring Artists Bookings (14)
  Symphony Orchestras:
    Baton Rouge Symphony, 22
    Louisiana Youth Orchestra, 3
  Opera Company:
    Baton Rouge Opera, 8

Dance Company:
Baton Rouge Ballet Theatre, 8
Places Rated Score: 425
Places Rated Rank: 169

Battle Creek, MI
Public Libraries (145 points):
7 branches, 244,350 volumes
Books added per year: 19,532
Art Museums/Galleries (150 points):
1 civic, 1 private, 1 university
Battle Creek Art Center
The Lively Arts Calendar (17 points):
Touring Artists Bookings (10)
Symphony Orchestra:
Battle Creek Symphony Orchestra, 7
Places Rated Score: 312
Places Rated Rank: 216

Beaumont–Port Arthur, TX
Fine Arts Broadcasting (84 points):
Concert Radio: KVLU-FM 91.3, 84 hours
Public Libraries (35 points):
14 branches, 646,863 volumes
Books added per year: 13,286
Art Museums/Galleries (100 points):
2 private
The Lively Arts Calendar (50 points):
Touring Artists Bookings (32)
Symphony Orchestra:
Beaumont Symphony Orchestra, 10
Dance Company:
Beaumont Civic Ballet Company, 8
Places Rated Score: 269
Places Rated Rank: 237

Beaver County, PA
Public Libraries (80 points):
11 branches, 303,458 volumes
Books added per year: 15,564
Art Museum/Gallery (50 points):
1 private
The Lively Arts Calendar (24 points):
Touring Artists Bookings (24)
CMSA Access: Pittsburgh–Beaver
County, PA (150 points)
Places Rated Score: 304
Places Rated Rank: 220

Bellingham, WA
Public Libraries (209 points):
14 branches, 380,411 volumes
Books added per year: 24,426
Art Museums/Galleries (150 points):
1 civic, 1 private, 1 university
Whatcom Museum of History and Art
The Lively Arts Calendar (16 points):
Touring Artists Bookings (16)
Places Rated Score: 375
Places Rated Rank: 187

Benton Harbor, MI
Fine Arts Broadcasting (164 points):
Concert Radio: WAUS-FM 90.7, 164 hours
Public Libraries (127 points):
13 branches, 451,003 volumes
Books added per year: 21,125
Art Museum/Gallery (50 points):
1 private
Krasl Art Center
The Lively Arts Calendar (12 points):
Touring Artists Bookings (12)
Places Rated Score: 353
Places Rated Rank: 195

★ Bergen–Passaic, NJ
Public Libraries (157 points):
77 branches, 4,780,261 volumes
Books added per year: 206,044

Art Museums/Galleries (100 points):
2 private
The Lively Arts Calendar (175 points):
Touring Artists Bookings (134)
Symphony Orchestras:
Bergen Philharmonic Orchestra, 4
Bergen Youth Orchestra, 3
Garden State Orchestra, 16
North Jersey Symphony Orchestra, 6
Ridgewood Symphony, 4
Wayne Chamber Orchestra, 4
Opera Company:
Opera Classics of New Jersey, 4
CMSA Access: New York–Northern
NJ–Long Island, NY–NJ–CT
(1,617 points):
Places Rated Score: 2,049
Places Rated Rank: 22

Billings, MT
Fine Arts Broadcasting (98 points):
Concert Radio: KEMC-FM 91.7, 98 hours
Public Libraries (101 points):
3 branches, 300,223 volumes
Books added per year: 12,000
Art Museum/Gallery (50 points):
1 civic
Yellowstone Art Center
The Lively Arts Calendar (93 points):
Touring Artists Bookings (81)
Symphony Orchestra:
Billings Symphony Orchestra, 12
Places Rated Score: 342
Places Rated Rank: 198

Biloxi–Gulfport, MS
Fine Arts Broadcasting (184 points):
Concert Radio: WMAH-FM 90.3, 84 hours
Non-Commercial TV: WMAH Channel 19
Public Libraries (78 points):
11 branches, 323,569 volumes
Books added per year: 16,493
Art Museum/Gallery (50 points):
1 civic
The Lively Arts Calendar (7 points):
Touring Artists Bookings (7)
Places Rated Score: 319
Places Rated Rank: 210

Binghamton, NY
Fine Arts Broadcasting (212 points):
Concert Radio: WSKG-FM 89.3, 112 hours
Non-Commercial TV: WSKG Channel 46
Public Libraries (179 points):
21 branches, 568,450 volumes
Books added per year: 46,920
Art Museums/Galleries (100 points):
1 private, 1 university
Robertson Center for the Arts and
Science
The Lively Arts Calendar (68 points):
Touring Artists Bookings (23)
Symphony Orchestras:
BC Pops, 15
Binghamton Symphony & Choral
Society, 12
Binghamton Youth Symphony, 4
Opera Company:
Tri-Cities Opera, 14
Places Rated Score: 559
Places Rated Rank: 128

Birmingham, AL
Fine Arts Broadcasting (268 points):
Concert Radio: WBHM-FM 90.3, 168
hours
Non-Commercial TV: WBIQ Channel 10

Public Libraries (68 points):
62 branches, 2,076,679 volumes
Books added per year: 63,027
Art Museums/Galleries (100 points):
1 private, 1 university
Birmingham Museum of Art
The Lively Arts Calendar (193 points):
Touring Artists Bookings (18)
Symphony Orchestras:
Alabama Symphony Orchestra, 120
Alabama Youth Symphony, 13
Opera Company:
Birmingham Opera Theater, 20
Dance Company:
State of Alabama Ballet, 22
Places Rated Score: 629
Places Rated Rank: 106

Bismarck, ND
Fine Arts Broadcasting (144 points):
Concert Radio: KCND-FM 90.5, 44 hours
Non-Commercial TV: KBME Channel 3
Public Libraries (139 points):
6 branches, 194,839 volumes
Books added per year: 12,347
The Lively Arts Calendar (6 points):
Symphony Orchestra:
Bismarck–Mandan Symphony
Orchestra, 6
Places Rated Score: 289
Places Rated Rank: 227

Bloomington, IN
Fine Arts Broadcasting (180 points):
Concert Radio: WFIU-FM 103.7, 80 hours
Non-Commercial TV: WTIU Channel 30
Public Libraries (120 points):
2 branches, 109,669 volumes
Books added per year: 12,478
Art Museums/Galleries (100 points):
1 civic, 1 university
Indiana University Art Museum
The Lively Arts Calendar (56 points):
Touring Artists Bookings (20)
Symphony Orchestras:
Bloomington Symphony Orchestra, 6
Indiana University Orchestras, 30
Places Rated Score: 456
Places Rated Rank: 157

Bloomington–Normal, IL
Fine Arts Broadcasting (62 points):
Concert Radio: WGLT-FM 89.1, 62 hours
Public Libraries (154 points):
13 branches, 328,156 volumes
Books added per year: 18,966
Art Museum/Gallery (50 points):
1 private
The Lively Arts Calendar (20 points):
Touring Artists Bookings (10)
Symphony Orchestra:
Bloomington–Normal and Springfield
Symphony, 10
Places Rated Score: 286
Places Rated Rank: 228

Boise City, ID
Fine Arts Broadcasting (130 points):
Concert Radio: KBSU-FM 91.3, 30 hours
Non-Commercial TV: KAID Channel 4
Public Libraries (193 points):
9 branches, 386,016 volumes
Books added per year: 38,596
Art Museum/Gallery (50 points):
1 private

The Lively Arts Calendar (171 points):
  Touring Artists Bookings (109)
  Symphony Orchestras:
    Boise Philharmonic, 17
    Treasure Valley Youth Symphony, 4
  Opera Company:
    Boise Opera, 11
  Dance Company:
    American Festival Ballet, 30
Places Rated Score: 544
Places Rated Rank: 132

★ **Boston, MA**
Fine Arts Broadcasting (492 points):
  Concert Radio: WBUR-FM 90.9, 56 hours
    WCRB-FM 103.5, 153 hours
    WGBH-FM 89.7, 83 hours
  Non-Commercial TV: WGBH Channel 2
    WGBX Channel 44
Public Libraries (204 points):
  168 branches, 15,398,851 volumes
  Books added per year: 578,371
Art Museums/Galleries (1,100 points):
  1 civic, 11 private, 10 university
  Busch-Reisinger Museum, Harvard
    University
  DeCordova and Dana Museum
  Fogg Art Museum, Harvard University
  Museum of Fine Arts
The Lively Arts Calendar (1,338 points):
  Touring Artists Bookings (733)
  Symphony Orchestras:
    Boston Symphony Orchestra, 70
    Boston University/Tanglewood Young
      Artists Orchestra, 5
    Concord Orchestra, 12
    Greater Boston Youth Symphony
      Orchestras, 15
    Handel and Haydn Society, 20
    Harvard-Radcliffe Orchestra, 6
    Indian Hill Symphony Orchestra, 4
    Jamaica Plain Symphony, 3
    Melrose Symphony Orchestra, 4
    MIT Symphony Orchestra, 6
    New England Conservatory Youth
      Philharmonic Orchestra, 3
    New England Philharmonic, 7
    Newton Symphony Orchestra, 7
    Plymouth Philharmonic Orchestra, 4
    Pro Arte Chamber Orchestra of
      Boston, 9
    SinfoNova, 6
    Symphony Pro Musica, 13
    Thayer Conservatory Orchestra, 13
    Waltham Philharmonic Orchestra, 6
    Wellesley Symphony Orchestra, 5
  Opera Companies:
    Boston Concert Opera, 10
    Boston Lyric Opera, 4
    Opera Company of Boston, 5
  Professional Theatres:
    American Repertory Theatre, 160
    Huntington Theatre Company, 100
  Dance Company:
    Boston Ballet, 108
CMSA Access: Boston-Lawrence-
  Salem, MA-NH (81 points)
Places Rated Score: 3,215
Places Rated Rank: 7

Boulder-Longmont, CO
Fine Arts Broadcasting (100 points):
  Non-Commercial TV: KBDI Channel 12
Public Libraries (164 points):
  6 branches, 667,077 volumes
  Books added per year: 36,645
Art Museums/Galleries (150 points):
  1 private, 2 university

The Lively Arts Calendar (90 points):
  Touring Artists Bookings (40)
  Symphony Orchestras:
    Boulder Philharmonic, 8
    Colorado Music Festival, 35
    Longmont Symphony Orchestra, 7
CMSA Access: Denver-Boulder, CO (84
  points)
Places Rated Score: 588
Places Rated Rank: 121

Bradenton, FL
Public Libraries (87 points):
  5 branches, 255,143 volumes
  Books added per year: 16,765
Art Museum/Gallery (50 points):
  1 private
Places Rated Score: 137
Places Rated Rank: 300

Brazoria, TX
Public Libraries (82 points):
  10 branches, 251,272 volumes
  Books added per year: 15,753
The Lively Arts Calendar (11 points):
  Touring Artists Bookings (4)
  Symphony Orchestra:
    Brazosport Symphony Orchestra, 7
CMSA Access: Houston-Galveston-
  Brazoria, TX (159 points)
Places Rated Score: 252
Places Rated Rank: 244

Bremerton, WA
Public Libraries (112 points):
  10 branches, 327,282 volumes
  Books added per year: 19,934
The Lively Arts Calendar (9 points):
  Symphony Orchestra:
    Bremerton Symphony Orchestra, 9
Places Rated Score: 121
Places Rated Rank: 308

★ **Bridgeport-Milford, CT**
Fine Arts Broadcasting (362 points):
  Concert Radio: WMNR-FM 88.1, 116
    hours
    WSHU-FM 91.1, 146 hours
  Non-Commercial TV: WEDW Channel 49
Public Libraries (153 points):
  20 branches, 1,430,497 volumes
  Books added per year: 69,277
Art Museums/Galleries (100 points):
  1 private, 1 university
  Museum of Art, Science and Industry
The Lively Arts Calendar (37 points):
  Touring Artists Bookings (12)
  Symphony Orchestras:
    Fairfield Chamber Orchestra, 14
    Greater Bridgeport Symphony
      Orchestra, 7
    Greater Bridgeport Symphony Youth
      Orchestra, 4
CMSA Access: New York-Northern
  NJ-Long Island, NY-NJ-CT (1,536
  points)
Places Rated Score: 2,188
Places Rated Rank: 16

Bristol, CT
Public Libraries (117 points):
  4 branches, 198,625 volumes
  Books added per year: 9,084
CMSA Access: Hartford-New
  Britain-Middletown, CT (103 points)
Places Rated Score: 220
Places Rated Rank: 258

Brockton, MA
Public Libraries (114 points):
  13 branches, 628,822 volumes
  Books added per year: 22,694
Art Museum/Gallery (50 points):
  1 private
  Brockton Art Center-Fuller Memorial
The Lively Arts Calendar (8 points):
  Touring Artists Bookings (8)
CMSA Access: Boston-Lawrence-Salem,
  MA-NH (293 points)
Places Rated Score: 465
Places Rated Rank: 151

Brownsville-Harlingen, TX
Fine Arts Broadcasting (100 points):
  Non-Commercial TV: KMBH Channel 60
Public Libraries (45 points):
  8 branches, 254,119 volumes
  Books added per year: 12,403
Art Museum/Gallery (50 points):
  1 private
The Lively Arts Calendar (2 points):
  Touring Artists Bookings (2)
Places Rated Score: 197
Places Rated Rank: 270

Bryan-College Station, TX
Fine Arts Broadcasting (156 points):
  Concert Radio: KAMU-FM 90.9, 56 hours
  Non-Commercial TV: KAMU Channel 15
Public Library (44 points):
  1 branch, 120,663 volumes
  Books added per year: 5,803
Art Museum/Gallery (50 points):
  1 university
The Lively Arts Calendar (32 points):
  Touring Artists Bookings (25)
  Symphony Orchestra:
    Brazos Valley Symphony, 7
Places Rated Score: 282
Places Rated Rank: 230

Buffalo, NY
Fine Arts Broadcasting (333 points):
  Concert Radio: WNED-FM 94.5, 133 hours
  Non-Commercial TV: WNED Channel 17
    WNEQ Channel 23
Public Libraries (183 points):
  57 branches, 3,513,376 volumes
  Books added per year: 177,501
Art Museums/Galleries (100 points):
  1 private, 1 university
  Albright-Knox Art Gallery
The Lively Arts Calendar (425 points):
  Touring Artists Bookings (98)
  Symphony Orchestras:
    Amherst Symphony Orchestra, 4
    Buffalo Philharmonic Orchestra, 160
    Greater Buffalo Youth Orchestra, 8
    Orchard Park Symphony, 5
  Professional Theatre:
    Studio Arena Theatre, 140
  Dance Company:
    Buffalo Ballet Theatre, 10
CMSA Access: Buffalo-Niagara Falls, NY
  (11 points)
Places Rated Score: 1,052
Places Rated Rank: 56

Burlington, NC
Public Libraries (61 points):
  2 branches, 90,000 volumes
  Books added per year: 6,376
The Lively Arts Calendar (8 points):
  Touring Artists Bookings (8)
Places Rated Score: 69
Places Rated Rank: 328

Burlington, VT
Fine Arts Broadcasting (100 points):
    Non-Commercial TV: WETK Channel 33
Public Libraries (111 points):
    14 branches, 225,988 volumes
    Books added per year: 14,788
Art Museums/Galleries (150 points):
    2 private, 1 university
The Lively Arts Calendar (84 points):
    Touring Artists Bookings (54)
    Symphony Orchestras:
        Vermont Symphony Orchestra, 22
        Vermont Youth Orchestra, 8
Places Rated Score: 445
Places Rated Rank: 161

Canton, OH
Fine Arts Broadcasting (100 points):
    Non-Commercial TV: WNEO Channel 45
Public Libraries (238 points):
    17 branches, 1,257,393 volumes
    Books added per year: 97,830
Art Museums/Galleries (100 points):
    2 private
    Canton Art Institute
The Lively Arts Calendar (61 points):
    Symphony Orchestras:
        Canton Symphony Orchestra, 47
        Canton Youth Symphony, 4
    Dance Company:
        Canton Ballet, 10
Places Rated Score: 499
Places Rated Rank: 141

Casper, WY
Public Libraries (81 points):
    2 branches, 144,503 volumes
    Books added per year: 5,936
Art Museum/Gallery (50 points):
    1 private
The Lively Arts Calendar (16 points):
    Touring Artists Bookings (10)
    Symphony Orchestra:
        Casper Symphony Orchestra, 6
Places Rated Score: 147
Places Rated Rank: 291

Cedar Rapids, IA
Public Libraries (132 points):
    13 branches, 464,845 volumes
    Books added per year: 22,370
Art Museums/Galleries (100 points):
    1 private, 1 university
    Cedar Rapids Museum of Art
The Lively Arts Calendar (29 points):
    Touring Artists Bookings (7)
    Symphony Orchestras:
        Cedar Rapids Symphony, 20
        Cedar Rapids Youth Orchestra, 2
Places Rated Score: 261
Places Rated Rank: 240

Champaign–Urbana–Rantoul, IL
Fine Arts Broadcasting (100 points):
    Non-Commercial TV: WILL Channel 12
Public Libraries (226 points):
    11 branches, 508,076 volumes
    Books added per year: 40,406
Art Museum/Gallery (50 points):
    1 university
    Krannert Art Museum, University of Illinois
The Lively Arts Calendar (83 points):
    Touring Artists Bookings (67)
    Symphony Orchestras:
        Champaign County Youth Symphony, 4
        Champaign–Urbana Symphony
            Orchestra, 12
Places Rated Score: 459
Places Rated Rank: 156

Charleston, SC
Fine Arts Broadcasting (100 points):
    Non-Commercial TV: WITV Channel 7
Public Libraries (98 points):
    14 branches, 573,742 volumes
    Books added per year: 49,796
Art Museums/Galleries (150 points):
    2 civic, 1 private
    Gibbs Art Gallery
The Lively Arts Calendar (124 points):
    Touring Artists Bookings (16)
    Symphony Orchestra:
        Charleston Symphony, 40
    Opera Company:
        Spoleto Festival U.S.A., 38
    Dance Company:
        Charleston Ballet Theatre, 30
Places Rated Score: 472
Places Rated Rank: 145

Charleston, WV
Public Libraries (96 points):
    16 branches, 688,984 volumes
    Books added per year: 25,848
Art Museum/Gallery (50 points):
    1 private
    Sunrise Museums
The Lively Arts Calendar (107 points):
    Touring Artists Bookings (64)
    Symphony Orchestras:
        Charleston Symphony Youth
            Orchestra, 2
        Lilliput Orchestra, 9
        West Virginia Symphony, 25
    Dance Company:
        Charleston Ballet, 7
Places Rated Score: 253
Places Rated Rank: 243

Charlotte–Gastonia–Rock Hill, NC–SC
Fine Arts Broadcasting (460 points):
    Concert Radio: WDAV-FM 89.9, 118 hours
        WFAE-FM 90.7, 42 hours
    Non-Commercial TV: WNSC Channel 30
        WTVI Channel 42
        WUNG Channel 58
Public Libraries (127 points):
    45 branches, 1,932,403 volumes
    Books added per year: 142,128
Art Museums/Galleries (300 points):
    1 civic, 4 private, 1 university
The Lively Arts Calendar (348 points):
    Touring Artists Bookings (103)
    Symphony Orchestras:
        Charlotte Symphony Orchestra, 225
        Charlotte Youth Symphony, 8
        Salisbury Symphony Orchestra, 4
    Opera Company:
        Opera Carolina, 8
Places Rated Score: 1,235
Places Rated Rank: 45

Charlottesville, VA
Public Libraries (173 points):
    6 branches, 253,531 volumes
    Books added per year: 21,569
Art Museums/Galleries (100 points):
    1 private, 1 university
The Lively Arts Calendar (51 points):
    Touring Artists Bookings (14)
    Symphony Orchestras:
        Charlottesville & University Symphony
            Orchestra, 10
        Youth Orchestra of
            Charlottesville–Albemarle, 2

Opera Company:
    Ash Lawn–Highland Summer
        Festival, 25
Places Rated Score: 324
Places Rated Rank: 206

Chattanooga, TN–GA
Fine Arts Broadcasting (173 points):
    Concert Radio: WSMC-FM 90.5, 19 hours
        WUTC-FM 88.1, 54 hours
    Non-Commercial TV: WTCI Channel 45
Public Libraries (65 points):
    15 branches, 653,602 volumes
    Books added per year: 27,981
Art Museums/Galleries (150 points):
    2 private, 1 university
    Hunter Museum of Art
The Lively Arts Calendar (61 points):
    Touring Artists Bookings (7)
    Symphony Orchestra:
        Chattanooga Symphony, 50
    Opera Company:
        Chattanooga Opera Association, 4
Places Rated Score: 449
Places Rated Rank: 159

Cheyenne, WY
Fine Arts Broadcasting (27 points):
    Concert Radio: KUWR-FM 91.9, 27 hours
Public Libraries (83 points):
    3 branches, 122,400 volumes
    Books added per year: 6,289
Art Museum/Gallery (50 points):
    1 state
    Wyoming Museum
The Lively Arts Calendar (16 points):
    Touring Artists Bookings (10)
    Symphony Orchestra:
        Cheyenne Symphony Orchestra, 6
Places Rated Score: 176
Places Rated Rank: 276

★ Chicago, IL
Fine Arts Broadcasting (540 points):
    Concert Radio: WFMT-FM 98.7, 154 hours
        WMWA-FM 88.5, 50 hours
        WNIB-FM 97.1, 136 hours
    Non-Commercial TV: WTTW Channel 11
        WYCC Channel 20
Public Libraries (167 points):
    211 branches, 14,469,133 volumes
    Books added per year: 1,043,012
Art Museums/Galleries (950 points):
    3 civic, 8 private, 8 university
    Art Institute of Chicago
    Museum of Contemporary Art
    Museum of Contemporary Photography
The Lively Arts Calendar (2,734 points):
    Touring Artists Bookings (580)
    Symphony Orchestras:
        Chicago Chamber Orchestra, 35
        Chicago Symphony Orchestra, 185
        Chicago Youth Symphony
            Orchestra, 12
        Civic Orchestra of Chicago, 8
        Civic Symphony of Oak Park–River
            Forest, 5
        Classical Symphony Orchestra, 6
        Grant Park Symphony, 40
        Illinois Philharmonic Orchestra, 9
        McHenry County Youth Orchestra, 3
        North Shore Youth Orchestra, 4
        Northbrook Symphony Orchestra, 5
        Skokie Valley Symphony Orchestra, 4
        Wheaton Summer Symphony, 2
    Opera Companies:
        American National Opera, 20

American Ritual Theater Company, 15
Chamber Opera Chicago, 15
Chicago Opera Theater, 28
Light Opera Works, 12
Lyric Opera of Chicago, 65
The Opera Factory, 6
Professional Theatres:
  Free Street Theater, 100
  Goodman Theatre, 120
  Northlight Theatre, 100
  Organic Theater Company, 200
  Remains Theatre, 60
  Steppenwolf Theatre Company, 100
  The Body Politic Theatre, 360
  Victory Gardens Theater, 400
  Wisdom Bridge Theatre, 80
Dance Companies:
  Chicago City Ballet, 85
  Hubbard Street Dance Company, 70
CMSA Access: Chicago–Gary–Lake
  County, IL–IN–WI (61 points)
Places Rated Score: 4,452
Places Rated Rank: 3

Chico, CA
Fine Arts Broadcasting (60 points):
  Concert Radio: KCHO-FM 91.7, 60 hours
Public Libraries (48 points):
  7 branches, 243,619 volumes
  Books added per year: 8,450
The Lively Arts Calendar (18 points):
  Touring Artists Bookings (13)
  Symphony Orchestra:
    Paradise Symphony Orchestra, 5
Places Rated Score: 126
Places Rated Rank: 304

Cincinnati, OH–KY–IN
Fine Arts Broadcasting (338 points):
  Concert Radio: WCUC-FM 90.9, 138
    hours
  Non-Commercial TV: WCET Channel 48
    WCVN Channel 54
Public Libraries (184 points):
  59 branches, 4,472,609 volumes
  Books added per year: 265,487
Art Museums/Galleries (200 points):
  3 private, 1 university
  Cincinnati Museum of Art
The Lively Arts Calendar (627 points):
  Touring Artists Bookings (36)
  Symphony Orchestras:
    Cincinnati Symphony Orchestra, 300
    Cincinnati Youth Symphony
      Orchestra, 6
    The Cincinnati Philharmonic & Concert
      Orchestras, 22
  Opera Company:
    Cincinnati Opera, 8
  Professional Theatre:
    Cincinnati Playhouse in the Park, 220
  Dance Company:
    Cincinnati/New Orleans Ballet, 35
CMSA Access: Cincinnati–Hamilton,
  OH–KY–IN (17 points)
Places Rated Score: 1,366
Places Rated Rank: 41

Clarksville–Hopkinsville, TN–KY
Public Libraries (50 points):
  3 branches, 198,491 volumes
  Books added per year: 8,001
Art Museum/Gallery (50 points):
  1 university
The Lively Arts Calendar (6 points):
  Touring Artists Bookings (6)
Places Rated Score: 106
Places Rated Rank: 312

★ Cleveland, OH
Fine Arts Broadcasting (244 points):
  Concert Radio: WCLV-FM 95.5, 144 hours
  Non-Commercial TV: WVIZ Channel 25
Public Libraries (311 points):
  89 branches, 6,561,133 volumes
  Books added per year: 576,367
Art Museums/Galleries (300 points):
  2 civic, 4 private
  Cleveland Museum of Art
The Lively Arts Calendar (1,130 points):
  Touring Artists Bookings (338)
  Symphony Orchestras:
    Cleveland Philharmonic Orchestra, 6
    Ohio Chamber Orchestra, 100
    The Cleveland Institute of Music, 3
    The Cleveland Orchestra, 185
    The Cleveland Orchestra Youth
      Orchestra, 6
  Opera Companies:
    Cleveland Opera, 24
    Lyric Opera Cleveland, 3
  Professional Theatres:
    Great Lakes Theater Festival, 200
    The Cleveland Play House, 220
  Dance Company:
    Cleveland/San Jose Ballet, 45
CMSA Access: Cleveland–Akron–Lorain,
  OH (66 points)
Places Rated Score: 2,051
Places Rated Rank: 21

Colorado Springs, CO
Fine Arts Broadcasting (240 points):
  Concert Radio: KCME-FM 88.1, 140 hours
  Non-Commercial TV: KTSC Channel 53
Public Libraries (138 points):
  9 branches, 705,798 volumes
  Books added per year: 55,186
Art Museums/Galleries (150 points):
  2 private, 1 university
  Colorado Springs Fine Arts Center
The Lively Arts Calendar (88 points):
  Touring Artists Bookings (23)
  Symphony Orchestra:
    Colorado Springs Symphony, 65
Places Rated Score: 616
Places Rated Rank: 110

Columbia, MO
Fine Arts Broadcasting (100 points):
  Concert Radio: KBIA-FM 91.3, 100 hours
Public Libraries (148 points):
  2 branches, 240,340 volumes
  Books added per year: 16,200
Art Museums/Galleries (150 points):
  1 private, 2 university
  University of Missouri Museum of Art
The Lively Arts Calendar (41 points):
  Touring Artists Bookings (15)
  Symphony Orchestras:
    Missouri Symphony Society, 20
    UMC Philharmonic Orchestra, 6
Places Rated Score: 439
Places Rated Rank: 164

Columbia, SC
Fine Arts Broadcasting (190 points):
  Concert Radio: WLTR-FM 91.3, 90 hours
  Non-Commercial TV: WRLK Channel 35
Public Libraries (212 points):
  15 branches, 651,742 volumes
  Books added per year: 98,971
Art Museums/Galleries (100 points):
  1 private, 1 university
  Museum of Art and Science

The Lively Arts Calendar (63 points):
  Touring Artists Bookings (14)
  Symphony Orchestras:
    Columbia Youth Orchestra, 2
    South Carolina Philharmonic &
      Chamber Orchestra, 10
  Opera Company:
    Columbia Lyric Opera, 15
  Dance Companies:
    Carolina Ballet Theatre, 8
    Columbia City Ballet, 14
Places Rated Score: 565
Places Rated Rank: 126

Columbus, GA–AL
Fine Arts Broadcasting (163 points):
  Concert Radio: WTJB-FM 91.7, 63 hours
  Non-Commercial TV: WJSP Channel 28
Public Libraries (68 points):
  6 branches, 549,984 volumes
  Books added per year: 17,293
Art Museum/Gallery (50 points):
  1 private
  Columbus Museum of Arts and Sciences
The Lively Arts Calendar (35 points):
  Symphony Orchestra:
    Columbus Symphony Orchestra, 35
Places Rated Score: 316
Places Rated Rank: 213

Columbus, OH
Fine Arts Broadcasting (338 points):
  Concert Radio: WCBE-FM 90.5, 70 hours
    WOSU-FM 89.7, 168 hours
  Non-Commercial TV: WOSU Channel 34
Public Libraries (232 points):
  46 branches, 3,514,958 volumes
  Books added per year: 308,720
Art Museums/Galleries (300 points):
  1 civic, 2 private, 3 university
  Columbus Museum of Art
The Lively Arts Calendar (304 points):
  Touring Artists Bookings (119)
  Symphony Orchestras:
    Central Ohio Symphony Orchestra, 7
    Columbus Symphony Orchestra, 100
    Columbus Symphony Youth
      Orchestra, 4
    Pro Musica Chamber Orchestra of
      Columbus, 6
    Westerville Civic Symphony, 3
  Opera Company:
    Opera/Columbus, 12
  Dance Company:
    BalletMet, 53
Places Rated Score: 1,174
Places Rated Rank: 50

Corpus Christi, TX
Fine Arts Broadcasting (251 points):
  Concert Radio: KKED-FM 90.3, 151 hours
  Non-Commercial TV: KEDT Channel 16
Public Libraries (51 points):
  15 branches, 466,910 volumes
  Books added per year: 18,826
Art Museums/Galleries (100 points):
  1 civic, 1 private
  Art Museum of South Texas
The Lively Arts Calendar (63 points):
  Touring Artists Bookings (21)
  Symphony Orchestra:
    Corpus Christi Symphony
      Orchestra, 22
  Dance Company:
    Corpus Christi Ballet, 20
Places Rated Score: 465
Places Rated Rank: 151

Cumberland, MD-WV
Public Libraries (75 points):
  8 branches, 224,008 volumes
  Books added per year: 7,819
The Lively Arts Calendar (4 points):
  Touring Artists Bookings (4)
Places Rated Score: 79
Places Rated Rank: 325

Dallas, TX
Fine Arts Broadcasting (311 points):
  Concert Radio: KERA-FM 90.1, 43 hours
    WRR-FM 101, 168 hours
  Non-Commercial TV: KERA Channel 13
Public Libraries (69 points):
  70 branches, 3,837,501 volumes
  Books added per year: 180,090
Art Museums/Galleries (200 points):
  2 private, 2 university
  Dallas Museum of Art
The Lively Arts Calendar (841 points):
  Touring Artists Bookings (319)
  Symphony Orchestras:
    AIMS Orchestra, 12
    Dallas Symphony Orchestra, 263
    Garland Symphony Orchestra, 6
    Greater Dallas Youth Orchestra, 7
    Irving Symphony Orchestra, 4
    New Philharmonic Orchestra of Irving, 5
    Richardson Symphony Orchestra, 6
  Opera Companies:
    Dallas Opera, 22
    Lyric Opera of Dallas, 12
  Professional Theatre:
    Dallas Theater Center, 120
  Dance Companies:
    Dallas Ballet, 55
    Dallas Black Dance Theatre, 10
CMSA Access: Dallas-Fort Worth, TX (60
points)
Places Rated Score: 1,481
Places Rated Rank: 39

★ Danbury, CT
Public Libraries (179 points):
  11 branches, 513,100 volumes
  Books added per year: 34,202
Art Museum/Gallery (50 points):
  1 private
The Lively Arts Calendar (20 points):
  Touring Artists Bookings (12)
  Symphony Orchestras:
    Ridgefield Symphony Orchestra, 5
    Ridgefield Youth Orchestra, 3
CMSA Access: New York-Northern
NJ-Long Island, NY-NJ-CT (1,606
points)
Places Rated Score: 1,855
Places Rated Rank: 26

Danville, VA
Public Libraries (102 points):
  4 branches, 146,445 volumes
  Books added per year: 11,310
Art Museum/Gallery (50 points):
  1 private
Places Rated Score: 152
Places Rated Rank: 288

Davenport-Rock Island-Moline, IA-IL
Fine Arts Broadcasting (224 points):
  Concert Radio: WVIK-FM 90.1, 124 hours
  Non-Commercial TV: WQPT Channel 24
Public Libraries (141 points):
  27 branches, 1,170,397 volumes
  Books added per year: 52,612

Art Museums/Galleries (100 points):
  1 civic, 1 university
  Davenport Museum of Art
The Lively Arts Calendar (71 points):
  Touring Artists Bookings (38)
  Symphony Orchestras:
    Augustana College Symphony
      Orchestra, 10
    Quad City Symphony Orchestra, 16
    Quad City Youth Symphony
      Orchestra, 7
Places Rated Score: 536
Places Rated Rank: 135

Dayton-Springfield, OH
Fine Arts Broadcasting (219 points):
  Concert Radio: WDPR-FM 89.5, 83 hours
    WYSO-FM 91.3, 36 hours
  Non-Commercial TV: WPTD Channel 16
Public Libraries (228 points):
  37 branches, 2,964,778 volumes
  Books added per year: 213,631
Art Museums/Galleries (250 points):
  1 civic, 3 private, 1 university
  Dayton Art Institute
  Springfield Art Center
The Lively Arts Calendar (379 points):
  Touring Artists Bookings (286)
  Symphony Orchestras:
    Dayton Philharmonic Orchestra, 31
    Dayton Philharmonic Youth
      Orchestra, 7
    Springfield Symphony Orchestra, 6
    Springfield Youth Symphony, 3
  Opera Company:
    Dayton Opera, 11
  Dance Company:
    Dayton Ballet, 35
Places Rated Score: 1,076
Places Rated Rank: 53

Daytona Beach, FL
Public Libraries (73 points):
  15 branches, 554,798 volumes
  Books added per year: 25,100
Art Museums/Galleries (150 points):
  2 private, 1 university
  Museum of Arts and Sciences
The Lively Arts Calendar (59 points):
  Touring Artists Bookings (59)
Places Rated Score: 282
Places Rated Rank: 230

Decatur, AL
Public Libraries (90 points):
  5 branches, 101,730 volumes
  Books added per year: 11,753
Art Museum/Gallery (50 points):
  1 university
The Lively Arts Calendar (12 points):
  Touring Artists Bookings (12)
Places Rated Score: 152
Places Rated Rank: 288

Decatur, IL
Public Libraries (171 points):
  12 branches, 280,642 volumes
  Books added per year: 21,647
Art Museum/Gallery (50 points):
  1 university
The Lively Arts Calendar (17 points):
  Touring Artists Bookings (12)
  Symphony Orchestra:
    Millikin-Decatur Symphony, 5
Places Rated Score: 238
Places Rated Rank: 253

Denver, CO
Fine Arts Broadcasting (377 points):
  Concert Radio: KCFR-FM 90.1, 88 hours
    KPOF-AM 910, 21 hours
    KVOD-FM 99.5, 168 hours
  Non-Commercial TV: KRMA Channel 6
Public Libraries (140 points):
  62 branches, 3,667,124 volumes
  Books added per year: 239,717
Art Museums/Galleries (300 points):
  1 civic, 4 private, 1 university
  Denver Museum of Art
The Lively Arts Calendar (708 points):
  Touring Artists Bookings (165)
  Symphony Orchestras:
    Denver Chamber Orchestra, 19
    Denver Symphony Orchestra, 164
    Denver Young Artists Orchestra, 3
    Jefferson Symphony Orchestra, 6
    National Repertory Orchestra, 48
  Opera Company:
    Opera Colorado, 8
  Professional Theatre:
    Denver Center Theatre Company, 240
  Dance Companies:
    Colorado Ballet, 25
    The David Taylor Dance Theatre, 30
CMSA Access: Denver-Boulder, CO (34
points)
Places Rated Score: 1,559
Places Rated Rank: 35

Des Moines, IA
Fine Arts Broadcasting (100 points):
  Non-Commercial TV: KDIN Channel 11
Public Libraries (72 points):
  32 branches, 1,015,660 volumes
  Books added per year: 28,034
Art Museums/Galleries (150 points):
  3 private
The Lively Arts Calendar (121 points):
  Touring Artists Bookings (25)
  Symphony Orchestras:
    Des Moines Community Orchestra, 4
    Des Moines Symphony Orchestra, 23
    Des Moines Youth Chamber Players, 7
    Drake University Symphony
      Orchestra, 4
    Greater Des Moines Youth
      Symphony, 4
  Opera Company:
    Des Moines Metro Opera, 24
  Dance Company:
    Des Moines Ballet, 30
Places Rated Score: 443
Places Rated Rank: 162

Detroit, MI
Fine Arts Broadcasting (268 points):
  Concert Radio: WQRS-FM 105.1, 168
    hours
  Non-Commercial TV: WTVS Channel 56
Public Libraries (100 points):
  145 branches, 8,461,908 volumes
  Books added per year: 432,617
Art Museums/Galleries (450 points):
  3 civic, 4 private, 2 university
  Cranbrook Academy of Art
  Detroit Institute of Arts
  Henry Ford Museum
The Lively Arts Calendar (726 points):
  Touring Artists Bookings (217)
  Symphony Orchestras:
    Birmingham-Bloomfield Symphony
      Orchestra, 12
    Dearborn Symphony Orchestra, 6
    Detroit Symphony Civic Orchestra, 3

Detroit Symphony Orchestra, 200
Lake St. Clair Symphony Orchestra, 6
Metropolitan Youth Symphony, 4
Pontiac–Oakland Symphony
  Orchestra, 8
Warren Symphony Orchestra, 21
Opera Company:
  Michigan Opera Theatre, 43
Professional Theatres:
  Attic Theatre, 120
  Detroit Repertory Theatre, 80
CMSA Access: Detroit–Ann Arbor, MI (71
points)
Places Rated Score: 1,615
Places Rated Rank: 32

Dothan, AL
Public Libraries (101 points):
  9 branches, 251,128 volumes
  Books added per year: 13,509
Places Rated Score: 101
Places Rated Rank: 315

Dubuque, IA
Public Libraries (97 points):
  3 branches, 46,587 volumes
  Books added per year: 8,842
Art Museum/Gallery (50 points):
  1 private
The Lively Arts Calendar (44 points):
  Touring Artists Bookings (27)
  Symphony Orchestra:
    Dubuque Symphony Orchestra, 17
Places Rated Score: 191
Places Rated Rank: 274

Duluth, MN–WI
Fine Arts Broadcasting (380 points):
  Concert Radio: WIRR-FM 90.9, 140 hours
    WSCD-FM 92.9, 140 hours
  Non-Commercial TV: WDSE Channel 8
Public Libraries (154 points):
  23 branches, 1,129,333 volumes
  Books added per year: 37,685
Art Museum/Gallery (50 points):
  1 university
The Lively Arts Calendar (55 points):
  Touring Artists Bookings (20)
  Symphony Orchestra:
    Duluth–Superior Symphony
      Orchestra, 15
  Dance Company:
    Duluth Ballet, 20
Places Rated Score: 639
Places Rated Rank: 104

Eau Claire, WI
Fine Arts Broadcasting (100 points):
  Non-Commercial TV: WHWC Channel 28
Public Libraries (184 points):
  11 branches, 366,349 volumes
  Books added per year: 25,860
The Lively Arts Calendar (38 points):
  Touring Artists Bookings (11)
  Symphony Orchestras:
    Chippewa Valley Symphony, 4
    University of Wisconsin Symphony, 23
Places Rated Score: 322
Places Rated Rank: 208

El Paso, TX
Fine Arts Broadcasting (141 points):
  Concert Radio: KTEP-FM 88.5, 41 hours
  Non-Commercial TV: KCOS Channel 13
Public Libraries (71 points):
  12 branches, 591,440 volumes
  Books added per year: 42,075

Art Museum/Gallery (50 points):
  1 private
  El Paso Museum of Art
The Lively Arts Calendar (51 points):
  Touring Artists Bookings (8)
  Symphony Orchestras:
    El Paso Philharmonic Strings, 4
    El Paso Symphony Orchestra, 25
    University of Texas Symphony, 6
  Dance Company:
    Ballet of the Americas, 8
Places Rated Score: 313
Places Rated Rank: 215

Elkhart–Goshen, IN
Fine Arts Broadcasting (168 points):
  Concert Radio: WGCS-FM 91.1, 68 hours
  Non-Commercial TV: WNIT Channel 34
Public Libraries (190 points):
  8 branches, 367,421 volumes
  Books added per year: 28,603
Art Museum/Gallery (50 points):
  1 private
The Lively Arts Calendar (10 points):
  Touring Artists Bookings (4)
  Symphony Orchestra:
    Elkhart Symphony Orchestra, 6
Places Rated Score: 418
Places Rated Rank: 171

Elmira, NY
Public Libraries (116 points):
  6 branches, 354,348 volumes
  Books added per year: 10,381
Art Museum/Gallery (50 points):
  1 private
  Arnot Art Museum
The Lively Arts Calendar (82 points):
  Touring Artists Bookings (75)
  Symphony Orchestra:
    Elmira Symphony & Choral Society, 7
Places Rated Score: 248
Places Rated Rank: 250

Enid, OK
Public Library (110 points):
  1 branch, 138,910 volumes
  Books added per year: 6,813
Art Museum/Gallery (50 points):
  1 university
The Lively Arts Calendar (35 points):
  Touring Artists Bookings (20)
  Symphony Orchestra:
    Enid–Phillips Symphony Orchestra, 15
Places Rated Score: 195
Places Rated Rank: 271

Erie, PA
Fine Arts Broadcasting (140 points):
  Concert Radio: WQLN-FM 91.3, 40 hours
  Non-Commercial TV: WQLN Channel 54
Public Libraries (189 points):
  10 branches, 545,040 volumes
  Books added per year: 53,026
Art Museum/Gallery (50 points):
  1 private
The Lively Arts Calendar (72 points):
  Touring Artists Bookings (54)
  Symphony Orchestras:
    Erie Philharmonic Orchestra, 16
    Erie Philharmonic Youth Orchestra, 2
Places Rated Score: 451
Places Rated Rank: 158

Eugene–Springfield, OR
Fine Arts Broadcasting (158 points):
  Concert Radio: KWAX-FM 91.1, 158 hours

Public Libraries (101 points):
  9 branches, 488,924 volumes
  Books added per year: 26,459
Art Museum/Gallery (50 points):
  1 university
  Museum of Art, University of Oregon
The Lively Arts Calendar (235 points):
  Touring Artists Bookings (7)
  Symphony Orchestras:
    Eugene Symphony Orchestra, 16
    Eugene Youth Symphony, 6
  Opera Company:
    Eugene Opera, 6
  Dance Company:
    Eugene Ballet Company, 200
Places Rated Score: 544
Places Rated Rank: 132

Evansville, IN–KY
Fine Arts Broadcasting (172 points):
  Concert Radio: WNIN-FM 88.3, 72 hours
  Non-Commercial TV: WNIN Channel 9
Public Libraries (166 points):
  17 branches, 989,490 volumes
  Books added per year: 46,666
Art Museums/Galleries (100 points):
  2 private
  Museum of Art and Sciences
The Lively Arts Calendar (30 points):
  Touring Artists Bookings (4)
  Symphony Orchestras:
    Evansville Philharmonic Orchestra, 22
    University of Evansville Symphony, 4
Places Rated Score: 468
Places Rated Rank: 149

Fall River, MA–RI
Public Libraries (97 points):
  8 branches, 615,939 volumes
  Books added per year: 15,692
CMSA Access: Providence–Pawtucket–
  Fall River, RI–MA (67 points)
Places Rated Score: 164
Places Rated Rank: 283

Fargo–Moorhead, ND–MN
Fine Arts Broadcasting (240 points):
  Concert Radio: KCCM-FM 91.9, 140 hours
  Non-Commercial TV: KFME Channel 13
Public Libraries (94 points):
  7 branches, 301,000 volumes
  Books added per year: 13,952
Art Museums/Galleries (100 points):
  1 private, 1 university
The Lively Arts Calendar (37 points):
  Touring Artists Bookings (20)
  Symphony Orchestra:
    Fargo–Moorhead Symphony
      Orchestra, 10
  Opera Company:
    Fargo–Moorhead Civic Opera, 7
Places Rated Score: 471
Places Rated Rank: 147

Fayetteville, NC
Public Libraries (95 points):
  7 branches, 257,429 volumes
  Books added per year: 25,166
Art Museums/Galleries (100 points):
  2 private
The Lively Arts Calendar (5 points):
  Symphony Orchestra:
    Fayetteville Symphony Orchestra, 5
Places Rated Score: 200
Places Rated Rank: 268

Fayetteville–Springdale, AR
Fine Arts Broadcasting (170 points):
Concert Radio: KUAF-FM 88.9, 70 hours
Non-Commercial TV: KAFT Channel 13
Public Libraries (80 points):
9 branches, 215,635 volumes
Books added per year: 8,797
The Lively Arts Calendar (29 points):
Touring Artists Bookings (9)
Symphony Orchestra:
North Arkansas Symphony Society, 20
Places Rated Score: 279
Places Rated Rank: 234

Fitchburg–Leominster, MA
Public Libraries (159 points):
6 branches, 390,266 volumes
Books added per year: 16,039
Art Museum/Gallery (50 points):
1 private
Fitchburg Art Museum
The Lively Arts Calendar (4 points):
Touring Artists Bookings (4)
Places Rated Score: 213
Places Rated Rank: 260

Flint, MI
Fine Arts Broadcasting (269 points):
Concert Radio: WFBE-FM 95.1, 57 hours
WFUM-FM 91.1, 112 hours
Non-Commercial TV: WFUM Channel 28
Public Libraries (354 points):
8 branches, 1,044,217 volumes
Books added per year: 158,218
Art Museum/Gallery (50 points):
1 private
Flint Institute of Arts
The Lively Arts Calendar (69 points):
Symphony Orchestras:
Flint School of the Performing Arts
Symphony, 20
Flint Symphony Orchestra, 6
Dance Companies:
Ballet Michigan, 40
Flint Ballet Theatre, 3
Places Rated Score: 742
Places Rated Rank: 85

Florence, AL
Fine Arts Broadcasting (100 points):
Non-Commercial TV: WFIQ Channel 36
Public Libraries (53 points):
9 branches, 135,703 volumes
Books added per year: 7,393
Art Museum/Gallery (50 points):
1 civic
The Lively Arts Calendar (5 points):
Touring Artists Bookings (5)
Places Rated Score: 208
Places Rated Rank: 264

Florence, SC
Fine Arts Broadcasting (100 points):
Non-Commercial TV: WJPM Channel 33
Public Libraries (91 points):
6 branches, 149,772 volumes
Books added per year: 10,859
Art Museum/Gallery (50 points):
1 private
The Lively Arts Calendar (8 points):
Touring Artists Bookings (8)
Places Rated Score: 249
Places Rated Rank: 248

Fort Collins–Loveland, CO
Public Libraries (135 points):
5 branches, 363,544 volumes
Books added per year: 24,824

The Lively Arts Calendar (41 points):
Touring Artists Bookings (26)
Symphony Orchestra:
Fort Collins Symphony Orchestra, 15
Places Rated Score: 176
Places Rated Rank: 276

Fort Lauderdale–Hollywood–Pompano Beach, FL
Public Libraries (199 points):
29 branches, 1,732,253 volumes
Books added per year: 244,925
Art Museums/Galleries (150 points):
1 civic, 2 private
Fort Lauderdale Museum of Art
The Lively Arts Calendar (293 points):
Touring Artists Bookings (105)
Symphony Orchestras:
Broward Community College Youth
Symphony, 19
Philharmonic Orchestra of Florida, 115
South Florida Symphony Orchestra, 45
Opera Company:
Gold Coast Opera, 9
CMSA Access: Miami–Fort Lauderdale,
FL (123 points)
Places Rated Score: 765
Places Rated Rank: 81

Fort Myers–Cape Coral, FL
Fine Arts Broadcasting (190 points):
Concert Radio: WSFP-FM 90.1, 90 hours
Non-Commercial TV: WSFP Channel 30
Public Libraries (177 points):
10 branches, 311,027 volumes
Books added per year: 56,712
Art Museum/Gallery (50 points):
1 university
The Lively Arts Calendar (197 points):
Touring Artists Bookings (180)
Symphony Orchestra:
Southwest Florida Symphony
Orchestra, 17
Places Rated Score: 614
Places Rated Rank: 112

Fort Pierce, FL
Fine Arts Broadcasting (52 points):
Concert Radio: WQCS-FM 88.9, 52 hours
Public Libraries (118 points):
6 branches, 221,292 volumes
Books added per year: 27,712
The Lively Arts Calendar (4 points):
Touring Artists Bookings (4)
Places Rated Score: 174
Places Rated Rank: 280

Fort Smith, AR–OK
Public Libraries (44 points):
21 branches, 258,650 volumes
Books added per year: 8,101
Art Museum/Gallery (50 points):
1 private
The Lively Arts Calendar (12 points):
Touring Artists Bookings (5)
Symphony Orchestra:
Fort Smith Symphony, 7
Places Rated Score: 106
Places Rated Rank: 312

Fort Walton Beach, FL
Public Libraries (20 points):
5 branches, 84,475 volumes
Books added per year: 3,169
The Lively Arts Calendar (34 points):
Symphony Orchestra:
Okaloosa Symphony Orchestra, 4

Dance Company:
Northwest Florida Ballet, 30
Places Rated Score: 54
Places Rated Rank: 331

Fort Wayne, IN
Fine Arts Broadcasting (95 points):
Concert Radio: WBNI-FM 89.1, 95 hours
Public Libraries (260 points):
19 branches, 2,128,937 volumes
Books added per year: 93,441
Art Museum/Gallery (50 points):
1 private
The Lively Arts Calendar (111 points):
Touring Artists Bookings (47)
Symphony Orchestra:
Fort Wayne Philharmonic, 44
Dance Company:
Fort Wayne Ballet, 20
Places Rated Score: 516
Places Rated Rank: 138

Fort Worth–Arlington, TX
Fine Arts Broadcasting (30 points):
Concert Radio: KTCU-FM 88.7, 30 hours
Public Libraries (95 points):
33 branches, 1,768,397 volumes
Books added per year: 124,774
Art Museums/Galleries (200 points):
3 private, 1 university
Amon Carter Museum of Western Art
Fort Worth Art Museum
Kimbell Art Museum
The Lively Arts Calendar (365 points):
Touring Artists Bookings (30)
Symphony Orchestras:
Fort Worth Civic Orchestra, 5
Fort Worth Symphony Orchestra, 50
Youth Orchestra of Greater Fort
Worth, 20
Opera Company:
Fort Worth Opera Association, 60
Professional Theatre:
Stage West, 180
Dance Company:
Fort Worth Ballet, 20
CMSA Access: Dallas–Fort Worth, TX
(135 points)
Places Rated Score: 825
Places Rated Rank: 74

Fresno, CA
Fine Arts Broadcasting (183 points):
Concert Radio: KVPR-FM 89.3, 83 hours
Non-Commercial TV: KMTF Channel 18
Public Libraries (48 points):
34 branches, 1,048,048 volumes
Books added per year: 28,824
Art Museums/Galleries (100 points):
2 private
Fresno Arts Center
The Lively Arts Calendar (62 points):
Touring Artists Bookings (30)
Symphony Orchestras:
Fresno Philharmonic Orchestra, 28
Fresno Youth Philharmonic Orchestra, 4
Places Rated Score: 393
Places Rated Rank: 178

Gadsden, AL
Public Libraries (99 points):
6 branches, 211,372 volumes
Books added per year: 10,193
Art Museum/Gallery (50 points):
1 private
The Lively Arts Calendar (9 points):
Touring Artists Bookings (9)
Places Rated Score: 158
Places Rated Rank: 285

Gainesville, FL
Fine Arts Broadcasting (184 points):
 Concert Radio: WUFT-FM 89.1, 84 hours
 Non-Commercial TV: WUFT Channel 5
Public Libraries (139 points):
 7 branches, 294,575 volumes
 Books added per year: 29,353
Art Museum/Gallery (50 points):
 1 university
 University of Florida Gallery
The Lively Arts Calendar (221 points):
 Touring Artists Bookings (15)
 Symphony Orchestra:
  University of Florida Symphony, 6
 Professional Theatre:
  The Hippodrome State Theatre, 200
Places Rated Score: 594
Places Rated Rank: 118

Galveston–Texas City, TX
Public Libraries (110 points):
 8 branches, 530,021 volumes
 Books added per year: 23,726
The Lively Arts Calendar (12 points):
 Touring Artists Bookings (12)
CMSA Access: Houston–Galveston–
 Brazoria, TX (159 points)
Places Rated Score: 281
Places Rated Rank: 232

Gary–Hammond, IN
Public Libraries (183 points):
 39 branches, 2,035,619 volumes
 Books added per year: 110,754
Art Museum/Gallery (50 points):
 1 university
The Lively Arts Calendar (30 points):
 Touring Artists Bookings (13)
 Symphony Orchestras:
  Northwest Indiana Symphony, 15
  Northwest Indiana Youth Orchestra, 2
CMSA Access: Chicago–Gary–Lake
 County, IL–IN–WI (428 points)
Places Rated Score: 691
Places Rated Rank: 94

Glens Falls, NY
Public Libraries (204 points):
 17 branches, 263,193 volumes
 Books added per year: 23,310
Art Museums/Galleries (150 points):
 3 private
The Lively Arts Calendar (94 points):
 Symphony Orchestras:
  Glens Falls Symphony Orchestra, 4
  Philharmonia Virtuosi, 90
Places Rated Score: 448
Places Rated Rank: 160

Grand Forks, ND
Fine Arts Broadcasting (175 points):
 Concert Radio: KFJM-FM 89.3, 75 hours
 Non-Commercial TV: KGFE Channel 2
Public Libraries (99 points):
 2 branches, 145,170 volumes
 Books added per year: 6,925
Art Museum/Gallery (50 points):
 1 university
The Lively Arts Calendar (20 points):
 Touring Artists Bookings (15)
 Symphony Orchestra:
  Greater Grand Forks Symphony, 5
Places Rated Score: 344
Places Rated Rank: 197

Grand Rapids, MI
Fine Arts Broadcasting (212 points):
 Concert Radio: WVGR-FM 104.1, 112
  hours
 Non-Commercial TV: WGVC Channel 35
Public Libraries (177 points):
 40 branches, 1,597,556 volumes
 Books added per year: 119,997
Art Museums/Galleries (100 points):
 1 private, 1 university
 Grand Rapids Art Museum
The Lively Arts Calendar (94 points):
 Touring Artists Bookings (6)
 Symphony Orchestras:
  Grand Rapids Symphony Orchestra, 65
  Grand Rapids Youth Symphony, 4
  Hope College Orchestra, 5
 Opera Company:
  Opera Grand Rapids, 4
 Dance Company:
  Grand Rapids Civic Ballet, 10
Places Rated Score: 583
Places Rated Rank: 122

Great Falls, MT
Public Libraries (91 points):
 3 branches, 189,712 volumes
 Books added per year: 7,221
Art Museums/Galleries (100 points):
 2 private
 C. W. Russell Museum
The Lively Arts Calendar (10 points):
 Symphony Orchestra:
  Great Falls Symphony Orchestra, 10
Places Rated Score: 201
Places Rated Rank: 267

Greeley, CO
Public Libraries (169 points):
 10 branches, 432,954 volumes
 Books added per year: 23,585
The Lively Arts Calendar (40 points):
 Touring Artists Bookings (40)
Places Rated Score: 209
Places Rated Rank: 263

Green Bay, WI
Fine Arts Broadcasting (100 points):
 Non-Commercial TV: WPNE Channel 38
Public Libraries (86 points):
 10 branches, 378,727 volumes
 Books added per year: 16,661
Art Museum/Gallery (50 points):
 1 private
 Neville Public Museum
The Lively Arts Calendar (25 points):
 Touring Artists Bookings (18)
 Symphony Orchestra:
  Green Bay Symphony Orchestra, 7
Places Rated Score: 261
Places Rated Rank: 240

Greensboro–Winston-Salem–High Point, NC
Fine Arts Broadcasting (177 points):
 Concert Radio: WFDD-FM 88.5, 77 hours
 Non-Commercial TV: WUNL Channel 26
Public Libraries (87 points):
 41 branches, 1,710,118 volumes
 Books added per year: 80,778
Art Museums/Galleries (250 points):
 1 civic, 3 private, 1 university
 Museum of Early Southern Decorative
  Arts
 Southeastern Center for Contemporary
  Art
The Lively Arts Calendar (322 points):
 Touring Artists Bookings (168)
 Symphony Orchestras:
  Eastern Philharmonic Orchestra, 11
  Greensboro Symphony Orchestra, 45
  Greensboro Symphony Youth
   Orchestra, 3
  Philharmonia of Greensboro, 7

Opera Companies:
  Greensboro Opera Company, 2
  Piedmont Opera Theatre, 6
 Dance Company:
  North Carolina Dance Theatre, 80
Places Rated Score: 836
Places Rated Rank: 72

Greenville–Spartanburg, SC
Fine Arts Broadcasting (223 points):
 Concert Radio: WMUU-FM 94.5, 23 hours
 Non-Commercial TV: WNTV Channel 29
  WRET Channel 49
Public Libraries (92 points):
 22 branches, 949,131 volumes
 Books added per year: 57,825
Art Museums/Galleries (300 points):
 3 private, 3 university
The Lively Arts Calendar (106 points):
 Touring Artists Bookings (68)
 Symphony Orchestras:
  Carolina Youth Symphony, 6
  Greenville County Youth Orchestra, 10
  Greenville Symphony Orchestra, 12
  Spartanburg Symphony Orchestra, 10
Places Rated Score: 721
Places Rated Rank: 87

Hagerstown, MD
Fine Arts Broadcasting (100 points):
 Non-Commercial TV: WWPB Channel 31
Public Libraries (113 points):
 6 branches, 235,036 volumes
 Books added per year: 13,168
Art Museum/Gallery (50 points):
 1 civic
 Washington County Museum of Fine Arts
The Lively Arts Calendar (103 points):
 Touring Artists Bookings (90)
 Symphony Orchestra:
  Maryland Symphony Orchestra, 13
Places Rated Score: 366
Places Rated Rank: 190

Hamilton–Middletown, OH
Fine Arts Broadcasting (100 points):
 Non-Commercial TV: WPTO Channel 14
Public Libraries (154 points):
 8 branches, 430,696 volumes
 Books added per year: 41,914
Art Museum/Gallery (50 points):
 1 university
The Lively Arts Calendar (20 points):
 Touring Artists Bookings (10)
 Symphony Orchestras:
  Hamilton–Fairfield Symphony, 4
  Middletown Symphony Orchestra, 6
CMSA Access: Cincinnati–Hamilton,
 OH–KY–IN (116 points)
Places Rated Score: 440
Places Rated Rank: 163

Harrisburg–Lebanon–Carlisle, PA
Fine Arts Broadcasting (319 points):
 Concert Radio: WITF-FM 89.5, 90 hours
  WMSP-FM 94.9, 129 hours
 Non-Commercial TV: WITF Channel 33
Public Libraries (74 points):
 26 branches, 784,160 volumes
 Books added per year: 43,395
Art Museum/Gallery (50 points):
 1 private
The Lively Arts Calendar (157 points):
 Touring Artists Bookings (117)
 Symphony Orchestras:
  Harrisburg Symphony Orchestra, 25
  Harrisburg Youth Symphony
   Orchestra, 5
  Hershey Symphony Orchestra, 10
Places Rated Score: 600
Places Rated Rank: 116

Hartford, CT
Fine Arts Broadcasting (219 points):
   Concert Radio: WNPR-FM 89.1, 119 hours
   Non-Commercial TV: WEDH Channel 24
Public Libraries (167 points):
   61 branches, 2,867,978 volumes
   Books added per year: 125,736
Art Museums/Galleries (300 points):
   5 private, 1 university
The Lively Arts Calendar (354 points):
   Touring Artists Bookings (73)
   Symphony Orchestras:
      Hartford Symphony Orchestra, 40
      Hartt Symphony Orchestra, 8
   Opera Company:
      Connecticut Opera, 13
   Professional Theatre:
      Hartford Stage Company, 120
   Dance Company:
      Hartford Ballet, 100
CMSA Access: Hartford-New
   Britain-Middletown, CT (16 points)
Places Rated Score: 1,056
Places Rated Rank: 55

Hickory, NC
Public Libraries (93 points):
   9 branches, 323,646 volumes
   Books added per year: 21,146
Art Museum/Gallery (50 points):
   1 private
The Lively Arts Calendar (9 points):
   Touring Artists Bookings (3)
   Symphony Orchestra:
      Western Piedmont Symphony, 6
Places Rated Score: 152
Places Rated Rank: 288

Honolulu, HI
Fine Arts Broadcasting (247 points):
   Concert Radio: KHPR-FM 88.1, 126 hours
      KTUH-FM 90.3, 21 hours
   Non-Commercial TV: KHET Channel 11
Public Libraries (83 points):
   22 branches, 1,408,743 volumes
   Books added per year: 70,000
Art Museums/Galleries (200 points):
   3 private, 1 university
   Honolulu Academy of Arts
The Lively Arts Calendar (417 points):
   Touring Artists Bookings (78)
   Symphony Orchestra:
      Honolulu Symphony Society, 150
   Opera Company:
      Hawaii Opera Theatre, 9
   Professional Theatre:
      Honolulu Theatre for Youth, 140
   Dance Company:
      Hawaii State Ballet, 40
Places Rated Score: 947
Places Rated Rank: 62

Houma-Thibodaux, LA
Public Libraries (95 points):
   16 branches, 280,575 volumes
   Books added per year: 18,371
Places Rated Score: 95
Places Rated Rank: 319

Houston, TX
Fine Arts Broadcasting (407 points):
   Concert Radio: KRTS-FM 92.1, 168 hours
      KUHF-FM 88.7, 139 hours
   Non-Commercial TV: KUHT Channel 8
Public Libraries (90 points):
   73 branches, 4,677,552 volumes
   Books added per year: 293,590
Art Museums/Galleries (250 points):
   3 private, 2 university

Contemporary Arts Museum
Museum of Fine Arts
The Lively Arts Calendar (919 points):
   Touring Artists Bookings (287)
   Symphony Orchestras:
      Clear Lake Symphony, 7
      Houston Symphony Orchestra, 175
      Houston Youth Symphony and Ballet, 9
      Symphony North of Houston, 7
   Opera Company:
      Houston Grand Opera, 68
   Professional Theatre:
      Alley Theatre, 280
   Dance Company:
      Houston Ballet, 85
CMSA Access: Houston-Galveston-
   Brazoria, TX (2 points)
Places Rated Score: 1,668
Places Rated Rank: 31

Huntington-Ashland, WV-KY-OH
Fine Arts Broadcasting (256 points):
   Concert Radio: WOUL-FM 89.1, 44 hours
      WVWV-FM 89.9, 12 hours
   Non-Commercial TV: WKAS Channel 25
      WPBY Channel 33
Public Libraries (73 points):
   19 branches, 574,249 volumes
   Books added per year: 24,356
Art Museum/Gallery (50 points):
   1 private
   Huntington Museum of Art
The Lively Arts Calendar (52 points):
   Touring Artists Bookings (46)
   Symphony Orchestra:
      Huntington Chamber Orchestra, 6
Places Rated Score: 431
Places Rated Rank: 167

Huntsville, AL
Fine Arts Broadcasting (170 points):
   Concert Radio: WLRH-FM 89.3, 70 hours
   Non-Commercial TV: WHIQ Channel 25
Public Libraries (67 points):
   4 branches, 229,724 volumes
   Books added per year: 16,480
Art Museums/Galleries (100 points):
   1 private, 1 university
   Huntsville Museum of Art
The Lively Arts Calendar (348 points):
   Touring Artists Bookings (311)
   Symphony Orchestras:
      Huntsville Symphony Orchestra, 11
      Huntsville Youth Orchestra, 5
      Metropolitan Youth Orchestra of
         Huntsville, 5
   Dance Company:
      Huntsville Civic Ballet, 17
Places Rated Score: 685
Places Rated Rank: 95

Indianapolis, IN
Fine Arts Broadcasting (282 points):
   Concert Radio: WAJC-FM 104.5, 30 hours
      WIAN-FM 90.1, 48 hours
      WICR-FM 88.7, 104 hours
   Non-Commercial TV: WFYI Channel 20
Public Libraries (163 points):
   52 branches, 3,124,899 volumes
   Books added per year: 201,997
Art Museums/Galleries (200 points):
   4 private
   Indianapolis Museum of Art
The Lively Arts Calendar (535 points):
   Touring Artists Bookings (90)
   Symphony Orchestras:
      Butler University Symphony, 4
      Carmel Symphony Orchestra, 15

Indianapolis Chamber Orchestra, 6
Indianapolis Symphony Orchestra, 180
   Opera Companies:
      Indiana Opera Theatre, 14
      Indianapolis Opera, 6
   Professional Theatre:
      Indiana Repertory Theatre, 120
   Dance Company:
      Indianapolis Ballet Theatre, 100
Places Rated Score: 1,180
Places Rated Rank: 49

Iowa City, IA
Fine Arts Broadcasting (215 points):
   Concert Radio: KSUI-FM 91.7, 115 hours
   Non-Commercial TV: KIIN Channel 12
Public Libraries (94 points):
   5 branches, 247,578 volumes
   Books added per year: 8,232
Art Museum/Gallery (50 points):
   1 university
   University of Iowa Museum of Art
The Lively Arts Calendar (40 points):
   Touring Artists Bookings (40)
Places Rated Score: 399
Places Rated Rank: 176

Jackson, MI
Public Libraries (99 points):
   15 branches, 205,885 volumes
   Books added per year: 14,312
The Lively Arts Calendar (46 points):
   Touring Artists Bookings (36)
   Symphony Orchestra:
      Jackson Symphony Orchestra, 10
Places Rated Score: 145
Places Rated Rank: 295

Jackson, MS
Fine Arts Broadcasting (184 points):
   Concert Radio: WMAA-FM 91.3, 84 hours
   Non-Commercial TV: WMAA Channel 29
Public Libraries (74 points):
   26 branches, 728,647 volumes
   Books added per year: 30,065
Art Museums/Galleries (100 points):
   1 private, 1 university
The Lively Arts Calendar (326 points):
   Touring Artists Bookings (9)
   Symphony Orchestras:
      Jackson Symphony Orchestra, 45
      Jackson Symphony Youth Orchestra, 3
   Opera Company:
      Mississippi Opera, 4
   Professional Theatre:
      New Stage Theatre, 140
   Dance Company:
      Ballet Mississippi, 25
Places Rated Score: 684
Places Rated Rank: 96

Jackson, TN
Public Library (38 points):
   1 branch, 103,427 volumes
   Books added per year: 3,009
The Lively Arts Calendar (12 points):
   Touring Artists Bookings (5)
   Symphony Orchestra:
      Jackson Symphony Orchestra, 7
Places Rated Score: 50
Places Rated Rank: 333

Jacksonville, FL
Fine Arts Broadcasting (226 points):
   Concert Radio: WJCT-FM 89.9, 126 hours
   Non-Commercial TV: WJCT Channel 7
Public Libraries (65 points):
   23 branches, 1,829,472 volumes
   Books added per year: 58,763

Art Museums/Galleries (150 points):
  2 private, 1 university
  Cummer Gallery of Art
  Jacksonville Art Museum
The Lively Arts Calendar (276 points):
  Touring Artists Bookings (91)
  Symphony Orchestra:
    Jacksonville Symphony Orchestra, 115
  Dance Company:
    The Florida Ballet, 70
Places Rated Score: 717
Places Rated Rank: 88

Jacksonville, NC
Fine Arts Broadcasting (100 points):
  Non-Commercial TV: WUNM Channel 19
Public Libraries (47 points):
  4 branches, 71,791 volumes
  Books added per year: 6,165
Places Rated Score: 147
Places Rated Rank: 291

Janesville–Beloit, WI
Public Libraries (171 points):
  7 branches, 369,836 volumes
  Books added per year: 23,670
Art Museum/Gallery (50 points):
  1 university
The Lively Arts Calendar (31 points):
  Touring Artists Bookings (17)
  Symphony Orchestra:
    Beloit–Janesville Symphony
      Orchestra, 14
Places Rated Score: 252
Places Rated Rank: 244

★ **Jersey City, NJ**
Public Libraries (110 points):
  10 branches, 1,723,527 volumes
  Books added per year: 61,005
Art Museums/Galleries (100 points):
  1 civic, 1 private
The Lively Arts Calendar (49 points):
  Touring Artists Bookings (34)
  Symphony Orchestra:
    The Hoboken Chamber Orchestra, 15
CMSA Access: New York–Northern
  NJ–Long Island, NY–NJ–CT (1,673
  points)
Places Rated Score: 1,932
Places Rated Rank: 25

Johnson City–Kingsport–Bristol, TN–VA
Fine Arts Broadcasting (54 points):
  Concert Radio: WETS-FM 89.5, 54 hours
Public Libraries (45 points):
  13 branches, 506,783 volumes
  Books added per year: 20,061
Art Museums/Galleries (100 points):
  2 university
  The Carroll Reece Museum
The Lively Arts Calendar (468 points):
  Touring Artists Bookings (13)
  Symphony Orchestras:
    Johnson City Symphony, 5
    Kingsport Symphony Orchestra, 10
  Professional Theatre:
    Barter Theatre, 440
Places Rated Score: 667
Places Rated Rank: 98

Johnstown, PA
Public Libraries (58 points):
  19 branches, 477,819 volumes
  Books added per year: 14,656
Art Museum/Gallery (50 points):
  1 university

The Lively Arts Calendar (28 points):
  Touring Artists Bookings (14)
  Symphony Orchestras:
    Johnstown Symphony Orchestra, 12
    Johnstown Youth Symphony, 2
Places Rated Score: 136
Places Rated Rank: 301

Joliet, IL
Public Libraries (150 points):
  17 branches, 725,335 volumes
  Books added per year: 57,003
The Lively Arts Calendar (55 points):
  Touring Artists Bookings (55)
CMSA Access: Chicago–Gary–Lake
  County, IL–IN–WI (445)
Places Rated Score: 650
Places Rated Rank: 102

Joplin, MO
Fine Arts Broadcasting (262 points):
  Concert Radio: KXMS-FM 88.7, 162 hours
  Non-Commercial TV: KOZJ Channel 26
Public Libraries (75 points):
  5 branches, 239,944 volumes
  Books added per year: 10,265
Art Museums/Galleries (100 points):
  1 civic, 1 university
Places Rated Score: 437
Places Rated Rank: 165

Kalamazoo, MI
Fine Arts Broadcasting (177 points):
  Concert Radio: WMUK-FM 102.1, 77
    hours
  Non-Commercial TV: WGVK Channel 52
Public Libraries (115 points):
  12 branches, 635,997 volumes
  Books added per year: 25,332
Art Museums/Galleries (100 points):
  1 private, 1 university
  Kalamazoo Institute of Arts
The Lively Arts Calendar (35 points):
  Touring Artists Bookings (15)
  Symphony Orchestras:
    Kalamazoo Junior Symphony, 5
    Kalamazoo Symphony Orchestra, 15
Places Rated Score: 427
Places Rated Rank: 168

Kankakee, IL
Public Libraries (101 points):
  6 branches, 153,880 volumes
  Books added per year: 9,851
The Lively Arts Calendar (5 points):
  Touring Artists Bookings (5)
Places Rated Score: 106
Places Rated Rank: 312

Kansas City, MO–KS
Fine Arts Broadcasting (308 points):
  Concert Radio: KWJC-FM 91.9, 40 hours
    KXTR-FM 96.5, 168 hours
  Non-Commercial TV: KCPT Channel 19
Public Libraries (141 points):
  62 branches, 2,971,426 volumes
  Books added per year: 217,909
Art Museums/Galleries (100 points):
  2 private
  Nelson-Atkins Museum of Art
The Lively Arts Calendar (522 points):
  Touring Artists Bookings (79)
  Symphony Orchestras:
    Independence Symphony Orchestra, 5
    Kansas City Civic Orchestra, 5
    Kansas City Symphony, 85
    Liberty Symphony Orchestra, 8
    Youth Symphony of Kansas City, 6

Opera Company:
    Lyric Opera of Kansas City, 30
  Professional Theatres:
    Missouri Repertory Theatre, 140
    Unicorn Theatre, 140
  Dance Company:
    State Ballet of Missouri, 24
Places Rated Score: 1,071
Places Rated Rank: 54

Kenosha, WI
Fine Arts Broadcasting (36 points):
  Concert Radio: WGTD-FM 91.1, 36 hours
Public Libraries (105 points):
  6 branches, 203,775 volumes
  Books added per year: 12,632
Art Museum/Gallery (100 points):
  1 private
  Kenosha Public Museum
The Lively Arts Calendar (15 points):
  Touring Artists Bookings (11)
  Symphony Orchestra:
    Kenosha Symphony, 4
CMSA Access: Chicago–Gary–Lake
  County, IL–IN–WI (439 points)
Places Rated Score: 695
Places Rated Rank: 93

Killeen–Temple, TX
Fine Arts Broadcasting (135 points):
  Concert Radio: KNCT-FM 91.3, 35 hours
  Non-Commercial TV: KNCT Channel 46
Public Libraries (30 points):
  8 branches, 211,158 volumes
  Books added per year: 7,239
The Lively Arts Calendar (17 points):
  Touring Artists Bookings (17)
Places Rated Score: 182
Places Rated Rank: 275

Knoxville, TN
Fine Arts Broadcasting (117 points):
  Concert Radio: WUOT-FM 91.9, 17 hours
  Non-Commercial TV: WSJK Channel 2
Public Libraries (66 points):
  27 branches, 1,086,149 volumes
  Books added per year: 40,144
Art Museums/Galleries (100 points):
  1 civic, 1 private
The Lively Arts Calendar (253 points):
  Touring Artists Bookings (51)
  Symphony Orchestras:
    Knoxville Symphony Orchestra, 100
    Knoxville Symphony Youth Orchestra, 3
    Maryville–Alcoa College Community
      Orchestra, 5
    Oak Ridge Symphony Orchestra, 6
  Opera Company:
    Knoxville Opera, 8
  Professional Theatre:
    Clarence Brown Theatre Company, 80
Places Rated Score: 536
Places Rated Rank: 135

Kokomo, IN
Public Libraries (221 points):
  6 branches, 289,599 volumes
  Books added per year: 22,841
The Lively Arts Calendar (6 points):
  Symphony Orchestra:
    Kokomo Symphony Orchestra, 6
Places Rated Score: 227
Places Rated Rank: 255

La Crosse, WI
Fine Arts Broadcasting (100 points):
  Non-Commercial TV: WHLA Channel 31

Public Libraries (225 points):
8 branches, 274,301 volumes
Books added per year: 21,631
The Lively Arts Calendar (51 points):
Touring Artists Bookings (39)
Symphony Orchestras:
La Crosse Symphony Orchestra, 10
La Crosse Youth Symphony, 2
Places Rated Score: 376
Places Rated Rank: 185

Lafayette, LA
Fine Arts Broadcasting (170 points):
Concert Radio: KRVS-FM 88.7, 70 hours
Non-Commercial TV: KLPB Channel 24
Public Libraries (91 points):
9 branches, 281,433 volumes
Books added per year: 19,905
Art Museum/Gallery (50 points):
1 university
The Lively Arts Calendar (18 points):
Touring Artists Bookings (11)
Symphony Orchestra:
Acadiana Symphony Association, 7
Places Rated Score: 329
Places Rated Rank: 204

Lafayette–West Lafayette, IN
Fine Arts Broadcasting (45 points):
Concert Radio: WBAA-AM 920, 45 hours
Public Libraries (194 points):
2 branches, 211,473 volumes
Books added per year: 24,297
Art Museums/Galleries (100 points):
1 private, 1 university
Greater Lafayette Museum of Art
The Lively Arts Calendar (36 points):
Touring Artists Bookings (15)
Symphony Orchestras:
Lafayette Symphony, 16
Purdue University Symphony
Orchestra, 5
Places Rated Score: 375
Places Rated Rank: 188

Lake Charles, LA
Fine Arts Broadcasting (100 points):
Non-Commercial TV: KLTL Channel 18
Public Libraries (62 points):
13 branches, 243,325 volumes
Books added per year: 10,867
Art Museum/Gallery (50 points):
1 private
The Lively Arts Calendar (8 points):
Symphony Orchestra:
Lake Charles Symphony Orchestra, 8
Places Rated Score: 220
Places Rated Rank: 258

Lake County, IL
Fine Arts Broadcasting (136 points):
Concert Radio: WNIZ-FM 96.9, 136 hours
Public Libraries (204 points):
19 branches, 1,772,702 volumes
Books added per year: 102,415
The Lively Arts Calendar (33 points):
Touring Artists Bookings (6)
Symphony Orchestras:
Lake Forest Symphony, 13
Waukegan Symphony Orchestra, 8
Zion Chamber Orchestra, 6
CMSA Access: Chicago–Gary–Lake
County, IL–IN–WI (452 points)
Places Rated Score: 825
Places Rated Rank: 74

Lakeland–Winter Haven, FL
Public Libraries (29 points):
10 branches, 376,625 volumes
Books added per year: 11,401
Art Museum/Gallery (50 points):
1 private
Polk Museum of Art
The Lively Arts Calendar (29 points):
Touring Artists Bookings (22)
Symphony Orchestra:
Imperial Symphony Orchestra, 7
Places Rated Score: 108
Places Rated Rank: 310

Lancaster, PA
Public Libraries (53 points):
14 branches, 512,582 volumes
Books added per year: 21,793
Art Museum/Gallery (50 points):
1 private
The Lively Arts Calendar (148 points):
Touring Artists Bookings (28)
Professional Theatre:
Fulton Opera House, 120
Places Rated Score: 251
Places Rated Rank: 246

Lansing–East Lansing, MI
Fine Arts Broadcasting (100 points):
Non-Commercial TV: WKAR Channel 23
Public Libraries (134 points):
20 branches, 574,708 volumes
Books added per year: 57,565
Art Museums/Galleries (150 points):
2 private, 1 university
Kresge Art Museum, Michigan State
University
The Lively Arts Calendar (331 points):
Touring Artists Bookings (55)
Symphony Orchestra:
Greater Lansing Symphony
Orchestra, 16
Professional Theatre:
BoarsHead: Michigan Public
Theater, 260
Places Rated Score: 715
Places Rated Rank: 89

Laredo, TX
Public Library (41 points):
1 branch, 49,372 volumes
Books added per year: 5,246
Art Museum/Gallery (50 points):
1 university
The Lively Arts Calendar (16 points):
Touring Artists Bookings (4)
Symphony Orchestra:
Laredo Philharmonic Orchestra, 12
Places Rated Score: 107
Places Rated Rank: 311

Las Cruces, NM
Fine Arts Broadcasting (152 points):
Concert Radio: KRWG-FM 90.7, 52 hours
Non-Commercial TV: KRWG Channel 32
Public Libraries (97 points):
2 branches, 151,173 volumes
Books added per year: 12,851
Art Museum/Gallery (50 points):
1 university
The Lively Arts Calendar (24 points):
Touring Artists Bookings (12)
Symphony Orchestra:
Las Cruces Symphony Orchestra, 12
Places Rated Score: 323
Places Rated Rank: 207

Las Vegas, NV
Fine Arts Broadcasting (188 points):
Concert Radio: KNPR-FM 89.5, 88 hours
Non-Commercial TV: KLVX Channel 10
Public Libraries (92 points):
23 branches, 717,527 volumes
Books added per year: 57,956
Art Museums/Galleries (100 points):
1 private, 1 university
The Lively Arts Calendar (102 points):
Touring Artists Bookings (53)
Symphony Orchestras:
Las Vegas Civic Symphony, 5
Las Vegas Symphonic & Chamber
Music Society, 9
Dance Company:
Nevada Dance Theatre, 35
Places Rated Score: 482
Places Rated Rank: 144

Lawrence, KS
Fine Arts Broadcasting (51 points):
Concert Radio: KANU-FM 91.5, 51 hours
Public Libraries (140 points):
3 branches, 192,495 volumes
Books added per year: 10,473
Art Museum/Gallery (50 points):
1 university
University of Kansas, Spencer Gallery
The Lively Arts Calendar (30 points):
Touring Artists Bookings (22)
Symphony Orchestras:
Lawrence Chamber Players, 4
Lawrence Symphony Orchestra, 4
Places Rated Score: 271
Places Rated Rank: 236

Lawrence–Haverhill, MA–NH
Public Libraries (167 points):
29 branches, 1,354,360 volumes
Books added per year: 64,380
Art Museum/Gallery (50 points):
1 private
The Lively Arts Calendar (35 points):
Touring Artists Bookings (31)
Symphony Orchestra:
Tri-Town Symphony Orchestra, 4
CMSA Access: Boston–Lawrence–Salem,
MA–NH (359 points)
Places Rated Score: 611
Places Rated Rank: 113

Lawton, OK
Public Library (55 points):
1 branch, 109,664 volumes
Books added per year: 6,725
The Lively Arts Calendar (19 points):
Touring Artists Bookings (7)
Symphony Orchestra:
Lawton Philharmonic Orchestra, 12
Places Rated Score: 74
Places Rated Rank: 327

Lewiston–Auburn, ME
Fine Arts Broadcasting (100 points):
Non-Commercial TV: WCBB Channel 10
Public Libraries (131 points):
7 branches, 289,228 volumes
Books added per year: 11,197
Art Museum/Gallery (50 points):
1 university
The Lively Arts Calendar (25 points):
Touring Artists Bookings (25)
Places Rated Score: 306
Places Rated Rank: 219

Lexington-Fayette, KY
Fine Arts Broadcasting (143 points):
  Concert Radio: WBKY-FM 91.3, 43 hours
  Non-Commercial TV: WKLE Channel 46
Public Libraries (121 points):
  11 branches, 530,789 volumes
  Books added per year: 40,758
Art Museums/Galleries (200 points):
  2 private, 2 university
  University of Kentucky Art Museum
The Lively Arts Calendar (88 points):
  Touring Artists Bookings (53)
  Symphony Orchestras:
    Central Kentucky Youth Orchestras, 6
    Lexington Philharmonic Orchestra, 25
  Dance Company:
    Lexington Ballet, 4
Places Rated Score: 552
Places Rated Rank: 129

Lima, OH
Fine Arts Broadcasting (146 points):
  Concert Radio: WGLE-FM 90.7, 146 hours
Public Libraries (176 points):
  10 branches, 523,739 volumes
  Books added per year: 27,631
The Lively Arts Calendar (24 points):
  Touring Artists Bookings (9)
  Symphony Orchestra:
    Lima Symphony Orchestra, 15
Places Rated Score: 346
Places Rated Rank: 196

Lincoln, NE
Fine Arts Broadcasting (200 points):
  Concert Radio: KUCV-FM 90.9, 100 hours
  Non-Commercial TV: KUON Channel 12
Public Libraries (114 points):
  6 branches, 170,000 volumes
  Books added per year: 24,000
Art Museums/Galleries (150 points):
  3 university
  Sheldon Gallery, University of Nebraska
The Lively Arts Calendar (128 points):
  Touring Artists Bookings (78)
  Symphony Orchestras:
    Lincoln Civic Orchestra, 2
    Lincoln Symphony Orchestra, 15
    Lincoln Youth Symphony Orchestra, 3
    Nebraska Chamber Orchestra, 30
Places Rated Score: 592
Places Rated Rank: 119

Little Rock-North Little Rock, AR
Fine Arts Broadcasting (200 points):
  Concert Radio: KLRE-FM 90.5, 100 hours
  Non-Commercial TV: KETS Channel 2
Public Libraries (45 points):
  13 branches, 832,699 volumes
  Books added per year: 23,572
Art Museum/Gallery (50 points):
  1 civic
  Arkansas Arts Center
The Lively Arts Calendar (252 points):
  Touring Artists Bookings (8)
  Symphony Orchestra:
    Arkansas Symphony Orchestra, 50
  Opera Company:
    Arkansas Opera Theatre, 10
  Professional Theatre:
    Arkansas Repertory Theatre, 180
  Dance Company:
    Ballet Arkansas, 4
Places Rated Score: 547
Places Rated Rank: 131

Longview-Marshall, TX
Public Libraries (38 points):
  6 branches, 217,014 volumes
  Books added per year: 6,546
Art Museum/Gallery (50 points):
  1 private
The Lively Arts Calendar (13 points):
  Touring Artists Bookings (13)
Places Rated Score: 101
Places Rated Rank: 315

Lorain-Elyria, OH
Public Libraries (163 points):
  6 branches, 706,411 volumes
  Books added per year: 43,838
Art Museums/Galleries (100 points):
  1 private, 1 university
The Lively Arts Calendar (39 points):
  Touring Artists Bookings (24)
  Symphony Orchestras:
    Northern Ohio Youth Orchestras, 3
    Oberlin College Symphony & Chamber
      Orchestra, 12
CMSA Access: Cleveland-Akron-Lorain,
  OH (167 points)
Places Rated Score: 469
Places Rated Rank: 148

★ Los Angeles-Long Beach, CA
Fine Arts Broadcasting (547 points):
  Concert Radio: KFAC-FM 92.3, 168 hours
    KUSC-FM 91.5, 154 hours
    KXLU-FM 88.9, 25 hours
  Non-Commercial TV: KCET Channel 28
    KLCS Channel 58
Public Libraries (87 points):
  269 branches, 16,292,637 volumes
  Books added per year: 761,867
Art Museums/Galleries (1,650 points):
  2 civic, 24 private, 7 university
  California State University Art Museum
  J. Paul Getty Museum
  Long Beach Museum of Art
  Los Angeles County Museum of Art
  Skirball Museum, Hebrew Union College
  Southwest Museum
  Wright Art Gallery, University of California
The Lively Arts Calendar (2,593 points):
  Touring Artists Bookings (1,259)
  Symphony Orchestras:
    American Youth Symphony, 8
    Claremont Chamber Orchestra, 10
    Claremont Symphony Orchestra, 6
    CSUN Youth Orchestra, 8
    Foothill Friends of Music, 4
    Glendale Symphony Orchestra, 6
    Long Beach Symphony Orchestra, 22
    Los Angeles Chamber Orchestra, 70
    Los Angeles Philharmonic, 200
    Los Angeles Pops Orchestra, 21
    Los Angeles Solo Repertory
      Orchestra, 10
    Palisades Symphony Orchestra, 6
    Pasadena Symphony, 5
    Pasadena Young Musicians
      Orchestra, 4
    Peninsula Symphony, 10
    Pomona College Symphony
      Orchestra, 8
    Seaver College Community
      Symphony, 4
    The New American Orchestra, 4
    University of Southern California
      Symphony, 6
    Young Musicians Foundation Debut
      Orchestra, 7
  Opera Companies:
    Casa Italiana Opera Company, 8

Desert Opera Theatre, 16
    Long Beach Civic Light Opera, 16
    Long Beach Opera, 16
    Los Angeles Music Center Opera, 50
  Professional Theatres:
    Bilingual Foundation of the Arts, 180
    Mark Taper Forum, 240
    Odyssey Theatre Ensemble, 120
    The Back Alley Theatre, 80
  Dance Companies:
    Bethune Theaterdanse, 35
    Lewitzky Dance Company, 50
    Long Beach Ballet, 32
    The John Pasqualetti Dance
      Company, 72
CMSA Access: Los Angeles-Anaheim-
  Riverside, CA (238 points)
Places Rated Score: 5,115
Places Rated Rank: 2

Louisville, KY-IN
Fine Arts Broadcasting (477 points):
  Concert Radio: WFPK-FM 91.9, 130 hours
    WUOL-FM 90.5, 147 hours
  Non-Commercial TV: WKMJ Channel 68
    WKPC Channel 15
Public Libraries (87 points):
  31 branches, 1,429,723 volumes
  Books added per year: 84,496
Art Museums/Galleries (200 points):
  3 private, 1 university
  J. B. Speed Art Museum
The Lively Arts Calendar (792 points):
  Touring Artists Bookings (15)
  Symphony Orchestras:
    Louisville Youth Orchestra, 18
    The Louisville Orchestra, 70
    University of Louisville Symphony, 7
  Opera Company:
    Kentucky Opera, 22
  Professional Theatres:
    Actors Theatre of Louisville, 440
    Stage One: The Louisville Children's
      Theatre, 160
  Dance Company:
    Louisville Ballet, 60
Places Rated Score: 1,556
Places Rated Rank: 36

Lowell, MA-NH
Public Libraries (124 points):
  11 branches, 610,508 volumes
  Books added per year: 31,662
Art Museum/Gallery (50 points):
  1 private
The Lively Arts Calendar (135 points):
  Touring Artists Bookings (15)
  Professional Theatre:
    Merrimack Repertory Theatre, 120
CMSA Access: Boston-Lawrence-Salem,
  MA-NH (315 points)
Places Rated Score: 624
Places Rated Rank: 109

Lubbock, TX
Fine Arts Broadcasting (100 points):
  Non-Commercial TV: KTXT Channel 5
Public Libraries (54 points):
  4 branches, 340,418 volumes
  Books added per year: 12,395
The Lively Arts Calendar (232 points):
  Touring Artists Bookings (222)
  Symphony Orchestra:
    Lubbock Symphony Orchestra, 10
Places Rated Score: 386
Places Rated Rank: 181

Lynchburg, VA
Public Libraries (114 points):
  6 branches, 209,381 volumes
  Books added per year: 16,624
Art Museums/Galleries (100 points):
  1 private, 1 university
The Lively Arts Calendar (10 points):
  Touring Artists Bookings (6)
  Symphony Orchestra:
    Lynchburg Symphony Orchestra, 4
Places Rated Score: 224
Places Rated Rank: 256

Macon–Warner Robins, GA
Fine Arts Broadcasting (188 points):
  Concert Radio: WDCO-FM 89.7, 88 hours
  Non-Commercial TV: WDCO Channel 15
Public Libraries (144 points):
  10 branches, 469,916 volumes
  Books added per year: 41,588
Art Museum/Gallery (50 points):
  1 private
  Museum of Arts and Sciences
The Lively Arts Calendar (35 points):
  Touring Artists Bookings (22)
  Symphony Orchestra:
    Macon Symphony Orchestra, 13
Places Rated Score: 417
Places Rated Rank: 172

Madison, WI
Fine Arts Broadcasting (135 points):
  Concert Radio: WERN-FM 88.7, 35 hours
  Non-Commercial TV: WHA Channel 21
Public Libraries (218 points):
  24 branches, 987,509 volumes
  Books added per year: 77,428
Art Museums/Galleries (150 points):
  1 civic, 1 private, 1 university
  Elvehjem Art Center, University of
    Wisconsin
  Madison Art Center
The Lively Arts Calendar (154 points):
  Touring Artists Bookings (90)
  Symphony Orchestras:
    Madison Symphony Orchestra, 16
    University of Wisconsin Symphony, 8
    Wisconsin Chamber Orchestra, 30
    Wisconsin Youth Symphony
      Orchestra, 5
  Opera Company:
    Madison Opera, 5
Places Rated Score: 657
Places Rated Rank: 100

Manchester, NH
Public Libraries (138 points):
  7 branches, 537,988 volumes
  Books added per year: 21,474
Art Museums/Galleries (100 points):
  2 private
  Currier Gallery of Art
The Lively Arts Calendar (71 points):
  Touring Artists Bookings (59)
  Symphony Orchestra:
    New Hampshire Symphony
      Orchestra, 12
Places Rated Score: 309
Places Rated Rank: 217

Mansfield, OH
Public Libraries (172 points):
  6 branches, 317,113 volumes
  Books added per year: 22,029
Art Museum/Gallery (50 points):
  1 private

The Lively Arts Calendar (18 points):
  Symphony Orchestras:
    Mansfield Symphony Orchestra, 16
    Mansfield Symphony Youth
      Orchestra, 2
Places Rated Score: 240
Places Rated Rank: 251

McAllen–Edinburg–Mission, TX
Public Libraries (40 points):
  10 branches, 393,926 volumes
  Books added per year: 15,399
Art Museum/Gallery (50 points):
  1 private
  International Museum
The Lively Arts Calendar (8 points):
  Touring Artists Bookings (4)
  Symphony Orchestra:
    Valley Symphony Orchestra, 4
Places Rated Score: 98
Places Rated Rank: 317

Medford, OR
Fine Arts Broadcasting (165 points):
  Concert Radio: KSOR-FM 90.1, 65 hours
  Non-Commercial TV: KSYS Channel 8
Public Libraries (121 points):
  15 branches, 298,184 volumes
  Books added per year: 17,387
Art Museum/Gallery (50 points):
  1 private
The Lively Arts Calendar (463 points):
  Touring Artists Bookings (8)
  Symphony Orchestra:
    Rogue Valley Symphony, 15
  Professional Theatre:
    Oregon Shakespearean Festival, 440
Places Rated Score: 799
Places Rated Rank: 77

Melbourne–Titusville–Palm Bay, FL
Public Libraries (144 points):
  13 branches, 621,264 volumes
  Books added per year: 54,836
Art Museum/Gallery (50 points):
  1 private
The Lively Arts Calendar (90 points):
  Touring Artists Bookings (52)
  Symphony Orchestras:
    Brevard Symphony Orchestra, 18
    Brevard Symphony Youth Orchestra, 5
    Florida Space Coast Philharmonic, 15
Places Rated Score: 284
Places Rated Rank: 229

Memphis, TN–AR–MS
Fine Arts Broadcasting (185 points):
  Concert Radio: WKNO-FM 91.0, 85 hours
  Non-Commercial TV: WKNO Channel 10
Public Libraries (100 points):
  36 branches, 1,853,679 volumes
  Books added per year: 98,073
Art Museums/Galleries (200 points):
  1 civic, 1 private, 2 university
  Brooks Memorial Art Gallery
  Dixon Gallery
The Lively Arts Calendar (259 points):
  Touring Artists Bookings (12)
  Symphony Orchestras:
    Memphis Symphony Orchestra, 56
    Memphis Youth Symphony Orchestra, 3
  Opera Company:
    Opera Memphis, 8
  Professional Theatre:
    Playhouse on the Square, 180
Places Rated Score: 744
Places Rated Rank: 84

Merced, CA
Public Libraries (76 points):
  21 branches, 313,807 volumes
  Books added per year: 13,092
Art Museum/Gallery (50 points):
  1 civic
The Lively Arts Calendar (15 points):
  Touring Artists Bookings (10)
  Symphony Orchestra:
    Merced Symphony Orchestra, 5
Places Rated Score: 141
Places Rated Rank: 297

Miami–Hialeah, FL
Fine Arts Broadcasting (350 points):
  Concert Radio: WLRN-FM 91.3, 20 hours
    WTMI-FM 93.1, 130 hours
  Non-Commercial TV: WLRN Channel 17
    WPBT Channel 2
Public Libraries (85 points):
  35 branches, 2,698,205 volumes
  Books added per year: 156,902
Art Museums/Galleries (350 points):
  1 civic, 4 private, 2 university
  Lowe Art Museum, University of Miami
The Lively Arts Calendar (528 points):
  Touring Artists Bookings (212)
  Symphony Orchestras:
    Greater Miami Youth Symphony, 6
    Miami Chamber Symphony, 6
    New World Symphony, 8
    South Florida Youth Symphony, 8
  Opera Company:
    Greater Miami Opera Association, 28
  Professional Theatre:
    Coconut Grove Playhouse, 140
  Dance Companies:
    Ballet Concerto Company of Miami, 10
    Linda Diamond & Company, 25
    Miami City Ballet, 85
CMSA Access: Miami–Fort Lauderdale, FL
  (44 points)
Places Rated Score: 1,357
Places Rated Rank: 44

★ Middlesex–Somerset–Hunterdon, NJ
Fine Arts Broadcasting (100 points):
  Non-Commercial TV: WNJB Channel 58
Public Libraries (157 points):
  42 branches, 2,969,042 volumes
  Books added per year: 157,591
Art Museums/Galleries (100 points):
  2 private
The Lively Arts Calendar (362 points):
  Touring Artists Bookings (161)
  Symphony Orchestra:
    Philharmonic Orchestra of New
      Jersey, 5
  Professional Theatres:
    Crossroads Theatre Company, 120
    George Street Playhouse, 100
  Dance Company:
    Princeton Ballet, 75
CMSA Access: New York–Northern
  NJ–Long Island, NY–NJ–CT (1,644
  points)
Places Rated Score: 2,363
Places Rated Rank: 15

Middletown, CT
Public Libraries (239 points):
  8 branches, 355,943 volumes
  Books added per year: 20,888
Art Museums/Galleries (100 points):
  1 private, 1 university
The Lively Arts Calendar (5 points):
  Touring Artists Bookings (5)

CMSA Access: Hartford–New Britain–
Middletown, CT (92 points)
Places Rated Score: 436
Places Rated Rank: 166

Midland, TX
Public Libraries (72 points):
2 branches, 168,403 volumes
Books added per year: 8,547
Art Museum/Gallery (50 points):
1 private
The Lively Arts Calendar (35 points):
Symphony Orchestra:
Midland–Odessa Symphony &
Chorale, 35
Places Rated Score: 157
Places Rated Rank: 286

★ Milwaukee, WI
Fine Arts Broadcasting (438 points):
Concert Radio: WFMR-FM 98.3, 168
hours
WUMW-FM 89.7, 70 hours
Non-Commercial TV: WMVS Channel 10
WMVT Channel 36
Public Libraries (171 points):
55 branches, 4,249,056 volumes
Books added per year: 236,680
Art Museums/Galleries (400 points):
5 private, 3 university
Milwaukee Art Museum
Milwaukee Public Museum
The Lively Arts Calendar (935 points):
Touring Artists Bookings (343)
Symphony Orchestras:
Milwaukee Symphony
Orchestra, 200
Milwaukee Youth Symphony
Orchestra, 6
Waukesha Symphony Orchestra, 5
Opera Companies:
Florentine Opera Company, 9
Skylight Comic Opera, 97
Professional Theatres:
Milwaukee Repertory Theater, 180
The Great American Children's Theatre
Company, 40
Dance Company:
Pennsylvania & Milwaukee Ballet, 55
CMSA Access: Milwaukee–Racine, WI (6
points)
Places Rated Score: 1,950
Places Rated Rank: 23

★ Minneapolis–St. Paul, MN–WI
Fine Arts Broadcasting (370 points):
Concert Radio: KSJN-FM 91.1, 140 hours
KUON-AM 770, 30 hours
Non-Commercial TV: KTCA Channel 2
KTCI Channel 17
Public Libraries (139 points):
114 branches, 5,558,315 volumes
Books added per year: 330,495
Art Museums/Galleries (500 points):
1 civic, 4 private, 5 university
Minneapolis Institute of Arts
Minnesota Museum of Art
Walker Art Center
The Lively Arts Calendar (2,101 points):
Touring Artists Bookings (416)
Symphony Orchestras:
Bloomington Symphony
Orchestra, 8
Civic Orchestra of Minneapolis, 12
Greater Twin Cities Youth
Symphonies, 60

Lakewood Orchestra, 10
Minnesota Youth Symphony, 10
Minnetonka Symphony Orchestra, 9
Saint Paul Chamber Orchestra, 160
The Minnesota Orchestra, 215
Opera Company:
Minnesota Opera Company, 16
Professional Theatres:
Actors Theatre of St. Paul, 300
Illusion Theater, 100
Mixed Blood Theatre Company, 80
The Children's Theatre
Company, 160
The Guthrie Theater, 180
The Playwrights' Center, 240
Theatre de la Jeune Lune, 100
Dance Company:
NorthWest Ballet, 25
Places Rated Score: 3,110
Places Rated Rank: 8

Mobile, AL
Fine Arts Broadcasting (114 points):
Concert Radio: WHIL-FM 91.3, 14 hours
Non-Commercial TV: WEIQ Channel 42
Public Libraries (66 points):
18 branches, 618,974 volumes
Books added per year: 31,774
Art Museums/Galleries (100 points):
2 private
The Lively Arts Calendar (20 points):
Touring Artists Bookings (10)
Opera Company:
Mobile Opera, 10
Places Rated Score: 300
Places Rated Rank: 222

Modesto, CA
Fine Arts Broadcasting (168 points):
Concert Radio: KHYV-AM 970, 168 hours
Public Libraries (70 points):
14 branches, 545,491 volumes
Books added per year: 22,827
The Lively Arts Calendar (42 points):
Symphony Orchestras:
Modesto Symphony Orchestra, 18
Modesto Symphony Youth Orchestra, 4
Dance Company:
Modesto Civic Ballet, 20
Places Rated Score: 280
Places Rated Rank: 233

★ Monmouth–Ocean, NJ
Public Libraries (122 points):
29 branches, 2,520,423 volumes
Books added per year: 121,163
Art Museum/Gallery (50 points):
1 private
Monmouth Museum and Cultural Center
The Lively Arts Calendar (106 points):
Touring Artists Bookings (88)
Symphony Orchestras:
Garden State Philharmonic
Orchestra, 7
Garden State Philharmonic Symphony
Society, 7
Monmouth Symphony Orchestra, 4
CMSA Access: New York–Northern
NJ –Long Island, NY–NJ–CT (1,522
points)
Places Rated Score: 1,800
Places Rated Rank: 30

Monroe, LA
Fine Arts Broadcasting (100 points):
Non-Commercial TV: KLTM Channel 13

Public Libraries (52 points):
5 branches, 243,988 volumes
Books added per year: 7,840
Art Museum/Gallery (50 points):
1 civic
The Lively Arts Calendar (10 points):
Touring Artists Bookings (10)
Places Rated Score: 212
Places Rated Rank: 261

Montgomery, AL
Fine Arts Broadcasting (100 points):
Non-Commercial TV: WAIQ Channel 26
Public Libraries (57 points):
16 branches, 334,029 volumes
Books added per year: 17,594
Art Museum/Gallery (50 points):
1 private
Montgomery Museum of Fine Arts
The Lively Arts Calendar (255 points):
Touring Artists Bookings (5)
Symphony Orchestra:
Montgomery Symphony, 10
Professional Theatre:
Alabama Shakespeare Festival, 220
Dance Company:
Montgomery Ballet, 20
Places Rated Score: 462
Places Rated Rank: 153

Muncie, IN
Fine Arts Broadcasting (213 points):
Concert Radio: WBST-FM 92.1, 113 hours
Non-Commercial TV: WIPB Channel 49
Public Libraries (99 points):
6 branches, 296,902 volumes
Books added per year: 12,012
Art Museum/Gallery (50 points):
1 university
Ball State University Art Gallery
The Lively Arts Calendar (19 points):
Touring Artists Bookings (7)
Symphony Orchestras:
East Central Indiana Youth Orchestra, 4
Muncie Symphony Orchestra, 8
Places Rated Score: 381
Places Rated Rank: 183

Muskegon, MI
Fine Arts Broadcasting (87 points):
Concert Radio: WBLV-FM 90.3, 87 hours
Public Libraries (61 points):
12 branches, 186,891 volumes
Books added per year: 9,719
Art Museum/Gallery (50 points):
1 private
Muskegon Museum of Art
The Lively Arts Calendar (51 points):
Touring Artists Bookings (25)
Symphony Orchestras:
West Shore Symphony
Orchestra, 20
West Shore Youth Symphony
Orchestra, 6
Places Rated Score: 249
Places Rated Rank: 248

Naples, FL
Public Libraries (79 points):
6 branches, 147,748 volumes
Books added per year: 10,900
The Lively Arts Calendar (9 points):
Touring Artists Bookings (9)
Places Rated Score: 88
Places Rated Rank: 323

Nashua, NH
Public Libraries (169 points):
  11 branches, 429,795 volumes
  Books added per year: 29,848
The Lively Arts Calendar (126 points):
  Touring Artists Bookings (16)
  Symphony Orchestra:
    Nashua Symphony Orchestra, 10
  Professional Theatre:
    American Stage Festival, 100
CMSA Access: Boston–Lawrence–Salem,
  MA–NH (321 points)
Places Rated Score: 616
Places Rated Rank: 110

Nashville, TN
Fine Arts Broadcasting (185 points):
  Concert Radio: WPLN-FM 90.3, 85 hours
  Non-Commercial TV: WDCN Channel 8
Public Libraries (51 points):
  30 branches, 1,125,405 volumes
  Books added per year: 49,579
Art Museums/Galleries (250 points):
  3 private, 2 university
The Lively Arts Calendar (121 points):
  Touring Artists Bookings (95)
  Symphony Orchestra:
    Nashville Youth Symphony, 6
  Opera Company:
    Nashville Opera Association, 8
  Dance Company:
    Nashville Ballet, 12
Places Rated Score: 607
Places Rated Rank: 115

★ Nassau–Suffolk, NY
Fine Arts Broadcasting (123 points):
  Concert Radio: WUSB-FM 90.1, 23 hours
  Non-Commercial TV: WLIW Channel 21
Public Libraries (278 points):
  121 branches, 10,996,671 volumes
  Books added per year: 753,031
Art Museums/Galleries (500 points):
  9 private, 1 university
  Parrish Art Museum, Southampton
The Lively Arts Calendar (601 points):
  Touring Artists Bookings (368)
  Symphony Orchestras:
    Camerata Youth Orchestra, 8
    Long Island Philharmonic, 32
    Long Island Youth Orchestra, 5
    Nassau Symphony, 6
    New York Virtuosi Chamber
      Symphony, 6
    Queens Festival Orchestra, 3
    Sound Symphony, 4
  Opera Company:
    National Grand Opera, 10
  Professional Theatre:
    Long Island Stage, 120
  Dance Companies:
    Eglevsky Ballet, 29
    New York Dance Theatre, 10
CMSA Access: New York–Northern
  NJ–Long Island, NY–NJ–CT (1,479
  points)
Places Rated Score: 2,981
Places Rated Rank: 9

New Bedford, MA
Public Libraries (115 points):
  12 branches, 750,568 volumes
  Books added per year: 20,196
Art Museum/Gallery (50 points):
  1 private

The Lively Arts Calendar (47 points):
  Touring Artists Bookings (40)
  Symphony Orchestra:
    New Bedford Symphony
      Orchestra, 7
Places Rated Score: 212
Places Rated Rank: 261

New Britain, CT
Public Libraries (54 points):
  7 branches, 446,239 volumes
  Books added per year: 7,945
Art Museum/Gallery (50 points):
  1 private
  New Britain Museum of American Art
The Lively Arts Calendar (4 points):
  Symphony Orchestra:
    New Britain Symphony Orchestra, 4
CMSA Access: Hartford–New Britain–
  Middletown, CT (98 points)
Places Rated Score: 206
Places Rated Rank: 265

New Haven–Meriden, CT
Fine Arts Broadcasting (200 points):
  Non-Commercial TV: WEDH Channel 12
    WEDY Channel 65
Public Libraries (137 points):
  32 branches, 1,786,490 volumes
  Books added per year: 71,666
Art Museums/Galleries (250 points):
  2 private, 3 university
  Yale University Art Museum
The Lively Arts Calendar (648 points):
  Touring Artists Bookings (213)
  Symphony Orchestras:
    Hamden Symphony Orchestra, 3
    New Haven Symphony
      Orchestra, 20
    Orchestra of New England, 50
    Philharmonia Orchestra of Yale, 10
    Shoreline Youth Symphony
      Orchestra, 4
    Wallingford Symphony Orchestra, 8
  Professional Theatres:
    Long Wharf Theatre, 140
    Yale Repertory Theatre, 200
Places Rated Score: 1,235
Places Rated Rank: 45

New London–Norwich, CT–RI
Fine Arts Broadcasting (100 points):
  Non-Commercial TV: WEDN Channel 53
Public Libraries (164 points):
  25 branches, 778,571 volumes
  Books added per year: 43,055
Art Museums/Galleries (200 points):
  4 private
  Lyman Allyn Museum
The Lively Arts Calendar (24 points):
  Touring Artists Bookings (19)
  Symphony Orchestra:
    Eastern Connecticut Symphony, 5
Places Rated Score: 488
Places Rated Rank: 143

New Orleans, LA
Fine Arts Broadcasting (318 points):
  Concert Radio: WWNO-FM 89.9, 118
    hours
  Non-Commercial TV: WLAE Channel 32
    WYES Channel 12
Public Libraries (68 points):
  45 branches, 1,993,887 volumes
  Books added per year: 93,398
Art Museums/Galleries (150 points):
  1 private, 2 university
  New Orleans Museum of Art

The Lively Arts Calendar (222 points):
  Touring Artists Bookings (45)
  Symphony Orchestras:
    New Orleans Symphony
      Orchestra, 150
    New Orleans Symphony Youth
      Orchestra, 3
  Opera Company:
    New Orleans Opera Association, 8
  Dance Company:
    Cincinnati/New Orleans Ballet, 16
Places Rated Score: 758
Places Rated Rank: 82

★ New York, NY
Fine Arts Broadcasting (700 points):
  Concert Radio: WFUV-FM 90.7, 35 hours
    WNCN-FM 104.3, 166 hours
    WNYC-FM 93.9, 131 hours
    WQXR-FM 96.3, 168 hours
  Non-Commercial TV: WNET Channel 13
    WNYE Channel 25
Public Libraries (203 points):
  277 branches, 25,857,634 volumes
  Books added per year: 1,734,370
Art Museums/Galleries (2,450 points):
  3 civic, 42 private, 4 university
  American Craft Museum
  Brooklyn Museum
  Frick Collection
  International Center for Photography
  Metropolitan Museum of Art
  Museum of Modern Art
  National Academy of Design Museum
  Pierpont Morgan Library and Art
    Museum
  Solomon R. Guggenheim Museum
  Whitney Museum of American Art
The Lively Arts Calendar (11,641 points):
  Touring Artists Bookings (2,257)
  Symphony Orchestras:
    American Composers Orchestra, 6
    American Symphony Orchestra, 30
    Bronx Arts Ensemble
      Orchestra, 100
    Bronx Symphony Orchestra, 6
    Brooklyn Neighborhood Chamber
      Orchestra, 8
    Brooklyn Philharmonic Symphony
      Orchestra, 70
    Chappaqua Orchestra, 4
    Columbia University Orchestra, 3
    Greater Westchester Youth
      Orchestras, 6
    Heritage Orchestra, 5
    Independent School Orchestra, 5
    Little Orchestra Society of New
      York, 30
    National Orchestra of New York, 8
    New Orchestra of Westchester, 25
    New York Chamber Players, 5
    New York City Symphony, 5
    New York Philharmonic, 190
    New York Youth Symphony, 6
    Orpheus Chamber Orchestra, 70
    Philharmonic Symphony of
      Westchester, 5
    Queens Symphony Orchestra, 30
    Staten Island Symphony, 7
    The Julliard Orchestra, 12
    West End Symphony, 24
    Westchester Conservatory Symphony
      Orchestra, 4
    Westchester Symphony
      Orchestra, 4
  Opera Companies:
    Amato Opera Theatre, 60

Bronx Opera Company, 8
Il Piccolo Teatro dell'Opera, 12
Light Opera of Manhattan, 364
Metropolitan Opera, 222
Music Theatre Group, 40
New York City Opera, 134
New York Gilbert & Sullivan
  Players, 75
New York Grand Opera, 5
Opera Ebony, 10
Opera Ensemble of New York, 5
Opera Northeast, 60
Operaworks, LTD, 48
Village Light Opera Group, 12
Professional Theatres:
  AMAS Repertory Theatre, 120
  American Jewish Theatre, 80
  Circle in the Square Theatre, 60
  Circle Repertory Company, 120
  Creative Arts Team, 40
  CSC Repertory Ltd.—The Classic
    Stage Company, 60
  Hudson Guild Theatre, 100
  INTAR Hispanic American Arts
    Center, 60
  Jean Cocteau Repertory, 100
  Lincoln Center Theater, 220
  Mabou Mines, 80
  Manhattan Punch Line Theatre, 240
  Manhattan Theatre Club, 140
  Music-Theatre Group, 60
  Musical Theatre Works, 80
  New Dramatists, 300
  New Federal Theatre, 100
  New York Shakespeare Festival, 240
  New York Theatre Workshop, 140
  O'Neill Theater Center, 740
  Pan Asian Repertory Theatre, 80
  Playwrights Horizons, 160
  Puerto Rican Traveling Theatre, 140
  Repertorio Espanol, 220
  The Acting Company, 60
  The American Place Theatre, 140
  The Ensemble Studio Theatre, 320
  The Second Stage, 80
  The Wooster Group, 100
  Theater for the New City, 340
  Theatre for a New Audience, 100
  Theatreworks/USA, 140
  Vineyard Theatre, 60
  WPA Theatre, 80
Dance Companies:
  Alvin Ailey American Dance
    Theatre, 175
  Alvin Ailey Repertory Ensemble, 150
  American Ballet Theatre, 200
  American Dancemachine, 100
  Ballet Hispanico of New York, 114
  Bill T. Jones/Arnie Zane &
    Company, 80
  Cohan/Suzeau Duet Company, 100
  Dance Theatre of Harlem, 200
  David Gordon Pickup Company, 30
  David Parsons Company, 60
  Dennis Wayne's Dancers, 50
  Desrosiers Dance Theatre, 100
  Gotta Dance, 50
  Joffrey Ballet, 150
  Joffrey II Dancers, 45
  Jose Greco Company, 100
  Laura Dean Dancers, 40
  Les Ballets Trockadero de Monte
    Carlo, 75
  Limon Dance Company, 63
  Martha Graham Dance Company, 100
  Merce Cunningham Dance
    Company, 75

New York Ballet, 215
Paul Tayler Dance Company, 89
Phyllis Lamhut Dance Company, 100
Rambert Dance Company, 125
Trisha Brown Company, 50
Universal Ballet Company, 25
CMSA Access: New York–Northern
NJ–Long Island, NY–NJ–CT (493
points)
Places Rated Score: 15,487
Places Rated Rank: 1

★ Newark, NJ
Fine Arts Broadcasting (100 points):
  Non-Commercial TV: WNJM Channel 50
Public Libraries (172 points):
  73 branches, 7,871,028 volumes
  Books added per year: 328,944
Art Museums/Galleries (200 points):
  4 private
  Montclair Art Museum
The Lively Arts Calendar (922 points):
  Touring Artists Bookings (163)
  Symphony Orchestras:
    Cathedral Symphony Orchestra, 15
    Colonial Symphony, 4
    Livingston Symphony Orchestra, 4
    Masterwork Orchestra, 12
    New Jersey Symphony
      Orchestra, 105
    New Jersey Youth Symphony, 4
    New Philharmonic of New Jersey, 9
    Plainfield Symphony Orchestra, 7
    Westfield Symphony Orchestra, 5
  Opera Companies:
    New Jersey State Opera, 10
    Opera of Florham, 9
  Professional Theatres:
    New Jersey Shakespeare Festival, 160
    Paper Mill Playhouse, 120
    Whole Theatre, 100
  Dance Companies:
    Garden State Ballet, 60
    New Jersey Ballet Company, 135
CMSA Access: New York–Northern
NJ–Long Island, NY–NJ–CT (1,578
points):
Places Rated Score: 2,972
Places Rated Rank: 10

Niagara Falls, NY
Public Libraries (122 points):
  11 branches, 558,259 volumes
  Books added per year: 26,536
Art Museums/Galleries (100 points):
  1 private, 1 university
The Lively Arts Calendar (10 points):
  Touring Artists Bookings (4)
  Opera Company:
    Artpark, 6
CMSA Access: Buffalo–Niagara Falls, NY
(86 points)
Places Rated Score: 318
Places Rated Rank: 212

Norfolk–Virginia Beach–Newport News, VA
Fine Arts Broadcasting (195 points):
  Concert Radio: WHRO-FM 89.5, 95 hours
  Non-Commercial TV: WHRO Channel 15
Public Libraries (164 points):
  43 branches, 2,357,299 volumes
  Books added per year: 224,249
Art Museums/Galleries (450 points):
  2 civic, 5 private, 2 university
  Chrysler Museum

The Lively Arts Calendar (408 points):
  Touring Artists Bookings (113)
  Symphony Orchestras:
    Old Dominion University
      Symphony, 3
    Peninsula Youth Orchestra, 2
    The Virginia Symphony, 103
    Virginia Beach Community
      Orchestra, 12
    Virginia Beach Pops, 46
    Williamsburg Symphonia, 14
  Opera Companies:
    Light Opera of Virginia, 10
    Virginia Opera, 20
  Professional Theatre:
    Virginia Stage Company, 80
  Dance Company:
    The Tidewater Ballet Association, 5
Places Rated Score: 1,217
Places Rated Rank: 48

★ Norwalk, CT
Public Libraries (246 points):
  7 branches, 500,794 volumes
  Books added per year: 32,283
The Lively Arts Calendar (106 points):
  Touring Artists Bookings (93)
  Symphony Orchestras:
    Norwalk Symphony Orchestra, 10
    Norwalk Youth Symphony, 3
CMSA Access: New York–Northern
NJ–Long Island, NY–NJ–CT (1,586
points)
Places Rated Score: 1,938
Places Rated Rank: 24

★ Oakland, CA
Fine Arts Broadcasting (45 points):
  Concert Radio: KSMC-FM 89.5, 45 hours
Public Libraries (112 points):
  70 branches, 4,162,616 volumes
  Books added per year: 226,901
Art Museums/Galleries (550 points):
  1 civic, 6 private, 4 university
  Oakland Museum
  University of California Art Museum
The Lively Arts Calendar (859 points):
  Touring Artists Bookings (344)
  Symphony Orchestras:
    Berkeley Youth Orchestra, 3
    Diablo Valley Philharmonic, 12
    Diablo Youth Symphony Orchestra, 4
    Livermore–Amador Symphony, 4
    Oakland Youth Orchestra, 3
    Philharmonic Society of
      Fremont-Newark, 5
    Young People's Symphony
      Orchestra, 5
  Opera Companies:
    Berkeley Opera, 18
    Oakland Opera, 11
  Professional Theatres:
    Berkeley Repertory Theatre, 160
    Berkeley Shakespeare Festival, 140
    Oakland Ensemble Theatre, 80
  Dance Companies:
    Berkeley Ballet Theatre, 20
    Oakland Ballet, 50
CMSA Access: San Francisco–Oakland–
San Jose, CA (503 points)
Places Rated Score: 2,069
Places Rated Rank: 20

Ocala, FL
Public Libraries (146 points):
  7 branches, 170,000 volumes
  Books added per year: 28,105

Art Museum/Gallery (50 points):
  1 private
The Lively Arts Calendar (4 points):
  Symphony Orchestra:
    Central Florida Community College
      Aeolian Players, 4
Places Rated Score: 200
Places Rated Rank: 268

Odessa, TX
Fine Arts Broadcasting (100 points):
  Non-Commercial TV: KOCV Channel 36
Public Library (32 points):
  1 branch, 148,082 volumes
  Books added per year: 4,333
Art Museum/Gallery (50 points):
  1 private
The Lively Arts Calendar (11 points):
  Touring Artists Bookings (11)
Places Rated Score: 193
Places Rated Rank: 273

Oklahoma City, OK
Fine Arts Broadcasting (299 points):
  Concert Radio: KCSC-FM 90.1, 154 hours
    KGOU-FM 106.3, 45 hours
  Non-Commercial TV: KETA Channel 13
Public Libraries (156 points):
  27 branches, 993,624 volumes
  Books added per year: 156,453
Art Museums/Galleries (250 points):
  4 private, 1 university
  Museum of Art, University of Oklahoma
  Oklahoma Art Center
The Lively Arts Calendar (128 points):
  Touring Artists Bookings (15)
  Symphony Orchestras:
    Chamber Orchestra of Oklahoma
      City, 8
    Oklahoma City Junior Symphony, 4
    Oklahoma Youth Orchestra, 6
  Opera Company:
    Lyric Theatre of Oklahoma, 55
  Dance Companies:
    Ballet Oklahoma, 15
    Oklahoma Festival Ballet, 25
Places Rated Score: 833
Places Rated Rank: 73

Olympia, WA
Public Libraries (123 points):
  5 branches, 309,934 volumes
  Books added per year: 19,414
Art Museums/Galleries (100 points):
  2 private
The Lively Arts Calendar (27 points):
  Touring Artists Bookings (16)
  Symphony Orchestras:
    Capital Area Youth Symphony, 6
    Olympia Symphony Orchestra, 5
Places Rated Score: 250
Places Rated Rank: 247

Omaha, NE–IA
Fine Arts Broadcasting (432 points):
  Concert Radio: KIOS-FM 91.5, 57 hours
    KIWR-FM 89.7, 91 hours
    KVNO-FM 90.7, 84 hours
  Non-Commercial TV: KBIN Channel 32
    KYNE Channel 26
Public Libraries (70 points):
  27 branches, 947,293 volumes
  Books added per year: 43,549
Art Museum/Gallery (50 points):
  1 private
  Joslyn Art Museum

The Lively Arts Calendar (391 points):
  Touring Artists Bookings (65)
  Symphony Orchestras:
    Omaha Area Youth Orchestra, 20
    Omaha Symphony Orchestra, 40
  Opera Company:
    Opera/Omaha, 36
  Professional Theatres:
    Emmy Gifford Children's Theater, 120
    Nebraska Theatre Caravan, 80
  Dance Company:
    Omaha Ballet, 30
Places Rated Score: 943
Places Rated Rank: 64

★ Orange County, NY
Public Libraries (114 points):
  18 branches, 514,996 volumes
  Books added per year: 33,561
Art Museums/Galleries (100 points):
  2 private
The Lively Arts Calendar (61 points):
  Touring Artists Bookings (61)
CMSA Access: New York–Northern
  NJ–Long Island, NY–NJ–CT (1,564
  points)
Places Rated Score: 1,839
Places Rated Rank: 27

Orlando, FL
Fine Arts Broadcasting (298 points):
  Concert Radio: WMFE-FM 90.7, 124 hours
    WPRK-FM 91.5, 74 hours
  Non-Commercial TV: WMFE Channel 24
Public Libraries (148 points):
  16 branches, 1,657,594 volumes
  Books added per year: 150,117
Art Museums/Galleries (250 points):
  4 private, 1 university
  Loch Haven Museum of Art
The Lively Arts Calendar (241 points):
  Touring Artists Bookings (18)
  Symphony Orchestras:
    Florida Symphony Orchestra, 140
    Florida Symphony Youth Orchestra, 7
    University of Central Florida
      Community Symphony, 6
  Opera Company:
    Orlando Opera Company, 10
  Dance Company:
    Southern Ballet Theatre, 60
Places Rated Score: 937
Places Rated Rank: 65

Owensboro, KY
Fine Arts Broadcasting (158 points):
  Concert Radio: WKWC-FM 90.3, 58 hours
  Non-Commercial TV: WKOH Channel 31
Public Libraries (70 points):
  2 branches, 115,425 volumes
  Books added per year: 6,146
Art Museum/Gallery (50 points):
  1 private
The Lively Arts Calendar (23 points):
  Touring Artists Bookings (5)
  Symphony Orchestras:
    Owensboro Symphony Orchestra, 15
    Owensboro Youth Symphony, 3
Places Rated Score: 301
Places Rated Rank: 221

Oxnard–Ventura, CA
Public Libraries (110 points):
  21 branches, 1,031,371 volumes
  Books added per year: 72,507
Art Museums/Galleries (100 points):
  1 civic, 1 private

The Lively Arts Calendar (35 points):
  Touring Artists Bookings (18)
  Symphony Orchestras:
    Conejo Symphony Orchestra, 11
    Ventura County Symphony
      Orchestra, 6
CMSA Access: Los Angeles–Anaheim–
  Riverside, CA (479 points)
Places Rated Score: 724
Places Rated Rank: 86

Panama City, FL
Fine Arts Broadcasting (90 points):
  Concert Radio: WKGC-FM 90.7, 90 hours
Public Libraries (46 points):
  6 branches, 164,858 volumes
  Books added per year: 5,982
The Lively Arts Calendar (10 points):
  Touring Artists Bookings (10)
Places Rated Score: 146
Places Rated Rank: 293

Parkersburg–Marietta, WV–OH
Fine Arts Broadcasting (77 points):
  Concert Radio: WMRT-FM 88.3, 65 hours
    WVPG-FM 90.3, 12 hours
Public Libraries (105 points):
  7 branches, 254,488 volumes
  Books added per year: 16,476
Art Museum/Gallery (50 points):
  1 private
The Lively Arts Calendar (30 points):
  Touring Artists Bookings (11)
  Symphony Orchestra:
    Marietta College Symphonette, 4
  Dance Company:
    Parkersburg/Wheeling Civic Ballet, 15
Places Rated Score: 262
Places Rated Rank: 239

Pascagoula, MS
Public Libraries (75 points):
  6 branches, 146,620 volumes
  Books added per year: 9,877
Places Rated Score: 75
Places Rated Rank: 326

Pawtucket–Woonsocket–Attleboro, RI–MA
Public Libraries (64 points):
  18 branches, 760,361 volumes
  Books added per year: 20,859
Art Museum/Gallery (50 points):
  1 private
CMSA Access: Providence–Pawtucket–
  Fall River, RI–MA (62 points)
Places Rated Score: 176
Places Rated Rank: 276

Pensacola, FL
Fine Arts Broadcasting (205 points):
  Concert Radio: WUWF-FM 88.1, 105
    hours
  Non-Commercial TV: WSRE Channel 23
Public Libraries (58 points):
  5 branches, 344,846 volumes
  Books added per year: 20,507
Art Museums/Galleries (150 points):
  2 private, 1 university
  Pensacola Museum of Art
The Lively Arts Calendar (157 points):
  Touring Artists Bookings (148)
  Symphony Orchestra:
    Greater Pensacola Symphony, 9
Places Rated Score: 570
Places Rated Rank: 125

Peoria, IL
Fine Arts Broadcasting (183 points):
  Concert Radio: WCBU-FM 89.9, 83 hours
  Non-Commercial TV: WTVP Channel 47
Public Libraries (202 points):
  30 branches, 1,377,013 volumes
  Books added per year: 67,850
Art Museum/Gallery (50 points):
  1 private
  Lakeview Museum of Arts and Sciences
The Lively Arts Calendar (140 points):
  Touring Artists Bookings (104)
  Symphony Orchestras:
    Central Illinois Youth Symphony, 5
    Peoria Symphony Orchestra, 18
  Opera Company:
    Peoria Civic Opera, 3
  Dance Company:
    Peoria Civic Ballet Company, 10
Places Rated Score: 575
Places Rated Rank: 124

★ Philadelphia, PA–NJ
Fine Arts Broadcasting (521 points):
  Concert Radio: WDUG-FM 90.5, 63 hours
    WFLN-FM 95.7, 168 hours
    WHYY-FM 90.9, 90 hours
  Non-Commercial TV: WHYY Channel 12
    WNJS Channel 23
Public Libraries (129 points):
  171 branches, 10,481,355 volumes
  Books added per year: 632,232
Art Museums/Galleries (1,100 points):
  1 civic, 12 private, 9 university
  Pennsylvania Academy of Fine Arts
  Philadelphia Museum of Art
The Lively Arts Calendar (1,937 points):
  Touring Artists Bookings (375)
  Symphony Orchestras:
    Ambler Symphony Orchestra, 4
    Concerto Soloists Chamber
      Orchestra, 150
    Haddonfield Symphony, 7
    Kennett Symphony Orchestra, 6
    North Penn Symphony Orchestra, 4
    Philadelphia Doctors' Symphony, 2
    Philadelphia Youth Orchestra, 2
    Pottstown Symphony Orchestra, 10
    Temple University Symphony
      Orchestra, 6
    The Philadelphia Chamber Orchestra, 4
    The Philadelphia Orchestra, 175
    Warminster Symphony Orchestra, 5
    West Chester University Orchestra, 4
    Youth Orchestra at Glassboro State
      College, 2
  Opera Companies:
    Opera Company of Philadelphia, 12
    Opera-North, 5
    Pennsylvania Opera Theater, 6
  Professional Theatres:
    Philadelphia Festival Theatre for New
      Plays, 120
    Philadelphia Drama Guild, 160
    Society Hill Playhouse, 80
    The People's Light and Theatre
      Company, 120
    The Philadelphia Theatre
      Company, 160
    The Walnut Street Theatre, 240
    The Wilma Theater, 80
  Dance Companies:
    Danceteller, 50
    Pennsylvania & Milwaukee Ballet, 88
    Philadelphia Dance Company, 60
CMSA Access: Philadelphia–Wilmington–
  Trenton, PA–NJ–DE–MD (97 points)
Places Rated Score: 3,784
Places Rated Rank: 6

Phoenix, AZ
Fine Arts Broadcasting (268 points):
  Concert Radio: KONC-FM 106.3, 168
    hours
  Non-Commercial TV: KAET Channel 8
Public Libraries (130 points):
  41 branches, 3,056,003 volumes
  Books added per year: 269,318
Art Museums/Galleries (400 points):
  1 civic, 6 private, 1 university
  Heard Museum
  Phoenix Art Museum
The Lively Arts Calendar (564 points):
  Touring Artists Bookings (329)
  Symphony Orchestras:
    Mesa Symphony Orchestra, 12
    Metropolitan Youth Symphony, 5
    Phoenix Symphony Guild Youth
      Orchestra, 6
    Phoenix Symphony Orchestra, 157
    Scottsdale Symphony Orchestra, 5
    Sun Cities Symphony Orchestra, 5
  Dance Company:
    Ballet Arizona, 45
Places Rated Score: 1,362
Places Rated Rank: 43

Pine Bluff, AR
Public Libraries (92 points):
  3 branches, 158,560 volumes
  Books added per year: 8,314
Art Museum/Gallery (50 points):
  1 civic
The Lively Arts Calendar (4 points):
  Symphony Orchestra:
    Pine Bluff Symphony Orchestra, 4
Places Rated Score: 146
Places Rated Rank: 293

Pittsburgh, PA
Fine Arts Broadcasting (336 points):
  Concert Radio: WQED-FM 89.3, 136
    hours
  Non-Commercial TV: WQED Channel 13
    WQEX Channel 16
Public Libraries (86 points):
  83 branches, 4,224,863 volumes
  Books added per year: 184,008
Art Museums/Galleries (600 points):
  1 civic, 10 private, 1 university
  Carnegie Museum of Art
  Westmoreland County Museum of Art
The Lively Arts Calendar (567 points):
  Touring Artists Bookings (103)
  Symphony Orchestras:
    McKeesport Symphony Orchestra, 6
    Pittsburgh Civic Orchestra, 4
    Pittsburgh Symphony Orchestra, 115
    Pittsburgh Youth Symphony
      Orchestra, 10
    Three Rivers Young Peoples'
      Orchestras, 7
    Westmoreland Symphony Orchestra, 7
  Opera Companies:
    Civic Light Opera, 51
    Pittsburgh Opera, 23
    Pittsburgh Opera Theater, 6
  Professional Theatre:
    Pittsburgh Public Theater, 120
  Dance Companies:
    American Dance Ensemble, 55
    Pittsburgh Ballet Theater, 60
CMSA Access: Pittsburgh–Beaver
  County, PA (7 points)
Places Rated Score: 1,596
Places Rated Rank: 33

Pittsfield, MA
Public Libraries (147 points):
  11 branches, 513,841 volumes
  Books added per year: 11,916
Art Museums/Galleries (150 points):
  3 private
The Lively Arts Calendar (253 points):
  Touring Artists Bookings (8)
  Opera Company:
    Berkshire Opera Company, 10
  Professional Theatre:
    Berkshire Theatre Festival, 160
  Dance Company:
    Berkshire Ballet, 75
Places Rated Score: 550
Places Rated Rank: 130

Portland, ME
Fine Arts Broadcasting (192 points):
  Concert Radio: WDCS-FM 106.3, 84
    hours
    WMEA-FM 90.1, 108 hours
Public Libraries (124 points):
  23 branches, 763,816 volumes
  Books added per year: 26,412
Art Museums/Galleries (150 points):
  2 private, 1 university
  Portland Museum of Art
The Lively Arts Calendar (212 points):
  Touring Artists Bookings (26)
  Symphony Orchestras:
    Portland Symphony Orchestra, 62
    Portland Symphony Youth Orchestra, 4
  Professional Theatre:
    Portland Stage Company, 120
Places Rated Score: 678
Places Rated Rank: 97

Portland, OR
Fine Arts Broadcasting (347 points):
  Concert Radio: KBPS-FM 89.9, 126 hours
    KOAP-FM 91.5, 54 hours
    KYTE-FM 101.1, 67 hours
  Non-Commercial TV: KOAP Channel 10
Public Libraries (147 points):
  41 branches, 1,359,247 volumes
  Books added per year: 172,830
Art Museums/Galleries (150 points):
  2 private, 1 university
  Portland Art Museum
The Lively Arts Calendar (365 points):
  Touring Artists Bookings (46)
  Symphony Orchestras:
    Little Orchestra of Portland, 4
    Oregon Symphony Orchestra, 135
    Portland Youth Philharmonic, 12
    West Coast Chamber Orchestra, 6
  Opera Company:
    Portland Opera, 12
  Dance Company:
    Ballet Oregon, 150
CMSA Access: Portland–Vancouver, OR
  (6 points)
Places Rated Score: 1,015
Places Rated Rank: 59

Portsmouth–Dover–Rochester, NH–ME
Fine Arts Broadcasting (200 points):
  Non-Commercial TV: WENH Channel 11
    WMEA Channel 26
Public Libraries (168 points):
  27 branches, 607,825 volumes
  Books added per year: 39,742
Art Museums/Galleries (250 points):
  4 private, 1 university
The Lively Arts Calendar (13 points):
  Touring Artists Bookings (13)
Places Rated Score: 631
Places Rated Rank: 105

Poughkeepsie, NY
Public Libraries (123 points):
22 branches, 431,357 volumes
Books added per year: 32,783
Art Museums/Galleries (150 points):
2 private, 1 university
The Lively Arts Calendar (114 points):
Touring Artists Bookings (80)
Symphony Orchestra:
Hudson Valley Philharmonic, 34
Places Rated Score: 387
Places Rated Rank: 180

Providence, RI
Fine Arts Broadcasting (100 points):
Non-Commercial TV: WSBE Channel 36
Public Libraries (126 points):
25 branches, 1,968,457 volumes
Books added per year: 81,865
Art Museums/Galleries (250 points):
3 private, 2 university
Museum of Art, Rhode Island School of
Design
The Lively Arts Calendar (265 points):
Touring Artists Bookings (19)
Symphony Orchestras:
Brown University Orchestra, 2
Rhode Island Philharmonic
Orchestra, 10
Rhode Island Philharmonic Youth
Orchestra, 5
Young Peoples Symphony of Rhode
Island, 6
Professional Theatre:
Trinity Repertory Company, 220
Dance Company:
State Ballet of Rhode Island, 3
CMSA Access: Providence–Pawtucket–
Fall River, RI–MA (5 points)
Places Rated Score: 746
Places Rated Rank: 83

Provo–Orem, UT
Fine Arts Broadcasting (257 points):
Concert Radio: KBYU-FM 88.9, 157 hours
Non-Commercial TV: KBYU Channel 11
Public Libraries (80 points):
9 branches, 432,077 volumes
Books added per year: 20,291
Art Museums/Galleries (100 points):
1 private, 1 university
The Lively Arts Calendar (24 points):
Touring Artists Bookings (20)
Symphony Orchestra:
Utah Valley Youth Symphony
Orchestra, 4
Places Rated Score: 461
Places Rated Rank: 155

Pueblo, CO
Fine Arts Broadcasting (100 points):
Non-Commercial TV: KTSC Channel 8
Public Library (115 points):
1 branch, 186,830 volumes
Books added per year: 14,940
Art Museum/Gallery (50 points):
1 private
The Lively Arts Calendar (49 points):
Touring Artists Bookings (42)
Symphony Orchestra:
Pueblo Symphony, 7
Places Rated Score: 314
Places Rated Rank: 214

Racine, WI
Public Libraries (141 points):
7 branches, 350,162 volumes
Books added per year: 24,306

Art Museum/Gallery (50 points):
1 private
Wustum Museum of Fine Arts
The Lively Arts Calendar (8 points):
Symphony Orchestra:
Racine Symphony Orchestra, 8
CMSA Access: Milwaukee–Racine, WI
(177 points)
Places Rated Score: 376
Places Rated Rank: 186

Raleigh–Durham, NC
Fine Arts Broadcasting (356 points):
Concert Radio: WCPE-FM 89.7, 168 hours
WUNC-FM 91.5, 88 hours
Non-Commercial TV: WUNC Channel 4
Public Libraries (256 points):
32 branches, 1,091,957 volumes
Books added per year: 180,005
Art Museums/Galleries (400 points):
3 private, 5 university
Ackland Museum, University of North
Carolina
Duke University Art Museum
North Carolina Museum of Art
The Lively Arts Calendar (533 points):
Touring Artists Bookings (79)
Symphony Orchestras:
Durham Symphony Orchestra, 4
North Carolina Symphony
Orchestra, 200
Raleigh Symphony Orchestra, 9
Opera Companies:
National Opera Company, 91
Triangle Music Theatre, 10
Professional Theatre:
PlayMakers Repertory Company, 140
Places Rated Score: 1,545
Places Rated Rank: 37

Rapid City, SD
Fine Arts Broadcasting (100 points):
Concert Radio: KBHE-FM 89.3, 100 hours
Public Libraries (95 points):
6 branches, 179,828 volumes
Books added per year: 7,400
Art Museums/Galleries (100 points):
2 private
The Lively Arts Calendar (40 points):
Touring Artists Bookings (34)
Symphony Orchestra:
Black Hills Symphony Orchestra, 6
Places Rated Score: 335
Places Rated Rank: 200

Reading, PA
Public Libraries (45 points):
10 branches, 415,849 volumes
Books added per year: 14,455
Art Museums/Galleries (100 points):
2 private
Reading Public Museum and Art Gallery
The Lively Arts Calendar (49 points):
Touring Artists Bookings (35)
Symphony Orchestra:
Reading Symphony Orchestra, 14
Places Rated Score: 194
Places Rated Rank: 272

Redding, CA
Fine Arts Broadcasting (100 points):
Non-Commercial TV: KIXE Channel 9
Public Libraries (63 points):
10 branches, 242,295 volumes
Books added per year: 8,936
Art Museum/Gallery (50 points):
1 private

The Lively Arts Calendar (18 points):
Touring Artists Bookings (13)
Symphony Orchestra:
Shasta Symphony, 5
Places Rated Score: 231
Places Rated Rank: 254

Reno, NV
Fine Arts Broadcasting (150 points):
Concert Radio: KUNR-FM 88.7, 50 hours
Non-Commercial TV: KNPB Channel 5
Public Libraries (53 points):
5 branches, 383,458 volumes
Books added per year: 12,540
Art Museums/Galleries (100 points):
1 private, 1 university
The Lively Arts Calendar (27 points):
Touring Artists Bookings (10)
Symphony Orchestras:
Reno Philharmonic Association, 12
Sierra Community Orchestra, 4
Opera Company:
Nevada Opera, 9
Places Rated Score: 330
Places Rated Rank: 203

Richland–Kennewick–Pasco, WA
Public Libraries (159 points):
7 branches, 357,315 volumes
Books added per year: 24,124
Places Rated Score: 159
Places Rated Rank: 284

Richmond–Petersburg, VA
Fine Arts Broadcasting (270 points):
Concert Radio: WRFK-FM 106.5, 70 hours
Non-Commercial TV: WCVE Channel 23
WCVW Channel 57
Public Libraries (128 points):
39 branches, 1,757,710 volumes
Books added per year: 107,459
Art Museums/Galleries (150 points):
1 civic, 1 private, 1 university
Virginia Museum of Fine Arts
The Lively Arts Calendar (817 points):
Touring Artists Bookings (31)
Symphony Orchestras:
Richmond Symphony Youth
Orchestra, 2
The Richmond Symphony, 300
Virginia Commonwealth University
Orchestra, 4
Professional Theatres:
Theatre IV, 300
TheatreVirginia, 160
Dance Company:
The Richmond Ballet, 20
Places Rated Score: 1,365
Places Rated Rank: 42

Riverside–San Bernardino, CA
Fine Arts Broadcasting (168 points):
Concert Radio: KUCR-FM 88.1, 20 hours
KVCR-FM 91.9, 48 hours
Non-Commercial TV: KVCR Channel 24
Public Libraries (62 points):
75 branches, 2,842,214 volumes
Books added per year: 136,820
Art Museums/Galleries (350 points):
2 civic, 3 private, 2 university
Palm Springs Desert Museum
The Lively Arts Calendar (304 points):
Touring Artists Bookings (216)
Symphony Orchestras:
Inland Empire Symphony, 16
Redlands Symphony Orchestra, 9
Riverside Symphony Orchestra, 10
San Bernardino Chamber Orchestra, 5

Opera Companies:
Riverside Opera Association, 4
San Bernardino Civic Light Opera, 44
CMSA Access: Los Angeles–Anaheim–
Riverside, CA (621 points)
Places Rated Score: 1,505
Places Rated Rank: 38

Roanoke, VA
Fine Arts Broadcasting (175 points):
Concert Radio: WVTF-FM 89.1, 75 hours
Non-Commercial TV: WBRA Channel 15
Public Libraries (130 points):
16 branches, 653,084 volumes
Books added per year: 29,420
Art Museum/Gallery (50 points):
1 private
Roanoke Museum of Fine Arts
The Lively Arts Calendar (38 points):
Touring Artists Bookings (25)
Symphony Orchestra:
Roanoke Symphony Orchestra, 13
Places Rated Score: 393
Places Rated Rank: 178

Rochester, MN
Fine Arts Broadcasting (140 points):
Concert Radio: KLSX-FM 90.7, 140 hours
Public Libraries (103 points):
2 branches, 159,179 volumes
Books added per year: 10,526
Art Museum/Gallery (50 points):
1 private
The Lively Arts Calendar (26 points):
Touring Artists Bookings (6)
Symphony Orchestra:
Rochester Symphony Orchestra, 20
Places Rated Score: 319
Places Rated Rank: 210

Rochester, NY
Fine Arts Broadcasting (264 points):
Concert Radio: WXXI-FM 91.5, 164 hours
Non-Commercial TV: WXXI Channel 21
Public Libraries (218 points):
66 branches, 2,745,110 volumes
Books added per year: 216,760
Art Museums/Galleries (150 points):
1 private, 2 university
University of Rochester Memorial Art
Gallery
The Lively Arts Calendar (587 points):
Touring Artists Bookings (112)
Symphony Orchestras:
Brighton Symphony Orchestra, 10
Eastman Philharmonia, 11
Penfield Symphony Orchestra, 6
Rochester Philharmonic Orchestra, 180
Rochester Philharmonic Youth
Orchestra, 8
Professional Theatre:
GeVa Theatre, 160
Dance Company:
Garth Fagan's Bucket Dance Theatre,
100
Places Rated Score: 1,219
Places Rated Rank: 47

Rockford, IL
Public Libraries (110 points):
12 branches, 469,497 volumes
Books added per year: 31,097
Art Museums/Galleries (100 points):
2 university
The Lively Arts Calendar (168 points):
Touring Artists Bookings (12)
Symphony Orchestras:
Rockford Area Youth Symphony, 7
Rockford Symphony Orchestra, 9

Professional Theatre:
New American Theater, 140
Places Rated Score: 378
Places Rated Rank: 184

Sacramento, CA
Fine Arts Broadcasting (185 points):
Concert Radio: KXPR-FM 90.9, 85 hours
Non-Commercial TV: KVIE Channel 6
Public Libraries (114 points):
53 branches, 2,236,758 volumes
Books added per year: 156,393
Art Museums/Galleries (100 points):
1 civic, 1 private
Crocker Museum of Art
The Lively Arts Calendar (679 points):
Touring Artists Bookings (80)
Symphony Orchestras:
Camellia Symphony Orchestra, 6
Sacramento Symphony Orchestra, 153
Sacramento Youth Symphony, 4
Opera Company:
Sacramento Opera Association, 6
Professional Theatre:
Sacramento Theatre Company, 360
Dance Companies:
Sacramento Ballet, 50
Theatre Ballet of Sacramento, 20
Places Rated Score: 1,078
Places Rated Rank: 52

Saginaw–Bay City–Midland, MI
Fine Arts Broadcasting (100 points):
Non-Commercial TV: WUCM Channel 19
Public Libraries (173 points):
22 branches, 945,697 volumes
Books added per year: 69,726
Art Museums/Galleries (150 points):
3 private
Saginaw Art Museum
The Lively Arts Calendar (84 points):
Touring Artists Bookings (41)
Symphony Orchestras:
Midland Symphony Orchestra, 9
Northwood Orchestra, 15
Saginaw Symphony Orchestra, 15
Saginaw Symphony Youth Orchestra, 4
Places Rated Score: 507
Places Rated Rank: 140

St. Cloud, MN
Fine Arts Broadcasting (116 points):
Concert Radio: KSJR-FM 90.1, 116 hours
Public Libraries (106 points):
12 branches, 290,075 volumes
Books added per year: 19,428
Art Museum/Gallery (50 points):
1 university
The Lively Arts Calendar (24 points):
Touring Artists Bookings (20)
Symphony Orchestra:
St. Cloud Symphony Orchestra, 4
Places Rated Score: 296
Places Rated Rank: 225

St. Joseph, MO
Public Libraries (41 points):
2 branches, 89,176 volumes
Books added per year: 3,594
Art Museum/Gallery (50 points):
1 private
Albrecht Art Museum
The Lively Arts Calendar (32 points):
Touring Artists Bookings (21)
Symphony Orchestras:
Missouri Western Philharmonia, 6
St. Joseph Symphony Orchestra, 5
Places Rated Score: 123
Places Rated Rank: 306

★ St. Louis, MO–IL
Fine Arts Broadcasting (338 points):
Concert Radio: KFUO-FM 99.1, 168 hours
KWMU 90.7, 70 hours
Non-Commercial TV: KETC Channel 9
Public Libraries (159 points):
83 branches, 6,301,736 volumes
Books added per year: 392,397
Art Museums/Galleries (400 points):
1 civic, 4 private, 3 university
Laumeier Sculpture Garden
St. Louis Art Museum
The Lively Arts Calendar (931 points):
Touring Artists Bookings (112)
Symphony Orchestras:
St. Louis Symphony Orchestra, 230
St. Louis Symphony Youth Orchestra, 4
The St. Louis Philharmonic
Orchestra, 5
Opera Company:
Opera Theatre of St. Louis, 40
Professional Theatres:
The Repertory Theatre of St. Louis, 240
Theatre Project company, 260
Dance Company:
Missouri Concert Ballet Company, 40
Places Rated Score: 1,828
Places Rated Rank: 29

Salem, OR
Public Libraries (161 points):
12 branches, 532,455 volumes
Books added per year: 42,607
Art Museum/Gallery (50 points):
1 private
The Lively Arts Calendar (11 points):
Touring Artists Bookings (11)
Places Rated Score: 222
Places Rated Rank: 257

Salem–Gloucester, MA
Fine Arts Broadcasting (168 points):
Concert Radio: WBOQ-FM 104.9, 168
hours
Public Libraries (212 points):
17 branches, 1,117,866 volumes
Books added per year: 56,276
Art Museums/Galleries (100 points):
2 private
Peabody Museum of Salem
The Lively Arts Calendar (70 points):
Touring Artists Bookingns (54)
Symphony Orchestras:
Cape Ann Symphony Orchestra, 6
Sinfonie-by-the-Sea, 10
CMSA Access: Boston–Lawrence–
Salem, MA–NH (302)
Places Rated Score: 852
Places Rated Rank: 69

Salinas–Seaside–Monterey, CA
Fine Arts Broadcasting (140 points):
Concert Radio: KBOQ-FM 92.7, 140 hours
Public Libraries (237 points):
23 branches, 1,104,664 volumes
Books added per year: 86,930
Art Museums/Galleries (300 points):
6 private
The Lively Arts Calendar (33 points):
Touring Artists Bookings (27)
Symphony Orchestra:
Monterey County Symphony, 6
Places Rated Score: 710
Places Rated Rank: 90

Salt Lake City–Ogden, UT
Fine Arts Broadcasting (169 points):
Concert Radio: KUER-FM 90.1, 69 hours
Non-Commercial TV: KUED Channel 7

Public Libraries (140 points):
34 branches, 2,235,828 volumes
Books added per year: 153,181
Art Museums/Galleries (250 points):
2 civic, 2 private, 1 university
Utah Museum of Fine Arts
The Lively Arts Calendar (1,015 points):
Touring Artists Bookings (335)
Symphony Orchestras:
  Murray Symphony Orchestra, 8
  Rocky Mountain Symphony, 6
  Utah Symphony Orchestra, 250
  Utah Youth Symphony, 6
Opera Company:
  Utah Opera, 15
Professional Theatres:
  Pioneer Theatre Company, 140
  The Salt Lake Acting Company, 140
Dance Company:
  Ballet West, 115
Places Rated Score: 1,574
Places Rated Rank: 34

San Angelo, TX
Public Libraries (61 points):
3 branches, 182,127 volumes
Books added per year: 6,069
Art Museum/Gallery (50 points):
1 private
The Lively Arts Calendar (13 points):
Touring Artists Bookings (4)
Symphony Orchestra:
  San Angelo Symphony Orchestra, 9
Places Rated Score: 124
Places Rated Rank: 305

San Antonio, TX
Fine Arts Broadcasting (373 points):
Concert Radio: KPAC-FM 99.9, 168 hours
  KRTU-FM 91.7, 105 hours
Non-Commercial TV: KLRN Channel 9
Public Libraries (67 points):
23 branches, 1,775,007 volumes
Books added per year: 90,635
Art Museums/Galleries (200 points):
4 private
McNay Art Institute
San Antonio Museum of Art
The Lively Arts Calendar (362 points):
Touring Artists Bookings (158)
Symphony Orchestras:
  Mid-Texas Symphony Orchestra, 8
  San Antonio Symphony Orchestra, 180
  Youth Orchestras of San Antonio, 4
Opera Company:
  Opera Theatre of San Antonio, 12
Places Rated Score: 1,002
Places Rated Rank: 60

★ San Diego, CA
Fine Arts Broadcasting (349 points):
Concert Radio: KFSD-FM 94.1, 168 hours
  KPBS-FM 89.5, 81 hours
Non-Commercial TV: KPBS Channel 15
Public Libraries (96 points):
74 branches, 3,252,671 volumes
Books added per year: 224,261
Art Museums/Galleries (400 points):
6 private, 2 university
La Jolla Museum of Contemporary Arts
Mingei Museum of World Folk Art
San Diego Museum of Art
The Lively Arts Calendar (1,308 points):
Touring Artists Bookings (139)
Symphony Orchestra:
  La Jolla Civic/University Symphony
    Orchestra, 6
  Pacific Chamber Ensemble, 4
  San Diego Chamber Orchestra, 30

San Diego Symphony Orchestra, 120
San Diego Youth Symphony, 12
Opera Companies:
  San Diego Civic Light Opera, 55
  San Diego Gilbert & Sullivan
    Company, 21
  San Diego Opera, 16
Professional Theatres:
  La Jolla Playhouse, 200
  Lamb's Players Theatre, 280
  Old Globe Theatre, 240
  San Diego Repertory Theatre, 160
Dance company:
  California Ballet Company, 25
Places Rated Score: 2,153
Places Rated Rank: 17

★ San Francisco, CA
Fine Arts Broadcasting (768 points):
Concert Radio: KCSM-FM 91.1, 20 hours
  KDFC-FM 102.1, 140 hours
  KKHI-FM 95.7, 168 hours
  KUSF-FM 90.3, 140 hours
Non-Commercial TV: KCSM Channel 60
  KQEC Channel 32
  KQED Channel 9
Public Libraries (177 points):
77 branches, 4,423,423 volumes
Books added per year: 293,226
Art Museums/Galleries (700 points):
5 civic, 7 private, 2 university
Asian Art Museum of San Francisco
Fine Arts Museums of San Francisco
San Francisco Museum of Modern Art
The Lively Arts Calendar (2,010 points):
Touring Artists Bookings (555)
Symphony Orchestras:
  Bay Area Women's Philharmonic, 4
  Bay Chamber Symphony Orchestra, 4
  Chamber Symphony of San Francisco, 4
  Marin Symphony Orchestra, 14
  Philharmonia Baroque Orchestra, 5
  San Francisco Chamber Players, 8
  San Francisco Conservatory of Music
    Orchestra, 5
  San Francisco State University
    Symphony Orchestra, 4
  San Francisco Symphony, 216
  San Francisco Symphony Youth
    Orchestra, 12
Opera Companies:
  Marin Civic Light Opera, 48
  Marin Opera, 6
  Pocket Opera, 60
  San Francisco Opera, 68
Professional Theatres:
  American Conservatory Theatre, 180
  Eureka Theatre Company, 120
  Magic Theatre, 220
  Marin Theatre Company, 120
  One Act Theatre Company of San
    Francisco, 160
  San Francisco Mime Troupe, 40
Dance Companies:
  ODC/San Francisco, 40
  Peninsula Ballet Theatre, 17
  San Francisco Ballet, 100
CMSA Access: San Francisco–Oakland–
San Jose, CA (351 points)
Places Rated Score: 4,006
Places Rated Rank: 5

★ San Jose, CA
Fine Arts Broadcasting (100 points):
Non-Commercial TV: KTEH Channel 54
Public Libraries (157 points):
39 branches, 3,249,430 volumes
Books added per year: 229,761

Art Museums/Galleries (450 points):
5 private, 4 university
The Lively Arts Calendar (901 points):
Touring Artists Bookings (148)
Symphony Orchestras:
  California Youth Symphony, 8
  El Camino Youth Symphony, 4
  Foothill-De Anza Orchestra, 4
  Nova Vista Symphony, 6
  San Jose Symphony Orchestra, 75
  South Valley Symphony, 12
Opera Companies:
  Opera San Jose, 24
  San Jose Civic Light Opera, 52
  West Bay Opera Association, 18
Professional Theatres:
  California Theatre Center, 360
  San Jose Repertory Company, 120
Dance Companies:
  Cleveland/San Jose Ballet, 45
  Santa Clara Ballet Company, 25
CMSA Access: San Francisco–Oakland–
San Jose, CA (521 points)
Places Rated Score: 2,129
Places Rated Rank: 18

Santa Barbara–Santa Maria–Lompoc, CA
Fine Arts Broadcasting (168 points):
Concert Radio: KDB-FM 93.7, 168 hours
Public Libraries (85 points):
17 branches, 513,245 volumes
Books added per year: 30,825
Art Museums/Galleries (100 points):
1 private, 1 university
Santa Barbara Museum of Art
The Lively Arts Calendar (212 points):
Touring Artists Bookings (63)
Symphony Orchestra:
  Santa Barbara Symphony, 25
Opera Company:
  Santa Barbara Civic Light Opera, 24
Professional Theatre:
  PCPA Theaterfest, 100
Places Rated Score: 565
Places Rated Rank: 126

Santa Cruz, CA
Fine Arts Broadcasting (71 points):
Concert Radio: KLZC-FM 107.5, 47 hours
  KUSP-FM 88.9, 24 hours
Public Libraries (75 points):
10 branches, 428,743 volumes
Books added per year: 17,866
Art Museums/Galleries (100 points):
2 private
The Lively Arts Calendar (111 points):
Touring Artists Bookings (80)
Symphony Orchestras:
  Cabrillo Music Festival, 11
  Santa Cruz County Symphony, 16
  Santa Cruz County Youth Symphony, 4
CMSA Access: San Francisco–Oakland–
San Jose, CA (493 points)
Places Rated Score: 850
Places Rated Rank: 71

Santa Fe, NM
Fine Arts Broadcasting (26 points):
Concert Radio: KLSK-FM 107.5, 26 hours
Public Libraries (222 points):
5 branches, 322,920 volumes
Books added per year: 25,110
Art Museums/Galleries (250 points):
2 civic, 3 private
The Lively Arts Calendar (142 points):
Touring Artists Bookings (76)
Symphony Orchestras:
  Orchestra of Santa Fe, 21
  The Santa Fe Symphony, 8

Opera Company:
  Santa Fe Opera, 37
Places Rated Score: 640
Places Rated Rank: 103

Santa Rosa–Petaluma, CA
Fine Arts Broadcasting (100 points):
  Non-Commercial TV: KRCB Channel 22
Public Libraries (111 points):
  13 branches, 631,612 volumes
  Books added per year: 41,643
Art Museum/Gallery (50 points):
  1 university
The Lively Arts Calendar (78 points):
  Touring Artists Bookings (16)
  Symphony Orchestras:
    Santa Rosa Symphony, 21
    Sonoma County Junior Symphony, 6
  Opera Company:
    Cinnabar Opera Theater, 35
CMSA Access: San Francisco–Oakland–San Jose, CA (358 points)
Places Rated Score: 697
Places Rated Rank: 92

Sarasota, FL
Public Libraries (62 points):
  5 branches, 318,064 volumes
  Books added per year: 16,664
Art Museum/Gallery (50 points):
  1 private
  Ringling Museum of Art
The Lively Arts Calendar (477 points):
  Touring Artists Bookings (104)
  Symphony Orchestra:
    Sarasota Community Orchestra, 7
  Opera Company:
    Sarasota Opera Association, 26
  Professional Theatres:
    Asolo Performing Arts Center, 200
    Florida Studio Theatre, 140
Places Rated Score: 589
Places Rated Rank: 120

Savannah, GA
Fine Arts Broadcasting (194 points):
  Concert Radio: WSVH-FM 91.1, 94 hours
  Non-Commercial TV: WVAN Channel 9
Public Libraries (121 points):
  17 branches, 454,316 volumes
  Books added per year: 29,456
Art Museum/Gallery (50 points):
  1 private
The Lively Arts Calendar (54 points):
  Touring Artists Bookings (9)
  Symphony Orchestra:
    Savannah Symphony Orchestra, 45
Places Rated Score: 419
Places Rated Rank: 170

Scranton–Wilkes-Barre, PA
Fine Arts Broadcasting (156 points):
  Concert Radio: WVIA-FM 89.9, 112 hours
  Non-Commercial TV: WVIA Channel 44
Public Libraries (68 points):
  34 branches, 1,024,542 volumes
  Books added per year: 49,888
Art Museums/Galleries (100 points):
  2 private
The Lively Arts Calendar (302 points):
  Touring Artists Bookings (30)
  Symphony Orchestras:
    Bloomsburg University-Community
      Orchestra, 7
    Northeastern Pennsylvania
      Philharmonic, 40
  Professional Theatre:
    The Bloomsburg Theatre Ensemble, 200

Dance Company:
    The Wilkes-Barre Ballet Theatre, 25
Places Rated Score: 626
Places Rated Rank: 108

★ Seattle, WA
Fine Arts Broadcasting (354 points):
  Concert Radio: KING-FM 98.1, 168 hours
    KUOW-FM 94.9, 86 hours
  Non-Commercial TV: KCTS Channel 9
Public Libraries (197 points):
  81 branches, 4,032,898 volumes
  Books added per year: 357,736
Art Museums/Galleries (250 points):
  4 private, 1 university
  Henry Art Gallery, University of
    Washington
  Seattle Art Museum
The Lively Arts Calendar (1,868 points):
  Touring Artists Bookings (202)
  Symphony Orchestras:
    Bellevue Philharmonic Orchestra, 22
    Cascade Symphony Orchestra, 4
    Everett Symphony Orchestra, 8
    Seattle Symphony Orchestra, 84
    Seattle Youth Symphony Orchestra, 3
  Opera Companies:
    Seattle Civic Light Opera, 30
    Seattle Opera Association, 36
  Professional Theatres:
    A Contemporary Theatre, 340
    Intiman Theatre Company, 200
    Seattle Children's Theatre, 120
    Seattle Repertory Theatre, 180
    The Bathhouse Theatre, 360
    The Empty Space Theatre, 100
    The Group Theatre Company, 120
  Dance Company:
    Pacific Northwest Ballet, 59
CMSA Access: Seattle–Tacoma, WA (45 points)
Places Rated Score: 2,714
Places Rated Rank: 11

Sharon, PA
Public Libraries (52 points):
  5 branches, 172,096 volumes
  Books added per year: 6,407
The Lively Arts Calendar (10 points):
  Touring Artists Bookings (5)
  Symphony Orchestra:
    Romanenko Chamber Players, 5
Places Rated Score: 62
Places Rated Rank: 330

Sheboygan, WI
Public Libraries (206 points):
  8 branches, 407,253 volumes
  Books added per year: 21,092
Art Museum/Gallery (50 points):
  1 private
  Kohler Arts Center
The Lively Arts Calendar (18 points):
  Touring Artists Bookings (13)
  Symphony Orchestra:
    Sheboygan Symphony Orchestra, 5
Places Rated Score: 274
Places Rated Rank: 235

Sherman–Denison, TX
Public Libraries (59 points):
  6 branches, 226,368 volumes
  Books added per year: 5,764
The Lively Arts Calendar (36 points):
  Touring Artists Bookings (36)
Places Rated Score: 95
Places Rated Rank: 319

Shreveport, LA
Fine Arts Broadcasting (202 points):
  Concert Radio: KDAQ-FM 89.9, 102 hours
  Non-Commercial TV: KLTS Channel 24
Public Libraries (92 points):
  25 branches, 448,975 volumes
  Books added per year: 33,801
Art Museums/Galleries (150 points):
  1 civic, 1 private, 1 university
  Meadows Museum of Art, Centenary
    College
The Lively Arts Calendar (72 points):
  Touring Artists Bookings (29)
  Symphony Orchestras:
    Ark-La-Tex Youth Symphony
      Orchestras, 5
    Shreveport Symphony Orchestra, 34
  Opera Company:
    Shreveport Opera, 4
Places Rated Score: 516
Places Rated Rank: 138

Sioux City, IA–NE
Fine Arts Broadcasting (200 points):
  Concert Radio: KWIT-FM 90.3, 100 hours
  Non-Commercial TV: KSIN Channel 27
Public Libraries (99 points):
  6 branches, 320,283 volumes
  Books added per year: 11,401
Art Museum/Gallery (50 points):
  1 civic
  Sioux City Art Center
The Lively Arts Calendar (13 points):
  Touring Artists Bookings (4)
  Symphony Orchestra:
    Sioux City Symphony Orchestra, 9
Places Rated Score: 362
Places Rated Rank: 192

Sioux Falls, SD
Fine Arts Broadcasting (100 points):
  Concert Radio: KCSD-FM 90.9, 100 hours
Public Libraries (91 points):
  10 branches, 245,192 volumes
  Books added per year: 11,600
Art Museum/Gallery (50 points):
  1 civic
The Lively Arts Calendar (23 points):
  Touring Artists Bookings (5)
  Symphony Orchestra:
    South Dakota Symphony, 18
Places Rated Score: 264
Places Rated Rank: 238

South Bend–Mishawaka, IN
Fine Arts Broadcasting (94 points):
  Concert Radio: WSND-FM 88.9, 84 hours
Public Libraries (271 points):
  11 branches, 574,441 volumes
  Books added per year: 65,092
Art Museums/Galleries (100 points):
  1 civic, 1 university
  Art Center, Inc.
  Snite Museum, University of Notre Dame
The Lively Arts Calendar (28 points):
  Touring Artists Bookings (13)
  Symphony Orchestra:
    South Bend Symphony, 15
Places Rated Score: 493
Places Rated Rank: 142

Spokane, WA
Fine Arts Broadcasting (185 points):
  Concert Radio: KPBX-FM 91.1, 85 hours
  Non-Commercial TV: KSPS Channel 7
Public Libraries (142 points):
  12 branches, 727,062 volumes
  Books added per year: 51,152

Art Museums/Galleries (100 points):
1 private, 1 university
The Lively Arts Calendar (171 points):
Touring Artists Bookings (23)
Symphony Orchestras:
Eastern Washington University
Symphony Orchestra, 2
Spokane Symphony Orchestra, 80
Spokane Youth Symphony, 6
Dance Company:
Spokane Ballet Theatre, 60
Places Rated Score: 598
Places Rated Rank: 117

Springfield, IL
Fine Arts Broadcasting (151 points):
Concert Radio: WSSR-FM 91.9, 51 hours
Non-Commercial TV: WJPT Channel 14
Public Libraries (104 points):
14 branches, 418,413 volumes
Books added per year: 20,058
Art Museums/Galleries (100 points):
1 private, 1 university
The Lively Arts Calendar (57 points):
Touring Artists Bookings (20)
Symphony Orchestra:
Bloomington–Normal and Springfield
Symphony, 10
Dance Company:
Springfield Ballet Company, 27
Places Rated Score: 412
Places Rated Rank: 174

Springfield, MA
Fine Arts Broadcasting (159 points):
Concert Radio: WFCR-FM 88.5, 102 hours
Non-Commercial TV: WGBY Channel 57
Public Libraries (130 points):
7 branches, 443,064 volumes
Books added per year: 30,577
Art Museums/Galleries (300 points):
4 private, 2 university
The Lively Arts Calendar (234 points):
Touring Artists Bookings (51)
Symphony Orchestras:
Holyoke College Civic Orchestra, 4
Springfield Symphony Orchestra, 55
Western Massachusetts Young
People's Symphony, 4
Professional Theatre:
StageWest, 120
Places Rated Score: 823
Places Rated Rank: 76

Springfield, MO
Fine Arts Broadcasting (168 points):
Concert Radio: KSMU-FM 91.1, 68 hours
Non-Commercial TV: KOZK Channel 21
Public Libraries (180 points):
37 branches, 2,113,648 volumes
Books added per year: 93,818
Art Museum/Gallery (50 points):
1 private
The Lively Arts Calendar (69 points):
Touring Artists Bookings (18)
Symphony Orchestras:
Southwest Missouri State Symphony, 6
Springfield Symphony Orchestra, 21
Opera Company:
Springfield Regional Opera, 9
Dance Company:
Springfield Ballet, 15
Places Rated Score: 467
Places Rated Rank: 150

★ Stamford, CT
Public Libraries (366 points):
10 branches, 978,196 volumes
Books added per year: 73,334
Art Museums/Galleries (200 points):
4 private
The Lively Arts Calendar (297 points):
Touring Artists Bookings (217)
Symphony Orchestras:
Connecticut Philharmonic Orchestra, 10
Greenwich Symphony Orchestra, 17
Stamford Symphony Orchestra, 14
Young Artists Philharmonic, 5
Opera Companies:
Connecticut Grand Opera-Stamford
State Opera, 8
New England Lyric Operetta, 6
Dance Company:
Ballet Today/Connecticut Ballet
Theatre, 20
CMSA Access: New York–Northern
NJ–Long Island, NY–NJ–CT (1,552
points)
Places Rated Score: 2,415
Places Rated Rank: 13

State College, PA
Fine Arts Broadcasting (100 points):
Non-Commercial TV: WPSX Channel 3
Public Libraries (85 points):
2 branches, 179,739 volumes
Books added per year: 9,922
Art Museums/Galleries (100 points):
1 private, 1 university
The Lively Arts Calendar (53 points):
Touring Artists Bookings (50)
Symphony Orchestra:
Nittany Valley Symphony, 3
Places Rated Score: 338
Places Rated Rank: 199

Steubenville–Weirton, OH–WV
Public Libraries (139 points):
13 branches, 338,999 volumes
Books added per year: 21,268
The Lively Arts Calendar (4 points):
Touring Artists Bookings (4)
Places Rated Score: 143
Places Rated Rank: 296

Stockton, CA
Fine Arts Broadcasting (30 points):
Concert Radio: KUOP-FM 91.3, 30 hours
Public Libraries (188 points):
26 branches, 825,303 volumes
Books added per year: 84,331
Art Museum/Gallery (50 points):
1 private
The Lively Arts Calendar (32 points):
Touring Artists Bookings (12)
Symphony Orchestra:
Stockton Symphony, 20
Places Rated Score: 300
Places Rated Rank: 222

Syracuse, NY
Fine Arts Broadcasting (250 points):
Concert Radio: WCNY-FM 91.3, 150 hours
Non-Commercial TV: WCNY Channel 24
Public Libraries (130 points):
48 branches, 1,383,404 volumes
Books added per year: 85,301
Art Museums/Galleries (250 points):
2 private, 3 university
Everson Museum of Art
Picker Art Gallery, Colgate University

The Lively Arts Calendar (415 points):
Touring Artists Bookings (77)
Symphony Orchestras:
Syracuse Symphony Orchestra, 325
Syracuse Symphony Youth Orchestra,
4
Opera Company:
Syracuse Opera Company, 9
Places Rated Score: 1,045
Places Rated Rank: 57

Tacoma, WA
Fine Arts Broadcasting (100 points):
Non-Commercial TV: KTPS Channel 28
Public Libraries (211 points):
25 branches, 1,078,579 volumes
Books added per year: 115,714
Art Museums/Galleries (100 points):
2 private
Tacoma Art Museum
The Lively Arts Calendar (252 points):
Touring Artists Bookings (36)
Symphony Orchestras:
Tacoma Symphony Orchestra, 18
Tacoma Youth Symphony, 60
Opera Company:
Tacoma Opera, 4
Dance Company:
Balletacoma, 14
CMSA Access: Seattle–Tacoma, WA (247
points):
Places Rated Score: 910
Places Rated Rank: 66

Tallahassee, FL
Fine Arts Broadcasting (223 points):
Concert Radio: WFSU-FM 91.5, 123 hours
Non-Commercial TV: WFSU Channel 11
Public Libraries (59 points):
6 branches, 238,619 volumes
Books added per year: 13,688
Art Museum/Gallery (50 points):
1 university
The Lively Arts Calendar (67 points):
Touring Artists Bookings (54)
Symphony Orchestras:
Florida State University Symphony, 8
Tallahassee Symphony Orchestra, 5
Places Rated Score: 399
Places Rated Rank: 176

★ Tampa–St. Petersburg–
Clearwater, FL
Fine Arts Broadcasting (314 points):
Concert Radio: WUSF-FM 89.7, 90 hours
WXCR-FM 92.1, 24 hours
Non-Commercial TV: WEDU Channel 3
WUSF Channel 16
Public Libraries (63 points):
49 branches, 2,428,521 volumes
Books added per year: 131,349
Art Museums/Galleries (450 points):
1 civic, 6 private, 2 university
Museum of Fine Arts
The Lively Arts Calendar (1,008 points):
Touring Artists Bookings (547)
Symphony Orchestras:
Pinellas Youth Symphony, 3
Tampa Bay Youth Orchestras, 4
The Florida Orchestra, 150
Opera Companies:
Florida Opera Company, 2
Spanish Lyric Theatre, 12
Professional Theatres:
The American Stage Company, 120
The Playmakers, 140
Dance Company:
The Tampa Ballet, 30
Places Rated Score: 1,835
Places Rated Rank: 28

Terre Haute, IN
Public Libraries (129 points):
6 branches, 303,571 volumes
Books added per year: 17,178
Art Museums/Galleries (100 points):
1 private, 1 university
Sheldon Swope Art Gallery
The Lively Arts Calendar (26 points):
Touring Artists Bookings (12)
Symphony Orchestra:
Terre Haute Symphony Orchestra, 14
Places Rated Score: 255
Places Rated Rank: 242

Texarkana, TX–Texarkana, AR
Fine Arts Broadcasting (65 points):
Concert Radio: KTXK-FM 91.5, 65 hours
Public Libraries (45 points):
3 branches, 155,705 volumes
Books added per year: 5,444
The Lively Arts Calendar (25 points):
Touring Artists Bookings (25)
Places Rated Score: 135
Places Rated Rank: 302

Toledo, OH
Fine Arts Broadcasting (346 points):
Concert Radio: WGTE-FM 91.3, 146 hours
Non-Commercial TV: WBGU Channel 27
WGTE Channel 30
Public Libraries (229 points):
35 branches, 2,191,025 volumes
Books added per year: 140,766
Art Museums/Galleries (100 points):
2 private
Toledo Museum of Art
The Lively Arts Calendar (107 points):
Touring Artists Bookings (32)
Symphony Orchestras:
Bowling Green Philharmonia, 7
Toledo Symphony Orchestra, 65
Opera company:
Toledo Opera, 3
Places Rated Score: 782
Places Rated Rank: 79

Topeka, KS
Fine Arts Broadcasting (100 points):
Non-Commercial TV: KTWU Channel 11
Public Libraries (110 points):
3 branches, 327,077 volumes
Books added per year: 17,803
Art Museums/Galleries (100 points):
1 private, 1 university
Mulvane Art Center
The Lively Arts Calendar (10 points):
Touring Artists Bookings (10)
Places Rated Score: 320
Places Rated Rank: 209

Trenton, NJ
Fine Arts Broadcasting (228 points):
Concert Radio: WPRB-FM 103.3, 29 hours
WWFM-FM 89.1, 99 hours
Non-Commercial TV: WJNT Channel 52
Public Libraries (206 points):
6 branches, 1,172,673 volumes
Books added per year: 67,335
Art Museums/Galleries (100 points):
1 civic, 1 university
Princeton University Museum of Art
The Lively Arts Calendar (235 points):
Touring Artists Bookings (87)
Symphony Orchestras:
Greater Princeton Youth Orchestra, 3
The Chamber Symphony of
Princeton, 5

Professional Theatre:
McCarter Theatre, 140
CMSA Access: Philadelphia–Wilmington–
Trenton, PA–NJ–DE–MD (356 points)
Places Rated Score: 1,125
Places Rated Rank: 51

Tucson, AZ
Fine Arts Broadcasting (289 points):
Concert Radio: KUAT-FM 90.5, 147 hours
KXCI-FM 91.7, 42 hours
Non-Commercial TV: KUAT Channel 6
Public Libraries (136 points):
19 branches, 820,067 volumes
Books added per year: 85,808
Art Museums/Galleries (300 points):
4 private, 2 university
Tucson Museum of Art
University of Arizona Museum of Art
The Lively Arts Calendar (248 points):
Touring Artists Bookings (48)
Symphony Orchestras:
Civic Orchestra of Tucson, 4
Philharmonia Orchestra of Tucson, 9
Tucson Symphony Orchestra, 51
Opera Company:
Arizona Opera Company, 16
Professional Theatre:
Arizona Theatre Company, 120
Places Rated Score: 973
Places Rated Rank: 61

Tulsa, OK
Fine Arts Broadcasting (369 points):
Concert Radio: KCMA-FM 92.1, 126 hours
KWGS-FM 89.5, 43 hours
Non-Commercial TV: KOED Channel 11
KXON Channel 35
Public Libraries (173 points):
21 branches, 1,040,759 volumes
Books added per year: 130,060
Art Museums/Galleries (100 points):
2 private
Gilcrease Institute
Philbrook Art Center
The Lively Arts Calendar (302 points):
Touring Artists Bookings (65)
Symphony Orchestras:
Oklahoma Sinfonia and Tulsa Pops, 12
Tulsa Philharmonic Orchestra, 40
Tulsa Youth Symphony Orchestra, 5
Opera Company:
Tulsa Opera, 10
Professional Theatre:
American Theatre Company, 120
Dance Company:
Tulsa Ballet Theater, 50
Places Rated Score: 944
Places Rated Rank: 63

Tuscaloosa, AL
Fine Arts Broadcasting (45 points):
Concert Radio: WUAL-FM 91.5, 45 hours
Public Libraries (24 points):
3 branches, 154,053 volumes
Books added per year: 3,474
Art Museum/Gallery (50 points):
1 university
The Lively Arts Calendar (22 points):
Touring Artists Bookings (15)
Symphony Orchestra:
Tuscaloosa Symphony Orchestra, 7
Places Rated Score: 141
Places Rated Rank: 297

Tyler, TX
Public Libraries (17 points):
2 branches, 112,080 volumes
Books added per year: 2,731
Art Museum/Gallery (50 points):
1 private
Tyler Museum of Art
The Lively Arts Calendar (20 points):
Touring Artists Bookings (10)
Symphony Orchestras:
East Texas Symphony Orchestra, 6
Tyler Youth Orchestra, 4
Places Rated Score: 87
Places Rated Rank: 324

Utica–Rome, NY
Fine Arts Broadcasting (150 points):
Concert Radio: WUNY-FM 89.5, 150 hours
Public Libraries (295 points):
34 branches, 659,335 volumes
Books added per year: 92,987
Art Museums/Galleries (150 points):
3 private
Munson-Williams-Proctor Institute
The Lively Arts Calendar (72 points):
Touring Artists Bookings (67)
Symphony Orchestra:
Utica Symphony, 5
Places Rated Score: 667
Places Rated Rank: 98

Vallejo–Fairfield–Napa, CA
Public Libraries (89 points):
13 branches, 870,059 volumes
Books added per year: 38,075
Art Museum/Gallery (50 points):
1 private
The Lively Arts Calendar (44 points):
Touring Artists Bookings (30)
Symphony Orchestra:
Napa Valley Symphony, 14
CMSA Access: San Francisco–Oakland–
San Jose, CA (516 points)
Places Rated Score: 704
Places Rated Rank: 91

Vancouver, WA
Public Libraries (189 points):
7 branches, 375,668 volumes
Books added per year: 41,852
Art Museum/Gallery (50 points):
1 private
The Lively Arts Calendar (6 points):
Touring Artists Bookings (6)
CMSA Access: Portland–Vancouver, OR
(86 points)
Places Rated Score: 331
Places Rated Rank: 202

Victoria, TX
Public Library (82 points):
1 branch, 111,261 volumes
Books added per year: 6,384
The Lively Arts Calendar (16 points):
Touring Artists Bookings (11)
Symphony Orchestra:
Victoria Symphony Society, 5
Places Rated Score: 98
Places Rated Rank: 317

Vineland–Millville–Bridgeton, NJ
Public Libraries (112 points):
6 branches, 393,104 volumes
Books added per year: 15,362

The Lively Arts Calendar (4 points):
  Symphony Orchestra:
    Bridgeton Symphony, 4
CMSA Access: Philadelphia–Wilmington–
  Trenton, PA–NJ–DE–MD (356 points)
Places Rated Score: 472
Places Rated Rank: 145

Visalia–Tulare–Porterville, CA
Public Libraries (52 points):
  23 branches, 573,542 volumes
  Books added per year: 15,280
Places Rated Score: 52
Places Rated Rank: 332

Waco, TX
Fine Arts Broadcasting (30 points):
  Concert Radio: KWBU-FM 107.5, 30 hours
Public Libraries (43 points):
  6 branches, 290,279 volumes
  Books added per year: 8,227
Art Museum/Gallery (50 points):
  1 private
The Lively Arts Calendar (16 points):
  Touring Artists Bookings (11)
  Symphony Orchestra:
    Waco Symphony Orchestra, 5
Places Rated Score: 139
Places Rated Rank: 299

★ Washington, DC–MD–VA
Fine Arts Broadcasting (816 points):
  Concert Radio: WGMS-FM 103.5, 168
    hours
    WGTS-FM 91.9, 148 hours
  Non-Commercial TV: WCPT Channel 36
    WETA Channel 26
    WFPT Channel 62
    WHMM Channel 32
    WNVC Channel 56
Public Libraries (142 points):
  134 branches, 6,862,429 volumes
  Books added per year: 531,862
Art Museums/Galleries (1,550 points):
  3 civic, 24 private, 4 university
  Corcoran Gallery of Art
  Hirshhorn Museum and Sculpture Garden
  National Gallery of Art
  National Museum of African Art
  National Museum of American Art
  National Portrait Gallery
  Phillips Collection
  University of Maryland Art Gallery
The Lively Arts Calendar (1,670 points):
  Touring Artists Bookings (622)
  Symphony Orchestras:
    Alexandria Symphony Orchestra, 12
    Amadeus Orchestra, 6
    Arlington Symphony, 8
    DC Youth Orchestra, 100
    District of Columbia Community
      Orchestra, 5
    Fairfax Symphony Orchestra, 30
    George Mason University Symphony
      Orchestra, 4
    Georgetown Symphony, 4
    Handel Festival Orchestra, 9
    Howard University Civic Orchestra, 4
    McLean Orchestra, 7
    Montgomery County Youth
      Orchestra, 8
    National Chamber Orchestra, 24
    National Symphony Orchestra, 180
    Northern Virginia Youth Symphony, 5
    Prince George's Philharmonic
      Orchestra, 7

Prince William Symphony Orchestra, 7
    The Virginia Chamber Orchestra, 6
    Urban Philharmonic Society, 4
    Youth Orchestra of Prince William, 2
  Opera Companies:
    Summer Opera Theatre, 11
    Washington Concert Opera, 2
    Washington Opera, 61
    Wolf Trap Opera Company, 8
  Professional Theatres:
    Arena Stage, 120
    Ford's Theatre, 40
    Living Stage Theatre Company, 40
    New Playwrights' Theatre, 20
    Round House Theatre, 100
    Shakespeare Theatre at the Folger, 80
    The Studio Theatre, 100
  Dance Company:
    Washington Ballet, 34
Places Rated Score: 4,178
Places Rated Rank: 4

Waterbury, CT
Public Libraries (119 points):
  13 branches, 474,674 volumes
  Books added per year: 25,784
Art Museum/Gallery (50 points):
  1 private
The Lively Arts Calendar (5 points):
  Symphony Orchestra:
    Waterbury Symphony Orchestra, 5
Places Rated Score: 174
Places Rated Rank: 280

Waterloo–Cedar Falls, IA
Fine Arts Broadcasting (226 points):
  Concert Radio: KHKE-FM 89.5, 84 hours
    KUNI-FM 90.9, 42 hours
  Non-Commercial TV: KRIN Channel 32
Public Libraries (98 points):
  13 branches, 505,718 volumes
  Books added per year: 14,810
Art Museums/Galleries (100 points):
  1 civic, 1 university
The Lively Arts Calendar (38 points):
  Touring Artists Bookings (14)
  Symphony Orchestras:
    Wartburg Community Symphony, 4
    Waterloo–Cedar Falls Symphony
      Orchestra, 20
Places Rated Score: 462
Places Rated Rank: 153

Wausau, WI
Fine Arts Broadcasting (100 points):
  Non-Commercial TV: WHRM Channel 20
Public Libraries (124 points):
  11 branches, 195,345 volumes
  Books added per year: 14,077
Art Museum/Gallery (50 points):
  1 private
  Woodson Art Museum
The Lively Arts Calendar (26 points):
  Touring Artists Bookings (20)
  Symphony Orchestra:
    The Wausau Symphony, 6
Places Rated Score: 300
Places Rated Rank: 222

West Palm Beach–Boca Raton–Delray Beach, FL
Fine Arts Broadcasting (200 points):
  Concert Radio: WXEL-FM 90.7, 100 hours
  Non-Commercial TV: WXEL Channel 42
Public Libraries (115 points):
  19 branches, 774,428 volumes
  Books added per year: 99,222

Art Museums/Galleries (250 points):
  5 private
  Norton Gallery and School of Art
  Society of the Four Arts Museum
The Lively Arts Calendar (220 points):
  Touring Artists Bookings (45)
  Symphony Orchestras:
    Boca Raton Symphonic Pops, 40
    Greater Palm Beach Symphony, 16
    Palm Beach Symphonette, 4
  Opera Company:
    Palm Beach Opera, 7
  Professional Theatre:
    Caldwell Theatre Company, 80
  Dance Company:
    Ballet Florida, 28
Places Rated Score: 785
Places Rated Rank: 78

Wheeling, WV–OH
Public Libraries (137 points):
  12 branches, 473,699 volumes
  Books added per year: 24,182
The Lively Arts Calendar (157 points):
  Touring Artists Bookings (120)
  Symphony Orchestras:
    Ovations Youth Orchestra, 2
    Wheeling Symphony Orchestra, 20
  Dance Company:
    Parkersburg/Wheeling Civic Ballet, 15
Places Rated Score: 294
Places Rated Rank: 226

Wichita, KS
Fine Arts Broadcasting (238 points):
  Concert Radio: KMUW-FM 89.1, 30 hours
    KSOF-FM 91.1, 108 hours
  Non-Commercial TV: KPTS Channel 8
Public Libraries (41 points):
  35 branches, 973,498 volumes
  Books added per year: 60,730
Art Museums/Galleries (250 points):
  4 private, 1 university
  Wichita Art Museum
The Lively Arts Calendar (80 points):
  Touring Artists Bookings (16)
  Symphony Orchestras:
    Wichita Symphony Orchestra, 60
    Wichita Youth Orchestras, 4
Places Rated Score: 609
Places Rated Rank: 114

Wichita Falls, TX
Public Libraries (142 points):
  4 branches, 174,855 volumes
  Books added per year: 5,246
Art Museum/Gallery (50 points):
  1 private
  Wichita Falls Art Center and Museum
The Lively Arts Calendar (12 points):
  Touring Artists Bookings (6)
  Symphony Orchestra:
    Wichita Falls Symphony Orchestra, 6
Places Rated Score: 204
Places Rated Rank: 266

Williamsport, PA
Public Libraries (73 points):
  5 branches, 157,603 volumes
  Books added per year: 8,505
The Lively Arts Calendar (16 points):
  Touring Artists Bookings (10)
  Symphony Orchestra:
    Williamsport Symphony Orchestra, 6
Places Rated Score: 89
Places Rated Rank: 322

Wilmington, DE–NJ–MD
Public Libraries (84 points):
  21 branches, 936,829 volumes
  Books added per year: 47,273
Art Museums/Galleries (150 points):
  2 private, 1 university
  Delaware Art Museum
The Lively Arts Calendar (261 points):
  Touring Artists Bookings (97)
  Symphony Orchestra:
    Delaware Symphony Orchestra, 55
  Opera Company:
    Opera Delaware, 9
  Professional Theatre:
    Delaware Theatre Company, 100
  CMSA Access: Philadelphia–Wilmington–
    Trenton, PA–NJ–DE–MD (356 points)
Places Rated Score: 851
Places Rated Rank: 70

Wilmington, NC
Fine Arts Broadcasting (175 points):
  Concert Radio: WHQR-FM 91.3, 75 hours
  Non-Commercial TV: WUNJ Channel 39
Public Libraries (148 points):
  3 branches, 185,240 volumes
  Books added per year: 17,767
Art Museum/Gallery (50 points):
  1 private
  St. John's Museum of Art
The Lively Arts Calendar (13 points):
  Touring Artists Bookings (8)
  Symphony Orchestra:
    Wilmington Symphony Orchestra, 5
Places Rated Score: 386
Places Rated Rank: 182

Worcester, MA
Fine Arts Broadcasting (40 points):
  Concert Radio: WICN-FM 90.5, 40 hours
Public Libraries (164 points):
  39 branches, 1,836,179 volumes
  Books added per year: 69,661
Art Museums/Galleries (100 points):
  1 civic, 1 private
  Worcester Art Museum
The Lively Arts Calendar (103 points):
  Touring Artists Bookings (99)
  Symphony Orchestra:
    Bach Society of Worcester, 4
Places Rated Score: 407
Places Rated Rank: 175

Yakima, WA
Fine Arts Broadcasting (100 points):
  Non-Commercial TV: KYVE Channel 47
Public Libraries (129 points):
  21 branches, 317,936 volumes
  Books added per year: 23,841
Art Museum/Gallery (50 points):
  1 private
The Lively Arts Calendar (30 points):
  Touring Artists Bookings (23)
  Symphony Orchestra:
    Yakima Symphony Orchestra, 7
Places Rated Score: 309
Places Rated Rank: 217

York, PA
Public Libraries (82 points):
  17 branches, 396,512 volumes
  Books added per year: 33,232

The Lively Arts Calendar (48 points):
  Touring Artists Bookings (31)
  Symphony Orchestras:
    Gettysburg College Community
      Orchestra, 2
    York Symphony Orchestra, 9
    York Youth Symphony, 6
Places Rated Score: 130
Places Rated Rank: 303

Youngstown–Warren, OH
Fine Arts Broadcasting (114 points):
  Concert Radio: WYSU-FM 88.5, 114 hours
Public Libraries (136 points):
  21 branches, 1,070,938 volumes
  Books added per year: 69,439
Art Museums/Galleries (100 points):
  1 private, 1 university
The Lively Arts Calendar (228 points):
  Touring Artists Bookings (135)
  Symphony Orchestras:
    Warren Chamber Orchestra, 10
    Youngstown State University
      Community Orchestra, 12
    Youngstown Symphony Orchestra, 23
  Dance Company:
    Ballet Western Reserve, 48
Places Rated Score: 578
Places Rated Rank: 123

Yuba City, CA
Public Libraries (86 points):
  6 branches, 238,354 volumes
  Books added per year: 9,985
The Lively Arts Calendar (9 points):
  Touring Artists Bookings (9)
Places Rated Score: 95
Places Rated Rank: 319

Et Cetera

FOLK ART IN AMERICA

Folk art is where you find it. And in one form or another—be it music, ethnic food traditions, games, sayings, rhymes, crafts, or simple street pastimes—that's just about everywhere you care to look.

The Midwest has festivals celebrating the customs of Germany, Sweden, Norway, Poland, and Lithuania. In the East, festivals honor Greeks, Italians, and Portuguese. Black Americans celebrate their history in ballads, blues, and gospel songs. In New Orleans, these oral traditions combine with instruments and modern city blues to create the renowned sound of New Orleans jazz.

Some festivals center on events. They celebrate the harvest, the making of wine, and the departure of fishing fleets. Some festivals are religious; others honor national or local heroes; still others reflect the workaday origins of a region, such as the logging festivals of the Northwest and the steam-thresher revivals on the Great Plains.

The list of festivals that follows has been compiled by the National Council for the Traditional Arts, in Washington, DC, and the various state folk arts coordinators.

Selected Folk Festivals, by State

ALABAMA
Mobile Jazz Festival
Mobile
Early May

Tennessee Valley Old Time Fiddlers
  Convention
Athens
Early October

ALASKA
Little Norway Festival
Petersburg
Mid-May

ARIZONA
"Tucson Meet Yourself"
A celebration of traditions of the Southwest

Tucson
2nd weekend in October

WA:K Annual Pow Wow
Authentic Indian ceremonies and crafts fair
Tucson
Early to mid-March

ARKANSAS
Arkansas Folk Festival
Traditional music, bluegrass
Mountain View
Mid-April

"Back in the Hills" Antique Show and
   Folklife Fair
Crafts, demonstrations, games
War Eagle (near Hindsville)
Early May

CALIFORNIA
Fiesta de la Primavera
Mexican mariachi bands and Spanish
   dancers
Old Town, San Diego
Mid-May

Ghost Mountain Bluegrass Festival
Pollock Pines
Late May

COLORADO
Colorado State Fair
Crafts, music, Western skills competition
Pueblo
Late August

Rocky Mountain Bluegrass Festival
Henderson
Late August

CONNECTICUT
Danbury State Fair
Danbury State Fairgrounds
Mid-July

DELAWARE
Delaware State Fair
Harrington
3rd week in July

DISTRICT OF COLUMBIA
Festival of American Folk Life
Sponsored by the Smithsonian Institution
Washington Monument grounds
Early October

FLORIDA
Florida Folk Festival
Native American folklore, crafts,
   demonstrations
White Springs
3rd week in May

Pioneer Days Festival
Traditional music, arts and crafts
Pine Castle Center of the Arts, Orlando
Last weekend in October

GEORGIA
Chattahoochee Folk Festival
Columbus
Last week in September

Georgia Sea Island Festival
Music of the Georgia coast
St. Simons Island
Mid-August

HAWAII
King Kamehameha Celebration
Traditional Hawaiian dances, storytelling
Honolulu
Early June

IDAHO
National Oldtime Fiddlers Contest
Weiser
Mid-June

ILLINOIS
International Folk Fair
Celebration of Chicago's ethnic diversity
Chicago
October

Pilsen Community *Fiesta del Sol*
Hispanic neighborhood celebration
Chicago
August

Southern Illinois Folk Festival
Emphasis on Indian and German-American
   traditions
Du Quoin
Late September

INDIANA
Annual Duneland Folk Festival
Chesterton and Porter
Mid-July

Annual Indiana Fiddlers Gathering
Battleground
Early September

Bean Blossom Festival
Bill Monroe's famous bluegrass festival
Bean Blossom
Mid-June

IOWA
Council Bluffs Old-Time Country Music
   Contest
Council Bluffs
Late August

Midwest Old Settlers and Threshers
   Reunion
Antique farm machinery, demonstrations,
   music
Mount Pleasant
Late August

Nordic Fest
One of the largest Norwegian-American
   celebrations in the country
Decorah
Late July

KANSAS
After Harvest Czech Festival
Wilson
3rd week in July

National Flat-Picking Championship
Guitar-playing competition
Winfield
Fall

Smoky Hill River Festival
Crafts, children's games
Salina
Mid-June

KENTUCKY
Celebration of Traditional Music
Berea
Late October

Kentucky Folklife Celebration
Traditional mountain music and dances
Louisville
Early June

LOUISIANA
Baton Rouge Blues Festival
Mostly black blues and gospel
Baton Rouge
Late April

Cajun Music Festival
Food, music
Lafayette
3rd week in September

Lagniappe on the Bayou
Cajun-Creole celebration
Chauvin
Mid-October

New Orleans Jazz and Heritage Festival
New Orleans
Mid-April

MAINE
Annual Fishermen's Festival
Blessing of the fleet, nautical contests
Boothbay Harbor
Late March

Heritage Days
Community celebration
Bath
Early July

MARYLAND
Colonial Highland Gathering
Scottish games, music, dances
Fair Hill
Early June

MASSACHUSETTS
Feast of St. Anthony
Italian religious feast
Boston (North End)
July

St. Peter's Fiesta
Italian-Portuguese fishing celebration
Gloucester
3rd week in June

MICHIGAN
Ann Arbor Council of Traditional Music and
   Dance
Ann Arbor
Early September

Wheatland Bluegrass and Old Time Music
   Festival
Remus
Early September

MINNESOTA
Forestville Arts and Crafts Festival
Forestville State Park, Preston
Early June

Laskiainen
Finnish celebration: logging, games, music
Palo–Markham
1st weekend in February

Paul Bunyan Festival
Brainerd
Late September

MISSISSIPPI
Delta Blues Festival
Black blues, spirituals
Greenville
Early September

Northeast Mississippi Blues and Gospel
   Festival
Traditional black music
Rust College, Holly Springs
Late September

MISSOURI
Frontier Folklife Festival
St. Louis
Mid-September

Missouri State Fiddling Championship
Columbia
Late August

Mountain Folks Music Festival
Music of the Ozarks
Silver Dollar City, Branson
Mid-June

MONTANA
Homesteaders Days
Hot Springs
Mid-June

NEBRASKA
Camp Creek Antique Machinery and
    Threshing Show
Old farm machinery, music, games, crafts
Waverly
3rd weekend in July

Kolachs Days
Czech celebration
Verdigre
Mid-June

Wilber Czech Festival
Wilber
Early August

NEVADA
Basque Festival
Elko
Early July

NEW HAMPSHIRE
Annual League of New Hampshire
    Craftsman's Fair
Carpentry, musical instruments, stained
    glass
Mount Sunapee State Park, Newbury
1st week in August

Canterbury Fair
Canterbury Center
Late July

New Hampshire Folk Festival
Concord
Last Sunday in August

NEW JERSEY
Middletown Folk Festival
Middletown
Mid-June

New Jersey Folk Festival at Douglass
    College
New Brunswick
Late April

NEW MEXICO
Feria de Artesanos
Arts and crafts show
Albuquerque
Late August

Indian Market
Native American crafts show
Santa Fe
Late August

Jickarilla Apache Tribal Fair
Dulce
Mid-July

Shalako Dance
Authentic religious ceremony
Zuni Pueblo
1st week in December

NEW YORK
Berkshire Mountains Bluegrass Festival
Ancram and Hillsdale
Late July

Festival of North Country Folklife
Robert Moses State Park, Massena
Early August

Scampagnata Folcloristica Italiana
Italian-American celebration
ARTPARK, Lewiston
Late June

NORTH CAROLINA
Annual Mountain Dance and Folk Festival
Asheville
Early August

Bascom Lamar Lunsford Mountain Music
    and Dance Festival
Mars Hill
Early October

World Champion Old Time Fiddlers
    Convention
Union Grove
1st week in April

NORTH DAKOTA
North Dakota Roughrider Days
Dickinson
Early July

OHIO
Gambier Folk Festival
Kenyon College, Gambier
Late October

Kent State Folk Festival
Kent
Late February

OKLAHOMA
American Indian Exposition
Anadarko
Mid-August

Grant's Annual Bluegrass and Oldtime
    Festival
Salt Creek Park, Hugo
Early August

World Series of Fiddling and Bluegrass
    Festival
Powderhorn Park, Langley
Late August

OREGON
State of Jefferson Days
Historic celebration
Klamath Falls
3 weekends in August

Willamette Valley Folk Festival
University of Oregon, Eugene
Mid-May

PENNSYLVANIA
Brandywine Mountain Music Convention
Concordville
Mid- to late July
Goshenhoppen Folk Festival
Small authentic Pennsylvania Dutch festival
East Greenville
2nd weekend in August

Harvest Days Festival
Landis Valley Farm Museum
Lancaster
Early October

Pittsburgh Folk Festival
Multi-ethnic celebration
Pittsburgh
Memorial Day weekend

RHODE ISLAND
Annual Usquepaug Johnnycake Festival
Historic festival
Richmond–South Kingstown
Late October

Blessing of the Fleet Festival
Newport
Late July

Cranberry Festival of the Tomaquag Indians
Exeter
Early October

SOUTH CAROLINA
Lee County Cotton Pickin Festival
Square dances, cotton picking, gospel
    music
Bishopville
Mid-October

Piccolo Spoleto Traditional Music Festival
One of the best festivals for fine arts
    lovers
Charleston
Late May–early June

SOUTH DAKOTA
Black Hills Bluegrass Festival
Nemo
July

Black Hills Steam Show and Threshing Bee
Antique farm machinery, music
Sturgis
Mid-August

South Dakota and Open Fiddling Contest
Yankton
3rd week in September

Steam Threshing Jamboree
Madison
3rd week in August

TENNESSEE
National Storytelling Festival
Jonesboro
Mid-September

Tennessee Grassroots Days
Centennial Park, Nashville
Late September–early October

Uncle Dave Macon Days
Traditional music and crafts
Murfreesboro
Early to mid-September

TEXAS
Annual Border Festival
Music, crafts, Mexican rodeo
El Paso
Early October

Texas Folklife Festival
Mexican and native American folklore,
    crafts
San Antonio
Late July

UTAH
Festival of the American West
Logan
Early August

Southern Utah Folklife Festival
Springdale
Early September

VERMONT
"Midsummer"
Traditional music, games, dances
Montpelier
Mid-July

Tunbridge Fair
Tunbridge
September

VIRGINIA
Blue Ridge Folklife Festival
Ferrum College, Ferrum
Late October

Sara–Maybelle Carter Memorial Festival
Abingdon
Late July–early August

WASHINGTON
The Festival of American Fiddle Tunes
Port Townsend
Late June–early July

Northwest Regional Folklife Festival
Seattle
3rd week in May

WEST VIRGINIA
Augusta Festival
Elkins
Early August

Vandalia Gathering
Traditional music, storytelling
State Capitol, Charleston
3rd week in May

WISCONSIN
Lakefront Summerfest
Multi-ethnic celebration
Summerfest Grounds, Milwaukee
Weekends, July-September

Polka Festival
Merrill
Mid-June

Swiss *Volksfest*
Swiss-American celebration
New Glarus
Early August

WYOMING
Cheyenne Frontier Days
Rodeo, horse racing, covered wagons
Cheyenne
3rd week in July

Wyoming State Fiddle Contest
Shoshoni
Memorial Day weekend

YWCA Ethnic Fest
Rock Springs
Mid-May

Recreation

After "Where's that?", the question people ask most often about an unfamiliar place is "Is there anything to do there?" Wherever they live, Americans want to make the most of their leisure time. This is evidenced by the billions of dollars spent each year on everything from video games to insulated jogging clothes, from season tickets at the ballpark to European vacations, from down-filled sleeping bags to graphite fishing rods.

But not everyone can take advantage of the myriad opportunities for recreation. A ski trip to Aspen or a golf weekend at Hilton Head Island is too costly for most people's budgets, and even a backpacking trip in a national park with nominal entrance fees and camping charges might be out of the question for the dollars and time it takes to get there and back.

Fortunately, there are many other things to do that are inexpensive and nearby. Movies, golf, bowling, and good restaurants are available almost everyplace in the country; in fact, people living in smaller metro areas usually have better access to these than residents of bigger metro areas. On the other hand, urban crowd pleasers such as zoos, family theme parks, professional sports arenas, and racetracks enhance leisure living in larger places. For more and more people, convenient outdoor recreation in a national forest or along a wild and scenic river is a lucky geographical circumstance;

the protected outdoors is a part of the landscape just as developed urban land is. *Places Rated Almanac* looks at each of these kinds of recreation in determining the best places to play in the United States.

COMMON DENOMINATORS

For scuba diving, the coasts of Florida, California, and Hawaii are your best bets. When it comes to skiing on powdery snow, certain parts of the country are better suited than others because of local topography and climate. The weather and the winds turn other areas into premier places for soaring in gliders. But there are certain kinds of recreation that you can find everywhere: dining out at a quality restaurant, a round of weekend golf, bowling at the local lanes, or moviegoing at a downtown picture palace or a suburban shopping mall.

Food, Glorious Food

If you're among the one in ten people who enjoys getting out of the house at least once a week for dinner, you might as well go to a worthwhile eatery instead of a portion-controlled Casa de la Maison where distantly prepared frozen packages of beef Wellington and veal *cordon bleu* are microwaved, dished out, and priced at ten times what the restaurant paid for them.

To determine the best metro areas in America for eating out, *Places Rated* consulted the seven-volume *Mobil Travel Guide*, which since 1958 has rated restaurants across the country. The ratings are derived from two sources: an extensive review of consumer comments, and the inspection reports of field representatives who dine anonymously at establishments throughout the year.

Restaurants are judged on the basis of their food, service, and ambience. Ratings range from one star for a "good, better-than-average" restaurant to five stars for "one of the country's best." Only a very few restaurants receive the coveted five stars in any given year; there were just nine top-rated restaurants across the nation in 1989.

Places Rated gauges access to good restaurants by dividing the resident population by the total number of quality stars awarded by *Mobil Travel Guide* to metro area restaurants. Four one-star restaurants and one three-star restaurant, for example, would yield seven quality stars. Therefore, even though Santa Fe has just 26 rated restaurants—not an overwhelming number when compared with the 182 found in New York, the most of any metro area—it can boast one quality star for every 1,886 residents, the best ratio among the metro areas. See the table below for the top 15 dining out areas.

The 15 Best Metro Areas for Dining Out

Metro Area	Quality Stars	Residents per Star
1. Santa Fe, NM	60	1,886
2. Pittsfield, MA	38	2,137
3. Salinas–Seaside–Monterey, CA	99	3,697
4. Reno, NV	64	3,730
5. Naples, FL	36	3,832
6. Billings, MT	27	4,421
7. Portsmouth–Dover–Rochester, NH–ME	49	4,825
8. Burlington, VT	26	5,103
9. Portland, ME	40	5,319
10. Glens Falls, NY	20	5,701
11. Fort Myers–Cape Coral, FL	52	6,152
12. Atlantic City, NJ	51	6,170
13. Rochester, MN	16	6,375
14. Elmira, NY	14	6,416
15. Las Vegas, NV	97	6,511

Source: Mobil Travel Guide (7 vols.), 1989.

Thirty-one metro areas have no restaurants awarded quality ratings by *Mobil Travel Guide*: Alexandria, LA; Anderson, IN; Anderson, SC; Athens, GA; Bloomington–Normal, IL; Brazoria, TX; Bristol, CT; Burlington, NC; Chico, CA; Danville, VA; Florence, SC; Gadsden, AL; Hickory, NC; Houma–Thibodaux, LA; Jacksonville, NC; Longview–Marshall, TX; Merced, CA; Midland, TX; New Britain, CT; Olympia, WA; Pine Bluff, AR; St. Joseph, MO; Sherman–Denison, TX; Steubenville–Weirton, OH–WV; Texarkana, TX–Texarkana, AR; Tyler, TX; Vancouver, WA; Victoria, TX; Vineland–Millville–Bridgeton, NJ; Yakima, WA; and Yuba City, CA.

Public Golf Links

Certainly golf is a common denominator; the game is played in every U.S. metro area, including Anchorage, AK. There are three options when it comes to finding a local golf course on an idle, sunny weekend: the private equity course, which is typically part of a country club

open only to members and their guests; daily-fee operations open to all players; and city-built and -operated courses, again open to everyone.

If you're a golfer who can afford to join a private country club with an 18-hole course, you've got one big advantage aside from all the dances and dinners you're paying dues for: You belong to the fortunate 14 percent of golfers who don't have to wait to tee off at a crowded municipal or daily-fee course. Two Florida metro areas (Fort Pierce and West Palm Beach–Boca Raton–Delray Beach) and two affluent suburban metro areas (Lake County, IL, north of Chicago, and Stamford, CT, near New York) have the most 18-hole private equity courses per capita in the nation.

On the other hand, if you're one of the country's 23 million golfers who've played a round at a local municipal or daily-fee course, only six out of every ten of the nation's 13,626 courses are open to you. Interestingly, the best access to city-owned and -operated courses is not in the upscale metro areas of Texas, California, or the Pacific Northwest but in the small metro areas of the Heartland, in Bismarck, ND; Terre Haute, IN; Waterloo–Cedar Falls, IA; and Rochester, MN.

Because access to public golf is an excellent reflection of recreation opportunities in metro areas, *Places Rated* counts the number of local municipal and daily-fee holes per capita. See the tables that follow for the 10 best and 10 worst areas for access to public golf.

Access to Public Links

The 10 Best Metro Areas	Residents per Golf Hole	The 10 Worst Metro Areas	Residents per Golf Hole
1. Jackson, MI	594	1. Bristol, CT	*
2. Sarasota, FL	683	2. Gadsden, AL	*
3. Kankakee, IL	771	3. Hagerstown, MD	*
4. Glens Falls, NY	792	4. Jackson, TN	*
5. Lorain–Elyria, OH	806	5. Jersey City, NJ	61,768
6. Kenosha, WI	836	6. New York, NY	20,243
7. Rochester, MN	872	7. Montgomery, AL	17,128
8. Battle Creek, MI	936	8. Albany, GA	13,331
9. Sheboygan, WI	947	9. Texarkana, TX–Texarkana, AR	13,320
10. Fort Myers–Cape Coral, FL	961	10. Modesto, CA	12,146

Source: Derived from National Golf Foundation, unpublished data, and Woods & Poole Economics, Inc., population forecasts, 1989.

The metro area average for public golf is one hole for every 3,147 people.

*These metro areas have no public golf courses.

Bowling

In "Rip Van Winkle," Washington Irving compared the sound of a hardwood ball striking hardwood pins to an ominous clap of thunder. This short story first appeared in 1819, a few years before the sport moved indoors to lanes built in the larger American cities for bowlers, typically Germans, who wanted to play year-round. Bowling has been around a long, long time indeed and, in all its variations—skittles, fivepins, ninepins, tenpins, candlepins, duckpins—is probably played by more of the world's people than any other game, with the possible exception of soccer.

Nearly 70 million people in the United States take a turn each year at tenpins, the dominant bowling variation. But if the 9,000 bowling centers in this country had to depend solely on this kind of casual participation, many might quickly convert to tanning salons or microcomputer showrooms for a steadier income. The credit for keeping bowling alleys in business goes to such highly organized competitive associations as the American Bowling Congress, the International Candlepin Bowling Association, and the National Duckpin Bowling Congress, which promote frequent tournaments throughout the country.

Access to Bowling

The 10 Best Metro Areas	Residents per Lane	The 10 Worst Metro Areas	Residents per Lane
1. Appleton–Oshkosh–Neenah, WI	522	1. Montgomery, AL	14,014
2. Wausau, WI	536	2. Sarasota, FL	11,265
3. Muskegon, MI	589	3. McAllen–Edinburg–Mission, TX	7,479
4. Glens Falls, NY	606	4. Jackson, MS	6,519
5. Erie, PA	634	5. Lynchburg, VA	5,195
6. Great Falls, MT	649	6. Florence, SC	4,962
7. Sharon, PA	664	7. Miami–Hialeah, FL	4,957
8. Sheboygan, WI	682	8. Tyler, TX	4,895
9. Racine, WI	683	9. Bradenton, FL	4,828
10. Mansfield, OH	704	10. Tuscaloosa, AL	4,491

Source: Derived from unpublished data from American Bowling Congress, International Candlepin Bowling Association, National Duckpin Bowling Congress, and Woods & Poole Economics, Inc., population forecasts, 1989.

The metro area average for bowling lanes is one for every 1,680 residents.

To rate metro areas for access to bowling, *Places Rated* compares the number of lanes with the local population (see the table entitled "Access to Bowling"). Metro areas that lead the country in this common denominator are typically smaller, blue-collar metro areas in the Frost Belt, where indoor sports and active teams thrive.

CROWD PLEASERS

At different times of the year, a resident of the Los Angeles–Long Beach, CA, metro area can view the animals at the Los Angeles Zoo; sample the varied offerings at Marineland of the Pacific and the Universal Studios Tour; watch auto racing at the Long Beach Grand Prix; bet on the horses at two thoroughbred racetracks; or take in professional baseball, football, basketball, and hockey, as well as NCAA Division I competition.

Few metro areas have as varied a supply of crowd pleasers as Los Angeles–Long Beach, but some of these opportunities are common in many of the larger metro areas. From Disneyland in Anaheim, CA, to New York's Bronx Zoo, these attractions offer Americans interesting ways to spend their leisure time.

Seeing the Animals: Zoos and Aquariums

The two best metro areas for seeing the animals are Chicago and San Diego. Each has not one but two of the country's top-ranked zoological parks. Altogether, 98 metro areas have at least one zoo accredited by the American Association of Zoological Parks and Aquari-

The 19 Most Popular Zoos and Aquariums

Zoo	Specimens	Annual Visitors	Zoo	Specimens	Annual Visitors
1. Lincoln Park Zoological Gardens — Chicago, IL	1,845	4,500,000	11. National Aquarium — Baltimore, MD	7,502	1,450,000
2. San Diego Zoo — San Diego, CA	3,888	3,800,000	12. Philadelphia Zoological Garden — Philadelphia, PA	1,526	1,300,000
3. National Zoological Park — Washington, DC	4,181	3,000,000	13. Cincinnati Zoo & Botanical Garden — Cincinnati, OH	407,402	1,287,037
4. New York Zoological Park — Bronx, NY	5,512	2,500,000	14. New England Aquarium — Boston, MA	7,606	1,200,000
5. St. Louis Zoological Park — St. Louis, MO	2,346	2,287,357	15. San Diego Wild Animal Park — Escondido, CA	2,444	1,200,000
6. Chicago Zoological Park — Brookfield, IL	2,200	1,950,000	16. Denver Zoological Gardens — Denver, CO	1,159	1,148,478
7. Houston Zoological Gardens — Houston, TX	2,464	1,771,029	17. San Francisco Zoological Gardens — San Francisco, CA	6,867	1,142,386
8. Milwaukee County Zoological Gardens — Milwaukee, WI	1,516	1,700,000	18. San Antonio Zoological Gardens — San Antonio, TX	3,612	1,000,000
9. Monterey Bay Aquarium — Monterey, CA	104,048	1,700,000	18. John G. Shedd Aquarium — Chicago, IL	7,658	1,000,000
10. Los Angeles Zoo — Los Angeles, CA	1,992	1,650,000			

Source: American Association of Zoological Parks and Aquariums, *Zoological Parks and Aquariums in the Americas*, 1989.

ums. The idea that zoos enhance people's lives is a European one that flourishes especially well in America's Midwest. Besides Chicago's two great zoos, the Cincinnati, Cleveland, Detroit, Milwaukee, and St. Louis zoological parks are among the best in the United States. It is not coincidental that the working-class citizens of these cities can trace their roots to European countries—particularly Germany—that also have great zoos.

"Postage-stamp collecting" is the name that zookeepers give to the assembling of colorful animal specimens without regard to whether the animals fit and thrive in a zoo's limited space. This was once a sure way of drawing more patrons and carving out a reputation as an outstanding institution. Today, professionally run zoos have fewer species on exhibit but more specimens of each. The standard phylogenetic exhibits (grouping African lions with Bengal tigers, timber wolves with hyenas) are being replaced with ecological displays (wildlife in desert or mountain environments) and behavioral exhibits (hibernation, burrowing, nocturnalism) that group specimens more creatively and openly.

This isn't to say that zoos no longer maintain large, diverse collections, for the best American zoos are those with the biggest animal populations. But today the benchmark of a zoo's quality isn't simply how many animals it can keep or breed; just as important is how creatively and naturally the animals are exhibited.

Nineteen American zoos and aquariums are visited by at least a million people each year. All of them are city- or society-owned, and several are so well known that they attract many tourists. These zoos and aquariums are listed on the previous page.

Aquariums are far less common than zoos in the United States; in fact, only 11 of the 333 metro areas can boast one: Baltimore, Boston, Chicago, Cleveland, Dallas, Honolulu, Monterey, New York, San Francisco, Seattle, and Tacoma. Not surprisingly, eight of these metro areas are found in states with ocean coastlines. Unlike the great zoological parks, which are run municipally or by societies, some of the best aquariums (including Boston's New England Aquarium) are owned and operated for profit by private firms.

Family Theme Parks

The person who started it all was Walter Elias Disney; his creation was Disneyland. Because he ignored such time-honored features as a waterfront location and games of chance and skill, the amusement park industry viewed his 180-acre playland skeptically when it opened in Anaheim, California, in 1954. Disney's purpose was to use his famous cartoon characters and feature films as themes to structure a family-centered park more carefully than such parks as Chicago's Riverview or Ocean Park in Santa Monica, places avoided by families because of

The 25 Most Popular Theme Parks

Park (Opening Year)	Operating Schedule	Annual Visitors	Park (Opening Year)	Operating Schedule	Annual Visitors
1. **Walt Disney World & Epcot Center** (1971)—Orlando, FL	365 days	12,560,000	14. **Opryland USA** (1972) Nashville, TN	140 days	2,290,000
2. **Disneyland** (1954) Anaheim, CA	303 days	10,420,000	15. **Six Flags Over Georgia** (1967)—Atlanta, GA	148 days	2,180,000
3. **Knott's Berry Farm** (1920) Buena Park, CA	365 days	4,000,000	16. **Busch Gardens—The Old Country** (1975) Williamsburg, VA	137 days	1,920,000
4. **Universal Studios Tour** (1964)—Los Angeles, CA	365 days	3,450,000	17. **Marriott's Great America** (1976)—Santa Clara, CA	141 days	1,760,000
5. **Busch Gardens—The Dark Continent** (1959)—Tampa, FL	365 days	3,080,000	18. **Astroworld** (1968) Houston, TX	159 days	1,660,000
6. **Sea World of Florida** (1973) Orlando, FL	365 days	3,000,000	19. **Hersheypark** (1907) Hershey, PA	120 days	1,480,000
7. **Six Flags Great Adventure** (1974)—Jackson, NJ	163 days	2,760,000	20. **Worlds of Fun** (1973) Kansas City, MO	140 days	1,400,000
8. **Cedar Point** (1960) Sandusky, OH	119 days	2,630,000	21. **Sea World of Ohio** (1970) Aurora, OH	100 days	1,170,000
9. **Kings Island** (1972) Cincinnati, OH	126 days	2,601,000	22. **Six Flags Over Mid-America** (1971)—St. Louis, MO	140 days	1,120,000
10. **Six Flags Magic Mountain** (1971)—Valencia, CA	185 days	2,570,000	23. **Carowinds** (1973) Charlotte, NC	121 days	1,113,000
11. **Sea World of California** (1964)—San Diego, CA	365 days	2,560,000	24. **Cypress Gardens** (1936) Winter Haven, FL	365 days	1,112,000
12. **Six Flags Great America** (1976)—Gurnee, IL	365 days	2,370,000	25. **Kings Dominion** (1975) Richmond, VA	121 days	1,011,000
13. **Six Flags Over Texas** (1961) Arlington, TX	146 days	2,330,000			

Source: Kings Entertainment Company, 1984, and Merrill Lynch, *Theme Park Industry Survey,* 1983.

their tawdriness and cheap, carny atmosphere. That he succeeded is obvious; today, Disneyland and Walt Disney World in Florida—which includes the Magic Kingdom, opened in 1971, Epcot Center, opened in 1982, and MGM Studios Tour, opened in 1989—together attract more than 30 million people a year.

Of the nearly 100 parks in the United States that market themselves as family theme parks, there are 25 that each draw more than one million visitors a year (see the table entitled "The 25 Most Popular Theme Parks"). Twenty-two metro areas have at least one theme park with this many annual visitors. These extremely popular parks are located near or in large metro areas, but they aren't havens for locals in the way that traditional parks such as Elitch Gardens in Denver, Salt Lake City's Lagoon Amusement Park, or Lake Pontchartrain Beach in New Orleans still are. Rather, theme parks are nationally advertised vacation-industry attractions.

Two "vacation" states—California and Florida—have ten of the top 25 theme parks, attracting more than half of the country's annual 75 million theme-park visitors. In these states, some theme park owners have chosen their locations strategically. The Orlando metro area, for example, is home not only to Walt Disney World, Epcot Center, and MGM Studios Tour, but also Sea World of Florida, which located there to take advantage of Disney World's draw. In Southern California, Knott's Berry Farm, a traditional roadside attraction since 1920, converted to theme-park format and joined Sea World of California and Six Flags Magic Mountain in trying to capitalize on Disneyland's crowds.

The Auto-Racing Circuit

America's celebrated love affair with fast cars started in Providence, RI, where the first automobile track race was sponsored in 1896. The love affair hasn't ended, at least not for cars that hit 200 miles an hour on oval tracks. Typically, the 250,000 reserved seats for the Indianapolis 500 are sold out weeks before the race, in most instances at $55 per ticket. Whether on a "short eight" crash track in rural Oregon or a banked concrete oval in the Deep South, auto racing in all its variations draws millions of dollars each year.

Of the 900 auto racetracks in the United States, only a fraction are sanctioned by one or more of the leading racing organizations: NASCAR, SCCA, USAC, and IMSA. NASCAR, the National Association for Stock Car Racing, sanctions late-model and modified stock-car racing; SCCA, the Sports Car Club of America, has jurisdiction over sports-car events; USAC, the United States Automobile Club, sanctions Indy, dirt-car, sprint-car, midget, and late-model racing; and IMSA, the International Motor Sports Association, sanctions urban Grand Prix events.

Among the 81 metro areas with sanctioned tracks, Indianapolis deserves its title of automobile-racing center. Besides the famous Brickyard—the Indianapolis Motor Speedway—the Hoosier capital has two other sanctioned tracks. Thirteen other metro areas have two tracks (see the table entitled "Metro Areas with Two Sanctioned Auto Tracks").

Metro Areas with Two Sanctioned Auto Tracks

Atlanta, GA
Charlotte–Gastonia–Rock Hill, NC–SC
Chicago, IL
Dallas, TX
Daytona Beach, FL
Los Angeles–Long Beach, CA
Nashville, TN
Phoenix, AZ
Portland, OR
Richmond–Petersburg, VA
Rockford, IL
Savannah, GA
Seattle, WA

Source: National Speedway Directory, 1989.

Pari-Mutuel Betting: Win, Place, or Show Payoffs

The biggest spectator sport in the United States is pari-mutuel racing at the track. Based on a system in which the players who bet on the first-, second-, and third-place finishers share the total amount of money bet, pari-mutuel racing draws nearly 100 million people each year. Eighty-six metro areas offer pari-mutuel betting.

Thoroughbred racing dominates the American racing scene. There are 5,695 days of racing at the country's 56 thoroughbred tracks, exclusive of county fairs. See the table, "The 10 Most Popular Thoroughbred Tracks." Ak-Sar-Ben (Nebraska spelled backwards), is an 85-day, nonprofit civic meet held near downtown Omaha that attracts nearly a million racegoers. In the Los Angeles–Long Beach metro area, Santa Anita Park's two-part season draws close to three million spectators. Aqueduct's three-part season is one of the longest in thoroughbred racing, and although attendance has fallen over the years, the track draws almost as many fans as do the New York Yankees across town in the Bronx.

Standardbred horses are entered in harness racing; jockeys ride behind the horses in small, two-wheeled carts. Harness racing competes with thoroughbred racing for the racegoer's wager in 15 states. Its annual following at the track is a good deal smaller than that of thoroughbred racing (44 million versus 18 million racegoers). Refer to the table "The 10 Most Popular Harness Tracks." However, in Delaware, upstate New York, Michigan, and the Chicago environs, pacing and trotting races attract more bettors and a greater cash total in bets than their thoroughbred competition, and in Canada they outdraw thoroughbred races two to one.

The country cousin of the more citified and patrician thoroughbred contests, quarter-horse racing usually takes place at state and county fairs. It gets its name from the wide-open quarter-mile sprint the horses run on the track. Fourteen states permit betting on quarter-horse races, usually on mixed programs with thoroughbred

The 10 Most Popular Thoroughbred Tracks

Track	Average Daily Attendance	Average Bet
Santa Anita Park (Arcadia, CA)	30,014	$206
Hollywood Park (Inglewood, CA)	28,891	180
Saratoga (Saratoga Springs, NY)	28,407	124
Oaklawn Jockey Club (Hot Springs, AR)	20,775	123
Del Mar (Del Mar, CA)	19,584	167
Belmont Park (Elmont, NY)	19,530	177
Aqueduct (New York)	14,749	204
Meadowlands (East Rutherford, NJ)	14,233	151
Gulfstream Park (Hallandale, FL)	14,074	151
Ak-Sar-Ben (Omaha)	13,655	118

Source: Thoroughbred Racing Associations of North America, Inc., *Directory and Record Book*, 1988.

The 10 Most Popular Harness Tracks

Track	Average Daily Attendance	Average Bet
Meadowlands (East Rutherford, NJ)	16,010	$145
Sportsman's Park (Cicero, IL)	8,988	132
Roosevelt Raceway (Westbury, NY)	7,873	168
Hollywood Park (Inglewood, CA)	7,805	127
Hawthorne (Cicero, IL)	7,179	150
Yonkers Raceway (Yonkers, NY)	6,441	204
Maywood Park (Maywood, IL)	6,135	139
Los Alamitos (Cypress, CA)	5,499	150
Pompano Park (Pompano Beach, FL)	5,492	88
Hazel Park (Hazel Park, MI)	5,200	140

Source: U.S. Trotting Association, *Trotting and Pacing Guide*, 1988.

races. The sport is more popular in the West and Northwest than in any other region.

Dog racing evolved from the early sport of coursing, in which two greyhounds were released together in pursuit of a hare. Modern greyhound racing stems from a 1904 coursing contest held in South Dakota. Its sponsor, Owen Patrick Smith, developed a strong distaste for the killing of hares and spent the next 15 years adapting a mechanical lure to the inside rail of an oval track. The lure now resembles a rabbit and moves around the track on an electric rail. Since greyhounds chase by sight rather than scent, it has proven to be effective.

Of the country's 50 greyhound tracks, just ten account for half of dog racing's 26 million annual attendance. Wonderland is a twenty-minute subway ride from downtown Boston. Plainfield Greyhound Park, near Hartford, is Connecticut's sole pari-mutuel racetrack. The only place where people in western Tennessee, northern Mississippi, and northeastern Arkansas can make a legal bet is at Southland Greyhound Park, on the Arkansas side of the Mississippi River, near Memphis.

Rooting for the Home Team

A frequent topic of discussion on talk shows, in bars, and at work is where the "good" sports towns are. The question is usually argued from one of two perspectives: whether a town has teams with winning records, or whether fans turn out to root for the teams. These two trends are often linked: Over the regular seasons, the clubs with the best attendance usually also have had some of the best records.

Another way to find the best sports towns is to measure the access that a metro area's fans have to regular-season games (see the following table, "Access to Professional Sports: The Top 15 Metro Areas"). "Game seats per capita" is an elementary measurement used most often in professional sports franchising and marketing, especially at expansion time. This figure is found by multiplying the number of home games played by all the teams in a metro area (for example, 81 baseball; 41 basketball; 8 football) by the combined seating capacity of the teams' playing arenas and then dividing that number by the metro area's population.

Professional Sports. In arriving at a figure for game seats per capita at professional sporting events, *Places Rated* surveyed each of the 141 metro areas with major-league or minor-league teams in any of four sports: baseball, basketball, football, and hockey. For example, the number of regular-season football games played by the Indianapolis Colts multiplied by the Hoosier Dome's capacity is 480,000. The same calculations yield a figure of 1,037,000 for NBA Pacers basketball and Ice minor-league hockey games played in Market Square Arena, and 995,918 for Indians minor-league baseball games played at Bush Stadium. The sum of these four figures divided by Indianapolis's metro area population is 1.944, or a little less than two game seats for everyone in the eight-county metro area. Other metro areas have better averages, and in each of them the presence of a baseball team, with its large stadium and long playing season, makes a good deal of difference.

The western Massachusetts metro area of Pittsfield has the highest figure for game seats per capita of any metro area, due to its New York Mets minor-league farm club, the Pittsfield Mets, who play in a market with a

Access to Professional Sports: The Top 15 Metro Areas

Metro Area	Game Seats per Capita	Metro Area	Game Seats per Capita
1. Pittsfield, MA*	4.547	10. San Francisco, CA	3.140
2. Elmira, NY*	4.428	11. Huntsville, AL*	3.007
3. Milwaukee, WI	4.284	12. Charleston, WV*	2.909
4. Denver, CO	4.116	13. Buffalo, NY	2.790
5. Cleveland, OH	4.034	14. Rapid City, SD*	2.759
6. Seattle, WA	3.890	15. Minneapolis–St. Paul, MN–WI	2.751
7. Cedar Rapids, IA*	3.617		
8. Hagerstown, MD*	3.612		
9. Cincinnati, OH–KY–IN	3.279		

Source: Derived from professional sports media guides and Woods & Poole, Inc., population forecasts, 1989.

One hundred forty-one metro areas have professional sports teams.

*These metro areas have only minor-league teams.

population of only 81,200. But if you're interested in major-league sports, consider Milwaukee. Its American League Brewers, NBA Bucks, NFL Green Bay Packers (who play half of their home games in Milwaukee County Stadium), plus a minor-league hockey club, give it the best game–seats rating of metro areas with major-league sports franchises.

Collegiate Sports. Among the biggest crowd pleasers around are the varsity teams fielded by American colleges and universities. The cream of those is generally found among the teams classified Division I (split into Divisions I–A and I–AA for football only) by the National Collegiate Athletic Association (NCAA). Eligibility for this division is based on the quality of a school's typical opponent, or "schedule strength," and game attendance figures. The top ten areas for access to NCAA Division I sports are detailed in the adjacent table.

Nearly 37 million fans attended the 3,353 regular-season games played by the 667 colleges and universities with varsity football teams in 1988. Although the 191 Division I–A and I–AA teams played only one third of these games, they drew 83 percent of the attendance that year. Basketball is even more widely available. More than 32 million fans came out for the 16,596 regular-season and tournament games played by the 1,277 schools that had men's varsity basketball teams in 1988.

Access to NCAA Division I Sports: The Top Ten Metro Areas

Metro Area	Game Seats per Capita	Metro Area	Game Seats per Capita
1. Iowa City, IA	6.020	6. Lafayette–West Lafayette, IN	4.053
2. Lawrence, KS	5.913	7. Athens, GA	3.734
3. Bloomington, IN	4.525	8. Tuscaloosa, AL	3.692
4. State College, PA	4.329	9. Fayetteville–Springdale, AR	3.514
5. Columbia, MO	4.204	10. Bryan–College Station, TX	3.422

Source: National Collegiate Athletic Association, *NCAA Basketball* and *NCAA Football*, 1988.

One hundred fifty-six metro areas have NCAA Division I football or basketball teams.

The 290 NCAA Division I teams played one-quarter of these games, yet they accounted for 65 percent of total attendance.

Division I football or basketball is on view in 150 of the 329 metro areas, from the Cowboys of Hardin-Simmons in Abilene to the Penguins of Youngstown State. Using game seats per capita as the criterion, the best metro area for NCAA Division I football and basketball is Lawrence, KS. The number of University of Kansas Jayhawks games played at home multiplied by the seating capacities of Memorial Stadium (football) and Allen Fieldhouse (basketball) yield a figure of

A Football Odyssey

The first NFL franchise in Cleveland, Ohio, belonged not to the Browns but to the Rams, who played such opponents as the Brooklyn Dodgers, Chicago Cardinals, and Pittsburgh Pirates back in the 1930s.

Organized professional football as we know it today began to take shape in 1922 with the establishment of the National Football League, although the early teams seem ragtag in comparison to the computerized juggernauts of the 1980s. Through a series of splits and mergers with other leagues over the years, the NFL has remained the dominant pro football organization, and presently consists of 28 teams. The list below recaps the moves and name changes of today's NFL teams since their founding date.*

Detroit Lions—*1930*, began as the NFL Portsmouth (OH) Spartans; *1934*, moved to Detroit and renamed Detroit Lions.
Indianapolis Colts—*1952*, defunct Dallas Texans of the All-America Football Conference moved to Baltimore, renamed Baltimore Colts, and joined the NFL; *1983*, moved to Indianapolis and renamed Indianapolis Colts.
Kansas City Chiefs—*1959*, began as the Dallas Texans of the American Football League; *1963*, moved to Kansas City and renamed Kansas City Chiefs; *1970*, joined NFL.
Los Angeles Raiders—*1959*, began as Oakland Raiders of the American Football League; *1970*, joined NFL; *1982*, moved to Los Angeles and renamed Los Angeles Raiders.

Los Angeles Rams—*1937*, began as Cleveland Rams; *1946*, moved to Los Angeles and renamed Los Angeles Rams.
New England Patriots—*1959*, began as the Boston Patriots of the American Football League; *1970*, joined NFL; *1971*, renamed New England Patriots.
New York Jets—*1959*, began as New York Titans of the American Football League; *1963*, renamed New York Jets; *1970*, joined NFL.
Phoenix Cardinals—*1913*, began as Racine Avenue (Chicago) Cardinals; *1922*, renamed Chicago Cardinals; *1960*, moved to St. Louis and renamed St. Louis Cardinals; *1988*, moved to Phoenix and renamed Phoenix Cardinals.
San Diego Chargers—*1959*, franchised as the AFL Los Angeles Chargers; *1961*, moved to San Diego and renamed San Diego Chargers; *1970*, joined NFL.
Washington Redskins—*1932*, began as Boston Braves; *1933*, renamed Boston Redskins; *1937*, moved to Washington and renamed Washington Redskins.

Source: NFL Properties, *NFL Record and Fact Book*, 1984.

*The Chicago Bears (1922), Green Bay Packers (1922), New York Giants (1925), Philadelphia Eagles (1933), Pittsburgh Steelers (1933), Dallas Cowboys (1960), Minnesota Vikings (1960), Atlanta Falcons (1965), New Orleans Saints (1966), Seattle Seahawks (1974), and Tampa Bay Buccaneers (1974) began as NFL teams and have neither moved nor changed their team name.

The Cleveland Browns (1946) and San Francisco 49ers (1946) are former All-America Football Conference teams that joined the NFL in 1949.

The Buffalo Bills (1959), Denver Broncos (1959), Houston Oilers (1959), Miami Dolphins (1965), and Cincinnati Bengals (1967) are former American Football League franchises that merged with the NFL in 1970.

465,498, or almost seven game seats for everyone in town and in surrounding Douglas County.

OUTDOOR RECREATION ASSETS

To many people, recreation is not something that takes place within four walls or in the middle of a crowded city. Instead, it means turning to the open spaces for fishing, boating, swimming, hiking, running, picnicking, or getting away from it all. Just as some metro areas have more to offer in urban recreation, others undeniably are richer in access to the great outdoors.

Coastlines and Inland Water

Sooners boast that Oklahoma has so many impounded lakes of every size that if you were to tip the state to the south a bit, the water would flow out and flood Texas for a good while. And Maryland crabbers point out to newcomers that the true length of estuarine shore reached by the Chesapeake Bay's tide would total more than 8,000 miles if all the bends and kinks were straightened out.

You'll spot inland water in nine out of ten of America's metro areas. Aside from being a basic necessity of life, water can be a scenic and recreational amenity if there is enough of it to fish in, boat on, and swim in if the temperature is right. Where would Reno be without Lake Tahoe? Or Nassau–Suffolk, NY, without Long Island Sound?

See the following table for metro areas with large inland water areas. Four of every five Americans today are congregated together in metro areas within 100 miles of an ocean or Great Lakes coastline; in less than ten years, the U.S. Department of the Interior predicts, three of every four Americans will live within 50 miles of a coastline. Ocean or Great Lakes coastlines form part of the peripheries of 85 metro areas and 100 percent of one, Honolulu.

Large Areas of Inland Water

Metro Area	Inland Water Area	Percent of Total Surface Area
New Orleans, LA	1175.2 sq mi	33
Jersey City, NJ	15.7	25
Burlington, VT	132.1	23
Melbourne–Titusville–Palm Bay, FL	299	23
Fort Myers–Cape Coral, FL	238	23
Salt Lake City–Ogden, UT	477.5	23
Brownsville–Harlingen, TX	262.9	22
Galveston–Texas City, TX	101.1	20
San Francisco, CA	253.3	20
Nassau–Suffolk, NY	288.2	19
Portland, ME	112.7	17
Wilmington, NC	35.7	16

Source: U.S. Bureau of the Census, unpublished area measurements, 1980.

Inland water area includes ponds and lakes of surface area greater than 40 acres; streams, canals, and rivers if width is one eighth of a mile or greater; water area along irregular Great Lakes and ocean coastlines, if bays, inlets, and estuaries are between one and ten miles wide.

A Baseball Odyssey

Quick—What major-league baseball team is descended from the old Beaneaters? It's not the Boston Red Sox; in fact, it's not even an American League team. It's the Atlanta Braves.

This is just one of many odd and intriguing changes major-league baseball teams have undergone since 1876, when eight professional clubs joined forces to form the National League. Twenty-five years later, in 1901, the American League began play, also with eight teams. Since that time, many of the teams have changed names and moved from one city to another, and the leagues have expanded the number of franchises. The list below shows which of today's American League (AL) and National League (NL) teams have moved to another city and/or changed their name since their founding date.*

Atlanta Braves (NL)—*1876*, began as Boston Red Caps; *1883*, renamed Beaneaters; *1907*, renamed Doves; *1909*, renamed Pilgrims; *1936*, renamed Bees; *1941*, renamed Braves; *1953*, moved to Milwaukee and renamed Milwaukee Braves; *1966*, moved to Atlanta and renamed Atlanta Braves.
Baltimore Orioles (AL)—*1901*, began as Milwaukee Brewers; *1902*, moved to St. Louis and renamed St. Louis Browns; *1954*, moved to Baltimore and renamed Baltimore Orioles.
Boston Red Sox (AL)—*1901*, began as Somersets; *1905*, renamed Puritans; *1907*, renamed Red Sox.
California Angels (AL)—*1961*, began as Los Angeles Angels; *1965*, renamed California Angels.
Chicago Cubs (NL)—*1876*, began as White Stockings; *1894*, renamed Colts; *1898*, renamed Orphans; *1899*, renamed Cubs.
Cleveland Indians (AL)—*1901*, began as Bronchos; *1902*, renamed Blues; *1905*, renamed Naps; *1912*, renamed Molly McGuires; *1914*, renamed Indians.
Houston Astros (NL)—*1962*, began as Houston Colt .45's; *1964*, renamed Astros.
Los Angeles Dodgers (NL)—*1890*, began as Brooklyn Bridegrooms; *1898*, renamed Superbas; *1911*, renamed Dodgers; *1958*, moved to Los Angeles and renamed Los Angeles Dodgers.
Milwaukee Brewers (AL)—*1969*, began as Seattle Pilots; *1970*, moved to Milwaukee and renamed Milwaukee Brewers.
Minnesota Twins (AL)—*1901*, began as Washington Senators; *1960*, moved to Minneapolis–St. Paul and renamed Minnesota Twins.
New York Yankees (AL)—*1901*, began as Baltimore Orioles; *1903*, moved to New York and renamed New York Highlanders; *1912*, renamed Yankees.
Oakland A's (AL)—*1901*, began as Philadelphia Athletics; *1955*, moved to Kansas City and renamed Kansas City Athletics; *1968*, moved to Oakland and renamed Oakland Athletics; *1974*, renamed Oakland A's.
Pittsburgh Pirates (NL)—*1887*, began as Alleghenys; *1890*, renamed Innocents; *1891*, renamed Pirates.
San Francisco Giants (NL)—*1879*, began as Troy (NY) Trojans; *1883*, moved to New York City and renamed New York Gothams; *1886*, renamed Giants; *1958*, moved to San Francisco and renamed San Francisco Giants.
Texas Rangers (AL)—*1961*, began as Washington Senators; *1971*, moved to Arlington and renamed Texas Rangers.

Source: Joseph L. Reichler, ed., *Baseball Encyclopedia*, 1982.

*The Cincinnati Reds (NL, 1876), Philadelphia Phillies (NL, 1883), St. Louis Cardinals (NL, 1892), Chicago White Sox (AL, 1901), Detroit Tigers (AL, 1901), New York Mets (NL, 1962), Kansas City Royals (AL, 1969), Montreal Expos (NL, 1969), San Diego Padres (NL, 1969), Seattle Mariners (AL, 1977), and Toronto Blue Jays (AL, 1977) have neither changed their name nor moved.

Outdoor Recreation Assets: 17 Outstanding Metro Areas

Metro Area	Coastline (mi)	Inland Water Area (sq mi)	Acres in National Parks, Forests, Wildlife Refuges
Anchorage, AK	90	36.0	275,000
Bellingham, WA	—	53.7	841,958
Brownsville–Harlingen, TX	31	262.9	45,451
Eugene–Springfield, OR	30	48.1	1,416,153
Fort Collins–Loveland, CO	—	29.7	766,568
Galveston–Texas City, TX	25	165.0	—
Houma–Thibodaux, LA	79	632.8	—
Melbourne–Titusville–Palm Bay, FL	72	299.0	35,733
Miami–Hialeah, FL	84	67.1	605,117
New Orleans, LA	75	1,265.2	32,948
Provo–Orem, UT	—	126.9	485,642
Salt Lake City–Ogden, UT	—	477.5	201,480
San Francisco, CA	75	249.6	127,278
Santa Barbara–Santa Maria–Lompoc, CA	78	7.5	754,425
Seattle, WA	70	89.1	966,533
Tacoma, WA	15	113.1	365,990
Visalia–Tulare–Porterville, CA	—	3.0	1,403,459

Listed above in alphabetical order are the metro areas earning the maximum 2,000 points for their supply of Outdoor Recreation Assets. (See the section "Scoring: Recreation," for an explanation of how *Places Rated* points are calculated.)

National Forests, Parks, and Wildlife Refuges

Some of the most popular outdoor activities—driving for pleasure, walking, picnicking, sight-seeing, bird watching, nature walking, and fishing—would probably be even more enjoyable in the country's splendid system of national forests, parks, and wildlife refuges.

There are 156 national forests and 19 national grasslands on 191 million acres in the United States. The main purpose of the National Forest System is silviculture: growing wood, harvesting it carefully, and preserving naturally beautiful areas. Within the forest system are more than a quarter of a million miles of roads, built not only for loggers but for everyone. They lead to a wide variety of recreation outlets: ski resorts, marinas, fishing lakes and streams, hiking trails, and campgrounds.

In contrast to the National Forest System, the National Park System is meant expressly for recreation. The founding of Yellowstone National Park in 1872 marked the beginning of the oldest and now the largest national park system in the world. It comprises 354 national parks, preserves, monuments, memorials, battlefields, seashores, riverways, and trails that together cover some 80 million acres.

Whereas the National Park System acts to keep irreplaceable geographical and historical treasures in the public domain, the national wildlife refuges protect native flora and fauna from people. There are 452 of these remarkable sanctuaries throughout the country, embracing more than 89 million acres. Most of them are open to the public for a variety of wildlife activities, particularly photography and nature observation. In certain refuges at irregular times, fishing and hunting are permitted, depending on the size of the wild populations. Although the majority of the nation's wildlife refuges are located in open, sometimes remote country, they aren't exclusively a rural amenity. Several can be found within metropolitan areas, such as the Nisqually National Wildlife Refuge in Olympia, WA, and San Pablo Bay National Wildlife Refuge in the California metro area of Santa Rosa–Petaluma.

The table "Outdoor Recreation Assets: 17 Outstanding Metro Areas" provides the metro areas that earned the highest scores for their supply of Outdoor Recreation Assets.

SCORING: RECREATION

Is there more to do in Houston than in Dallas? How do the California rivals of Los Angeles and San Francisco compare for recreation? Or Jacksonville and Tampa–St. Pete? To answer these questions, *Places Rated Almanac* examines three categories of assets—Common Denominators (quality restaurants, golf, and bowling), Crowd Pleasers (zoos, aquariums, theme parks, automobile racing, pari-mutuel betting, and professional and collegiate sports), and Outdoor Recreation Assets (miles of coastline, inland water area, and acreage in national forests, parks, and wildlife refuges).

Like the chapters on education, health care, transportation, and the arts, this chapter's rating system now allows for bonus points to be awarded to metro areas that are part of a Consolidated Metropolitan Statistical Area (CMSA)—see the Appendix for a complete listing of CMSAs. CMSA Access points are *Places Rated*'s way of recognizing that certain outstanding facilities can be enjoyed by people within a relatively wide radius. In the case of recreation, each metro area that is part of a CMSA is eligible to receive points for the Crowd Pleasers assets located in neighboring metro areas, as explained in item 15 below.

In the categories of Common Denominators and Crowd Pleasers, metro areas are awarded points not for their number of facilities but rather for the availability of these facilities to residents. Access to these different events is given a rating of AA, A, B, or C (AA indicating the best access and C the worst), and those ratings mean a certain number of points for the metro area: 400 for an AA rating, 300 for A, 200 for B, and 100 for C. The exceptions to this rule—zoos, aquariums, and auto racing—are explained on the next page. For Outdoor Recreation Assets, metro areas earn points according to a different system, also delineated on the next page.

Each metro area starts with a base score of zero, to which points are added according to the following criteria:

1. *Good restaurants.*

A metro area gets a rating of:	If there is one quality star for every:
AA	14,000 or fewer people
A	14,001–20,000 people
B	20,001–32,500 people
C	32,501 or more people

2. *Public golf courses.*

A metro area gets a rating of:	If there is one hole for every:
AA	1,750 or fewer people
A	1,751–2,750 people
B	2,751–4,250 people
C	4,251 or more people

3. *Bowling lanes.*

A metro area gets a rating of:	If there is one lane for every:
AA	1,000 or fewer people
A	1,001–1,500 people
B	1,501–2,500 people
C	2,501 or more people

4. *Zoos.* Metro areas with zoos are rated by the size of their annual budgets as listed in the directory of zoos that are members of the American Association of Zoological Parks and Aquariums.

A metro area gets a rating of:	If the annual operating budget for its zoo(s):
AA	exceeds $4 million
A	falls between $1.5 and $3.9 million
B	falls between $750,000 and $1.49 million
C	is less than $749,999

5. *Aquariums.* Eleven metro areas receive an A rating for having an aquarium certified by the American Association of Zoological Parks and Aquariums.

6. *Family theme parks.* Theme parks drawing more than one million visitors per year are awarded points as follows:

A metro area gets a rating of:	If there is one open day for every:
AA	4,500 or fewer people
A	4,501–6,500 people
B	6,501–10,000 people
C	10,001 or more people

7. *Auto racing.* Metro areas earn points for having one or more sanctioned speedways as follows: AA for three speedways, A for two speedways, and B for one speedway.

8. *Pari-mutuel betting.* Tracks for thoroughbred, harness, and greyhound racing, as well as jai alai frontons, are scored as follows:

A metro area gets a rating of:	If there is one racing/open day for every:
AA	2,000 or fewer people
A	2,001–3,500 people
B	3,501–9,500 people
C	9,501 or more people

9. *Professional sports.*

A metro area gets a rating of:	If local major- and minor-league teams provide:
AA	2.500 or more game seats per capita
A	1.500–2.499 game seats per capita
B	.750–1.499 game seats per capita
C	.749 or fewer game seats per capita

10. *NCAA Division I football and basketball.*

A metro area gets a rating of:	If local NCAA Division I teams provide:
AA	1.500 or more game seats per capita
A	.700–1.499 game seats per capita
B	.300–.699 game seats per capita
C	.299 or fewer game seats per capita

11. *Coastlines.* Each mile of general coastline, whether on the ocean or on the Great Lakes, gets 10 points. For example, the 55 miles of Pacific coastline west of San Diego earn the California metro area 550 points.

12. *Inland water area.* The percent of a metro area's total surface area that is classified as inland water is multiplied by 50. In Chicago, 9.6 of the 1,902 square miles of surface area are inland water. That works out to 0.5 percent inland water, or 25 points.

13. *National forests, parks, and wildlife refuges.* The percent of a metro area's total acreage that is set aside for national forests, parks, or wildlife refuges is multiplied by 50. Seattle has more than 2,704,640 total acres, 36.29 percent of which composes the Mount Baker and Snoqualmie national forests (981,515 acres), giving the Washington metro area 1,814 points.

14. *CMSA Access.* The 71 metro areas that are part of America's 20 CMSA complexes are eligible for bonus points based on the total number of points amassed for Crowd Pleasers by the other metro areas in its CMSA. A metro area's own points are not considered in calculating its access bonus.

A metro area gets a rating of:	If points for Crowd Pleasers earned by CMSA partner(s) total:
AA	1,000 or more
A	700–999
B	400–699
C	100–399

Four eligible metro areas receive no access bonus because the other area or areas in their CMSA have no Crowd Pleasers.

To maintain relative parity among the three major recreation categories—Common Denominators,

Crowd Pleasers, and Outdoor Recreation Assets—a ceiling of 2,000 points is applied to the total for outdoor assets (items 11, 12, and 13).

Sample Comparison: Seattle, WA, and Danville, VA

As it did in the first edition of *Places Rated Almanac,* Seattle wins top honors among the metro areas for recreational facilities. Danville—a much smaller area— finishes near the bottom, with just more than a twelfth of the points earned by Seattle.

The Washington metro area receives either A or B ratings for all its Common Denominators, adding up to 1,000 points for this category. Its Crowd Pleasers are equally impressive: There is a premier AA-rated zoo, Woodland Park; an AA-rated aquarium; and supplies of auto racing and pari-mutuel betting that earn A and C ratings, respectively. Seattle's ratio of game seats to local residents ranks seventh among the 132 metro areas with major- and minor-league professional sports. The AL Mariners, NFL Seahawks, and NBA SuperSonics play a total of 130 home games in the Kingdome; and 25 miles north of downtown, the Everett Giants, a San Francisco Giants farm club, play 38 baseball games in Memorial Stadium. Although the University of Washington Huskies play the only NCAA Division I basketball and football games in town, the crowds at Husky Stadium and Edmundson Fieldhouse on the west bank of Lake Washington add to Seattle's reputation as a partisan sports town. The access to all these Crowd Pleasers earns Seattle a hefty 1,700 points for this category.

Manufactured recreation amenities tend to crop up with population density; that's an elementary marketing rule. But no other populous metro area has as splendid a combination of outdoor recreation endowments as Seattle. For openers, there's a 70-mile shoreline frontage on Puget Sound and nearly 90 square miles of inland water, including giant Lake Washington and suburban Lake Sammamish. An hour's drive east on I-90 will bring you to several challenging Cascade ski slopes in the midst of Snoqualmie National Forest. North on I-5 and then east on state roads is a big chunk of Mount Baker National Forest. Taken together, these natural facilities earn Seattle 2,000 points, the maximum for Outdoor Recreation Assets. Seattle also is eligible for a bonus of 90 points because it shares the Crowd Pleasers of nearby Tacoma, its partner in the Seattle–Tacoma consolidated area. The total recreation score for Seattle, then, is 4,390.

Danville, in contrast, ranks 328th in recreation outlets. There are no restaurants here rated for quality by the *Mobil Travel Guide,* nor are there any municipal golf courses. The 27 holes of daily-fee golf and 44 lanes of tenpin bowling give the Virginia metro area B and C ratings, respectively, in those categories, bringing Danville's total for Common Denominators to 300 points. In Crowd Pleasers, the metro area comes up empty; it has no zoos, aquariums, theme parks, racetracks, not even a Class A Carolina League baseball team like the ones in Lynchburg and Roanoke.

Although Danville's natural setting east of the Blue Ridge Mountains is pleasant, there are few lakes for water sports in surrounding Pittsylvania County; the metro area's ten square miles of inland water are good for just 49 points. Likewise, there are no acres set aside as national parks, national forests, or national wildlife refuges. Danville's 49 points for outdoor recreation, added to its previous total of 300 points, yield a recreation score of 349.

Rankings: Recreation

Thirteen criteria are used to rate a metro area's supply of recreation assets: (1) good restaurants, (2) public golf courses, (3) bowling lanes, (4) zoos, (5) aquariums, (6) family theme parks, (7) sanctioned automobile racetracks, (8) pari-mutuel betting attractions, (9) major- and minor-league professional sports teams, (10) NCAA Division I football and basketball teams, (11) miles of ocean or Great Lakes coastline, (12) inland water area, and (13) national forests, national parks, or national wildlife refuges. The 71 metro areas that belong to a Consolidated Metropolitan Statistical Area (CMSA) can also earn points for shared recreation assets found in other metro areas within that consolidated area. Metro areas that receive tie scores are given the same rank and listed alphabetically.

Metro Areas from Best to Worst

Places Rated Rank	Places Rated Score			

Places Rated Rank	Places Rated Score	Places Rated Rank	Places Rated Score	Places Rated Rank	Places Rated Score
1. Seattle, WA	4,390	53. Sacramento, CA	2,368	109. Kenosha, WI	1,812
2. San Francisco, CA	3,820	54. Knoxville, TN	2,366	110. Erie, PA	1,790
3. San Diego, CA	3,640	55. Buffalo, NY	2,350		
4. Los Angeles–Long Beach, CA	3,633			111. Peoria, IL	1,787
5. Tacoma, WA	3,570	56. Cincinnati, OH–KY–IN	2,299	112. Bergen–Passaic, NJ	1,786
		57. Boston, MA	2,277	113. Bloomington, IN	1,771
6. Miami–Hialeah, FL	3,520	58. Muskegon, MI	2,272	114. Greensboro–Winston–Salem–High Point, NC	1,770
7. Fort Collins–Loveland, CO	3,500	59. Burlington, VT	2,268		
7. New Orleans, LA	3,500	59. Portland, OR	2,268	115. Salem, OR	1,767
9. Nassau–Suffolk, NY	3,450				
10. Tucson, AZ	3,431	61. Atlantic City, NJ	2,267	116. Oklahoma City, OK	1,759
		62. Redding, CA	2,256	117. Pittsburgh, PA	1,746
11. Charleston, SC	3,333	63. Sarasota, FL	2,214	118. Pascagoula, MS	1,732
12. Salinas–Seaside–Monterey, CA	3,305	64. Albuquerque, NM	2,212	119. La Crosse, WI	1,731
13. Eugene–Springfield, OR	3,300	65. Santa Fe, NM	2,208	120. South Bend–Mishawaka, IN	1,727
14. Norfolk–Virginia Beach–Newport News, VA	3,236	66. Omaha, NE–IA	2,195	121. Appleton–Oshkosh–Neenah, WI	1,726
15. New York, NY	3,209	67. Pensacola, FL	2,190	122. Harrisburg–Lebanon–Carlisle, PA	1,713
16. Chicago, IL	3,205	68. Portsmouth–Dover–Rochester, NH–ME	2,184	122. Tallahassee, FL	1,713
17. Santa Barbara–Santa Maria–Lompoc, CA	3,200	69. Toledo, OH	2,151	124. Grand Rapids, MI	1,708
18. Salt Lake City–Ogden, UT	3,188	70. Wichita, KS	2,150	125. Glens Falls, NY	1,676
19. Baltimore, MD	3,099				
20. Boulder–Longmont, CO	3,098	71. Utica–Rome, NY	2,144	126. Fort Smith, AK–OK	1,675
		72. Panama City, FL	2,142	127. Atlanta, GA	1,656
21. Rapid City, SD	3,082	73. Clarksville–Hopkinsville, TN–KY	2,118	128. Mobile, AL	1,654
22. Fort Myers–Cape Coral, FL	3,066	74. Waterloo–Cedar Falls, IA	2,100	129. Houston, TX	1,653
23. Rochester, NY	3,064	75. Lake County, IL	2,096	130. Johnson City–Kingsport–Bristol, TN–VA	1,650
24. Bellingham, WA	3,000				
24. Naples, FL	3,000	76. Niagara Falls, NY	2,091	131. Richmond–Petersburg, VA	1,639
24. Provo–Orem, UT	3,000	77. Houma–Thibodaux, LA	2,082	132. Pittsfield, MA	1,633
27. Daytona Beach, FL	2,977	78. Colorado Springs, CO	2,074	133. Des Moines, IA	1,630
28. Tampa–St. Petersburg–Clearwater, FL	2,902	79. Lakeland–Winter Haven, FL	2,066	134. Sheboygan, WI	1,617
29. Melbourne–Titusville–Palm Bay, FL	2,900	80. Washington, DC–MD–VA	2,051	135. Davenport–Rock Island–Moline, IA–IL	1,616
30. Las Vegas, NV	2,854	81. Bangor, ME	2,044	136. Lafayette, LA	1,613
		82. Indianapolis, IN	2,019	137. Las Cruces, NM	1,609
31. Syracuse, NY	2,842	83. Salem–Gloucester, MA	2,010	138. Fall River, MA–RI	1,606
32. Honolulu, HI	2,769	84. Akron, OH	1,995	139. Fort Worth–Arlington, TX	1,605
33. Fort Pierce, FL	2,756	85. Wilmington, NC	1,971	140. Cedar Rapids, IA	1,603
34. Detroit, MI	2,721	86. Reno, NV	1,968		
35. Oxnard–Ventura, CA	2,720	87. Galveston–Texas City, TX	1,961	141. Springfield, MA	1,603
		88. Kansas City, MO–KS	1,945	142. Beaumont–Port Arthur, TX	1,598
36. Fresno, CA	2,673	89. Louisville, KY–IN	1,943	143. Hartford, CT	1,588
37. Jacksonville, FL	2,657	90. Madison, WI	1,940	144. Bridgeport–Milford, CT	1,587
38. Monmouth–Ocean, NJ	2,649			145. Lawrence–Haverhill, MA–NH	1,585
39. Brownsville–Harlingen, TX	2,639	91. Jackson, MI	1,930		
40. Portland, ME	2,622	91. Jersey City, NJ	1,930	146. Lewiston–Auburn, ME	1,583
		93. Great Falls, MT	1,925	146. Memphis, TN–AR–MS	1,583
41. Orlando, FL	2,620	94. St. Louis, MO–IL	1,920	146. Santa Rosa–Petaluma, CA	1,583
42. Anchorage, AK	2,600	95. Spokane, WA	1,916	149. Corpus Christi, TX	1,576
43. Minneapolis–St. Paul, MN–WI	2,573	96. Nashville, TN	1,894	150. Fort Walton Beach, FL	1,570
44. Milwaukee, WI	2,518	97. Biloxi–Gulfport, MS	1,893		
45. Phoenix, AZ	2,511	98. Providence, RI	1,885	151. Tulsa, OK	1,551
		99. Dallas, TX	1,873	152. Lawrence, KS	1,546
46. West Palm Beach–Boca Raton–Delray Beach, FL	2,508	99. Green Bay, WI	1,873	152. Springfield, IL	1,546
47. Visalia–Tulare–Porterville, CA	2,500	101. Denver, CO	1,871	154. Norwalk, CT	1,545
48. Ocala, FL	2,448	102. Saginaw–Bay City–Midland, MI	1,869	155. Yakima, WA	1,540
49. Anaheim–Santa Ana, CA	2,437	103. Waco, TX	1,864	156. San Jose, CA	1,533
50. Duluth, MN–WI	2,404	104. Riverside–San Bernardino, CA	1,838	157. Rockford, IL	1,524
		105. Roanoke, VA	1,834	158. Wilmington, DE–NJ–MD	1,518
51. Savannah, GA	2,398			159. Lafayette–West Lafayette, IN	1,514
52. Cleveland, OH	2,391	106. Columbus, OH	1,831	160. Albany–Schenectady–Troy, NY	1,512
		107. Oakland, CA	1,828		
		108. Bremerton, WA	1,827	161. Elmira, NY	1,500

Places Rated Rank	Places Rated Score	Places Rated Rank	Places Rated Score	Places Rated Rank	Places Rated Score
162. Gary–Hammond, IN	1,492	219. Hamilton–Middletown, OH	1,223	276. El Paso, TX	900
163. Scranton–Wilkes-Barre, PA	1,484	220. Decatur, AL	1,215	277. San Angelo, TX	886
164. Charlotte–Gastonia–Rock				278. Fitchburg–Leominster, MA	881
Hill, NC–SC	1,482	221. New London–Norwich,		279. Florence, AL	867
165. Vallejo–Fairfield–Napa, CA	1,468	CT–RI	1,211	280. Huntington–Ashland,	
		221. Raleigh–Durham, NC	1,211	WV–KY–OH	858
166. Bradenton, FL	1,467	223. Bloomington–Normal, IL	1,210		
167. Lincoln, NE	1,444	223. Lansing–East Lansing, MI	1,210	281. Vancouver, WA	854
168. Evansville, IN–KY	1,426	225. Wichita Falls, TX	1,209	282. Nashua, NH	849
169. Fayetteville–Springdale, AR	1,418			283. Cumberland, MD–WV	839
170. Ann Arbor, MI	1,416	226. Baton Rouge, LA	1,206	284. Allentown–Bethlehem, PA–NJ	838
		227. Eau Claire, WI	1,195	284. Decatur, IL	838
171. Fort Wayne, IN	1,413	228. Lorain–Elyria, OH	1,192		
172. Charlottesville, VA	1,407	229. Brazoria, TX	1,187	286. Williamsport, PA	826
173. Lexington–Fayette, KY	1,403	230. Danbury, CT	1,186	287. Sioux Falls, SD	824
174. Fort Lauderdale–Hollywood–				288. Abilene, TX	816
Pompano Beach, FL	1,402	231. Newark, NJ	1,183	289. Augusta, GA–SC	811
174. Joliet, IL	1,402	232. Shreveport, LA	1,182	289. Fargo–Moorhead, ND–MN	811
		233. Sharon, PA	1,178		
176. Champaign–Urbana–		234. St. Cloud, MN	1,163	291. Altoona, PA	810
Rantoul, IL	1,401	235. Flint, MI	1,162	292. Tuscaloosa, AL	809
177. Dubuque, IA	1,386			293. Kokomo, IN	808
178. Little Rock–North Little		236. Sioux City, IA–NE	1,159	294. Enid, OK	800
Rock, AR	1,380	237. Canton, OH	1,157	295. Vineland–Millville–Bridgeton,	
179. Benton Harbor, MI	1,377	238. Wausau, WI	1,154	NJ	783
180. Huntsville, AL	1,375	239. Jacksonville, NC	1,151		
		240. Billings, MT	1,146	296. Columbus, GA–AL	777
181. Boise City, ID	1,372			297. Anniston, AL	769
182. Pawtucket–Woonsocket–		241. Monroe, LA	1,140	298. Kalamazoo, MI	758
Attleboro, RI–MA	1,365	242. Mansfield, OH	1,133	299. Anderson, SC	752
183. San Antonio, TX	1,363	243. Jackson, MS	1,130	300. Owensboro, KY	748
184. Youngstown–Warren, OH	1,355	243. Johnstown, PA	1,130		
185. Philadelphia, PA–NJ	1,349	245. Bismarck, ND	1,128	301. Hickory, NC	738
				302. Medford, OR	726
186. Pueblo, CO	1,345	246. Aurora–Elgin, IL	1,120	303. Amarillo, TX	706
187. Charleston, WV	1,344	247. Bryan–College Station, TX	1,119	304. Lancaster, PA	660
188. Lynchburg, VA	1,341	248. Chico, CA	1,101	305. Lowell, MA–NH	655
189. Greenville–Spartanburg, SC	1,334	249. Beaver County, PA	1,089		
190. Binghamton, NY	1,331	250. Alexandria, LA	1,055	306. Waterbury, CT	644
				307. Fayetteville, NC	609
190. Columbia, MO	1,331	251. Birmingham, AL	1,040	308. Merced, CA	607
192. State College, PA	1,327	252. Lima, OH	1,038	309. Joplin, MO	601
193. New Haven–Meriden, CT	1,320	252. Stockton, CA	1,038	310. Anderson, IN	600
194. Janesville–Beloit, WI	1,314	254. Chattanooga, TN–GA	1,036		
195. Orange County, NY	1,313	255. Trenton, NJ	1,032	311. Tyler, TX	592
				312. Killeen–Temple, TX	574
196. Rochester, MN	1,307	256. Macon–Warner Robins, GA	1,017	313. McAllen–Edinburg–Mission,	
197. Racine, WI	1,304	256. New Britain, CT	1,017	TX	558
198. New Bedford, MA	1,298	258. Richland–Kennewick–Pasco,		314. Greeley, CO	539
199. Gainesville, FL	1,297	WA	1,012	315. Modesto, CA	533
199. Santa Cruz, CA	1,297	258. Worcester, MA	1,012		
		260. Grand Forks, ND	1,004	316. Sherman–Denison, TX	526
201. Hagerstown, MD	1,283			317. Burlington, NC	522
202. Wheeling, WV–OH	1,275	260. Lubbock, TX	1,004	318. Yuba City, CA	517
203. Columbia, SC	1,274	262. Middletown, CT	972	319. Midland, TX	502
204. Iowa City, IA	1,273	263. Middlesex–Somerset–		320. Odessa, TX	500
205. Bakersfield, CA	1,267	Hunterdon, NJ	964		
		264. Austin, TX	963	321. Bristol, CT	463
206. Poughkeepsie, NY	1,265	265. Steubenville–Weirton,		321. Texarkana, TX–Texarkana,	
207. Lawton, OK	1,262	OH–WV	958	AR	463
208. Topeka, KS	1,260			323. Albany, GA	458
208. Reading, PA	1,260	266. Parkersburg–Marietta,		324. Longview–Marshall, TX	434
210. Lake Charles, LA	1,255	WV–OH	947	325. Laredo, TX	405
		267. Manchester, NH	946		
211. Muncie, IN	1,253	268. York, PA	945	326. Jackson, TN	400
212. Battle Creek, MI	1,248	269. Dayton–Springfield, OH	933	327. Pine Bluff, AR	388
213. Stamford, CT	1,242	270. Elkhart–Goshen, IN	922	328. Danville, VA	349
213. Asheville, NC	1,242			329. Dothan, AL	325
215. Casper, WY	1,236	271. Kankakee, IL	919	330. Victoria, TX	310
		272. Montgomery, AL	917		
215. Springfield, MO	1,236	273. Brockton, MA	906	331. St. Joseph, MO	264
215. Terre Haute, IN	1,236	274. Athens, GA	904	332. Florence, SC	204
218. Olympia, WA	1,230	274. Cheyenne, WY	904	333. Gadsden, AL	177

The following profiles are a selective catalogue of recreation features in each metro area.

The profiles begin with the category Common Denominators, specific options for urban recreation that ought to be available everywhere; the access rating for each item is shown in the right-hand column. The Good Restaurants entry tells how many restaurants at each quality level are in a metro area ("4 ★★" means, for example, that the place has four two-star restaurants).

The Crowd Pleasers category lists local zoos, aquariums, theme parks, automobile racecourses (along with sanctioning organization), and pari-mutuel betting attractions. Also included are the days per year that theme parks and pari-mutuel tracks are open, along with their access rating. Under the heading Professional Sports, the names of major- and minor-league baseball, basketball, football, and hockey teams are given along with the total game seats per capita and access rating. Local colleges and universities that field NCAA Division I teams in football and/or basketball are also listed, with separate total game seats per capita and access rating.

The third category, Outdoor Recreation Assets, counts the metro area's number of miles of ocean or Great Lakes coastline, its square miles of inland water, and the acreage for all national forests, parks, and wildlife refuges located there. Ponds and lakes are counted if their surface areas are 40 acres or more; streams, canals, and rivers are also counted if their width is one eighth of a mile or more. The water area along irregular Great Lakes and ocean coastlines is counted, too, if the bays, inlets, and estuaries are between one and ten miles in width. Lengths of ocean and Great Lakes coastlines are estimated from state totals measured by the National Oceanic and Atmospheric Administration. A number of abbreviations are used in this section:

NF	National Forest	NP	National Park
NHP	National Historic Park	NRA	National Recreation Area
NHS	National Historic Site	NSR	National Scenic River
NMP	National Military Park	NS	National Seashore
NM	National Monument	NWR	National Wildlife Refuge

The figure in parentheses beside each major heading represents the number of *Places Rated* points awarded the metro area for assets in that category. If the metro area is part of a CMSA complex and receives bonus points for shared recreation assets, the number of access points is shown in parentheses following the name of the consolidated area. A star preceding a metro area's name highlights it as one of the top 30 places for recreation.

Information comes from these sources: American Association of Zoological Parks and Aquariums, *Zoological Parks and Aquariums in the Americas, 1988–1989*, 1988; American Baseball League, unpublished data, 1989; American Bowling Congress, unpublished data, 1989; American Greyhound Track Operators Association, *Directory*, 1988; American Hockey League, *Media Guide*, 1988; Baseball America, *Directory*, 1989; Brown Publishing Company, *National Speedway Directory*, 1989; Continental Basketball Association, unpublished data, 1989; International Hockey League, *Media Guide*, 1989; Kings Entertainment Company, 1989; Merrill Lynch, *Theme Park Industry Survey*, 1987; National Association of Collegiate Directors of Athletics, *The 1988–1989 National Directory of College Athletics*, 1988; National Association of Professional Baseball Leagues, unpublished data, 1988; National Basketball Association, *Media Guide*, 1988; National Collegiate Athletic Association, *National Collegiate Championships*, 1989, *NCAA Basketball*, 1988, and *NCAA Football*, 1988; National Football League, unpublished data, 1988; National Golf Foundation, unpublished data, 1989; National Hockey League, unpublished data, 1988; National League of Professional Baseball Teams, unpublished data, 1988; Prentice Hall Press, *Mobil Travel Guide* (7 vols.), 1989; Thoroughbred Racing Associations of North America, Inc., *Directory and Record Book*, 1988; U.S. Department of Agriculture, Forest Service, *Land Areas of the National Forest System*, 1988; U.S. Department of Commerce: Bureau of the Census, unpublished data measurements, 1980, National Oceanic and Atmospheric Administration, *The Coastline of the United States*, 1975; U.S. Department of the Interior: Fish and Wildlife Service, unpublished master deed listing, 1988, and National Park Service, *Index to the National Park System and Related Areas*, 1988, and unpublished master deed listing, 1989; and U.S. Trotting Association, *Trotting and Pacing Guide*, 1988.

	Rating
Abilene, TX	
Common Denominators (600 points)	
Good restaurants: 2 ★, 1 ★★	B
Golf courses: 4 private (63 holes); 1 municipal (18 holes)	C
Bowling centers: 5 (114 lanes, tenpins)	A
Crowd Pleasers (200 points)	

	Rating
Zoo: Abilene Zoological Gardens—159 species, 495 specimens	C
NCAA Division I: 0.284 game seats per capita Hardin–Simmons Cowboys	C
Outdoor Recreation Assets (16)	
Inland Water Area: 2.9 square miles	
Places Rated Score: 816	Places Rated Rank: 288

Rating

Akron, OH
Common Denominators (1,000 points)
Good restaurants: 2 *, 7 **, 3 ***   **B**
Golf courses: 13 private (243 holes); 28 daily fee   **AA**
  (558 holes); 3 municipal (45 holes)
Bowling centers: 37 (912 lanes, tenpins)   **AA**
Crowd Pleasers (800 points)
Theme Park: Sea World of Ohio (100 days)   **B**
Pari-Mutuel Betting: **A**
  Northfield Park (harness, 213 races)
NCAA Division I: 0.741 game seats per capita   **A**
  Kent State Golden Flashes, University of Akron
  Zips
Outdoor Recreation Assets (105)
Inland Water Area: 19.3 square miles
National Forests, Parks, Wildlife Refuges:
  Cuyahoga Valley NRA (16,074 acres)
CMSA Access: Cleveland–Akron–Lorain, OH (90
points
Places Rated Score: 1,995   Places Rated Rank: 84

Albany, GA
Common Denominators (400 points)
Good restaurant: 1 **   **C**
Golf courses: 3 private (45 holes): 1 municipal (9   **C**
  holes)
Bowling centers: 2 (54 lanes, tenpins)   **B**
Outdoor Recreation Assets (58)
Inland Water Area: 8.1 square miles
Places Rated Score: 458   Places Rated Rank: 323

Albany–Schenectady–Troy, NY
Common Denominators (1,000 points)
Good restaurants: 4 *, 12 **, 9 ***   **A**
Golf courses: 19 private (315 holes); 22 daily fee   **A**
  (324 holes); 6 municipal (117 holes)
Bowling centers: 54 (1042 lanes, tenpins)   **AA**
Crowd Pleasers (400 points)
Pari-Mutuel Betting: **B**
  Saratoga Raceway (mixed meetings, 219 races)
Professional Sports: 0.565 game seats per capita   **C**
  Patroons (CBA Basketball), Yankees (Double A
  Baseball)
NCAA Division I: 0.0700 game seats per capita   **C**
  Siena College Indians
Outdoor Recreation Assets (112)
Inland Water Area: 69.9 square miles
National Forests, Parks, Wildlife Refuges:
  Saratoga NHP (2,605 acres)
Places Rated Score: 1,512   Places Rated Rank: 160

Albuquerque, NM
Common Denominators (600 points)
Good restaurants: 3 *, 17 **, 5 ***   **AA**
Golf courses: 5 private (99 holes); 1 daily fee (27   **C**
  holes); 4 municipal (63 holes)
Bowling centers: 9 (264 lanes, tenpins)   **B**
Crowd Pleasers (1,100 points)
Zoo: Rio Grande Zoological Park—253 species,   **A**
  1,063 specimens
Pari-Mutuel Betting: **B**
  Downs at Albuquerque (mixed meetings, 78
  races)
Professional Sports: 1.530 game seats per capita   **A**
  Dukes (Triple A Baseball)
NCAA Division I: 0.725 game seats per capita   **A**
  University of New Mexico Lobos
Outdoor Recreation Assets (512)
National Forests, Parks, Wildlife Refuges:
  Cibola NF (76,588 acres)
Places Rated Score: 2,212   Places Rated Rank: 64

Alexandria, LA
Common Denominators (300 points)
Golf courses: 3 private (45 holes); 2 daily fee (18   **C**
  holes)

Rating

Bowling centers: 2 (60 lanes, tenpins)   **B**
Crowd Pleasers (100 points)
Zoo: Alexandria Zoological Park—103 species, 377   **C**
  specimens
Outdoor Recreation Assets (655)
Inland Water Area: 20.3 square miles
National Forests, Parks, Wildlife Refuges:
  Kisatchie NF (101,221 acres)
Places Rated Score: 1,055   Places Rated Rank: 250

Allentown–Bethlehem, PA–NJ
Common Denominators (400 points)
Good restaurants: 1 **, 1 ***, 1 ****   **C**
Golf courses: 9 private (207 holes); 12 daily fee   **B**
  (180 holes); 2 municipal (36 holes)
Bowling centers: 58 (650 lanes, tenpins)   **A**
Crowd Pleasers (300 points)
Auto Racing: Pennsylvania International Speedway   **C**
  (NASCAR)
NCAA Division I: 0.311 game seats per capita   **B**
  Lafayette College Leopards, Lehigh Engineers
Outdoor Recreation Assets (138)
Inland Water Area: 8.7 square miles
National Forests, Parks, Wildlife Refuges:
  Appalachian Trail (4,079 acres)
  Delaware NSR (368 acres)
  Delaware Water Gap NRA (16,066 acres)
Places Rated Score: 838   Places Rated Rank: 284

Altoona, PA
Common Denominators (800 points)
Good restaurants: 1 *, 2 **, 1 ***   **A**
Golf courses: 4 private (72 holes); 3 daily fee (27   **C**
  holes)
Bowling centers: 11 (137 lanes, tenpins)   **AA**
Outdoor Recreation Assets (10)
Inland Water Area: 0.2 square miles
National Forests, Parks, Wildlife Refuges:
  Allegheny Portage NHS (517 acres)
Places Rated Score: 810   Places Rated Rank: 291

Amarillo, TX
Common Denominators (500 points)
Good restaurants: 4 **, 1 ***   **A**
Golf courses: 4 private (63 holes); 4 daily fee (63   **A**
  holes); 1 municipal (36 holes)
Bowling centers: 4 (96 lanes, tenpins)   **B**
Outdoor Recreation Assets (206)
Inland Water Area: 25.9 square miles
National Forests, Parks, Wildlife Refuges:
  Alibates Flint Quarries NM (1,079 acres)
  Buffalo Lake NWR (7,664 acres)
  Lake Meredith NRA (23,379 acres)
Places Rated Score: 706   Places Rated Rank: 303

Anaheim–Santa Ana, CA
Common Denominators (300 points)
Good restaurants: 16 *, 20 **, 12 ***, 2 ****   **B**
Golf courses: 16 private (306 holes); 10 daily fee   **C**
  (180 holes); 6 municipal (126 holes)
Bowling centers: 24 (822 lanes, tenpins)   **C**
Crowd Pleasers (1,000 points)
Zoo: Santa Ana Zoo—96 species, 243 specimens   **C**
Theme Parks: **AA**
  Disneyland (303 days)
  Knott's Berry Farm (365 days)
  Six Flags Magic Mountain (185 days)
Pari-Mutuel Betting: **C**
  Los Alamitos (mixed meetings, 240 races)
Professional Sports: 2.467 game seats per capita   **A**
  California Angels (AL Baseball), Rams (NFC
  Football
NCAA Division I: 0.026 game seats per capita   **C**
  University of California Anteaters

Rating

Outdoor Recreation Assets (967)
 Pacific Coastline: 40 miles
 Inland Water Area: 6.3 square miles
 National Forests, Parks, Wildlife Refuges:
  Cleveland NF (53,893 acres)
 CMSA Access: Los Angeles–Anaheim–Riverside,
  CA (170 points)
Places Rated Score: 2,437   Places Rated Rank: 49

Anchorage, AK
Common Denominators (500 points)
 Golf courses: 1 private (18 holes); 1 daily fee (18   C
  holes); 1 municipal (18 holes)
 Bowling centers: 9 (270 lanes, tenpins)   AA
Crowd Pleasers (100 points)
 Zoo: Alaska Zoo—47 species, 102 specimens   C
Outdoor Recreation Assets (2,000)
 Pacific Coastline: 90 miles
 Inland Water Area: 36 square miles
 National Forests, Parks, Wildlife Refuges:
  Chugach NF (275,000 acres)
Places Rated Score: 2,600   Places Rated Rank: 42

Anderson, IN
Common Denominators (600 points)
 Golf courses: 5 private (81 holes); 2 daily fee (27   B
  holes); 1 municipal (18 holes)
 Bowling centers: 8 (164 lanes, tenpins):   AA
Places Rated Score: 600   Places Rated Rank: 310

Anderson, SC
Common Denominators (400 points)
 Golf courses: 3 private (45 holes); 3 daily fee (54   A
  holes)
 Bowling centers: 2 (56 lanes, tenpins)   C
Crowd Pleasers (100 points)
 Auto Racing: Anderson Speedway (NASCAR)   C
Outdoor Recreation Assets (252)
 Inland Water Area: 38.1 square miles
Places Rated Score: 752   Places Rated Rank: 299

Ann Arbor, MI
Common Denominators (800 points)
 Good restaurants: 3 *, 6 **, 2 ***   AA
 Golf courses: 7 private (108 holes); 9 daily fee (144 AA
  holes); 4 municipal (81 holes)
 Bowling centers: 13 (350 lanes, tenpins)   AA
Crowd Pleasers (400 points)
 NCAA Division I: 3.076 game seats per capita   AA
  Eastern Michigan University Hurons, University of
  Michigan Wolverines
Outdoor Recreation Assets (86)
 Inland Water Area: 12.5 square miles
 CMSA Access: Detroit–Ann Arbor, MI (130 points)
Places Rated Score: 1,416   Places Rated Rank: 170

Anniston, AL
Common Denominators (500 points)
 Good restaurant: 1 **   C
 Golf courses: 3 private (54 holes); 2 daily fee (36   B
  holes); 1 municipal (9 holes)
 Bowling centers: 2 (44 lanes, tenpins):   C
Outdoor Recreation Assets (269)
 Inland Water Area: 1.7 square miles
 National Forests, Parks, Wildlife Refuges:
  Talledega NF (19,985 acres)
Places Rated Score: 769   Places Rated Rank: 297

Appleton–Oshkosh–Neenah, WI
Common Denominators (900 points)
 Good restaurants: 2 **   C
 Golf courses: 6 private (99 holes); 14 daily fee (216 AA
  holes); 2 municipal (36 holes)
 Bowling Centers: 40 (601 lanes, tenpins)
Crowd Pleasers (200 points)

Rating

 Professional Sports: 0.959 game seats per capita   B
  Appleton Foxes (Class A Baseball)
Outdoor Recreation Assets (626)
 Inland Water Area: 202.9 square miles
Places Rated Score: 1,726   Places Rated Rank: 121

Asheville, NC
Common Denominators (400 points)
 Good restaurants: 1 *, 2 **   C
 Golf courses: 5 private (90 holes); 2 daily fee (27   B
  holes); 2 municipal (36 holes)
 Bowling centers: 2 (48 lanes, tenpins)   C
Crowd Pleasers (400 points)
 Auto Racing: New Asheville Speedway (NASCAR)   C
 Professional Sports: 1.404 game sets per capita   B
  Tourists (Class A Baseball)
 NCAA Division I: 0.172 game seats per capita   C
  University of North Carolina Bulldogs
Outdoor Recreation assets (442)
 Inland Water Area: 0.8 square miles
 National Forests, Parks, Wildlife Refuges:
  Blue Ridge Parkway (5,411 acres)
  Pisgah NF (31,464 acres)
Places Rated Score: 1,242   Places Rated Rank: 213

Athens, GA
Common Denominators (500 points)
 Golf courses: 2 private (45 holes); 4 daily fee (54   A
  holes)
 Bowling centers: 3 (68 lanes, tenpins)   B
Crowd Pleasers (400 points)
 NCAA Division I: 3.734 game seats per capita   AA
  University of Georgia Bulldogs
Outdoor Recreation Assets (4)
 Inland Water Area: 0.6 square miles
 National Forests, Parks, Wildlife Refuges:
  Oconee NF (112 acres)
Places Rated Score: 904   Places Rated Rank: 274

Atlanta, GA
Common Denominators (500 points)
 Good restaurants: 5 *, 29 **, 25 ***, 1 ****   A
 Golf courses: 46 private (846 holes); 19 daily fee   C
  (315 holes); 9 municipal (144 holes)
 Bowling centers: 29 (820 lanes, tenpins)   C
Crowd Pleasers (1,100 points)
 Zoo: Zoo Atlanta—278 species, 951 specimens   A
 Theme Park: Six Flags over Georgia (148 days)   C
 Auto Racing: A
  Atlanta International Raceway (NASCAR)
  Seven Flags Speedway (NASCAR)
 Professional Sports: 1.917 game seats per capita   A
  Braves (NL Baseball), Falcons (NFC Football),
  Hawks (NBA Basketball)
 NCAA Division I: 0.15 game seats per capita   C
  Georgia State Crimson Panthers, Georgia Tech
  Yellow Jackets
Outdoor Recreation Assets (56)
 Inland Water Area: 44.3 square miles
 National Forests, Parks, Wildlife Refuges:
  Chattahoochee River NRA (5,968 acres)
  Kennesaw Mountain National Battlefield Park
  (2,884 acres)
  Martin Luther King, Jr., NHS (8 acres)
Places Rated Score: 1,656   Places Rated Rank: 127

Atlantic City, NJ
Common Denominators (1,000 points)
 Good restaurants: 1 *, 16 **, 6 ***   AA
 Golf courses: 5 private (108 holes); 7 daily fee (117 A
  holes); 1 municipal (9 holes)
 Bowling centers: 8 (242 lanes, tenpins)   A
Crowd Pleasers (200 points)
 Pari-Mutuel Betting: B
  Atlantic City (thoroughbred, 64 races)

	Rating
Outdoor Recreation Assets (1,067)	
Atlantic Coastline: 67.2 miles	
National Forests, Parks, Wildlife Refuges:	
Forsythe NWR (19,840 acres)	
Places Rated Score: 2,267	Places Rated Rank: 61

Augusta, GA–SC
	Rating
Common Denominators (500 points)	
Good restaurants: 3 **	C
Golf courses: 11 private (198 holes); 9 daily fee (135 holes); 1 municipal (18 holes)	A
Bowling centers: 6 (142 lanes, tenpins)	C
Crowd Pleasers (200 points)	
Professional Sports: 0.682 game seats per capita	C
Pirates (Class A Baseball)	
NCAA Division I: 0.21 game seats per capita	C
Augusta College Jaguars	
Outdoor Recreation Assets (111)	
Inland Water Area: 35 square miles	
National Forests, Parks, Wildlife Refuges:	
Sumter NF (6,021 acres)	
Places Rated Score: 811	Places Rated Rank: 289

Aurora–Elgin, IL
	Rating
Common Denominators (900 points)	
Good restaurants: 1 *, 7 **, 2 ***	A
Golf courses: 4 private (63 holes); 6 daily fee (81 holes); 7 municipal (108 holes)	A
Bowling centers: 12 (328 lanes, tenpins)	A
CMSA Access: Chicago–Gary–Lake County, IL–IN–WI (220 points)	
Places Rated Score: 1,120	Places Rated Rank: 246

Austin, TX
	Rating
Common Denominators (400 points)	
Good restaurants: 3 *, 4 **, 4 ***	C
Golf courses: 14 private (279 holes); 11 daily fee (189 holes); 4 municipal (63 holes)	B
Bowling centers: 12 (266 lanes, tenpins)	C
Crowd Pleasers (500 points)	
Auto Racing: San Marcos Airport (SCCA)	B
NCAA Division I: 0.963 game seats per capita	A
Southwest Texas State Bobcats, University of Texas Longhorns	
Outdoor Recreation Assets (63)	
Inland Water Area: 35.3 square miles	
Places Rated Score: 963	Places Rated Rank: 264

Bakersfield, CA
	Rating
Common Denominators (500 points)	
Good restaurants: 1 *, 3 **, 2 ***	C
Golf courses: 5 private (90 holes); 6 daily fee (99 holes); 5 municipal (81 holes)	B
Bowling centers: 12 (274 lanes, tenpins)	B
Crowd Pleasers (400 points)	
Auto Racing: Bakersfield Speedway (NASCAR)	B
Pari-Mutuel Betting:	C
Kern County Fair (mixed meetings, 13 races)	
Professional Sports: 0.414 game seats per capita	C
Dodgers (Class A Baseball)	
Outdoor Recreation Assets (367)	
Inland Water Area: 19.6 square miles	
National Forests, Parks, Wildlife Refuges:	
Kern-Pixley NWR (10,618 acres)	
Los Padres NF (64,803 acres)	
Sequoia NF (294,917 acres)	
Places Rated Score: 1,267	Places Rated Rank: 205

★ Baltimore, MD
	Rating
Common Denominators (600 points)	
Good restaurants: 6 *, 24 **, 11 ***	B
Golf courses: 27 private (540 holes); 7 daily fee (108 holes); 9 municipal (153 holes)	C
Bowling centers: 70 (1844 lanes, mixed)	A
Crowd Pleasers (1,300 points)	

	Rating
Zoo: Baltimore Zoo—238 species, 1,040 specimens	AA
Aquarium: National Aquarium in Baltimore—520 species, 7,502 specimens	AA
Pari-Mutuel Betting:	C
Pimlico (thoroughbred, 148 races)	
Timonium (thoroughbred, 10 races)	
Professional Sports: 2.065 game seats per capita	A
Orioles (AL Baseball), Skip Jacks (AHL Hockey)	
NCAA Division I: 0.239 game seats per capita	C
Coppin State Eagles, Loyola College Greyhounds, Morgan State Bears, Towson State Tigers, U.S. Naval Academy Midshipmen, University of Maryland Retrievers	
Outdoor Recreation Assets (1,199)	
Chesapeake Bay Coastline: 96 miles	
Inland Water Area: 137.9 square miles	
National Forests, Parks, Wildlife Refuges:	
Fort McHenry NM (43 acres)	
Hampton NHS (59 acres)	
National Capital Park (432 acres)	
Patuxent NWR (432 acres)	
Susquehanna NWR (4 acres)	
Places Rated Score: 3,099	Places Rated Rank: 19

Bangor, ME
	Rating
Common Denominators (1,000 points)	
Good restaurants: 3 **, 2 ***	AA
Golf courses: 5 daily fee (63 holes); 1 municipal (18 holes)	AA
Bowling centers: 3 (56 lanes, mixed)	B
Crowd Pleasers (700 points)	
Pari-Mutuel Betting:	AA
Bangor Raceway (harness, 45 races)	
NCAA Division I: 0.852 game seats per capita	A
University of Maine Black Bears	
Outdoor Recreation Assets (344)	
Inland Water Area: 25.3 square miles	
Places Rated Score: 2,044	Places Rated Rank: 81

Baton Rouge, LA
	Rating
Common Denominators (500 points)	
Good restaurants: 1 *, 9 **, 2 ***, 1 ****	A
Golf courses: 12 private (180 holes); 1 daily fee (18 holes); 4 municipal (54 holes)	C
Bowling centers: 5 (160 lanes, tenpins)	C
Crowd Pleasers (500 points)	
Zoo: Greater Baton Rouge Zoo—212 species, 993 specimens	B
NCAA Division I: 1.368 game seats per capita	A
Louisiana State Fighting Tigers, Southern University Jaguars	
Outdoor Recreation Assets (206)	
Inland Water Area: 68.4 square miles	
Places Rated Score: 1,206	Places Rated Rank: 226

Battle Creek, MI
	Rating
Common Denominators (1,100 points)	
Good restaurants: 3 *, 2 **	A
Golf courses: 5 private (90 holes); 8 daily fee (117 holes); 2 municipal (27 holes)	AA
Bowling centers: 5 (160 lanes, tenpins)	AA
Crowd Pleasers (100 points)	
Zoo: Binder Park Zoo—73 species, 264 specimens	C
Outdoor Recreation Assets (48)	
Inland Water Area: 6.9 square miles	
Places Rated Score: 1,248	Places Rated Rank: 212

Beaumont–Port Arthur, TX
	Rating
Common Denominators (600 points)	
Good restaurants: 2 *, 4 **	C
Golf courses: 8 private (135 holes); 5 daily fee (81 holes); 4 municipal (72 holes)	A
Bowling centers: 5 (174 lanes, tenpins)	B
Crowd Pleasers (200 points)	
NCAA Division I: 0.563 game seats per capita	B
Lamar University Cardinals	

Rating

Outdoor Recreation Assets (798)
   Gulf of Mexico Coastline: 32 miles
   Inland Water Area: 72.3 square miles
   National Forests, Parks, Wildlife Refuges:
      Big Thicket National Preserve (41,730 acres)
      McFaddin NWR (41,682 acres)
      Texas Point NWR (8,952 acres)
Places Rated Score: 1,598   Places Rated Rank: 142

Beaver County, PA

Common Denominators (900 points)
   Good restaurant: 1***   C
   Golf courses: 4 private (63 holes); 7 daily fee (126   AA
      holes)
   Bowling centers: 13 (216 lanes, tenpins)   AA
Outdoor Recreation Assets (89)
   Inland Water Area: 7 square miles
CMSA Access: Pittsburgh–Beaver County, PA
   (100 points)
Places Rated Score: 1,089   Places Rated Rank: 249

★ Bellingham, WA

Common Denominators (800 points)
   Good restaurants: 2 **   B
   Golf courses: 1 private (18 holes); 5 daily fee (72   AA
      holes); 1 municipal (18 holes)
   Bowling centers: 3 (60 lanes, tenpins)   B
Crowd Pleasers (200 points)
   Professional Sports: 0.975 game seats per capita   B
      Mariners (Class A Baseball)
Outdoor Recreation Assets (2,000)
   Inland Water Area: 53.7 square miles
   National Forests, Parks, Wildlife Refuges:
      Mount Baker NF (452,909 acres)
      North Cascades NP (281,413 acres)
      Ross Lake NRA (107,633 acres)
      San Juan Island NWR (3 acres)
Places Rated Score: 3,000   Places Rated Rank: 24

Benton Harbor, MI

Common Denominators (900 points)
   Good restaurants: 1 **, 1 ***   C
   Golf courses: 5 private (81 holes); 9 daily fee (153   AA
      holes); 2 municipal (18 holes)
   Bowling centers: 11 (236 lanes, tenpins)   AA
Outdoor Recreation Assets (477)
   Great Lakes Coastline: 44 miles
   Inland Water Area: 4.3 square miles
Places Rated Score: 1,377   Places Rated Rank: 179

Bergen–Passaic, NJ

Common Denominators (500 points)
   Good restaurants: 2 *, 11 **, 3 ***,
      1 ****, 1 *****   B
   Golf courses: 17 private (288 holes); 5 daily fee (90   C
      holes); 5 municipal (117 holes)
   Bowling centers: 22 (562 lanes, tenpins)   B
Crowd Pleasers (900 points)
   Zoo: Van Saun Park Zoo—62 species, 200   C
      specimens
   Auto Racing: Meadowlands Grand Prix (SCCA)   B
   Pari-Mutuel Betting: B
      The Meadowlands (mixed meetings, 288 races)
   Professional Sports: 2.165 game seats per capita   A
      Giants (NFC Football), Jets (AFC Football), Devils
      (NHL Hockey), Nets (NBA Basketball)
   NCAA Division I: 0.055 game seats per capita   C
      Fairleigh Dickinson Knights
Outdoor Recreation Assets (226)
   Inland Water Area: 19.7 square miles
   National Forests, Parks, Wildlife Refuges:
      Appalachian Trail (255 acres)
CMSA Access: New York–Northern NJ–Long
   Island, NY–NJ–CT (160 points)
Places Rated Score: 1,786   Places Rated Rank: 112

Rating

Billings, MT

Common Denominators (800 points)
   Good restaurants: 3 *, 9 **, 2 ***   AA
   Golf courses: 5 private (81 holes); 3 daily fee (36   B
      holes)
   Bowling centers: 5 (76 lanes, tenpins)   B
Crowd Pleasers (300 points)
   Pari-Mutuel Betting: A
      Metrapark (thoroughbred, 35 races)
Outdoor Recreation Assets (46)
   Inland Water Area: 24.1 square miles
Places Rated Score: 1,146   Places Rated Rank: 240

Biloxi–Gulfport, MS

Common Denominators (900 points)
   Good restaurants: 3 *, 4 **, 3 ***   AA
   Golf courses: 5 private (99 holes); 4 daily fee (90   A
      holes)
   Bowling centers: 5 (100 lanes, tenpins)   B
Outdoor Recreation Assets (993)
   Gulf of Mexico Coastline: 30 miles
   Inland Water Area: 22.4 square miles
   National Forests, Parks, Wildlife Refuges:
      De Soto NF (61,389 acres)
      Gulf Islands NS (19,997 acres)
Places Rated Score: 1,893   Places Rated Rank: 97

Binghamton, NY

Common Denominators (900 points)
   Good restaurants: 1 *, 4 **, 1 ***   B
   Golf courses: 3 private (63 holes); 10 daily fee (162   AA
      holes); 3 municipal (54 holes)
   Bowling centers: 11 (242 lanes, tenpins)   A
Crowd Pleasers (400 points)
   Zoo: Ross Park Zoo—54 species, 113 specimens   C
   Auto Racing: Shangri-La Motor Speedway   B
      (NASCAR)
   Professional Sports: 0.740 game seats per capita   C
      Whalers (AHL Hockey)
Outdoor Recreation Assets (31)
   Inland Water Area: 7.6 square miles
Places Rated Score: 1,331   Places Rated Rank: 190

Birmingham, AL

Common Denominators (400 points)
   Good restaurants: 2 *, 12 **, 2 ***   B
   Golf courses: 20 private (351 holes); 7 daily fee (90   C
      holes); 6 municipal (99 holes)
   Bowling centers: 9 (236 lanes, tenpins)   C
Crowd Pleasers (600 points)
   Zoo: Birmingham Zoo—223 species, 793
      specimens   A
   Professional Sports: 0.780 game seats per capita   B
      Barons (Double A Baseball)
   NCAA Division I: 0.273 game seats per capita   C
      Samford University Bulldogs, University of
      Alabama Blazers
Outdoor Recreation Assets (40)
   Inland Water Area: 32 square miles
   National Forests, Parks, Wildlife Refuges:
      Watercress NWR (7 acres)
Places Rated Score: 1,040   Places Rated Rank: 251

Bismarck, ND

Common Denominators (1,000 points)
   Good restaurants: 3 **, 1 ***   AA
   Golf courses: 1 private (18 holes); 4 municipal (45   A
      holes)
   Bowling centers: 4 (68 lanes, tenpins)   A
Outdoor Recreation Assets (128)
   Inland Water Area: 73.5 square miles
   National Forests, Parks, Wildlife Refuges:
      Canfield Lake NWR (3 acres)
      Florence Lake NWR (1,468 acres)
      Long Lake NWR (10,330 acres)
Places Rated Score: 1,128   Places Rated Rank: 245

Rating

Bloomington, IN
Common Denominators (700 points)
 Good restaurants: 1 **, 1 ***   **B**
 Golf courses: 1 private (18 holes); 2 daily fee (36 **A**
  holes); 1 municipal (18 holes)
 Bowling centers: 3 (68 lanes, tenpins)   **B**
Crowd Pleasers (400 points)
 NCAA Division I: 4.525 game seats per capita **AA**
  Indiana University Fightin' Hoosiers
Outdoor Recreation Assets (671)
 Inland Water Area: 26.6 square miles
 National Forests, Parks, Wildlife Refuges:
  Hoosier NF (18,317 acres)
Places Rated Score: 1,771   Places Rated Rank: 113

Bloomington–Normal, IL
Common Denominators (700 points)
 Golf courses: 3 private (45 holes); 4 daily fee (36 **AA**
  holes); 2 municipal (36 holes)
 Bowling centers: 7 (106 lanes, tenpins)   **A**
Crowd Pleasers (500 points)
 Zoo: Miller Park Zoo—86 species, 241 specimens **C**
 NCAA Division I: 1.587 game seats per capita **AA**
  Illinois State Redbirds
Outdoor Recreation Assets (10)
 Inland Water Area: 2.3 square miles
Places Rated Score: 1,210   Places Rated Rank: 223

Boise City, ID
Common Denominators (600 points)
 Good restaurants: 3 **   **C**
 Golf courses: 4 private (72 holes); 4 daily fee (63 **B**
  holes); 1 municipal (9 holes)
 Bowling centers: 6 (138 lanes, tenpins)   **A**
Crowd Pleasers (700 points)
 Pari-Mutuel Betting: **B**
  Les Bois Park (thoroughbred, 51 races)
 Professional Sports: 1.139 game seats per capita **B**
  Hawks (Class A Baseball)
 NCAA Division I: 1.257 game seats per capita **A**
  Boise State Broncos
Outdoor Recreation Assets (72)
 Inland Water Area: 8.6 square miles
 National Forests, Parks, Wildlife Refuges:
  Boise NF (4,211 acres)
Places Rated Score: 1,372   Places Rated Rank: 181

Boston, MA
Common Denominators (500 points)
 Good restaurants: 9 *, 30 **, 30 ***, 3 **** **A**
 Golf courses: 47 private (774 holes); 26 daily fee **C**
  (396 holes); 16 municipal (252 holes)
 Bowling centers: 48 (1,079 lanes, mixed)   **C**
Crowd Pleasers (900 points)
 Aquarium: New England Aquarium—412 species, **AA**
  7,606 specimens
 Pari-Mutuel Betting: **C**
  Raynham Taunton Park (greyhound, 520 races)
  Suffolk Downs (thoroughbred, 250 races)
  Wonderland Park (greyhound, 460 races)
 Professional Sports: 1.562 game seats per capita **A**
  Bruins (NHL Hockey), Celtics (NBA Basketball),
  New England Patriots (AFC Football), Red Sox
  (AL Baseball)
 NCAA Division I: 0.260 game seats per capita **C**
  Boston College Eagles, Boston University Terriers,
  Harvard Crimson
Outdoor Recreation Assets (737)
 Atlantic Coastline: 41 miles
 Inland Water Area: 115.4 square miles
 National Forests, Parks, Wildlife Refuges:
  Adams NHS (9 acres)
  Boston NHP (41 acres)
  Frederick Law Olmstead NHS (2 acres)
  Great Meadows NWR (1,526 acres)

Rating

  John F. Kennedy NHS (0.09 acres)
  Longfellow NHS (2 acres)
  Massasoit NWR (184 acres)
  Minute Man NHP (712 acres)
  Oxbow NWR (662 acres)
  Saugus Iron Works NHS (9 acres)
 CMSA Access: Boston–Lawrence–Salem, MA–NH
  (140 points)
Places Rated Score: 2,277   Places Rated Rank: 57

★ Boulder–Longmont, CO
Common Denominators (800 points)
 Good restaurants: 5 **, 1 ***, 1 ****   **AA**
 Golf courses: 2 private (36 holes); 3 daily fee (45 **A**
  holes); 3 municipal (45 holes)
 Bowling centers: 4 (82 lanes, tenpins)   **C**
Crowd Pleasers (400 points)
 NCAA Division I: 1.753 game seats per capita **AA**
  University of Colorado Buffalos
Outdoor Recreation Assets (1,788)
 Inland Water Area: 9.7 square miles
 National Forests, Parks, Wildlife Refuges:
  Rocky Mountain NP (27,259 acres)
  Roosevelt NF (138,624 acres)
 CMSA Access: Denver–Boulder, CO (110 points)
Places Rated Score: 3,098   Places Rated Rank: 20

Bradenton, FL
Common Denominators (700 points)
 Good restaurants: 5 **   **A**
 Golf courses: 4 private (72 holes); 3 daily fee (72 **A**
  holes); 2 municipal (36 holes)
 Bowling center: 1 (40 lanes, tenpins)   **C**
Crowd Pleasers (200 points)
 Auto Racing: DeSoto Memorial Speedway   **B**
  (NASCAR)
Outdoor Recreation Assets (567)
 Gulf of Mexico Coastline: 24 miles
 Inland Water Area: 52.2 square miles
 National Forests, Parks, Wildlife Refuges:
  DeSoto National Monument (25 acres)
  Passage Key NWR (36 acres)
Places Rated Score: 1,467   Places Rated Rank: 166

Brazoria, TX
Common Denominators (300 points)
 Golf courses: 6 private (81 holes); 2 daily fee (27 **C**
  holes); 1 municipal (18 holes)
 Bowling centers: 3 (84 lanes, tenpins)   **B**
Outdoor Recreation Assets (787)
 Gulf of Mexico Coastline: 35 miles
 Inland Water Area: 79.8 square miles
 National Forests, Parks, Wildlife Refuges:
  Brazoria NWR (10,361 acres)
  San Bernard NWR (21,783 acres)
 CMSA Access: Houston–Galveston–Brazoria, TX
  (100 points)
Places Rated Score: 1,187   Places Rated Rank: 229

Bremerton, WA
Common Denominators (800 points)
 Good restaurant: 1 ***   **C**
 Golf courses: 3 private (36 holes); 3 daily fee (54 **A**
  holes); 1 municipal (18 holes)
 Bowling centers: 8 (202 lanes, tenpins)   **AA**
Outdoor Recreation Assets (1,027)
 Puget Sound Coastline: 30 miles
 Inland Water Area: 66.8 square miles
Places Rated Score: 1,827   Places Rated Rank: 108

Bridgeport–Milford, CT
Common Denominators (500 points)
 Good restaurants: 2 **   **C**
 Golf courses: 8 private (135 holes); 3 daily fee (36 **B**
  holes); 4 municipal (90 holes)

	Rating
Bowling centers: 8 (278 lanes, mixed)	**B**

Crowd Pleasers (600 points)
Zoo: Beardsley Zoological Gardens—74 species, 244 specimens	**C**
Pari-Mutuel Betting:	**AA**
Bridgeport Jai Alai (243 matches)	
Milford Jai Alai (231 matches)	
NCAA Division I: 0.079 game seats per capita	**C**
Fairfield University Stags	

Outdoor Recreation Assets (337)
Atlantic Coastline: 17 miles
Inland Water Area: 7.9 square miles
National Forests, Parks, Wildlife Refuges:
S.B. McKinney NWR (22 acres)
CMSA Access: New York–Northern NJ–Long
Island, NY–NJ–CT (150 points)
Places Rated Score: 1,587   Places Rated Rank: 144

Bristol, CT

Common Denominators (300 points)
Golf course: 1 private (18 holes)	—
Bowling centers: 2 (64 lanes, mixed)	**A**

Outdoor Recreation Assets (63)
Inland Water Area: 1.0 square miles
CMSA Access: Hartford–New Britain–Middletown,
CT (100 points)
Places Rated Score: 463   Places Rated Rank: 321

Brockton, MA

Common Denominators (600 points)
Good restaurant: 1 **	**C**
Golf courses: 2 private (27 holes); 6 daily fee (81 holes); 1 municipal (18 holes)	**A**
Bowling centers: 6 (130 lanes, mixed)	**B**

Crowd Pleasers (100 points)
Pari-Mutuel Betting:	**C**
Marshfield Fair (thoroughbred, 10 races)	

Outdoor Recreation Assets (116)
Inland Water Area: 3.5 square miles
CMSA Access: Boston–Lawrence–Salem, MA–NH
(90 points)
Places Rated Score: 906   Places Rated Rank: 273

Brownsville–Harlingen, TX

Common Denominators (600 points)
Good restaurants: 2 *, 6 **, 1 ***	**A**
Golf courses: 6 private (108 holes); 2 daily fee (27 holes); 1 municipal (27 holes)	**C**
Bowling centers: 7 (146 lanes, tenpins)	**B**

Crowd Pleasers (300 points)
Zoo: Gladys Porter Zoo—371 species, 1,516 specimens	**A**

Outdoor Recreation Assets (1,739)
Gulf of Mexico Coastline: 31 miles
Inland Water Area: 262.9 square miles
National Forests, Parks, Wildlife Refuges:
Laguna Atascosa NWR (44,940 acres)
Lower Rio Grande Valley NWR (511 acres)
Places Rated Score: 2,639   Places Rated Rank: 39

Bryan–College Station, TX

Common Denominators (500 points)
Good restaurants: 2 *, 1**	**C**
Golf courses: 1 private (18 holes); 1 daily fee (18 holes); 1 municipal (18 holes)	**B**
Bowling centers: 3 (76 lanes, tenpins)	**B**

Crowd Pleasers (600 points)
Auto Racing: Texas World Speedway (SCCA)	**B**
NCAA Division I: 3.422 game seats per capita	**AA**
Texas A & M Aggies	

Outdoor Recreation Assets (19)
Inland Water Area: 1.5 square miles
Places Rated Score: 1,119   Places Rated Rank: 247

Buffalo, NY

Common Denominators (800 points)
Good restaurants: 3 *, 11 **, 5 ***	**B**
Golf courses: 12 private (216 holes); 10 daily fee (171 holes); 11 municipal (162 holes)	**B**
Bowling centers: 57 (1208 lanes, tenpins)	**AA**

Crowd Pleasers (1,200 points)
Zoo: Buffalo Zoological Gardens—272 species, 1,441 specimens	**A**
Auto Racing: Holland International Speedway (NASCAR)	**B**
Pari-Mutuel Betting:	**B**
Buffalo Raceway (harness, 128 races)	
Professional Sports: 2.790 game seats per capita	**AA**
Bills (AFC Football), Bisons (Triple A Baseball), Sabres (NHL Hockey)	
NCAA Division I: 0.204 game seats per capita	**C**
Canisius College Golden Griffins	

Outdoor Recreation Assets (340)
Great Lakes Coastline: 29 miles
Inland Water Area: 10.6 square miles
National Forests, Parks, Wildlife Refuges:
Theodore Roosevelt Inaugural NHS (1 acre)
CMSA Access: Buffalo–Niagara Falls, NY (10 points)
Places Rated Score: 2,350   Places Rated Rank: 55

Burlington, NC

Common Denominators (500 points)
Golf courses: 1 private (18 holes); 5 daily fee (90 holes); 1 municipal (18 holes)	**AA**
Bowling center: 1 (32 lanes, tenpins)	**C**

Outdoor Recreation Assets (22)
Inland Water Area: 1.9 square mile
Places Rated Score: 522   Places Rated Rank: 317

Burlington, VT

Common Denominators (1,000 points)
Good restaurants: 1 *, 8 **, 3 ***	**AA**
Golf courses: 1 private (18 holes); 4 daily fee (63 holes)	**A**
Bowling centers: 6 (118 lanes, tenpins)	**A**

Crowd Pleasers (100 points)
NCAA Division I: 0.288 game seats per capita	**C**
University of Vermont Catamounts	

Outdoor Recreation Assets (1,168)
Inland Water Area: 132.3 square miles
Places Rated Score: 2,268   Places Rated Rank: 59

Canton, OH

Common Denominators (900 points)
Good restaurants: 1 *, 3 **, 1 ***	**C**
Golf courses: 5 private (90 holes); 17 daily fee (333 holes)	**AA**
Bowling centers: 26 (540 lanes, tenpins)	**AA**

Crowd Pleasers (200 points)
Professional Sports: 0.955 game seats per capita	**B**
Indians (Double A Baseball)	

Outdoor Recreation Assets (57)
Inland Water Area: 11.1 square miles
Places Rated Score: 1,157   Places Rated Rank: 237

Casper, WY

Common Denominators (1,000 points)
Good restaurants: 1 **, 1 ***	**A**
Golf courses: 2 private (36 holes); 1 daily fee (9 holes); 1 municipal (18 holes)	**A**
Bowling centers: 5 (84 lanes, tenpins)	**AA**

Crowd Pleasers (200 points)
Pari-Mutuel Betting:	**B**
Central Wyoming Fair (mixed meetings, 9 races)	

Outdoor Recreation Assets (36)
Inland Water Area: 26.7 square miles
National Forests, Parks, Wildlife Refuges:
Medicine Bow NF (5,614 acres)
Pathfinder NWR (1,535 acres)
Places Rated Score: 1,236   Places Rated Rank: 215

	Rating
Cedar Rapids, IA	
Common Denominators (1,000 points)	
Good restaurants: 2 ★, 2 ★★	B
Golf courses: 3 private (45 holes); 4 daily fee (36 holes); 4 municipal (63 holes)	AA
Bowling centers: 9 (172 lanes, tenpins)	AA
Crowd Pleasers (600 points)	
Auto Racing: Hawkeye Downs Speedway (NASCAR)	B
Professional Sports: 3.617 game seats per capita Reds (Class A Baseball), Silver Bullets (CBA Basketball)	AA
Outdoor Recreation Assets (3)	
Inland Water Area: 0.2 square miles	
Places Rated Score: 1,603 Places Rated Rank: 140	

Champaign–Urbana–Rantoul, IL	
Common Denominators (1,000 points)	
Good restaurants: 7 ★★, 1 ★★★	AA
Golf courses: 4 private (72 holes); 1 daily fee (36 holes); 2 municipal (36 holes)	A
Bowling centers: 7 (134 lanes, tenpins)	A
Crowd Pleasers (400 points)	
NCAA Division I: 3.016 game seats per capita University of Illinois Fighting Illini	AA
Outdoor Recreation Assets (1)	
Inland Water Area: 0.1 square miles	
Places Rated Score: 1,401 Places Rated Rank: 176	

★ **Charleston, SC**	
Common Denominators (800 points)	
Good restaurants: 1 ★, 9 ★★, 9 ★★★	AA
Golf courses: 10 private (189 holes); 7 daily fee (162 holes); 1 municipal (18 holes)	B
Bowling centers: 9 (244 lanes, tenpins)	B
Crowd Pleasers (600 points)	
Auto Racing: Summerville Speedway (NASCAR)	B
Professional Sports: 0.823 game seats per capita Rainbows (Class A Baseball)	B
NCAA Division I: 0.397 game seats per capita Baptist College Buccaneers, The Citadel Bulldogs	B
Outdoor Recreation Assets (1,933)	
Atlantic Coastline: 75 miles	
Inland Water Area: 230.6 square miles	
National Forests, Parks, Wildlife Refuges:	
Cape Romain NWR (34,049 acres)	
Fort Sumter NM (67 acres)	
Francis Marion NF (250,005 acres)	
Santee NWR (2 acres)	
Places Rated Score: 3,333 Places Rated Rank: 11	

Charleston, WV	
Common Denominators (500 points)	
Good restaurants: 2 ★★, 3 ★★★	B
Golf courses: 6 private (108 holes); 3 municipal (45 holes)	C
Bowling centers: 5 (116 lanes, tenpins)	B
Crowd Pleasers (800 points)	
Pari-Mutuel Betting:	AA
Tri-State Greyhound Park (310 greyhound races)	
Professional Sports: 2.909 game seats per capita Gunners (CBA Basketball), Wheelers (Class A Baseball)	AA
Outdoor Recreation Assets (44)	
Inland Water Area: 11.1 square miles	
Places Rated Score: 1,344 Places Rated Rank: 187	

Charlotte–Gastonia–Rock Hill, NC–SC	
Common Denominators (500 points)	
Good restaurants: 1 ★, 8 ★★, 5 ★★★	C
Golf courses: 23 private (450 holes); 25 daily fee (423 holes); 3 municipal (45 holes)	A
Bowling centers: 14 (416 lanes, tenpins)	C
Crowd Pleasers (900 points)	
Theme Park: Carowinds (121 days)	B

	Rating
Auto Racing:	A
Charlotte Motor Speedway (NASCAR)	
Concord Motor Speedway (NASCAR)	
Professional Sports: 1.340 game seats per capita Gastonia Rangers (Class A Baseball), Hornets (NBA Basketball), Knights (Double A Baseball)	B
NCAA Division I: 0.382 game seats per capita Davidson Wildcats, University of North Carolina 49ers, Winthrop College Eagles	B
Outdoor Recreation Assets (82)	
Inland Water Area: 52.5 square miles	
National Forests, Parks, Wildlife Refuges:	
Kings Mountain NMP (2,529 acres)	
Places Rated Score: 1,482 Places Rated Rank: 164	

Charlottesville, VA	
Common Denominators (800 points)	
Good restaurants: 2 ★★, 3 ★★★	AA
Golf courses: 4 private (81 holes); 1 daily fee (18 holes); 2 municipal (18 holes)	B
Bowling centers: 2 (52 lanes, mixed)	B
Crowd Pleasers (400 points)	
NCAA Division I: 2.467 game seats per capita University of Virginia Cavaliers	AA
Outdoor Recreation Assets (207)	
Inland Water Area: 1.1 square miles	
National Forests, Parks, Wildlife Refuges:	
Appalachian Trail (926 acres)	
Shenandoah NP (29,786 acres)	
Places Rated Score: 1,407 Places Rated Rank: 172	

Chattanooga, TN–GA	
Common Denominators (500 points)	
Good restaurants: 2 ★, 8 ★★, 4 ★★★	A
Golf courses: 9 private (153 holes); 5 daily fee (63 holes); 2 municipal (27 holes)	C
Bowling centers: 4 (120 lanes, tenpins)	C
Crowd Pleasers (400 points)	
Professional Sports: 1.343 game seats per capita Lookouts (Double A Baseball)	B
NCAA Division I: 0.436 game seats per capita University of Tennessee Moccasins	B
Outdoor Recreation Assets (136)	
Inland Water Area: 45.3 square miles	
National Forests, Parks, Wildlife Refuges:	
Chickamauga and Chattanooga NMP (8,085 acres)	
Places Rated Score: 1,036 Places Rated Rank: 254	

Cheyenne, WY	
Common Denominators (900 points)	
Good restaurants: 1 ★★, 1 ★★★	A
Golf courses: 2 private (36 holes); 2 municipal (27 holes)	B
Bowling centers: 5 (84 lanes, tenpins)	AA
Outdoor Recreation Assets (4)	
Inland Water Area: 2.0 square miles	
Places Rated Score: 904 Places Rated Rank: 274	

★ **Chicago, IL**	
Common Denominators (1,100 points)	
Good restaurants: 49 ★, 6 ★★, 41 ★★★, 4 ★★★★, 2 ★★★★★	A
Golf courses: 49 private (909 holes); 42 daily fee (864 holes); 39 municipal (657 holes)	B
Bowling centers: 175 (3,976 lanes, tenpins)	B
Crowd Pleasers (1,500 points)	
Zoos: Chicago (Brookfield) Zoological Park—426 species, 2,200 specimens	AA
Lincoln Park Zoological Gardens—389 species, 1,845 specimens	AA
Aquarium: John G. Shedd Aquarium—815 species, 7,658 specimens	AA
Auto Racing:	A
Chicagoland Grand Prix (USAC)	
Santa Fe Speedway (NASCAR)	

Rating

Pari-Mutuel Betting: **C**
    Arlington Park (thoroughbred, 95 races)
    Hawthorne Race Course (mixed meetings, 136
    races)
    Maywood Park (harness, 174 races)
    Sportsman's Park (mixed meetings, 175 races)
Professional Sports: 1.377 game seats per capita   **B**
    Bears (NFC Football), Black Hawks (NHL Hockey),
    Bulls (NBA Basketball), Cubs (NL Baseball),
    White Sox (AL Baseball)
NCAA Division I: 0.097 game seats per capita   **C**
    Chicago State Cougars, DePaul Blue Demons,
    Loyola University Ramblers, Northwestern
    University Wildcats, University of Illinois Flames
Outdoor Recreation Assets (355)
  Great Lakes Coastline: 33 miles
  Inland Water Area: 9.6 square miles
  National Forests, Parks, Wildlife Refuges:
    Chicago Portage NHS (91 acres)
CMSA Access: Chicago–Gary–Lake County,
  IL–IN–WI (250 points)
Places Rated Score: 3,205   Places Rated Rank: 16

Chico, CA
Common Denominators (400 points)
  Golf courses: 1 private (18 holes); 2 daily fee (18   **B**
    holes); 2 municipal (36 holes)
  Bowling centers: 3 (74 lanes, tenpins)   **B**
Outdoor Recreation Assets (701)
  Inland Water Area: 30.1 square miles
  National Forests, Parks, Wildlife Refuges:
    Lassen NF (49,239 acres)
    Plumas NF (81,972 acres)
Places Rated Score: 1,101   Places Rated Rank: 248

Cincinnati, OH–KY–IN
Common Denominators (1,000 points)
  Good restaurants: 6 ★, 24 ★★, 15 ★★★,   **AA**
    1 ★★★★, 1 ★★★★★
  Golf courses: 30 private (504 holes); 13 daily fee   **A**
    (198 holes); 19 municipal (333 holes)
  Bowling centers: 53 (1186 lanes, tenpins)   **A**
Crowd Pleasers (1,200 points)
  Zoo: Cincinnati Zoo & Botanical Garden—734   **AA**
    species, 407,402 specimens
  Theme Park: King's Island (126 days)   **C**
  Pari-Mutuel Betting: **C**
    Lebanon Raceway (harness, 132 races)
    River Downs (thoroughbred, 147 races)
    Turfway Park (thoroughbred, 125 races)
  Professional Sports: 3.279 game seats per capita   **AA**
    Reds (NL Baseball), Bengals (AFC Football)
  NCAA Division I: 0.407 game seats per capita   **B**
    University of Cincinnati Bearcats, Xavier
    University Musketeers
Outdoor Recreation Assets (69)
  Inland Water Area: 29.9 square miles
  National Forests, Parks, Wildlife Refuges:
    William Howard Taft NHS (3 acres)
CMSA Access: Cincinnati–Hamilton, OH–KY–IN
  (30 points)
Places Rated Score: 2,299   Places Rated Rank: 56

Clarksville–Hopkinsville, TN–KY
Common Denominators (600 points)
  Good restaurants: 1 ★, 1 ★★   **C**
  Golf courses: 4 private (63 holes); 5 municipal (63   **A**
    holes)
  Bowling centers: 4 (84 lanes, tenpins)   **B**
Crowd Pleasers (300 points)
  NCAA Division I: 0.994 game seats per capita   **A**
    Austin Peay State Governors
Outdoor Recreation Assets (1,218)
  Inland Water Area: 4.8 square miles
  National Forests, Parks, Wildlife Refuges:
    Cherokee NF (193,640 acres)
Places Rated Score: 2,118   Places Rated Rank: 73

Rating

Cleveland, OH
Common Denominators (800 points)
  Good restaurants: 6 ★, 20 ★★, 6 ★★★   **B**
  Golf courses: 24 private (459 holes); 31 daily fee   **A**
    (522 holes); 12 municipal (234 holes)
  Bowling centers: 83 (1,832 lanes, tenpins)   **A**
Crowd Pleasers (900 points)
  Zoo: Cleveland Metroparks Zoological Park—506   **A**
    species, 3,344 specimens
  Pari-Mutuel Betting: **C**
    Thistledown (thoroughbred, 188 races)
  Professional Sports: 4.034 game seats per capita   **AA**
    Browns (AFC Football), Cavaliers (NBA Basketball),
    Indians (AL Baseball)
  NCAA Division I: 0.019 game seats per capita   **C**
    Cleveland State Vikings
Outdoor Recreation Assets (611)
  Great Lakes Coastline: 56 miles
  Inland Water Area: 5.5 square miles
  National Forests, Parks, Wildlife Refuges:
    Cuyahoga Valley NRA (6,469 acres)
CMSA Access: Cleveland–Akron–Lorain, OH (80
  points)
Places Rated Score: 2,391   Places Rated Rank: 52

Colorado Springs, CO
Common Denominators (800 points)
  Good restaurants: 5 ★, 10 ★★, 2 ★★★   **AA**
  Golf courses: 10 private (225 holes); 3 daily fee (45   **C**
    holes); 2 municipal (45 holes)
  Bowling centers: 12 (302 lanes, tenpins)   **A**
Crowd Pleasers (900 points)
  Zoo: Cheyenne Mountain Zoological Park—147   **A**
    species, 657 specimens
  Pari-Mutuel Betting: **C**
    Pikes Peak Meadows (thoroughbred, 90 races)
    Rocky Mountain Greyhound Park (74 greyhound
    races)
  Professional Sports: 1.100 game seats per capita   **B**
    Sky Sox (Triple A Baseball)
  NCAA Division I: 0.830 game seats per capita   **A**
    U.S. Air Force Academy Falcons
Outdoor Recreation Assets (374)
  Inland Water Area: 2.1 square miles
  National Forests, Parks, Wildlife Refuges:
    Pike NF (100,726 acres)
Places Rated Score: 2,074   Places Rated Rank: 78

Columbia, MO
Common Denominators (900 points)
  Good restaurants: 2 ★★   **B**
  Golf courses: 4 private (45 holes); 1 daily fee (18   **A**
    holes); 2 municipal (36 holes)
  Bowling centers: 7 (130 lanes, tenpins)   **AA**
Crowd Pleasers (400 points)
  NCAA Division I: 4.204 game seats per capita   **AA**
    University of Missouri Tigers
Outdoor Recreation Assets (31)
  Inland Water Area: 4.2 square miles
Places Rated Score: 1,331   Places Rated Rank: 190

Columbia, SC
Common Denominators (300 points)
  Good restaurants: 4 ★★, 2 ★★★   **C**
  Golf courses: 9 private (171 holes); 5 daily fee (72   **C**
    holes); 1 municipal (18 holes)
  Bowling centers: 5 (152 lanes, tenpins)   **C**
Crowd Pleasers (700 points)
  Zoo: Riverbanks Zoological Park—196 species, 744   **A**
    specimens
  Professional Sports: 0.599 game seats per capita   **C**
    Mets (Class A Baseball)
  NCAA Division I: 1.093 game seats per capita   **A**
    University of South Carolina Fighting Gamecocks
Outdoor Recreation Assets (274)
  Inland Water Area: 59.9 square miles

	Rating
National Forests, Parks, Wildlife Refuges:	
Congaree Swamp NM (15,138 acres)	

Places Rated Score: 1,274   Places Rated Rank: 203

Columbus, GA–AL
Common Denominators (400 points)
Good restaurant: 1 **	C
Golf courses: 4 private (81 holes); 1 daily fee (9 holes); 2 municipal (36 holes)	C
Bowling centers: 4 (144 lanes, tenpins)	B

Crowd Pleasers (300 points)
Professional Sports: 1.697 game seats per capita	A
Mudcats (Double A Baseball)	

Outdoor Recreation Assets (77)
Inland Water Area: 17.2 square miles

Places Rated Score: 777   Places Rated Rank: 296

Columbus, OH
Common Denominators (700 points)
Good restaurants: 6 **, 7 ***	C
Golf courses: 22 private (369 holes); 31 daily fee (468 holes); 7 municipal (108 holes)	A
Bowling centers: 40 (1094 lanes, tenpins)	A

Crowd Pleasers (1,100 points)
Zoo: Columbus Zoological Gardens—680 species, 8,260 specimens	AA
Auto Racing: Columbus Grand Prix (IMSA)	B
Pari-Mutuel Betting:	C
Beulah Park (thoroughbred, 138 races)	
Scioto Downs (harness, 115 races)	
Professional Sports: 0.799 game seats per capita	B
Clippers (Triple A Baseball)	
NCAA Division I: 0.442 game seats per capita	B
Ohio State Buckeyes	

Outdoor Recreation Assets (31)
Inland Water Area: 22.7 square miles

Places Rated Score: 1,831   Places Rated Rank: 106

Corpus Christi, TX
Common Denominators (600 points)
Good restaurants: 3 *, 3 **, 1 ***	B
Golf courses: 10 private (144 holes); 2 daily fee (36 holes); 3 municipal (54 holes)	B
Bowling centers: 6 (184 lanes, tenpins)	B

Outdoor Recreation Assets (976)
Gulf of Mexico Coastline: 25 miles
Inland Water Area: 273.3 square miles

Places Rated Score: 1,576   Places Rated Rank: 149

Cumberland, MD–WV
Common Denominators (800 points)
Good restaurants: 1 *, 1 **, 2 ***	AA
Golf courses: 2 private (39 holes); 2 daily fee (18 holes)	C
Bowling centers: 5 (86 lanes, tenpins)	A

Outdoor Recreation Assets (39)
Inland Water Area: 0.4 square miles
National Forests, Parks, Wildlife Refuges:
Chesapeake and Ohio Canal NHP (3,494 acres)

Places Rated Score: 839   Places Rated Rank: 283

Dallas, TX
Common Denominators (300 points)
Good restaurants: 4 **, 17 **, 11 ***, 2 ****	C
Golf courses: 33 private (657 holes); 7 daily fee (135 holes); 16 municipal (342 holes)	C
Bowling centers: 24 (796 lanes, tenpins)	C

Crowd Pleasers (1,300 points)
Zoo: Dallas Zoo—401 species, 1,519 specimens	AA
Aquarium: Dallas Aquarium—296 species, 1,443 specimens	AA
Auto Racing:	A
Grand Prix of Dallas (SCCA)	
North Texas Motor Speedway (NASCAR)	
Professional Sports: 0.463 game seats per capita	C
Cowboys (NFC Football), Mavericks (NBA Basketball)	

NCAA Division I: 0.126 game seats per capita	C
Southern Methodist Mustangs, University of North Texas Mean Green Eagles	

Outdoor Recreation Assets (173)
Inland Water Area: 161.3 square miles
CMSA Access: Dallas–Fort Worth, TX (100 points)

Places Rated Score: 1,873   Places Rated Rank: 99

Danbury, CT
Common Denominators (800 points)
Good restaurants: 1 *, 3 **, 4 ***	AA
Golf courses: 4 private (63 holes); 2 daily fee (27 holes); 2 municipal (36 holes)	B
Bowling centers: 4 (110 lanes, mixed)	B

Outdoor Recreation Assets (176)
Inland Water Area: 11.9 square miles
CMSA Access: New York–Northern NJ–Long Island, NY–NJ–CT (210 points)

Places Rated Score: 1,186   Places Rated Rank: 230

Danville, VA
Common Denominators (300 points)
Golf courses: 5 private (72 holes); 2 daily fee (27 holes)	B
Bowling centers: 2 (44 lanes, tenpins)	C

Outdoor Recreation Assets (49)
Inland Water Area: 10 square miles

Places Rated Score: 349   Places Rated Rank: 328

Davenport–Rock Island–Moline, IA–IL
Common Denominators (1,000 points)
Good restaurants: 1 *, 3 **, 2 ***	B
Golf courses: 7 private (126 holes); 8 daily fee (108 holes); 7 municipal (126 holes)	AA
Bowling centers: 21 (496 lanes, tenpins)	AA

Crowd Pleasers (500 points)
Pari-Mutuel Betting:	A
Quad City Downs (harness, 144 races)	
Professional Sports: 1.374 game seats per capita	B
Quad City Thunder (CBA Basketball), Quad City Angels (Class A Baseball)	

Outdoor Recreation Assets (116)
Inland Water Area: 40.3 square miles
National Forests, Parks, Wildlife Refuges:
Upper Mississippi NWR (398 acres)

Places Rated Score: 1,616   Places Rated Rank: 135

Dayton–Springfield, OH
Common Denominators (800 points)
Good restaurants: 3 *, 6 **, 4 ***, 2 ****	B
Golf courses: 16 private (297 holes); 9 daily fee (135 holes); 9 municipal (198 holes)	B
Bowling centers: 42 (1072 lanes, tenpins)	AA

Crowd Pleasers (100 points)
NCAA Division I: 0.208 game seats per capita	C
University of Dayton Flyers, Wright State Raiders	

Outdoor Recreation Assets (33)
Inland Water Area: 11.1 square miles

Places Rated Score: 933   Places Rated Rank: 269

★ Daytona Beach, FL
Common Denominators (900 points)
Good restaurants: 4 **, 2 ***	B
Golf courses: 4 private (72 holes); 9 daily fee (180 holes); 2 municipal (54 holes)	AA
Bowling centers: 8 (240 lanes, tenpins)	A

Crowd Pleasers (700 points)
Auto Racing:	A
Daytona International Speedway (NASCAR)	
Volusia County Speedway (NASCAR)	
Pari-Mutuel Betting:	B
Daytona Beach Kennel Club (greyhound, 166 races)	
Volusia Jai Alai (229 matches)	
NCAA Division I: 0.389 game seats per capita	B
Bethune–Cookman College Wildcats, Stetson	

Rating

University Hatters
Outdoor Recreation Assets (1,377)
  Atlantic Coastline: 49 miles
  Inland Water Area: 151.9 square miles
  National Forests, Parks, Wildlife Refuges:
    Canaveral NS (28,148 acres)
    Lake Woodruff NWR (18,225 acres)
Places Rated Score: 2,977   Places Rated Rank: 27

Decatur, AL
Common Denominators (500 points)
  Good restaurant: 1 **   C
  Golf courses: 2 private (36 holes); 2 daily fee (27   A
    holes); 2 municipal (27 holes)
  Bowling centers: 2 (44 lanes, tenpins)   C
Outdoor Recreation Assets (715)
  Inland Water Area: 48.3 square miles
  National Forests, Parks, Wildlife Refuges:
    Bankhead NF (89,558 acres)
Places Rated Score: 1,215   Places Rated Rank: 220

Decatur, IL
Common Denominators (800 points)
  Good restaurants: 2 **   B
  Golf courses: 2 private (36 holes); 3 municipal (54   A
    holes)
  Bowling centers: 5 (92 lanes, tenpins)   A
Outdoor Recreation Assets (38)
  Inland Water Area: 4.4 square miles
Places Rated Score: 838   Places Rated Rank: 284

Denver, CO
Common Denominators (700 points)
  Good restaurants: 6 *, 16 **, 9 ***   B
  Golf courses: 25 private (468 holes); 7 daily fee   B
    (117 holes); 17 municipal (324 holes)
  Bowling centers: 45 (1,228 lanes, tenpins)   A
Crowd Pleasers (1,100 points)
  Zoo: Denver Zoological Gardens—295 species,   AA
    1,159 specimens
  Auto Racing: Second Creek Raceway (SCCA)   B
  Pari-Mutuel Betting: C
    Colorado Horse Racing Association (mixed
      meetings, 15 races)
    Interstate Kennel Club (greyhound, 76 races)
    Mile High Kennel Club (greyhound, 74 races)
    Rocky Mountain Paint Racing (mixed meetings,
      15 races)
  Professional Sports: 4.116 game seats per capita   AA
    Broncos (AFC Football), Nuggets (NBA
    Basketball), Rangers (IHL Hockey), Zephyrs (Triple
    A Baseball)
Outdoor Recreation Assets (31)
  Inland Water Area: 23.2 square miles
CMSA Access: Denver–Boulder, CO (40 points)
Places Rated Score: 1,871   Places Rated Rank: 101

Des Moines, IA
Common Denominators (800 points)
  Good restaurants: 8 **, 1 ***   B
  Golf courses: 10 private (153 holes); 8 daily fee   A
    (117 holes); 4 municipal (72 holes)
  Bowling centers: 16 (354 lanes, tenpins)   A
Crowd Pleasers (800 points)
  Zoo: Blank Park Zoo of Des Moines—107 species,   C
    633 specimens
  Pari-Mutuel Betting: A
    Prairie Meadows (mixed meetings, 169 races)
  Professional Sports: 1.389 game seats per capita   B
    Iowa Cubs (Triple A Baseball)
  NCAA Division I: 0.417 game seats per capita   B
    Drake University Bulldogs
Outdoor Recreation Assets (30)
  Inland Water Area: 10.6 square miles
Places Rated Score: 1,630   Places Rated Rank: 133

Detroit, MI
Common Denominators (800 points)
  Good restaurants: 10 *, 26 **, 8 ***   C
  Golf courses: 42 private (792 holes); 76 daily fee   A
    (1332 holes); 31 municipal (495 holes)
  Bowling centers: 181 (5045 lanes, tenpins)   AA
Crowd Pleasers (1,300 points)
  Zoos: Belle Isle Zoo & Aquarium—164 species, 893   B
    specimens
    Detroit Zoological Park—255 species, 1,213   AA
    specimens
  Auto Racing: Detroit Grand Prix (SCCA)   B
  Pari-Mutuel Betting: C
    Detroit Race Course (thoroughbred, 123 races)
    Hazel Park (harness, 168 races)
    Northville Downs (harness, 143 races)
  Professional Sports: 1.525 game seats per capita   A
    Lions (NFC Football), Pistons (NBA Basketball),
    Red Wings (NHL Hockey), Tigers (AL Baseball)
  NCAA Division I: 0.023 game seats per capita   C
    University of Detroit Titans
Outdoor Recreation Assets (581)
  Great Lakes Coastline: 48 miles
  Inland Water Area: 92.9 square miles
CMSA Access: Detroit–Ann Arbor, MI (40 points)
Places Rated Score: 2,721   Places Rated Rank: 34

Dothan, AL
Common Denominators (300 points)
  Good restaurants: 2 **   C
  Golf courses: 5 private (72 holes); 1 daily fee (18   C
    holes)
  Bowling centers: 2 (48 lanes, tenpins)   C
Outdoor Recreation Assets (25)
  Inland Water Area: 5.8 square miles
Places Rated Score: 325   Places Rated Rank: 329

Dubuque, IA
Common Denominators (900 points)
  Good restaurants: 2 **, 1 ***   AA
  Golf courses: 3 private (45 holes); 2 daily fee (27   AA
    holes); 2 municipal (27 holes)
  Bowling centers: 4 (32 lanes, tenpins)   C
Crowd Pleasers (400 points)
  Pari-Mutuel Betting: AA
    Dubuque Greyhound Park (238 greyhound races)
Outdoor Recreation Assets (86)
  Inland Water Area: 9.8 square miles
  National Forests, Parks, Wildlife Refuges:
    Upper Mississippi NWR (476 acres)
Places Rated Score: 1,386   Places Rated Rank: 177

Duluth, MN–WI
Common Denominators (900 points)
  Good restaurants: 1 *, 4 **, 1 ***   B
  Golf courses: 5 private (72 holes); 4 daily fee (36   AA
    holes); 7 municipal (108 holes)
  Bowling centers: 13 (208 lanes, tenpins)   A
Crowd Pleasers (100 points)
  Zoo: Lake Superior Zoological Garden—122   C
    species, 524 specimens
Outdoor Recreation Assets (1,404)
  Great Lakes Coastline: 36 miles
  Inland Water Area: 656.1 square miles
  National Forests, Parks, Wildlife Refuges:
    Superior NF (670,753 acres)
Places Rated Score: 2,404   Places Rated Rank: 50

Eau Claire, WI
Common Denominators (1,100 points)
  Good restaurants: 2 *, 4 **   A
  Golf courses: 3 private (45 holes); 5 daily fee (63   AA
    holes); 2 municipal (18 holes)
  Bowling centers: 10 (148 lanes, tenpins)   AA
Outdoor Recreation Assets (95)
  Inland Water Area: 32.1 square miles
Places Rated Score: 1,195   Places Rated Rank: 227

Rating

El Paso, TX
Common Denominators (500 points)
Good restaurants: 3 ★, 7 ★★, 1 ★★★   **B**
Golf courses: 5 private (90 holes); 1 daily fee (9   **C**
   holes); 2 municipal (45 holes)
Bowling centers: 9 (238 lanes, tenpins)   **B**
Crowd Pleasers (400 points)
Zoo: El Paso Zoological Park—129 species, 462   **C**
   specimens
Professional Sports: 0.808 game seats per capita   **B**
   Diablos (Double A Baseball)
NCAA Division I: 0.289 game seats per capita   **C**
   University of Texas Miners
Places Rated Score: 900   Places Rated Rank: 276

Elkhart–Goshen, IN
Common Denominators (900 points)
Good restaurants: 2 ★, 1 ★★, 1 ★★★   **B**
Golf courses: 3 private (54 holes); 3 daily fee (63   **AA**
   holes); 2 municipal (27 holes)
Bowling centers: 8 (148 lanes, tenpins)   **A**
Outdoor Recreation Assets (22)
Inland Water Area: 2.1 square miles
Places Rated Score: 922   Places Rated Rank: 270

Elmira, NY
Common Denominators (1,100 points)
Good restaurants: 1 ★, 3 ★★, 1 ★★★, 1 ★★★★   **AA**
Golf courses: 2 private (36 holes); 3 daily fee (63   **AA**
   holes); 2 municipal (27 holes)
Bowling centers: 3 (86 lanes, tenpins)   **A**
Crowd Pleasers (400 points)
Professional Sports: 4.428 game seats per capita   **AA**
   Pioneers (Class A Baseball)
Places Rated Score: 1,500   Places Rated Rank: 161

Enid, OK
Common Denominators (800 points)
Good restaurant: 1 ★★   **B**
Golf courses: 1 private (18 holes); 1 daily fee (9   **A**
   holes); 1 municipal (18 holes)
Bowling centers: 2 (48 lanes, tenpins)   **A**
Places Rated Score: 800   Places Rated Rank: 294

Erie, PA
Common Denominators (900 points)
Good restaurants: 1 ★, 1 ★★   **C**
Golf courses: 6 private (90 holes); 8 daily fee (117   **AA**
   holes); 4 municipal (63 holes)
Bowling centers: 37 (442 lanes, tenpins)   **AA**
Crowd Pleasers (500 points)
Zoo: Erie Zoological Gardens—77 species, 330   **C**
   specimens
Pari-Mutuel Betting: **B**
   Erie Downs (thoroughbred, 79 races)
Professional Sports: 0.752 game seats per capita   **B**
   Orioles (Class A Baseball)
Outdoor Recreation Assets (390)
Inland Water Area: 6.4 square miles
Places Rated Score: 1,790   Places Rated Rank: 110

★ Eugene–Springfield, OR
Common Denominators (700 points)
Good restaurants: 2 ★, 5 ★★, 1 ★★★   **A**
Golf courses: 3 private (45 holes); 6 daily fee (81   **B**
   holes); 1 municipal (9 holes)
Bowling centers: 10 (154 lanes, tenpins)   **B**
Crowd Pleasers (600 points)
Professional Sports: 1.857 game seats per capita   **A**
   Eugene Emeralds (Class A Baseball)
NCAA Division I: 1.241 game seats per capita   **A**
   University of Oregon Ducks
Outdoor Recreation Assets (2,000)
Pacific Coastline: 30 miles
Inland Water Area: 58.2 square miles

National Forests, Parks, Wildlife Refuges:
   Oregon Islands NWR (6 acres)
   Siuslaw NF (242,790 acres)
   Umpqua NF (151,588 acres)
   Willamette NF (1,021,769 acres)
Places Rated Score: 3,300   Places Rated Rank: 13

Evansville, IN–KY
Common Denominators (700 points)
Good restaurants: 3 ★★   **C**
Golf courses: 6 private (81 holes); 4 daily fee (72   **A**
   holes); 3 municipal (45 holes)
Bowling centers: 11 (210 lanes, tenpins)   **A**
Crowd Pleasers (600 points)
Zoo: Mesker Park Zoo—207 species, 640   **B**
   specimens
Pari-Mutuel Betting: **B**
   Ellis Park (thoroughbred, 59 races)
   Riverside Downs (quarter horse, 64 races)
NCAA Division I: 0.473 game seats per capita   **B**
   University of Evansville Aces
Outdoor Recreation Assets (126)
Inland Water Area: 36 square miles
Places Rated Score: 1,426   Places Rated Rank: 168

Fall River, MA–RI
Common Denominators (600 points)
Good restaurant: 1 ★★   **C**
Golf courses: 3 private (45 holes); 5 daily fee (54   **B**
   holes)
Bowling centers: 4 (110 lanes, mixed)   **A**
Outdoor Recreation Assets (906)
Atlantic Coastline: 18 miles
Inland Water Area: 27.9 square miles
CMSA Access: Providence–Pawtucket–Fall River,
RI–MA (100 points)
Places Rated Score: 1,606   Places Rated Rank: 138

Fargo–Moorhead, ND–MN
Common Denominators (800 points)
Good restaurants: 3 ★   **C**
Golf courses: 4 private (63 holes); 3 daily fee (36   **AA**
   holes); 4 municipal (54 holes)
Bowling centers: 10 (148 lanes, tenpins)   **A**
Outdoor Recreation Assets (11)
Inland Water Area: 7.7 square miles
Places Rated Score: 811   Places Rated Rank: 289

Fayetteville, NC
Common Denominators (400 points)
Good restaurants: 2 ★★   **C**
Golf courses: 6 private (108 holes); 2 daily fee (36   **C**
   holes)
Bowling centers: 6 (168 lanes, tenpins)   **B**
Crowd Pleasers (200 points)
Professional Sports: 0.794 game seats per capita   **B**
   Generals (Class A Baseball)
Outdoor Recreation Assets (9)
Inland Water Area: 1.2 square miles
Places Rated Score: 609   Places Rated Rank: 307

Fayetteville–Springdale, AR
Common Denominators (800 points)
Good restaurants: 1 ★, 1 ★★, 2 ★★★   **AA**
Golf courses: 1 private (18 holes); 3 daily fee (36   **B**
   holes)
Bowling centers: 2 (68 lanes, tenpins)   **B**
Crowd Pleasers (400 points)
NCAA Division I: 3.514 game seats per capita   **AA**
   University of Arkansas Razorbacks
Outdoor Recreation Assets (218)
Inland Water Area: 5.3 square miles
National Forests, Parks, Wildlife Refuges:
   Ozark NF (23,247 acres)
Places Rated Score: 1,418   Places Rated Rank: 169

Rating

Fitchburg–Leominster, MA
Common Denominators (700 points)
Good restaurant: 1 ***   C
Golf courses: 1 private (18 holes); 5 daily fee (63   AA
holes)
Bowling centers: 3 (54 lanes, mixed)   B
Outdoor Recreation Assets (181)
Inland Water Area: 6.8 square miles
Places Rated Score: 881   Places Rated Rank: 278

Flint, MI
Common Denominators (700 points)
Good restaurants: 1 *, 1 **   C
Golf courses: 10 private (180 holes); 9 daily fee   A
(162 holes); 4 municipal (72 holes)
Bowling centers: 15 (350 lanes, tenpins)   A
Crowd Pleasers (400 points)
Pari-Mutuel Betting: A
Sports Creek Raceway (harness, 143 races)
Professional Sports: 0.369 game seats per capita   C
Spirits (IHL Hockey)
Outdoor Recreation Assets (62)
Inland Water Area: 7 square miles
Places Rated Score: 1,162   Places Rated Rank: 235

Florence, AL
Common Denominators (500 points)
Good restaurants: 2 **   C
Golf courses: 5 private (72 holes); 1 daily fee (9   A
holes); 3 municipal (45 holes)
Bowling center: 1 (32 lanes, tenpins)   C
Outdoor Recreation Assets (367)
Inland Water Area: 92.1 square miles
National Forests, Parks, Wildlife Refuges:
Natchez Trace Parkway (4,176 acres)
Places Rated Score: 867   Places Rated Rank: 279

Florence, SC
Common Denominators (200 points)
Golf courses: 5 private (90 holes); 1 daily fee (18   C
holes)
Bowling center: 1 (24 lanes, tenpins)   C
Outdoor Recreation Assets (4)
Inland Water Area: 0.6 square miles
Places Rated Score: 204   Places Rated Rank: 332

★ Fort Collins–Loveland, CO
Common Denominators (900 points)
Good restaurants: 3 *, 4 **   A
Golf courses: 3 private (45 holes); 2 daily fee (36   A
holes); 4 municipal (63 holes)
Bowling centers: 8 (136 lanes, tenpins)   A
Crowd Pleasers (600 points)
Pari-Mutuel Betting: A
Cloverleaf Kennel Club (greyhound, 75 races)
NCAA Division I: 1.467 game seats per capita   A
Colorado State Rams
Outdoor Recreation Assets (2,000)
Inland Water Area: 29.7 square miles
National Forests, Parks, Wildlife Refuges:
Rocky Mountain NP (143,434 acres)
Roosevelt NF (623,134 acres)
Places Rated Score: 3,500   Places Rated Rank: 7

Fort Lauderdale–Hollywood– Pompano Beach, FL
Common Denominators (800 points)
Good restaurants: 1 *, 19 **, 22 ***, 2 ****   AA
Golf courses: 19 private (432 holes); 20 daily fee   A
(459 holes); 2 municipal (72 holes)
Bowling centers: 16 (478 lanes, tenpins)   C
Crowd Pleasers (200 points)
Pari-Mutuel Betting: C
Dania Jai Alai (301 matches)
Gulfstream Park (thoroughbred, 50 races)
Hollywood Greyhound Track (greyhound, 158
races)

Pompano Park (harness, 175 races)
Professional Sports: 0.410 game seats per capita   C
Fort Lauderdale Yankees (Class A Baseball)
Outdoor Recreation Assets (292)
Atlantic Coastline: 25 miles
Inland Water Area: 10.2 square miles
CMSA Access: Miami–Fort Lauderdale, FL (110 points)
Places Rated Score: 1,402   Places Rated Rank: 174

★ Fort Myers–Cape Coral, FL
Common Denominators (1,100 points)
Good restaurants: 3 *, 20 **, 3 ***   AA
Golf courses: 9 private (189 holes); 15 daily fee   AA
(261 holes); 4 municipal (72 holes)
Bowling centers: 10 (248 lanes, tenpins)   A
Crowd Pleasers (400 points)
Pari-Mutuel Betting: AA
Naples–Fort Myers Track (greyhound, 463 races)
Outdoor Recreation Assets (1,566)
Gulf of Mexico Coastline: 38 miles
Inland Water Area: 238 square miles
National Forests, Parks, Wildlife Refuges:
Caloosahatchee NWR (140 acres)
J.N. "Ding" Darling NWR (4,960 acres)
Matlacha Pass NWR (231 acres)
Pine Island NWR (404 acres)
Places Rated Score: 3,066   Places Rated Rank: 22

Fort Pierce, FL
Common Denominators (1,000 points)
Good restaurants: 2 *, 8 **, 3 ***   AA
Golf courses: 19 private (432 holes); 8 daily fee   AA
(180 holes)
Bowling centers: 4 (124 lanes, tenpins)   B
Crowd Pleasers (700 points)
Pari-Mutuel Betting: AA
Fort Pierce Jai Alai (260 matches)
Professional Sports: 2.198 game seats per capita   A
St. Lucie Mets (Class A Baseball)
Outdoor Recreation Assets (1,056)
Atlantic Coastline: 45 miles
Inland Water Area: 155 square miles
National Forests, Parks, Wildlife Refuges:
Hobe Sound NWR (960 acres)
Places Rated Score: 2,756   Places Rated Rank: 33

Fort Smith, AR–OK
Common Denominators (700 points)
Good restaurants: 1 *, 2 **, 1 ***   B
Golf courses: 3 private (45 holes); 7 daily fee (99   AA
holes); 1 municipal (18 holes)
Bowling centers: 2 (68 lanes, tenpins)   C
Crowd Pleasers (400 points)
Pari-Mutuel Betting: AA
Blue Ribbon Downs (mixed meetings, 165 races)
Outdoor Recreation Assets (575)
Inland Water Area: 58.8 square miles
National Forests, Parks, Wildlife Refuges:
Fort Smith NHS (23 acres)
Ouachita NF (15,128 acres)
Ozark NF (84,547 acres)
Places Rated Score: 1,675   Places Rated Rank: 126

Fort Walton Beach, FL
Common Denominators (900 points)
Good restaurants: 4 **, 1 ***   A
Golf courses: 2 private (45 holes); 6 daily fee (135   AA
holes); 1 municipal (27 holes)
Bowling centers: 4 (68 lanes, tenpins)   B
Outdoor Recreation Assets (670)
Gulf of Mexico Coastline: 24 miles
Inland Water Area: 58.7 square miles
National Forests, Parks, Wildlife Refuges:
Choctawhatchee NF (675 acres)
Gulf Islands NS (15,910 acres)
Places Rated Score: 1,570   Places Rated Rank: 150

Rating

Fort Wayne, IN
Common Denominators (1,000 points)
Good restaurants: 5 **, 1 **** — **B**
Golf courses: 4 private (72 holes); 14 daily fee (225 — **AA**
holes); 1 municipal (18 holes)
Bowling centers: 20 (392 lanes, tenpins) — **AA**
Crowd Pleasers (400 points)
Zoo: Fort Wayne Children's Zoo—199 species, 812 — **B**
specimens
Professional Sports: 0.915 game seats per capita — **B**
Komets (IHL Hockey)
Outdoor Recreation Assets (13)
Inland Water Area: 3.5 square miles
Places Rated Score: 1,413 — Places Rated Rank: 171

Fort Worth–Arlington, TX
Common Denominators (400 points)
Good restaurants: 6 *, 9 **, 3 *** — **C**
Golf courses: 22 private (378 holes); 5 daily fee (99 — **C**
holes); 8 municipal (144 holes)
Bowling centers: 18 (574 lanes, tenpins) — **B**
Crowd Pleasers (1,000 points)
Zoo: Fort Worth Zoological Park—758 species, — **A**
4,408 specimens
Theme Park: Six Flags over Texas (146 days) — **B**
Professional Sports: 2.679 game seats per capita — **AA**
Texas Rangers (AL Baseball)
NCAA Division I: 0.255 game seats per capita — **C**
Texas Christian Horned Frogs, University of Texas
Mavericks
Outdoor Recreation Assets (75)
Inland Water Area: 37.9 square miles
CMSA Access: Dallas–Fort Worth, TX (120 points)
Places Rated Score: 1,605 — Places Rated Rank: 139

Fresno, CA
Common Denominators (400 points)
Good restaurants: 3 ** — **C**
Golf courses: 5 private (90 holes); 5 daily fee (81 — **C**
holes); 3 municipal (54 holes)
Bowling centers: 10 (258 lanes, tenpins) — **B**
Crowd Pleasers (500 points)
Zoo: Fresno Zoo—165 species, 465 specimens — **B**
Pari-Mutuel Betting: — **C**
Fresno District Fair (mixed meetings, 13 races)
NCAA Division I: 0.448 game seats per capita — **B**
Cal State Fresno Bulldogs
Outdoor Recreation Assets (1,773)
Inland Water Area: 37.6 square miles
National Forests, Parks, Wildlife Refuges:
Kings Canyon NP (354,828 acres)
Sequoia NF (130,641 acres)
Sierra NF (855,231 acres)
Places Rated Score: 2,673 — Places Rated Rank: 36

Gadsden, AL
Common Denominators (100 points)
Golf courses: 5 private (90 holes) — —
Bowling center: 1 (32 lanes, tenpins) — **C**
Outdoor Recreation Assets (77)
Inland Water Area: 8.5 square miles
Places Rated Score: 177 — Places Rated Rank: 333

Gainesville, FL
Common Denominators (500 points)
Good restaurants: 1 *, 1 **, 2 *** — **B**
Golf courses: 3 private (54 holes); 3 daily fee (45 — **C**
holes)
Bowling centers: 4 (104 lanes, tenpins) — **B**
Crowd Pleasers (500 points)
Zoo: Santa Fe Teaching Zoo—77 species, 226 — **C**
specimens
NCAA Division I: 2.386 game seats per capita — **AA**
University of Florida Gators
Outdoor Recreation Assets (297)
Inland Water Area: 75.3 square miles
Places Rated Score: 1,297 — Places Rated Rank: 199

Rating

Galveston–Texas City, TX
Common Denominators (600 points)
Good restaurants: 3 **, 3 *** — **A**
Golf courses: 5 private (72 holes); 1 daily fee (18 — **B**
holes); 3 municipal (54 holes)
Bowling centers: 2 (56 lanes, tenpins) — **C**
Outdoor Recreation Assets (1,261)
Gulf of Mexico Coastline: 25 miles
Inland Water Area: 101.1 square miles
CMSA Access: Houston–Galveston–Brazoria, TX
(100 points)
Places Rated Score: 1,961 — Places Rated Rank: 87

Gary–Hammond, IN
Common Denominators (800 points)
Good restaurants: 2 *, 6 **, 1 *** — **C**
Golf courses: 7 private (126 holes); 15 daily fee — **A**
(261 holes); 4 municipal (72 holes)
Bowling centers: 27 (652 lanes, tenpins) — **AA**
Crowd Pleasers (100 points)
NCAA Division I: 0.085 game seats per capita — **C**
Valparaiso Crusaders
Outdoor Recreation Assets (442)
Great Lakes Coastline: 32 miles
Inland Water Area: 5 square miles
National Forests, Parks, Wildlife Refuges:
Indiana Dunes National Lakeshore (10,948 acres)
CMSA Access: Chicago–Gary–Lake County,
IL–IN–WI (150 points)
Places Rated Score: 1,492 — Places Rated Rank: 162

Glens Falls, NY
Common Denominators (1,200 points)
Good restaurants: 3 *, 4 **, 3 *** — **AA**
Golf courses: 1 private (18 holes); 11 daily fee (144 — **AA**
holes)
Bowling centers: 11 (188 lanes, tenpins) — **AA**
Crowd Pleasers (300 points)
Professional Sports: 1.673 game seats per capita — **A**
Adirondack Red Wings (AHL Hockey)
Outdoor Recreation Assets (176)
Inland Water Area: 63 square miles
Places Rated Score: 1,676 — Places Rated Rank: 125

Grand Forks, ND
Common Denominators (1,000 points)
Good restaurant: 1 *** — **B**
Golf courses: 2 private (27 holes); 2 daily fee (18 — **AA**
holes); 2 municipal (27 holes)
Bowling centers: 6 (78 lanes, tenpins) — **AA**
Outdoor Recreation Assets (4)
National Forests, Parks, Wildlife Refuges:
Kelly's Slough NWR (680 acres)
Places Rated Score: 1,004 — Places Rated Rank: 260

Grand Rapids, MI
Common Denominators (1,200 points)
Good restaurants: 4 *, 14 **, 6 *** — **AA**
Golf courses: 11 private (189 holes); 29 daily fee — **AA**
(576 holes); 3 municipal (54 holes)
Bowling centers: 32 (758 lanes, tenpins) — **AA**
Crowd Pleasers (200 points)
Zoo: John Ball Zoological Gardens—185 species, — **B**
553 specimens
Outdoor Recreation Assets (308)
Great Lakes Coastline: 24 miles
Inland Water Area: 19.6 square miles
Places Rated Score: 1,708 — Places Rated Rank: 124

Great Falls, MT
Common Denominators (1,000 points)
Good restaurants: 1*, 3 ** — **AA**
Golf courses: 1 private (18 holes); 2 municipal (27 — **B**
holes)
Bowling centers: 9 (122 lanes, tenpins) — **AA**
Crowd Pleasers (300 points)

	Rating
Pari-Mutuel Betting:	**A**
Montana State Fair (thoroughbred, 32 races)	

Outdoor Recreation Assets (625)
Inland Water Area: 12.4 square miles
National Forests, Parks, Wildlife Refuges:
  Benton Lake NWR (11,955 acres)
  Lewis and Clark NF (197,103 acres)

Places Rated Score: 1,925   Places Rated Rank: 93

Greeley, CO

Common Denominators (500 points)

Good restaurant: 1 ✱✱	**C**
Golf courses: 2 private (36 holes); 1 municipal (18 holes)	**C**
Bowling centers: 7 (96 lanes, tenpins)	**A**

Outdoor Recreation Assets (39)
Inland Water Area: 31.5 square miles

Places Rated Score: 539   Places Rated Rank: 314

Green Bay, WI

Common Denominators (1,000 points)

Good restaurants: 4 ✱✱	**B**
Golf courses: 1 private (18 holes); 9 daily fee (126 holes); 1 municipal (18 holes)	**AA**
Bowling centers: 15 (274 lanes, tenpins)	**AA**

Crowd Pleasers (500 points)

Professional Sports: 2.353 game seats per capita	**A**
Packers (NFC Football)	
NCAA Division I: 0.371 game seats per capita	**B**
University of Wisconsin Phoenix	

Outdoor Recreation Assets (373)
Great Lakes Coastline: 21.1 miles
Inland Water Area: 4.7 square miles

Places Rated Score: 1,873   Places Rated Rank: 99

Greensboro–Winston-Salem–High Point, NC

Common Denominators (600 points)

Good restaurants: 2 ✱✱, 2 ✱✱✱	**C**
Golf courses: 19 private (333 holes); 25 daily fee (396 holes); 9 municipal (162 holes)	**AA**
Bowling centers: 11 (278 lanes, tenpins)	**C**

Crowd Pleasers (1,100 points)

Zoo: North Carolina Zoological Park—154 species, 792 specimens	**AA**
Auto Racing: Bowman Gray Stadium (NASCAR)	**B**
Professional Sports: 1.074 game seats per capita	**A**
Greensboro Hornets (Class A Baseball), Winston-Salem Spirits (Class A Baseball)	
NCAA Division I: 0.453 game seats per capita	**B**
North Carolina A & T Aggies, Wake Forest Demon Deacons	

Outdoor Recreation Assets (70)
Inland Water Area: 33.1 square miles
National Forests, Parks, Wildlife Refuges:
  Guilford Courthouse NMP (220 acres)
  Uwharrie NF (9,807 acres)

Places Rated Score: 1,770   Places Rated Rank: 114

Greenville–Spartanburg, SC

Common Denominators (500 points)

Good restaurants: 4 ✱✱, 2 ✱✱✱	**C**
Golf courses: 13 private (252 holes); 13 daily fee (225 holes)	**B**
Bowling centers: 10 (288 lanes, tenpins)	**B**

Crowd Pleasers (800 points)

Zoo: Greenville Zoo—115 species, 432 specimens	**C**
Auto Racing: Greenville–Pickens Speedway (NASCAR)	**B**
Professional Sports: 1.235 game seats per capita	**B**
Braves (Double A Baseball), Spartanburg Phillies (Class A Baseball)	
NCAA Division I: 1.080 game seats per capita	**A**
Clemson Tigers, Furman Paladins	

Outdoor Recreation Assets (34)
Inland Water Area: 14.4 square miles

Places Rated Score: 1,334   Places Rated Rank: 189

Hagerstown, MD

Common Denominators (600 points)

Good restaurants: 2 ✱✱	**B**
Golf courses: 2 private (36 holes)	**—**
Bowling centers: 6 (118 lanes, mixed)	**AA**

Crowd Pleasers (400 points)

Professional Sports: 3.612 game seats per capita	**AA**
Suns (Double A Baseball)	

Outdoor Recreation Assets (283)
Inland Water Area: 12.1 square miles
National Forests, Parks, Wildlife Refuges:
  Antietam National Battlefield (1,764 acres)
  Appalachian Trail (22 acres)
  Catoctin Mountain Park (75 acres)
  Chesapeake and Ohio Canal NHP (6,557 acres)
  Harper's Ferry NHP (765 acres)

Places Rated Score: 1,283   Places Rated Rank: 201

Hamilton–Middletown, OH

Common Denominators (800 points)

Good restaurants: 2 ✱, 1 ✱✱	**C**
Golf courses: 4 private (72 holes); 6 daily fee (90 holes); 4 municipal (90 holes)	**AA**
Bowling centers: 7 (192 lanes, tenpins)	**A**

Crowd Pleasers (300 points)

NCAA Division I: 0.866 game seats per capita	**A**
Miami University Redskins	

Outdoor Recreation Assets (3)
Inland Water Area: 0.4 square miles
CMSA Access: Cincinnati–Hamilton, OH–KY–IN (120 points)

Places Rated Score: 1,223   Places Rated Rank: 219

Harrisburg–Lebanon–Carlisle, PA

Common Denominators (800 points)

Good restaurants: 7 ✱✱, 2 ✱✱✱	**B**
Golf courses: 11 private (171 holes); 13 daily fee (234 holes); 2 municipal (36 holes)	**A**
Bowling centers: 29 (404 lanes, tenpins)	**A**

Crowd Pleasers (800 points)

Theme Park: Hersheypark (120 days)	**A**
Pari-Mutuel Betting:	**A**
Penn National Race Course (thoroughbred, 200 races)	
Professional Sports: 1.111 game seats per capita	**B**
Hershey Bears (AHL Hockey), Senators (Double A Baseball)	

Outdoor Recreation Assets (113)
Inland Water Area: 32.6 square miles
National Forests, Parks, Wildlife Refuges:
  Appalachian Trail (8,363 acres)

Places Rated Score: 1,713   Places Rated Rank: 122

Hartford, CT

Common Denominators (900 points)

Good restaurants: 1 ✱, 8 ✱✱, 9 ✱✱✱	**A**
Golf courses: 12 private (234 holes); 18 daily fee (288 holes); 5 municipal (99 holes)	**A**
Bowling centers: 20 (616 lanes, mixed)	**A**

Crowd Pleasers (500 points)

Pari-Mutuel Betting:	**B**
Hartford Jai Alai (274 matches)	
Professional Sports: 0.806 game seats per capita	**B**
Whalers (NHL Hockey)	
NCAA Division I: 0.249 game seats per capita	**C**
University of Hartford Hawks	

Outdoor Recreation Assets (88)
Inland Water Area: 19.4 square miles
CMSA Access: Hartford–New Britain–Middletown, CT (100 points)

Places Rated Score: 1,588   Places Rated Rank: 143

Hickory, NC

Common Denominators (400 points)

Golf courses: 6 private (99 holes); 7 daily fee (117 holes)	**A**

	Rating
Bowling centers: 4 (80 lanes, tenpins)	C

Crowd Pleasers (200 points)
| Auto Racing: Hickory Speedway (NASCAR) | B |

Outdoor Recreation Assets (138)
Inland Water Area: 32.9 square miles
Places Rated Score: 738   Places Rated Rank: 301

Honolulu, HI
Common Denominators (400 points)
| Golf courses: 12 private (225 holes); 11 daily fee (189 holes); 4 municipal (63 holes) | B |
| Bowling centers: 28 (550 lanes, tenpins) | B |

Crowd Pleasers (800 points)
Zoo: Honolulu Zoo—252 species, 906 specimens	B
Aquarium: Waikiki Aquarium—395 species, 1,194 specimens	AA
NCAA Division I: 0.360 game seats per capita University of Hawaii Rainbow Warriors	B

Outdoor Recreation Assets (1,569)
Pacific Coastline: 135 miles
Inland Water Area: 24.2 square miles
National Forests, Parks, Wildlife Refuges:
Hawaiian Islands NWR (1,907 acres)
Places Rated Score: 2,769   Places Rated Rank: 32

Houma–Thibodaux, LA
Common Denominators (400 points)
| Golf courses: 4 private (54 holes); 2 daily fee (18 holes) | C |
| Bowling centers: 6 (136 lanes, tenpins) | A |

Crowd Pleasers (200 points)
| NCAA Division I: 0.505 game seats per capita Nicholls State Colonels | B |

Outdoor Recreation Assets (1,482)
Gulf of Mexico Coastline: 79 miles
Inland Water Area: 403 square miles
Places Rated Score: 2,082   Places Rated Rank: 77

Houston, TX
Common Denominators (500 points)
Good restaurants: 6 *, 22 **, 21 ***, 3 ****	B
Golf courses: 52 private (1080 holes); 15 daily fee (288 holes); 8 municipal (144 holes)	C
Bowling centers: 44 (1388 lanes, tenpins)	B

Crowd Pleasers (1,000 points)
Zoo: Houston Zoological Gardens—829 species, 2,464 specimens	A
Theme Park: Astroworld (159 days)	C
Auto Racing: Battle Ground Speedway (NASCAR)	B
Professional Sports: 1.440 game seats per capita Astros (NL Baseball), Oilers (AFC Football), Rockets (NBA Basketball)	B
NCAA Division I: 0.361 game seats per capita Houston Baptist Huskies, Prairie View A & M Panthers, Rice University Owls, Texas Southern Tigers, University of Houston Cougars	B

Outdoor Recreation Assets (153)
Inland Water Area: 90.5 square miles
National Forests, Parks, Wildlife Refuges:
Big Thicket National Preserve (1,348 acres)
Sam Houston NF (47,358 acres)
Places Rated Score: 1,653   Places Rated Rank: 129

Huntington–Ashland, WV–KY–OH
Common Denominators (600 points)
Good restaurants: 2 **	C
Golf courses: 5 private (81 holes); 12 daily fee (135 holes)	A
Bowling centers: 9 (192 lanes, tenpins)	B

Crowd Pleasers (200 points)
| NCAA Division I: 0.630 game seats per capita Marshall University Thundering Herd | B |

Outdoor Recreation Assets (58)
Inland Water Area: 25.5 square miles
Places Rated Score: 858   Places Rated Rank: 280

Huntsville, AL
Common Denominators (700 points)
Good restaurants: 5 **, 2 ***	A
Golf courses: 3 private (63 holes); 3 daily fee (45 holes); 2 municipal (36 holes)	B
Bowling centers: 5 (118 lanes, tenpins)	B

Crowd Pleasers (600 points)
| Auto Racing: Huntsville Motor Speedway (NASCAR) | B |
| Professional Sports: 3.007 game seats per capita Stars (Double A Baseball) | AA |

Outdoor Recreation Assets (75)
Inland Water Area: 7.4 square miles
National Forests, Parks, Wildlife Refuges:
Wheeler NWR (3,019 acres)
Places Rated Score: 1,375   Places Rated Rank: 180

Indianapolis, IN
Common Denominators (800 points)
Good restaurants: 2 *, 11 **, 8 ***	B
Golf courses: 24 private (378 holes); 23 daily fee (297 holes); 13 municipal (207 holes)	A
Bowling centers: 31 (960 lanes, tenpins)	A

Crowd Pleasers (1,200 points)
| Zoo: Indianapolis Zoo—163 species, 584 specimens | AA |
| Auto Racing: | AA |
| Indiana State Fairgrounds (USAC) |
| Indianapolis Motor Speedway (USAC) |
| Indianapolis Raceway Park (NASCAR, SCCA) |
| Professional Sports: 1.944 game seats per capita Colts (AFC Football), Ice (IHL Hockey), Indians (Triple A Baseball), Pacers (NBA Basketball) | A |
| NCAA Division I: 0.145 game seats per capita Butler University Bulldogs | C |

Outdoor Recreation Assets (19)
Inland Water Area: 11.8 square miles
Places Rated Score: 2,019   Places Rated Rank: 82

Iowa City, IA
Common Denominators (800 points)
Good restaurants: 2 **	B
Golf courses: 1 private (9 holes); 3 daily fee (27 holes); 1 municipal (18 holes)	A
Bowling centers: 3 (60 lanes, tenpins)	A

Crowd Pleasers (400 points)
| NCAA Division I: 6.020 game seats per capita University of Iowa Hawkeyes | AA |

Outdoor Recreation Assets (73)
Inland Water Area: 9.1 square miles
Places Rated Score: 1,273   Places Rated Rank: 204

Jackson, MI
Common Denominators (900 points)
Good restaurants: 1 *, 2 **	B
Golf courses: 3 private (45 holes); 14 daily fee (207 holes); 2 municipal (36 holes)	AA
Bowling centers: 5 (118 lanes, tenpins)	A

Crowd Pleasers (900 points)
| Auto Racing: Michigan International Speedway (NASCAR) | B |
| Pari-Mutuel Betting: | AA |
| Jackson Raceway (harness, 85 races) |
| NCAA Division I: 0.996 game seats per capita Jackson State Tigers | A |

Outdoor Recreation Assets (130)
Inland Water Area: 18.8 square miles
Places Rated Score: 1,930   Places Rated Rank: 91

Jackson, MS
Common Denominators (600 points)
Good restaurants: 1 *, 10 **, 4 ***	AA
Golf courses: 12 private (207 holes); 1 daily fee (18 holes); 3 municipal (36 holes)	C
Bowling centers: 3 (62 lanes, tenpins)	C

Crowd Pleasers (400 points)

Rating

Zoo: Jackson Zoological Park—131 species, 425 specimens ... **B**

Professional Sports: 0.875 game seats per capita ... **B**
Mets (Double A Baseball)

Outdoor Recreation Assets (130)
Inland Water Area: 51.6 square miles
National Forests, Parks, Wildlife Refuges:
Natchez Trace Parkway (7,352 acres)

Places Rated Score: 1,130   Places Rated Rank: 243

Jackson, TN
Common Denominators (400 points)
Good restaurants: 1 *, 1 ** ... **B**
Golf courses: 3 private (45 holes) ... **—**
Bowling centers: 2 (34 lanes, tenpins) ... **B**

Places Rated Score: 400   Places Rated Rank: 326

Jacksonville, FL
Common Denominators (700 points)
Good restaurants: 2 *, 15 **, 5 *** ... **A**
Golf courses: 21 private (405 holes); 13 daily fee (216 holes); 2 municipal (45 holes) ... **B**
Bowling centers: 16 (424 lanes, tenpins) ... **B**
Crowd Pleasers (800 points)
Zoo: Jacksonville Zoological Park—171 species, 587 specimens ... **A**
Auto Racing: Jax Raceways (NASCAR) ... **B**
Pari-Mutuel Betting: ... **C**
Bayard Greyhound Track (greyhound, 130 races)
Jacksonville Kennel Club (greyhound, 146 races)
Orange Park Kennel Club (greyhound, 148 races)
Professional Sports: 0.650 game seats per capita ... **C**
Expos (Double A Baseball)
NCAA Division I: 0.132 game seats per capita ... **C**
Jacksonville University Dolphins
Outdoor Recreation Assets (1,157)
Atlantic Coastline: 80 miles
Inland Water Area: 201.6 square miles
National Forests, Parks, Wildlife Refuges:
Castillo de San Marcos NM (21 acres)
Fort Caroline National Memorial (132 acres)
Fort Matanzas NM (299 acres)

Places Rated Score: 2,657   Places Rated Rank: 37

Jacksonville, NC
Common Denominators (500 points)
Golf courses: 2 private (54 holes); 3 daily fee (63 holes) ... **A**
Bowling centers: 3 (80 lanes, tenpins) ... **B**
Outdoor Recreation Assets (651)
Atlantic Coastline: 30 miles
Inland Water Area: 57.6 square miles

Places Rated Score: 1,151   Places Rated Rank: 239

Janesville–Beloit, WI
Common Denominators (1,000 points)
Good restaurants: 5 ** ... **AA**
Golf courses: 2 private (36 holes); 4 daily fee (54 holes); 2 municipal (27 holes) ... **AA**
Bowling centers: 5 (60 lanes, tenpins) ... **B**
Crowd Pleasers (300 points)
Professional Sports: 1.927 game seats per capita ... **A**
Beloit Brewers (Class A Baseball)
Outdoor Recreation Assets (14)
Inland Water Area: 2.1 square miles

Places Rated Score: 1,314   Places Rated Rank: 194

Jersey City, NJ
Common Denominators (400 points)
Good restaurants: 1 *, 1 **, 2 *** ... **C**
Golf courses: 1 daily fee (9 holes) ... **C**
Bowling centers: 8 (224 lanes, tenpins) ... **B**
Crowd Pleasers (100 points)
NCAA Division I: 0.078 game seats per capita ... **C**
St. Peters College Peacocks
Outdoor Recreation Assets (1,270)

Inland Water Area: 15.7 square miles
National Forests, Parks, Wildlife Refuges:
Statue of Liberty NM (45 acres)
CMSA Access: New York–Northern NJ–Long Island, NY–NJ–CT (160 points)

Places Rated Score: 1,930   Places Rated Rank: 91

Johnson City–Kingsport–Bristol, TN–VA
Common Denominators (500 points)
Good restaurants: 3 *, 6 **, 1 *** ... **B**
Golf courses: 5 private (81 holes); 7 daily fee (81 holes); 5 municipal (72 holes) ... **B**
Bowling centers: 9 (172 lanes, tenpins) ... **C**
Crowd Pleasers (400 points)
Auto Racing: Bristol International Raceway (NASCAR) ... **B**
NCAA Division I: 0.348 game seats per capita ... **B**
East Tennessee State Buccaneers
Outdoor Recreation Assets (750)
Inland Water Area: 44.5 square miles
National Forests, Parks, Wildlife Refuges:
Appalachian Trail (966 acres)
Cherokee NF (193,640 acres)
Jefferson NF (55,961 acres)

Places Rated Score: 1,650   Places Rated Rank: 130

Johnstown, PA
Common Denominators (800 points)
Good restaurants: 1 *, 1 ** ... **C**
Golf courses: 5 private (72 holes); 13 daily fee (144 holes); 1 municipal (9 holes) ... **AA**
Bowling centers: 17 (188 lanes, tenpins) ... **A**
Crowd Pleasers (300 points)
Auto Racing: Jennerstown Speedway (NASCAR) ... **B**
NCAA Division I: 0.190 game seats per capita ... **C**
St. Francis College Red Flash
Outdoor Recreation Assets (30)
Inland Water Area: 9.8 square miles
National Forests, Parks, Wildlife Refuges:
Allegheny Portage Railroad NHS (330 acres)
Appalachian Trail (79 acres)
Johnstown Flood National Memorial (164 acres)

Places Rated Score: 1,130   Places Rated Rank: 243

Joliet, IL
Common Denominators (900 points)
Good restaurants: 1 *, 3 **, 1 *** ... **C**
Golf courses: 6 private (108 holes); 12 daily fee (225 holes); 3 municipal (54 holes) ... **AA**
Bowling centers: 22 (392 lanes, tenpins) ... **AA**
Crowd Pleasers (300 points)
Pari-Mutuel Betting: ... **A**
Balmoral Park (mixed meetings, 165 races)
Outdoor Recreation Assets (52)
Inland Water Area: 13.2 square miles
CMSA Access: Chicago–Gary–Lake County, IL–IN–WI (150 points)

Places Rated Score: 1,402   Places Rated Rank: 174

Joplin, MO
Common Denominators (600 points)
Good restaurant: 1 ** ... **C**
Golf courses: 4 private (63 holes); 3 municipal (36 holes) ... **B**
Bowling centers: 6 (134 lanes, tenpins) ... **A**
Outdoor Recreation Assets (1)
National Forests, Parks, Wildlife Refuges:
George Washington Carver NM (210 acres)

Places Rated Score: 601   Places Rated Rank: 309

Kalamazoo, MI
Common Denominators (100 points)
Good restaurants: 2 *, 3 **, 2 *** ... **A**
Golf courses: 4 private (72 holes); 9 daily fee (162 holes); 2 municipal (45 holes) ... **AA**
Bowling centers: 9 (264 lanes, tenpins) ... **AA**

	Rating
Crowd Pleasers (500 points)	
Professional Sports: 0.954 game seats per capita	**B**
Wings (IHL Hockey)	
NCAA Division I: 1.008 game seats per capita	**A**
Western Michigan University Broncos	
Outdoor Recreation Assets (158)	
Inland Water Area: 18.3 square miles	
Places Rated Score: 758 Places Rated Rank: 298	

Kankakee, IL
	Rating
Common Denominators (900 points)	
Good restaurants: 1 ★, 2 ★★	**A**
Golf courses: 1 private (18 holes); 6 daily fee (108 holes); 1 municipal (18 holes)	**AA**
Bowling centers: 4 (44 lanes, tenpins)	**B**
Outdoor Recreation Assets (19)	
Inland Water Area: 2.6 square miles	
Places Rated Score: 919 Places Rated Rank: 271	

Kansas City, MO–KS
	Rating
Common Denominators (700 points)	
Good restaurants: 8 ★, 15 ★★, 11 ★★★, 3 ★★★★	**A**
Golf courses: 28 private (468 holes); 15 daily fee (252 holes); 14 municipal (243 holes)	**B**
Bowling centers: 50 (1010 lanes, tenpins)	**B**
Crowd Pleasers (1,200 points)	
Zoo: Kansas City Zoological Gardens—176 species, 614 specimens	**A**
Theme Park: Worlds of Fun (140 days)	**B**
Auto Racing: Lakeside Speedway (NASCAR)	**B**
Pari-Mutuel Betting:	**C**
Woodlands (greyhound, 109 races)	
Professional Sports: 2.525 game seats per capita	**AA**
Chiefs (AFC Football), Royals (AL Baseball)	
Outdoor Recreation Assets (45)	
Inland Water Area: 45.3 square miles	
Places Rated Score: 1,945 Places Rated Rank: 88	

Kenosha, WI
	Rating
Common Denominators (1,200 points)	
Good restaurants: 1 ★, 1 ★★, 2 ★★★	**AA**
Golf courses: 1 private (18 holes); 5 daily fee (90 holes); 3 municipal (54 holes)	**AA**
Bowling centers: 7 (156 lanes, tenpins)	**AA**
Crowd Pleasers (200 points)	
Professional Sports: 1.454 game seats per capita	**B**
Twins (Class A Baseball)	
Outdoor Recreation Assets (222)	
Great Lakes Coastline: 12 miles	
Inland Water Area: 5.7 square miles	
CMSA Access: Chicago–Gary–Lake County, IL–IN–WI (190 points)	
Places Rated Score: 1,812 Places Rated Rank: 109	

Killeen–Temple, TX
	Rating
Common Denominators (500 points)	
Good restaurant: 1 ★★	**C**
Golf courses: 6 private (99 holes); 2 daily fee (36 holes); 3 municipal (36 holes)	**B**
Bowling centers: 5 (120 lanes, tenpins)	**B**
Outdoor Recreation Assets (74)	
Inland Water Area: 31.7 square miles	
Places Rated Score: 574 Places Rated Rank: 312	

Knoxville, TN
	Rating
Common Denominators (700 points)	
Good restaurants: 2 ★, 14 ★★, 3 ★★★, 1 ★★★★	**A**
Golf courses: 7 private (126 holes); 14 daily fee (252 holes); 2 municipal (36 holes)	**A**
Bowling centers: 8 (154 lanes, tenpins)	**C**
Crowd Pleasers (800 points)	
Zoo: Knoxville Zoological Park—244 species, 855 specimens	**A**
Professional Sports: 0.951 game seats per capita	**B**
Blue Jays (Double A Baseball)	

	Rating
NCAA Division I: 1.247 game seats per capita	**A**
University of Tennessee Volunteers	
Outdoor Recreation Assets (866)	
Inland Water Area: 149.1 square miles	
National Forests, Parks, Wildlife Refuges:	
Appalachian Trail (640 acres)	
Great Smoky Mountains NP (225,193 acres)	
Places Rated Score: 2,366 Places Rated Rank: 54	

Kokomo, IN
	Rating
Common Denominators (800 points)	
Good restaurant: 1 ★★	**C**
Golf courses: 1 private (18 holes); 3 daily fee (54 holes); 1 municipal (18 holes)	**AA**
Bowling centers: 4 (76 lanes, tenpins)	**A**
Outdoor Recreation Assets (8)	
Inland Water Area: 0.9 square miles	
Places Rated Score: 808 Places Rated Rank: 293	

La Crosse, WI
	Rating
Common Denominators (1,000 points)	
Good restaurants: 1 ★, 3 ★★	**AA**
Golf courses: 1 private (18 holes); 3 daily fee (45 holes)	**A**
Bowling centers: 9 (94 lanes, tenpins)	**A**
Crowd Pleasers (300 points)	
Professional Sports: 1.689 game seats per capita	**A**
Catbirds (CBA Basketball)	
Outdoor Recreation Assets (431)	
Inland Water Area: 23.2 square miles	
National Forests, Parks, Wildlife Refuges:	
Upper Mississippi River NWR (11,666 acres)	
Places Rated Score: 1,731 Places Rated Rank: 119	

Lafayette, LA
	Rating
Common Denominators (700 points)	
Good restaurants: 1 ★, 5 ★★, 5 ★★★	**AA**
Golf courses: 4 private (72 holes); 2 municipal (36 holes)	**C**
Bowling centers: 4 (120 lanes, tenpins)	**B**
Crowd Pleasers (600 points)	
Pari-Mutuel Betting:	**A**
Evangeline Downs (thoroughbred, 92 races)	
NCAA Division I: 1.373 game seats per capita	**A**
Southwestern Louisiana University Ragin' Cajuns	
Outdoor Recreation Assets (313)	
Inland Water Area: 68 square miles	
National Parks, Forests, Wildlife Refuges:	
Atchafalaya NWR (1,472 acres)	
Places Rated Score: 1,613 Places Rated Rank: 136	

Lafayette–West Lafayette, IN
	Rating
Common Denominators (1,100 points)	
Good restaurants: 1 ★, 3 ★★, 1 ★★★	**AA**
Golf courses: 2 private (45 holes); 2 daily fee (54 holes); 1 municipal (18 holes)	**AA**
Bowling centers: 5 (104 lanes, tenpins)	**A**
Crowd Pleasers (400 points)	
NCAA Division I: 4.053 game seats per capita	**AA**
Purdue Boilermakers	
Outdoor Recreation Assets (14)	
Inland Water Area: 1.4 square miles	
Places Rated Score: 1,514 Places Rated Rank: 159	

Lake Charles, LA
	Rating
Common Denominators (500 points)	
Good restaurants: 1 ★★, 1 ★★★	**C**
Golf courses: 2 private (36 holes); 1 daily fee (18 holes); 2 municipal (36 holes)	**B**
Bowling centers: 3 (84 lanes, tenpins)	**B**
Crowd Pleasers (700 points)	
Pari-Mutuel Betting:	**AA**
Delta Downs (mixed meetings, 200 races)	
NCAA Division I: 1.120 game seats per capita	**A**
McNeese State Cowboys	

Rating

Outdoor Recreation Assets (55)
Inland Water Area: 12 square miles
Places Rated Score: 1,255   Places Rated Rank: 210

Lake County, IL
Common Denominators (1,100 points)
Good restaurants: 4 *, 13 **, 3 ***, 1 *****   AA
Golf courses: 26 private (468 holes); 12 daily fee   AA
(198 holes); 12 municipal (189 holes)
Bowling centers: 23 (476 lanes, tenpins)   A
Crowd Pleasers (400 points)
Theme Park: Great America (120 days)   AA
Outdoor Recreation Assets (426)
Great Lakes Coastline: 25 miles
Inland Water Area: 16.8 square miles
CMSA Access: Chicago–Gary–Lake County,
IL–IN–WI (170 points)
Places Rated Score: 2,096   Places Rated Rank: 75

Lakeland–Winter Haven, FL
Common Denominators (900 points)
Good restaurants: 1 *, 3 **, 4 ***, 1 ****   A
Golf courses: 8 private (144 holes); 9 daily fee (171   AA
holes); 3 municipal (63 holes)
Bowling centers: 7 (240 lanes, tenpins)   B
Crowd Pleasers (700 points)
Theme Park: Cypress Gardens (365 days)   AA
Professional Sports: 2.027 game seats per capita   A
Lakeland Tigers (Class A Baseball), Winter Haven
Red Sox (Class A Baseball)
Outdoor Recreation Assets (466)
Inland Water Area: 187.2 square miles
Places Rated Score: 2,066   Places Rated Rank: 79

Lancaster, PA
Common Denominators (500 points)
Good restaurants: 1 *, 8 **, 1 ***   B
Golf courses: 5 private (81 holes); 5 daily fee (90   C
holes)
Bowling centers: 10 (242 lanes, tenpins)   B
Outdoor Recreation Assets (160)
Inland Water Area: 31.5 square miles
Places Rated Score: 660   Places Rated Rank: 304

Lansing–East Lansing, MI
Common Denominators (800 points)
Good restaurants: 3 *, 5 **   C
Golf courses: 3 private (45 holes); 25 daily fee (360   AA
holes); 3 municipal (36 holes)
Bowling centers: 20 (422 lanes, tenpins)   A
Crowd Pleasers (400 points)
Zoo: Potter Park Zoological Gardens—123 species,   C
346 specimens
NCAA Division I: 1.160 game seats per capita   A
Michigan State Spartans
Outdoor Recreation Assets (10)
Inland Water Area: 3.1 square miles
Places Rated Score: 1,210   Places Rated Rank: 223

Laredo, TX
Common Denominators (400 points)
Good restaurants: 3 **   B
Golf courses: 1 private (18 holes); 1 municipal (18   C
holes)
Bowling centers: 2 (44 lanes, tenpins)   C
Outdoor Recreation Assets (5)
Inland Water Area: 3.5 square miles
Places Rated Score: 405   Places Rated Rank: 325

Las Cruces, NM
Common Denominators (700 points)
Good restaurants: 2 **, 2 ***   AA
Golf courses: 5 private (90 holes); 2 daily fee (36   B
holes)
Bowling centers: 2 (42 lanes, tenpins)   C
Crowd Pleasers (800 points)

Rating

Pari-Mutuel Betting: AA
Sunland Park (mixed meetings, 114 races)
NCAA Division I: 2.340 game seats per capita   AA
New Mexico State Aggies
Outdoor Recreation Assets (109)
National Forests, Parks, Wildlife Refuges:
San Andres NWR (2 acres)
White Sands NM (53,059 acres)
Places Rated Score: 1,609   Places Rated Rank: 137

★ Las Vegas, NV
Common Denominators (900 points)
Good restaurants: 2 *, 15 **, 19 ***, 2 ****   AA
Golf courses: 3 private (54 holes); 8 daily fee (144   B
holes); 3 municipal (45 holes)
Bowling centers: 12 (454 lanes, tenpins)   A
Crowd Pleasers (400 points)
Professional Sports: 1.068 game seats per capita   B
Stars (Triple A Baseball)
NCAA Division I: 0.605 game seats per capita   B
University of Nevada Rebels
Outdoor Recreation Assets (1,554)
Inland Water Area: 209.8 square miles
National Forests, Parks, Wildlife Refuges:
Desert NWR (828,766 acres)
Lake Mead NRA (588,785 acres)
Moapa Valley NWR (11 acres)
Toiyabe NF (58,040 acres)
Places Rated Score: 2,854   Places Rated Rank: 30

Lawrence, KS
Common Denominators (1,000 points)
Good restaurant: 1 ***   B
Golf courses: 1 private (18 holes); 2 daily fee (45   AA
holes)
Bowling centers: 4 (80 lanes, tenpins)   AA
Crowd Pleasers (400 points)
NCAA Division I: 5.913 game seats per capita   AA
University of Kansas Jayhawks
Outdoor Recreation Assets (146)
Inland Water Area: 13.9 square miles
Places Rated Score: 1,546   Places Rated Rank: 152

Lawrence–Haverhill, MA–NH
Common Denominators (700 points)
Good restaurants: 1 *, 4 **, 2 ***   B
Golf courses: 3 private (45 holes); 11 daily fee (144   A
holes)
Bowling centers: 7 (148 lanes, mixed)   C
Crowd Pleasers (400 points)
Pari-Mutuel Betting: AA
Rockingham Park (thoroughbred, 262 races)
Outdoor Recreation Assets (395)
Atlantic Coastline: 13 miles
Inland Water Area: 21.8 square miles
National Forests, Parks, Wildlife Refuges:
Parker River NWR (2,321 acres)
CMSA Access: Boston–Lawrence–Salem, MA–HN
(90 points)
Places Rated Score: 1,585   Places Rated Rank: 145

Lawton, OK
Common Denominators (800 points)
Good restaurants: 3 **, 1 ***   AA
Golf courses: 2 private (36 holes); 1 daily fee (18   B
holes); 1 municipal (18 holes)
Bowling centers: 2 (60 lanes, tenpins)   B
Outdoor Recreation Assets (462)
Inland Water Area: 8 square miles
National Forests, Parks, Wildlife Refuges:
Wichita Mountains NWR (59,019 acres)
Places Rated Score: 1,262   Places Rated Rank: 207

Lewiston–Auburn, ME
Common Denominators (900 points)
Good restaurants: 3 **   A

	Rating
Golf courses: 1 private (18 holes); 5 daily fee (72 holes)	**AA**
Bowling centers: 2 (48 lanes, mixed)	**B**
Crowd Pleasers (400 points)	
Pari-Mutuel Betting:	**AA**
Lewiston Raceway (harness, 112 races)	
Outdoor Recreation Assets (283)	
Inland Water Area: 12.1 square miles	
Places Rated Score: 1,583 Places Rated Rank: 146	

Lexington–Fayette, KY
Common Denominators (900 points)
Good restaurants: 6 **, 6 ***	**AA**
Golf courses: 11 private (171 holes); 6 daily fee (99 holes); 2 municipal (36 holes)	**A**
Bowling centers: 6 (136 lanes, tenpins)	**B**

Crowd Pleasers (500 points)
Pari-Mutuel Betting:	**C**
Keeneland (thoroughbred, 32 races)	
The Red Mile (harness, 67 races)	
NCAA Division I: 1.677 game seats per capita	**AA**
University of Kentucky Wildcats	

Outdoor Recreation Assets (3)
  Inland Water Area: 0.8 square miles
Places Rated Score: 1,403   Places Rated Rank: 173

Lima, OH
Common Denominators (1,000 points)
Good restaurants: 2 *, 2 **	**B**
Golf courses: 4 private (63 holes); 7 daily fee (117 holes)	**AA**
Bowling centers: 12 (198 lanes, tenpins)	**AA**

Outdoor Recreation Assets (38)
  Inland Water Area: 6.1 square miles
Places Rated Score: 1,038   Places Rated Rank: 252

Lincoln, NE
Common Denominators (800 points)
Good restaurants: 2 *, 3 ***	**A**
Golf courses: 5 private (90 holes); 1 daily fee (18 holes); 3 municipal (54 holes)	**B**
Bowling centers: 7 (142 lanes, tenpins)	**A**

Crowd Pleasers (600 points)
Pari-Mutuel Betting:	**B**
State Fair Park (thoroughbred, 43 races)	
NCAA Division I: 2.575 game seats per capita	**AA**
University of Nebraska Cornhuskers	

Outdoor Recreation Assets (44)
  Inland Water Area: 7.4 square miles
Places Rated Score: 1,444   Places Rated Rank: 167

Little Rock–North Little Rock, AR
Common Denominators (600 points)
Good restaurants: 1 *, 3 **, 3 ***	**B**
Golf courses: 15 private (234 holes); 4 daily fee (54 holes); 4 municipal (90 holes)	**B**
Bowling centers: 8 (222 lanes, tenpins)	**B**

Crowd Pleasers (500 points)
Zoo: Little Rock Zoological Gardens—216 species, 629 specimens	**B**
Professional Sports: 0.828 game seats per capita	**B**
Arkansas Travelers (Double A Baseball)	
NCAA Division I: 0.192 game seats per capita	**C**
University of Arkansas Trojans	

Outdoor Recreation Assets (280)
  Inland Water Area: 85.1 square miles
  National Forests, Parks, Wildlife Refuges:
    Ouachita NF (53,357 acres)
Places Rated Score: 1,380   Places Rated Rank: 178

Longview–Marshall, TX
Common Denominators (400 points)
Golf courses: 6 private (81 holes); 3 daily fee (45 holes)	**B**
Bowling centers: 3 (72 lanes, tenpins)	**B**

	Rating
Outdoor Recreation Assets (34)	
Inland Water Area: 8.1 square miles	
Places Rated Score: 434 Places Rated Rank: 324	

Lorain–Elyria, OH
Common Denominators (900 points)
Good restaurants: 1 *, 2 **	**C**
Golf courses: 7 private (126 holes); 19 daily fee (315 holes); 1 municipal (18 holes)	**AA**
Bowling centers: 19 (336 lanes, tenpins)	**AA**

Outdoor Recreation Assets (202)
  Great Lakes Coastline: 20 miles
  Inland Water Area: 0.2 square miles
CMSA Access: Cleveland–Akron–Lorain, OH (90 points)
Places Rated Score: 1,192   Places Rated Rank: 228

★ Los Angeles–Long Beach, CA
Common Denominators (400 points)
Good restaurants: 28 *, 59 **, 40 ***, 2 ****	**B**
Golf courses: 32 private (639 holes); 11 daily fee (171 holes); 34 municipal (648 holes)	**C**
Bowling centers: 74 (2289 lanes, tenpins)	**C**

Crowd Pleasers (1,200 points)
Zoo: Los Angeles Zoo—471 species, 1,992 specimens	**AA**
Theme Parks:	**C**
Marineland of the Pacific (300 days)	
Universal Studios Tour (365 days)	
Auto Racing:	**A**
Ascot Park (NASCAR)	
Grand Prix of Long Beach (SCCA)	
Pari-Mutuel Betting:	**C**
Antelope Valley Fair (mixed meetings, 13 races)	
Hollywood Park (thoroughbred, 110 races)	
Santa Anita (thoroughbred, 120 races)	
Professional Sports: 0.836 game seats per capita	**B**
Clippers (NBA Basketball), Dodgers (NL Baseball), Kings (NHL Hockey), Lakers (NBA Basketball), Raiders (AFC Football)	
NCAA Division I: 0.186 game seats per capita	**C**
Cal State Long Beach 49ers, Loyola Marymount Lions, Pepperdine University Waves, University of California Bruins, University of Southern California Trojans	

Outdoor Recreation Assets (1,873)
  Pacific Coastline: 55 miles
  Inland Water Area: 42.8 square miles
  National Forests, Parks, Wildlife Refuges:
    Angeles NF (642,260 acres)
    Santa Monica Mountains NRA (26,734 acres)
CMSA Access: Los Angeles–Anaheim–Riverside, CA (160 points)
Places Rated Score: 3,633   Places Rated Rank: 4

Louisville, KY–IN
Common Denominators (800 points)
Good restaurants: 11 **, 10 ***, 1 ****	**A**
Golf courses: 19 private (297 holes); 9 daily fee (108 holes); 10 municipal (144 holes)	**B**
Bowling centers: 28 (766 lanes, tenpins)	**A**

Crowd Pleasers (1,100 points)
Zoo: Louisville Zoological Garden—236 species, 703 specimens	**A**
Auto Racing: Louisville Motor Speedway (NASCAR)	**B**
Pari-Mutuel Betting:	**C**
Churchill Downs (thoroughbred, 79 races)	
Louisville Downs (harness, 168 races)	
Professional Sports: 2.454 game seats per capita	**A**
Redbirds (Triple A Baseball)	
NCAA Division I: 0.418 game seats per capita	**B**
University of Louisville Cardinals	

Outdoor Recreation Assets (43)
  Inland Water Area: 19.3 square miles
Places Rated Score: 1,943   Places Rated Rank: 89

Rating

Lowell, MA–NH
Common Denominators (400 points)
Good restaurant: 1 **   C
Golf courses: 3 private (36 holes); 7 daily fee (72 holes)   B
Bowling centers: 4 (80 lanes, mixed)   C
Outdoor Recreation Assets (125)
Inland Water Area: 5.6 square miles
National Forests, Parks, Wildlife Refuges:
Great Meadows NWR (65 acres)
Lowell NHP (4 acres)
CMSA Access: Boston–Lawrence–Salem, NA–NH (130 points)
Places Rated Score: 655   Places Rated Rank: 305

Lubbock, TX
Common Denominators (700 points)
Good restaurants: 5 **, 1 ***   A
Golf courses: 3 private (36 holes); 3 daily fee (45 holes); 1 municipal (36 holes)   B
Bowling centers: 5 (138 lanes, tenpins)   B
Crowd Pleasers (300 points)
NCAA Division I: 1.443 game seats per capita   A
Texas Tech Red Raiders
Outdoor Recreation Assets (4)
Inland Water Area: 0.6 square miles
National Forests, Parks, Wildlife Refuges:
Lower Rio Grande Valley NWR (118 acres)
Places Rated Score: 1,004   Places Rated Rank: 260

Lynchburg, VA
Common Denominators (400 points)
Good restaurants: 2 **   C
Golf courses: 2 private (36 holes); 3 daily fee (36 holes)   B
Bowling center: 1 (28 lanes, tenpins)   C
Crowd Pleasers (500 points)
Professional Sports: 2.021 game seats per capita   A
Red Sox (Class A Baseball)
NCAA Division I: 0.330 game seats per capita   B
Liberty University Flames
Outdoor Recreation Assets (441)
Inland Water Area: 1.1 square miles
National Forests, Parks, Wildlife Refuges:
Blue Ridge Parkway (2,037 acres)
George Washington NF (55,587 acres)
Places Rated Score: 1,341   Places Rated Rank: 188

Macon–Warner Robins, GA
Common Denominators (500 points)
Good restaurants: 1 *, 2 **, 1 ***   C
Golf courses: 7 private (117 holes); 3 daily fee (45 holes); 2 municipal (36 holes)   B
Bowling centers: 5 (116 lanes, tenpins)   B
Crowd Pleasers (200 points)
NCAA Division I: 0.375 game seats per capita   B
Mercer University Bears
Outdoor Recreation Assets (317)
Inland Water Area: 3.4 square miles
National Forests, Parks, Wildlife Refuges:
Ocmulgee NM (683 acres)
Oconee NF (16,570 acres)
Piedmont NWR (28,503 acres)
Places Rated Score: 1,017   Places Rated Rank: 256

Madison, WI
Common Denominators (1,000 points)
Good restaurants: 2 *, 5 **, 2 ***   A
Golf courses: 6 private (90 holes); 7 daily fee (117 holes); 3 municipal (63 holes)   A
Bowling centers: 24 (416 lanes, tenpins)   AA
Crowd Pleasers (800 points)
Zoo: Henry Vilas Zoo—178 species, 712 specimens   B
Professional Sports: 0.772 game seats per capita   B
Muskies (Class A Baseball)
NCAA Division I: 1.507 game seats per capita   AA
University of Wisconsin Badgers

Rating

Outdoor Recreation Assets (140)
Inland Water Area: 34.7 square miles
Places Rated Score: 1,940   Places Rated Rank: 90

Manchester, NH
Common Denominators (800 points)
Good restaurants: 1 *, 4 **, 1 ***   AA
Golf courses: 1 private (18 holes); 3 daily fee (36 holes); 1 municipal (18 holes)   B
Bowling centers: 3 (68 lanes, mixed)   B
Outdoor Recreation Assets (146)
Inland Water Area: 6.5 square miles
Places Rated Score: 946   Places Rated Rank: 267

Mansfield, OH
Common Denominators (900 points)
Good restaurants: 2 **   B
Golf courses: 2 private (36 holes); 4 daily fee (63 holes)   A
Bowling centers: 6 (182 lanes, tenpins)   AA
Crowd Pleasers (200 points)
Auto Racing: Mid-Ohio Sports Car Course (IMSA, SCCA)   B
Outdoor Recreation Assets (33)
Inland Water Area: 3.3 square miles
Places Rated Score: 1,133   Places Rated Rank: 242

McAllen–Edinburg–Mission, TX
Common Denominators (400 points)
Good restaurants: 2 *, 2 **   C
Golf courses: 5 private (81 holes); 4 daily fee (45 holes); 3 municipal (54 holes)   B
Bowling centers: 3 (52 lanes, tenpins)   C
Crowd Pleasers (100 points)
NCAA Division I: 0.154 game seats per capita   C
Pan American University Broncs
Outdoor Recreation Assets (58)
Inland Water Area: 12.4 square miles
National Forests, Parks, Wildlife Refuges:
Lower Rio Grande Valley NWR (7,640 acres)
Santa Anna NWR (3,769 acres)
Places Rated Score: 558   Places Rated Rank: 313

Medford, OR
Common Denominators (400 points)
Good restaurant: 1 ***   C
Golf courses: 1 private (27 holes); 1 daily fee (18 holes); 1 municipal (9 holes)   C
Bowling centers: 3 (74 lanes, tenpins)   B
Crowd Pleasers (300 points)
Professional Sports: 1.530 game seats per capita   A
A's (Class A Baseball)
Outdoor Recreation Assets (26)
Inland Water Area: 14.4 square miles
Places Rated Score: 726   Places Rated Rank: 302

★ Melbourne–Titusville–Palm Bay, FL
Common Denominators (500 points)
Good restaurants: 2 *, 3 **, 1 ***   C
Golf courses: 5 private (108 holes); 3 daily fee (54 holes); 4 municipal (72 holes)   B
Bowling centers: 8 (176 lanes, tenpins)   B
Crowd Pleasers (400 points)
Pari-Mutuel Betting: AA
Melbourne Jai Alai (233 matches)
Outdoor Recreation Assets (2,000)
Atlantic Coastline: 72 miles
Inland Water Area: 299 square miles
National Forests, Parks, Wildlife Refuges:
Canaveral NS (29,479 acres)
St. John's NWR (6,254 acres)
Places Rated Score: 2,900   Places Rated Rank: 29

Memphis, TN–AR–MS
Common Denominators (400 points)
Good restaurants: 6 **, 5 ***   C

	Rating
Golf courses: 19 private (414 holes); 2 daily fee (36 holes); 10 municipal (162 holes)	C
Bowling centers: 15 (416 lanes, tenpins)	B

Crowd Pleasers (1,000 points)

Zoo: Memphis Zoological Garden & Aquarium—418 species, 2,815 specimens	A
Auto Racing: Memphis International Motorsports Park (SCCA)	B
Pari-Mutuel Betting: Southland Greyhound Park (greyhound, 218 races)	B
Professional Sports: 0.733 game seats per capita Chicks (Double A Baseball)	C
NCAA Division I: 0.459 game seats per capita Memphis State Tigers	B

Outdoor Recreation Assets (183)
Inland Water Area: 78.4 square miles
National Forests, Parks, Wildlife Refuges:
Lower Hatchie NWR (346 acres)
Wapanocca NWR (5,484 acres)

Places Rated Score: 1,583   Places Rated Rank: 146

Merced, CA

Common Denominators (300 points)

Golf courses: 2 private (36 holes); 2 daily fee (27 holes)	C
Bowling centers: 4 (72 lanes, tenpins)	B

Crowd Pleasers (200 points)

Auto Racing: Merced Fairgrounds Speedway (NASCAR)	B

Outdoor Recreation Assets (107)
Inland Water Area: 26.4 square miles
National Forests, Parks, Wildlife Refuges:
Merced NWR (2,562 acres)
San Luis NWR (7,422 acres)

Places Rated Score: 607   Places Rated Rank: 308

★ Miami–Hialeah, FL

Common Denominators (400 points)

Good restaurants: 6 *, 18 **, 13 ***, 2 ****	B
Golf courses: 13 private (270 holes); 7 daily fee (225 holes); 9 municipal (225 holes)	C
Bowling centers: 10 (374 lanes, tenpins)	C

Crowd Pleasers (1,100 points)

Zoo: Miami Metrozoo—241 species, 3,036 specimens	AA
Auto Racing: Miami Grand Prix (IMSA)	B
Pari-Mutuel Betting:	C
Biscayne Dog Track (greyhound, 158 races)	
Calder Race Course (thoroughbred, 171 races)	
Flagler Greyhound Track (greyhound, 159 races)	
Hialeah Park (thoroughbred, 50 races)	
Miami Jai Alai (329 matches)	
Professional Sports: 1.022 game seats per capita Dolphins (AFC Football), Heat (NBA Basketball), Miami Marlins (Class A Baseball)	B
NCAA Division I: 0.334 game seats per capita Florida International University Golden Panthers, University of Miami Hurricanes	B

Outdoor Recreation Assets (2,000)
Atlantic Coastline: 84 miles
Inland Water Area: 64.2 square miles
National Forests, Parks, Wildlife Refuges:
Big Cypress National Preserve (18,628 acres)
Biscayne NP (170,773 acres)
Everglades NP (415,716 acres)
CMSA Access: Miami–Fort Lauderdale, FL (20 points)

Places Rated Score: 3,520   Places Rated Rank: 6

Middlesex–Somerset–Hunterdon, NJ

Common Denominators (400 points)

Good restaurants: 2 *, 8 **, 2 ***	C
Golf courses: 13 private (252 holes); 7 daily fee (117 holes); 5 municipal (99 holes)	C
Bowling centers: 13 (414 lanes, tenpins)	B

Crowd Pleasers (200 points)

NCAA Division I: 0.490 game seats per capita Rutgers Scarlet Knights	B

Outdoor Recreation Assets (144)
Atlantic Coastline: 6 miles
Inland Water Area: 17.6 square miles
National Forests, Parks, Wildlife Refuges:
Morristown NHP (188 acres)
CMSA Access: New York–Northern NJ–Long Island, NY–NJ–CT (220 points)

Places Rated Score: 964   Places Rated Rank: 263

Middletown, CT

Common Denominators (700 points)

Good restaurant: 1 ***	B
Golf courses: 1 private (18 holes); 3 daily fee (45 holes)	A
Bowling center: 1 (36 lanes, tenpins)	B

Outdoor Recreation Assets (172)
Inland Water Area: 6.9 square miles
CMSA Access: Hartford–New Britain–Middletown, CT (100 points)

Places Rated Score: 972   Places Rated Rank: 262

Midland, TX

Common Denominators (200 points)

Golf courses: 3 private (63 holes); 1 municipal (27 holes)	C
Bowling center: 1 (30 lanes, tenpins)	C

Crowd Pleasers (300 points)

Professional Sports: 1.884 game seats per capita Angels (Double A Baseball)	A

Outdoor Recreation Assets (2)
Inland Water Area: 0.3 square miles

Places Rated Score: 502   Places Rated Rank: 319

Milwaukee, WI

Common Denominators (1,000 points)

Good restaurants: 5 *, 25 **, 8 ***, 1 ****	A
Golf courses: 16 private (297 holes); 28 daily fee (441 holes); 13 municipal (225 holes)	A
Bowling centers: 100 (1514 lanes, tenpins)	AA

Crowd Pleasers (900 points)

Zoo: Milwaukee County Zoological Gardens—297 species, 1,516 specimens	AA
Professional Sports: 4.284 game seats per capita Admirals (IHL Hockey), Brewers (AL Baseball), Bucks (NBA Basketball), Packers (NFC Football)	AA
NCAA Division I: 0.156 game seats per capita Marquette Warriors	C

Outdoor Recreation Assets (608)
Great Lakes Coastline: 49 miles
Inland Water Area: 32.6 square miles
CMSA Access: Milwaukee–Racine, WI (10 points)

Places Rated Score: 2,518   Places Rated Rank: 44

Minneapolis–St. Paul, MN–WI

Common Denominators (900 points)

Good restaurants: 8 *, 40 **, 15 ***, 1 ****	A
Golf courses: 32 private (558 holes); 41 daily fee (603 holes); 25 municipal (414 holes)	A
Bowling centers: 113 (1999 lanes, tenpins)	A

Crowd Pleasers (1,400 points)

Zoos: Minnesota Zoological Garden—398 species, 1,378 specimens	AA
St. Paul's Como Zoo—107 species, 361 specimens	C
Auto Racing:	A
Elko Speedway (NASCAR)	
Shakopee Raceway Park (NASCAR)	
Pari-Mutuel Betting: Canterbury Downs (mixed meetings, 125 races)	C
Professional Sports: 2.751 game seats per capita Minnesota North Stars (NHL Hockey), Minnesota Timberwolves (NBA Basketball), Minnesota Twins (AL Baseball), Minnesota Vikings (NFC Football)	AA
NCAA Division I: 0.217 game seats per capita University of Minnesota Golden Gophers	C

Rating

Outdoor Recreation Assets (273)
Inland Water Area: 273.3 square miles
National Forests, Parks, Wildlife Refuges:
Lower St. Croix NSR (5,178 acres)
Minnesota Valley NWR (4,636 acres)
St. Croix NSR (5,673 acres)
Places Rated Score: 2,573   Places Rated Rank: 43

Mobile, AL
Common Denominators (400 points)
Good restaurants: 1 ★, 1 ★★, 3 ★★★   C
Golf courses: 9 private (180 holes); 5 daily fee (81   B
holes); 5 municipal (81 holes)
Bowling centers: 7 (162 lanes, tenpins)   C
Crowd Pleasers (500 points)
Pari-Mutuel Betting: AA
Mobile Greyhound Park (greyhound, 300 races)
NCAA Division I: 0.255 game seats per capita   C
University of South Alabama Jaguars
Outdoor Recreation Assets (754)
Gulf of Mexico Coastline: 53 miles
Inland Water Area: 128.9 square miles
National Forests, Parks, Wildlife Refuges:
Bon Secour NWR (2,168 acres)
Places Rated Score: 1,654   Places Rated Rank: 128

Modesto, CA
Common Denominators (400 points)
Good restaurants: 1 ★, 1 ★★   C
Golf courses: 2 private (36 holes); 2 municipal (27   C
holes)
Bowling centers: 4 (138 lanes, tenpins)   B
Crowd Pleasers (100 points)
Professional Sports: 0.541 game seats per capita   C
A's (Class A Baseball)
Outdoor Recreation Assets (33)
Inland Water Area: 10 square miles
Places Rated Score: 533   Places Rated Rank: 315

Monmouth–Ocean, NJ
Common Denominators (600 points)
Good restaurants: 15 ★★, 2 ★★★   B
Golf courses: 15 private (261 holes); 12 daily fee   B
(189 holes); 7 municipal (126 holes)
Bowling centers: 23 (582 lanes, tenpins)   B
Crowd Pleasers (500 points)
Theme Park: Great Adventure (163 days)   A
Pari-Mutuel Betting: C
Freehold Raceway (harness, 258 races)
Monmouth Park (thoroughbred, 80 races)
NCAA Division I: 0.034 game seats per capita   C
Monmouth College Hawks
Outdoor Recreation Assets (1,379)
Atlantic Coastline: 80 miles
Inland Water Area: 124.8 square miles
National Forests, Parks, Wildlife Refuges:
Barnegat NWR (7,427 acres)
Forsythe NWR (10,000 acres)
Gateway NRA (4,169 acres)
CMSA Access: New York–Northern NJ–Long
Island, NY–NJ–CT (170 points)
Places Rated Score: 2,649   Places Rated Rank: 38

Monroe, LA
Common Denominators (700 points)
Good restaurants: 3 ★★, 1 ★★★   A
Golf courses: 4 private (54 holes); 3 municipal (36   B
holes)
Bowling centers: 3 (72 lanes, tenpins)   B
Crowd Pleasers (300 points)
NCAA Division I: 1.422 game seats per capita   A
Northeast Louisiana University Indians
Outdoor Recreation Assets (140)
Inland Water Area: 5.4 square miles
National Forests, Parks, Wildlife Refuges:
D'Arbonne NWR (7,859 acres)
Places Rated Score: 1,140   Places Rated Rank: 241

Rating

Montgomery, AL
Common Denominators (500 points)
Good restaurants: 4 ★★, 3 ★★★   A
Golf courses: 11 private (198 holes); 1 municipal
(18 holes)   C
Bowling centers: 6 (88 lanes, tenpins)   C
Crowd Pleasers (300 points)
Zoos: Montgomery Zoo   B
NCAA Division I: 0.172 game seats per capita   C
Alabama State Hornets
Outdoor Recreation Assets (117)
Inland Water Area: 45.1 square miles
Places Rated Score: 917   Places Rated Rank: 272

Muncie, IN
Common Denominators (900 points)
Good restaurants: 1 ★, 1 ★★   C
Golf courses: 2 private (36 holes); 5 daily fee (81   AA
holes)
Bowling centers: 4 (156 lanes, tenpins)   AA
Crowd Pleasers (300 points)
NCAA Division I: 1.371 game seats per capita   A
Ball State Cardinals
Outdoor Recreation Assets (53)
Inland Water Area: 4.2 square miles
Places Rated Score: 1,253   Places Rated Rank: 211

Muskegon, MI
Common Denominators (1,000 points)
Good restaurants: 2 ★, 2 ★★   B
Golf courses: 4 private (72 holes); 7 daily fee (108   AA
holes); 1 municipal (18 holes)
Bowling centers: 14 (270 lanes, tenpins)   AA
Crowd Pleasers (600 points)
Pari-Mutuel Betting: AA
Muskegon Race Track (harness, 109 races)
Professional Sports: 1.299 game seats per capita   B
Lumberjacks (IHL Hockey)
Outdoor Recreation Assets (672)
Great Lakes Coastline: 30 miles
Inland Water Area: 19.7 square miles
National Forests, Parks, Wildlife Refuges:
Manistee NF (12,500 acres)
Places Rated Score: 2,272   Places Rated Rank: 58

★ Naples, FL
Common Denominators (1,000 points)
Good restaurants: 2 ★, 5 ★★, 8 ★★★   AA
Golf courses: 16 private (351 holes); 6 daily fee   AA
(108 holes)
Bowling centers: 3 (72 lanes, tenpins)   B
Outdoor Recreation Assets (2,000)
Gulf of Mexico Coastline: 65 miles
Inland Water Area: 112.8 square miles
National Forests, Parks, Wildlife Refuges:
Big Cypress National Preserve (395,048 acres)
Everglades NP (39,262 acres)
Places Rated Score: 3,000   Places Rated Rank: 24

Nashua, NH
Common Denominators (700 points)
Good restaurants: 2 ★, 1 ★★★   C
Golf courses: 1 private (18 holes); 5 daily fee (81   A
holes)
Bowling centers: 4 (120 lanes, mixed)   A
Outdoor Recreation Assets (19)
Inland Water Area: 1.2 square miles
CMSA Access: Boston–Lawrence–Salem, MA–NH (130)
Places Rated Score: 849   Places Rated Rank: 282

Nashville, TN
Common Denominators (700 points)
Good restaurants: 3 ★, 7 ★★, 10 ★★★, 3 ★★★★   A
Golf courses: 18 private (252 holes); 6 daily fee (99   B
holes); 11 municipal (180 holes)
Bowling centers: 17 (422 lanes, tenpins)   B
Crowd Pleasers (1,100 points)
Theme Park: Opryland (140 days)   A

	Rating
Auto Racing:	**A**
Highland Rim Speedway (NASCAR)	
Nashville Motor Speedway (NASCAR)	
Professional Sports: 1.311 game seats per capita	**B**
Sounds (Triple A Baseball)	
NCAA Division I: 0.826 game seats per capita	**A**
Middle Tennessee State Blue Raiders, Tennessee State Tigers, Vanderbilt Commodores	

Outdoor Recreation Assets (94)
Inland Water Area: 75.1 square miles
National Forests, Parks, Wildlife Refuges:
Natchez Trace Parkway (1,132 acres)
Stones River National Battlefield (351 acres)
Places Rated Score: 1,894   Places Rated Rank: 96

★ Nassau–Suffolk, NY

Common Denominators (800 points)	
Good restaurants: 13 ★, 36 ★★, 19 ★★★	**A**
Golf courses: 59 private (1,035 holes); 17 daily fee (279 holes); 17 municipal (414 holes)	**B**
Bowling centers: 65 (1,870 lanes, tenpins)	**A**
Crowd Pleasers (500 points)	
Auto Racing: Riverhead Raceway (NASCAR)	**B**
Pari-Mutuel Betting:	**C**
Belmont Park (thoroughbred, 114 races)	
Professional Sports: 0.240 game seats per capita	**C**
New York Islanders (NHL Hockey)	
NCAA Division I: 0.019 game seats per capita	**C**
Hofstra Flying Dutchmen	

Outdoor Recreation Assets (2,000)
Atlantic Coastline: 170 miles
Inland Water Area: 288.2 square miles
National Forests, Parks, Wildlife Refuges:
Amagansett NWR (36 acres)
Conscience Point NWR (60 acres)
E.A. Norton NWR (187 acres)
Fire Island NS (18,606 acres)
Oyster Bay NWR (3,204 acres)
Sagamore Hill NHS (78 acres)
Seatuck NWR (183 acres)
Target Rock NWR (80 acres)
Wertheim NWR (2,235 acres)
CMSA Access: New York–Northern NJ–Long
Island, NY–NJ–CT (150 points)
Places Rated Score: 3,450   Places Rated Rank: 9

New Bedford, MA

Common Denominators (600 points)	
Good restaurants: 1 ★, 1 ★★	**C**
Golf courses: 5 private (72 holes); 3 daily fee (27 holes); 1 municipal (18 holes)	**B**
Bowling centers: 6 (136 lanes, mixed)	**A**

Outdoor Recreation Assets (698)
Atlantic Coastline: 26 miles
Inland Water Area: 20.4 square miles
Places Rated Score: 1,298   Places Rated Rank: 198

New Britain, CT

Common Denominators (400 points)	
Golf courses: 2 daily fee (36 holes); 1 municipal (27 holes)	**A**
Bowling centers: 3 (36 lanes, mixed)	**C**
Crowd Pleasers (500 points)	
Professional Sports: 1.915 game seats per capita	**A**
Red Sox (Double A Baseball)	
NCAA Division I: 0.369 game seats per capita	**B**

Outdoor Recreation Assets (17)
Inland Water Area: 0.3 square miles
CMSA Access: Hartford–New Britain–Middletown,
CT (100)
Places Rated Score: 1,017   Places Rated Rank: 256

New Haven–Meriden, CT

Common Denominators (500 points)	
Good restaurants: 2 ★, 7 ★★, 1 ★★★	**B**
Golf courses: 11 private (198 holes); 3 daily fee (36 holes); 4 municipal (63 holes)	**C**

	Rating
Bowling centers: 10 (294 lanes, mixed)	**B**
Crowd Pleasers (400 points)	
Professional Sports: 0.455 game seats per capita	**C**
Nighthawks (AHL Hockey)	
NCAA Division I: 0.751 game seats per capita	**A**
Yale Bulldogs	

Outdoor Recreation Assets (420)
Atlantic Coastline: 30 miles
Inland Water Area: 8.7 square miles
National Forests, Parks, Wildlife Refuges:
S.B. McKinney NWR (5 acres)
Places Rated Score: 1,320   Places Rated Rank: 193

New London–Norwich, CT–RI

Common Denominators (600 points)	
Good restaurants: 1 ★, 1 ★★, 4 ★★★	**A**
Golf courses: 4 private (54 holes); 1 daily fee (18 holes); 2 municipal (36 holes)	**C**
Bowling centers: 7 (162 lanes, mixed)	**B**

Outdoor Recreation Assets (611)
Atlantic Coastline: 35 miles
Inland Water Area: 33.4 square miles
Places Rated Score: 1,211   Places Rated Rank: 221

★ New Orleans, LA

Common Denominators (700 points)	
Good restaurants: 4 ★, 23 ★★, 18 ★★★, 4 ★★★★	**AA**
Golf courses: 19 private (351 holes); 4 daily fee (72 holes); 3 municipal (108 holes)	**C**
Bowling centers: 20 (562 lanes, tenpins)	**B**
Crowd Pleasers (800 points)	
Zoo: Audubon Park & Zoological Garden—401 species, 1,535 specimens	**AA**
Pari-Mutuel Betting:	**C**
Fair Grounds (thoroughbred, 96 races)	
Jefferson Downs (thoroughbred, 137 races)	
Professional Sports: 0.404 game seats per capita	**C**
Saints (NFC Football)	
NCAA Division I: 0.351 game seats per capita	**B**
Tulane Green Wave, University of New Orleans Privateers	

Outdoor Recreation Assets (2,000)
Gulf of Mexico Coastline: 75 miles
Inland Water Area: 1,175.2 square miles
National Forests, Parks, Wildlife Refuges:
Boguechito NWR (16,792 acres)
Breton NWR (8,402 acres)
Jean Lafitte NHP (7,754 acres)
Places Rated Score: 3,500   Places Rated Rank: 7

★ New York, NY

Common Denominators (400 points)	
Good restaurants: 28 ★, 86 ★★, 55 ★★★, 12 ★★★★, 1 ★★★★★	**B**
Golf courses: 48 private (891 holes); 5 daily fee (63 holes); 19 municipal (360 holes)	**C**
Bowling centers: 83 (2,352 lanes, tenpins)	**C**
Crowd Pleasers (1,500 points)	
Zoos: New York (Bronx) Zoological Park—658 species, 5,512 specimens	**AA**
Staten Island Zoo—202 species, 457 specimens	**A**
Aquarium: New York Aquarium—304 species, 22,577 specimens	**AA**
Pari-Mutuel Betting:	**C**
Aqueduct (thoroughbred, 174 races)	
Yonkers Raceway (harness, 321 races)	
Professional Sports: 1.248 game seats per capita	**B**
Knicks (NBA Basketball), Mets (NL Baseball), Rangers (NHL Hockey), Yankees (AL Baseball)	
NCAA Division I: 0.046 game seats per capita	**C**
Brooklyn College Kingsmen, Columbia Lions, Fordham University Rams, Iona Gaels, Long Island University-Brooklyn Blackbirds, Manhattan College Jaspers, St. Francis College Terriers, St. John's University Redmen, Wagner College Seahawks	

Rating

Outdoor Recreation Assets (989)
Atlantic Coastline: 27 miles
Inland Water Area: 149.8 square miles
National Forests, Parks, Wildlife Refuges:
Appalachian Trail (960 acres)
Castle Clinton NM (1 acre)
Federal Hall NM (0.45 acres)
Gateway NRA (21,715 acres)
General Grant NM (0.76 acres)
Hamilton Grange NM (0.71 acres)
Statue of Liberty NM (13 acres)
Theodore Roosevelt Birthplace NHS (0.11 acres)
CMSA Access: New York–Northern NJ–Long
Island, NY–NJ–CT (320 points)
Places Rated Score: 3,209   Places Rated Rank: 15

Newark, NJ
Common Denominators (400 points)

	Rating
Good restaurants: 9 **, 8 ***, 2 ****	C
Golf courses: 32 private (603 holes); 9 daily fee (144 holes); 13 municipal (234 holes)	C
Bowling centers: 34 (931 lanes, tenpins)	B

Crowd Pleasers (100 points)

	Rating
NCAA Division I: 0.020 game seats per capita	C

Seton Hall Pirates
Outdoor Recreation Assets (413)
Inland Water Area: 25 square miles
National Forests, Parks, Wildlife Refuges:
Appalachian Trail (3,211 acres)
Delaware NSR (684 acres)
Delaware Water Gap NRA (37,398 acres)
Edison NHS (21 acres)
Great Swamp NWR (6,792 acres)
Morristown NHP (1,488 acres)
CMSA Access: New York–Northern NJ–Long
Island, NY–NJ–CT (270 points)
Places Rated Score: 1,183   Places Rated Rank: 231

Niagara Falls, NY
Common Denominators (1,100 points)

	Rating
Good restaurants: 1 *, 4 **, 1 ***	A
Golf courses: 5 private (72 holes); 4 daily fee (54 holes); 3 municipal (72 holes)	AA
Bowling centers: 11 (226 lanes, tenpins)	AA

Crowd Pleasers (500 points)

	Rating
Auto Racing: Grand Prix of Niagara Falls (SCCA)	B
Professional Sports: 1.302 game seats per capita	B

Tigers (Class A Baseball)

	Rating
NCAA Division I: 0.204 game seats per capita	C

Niagara University Purple Eagles
Outdoor Recreation Assets (371)
Great Lakes Coastline: 31 miles
Inland Water Area: 6.6 square miles
CMSA Access: Buffalo–Niagara Falls, NY (120 points)
Places Rated Score: 2,091   Places Rated Rank: 76

★ Norfolk–Virginia Beach–Newport News, VA
Common Denominators (700 points)

	Rating
Good restaurants: 9 *, 27 **, 10 ***, 1 ****	A
Golf courses: 14 private (288 holes); 8 daily fee (144 holes); 8 municipal (153 holes)	C
Bowling centers: 38 (980 lanes, mixed)	A

Crowd Pleasers (800 points)

	Rating
Zoo: Virginia Zoological Park—108 species, 322 specimens	B
Theme Park: Busch Gardens—The Old Country (137 days)	B
Auto Racing: Langley Speedway (NASCAR)	B
Professional Sports: 0.543 game seats per capita	C

Peninsula Pilots (Class A Baseball), Tidewater
Tides (Triple A Baseball)

	Rating
NCAA Division I: 0.238 game seats per capita	C

College of William and Mary Indians, Old
Dominion Monarchs
Outdoor Recreation Assets (1,736)
Atlantic Coastline: 69 miles

Rating

Inland Water Area: 265.9 square miles
National Forests, Parks, Wildlife Refuges:
Back Bay NWR (4,589 acres)
Colonial NHP (8,814 acres)
Great Dismal Swamp NWR (77,733 acres)
Jamestown NHS (21 acres)
Mackay Island NWR (874 acres)
Nansemond NWR (208 acres)
Plum Tree Island NWR (3,276 acres)
Yorktown National Cemetery (3 acres)
Places Rated Score: 3,236   Places Rated Rank: 14

Norwalk, CT
Common Denominators (900 points)

	Rating
Good restaurants: 3 *, 6 **, 1 ***	AA
Golf courses: 5 private (81 holes); 2 municipal (36 holes)	B
Bowling centers: 2 (88 lanes, tenpins)	A

Crowd Pleasers (435 points)
Outdoor Recreation Assets (568)
Atlantic Coastline: 9 miles
Inland Water Area: 8.5 square miles
National Forests, Parks, Wildlife Refuges:
S.B. McKinney NWR (119 acres)
CMSA Access: New York–Northern NJ–Long
Island, NY–NJ–CT (210)
Places Rated Score: 1,545   Places Rated Rank: 154

Oakland, CA
Common Denominators (400 points)

	Rating
Good restaurants: 4 *, 5 **, 9 ***	C
Golf courses: 13 private (279 holes); 12 daily fee (207 holes); 10 municipal (207 holes)	C
Bowling centers: 33 (938 lanes, tenpins)	B

Crowd Pleasers (700 points)

	Rating
Auto Racing: Antioch Speedway (NASCAR)	B
Pari-Mutuel Betting:	C

Alameda County Fair (mixed meetings, 13 races)
Golden Gate Fields (thoroughbred, 101 races)

	Rating
Professional Sports: 2.231 game seats per capita	A

A's (AL Baseball), Golden State Warriors (NBA
Basketball)

	Rating
NCAA Division I: 0.246 game seats per capita	C

St. Mary's College Gaels, University of California
Golden Bears
Outdoor Recreation Assets (538)
Inland Water Area: 157.4 square miles
National Forests, Parks, Wildlife Refuges:
Antioch Dunes NWR (55 acres)
Eugene O'Neill NHS (13 acres)
John Muir NHS (9 acres)
San Francisco Bay NWR (10,620 acres)
CMSA Access: San Francisco–Oakland–San Jose,
CA (190 points)
Places Rated Score: 1,828   Places Rated Rank: 107

Ocala, FL
Common Denominators (800 points)

	Rating
Good restaurants: 2 **, 1 ***	B
Golf courses: 2 private (36 holes); 3 daily fee (54 holes); 2 municipal (45 holes)	A
Bowling centers: 6 (130 lanes, mixed)	A

Crowd Pleasers (200 points)

	Rating
Pari-Mutuel Betting:	B

Classic Mile (quarter horse, 68 races)
Ocala Jai Alai (192 matches)
Outdoor Recreation Assets (1,448)
Inland Water Area: 52.5 square miles
National Forests, Parks, Wildlife Refuges:
Ocala NF (274,383 acres)
Places Rated Score: 2,448   Places Rated Rank: 48

Odessa, TX
Common Denominators (500 points)

	Rating
Good restaurants: 6 *	B
Golf courses: 2 private (36 holes); 1 daily fee (18 holes)	C

	Rating
Bowling centers: 3 (80 lanes, tenpins)	B
Places Rated Score: 500	Places Rated Rank: 320

Oklahoma City, OK
Common Denominators (700 points)
- Good restaurants: 4 *, 9 **, 11 *** — **A**
- Golf courses: 13 private (225 holes); 5 daily fee (99 holes); 11 municipal (207 holes) — **B**
- Bowling centers: 23 (610 lanes, tenpins) — **B**

Crowd Pleasers (1,000 points)
- Zoo: Oklahoma City Zoological Park—477 species, 1,819 specimens — **AA**
- Pari-Mutuel Betting: — **B**
  Remington Park (mixed meetings, 153 races)
- Professional Sports: 0.850 game seats per capita — **B**
  89ers (Triple A Baseball)
- NCAA Division I: 0.504 game seats per capita — **B**
  University of Oklahoma Sooners

Outdoor Recreation Assets (59)
- Inland Water Area: 50.8 square miles

Places Rated Score: 1,759 — Places Rated Rank: 116

Olympia, WA
Common Denominators (600 points)
- Golf courses: 1 private (18 holes); 5 daily fee (90 holes) — **AA**
- Bowling centers: 4 (64 lanes, tenpins) — **B**

Crowd Pleasers (200 points)
- Auto Racing: Olympia–Tenino Raceway (NASCAR) — **B**

Outdoor Recreation Assets (430)
- Puget Sound Coastline: 10 miles
- Inland Water Area: 47 square miles
- National Forests, Parks, Wildlife Refuges:
  - Nisqually NWR (1,985 acres)
  - Olympic NF (10 acres)
  - Snoqualmie NF (612 acres)

Places Rated Score: 1,230 — Places Rated Rank: 218

Omaha, NE–IA
Common Denominators (1,000 points)
- Good restaurants: 2 *, 13 **, 7 *** — **AA**
- Golf courses: 11 private (171 holes); 6 daily fee (81 holes); 10 municipal (135 holes) — **B**
- Bowling centers: 32 (649 lanes, tenpins) — **AA**

Crowd Pleasers (1,100 points)
- Zoo: Omaha's Henry Doorly Zoo—385 species, 7,041 specimens — **A**
- Auto Racing: Sunset Speedway (NASCAR) — **B**
- Pari-Mutuel Betting: — **B**
  - Ak-Sar-Ben (thoroughbred, 85 races)
  - Bluffs Run (greyhound, 462 races)
- Professional Sports: 1.705 game seats per capita — **A**
  Royals (Triple A Baseball)
- NCAA Division I: 0.192 game seats per capita — **C**
  Creighton Bluejays

Outdoor Recreation Assets (95)
- Inland Water Area: 29.5 square miles
- National Forests, Parks, Wildlife Refuges:
  - De Soto NWR (4,324 acres)

Places Rated Score: 2,195 — Places Rated Rank: 66

Orange County, NY
Common Denominators (700 points)
- Good restaurants: 2 *, 2 **, 1 *** — **C**
- Golf courses: 9 private (135 holes); 7 daily fee (90 holes); 1 municipal (18 holes) — **A**
- Bowling centers: 10 (240 lanes, tenpins) — **A**

Crowd Pleasers (300 points)
- NCAA Division I: 0.879 game seats per capita — **A**
  U.S. Military Academy Black Knights

Outdoor Recreation Assets (163)
- Inland Water Area: 13.4 square miles
- National Forests, Parks, Wildlife Refuges:
  - Appalachian Trail (2,422 acres)
  - Upper Delaware NSR (6,559 acres)

CMSA Access: New York–Northern NJ–Long Island, NY–NJ–CT (150 points)

Places Rated Score: 1,313 — Places Rated Rank: 195

Orlando, FL
Common Denominators (900 points)
- Good restaurants: 5 *, 15 **, 17 ***, 1 **** — **AA**
- Golf courses: 16 private (324 holes); 32 daily fee (549 holes); 1 municipal (18 holes) — **A**
- Bowling centers: 21 (574 lanes, tenpins) — **B**

Crowd Pleasers (1,200 points)
- Zoos: Central Florida Zoological Park—179 species, 455 specimens — **B**
  Discovery Island Zoological Park—118 species, 470 specimens — **C**
- Theme Parks: — **AA**
  - Sea World of Florida (365 days)
  - Walt Disney World and Epcot Center
- Pari-Mutuel Betting: — **C**
  - Florida Jai Alai (282 matches)
  - Sanford–Orlando Kennel Club (greyhound, 239 races)
  - Seminole Greyhound Park (greyhound, 234 races)
- Professional Sports: 1.849 game seats per capita — **A**
  Baseball City Royals (Class A Baseball), Magic (NBA Basketball), Osceola Astros (Class A Baseball), Twins (Double A Baseball)
- NCAA Division I: 0.035 game seats per capita — **C**
  University of Central Florida Knights

Outdoor Recreation Assets (520)
- Inland Water Area: 297.1 square miles

Places Rated Score: 2,620 — Places Rated Rank: 41

Owensboro, KY
Common Denominators (400 points)
- Good restaurants: 1 *, 1 ** — **B**
- Golf courses: 2 private (36 holes); 2 daily fee (27 holes); 1 municipal (9 holes) — **A**
- Bowling center: 1 (24 lanes, tenpins) — **C**

Crowd Pleasers (200 points)
- Auto Racing: Kentucky Motor Speedway (NASCAR) — **B**

Outdoor Recreation Assets (148)
- Inland Water Area: 14.1 square miles

Places Rated Score: 748 — Places Rated Rank: 300

Oxnard–Ventura, CA
Common Denominators (500 points)
- Good restaurants: 1 *, 3 **, 2 *** — **C**
- Golf courses: 6 private (99 holes); 5 daily fee (81 holes); 5 municipal (90 holes) — **B**
- Bowling centers: 14 (330 lanes, tenpins) — **B**

Crowd Pleasers (100 points)
- Pari-Mutuel Betting: — **C**
  Ventura County Fair (mixed meetings, 13 races)

Outdoor Recreation Assets (2,000)
- Pacific Coastline: 37 miles
- Inland Water Area: 5.5 square miles
- National Forests, Parks, Wildlife Refuges:
  - Angeles NF (1,473 acres)
  - Bitter Creek NWR (122 acres)
  - Channel Islands NP (9,905 acres)
  - Hopper Mountain NWR (1,871 acres)
  - Los Padres NF (556,632 acres)
  - Santa Monica Mountains NRA (17,165 acres)

CMSA Access: Los Angeles–Anaheim–Riverside, CA (120 points)

Places Rated Score: 2,720 — Places Rated Rank: 35

Panama City, FL
Common Denominators (1,000 points)
- Good restaurants: 1 *, 1 **, 4 *** — **AA**
- Golf courses: 2 private (36 holes); 4 daily fee (81 holes) — **AA**
- Bowling centers: 3 (56 lanes, tenpins) — **B**

Outdoor Recreation Assets (1,142)

Rating

Gulf of Mexico Coastline: 44 miles
Inland Water Area: 123.8 square miles
Places Rated Score: 2,142   Places Rated Rank: 72

Parkersburg–Marietta, WV–OH
Common Denominators (900 points)
  Good restaurants: 1 **, 3 ***   **A**
  Golf courses: 2 private (36 holes); 5 daily fee (90   **AA**
    holes)
  Bowling centers: 4 (85 lanes, tenpins)   **B**
Outdoor Recreation Assets (47)
  Inland Water Area: 9.6 square miles
Places Rated Score: 947   Places Rated Rank: 266

Pascagoula, MS
Common Denominators (800 points)
  Good restaurants: 2 **, 1 ***   **A**
  Golf courses: 2 private (27 holes); 3 daily fee (54   **A**
    holes); 1 municipal (9 holes)
  Bowling centers: 4 (84 lanes, tenpins)   **B**
Outdoor Recreation Assets (932)
  Gulf of Mexico Coastline: 25 miles
  Inland Water Area: 25.3 square miles
  National Forests, Parks, Wildlife Refuges:
    Gulf Islands NS (49,873 acres)
    Mississippi Sandhill Crane NWR (17,190 acres)
Places Rated Score: 1,732   Places Rated Rank: 118

Pawtucket–Woonsocket–Attleboro, RI–MA
Common Denominators (600 points)
  Good restaurant: 1 **   **C**
  Golf courses: 7 private (108 holes); 14 daily fee   **A**
    (171 holes)
  Bowling centers: 6 (156 lanes, mixed)   **B**
Crowd Pleasers (600 points)
  Pari-Mutuel Betting: **AA**
    Lincoln Greyhound Park (greyhound, 470 races)
  Professional Sports: 1.316 game seats per capita   **B**
    Red Sox (Triple A Baseball)
Outdoor Recreation Assets (125)
  Inland Water Area: 7 square miles
  National Forests, Parks, Wildlife Refuges:
    Trustom Pond NWR (579 acres)
CMSA Access: Providence–Pawtucket–Fall River,
  RI–MA (40 points)
Places Rated Score: 1,365   Places Rated Rank: 182

Pensacola, FL
Common Denominators (700 points)
  Good restaurants: 2 *, 3 **, 2 ***   **B**
  Golf courses: 7 private (126 holes); 3 daily fee (72   **B**
    holes); 1 municipal (18 holes)
  Bowling centers: 11 (242 lanes, tenpins)   **A**
Crowd Pleasers (500 points)
  Pari-Mutuel Betting: **AA**
    Pensacola Greyhound Track (greyhound, 398
    races)
  Professional Sports: 0.746 game seats per capita   **C**
    Tornados (CBA Basketball)
Outdoor Recreation Assets (990)
  Gulf of Mexico Coastline: 43 miles
  Inland Water Area: 212.2 square miles
Places Rated Score: 2,190   Places Rated Rank: 67

Peoria, IL
Common Denominators (900 points)
  Good restaurants: 2 **, 2 ***   **C**
  Golf courses: 7 private (108 holes); 7 daily fee (126   **AA**
    holes); 6 municipal (117 holes)
  Bowling centers: 28 (422 lanes, tenpins)   **AA**
Crowd Pleasers (800 points)
  Zoo: Glen Oak Zoo—112 species, 279 specimens   **C**
  Auto Racing: Peoria Speedway (NASCAR)   **B**
  Professional Sports: 2.152 game seats per capita   **A**
    Chiefs (Class A Baseball), Rivermen (IHL Hockey)
  NCAA Division I: 0.368 game seats per capita   **B**

Rating

  Bradley University Braves
Outdoor Recreation Assets (87)
  Inland Water Area: 31.8 square miles
Places Rated Score: 1,787   Places Rated Rank: 111

Philadelphia, PA–NJ
Common Denominators (400 points)
  Good restaurants: 11 *, 35 **, 13 ***, 1 ****,   **C**
    1 *****
  Golf courses: 72 private (1,233 holes); 49 daily fee   **C**
    (900 holes); 13 municipal (234 holes)
  Bowling centers: 101 (2,188 lanes, tenpins)   **B**
Crowd Pleasers (800 points)
  Zoo: Philadelphia Zoological Garden—459 species,   **AA**
    1,526 specimens
  Pari-Mutuel Betting: **C**
    Garden State Park (mixed meetings, 169 races)
    Philadelphia Park (thoroughbred, 199 races)
  Professional Sports: 1.471 game seats per capita   **B**
    76ers (NBA Basketball), Eagles (NFC Football),
    Flyers (NHL Hockey), Phillies (NL Baseball)
  NCAA Division I: 0.225 game seats per capita   **C**
    Drexel University Dragons, LaSalle Explorers, St.
    Joseph's University Hawks, Temple University
    Owls, University of Pennsylvania Quakers,
    Villanova Wildcats
Outdoor Recreation Assets (89)
  Inland Water Area: 53.9 square miles
  National Forests, Parks, Wildlife Refuges:
    Brigantine NWR (97 acres)
    Edgar Allen Poe House NHS (0.52 acres)
    Hopewell Village NHS (320 acres)
    Independence NHP (2,814 acres)
    Thaddeus Kosciuszko NM (0.02 acres)
    Tinicum NWR (930 acres)
    Valley Forge NHP (2,988 acres)
CMSA Access: Philadelphia–Wilmington–Trenton,
  PA–NJ–DE–MD (60 points)
Places Rated Score: 1,349   Places Rated Rank: 185

Phoenix, AZ
Common Denominators (800 points)
  Good restaurants: 12 *, 20 **, 13 ***, 4 ****   **A**
  Golf courses: 35 private (720 holes); 34 daily fee   **A**
    (684 holes); 9 municipal (171 holes)
  Bowling centers: 34 (1014 lanes, tenpins)   **B**
Crowd Pleasers (1,100 points)
  Zoo: The Phoenix Zoo—293 species, 2,270   **AA**
    specimens
  Auto Racing: **A**
    Firebird International Raceway (IMSA, SCCA)
    Phoenix International Raceway (NASCAR, SCCA,
    USAC)
  Pari-Mutuel Betting: **C**
    Phoenix Greyhound Park (greyhound, 460 races)
    Turf Paradise (thoroughbred, 161 races)
  Professional Sports: 0.850 game seats per capita   **B**
    Cardinals (NFC Football), Firebirds (Triple A
    Baseball), Suns (NBA Basketball)
  NCAA Division I: 0.252 game seats per capita   **C**
    Arizona State Sun Devils
Outdoor Recreation Assets (611)
  Inland Water Area: 14.9 square miles
  National Forests, Parks, Wildlife Refuges:
    Tonto NF (658,436 acres)
Places Rated Score: 2,511   Places Rated Rank: 45

Pine Bluff, AR
Common Denominators (200 points)
  Golf courses: 2 private (36 holes); 1 municipal (18   **C**
    holes)
  Bowling center: 1 (24 lanes, tenpins)   **C**
Outdoor Recreation Assets (188)
  Inland Water Area: 34.1 square miles
Places Rated Score: 388   Places Rated Rank: 327

	Rating

Pittsburgh, PA
Common Denominators (700 points)
  Good restaurants: 4 ★, 26 ★★, 13 ★★★ — **B**
  Golf courses: 39 private (711 holes); 46 daily fee — **B**
    (738 holes); 5 municipal (90 holes)
  Bowling centers: 105 (1852 lanes, tenpins) — **B**
Crowd Pleasers (1,000 points)
  Zoos: Pittsburgh Aviary—276 species, 1,025 — **C**
    specimens
    Pittsburgh Zoo—357 species, 1,901 specimens — **A**
  Pari-Mutuel Betting: — **C**
    The Meadows (harness, 208 races)
  Professional Sports: 2.599 game seats per capita — **AA**
    Penguins (NHL Hockey), Pirates (NL Baseball),
    Steelers (NFC Football)
  NCAA Division I: 0.218 game seats per capita — **C**
    Duquesne Dukes, Robert Morris Colonials,
    University of Pittsburgh Panthers
Outdoor Recreation Assets (46)
  Inland Water Area: 28.1 square miles
  National Forests, Parks, Wildlife Refuges:
    Fort Necessity National Battlefield (903 acres)
    Friendship Hill NHS (661 acres)
Places Rated Score: 1,746   Places Rated Rank: 117

Pittsfield, MA
Common Denominators (1,100 points)
  Good restaurants: 8 ★★, 6 ★★★, 1 ★★★★ — **AA**
  Golf courses: 4 private (72 holes); 6 daily fee (72 — **AA**
    holes)
  Bowling centers: 2 (58 lanes, tenpins) — **A**
Crowd Pleasers (400 points)
  Professional Sports: 4.547 game seats per capita — **AA**
    Mets (Class A Baseball)
Outdoor Recreation Assets (133)
  Inland Water Area: 6.3 square miles
Places Rated Score: 1,633   Places Rated Rank: 132

Portland, ME
Common Denominators (900 points)
  Good restaurants: 2 ★, 10 ★★, 6 ★★★ — **AA**
  Golf courses: 3 private (54 holes); 9 daily fee (99 — **AA**
    holes); 3 municipal (45 holes)
  Bowling centers: 4 (80 lanes, mixed) — **C**
Crowd Pleasers (500 points)
  Pari-Mutuel Betting: — **A**
    Scarborough Downs (harness, 100 races)
  Professional Sports: 1.265 game seats per capita — **B**
    Maine Mariners (AHL Hockey)
Outdoor Recreation Assets (1,222)
  Atlantic Coastline: 36 miles
  Inland Water Area: 112.7 square miles
  National Forests, Parks, Wildlife Refuges:
    Rachel Carson NWR (144 acres)
Places Rated Score: 2,622   Places Rated Rank: 40

Portland, OR
Common Denominators (800 points)
  Good restaurants: 12 ★, 23 ★★, 13 ★★★ — **AA**
  Golf courses: 11 private (198 holes); 17 daily fee — **B**
    (279 holes); 4 municipal (81 holes)
  Bowling centers: 30 (634 lanes, tenpins) — **B**
Crowd Pleasers (1,200 points)
  Zoo: Washington Park Zoo—142 species, 620 — **AA**
    specimens
  Auto Racing: — **A**
    Portland International Raceway (IMSA, SCCA)
    Portland Speedway (NASCAR)
  Pari-Mutuel Betting: — **C**
    Multnomah Kennel Club (greyhound, 133 races)
    Portland Meadows (thoroughbred, 90 races)
  Professional Sports: 2.059 game seats per capita — **A**
    Beavers (Triple A Baseball), Trail Blazers (NBA
    Basketball)
  NCAA Division I: 0.051 game seats per capita — **C**
    University of Portland Pilots

Outdoor Recreation Assets (268)
  Inland Water Area: 46.4 square miles
  National Forests, Parks, Wildlife Refuges:
    Eagle Creek NWR (166 acres)
    McLoughlin House NHS (0.63 acres)
    Mount Hood NF (72,415 acres)
    Siuslaw NF (25,440 acres)
    Willamette NF (856 acres)
Places Rated Score: 2,268   Places Rated Rank: 59

Portsmouth–Dover–Rochester, NH–ME
Common Denominators (900 points)
  Good restaurants: 1 ★, 15 ★★, 6 ★★★ — **AA**
  Golf courses: 5 private (90 holes); 7 daily fee (81 — **B**
    holes)
  Bowling centers: 9 (158 lanes, mixed) — **A**
Crowd Pleasers (800 points)
  Auto Racing: Star Speedway (NASCAR) — **B**
  Pari-Mutuel Betting: — **AA**
    Seabrook Greyhound Park (greyhound, 427 races)
  NCAA Division I: 0.463 game seats per capita — **B**
    University of New Hampshire Wildcats
Outdoor Recreation Assets (484)
  Atlantic Coastline: 26 miles
  Inland Water Area: 28.6 square miles
  National Forests, Parks, Wildlife Refuges:
    Rachel Carson NWR (1,748 acres)
Places Rated Score: 2,184   Places Rated Rank: 68

Poughkeepsie, NY
Common Denominators (1,000 points)
  Good restaurants: 3 ★, 6 ★★, 5 ★★★, 1 ★★★★, — **AA**
    1 ★★★★★
  Golf courses: 8 private (81 holes); 6 daily fee (81 — **A**
    holes); 4 municipal (63 holes)
  Bowling centers: 9 (210 lanes, tenpins) — **A**
Crowd Pleasers (100 points)
  NCAA Division I: 0.178 game seats per capita — **C**
    Marist College Red Foxes
Outdoor Recreation Assets (165)
  Inland Water Area: 20.7 square miles
  National Forests, Parks, Wildlife Refuges:
    Appalachian Trail (3,619 acres)
    Eleanor Roosevelt NHS (181 acres)
    Home of Franklin D. Roosevelt NHS (264 acres)
    Vanderbilt Mansion NHS (212 acres)
Places Rated Score: 1,265   Places Rated Rank: 206

Providence, RI
Common Denominators (600 points)
  Good restaurants: 6 ★★, 6 ★★★ — **B**
  Golf courses: 11 private (180 holes); 13 daily fee — **B**
    (153 holes); 3 municipal (45 holes)
  Bowling centers: 12 (352 lanes, mixed) — **B**
Crowd Pleasers (400 points)
  Zoo: Roger Williams Park Zoo—132 species, 325 — **B**
    specimens
  NCAA Division I: 0.430 game seats per capita — **B**
    Brown University Bears, Providence College Friars
Outdoor Recreation Assets (825)
  Atlantic Coastline: 12 miles
  Inland Water Area: 100.6 square miles
  National Forests, Parks, Wildlife Refuges:
    Roger Williams National Memorial (5 acres)
    Trustom Pond NWR (642 acres)
  CMSA Access: Providence–Pawtucket–Fall River,
    RI–MA (60 points)
Places Rated Score: 1,885   Places Rated Rank: 98

★ Provo–Orem, UT
Common Denominators (600 points)
  Good restaurants: 1 ★, 1 ★★, 1 ★★★ — **C**
  Golf courses: 3 private (54 holes); 2 daily fee (27 — **A**
    holes); 5 municipal (99 holes)
  Bowling centers: 7 (126 lanes, tenpins) — **B**
Crowd Pleasers (400 points)

	Rating
NCAA Division I: 2.355 game seats per capita Brigham Young Cougars	AA

Outdoor Recreation Assets (2,000)
Inland Water Area: 126.9 square miles
National Forests, Parks, Wildlife Refuges:
Ashley NF (3,885 acres)
Manti-La Sal NF (91,292 acres)
Timpanogos Cave NM (250 acres)
Uinta NF (390,215 acres)
Places Rated Score: 3,000   Places Rated Rank: 24

Pueblo, CO

Common Denominators (700 points)

	Rating
Good restaurants: 2 *	C
Golf courses: 1 private (18 holes); 2 daily fee (27 holes); 3 municipal (45 holes)	A
Bowling centers: 5 (118 lanes, tenpins)	A

Crowd Pleasers (600 points)

	Rating
Auto Racing: Pueblo Motorsports Park (SCCA)	B
Pari-Mutuel Betting: Pueblo Greyhound Park (greyhound, 74 races)	AA

Outdoor Recreation Assets (45)
Inland Water Area: 21.6 square miles
Places Rated Score: 1,345   Places Rated Rank: 186

Racine, WI

Common Denominators (900 points)

	Rating
Good restaurants: 3 *, 1 **	C
Golf courses: 2 private (36 holes); 2 daily fee (36 holes); 5 municipal (72 holes)	AA
Bowling centers: 13 (252 lanes, tenpins)	AA

Crowd Pleasers (100 points)

	Rating
Zoo: Racine Zoological Garden—102 species, 371 specimens	C

Outdoor Recreation Assets (214)
Great Lakes Coastline: 12 miles
Inland Water Area: 6.4 square miles
CMSA Access: Milwaukee–Racine, WI (90 points)
Places Rated Score: 1,304   Places Rated Rank: 197

Raleigh–Durham, NC

Common Denominators (700 points)

	Rating
Good restaurants: 9 **, 9 ***	A
Golf courses: 12 private (216 holes); 19 daily fee (324 holes)	A
Bowling centers: 8 (204 lanes, tenpins)	C

Crowd Pleasers (500 points)

	Rating
Professional Sports: 0.498 game seats per capita Durham Bulls (Class A Baseball)	C
NCAA Division I: 1.725 game seats per capita Duke Blue Devils, North Carolina State Wolfpack, University of North Carolina Tarheels	AA

Outdoor Recreation Assets (11)
Inland Water Area: 4.7 square miles
Places Rated Score: 1,211   Places Rated Rank: 221

★ Rapid City, SD

Common Denominators (900 points)

	Rating
Good restaurants: 3 *, 1 **	A
Golf courses: 3 private (36 holes); 3 municipal (36 holes)	A
Bowling centers: 4 (64 lanes, tenpins)	A

Crowd Pleasers (800 points)

	Rating
Pari-Mutuel Betting: Black Hills Greyhound Track (greyhound, 130 races)	AA
Professional Sports: 2.759 game seats per capita Thrillers (CBA Basketball)	AA

Outdoor Recreation Assets (1,382 points)
Inland Water Area: 2.8 square miles
National Forests, Parks, Wildlife Refuges:
Badlands NP (94,713 acres)
Black Hills NF (394,905 acres)
Mount Rushmore NM (1,238 acres)
Places Rated Score: 3,082   Places Rated Rank: 21

Reading, PA

Common Denominators (900 points)

	Rating
Good restaurants: 2 *, 2 **, 2 ****	B
Golf courses: 5 private (90 holes); 11 daily fee (198 holes)	AA
Bowling centers: 26 (270 lanes, tenpins)	A

Crowd Pleasers (300 points)

	Rating
Professional Sports: 1.778 game seats per capita Phillies (Double A Baseball)	A

Outdoor Recreation Assets (60)
Inland Water Area: 3.7 square miles
National Forests, Parks, Wildlife Refuges:
Appalachian Trail (3,703 acres)
Hopewell Village NHS (529 acres)
Places Rated Score: 1,260   Places Rated Rank: 208

Redding, CA

Common Denominators (600 points)

	Rating
Good restaurants: 1 *, 2 **, 1 ***	A
Golf courses: 2 private (36 holes); 4 daily fee (45 holes)	B
Bowling centers: 3 (38 lanes, tenpins)	C

Crowd Pleasers (300 points)

	Rating
Auto Racing: Shasta Speedway (NASCAR)	B
Pari-Mutuel Betting: Shasta District Fair (mixed meetings, 13 races)	C

Outdoor Recreation Assets (1,356)
Inland Water Area: 67.8 square miles
National Forests, Parks, Wildlife Refuges:
Lassen NF (149,931 acres)
Lassen Volcanic NP (4,200 acres)
Shasta NF (471,224 acres)
Trinity NF (30,626 acres)
Whiskeytown-Shasta-Trinity NRA (42,488 acres)
Places Rated Score: 2,256   Places Rated Rank: 62

Reno, NV

Common Denominators (1,000 points)

	Rating
Good restaurants: 5 *, 14 **, 9 ***, 1 ****	AA
Golf courses: 1 private (18 holes); 3 daily fee (54 holes); 4 municipal (63 holes)	A
Bowling centers: 7 (174 lanes, tenpins)	A

Crowd Pleasers (500 points)

	Rating
Professional Sports: 1.338 game seats per capita Silver Sox (Class A Baseball)	B
NCAA Division I: 0.882 game seats per capita University of Nevada Wolf Pack	A

Outdoor Recreation Assets (468)
Inland Water Area: 232.9 square miles
National Forests, Parks, Wildlife Refuges:
Anaho Island NWR (248 acres)
Sheldon NWR (187,200 acres)
Toiyabe NF (56,087 acres)
Places Rated Score: 1,968   Places Rated Rank: 86

Richland–Kennewick–Pasco, WA

Common Denominators (700 points)

	Rating
Good restaurants: 1 **, 1 ***	B
Golf courses: 2 private (36 holes); 4 daily fee (54 holes); 1 municipal (18 holes)	A
Bowling centers: 3 (68 lanes, tenpins)	B

Crowd Pleasers (200 points)

	Rating
Pari-Mutuel Betting: Sun Downs (mixed meetings, 20 races)	B

Outdoor Recreation Assets (112)
Inland Water Area: 68 square miles
National Forests, Parks, Wildlife Refuges:
Umatilla NWR (1466 acres)
Places Rated Score: 1,012   Places Rated Rank: 258

Richmond–Petersburg, VA

Common Denominators (500 points)

	Rating
Good restaurants: 3 *, 4 **, 2 ***	C
Golf courses: 12 private (243 holes); 12 daily fee (189 holes); 1 municipal (18 holes)	B
Bowling centers: 13 (414 lanes, mixed)	B

	Rating
Crowd Pleasers (1,000 points)	
Theme Park: King's Dominion (121 days)	**A**
Auto Racing:	**A**
Richmond Fairgrounds Raceway (NASCAR)	
Southside Speedway (NASCAR)	
Professional Sports: 1.013 game seats per capita	**B**
Braves (Triple A Baseball)	
NCAA Division I: 0.429 game seats per capita	**B**
University of Richmond Spiders, Virginia	
Commonwealth University Rams	

Outdoor Recreation Assets (139)
Inland Water Area: 78.2 square miles
National Forests, Parks, Wildlife Refuges:
Harrison Lake NWR (445 acres)
Maggie L. Walker NHS (1.28 acres)
Petersburg National Battlefield (1,524 acres)
Poplar Grove National Cemetery (9 acres)
Presquile NWR (1,329 acres)
Richmond National Battlefield Park (771 acres)
Places Rated Score: 1,639   Places Rated Rank: 131

Riverside–San Bernardino, CA

Common Denominators (700 points)	
Good restaurants: 13 *, 18 **, 8 ***	**B**
Golf courses: 55 private (1053 holes); 35 daily fee	**A**
(756 holes); 8 municipal (117 holes)	
Bowling centers: 39 (980 lanes, tenpins)	**B**
Crowd Pleasers (500 points)	
Zoo: The Living Desert—110 species, 846 specimens	**B**
Auto Racing: Orange Show Speedway (NASCAR)	**B**
Professional Sports: 0.374 game seats per capita	**C**
Palm Springs Angels (Class A Baseball),	
Riverside Red Wave (Class A Baseball),	
San Bernardino Spirit (Class A Baseball)	

Outdoor Recreation Assets (418)
Inland Water Area: 117.6 square miles
National Forests, Parks, Wildlife Refuges:
Angeles NF (10,129 acres)
Cleveland NF (77,977 acres)
Death Valley NM (85,152 acres)
Joshua Tree NM (556,995 acres)
San Bernardino NF (658,645 acres)
CMSA Access: Los Angeles–Anaheim–Riverside,
CA (220 points)
Places Rated Score: 1,838   Places Rated Rank: 104

Roanoke, VA

Common Denominators (700 points)	
Good restaurants: 2 **, 2 ***, 1 ****	**A**
Golf courses: 6 private (117 holes); 3 daily fee (45	**C**
holes)	
Bowling centers: 6 (188 lanes, tenpins)	**A**
Crowd Pleasers (300 points)	
Professional Sports: 1.544 game seats per capita	**A**
Salem Buccaneers (Class A Baseball)	

Outdoor Recreation Assets (834)
Inland Water Area: 1.2 square miles
National Forests, Parks, Wildlife Refuges:
Appalachian Trail (3,458 acres)
Blue Ridge Parkway (5,661 acres)
George Washington NF (13,520 acres)
Jefferson NF (67,819 acres)
Places Rated Score: 1,834   Places Rated Rank: 105

Rochester, MN

Common Denominators (1,100 points)	
Good restaurants: 2 *, 4 **, 2 ***	**AA**
Golf courses: 1 private (18 holes); 2 daily fee (36	**AA**
holes); 4 municipal (81 holes)	
Bowling centers: 5 (80 lanes, tenpins)	**A**
Crowd Pleasers (200 points)	
Professional Sports: 1.343 game seats per capita	**B**
Flyers (CBA Basketball)	

Outdoor Recreation Assets (7)
Inland Water Area: 0.9 square miles
Places Rated Score: 1,307   Places Rated Rank: 196

★ Rochester, NY

Common Denominators (1,200 points)	
Good restaurants: 6 *, 22 **, 13 ***	**AA**
Golf courses: 19 private (324 holes); 32 daily fee	**AA**
(504 holes); 4 municipal (90 holes)	
Bowling centers: 63 (1292 lanes, tenpins)	**AA**
Crowd Pleasers (900 points)	
Zoo: Seneca Park Zoo—217 species, 654 specimens	**A**
Auto Racing: Spencer Speedway (NASCAR)	**B**
Pari-Mutuel Betting:	**B**
Finger Lakes (thoroughbred, 171 races)	
Professional Sports: 1.175 game seats per capita	**B**
Americans (AHL Hockey), Red Wings (Triple A	
Baseball)	

Outdoor Recreation Assets (964)
Great Lakes Coastline: 90 miles
Inland Water Area: 38.3 square miles
National Forests, Parks, Wildlife Refuges:
Iroquois NWR (5,374 acres)
Places Rated Score: 3,064   Places Rated Rank: 23

Rockford, IL

Common Denominators (900 points)	
Good restaurants: 5 **, 1 ***	**B**
Golf courses: 4 private (72 holes); 7 municipal (117	**A**
holes)	
Bowling centers: 18 (354 lanes, tenpins)	**AA**
Crowd Pleasers (600 points)	
Auto Racing:	**A**
Blackhawk Farms Raceway (SCCA)	
Rockford Speedway (NASCAR)	
Professional Sports: 1.888 game seats per capita	**A**
Expos (Class A Baseball), Lightning (CBA	
Basketball)	

Outdoor Recreation Assets (24)
Inland Water Area: 3.8 square miles
Places Rated Score: 1,524   Places Rated Rank: 157

Sacramento, CA

Common Denominators (400 points)	
Good restaurants: 3 *, 5 **, 3 ***	**C**
Golf courses: 14 private (225 holes); 10 daily fee	**C**
(171 holes); 7 municipal (135 holes)	
Bowling centers: 23 (642 lanes, tenpins)	**B**
Crowd Pleasers (600 points)	
Zoo: Sacramento Zoo—150 species, 742 specimens	**B**
Auto Racing: Placer County Speedway (NASCAR)	**B**
Pari-Mutuel Betting:	**C**
Cal-Expo (mixed meetings, 50 races)	
Professional Sports: 0.489 game seats per capita	**C**
Kings (NBA Basketball)	

Outdoor Recreation Assets (1,368)
Inland Water Area: 186.8 square miles
National Forests, Parks, Wildlife Refuges:
Eldorado NF (539,658 acres)
Tahoe NF (269,335 acres)
Places Rated Score: 2,368   Places Rated Rank: 53

Saginaw–Bay City–Midland, MI

Common Denominators (1,100 points)	
Good restaurants: 3 *, 8 **, 1 ***	**A**
Golf courses: 6 private (99 holes); 16 daily fee (261	**AA**
holes); 2 municipal (45 holes)	
Bowling centers: 18 (496 lanes, tenpins)	**AA**
Crowd Pleasers (300 points)	
Pari-Mutuel Betting:	**B**
Saginaw Valley Downs (harness, 86 races)	
Professional Sports: 0.554 game seats per capita	**C**
Hawks (IHL Hockey)	

Outdoor Recreation Assets (469)
Great Lakes Coastline: 40 miles
Inland Water Area: 10.9 square miles
National Forests, Parks, Wildlife Refuges:
Shiawassee NWR (8,984 acres)
Places Rated Score: 1,869   Places Rated Rank: 102

Rating

St. Cloud, MN
Common Denominators (900 points)
- Good restaurants: 1 *, 2 ** — C
- Golf courses: 2 private (27 holes); 9 daily fee (117 holes); 1 municipal (18 holes) — AA
- Bowling centers: 22 (230 lanes, tenpins) — AA

Outdoor Recreation Assets (263)
- Inland Water Area: 72.8 square miles
- National Forests, Parks, Wildlife Refuges:
  - Sherburne NWR (29,406 acres)

Places Rated Score: 1,163   Places Rated Rank: 234

St. Joseph, MO
Common Denominators (200 points)
- Golf courses: 1 private (18 holes); 1 municipal (18 holes) — C
- Bowling center: 1 (24 lanes, tenpins) — C

Outdoor Recreation Assets (64)
- Inland Water Area: 5.3 square miles

Places Rated Score: 264   Places Rated Rank: 331

St. Louis, MO–IL
Common Denominators (600 points)
- Good restaurants: 15 **, 19 ***, 5 ****, 1 ***** — B
- Golf courses: 23 private (396 holes); 34 daily fee (459 holes); 7 municipal (99 holes) — C
- Bowling centers: 85 (1,780 lanes, tenpins) — A

Crowd Pleasers (1,200 points)
- Zoo: St. Louis Zoological Park—619 species, 2,346 specimens — AA
- Theme Park: Six Flags over Mid-America (140 days) — C
- Auto Racing: Gateway International Raceway (SCCA) — B
- Pari-Mutuel Betting: — C
  - Fairmount Park (mixed meetings, 255 races)
- Professional Sports: 2.040 game seats per capita — A
  - Blues (NHL Hockey), Cardinals (NL Baseball)
- NCAA Division I: 0.045 game seats per capita — C
  - St. Louis University Billikens

Outdoor Recreation Assets (120)
- Inland Water Area: 130.9 square miles
- National Forests, Parks, Wildlife Refuges:
  - Jefferson National Expansion Memorial NHS (91 acres)

Places Rated Score: 1,920   Places Rated Rank: 94

Salem, OR
Common Denominators (700 points)
- Good restaurants: 1 *, 2 ** — C
- Golf courses: 2 private (36 holes); 7 daily fee (99 holes) — A
- Bowling centers: 9 (182 lanes, tenpins) — A

Crowd Pleasers (200 points)
- Pari-Mutuel Betting: — C
  - Lone Oak Track (thoroughbred, 14 races)
- Professional Sports: 0.710 game seats per capita — C
  - Dodgers (Class A Baseball)

Outdoor Recreation Assets (867)
- Inland Water Area: 14 square miles
- National Forests, Parks, Wildlife Refuges:
  - Ankeny NWR (2,796 acres)
  - Baskett Slough NWR (2,492 acres)
  - Mount Hood NF (65,872 acres)
  - Willamette NF (135,004 acres)

Places Rated Score: 1,767   Places Rated Rank: 115

Salem–Gloucester, MA
Common Denominators (1,000 points)
- Good restaurants: 3 *, 8 **, 4 *** — AA
- Golf courses: 8 private (126 holes); 6 daily fee (72 holes); 2 municipal (27 holes) — A
- Bowling centers: 7 (194 lanes, mixed) — A

Outdoor Recreation Assets (880)
- Atlantic Coastline: 33 miles
- Inland Water Area: 22.3 square miles
- National Forests, Parks, Wildlife Refuges:
  - Parker River NWR (2,330 acres)
  - Salem Maritime NHS (9 acres)
  - Thatcher Island NWR (22 acres)
- CMSA Access: Boston–Lawrence–Salem, MA–NH (130 points)

Places Rated Score: 2,010   Places Rated Rank: 83

★ Salinas–Seaside–Monterey, CA
Common Denominators (900 points)
- Good restaurants: 13 *, 18 **, 14 ***, 2 **** — AA
- Golf courses: 8 private (180 holes); 11 daily fee (207 holes); 3 municipal (45 holes) — AA
- Bowling centers: 6 (102 lanes, tenpins) — C

Crowd Pleasers (800 points)
- Aquarium: Monterey Bay Aquarium—388 species, 104,048 specimens — AA
- Auto Racing: Laguna Seca Raceway (SCCA) — B
- Pari-Mutuel Betting: — C
  - Monterey County Fair (mixed meetings, 13 races)
- Professional Sports: 0.687 game seats per capita — C
  - Salinas Spurs (Class A Baseball)

Outdoor Recreation Assets (1,605)
- Pacific Coastline: 85 miles
- Inland Water Area: 24 square miles
- National Forests, Parks, Wildlife Refuges:
  - Los Padres NF (304,578 acres)
  - Pinnacles NM (1,283 acres)
  - Salinas River NWR (364 acres)

Places Rated Score: 3,305   Places Rated Rank: 12

★ Salt Lake City–Ogden, UT
Common Denominators (600 points)
- Good restaurants: 3 *, 12 **, 7 *** — B
- Golf courses: 12 private (198 holes); 8 daily fee (90 holes); 14 municipal (225 holes) — B
- Bowling centers: 26 (590 lanes, tenpins) — B

Crowd Pleasers (700 points)
- Zoo: Hogle Zoological Garden—311 species, 1,164 specimens — A
- Professional Sports: 0.851 game seats per capita — B
  - Golden Eagles (IHL Hockey), Jazz (NBA Basketball)
- NCAA Division I: 0.535 game seats per capita — B
  - University of Utah Utes, Weber State Wildcats

Outdoor Recreation Assets (1,888)
- Inland Water Area: 477.5 square miles
- National Forests, Parks, Wildlife Refuges:
  - Cache NF (67,554 acres)
  - Wasatch NF (133,926 acres)

Places Rated Score: 3,188   Places Rated Rank: 18

San Angelo, TX
Common Denominators (800 points)
- Good restaurants: 1 *, 4 ** — AA
- Golf courses: 2 private (36 holes); 1 daily fee (18 holes) — C
- Bowling centers: 3 (68 lanes, tenpins) — A

Outdoor Recreation Assets (86)
- Inland Water Area: 26.6 square miles

Places Rated Score: 886   Places Rated Rank: 277

San Antonio, TX
Common Denominators (500 points)
- Good restaurants: 10 *, 12 **, 7 *** — B
- Golf courses: 18 private (351 holes); 1 daily fee (18 holes); 6 municipal (108 holes) — C
- Bowling centers: 21 (572 lanes, tenpins) — B

Crowd Pleasers (800 points)
- Zoo: San Antonio Zoological Gardens & Aquarium—674 species, 3,612 specimens — AA
- Auto Racing: San Antonio Grand Prix (IMSA) — B
- Professional Sports: 0.651 game seats per capita — C
  - Missions (Double A Baseball), Spurs (NBA Basketball)

	Rating
NCAA Division I: 0.040 game seats per capita	**C**
University of Texas Roadrunners	
Outdoor Recreation Assets (63)	
Inland Water Area: 31.4 square miles	
National Forests, Parks, Wildlife Refuges:	
San Antonio Missions NHP (463 acres)	
Places Rated Score: 1,363 Places Rated Rank: 183	

★ San Diego, CA

	Rating
Common Denominators (600 points)	
Good restaurants: 6 ★, 35 ★★, 20 ★★★	**A**
Golf courses: 24 private (477 holes); 23 daily fee (441 holes); 5 municipal (108 holes)	**C**
Bowling centers: 28 (940 lanes, tenpins)	**B**
Crowd Pleasers (1,900 points)	
Zoos: San Diego Wild Animal Park—330 species, 2,444 specimens	**AA**
San Diego Zoo—845 species, 3,888 specimens	**AA**
Theme Park: Sea World of California (365 days)	**A**
Auto Racing:	**A**
Cajon Speedway (NASCAR)	
Grand Prix of Del Mar (IMSA)	
Pari-Mutuel Betting:	**C**
22nd District Fair (mixed meetings, 13 races)	
Del Mar (thoroughbred, 43 races)	
Professional Sports: 2.223 game seats per capita	**A**
Chargers (NFC Football), Padres (NL Baseball)	
NCAA Division I: 0.218 game seats per capita	**C**
San Diego State Aztecs, U.S. International University Soaring Gulls, University of San Diego Toreros	
Outdoor Recreation Assets (1,140)	
Pacific Coastline: 55 miles	
Inland Water Area: 52.2 square miles	
National Forests, Parks, Wildlife Refuges:	
Cabrillo NM (144 acres)	
Cleveland NF (288,125 acres)	
Tijuana Slough NWR (407 acres)	
Places Rated Score: 3,640 Places Rated Rank: 3	

★ San Francisco, CA

	Rating
Common Denominators (600 points)	
Good restaurants: 20 ★, 34 ★★, 14 ★★★, 9 ★★★★, 1 ★★★★★	**AA**
Golf courses: 12 private (234 holes); 7 daily fee (108 holes); 5 municipal (81 holes)	**C**
Bowling centers: 19 (510 lanes, tenpins)	**C**
Crowd Pleasers (1,000 points)	
Zoo: San Francisco Zoological Gardens—351 species, 6,867 specimens	**AA**
Pari-Mutuel Betting:	**C**
Bay Meadows (mixed meetings, 148 races)	
Professional Sports: 3.140 game seats per capita	**AA**
49ers (NFC Football), Giants (NL Baseball)	
NCAA Division I: 0.038 game seats per capita	**C**
University of San Francisco Dons	
Outdoor Recreation Assets (2,000)	
Pacific Coastline: 75 miles	
Inland Water Area: 253.3 square miles	
National Forests, Parks, Wildlife Refuges:	
Farallon NWR (91 acres)	
Fort Point NHS (29 acres)	
Golden Gate NRA (60,788 acres)	
Muir Woods NM (554 acres)	
Point Reyes NS (63,953 acres)	
San Francisco Bay NWR (1,863 acres)	
CMSA Access: San Francisco–Oakland–San Jose, CA (220 points)	
Places Rated Score: 3,820 Places Rated Rank: 2	

★ San Jose, CA

	Rating
Common Denominators (500 points)	
Good restaurants: 2 ★, 14 ★★, 6 ★★★	**B**
Golf courses: 9 private (153 holes); 7 daily fee (126 holes); 7 municipal (117 holes)	**C**
Bowling centers: 21 (674 lanes, tenpins)	**B**

	Rating
Crowd Pleasers (800 points)	
Theme Park: Great America (141 days)	**B**
Auto Racing: San Jose Fairgrounds Speedway (NASCAR)	**B**
Pari-Mutuel Betting:	**C**
Santa Clara County Fair (mixed meetings, 13 races)	
Professional Sports: 0.253 game seats per capita	**C**
Giants (Class A Baseball)	
NCAA Division I: 0.530 game seats per capita	**B**
San Jose State Spartans, Santa Clara University Broncos, Stanford University Cardinals	
Outdoor Recreation Assets (63)	
Inland Water Area: 11.6 square miles	
National Forests, Parks, Wildlife Refuges:	
San Francisco NWR (3,156 acres)	
CMSA Access: San Francisco–Oakland–San Jose, CA (170 points)	
Places Rated Score: 1,533 Places Rated Rank: 156	

★ Santa Barbara–Santa Maria–Lompoc, CA

	Rating
Common Denominators (800 points)	
Good restaurants: 1 ★, 8 ★★, 4 ★★★	**AA**
Golf courses: 9 private (153 holes); 5 daily fee (72 holes); 1 municipal (18 holes)	**B**
Bowling centers: 6 (172 lanes, tenpins)	**B**
Crowd Pleasers (400 points)	
Zoo: Santa Barbara Zoological Gardens—131 species, 479 specimens	**B**
Pari-Mutuel Betting:	**C**
Santa Barbara County Fair (mixed meetings, 13 races)	
NCAA Division I: 0.189 game seats per capita	**C**
University of California Gauchos	
Outdoor Recreation Assets (2,000)	
Pacific Coastline: 78 miles	
Inland Water Area: 10 square miles	
National Forests, Parks, Wildlife Refuges:	
Channel Islands NP (125,539 acres)	
Los Padres NF (628,886 acres)	
Places Rated Score: 3,200 Places Rated Rank: 17	

Santa Cruz, CA

	Rating
Common Denominators (500 points)	
Good restaurants: 1 ★, 1 ★★, 1 ★★★	**C**
Golf courses: 5 daily fee (81 holes); 1 municipal (18 holes)	**A**
Bowling centers: 3 (60 lanes, tenpins)	**C**
Crowd Pleasers (200 points)	
Auto Racing: Watsonville Fairgrounds Speedway (NASCAR)	**B**
Outdoor Recreation Assets (417)	
Pacific Coastline: 40 miles	
Inland Water Area: 1.5 square miles	
National Forests, Parks, Wildlife Refuges:	
Ellicott Slough (126 acres)	
CMSA Access: San Francisco–Oakland–San Jose, CA (180 points)	
Places Rated Score: 1,297 Places Rated Rank: 199	

Santa Fe, NM

	Rating
Common Denominators (800 points)	
Good restaurants: 1 ★, 17 ★★, 7 ★★★, 1 ★★★★	**AA**
Golf courses: 1 private (9 holes); 1 daily fee (18 holes); 1 municipal (18 holes)	**B**
Bowling centers: 3 (72 lanes, tenpins)	**B**
Crowd Pleasers (300 points)	
Pari-Mutuel Betting:	**A**
Downs at Santa Fe (mixed meetings, 52 races)	
Outdoor Recreation Assets (1,108)	
Inland Water Area: 6.9 square miles	
National Forests, Parks, Wildlife Refuges:	
Bandelier NM (7,309 acres)	
Santa Fe NF (275,070 acres)	
Places Rated Score: 2,208 Places Rated Rank: 65	

Rating

Santa Rosa–Petaluma, CA
Common Denominators (600 points)
  Good restaurants: 6 *, 5 **, 1 *** A
  Golf courses: 1 private (18 holes); 7 daily fee (99 holes); 3 municipal (63 holes) A
  Bowling centers: 9 (180 lanes, tenpins) B
Crowd Pleasers (400 points)
  Auto Racing: A
    Petaluma Fairgrounds Speedway (NASCAR)
    Sears Point International Raceway (IMSA, NASCAR, SCCA)
  Pari-Mutuel Betting: C
    Sonoma County Fair (mixed meetings, 13 races)
Outdoor Recreation Assets (473)
  Pacific Coastline: 44 miles
  Inland Water Area: 10.2 square miles
  National Forests, Parks, Wildlife Refuges:
    San Pablo Bay NWR (249 acres)
CMSA Access: San Francisco–Oakland–San Jose, CA (110 points)
Places Rated Score: 1,583   Places Rated Rank: 146

Sarasota, FL
Common Denominators (900 points)
  Good restaurants: 3 *, 9 **, 6 *** AA
  Golf courses: 9 private (216 holes); 15 daily fee (333 holes); 2 municipal (63 holes) AA
  Bowling center: 1 (24 lanes, tenpins) C
Crowd Pleasers (700 points)
  Pari-Mutuel Betting: AA
    Sarasota Kennel Club (greyhound, 158 races)
  Professional Sports: 1.942 game seats per capita A
    White Sox (Class A Baseball)
Outdoor Recreation Assets (614)
  Gulf of Mexico Coastline: 35 miles
  Inland Water Area: 31.9 square miles
Places Rated Score: 2,214   Places Rated Rank: 63

Savannah, GA
Common Denominators (1,000 points)
  Good restaurants: 3 *, 9 **, 3 *** AA
  Golf courses: 4 private (54 holes); 3 daily fee (117 holes); 1 municipal (27 holes) AA
  Bowling centers: 5 (148 lanes, tenpins) B
Crowd Pleasers (600 points)
  Auto Racing: A
    Oglethorpe Speedway Park (NASCAR)
    Roebling Road Raceway (SCCA)
  Professional Sports: 2.150 game seats per capita A
    Cardinals (Class A Baseball)
Outdoor Recreation Assets (798)
  Atlantic Coastline: 30 miles
  Inland Water Area: 55.2 square miles
  National Forests, Parks, Wildlife Refuges:
    Fort Pulaski NM (5,623 acres)
    Savannah NWR (11,499 acres)
    Wassaw NWR (10,050 acres)
Places Rated Score: 2,398   Places Rated Rank: 51

Scranton–Wilkes-Barre, PA
Common Denominators (800 points)
  Good restaurants: 4 **, 3 *** C
  Golf courses: 14 private (234 holes); 30 daily fee (459 holes); 2 municipal (27 holes) AA
  Bowling centers: 35 (564 lanes, tenpins) A
Crowd Pleasers (600 points)
  Auto Racing: Pocono International Raceway (NASCAR) B
  Pari-Mutuel Betting: B
    Pocono Downs (harness, 150 races)
  Professional Sports: 0.972 game seats per capita B
    Red Barons (Triple A Baseball)
Outdoor Recreation Assets (84)
  Inland Water Area: 37.5 square miles
  National Forests, Parks, Wildlife Refuges:

Delaware NSR (372 acres)
Delaware Water Gap NRA (6,662 acres)
Places Rated Score: 1,484   Places Rated Rank: 163

★ Seattle, WA
Common Denominators (600 points)
  Good restaurants: 6 *, 20 **, 16 ***, 1 **** A
  Golf courses: 19 private (306 holes); 11 daily fee (180 holes); 13 municipal (225 holes) C
  Bowling centers: 37 (918 lanes, tenpins) B
Crowd Pleasers (1,700 points)
  Zoo: Woodland Park Zoological Gardens—257 species, 2,283 specimens AA
  Aquarium: The Seattle Aquarium—313 species, 17,263 specimens AA
  Auto Racing: A
    Evergreen Speedway (NASCAR)
    Seattle International Raceway (SCCA)
  Pari-Mutuel Betting: C
    Longacres (thoroughbred, 135 races)
  Professional Sports: 3.890 game seats per capita AA
    Everett Giants (Class A Baseball), Mariners (AL Baseball), Seahawks (NFC Football), Supersonics (NBA Basketball)
  NCAA Division I: 0.252 game seats per capita C
    University of Washington Huskies
Outdoor Recreation Assets (2,000)
  Puget Sound Coastline: 70 miles
  Inland Water Area: 89.1 square miles
  National Forests, Parks, Wildlife Refuges:
    Mount Baker NF (462,209 acres)
    Snoqualmie NF (504,324 acres)
CMSA Access: Seattle–Tacoma, WA (90 points)
Places Rated Score: 4,390   Places Rated Rank: 1

Sharon, PA
Common Denominators (1,100 points)
  Good restaurants: 1 *, 3 ** A
  Golf courses: 4 private (63 holes); 7 daily fee (108 holes) AA
  Bowling centers: 11 (186 lanes, tenpins) AA
Outdoor Recreation Assets (78)
  Inland Water Area: 10.6 square miles
Places Rated Score: 1,178   Places Rated Rank: 233

Sheboygan, WI
Common Denominators (1,100 points)
  Good restaurants: 2 **, 1 *** A
  Golf courses: 2 private (36 holes); 5 daily fee (108 holes) AA
  Bowling centers: 12 (150 lanes, tenpins) AA
Crowd Pleasers (200 points)
  Auto Racing: Road America (IMSA, SCCA) B
Outdoor Recreation Assets (317)
  Great Lakes Coastline: 29 miles
  Inland Water Area: 2.7 square miles
Places Rated Score: 1,617   Places Rated Rank: 134

Sherman–Denison, TX
Common Denominators (300 points)
  Golf courses: 4 private (72 holes); 1 daily fee (18 holes) C
  Bowling centers: 2 (56 lanes, tenpins) B
Outdoor Recreation Assets (226)
  Inland Water Area: 44.2 square miles
Places Rated Score: 526   Places Rated Rank: 316

Shreveport, LA
Common Denominators (400 points)
  Good restaurants: 1 *, 4 **, 1 ***, 1**** B
  Golf courses: 6 private (99 holes); 2 daily fee (18 holes); 3 municipal (45 holes) C
  Bowling centers: 5 (132 lanes, tenpins) C
Crowd Pleasers (600 points)
  Pari-Mutuel Betting: A
    Louisiana Downs (thoroughbred, 145 races)

	Rating
Professional Sports: 0.994 game seats per capita	B
Captains (Double A Baseball)	
NCAA Division I: 0.130 game seats per capita	C
Centenary College Gentlemen	

Outdoor Recreation Assets (182)
Inland Water Area: 65.6 square miles
Places Rated Score: 1,182   Places Rated Rank: 232

Sioux City, IA–NE
Common Denominators (900 points)

	Rating
Good restaurants: 1 *, 1 **, 1 ***	A
Golf courses: 6 private (72 holes); 4 daily fee (45 holes); 1 municipal (18 holes)	A
Bowling centers: 6 (82 lanes, tenpins)	A

Crowd Pleasers (200 points)

	Rating
Pari-Mutuel Betting:	B
Atokad Park (thoroughbred, 24 races)	

Outdoor Recreation Assets (59)
Inland Water Area: 13.4 square miles
Places Rated Score: 1,159   Places Rated Rank: 236

Sioux Falls, SD
Common Denominators (800 points)

	Rating
Good restaurants: 2 **	B
Golf courses: 4 private (54 holes); 1 daily fee (9 holes); 2 municipal (36 holes)	B
Bowling centers: 7 (136 lanes, tenpins)	AA

Outdoor Recreation Assets (24)
Inland Water Area: 3.9 square miles
Places Rated Score: 824   Places Rated Rank: 287

South Bend–Mishawaka, IN
Common Denominators (1,000 points)

	Rating
Good restaurants: 4 *, 3 **, 1 ***	A
Golf courses: 2 private (36 holes); 4 daily fee (54 holes); 3 municipal (54 holes)	A
Bowling centers: 20 (338 lanes, tenpins)	AA

Crowd Pleasers (700 points)

	Rating
Zoo: Potawwatomi Zoo—73 species, 506 specimens	C
Professional Sports: 1.460 game seats per capita	B
White Sox (Class A Baseball)	
NCAA Division I: 1.803 game seats per capita	AA
University of Notre Dame Fighting Irish	

Outdoor Recreation Assets (27)
Inland Water Area: 2.5 square miles
Places Rated Score: 1,727   Places Rated Rank: 120

Spokane, WA
Common Denominators (800 points)

	Rating
Good restaurants: 5 *, 2 **, 3 ***	B
Golf courses: 2 private (36 holes); 2 daily fee (36 holes); 6 municipal (108 holes)	A
Bowling centers: 12 (256 lanes, tenpins)	A

Crowd Pleasers (1,000 points)

	Rating
Auto Racing: Grand Prix of Spokane (NASCAR, SCCA)	B
Pari-Mutuel Betting:	B
Playfair Race Course (thoroughbred, 90 races)	
Professional Sports: 2.102 game seats per capita	A
Indians (Class A Baseball)	
NCAA Division I: 0.744 game seats per capita	A
Eastern Washington University Eagles, Gonzaga Zags	

Outdoor Recreation Assets (116)
Inland Water Area: 18.6 square miles
National Forests, Parks, Wildlife Refuges:
Turnbull NWR (14,489 acres)
Places Rated Score: 1,916   Places Rated Rank: 95

Springfield, IL
Common Denominators (1,000 points)

	Rating
Good restaurants: 8 **, 1 ***	AA
Golf courses: 2 private (36 holes); 3 daily fee (45 holes); 3 municipal (45 holes)	A

	Rating
Bowling centers: 7 (148 lanes, tenpins)	A

Crowd Pleasers (500 points)

	Rating
Zoo: Henson Robinson Zoo—81 species, 230 specimens	C
Professional Sports: 1.820 game seats per capita	A
Cardinals (Class A Baseball)	

Outdoor Recreation Assets (46)
Inland Water Area: 10.9 square miles
National Forests, Parks, Wildlife Refuges:
Lincoln Home NHS (12 acres)
Places Rated Score: 1,546   Places Rated Rank: 152

Springfield, MA
Common Denominators (700 points)

	Rating
Good restaurants: 5 **, 3 ***	B
Golf courses: 11 private (180 holes); 15 daily fee (225 holes); 4 municipal (72 holes)	A
Bowling centers: 12 (288 lanes, mixed)	B

Crowd Pleasers (800 points)

	Rating
Theme Park: Riverside (120 days)	AA
Auto Racing: Riverside Park Speedway (NASCAR)	B
Pari-Mutuel Betting:	C
Tri-County Fair (thoroughbred, 9 races)	
Professional Sports: 0.584 game seats per capita	C
Indians (AHL Hockey)	

Outdoor Recreation Assets (103)
Inland Water Area: 12.2 square miles
National Forests, Parks, Wildlife Refuges:
Springfield Armory NHS (55 acres)
Places Rated Score: 1,603   Places Rated Rank: 141

Springfield, MO
Common Denominators (500 points)

	Rating
Good restaurants: 2 **, 3 ***	A
Golf courses: 5 private (72 holes); 1 daily fee (18 holes); 2 municipal (36 holes)	C
Bowling centers: 4 (62 lanes, tenpins)	C

Crowd Pleasers (400 points)

	Rating
Zoo: Dickerson Park Zoo—176 species, 544 specimens	B
NCAA Division I: 0.601 game seats per capita	B
Southwest Missouri State Bears	

Outdoor Recreation Assets (336)
Inland Water Area: 0.6 square miles
National Forests, Parks, Wildlife Refuges:
Mark Twain NF (51,327 acres)
Wilson's Creek National Battlefield (1,749 acres)
Places Rated Score: 1,236   Places Rated Rank: 215

Stamford, CT
Common Denominators (700 points)

	Rating
Good restaurants: 1 *, 2 **, 6 ***	AA
Golf courses: 14 private (243 holes); 3 municipal (54 holes)	B
Bowling centers: 3 (80 lanes, tenpins)	C

Crowd Pleasers (0000 points)
Outdoor Recreation Assets (332)
Atlantic Coastline: 11 miles
Inland Water Area: 5.6 square miles
CMSA Access: New York–Northern NJ–Long Island, NY–NJ–CT (210 points)
Places Rated Score: 1,242   Places Rated Rank: 213

State College, PA
Common Denominators (900 points)

	Rating
Good restaurants: 1 **, 3 ***	AA
Golf courses: 4 private (54 holes); 2 daily fee (54 holes)	A
Bowling centers: 4 (71 lanes, tenpins)	B

Crowd Pleasers (400 points)

	Rating
NCAA Division I: 4.329 game seats per capita	AA
Penn State Nittany Lions	

Outdoor Recreation Assets (27)
Inland Water Area: 6.1 square miles
Places Rated Score: 1,327   Places Rated Rank: 192

Rating

Steubenville–Weirton, OH–WV
Common Denominators (500 points)
Golf courses: 5 private (63 holes); 4 daily fee (54 holes); 1 municipal (9 holes) **A**
Bowling centers: 6 (102 lanes, tenpins) **B**
Crowd Pleasers (400 points)
Pari-Mutuel Betting: **AA**
Mountaineer Park (thoroughbred, 220 races)
Outdoor Recreation Assets (58)
Inland Water Area: 7 square miles
Places Rated Score: 958   Places Rated Rank: 265

Stockton, CA
Common Denominators (300 points)
Good restaurants: 1 *, 1 **, 1 *** **C**
Golf courses: 6 private (108 holes); 3 municipal (54 holes) **C**
Bowling centers: 7 (170 lanes, tenpins) **C**
Crowd Pleasers (700 points)
Auto Racing: Stockton 99 Speedway (NASCAR) **B**
Pari-Mutuel Betting: **C**
San Joaquin County Fair (mixed meetings, 13 races)
Professional Sports: 0.951 game seats per capita **B**
Ports (Class A Baseball)
NCAA Division I: 0.498 game seats per capita **B**
University of the Pacific Tigers
Outdoor Recreation Assets (38)
Inland Water Area: 10.9 square miles
Places Rated Score: 1,038   Places Rated Rank: 252

Syracuse, NY
Common Denominators (1,200 points)
Good restaurants: 5 *, 25 **, 8 *** **AA**
Golf courses: 17 private (288 holes); 36 daily fee (495 holes); 2 municipal (36 holes) **AA**
Bowling centers: 46 (678 lanes, tenpins) **AA**
Crowd Pleasers (1,100 points)
Zoo: Burnet Park Zoo—226 species, 997 specimens **A**
Auto Racing: Oswego Speedway (NASCAR) **B**
Pari-Mutuel Betting: **C**
Syracuse Mile (harness, 7 races)
Professional Sports: 1.133 game seats per capita **B**
Chiefs (Triple A Baseball)
NCAA Division I: 0.703 game seats per capita **A**
Colgate Red Raiders, Syracuse University Orangemen
Outdoor Recreation Assets (542)
Great Lakes Coastline: 36 miles
Inland Water Area: 91.5 square miles
Places Rated Score: 2,842   Places Rated Rank: 31

★ Tacoma, WA
Common Denominators (500 points)
Good restaurants: 1 *, 5 **, 1 *** **C**
Golf courses: 7 private (126 holes); 7 daily fee (108 holes); 4 municipal (63 holes) **B**
Bowling centers: 13 (334 lanes, tenpins) **B**
Crowd Pleasers (900 points)
Zoos: Northwest Trek Wildlife Park—77 species, 335 specimens **B**
Point Defiance Zoo & Aquarium—279 species, 4,572 specimens **A**
Auto Racing: Tacoma Grand Prix (NASCAR, SCCA) **B**
Professional Sports: 1.049 game seats per capita **B**
Tigers (Triple A Baseball)
Outdoor Recreation Assets (2,000)
Puget Sound Coastline: 15 miles
Inland Water Area: 113.1 square miles
National Forests, Parks, Wildlife Refuges:
Mount Rainier NP (235,239 acres)
Nisqually NWR (813 acres)
Snoqualmie NF (129,938 acres)
CMSA Access: Seattle–Tacoma, WA (170 points)
Places Rated Score: 3,570   Places Rated Rank: 5

Rating

Tallahassee, FL
Common Denominators (500 points)
Good restaurants: 4 *, 1 *** **B**
Golf courses: 4 private (72 holes); 2 daily fee (36 holes); 3 municipal (36 holes) **B**
Bowling centers: 2 (64 lanes, tenpins) **C**
Crowd Pleasers (400 points)
NCAA Division I: 2.792 game seats per capita **AA**
Florida A & M Rattlers, Florida State Seminoles
Outdoor Recreation Assets (813)
Inland Water Area: 36.5 square miles
National Forests, Parks, Wildlife Refuges:
Apalachicola NF (104,405 acres)
Places Rated Score: 1,713   Places Rated Rank: 122

★ Tampa–St. Petersburg–Clearwater, FL
Common Denominators (800 points)
Good restaurants: 11 *, 22 **, 13 ***, 2 **** **B**
Golf courses: 26 private (630 holes); 41 daily fee (792 holes); 5 municipal (90 holes) **A**
Bowling centers: 46 (1440 lanes, tenpins) **A**
Crowd Pleasers (1,000 points)
Theme Park: Busch Gardens—The Dark Continent (365 days) **AA**
Auto Racing: St. Petersburg Grand Prix (SCCA) **B**
Pari-Mutuel Betting: **C**
St. Petersburg Kennel Club (greyhound, 162 races)
Tampa Bay Downs (thoroughbred, 97 races)
Tampa Greyhound Track (greyhound, 162 races)
Tampa Jai Alai (398 matches)
Professional Sports: 0.829 game seats per capita **B**
Buccaneers (NFC Football), Clearwater Phillies (Class A Baseball), Dunedin Blue Jays (Class A Baseball), St. Petersburg Cardinals (Class A Baseball)
NCAA Division I: 0.059 game seats per capita **C**
University of South Florida Bulls
Outdoor Recreation Assets (1,102)
Gulf of Mexico Coastline: 78 miles
Inland Water Area: 164.3 square miles
National Forests, Parks, Wildlife Refuges:
Chassahowitzka NWR (6,707 acres)
Egmont Key NWR (328 acres)
Pinellas NWR (15 acres)
Places Rated Score: 2,902   Places Rated Rank: 28

Terre Haute, IN
Common Denominators (800 points)
Good restaurants: 2 ** **C**
Golf courses: 3 private (45 holes); 1 daily fee (9 holes); 4 municipal (63 holes) **A**
Bowling centers: 7 (138 lanes, tenpins) **AA**
Crowd Pleasers (400 points)
NCAA Division I: 1,686 game seats per capita **AA**
Indiana State Sycamores
Outdoor Recreation Assets (36)
Inland Water Area: 5.5 square miles
Places Rated Score: 1,236   Places Rated Rank: 215

Texarkana, TX–Texarkana, AR
Common Denominators (300 points)
Golf courses: 2 private (36 holes); 1 daily fee (9 holes) **C**
Bowling centers: 4 (74 lanes, tenpins) **B**
Outdoor Recreation Assets (163)
Inland Water Area: 51 square miles
Places Rated Score: 463   Places Rated Rank: 321

Toledo, OH
Common Denominators (900 points)
Good restaurants: 3 *, 7 **, 2 *** **B**
Golf courses: 8 private (144 holes); 11 daily fee (180 holes); 4 municipal (54 holes) **A**
Bowling centers: 26 (624 lanes, tenpins) **AA**
Crowd Pleasers (1,000 points)

	Rating
Zoo: Toledo Zoological Gardens—393 species, 1,879 specimens	**AA**
Pari-Mutuel Betting:	**B**
Raceway Park (harness, 152 races)	
Professional Sports: 1.160 game seats per capita	**B**
Mud Hens (Triple A Baseball)	
NCAA Division I: 0.682 game seats per capita	**B**
Bowling Green State Falcons, University of Toledo Rockets	

Outdoor Recreation Assets (251)
Great Lakes Coastline: 19 miles
Inland Water Area: 9.7 square miles
National Forests, Parks, Wildlife Refuges:
  Cedar Point NWR (2,445 acres)
  Ottawa NWR (2,078 acres)
  West Sister Island NWR (82 acres)
Places Rated Score: 2,151   Places Rated Rank: 69

Topeka, KS

Common Denominators (600 points)

	Rating
Good restaurants: 2 **	**C**
Golf courses: 4 private (63 holes); 1 daily fee (9 holes); 3 municipal (45 holes)	**B**
Bowling centers: 5 (126 lanes, tenpins)	**A**

Crowd Pleasers (600 points)

	Rating
Zoo: Topeka Zoological Park—134 species, 400 specimens	**B**
Auto Racing: Topeka Raceway Park (NASCAR)	**B**
Professional Sports: 1.355 game seats per capita	**B**
Sizzlers (CBA Basketball)	

Outdoor Recreation Assets (60)
Inland Water Area: 6.7 square miles
Places Rated Score: 1,260   Places Rated Rank: 208

Trenton, NJ

Common Denominators (600 points)

	Rating
Good restaurants: 3 *, 6 **, 1 ***	**A**
Golf courses: 8 private (126 holes); 2 daily fee (36 holes); 2 municipal (36 holes)	**C**
Bowling centers: 6 (192 lanes, tenpins)	**B**

Crowd Pleasers (300 points)

	Rating
NCAA Division I: 1.056 game seats per capita	**A**
Princeton University Tigers, Rider College Broncs	

Outdoor Recreation Assets (52)
Inland Water Area: 2.4 square miles
CMSA Access: Philadelphia–Wilmington–Trenton, PA–NJ–DE–MD (80 points)
Places Rated Score: 1,032   Places Rated Rank: 255

★ Tucson, AZ

Common Denominators (900 points)

	Rating
Good restaurants: 7 *, 8 **, 13 ***, 1 ****, 1 *****	**AA**
Golf courses: 11 private (234 holes); 9 daily fee (162 holes); 5 municipal (108 holes)	**A**
Bowling centers: 13 (380 lanes, tenpins)	**B**

Crowd Pleasers (1,500 points)

	Rating
Zoos: Arizona-Sonora Desert Museum—289 species, 4,792 specimens	**A**
Reid Park Zoo—88 species, 716 specimens	**B**
Auto Racing: Raven Raceway (USAC)	**B**
Pari-Mutuel Betting:	**AA**
Tucson Greyhound Park (greyhound, 470 races)	
Professional Sports: 1.086 game seats per capita	**B**
Toros (Triple A Baseball)	
NCAA Division I: 0.688 game seats per capita	**B**
University of Arizona Wildcats	

Outdoor Recreation Assts (1,031)
Inland Water Area: 1.1 square miles
National Forests, Parks, Wildlife Refuges:
  Buenos Aires NWR (21,281 acres)
  Cabeza Prieta NWR (416,210 acres)
  Coronado NF (382,093 acres)
  Organ Pipe Cactus NM (330,479 acres)
  Saguaro NM (83,337 acres)
Places Rated Score: 3,431   Places Rated Rank: 10

Tulsa, OK

Common Denominators (700 points)

	Rating
Good restaurants: 1 *, 15 **, 6 ***	**A**
Golf courses: 8 private (144 holes); 8 daily fee (108 holes); 5 municipal (126 holes)	**B**
Bowling centers: 11 (364 lanes, tenpins)	**B**

Crowd Pleasers (700 points)

	Rating
Zoo: Tulsa Zoological Park—332 species, 1,288 specimens	**A**
Pari-Mutuel Betting:	**C**
Tulsa State Fair (mixed meetings, 14 races)	
Will Rogers Downs (mixed meetings, 13 races)	
Professional Sports: 0.978 game seats per capita	**B**
Drillers (Double A Baseball), Fast Breakers (CBA Basketball)	
NCAA Division I: 0.585 game seats per capita	**B**
Oral Roberts Titans, University of Tulsa Golden Hurricane	

Outdoor Recreation Assets (151)
Inland Water Area: 156.2 square miles
Places Rated Score: 1,551   Places Rated Rank: 151

Tuscaloosa, AL

Common Denominators (300 points)

	Rating
Good restaurants: 1 *, 1 **	**C**
Golf courses: 5 private (90 holes); 1 municipal (18 holes)	**C**
Bowling center: 1 (32 lanes, tenpins)	**C**

Crowd Pleasers (400 points)

	Rating
NCAA Division I: 3.692 game seats per capita	**AA**
University of Alabama Crimson Tide	

Outdoor Recreation Assets (109)
Inland Water Area: 16.1 square miles
National Forests, Parks, Wildlife Refuges:
  Talladega NF (8,562 acres)
Places Rated Score: 809   Places Rated Rank: 292

Tyler, TX

Common Denominators (300 points)

	Rating
Golf courses: 6 private (99 holes); 3 daily fee (54 holes)	**B**
Bowling center: 1 (32 lanes, tenpins)	**C**

Crowd Pleasers (200 points)

	Rating
Zoo: Caldwell Zoo—219 species, 1,030 specimens	**B**

Outdoor Recreation Assets (92)
Inland Water Area: 17.5 square miles
Places Rated Score: 592   Places Rated Rank: 311

Utica–Rome, NY

Common Denominators (1,200 points)

	Rating
Good restaurants: 2 *, 7 **, 4 ***	**AA**
Golf courses: 13 private (180 holes); 21 daily fee (261 holes); 3 municipal (36 holes)	**AA**
Bowling centers: 29 (404 lanes, tenpins)	**AA**

Crowd Pleasers (800 points)

	Rating
Zoo: Utica Zoo—108 species, 224 specimens	**C**
Pari-Mutuel Betting:	**AA**
Vernon Downs (harness, 159 races)	
Professional Sports: 1.741 game seats per capita	**A**
Devils (AHL Hockey), Utica Blue Sox (Class A Baseball)	

Outdoor Recreation Assets (144)
Inland Water Area: 78.9 square miles
National Forests, Parks, Wildlife Refuges:
  Fort Stanwix NM (16 acres)
Places Rated Score: 2,144   Places Rated Rank: 71

Vallejo–Fairfield–Napa, CA

Common Denominators (800 points)

	Rating
Good restaurants: 7 *, 8 **, 3 ***, 2 ****	**AA**
Golf courses: 5 private (90 holes); 4 daily fee (63 holes); 3 municipal (45 holes)	**B**
Bowling centers: 9 (226 lanes, tenpins)	**B**

Crowd Pleasers (100 points)

	Rating
Pari-Mutuel Betting:	**C**
Solano County Fair (mixed meetings, 13 races)	

Rating

Outdoor Recreation Assets (358)
  Inland Water Area: 121.8 square miles
  National Forests, Parks, Wildlife Refuges:
    San Pablo Bay NWR (248 acres)
CMSA Access: San Francisco–Oakland–San Jose,
  CA (210)
Places Rated Score: 1,468   Places Rated Rank: 165

Vancouver, WA
Common Denominators (500 points)
Golf courses: 2 private (36 holes); 4 daily fee (63 holes)	B
Bowling centers: 8 (164 lanes, tenpins)	A

Outdoor Recreation Assets (234)
  Inland Water Area: 28.6 square miles
  National Forests, Parks, Wildlife Refuges:
    Fort Vancouver NHS (209 acres)
    Gifford Pinchot NF (1,150 acres)
    Ridgefield NWR (4,627 acres)
    Steigerwold NWR (27 acres)
CMSA Access: Portland–Vancouver, OR–WA (120 points)
Places Rated Score: 854   Places Rated Rank: 281

Victoria, TX
Common Denominators (300 points)
Golf courses: 3 private (45 holes); 1 municipal (18 holes)	C
Bowling centers: 1 (32 lanes, tenpins)	B

Outdoor Recreation Assets (10)
  Inland Water Area: 1.8 square miles
Places Rated Score: 310   Places Rated Rank: 330

Vineland–Millville–Bridgeton, NJ
Common Denominators (300 points)
Golf course: 1 daily fee (18 holes)	C
Bowling centers: 3 (72 lanes, tenpins)	B

Outdoor Recreation Assets (373)
  Atlantic Coastline: 30 miles
  Inland Water Area: 7.4 square miles
CMSA Access: Philadelphia–Wilmington–Trenton,
  PA–NJ–DE–MD (110 points)
Places Rated Score: 783   Places Rated Rank: 295

Visalia–Tulare–Porterville, CA
Common Denominators (400 points)
Good restaurants: 1 **, 1 ***	C
Golf courses: 2 private (36 holes); 3 daily fee (45 holes); 2 municipal (27 holes)	B
Bowling centers: 5 (104 lanes, tenpins)	C

Crowd Pleasers (100 points)
Professional Sports: 0.479 game seats per capita	C
Visalia Oaks (Class A Baseball)	

Outdoor Recreation Assets (2,000)
  Inland Water Area: 35.1 square miles
  National Forests, Parks, Wildlife Refuges:
    Blue Ridge NWR (577 acres)
    Inyo NF (190,574 acres)
    Kings Canyon NP (105,252 acres)
    Pixley NWR (5,147 acres)
    Sequoia NF (700,135 acres)
    Sequoia NP (401,774 acres)
Places Rated Score: 2,500   Places Rated Rank: 47

Waco, TX
Common Denominators (600 points)
Good restaurants: 5 *, 2 **	B
Golf courses: 3 private (54 holes); 3 daily fee (54 holes); 2 municipal (36 holes)	A
Bowling centers: 2 (44 lanes, tenpins)	C

Crowd Pleasers (700 points)
Zoo: Central Texas Zoo—145 species, 393 specimens	C
Auto Racing: Heart O' Texas Speedway (NASCAR)	B
NCAA Division I: 1.888 game seats per capita	AA
Baylor University Bears	

Rating

Outdoor Recreation Assets (564)
  Inland Water Area: 30.6 square miles
Places Rated Score: 1,864   Places Rated Rank: 103

Washington, DC–MD–VA
Common Denominators (1,000 points)
Good restaurants: 27 *, 89 **, 30 ***, 7 ****	AA
Golf courses: 55 private (1,008 holes); 13 daily fee (225 holes); 17 municipal (288 holes)	A
Bowling centers: 71 (1,759 lanes, mixed)	A

Crowd Pleasers (900 points)
Zoo: National Zoological Park—509 species, 4,181 specimens	AA
Auto Racing: Old Dominion Speedway (NASCAR)	B
Pari-Mutuel Betting:	C
Freestate Raceway (harness, 115 races)	
Laurel Race Course (thoroughbred, 148 races)	
Rosecroft Raceway (harness, 145 races)	
Professional Sports: 0.706 game seats per capita	C
Bullets (NBA Basketball), Capitols (NHL Hockey), Frederick Keys (Class A Baseball), Prince William Cannons (Class A Baseball), Redskins (NFC Football)	
NCAA Division I: 0.215 game seats per capita	C
American University Eagles, George Mason University Patriots, George Washington University Colonials, Georgetown Hoyas, Howard University Bisons, Mount St. Mary's Mountaineers, University of Maryland Terps	

Outdoor Recreation Assets (151)
  Inland Water Area: 123.3 square miles
  National Forests, Parks, Wildlife Refuges:
    Antietam National Battlefield (0.22 acres)
    Appalachian Trail (1,061 acres)
    Battleground National Cemetery (1 acre)
    Catoctin Mountain Park (5,694 acres)
    Chesapeake and Ohio Canal NHP (4,761 acres)
    Clara Barton NHS (9 acres)
    Featherstone NWR (164 acres)
    Ford's Theatre NHS (0.29 acres)
    Fort Washington Park (341 acres)
    Frederick Douglass Home (8 acres)
    Fredericksburg and Spotsylvania Country
      Battlefields NMP (84 acres)
    George Washington Parkway (7,045 acres)
    Greenbelt Park (1,176 acres)
    Harpers Ferry NHP (370 acres)
    John F. Kennedy Center for the Performing Arts
      (18 acres)
    Lincoln Memorial (164 acres)
    Lyndon B. Johnson Memorial Grove (17 acres)
    Manassas National Battlefield Park (3,021 acres)
    Marumsco NWR (63 acres)
    Mason Neck NWR (1,131 acres)
    Monocacy National Battlefield (422 acres)
    National Capital Parks (6,036 acres)
    National Mall (146 acres)
    Patuxent NWR (4,250 acres)
    Piscataway Park (4,210 acres)
    Presquile NWR (1,329 acres)
    Prince William Forest Park (17,410 acres)
    Robert E. Lee Memorial (28 acres)
    Rock Creek Park (1,754 acres)
    Theodore Roosevelt Island (89 acres)
    Thomas Jefferson Memorial (18 acres)
    Thomas Stone NHS (322 acres)
    Washington Monument (106 acres)
    White House (18 acres)
    Wolf Trap Farm Park for the Performing Arts (130
      acres)
Places Rated Score: 2,051   Places Rated Rank: 80

Waterbury, CT
Common Denominators (600 points)
Good restaurant: 1 ***	C

	Rating
Golf courses: 4 private (72 holes); 1 daily fee (9 holes); 5 municipal (72 holes)	A
Bowling centers: 5 (122 lanes, mixed)	B

Outdoor Recreation Assets (44)
Inland Water Area: 2.1 square miles
Places Rated Score: 644   Places Rated Rank: 305

Waterloo–Cedar Falls, IA

Common Denominators (1,000 points)

	Rating
Good restaurants: 1 *, 1 **, 1 ***	B
Golf courses: 5 private (63 holes); 1 daily fee (18 holes); 7 municipal (108 holes)	AA
Bowling centers: 9 (166 lanes, tenpins)	AA

Crowd Pleasers (1,100 points)

	Rating
Pari-Mutuel Betting: Waterloo Greyhound Park (greyhound, 222 races)	AA
Professional Sports: 2.557 game seats per capita Waterloo Diamonds (Class A Baseball)	AA
NCAA Division I: 1.421 game seats per capita University of Northern Iowa Panthers	A

Places Rated Score: 2,100   Places Rated Rank: 74

Wausau, WI

Common Denominators (800 points)

	Rating
Good restaurants: 1 **	C
Golf courses: 1 private (18 holes); 4 daily fee (45 holes)	A
Bowling centers: 15 (212 lanes, tenpins)	AA

Crowd Pleasers (300 points)

	Rating
Professional Sports: 1.541 game seats per capita Timbers (Class A Baseball)	A

Outdoor Recreation Assets (54)
Inland Water Area: 16.7 square miles
Places Rated Score: 1,154   Places Rated Rank: 238

West Palm Beach–Boca Ranton–Delray Beach, FL

Common Denominators (900 points)

	Rating
Good restaurants: 13 *, 23 **, 17 ***, 1 ****, 1 *****	AA
Golf courses: 56 private (1557 holes); 14 daily fee (261 holes); 8 municipal (144 holes)	A
Bowling centers: 13 (408 lanes, tenpins)	B

Crowd Pleasers (600 points)

	Rating
Auto Racing: Grand Prix of Palm Beach (IMSA) Moroso Motorsports Park (SCCA)	A
Pari-Mutuel Betting: Palm Beach Jai Alai (223 matches) Palm Beach Kennel Club (greyhound, 321 races)	B
Professional Sports: 0.407 game seats per capita West Palm Beach Expos (Class A Baseball)	C

Outdoor Recreation Assets (1,008)
Atlantic coastline: 47 miles
Inland Water Area: 235.9 square miles
National Forests, Parks, Wildlife Refuges: Loxahatchee NWR (2,550 acres)
Places Rated Score: 2,508   Places Rated Rank: 46

Wheeling, WV–OH

Common Denominators (700 points)

	Rating
Good restaurants: 1 *, 1 **, 1 ***	B
Golf courses: 3 private (54 holes); 1 daily fee (9 holes); 3 municipal (45 holes)	B
Bowling centers: 13 (174 lanes, tenpins)	A

Crowd Pleasers (500 points)

	Rating
Zoo: Oglebay's Good Children's Zoo—81 species, 445 specimens	C
Pari-Mutuel Betting: Wheeling Downs (greyhound, 310 races)	AA

Outdoor Recreation Assets (75)
Inland Water Area: 14.5 square miles
Places Rated Score: 1,275   Places Rated Rank: 202

Wichita, KS

Common Denominators (1,000 points)

	Rating
Good restaurants: 1 *, 6 **, 4 ***	A

	Rating
Golf courses: 9 private (153 holes); 8 daily fee (99 holes); 6 municipal (99 holes)	A
Bowling centers: 20 (432 lanes, tenpins)	AA

Crowd Pleasers (1,100 points)

	Rating
Zoo: Sedgwick County Zoo & Botanical Gardens—287 species, 1,359 specimens	A
Auto Racing: Lake Afton Grand Prix (SCCA)	B
Pari-Mutuel Betting: Wichita Greyhound Park (greyhound, 137 races)	A
Professional Sports: 1.188 game seats per capita Wranglers (Double A Baseball)	B
NCAA Division I: 0.299 game seats per capita Wichita State Shockers	C

Outdoor Recreation Assets (50)
Inland Water Area: 5.2 square miles
Places Rated Score: 2,150   Places Rated Rank: 70

Wichita Falls, TX

Common Denominators (1,000 points)

	Rating
Good restaurants: 1 *, 2 **, 1 ***	A
Golf courses: 2 private (36 holes); 2 daily fee (27 holes); 2 municipal (36 holes)	A
Bowling centers: 6 (132 lanes, tenpins)	AA

Crowd Pleasers (200 points)

	Rating
Professional Sports: 1.259 game seats per capita Texans (CBA Basketball)	B

Outdoor Recreation Assets (9)
Inland Water Area: 6.1 square miles
Places Rated Score: 1,209   Places Rated Rank: 225

Williamsport, PA

Common Denominators (500 points)

	Rating
Good restaurants: 1 *, 2 **	B
Golf courses: 1 private (18 holes); 1 municipal (18 holes)	C
Bowling centers: 5 (74 lanes, tenpins)	B

Crowd Pleasers (300 points)

	Rating
Professional Sports: 2.100 game seats per capita Bills (Double A Baseball)	A

Outdoor Recreation Assets (26)
Inland Water Area: 6.5 square miles
Places Rated Score: 826   Places Rated Rank: 286

Wilmington, DE–NJ–MD

Common Denominators (700 points)

	Rating
Good restaurants: 3 *, 5 **, 3 ***	B
Golf courses: 11 private (207 holes); 6 daily fee (117 holes); 2 municipal (36 holes)	B
Bowling centers: 13 (426 lanes, tenpins)	A

Crowd Pleasers (300 points)

	Rating
Zoo: Brandywine Zoo—56 species, 184 specimens	C
Pari-Mutuel Betting: Brandywine Raceway (harness, 163 races) Delaware Park (thoroughbred, 100 races) Fair Hill (harness, 5 races)	C
NCAA Division I: 0.268 game seats per capita University of Delaware Fightin' Blue Hens	C

Outdoor Recreation Assets (438)
Inland Water Area: 101.9 square miles
National Forests, Parks, Wildlife Refuges: Supawna Meadow NWR (1,716 acres)
CMSA Access: Philadelphia–Wilmington–Trenton, PA–NJ–DE–MD (80 points)
Places Rated Score: 1,518   Places Rated Rank: 158

Wilmington, NC

Common Denominators (700 points)

	Rating
Good restaurants: 1 *, 1 **	C
Golf courses: 3 private (54 holes); 3 daily fee (54 holes); 1 municipal (18 holes)	AA
Bowling centers: 4 (74 lanes, tenpins)	B

Crowd Pleasers (200 points)

	Rating
NCAA Division I: 0.610 game seats per capita University of North Carolina Seahawks	B

Outdoor Recreation Assets (1,071)

Rating

Atlantic Coastline: 26 miles
Inland Water Area: 35.7 square miles
Places Rated Score: 1,971   Places Rated Rank: 85

Worcester, MA
Common Denominators (600 points)
  Good restaurants: 4 **, 1 ***   **C**
  Golf courses: 5 private (81 holes); 14 daily fee (180   **A**
    holes); 3 municipal (36 holes)
  Bowling centers: 8 (244 lanes, mixed)   **B**
Crowd Pleasers (200 points)
  NCAA Division I: 0.391 game seats per capita   **B**
    Holy Cross Crusaders
Outdoor Recreation Assets (212)
  Inland Water Area: 31.1 square miles
Places Rated Score: 1,012   Places Rated Rank: 258

Yakima, WA
Common Denominators (300 points)
  Golf courses: 3 private (54 holes); 3 daily fee (36   **C**
    holes)
  Bowling centers: 7 (110 lanes, tenpins)   **B**
Crowd Pleasers (300 points)
  Pari-Mutuel Betting: **A**
    Yakima Meadows (mixed meeetings, 76 races)
Outdoor Recreation Assets (940)
  Inland Water Area: 18.4 square miles
  National Forests, Parks, Wildlife Refuges:
    Gifford Pinchot NF (37,552 acres)
    Snoqualmie NF (466,801 acres)
    Toppenish NWR (1,763 acres)
Places Rated Score: 1,540   Places Rated Rank: 155

York, PA
Common Denominators (900 points)
  Good restaurants: 1 *, 5 **, 4 ***   **A**
  Golf courses: 7 private (99 holes); 9 daily fee (162   **A**
    holes)

Rating

Bowling centers: 20 (330 lanes, tenpins)   **A**
Outdoor Recreation Assets (45)
  Inland Water Area: 6 square miles
  National Forests, Parks, Wildlife Refuges:
    Eisenhower NHS (690 acres)
    Gettysburg National Cemetery (21 acres)
    Gettysburg NMP (3,689 acres)
Places Rated Score: 945   Places Rated Rank: 268

Youngstown–Warren, OH
Common Denominators (800 points)
  Good restaurants: 7 **   **C**
  Golf courses: 7 private (108 holes); 25 daily fee   **AA**
    (378 holes); 2 municipal (45 holes)
  Bowling centers: 19 (442 lanes, tenpins)   **A**
Crowd Pleasers (400 points)
  Auto Racing: Nelson Ledges Road Course (SCCA) **B**
  NCAA Division I: 0.327 game seats per capita **B**
    Youngstown State Penguins
Outdoor Recreation Assets (155)
  Inland Water Area: 32.9 square miles
Places Rated Score: 1,355   Places Rated Rank: 184

Yuba City, CA
Common Denominators (200 points)
  Golf courses: 2 private (27 holes); 1 daily fee (9   **C**
    holes); 1 municipal (18 holes)
  Bowling centers: 2 (40 lanes, tenpins)   **C**
Outdoor Recreation Assets (317)
  Inland Water Area: 10.1 square miles
  National Forests, Parks, Wildlife Refuges:
    Butte Sink NWR (658 acres)
    Plumas NF (23,885 acres)
    Sutter NWR (2590 acres)
    Tahoe NF (20,494 acres)
Places Rated Score: 517   Places Rated Rank: 318

Et Cetera

WHERE ARE THE BEST SPORTS TOWNS?

Ask 100 sports fans to describe the ideal sports town and you'll probably get 100 different answers. Earlier in this chapter, *Places Rated* looked at major spectator sports from the point of view of easy accessibility and on this basis found the best metro areas to be Pittsfield, MA; Elmira, NY; and Milwaukee, WI.

Obviously, though, being able to attend a game easily is not the only thing a fan wants. Rooting for the home team is fun, but rooting for a *winning* home team is ecstasy. In the lists that follow, *Places Rated* looks at the metro areas with the winningest teams.

Major-League Title Towns

For baseball fans in the mid-1970s, the place to be was Oakland, CA, as the A's hauled in three straight World Series championships. In the 1960s, football fans found a warm welcome in frosty Green Bay, WI, where the Packers took five NFL Championships over a seven-year span. No baseball team can really be called a dominant World Series champ for the 1980s. Neither has any football team topped the Packer's record for the 1960s, but both the San Francisco 49ers, with three Super Bowl wins, and the Washington Redskins, with two, have inspired devotion among fans in the 1980s.

Basketball lovers, on the other hand, won't ever go far wrong if they back the Boston Celtics, winners of more titles then any other team in NBA history. With all their tradition and mystique—not to mention the renowned parquet floor of the Boston Garden, where they play—they have left many opponents over the years bewitched, bothered, and bewildered. Still, in the 1980s the L.A. Lakers aren't doing too badly either, with more championships in this decade than any other team.

Our survey of metro areas with major professional

championships (in the list just below) looks at the winners in four team sports: baseball, football, basketball, and ice hockey. In the cases of baseball and ice hockey, we include the winners of the World Series (since 1903) and Stanley Cup (since 1894). For football and basketball, we include the Super Bowl and NBA Championship winners. Going back a little more toward the roots, we also list the winning teams from the leagues that preceded the modern NFL (the National Football League, 1933–1969, and American Football League, 1960–1969) and the NBA (the Basketball Association of America, 1947–1949). The NFL and AFL champions of 1966, 1967, and 1968 met in the Super Bowls of 1967, 1968, and 1969, before the formation of the modern NFL; for those years, we name the winners of both the individual league championships and the Super Bowl.

If a team has changed names or towns, we list it with the name it used and in the town it played at the time it won the championship.

Professional Championships in the Metro Areas

Anaheim–Santa Ana, CA
NFL Championship: Los Angeles Rams, 1951

Baltimore, MD
World Series: Orioles, 1966, 1970, 1983
Super Bowl: Colts, 1971
NFL Championship: Colts, 1958, 1959, 1968
BAA Championship: Bullets, 1948

Boston, MA
World Series: Somersets, 1903; Pilgrims, 1911; Red Sox, 1912, 1914, 1915, 1916, 1918
NBA Championship: Celtics, 1957, 1959, 1960, 1961, 1962, 1963, 1964, 1965, 1966, 1968, 1969, 1974, 1976, 1981, 1984, 1986
Stanley Cup: Bruins, 1929, 1939, 1941, 1970, 1972

Buffalo, NY
AFL Championship: Bills, 1964, 1965

Chicago, IL
World Series: White Sox, 1906, 1917; Cubs, 1907, 1908
NFL Championship: Bears, 1933, 1940, 1941, 1943, 1946, 1963; Cardinals, 1947
Stanley Cup: Black Hawks, 1934, 1938, 1961
Super Bowl: Bears, 1986

Cincinnati, OH–KY–IN
World Series: Reds, 1919, 1940, 1975, 1976

Cleveland, OH
World Series: Indians, 1920, 1948
NFL Championship: Rams, 1945; Browns, 1950, 1954, 1955, 1964

Dallas, TX
Super Bowl: Cowboys, 1972, 1978
AFL Championship: Texans, 1962

Detroit, MI
World Series: Tigers, 1935, 1945, 1968, 1984
NFL Championship: Lions, 1935, 1952, 1953, 1957
Stanley Cup: Red Wings, 1936, 1937, 1943, 1950, 1952, 1954, 1955

Green Bay, WI
Super Bowl: Packers, 1967, 1968
NFL Championship: Packers, 1936, 1937, 1939, 1944, 1961, 1962, 1965, 1966, 1967

Houston, TX
AFL Championship: Oilers, 1960, 1961

Kansas City, MO
Super Bowl: Chiefs, 1970
AFL Championship: Chiefs, 1966, 1969
World Series: Royals, 1985

Los Angeles–Long Beach, CA
World Series: Dodgers, 1959, 1963, 1965, 1981, 1988
Super Bowl: Raiders, 1984
NFL Championship: Rams, 1951
NBA Championship: Lakers, 1972, 1980, 1982, 1985, 1987, 1988

Miami–Hialeah, FL
Super Bowl: Dolphins, 1973, 1974

Milwaukee, WI
World Series: Braves, 1957
NBA Championship: Bucks, 1971

Minneapolis–St. Paul, MN–WI
NFL Championship: Minnesota Vikings, 1969

Pro Sports Franchising

Only 38 of the country's 333 metro areas have the privilege of being called "home" by one of the 88 major-league professional sports teams in the United States. The greatest number of franchises, six, is found in the Los Angeles–Long Beach, CA, metro area.

In professional sports marketing, the largest metro areas get the teams. Only in such mega-communities as Los Angeles–Long Beach can local governments afford to underwrite stadiums and arenas. There, too, ticket-buying fans can be found in the greatest numbers—an important element in the equation.

So how does a small major-league metro area, such as Green Bay, WI, fit into this picture? Without conforming to the typical profile, Green Bay has the Packers, one of the oldest franchises in the NFL. The team divides its eight regular-season home games between Milwaukee's County Stadium and Lambeau Field in Green Bay—a strategy that provides it some of the benefits of a team located in a large metro area. The "Pack" is also the only municipally owned team in professional sports and, therefore, the only club whose owners can't threaten to move it.

Certain large metro areas have no professional sports franchises; others could support more teams than they already do. With this in mind, the owners of major-league baseball's 26 franchises appointed a committee to identify metro areas that might have the means to put together publicly financed stadiums and blue-ribbon groups of prospective owners. Nine cities were mentioned: Denver, CO; Phoenix, AZ; Washington, DC; Miami, FL; Buffalo, NY; New Orleans, LA; Indianapolis, IN; Vancouver, WA; and Tampa, FL.

While it may be true, as some studies show, that big-time professional football could easily expand into eight more cities, and major-league baseball into six, the number of franchises is strictly controlled by owners. In fact, they have so much control that professional sports has been called the only unregulated monopoly allowed to operate in the United States. If there is to be any expansion, it is likely to occur at a glacial rate (i.e., slowly), because club owners, like classic monopolists, do not care to have anyone encroaching on their territorial rights.

BAA Championship: Minneapolis Lakers, 1949
NBA Championship: Minneapolis Lakers, 1950, 1952, 1953, 1954
World Series: Twins, 1985

Nassau–Suffolk, NY
Stanley Cup: New York Islanders, 1980, 1981, 1982, 1983

New York, NY
World Series: Giants, 1905, 1921, 1922, 1933, 1954; Yankees, 1923, 1927, 1928, 1932, 1936, 1937, 1938, 1939, 1941, 1943, 1947, 1949, 1950, 1951, 1952, 1953, 1956, 1958, 1961, 1962, 1977, 1978; Brooklyn Dodgers, 1955; Mets, 1969
Super Bowl: Jets, 1969; Giants, 1987
AFL Championship: Jets, 1968
NFL Championship: Giants, 1934, 1938, 1944, 1956
NBA Championship: Knickerbockers, 1970, 1973
Stanley Cup: Rangers, 1928, 1933, 1940

Oakland, CA
World Series: Athletics, 1972, 1973; A's, 1974
Super Bowl: Raiders, 1977, 1981
AFL Championship: Raiders, 1967
NBA Championship: Golden State Warriors, 1975

Philadelphia, PA–NJ
World Series: Athletics, 1910, 1911, 1913, 1929, 1930; Phillies, 1980
NFL Championship: Eagles, 1948, 1949, 1960
BAA Championship: Warriors, 1947
NBA Championship: Warriors, 1956; 76ers, 1967, 1983
Stanley Cup: Flyers, 1974, 1975

Pittsburgh, PA
World Series: Pirates, 1909, 1925, 1960, 1971, 1979
Super Bowl: Steelers, 1975, 1976, 1979, 1980

Portland, OR
NBA Championship: Trail Blazers, 1977

Rochester, NY
NBA Championship: Royals, 1951

St. Louis, MO–IL
World Series: Cardinals, 1926, 1931, 1934, 1942, 1944, 1946, 1964, 1967, 1982
NBA Championship: Hawks, 1958

San Diego, CA
AFL Championship: Chargers, 1963

San Francisco, CA
Super Bowl: 49ers, 1982, 1985, 1989

Seattle, WA
NBA Championship: SuperSonics, 1979
Stanley Cup: Metropolitans, 1917

Syracuse, NY
NBA Championship: Nationals, 1955

Washington, DC–MD–VA
World Series: Senators, 1924
Super Bowl: Redskins, 1983, 1988
NFL Championship: Redskins, 1937, 1942
NBA Championship: Bullets, 1978

Source: Official league histories.

Collegiate Title Towns

The 1988–1989 academic year marks the 107th season of college athletic championships that began all the way back when Harvard University's J. S. Clark captured the first singles title in college tennis in 1883. Founded in 1906, the National Collegiate Athletic Association (NCAA) began sponsoring college athletic championships in 1921, beginning with its first outdoor track meet. It was not until 1981, however, that the association initiated women's championships. Over the years, some 600 colleges and universities have been named national champions in each of the NCAA's three divi-

sions. What follows is a list covering the past decade that shows 56 metro areas with Division I champions.

Many NCAA sports, such as basketball and volleyball, have both men's and women's championships. An M or W after the sport in the list below indicates whether the title was in men's or women's competition. Sports such as baseball, football, and wrestling are played at the championship level by men only, whereas field hockey and softball championships are for women only; accordingly, no M or W designation is given for those sports. Ski teams are coed.

NCAA Division I Championships in the Metro Areas

Albany–Schenectady–Troy, NY
Rensselaer Polytechnic Institute: Hockey, 1985

Anaheim–Santa Ana, CA
California State University, Fullerton: Baseball, 1984; Softball, 1986
University of California, Irvine: Water Polo, 1982

Ann Arbor, MI
University of Michigan: Basketball (M), 1989

Athens, GA
University of Georgia: Football (Division I–A), 1980; Tennis (M), 1987

Austin, TX
University of Texas: Baseball, 1983, 1986; Cross-Country Track, 1986; Gymnastics (W), 1987; Swimming and Diving (M), 1981, 1988; Swimming and Diving (W), 1984, 1985, 1986, 1987, 1988

Baltimore, MD
Johns Hopkins University: Lacrosse (M), 1980, 1984

Bloomington, IN
Indiana University: Basketball (M), 1981, 1987; Soccer (M), 1982, 1983, 1984

Boise City, ID
Boise State University: Football (Division I–AA), 1980

Boston, MA
Harvard University: Hockey, 1989

Boulder–Longmont, CO
University of Colorado: Skiing, 1982

Bryan–College Station, TX
Texas A & M University: Softball, 1983, 1987

Burlington, VT
University of Vermont: Skiing (M), 1980

Charlottesville, VA
University of Virginia: Cross-Country Track (W), 1981, 1982

Chattanooga, TN
University of Tennessee: Basketball (W), 1987

Columbus, OH
Ohio State University: Gymnastics (M), 1985

Dallas, TX
Southern Methodist University: Outdoor Track (M), 1983, 1986

Denver, CO
University of Denver: Gymnastics (W), 1983

Detroit, MI
Wayne State University: Fencing (M), 1980, 1982, 1983, 1984; Fencing (W), 1982, 1984

El Paso, TX
University of Texas, El Paso: Cross-Country Track (M), 1980, 1981, 1983; Outdoor Track (M), 1980, 1981, 1982

Eugene–Springfield, OR
University of Oregon: Cross-Country Track (W), 1983, 1987; Outdoor Track (M), 1984

Fayetteville, AR
Universtity of Arkansas: Cross Country Track (M), 1986, 1987; Outdoor Track (M), 1988

Fort Worth–Arlington, TX
Texas Christian University: Golf (W), 1983

Gainesville, FL
University of Florida: Swimming and Diving (M), 1983, 1984; Swimming and Diving (W), 1982

Grand Forks, ND
University of North Dakota: Ice Hockey, 1980, 1982, 1987

Greensboro–Winston-Salem–High Point, NC
Wake Forest University: Golf (M), 1986

Greenville–Spartanburg, SC
Clemson University: Football (Division I-A), 1981; Soccer, 1984, 1987

Honolulu, HI
University of Hawaii: Volleyball (W), 1982

Houston, TX
University of Houston: Golf (M), 1982, 1984, 1987

Iowa City, IA
University of Iowa: Field Hockey, 1986; Wrestling, 1980, 1981, 1982, 1983, 1984, 1985, 1986

Lansing–East Lansing, MI
Michigan State University: Hockey, 1986

Lawrence, KS
Kansas University: Basketball (M), 1988

Lincoln, NE
University of Nebraska: Gymnastics (M), 1980, 1981, 1982, 1983, 1988

Los Angeles–Long Beach, CA
California State University, Northridge: Gymnastics (W), 1982
Pepperdine University: Volleyball (M), 1985, 1986
University of California, Los Angeles: Gymnastics (M), 1984, 1987; Golf (M), 1988; Soccer, 1985; Outdoor Track (M), 1987, 1988; Softball, 1982, 1984, 1985, 1988; Swimming and Diving (M), 1982; Tennis (M), 1982, 1984; Volleyball (M), 1981, 1982, 1983, 1984, 1987
University of Southern California: Basketball (W), 1983, 1984; Outdoor Track (W), 1982, 1983; Tennis (W), 1983, 1985; Volleyball (W), 1983; Volleyball (W), 1980, 1988

Louisville, KY–IN
University of Louisville: Basketball (M), 1980, 1986

Madison, WI
University of Wisconsin: Cross-Country Track (M), 1982; Cross-Country Track (W), 1984, 1985; Ice Hockey, 1981, 1983

Miami–Hialeah, FL
University of Miami: Baseball, 1982, 1985; Football (Division I-A), 1983, 1987; Golf (W), 1984

Monroe, LA
Northeast Louisiana University: Football (Division I-AA), 1987

Norfolk–Virginia Beach–Newport News, VA
Old Dominion University: Field Hockey, 1982, 1983, 1984, Basketball (W), 1985

Oakland, CA
University of California, Berkeley: Swimming and Diving (M), 1980

Philadelphia, PA–NJ
Temple University: Lacrosse (W), 1984
University of Pennsylvania: Fencing (M), 1981
Villanova University: Basketball (M), 1985

Phoenix, AZ
Arizona State University: Baseball, 1981; Gymnastics (M), 1986; Wrestling, 1988

Provo–Orem, UT
Brigham Young University: Golf (M), 1981; Football, 1984

Raleigh–Durham, NC
Duke University: Soccer, 1986
North Carolina State University: Basketball (M), 1983
University of North Carolina: Basketball (M), 1982; Lacrosse (M), 1981, 1982; Soccer (W), 1982

Salt Lake City–Ogden, UT
University of Utah: Gymnastics (W), 1982, 1983, 1984, 1985, 1986 Skiing, 1981, 1983, 1984, 1986, 1987, 1988

San Francisco, CA
University of San Francisco: Soccer (M), 1980

San Jose, CA
Stanford University: Baseball, 1987, 1988; Tennis (M), 1980, 1981, 1982, 1983, 1986, 1988; Tennis (W), 1982, 1984, 1986, 1987, 1988; Swimming, 1985, 1986, 1987; Swimming and Diving (W), 1983; Water Polo (M), 1980, 1981

South Bend–Mishawaka, IN
University of Notre Dame: Football (Division I-A), 1988

State College, PA
Pennsylvania State University: Fencing (W), 1983; Football (Division I-A), 1982, 1986

Syracuse, NY
Syracuse University: Lacrosse (M), 1983

Tallahassee, FL
Florida State University: Outdoor Track (W), 1984

Toledo, OH
Bowling Green University: Hockey, 1984

Tucson, AZ
University of Arizona: Baseball, 1980, 1986

Tulsa, OK
University of Tulsa: Golf (W), 1982

Tuscaloosa, AL
University of Alabama: Football (Division I-A), 1979; Gymnastics (W), 1988

Washington, DC–MD–VA
Georgetown University: Basketball (M), 1984
University of Maryland: Field Hockey, 1987

Wilmington, DE–NJ–MD
University of Delaware: Lacrosse (W), 1983

Source: National Collegiate Athletic Association, *College Champions,* 1988.

In Division I-A Football, the NCAA recognizes as unofficial national champion the team selected each year by the Associated Press poll of sportswriters and the United Press International poll of coaches.

LEGAL HOLIDAYS

Properly speaking, the United States doesn't have any national holidays. A day off on Independence Day, Thanksgiving, or Christmas comes by the grace of state legislatures rather than a presidential proclamation or an act of Congress.

The only thing "national" about your holiday calendar is the ten days off given to everyone who works for the federal government: Christmas, Independence Day, Labor Day, New Year's Day, Thanksgiving, and five Mondays—Columbus Day, Memorial Day, Veterans Day, Washington's Birthday, and Martin Luther King Day. The first four holiday Mondays were approved in 1968 to create predictable long weekends. The fifth, approved in 1986, honors the great hero Martin Luther King, Jr. each year on the third Monday of January.

Although lawmakers in many states have since adopted these same days as legal holidays for their local constituencies, many have not. In 1978, for instance, the federal government moved Veterans Day from the second Monday in November back to its original date, November 11, while four states have simply decided to celebrate it in October.

The Civil War era gave us more events and heroes to honor with holidays than any other period in American history. However, they aren't all celebrated nationwide.

Just as no former secessionist state takes notice of Lincoln's birthday, so none of the Union states honors Robert E. Lee's birthday. Memorial Day, a date originally created to mourn those who died for the Union cause, isn't observed in Alabama, Mississippi, or South Carolina. Those states, as well as Florida, Georgia, Kentucky, and Louisiana, celebrate Confederate Memorial Day instead. So if the calendars of some states have more holidays on them than others, it reflects the decisions of their lawmakers as to which local heroes and events are worthy of commemoration.

For traveling salespeople who have found themselves all dressed up with no place to go in Boston on Evacuation Day or in Omaha on Arbor Day, and for anyone who wonders whether Florida has more long weekends than California or Texas, we present the following comprehensive list of days, fixed and movable, that are legal holidays somewhere in the United States.

An American List of Days

JANUARY

Fixed Dates

January 1, New Year's Day: All states
January 8, Battle of New Orleans Day: Louisiana
January 15, Martin Luther King Day: All states
January 19, Robert E. Lee's Birthday: Arkansas, Florida, Kentucky, Louisiana, South Carolina
  Confederate Heroes Day: Texas
January 30, Franklin D. Roosevelt's Birthday: Kentucky

Movable Feasts

Third Monday, Robert E. Lee's Birthday: Alabama, Mississippi
  Lee-Jackson-King Day: Virginia

FEBRUARY

Fixed Dates

February 12, Lincoln's Birthday: Alaska, California, Colorado, Connecticut, Florida, Illinois, Indiana, Iowa, Kansas, Kentucky, Maryland, Missouri, Montana, New Jersey, New Mexico, New York, Utah, Vermont, Washington, West Virginia
February 15, Susan B. Anthony's Birthday: Florida, Minnesota
February 19, Robert E. Lee Day: Kentucky

Movable Feasts

First Monday, Lincoln's Birthday: Delaware, Oregon
Second Monday, Lincoln Day: Arizona
Third Monday, Washington's Birthday: All states
Tuesday before Ash Wednesday, Mardi Gras: Alabama, Florida (some counties), Louisiana (some parishes)

MARCH

Fixed Dates

March 2, Texas Independence Day: Texas
March 17, Evacuation Day: Massachusetts (Suffolk County only)
March 20, Youth Day: Oklahoma
March 25, Maryland Day: Maryland
March 26, Prince Jonah Kuhio Kalanianaole Day: Hawaii

Movable Feasts

First Monday, Casimir Pulaski's Birthday: Illinois
First Tuesday, Town Meeting Day: Vermont
Two days before Easter, Good Friday: Connecticut, Delaware, Florida, Hawaii, Indiana, Louisiana, Maryland, New Jersey, North Dakota, Pennsylvania, Tennessee, Wisconsin (11 A.M.–3 P.M.)
One day after Easter, Easter Monday: North Carolina
Last Monday, Seward's Day: Alaska

APRIL

Fixed Dates

April 2, Pascua Florida Day: Florida
April 3, Arbor Day: Arizona
April 13, Thomas Jefferson's Birthday: Alabama, Oklahoma
April 21, San Jacinto Day: Texas
April 22, Arbor Day: Nebraska
  Oklahoma Day: Oklahoma
April 26, Confederate Memorial Day: Florida, Georgia

Movable Feasts

Third Monday, Patriots' Day: Maine, Massachusetts
Fourth Monday, Fast Day: New Hampshire
Last Monday, Confederate Memorial Day: Alabama, Mississippi

MAY

Fixed Dates

May 1, Bird Day: Oklahoma
May 4, Rhode Island Independence Day: Rhode Island
May 8, Truman Day: Missouri
May 10, Confederate Memorial Day: South Carolina
May 11, Minnesota Day: Minnesota
May 20, Mecklenburg Independence Day: North Carolina
May 25, Memorial Day: New Mexico, South Dakota, Vermont
May 30, Memorial Day: Delaware, Illinois, Maryland, New Hampshire

Movable Feasts

First Tuesday after first Monday, Primary Election Day: Indiana
Second Sunday, Mother's Day: Arizona, Oklahoma
Last Monday, Memorial Day: All states except Alabama, Mississippi, South Carolina, and those celebrating on May 30

JUNE

Fixed Dates

June 3, Jefferson Davis's Birthday: Florida, South Carolina
  Confederate Memorial Day: Kentucky, Louisiana
June 9, Senior Citizens Day: Oklahoma
June 11, King Kamehameha I Day: Hawaii
June 14, Flag Day: Pennsylvania
June 15, Separation Day: Delaware
June 17, Bunker Hill Day: Massachusetts (Suffolk County only)
June 19, Emancipation Day: Texas
June 20, West Virginia Day: West Virginia

Movable Feasts

First Monday, Jefferson Davis's Birthday: Alabama, Mississippi
Second Sunday, Flag Day: New York
Third Sunday, Father's Day: Arizona

JULY

Fixed Dates

July 4, Independence Day: All states
July 24, Pioneer Day: Utah

Movable Feasts: *None*

AUGUST

Fixed Dates

August 16, Bennington Battle Day: Vermont
August 27, Lyndon B. Johnson's Birthday: Texas
August 30, Huey P. Long Day: Louisiana

Movable Feasts

First Sunday, American Family Day: Arizona
First Monday, Colorado Day: Colorado
Second Monday, Victory Day: Rhode Island
Third Friday, Admission Day: Hawaii

SEPTEMBER

Fixed Dates

September 9, Admission Day: California
September 12, Defenders' Day: Maryland
September 16, Cherokee Strip Day: Oklahoma

Movable Feasts

First Monday, Labor Day: All states
First Tuesday, Primary Election Day: Wisconsin
Second Tuesday, Primary Election Day: Wyoming
First Saturday after full moon, Indian Day: Oklahoma

OCTOBER

Fixed Dates

October 10, Oklahoma Historical Day: Oklahoma
 Leif Erickson Day: Minnesota
October 12, Columbus Day: Maryland
October 18, Alaska Day: Alaska
October 31, Nevada Day: Nevada

Movable Feasts

Second Monday, Columbus Day: All states except Alaska, Iowa, Maryland, Michigan, Mississippi, Nevada, North Carolina, North Dakota, Oregon, South Carolina, Washington
Fourth Monday, Veterans Day: Arkansas, Montana, North Carolina, Utah

NOVEMBER

Fixed Dates

November 1, All Saints' Day: Louisiana
November 4, Will Rogers Day: Oklahoma
November 11, Veterans Day: All states except those celebrating in October
Week of November 16, Oklahoma Heritage Week: Oklahoma
November 29, Nellie Tayloe Ross's Birthday: Wyoming

Movable Feasts

First Tuesday after first Monday, General Election Day: Arkansas, California, Colorado, District of Columbia, Delaware, Florida, Hawaii, Idaho, Illinois, Kentucky, Louisiana, Maryland, Missouri, Montana, New Jersey, New York, Oklahoma, Pennsylvania, Rhode Island, South Carolina, Tennessee, Texas, Virginia, West Virginia, Wisconsin, Wyoming

DECEMBER

Fixed Dates

December 7, Delaware Day: Delaware
December 10, Wyoming Day: Wyoming
December 25, Christmas: All states

Movable Feasts: None

LEGALIZED GAMBLING IN THE STATES

None of the 50 states has completely unrestricted legalized gambling. What 46 of them do is to make certain forms of gambling legitimate and to authorize the state's right to run them as profitable enterprises, a right they steadfastly withhold from others. Nevada's constitution prohibits lotteries not because they are another form of gambling but because they would compete with the state's cut from casino gambling. A bettor who places twenty dollars on a horse with a bookie would break the law in New York or California—the number-one and number-two horse-racing states—just as he or she would anywhere else.

Gambling raises revenue, and this is the main reason that many states permit it in some form. For a complete list of states that have legalized gambling, check the

The Video Revolution

Although showcase cinemas are suburban phenomena, electronic communication has made another sort of cultural experience—video—accessible to all Americans, regardless of where they live.

In 1977, a Detroit businessman named Andre Blay became convinced that he could use his VCR for something more innovative than simply recording programs off his television. He attempted to sell Hollywood the idea of releasing some feature films for a home-video audience. Every major studios turned him down, except for 20th Century-Fox, which leased him the rights to a dozen movies, including *Gone with the Wind.* Soon after successfully launching his concept, Blay sold his business to Fox for $7.2 million. Hollywood's reaction followed a pattern familiar from talking movies, color films, and television: initial suspicion and resistance, then a rush to cash in on overwhelming success.

Nearly 80 percent of the households in America now own VCRs. A more startling statistic is that by the end of 1989, it's expected that half of all households will have *two* VCRs.

Once, movies were only shown in theatres, which people flocked to like large temples where the images of Hollywood were collectively experienced. TV changed habits, and VCRs brought an even more radical option. Now people have become their own programmers. All of film history is available by buying or renting videos. People now can privately screen festivals of foreign films of their choice, or John Ford westerns, or *film noir* classics, not to mention the chance to see Astaire dance or the Marx Brothers clown in fast forward.

It's unlikely that the video revolution will spell the end of movie theatres. The revolution *does* mean that Hollywood has yet another source of revenue, and a lucrative one at that. Home video sales now account for three times the earnings of theatrical releases. Producers now conceive of movies with TV and videocassettes in mind. That means that the *nature* of movies, the way they look, will continue to change. The image is shrinking to fit the small screen, as directors rely upon medium and close shots. The panorama is becoming a visual dinosaur.

Industry analysts predict the next wave of technology will be video laser discs, a cousin to the music industry's laser compact discs, which have already changed the musical market. Some analysts are even predicting that digital imaging in the 1990s will allow home viewers to alter movies at a whim. You might, for instance, decide to delete John Wayne from "Stagecoach," and substitute an image of yourself instead.

Legalized Gambling by State

	Horse Racing	Off-Track Betting	Dog Racing	Jai Alai	Lotteries	Bingo	Raffles	Casinos	Numbers	Sports Betting
Alabama	•		•			•				
Alaska						•	•			
Arizona	•		•	•	•	•				
Arkansas	•		•							
California	•				•	•	•		•	
Colorado	•		•		•	•	•			
Connecticut	•	•	•	•	•	•	•		•	
Delaware	•				•	•			•	•
Florida	•		•	•	•	•				
Georgia						•				
Hawaii										
Idaho	•					•				
Illinois	•	•			•	•	•		•	
Indiana										
Iowa	•		•		•	•		•		
Kansas	•		•		•	•				
Kentucky	•					•	•			
Louisiana	•	•				•	•			
Maine	•				•	•	•		•	
Maryland	•				•	•	•			
Massachusetts	•		•		•	•	•		•	
Michigan	•				•	•	•		•	
Minnesota	•					•	•			
Mississippi						•				
Missouri	•				•	•			•	
Montana	•					•	•			•
Nebraska	•					•	•			
Nevada	•	•	•	•		•		•		•
New Hampshire	•		•		•	•			•	
New Jersey	•				•	•		•	•	
New Mexico	•					•	•			
New York	•	•			•	•			•	
North Carolina						•				
North Dakota	•					•	•			
Ohio	•				•	•	•		•	
Oklahoma	•					•				
Oregon	•	•	•		•	•	•			•
Pennsylvania	•				•	•	•		•	
Rhode Island	•		•	•	•	•	•		•	
South Carolina						•				
South Dakota	•		•			•		•		
Tennessee	•					•				
Texas	•		•			•	•			
Utah										
Vermont			•		•	•			•	
Virginia						•	•			
Washington	•				•	•	•		•	•
West Virginia	•		•		•	•			•	
Wisconsin	•		•			•				
Wyoming						•				

Source: Gaming and Wagering Magazine, 1989; National Association of State Racing Commissioners, 1989.

table above, which also shows the forms of legalized gambling available. It may seem remarkable, but each of seven states—California, Connecticut, Florida, Illinois,

Massachusetts, New Jersey, and New York—takes in more money from lotteries or pari-mutuel betting on horses and dogs than Nevada does from its amusement tax on the tables, slot machines, sports-card betting shops, jai alai matches, and occasional horse races combined.

Another reason states sanction certain forms of gambling is to reduce illegal betting by offering comparable alternatives. But it is very difficult for states to raise money through legal gambling and control illegal operations at the same time. To start with, the illicit forms of gambling are usually more popular; the payoff from an illegal bookmaking shop, floating dice and card games, or the numbers game is greater than that from sanctioned operations for two reasons. First, there is no government takeout, and second the winnings are hidden from the tax collector. The stories about bookmakers setting up shop next door to New York City Off-Track Betting parlors are true, just as illegal numbers games still thrive in Massachusetts and New Jersey, two states with daily numbers games of their own.

LOOKING FOR THE BEST SKIING?

If you were to draw a line on a map of the United States separating states with the best conditions for skiing from those with poor conditions or no facilities, the result would be a jagged northward arc. It would begin in the Great Smoky Mountains of North Carolina and run due north to Lake Erie, west to the foothills of the Rockies, and then south along the Rocky Mountain cordillera to northern New Mexico and Arizona. Next it would reappear in the California Sierra Nevada, dropping southwest to end in the San Bernardino National Forest an hour and a half out of Los Angeles. Although ski areas exist south of this imaginary curve, the ideal conditions are north of it, in the rolling, rugged terrain and predictable winter weather that everyone except skiers would call bad.

By definition, a ski area is a hill or mountain with some form of developed trails and lift machinery. Usually there is a lodge for meals and overnight stays. If the area is large and popular, it also has après-ski—nighttime entertainment that can range from music to movies to disco—that to many skiers is as critical as fresh snow and challenging runs.

Of the 587 U.S. ski areas, more than half are found in eight northeastern and Great Lakes states—Massachusetts, Michigan, Minnesota, New Hampshire, New York, Pennsylvania, Vermont, and Wisconsin—because of harsh, long winters and large, recreation-hungry urban populations. As you can see on the table on the following page, these eight states are among the ten ranked as particularly rich in ski areas.

But if you're a skier with time and money, skiing Hanley's Happy Hill in Pennsylvania, Little Switzerland in Wisconsin, or even Vermont's Killington or Stowe

---

The 15 Busiest Ski Areas

America's busiest ski areas, determined by a measurement known as a ski occasion (one ascent and descent of the mountain by a skier), are all located within national forests.

Ski Area	Ski Occasions
1. Mammoth Mountain, CA	1,536,214
2. Breckenridge, CO	763,200
3. Steamboat, CO	743,200
4. Keystone, CO	732,200
5. Snowmass, CO	679,800
6. Copper Mountain, CO	651,800
7. Taos Ski Valley, NM	624,235
8. Mount Bachelor, OR	603,918
9. Crystal Mountain, WA	600,000
10. Santa Fe Ski Area, NM	590,000
11. Alta, UT	533,536
12. Snow Summit, CA	503,571
13. Sugarbush Valley, VT	501,000
14. Bald Mountain, ID	444,227
15. Snowbird, UT	415,111

Source: U.S. Forest Service, *National Forest Recreation Use Reports*, 1984.

---

isn't quite the same as skiing "destination" areas in the West such as Aspen, Park City, or Jackson Hole. Ski areas are where you find them, but the best *skiing* is in the highest part of the country: the Rocky Mountain West and the Sierra Nevada near Lake Tahoe.

This statement is not purely a matter of opinion. According to ski-industry surveys, most of the eight to ten million skiers in the United States are of intermediate ability, tending toward advanced. If they could ski anywhere, they would choose areas that enhance their ability; that is, places with high mountains, great vertical rises, long runs, and heavy powder snowfalls that begin early in winter and last into spring. You'll find more of these qualities within short drives of Denver, Boulder, Reno, Salt Lake City, Seattle, Tacoma, and Spokane than anywhere else. And as the table above indicates, the busiest 15 ski areas are indeed located near some of these cities.

The 10 States with the Most Ski Areas

State	Ski Areas
1. New York	56
2. Michigan	47
3. Wisconsin	35
4. California	34
5. Colorado	30
5. Pennsylvania	29
7. New Hampshire	26
8. Vermont	25
9. Minnesota	22
10. Massachusetts	17

Source: Inter-Ski Services, *The White Book of Ski Areas*, 1988.

Vertical Rise . . .

The perpendicular distance from the base to the highest skiable point on a hill or mountain is a ski area's "vertical." Utah's 14 ski areas average 1,826 feet, whereas Alabama's single ski area has a rise of only 150 feet. The table below shows the 20 ski areas with the greatest vertical rises. Although vertical rise has little to do with the quality of the trails, it is a good indication of length of the runs and the mountain's challenge. More than one optimistic ski-area promoter has stretched the distance a bit—some, allegedly, by measuring from the top of the tallest tree on the crest to the surface of the highway below the base lodge.

The 20 Greatest Vertical Rises

Ski Area	Height
1. Jackson Hole, WY	4,139 ft
2. Aspen Highlands, CO	3,800
3. Snowmass, CO	3,615
4. Steamboat, CO	3,600
5. Sun Valley, ID	3,400
6. Beaver Creek, CO	3,340
7. Aspen, CO	3,267
8. Whiteface Mountain, NY	3,216
9. Vail, CO	3,200
10. Killington, VT	3,175
11. Telluride, CO	3,155
12. Crystal Mountain, WA	3,100
12. Mammoth Mountain, CA	3,100
12. Mt. Bachelor, OR	3,100
12. Park City, UT	3,100
12. Snowbird, UT	3,100
17. Heavenly Valley, CA	2,900
18. Alyeska, AK	2,850
18. Squaw Valley, CA	2,850
20. Big Sky, MT	2,800

Source: Inter-Ski Services, *The White Book of Skiing*, 1988.

. . . and Longest Runs . . .

The highest vertical is found at Wyoming's Jackson Hole, but, as can be seen in the following table, the longest ski run is at Killington, in Vermont. The longest run is the longest continuous trail on the mountain, from the top to the runout, which is usually in the base lodge's parking lot.

The 9 Longest Ski Runs

Ski Area	Length
1. Killington, VT	10.2 mi
2. Jackson Hole, WY	7.0
3. Heavenly Valley, CA	5.5
3. Taos Ski Valley, NM	5.5
5. Mission Ridge, WA	5.0
6. Okemo Mountain, VT	4.5
6. Stowe, VT	4.5
6. Vail, CO	4.5
9. Stratton, VT	4.0

Source: Inter-Ski Services, *The White Book of Ski Areas,* 1988.

. . . and Lift Capacities

A ski area's lift capacity is the number of people its lifts can move up the mountain in one hour. Lifts can be elementary rope or cable tows, bars (T-bars, J-bars, pomalifts, or platterpulls), chairs, trams, or gondolas. Whatever the mix of lifts at a ski resort, the total lift capacity is a good indication of how developed the ski area is and often of how efficient the lift lines are. Twenty-five U.S. ski areas have lift capacities of at least 15,000 skiers per hour, and ten of these can move 20,000 or more up the mountain every hour. At Mammoth Mountain, CA, an amazing 42,000 skiers per hour can be moved up the mountain. The table below lists the other ski areas that, with Mammoth Mountain, have the greatest lift capacities.

The 20 Best Ski Areas for Lift Capacity

Ski Area	Skiers per Hour
1. Mammoth Mountain, CA	42,000
2. Squaw Valley, CA	39,380
3. Vail, CO	35,020
4. Killington, VT	30,827
5. Heavenly Valley, CA	30,000
6. Steamboat, CO	28,730
7. Winter Park, CO	28,310
8. Alpental/Snoqualmie, WA	27,940
9. Copper Mountain, CO	27,050
10. Sun Valley, ID	24,644
11. Mount Snow, VT	23,955
12. Breckenridge, CO	22,650
13. Snowmass, CO	20,535
14. Seven Springs, PA	20,400
15. Afton Alps, MN	20,000
16. Sunday River, ME	19,550
17. Park City, UT	18,700
18. Snow Valley, CA	18,550
19. Mt. Bachelor, OR	18,140
20. Hunter Mountain, NY	18,000

Source: Inter-Ski Services, *The White Book of Ski Areas,* 1988.

Climate

"The Fortunate people of the planet," John Kenneth Galbraith wrote years ago in *Harper's*, "are those who live by the seasons. There is far more difference between a Vermont farm in the summer and that farm in the winter than there is between San Diego and São Paulo. This means that people who live where the seasons are good and strong have no need to travel; they can stay at home and let change come to them. This simple truth will one day be recognized and then we will see a great reverse migration from Florida to Maine and on into Quebec."

Galbraith's forecast may still be too optimistic. The migration to the sun continues—and it will continue, some experts predict, well into the 21st century. Why shouldn't it? Americans say they prefer mild, sunny climates, and when asked where in the country these climates are, they point to the fast-growing lower half of the Pacific Coast, Florida, and anywhere along the South Atlantic and Gulf Coast Shore. Certainly this area, between 25 degrees and 35 degrees latitude, has been drawing migrants for decades.

But other places north of the Mason-Dixon line and hundreds of miles from ocean beaches benefit from population growth, and many of these enjoy mild climates, too. Some of these places might surprise you.

What has always been surprising is the enormous variety of global climates found right here at home. Northern maritime, extremely mild Mediterranean, southerly mountain, lowland desert, tropical "paradise," desert highland, rugged northern continental, windward slope, leeward slope, and humid subtropical climates—you name it, and you'll meet up with it somewhere in the United States.

The weather events that make up a place's climate—rain, snow, heat, cold, drought, wind—can vary, sometimes dramatically, from year to year. But climate is a part of your circumstances that can't be bought, built, remodeled, or relocated. A place's climate is there for keeps, and its seasonal patterns may have a profound effect on your life.

FACTORS THAT DETERMINE CLIMATE

Five geographic factors are major determinants of any area's climate: water, latitude, elevation, prevailing winds, and mountain ranges.

Large bodies of water, particularly oceans, take the edge off temperature. Water warms up slowly, holds much more heat than does land, and cools more slowly. Places near or surrounded by water tend to be cooler in summer and warmer in winter than others far from water. San Francisco, with water on three sides, experiences a marine climate that is one of the mildest and least changing in North America.

Places located in the middle of large land masses, away from the moderating effects of water, experience wide swings of temperature. These continental climates tend to be more rigorous in the higher latitudes. The closer to the poles you get, the more exaggerated are the seasonal shifts, because polar (and very northerly locations) undergo the greatest seasonal variation in the amount and intensity of sunlight. In Fairbanks, Alaska, for example, the average period between the sun's rising and setting during December is just 4 hours. But in late June, the period lengthens to more than 18 hours, and the sun's heat is intense. Places in the North and far North, then, can experience not only Siberian winters but also sun-baked summers.

Elevation, or height above sea level, has the same effect as a higher latitude. Each 1,000 feet of elevation lowers the average temperature by 3.3 degrees Fahrenheit. In New Mexico, for example, there are just 3 degrees of difference in annual average temperature between two weather stations at similar elevations, one in the extreme northeast and the other in the extreme southwest. However, at two weather stations just 15 miles apart, but differing in elevation by 4,700 feet, the average annual temperatures differ by 16 degrees.

In the United States, places that combine high altitudes with southerly latitudes seem to get the best of both North and South, enjoying the mild, short winters of the South and the cooler nights and crisp falls of the North. Asheville, North Carolina, in the southern Appa-

lachians, and Sante Fe, New Mexico, in the southern Rockies, have long been known for their mild, four-season climates.

To understand how prevailing winds influence climate, look at a pair of metro areas: Portland, Oregon, and Portland, Maine. Each is located at a rather northerly latitude. Both are also situated on ocean coasts. Thus one would naturally suppose that the two Portlands would be roughly the same type of climate. Why, then, is Portland, Oregon, so much milder? The answer lies in the prevailing winds that sweep across our continent. America's prevailing winds blow from west to east. Places along the West Coast receive the full impact of winds that have moved thousands of miles over water; cities even hundreds of miles inland still feel some of the beneficial effects of the Pacific winds. But inland cities in the East feel few consequences of the Atlantic save on those rare occasions when the prevailing wind direction *doesn't* prevail. And, sad to say, this reversal of wind direction often means a storm.

Mountain ranges help determine climate and weather because they act as giant barriers that deflect and channel winds and weather. The weather—and also climate—on one side of a mountain range is often radically different from that on the other. Because of this, mountain ranges are natural dividing points between climate zones.

Climatic Regions of the United States

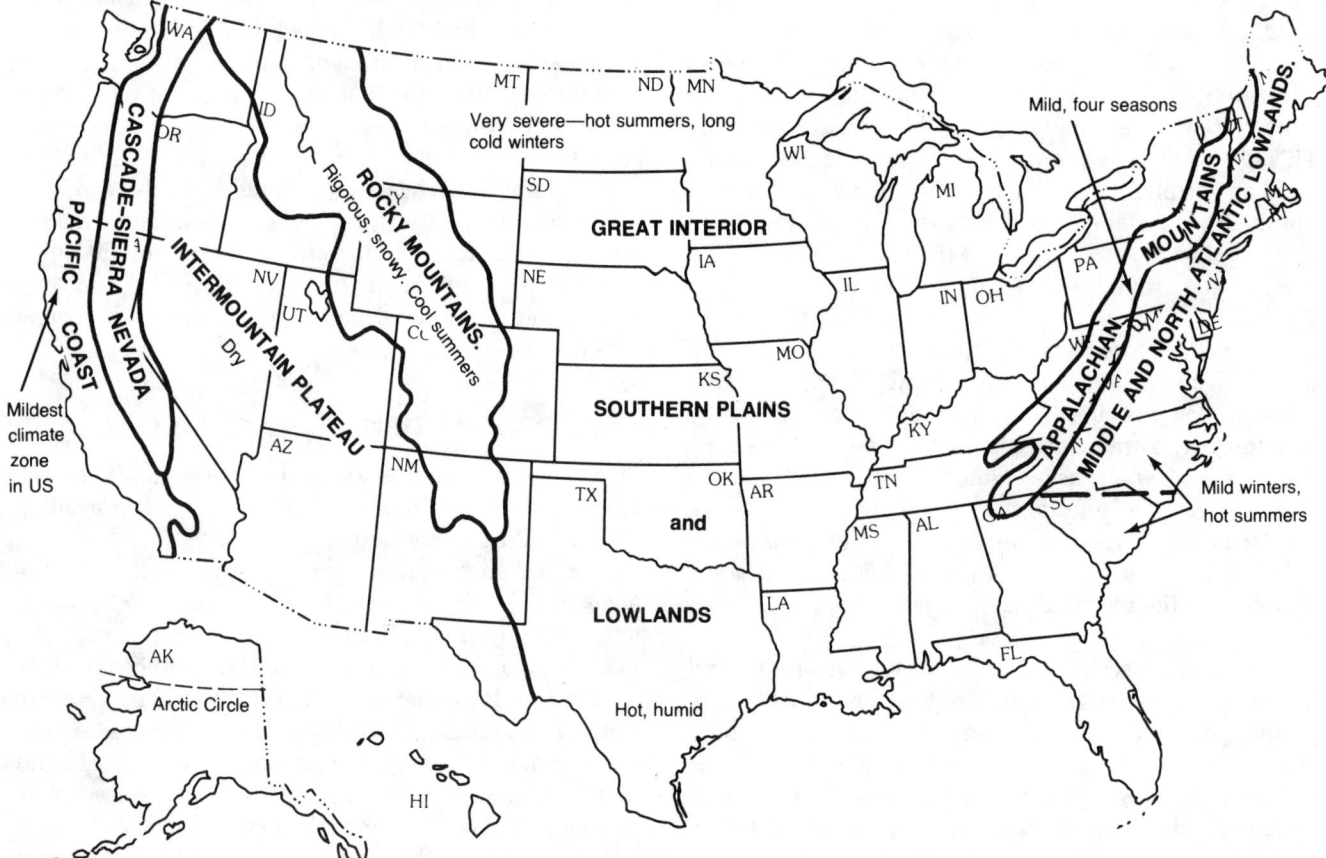

AMERICA'S MAJOR CLIMATIC REGIONS

Mountain ranges delineate the seven major climatic regions of the continental United States. The Pacific Coast is the mildest of these regions, and the northern portion of the Great Interior is the most rigorous. The Intermountain Plateau (which is also called the Great Basin), lying between the Sierra Nevada to the west and the Rocky Mountains to the east, is noted primarily for its dryness. Some of the best climates for variety and mildness are found in the southern portion of this area. The southern half of the Appalachian Mountains region also offers climates that are both mild and variable.

Most Americans live in the large climatic zone that includes the Great Interior, Southern Plains, and Low-lands regions. This zone, ironically, also happens to be the least desirable as far as mildness and human comfort are concerned. Those who live in its northern part are plagued by severe winters and hot, humid summers with very short springs and autumns. In the southern portion, winters are mild while springs and autumns are longer, but the steam-bath summers are very uncomfortable and debilitating. The climate of the East Coast, called the Middle and North Atlantic Lowlands, is similar to that of the Great Interior, but milder and somewhat damper. Right on the coast, winters are milder and summers are noticeably cooler. There are some excellent climates to be found in this region, especially in coastal locations.

The high-altitude regions that include the Rocky Mountains, the Cascades and Sierra Nevada, and the northern half of the Appalachian Mountains are resort areas because they all have cool, crisp, sunny summers with cold nights, and winters that provide plenty of snow for outdoor sports. These places are popular with people who enjoy a stimulating yet not too mild climate.

The Alaskan climate varies from bitterly cold in the northern tundra area—about one-fifth of the state lies north of the Arctic Circle—to relatively mild temperatures in the interior and southern regions. The southern area experiences abundant rainfall, the Aleutian Islands chain being one of the stormiest regions in the world.

Hawaii is the only state situated in the tropical zone. The islands undergo relatively small temperature changes, with summer temperatures averaging only 4 degrees to 8 degrees higher than those in winter. Moisture-bearing trade winds from over the Pacific have a moderating effect on the heat associated with a tropical climate.

SCORING: CLIMATE

Temperature affects human comfort and our daily range of activities more than any other climate-related variable. Bioclimatologists—scientists who study the connection between weather and health—generally agree that an average temperature of 65 degrees Fahrenheit with 65 percent humidity is ideal for work, play, and general well-being. *Places Rated* uses 65 degrees Fahrenheit as a

The 8 Coldest Metro Areas

	Zero-Degree Days per Year	Freezing Days per Year
Fargo–Moorhead, ND–MN	54	181
Duluth, MN–WI	51	187
Bismarck, ND	51	186
Anchorage, AK	41	192
Rochester, MN	35	165
Minneapolis–St. Paul, MN–WI	34	158
Sioux Falls, SD	33	171
Waterloo–Cedar Falls, IA	31	159

Listed above are those metro areas described in the Place Profiles that combine more than 30 zero-degree days per year with more than 150 freezing days.

The 12 Hottest Metro Areas

	90-Degree Days per Year	July Noon Relative Humidity
San Antonio, TX	111	55%
Fort Myers, FL	106	65
Orlando, FL	104	65
Brownsville–Harlingen, TX	102	55
Austin, TX	101	55
Corpus Christi, TX	96	65
Tallahassee, FL	87	65
Shreveport, LA	87	55
Jacksonville, FL	82	65
Mobile, AL	81	65
Tampa–St. Petersburg–Clearwater, FL	81	65
Houston, TX	81	60

Listed above are those metro areas described in the Place Profiles that combine 80 or more 90-degree days with a July noon relative humidity of 55 percent or higher. Three metro areas have more than 130 ninety-degree days per year—Phoenix, AZ (164); Tucson, AZ (139); and Las Vegas, NV (131)—but all of them have a July relative humidity of less than 30 percent.

The 10 Sunniest Metro Areas   ... and the 11 Drizzliest

	Clear Days per Year		Precipitation Days per Year
Chico, CA	219	Saginaw–Bay City–Midland, MI	181
Las Vegas, NV	216	Buffalo, NY	168
Phoenix, AZ	214	Syracuse, NY	168
Bakersfield, CA	202	Binghamton, NY	163
Fresno, CA	200	Olympia, WA	163
Tucson, AZ	198	Seattle, WA	160
El Paso, TX	194	Cleveland, OH	156
Sacramento, CA	193	Akron, OH	153
Santa Barbara–Santa Maria–Lompoc, CA	177	Burlington, VT	153
Santa Rosa–Petaluma, CA	176	Pittsburgh, PA	152
		Portland, OR	152

Listed above are those metro areas described in the Place Profiles that have more than 175 clear days per year or more than 150 precipitation days per year. A precipitation day is one on which at least .01 inch of precipitation falls.

standard for mildness in the discussions that follow.

Because most people tend to favor mild, sunny climates, *Places Rated* compares the 333 metro areas on the basis of climate mildness, using a combination of temperature and humidity factors. "Mild," as we use the term, does not necessarily mean warm but simply refers to the absence of great variations or extremes of temperature. A mild climate is characterized by cool summers and warm winters, with long falls and springs. *Places Rated* defines the mildest climates as those whose mean temperatures remain closest to 65 degrees Fahrenheit for the greatest percentage of time. Any deviations from this mean are labeled negative indicators, and are scored as such. Each place's final score indicates its climate mildness.

Nearly all climate and weather data presented in this chapter are from the National Oceanic and Atmospheric Administration (NOAA), the National Climatic Center, Asheville, North Carolina, and its three-volume publication *Local Climatological Data*. The National Climatic Center houses the world's largest climate data bank, with the equivalent of 25 miles of shelf space devoted solely to worldwide climate and weather data and research.

Some of the figures we present are referred to by the NOAA as 30-year normals—mean averages collected over three decades. Each ten years, the data for the new decade are added into the normal, and the data for the earliest ten years are dropped. Data are collected and averaged over this rather long period to flatten out irregularities and weather extremes. Atypical events such as blizzards and heat waves have little overall effect on a 30-year normal. Other figures are the means of annual records kept for periods ranging from a few years to more than 100 years. Mean temperatures are the average of the highest and lowest readings during a given period. For example, to determine the mean temperature for a particular month, the mean maximum temperature (the average of the highest daily readings during the month) and the mean minimum temperature (the average of the lowest) are averaged.

Each metro area is given a base number of 1,000 points, from which points are subtracted according to the following indicators, based on yearly averages:

1. *Very hot and very cold months.* Ten points are subtracted for each month in which the mean temperature is above 70 degrees or below 32. An additional 10 points are subtracted, for a total of 20 points, if the mean temperature is above 80 degrees or below 20.
2. *Seasonal temperature variation.* The difference in degrees Fahrenheit between the summer mean maximum temperature and the winter mean minimum is subtracted from the base score.
3. *Heating- and cooling-degree days.* The total number of these days per year is divided by 50, and the result is subtracted from the score. The base temperature for arriving at heating- and cooling-degree days is 65 degrees, the standard established by the American gas industry. If, for example, the average temperature on a summer day is 66 degrees, 1 degree of cooling is necessary, which counts as 1 cooling-degree day. Similarly, if the average temperature on a particular winter day is 55 degrees, 10 degrees of heating are needed, yielding 10 heating-degree days.
4. *Freezing days.* One point is subtracted for each day on which the average temperature is 32 degrees or below.
5. *Zero-degree days.* Five additional points are subtracted for each day the temperature drops to zero or below.
6. *Ninety-degree days.* Since relative humidity has a profound effect on felt heat and daily temperature range, points are subtracted in accordance with each location's mean relative humidity at noon in July, when high temperatures are most likely to occur (see the map on page 379). For each day with a high of at least 90 degrees, 4 points are subtracted if the metro area's July relative humidity is more than 60 percent, 3 points if relative humidity is 51 percent to 60 percent, 2 points if relative humidity is 41 percent to 50 percent, and 1 point if relative humidity is 40 percent or lower.

SCORING EXAMPLES

Phoenix and San Francisco experience dramatically contrasting climate types: desert and marine.

Phoenix, AZ (#176)

If Phoenix's summertime temperatures of 40 years ago were to have persisted to this day, the Arizona capital might be rated much higher than the ranking of 176 by *Places Rated's* standards for climate mildness.

According to climatologists at Arizona State University (ASU), afternoon high temperatures during June, July, and August have remained constant over the years, but low temperatures during those months are now 8 degrees hotter than they were in 1948. These 8 degrees make the difference between formerly bearable warm nights and currently oppressive, hot ones. The change is due to the extraordinary twelvefold increase in population since the end of World War II.

Long-time residents who recall the old desert-cowtown days blame the heat on humidity caused by evaporating surface water in swimming pools, fountains, and man-made lakes. Actually, atmospheric moisture hasn't changed much since the late 1940s.

According to the ASU scientists, modern Phoenix, with a population of 1.8 million, has classic "urban heat island" characteristics: (1) the ability of concrete and asphalt to absorb and store more radiant energy than natural vegetation and soil, (2) low winds, (3) man-made sources of heat, especially the automobile, and (4) a persistent high-pressure cell that traps air pollution, creating a blanket effect.

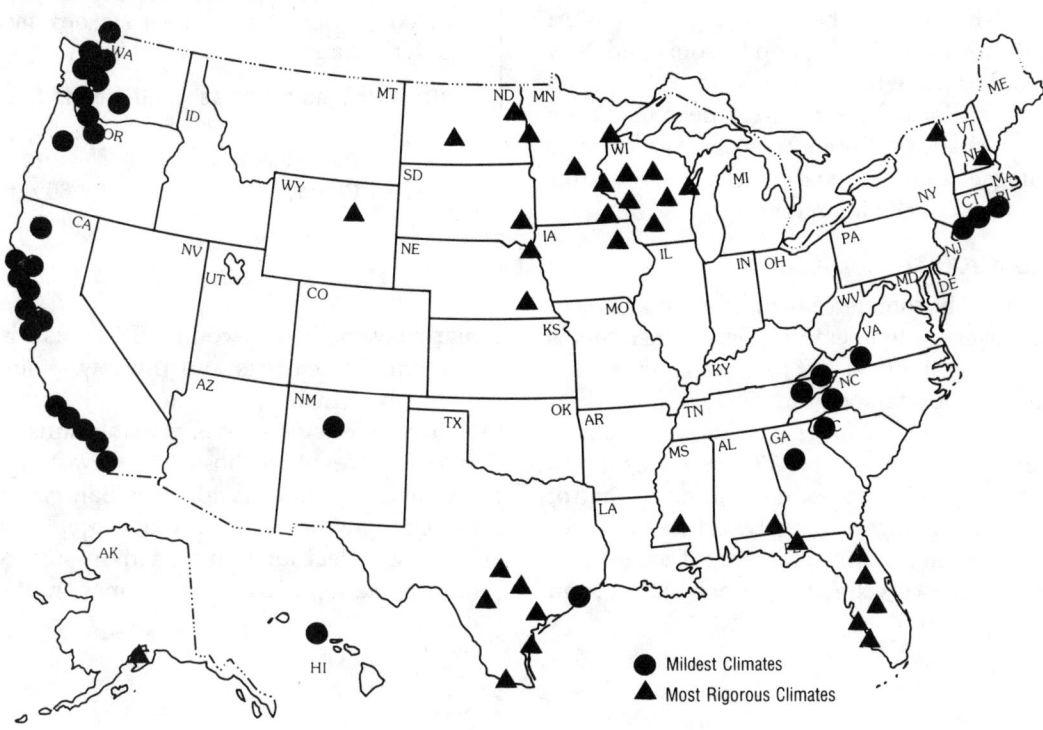

Places Rated's Mildest and Wildest Metro Areas

● Mildest Climates
▲ Most Rigorous Climates

Mild and Wild

With such a large variety of climates in the United States, there naturally is a mix of places around the country qualifying for the descriptions "mild" and "wild."

The area of greatest mildness is the Pacific Coast, as the map "Places Rated's Mildest and Wildest Metro Areas" illustrates. This region contains 23 of the 35 top-ranked climates. The California metro areas owe their high ratings in part to their southerly locations, but all 23 (as well as the Honolulu metro area) are indebted to the moderating influence of the Pacific, which reduces their seasonal shifts to a minimum and practically rules out any zero-degree or 90-degree days.

The second mildest region in America is located in the southern Appalachian Mountains, in sections of Georgia, North and South Carolina, Tennessee, and Virginia. Here, southerly latitudes provide mild winters and long springs and falls, while high elevations offer relief from the hot, muggy summers that plague most other southern locations.

Other mild areas are to be found along the Atlantic coast in New York and Connecticut, and in the southern tip of the Rocky Mountains, near Albuquerque. This mountain region resembles the southern Appalachians, except that it is noticeably drier.

The climates of America's most rigorous metro areas are characterized by great swings in temperature from season to season and from day to day. They have either a winter that is cold and long, a summer that is long, hot, and humid, or both. Most of these rigorous places are located inside the wide band stretching up the center of the continent that is known as the Great Interior.

Besides the northern and southern extremes of the Great Interior, rigorous climates are found in Alaska, northern New England, the northern Rockies, and the Florida peninsula. A characteristic of all these places is an excessive number of 90-degree days and/or zero-degree days.

In a few areas, good and bad weather bump up against each other. Metro areas located in northern New England experience long, cold, snowy winters and a lot of cloudiness, and thus we find Burlington, Vermont, and Manchester, New Hampshire, near the bottom of the Places Rated climate list. However, not far from up-country New Hampshire are the coastal waters of Cape Ann, Massachusetts, and the mild climate of Salem–Gloucester.

Similarly, although the neighboring Texas metro areas of Brownsville–Harlingen and McAllen–Edinburg–Mission have rigorous climates because of the excessive heat and humidity during the summer, Galveston–Texas City, with its coastal location and sea breezes, ranks as one of America's mildest metro areas.

There can be no doubt that temperatures in the Valley of the Sun are mild much of the year. Catch a televised Phoenix Cardinals football game in November and you may wish you were there. The biggest comfort liability here, however, is a period from mid-May through September when temperatures rarely drop to 65 degrees at night and usually exceed 100 degrees during the day. More than any other climate factor, it is Phoenix's intense summer heat that influences this metro area's mediocre climate rating.

San Francisco, CA (#1)

Beware of chamber of commerce blandishments about a place's annual average temperature. San Francisco's is 57 degrees. So is St. Louis's. But San Francisco enjoys both a diurnal (24 hour) temperature range of 12 degrees and an annual range (the difference between January's and July's average temperatures) of 12 degrees. St. Louis has a diurnal range of 17 degrees and an annual range of 47. The temperature swings in these two cities highlight the difference between a marine climate and a continental climate. San Francisco's climate is somewhat cool and

remarkably stable year-round. St. Louis's is neither.

In spite of sea fogs and the low stratus associated with them (which appeals to many San Franciscans), this metro area's percent of possible sunshine is greater than that of New York, Boston, and Washington, DC. But more than any other factor, it is San Francisco's infrequent extremes of heat and cold, coupled with a temperature range ideal for human activity and comfort, that produces the top *Places Rated* climate rating.

> ### Behind Every Silver Lining . . .
>
> The National Oceanic and Atomospheric Administration (NOAA), at each of its weather stations, measures local cloudiness during daylight hours only.
>
> **NOAA defines a day as . . . if clouds form**
>
> | | |
> |---|---|
> | Clear | 0% to 30% |
> | Partly cloudy | 40% to 70% |
> | Cloudy | 80% to 100% |
> | | **of the sky cover.** |

Rankings: Climate

Six criteria are used to determine a score for climate mildness: (1) very hot and very cold months, (2) seasonal temperature variation, (3) heating- and cooling-degree days, (4) freezing days, (5) zero-degree days, and (6) ninety-degree days.

Because the NOAA publication *Local Climatological Data* does not provide specific data for all metro areas, the scores for some places are calculated from data for

the nearest substation (this information appears in the *NOAA Series 20*). Scores arrived at in this way are enclosed in parentheses. Metro areas that receive tie scores are given the same rank and are listed in alphabetical order.

Those metro areas described in the Place Profiles later on in this chapter are shown in boldface type in the lists below.

Metro Areas from Best to Worst

Places Rated Rank	Places Rated Score	Places Rated Rank	Places Rated Score	Places Rated Rank	Places Rated Score
1. Oakland, CA	(910)	12. **Seattle, WA**	808	27. Redding, CA	664
1. **San Francisco, CA**	910	12. Tacoma, WA	(808)	27. Richland–Kennewick–Pasco, WA	(664)
3. **San Diego, CA**	903	15. Bellingham, WA	(772)	29. **Johnson City–Kingsport–Bristol, TN–VA**	663
4. Oxnard–Ventura, CA	(890)			30. **Albuquerque, NM**	659
5. Anaheim–Santa Ana, CA	885	16. **Portland, OR**	768		
		16. Vancouver, WA	(768)	31. Nassau–Suffolk, NY	(656)
5. **Los Angeles–Long Beach, CA**	885	18. Eugene–Springfield, OR	741	32. **Greenville–Spartanburg, SC**	655
5. **Santa Barbara–Santa Maria–Lompoc, CA**	885	19. Santa Rosa–Petaluma, CA	(732)	33. **Roanoke, VA**	652
		20. Galveston–Texas City, TX	(727)	34. Bridgeport–Milford, CT	648
8. San Jose, CA	(850)	21. **Olympia, WA**	726	34. Norwalk, CT	(648)
9. Salinas–Seaside–Monterey, CA	(843)	22. **Honolulu, HI**	717		
9. Santa Cruz, CA	(843)	23. Salem, OR	716	34. Stamford, CT	(648)
		24. **Atlanta, GA**	696	37. **Raleigh–Durham, NC**	647
		25. Asheville, NC	694	38. **Charlotte–Gastonia–Rock Hill, NC–SC**	644
11. Vallejo–Fairfield–Napa, CA	(821)				
12. Bremerton, WA	(808)	26. **Knoxville, TN**	670		

Places Rated Rank	Places Rated Score	Places Rated Rank	Places Rated Score	Places Rated Rank	Places Rated Score
38. Salem–Gloucester, MA	(644)	94. Richmond–Petersburg, VA	585	151. Fayetteville–Springdale, AR	(549)
40. Fall River, MA–RI	(643)	95. Biloxi–Gulfport, MS	(584)	151. Kansas City, MO–KS	549
				153. Lawrence–Haverhill, MA–NH	(548)
40. New Bedford, MA	(643)	95. Cincinnati, OH–KY–IN	584	153. Syracuse, NY	548
42. Lynchburg, VA	642	95. Pascagoula, MS	(584)	153. Utica–Rome, NY	(548)
43. Modesto, CA	(639)	98. New Haven–Meriden, CT	(583)		
44. New York, NY	638	98. New London–Norwich, CT–RI	(583)	156. Johnstown, PA	(547)
45. Burlington, NC	(637)			157. Ann Arbor, MI	(546)
		100. Melbourne–Titusville–Palm Bay, FL	(582)	157. Florence, AL	(546)
46. Huntington–Ashland, WV–KY–OH	636			159. Danville, VA	(545)
46. Trenton, NJ	(636)	101. Joplin, MO	(580)	159. South Bend–Mishawaka, IN	(545)
48. Lexington–Fayette, KY	635	101. Merced, CA	(580)		
49. Miami–Hialeah, FL	634	101. Muskegon, MI	580	161. Clarksville–Hopkinsville, TN–KY	(544)
50. Norfolk–Virginia Beach–Newport News, VA	632	104. Cleveland, OH	579	161. Dallas, TX	544
		104. Lorain–Elyria, OH	(579)	161. Dayton–Springfield, OH	544
51. Washington, DC–MD–VA	631			161. Springfield, MO	544
52. Philadelphia, PA–NJ	630	106. Chattanooga, TN–GA	576	165. Visalia–Tulare–Porterville, CA	(543)
53. Charleston, WV	627	106. Sacramento, CA	576		
54. Greensboro–Winston-Salem–High Point, NC	626	108. Akron, OH	575		
55. Stockton, CA	625	108. Brockton, MA	(575)	166. Hamilton–Middletown, OH	(542)
		108. Canton, OH	(575)	166. Savannah, GA	542
56. Boston, MA	623			166. Steubenville–Weirton, OH–WV	(542)
56. Hickory, NC	(623)	108. Scranton–Wilkes-Barre, PA	575	166. Wheeling, WV–OH	(542)
58. Charlottesville, VA	(618)	108. State College, PA	(575)	170. Columbia, MO	(541)
59. Parkersburg–Marietta, WV–OH	617	113. Spokane, WA	574		
60. Louisville, KY–IN	616	114. Fort Lauderdale–Hollywood–Pompano Beach, FL	(572)	170. Salt Lake City–Ogden, UT	541
		115. Buffalo, NY	571	172. Flint, MI	540
61. Atlantic City, NJ	615			172. York, PA	(540)
61. Monmouth–Ocean, NJ	(615)	116. Sharon, PA	(570)	174. Nashua, NH	(538)
61. Riverside–San Bernardino, CA	(615)	116. Youngstown–Warren, OH	570	175. St. Louis, MO–IL	537
61. Sante Fe, NM	(615)	118. Charleston, SC	569		
61. Vineland–Millville–Bridgeton, NJ	(615)	118. Danbury, CT	(569)	176. Detroit, MI	536
		118. Waterbury, CT	(569)	176. Fort Walton Beach, FL	(536)
66. Reading, PA	(614)			176. Panama City, FL	536
67. Birmingham, AL	612	121. Hagerstown, MD	(568)	176. Pensacola, FL	536
68. Medford, OR	611	122. Baltimore, MD	567	176. Phoenix, AZ	536
69. Amarillo, TX	609	123. Benton Harbor, MI	(566)		
70. Yuba City, CA	(608)	124. Jacksonville, NC	(564)	176. Rochester, NY	536
		124. Wilmington, NC	564	182. Reno, NV	535
71. Erie, PA	605			182. Yakima, WA	535
72. Lubbock, TX	604	126. Worcester, MA	562	184. Augusta, GA–SC	534
73. Chico, CA	(603)	127. Altoona, PA	(561)	185. Anderson, IN	(530)
73. Midland, TX	603	127. Daytona Beach, FL	(561)		
73. Odessa, TX	(603)	127. Fayetteville, NC	(561)	185. Muncie, IN	(530)
		130. Anniston, AL	(560)	185. Tulsa, OK	530
76. Fort Pierce, FL	(602)			188. Fort Worth–Arlington, TX	(528)
77. Athens, GA	601	130. Bakersfield, CA	560	189. Battle Creek, MI	(527)
77. Jersey City, NJ	(601)	132. Allentown–Bethlehem, PA–NJ	559	189. Kalamazoo, MI	(527)
77. Newark, NJ	601	132. Bergen–Passaic, NJ	(559)		
80. Decatur, AL	(600)	132. Fresno, CA	559	191. Colorado Springs, CO	526
		132. Lancaster, PA	559	191. Columbia, SC	526
80. Huntsville, AL	600			191. Gadsden, AL	(526)
80. Nashville, TN	600	132. Middlesex–Somerset–Hunterdon, NJ	(559)	191. Lowell, MA–NH	526
83. Wilmington, DE–NJ–MD	597	137. Bloomington, IN	(558)	195. Champaign–Urbana–Rantoul, IL	(525)
84. Middletown, CT	(593)	137. Columbus, OH	558		
85. Boise City, ID	592	137. Mansfield, OH	558	196. Owensboro, KY	(524)
		137. Williamsport, PA	558	196. Sherman–Denison, TX	(524)
85. El Paso, TX	592			196. Springfield, IL	524
87. Anderson, SC	(591)	141. Indianapolis, IN	557	199. Lima, OH	(522)
87. Cumberland, MD–WV	(591)	141. Terre Haute, IN	(557)	200. Abilene, TX	521
89. Tucson, AZ	589	143. Harrisburg–Lebanon–Carlisle, PA	(556)		
90. Beaver County, PA	(586)	143. Las Vegas, NV	556	200. Denver, CO	521
		145. Niagara Falls, NY	(554)	200. Elkhart–Goshen, IN	(521)
90. Pawtucket–Woonsocket–Attleboro, RI–MA	(586)			203. Alexandria, LA	520
		145. Oklahoma City, OK	554	204. Jackson, MI	(518)
90. Pittsburgh, PA	586	147. Florence, SC	(552)	204. Toledo, OH	518
90. Providence, RI	586	147. Las Cruces, NM	(552)		
		149. Binghamton, NY	550	206. Columbus, GA–AL	(517)
		149. Evansville, IN–KY	550	207. Bristol, CT	(516)
				207. Hartford, CT	516

Places Rated Rank	Places Rated Score
207. New Britain, CT	(516)
210. **Saginaw–Bay City–Midland, MI**	(515)
211. **Chicago, IL**	514
211. Lake County, IL	514
211. **Memphis, TN–AR–MS**	514
214. **Grand Rapids, MI**	513
214. Lawrence, KS	(513)
216. Kokomo, IN	(512)
217. Cheyenne, WY	(509)
217. **Fort Wayne, IN**	509
217. Orange County, NY	(509)
217. West Palm Beach–Boca Raton–Delray Beach, FL	509
221. **Shreveport, LA**	508
222. Fitchburg–Leominster, MA	(507)
223. Topeka, KS	501
224. Longview–Marshall, TX	(500)
224. Provo–Orem, UT	(500)
224. Tyler, TX	(500)
227. **New Orleans, LA**	498
228. **Little Rock–North Little Rock, AR**	497
228. Pueblo, CO	497
230. Kenosha, WI	(496)
230. Racine, WI	(496)
232. Lafayette–West Lafayette, IN	(494)
232. **Wichita, KS**	494
234. **Peoria, IL**	491
235. Fort Collins–Loveland, CO	(490)
235. Greeley, CO	(490)
235. Lewiston–Auburn, ME	(490)
238. Jackson, TN	(488)
238. Poughkeepsie, NY	(488)
238. **San Angelo, TX**	488
241. Bloomington–Normal, IL	(487)
242. Gary–Hammond, IN	(483)
242. Kankakee, IL	(483)
242. **Montgomery, AL**	483
242. **Portland, ME**	483
246. **Fort Smith, AR–OK**	482
246. Pittsfield, MA	(482)
248. Decatur, IL	(480)
248. Lansing–East Lansing, MI	480
250. Joliet, IL	(479)
250. Lawton, OK	(479)

Places Rated Rank	Places Rated Score
252. **Albany–Schenectady–Troy, NY**	476
252. Glens Falls, NY	(476)
254. St. Joseph, MO	(475)
255. Aurora–Elgin, IL	(474)
256. Tuscaloosa, AL	(470)
257. Lake Charles, LA	469
257. Portsmouth–Dover–Rochester, NH–ME	(469)
259. Albany, GA	(468)
260. Elmira, NY	(467)
260. Texarkana, TX–Texarkana, AR	(467)
262. Janesville–Beloit, WI	(466)
262. **Rockford, IL**	466
264. Pine Bluff, AR	(463)
265. Enid, OK	(461)
266. **Milwaukee, WI**	460
267. Boulder–Longmont, CO	(459)
268. **Jacksonville, FL**	457
268. **Orlando, FL**	457
270. Wichita Falls, TX	456
271. Monroe, LA	(455)
272. Springfield, MA	(453)
273. **Billings, MT**	452
274. **Bangor, ME**	(451)
275. Macon–Warner Robins, GA	(447)
276. **Des Moines, IA**	444
277. **Mobile, AL**	442
277. Sheboygan, WI	(442)
279. Bradenton, FL	(440)
279. **Brownsville–Harlingen, TX**	440
279. **Davenport–Rock Island–Moline, IA–IL**	440
279. **Omaha, NE–IA**	440
279. **Tampa–St. Petersburg–Clearwater, FL**	440
284. **Austin, TX**	435
285. Cedar Rapids, IA	(434)
285. Iowa City, IA	(434)
287. Lafayette, LA	(429)
288. Baton Rouge, LA	427
288. Houma–Thibodaux, LA	(427)
290. **Houston, TX**	424
290. Laredo, TX	(424)

Places Rated Rank	Places Rated Score
292. Beaumont–Port Arthur, TX	423
292. Brazoria, TX	(423)
294. Dubuque, IA	419
295. **Jackson, MS**	412
295. Waco, TX	412
297. **Great Falls, MT**	410
298. **Manchester, NH**	(404)
298. **Tallahassee, FL**	404
300. Gainesville, FL	(402)
301. **Casper, WY**	401
302. **Lincoln, NE**	398
302. **San Antonio, TX**	398
304. Appleton–Oshkosh–Neenah, WI	(396)
305. Sarasota, FL	(391)
306. Sioux City, IA–NE	385
307. **Bryan–College Station, TX**	(383)
307. **Burlington, VT**	383
309. **Madison, WI**	378
310. Rapid City, SD	(373)
311. **Green Bay, WI**	367
312. Killeen–Temple, TX	(365)
313. **Corpus Christi, TX**	362
314. **La Crosse, WI**	352
315. Naples, FL	(348)
316. **Waterloo–Cedar Falls, IA**	(347)
317. **Fort Myers–Cape Coral, FL**	(342)
318. Dothan, AL	(336)
318. Victoria, TX	336
320. Ocala, FL	(333)
321. **Rochester, MN**	308
321. Wausau, WI	(308)
323. Lakeland–Winter Haven, FL	(307)
324. **Minneapolis–St. Paul, MN–WI**	293
325. **Sioux Falls, SD**	276
326. Eau Claire, WI	257
327. McAllen–Edinburg–Mission, TX	(238)
328. **Anchorage, AK**	195
329. St. Cloud, MN	(195)
330. **Duluth, MN–WI**	193
331. **Bismarck, ND**	149
332. **Fargo–Moorhead, ND–MN**	148
333. Grand Forks, ND	(105)

RELOCATION RESOURCES

If climate is a factor in your decision about where to move, these publications may be helpful.

How does your climate compare? Meteorologists at the National Climatic Data Center can take your order for comparative data the center publishes for any of thousands of locations in this country.

The Center's best-seller is the annual *Comparative Climatic Data for the United States*, a collection of month-by-month and annual summaries for normal daily maximum and minimum temperature, average and maximum wind speed, percentage of possible sunshine, rainfall, snowfall, and morning and afternoon humidity at each of 300 "first order" weather stations in this country. The cost is $3, plus $5 handling and shipping.

If the place you have in mind doesn't have a first order weather station, it may yet be one of the 1,063 locations with a "cooperative" weather station. Their data are in *Climatography of the United States, Series 20,* a two-page publication for each location containing freeze and precipitation probability data; tables of long-term monthly and annual mean maximum, mean minimum, and average temperature; and tables of monthly and annual total precipitation and total snowfall. The cost is $1 per location, plus $5 handling and shipping.

All orders must be prepaid by check, MasterCard, Visa, or American Express. Call or write

National Climatic Data Center
Federal Building
Asheville, NC 28801
(704) 259-0682

Place Profiles: Climate

The pages that follow are brief profiles of 141 weather stations, which were carefully selected to present a sampling of reports from weather stations all over the country. The figures given in each profile come from extensive government data tables. The narrative summaries, describing climate and terrain, are condensations of those that appear in the NOAA publication *Local Climatological Data*.

These summaries provide brief descriptions of each location and point out important or distinctive features of the climate and the local terrain. When terrain is described in the profiles, it is usually in connection with the effect—if any—it has on the climate in the immediate area. But few people would deny that terrain is an important element in its own right; to many it's as important as climate. Some people prefer mountains or seacoast, others rolling plains or forest. Rather than attempt to judge, rate, or score terrain, *Places Rated* simply describes it briefly and lets you decide.

The table of average temperatures on the right-hand side of each profile is a detailed and extremely useful set of data, from which you can get a clear idea of the temperature ranges, averages, and extremes of each place. For example, if you want to know how hot it gets in Albuquerque in July, simply look at the table in Albuquerque's profile. There you'll see that in July the daily high temperatures (which usually occur in midafternoon) average 92.2 degrees Fahrenheit. That sounds hot, and it is. But note that the average low, or minimum, temperature for the same month is only 65.2 degrees. The minimum temperature generally occurs in the early hours of the morning. Even a quick glance at these temperatures will tell you that Albuquerque in the

summer has hot days and cool nights, with a mean temperature of less than 80 degrees (78.7). This is in keeping with Albuquerque's dry, desert location and altitude of about 5,000 feet.

Rounding out the weather picture of each locale are data such as wind speed, amount of snow and rain, number of heating- and cooling-degree days, clear and cloudy days, storms, very hot and cold days, and precipitation days (days on which there is at least .01 inch of precipitation). To derive the greatest benefit from these assorted indicators, compare two or more metro areas. Which has more snow? More rain? More 90-degree days? Comparing two places you're interested in may help you decide which to visit first.

A unique visual device in each profile is the circular graph showing the length of each season. These graphs are prepared from a formula developed by *Places Rated* and reflect the theory that seasonal change should be defined and measured by weather conditions, human activities, and growth or dormancy of plant life rather than by the calendar. In *Places Rated Almanac*, the seasons are defined as follows: Summer begins when the mean monthly temperature rises above 60 degrees Fahrenheit; summer ends when it falls below 60. Winter begins when the average daily low falls below 32 degrees and ends when it rises above that mark. The remaining portions of the year constitute fall and spring. (In the seasonal graphs, winter is shown by the black segments, spring and fall appear as gray, and summer is white.)

A star (★) preceding a metro area's name highlights it as one of the top 30 places in the country for climate mildness.

Abilene, TX

Terrain: Rolling plains, treeless except for mesquite, broken by low hills to the south and west. Land rises gently to the south and east. Primarily cattle-grazing terrain, with some dry-land cotton and feed.

Climate: Lies roughly midway between the humid climate of East Texas and the semiarid climate to the west and north. Most rain occurs in thunderstorms during April, May, June, September, and October. Severe storms or tornadoes are rare. Summer brings hot days and cool nights, with temperatures dropping to the 60s or 70s most nights. High summer temperatures are usually associated with clear skies, southwesterly winds, and dry air. Low relative humidity, however, makes the climate comfortable. The region receives almost 70% of possible sunshine over the year. Rapid temperature changes occur in winter, as polar air replaces warm, moist tropical air. Temperatures may fall 30 degrees in one hour. Strongest winds come from the north and often bring cold and severe weather.

Pluses: Warm, sunny, and dry.

Minuses: Hot summer days; can be dusty.

Places Rated Score: 521   **Places Rated Rank: 200**

Elevation: 1,790 feet

Relative Humidity: 59%
Wind Speed: 12.2 mph

Seasonal Change

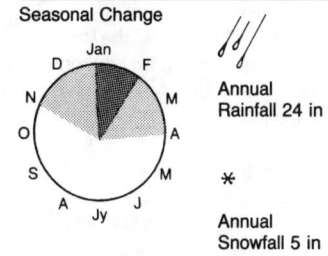

Annual Rainfall 24 in

Annual Snowfall 5 in

Clear 148 days   Partly Cloudy 98 days   Cloudy 119 days

Precipitation Days: 65   Storm Days: 42

Average Temperatures			
	Daily High	Daily Low	Monthly Mean
January	55.7	31.7	43.7
February	59.9	35.9	47.9
March	67.3	41.7	54.5
April	77.7	52.7	65.2
May	83.9	60.8	72.4
June	91.6	69.0	80.3
July	95.3	72.4	83.9
August	95.3	71.9	83.6
September	87.5	64.6	76.1
October	78.0	54.2	66.1
November	66.2	42.0	54.1
December	58.2	34.5	46.4

Zero-Degree Days: 0
Freezing Days: 56
90-Degree Days: 89
Heating- and Cooling-Degree Days: 5,076

Akron, OH

Terrain: Rolling, with highest elevations almost 1,300 feet above sea level. Many small lakes provide water for local industry as well as recreation for the densely populated region. The area is mainly industrial; the number of agricultural operations has diminished rapidly in recent years.

Climate: Lake Erie has a considerable effect on area weather, tempering cold air masses during the winter and contributing to brief but heavy snow squalls until the lake freezes over. Snowfall is much heavier north of the weather station near the lake, in the area commonly referred to as the Snow Belt. Spring comes late here. Summers are moderately warm, though humid. September, October, and November are pleasant, but there is considerable morning fog. Average date of last freeze: April 30. First freeze: October 22.

Pluses: Pleasant falls.

Minuses: Cold, wet winters with heavy snowfalls; damp and cloudy.

Places Rated Score: 575   **Places Rated Rank: 108**

Elevation: 1,027 feet

Relative Humidity: 71%
Wind Speed: 9.9 mph

Seasonal Change

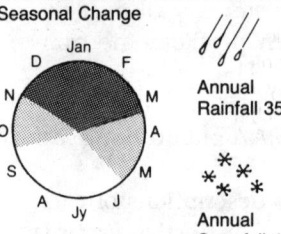

Annual
Rainfall 35 in

Annual
Snowfall 48 in

Clear
70 days

Partly Cloudy
101 days

Cloudy
194 days

Precipitation Days: 153 Storm Days: 40

Average Temperatures			
	Daily High	Daily Low	Monthly Mean
January	33.9	18.6	26.3
February	36.0	19.4	27.7
March	45.4	26.9	36.2
April	59.3	37.7	48.5
May	69.8	47.5	58.7
June	79.4	57.1	68.3
July	82.6	60.8	71.7
August	81.3	59.3	70.3
September	74.7	52.7	63.7
October	63.7	42.8	53.3
November	48.6	32.7	40.7
December	36.5	22.2	29.4

Zero-Degree Days: 5
Freezing Days: 128
90-Degree Days: 7
Heating- and Cooling-Degree Days: 6,858

Albany–Schenectady–Troy, NY

Terrain: On the west bank of the Hudson River 150 miles north of New York City and 8 miles south of the confluence of the Hudson and Mohawk Rivers. The point at which the city meets the river is only a few feet above sea level. Eleven miles west, the Helderberg escarpment rises to between 1,400 and 1,800 feet. To the east is a rugged valley floor rising to hills 1,600 to 2,000 feet high. The valley floor on which the city is located is gently rolling.

Climate: Harsh continental but subject to some moderating influences from the Atlantic, to the south. Winters are cold and occasionally severe. Maximum temperatures during cold months often do not rise above 32° F. In the warmer months, temperatures rise quickly during the day to moderate levels, then fall rapidly at night to moderate to cool. Occasional hot spells of a week or so occur during the summer. The growing season is about 160 days, long for a city in this latitude. Average date of last freeze: April 27. First freeze: October 13.

Pluses: Cool summer nights.

Minuses: Cold, snowy winters.

Places Rated Score: 476   **Places Rated Rank: 252**

Elevation: 292 feet

Relative Humidity: 71%
Wind Speed: 8.9 mph

Seasonal Change

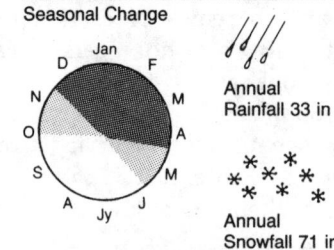

Annual
Rainfall 33 in

Annual
Snowfall 71 in

Clear
71 days

Partly Cloudy
111 days

Cloudy
183 days

Precipitation Days: 135 Storm Days: 28

Average Temperatures			
	Daily High	Daily Low	Monthly Mean
January	30.4	12.5	21.5
February	32.7	14.3	23.5
March	42.6	24.2	33.4
April	58.0	35.7	46.9
May	69.7	45.7	57.7
June	79.4	55.6	67.5
July	83.9	60.1	72.0
August	81.4	57.8	69.6
September	73.7	50.1	61.9
October	62.8	40.0	51.4
November	48.1	31.1	39.6
December	34.1	17.7	25.9

Zero-Degree Days: 17
Freezing Days: 155
90-Degree Days: 8
Heating- and Cooling-Degree Days: 7,462

★ Albuquerque, NM

Terrain: Rests in the Rio Grande Valley 55 miles southwest of Santa Fe, and is surrounded by mountains, most of them to the east. These mountainous areas receive more precipitation than does the city proper. With an annual rainfall of 8 inches, only the most hardy desert flora can grow. However, successful farming—primarily fruit and produce—is carried out in the valley by irrigation.

Climate: Arid continental. No muggy days. Half the moisture falls between July and September in the form of brief but severe thunderstorms. Long drizzles are unknown. These storms do not greatly interfere with outdoor activities, and they have a moderating effect on the heat. The hottest month is July, with temperatures reaching 90° F almost constantly. However, the low humidity and cool nights make the heat much less felt.

Pluses: Sunny and dry, with mild winters.

Minuses: Dust storms.

Places Rated Score: 659   **Places Rated Rank: 30**

Elevation: 5,314 feet

Relative Humidity: 43%
Wind Speed: 9 mph

Seasonal Change

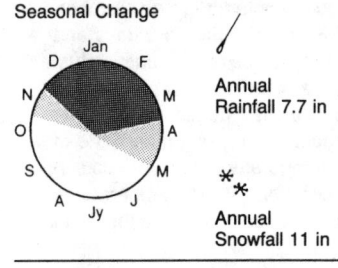

Annual
Rainfall 7.7 in

Annual
Snowfall 11 in

Clear
172 days

Partly Cloudy
111 days

Cloudy
82 days

Precipitation Days: 59 Storm Days: 43

Average Temperatures			
	Daily High	Daily Low	Monthly Mean
January	46.9	23.5	35.2
February	52.6	27.4	40.0
March	59.2	32.3	45.8
April	70.1	41.4	55.8
May	79.9	50.7	65.3
June	89.5	59.7	74.6
July	92.2	65.2	78.7
August	89.7	63.4	76.6
September	83.4	56.7	70.1
October	71.7	44.7	58.2
November	57.1	31.8	44.5
December	47.5	24.9	36.2

Zero-Degree Days: 1
Freezing Days: 123
90-Degree Days: 61
Heating- and Cooling-Degree Days: 5,608

Alexandria, LA

Terrain: Located along the Red River in the geographic center of the state. The area is heavily wooded and is the site of the Kisatchie National Forest. The river is lined by high levees, which protect the surrounding land and cities from floods. The terrain is mostly flat.
Climate: Generally subtropical and humid. The winter months are mild, with short cold spells that occur when severely cold air moving across the Plains and the Mississippi Valley invades the city. Snowfall here is negligible, averaging less than an inch a year. Rainfall is heavy in all seasons. Summers are hot, humid, and uncomfortable, but temperatures in April, May, and especially late September through November are pleasant. Severe storms, including hailstorms and tornadoes, occur in all seasons.

Pluses: Mild winters.

Minuses: Hot and humid; stormy.

Places Rated Score: 520   **Places Rated Rank: 203**

Elevation: 118 feet

Relative Humidity: 77%
Wind Speed: 6.2 mph

Seasonal Change

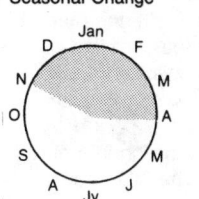

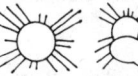
Annual Rainfall 54 in

Annual Snowfall .7 in

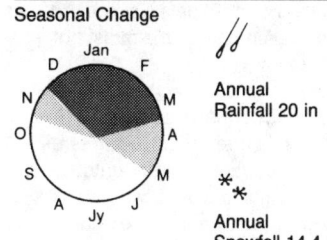

Clear	Partly Cloudy	Cloudy
110 days	109 days	146 days

Precipitation Days: 106   Storm Days: 69

Average Temperatures			
	Daily High	Daily Low	Monthly Mean
January	58.6	36.7	47.7
February	61.8	39.2	50.5
March	68.3	44.3	56.3
April	76.9	54.1	65.5
May	83.7	60.8	72.3
June	89.6	67.5	78.6
July	91.4	70.4	80.9
August	91.8	69.6	80.7
September	87.0	64.0	75.5
October	79.6	51.9	65.8
November	68.6	42.5	55.6
December	61.0	37.8	49.4

Zero-Degree Days: 0
Freezing Days: 43
90-Degree Days: 75
Heating- and Cooling-Degree Days: 4,393

Amarillo, TX

Terrain: Located in the heart of the Panhandle, Amarillo sits on the cap rock, or High Plains, of the Southwest. The area, which includes part of Oklahoma and northern Mexico, has often been called the Dust Bowl. It is a plateau with scrubby growth; cotton and sorghum are the primary crops. Amarillo lies between the Canadian and Red rivers.
Climate: The area is generally dry, but thunderstorms occur between April and September. This, however, can vary greatly from year to year, and droughts are fairly frequent. The area is subject to rapid and great temperature changes, especially in winter, when cold air comes down from the Plains and the Rocky Mountains at high speed. Nearness to paths of moving pressure systems causes strong winds, especially in March and April. Though summer days are hot, the low humidity lessens the felt heat and makes for pleasant mornings and nights.

Pluses: Sunny, dry, and mild, with distinct seasons.

Minuses: Hot; can be dusty.

Places Rated Score: 609   **Places Rated Rank: 69**

Elevation: 3,604 feet

Relative Humidity: 55%
Wind Speed: 13.7 mph

Seasonal Change

Annual Rainfall 20 in

Annual Snowfall 14.4 in

Clear	Partly Cloudy	Cloudy
163 days	102 days	100 days

Precipitation Days: 67   Storm Days: 48

Average Temperatures			
	Daily High	Daily Low	Monthly Mean
January	49.4	22.5	36.0
February	53.0	26.4	39.7
March	60.0	31.2	45.6
April	70.9	42.1	56.5
May	79.2	51.9	65.6
June	88.0	61.2	74.6
July	91.4	65.9	78.7
August	90.4	64.7	77.6
September	82.9	56.7	69.8
October	72.9	46.1	59.5
November	60.0	32.5	46.3
December	51.5	25.5	38.5

Zero-Degree Days: 2
Freezing Days: 108
90-Degree Days: 63
Heating- and Cooling-Degree Days: 5,616

Anchorage, AK

Terrain: Situated in a broad valley with adjacent narrow bodies of water. Terrain rises gradually to the east with marshes interspersed with glacial moraines, depressions, streams, and knolls. Beyond this area, the Chugach Mountains rise sharply to between 4,000 feet and 5,000 feet, with some peaks 8,000 feet to 10,000 feet high. These mountains block the warm air and the moisture from the Gulf of Alaska. Approximately 100 miles north lies the Alaska Range, which keeps much of the very cold air from the interior. Consequently, when temperatures in the interior are −50° F or −60° F, they will be −15° F to −30° F in Anchorage. The two ranges can also act as a trap, stalling very cold air when winds are light.
Climate: The four seasons are well marked in Anchorage, though in length and other characteristics they differ considerably from the standards of the middle latitudes. The rivers and lakes thaw in mid-April to early May. Snow arrives in October, leaves in mid-April.

Pluses: Well-defined, four-season climate.

Minuses: Rigorous.

Places Rated Score: 195   **Places Rated Rank: 328**

Elevation: 132 feet

Relative Humidity: 71%
Wind Speed: 6.7 mph

Seasonal Change

Annual Rainfall 14 in

Annual Snowfall 70 in

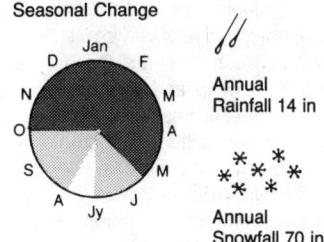

Clear	Partly Cloudy	Cloudy
64 days	67 days	234 days

Precipitation Days: 113   Storm Days: 1

Average Temperatures			
	Daily High	Daily Low	Monthly Mean
January	20.0	3.5	11.8
February	26.6	8.9	17.8
March	32.8	14.6	23.7
April	43.8	26.8	35.3
May	55.2	37.2	46.2
June	62.9	46.2	54.6
July	65.6	50.1	57.9
August	63.8	48.0	55.9
September	55.7	40.4	48.1
October	41.8	27.8	34.8
November	28.3	13.9	21.1
December	20.6	5.3	13.0

Zero-Degree Days: 41
Freezing Days: 192
90-Degree Days: 12
Heating- and Cooling-Degree Days: 10,911

★ Asheville, NC

Terrain: Located on both banks of the French Broad River, near the center of the basin of the same name. Two miles upstream from Asheville, the Swannanoa River joins the French Broad River from the east. The entire valley is called the Asheville Plateau and is flanked on the east and west by mountain ranges. Thirty miles south, the Blue Ridge Mountains form an escarpment, with an average elevation of 2,700 feet. Tallest peaks near Asheville are Mount Mitchell (6,684 feet), 20 miles northeast, and Big Pisgah (5,721 feet), 16 miles southwest.

Climate: Temperate but invigorating. Considerable variation in temperature occurs from day to day throughout the year. The valley has a pronounced effect on wind direction, which is mostly from the northwest. Destructive weather events are rare. However, the French Broad Valley is subject to flooding, with especially high flooding occurring in 12-year cycles.

Pluses: Long spring, beginning early.

Minuses: Drizzly, flood-prone.

Places Rated Score: 694   **Places Rated Rank: 25**

Elevation: 2,207 feet

Relative Humidity: 77%
Wind Speed: 7.8 mph

Seasonal Change

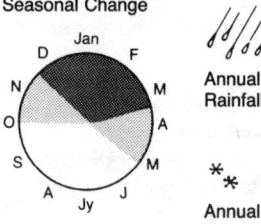

Annual
Rainfall 45 in

Annual
Snowfall 18 in

Clear
102 days

Partly Cloudy
107 days

Cloudy
156 days

Precipitation Days: 128   Storm Days: 49

Average Temperatures			
	Daily High	Daily Low	Monthly Mean
January	48.4	27.3	37.9
February	50.6	28.2	39.4
March	58.3	33.5	45.9
April	69.4	42.4	55.9
May	76.8	50.6	63.7
June	82.5	58.7	70.6
July	84.3	62.6	73.5
August	83.8	61.8	72.8
September	78.0	55.4	66.7
October	69.1	44.5	56.8
November	58.2	34.3	46.3
December	49.3	28.1	38.7

Zero-Degree Days: 1
Freezing Days: 106
90-Degree Days: 5
Heating- and Cooling-Degree Days: 5,109

★ Atlanta, GA

Terrain: Located in the foothills of the southern Appalachians in north central Georgia. Terrain is rolling to hilly and slopes downward toward the east, west, and south. With a mean elevation of 1,000 feet and a location on a plateau with mountains to the north, Atlanta's exposure to the cold north air is blocked, and its elevation retards the moist hot air from the Gulf of Mexico.

Climate: Abundant rainfall fosters natural vegetation and growth of crops. In summer, afternoon high temperatures equal or exceed 90° F one day in five, but a temperature of 100° F is rare. Atlanta's winters are mild. Cold spells are not unusual, but they rarely disrupt outdoor activities for extended periods. Snow is very light and usually does not stay on the ground long. Ice storms, however, occur about one year in ten and cause heavy damage. Atlanta averages 50 thunderstorms a year, which occur mostly in the spring, sometimes spinning off destructive tornadoes. Average date of last freeze: March 24. First freeze: November 12. Average growing period: 233 days.

Pluses: Mild, sunny, pleasant.

Minuses: Hot summers, stormy.

Places Rated Score: 696   **Places Rated Rank: 24**

Elevation: 1,034 feet

Relative Humidity: 70%
Wind Speed: 9.1 mph

Seasonal Change

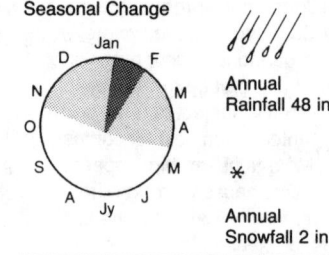

Annual
Rainfall 48 in

Annual
Snowfall 2 in

Clear
108 days

Partly Cloudy
111 days

Cloudy
146 days

Precipitation Days: 116   Storm Days: 50

Average Temperatures			
	Daily High	Daily Low	Monthly Mean
January	51.4	33.4	42.4
February	54.5	35.5	45.0
March	61.1	41.1	51.1
April	71.4	50.7	61.1
May	79.0	59.2	69.1
June	84.6	66.6	75.6
July	86.5	69.4	78.0
August	86.4	68.6	77.5
September	81.2	63.4	72.3
October	72.5	52.3	62.4
November	61.9	40.8	51.4
December	52.7	34.3	43.5

Zero-Degree Days: 0
Freezing Days: 59
90-Degree Days: 19
Heating- and Cooling-Degree Days: 4,684

Atlantic City, NJ

Terrain: Located on a sand island south of Absecon Inlet on the southeast coast of New Jersey. Surrounding terrain, composed of tidal marshes and beach sand, is flat and lies slightly above sea level.

Climate: Continental, but the moderating influence of the Atlantic Ocean is apparent throughout the year. Summers are relatively cooler, winters warmer than those of other places at the same latitude. During the warm season, sea breezes in the late morning and afternoon prevent excessive heat. On occasion, sea breezes may lower the temperature between 15 degrees and 20 degrees within a half hour. Temperatures of 90° F or higher are recorded only about three times a year here. Fall is long, lasting until almost mid-November. On the other hand, warming is somewhat delayed in the spring. Ocean temperatures range from an average near 37° F in winter to 72° F in August. Precipitation is moderate and well distributed throughout the year, but great variation is seen from year to year in precipitation during the late summer and early fall (August, September, and October).

Pluses: Moderate temperatures.   **Minuses:** Late springs.

Places Rated Score: 615   **Places Rated Rank: 61**

Elevation: 10 feet

Relative Humidity: 73%
Wind Speed: 10.7 mph

Seasonal Change

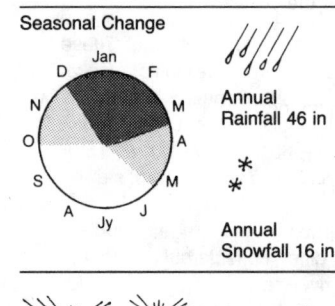

Annual
Rainfall 46 in

Annual
Snowfall 16 in

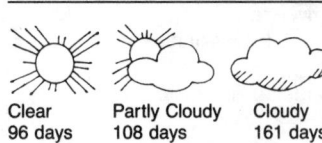

Clear
96 days

Partly Cloudy
108 days

Cloudy
161 days

Precipitation Days: 112   Storm Days: 25

Average Temperatures			
	Daily High	Daily Low	Monthly Mean
January	41.4	24.0	32.7
February	42.9	24.9	33.9
March	50.7	31.5	41.1
April	62.3	41.0	51.7
May	72.4	50.7	61.6
June	80.8	59.7	70.3
July	84.7	65.4	75.1
August	83.0	63.8	73.4
September	77.3	56.8	67.1
October	67.5	45.9	56.7
November	55.9	36.1	46.0
December	44.2	26.0	35.1

Zero-Degree Days: 1
Freezing Days: 15
90-Degree Days: 16
Heating- and Cooling-Degree Days: 5,810

Augusta, GA–SC

Terrain: Located in eastern Georgia on the Savannah River, which forms part of the boundary between Georgia and South Carolina. The dividing line between the Piedmont Plateau and the Coastal Plain, which is known as the fall line, passes through the Savannah River basin in a northeast-southwest direction near Augusta. The terrain consists of low hills to the western half of the city and swampland immediately to the north and east.

Climate: Warm and mild, with occasional hot spells. In the winter, measurable snow is a rarity and remains on the ground only a short time. In 100 years of weather records, a temperature of zero or colder has never been reached. The growing season averages 241 days, from March 16 to November 16, although frosts have been reported as late as April 21 and as early as October 17. Although Augusta is protected from flooding of the Savannah River by two multipurpose dams, the potential for flooding still exists in some low-lying areas.

Pluses: Very brief winters.

Minuses: Can be hot, flood-prone.

Places Rated Score: 534   **Places Rated Rank: 184**

Elevation: 136 feet

Relative Humidity: 72%
Wind Speed: 6.6 mph

Seasonal Change

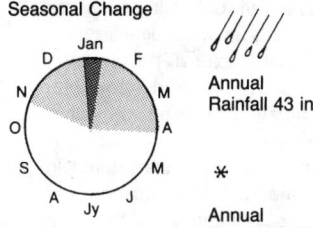

Annual Rainfall 43 in

Annual Snowfall 1.3 in

Clear 110 days   Partly Cloudy 107 days   Cloudy 148 days

Precipitation Days: 107   Storm Days: 55

Average Temperatures			
	Daily High	Daily Low	Monthly Mean
January	56.7	34.0	45.8
February	60.5	36.1	48.3
March	67.1	42.0	54.6
April	76.9	50.7	63.8
May	84.2	59.1	71.7
June	89.6	66.7	78.2
July	90.8	69.9	80.4
August	90.2	69.0	79.6
September	85.2	63.2	74.2
October	77.0	51.2	64.1
November	67.1	40.2	53.7
December	58.7	34.1	46.4

Zero-Degree Days: 0
Freezing Days: 59
90-Degree Days: 63
Heating- and Cooling-Degree Days: 4,542

Austin, TX

Terrain: Located on the Colorado River where it crosses the Balcones escarpment, which separates the Texas hill country from the blackland prairies of East Texas. Elevations within the city limits vary from 400 feet to 900 feet above sea level. Native trees include cedar, oak, walnut, mesquite, and pecan.

Climate: Subtropical. Although summers are hot, the nights are a bit cooler, with temperatures usually dropping into the 70s. Winters are mild, with below-freezing temperatures on fewer than 25 days; strong northers may bring cold spells, but these rarely last more than a few days. Precipitation is well distributed but heaviest in late spring, with a secondary rainfall peak in September. With summer come heavy thunderstorms; in winter, the rain tends to be slow and steady. Snowfall (1 inch per year) is inconsequential. Prevailing winds are southerly. Destructive weather is infrequent. Freeze-free season: 270 days. Average date of last freeze: March 3. First freeze: November 28.

Pluses: Mild winters.

Minuses: Hot.

Places Rated Score: 435   **Places Rated Rank: 284**

Elevation: 570 feet

Relative Humidity: 67%
Wind Speed: 9.4 mph

Seasonal Change

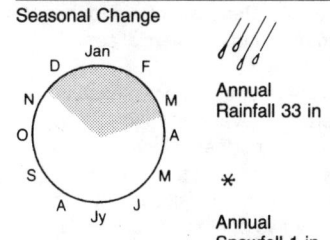

Annual Rainfall 33 in

Annual Snowfall 1 in

Clear 115 days   Partly Cloudy 116 days   Cloudy 134 days

Precipitation Days: 82   Storm Days: 41

Average Temperatures			
	Daily High	Daily Low	Monthly Mean
January	60.0	39.3	49.7
February	63.8	42.8	53.3
March	70.7	48.2	59.5
April	79.0	58.2	68.6
May	85.2	65.1	75.2
June	91.7	71.4	81.6
July	95.4	73.7	84.6
August	95.9	73.5	84.7
September	89.4	68.4	78.9
October	81.3	58.9	70.1
November	70.2	48.0	59.1
December	63.0	41.6	52.3

Zero-Degree Days: 0
Freezing Days: 23
90-Degree Days: 101
Heating- and Cooling-Degree Days: 4,645

Bakersfield, CA

Terrain: Situated in the extreme southern end of the great San Joaquin Valley, the city is partially surrounded by a horseshoe-shaped rim of mountains with an opening at the northwest. The Sierra Nevada to the northeast block much of the cold air that flows southward over the country in the winter. This range also catches and stores snow, which is used for irrigation in the valley below. The valley is suited for Mediterranean and specialized forms of agriculture.

Climate: Because of the surrounding topography, there are three different climates within short distances of each other: valley, mountain, and desert. The overall climate, however, is warm and semiarid. Ninety percent of the precipitation falls between October and April, typical of the southern half of California. Thunderstorms and snow are rare in the valley. Summers are hot, cloudless, and dry but occasionally relieved by ocean breezes from the west. Winters are mild. Average growing season: 265 days.

Pluses: Dry; mild winters.

Minuses: Hot summers.

Places Rated Score: 560   **Places Rated Rank: 130**

Elevation: 492 feet

Relative Humidity: 52%
Wind Speed: 6.4 mph

Seasonal Change

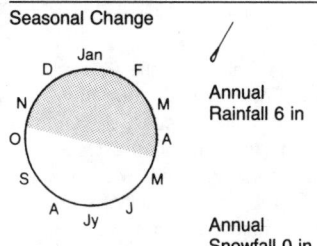

Annual Rainfall 6 in

Annual Snowfall 0 in

Clear 202 days   Partly Cloudy 79 days   Cloudy 84 days

Precipitation Days: 36   Storm Days: 3

Average Temperatures			
	Daily High	Daily Low	Monthly Mean
January	57.5	37.4	47.5
February	63.3	41.4	52.4
March	68.6	44.5	56.6
April	75.5	49.9	62.7
May	83.6	56.0	69.8
June	91.5	62.3	76.9
July	99.1	68.7	83.9
August	96.5	66.6	81.6
September	91.1	62.1	76.6
October	80.5	53.3	66.9
November	67.8	44.2	56.0
December	57.4	38.4	47.9

Zero-Degree Days: 0
Freezing Days: 11
90-Degree Days: 110
Heating- and Cooling-Degree Days: 4,364

Baltimore, MD

Terrain: Baltimore lies in a region about midway between the rigorous climates of the North and the mild ones of the South. It is also adjacent to the modifying influences of Chesapeake Bay and the Atlantic Ocean. Since this region is near the usual path of the low-pressure systems that move across the country, shifts in wind direction are frequent and contribute to the changeable character of the weather. The net effect of the Appalachian Mountains to the west and the ocean to the east is to produce an equable climate compared with other locations farther inland at the same latitude.

Climate: Rainfall is fairly uniform throughout the year but is greatest in late summer and early fall. This is also the time of hurricanes and severe thunderstorms. In summer, Baltimore is influenced by the great high-pressure system known as the Bermuda High. This high brings a constant flow of warm, humid air masses from the Deep South. These air masses, as well as the proximity of water, account for the high humidity here.

Pluses: Mild for its latitude.   **Minuses:** Humid, stormy.

Places Rated Score: 567   **Places Rated Rank: 122**

Elevation: 155 feet

Relative Humidity: 67%
Wind Speed: 9.5 mph

Seasonal Change

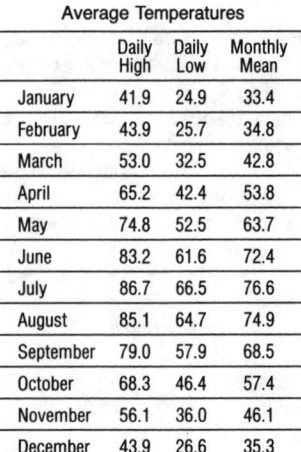

Annual Rainfall 40 in

Annual Snowfall 22 in

Clear 106 days   Partly Cloudy 109 days   Cloudy 150 days

Precipitation Days: 112 Storm Days: 26

Average Temperatures			
	Daily High	Daily Low	Monthly Mean
January	41.9	24.9	33.4
February	43.9	25.7	34.8
March	53.0	32.5	42.8
April	65.2	42.4	53.8
May	74.8	52.5	63.7
June	83.2	61.6	72.4
July	86.7	66.5	76.6
August	85.1	64.7	74.9
September	79.0	57.9	68.5
October	68.3	46.4	57.4
November	56.1	36.0	46.1
December	43.9	26.6	35.3

Zero-Degree Days: 0
Freezing Days: 100
90-Degree Days: 31
Heating- and Cooling-Degree Days: 5,837

Bangor, ME

Terrain: Located in east-central Maine at the navigable head of the Penobscot River, about 80 miles northeast of the state capital, Augusta. By means of the Penobscot River, Bangor links the vast timber forests of Maine's northern interior with Penobscot Bay, to the south. It has always been an important trading and commercial center, especially for the lumber industry.

Climate: Decidedly continental in character; summers are pleasant, with cool nights, and winters are moderately severe and fairly long. The extremes of weather caused by this northerly location are somewhat modified by Bangor's setting less than 50 miles from the Atlantic Ocean. The tempering effect of the Atlantic is felt most during the summer, when southerly winds bring ocean-cooled air northward. In the winter, westerly and northerly winds predominate, enhancing the cold. Precipitation is dependable and abundant, with an average of 43 inches of rain and almost 100 inches of snow each year.

Pluses: Comfortable summers.   **Minuses:** Long, cold winters.

Places Rated Score: 451   **Places Rated Rank: 274**

Elevation: 202 feet

Relative Humidity: 74%
Wind Speed: 8.8 mph

Seasonal Change

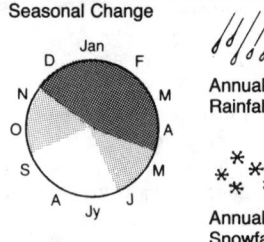

Annual Rainfall 43 in

Annual Snowfall 97 in

Clear 107 days   Partly Cloudy 98 days   Cloudy 160 days

Precipitation Days: 136 Storm Days: 17

Average Temperatures			
	Daily High	Daily Low	Monthly Mean
January	26.9	9.8	18.4
February	29.5	10.4	20.0
March	38.0	21.3	29.7
April	50.8	32.5	41.7
May	63.4	42.3	52.9
June	73.3	52.3	62.8
July	77.7	57.6	67.7
August	76.0	55.8	65.9
September	67.9	47.9	57.9
October	57.3	39.0	48.2
November	44.6	30.2	37.4
December	31.3	15.8	23.6

Zero-Degree Days: 18
Freezing Days: 157
90-Degree Days: 3
Heating- and Cooling-Degree Days: 8,113

Billings, MT

Terrain: Situated on the border between the Great Plains and the Rocky Mountains, and located on the west bank of the Yellowstone River. Billings is the center of a vast, rich agricultural belt; irrigation and sufficient rain during early spring and fall make it possible to raise a variety of crops here.

Climate: Takes on the character of both the Plains and the Rockies but is classified as semiarid. About a third of the yearly total of 14 inches of rain falls during May and June. The winter is usually dry and cold, although heavy snows can occur anytime during the winter months. The heaviest snows come either in spring or fall, when the temperature may take an unexpected drop. Blizzard conditions are expected. Severe cold spells are sometimes relieved by the Chinook, or "drainage," winds moving down Yellowstone Valley and bringing warm Pacific air. Springs: changeable, cloudy, cool. Summers: mild, dry, sunny, with cool to cold nights.

Pluses: Cool summers.   **Minuses:** Fairly rugged.

Places Rated Score: 452   **Places Rated Rank: 273**

Elevation: 3,570 feet

Relative Humidity: 55%
Wind Speed: 11.5 mph

Seasonal Change

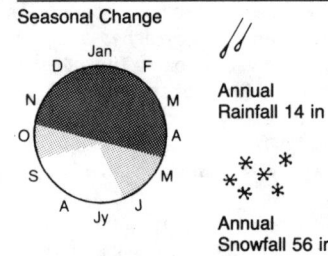

Annual Rainfall 14 in

Annual Snowfall 56 in

Clear 90 days   Partly Cloudy 116 days   Cloudy 159 days

Precipitation Days: 95 Storm Days: 29

Average Temperatures			
	Daily High	Daily Low	Monthly Mean
January	31.2	12.5	21.9
February	37.1	17.7	27.4
March	42.1	23.1	32.6
April	55.8	33.4	44.6
May	65.7	43.3	54.5
June	73.7	51.5	62.6
July	85.6	58.0	71.8
August	83.8	56.3	70.1
September	71.3	46.5	58.9
October	61.0	37.5	49.3
November	45.0	26.4	35.7
December	35.8	17.7	26.8

Zero-Degree Days: 18
Freezing Days: 152
90-Degree Days: 28
Heating- and Cooling-Degree Days: 7,763

Biloxi–Gulfport, MS

Terrain: In speaking of the Mississippi Gulf Coast, one usually thinks of the thickly settled area stretching from St. Louis Bay at Pass Christian to Biloxi Bay and Ocean Springs. This area is climatologically homogeneous, and a summary of any town (in this case, Biloxi–Gulfport) is applicable to the others. The terrain is flat, consisting of low-lying delta floodplains sloping down to sand beaches and rather shallow harbors and bays.

Climate: The Gulf waters have a modifying effect on the local climate that is not felt farther inland. Temperatures of 90° F or higher occur only half as often here as they do in Hattiesburg, 60 miles north. However, there is no such reverse effect on cold air moving down from the north in winter. Rainfall is plentiful and is heaviest in July, with totals in March and September following close behind. Damage from hurricanes and tropical storms can occur six to seven times a year.

Pluses: Warm, mild beach climate.

Minuses: Winters relatively chilly; hurricane-prone.

Places Rated Score: 584   **Places Rated Rank: 95**

Elevation: 15 feet

Relative Humidity: 77%
Wind Speed: 9.1 mph

Seasonal Change

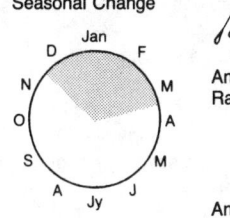

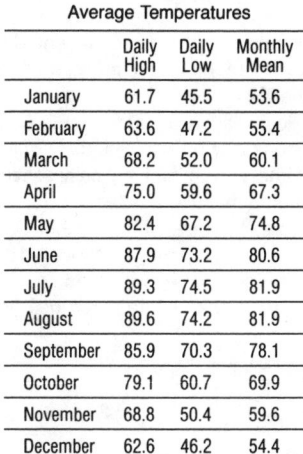

Annual Rainfall 59 in

Annual Snowfall 0 in

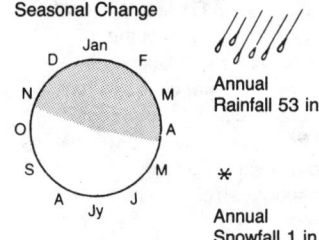

Clear	Partly Cloudy	Cloudy
100 days	119 days	146 days

Precipitation Days: 75   Storm Days: 94

Average Temperatures			
	Daily High	Daily Low	Monthly Mean
January	61.7	45.5	53.6
February	63.6	47.2	55.4
March	68.2	52.0	60.1
April	75.0	59.6	67.3
May	82.4	67.2	74.8
June	87.9	73.2	80.6
July	89.3	74.5	81.9
August	89.6	74.2	81.9
September	85.9	70.3	78.1
October	79.1	60.7	69.9
November	68.8	50.4	59.6
December	62.6	46.2	54.4

Zero-Degree Days: 0
Freezing Days: 11
90-Degree Days: 52
Heating- and Cooling-Degree Days: 3,652

Binghamton, NY

Terrain: Binghamton, in south-central New York State, lies in a narrow valley at the confluence of the Susquehanna and Chenango rivers. Within a radius of approximately 5 miles around the city, hills rise to some 1,400 feet to 1,600 feet. In the spring, melting snow and rains sometimes cause flooding along the riverbanks.

Climate: Representative of the humid area of the northeastern United States and decidedly continental in character. Since the area is adjacent to the so-called St. Lawrence Valley storm track and is also subject to intruding Arctic air masses that approach from the west and north, the local weather undergoes frequent and rapid changes. Winters are cold but usually not severe. However, moisture-laden winds from the Great Lakes bring much snow. Summers are pleasantly cool and invigorating.

Pluses: Nice summers.

Minuses: Cloudy, snowy.

Places Rated Score: 550   **Places Rated Rank: 149**

Elevation: 1,590 feet

Relative Humidity: 74%
Wind Speed: 10.3 mph

Seasonal Change

Annual Rainfall 37 in

Annual Snowfall 86 in

Clear	Partly Cloudy	Cloudy
49 days	102 days	214 days

Precipitation Days: 163   Storm Days: 31

Average Temperatures			
	Daily High	Daily Low	Monthly Mean
January	28.7	15.2	22.0
February	30.1	15.4	22.8
March	38.9	23.7	31.3
April	54.0	35.3	44.7
May	65.0	45.2	55.1
June	74.5	55.1	64.8
July	78.5	59.6	69.1
August	76.8	57.8	67.3
September	69.4	50.9	60.2
October	59.2	41.4	50.3
November	44.5	31.8	38.2
December	31.3	19.4	25.4

Zero-Degree Days: 8
Freezing Days: 147
90-Degree Days: 2
Heating- and Cooling-Degree Days: 7,654

Birmingham, AL

Terrain: Hilly and located in a valley between a ridge of hills, extending from the northeast to the west, and the Red Mountain ridge, covering the east to the southwest. This valley is 8 miles long and 2 miles to 4 miles wide. The Red Mountain ridge approaches a height of 600 feet above the valley floor. Rolling terrain extends to the southwest and west. The hills in the Birmingham area, which extend to the northeast and north, are the foothills of the Appalachians and the Cumberland Plateau.

Climate: Ideal solar radiation and cold-air drainage produce extreme temperature inversions and low minimum temperatures. Located 300 miles from the Gulf of Mexico, Birmingham is safe from the direct effects of tropical hurricanes, although it does receive heavy rains from these storms. Birmingham occasionally receives very low temperatures. Average growing season: 239 days.

Pluses: Mild winters.

Minuses: Humid, rainy.

Places Rated Score: 612   **Places Rated Rank: 67**

Elevation: 630 feet

Relative Humidity: 72%
Wind Speed: 7.4 mph

Seasonal Change

Annual Rainfall 53 in

Annual Snowfall 1 in

Clear	Partly Cloudy	Cloudy
99 days	111 days	155 days

Precipitation Days: 118   Storm Days: 58

Average Temperatures			
	Daily High	Daily Low	Monthly Mean
January	54.3	34.1	44.2
February	57.7	36.1	46.9
March	64.8	41.8	53.3
April	75.3	51.0	63.2
May	82.5	58.4	70.5
June	88.4	66.4	77.4
July	90.3	69.5	79.9
August	89.7	68.7	79.2
September	84.7	63.0	73.9
October	75.8	50.8	63.3
November	64.0	40.1	52.1
December	55.5	34.9	45.2

Zero-Degree Days: 0
Freezing Days: 60
90-Degree Days: 39
Heating- and Cooling-Degree Days: 4,772

Bismarck, ND

Terrain: Located in south central North Dakota, near the center of the North American land mass, on the east bank of the Missouri River in a shallow basin 7 miles wide and 11 miles long. The closest hills, about 3 miles away, are 200 feet or 300 feet high. West, across the river, the land is hilly and considerably higher.

Climate: Semiarid, typically continental in character, and invigorating. The normal average temperature range from summer to winter is 135 degrees, typical of the northern Great Plains. In summer, readings of 100° F or more may be expected six years out of ten. Readings of –30° F in winter are experienced seven years out of ten. On seven days of the year, the temperature does not rise above zero.

Pluses: Invigorating, variable.

Minuses: Rugged, rigorous; Bismarck has one of the most extreme climates in America.

Places Rated Score: 149   **Places Rated Rank: 331**

Elevation: 1,660 feet

Relative Humidity: 66%
Wind Speed: 10.6 mph

Seasonal Change

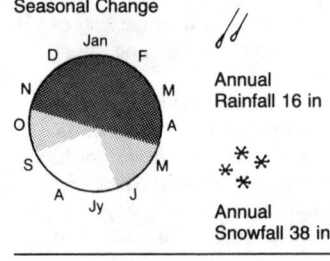

Annual Rainfall 16 in

Annual Snowfall 38 in

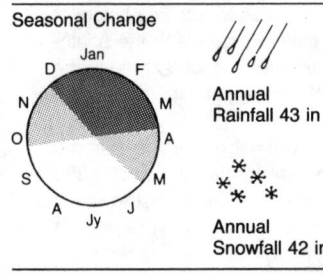

Clear 94 days   Partly Cloudy 105 days   Cloudy 166 days

Precipitation Days: 96   Storm Days: 34

Average Temperatures			
	Daily High	Daily Low	Monthly Mean
January	19.1	–2.8	8.2
February	24.5	2.4	13.5
March	35.4	14.7	25.1
April	54.8	31.1	43.0
May	67.1	41.7	54.4
June	75.8	51.8	63.8
July	84.3	57.3	70.8
August	83.5	54.9	69.2
September	71.3	43.7	57.5
October	60.3	33.2	46.8
November	39.4	18.3	28.9
December	26.0	5.2	15.6

Zero-Degree Days: 51
Freezing Days: 186
90-Degree Days: 22
Heating- and Cooling-Degree Days: 9,531

Boise City, ID

Terrain: Cradled in the valley of the Boise River about 8 miles below the mouth of a mountain canyon, where this valley widens. The Boise Mountains rise to a height of 5,000 feet to 6,000 feet within 8 miles. Their slopes are partially mantled with sagebrush and chaparral, changing to stands of fir, spruce, and pine trees higher up.

Climate: Almost a typical upland continental climate in summer but one tempered by periods of cloudy or stormy and mild weather during almost every winter. The cause of this modification in the winter months is the flow of warm, moist Pacific air, called Chinook winds. While this air is considerably moderated by the time it reaches Boise, its effect is nonetheless felt. Summer hot spells rarely last longer than a few days, but temperatures may reach 100° F each year. However, due to the low humidity, the average 5:00 PM July temperature of 62° F is comfortable. In general, the climate is dry and temperate, with enough variation to be stimulating.

Pluses: Mild; low humidity.

Minuses: Stormy winters.

Places Rated Score: 592   **Places Rated Rank: 85**

Elevation: 2,868 feet

Relative Humidity: 57%
Wind Speed: 9 mph

Seasonal Change

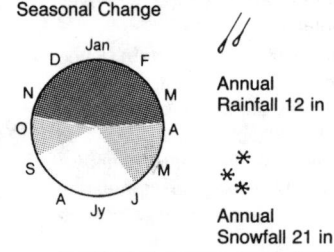

Annual Rainfall 12 in

Annual Snowfall 21 in

Clear 124 days   Partly Cloudy 90 days   Cloudy 151 days

Precipitation Days: 91   Storm Days: 15

Average Temperatures			
	Daily High	Daily Low	Monthly Mean
January	36.5	21.4	29.0
February	43.8	27.2	35.5
March	51.6	30.5	41.1
April	61.4	36.5	49.0
May	70.6	44.1	57.4
June	78.3	51.2	64.8
July	90.5	58.5	74.5
August	87.6	56.7	72.2
September	77.6	48.5	63.1
October	64.7	39.4	52.1
November	48.9	30.7	39.8
December	39.1	25.0	32.1

Zero-Degree Days: 2
Freezing Days: 124
90-Degree Days: 43
Heating- and Cooling-Degree Days: 6,547

Boston, MA

Terrain: Located in Massachusetts Bay at the mouths of the Mystic and Charles rivers. The western section of Massachusetts Bay is called Boston Bay, and its innermost part is called Boston Harbor, a large, sheltered body of water studded with many small islands, known as the Harbor Islands. Sections of Boston are rolling; two of the more famous hills are Beacon Hill in Boston and Bunker Hill in Charlestown.

Climate: Boston's proximity to the ocean greatly influences its climate —roughly described as damp, changeable, and relatively mild, considering its northern location. Sea breezes from the Atlantic do a great deal to moderate the temperature in both summer and winter. Hot summer afternoons as well as winter cold snaps (which may be severe and aggravated by high winds) are frequently relieved by these breezes. Rain is plentiful and well distributed throughout the year. Boston receives a great amount of snow, although in the city proper and to the south it often falls as sleet with no accumulation.

Pluses: Great variety, frequent changes.

Minuses: Rainy, snowy.

Places Rated Score: 623   **Places Rated Rank: 56**

Elevation: 29 feet

Relative Humidity: 67%
Wind Speed: 12.6 mph

Seasonal Change

Annual Rainfall 43 in

Annual Snowfall 42 in

Clear 99 days   Partly Cloudy 106 days   Cloudy 160 days

Precipitation Days: 128   Storm Days: 19

Average Temperatures			
	Daily High	Daily Low	Monthly Mean
January	35.9	22.5	29.2
February	37.5	23.3	30.4
March	44.6	31.5	38.1
April	56.3	40.8	48.6
May	67.1	50.1	58.6
June	76.6	59.3	68.0
July	81.4	65.1	73.3
August	79.3	63.3	71.3
September	72.2	56.7	64.5
October	63.2	47.5	55.4
November	51.7	38.7	45.2
December	39.3	26.6	33.0

Zero-Degree Days: 1
Freezing Days: 99
90-Degree Days: 12
Heating- and Cooling-Degree Days: 6,282

Brownsville–Harlingen, TX

Terrain: Situated at the extreme southern tip of Texas, on the Mexican border, and on the alluvial soils of the Rio Grande. The only more southerly city in America is Key West, Florida. The Gulf of Mexico is 18 miles to the east, and more than half the land toward the coast consists of tidal marshlands, which have the net effect of "moving" the coast 10 miles nearer to the city.

Climate: Humid subtropical. It's always summer here, accounting for the area's agricultural importance in growing citrus fruits, cotton, and warm-weather vegetables. Part of the climate is man-made: Irrigation, used for all the crops, adds considerably to the humidity. Summer temperatures follow a predictable pattern of lower 90s in the day and middle 70s at night. Gulf breezes help temper the summer heat. This is a popular tourist spot in the winter months. The normal daily January minimum temperature is 51° F.

Pluses: Long growing season.   **Minuses:** Hot.

Places Rated Score: 440   **Places Rated Rank: 279**

Elevation: 20 feet

Relative Humidity: 76%
Wind Speed: 11.8 mph

Seasonal Change

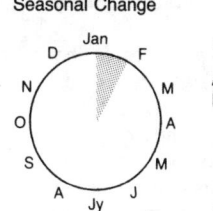

Annual
Rainfall 25 in

Annual
Snowfall 0 in

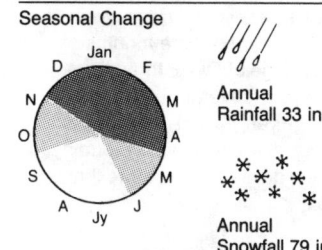

Clear
96 days

Partly Cloudy
138 days

Cloudy
131 days

Precipitation Days: 73   Storm Days: 24

Average Temperatures			
	Daily High	Daily Low	Monthly Mean
January	69.5	51.0	60.3
February	72.7	54.1	63.4
March	76.6	58.8	67.7
April	83.1	66.7	74.9
May	87.1	71.4	79.3
June	90.6	75.0	82.8
July	92.8	75.9	84.4
August	93.0	75.7	84.4
September	89.9	73.2	81.6
October	84.7	66.6	75.7
November	77.5	58.7	68.1
December	72.3	53.3	62.8

Zero-Degree Days: 0
Freezing Days: 2
90-Degree Days: 102
Heating- and Cooling-Degree Days: 4,524

Buffalo, NY

Terrain: The surrounding country is comparatively low and level to the west, and gently rolling to the east and south, rising to pronounced hills within 12 miles to 18 miles, and to 1,000 feet above Lake Erie at a point 35 miles south-southeast of the city. The eastern end of Lake Erie is 9 miles to the west-southwest, and Lake Ontario is 25 miles to the north. The two lakes are connected by the Niagara River and the famous falls of the same name.

Climate: The weather here is varied and changeable. Wide seasonal swings of temperature are tempered somewhat by the surrounding lakes. Spring comes late, primarily because of the ice buildup and cold water on Lake Erie. Summers are mild, with more sun here than anywhere else in the state. Thunderstorms are infrequent. Autumn has long, dry periods and is frost-free until mid-October. Winters are famous for snow: 90 inches are expected each year.

Pluses: Pleasant summers.   **Minuses:** Snowy, cloudy.

Places Rated Score: 571   **Places Rated Rank: 115**

Elevation: 706 feet

Relative Humidity: 73%
Wind Speed: 12.3 mph

Seasonal Change

Annual
Rainfall 36 in

Annual
Snowfall 90 in

Clear
55 days

Partly Cloudy
104 days

Cloudy
206 days

Precipitation Days: 168   Storm Days: 31

Average Temperatures			
	Daily High	Daily Low	Monthly Mean
January	29.8	17.6	23.7
February	31.0	17.7	24.4
March	39.0	25.2	32.1
April	53.3	36.4	44.9
May	64.3	45.9	55.1
June	75.1	56.3	65.7
July	79.5	60.7	70.1
August	77.6	59.1	68.4
September	70.8	52.3	61.6
October	60.2	42.7	51.5
November	46.1	33.5	39.8
December	33.6	22.2	27.9

Zero-Degree Days: 5
Freezing Days: 137
90-Degree Days: 2
Heating- and Cooling-Degree Days: 7,364

Burlington, VT

Terrain: Located on the eastern shore of Lake Champlain at the widest part of that lake. About 35 miles to the west lie the highest peaks of the Adirondacks; the foothills of the Green Mountains begin 10 miles to the east and southeast.

Climate: Burlington's northerly latitude assures the variety and vigor of a true New England climate. Lake Champlain, however, has a tempering effect; during the winter months, temperatures along the lakeshore often run from 5 degrees to 10 degrees warmer than those at the airport 3.5 miles away. The summer, while not long compared with most, is quite pleasant, with only four 90-degree days per year on the average. Fall is cool, extending through October. Winters are cold, with intense cold snaps (usually not lasting long) formed by high-pressure systems moving down from central Canada and Hudson Bay. Because of its location in the path of the St. Lawrence Valley storm track and the effects of the lake, Burlington is one of the cloudiest cities in the United States.

Pluses: Cool summers.   **Minuses:** Long, cold winters.

Places Rated Score: 383   **Places Rated Rank: 307**

Elevation: 340 feet

Relative Humidity: 71%
Wind Speed: 8.8 mph

Seasonal Change

Annual
Rainfall 33 in

Annual
Snowfall 79 in

Clear
58 days

Partly Cloudy
103 days

Cloudy
204 days

Precipitation Days: 153   Storm Days: 25

Average Temperatures			
	Daily High	Daily Low	Monthly Mean
January	25.9	7.6	16.8
February	28.2	8.9	18.6
March	38.0	20.1	29.1
April	53.3	32.6	43.0
May	66.1	43.5	54.8
June	76.5	53.9	65.2
July	81.0	58.5	69.8
August	78.3	56.4	67.4
September	70.0	48.6	59.3
October	58.7	38.8	48.8
November	44.3	29.7	37.0
December	30.3	14.8	22.6

Zero-Degree Days: 28
Freezing Days: 163
90-Degree Days: 5
Heating- and Cooling-Degree Days: 8,272

Casper, WY

Terrain: Located in the central part of the state in the North Platte River valley. The nearby countryside is rolling and hilly with considerable flat prairie land in all directions except south, where Casper Mountain rises 3,500 feet above the valley floor. The prairie land is used mostly for grazing.

Climate: Rather dry due to the effective moisture barrier of the Cascades, the Sierra Nevada, and the Rocky Mountains, which block most of the moist Pacific winds. Summertime precipitation is almost all in the form of thunderstorms, which generally provide ample moisture for grasslands. Annual snowfall averages 77 inches, but the winter season is not severe, contrary to common belief. The dryness of the air prevents discomfort during both the warm summer months and winter cold snaps. Summer highs average 84° F, winter lows 15° F.

Pluses: Invigorating.

Minuses: Short summers, long winters.

Places Rated Score: 401

Places Rated Rank: 301

Elevation: 5,338 feet

Relative Humidity: 56%
Wind Speed: 13 mph

Seasonal Change

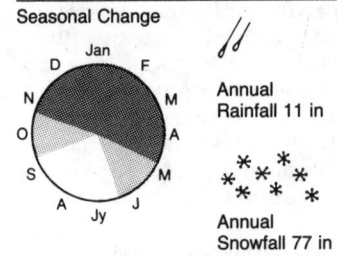

Annual Rainfall 11 in

Annual Snowfall 77 in

Clear 109 days   Partly Cloudy 110 days   Cloudy 146 days

Precipitation Days: 93   Storm Days: 34

Average Temperatures			
	Daily High	Daily Low	Monthly Mean
January	33.6	12.7	23.2
February	37.7	15.9	26.8
March	42.6	19.4	31.0
April	55.5	29.9	42.7
May	66.1	39.3	52.7
June	76.3	47.4	61.9
July	87.1	54.9	71.0
August	85.6	53.5	69.6
September	74.1	43.3	58.7
October	61.4	33.9	47.7
November	44.8	22.9	33.9
December	36.2	16.2	26.2

Zero-Degree Days: 21
Freezing Days: 185
90-Degree Days: 25
Heating- and Cooling-Degree Days: 8,013

Charleston, SC

Terrain: Before the expansion begun in 1960, Charleston was limited to the peninsula bounded on the west and south by the Ashley River, on the east by the Cooper River, and on the southeast by a spacious harbor that contains historic Fort Sumter. The terrain is generally level and the soil sandy to sandy loam. Because of the low elevation, a portion of the city and nearby coastal islands are vulnerable to tidal flooding.

Climate: Generally temperate, modified considerably by the ocean. Summer is warm and humid, but temperatures over 100° F are infrequent. Most rain—41% of the annual total—occurs then. The fall passes from an Indian summer to the prewinter cold spells that begin in November. From late September to early November, the weather is very pleasant, being cool and sunny. Winters are mild; temperatures of 20° F or less are very unusual. Spring is warm, windy, and changeable. Most storms occur then.

Pluses: Pleasant falls, mild winters.

Minuses: Hot, humid, stormy.

Places Rated Score: 569

Places Rated Rank: 118

Elevation: 48 feet

Relative Humidity: 76%
Wind Speed: 8.8 mph

Seasonal Change

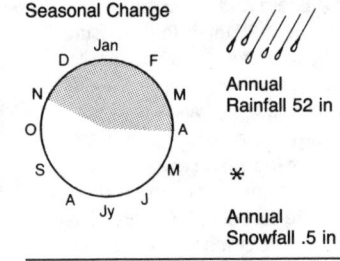

Annual Rainfall 52 in

Annual Snowfall .5 in

Clear 101 days   Partly Cloudy 113 days   Cloudy 151 days

Precipitation Days: 115   Storm Days: 56

Average Temperatures			
	Daily High	Daily Low	Monthly Mean
January	59.8	37.3	48.6
February	61.9	39.0	50.5
March	67.8	45.1	56.5
April	76.2	53.0	64.6
May	83.1	61.1	72.1
June	87.7	68.1	77.9
July	89.1	71.2	80.2
August	88.6	70.6	79.6
September	84.5	65.9	75.2
October	77.1	55.1	66.1
November	68.4	44.1	56.3
December	60.8	37.7	49.3

Zero-Degree Days: 0
Freezing Days: 36
90-Degree Days: 47
Heating- and Cooling-Degree Days: 4,224

Charleston, WV

Terrain: Situated in the western foothills of the Appalachians at the junction of the Kanawha and Elk rivers.

Climate: Characterized by sharp temperature contrasts, both seasonal and day-to-day. May through September is generally warm; November through March moderately cold. April and October are months of rapid transition. Cold spells occur on the average of two or three times each winter, but they seldom last longer than several days. Ample precipitation is well distributed throughout the year, with a maximum in July and a minimum in October. Because of the conditions of terrain and air flow, Charleston experiences 111 fog days per year, more than any other major city in the United States.

Pluses: Changeable climate.

Minuses: Foggy, rainy.

Places Rated Score: 627

Places Rated Rank: 53

Elevation: 951 feet

Relative Humidity: 70%
Wind Speed: 6.5 mph

Seasonal Change

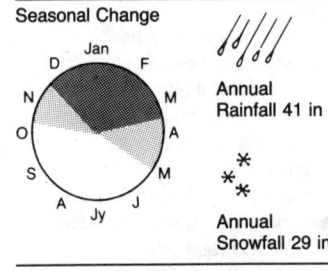

Annual Rainfall 41 in

Annual Snowfall 29 in

Clear 59 days   Partly Cloudy 116 days   Cloudy 190 days

Precipitation Days: 149   Storm Days: 43

Average Temperatures			
	Daily High	Daily Low	Monthly Mean
January	43.6	25.3	34.5
February	46.2	26.8	36.5
March	55.2	33.8	44.5
April	67.9	43.8	55.9
May	76.6	52.3	64.5
June	83.4	60.6	72.0
July	85.6	64.3	75.0
August	84.4	62.8	73.6
September	79.0	55.9	67.5
October	69.1	44.8	57.0
November	55.8	35.0	45.4
December	45.2	27.2	36.2

Zero-Degree Days: 1
Freezing Days: 101
90-Degree Days: 21
Heating- and Cooling-Degree Days: 5,645

Charlotte–Gastonia–Rock Hill, NC–SC

Terrain: Charlotte is located in the southern Piedmont, an area of rolling country between the mountains to the west and the Coastal Plain to the east. The mountains extend from southwest to northeast, being about 80 miles to 90 miles from the city to the west and north. The ocean is approximately 160 miles to the southeast. The mountains have a moderating effect on winter temperatures, causing appreciable warming of cold air coming from the west and northwest. The ocean is too distant to affect summer weather, but it moderates winter weather.
Climate: Moderate, characterized by cool winters and summers that are quite warm. Winter weather is changeable, alternating between mild and cool spells, with occasional cold periods. Extreme cold is rare. Snow is infrequent, occurring, on the average, once a month from December through March. Summers are long and warm, with after-noon temperatures frequently in the 90s. Nights are cooler, with temperatures dropping into the low 70s even in the warmest months.

Pluses: Moderate, mild winters.   **Minuses:** Long summers.

Places Rated Score: 644   **Places Rated Rank: 38**

Elevation: 769 feet

Relative Humidity: 69%
Wind Speed: 7.6 mph

Seasonal Change

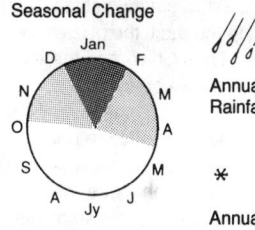

Annual
Rainfall 43 in

✳
Annual
Snowfall 6 in

Clear 111 days   Partly Cloudy 103 days   Cloudy 151 days

Precipitation Days: 111   Storm Days: 42

Average Temperatures			
	Daily High	Daily Low	Monthly Mean
January	52.1	32.1	42.1
February	54.9	33.1	44.0
March	62.2	39.0	50.6
April	72.7	48.9	60.8
May	80.2	57.4	68.8
June	86.4	65.3	75.9
July	88.3	68.7	78.5
August	87.4	67.9	77.7
September	82.0	61.9	72.0
October	73.1	50.3	61.7
November	62.4	39.6	51.0
December	52.5	32.4	42.5

Zero-Degree Days: 0
Freezing Days: 71
90-Degree Days: 31
Heating- and Cooling-Degree Days: 4,814

Chattanooga, TN–GA

Terrain: Local topography is complex, with the difference in elevation between minor valleys and ridges being as much as 500 feet. The city is located in the southern portion of the Great Valley of the Tennessee, an area of the Tennessee River between the Cumberland Mountains to the west and the Appalachian Mountains to the east. Most of the city lies south of the river. In winter the Cumberlands have a moderating influence on the local climate, retarding the flow of cold air from the north and west.
Climate: Moderate, characterized by cool winters and summers that are quite warm. Winter weather is changeable and alternates between cool spells and an occasional cold period. Extreme or prolonged cold is rare. Summer temperatures average in the high 80s or low 90s. Most afternoon summer temperatures are modified by brief thunder-showers, which cause the mercury to drop 10 degrees to 15 degrees.

Pluses: Mild winters.   **Minuses:** Can be hot and muggy.

Places Rated Score: 576   **Places Rated Rank: 106**

Elevation: 665 feet

Relative Humidity: 72%
Wind Speed: 6.2 mph

Seasonal Change

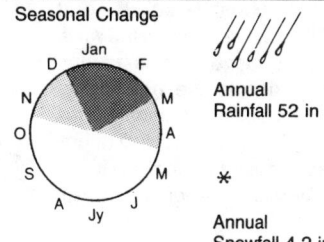

Annual
Rainfall 52 in

✳
Annual
Snowfall 4.2 in

Clear 107 days   Partly Cloudy 106 days   Cloudy 152 days

Precipitation Days: 121   Storm Days: 56

Average Temperatures			
	Daily High	Daily Low	Monthly Mean
January	49.9	30.5	40.2
February	53.4	32.3	42.9
March	61.2	38.4	49.8
April	72.9	48.1	60.5
May	81.0	56.0	68.5
June	87.5	64.5	76.0
July	89.5	68.1	78.8
August	89.0	67.0	78.0
September	83.4	60.4	71.9
October	73.5	48.1	60.8
November	60.7	37.1	48.9
December	50.9	31.4	41.2

Zero-Degree Days: 0
Freezing Days: 75
90-Degree Days: 49
Heating- and Cooling-Degree Days: 5,141

Chicago, IL

Terrain: Sprawls along the southwest shore of Lake Michigan on a plain that, for the most part, is only some tens of feet above the lake. Topography does not significantly affect air flow in or near the city, except that lower frictional drag over Lake Michigan permits winds to be frequently stronger along the lakeshore. Terrain is basically flat.
Climate: Predominantly continental, with warm to hot summers and cold winters. The climate of the city proper is modified by the lake, with summer temperatures near the shore often 10 degrees cooler than elsewhere. Summer hot spells—an uncomfortable combination of high temperature and high humidity—may last for several days, then end abruptly with a shift of winds to the north or northwest. They are often accompanied by thunderstorms. The normal heating season lasts from mid-September to early June. The air-conditioning season lasts from mid-June to early September.

Pluses: Changeable; pleasant falls.   **Minuses:** Hot summers, cold winters, cloudy.

Places Rated Score: 514   **Places Rated Rank: 211**

Elevation: 623 feet

Relative Humidity: 67%
Wind Speed: 10.4 mph

Seasonal Change

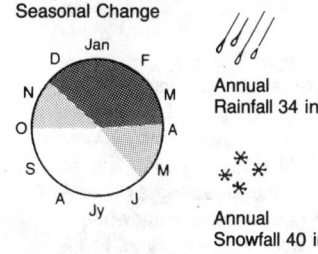

Annual
Rainfall 34 in

✳ ✳
✳
Annual
Snowfall 40 in

Clear 94 days   Partly Cloudy 103 days   Cloudy 168 days

Precipitation Days: 123   Storm Days: 40

Average Temperatures			
	Daily High	Daily Low	Monthly Mean
January	31.5	17.0	24.3
February	34.6	20.2	27.4
March	44.6	29.0	36.8
April	59.3	40.4	49.9
May	70.3	49.7	60.0
June	80.5	60.3	70.5
July	84.4	65.0	74.7
August	83.3	64.1	73.7
September	75.8	56.0	65.9
October	65.1	45.6	55.4
November	48.1	32.6	40.4
December	35.3	21.6	28.5

Zero-Degree Days: 7
Freezing Days: 119
90-Degree Days: 21
Heating- and Cooling-Degree Days: 7,052

Chico, CA

Terrain: Lies in the northern third of the Sacramento River valley in the foothills of the Sierra Nevada. The city itself is about 6 miles east of the Sacramento River. The lower slopes of the nearby Sierra foothills are cut by well-defined canyons draining from northeast to southwest. To the west the Coast Ranges rise up to 7,000 feet; to the east, the peaks of the Sierra Nevada reach as high as 9,000 feet. Thus Chico and the other towns of the upper valley are sheltered from ocean breezes and the extreme dryness of the Great Basin.

Climate: As a result of its inland location, Chico experiences a considerable range of temperature. However, even in winter the average low temperature is not below freezing, which enhances the region's agricultural productivity, particularly in fruit- and nut-growing. Chico receives 26 inches of rain per year, most of it in the cooler winter months.

Pluses: Mild, sunny, variable. **Minuses:** Hot summer days.

Places Rated Score: 603 **Places Rated Rank: 73**

Elevation: 230 feet

Relative Humidity: 68%
Wind Speed: 8 mph

Seasonal Change

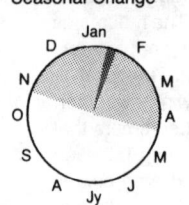

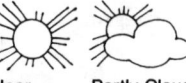

Annual Rainfall 26 in

Annual Snowfall .6 in

Clear 219 days   Partly Cloudy 57 days   Cloudy 89 days

Precipitation Days: 62   Storm Days: 7

Average Temperatures			
	Daily High	Daily Low	Monthly Mean
January	53.3	35.7	44.6
February	59.1	38.4	48.8
March	65.2	40.9	53.1
April	72.8	45.3	59.1
May	80.6	50.9	65.8
June	89.0	56.4	72.7
July	96.5	60.7	78.6
August	94.5	58.2	76.4
September	89.8	54.8	72.3
October	78.3	48.1	63.2
November	65.6	39.9	52.8
December	55.0	36.7	45.9

Zero-Degree Days: 0
Freezing Days: 36
90-Degree Days: 92
Heating- and Cooling-Degree Days: 3,816

Cincinnati, OH–KY–IN

Terrain: Located on the bank of the Ohio River in extreme southwestern Ohio. It extends over two ranges of hills bisected by the Mill Creek Valley, with hills extending some 400 feet above the valley floor. The city incorporates the lower portion of the Little Miami Valley to the east and extends to within 5 or 6 miles of the Great Miami Valley to the west.

Climate: Basically continental, with a wide range in temperature. Subject to frequent changes in weather due to the passage of numerous cyclonic storms in winter and spring, and thunderstorms during the summer. Fall is very pleasant, with the least rainfall of any season, an abundance of sunshine, and comfortable temperatures. Average freeze-free period: 198 days. Average date of last freeze: April 10. First freeze: October 25.

Pluses: Milder version of continental climate. **Minuses:** Summers can be hot; flooding approximately every three years.

Places Rated Score: 584 **Places Rated Rank: 95**

Elevation: 869 feet

Relative Humidity: 70%
Wind Speed: 7.1 mph

Seasonal Change

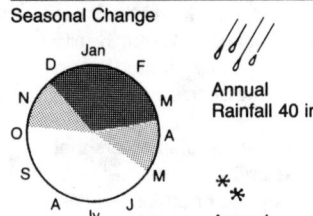

Annual Rainfall 40 in

Annual Snowfall 19 in

Clear 80 days   Partly Cloudy 97 days   Cloudy 188 days

Precipitation Days: 131   Storm Days: 50

Average Temperatures			
	Daily High	Daily Low	Monthly Mean
January	39.8	24.3	32.1
February	42.9	25.8	34.4
March	52.2	33.5	42.9
April	65.5	44.6	55.1
May	75.2	53.6	64.4
June	83.6	62.5	73.1
July	86.6	65.8	76.2
August	86.0	64.1	75.1
September	79.8	57.0	68.4
October	68.8	46.7	57.8
November	53.0	36.2	44.6
December	41.8	27.1	34.4

Zero-Degree Days: 2
Freezing Days: 98
90-Degree Days: 28
Heating- and Cooling-Degree Days: 6,032

Cleveland, OH

Terrain: Situated on the south shore of Lake Erie, with a lake frontage of 31 miles. The surrounding terrain is mostly level, except for a ridge of the southeastern edge of the city rising some 500 feet above shore level. A rather deep north-south valley, in which flows the Cuyahoga River, approximately bisects the city. Local topography is of minor importance to the climate.

Climate: In the winter, Cleveland lies in the path of many cold air masses advancing south and east out of Canada, but the low temperatures are somewhat modified by the air having passed over the comparatively warm water of the lake. But this also means considerable winter cloudiness and frequent snows. Spring is generally a brief transition period. Summer heat is moderated somewhat by the lake, since breezes are felt a considerable distance inland. Fall is the most pleasant season, with mild, sunny weather often extending into November or even early December. Average growing season: 195 days.

Pluses: Long, sunny falls. **Minuses:** Cloudy, snowy.

Places Rated Score: 579 **Places Rated Rank: 104**

Elevation: 805 feet

Relative Humidity: 72%
Wind Speed: 10.8 mph

Seasonal Change

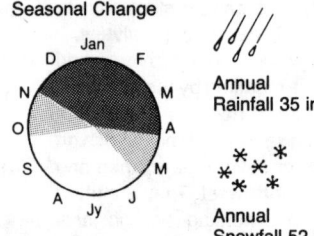

Annual Rainfall 35 in

Annual Snowfall 52 in

Clear 70 days   Partly Cloudy 98 days   Cloudy 197 days

Precipitation Days: 156   Storm Days: 36

Average Temperatures			
	Daily High	Daily Low	Monthly Mean
January	33.4	20.3	26.9
February	35.0	20.8	27.9
March	44.1	28.1	36.1
April	58.0	38.5	48.3
May	68.4	48.1	58.3
June	78.2	57.5	67.9
July	81.6	61.2	71.4
August	80.4	59.6	70.0
September	74.2	53.5	63.9
October	63.6	43.9	53.8
November	48.8	34.4	41.6
December	36.4	24.1	30.3

Zero-Degree Days: 5
Freezing Days: 125
90-Degree Days: 8
Heating- and Cooling-Degree Days: 6,767

Colorado Springs, CO

Terrain: At an elevation of more than 6,000 feet, Colorado Springs is located in relatively flat semiarid country on the eastern slope of the Rocky Mountains. Immediately to the west, the mountains rise abruptly to heights ranging from 10,000 feet to 14,000 feet. To the east lies the gently undulating prairie land of eastern Colorado. The land slopes upward to the north, reaching an average height of 8,000 feet within 20 miles, at the top of Palmer Lake Divide.

Climate: The terrain of the area, particularly its wide range of elevations, helps to give Colorado Springs the pleasant plains-and-mountain mixture of climate that has established it as a desirable place to live. Precipitation is generally light, with 80% of it falling between April 1 and September 30. Heavy downpours accompany summer thunderstorms. Temperatures are on the mild side for a city in this latitude and at this elevation.

Pluses: Dry, sunny, variable. **Minuses:** Long winters.

Elevation: 6,170 feet

Relative Humidity: 49%
Wind Speed: 10.4 mph

Seasonal Change

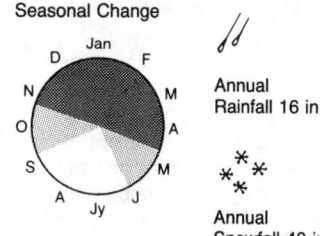

Annual Rainfall 16 in

Annual Snowfall 40 in

Clear 130 days   Partly Cloudy 119 days   Cloudy 116 days

Precipitation Days: 87   Storm Days: 59

Average Temperatures			
	Daily High	Daily Low	Monthly Mean
January	41.0	16.1	28.6
February	43.6	18.9	31.3
March	47.7	22.8	35.3
April	59.2	33.1	46.2
May	68.4	42.6	55.5
June	78.1	51.1	64.6
July	84.4	57.0	70.7
August	82.4	55.8	69.1
September	74.9	46.9	60.9
October	64.2	36.8	50.5
November	49.8	25.1	37.5
December	43.1	18.9	31.0

Zero-Degree Days: 7
Freezing Days: 162
90-Degree Days: 15
Heating- and Cooling-Degree Days: 6,934

Places Rated Score: 526 **Places Rated Rank: 191**

Columbia, MO

Terrain: Columbia, a university town, is located on the broad, gently rolling plains of northern Missouri in the valley of the Missouri River. Its elevation is almost 900 feet, and its location dictates a continental climate.

Climate: With its interior location, Columbia experiences moderately cold winters and warm, often humid summers. Each summer brings some temperatures over 100° F, and winter lows reach zero an average of eight times annually. Yet summer hot spells are relieved by thunderstorms, and winter cold snaps are often interrupted by days that are almost balmy, with temperatures as high as the 50s and 60s. The late spring and early summer months are the rainiest, but by late summer the rain diminishes so that by middle or late August, the moisture in the top two feet of soil is often depleted. The last spring freeze is usually on April 9; first autumn frost is October 24.

Pluses: Variable, sunny. **Minuses:** Tornado-prone.

Elevation: 887 feet

Relative Humidity: 69%
Wind Speed: 9.8 mph

Seasonal Change

Annual Rainfall 37 in

Annual Snowfall 24 in

Clear 100 days   Partly Cloudy 91 days   Cloudy 174 days

Precipitation Days: 109   Storm Days: 51

Average Temperatures			
	Daily High	Daily Low	Monthly Mean
January	38.0	20.6	29.3
February	42.7	24.5	33.6
March	51.3	32.0	41.7
April	65.3	44.6	55.0
May	74.5	54.3	64.4
June	82.7	63.3	73.0
July	87.4	67.1	77.3
August	86.4	65.5	76.0
September	79.4	57.2	68.3
October	69.2	46.7	58.0
November	53.6	34.2	43.9
December	41.1	24.5	32.8

Zero-Degree Days: 8
Freezing Days: 108
90-Degree Days: 39
Heating- and Cooling-Degree Days: 6,352

Places Rated Score: 541 **Places Rated Rank: 170**

Columbia, SC

Terrain: Located on the Congaree River in the center of the state, near the confluence of the Broad and Saluda rivers. The fall line, or division between the Piedmont and the Coastal Plain, is near Columbia. The soil ranges from sand to clay loam. Terrain is rolling, sloping from about 350 feet above sea level in the northern part of the city to about 200 feet at the city's southeastern edge.

Climate: Although the Appalachian chain to the north shields the city from northern cold fronts in the winter, the surrounding gently rolling terrain offers little moderating effect on summer heat. Summers are long and hot, with high temperatures from May to September. Temperatures will surpass 100° F an average of six times a year. Winters are mild: Only about a third of the days have freezing temperatures. Snow accumulation is very rare. Spring is changeable and may bring some violent weather. Fall is cool, pleasant, and very sunny. Some grazing crops are grown year-round. Average growing period: 217 days.

Pluses: Cool, sunny falls. **Minuses:** Long, hot summers.

Elevation: 225 feet

Relative Humidity: 73%
Wind Speed: 6.9 mph

Seasonal Change

Annual Rainfall 46 in

Annual Snowfall 2 in

Clear 120 days   Partly Cloudy 103 days   Cloudy 142 days

Precipitation Days: 111   Storm Days: 54

Average Temperatures			
	Daily High	Daily Low	Monthly Mean
January	56.9	33.9	45.4
February	59.7	35.5	47.6
March	66.5	41.9	54.2
April	76.9	51.3	64.1
May	84.5	59.6	72.1
June	90.3	67.2	78.8
July	92.0	70.3	81.2
August	91.0	69.4	80.2
September	85.4	63.5	74.5
October	77.1	51.3	64.2
November	66.9	40.6	53.8
December	57.9	34.1	46.0

Zero-Degree Days: 0
Freezing Days: 60
90-Degree Days: 64
Heating- and Cooling-Degree Days: 4,685

Places Rated Score: 526 **Places Rated Rank: 191**

Columbus, GA–AL

Terrain: Located on the Chattahoochee River at the western boundary of Georgia, about 225 miles west of the Atlantic and 170 miles north of the Gulf of Mexico. Elevation ranges from between 200 feet to 500 feet. The terrain is basically level, and effects of terrain on climate are therefore negligible.

Climate: Humid and warm, with pronounced maritime effects at some periods and equally pronounced continental effects at others. Rainfall averages an abundant 51 inches a year; the wettest months are March and July, the driest October. Snow is rare but by no means unknown, with each winter usually bringing at least a few flakes. Most days in June, July, and August will see a high of 90° F or higher, with accompanying high humidity. The unpleasant effects of this heat are perhaps balanced by the mild winters, during which temperatures seldom drop below 20° F.

Pluses: Very mild winters.

Minuses: Hot summers; humid.

Places Rated Score: 517   **Places Rated Rank: 206**

Elevation: 445 feet

Relative Humidity: 73%
Wind Speed: 6.8 mph

Seasonal Change

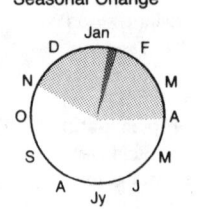

Annual Rainfall 51 in

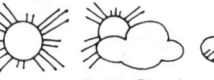

Annual Snowfall .5 in

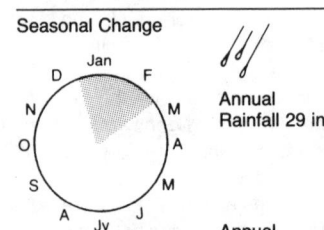

Clear 113 days	Partly Cloudy 103 days	Cloudy 149 days

Precipitation Days: 111 Storm Days: 58

Average Temperatures			
	Daily High	Daily Low	Monthly Mean
January	57.8	35.9	46.9
February	60.9	37.8	49.4
March	67.4	43.3	55.4
April	77.3	51.8	64.4
May	84.7	60.0	72.4
June	89.9	67.5	78.7
July	90.8	70.4	80.6
August	90.8	69.8	80.3
September	85.8	65.1	75.5
October	77.4	53.4	65.4
November	66.8	41.9	54.4
December	59.0	36.3	47.7

Zero-Degree Days: 0
Freezing Days: 46
90-Degree Days: 74
Heating- and Cooling-Degree Days: 4,521

Columbus, OH

Terrain: Situated in the center of the state and in the drainage area of the Ohio River. Four small rivers—the Scioto, Alum, Big Walnut, and Olentangy—flow through and near the city.

Climate: The city is located in an area of changeable weather. Cold air masses from central and northwest Canada frequently invade the region. Tropical Gulf masses often reach central Ohio during the summer but to a much lesser extent in fall and winter. Columbus's four rivers provide variations in the microclimate of the area, contributing to the formation of shallow ground fog at daybreak in the summer and fall.

Pluses: Changeable climate.

Minuses: Cold spells.

Places Rated Score: 558   **Places Rated Rank: 137**

Elevation: 833 feet

Relative Humidity: 70%
Wind Speed: 8.7 mph

Seasonal Change

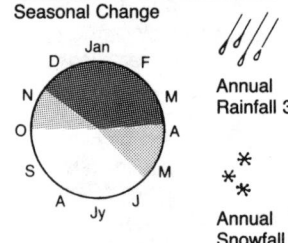

Annual Rainfall 37 in

Annual Snowfall 28 in

Clear 75 days	Partly Cloudy 106 days	Cloudy 184 days

Precipitation Days: 136 Storm Days: 42

Average Temperatures			
	Daily High	Daily Low	Monthly Mean
January	36.4	20.4	28.4
February	39.2	21.4	30.3
March	49.3	29.1	39.2
April	62.8	39.5	51.2
May	72.9	49.3	61.1
June	81.9	58.9	70.4
July	84.8	62.4	73.6
August	83.7	60.1	71.9
September	77.6	52.7	65.2
October	66.4	42.0	54.2
November	50.9	32.4	41.7
December	38.7	22.7	30.7

Zero-Degree Days: 4
Freezing Days: 122
90-Degree Days: 15
Heating- and Cooling-Degree Days: 6,511

Corpus Christi, TX

Terrain: Located on Corpus Christi Bay, an inlet in the Gulf of Mexico. It is in the southern part of the Texas Gulf coastline, roughly halfway between Galveston to the north and Brownsville to the south. Padre Island National Seashore adjoins the city. Climate and abundant beaches make the area a major resort center.

Climate: Although located on the Gulf, Corpus Christi has a climate midway between humid subtropical conditions to the northeast along the Gulf Coast and the semiarid ones to the west and southwest. Peak rainfall months are May and September, with the winter months being the driest. Tropical storms, which may occur from June through November, add a large portion to the total rainfall. There is little variation in the summer temperature from day to day, which averages in the high 80s or low 90s. But nights are cooler, even pleasant, with temperatures dropping into the low 70s because of sea breezes.

Pluses: Winter vacation spot.

Minuses: Storms.

Places Rated Score: 362   **Places Rated Rank: 313**

Elevation: 44 feet

Relative Humidity: 77%
Wind Speed: 12 mph

Seasonal Change

Annual Rainfall 29 in

Annual Snowfall 0 in

Clear 104 days	Partly Cloudy 118 days	Cloudy 143 days

Precipitation Days: 77 Storm Days: 31

Average Temperatures			
	Daily High	Daily Low	Monthly Mean
January	66.5	46.1	56.3
February	69.8	49.3	59.6
March	75.5	54.2	64.9
April	82.1	63.4	72.8
May	86.6	69.1	77.9
June	91.2	73.6	82.4
July	94.4	75.2	84.8
August	94.8	75.4	85.1
September	90.0	72.0	81.0
October	84.1	63.7	73.9
November	75.2	54.6	64.9
December	69.3	48.9	59.1

Zero-Degree Days: 0
Freezing Days: 7
90-Degree Days: 96
Heating- and Cooling-Degree Days: 4,404

Cumberland, MD–WV

Terrain: Cumberland, the seat of Allegany County and Maryland's third largest city, is located in what is called the Ridge and Valley Physiographic Province, with the valleys and ridges running from northeast to southwest. The valleys drain southward into the Potomac Basin and vary from narrow, steep-sided trenches to broad, gently sloping valleys. Most of Cumberland lies on the valley floor, but nearby elevations range from 600 feet to 900 feet. The surrounding terrain is fairly rugged.

Climate: A variable continental-type climate on the mild side. The ridge-and-valley terrain exerts strong influences on local weather, with considerable variation observed over short distances. The annual rainfall of 37 inches is evenly distributed throughout the year. June is usually the wettest month and November the driest. Prevailing winds are from the northwest. There are about 35 thunderstorms a year on the average.

Pluses: Mild and variable. **Minuses:** Cloudy.

Places Rated Score: 591 **Places Rated Rank: 87**

Elevation: 945 feet

Relative Humidity: 70%
Wind Speed: 8 mph

Seasonal Change

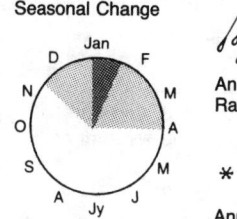

Annual Rainfall 37 in

Annual Snowfall 33 in

Clear 102 days Partly Cloudy 114 days Cloudy 149 days

Precipitation Days: 122 Storm Days: 35

Average Temperatures

	Daily High	Daily Low	Monthly Mean
January	40.8	23.6	32.2
February	43.8	25.3	34.6
March	51.2	30.8	41.0
April	64.8	41.3	53.1
May	75.7	50.0	62.9
June	82.7	57.5	70.1
July	86.5	61.3	73.9
August	84.8	60.3	72.6
September	78.4	53.3	65.9
October	68.6	43.4	56.0
November	53.2	34.3	43.8
December	41.2	25.0	33.1

Zero-Degree Days: 1
Freezing Days: 114
90-Degree Days: 27
Heating- and Cooling-Degree Days: 5,788

Dallas, TX

Terrain: Located in north central Texas, about 250 miles north of the Gulf of Mexico, near the headwaters of the Trinity River. This hilly area marks the upper boundary of the Coastal Plain. Grasses, live oaks, and coniferous trees compose most of the local vegetation.

Climate: Humid, subtropical, with hot summers. It is also continental, characterized by a wide range in annual temperature. Winters tend to be mild, but "northers" occur, bringing cold air masses down from the Great Plains and the Rocky Mountains. These cold snaps are not prolonged, however. Much of the rain falls at night; downpours may accompany thunderstorms during April and May. July and August are relatively dry. Hail falls about two or three times a year. Snowfall is slight and doesn't accumulate. Average freeze-free growing period: 249 days.

Pluses: Wide range of weather. **Minuses:** Hot summers.

Places Rated Score: 544 **Places Rated Rank: 161**

Elevation: 596 feet

Relative Humidity: 67%
Wind Speed: 11 mph

Seasonal Change

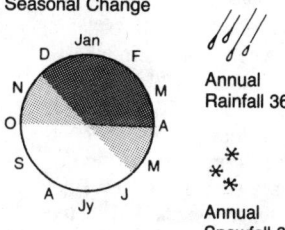

Annual Rainfall 32 in

Annual Snowfall 3 in

Clear 138 days Partly Cloudy 95 days Cloudy 132 days

Precipitation Days: 79 Storm Days: 46

Average Temperatures

	Daily High	Daily Low	Monthly Mean
January	55.7	33.9	44.8
February	59.8	37.6	48.7
March	66.6	43.3	55.0
April	76.3	54.1	65.2
May	82.8	62.1	72.5
June	90.8	70.3	80.6
July	95.5	74.0	84.8
August	96.1	73.7	84.9
September	88.5	66.8	77.7
October	79.2	56.0	67.6
November	67.5	44.1	55.8
December	58.7	37.0	47.9

Zero-Degree Days: 0
Freezing Days: 39
90-Degree Days: 88
Heating- and Cooling-Degree Days: 4,969

Davenport–Rock Island–Moline, IA–IL

Terrain: Located on the banks of the Mississippi River. Topography characterized by rolling agricultural prairie. Close to the river there is considerable truck gardening and dairying. Field production of grains and livestock is greater in rolling prairie, away from the large streams.

Climate: Temperate continental, with a wide temperature range throughout the year. Some intensely hot, usually humid periods in summer and severely cold periods in winter. Proximity to major storm tracks brings substantial weather changes, frequently occurring at three- or four-day intervals. Maxima of 90° F or higher have occurred as frequently as 55 days a year (1936), but in 1882 there were none. Readings of zero or below have been made during every winter, ranging from 37 times in 1874–75 to one time during four other winters.

Pluses: Variable climate with average growing season and even precipitation.

Minuses: Unpredictable climate, long winters, hot summer stretches.

Places Rated Score: 440 **Places Rated Rank: 279**

Elevation: 594 feet

Relative Humidity: 70%
Wind Speed: 9.9 mph

Seasonal Change

Annual Rainfall 36 in

Annual Snowfall 30 in

Clear 101 days Partly Cloudy 101 days Cloudy 163 days

Precipitation Days: 112 Storm Days: 47

Average Temperatures

	Daily High	Daily Low	Monthly Mean
January	30.0	13.0	21.5
February	34.3	17.0	25.7
March	45.0	26.4	35.7
April	61.3	39.8	50.6
May	72.0	50.2	61.1
June	81.4	60.2	70.8
July	85.2	63.8	74.5
August	83.8	62.0	72.9
September	76.0	53.2	64.6
October	66.0	42.8	54.4
November	48.1	30.2	39.2
December	34.6	18.5	26.6

Zero-Degree Days: 16
Freezing Days: 136
90-Degree Days: 22
Heating- and Cooling-Degree Days: 7,288

Denver, CO

Terrain: The Mile-High City rests on the eastern slope of the Rocky Mountains. It is far from any source of moisture and is isolated from the Pacific Ocean by three mountain ranges: the Coastal Ranges, the Sierra Nevada, and the Rockies.

Climate: A mild, sunny, semiarid climate, reaching over much of the central Rocky Mountain region. This tempered climate lacks the extremely cold winter mornings of the high elevations and remote mountain valleys, as well as the hot summer afternoons of lower altitudes. There is little humidity or precipitation, and lots of sunshine. During the cold months, invasion of cold air from the north can be abrupt and severe. Yet many of these air masses from Canada are too low to reach Denver and so are deflected off to the east by the mountains. For this reason, Denver often has milder winters than cities of comparable latitude on the Great Plains. Spring is wet, cloudy, and windy. Summers are cool. Fall is the most pleasant season.

Pluses: Sunny; dry; comparatively mild winters.

Minuses: Cold snaps in winter, stormy springs.

Places Rated Score: 521   **Places Rated Rank: 200**

Elevation: 5,332 feet

Relative Humidity: 53%
Wind Speed: 9.1 mph

Seasonal Change

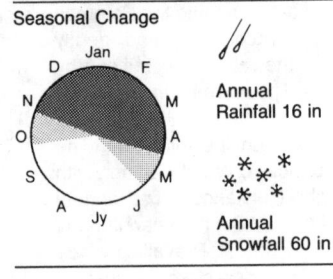

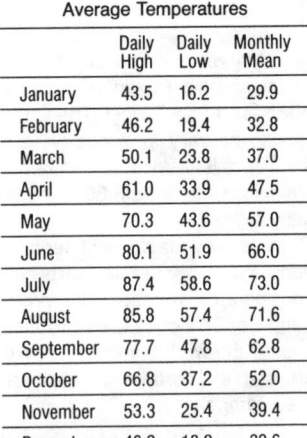

Annual Rainfall 16 in

Annual Snowfall 60 in

Clear 115 days   Partly Cloudy 131 days   Cloudy 119 days

Precipitation Days: 88   Storm Days: 41

Average Temperatures			
	Daily High	Daily Low	Monthly Mean
January	43.5	16.2	29.9
February	46.2	19.4	32.8
March	50.1	23.8	37.0
April	61.0	33.9	47.5
May	70.3	43.6	57.0
June	80.1	51.9	66.0
July	87.4	58.6	73.0
August	85.8	57.4	71.6
September	77.7	47.8	62.8
October	66.8	37.2	52.0
November	53.3	25.4	39.4
December	46.2	18.9	32.6

Zero-Degree Days: 10
Freezing Days: 163
90-Degree Days: 32
Heating- and Cooling-Degree Days: 6,641

Des Moines, IA

Terrain: Located close to the center of Iowa, and roughly in the geographic center of the continental United States. The terrain is flat to gently rolling prairie, ideally suited to agriculture. Most of the soil in Iowa is dark, rich, sandy loam with good drainage. The state has the highest rate of agricultural production per acre in the nation.

Climate: Situated in the center of the country far from any large body of water, Des Moines, not surprisingly, has a continental climate, characterized by rather long, cold winters, hot summers, and short springs and falls. Winter cold is often intensified by the winds that sweep over the flat land.

Pluses: Sunny falls.

Minuses: Climate tending toward rigorous.

Places Rated Score: 444   **Places Rated Rank: 276**

Elevation: 963 feet

Relative Humidity: 69%
Wind Speed: 11.1 mph

Seasonal Change

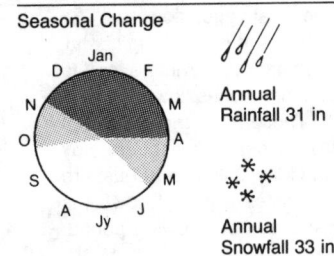

Annual Rainfall 31 in

Annual Snowfall 33 in

Clear 103 days   Partly Cloudy 96 days   Cloudy 166 days

Precipitation Days: 106   Storm Days: 50

Average Temperatures			
	Daily High	Daily Low	Monthly Mean
January	27.5	11.3	19.4
February	32.5	15.8	24.2
March	42.5	25.2	33.9
April	59.7	39.2	49.5
May	70.9	50.9	60.9
June	79.8	61.1	70.5
July	84.9	65.3	75.1
August	83.2	63.4	73.3
September	74.6	54.0	64.3
October	64.9	43.6	54.3
November	46.4	29.2	37.8
December	32.8	17.2	25.0

Zero-Degree Days: 16
Freezing Days: 137
90-Degree Days: 21
Heating- and Cooling-Degree Days: 7,638

Detroit, MI

Terrain: Detroit is located in the southeastern corner of the state, across the St. Clair River from Windsor, Ontario. Consequently, it is one of the few metro areas that cross international boundaries. Detroit lies on an important waterway that connects Lake Huron to Lake Erie. Nearly flat land slopes up gently from the water's edge northwestward for about 10 miles, then gives way to increasingly rolling terrain. The Irish Hills, about 40 miles northwest, are more than 1,000 feet high.

Climate: The winters, while cold, are modified by the Great Lakes, which warm and moisten the cold Arctic air that passes over the northern Plains. As a result, however, the area is quite cloudy, especially in the winter. Summers in the city are warm and sunny. Brief showers usually occur every few days but often fall on only part of the city. Winter storms may bring rain, snow, or both. Freezing rain and sleet are common. Though cloudy, Detroit's proximity to the Great Lakes helps give it a milder climate than one would expect in a place so far north.

Pluses: Mild for its latitude.

Minuses: Cold winters, cloudy.

Places Rated Score: 536   **Places Rated Rank: 176**

Elevation: 664 feet

Relative Humidity: 72%
Wind Speed: 10.4 mph

Seasonal Change

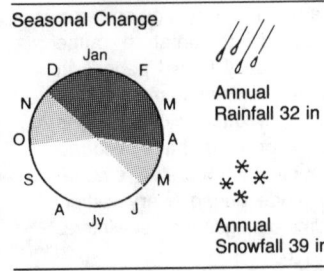

Annual Rainfall 32 in

Annual Snowfall 39 in

Clear 75 days   Partly Cloudy 110 days   Cloudy 180 days

Precipitation Days: 133   Storm Days: 33

Average Temperatures			
	Daily High	Daily Low	Monthly Mean
January	31.9	17.3	24.6
February	34.3	18.8	26.6
March	43.8	26.7	35.3
April	58.1	37.3	47.7
May	69.1	47.0	58.1
June	79.4	57.2	68.3
July	83.4	61.1	72.3
August	82.0	59.5	70.8
September	74.8	52.3	63.6
October	64.1	42.1	53.1
November	47.8	32.3	40.1
December	35.4	21.5	28.5

Zero-Degree Days: 7
Freezing Days: 139
90-Degree Days: 11
Heating- and Cooling-Degree Days: 7,073

Duluth, MN–WI

Terrain: Located at Lake Superior's western tip, Duluth lies at the base of a range of hills that rise abruptly to between 600 feet and 800 feet above the lake level. Two or 3 miles back from the waterfront, however, the country assumes the character of a slightly rolling plateau. Directly opposite, on the flats occupying the east banks of St. Louis Bay, lies the city of Superior, Wisconsin. These two cities are referred to as the Twin Ports.

Climate: Rugged continental in character. Winters are long and quite cold. Snow comes early and remains on the ground until springtime. While the airport area receives more than 75 inches of snow a year, the city proper receives only about 55 inches. Summers are seldom hot, due to the northerly latitude and proximity of Lake Superior.

Pluses: Cool summers, rugged four-season climate.

Minuses: Cold.

Places Rated Score: 193

Places Rated Rank: 330

Elevation: 1,417 feet

Relative Humidity: 71%
Wind Speed: 11.4 mph

Seasonal Change

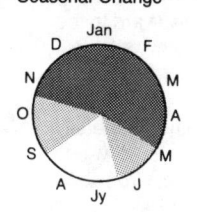

Annual Rainfall 30 in

Annual Snowfall 78 in

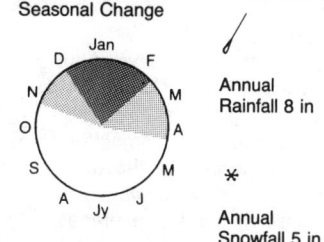

| Clear 77 days | Partly Cloudy 103 days | Cloudy 185 days |

Precipitation Days: 135   Storm Days: 35

Average Temperatures			
	Daily High	Daily Low	Monthly Mean
January	17.6	-.6	8.5
February	22.1	2.0	12.1
March	32.6	14.4	23.5
April	47.8	29.3	38.6
May	60.0	38.8	49.4
June	69.7	48.3	59.0
July	76.4	54.7	65.6
August	74.4	53.7	64.1
September	64.0	44.8	54.4
October	54.3	36.2	45.3
November	35.3	21.4	28.4
December	22.5	6.3	14.4

Zero-Degree Days: 51
Freezing Days: 187
90-Degree Days: 2
Heating- and Cooling-Degree Days: 9,932

El Paso, TX

Terrain: Located at the extreme western tip of Texas at an elevation of 3,700 feet. Across the Rio Grande to the south lies Ciudad Juárez, Mexico. The Franklin Mountains begin within the city limits and extend northward for about 16 miles. Some of these peaks reach as high as 4,500 feet to 5,000 feet above sea level. The general terrain is composed of mountains and mesas characteristic of western Texas and New Mexico.

Climate: Dry and sunny. Summer temperatures are high but not extreme. The very low relative humidity (39%) lessens the felt heat. The winter is mild, typical of arid areas at low altitudes. Rainfall is scarce year-round and fosters only scrublike desert vegetation. Irrigation is necessary for crops, gardens, and lawns. Winter nights can be cold, but the days are warm, averaging in the 50s. Similarly, summer days are hot but the nights cool, averaging in the 60s.

Pluses: Mild winters, low humidity.

Minuses: Dust storms and sandstorms.

Places Rated Score: 592

Places Rated Rank: 85

Elevation: 3,700 feet

Relative Humidity: 39%
Wind Speed: 9.6 mph

Seasonal Change

Annual Rainfall 8 in

Annual Snowfall 5 in

| Clear 194 days | Partly Cloudy 100 days | Cloudy 71 days |

Precipitation Days: 45   Storm Days: 36

Average Temperatures			
	Daily High	Daily Low	Monthly Mean
January	57.0	30.2	43.6
February	62.5	34.3	48.4
March	68.9	40.3	54.6
April	78.5	49.3	63.9
May	87.2	57.2	72.2
June	94.9	65.7	80.3
July	94.6	69.9	82.3
August	92.8	68.2	80.5
September	87.4	61.0	74.2
October	78.5	49.5	64.0
November	66.1	37.0	51.6
December	57.8	30.9	44.4

Zero-Degree Days: 0
Freezing Days: 64
90-Degree Days: 103
Heating- and Cooling-Degree Days: 4,776

★ Eugene–Springfield, OR

Terrain: Situated at the southern end of the fertile Willamette Valley. This valley is bounded on both sides by mountain ranges: the Cascades to the east and the Coast Ranges to the west. To the north, the valley widens and levels out. Hills of the rolling, wooded Coast Ranges begin about 5 miles west of the airport and rise to between 1,500 feet and 2,000 feet midway between the city and the Pacific, 50 miles to the west. The Cascades, 75 miles east, reach heights of 10,000 feet. These sheltering ranges and the proximity of the ocean contribute heavily to Eugene's extremely mild climate. This is one of the nation's most important agricultural and lumbering areas.

Climate: Very mild maritime climate. Temperature minima below 20° F occur only five times a year. The temperature rarely reaches the mid-90s. Seasonal change is gradual, with intermediate seasons being as long as summer and winter.

Pluses: Mild; gradual change of seasons.

Minuses: Cloudy, damp.

Places Rated Score: 741

Places Rated Rank: 18

Elevation: 373 feet

Relative Humidity: 77%
Wind Speed: 7.6 mph

Seasonal Change

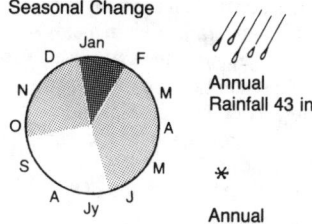

Annual Rainfall 43 in

Annual Snowfall 7 in

| Clear 77 days | Partly Cloudy 81 days | Cloudy 207 days |

Precipitation Days: 137   Storm Days: 5

Average Temperatures			
	Daily High	Daily Low	Monthly Mean
January	45.6	33.1	39.4
February	51.7	35.2	43.5
March	55.2	36.5	45.9
April	61.2	39.4	50.3
May	67.8	43.7	55.8
June	74.1	48.7	61.4
July	82.6	51.1	66.9
August	81.3	50.9	66.1
September	76.5	47.4	62.0
October	64.0	42.3	53.2
November	53.1	38.1	45.6
December	47.4	35.6	41.5

Zero-Degree Days: 0
Freezing Days: 54
90-Degree Days: 15
Heating- and Cooling-Degree Days: 4,739

Evansville, IN–KY

Terrain: Located on the Ohio River near the juncture of Indiana, Illinois, and Kentucky. The country around Evansville ranges from level to rolling. Dress Regional Airport, where weather observations have been made since 1940, is in a shallow valley with low hills to the east and west that run parallel to the valley but slope downward to the south. The open end of this valley slopes down to the south-southwest toward Evansville and the Ohio River.

Climate: Prevailing wind here is from the south, and, although Evansville is 550 miles from the Gulf of Mexico, its weather generally resembles that of its neighbors to the south. Strong cold winds sometimes blow from the north and northwest following cold fronts. As soon as the high-pressure ridge moves by, the wind backs around again from the south. Snowfall varies a great deal from year to year; accumulation is rare. Average growing season: 199 days. Average date of last freeze: April 7. First freeze: October 23.

Pluses: Influenced by Gulf winds.

Minuses: Summers can be hot and humid.

Places Rated Score: 550

Places Rated Rank: 149

Elevation: 388 feet

Relative Humidity: 70%
Wind Speed: 8.3 mph

Seasonal Change

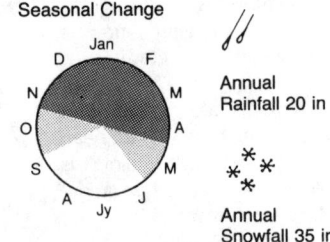

Annual Rainfall 42 in

Annual Snowfall 13 in

Clear 103 days   Partly Cloudy 100 days   Cloudy 162 days

Precipitation Days: 114   Storm Days: 45

Average Temperatures			
	Daily High	Daily Low	Monthly Mean
January	41.5	23.7	32.6
February	45.4	26.4	35.9
March	54.6	34.0	44.3
April	67.9	45.5	56.7
May	77.0	54.4	65.7
June	86.0	63.4	74.7
July	88.9	66.7	77.8
August	88.0	64.4	76.2
September	81.4	56.7	69.1
October	71.2	45.2	58.2
November	55.2	34.5	44.9
December	44.0	26.5	35.3

Zero-Degree Days: 3
Freezing Days: 103
90-Degree Days: 39
Heating- and Cooling-Degree Days: 5,993

Fargo–Moorhead, ND–MN

Terrain: Moorhead, Minnesota, and Fargo, North Dakota, are twin cities in the Red River valley of the north. This river flows between the two cities and is part of the Hudson Bay drainage area. The river has no effect on the climate but does cause occasional severe spring flooding. Surrounding terrain is flat and open.

Climate: Summers are generally comfortable, with a few days of hot and humid weather; nights are cool. Winter months are cold and dry, with maximum temperatures rising above freezing only six times per month. At night, the temperature drops below zero half the time. With the flat terrain, surface friction has little slowing effect on the wind, contributing to the legendary Dakota blizzards. Strong winds with even light snowfall cause heavy snowdrifts. Surprisingly, the area averages only 35 inches of snow per year.

Pluses: Pleasant, dry summers.

Minuses: Extremely rigorous; ranks next to last in mildness of the 333 metro areas.

Places Rated Score: 148

Places Rated Rank: 332

Elevation: 899 feet

Relative Humidity: 71%
Wind Speed: 12.7 mph

Seasonal Change

Annual Rainfall 20 in

Annual Snowfall 35 in

Clear 87 days   Partly Cloudy 112 days   Cloudy 166 days

Precipitation Days: 102   Storm Days: 33

Average Temperatures			
	Daily High	Daily Low	Monthly Mean
January	15.4	−3.6	5.9
February	20.6	.8	10.7
March	33.5	14.9	24.2
April	52.6	31.9	42.3
May	66.8	42.3	54.6
June	75.9	53.4	64.7
July	82.8	58.6	70.7
August	81.6	56.8	69.2
September	69.6	46.2	57.9
October	58.4	35.5	47.0
November	37.2	20.0	28.6
December	21.9	4.1	13.0

Zero-Degree Days: 54
Freezing Days: 181
90-Degree Days: 15
Heating- and Cooling-Degree Days: 9,744

Fort Myers–Cape Coral, FL

Terrain: Located on the south bank of the Caloosahatchee River, about 15 miles from the Gulf of Mexico, Fort Myers sits on land that is level and low, with lush greenery.

Climate: Subtropical, with temperature extremes of both summer and winter checked by the influence of the Gulf. The average annual mean temperature is a warm 74° F, with averages ranging from the low 60s in January to the low 80s in the summer months. Winters are mild, with many bright, warm days and moderately cool nights. Maximum temperatures average in the low 90s from June through the first part of September, with daily highs of 90° F or greater on 80% of the days. Rainfall averages more than 50 inches annually, with two thirds of this total coming between June and September. Most rain falls as late afternoon or early evening thunderstorms, which in the summer bring welcome relief from the heat and occur almost every day.

Pluses: Mild, sunny winters.

Minuses: Hot, humid, stormy.

Places Rated Score: 342

Places Rated Rank: 317

Elevation: 15 feet

Relative Humidity: 76%
Wind Speed: 8.2 mph

Seasonal Change

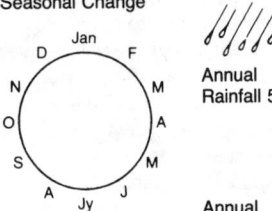

Annual Rainfall 54 in

Annual Snowfall 0 in

Clear 103 days   Partly Cloudy 161 days   Cloudy 101 days

Precipitation Days: 112   Storm Days: 93

Average Temperatures			
	Daily High	Daily Low	Monthly Mean
January	74.7	52.3	63.5
February	76.0	53.3	64.7
March	79.7	57.3	68.5
April	84.8	61.8	73.3
May	89.0	66.4	77.7
June	90.5	71.7	81.1
July	91.1	73.8	82.5
August	91.5	74.1	82.8
September	89.8	73.4	81.6
October	85.3	67.5	76.4
November	79.9	58.8	69.4
December	75.9	53.6	64.8

Zero-Degree Days: 0
Freezing Days: 1
90-Degree Days: 106
Heating- and Cooling-Degree Days: 4,168

Fort Smith, AR–OK

Terrain: Located at the confluence of the Poteau and Arkansas rivers. About 20 miles to the northwest are the Cookson Hills, which have an elevation of 1,500 feet. To the northeast are the Boston Mountains (in the Ozark region of Arkansas), 2,700 feet high. To the west, south, and east, the terrain is broken hills separated by creek- and river-bottom land. The bottomlands are very fertile and produce large yields of hay, beans, and spinach. Small wild game is plentiful; lakes and streams have an abundance of game fish.

Climate: Well-suited to raising fruits and berries. The climate is generally mild, except during the summer, which can be hot.

Pluses: Mild.

Minuses: Hot summers.

Elevation: 463 feet

Relative Humidity: 68%
Wind Speed: 7.6 mph

Seasonal Change

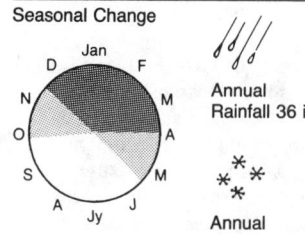

Annual Rainfall 42 in

Annual Snowfall 6 in

Clear 124 days   Partly Cloudy 96 days   Cloudy 145 days

Precipitation Days: 96   Storm Days: 57

Average Temperatures			
	Daily High	Daily Low	Monthly Mean
January	49.9	28.0	39.0
February	54.6	32.0	43.3
March	62.1	38.5	50.3
April	74.2	50.2	62.2
May	81.3	58.8	70.1
June	89.0	67.0	78.0
July	93.8	70.5	82.2
August	93.5	69.3	81.4
September	86.3	61.7	74.0
October	76.5	49.9	63.2
November	62.7	38.0	50.4
December	52.2	30.8	41.5

Zero-Degree Days: 0
Freezing Days: 80
90-Degree Days: 65
Heating- and Cooling-Degree Days: 5,358

Places Rated Score: 482   **Places Rated Rank: 246**

Fort Wayne, IN

Terrain: Located at the junction of the St. Mary's, St. Joseph, and Maumee rivers in northeastern Indiana. Terrain is generally level south and east of the city. Southwest and west, the land is somewhat rolling, while to the northwest and north it becomes slightly hilly. The highest point in the area is 40 miles north, near the town of Angola, where the elevation is 1,060 feet above sea level.

Climate: Similar to that of other midwestern cities at the same latitude. Precipitation is well distributed throughout the year, varying from a monthly rate of 2 inches in February to 4 inches in May. Damaging hailstorms may be expected twice a year. Snow usually covers the ground for 30 days each winter, but heavy snowstorms are rare. Average date of last freeze: April 26. First freeze: October 17.

Pluses: Milder version of Great Interior climate.

Minuses: Cold winters, hot summers.

Elevation: 828 feet

Relative Humidity: 72%
Wind Speed: 10.3 mph

Seasonal Change

Annual Rainfall 36 in

Annual Snowfall 31 in

Clear 77 days   Partly Cloudy 105 days   Cloudy 183 days

Precipitation Days: 131   Storm Days: 41

Average Temperatures			
	Daily High	Daily Low	Monthly Mean
January	32.6	17.9	25.3
February	35.5	19.7	27.6
March	45.1	27.9	36.5
April	59.5	39.0	49.3
May	70.2	48.9	59.6
June	80.1	58.8	69.5
July	83.6	62.4	73.0
August	82.2	60.4	71.3
September	75.9	53.0	64.5
October	64.6	42.5	53.6
November	48.3	32.0	40.2
December	35.7	21.4	28.6

Zero-Degree Days: 10
Freezing Days: 134
90-Degree Days: 14
Heating- and Cooling-Degree Days: 6,957

Places Rated Score: 509   **Places Rated Rank: 217**

Fresno, CA

Terrain: Rests in the middle of the San Joaquin Valley, near its eastern edge. The valley runs northwest to southeast and is about 225 miles long, with an average width of about 50 miles. The terrain around Fresno is generally level, with an abrupt upward slope 15 miles eastward to the foothills of the Sierra Nevada. This mountain range lies 50 miles to the east and has elevations from 12,000 feet to 14,000 feet. Forty-five miles to the west lie the foothills of the Coast Ranges.

Climate: Dry and sunny. Winters are mild, summers are hot. Ninety percent of the city's precipitation falls between November and April. Summers are virtually rainless. Because of the great amount of sunshine the valley receives, and the blockage of cooler moist air from the Pacific, daily maximum temperatures in July climb to the upper 90s. But on summer afternoons, the relative humidity is only 5% to 8%; on winter mornings, it is 90%.

Pluses: Sunny; nice springs and falls.

Minuses: Hot summers.

Elevation: 327 feet

Relative Humidity: 61%
Wind Speed: 6.3 mph

Seasonal Change

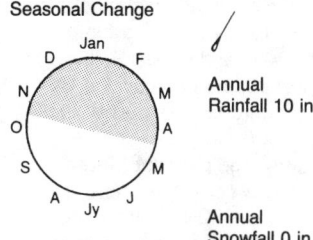

Annual Rainfall 10 in

Annual Snowfall 0 in

Clear 200 days   Partly Cloudy 71 days   Cloudy 94 days

Precipitation Days: 44   Storm Days: 6

Average Temperatures			
	Daily High	Daily Low	Monthly Mean
January	54.8	35.8	45.3
February	60.8	39.0	49.9
March	66.6	41.2	53.9
April	74.3	46.2	60.3
May	82.9	51.9	67.4
June	90.3	57.5	73.9
July	98.2	62.9	80.6
August	96.0	60.6	78.3
September	91.0	56.5	73.8
October	79.8	48.6	64.2
November	66.1	40.8	53.5
December	54.6	36.9	45.8

Zero-Degree Days: 0
Freezing Days: 29
90-Degree Days: 107
Heating- and Cooling-Degree Days: 4,321

Places Rated Score: 559   **Places Rated Rank: 132**

★ Galveston–Texas City, TX

Terrain: Located on Galveston Island, off the southeast coast of Texas. The island is nearly 3 miles across at its widest point and 29 miles long. It is bounded on the southeast by the Gulf of Mexico and on the northwest by Galveston Bay, which is about 3 miles wide at this point. The island's low-lying terrain makes it especially vulnerable to tidal surges.

Climate: Predominantly marine, with periods of modified continental influence during the colder months, when cold fronts from the Northwest sometimes reach the coast. Winters are very mild, with temperatures below 34° F recorded only about four times each winter. Normal daily maximum temperatures range from 60° F in January to 88° F in August, while minima range from 48° F in January to the upper 70s in the summer. The Great Hurricane of 1900, which swept over the island and killed approximately 6,000 people, was the worst natural disaster in American history. It also made inland Houston the major regional city, relegating Galveston to a resort community.

Pluses: Mild maritime climate.

Minuses: Hot summer spells.

Places Rated Score: 727

Places Rated Rank: 20

Elevation: 7 feet

Relative Humidity: 78%
Wind Speed: 11 mph

Seasonal Change

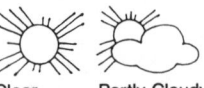

Annual Rainfall 42 in

Annual Snowfall 0 in

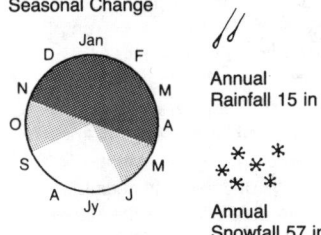

Clear 94 days   Partly Cloudy 109 days   Cloudy 162 days

Precipitation Days: 96   Storm Days: 70

Average Temperatures			
	Daily High	Daily Low	Monthly Mean
January	59.4	48.3	53.9
February	61.5	50.9	56.2
March	66.0	55.9	61.0
April	73.3	65.0	69.2
May	80.0	71.8	75.9
June	85.2	77.4	81.3
July	87.4	79.0	83.2
August	87.6	78.9	83.3
September	84.6	75.3	80.0
October	78.0	68.1	73.1
November	68.8	58.2	63.5
December	62.7	51.5	57.1

Zero-Degree Days: 0
Freezing Days: 4
90-Degree Days: 11
Heating- and Cooling-Degree Days: 4,228

Grand Rapids, MI

Terrain: Located in the Grand River valley 30 miles east of Lake Michigan. The Grand River, Michigan's largest stream, bisects the city. The valley has tall hills and bluffs rising on all sides, ranging in elevation from 600 feet to 1,000 feet. The area is known for fruit growing, especially peaches and cherries.

Climate: Largely determined by the proximity of Lake Michigan. In spring, the cooling effect of the lake retards the growth of vegetation until the danger of frost is past. In the fall, the warming effect holds off frost until the crops have matured. Summer days are warm and pleasant, with cooler nights. Winters are snowy and cold, but extremely cold temperatures or prolonged cold spells are rare because of the warm lake breeze. Average growing season: 170 days. Average date of last freeze: April 25. First freeze: October 12.

Pluses: Pleasant summers, temperatures moderated by Lake Michigan.

Minuses: Very cloudy, lots of snow.

Places Rated Score: 513

Places Rated Rank: 214

Elevation: 803 feet

Relative Humidity: 73%
Wind Speed: 9.9 mph

Seasonal Change

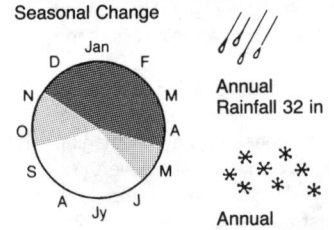

Annual Rainfall 32 in

Annual Snowfall 77 in

Clear 67 days   Partly Cloudy 96 days   Cloudy 202 days

Precipitation Days: 144 Storm Days: 37

Average Temperatures			
	Daily High	Daily Low	Monthly Mean
January	30.3	16.0	23.2
February	32.6	16.4	24.5
March	42.0	24.2	33.1
April	57.3	35.6	46.5
May	68.8	45.4	57.1
June	79.1	55.6	67.4
July	83.3	59.6	71.5
August	81.9	58.1	70.0
September	73.9	50.8	62.4
October	63.1	40.8	52.0
November	46.2	31.1	38.7
December	33.9	20.8	27.4

Zero-Degree Days: 8
Freezing Days: 149
90-Degree Days: 11
Heating- and Cooling-Degree Days: 7,376

Great Falls, MT

Terrain: Located astride the main stem of the Missouri River at its confluence with the Sun River. Except to the north and northeast, the valley is bordered by mountain ranges, which lie about 30 miles away from east to south, 40 miles to the southwest, and 60 miles to 100 miles from west to northwest. Terrain plays an important part in the climate here: The Continental Divide to the west and the Big Belt and Little Belt mountains to the south are major factors in producing the frequent wintertime Chinook winds blowing through this part of the state.

Climate: Semiarid. Summers are cool, sunny, and pleasant. Seventy percent of the annual rainfall occurs between April and September, the growing season. Winters are cold but continually modified by Chinook winds, which bear warm air from the Pacific, causing rapid warming and preventing accumulation of snow.

Pluses: Good, rigorous climate.

Minuses: Long winters.

Places Rated Score: 410

Places Rated Rank: 297

Elevation: 702 feet

Relative Humidity: 55%
Wind Speed: 13.1 mph

Seasonal Change

Annual Rainfall 15 in

Annual Snowfall 57 in

Clear 81 days   Partly Cloudy 106 days   Cloudy 178 days

Precipitation Days: 100 Storm Days: 26

Average Temperatures			
	Daily High	Daily Low	Monthly Mean
January	29.3	11.6	20.5
February	35.9	17.2	26.6
March	40.4	20.6	30.5
April	54.5	32.3	43.4
May	65.0	41.5	53.3
June	72.1	49.5	60.8
July	83.7	54.9	69.3
August	81.8	53.0	67.4
September	70.0	44.6	57.3
October	59.4	37.1	48.3
November	43.4	25.7	34.6
December	34.7	18.2	36.5

Zero-Degree Days: 28
Freezing Days: 156
90-Degree Days: 22
Heating- and Cooling-Degree Days: 7,991

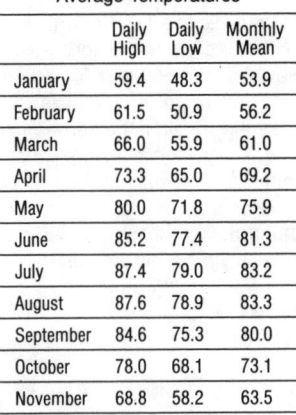

Green Bay, WI

Terrain: Located at the mouth of the Fox River, which empties into the southernmost end of Green Bay, a long and narrow bay off Lake Michigan in northeastern Wisconsin. The comparatively small temperature variation and the fact that the majority of precipitation falls during the growing periods contribute to successful dairy farming, as well as large acreages of vegetables, grown mostly for canning. Apple and cherry orchards predominate locally, with potatoes grown widely farther west.

Climate: Continental, modified somewhat by the proximity of Lake Superior to the northwest and Lake Michigan and Green Bay to the east. Summers are pleasant, with cool evenings and nights. Winters tend to be long and cold. Has a moderate amount of snow for a city in this region and latitude.

Pluses: Cool summers.

Minuses: Long winters.

Places Rated Score: 367

Places Rated Rank: 311

Elevation: 702 feet

Relative Humidity: 73%
Wind Speed: 10.2 mph

Seasonal Change

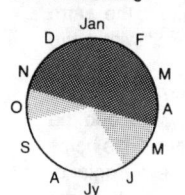

Annual Rainfall 27 in

Annual Snowfall 43 in

Clear 90 days
Partly Cloudy 102 days
Cloudy 173 days

Precipitation Days: 120 Storm Days: 35

Average Temperatures			
	Daily High	Daily Low	Monthly Mean
January	23.9	6.9	15.4
February	27.2	8.8	18.0
March	37.1	20.1	28.6
April	54.1	33.5	43.8
May	65.8	43.1	54.5
June	75.8	53.2	64.5
July	80.7	57.7	69.2
August	79.1	56.3	67.7
September	69.8	48.0	58.9
October	59.6	38.7	49.2
November	41.8	26.4	34.1
December	28.6	13.2	20.9

Zero-Degree Days: 29
Freezing Days: 163
90-Degree Days: 7
Heating- and Cooling-Degree Days: 8,484

Greenville–Spartanburg, SC

Terrain: Located on the Piedmont Plateau, on the eastern slope of the southern Appalachian Mountains. It is rolling country with the first ridge of mountains about 20 miles to the northwest. These mountains usually protect the area from the full force of the cold air masses that move southeastward from central Canada during the winter.

Climate: The area's elevation is conducive to cool nights, even during the summer months. The temperature rises to 90° F or above on almost half of the days during the summer but usually falls to 70° F or lower at night. Winters are mild and pleasant, with the temperature falling below freezing during daylight hours only several times annually, though the nights are colder. There are usually two freezing rainstorms and two or three small snowstorms each winter. Rainfall is abundant and well distributed throughout the year. The region is fairly stormy, but tornadoes are infrequent. Average growing season: 225 days.

Pluses: Mildness coupled with variety.

Minuses: Hot summers.

Places Rated Score: 655

Places Rated Rank: 32

Elevation: 971 feet

Relative Humidity: 70%
Wind Speed: 6.8 mph

Seasonal Change

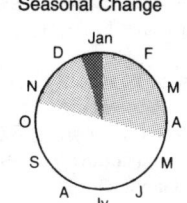

Annual Rainfall 48 in

Annual Snowfall 6 in

Clear 117 days
Partly Cloudy 104 days
Cloudy 144 days

Precipitation Days: 119 Storm Days: 44

Average Temperatures			
	Daily High	Daily Low	Monthly Mean
January	51.6	33.0	42.3
February	54.1	34.7	44.4
March	61.6	40.2	50.9
April	72.0	49.9	61.0
May	79.9	58.3	69.1
June	85.9	65.9	75.9
July	87.6	69.0	78.3
August	86.8	68.1	77.5
September	81.0	62.3	71.7
October	72.4	50.9	61.7
November	61.8	40.1	51.0
December	52.4	33.3	42.9

Zero-Degree Days: 0
Freezing Days: 68
90-Degree Days: 29
Heating- and Cooling-Degree Days: 4,736

Harrisburg–Lebanon–Carlisle, PA

Terrain: Situated on the east bank of the Susquehanna River in the Great Valley formed by the eastern foothills of the Appalachian chain and about 60 miles southeast of the state's geographic center. It is nestled in a saucerlike depression 8 miles to 10 miles south of the Blue Mountains. This serves as a barrier to severe winter weather experienced 50 miles to 100 miles to the north and west. Although Harrisburg is too far inland (150 miles) to derive full benefits of the coastal climate, it does receive precipitation produced when warm, maritime air from the Atlantic is forced upslope to cross the Blue Ridge Mountains.

Climate: Although the saucer-shaped valley protects the area from generally severe winter weather, it often traps cool air, which causes the accumulation of heavy fog and industrial smoke. Fortunately, the weather is changeable enough so that this trapped air does not remain for long. Average growing season: 201 days.

Pluses: Relatively mild winters, changeable weather.

Minuses: Damp, foggy.

Places Rated Score: 556

Places Rated Rank: 143

Elevation: 351 feet

Relative Humidity: 67%
Wind Speed: 7.7 mph

Seasonal Change

Annual Rainfall 36 in

Annual Snowfall 35 in

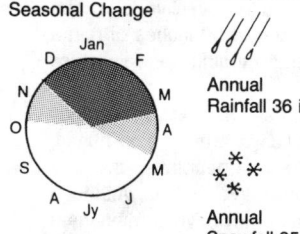
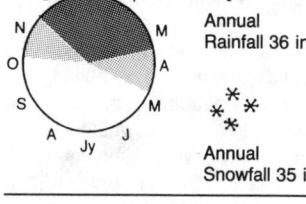

Clear 86 days
Partly Cloudy 107 days
Cloudy 172 days

Precipitation Days: 125 Storm Days: 33

Average Temperatures			
	Daily High	Daily Low	Monthly Mean
January	37.7	22.5	30.1
February	40.5	24.0	32.3
March	50.7	31.2	41.0
April	64.1	41.5	52.8
May	74.5	51.6	63.1
June	83.0	61.0	72.0
July	86.8	65.4	76.1
August	84.6	63.2	73.9
September	78.0	56.0	67.0
October	66.9	44.6	55.8
November	52.9	34.7	43.8
December	40.1	25.0	32.6

Zero-Degree Days: 1
Freezing Days: 107
90-Degree Days: 24
Heating- and Cooling-Degree Days: 6,249

Hartford, CT

Terrain: Located on the Connecticut River on a slight rise of ground between north-south mountain ranges whose heights do not exceed 1,200 feet. It is near the state's geographic center, about 30 miles due north of Long Island Sound.

Climate: Varies from the cold continental climate in winter to the warm maritime air of summer. Hartford's latitude places it well within the northern temperate climate zone, with westerly winds bearing the majority of weather systems. The average wintertime polar front, which is the boundary between masses of cold, dry polar air and the warm, moist air of the tropics, is just south of New England. This helps explain the great changeability of the weather in New England, characterized by rapidly shifting winds and temperatures, and frequent storms. Hartford's proximity to the ocean is also significant, since many storms move upward along the Atlantic Coast, frequently producing strong and persistent northeast winds.

Pluses: Changeable, varied, yet relatively mild.

Minuses: Stormy.

Places Rated Score: 516

Places Rated Rank: 207

Elevation: 179 feet

Relative Humidity: 68%
Wind Speed: 9 mph

Seasonal Change

Annual Rainfall 43 in

Annual Snowfall 53 in

Clear 78 days | Partly Cloudy 110 days | Cloudy 177 days

Precipitation Days: 128   Storm Days: 22

Average Temperatures			
	Daily High	Daily Low	Monthly Mean
January	33.4	16.1	24.8
February	35.7	17.9	26.8
March	44.6	26.6	35.6
April	58.9	36.5	47.7
May	70.3	46.2	58.3
June	79.5	56.0	67.8
July	84.1	61.2	72.7
August	81.9	58.9	70.4
September	74.5	51.0	62.8
October	64.3	40.8	52.6
November	50.6	31.9	41.3
December	36.8	19.6	28.2

Zero-Degree Days: 6
Freezing Days: 36
90-Degree Days: 20
Heating- and Cooling-Degree Days: 6,934

★ Honolulu, HI

Terrain: Oahu, the island on which Honolulu is located, is the third largest of the Hawaiian Islands. The Koolau Range, at an average height of 2,000 feet, parallels the northeast coast. The Waianae Mountains, somewhat higher in elevation, parallel the west coast. Much of the city lies along the coastal plain, leeward (relative to the trade winds) of the Koolaus.

Climate: Mild marine tropical. Honolulu shows the least seasonal temperature change of any American city: The difference between the mean January minimum temperature and the August maximum mean temperature is only about 22 degrees. Honolulu's location just south of the Tropic of Cancer in the Pacific Ocean assures this mildness. It has no snow, fog, or freezing weather, and an average of only nine 90-degree days and seven thunderstorms a year. There are no heating-degree days here. Although it can be uncomfortably warm occasionally, the persistent trade winds give relief.

Pluses: Extremely mild.

Minuses: A bit monotonous.

Places Rated Score: 717

Places Rated Rank: 22

Elevation: 15 feet

Relative Humidity: 67%
Wind Speed: 11.8 mph

Seasonal Change

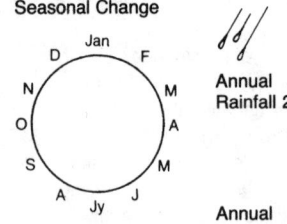

Annual Rainfall 23 in

Annual Snowfall 0 in

Clear 90 days | Partly Cloudy 174 days | Cloudy 101 days

Precipitation Days: 102   Storm Days: 7

Average Temperatures			
	Daily High	Daily Low	Monthly Mean
January	79.3	65.3	72.3
February	79.2	65.3	72.3
March	79.7	66.3	73.0
April	81.4	68.1	74.8
May	83.6	70.2	76.9
June	85.6	72.2	78.9
July	86.8	73.4	80.1
August	87.4	74.0	80.7
September	87.4	73.4	80.4
October	85.8	72.0	78.9
November	83.2	69.8	76.5
December	80.3	67.1	73.7

Zero-Degree Days: 0
Freezing Days: 0
90-Degree Days: 9
Heating- and Cooling-Degree Days: 4,221

Houston, TX

Terrain: Located in the flat Coastal Plain of the state, about 50 miles inland from the Gulf of Mexico and 25 miles from Galveston Bay. The surrounding numerous small streams and bayous, together with the bay, favor the development of both ground and advective fogs. The land is low and flat and, since it receives almost 50 inches of rain a year, is ideal for agriculture—especially fruit farming—and livestock raising.

Climate: Predominantly marine. Temperatures are modified by winds from the Gulf. Winters are mild. Summer days are hot and humid, though the evenings are relatively cool. Polar air penetrates the area frequently enough to provide some stimulating variety. Although temperatures dip below freezing occasionally, they never remain there long, accounting for a year-round growing season. Destructive windstorms are fairly infrequent, but thunderstorms and hurricanes occur occasionally.

Pluses: Mild winters.

Minuses: Hot and humid.

Places Rated Score: 424

Places Rated Rank: 290

Elevation: 108 feet

Relative Humidity: 77%
Wind Speed: 6.1 mph

Seasonal Change

Annual Rainfall 48 in

Annual Snowfall 0 in

Clear 94 days | Partly Cloudy 109 days | Cloudy 162 days

Precipitation Days: 107   Storm Days: 69

Average Temperatures			
	Daily High	Daily Low	Monthly Mean
January	62.6	41.5	52.1
February	66.0	44.6	55.3
March	71.8	49.8	60.8
April	79.4	59.3	69.4
May	85.9	65.6	75.8
June	91.3	70.9	81.1
July	93.8	72.8	83.3
August	94.3	72.4	83.4
September	90.1	68.2	79.2
October	83.5	58.3	70.9
November	73.0	49.1	61.1
December	65.8	43.4	54.6

Zero-Degree Days: 0
Freezing Days: 24
90-Degree Days: 81
Heating- and Cooling-Degree Days: 4,323

Huntsville, AL

Terrain: The city is almost surrounded by the foothills of the Appalachian Mountains. The Tennessee River winds its way westward about 7 miles south of the city, and the broad and fertile Tennessee Valley, with flat to gently rolling terrain, extends to the west.

Climate: Cold air masses from the north predominate during the winter, but at times mild air from the Gulf of Mexico, spreading northward to Huntsville and beyond, may persist for several days. There are very few severely cold days. Temperatures drop below zero on an average of once a year. Springs are variable and can be stormy as cold polar air and warm Gulf air meet. Summers are hot and humid, relieved only by the showers that come about every three days. Falls are dry, cooler, and pleasant. The length of the growing season, 241 days, and high rainfall make the area suitable for truck farming.

Pluses: Mild yet variable winter through spring.

Minuses: Hot, humid summers.

Places Rated Score: 600

Places Rated Rank: 80

Elevation: 644 feet

Relative Humidity: 73%
Wind Speed: 8 mph

Seasonal Change

Annual Rainfall 52 in

Annual Snowfall 3 in

Clear 106 days   Partly Cloudy 101 days   Cloudy 158 days

Precipitation Days: 121   Storm Days: 58

Average Temperatures			
	Daily High	Daily Low	Monthly Mean
January	50.5	31.3	40.9
February	54.0	33.2	43.6
March	61.7	39.8	50.8
April	73.1	50.2	61.7
May	80.9	58.3	69.6
June	87.9	65.9	76.9
July	90.2	68.8	79.5
August	90.2	67.7	79.0
September	84.2	61.6	72.9
October	74.5	49.8	62.2
November	61.6	38.9	50.3
December	52.1	32.7	42.4

Zero-Degree Days: 0
Freezing Days: 65
90-Degree Days: 38
Heating- and Cooling-Degree Days: 5,110

Indianapolis, IN

Terrain: Located in the central part of the state on mostly level or slightly rolling terrain. The greater part of the city lies east of the White River, which flows approximately from north to south. From Weir Cook Airport, 7 miles southwest of the city, the terrain slopes gradually downward to the city, then upward again past the city to the east.

Climate: Continental. Rather warm summers, moderately cold winters, and occasional wide variations in temperatures, especially during the cold season. Snowfalls of 3 inches or more occur about three times annually. Periods of muggy weather can occur in summer, although usually air masses from the Gulf of Mexico are soon replaced by cooler air from the northern Plains and Great Lakes. Occasionally, hot dry winds from the Southwest prevail. Late spring and fall are the most pleasant seasons. Precipitation, well distributed throughout the year, is normally adequate for good crops. Several flood-control reservoirs protect most formerly flood-prone areas.

Pluses: Pleasant springs and falls.

Minuses: Humid spells in summer, cold winters.

Places Rated Score: 557

Places Rated Rank: 141

Elevation: 808 feet

Relative Humidity: 73%
Wind Speed: 9.7 mph

Seasonal Change

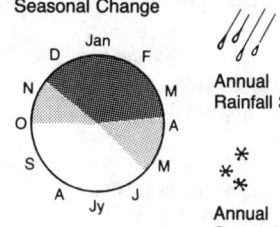

Annual Rainfall 39 in

Annual Snowfall 21 in

Clear 90 days   Partly Cloudy 101 days   Cloudy 174 days

Precipitation Days: 122   Storm Days: 45

Average Temperatures			
	Daily High	Daily Low	Monthly Mean
January	36.0	19.7	27.9
February	39.3	22.1	30.7
March	49.0	30.3	39.7
April	62.8	41.8	52.3
May	72.9	51.5	62.2
June	82.3	61.1	71.7
July	85.4	64.6	75.0
August	84.0	62.4	73.2
September	77.7	54.9	66.3
October	67.0	44.3	55.7
November	50.5	32.8	41.7
December	38.7	23.1	30.9

Zero-Degree Days: 7
Freezing Days: 122
90-Degree Days: 15
Heating- and Cooling-Degree Days: 6,551

Jackson, MS

Terrain: Jackson is about 45 miles east of the Mississippi River on the west bank of the Pearl River and about 150 miles north of the Gulf of Mexico. The terrain is gently rolling, with no local topographic features that appreciably influence the weather. Alluvial plains up to 3 miles wide extend along the river near Jackson. Some levees have been built on both sides of the river.

Climate: Significantly humid during most of the year, with one short cold season and one long warm one. In summer, the southerly winds and accompanying warm Gulf air masses predominate, resulting in a warm, humid maritime climate. Summer days are hot and humid, and often so are the nights. In winter, colder northern air occasionally invades the area, causing rapid and sometimes dramatic temperature shifts. Average freeze-free period: 235 days.

Pluses: Long summers.

Minuses: Hot, humid, stormy.

Places Rated Score: 412

Places Rated Rank: 295

Elevation: 331 feet

Relative Humidity: 75%
Wind Speed: 7.6 mph

Seasonal Change

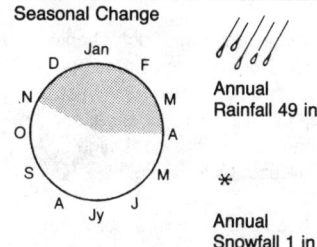

Annual Rainfall 49 in

Annual Snowfall 1 in

Clear 109 days   Partly Cloudy 108 days   Cloudy 148 days

Precipitation Days: 112   Storm Days: 65

Average Temperatures			
	Daily High	Daily Low	Monthly Mean
January	58.4	35.8	47.1
February	61.7	37.8	49.8
March	68.7	43.4	56.1
April	78.2	53.1	65.7
May	85.0	60.4	72.7
June	91.0	67.7	79.4
July	92.7	70.6	81.7
August	92.6	69.8	81.2
September	88.0	64.0	76.0
October	80.1	51.5	65.8
November	68.5	42.0	55.3
December	60.5	37.3	48.9

Zero-Degree Days: 0
Freezing Days: 47
90-Degree Days: 78
Heating- and Cooling-Degree Days: 4,621

Jacksonville, FL

Terrain: Jacksonville, located on the St. Johns River about 16 miles inland from the Atlantic Ocean, is near the northern boundary of the trade winds. The surrounding terrain is level.

Climate: Humid subtropical. The atmosphere is moist, with an average relative humidity of about 75%, ranging from a high of 90% in early morning to about 55% in late afternoon. The average daily sunshine ranges from five and one-half hours in December to nine hours in May. The greatest amount of rain, mostly in the form of local thundershowers, falls during the last summer months, when a measurable amount can be expected every other day.

Pluses: Pleasant winters.

Minuses: Hot, stormy summers.

Places Rated Score: 457

Places Rated Rank: 268

Elevation: 31 feet

Relative Humidity: 75%
Wind Speed: 8.5 mph

Seasonal Change

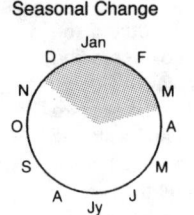

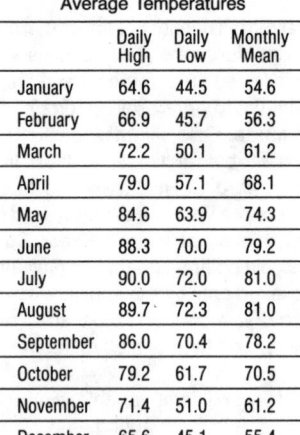

Annual Rainfall 54 in

Annual Snowfall 0 in

Clear 98 days | Partly Cloudy 128 days | Cloudy 139 days

Precipitation Days: 116 Storm Days: 64

	Average Temperatures		
	Daily High	Daily Low	Monthly Mean
January	64.6	44.5	54.6
February	66.9	45.7	56.3
March	72.2	50.1	61.2
April	79.0	57.1	68.1
May	84.6	63.9	74.3
June	88.3	70.0	79.2
July	90.0	72.0	81.0
August	89.7	72.3	81.0
September	86.0	70.4	78.2
October	79.2	61.7	70.5
November	71.4	51.0	61.2
December	65.6	45.1	55.4

Zero-Degree Days: 0
Freezing Days: 12
90-Degree Days: 82
Heating- and Cooling-Degree Days: 3,923

★ Johnson City–Kingsport–Bristol, TN–VA

Terrain: This tri-city area is located in the extreme upper east Tennessee Valley. Mountain ranges begin about 10 miles to the southeast and 15 miles to the west and north, with many peaks and ridges rising to 4,000 feet, and some to 6,000 feet in the southeast.

Climate: The topography has considerable influence on the weather changes peculiar to this area. Moist easterly air flow in the lower levels of the atmosphere is more or less blocked on the eastern slopes of the mountains, thus producing an abundance of precipitation in these higher ridges and reaching the tri-city area drier and slightly warmer. Although average annual rainfall is 41 inches in the vicinity, annual amounts of 80 inches have been recorded in mountainous sections to the east and south. Snowfall seldom begins before November and rarely remains on the ground more than a few days. Mountainous regions to the southeast, however, are frequently blanketed for long periods.

Pluses: Mild winters.

Minuses: Can be drizzly.

Places Rated Score: 663

Places Rated Rank: 29

Elevation: 1,525 feet

Relative Humidity: 72%
Wind Speed: 5.6 mph

Seasonal Change

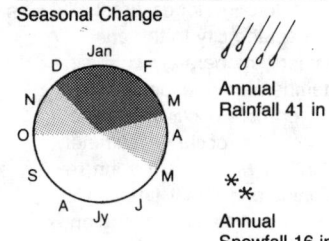

Annual Rainfall 41 in

Annual Snowfall 16 in

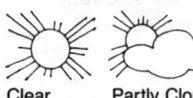

Clear 90 days | Partly Cloudy 112 days | Cloudy 163 days

Precipitation Days: 134 Storm Days: 45

	Average Temperatures		
	Daily High	Daily Low	Monthly Mean
January	46.0	26.7	36.4
February	48.9	28.4	38.7
March	57.1	34.5	45.8
April	68.3	44.2	56.3
May	77.1	52.6	64.9
June	84.0	60.7	72.4
July	85.9	64.4	75.2
August	85.3	63.1	74.2
September	80.4	56.6	68.5
October	70.4	45.3	57.9
November	56.9	34.5	45.7
December	47.3	28.0	37.7

Zero-Degree Days: 1
Freezing Days: 96
90-Degree Days: 13
Heating- and Cooling-Degree Days: 5,413

Kansas City, MO-KS

Terrain: Kansas City is very near the geographic center of the United States. The surrounding terrain is gently rolling. Its continental climate is modified by a lack of natural obstructions to the free sweep of air currents from all directions.

Climate: Early spring brings a period of frequent and rapid fluctuations of weather, tapering off as spring progresses. Summer days are warm, sometimes hot, but nights are mild with moderate humidity. As with so many locations in America's heartland, fall is the most pleasant season, characterized by many mild sunny days and cool nights. Average date of last freeze: April 7. First freeze: October 26.

Pluses: Sunny; good four-season climate.

Minuses: Variable weather in early spring; winters can be cold, summers hot.

Places Rated Score: 549

Places Rated Rank: 151

Elevation: 1,025 feet

Relative Humidity: 68%
Wind Speed: 10.3 mph

Seasonal Change

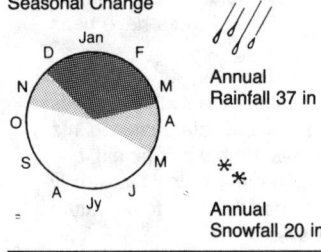

Annual Rainfall 37 in

Annual Snowfall 20 in

Clear 132 days | Partly Cloudy 85 days | Cloudy 148 days

Precipitation Days: 97 Storm Days: 47

	Average Temperatures		
	Daily High	Daily Low	Monthly Mean
January	36.2	19.3	27.8
February	41.9	24.2	33.1
March	50.5	31.8	41.2
April	64.8	45.1	55.0
May	74.3	55.7	65.0
June	82.6	65.2	73.9
July	88.0	69.6	78.8
August	86.7	68.1	77.4
September	78.8	58.8	68.8
October	68.9	48.3	58.6
November	52.7	34.5	43.6
December	40.4	24.1	32.3

Zero-Degree Days: 5
Freezing Days: 105
90-Degree Days: 40
Heating- and Cooling-Degree Days: 6,581

★ Knoxville, TN

Terrain: Located in a broad valley between the Cumberland Mountains to the northwest and the Great Smoky Mountains to the southeast. The Cumberland Mountains serve to retard and weaken the force of the cold winter air moving down from the northern Plains during the colder months, and the Smoky Mountains shelter Knoxville from much of the hot, humid tropical air that moves northward during the summertime.

Climate: Moderate, thanks to the sheltering effects of the two mountain ranges. Though summers are long, the nights are almost always cool, with the average diurnal variation being about 20 degrees. The mean daytime temperature for July is 81° F, but nighttime temperatures are in the mid-70s.

Pluses: Mild mountain climate.   **Minuses:** Somewhat stormy in summer.

Places Rated Score: 670   **Places Rated Rank: 26**

Elevation: 980 feet

Relative Humidity: 71%
Wind Speed: 7.3 mph

Seasonal Change

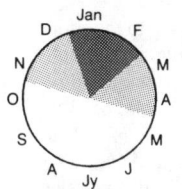

Annual Rainfall 46 in

Annual Snowfall 12 in

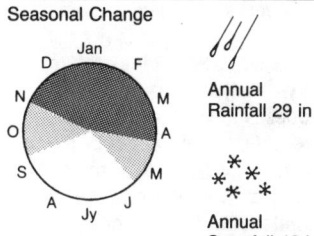

Clear 95 days   Partly Cloudy 107 days   Cloudy 163 days

Precipitation Days: 128   Storm Days: 47

	Average Temperatures		
	Daily High	Daily Low	Monthly Mean
January	48.9	32.2	40.6
February	52.0	33.5	42.8
March	60.4	39.4	49.9
April	72.0	48.6	60.3
May	79.8	56.9	68.4
June	86.1	64.8	75.5
July	88.0	68.3	78.2
August	87.3	67.2	77.3
September	82.0	61.2	71.6
October	71.8	50.0	60.9
November	58.9	39.4	49.2
December	49.8	33.1	41.5

Zero-Degree Days: 1
Freezing Days: 71
90-Degree Days: 19
Heating- and Cooling-Degree Days: 5,047

La Crosse, WI

Terrain: Situated on the east bank of the Mississippi River at the confluence of the Mississippi, Black, and La Crosse rivers. The town is on a level, sandy plain, but steep-sided hills with narrow valleys are characteristic of most of the surrounding area. The leading field crops are corn, hay, and oats. Dairying is the principal farm activity.

Climate: The location of the city in a natural bowl between the hills results in colder temperatures at night due to air drainage and in valley fogs that often persist through forenoon. The continental climate means frequent variations in temperature. Winters are cold and humid; snows are frequent. Summers are warm and moderately humid. Most of the annual precipitation falls during the main growing season extending from May to September.

Pluses: Five-month growing season with above-average rainfall.   **Minuses:** Long, cold winters with frequent snow.

Places Rated Score: 352   **Places Rated Rank: 314**

Elevation: 672 feet

Relative Humidity: 72%
Wind Speed: 8.9 mph

Seasonal Change

Annual Rainfall 29 in

Annual Snowfall 43 in

Clear 95 days   Partly Cloudy 97 days   Cloudy 173 days

Precipitation Days: 109   Storm Days: 40

	Average Temperatures		
	Daily High	Daily Low	Monthly Mean
January	25.0	7.1	16.1
February	29.7	10.3	20.0
March	40.0	22.1	31.1
April	57.8	37.4	47.6
May	69.3	48.7	59.0
June	78.4	58.5	68.5
July	83.0	62.5	72.8
August	81.7	61.0	71.4
September	71.8	51.8	61.8
October	61.8	41.7	51.8
November	43.0	27.8	35.4
December	29.6	14.0	21.8

Zero-Degree Days: 26
Freezing Days: 152
90-Degree Days: 16
Heating- and Cooling-Degree Days: 8,112

Las Vegas, NV

Terrain: Situated near the center of a broad desert valley surrounded by mountains ranging from 2,000 feet to 10,000 feet higher than the valley's floor. These mountains act as effective barriers to moisture-laden storms moving eastward from the Pacific Ocean, so that Las Vegas sees very few overcast or rainy days.

Climate: Summers are typical of a desert climate—low humidity with maximum temperatures in the 100-degree levels. Nearby mountains contribute to relatively cool nights, with minimums between 70° F and 75° F. Springs and falls are ideal: Outdoor activities are rarely interrupted by adverse weather conditions. Winters, too, are mild, with daytime averages of 60° F, clear skies, and warm sunshine.

Pluses: Mild year-round climate with especially pleasant springs and falls.   **Minuses:** High winds, though infrequent, bring dust and sand.

Places Rated Score: 556   **Places Rated Rank: 143**

Elevation: 2,180 feet

Relative Humidity: 29%
Wind Speed: 9 mph

Seasonal Change

Annual Rainfall 4 in

Annual Snowfall 1.5 in

Clear 216 days   Partly Cloudy 84 days   Cloudy 65 days

Precipitation Days: 24   Storm Days: 15

	Average Temperatures		
	Daily High	Daily Low	Monthly Mean
January	55.7	32.6	44.2
February	61.3	36.9	49.1
March	67.8	41.7	54.8
April	77.5	50.0	63.8
May	87.5	59.0	73.3
June	97.2	67.4	82.3
July	103.9	75.3	89.6
August	101.5	73.3	87.4
September	94.8	65.4	80.1
October	81.0	53.1	67.1
November	65.7	40.8	53.3
December	56.7	33.7	45.2

Zero-Degree Days: 0
Freezing Days: 41
90-Degree Days: 131
Heating- and Cooling-Degree Days: 5,547

Lexington–Fayette, KY

Terrain: Located in the heart of the Kentucky Bluegrass region on a gently rolling plateau with varying elevations of 900 feet to 1,050 feet. The surrounding country is noted for its beauty, fertile soil, excellent grass, stock farms, and burley tobacco. There are no bodies of water nearby that are large enough to have an effect on climate.
Climate: Decidedly continental, temperate, yet subject to sudden large but brief changes in temperature. Precipitation is evenly distributed throughout the winter, spring, and summer, with an average of 12 inches falling in each of these seasons. Snowfall is variable, but the ground does not retain snow for more than a few days at a time. The months of September and October are the most pleasant of the year; they have the least precipitation, the most clear days, and generally comfortable temperatures.

Pluses: Temperate, four-season climate with pleasant falls.

Minuses: Large diurnal temperature range.

Places Rated Score: 635

Places Rated Rank: 48

Elevation: 989 feet

Relative Humidity: 70%
Wind Speed: 9.7 mph

Seasonal Change

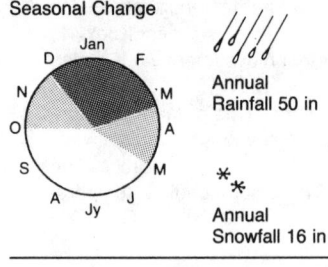

Annual Rainfall 50 in

Annual Snowfall 16 in

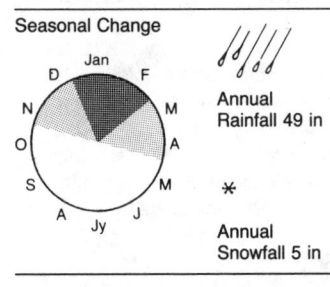

Clear 95 days
Partly Cloudy 102 days
Cloudy 168 days

Precipitation Days: 130   Storm Days: 47

Average Temperatures			
	Daily High	Daily Low	Monthly Mean
January	41.3	24.5	32.9
February	44.3	26.2	35.3
March	53.4	33.7	43.6
April	66.0	44.6	55.3
May	75.5	53.8	64.7
June	83.5	62.5	73.0
July	86.4	65.9	76.2
August	85.5	64.4	75.0
September	79.6	57.6	68.6
October	68.8	46.8	57.8
November	53.9	35.3	44.6
December	43.7	27.2	35.5

Zero-Degree Days: 2
Freezing Days: 97
90-Degree Days: 16
Heating- and Cooling-Degree Days: 5,926

Lincoln, NE

Terrain: Lies on rolling prairie in southeastern Nebraska beyond the edge of the tornado and hail belt.
Climate: The majority of winter outbreaks of severely cold air from Canada move over the Lincoln area. However, the centers of some cold air masses move so far to the east that their full effect is not felt here. The Chinook effect often produces rapid rises in temperature during the winter, with a shift of the wind to westerly. An average winter brings 26 inches of snow, most of which doesn't melt until spring. The crop season, April through September, receives three fourths of the yearly precipitation. Nighttime showers occur mostly in the summer. There is much sunshine—Lincoln receives an average of 64% of possible sunlight—with humidity at a comfortable level, except for short periods during the summer.

Pluses: Varied but not too rigorous continental climate.

Minuses: Occasional high winds and high temperature combinations; long winters.

Places Rated Score: 398

Places Rated Rank: 302

Elevation: 1,189 feet

Relative Humidity: 68%
Wind Speed: 10.5 mph

Seasonal Change

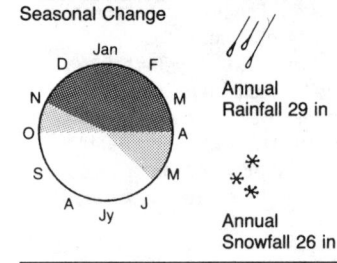

Annual Rainfall 29 in

Annual Snowfall 26 in

Clear 115 days
Partly Cloudy 97 days
Cloudy 153 days

Precipitation Days: 88   Storm Days: 9

Average Temperatures			
	Daily High	Daily Low	Monthly Mean
January	32.8	11.7	22.2
February	38.3	17.4	27.9
March	47.0	26.0	36.5
April	63.4	39.2	51.3
May	73.4	50.6	62.0
June	83.1	60.9	72.0
July	88.9	65.7	77.3
August	87.0	64.2	75.6
September	77.5	53.6	65.6
October	67.6	44.2	54.9
November	50.3	27.8	39.0
December	37.7	16.9	27.3

Zero-Degree Days: 17
Freezing Days: 146
90-Degree Days: 43
Heating- and Cooling-Degree Days: 7,366

Little Rock–North Little Rock, AR

Terrain: Located on the Arkansas River near the geographic center of the state. To the west lie the Ouachita Mountains and to the east the flat lowlands of the Mississippi River valley.
Climate: Modified four-season continental climate. The area is exposed to all North American air-mass types, but the Gulf of Mexico gives the summer season prolonged periods of warm and humid weather. Sixty-two percent of the normal annual precipitation occurs during the growing season, averaging 233 days. Winters are mild, but polar and Arctic outbreaks are not uncommon. Glaze and ice storms, though infrequent, can be severe.

Pluses: Negligible snow, long growing season, sufficient precipitation.

Minuses: Long periods of warm, humid days in summer.

Places Rated Score: 497

Places Rated Rank: 228

Elevation: 265 feet

Relative Humidity: 70%
Wind Speed: 8.2 mph

Seasonal Change

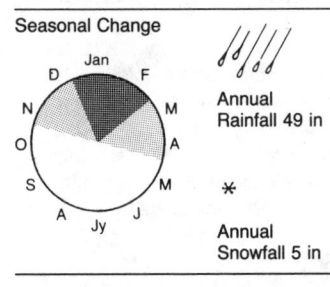

Annual Rainfall 49 in

Annual Snowfall 5 in

Clear 120 days
Partly Cloudy 100 days
Cloudy 145 days

Precipitation Days: 104   Storm Days: 57

Average Temperatures			
	Daily High	Daily Low	Monthly Mean
January	50.1	28.9	39.5
February	53.8	31.9	42.9
March	61.8	38.7	50.3
April	73.5	49.9	61.7
May	81.4	58.1	69.8
June	89.3	66.8	78.1
July	92.6	70.1	81.4
August	92.6	68.6	80.6
September	85.8	60.8	73.3
October	76.0	48.7	62.4
November	62.4	38.1	50.3
December	52.1	31.1	41.6

Zero-Degree Days: 0
Freezing Days: 63
90-Degree Days: 70
Heating- and Cooling-Degree Days: 5,279

★ Los Angeles–Long Beach, CA

Terrain: Predominating influences on the climate of Los Angeles are the Pacific Ocean, 3 miles to the west, and the southern California coastal mountain ranges, which line the inland side of the coastal plain of the city and act as buffers to the more extreme conditions of the interior.

Climate: The most characteristic features of this mild, two-season climate are low clouds at night and morning, and sunny afternoons that prevail during the spring and summer and occur often during the remainder of the year. Combined with a sea breeze, the coastal cloudiness is associated with mild temperatures throughout the year. Pronounced differences in temperature, humidity, fog, sunshine, and rain occur over fairly short distances on the coastal plains and adjoining foothills. Temperature ranges are least and humidity higher close to the coast; precipitation increases with elevation.

Pluses: Positive benefits from Pacific Ocean and surrounding foothills.

Minuses: Frequent haze, fog, and smoke; dry Santa Ana winds.

Places Rated Score: 885

Places Rated Rank: 5

Elevation: 104 feet

Relative Humidity: 71%
Wind Speed: 7.4 mph

Seasonal Change

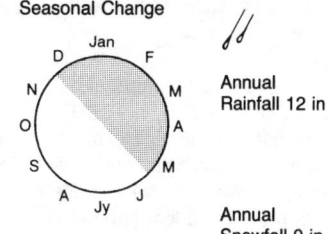

Annual Rainfall 12 in

Annual Snowfall 0 in

Clear 143 days

Partly Cloudy 115 days

Cloudy 107 days

Precipitation Days: 35   Storm Days: 3

Average Temperatures			
	Daily High	Daily Low	Monthly Mean
January	63.5	45.4	54.5
February	64.1	47.0	55.6
March	64.3	48.6	56.5
April	65.9	51.7	58.8
May	68.4	55.3	61.9
June	70.3	58.6	64.5
July	74.8	62.1	68.5
August	75.8	63.2	69.5
September	75.7	61.6	68.7
October	72.9	57.5	65.2
November	69.6	51.3	60.5
December	66.5	47.3	56.9

Zero-Degree Days: 0
Freezing Days: 0
90-Degree Days: 5
Heating- and Cooling-Degree Days: 2,437

Louisville, KY–IN

Terrain: Located on the south bank of the Ohio River, about 400 miles southwest of Pittsburgh. The eastern part of the city is residential and consists of rolling hills and plateaus. The western, industrial part lies on the river's floodplain. A low range of hills on the Indiana bank provides a partial barrier to icy blasts of winter.

Climate: Continental, but more variable because of its position in midlatitudes, in the belt of westerly winds, not completely shut off from the Gulf of Mexico. Winters are moderately cold. Snows, although seldom heavy, are a usual occurrence from November through March. Summers are quite warm, with high relative humidity and rainstorms of high intensity common during both springs and summers.

Pluses: Well-defined seasons with good precipitation.

Minuses: Humid summers, intense rainfalls.

Places Rated Score: 616

Places Rated Rank: 60

Elevation: 488 feet

Relative Humidity: 69%
Wind Speed: 8.4 mph

Seasonal Change

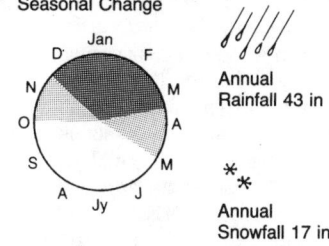

Annual Rainfall 43 in

Annual Snowfall 17 in

Clear 94 days

Partly Cloudy 103 days

Cloudy 168 days

Precipitation Days: 124   Storm Days: 45

Average Temperatures			
	Daily High	Daily Low	Monthly Mean
January	42.0	24.5	33.3
February	45.0	26.5	35.8
March	54.0	34.0	44.0
April	66.9	44.8	55.9
May	75.6	53.9	64.8
June	83.7	62.9	73.3
July	87.3	66.4	76.9
August	86.8	64.9	76.9
September	80.5	57.7	69.1
October	70.3	45.9	58.1
November	54.9	35.1	45.0
December	44.1	27.1	35.6

Zero-Degree Days: 2
Freezing Days: 92
90-Degree Days: 24
Heating- and Cooling-Degree Days: 5,908

Lubbock, TX

Terrain: Located in a plateau area of northwestern Texas that is often referred to as the South Plains region. It is an essentially level area with numerous small playas, small stream valleys, and low hummocks. There are no appreciable terrain features that affect wind flow across the plateau.

Climate: Semiarid, transitional between desert conditions to the west and humid climates to the east. Normal precipitation is 18 inches per year, with maximum precipitation occurring during May, June, and July, when warm tropical air is carried inland from the Gulf of Mexico. This air mass produces moderate to heavy afternoon and evening convective thunderstorms, sometimes with hail. Dry daytime winds help alleviate summer heat.

Pluses: Generally pleasant climate year-round.

Minuses: During dry spells, high winds cause dusty conditions.

Places Rated Score: 604

Places Rated Rank: 72

Elevation: 3,241 feet

Relative Humidity: 56%
Wind Speed: 10.8 mph

Seasonal Change

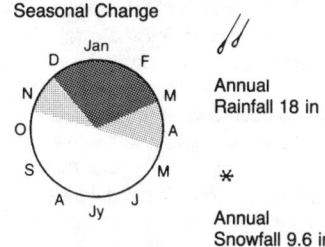

Annual Rainfall 18 in

Annual Snowfall 9.6 in

Clear 164 days

Partly Cloudy 103 days

Cloudy 98 days

Precipitation Days: 60   Storm Days: 45

Average Temperatures			
	Daily High	Daily Low	Monthly Mean
January	53.4	24.8	39.1
February	57.0	28.3	42.7
March	63.8	34.0	48.9
April	74.8	45.1	60.0
May	82.5	54.5	68.5
June	90.6	63.6	77.1
July	92.4	66.9	79.7
August	91.3	65.5	78.4
September	83.8	58.2	71.0
October	74.7	47.3	61.0
November	63.1	34.4	48.8
December	55.2	27.4	41.3

Zero-Degree Days: 0
Freezing Days: 98
90-Degree Days: 77
Heating- and Cooling-Degree Days: 5,192

Madison, WI

Terrain: Madison sits on a narrow isthmus of land between Lakes Mendota (15 square miles) and Monona (5 square miles). Normally these lakes are frozen from December 17 to April 5. Most farming is dairying, with field crops mainly of corn, oats, and alfalfa. The majority of fruits grown are apples, strawberries, and raspberries.

Climate: Continental, typical of interior North America, with a large annual temperature range and frequent short periods of temperature changes. The absolute temperature range is from 107° F to −37° F. Winter temperatures average 20° F and summer ones 68° F. The most common air masses are of polar origin, with occasional outbreaks of Arctic air during the winter. Much of the precipitation falls between May and September. Lighter winter precipitation falls over a longer period of time. Average growing season: 175 days.

Pluses: Pleasant summers with moderate growing season; even precipitation.

Minuses: Long, severe winters.

Places Rated Score: 378

Places Rated Rank: 309

Elevation: 866 feet

Relative Humidity: 73%
Wind Speed: 9.9 mph

Seasonal Change

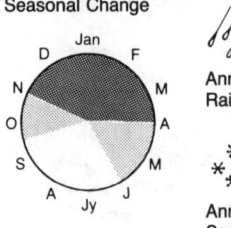

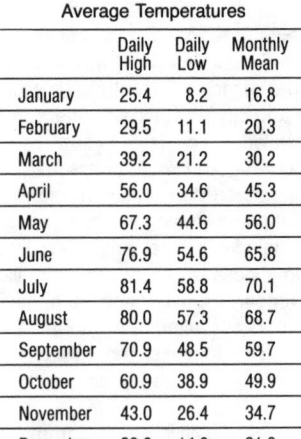

Annual Rainfall 30 in

Annual Snowfall 39 in

Clear 94 days
Partly Cloudy 96 days
Cloudy 175 days

Precipitation Days: 117 Storm Days: 40

Average Temperatures			
	Daily High	Daily Low	Monthly Mean
January	25.4	8.2	16.8
February	29.5	11.1	20.3
March	39.2	21.2	30.2
April	56.0	34.6	45.3
May	67.3	44.6	56.0
June	76.9	54.6	65.8
July	81.4	58.8	70.1
August	80.0	57.3	68.7
September	70.9	48.5	59.7
October	60.9	38.9	49.9
November	43.0	26.4	34.7
December	29.8	14.0	21.9

Zero-Degree Days: 25
Freezing Days: 164
90-Degree Days: 12
Heating- and Cooling-Degree Days: 8,190

Manchester, NH

Terrain: Surrounded by hills, with many lakes and ponds. Manchester is situated on the Merrimack River near the geographic center of the New England region. The countryside is generously wooded, most of it land that was formerly used for farming. Mount Washington, the highest peak in the Presidential Chain of the White Mountains (and the site of perhaps the most violent weather in the continental United States), is 75 miles north.

Climate: Northwesterly winds prevail here, bringing cold, dry air during the winter and pleasantly cool, dry air in the summer. Although the winters here are long, cold, and snowy, the summers are ideal, with warm sunny days and cool nights. Thus the Manchester area and New Hampshire in general offer year-round recreation. Ski areas and other resorts dot the countryside. Agriculture is limited to freeze-resistant crops, such as potatoes and apples, and to forage crops for the dairy industry.

Pluses: Good rugged climate, pleasant summers.

Minuses: Long, cold, snowy winters.

Places Rated Score: 404

Places Rated Rank: 298

Elevation: 346 feet

Relative Humidity: 73%
Wind Speed: 6.7 mph

Seasonal Change

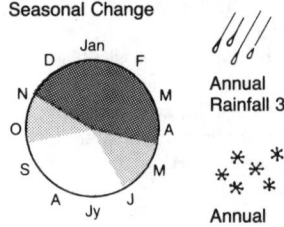

Annual Rainfall 36 in

Annual Snowfall 64 in

Clear 92 days
Partly Cloudy 113 days
Cloudy 160 days

Precipitation Days: 125 Storm Days: 21

Average Temperatures			
	Daily High	Daily Low	Monthly Mean
January	31.3	9.9	20.6
February	33.8	11.3	22.6
March	42.4	22.1	32.3
April	56.7	31.7	44.2
May	68.6	41.5	55.1
June	77.7	51.6	64.7
July	82.6	56.7	69.7
August	80.1	54.2	67.2
September	72.4	46.5	59.5
October	62.3	36.3	49.3
November	47.9	28.1	38.0
December	34.6	14.9	24.8

Zero-Degree Days: 26
Freezing Days: 176
90-Degree Days: 11
Heating- and Cooling-Degree Days: 7,709

Medford, OR

Terrain: Located in a mountain valley formed by the famous Rogue River and one of its tributaries, Bear Creek. Most of the valley ranges in elevation from 1,300 feet to 1,400 feet above sea level. The valley's outlet to the ocean 80 miles west is the narrow canyon of the Rogue.

Climate: Moderate, with marked seasonal characteristics. Late fall, winter, and early spring are cloudy, damp, and cool. The remainder of the year is warm, dry, and sunny. The rain shadow afforded by the Siskiyous and the Coast Ranges results in relatively light rainfall, most of which falls in the wintertime. Snowfalls are very light and seldom remain on the ground more than 24 hours. Winters are mild, with the temperatures just dipping below freezing during December and January. Summer days can reach 90° F, but nights are cool. The climate is ideal for truck and fruit farming, and the area is dotted with orchards.

Pluses: Very mild four-season climate; sunny summers.

Minuses: Half the year is damp and cloudy.

Places Rated Score: 611

Places Rated Rank: 68

Elevation: 1,298 feet

Relative Humidity: 67%
Wind Speed: 4.8 mph

Seasonal Change

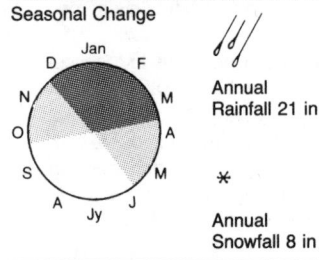

Annual Rainfall 21 in

Annual Snowfall 8 in

Clear 117 days
Partly Cloudy 79 days
Cloudy 169 days

Precipitation Days: 101 Storm Days: 9

Average Temperatures			
	Daily High	Daily Low	Monthly Mean
January	44.2	29.0	36.6
February	51.8	30.7	41.3
March	56.7	32.8	44.8
April	63.8	36.6	50.2
May	71.7	42.8	57.3
June	79.4	49.1	64.3
July	89.5	53.8	71.7
August	87.8	52.9	70.4
September	82.1	46.7	64.4
October	67.4	39.1	53.4
November	52.7	34.2	43.5
December	44.2	31.1	37.7

Zero-Degree Days: 0
Freezing Days: 90
90-Degree Days: 54
Heating- and Cooling-Degree Days: 5,492

Memphis, TN–AR–MS

Terrain: Located on the east bank of the Mississippi River in slightly rolling topography, across from the level alluvial area on the Arkansas side. Major crops are cotton, corn, peaches, apples, and vegetables. The climate is favorable for dairying and for raising cattle and hogs.
Climate: Though not in the normal paths of storms coming from the Gulf of Mexico or from Canada, Memphis is affected by both and therefore has comparatively frequent changes in weather. Extremes in highs and lows are relatively rare; the average annual temperature is in the low 60s and varies from the low 40s in January to the low 80s in July. Average growing season: 230 days.

Pluses: Short winters, long summers, moderate temperature variation.

Minuses: Frequent weather changes, occasional humid periods in summer.

Places Rated Score: 514   **Places Rated Rank: 211**

Elevation: 284 feet

Relative Humidity: 69%
Wind Speed: 9.2 mph

Seasonal Change

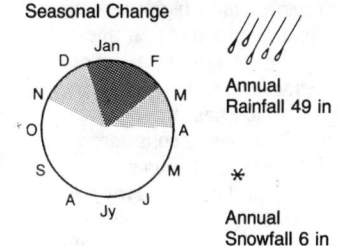

Annual Rainfall 49 in

Annual Snowfall 6 in

Clear 118 days   Partly Cloudy 99 days   Cloudy 148 days

Precipitation Days: 106   Storm Days: 53

Average Temperatures			
	Daily High	Daily Low	Monthly Mean
January	49.4	31.6	40.5
February	53.1	34.4	43.8
March	60.8	41.1	51.0
April	72.7	52.3	62.5
May	81.2	60.6	70.9
June	88.7	68.5	78.6
July	91.6	71.5	81.6
August	90.6	70.1	80.4
September	84.3	62.8	73.6
October	74.9	51.1	63.0
November	61.5	40.3	50.9
December	51.7	33.7	42.7

Zero-Degree Days: 0
Freezing Days: 59
90-Degree Days: 64
Heating- and Cooling-Degree Days: 5,256

Miami–Hialeah, FL

Terrain: Located on the lower east coast of Florida. To the east lies Biscayne Bay, and east of it Miami Beach. The surrounding countryside is level and sparsely wooded.
Climate: Essentially subtropical marine, characterized by a long, warm summer with abundant rainfall and a mild, dry winter. The Atlantic Ocean greatly influences the city's small range of daily temperature and aids the rapid warming of colder air masses that pass to the east of the state. During the early morning hours, more rainfall occurs at Miami Beach than at the airport (9 miles inland), while during the afternoon the reverse is true. Even more striking is the difference in the annual number of days over 90° F: at Miami Beach, 15 days; at the airport, 60. Freezing temperatures occur occasionally in surrounding farming districts but almost never near the ocean. In 1977, for the first time in Miami's history, traces of snow were reported. Tropical hurricanes affect the area and are most frequent in early fall.

Pluses: Single-season, subtropical climate.

Minuses: Hurricanes, frequent thunderstorms.

Places Rated Score: 634   **Places Rated Rank: 49**

Elevation: 12 feet

Relative Humidity: 75%
Wind Speed: 9.1 mph

Seasonal Change

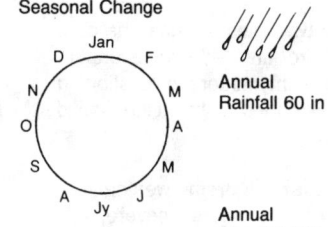

Annual Rainfall 60 in

Annual Snowfall 0 in

Clear 76 days   Partly Cloudy 172 days   Cloudy 117 days

Precipitation Days: 129   Storm Days: 75

Average Temperatures			
	Daily High	Daily Low	Monthly Mean
January	75.6	58.7	67.2
February	76.6	59.0	67.8
March	79.5	63.0	71.3
April	82.7	67.3	75.0
May	85.3	70.7	78.0
June	88.0	73.9	81.0
July	89.1	75.5	82.3
August	89.9	75.8	82.9
September	88.3	75.0	81.7
October	84.6	71.0	77.8
November	79.9	64.5	72.2
December	76.6	60.0	68.3

Zero-Degree Days: 0
Freezing Days: 0
90-Degree Days: 30
Heating- and Cooling-Degree Days: 4,244

Midland, TX

Terrain: Located on the southern extension of the South Plains region of Texas. Topography is level, with only slight and infrequent undulations. Vegetation consists mainly of grasses, and there are very few trees in the area, most of them mesquite.
Climate: Semiarid. Droughts occur with monotonous frequency, resulting in dust storms so severe that suspended dust remains in the air several days after the storm has passed. Though summer afternoon temperatures are frequently above 90° F, low humidity and rapid evaporation have a cooling effect. The climate is generally pleasant, with the most disagreeable weather concentrated in late winter and spring.

Pluses: Short winters; long, pleasant summers and falls.

Minuses: Severe drought conditions, frequent dust storms.

Places Rated Score: 603   **Places Rated Rank: 73**

Elevation: 2,862 feet

Relative Humidity: 53%
Wind Speed: 10.8 mph

Seasonal Change

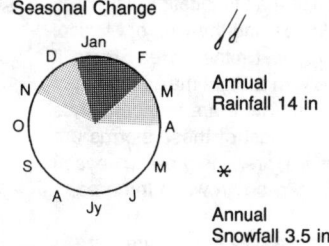

Annual Rainfall 14 in

Annual Snowfall 3.5 in

Clear 167 days   Partly Cloudy 97 days   Cloudy 101 days

Precipitation Days: 51   Storm Days: 36

Average Temperatures			
	Daily High	Daily Low	Monthly Mean
January	57.8	29.4	43.6
February	62.1	33.5	47.8
March	69.4	39.2	54.3
April	79.1	49.4	64.3
May	86.5	58.1	72.3
June	92.8	66.9	79.9
July	95.0	69.5	82.3
August	94.4	69.1	81.8
September	87.9	62.8	75.4
October	79.2	52.4	65.8
November	67.5	39.1	53.3
December	60.1	31.6	45.9

Zero-Degree Days: 0
Freezing Days: 65
90-Degree Days: 89
Heating- and Cooling-Degree Days: 4,871

Milwaukee, WI

Terrain: Milwaukee is situated on the west shore of Lake Michigan, 50 miles north of Chicago.

Climate: Influenced by storms that move eastward across the upper Ohio River valley and the Great Lakes region. Large high-pressure systems moving southeastward out of Canada also have an effect, and it is seldom that two or three days will pass without a distinct change in the weather, particularly during winter and spring. The major influence on the climate is Lake Michigan, which has a particularly marked effect when the temperature of the water differs considerably from that of the air. Generally, the lake cools the shoreline in summer and warms it in winter. Thunderstorms occur less frequently in Milwaukee than in areas to the south and west. Winters are cloudy. Summers are usually clear, receiving an average of 70% of possible sunshine.

Pluses: Lake Michigan has a moderating effect on temperature extremes.

Minuses: Subject to severe winter storm systems.

Places Rated Score: 460

Places Rated Rank: 266

Elevation: 693 feet

Relative Humidity: 73%
Wind Speed: 11.8 mph

Seasonal Change

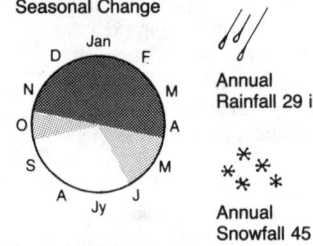

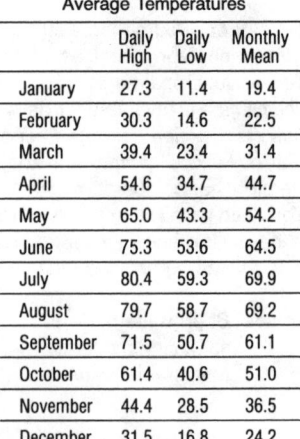

Annual Rainfall 29 in

Annual Snowfall 45 in

Clear 96 days

Partly Cloudy 99 days

Cloudy 170 days

Precipitation Days: 122   Storm Days: 36

Average Temperatures			
	Daily High	Daily Low	Monthly Mean
January	27.3	11.4	19.4
February	30.3	14.6	22.5
March	39.4	23.4	31.4
April	54.6	34.7	44.7
May	65.0	43.3	54.2
June	75.3	53.6	64.5
July	80.4	59.3	69.9
August	79.7	58.7	69.2
September	71.5	50.7	61.1
October	61.4	40.6	51.0
November	44.4	28.5	36.5
December	31.5	16.8	24.2

Zero-Degree Days: 16
Freezing Days: 146
90-Degree Days: 9
Heating- and Cooling-Degree Days: 7,894

Minneapolis–St. Paul, MN–WI

Terrain: The Twin Cities are located at the confluence of the Mississippi and Minnesota rivers over the heart of an artesian water basin. The topography is flat or gently rolling with numerous lakes that are small, shallow, and ice-covered in winter.

Climate: Predominantly continental (the two cities are near the geographic center of North America). There are wide variations in temperature, ample summer rainfall, and scanty winter precipitation. In general, there exists a tendency toward extremes in almost all climatic features.

Pluses: Changeable weather that many find stimulating and invigorating.

Minuses: Extreme weather features; severe, long winters.

Places Rated Score: 293

Places Rated Rank: 324

Elevation: 838 feet

Relative Humidity: 69%
Wind Speed: 10.5 mph

Seasonal Change

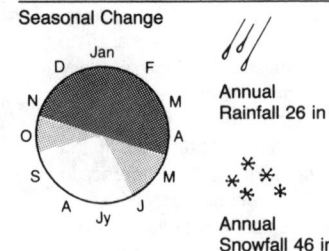

Annual Rainfall 26 in

Annual Snowfall 46 in

Clear 100 days

Partly Cloudy 100 days

Cloudy 165 days

Precipitation Days: 113   Storm Days: 36

Average Temperatures			
	Daily High	Daily Low	Monthly Mean
January	21.2	3.2	12.2
February	25.9	7.1	16.5
March	36.9	19.6	28.3
April	55.5	34.7	45.1
May	67.9	46.3	57.1
June	77.1	56.7	66.9
July	82.4	61.4	71.9
August	80.8	59.6	70.2
September	70.7	49.3	60.0
October	60.7	39.2	50.0
November	40.6	24.2	32.4
December	26.6	10.6	18.6

Zero-Degree Days: 34
Freezing Days: 158
90-Degree Days: 15
Heating- and Cooling-Degree Days: 8,744

Mobile, AL

Terrain: Located at the head of Mobile Bay, approximately 30 miles from the Gulf of Mexico.

Climate: Although Mobile has not had a destructive hurricane since 1926, this seems to be due more to chance than to location. The area is subject to hurricanes from the West Indies and the Gulf of Mexico. The normal annual rainfall is among the highest in the United States. It is evenly distributed throughout the year, with a slight maximum at the height of the summer thunderstorm season (there are thunderstorms every other day during July and August). Most of these storms are showers; long periods of continuous rain are rare. The growing season averages 274 days, enough for citrus fruit to be grown in the area.

Pluses: Mild winters, ample and even precipitation.

Minuses: Summers are hot and muggy with frequent thunderstorms; area prone to hurricanes.

Places Rated Score: 442

Places Rated Rank: 277

Elevation: 221 feet

Relative Humidity: 73%
Wind Speed: 9.2 mph

Seasonal Change

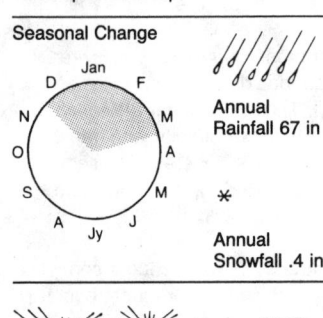

Annual Rainfall 67 in

Annual Snowfall .4 in

Clear 100 days

Partly Cloudy 117 days

Cloudy 148 days

Precipitation Days: 124   Storm Days: 80

Average Temperatures			
	Daily High	Daily Low	Monthly Mean
January	61.1	41.3	51.2
February	64.1	43.9	54.0
March	69.5	49.2	59.4
April	78.0	57.7	67.9
May	85.0	64.5	74.8
June	89.8	70.7	80.3
July	90.5	72.6	81.6
August	90.6	72.3	81.5
September	86.5	68.4	77.5
October	79.7	58.0	68.9
November	69.5	47.5	58.5
December	63.0	42.8	52.9

Zero-Degree Days: 0
Freezing Days: 19
90-Degree Days: 81
Heating- and Cooling-Degree Days: 4,261

Montgomery, AL

Terrain: Located in a gently rolling area of southern Alabama. No local topographic features appreciably influence climate.

Climate: From June through September, humidity and temperature conditions show little daily change. During summer, 100-degree readings are infrequent. From April through September, all precipitation is from local heat thundershowers in the afternoon. Rain is abundant and includes all types and intensities from December through March. During the coldest months (December, January, and February), there are frequent shifts between mild, moist air from the Gulf of Mexico and dry, cool continental air. Hard freezes are infrequent during winter; snow is rare enough to be a curiosity.

Pluses: Mild, two-season climate wih abundant rainfall.

Minuses: Humid summers and falls, lots of cloudy days.

Places Rated Score: 483　　　　**Places Rated Rank: 242**

Elevation: 202 feet

Relative Humidity: 73%
Wind Speed: 6.8 mph

Seasonal Change

Annual Rainfall 50 in

Annual Snowfall .2 in

Clear 107 days　　Partly Cloudy 109 days　　Cloudy 149 days

Precipitation Days: 109　Storm Days: 62

	Average Temperatures		
	Daily High	Daily Low	Monthly Mean
January	57.9	37.1	47.5
February	61.4	39.7	50.6
March	67.7	45.2	56.5
April	76.8	53.6	65.2
May	83.6	61.2	72.4
June	89.2	68.6	78.9
July	90.5	71.5	81.0
August	90.7	70.7	80.7
September	86.5	65.5	76.0
October	78.0	53.5	65.8
November	67.2	42.7	55.0
December	59.3	37.7	48.5

Zero-Degree Days: 0
Freezing Days: 39
90-Degree Days: 66
Heating- and Cooling-Degree Days: 4,507

Nashville, TN

Terrain: Located on the Cumberland River in the northwestern corner of the Nashville Basin, near the escarpment of the Highland Rim. The rim rises 400 feet above the mean elevation of the basin, forming an amphitheater around the city from the southwest to the southeast.

Climate: Moderate temperatures. Extremes of heat or cold are rare, yet fairly frequent changes give variety. The humidity is moderate compared with other locations east of the Mississippi River and south of the Ohio River. The city is not in the most highly traveled path of general storm systems that cross the country; however, it is in a zone that experiences thunderstorms moderately often. Average growing season: 211 days.

Pluses: Fairly mild four-season climate, long summers.

Minuses: Relatively few clear days.

Places Rated Score: 600　　　　**Places Rated Rank: 80**

Elevation: 605 feet

Relative Humidity: 71%
Wind Speed: 7.9 mph

Seasonal Change

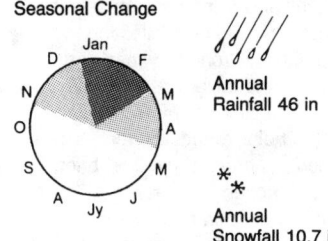

Annual Rainfall 46 in

Annual Snowfall 10.7 in

Clear 103 days　　Partly Cloudy 107 days　　Cloudy 155 days

Precipitation Days: 119　Storm Days: 55

	Average Temperatures		
	Daily High	Daily Low	Monthly Mean
January	47.6	29.0	38.3
February	50.9	31.0	41.0
March	59.2	38.1	48.7
April	71.3	48.8	60.1
May	79.8	57.3	68.5
June	87.5	65.7	76.6
July	90.2	69.0	79.6
August	89.2	67.7	78.5
September	83.5	60.5	72.0
October	73.2	48.6	60.9
November	59.0	37.7	48.4
December	49.6	31.1	40.4

Zero-Degree Days: 1
Freezing Days: 75
90-Degree Days: 37
Heating- and Cooling-Degree Days: 5,390

New Bedford, MA

Terrain: New Bedford, one of America's most famous whaling ports, lies at the mouth of the Acushnet River in Buzzards Bay. The terrain is relatively flat and low-lying, which makes New Bedford especially vulnerable to tidal hurricane surges. Because of severe hurricanes that have struck the area over the last 50 years, huge floodgates have been installed around the city and remain an interesting sight.

Climate: Although this fishing port and manufacturing center is only an hour and a half south of Boston, there's a great difference between the climates of the two cities. New Bedford, located on the northern portion of Rhode Island Sound in a large bay, is almost surrounded by ocean. Thus, it enjoys a modified maritime climate characterized by cool summer ocean breezes and warm ocean air in the wintertime. When Boston is in the midst of a blizzard, New Bedford is usually experiencing rain or sleet that melts away in a few days. Similarly, when Boston and points north simmer in a summer heat wave, New Bedford is usually cooler.

Pluses: Mild maritime climate.

Minuses: Ice storms.

Places Rated Score: 643　　　　**Places Rated Rank: 40**

Elevation: 60 feet

Relative Humidity: 76%
Wind Speed: 10 mph

Seasonal Change

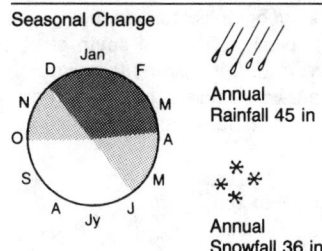

Annual Rainfall 45 in

Annual Snowfall 36 in

Clear 97 days　　Partly Cloudy 114 days　　Cloudy 154 days

Precipitation Days: 79　Storm Days: 14

	Average Temperatures		
	Daily High	Daily Low	Monthly Mean
January	36.3	21.6	29.0
February	38.4	22.7	30.6
March	45.2	29.6	37.4
April	56.8	38.5	47.7
May	67.3	47.6	57.5
June	76.6	57.6	67.1
July	81.7	63.8	72.8
August	80.3	62.4	71.3
September	73.4	55.2	64.3
October	63.3	45.7	54.5
November	51.0	36.3	43.7
December	40.2	25.8	33.1

Zero-Degree Days: 0
Freezing Days: 110
90-Degree Days: 5
Heating- and Cooling-Degree Days: 6,373

New Orleans, LA

Terrain: The metropolitan area is surrounded by water: Lake Pontchartrain (610 square miles) to the north; the Mississippi River to the east and south; bayous, lakes, and marshy delta land to the west and south. Elevations in the city vary from a few feet above mean sea level to a few feet below. A massive levee system offers protection from river flooding and tidal surges.

Climate: Best described as humid with surrounding water modifying the temperature and decreasing the range of temperatures. Heavy and frequent rains are typical, and there are daily afternoon thunderstorms from mid-June through September. From December to March, precipitation is likely to be steady rain of two or three days' duration, instead of showers. During winter and spring, cold rain forms fogs that inhibit air and river transportation. The city has been hard hit by three hurricanes since 1900.

Pluses: Tropical climate moderated by water.

Minuses: Hot and humid, heavy rains and fogs, hurricanes.

Places Rated Score: 498

Places Rated Rank: 227

Elevation: 30 feet

Relative Humidity: 77%
Wind Speed: 8.4 mph

Seasonal Change

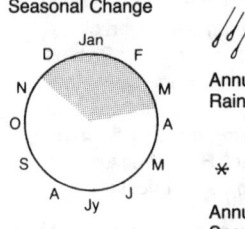

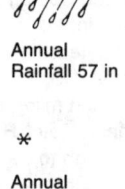

Annual Rainfall 57 in

Annual Snowfall .2 in

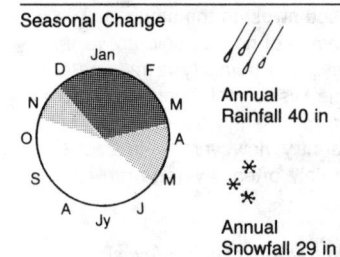

Clear 109 days Partly Cloudy 120 days Cloudy 136 days

Precipitation Days: 113 Storm Days: 68

Average Temperatures			
	Daily High	Daily Low	Monthly Mean
January	62.3	43.5	52.9
February	65.1	46.0	55.6
March	70.4	50.9	60.7
April	78.4	58.8	68.6
May	84.9	65.3	75.1
June	89.6	71.2	80.4
July	90.4	73.3	81.9
August	90.6	73.1	81.9
September	86.6	69.7	78.2
October	79.9	59.6	69.8
November	70.3	49.8	60.1
December	64.2	45.3	54.8

Zero-Degree Days: 0
Freezing Days: 13
90-Degree Days: 67
Heating- and Cooling-Degree Days: 4,171

New York, NY

Terrain: Located on the Atlantic Coastal Plain at the mouth of the Hudson River. Topography is diversified by numerous waterways: All but one of the city's five boroughs are situated on islands.

Climate: Close to the path of most storm and frontal systems that move across the continent. Therefore, weather conditions affecting the city approach from a westerly direction. New York City can thus experience higher temperatures in summer and lower ones in winter than would otherwise be expected in a coastal area. However, the frequent passage of weather systems often helps reduce the length of warm and cold spells and also keeps periods of air stagnation brief. Although continental influence is dominant, ocean influence is by no means absent. Sea breezes moderate the afternoon heat of summer and delay the advent of winter snows. The Atlantic's influence is also measured in the length of the frost-free season—more than 200 days.

Pluses: Moderating ocean influence, mild summers and falls.

Minuses: Coastal storms bring record snow and rain.

Places Rated Score: 638

Places Rated Rank: 44

Elevation: 87 feet

Relative Humidity: 65%
Wind Speed: 9.4 mph

Seasonal Change

Annual Rainfall 40 in

Annual Snowfall 29 in

Clear 107 days Partly Cloudy 125 days Cloudy 133 days

Precipitation Days: 121 Storm Days: 20

Average Temperatures			
	Daily High	Daily Low	Monthly Mean
January	38.5	25.9	32.2
February	40.2	26.5	33.4
March	48.4	33.7	41.1
April	60.7	43.5	52.1
May	71.4	53.1	62.3
June	80.5	62.6	71.6
July	85.2	68.0	76.6
August	83.4	66.4	74.9
September	76.8	59.9	68.4
October	66.8	50.6	58.7
November	54.0	40.8	47.4
December	41.4	29.5	35.5

Zero-Degree Days: 0
Freezing Days: 81
90-Degree Days: 16
Heating- and Cooling-Degree Days: 5,916

Norfolk–Virginia Beach–Newport News, VA

Terrain: Located on low level land, with Chesapeake Bay immediately to the north, Hampton Roads to the west, and the Atlantic Ocean to the east.

Climate: The metro area is in a favorable geographic position, being north of the track of hurricanes and tropical storms and south of high-latitude storm systems. Winters are mild. Springs and falls are especially pleasant. Summers, though, are warm, humid, and long. A temperature of zero has never been recorded here, although there is occasional snow.

Pluses: Four-season climate suited for year-round outdoor activities.

Minuses: Long, humid summers.

Places Rated Score: 632

Places Rated Rank: 50

Elevation: 30 feet

Relative Humidity: 71%
Wind Speed: 10.6 mph

Seasonal Change

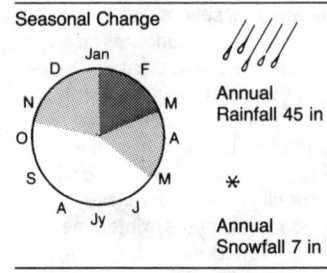

Annual Rainfall 45 in

Annual Snowfall 7 in

Clear 110 days Partly Cloudy 102 days Cloudy 153 days

Precipitation Days: 115 Storm Days: 37

Average Temperatures			
	Daily High	Daily Low	Monthly Mean
January	48.8	32.2	40.5
February	50.0	32.7	41.4
March	57.3	38.9	48.1
April	67.7	47.9	57.8
May	76.2	57.2	66.7
June	83.5	65.5	74.5
July	86.6	69.9	78.3
August	84.9	68.9	76.9
September	79.6	63.9	71.8
October	70.1	53.3	61.7
November	60.5	42.6	51.6
December	50.6	34.0	42.3

Zero-Degree Days: 0
Freezing Days: 54
90-Degree Days: 30
Heating- and Cooling-Degree Days: 4,929

Oklahoma City, OK

Terrain: Situated along the North Canadian River at the geographic center of the state. The countryside is rolling, with the nearest hills, the Arbuckles, 80 miles south.

Climate: Although some influence is exerted at times by warm, moist air from the Gulf of Mexico, the climate of the city falls mainly under continental controls characteristic of the Great Plains. The continental effect produces pronounced daily and seasonal temperature changes and considerable variation in seasonal and annual precipitation. Summers are long and usually hot. Winters are comparatively mild and short.

Pluses: Clear days, mild winters.

Minuses: Long, hot summers; tornadoes.

Places Rated Score: 554

Places Rated Rank: 145

Elevation: 1,304 feet

Relative Humidity: 65%
Wind Speed: 12.8 mph

Seasonal Change

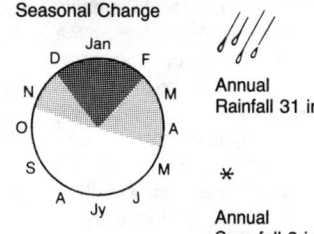

Annual Rainfall 31 in

Annual Snowfall 9 in

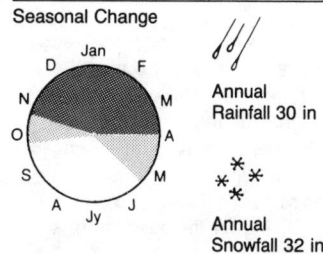

Clear	Partly Cloudy	Cloudy
141 days	96 days	128 days

Precipitation Days: 81   Storm Days: 51

Average Temperatures			
	Daily High	Daily Low	Monthly Mean
January	47.6	26.0	36.8
February	52.6	30.0	41.3
March	59.8	36.5	48.2
April	71.6	49.1	60.4
May	78.7	57.9	68.3
June	87.0	66.6	76.8
July	92.6	70.4	81.5
August	92.5	69.6	81.1
September	84.7	61.3	73.0
October	74.2	50.6	62.4
November	60.9	37.4	49.2
December	50.7	29.2	40.0

Zero-Degree Days: 0
Freezing Days: 80
90-Degree Days: 64
Heating- and Cooling-Degree Days: 5,571

★ Olympia, WA

Terrain: The capital of the state of Washington, Olympia lies at the southernmost end of Puget Sound, some 60 miles south-southwest of Seattle. The Olympic Peninsula, with its fine remnants of the Pacific Northwest rain forests, active glaciers, and alpine meadows, lies to the northwest. The city and vicinity are well protected by the Coast Ranges from the strong south and southwest winds accompanying many Pacific storms during the fall and winter.

Climate: Characterized by warm, generally dry summers and wet, mild winters. Fall rains begin in October and continue with few interruptions until spring. During the rainy season there is little variation in temperature, with days in the 40s and 50s and nights in the 30s, and constant cloud cover. The summer highs are between 60° F and 80° F, with up to 20 days without rain. The summer is marked by clear skies at night and frequent morning fog.

Pluses: Mild winters, dry summers.

Minuses: Cloudy, damp, rainy.

Places Rated Score: 726

Places Rated Rank: 21

Elevation: 195 feet

Relative Humidity: 71%
Wind Speed: 6.7 mph

Seasonal Change

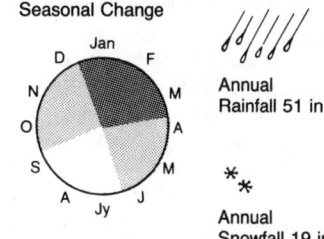

Annual Rainfall 51 in

Annual Snowfall 19 in

Clear	Partly Cloudy	Cloudy
49 days	88 days	228 days

Precipitation Days: 163   Storm Days: 5

Average Temperatures			
	Daily High	Daily Low	Monthly Mean
January	44.0	30.4	37.2
February	49.0	32.4	41.0
March	53.6	32.8	43.2
April	59.9	36.5	48.2
May	67.2	40.8	54.0
June	71.9	45.9	58.9
July	78.4	48.7	63.6
August	77.2	48.4	62.8
September	72.1	45.0	58.6
October	61.2	40.0	50.6
November	51.3	35.2	43.3
December	45.8	33.1	39.5

Zero-Degree Days: 0
Freezing Days: 89
90-Degree Days: 6
Heating- and Cooling-Degree Days: 5,631

Omaha, NE–IA

Terrain: Situated on the west bank of the Missouri River among rolling hills that rise 300 feet above the riverbank.

Climate: Typically continental, with relatively warm summers and cold, dry winters. It is situated midway between two climates, those of the humid East and the dry West, and receives weather conditions characteristic of both. Omaha is also affected by most storms, or "lows," that cross the country. This causes periodic and rapid changes in weather, especially during the winter.

Pluses: Moderate growing season with adequate rainfall.

Minuses: Long, cold winters.

Places Rated Score: 440

Places Rated Rank: 279

Elevation: 982 feet

Relative Humidity: 68%
Wind Speed: 10.9 mph

Seasonal Change

Annual Rainfall 30 in

Annual Snowfall 32 in

Clear	Partly Cloudy	Cloudy
113 days	107 days	145 days

Precipitation Days: 99   Storm Days: 48

Average Temperatures			
	Daily High	Daily Low	Monthly Mean
January	32.7	12.4	22.6
February	38.5	17.4	28.0
March	47.7	26.4	37.1
April	64.4	40.1	52.3
May	74.4	51.5	63.0
June	83.1	61.3	72.2
July	88.6	65.8	77.2
August	87.2	64.0	75.6
September	78.6	54.0	66.3
October	69.1	42.6	55.9
November	50.9	29.1	40.0
December	37.8	18.1	28.0

Zero-Degree Days: 13
Freezing Days: 138
90-Degree Days: 38
Heating- and Cooling-Degree Days: 7,222

Orlando, FL

Terrain: Located in the central section of the Florida peninsula, almost surrounded by lakes. The countryside is flat, with no natural barriers to exterior weather systems.

Climate: Because of the surrounding water, relative humidity remains high year-round, hovering near 90% at night and dipping to 50% in the afternoon. The rainy season extends from June through September; afternoon thundershowers occur daily. Rain is light during the winter, and snow and sleet are rare. Winter temperatures may drop to freezing at night, but days are usually pleasant, with brilliant sunshine.

Pluses: Mild.

Minuses: Humid year-round; hot summers with daily thunder-showers.

Elevation: 106 feet

Relative Humidity: 74%
Wind Speed: 8.7 mph

Seasonal Change

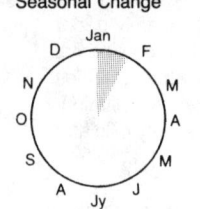

Annual Rainfall 51 in

Annual Snowfall 0 in

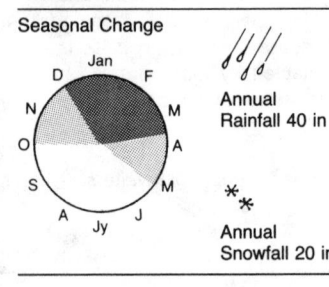

Clear 94 days   Partly Cloudy 148 days   Cloudy 123 days

Precipitation Days: 116   Storm Days: 81

Average Temperatures			
	Daily High	Daily Low	Monthly Mean
January	70.5	50.0	60.3
February	71.8	51.2	61.5
March	76.0	55.7	65.9
April	81.5	61.1	71.3
May	86.7	66.1	76.4
June	89.3	71.1	80.2
July	89.8	72.9	81.4
August	90.0	73.5	81.8
September	87.9	72.3	80.1
October	82.5	66.0	74.3
November	76.2	56.9	66.6
December	71.5	51.5	61.5

Zero-Degree Days: 0
Freezing Days: 2
90-Degree Days: 104
Heating- and Cooling-Degree Days: 3,959

Places Rated Score: 457   **Places Rated Rank: 268**

Peoria, IL

Terrain: Located on the Illinois River, with gently rising topography extending to level tableland.

Climate: Typically continental, characterized by changeable weather and a wide range of temperatures. For example, 1936 had 17 days with temperatures of 100° F or higher in July, while the early part of that same year had 26 days within a 31-day period when the temperature was zero. The same year had the absolute maximum record of 113° F, set on July 15. June and September are usually the most pleasant months of the year. During October and early November, residents enjoy Indian summer, with its extended period of warm, dry weather.

Pluses: Invigorating continental climate, with especially pleasant falls.

Minuses: Periods of extreme cold and extreme heat.

Elevation: 662 feet

Relative Humidity: 72%
Wind Speed: 10.3 mph

Seasonal Change

Annual Rainfall 35 in

Annual Snowfall 23 in

Clear 97 days   Partly Cloudy 100 days   Cloudy 168 days

Precipitation Days: 111   Storm Days: 49

Average Temperatures			
	Daily High	Daily Low	Monthly Mean
January	31.9	15.7	23.8
February	36.0	19.3	27.7
March	46.5	28.1	37.3
April	61.7	40.8	51.3
May	72.3	50.7	61.5
June	81.7	60.9	71.3
July	85.5	64.6	75.1
August	84.0	62.9	73.5
September	76.4	54.6	65.5
October	65.9	44.0	55.0
November	48.7	31.1	39.9
December	35.7	20.3	28.0

Zero-Degree Days: 11
Freezing Days: 132
90-Degree Days: 17
Heating- and Cooling-Degree Days: 7,066

Places Rated Score: 491   **Places Rated Rank: 234**

Philadelphia, PA–NJ

Terrain: Situated on the Schuylkill and Delaware rivers on the eastern border of Pennsylvania. The Appalachian Mountains to the west and the Atlantic Ocean to the east have a moderating effect on the city's climate.

Climate: Sustained periods of very high or very low temperatures seldom last for more than three or four days. Occasionally during the summer, the area becomes engulfed in marine air, so that high humidity adds to the discomfort of warm temperatures. Precipitation is evenly distributed throughout the year, with maximum amounts during late summer. Snowfall often is considerably higher in the northern suburbs than in the city, where sometimes rain will fall instead. Winters often bring high winds, accompanying cold air after the passage of a deep low-pressure system.

Pluses: Four-season climate moderated by the proximity of the Atlantic Ocean.

Minuses: Humid summer periods; high winter winds accentuate the cold.

Elevation: 28 feet

Relative Humidity: 67%
Wind Speed: 9.6 mph

Seasonal Change

Annual Rainfall 40 in

Annual Snowfall 20 in

Clear 92 days   Partly Cloudy 113 days   Cloudy 160 days

Precipitation Days: 116   Storm Days: 27

Average Temperatures			
	Daily High	Daily Low	Monthly Mean
January	40.1	24.4	32.3
February	42.2	25.5	33.9
March	51.2	32.5	41.9
April	63.5	42.3	52.9
May	74.1	52.3	63.2
June	83.0	61.6	72.3
July	86.8	66.7	76.8
August	84.8	64.7	74.8
September	78.4	57.8	68.1
October	67.9	46.9	57.4
November	55.5	36.9	46.2
December	43.2	27.2	35.2

Zero-Degree Days: 0
Freezing Days: 101
90-Degree Days: 19
Heating- and Cooling-Degree Days: 5,969

Places Rated Score: 630   **Places Rated Rank: 52**

Phoenix, AZ

Terrain: Located in the center of the Salt River valley, on a broad, oval, nearly flat plain. To the south, west, and north are nearby mountain ranges, and 35 miles to the east are the famous Superstition Mountains, which rise to 5,000 feet.
Climate: Typical desert, with low annual rainfall and low humidity. Daytime temperatures are high throughout the summer. Winters are mild, but nighttime temperatures frequently drop below freezing during December, January, and February. The valley floor is generally free of wind except during the thunderstorm season, in July and August, when local gusts flow from the east. The majority of days are clear and sunny, except for July and August; then, considerable afternoon cloudiness builds up over nearby mountains.

Pluses: Dry, two-season desert climate.

Minuses: Hot summers.

Places Rated Score: 536   **Places Rated Rank: 176**

Elevation: 1,107 feet

Relative Humidity: 36%
Wind Speed: 6.2 mph

Seasonal Change

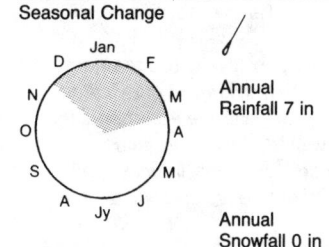

Annual Rainfall 7 in

Annual Snowfall 0 in

Clear 214 days   Partly Cloudy 81 days   Cloudy 70 days

Precipitation Days: 34   Storm Days: 23

Average Temperatures			
	Daily High	Daily Low	Monthly Mean
January	64.8	37.6	51.2
February	69.3	40.8	55.1
March	74.5	44.8	59.7
April	83.6	51.8	67.7
May	92.9	59.6	76.3
June	101.5	67.7	84.6
July	104.8	77.5	91.2
August	102.2	76.0	89.1
September	98.4	69.1	83.8
October	87.6	56.8	72.2
November	74.7	44.8	59.8
December	66.4	38.5	52.5

Zero-Degree Days: 0
Freezing Days: 32
90-Degree Days: 164
Heating- and Cooling-Degree Days: 5,060

Pittsburgh, PA

Terrain: Lies at the foothills of the Allegheny Mountains at the confluence of the Allegheny and Monongahela rivers, forming the Ohio. The city is approximately 100 miles south of Lake Erie.
Climate: Humid, continental type, modified only slightly by its nearness to the Atlantic Seaboard and the Great Lakes. The predominant air is of polar origin from Canada and moves in by way of storm tracks, which vary in origin from Hudson Bay to the Rockies. There are frequent inversions of air from the Gulf of Mexico during the summer, resulting in spells of warm, humid weather. Precipitation is well distributed; during the winter, one fourth of it is snow, and there is a 50% chance of measurable precipitation on any given day.

Pluses: Variable continental climate.

Minuses: Cloudy, wet, cold winters; occasional humid summer days.

Places Rated Score: 586   **Places Rated Rank: 90**

Elevation: 1,223 feet

Relative Humidity: 68%
Wind Speed: 9.4 mph

Seasonal Change

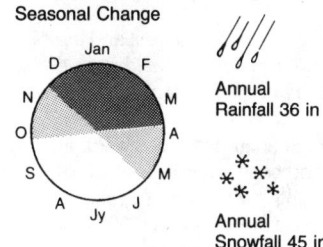

Annual Rainfall 36 in

Annual Snowfall 45 in

Clear 59 days   Partly Cloudy 102 days   Cloudy 204 days

Precipitation Days: 152   Storm Days: 36

Average Temperatures			
	Daily High	Daily Low	Monthly Mean
January	35.3	20.8	28.1
February	37.3	21.3	29.3
March	47.2	29.0	38.1
April	60.9	39.4	50.2
May	70.8	48.7	59.8
June	79.5	57.7	68.6
July	82.5	61.3	71.9
August	80.9	59.4	70.2
September	74.9	52.7	63.8
October	63.9	42.4	53.2
November	49.3	33.3	41.3
December	37.3	23.6	30.5

Zero-Degree Days: 5
Freezing Days: 124
90-Degree Days: 7
Heating- and Cooling-Degree Days: 6,577

Portland, ME

Terrain: Located on a hilly section of the southern coast of Maine, some 45 miles southeast of the White Mountains.
Climate: As a rule, the city has very pleasant summers and falls, cold winters with frequent thaws, and disagreeable springs. Autumn has the greatest number of sunny days. Winters are severe: They begin late but extend deep into what is normally considered springtime, and temperatures well below zero are recorded frequently. Normal monthly precipitation is uniform throughout the year, but heavy snowfalls, sometimes totaling more than 100 inches per year, do occur.

Pluses: Northern marine setting with extremely pleasant summers and falls.

Minuses: Severe winters, with heavy snows, extending well into normal springtime.

Places Rated Score: 483   **Places Rated Rank: 242**

Elevation: 63 feet

Relative Humidity: 74%
Wind Speed: 8.8 mph

Seasonal Change

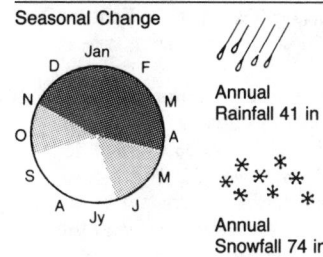

Annual Rainfall 41 in

Annual Snowfall 74 in

Clear 107 days   Partly Cloudy 98 days   Cloudy 160 days

Precipitation Days: 127   Storm Days: 18

Average Temperatures			
	Daily High	Daily Low	Monthly Mean
January	31.2	11.7	21.5
February	33.3	12.5	22.9
March	40.8	22.8	31.8
April	52.8	32.5	42.7
May	63.6	41.7	52.7
June	73.2	51.1	62.2
July	79.1	56.9	68.0
August	77.6	55.2	66.4
September	69.9	47.4	58.7
October	60.2	38.0	49.1
November	47.5	29.7	38.6
December	34.9	16.4	25.7

Zero-Degree Days: 15
Freezing Days: 160
90-Degree Days: 5
Heating- and Cooling-Degree Days: 7,750

★ Portland, OR

Terrain: Situated 65 miles inland from the Pacific Ocean and midway between the northerly oriented low Coast Ranges on the west and the higher Cascade Range on the east, each 30 miles distant. The long growing season, with its mild temperatures and ample moisture, favors local nursery and seed industries.

Climate: A rain climate in winter, marked by relatively mild temperatures and cloudy skies. Summers are pleasantly mild with northwesterly winds and very little precipitation. Fall and spring are transitional in nature. Fog occurs frequently in fall and winter. At all times, incursions of marine air are a moderating influence. Extremes in winter and summer come from the continental interior. Destructive winds are infrequent.

Pluses: Short winters; long, pleasant summers; ample precipitation.

Minuses: Daily rains during winter and part of spring; often cloudy.

Places Rated Score: 768

Places Rated Rank: 16

Elevation: 39 feet

Relative Humidity: 74%
Wind Speed: 7.8 mph

Seasonal Change

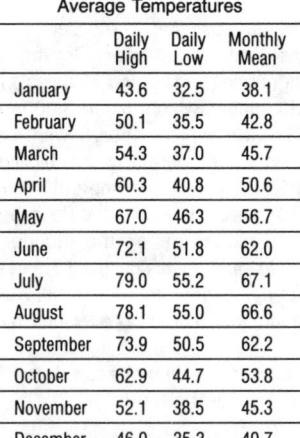

Annual Rainfall 38 in

Annual Snowfall 7 in

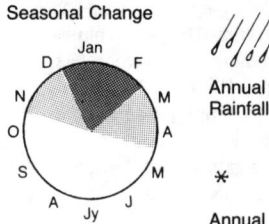

Clear 69 days
Partly Cloudy 68 days
Cloudy 228 days

Precipitation Days: 152   Storm Days: 7

Average Temperatures			
	Daily High	Daily Low	Monthly Mean
January	43.6	32.5	38.1
February	50.1	35.5	42.8
March	54.3	37.0	45.7
April	60.3	40.8	50.6
May	67.0	46.3	56.7
June	72.1	51.8	62.0
July	79.0	55.2	67.1
August	78.1	55.0	66.6
September	73.9	50.5	62.2
October	62.9	44.7	53.8
November	52.1	38.5	45.3
December	46.0	35.3	40.7

Zero-Degree Days: 0
Freezing Days: 44
90-Degree Days: 10
Heating- and Cooling-Degree Days: 5,092

Raleigh–Durham, NC

Terrain: Situated in the transition zone between the Coastal Plain and the Piedmont Plateau of North Carolina. The surrounding topography is rolling, with elevations from 200 feet to 500 feet within a 10-mile radius.

Climate: Because it is located between mountains to the west and the Atlantic Coast to the east and south, the metro area enjoys a favorable climate. The mountains form a partial barrier to cold air masses moving eastward from the nation's interior, so that there are very few days in the heart of the winter when the temperature falls below 20° F. Tropical air is present over the eastern and central sections of North Carolina during much of the summer, bringing warm temperatures and high humidity. In midsummer, afternoon temperatures reach 90° F or higher on an average of every fourth day. Rainfall is well distributed throughout the year. July has, on the average, the greatest amount of rainfall, and November the least.

Pluses: Mild four-season climate.

Minuses: Long, humid summers.

Places Rated Score: 647

Places Rated Rank: 37

Elevation: 441 feet

Relative Humidity: 71%
Wind Speed: 7.9 mph

Seasonal Change

Annual Rainfall 43 in

Annual Snowfall 7 in

Clear 113 days
Partly Cloudy 107 days
Cloudy 145 days

Precipitation Days: 112   Storm Days: 46

Average Temperatures			
	Daily High	Daily Low	Monthly Mean
January	51.0	30.0	40.5
February	53.2	31.1	42.2
March	61.0	37.4	49.2
April	72.2	46.7	59.5
May	79.4	55.4	67.4
June	85.6	63.1	74.4
July	87.7	67.2	77.5
August	86.8	66.2	76.5
September	81.5	59.7	70.6
October	72.4	48.0	60.2
November	62.1	37.8	50.0
December	51.9	30.5	41.2

Zero-Degree Days: 0
Freezing Days: 82
90-Degree Days: 25
Heating- and Cooling-Degree Days: 4,908

Reno, NV

Terrain: Located at the west edge of Truckee Meadows in a semiarid plateau lying in the lee of the Sierra Nevada. To the west, this range rises to elevations of 9,000 feet to 10,000 feet, and hills to the east reach 6,000 feet to 7,000 feet. The Truckee River, flowing from the Sierra Nevada eastward through Reno, drains into Pyramid Lake to the northeast.

Climate: Sunshine is abundant throughout the year. Temperatures are mild, but the daily range may exceed 45 degrees. Even when afternoons reach the upper 90s, a light jacket is needed shortly after sunset. Nights with a minimum temperature over 60° F are rare. Afternoon temperatures are moderate, and only about ten days a year fail to reach a level above freezing. Humidity is very low during the summer months and moderately low during winter.

Pluses: Mild, sunny climate in alpine setting.

Minuses: Considerable daily temperature variation, little precipitation.

Places Rated Score: 535

Places Rated Rank: 182

Elevation: 4,400 feet

Relative Humidity: 50%
Wind Speed: 6.3 mph

Seasonal Change

Annual Rainfall 7 in

Annual Snowfall 27 in

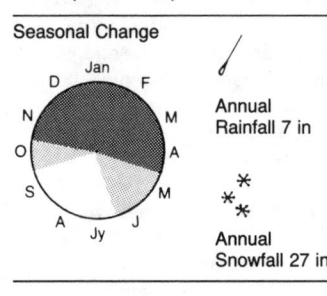

Clear 165 days
Partly Cloudy 90 days
Cloudy 110 days

Precipitation Days: 49   Storm Days: 13

Average Temperatures			
	Daily High	Daily Low	Monthly Mean
January	45.4	18.3	31.9
February	51.1	23.0	37.1
March	56.0	24.6	40.3
April	64.0	29.6	46.8
May	72.2	37.0	54.6
June	80.4	42.5	61.5
July	91.1	47.4	69.3
August	89.0	44.8	66.9
September	81.8	38.6	60.2
October	70.0	30.5	50.3
November	56.3	23.9	40.1
December	46.4	19.6	33.0

Zero-Degree Days: 3
Freezing Days: 189
90-Degree Days: 52
Heating- and Cooling-Degree Days: 6,351

Richmond–Petersburg, VA

Terrain: Located in east-central Virginia at the head of navigation on the James River between Tidewater Virginia and the Piedmont. The Blue Ridge Mountains lie about 90 miles to the west and the Chesapeake Bay 60 miles to the east.

Climate: Water- and mountain-modified continental, with warm, humid summers and generally mild winters. The mountains to the west act as a barrier to outbreaks of cold, continental air in winter; the open waters of the Chesapeake Bay and the Atlantic also contribute to mild winters and to humid summers. Coldest weather usually occurs in late December and in January, with a normal temperature range from 20° F to 50° F. Precipitation is uniformly distributed throughout the year, though dry periods do occur in the autumn, when long periods of pleasant, mild weather are most common.

Pluses: Modified continental climate with long growing season.

Minuses: Humid summers, severe thunderstorms, hurricanes.

Places Rated Score: 585   **Places Rated Rank: 94**

Elevation: 177 feet

Relative Humidity: 72%
Wind Speed: 7.5 mph

Seasonal Change

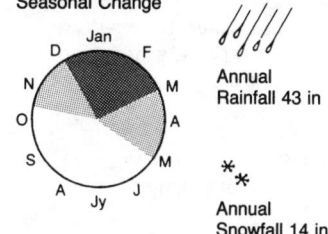

Annual Rainfall 43 in

Annual Snowfall 14 in

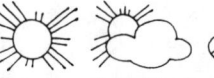

Clear 103 days   Partly Cloudy 107 days   Cloudy 155 days

Precipitation Days: 113 Storm Days: 37

Average Temperatures			
	Daily High	Daily Low	Monthly Mean
January	47.4	27.6	37.5
February	49.9	28.8	39.4
March	58.2	35.5	46.9
April	70.3	45.2	57.8
May	78.4	54.5	66.5
June	85.4	62.9	74.2
July	88.2	67.5	77.9
August	86.6	65.9	76.3
September	80.9	59.0	70.0
October	71.2	47.4	59.3
November	60.6	37.3	49.0
December	49.1	28.8	39.0

Zero-Degree Days: 0
Freezing Days: 85
90-Degree Days: 41
Heating- and Cooling-Degree Days: 5,292

Roanoke, VA

Terrain: Located in the part of the Great Valley that runs from the northernmost part of Virginia southwest to Scott County. The Blue Ridge Mountains are to the west, the Allegheny Mountains to the north.

Climate: Mild. The mountain barrier moderates cold air from the north before it reaches the area. The elevation of the city usually produces cool summer nights. Rainfall is well distributed throughout the year, with an average of 23 inches in the warm season. Snow usually falls each winter, with extremes ranging from a trace to 60 inches.

Pluses: Invigorating, but rare extremes of temperature do occur.

Minuses: Roanoke River liable to flood.

Places Rated Score: 652   **Places Rated Rank: 33**

Elevation: 1,176 feet

Relative Humidity: 65%
Wind Speed: 8.3 mph

Seasonal Change

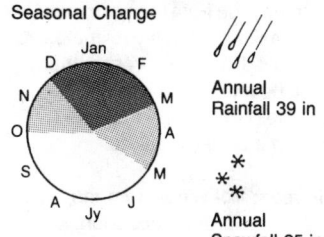

Annual Rainfall 39 in

Annual Snowfall 25 in

Clear 103 days   Partly Cloudy 114 days   Cloudy 148 days

Precipitation Days: 121 Storm Days: 38

Average Temperatures			
	Daily High	Daily Low	Monthly Mean
January	45.6	27.2	36.4
February	47.9	28.3	38.1
March	56.3	34.3	45.3
April	67.9	43.9	55.9
May	76.1	52.7	64.4
June	83.0	60.4	71.7
July	85.9	64.4	75.2
August	84.9	63.3	74.1
September	79.5	56.5	68.0
October	69.9	45.6	57.8
November	57.6	35.8	46.7
December	46.6	28.1	37.4

Zero-Degree Days: 0
Freezing Days: 92
90-Degree Days: 20
Heating- and Cooling-Degree Days: 5,337

Rochester, MN

Terrain: Located in the Zumbro River valley in southeastern Minnesota amid rolling farmland.

Climate: Continental weather pattern with four definite seasons. Winters are cold, but summers are pleasant, with temperatures reaching as high as 90° F on only seven days in an average summer. Thunderstorms (sometimes heavy downpours) occur about once every three days, on the average, during the growing season. These storms often cause high winds. About four times each year, hail will fall. Tornadoes are rare but do occur. Heavy fog occurs 35 times a year on the average.

Pluses: Invigorating four seasons with especially pleasant summers.

Minuses: Cold winters lasting at least five months.

Places Rated Score: 308   **Places Rated Rank: 321**

Elevation: 1,320 feet

Relative Humidity: 74%
Wind Speed: 12.7 mph

Seasonal Change

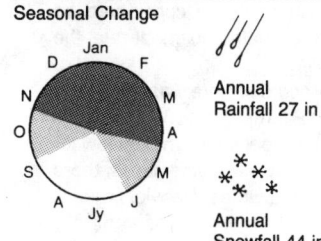

Annual Rainfall 27 in

Annual Snowfall 44 in

Clear 91 days   Partly Cloudy 96 days   Cloudy 178 days

Precipitation Days: 115 Storm Days: 41

Average Temperatures			
	Daily High	Daily Low	Monthly Mean
January	21.9	3.9	12.9
February	26.4	7.4	16.9
March	36.5	19.1	27.8
April	54.9	34.1	44.5
May	67.1	45.3	56.2
June	76.4	55.5	66.0
July	80.7	59.5	70.1
August	79.4	57.7	68.6
September	70.2	48.3	59.3
October	60.4	38.7	49.6
November	40.9	24.2	32.6
December	26.9	10.9	18.9

Zero-Degree Days: 35
Freezing Days: 165
90-Degree Days: 7
Heating- and Cooling-Degree Days: 8,701

Rockford, IL

Terrain: Located northwest of the Chicago area in rolling prairie.
Climate: When winter winds blow from Lake Michigan, cloudiness is often increased, and temperatures are somewhat higher than those to the west around the Mississippi. The lake can also be a moderating influence in summer, sometimes lowering temperatures. Summers are usually hot, however, but oppressive heat seldom prevails for extended periods. Winters are cold, and snow cover is continuous from late December through February.

Pluses: Adequate snow cover for diversified winter sports.

Minuses: Long, cold winters; hot summers.

Elevation: 743 feet

Relative Humidity: 72%
Wind Speed: 9.9 mph

Seasonal Change

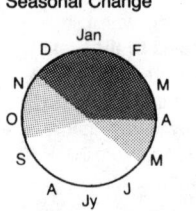

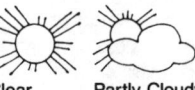
Annual Rainfall 37 in

Annual Snowfall 33 in

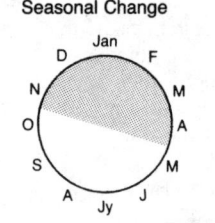

Clear 96 days   Partly Cloudy 100 days   Cloudy 169 days

Precipitation Days: 114   Storm Days: 42

Average Temperatures			
	Daily High	Daily Low	Monthly Mean
January	28.9	11.5	20.2
February	32.6	15.3	24.0
March	43.1	25.0	34.1
April	59.1	37.3	48.2
May	70.3	47.2	58.8
June	79.9	57.7	68.8
July	84.2	61.4	72.8
August	82.8	60.1	71.5
September	74.7	51.8	63.3
October	64.3	41.1	52.7
November	46.5	28.7	37.6
December	33.1	16.7	24.9

Zero-Degree Days: 16
Freezing Days: 142
90-Degree Days: 13
Heating- and Cooling-Degree Days: 7,559

Places Rated Score: 466   **Places Rated Rank: 262**

Sacramento, CA

Terrain: Located in the heart of a broad, flat valley between California's Coast Ranges and the Sierra Nevada. The land is tabletop-flat and, when irrigated, perfect for growing fruits and vegetables.
Climate: The two mountain ranges shelter the area from many storms and violent weather, thus adding to the mildness of the climate. Occasionally, however, northerly winds, called northers, reach the valley over the Siskiyou Mountains, causing heat waves. Summers are sunny and hot, but low humidity lessens the felt heat. Winters are mild, and snow is rare enough to not be regarded a climatic feature.

Pluses: Sunny, mild.

Minuses: Hot winds from the north on occasion, hot summers.

Elevation: 25 feet

Relative Humidity: 66%
Wind Speed: 8.3 mph

Seasonal Change

Annual Rainfall 17 in

Annual Snowfall .1 in

Clear 193 days   Partly Cloudy 72 days   Cloudy 100 days

Precipitation Days: 57   Storm Days: 5

Average Temperatures			
	Daily High	Daily Low	Monthly Mean
January	53.0	37.1	45.1
February	59.1	40.4	49.8
March	64.1	41.9	53.0
April	71.3	45.3	58.3
May	78.8	49.8	64.3
June	86.4	54.6	70.5
July	92.9	57.5	75.2
August	91.3	56.9	74.1
September	87.7	55.3	71.5
October	77.1	49.5	63.3
November	63.6	42.4	53.0
December	53.3	38.3	45.8

Zero-Degree Days: 0
Freezing Days: 17
90-Degree Days: 77
Heating- and Cooling-Degree Days: 4,002

Places Rated Score: 576   **Places Rated Rank: 106**

Saginaw–Bay City–Midland, MI

Terrain: Located south of the tip of Saginaw Bay on the Saginaw River, which flows into the bay. To the west, the land is level and sandy; to the east, it is heavy and fertile lake-bed clay. The metro area is far enough from the bay (and Lake Huron) to be considered an inland location. However, these bodies of water do moderate the climate somewhat.
Climate: The highest temperature ever recorded here was 111° F on July 13, 1936. The coldest was –18° F on February 9, 1934. However, the area averages only five zero-degree days per year, which is low for a location this far north away from an ocean. On the other hand, there are 16 ninety-degree days each summer, on average. Heaviest rainfall is in May. Cloud cover is most frequent in November but is generally less so than that in other places in the state nearer Lake Michigan. The driest month is usually January.

Pluses: Pleasant summers with cool nights.

Minuses: Long winters, cloudy.

Elevation: 662 feet

Relative Humidity: 76%
Wind Speed: 10 mph

Seasonal Change

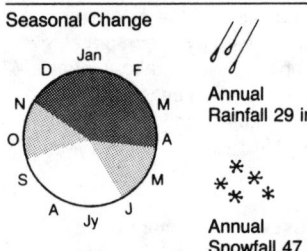

Annual Rainfall 29 in

Annual Snowfall 47 in

Clear 67 days   Partly Cloudy 96 days   Cloudy 202 days

Precipitation Days: 181   Storm Days: 38

Average Temperatures			
	Daily High	Daily Low	Monthly Mean
January	30.4	16.5	23.5
February	31.3	16.1	23.7
March	40.1	24.4	32.3
April	54.9	34.6	44.8
May	67.5	45.1	56.3
June	78.1	55.6	66.9
July	83.8	59.8	71.8
August	81.2	57.9	69.6
September	72.7	50.7	61.7
October	61.4	40.8	51.1
November	45.1	30.7	37.9
December	33.5	20.9	27.2

Zero-Degree Days: 5
Freezing Days: 147
90-Degree Days: 16
Heating- and Cooling-Degree Days: 7,362

Places Rated Score: 515   **Places Rated Rank: 210**

St. Louis, MO–IL

Terrain: Located at the confluence of the Missouri and Mississippi rivers and slightly east of the geographic center of the United States. The surrounding terrain is gently rolling, with occasional high bluffs characteristic of parts of the Mississippi Valley.

Climate: Modified continental. St. Louis is in the enviable position of having a changeable, four-season climate without prolonged periods of extreme cold, heat, or humidity. To the south is the warm, moist air of the Gulf of Mexico and to the north the region of cold polar air masses. Alternating invasions by these influences, and the conflict along the frontal zones where they meet, produce a great variety of weather conditions, but none lasting long enough to become monotonous. Winters are brisk but seldom severe. Snowfall averages less than 20 inches per season. Summers are quite warm, often uncomfortably so when coupled with high humidity. These oppressive spells usually are relieved by storms.

Pluses: Changeable weather, relatively mild winters.

Minuses: Hot, humid summers.

Places Rated Score: 537

Places Rated Rank: 175

Elevation: 564 feet

Relative Humidity: 70%
Wind Speed: 9.5 mph

Seasonal Change

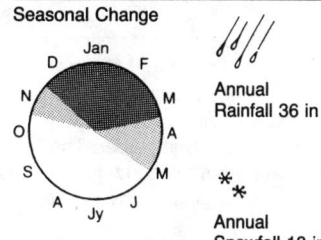

Annual Rainfall 36 in

Annual Snowfall 18 in

Clear 105 days Partly Cloudy 101 days Cloudy 159 days

Precipitation Days: 108 Storm Days: 45

Average Temperatures	Daily High	Daily Low	Monthly Mean
January	39.9	22.6	31.3
February	44.2	26.0	35.1
March	53.0	33.5	43.3
April	67.0	46.0	56.5
May	76.0	55.5	65.8
June	84.9	64.8	74.9
July	88.4	68.8	78.6
August	87.2	67.1	77.2
September	80.1	59.1	69.6
October	69.8	48.4	59.1
November	54.1	35.9	45.0
December	42.7	26.5	34.6

Zero-Degree Days: 3
Freezing Days: 107
90-Degree Days: 37
Heating- and Cooling-Degree Days: 6,225

Salt Lake City–Ogden, UT

Terrain: Spectacular setting. To the east, the Wasatch Mountains rise from heights of 8,000 feet to 12,000 feet; to the southwest, the Oguirrh Mountains climb to 10,000 feet.

Climate: Though by no means mild, it is modified by the surrounding mountains, which deflect stormy weather elsewhere. There are four well-defined seasons, including a long winter. Summers are hot, but the dry air lessens felt heat, and nights are cool. Winters are cold but not severe. Most of the precipitation is snow, with accumulations staying on the ground for most of the winter. Fall is short, with spring longer and sometimes stormy. Nearby Great Salt Lake also helps modify the climate.

Pluses: Scenic setting, good rigorous climate.

Minuses: Cold, snowy winters.

Places Rated Score: 541

Places Rated Rank: 170

Elevation: 4,227 feet

Relative Humidity: 54%
Wind Speed: 8.7 mph

Seasonal Change

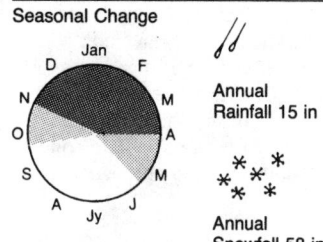

Annual Rainfall 15 in

Annual Snowfall 58 in

Clear 129 days Partly Cloudy 103 days Cloudy 133 days

Precipitation Days: 88 Storm Days: 35

Average Temperatures	Daily High	Daily Low	Monthly Mean
January	37.4	18.5	28.0
February	43.4	23.3	33.4
March	50.8	28.3	39.6
April	61.8	36.6	49.2
May	72.4	44.2	58.3
June	81.3	51.1	66.2
July	92.8	60.5	76.7
August	90.2	58.7	74.5
September	80.3	43.3	64.8
October	66.4	38.4	52.4
November	50.0	28.1	39.1
December	39.0	21.5	30.3

Zero-Degree Days: 3
Freezing Days: 134
90-Degree Days: 58
Heating- and Cooling-Degree Days: 6,910

San Angelo, TX

Terrain: Lies on the northern edge of the Edwards Plateau. The land is flat, sometimes slightly rolling, and is classified as semiarid, or steppe, covered with grass, thorny bush, and cacti.

Climate: San Angelo is situated between the humid climate of eastern Texas and the dry High Plains and the Basin and Range region of western Texas. It is hot, though usually dry. However, uncomfortable hot spells with humid air permeate the area occasionally. The wind is brisk, modifying summer heat. Summers are long, winters short and mild.

Pluses: Dry sunny climate, long summers, short winters.

Minuses: Can be dusty; humid hot spells.

Places Rated Score: 488

Places Rated Rank: 238

Elevation: 1,908 feet

Relative Humidity: 59%
Wind Speed: 10.5 mph

Seasonal Change

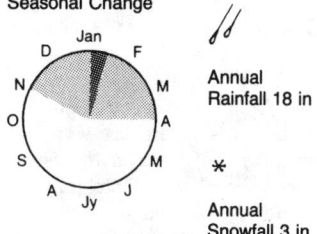

Annual Rainfall 18 in

Annual Snowfall 3 in

Clear 157 days Partly Cloudy 97 days Cloudy 111 days

Precipitation Days: 57 Storm Days: 37

Average Temperatures	Daily High	Daily Low	Monthly Mean
January	59.1	33.6	46.4
February	63.2	37.5	50.4
March	70.7	43.5	57.1
April	80.4	54.0	67.2
May	86.5	62.4	74.5
June	93.4	69.8	81.6
July	96.9	72.4	84.7
August	96.9	72.0	84.5
September	88.4	65.1	76.8
October	79.6	54.7	67.2
November	68.5	42.5	55.5
December	61.4	35.2	48.3

Zero-Degree Days: 0
Freezing Days: 52
90-Degree Days: 109
Heating- and Cooling-Degree Days: 4,942

San Antonio, TX

Terrain: Located between the Edwards Plateau and the Gulf Coastal Plain of south central Texas. Terrain is rolling. Vegetation consists of grasses and live oak trees, along with mesquite and cacti. Soils are blackland clay and silty loam.

Climate: Two-season, with mild weather during normal winter months and a long, hot summer. Though 140 miles from the Gulf of Mexico, the city feels the influence of its hot moist air. Thunderstorms and rains have occurred in every month of the year, but they are most common during the summer, with most rain falling in May and September. The winds during the winter are from the north, and from the south in the summer. Skies are clear more than 30% of the time, and cloudy about 30%.

Pluses: No winter, attractive terrain.

Minuses: Hot, muggy summers.

Places Rated Score: 398

Places Rated Rank: 302

Elevation: 794 feet

Relative Humidity: 67%
Wind Speed: 9.3 mph

Seasonal Change

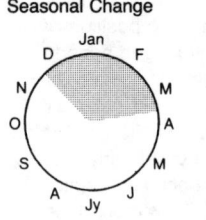

Annual Rainfall 28 in

Annual Snowfall .5 in

Clear 110 days | Partly Cloudy 117 days | Cloudy 138 days

Precipitation Days: 81   Storm Days: 36

Average Temperatures			
	Daily High	Daily Low	Monthly Mean
January	61.6	39.8	50.7
February	65.6	43.4	54.5
March	72.5	49.1	60.8
April	80.3	58.8	69.6
May	86.2	65.7	76.0
June	92.4	72.0	82.2
July	95.6	73.8	84.7
August	95.9	73.4	84.7
September	89.8	68.8	79.3
October	81.8	59.2	70.5
November	71.1	48.2	59.7
December	64.4	41.8	53.2

Zero-Degree Days: 0
Freezing Days: 22
90-Degree Days: 111
Heating- and Cooling-Degree Days: 4,564

★ San Diego, CA

Terrain: Located on San Diego Bay in the southwest corner of California near the Mexican border. Its coastal location is backed by coastal foothills and mountains to the east.

Climate: One of the mildest in North America: typically marine, sometimes called Mediterranean. There are no freezing days and an average of only three 90-degree days each year. San Diego has abundant sunshine and mild sea breezes. Only two seasons occur here: a dry, mild summer and a spring that is cooler, with some rain. Storms are practically unknown, though there is considerable fog along the coast, and many low clouds in early morning and evening during the summer.

Pluses: One of the best climates for sun and mildness.

Minuses: Paradise climate lacking variety and seasonal contrasts.

Places Rated Score: 903

Places Rated Rank: 3

Elevation: 28 feet

Relative Humidity: 68%
Wind Speed: 6.7 mph

Seasonal Change

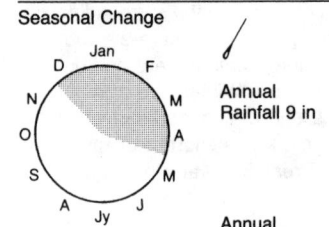

Annual Rainfall 9 in

Annual Snowfall 0 in

Clear 150 days | Partly Cloudy 117 days | Cloudy 98 days

Precipitation Days: 41   Storm Days: 3

Average Temperatures			
	Daily High	Daily Low	Monthly Mean
January	64.6	45.8	55.2
February	65.6	47.8	56.7
March	66.0	50.1	58.1
April	67.6	53.8	60.7
May	69.4	57.2	63.3
June	71.1	59.9	65.5
July	75.3	63.9	69.6
August	77.3	65.4	71.4
September	76.5	63.2	69.9
October	73.8	58.4	66.1
November	70.1	51.5	60.8
December	66.1	55.4	62.9

Zero-Degree Days: 0
Freezing Days: 0
90-Degree Days: 3
Heating- and Cooling-Degree Days: 2,229

★ San Francisco, CA

Terrain: Unique location—at the northern end of a narrow peninsula that separates San Francisco Bay from the Pacific Ocean and forms the southern shore of the Golden Gate Bridge—causes San Francisco to be known as the Air-Conditioned City.

Climate: Two-season climate: a cool, pleasant summer and a mild spring. Flowers bloom throughout the year, and warm clothing is needed every month. Sea fogs and associated low stratus clouds are a striking characteristic of the city's climate. On the average, though, the sun shines during 66% of the daylight hours. There are wide contrasts in climate within short distances of the bay; nearby communities of Marin County, to the north across the Golden Gate and sheltered from the prevailing winds by high peaks and ridges of the Coast Ranges, enjoy warmer and sunnier weather than the city.

Pluses: Mild, springlike weather ten months of the year; ranks first among the 333 metro areas.

Minuses: Invariable climate patterns; fogs and cloudy days.

Places Rated Score: 910

Places Rated Rank: 1

Elevation: 155 feet

Relative Humidity: 75%
Wind Speed: 8.7 mph

Seasonal Change

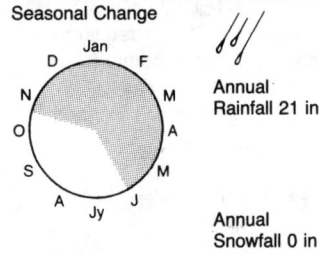

Annual Rainfall 21 in

Annual Snowfall 0 in

Clear 162 days | Partly Cloudy 103 days | Cloudy 100 days

Precipitation Days: 67   Storm Days: 2

Average Temperatures			
	Daily High	Daily Low	Monthly Mean
January	55.3	41.2	48.3
February	58.6	43.8	51.2
March	61.0	44.9	53.0
April	63.5	47.0	55.3
May	66.6	49.9	58.3
June	70.2	53.0	61.6
July	70.9	54.0	62.5
August	71.6	54.3	63.0
September	73.6	54.5	64.1
October	70.3	51.6	61.0
November	63.3	47.2	55.3
December	56.5	42.9	49.7

Zero-Degree Days: 0
Freezing Days: 0
90-Degree Days: 1
Heating- and Cooling-Degree Days: 3,119

★ Santa Barbara–Santa Maria–Lompoc, CA

Terrain: Located in the Santa Maria Valley 150 miles north of Los Angeles and 250 miles south of San Francisco. The valley is flat and fertile, opening onto the Pacific Ocean at its widest point and tapering inland at a distance of 30 miles from the coast. It is bounded by the foothills of the San Rafael Mountains, the Solomon Hills, and the Casmalia Hills.

Climate: Rainfall season, typical of the California coast, is winter. During the rest of the year, particularly from June to October, there is little or no precipitation. Clear, sunshiny afternoons prevail on most days. At night and in the morning, however, the California stratus and fog appear.

Pluses: Year-round mildness moving through gradual transitions.

Minuses: No distinct seasonal changes, night and morning fogs.

Places Rated Score: 885

Places Rated Rank: 5

Elevation: 238 feet

Relative Humidity: 74%
Wind Speed: 7 mph

Seasonal Change

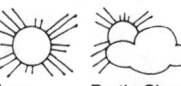

Annual Rainfall 12 in

Annual Snowfall 0 in

Clear 177 days

Partly Cloudy 108 days

Cloudy 80 days

Precipitation Days: 45   Storm Days: 2

Average Temperatures			
	Daily High	Daily Low	Monthly Mean
January	62.7	38.3	50.5
February	63.6	40.3	52.0
March	64.3	41.3	52.8
April	66.0	43.7	54.9
May	67.4	46.7	57.1
June	69.7	49.5	59.6
July	71.8	52.4	62.1
August	72.1	52.5	62.3
September	73.9	51.2	62.6
October	73.3	47.5	60.4
November	69.2	42.9	56.1
December	64.2	39.3	51.8

Zero-Degree Days: 0
Freezing Days: 24
90-Degree Days: 6
Heating- and Cooling-Degree Days: 3,137

Santa Fe, NM

Terrain: This historic city, the capital of New Mexico and seat of Santa Fe County, sits in the Rio Grande Valley in the north central section of the state. It is situated amid the rolling foothills of the Sangre de Cristo Mountains, which rise to peaks of 10,000 feet. Westward the terrain slopes downward to the Rio Grande River, some 20 miles away. The high mountains to the east protect the city from much of the cold air of winter. The city's historic legacy, cultural facilities, and fine climate have long attracted tourists and retired people.

Climate: Semiarid continental, with cool and pleasant summers. Days are in the 80s, but nights in the 50s. Long cloudy periods are unknown. Winters are crisp, clear, and sunny, with considerable daytime warming.

Pluses: Beautiful scenery. Mild, sunny four-season climate.

Minuses: Wide temperature range and high altitude may present health problems for some persons.

Places Rated Score: 615

Places Rated Rank: 61

Elevation: 7,200 feet

Relative Humidity: 50%
Wind Speed: 9 mph

Seasonal Change

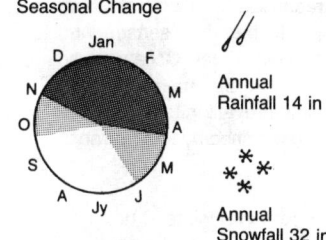

Annual Rainfall 14 in

Annual Snowfall 32 in

Clear 172 days

Partly Cloudy 110 days

Cloudy 83 days

Precipitation Days: 37   Storm Days: 54

Average Temperatures			
	Daily High	Daily Low	Monthly Mean
January	41.0	19.3	29.9
February	44.9	22.5	33.7
March	51.6	26.8	39.2
April	61.7	34.5	48.0
May	70.7	42.9	56.6
June	81.4	52.1	66.4
July	84.3	56.7	70.4
August	82.2	55.0	68.6
September	76.5	49.1	62.9
October	65.2	38.7	52.0
November	51.5	26.5	39.0
December	43.3	21.2	32.0

Zero-Degree Days: 1
Freezing Days: 152
90-Degree Days: 7
Heating- and Cooling-Degree Days: 6,809

★ Santa Rosa–Petaluma, CA

Terrain: Located in the east-central portion of the Petaluma–Santa Rosa–Russian River valley, which extends northwestward from San Pablo Bay, about 45 miles from the Golden Gate Bridge. This valley runs parallel to the Pacific Coast, with only low hills (300 feet to 500 feet) between it and the ocean 25 miles southwest. Higher hills rise to the east of the metro area, with greater elevations about 10 miles farther east, in the foothills of the Coast Ranges.

Climate: The nearness of the ocean and the surrounding topography join with the prevailing westerly circulation to produce a predominantly southerly air flow year-round. However, the area is sufficiently far inland to assure it a more varied climate than San Francisco's. Summers are warmer, winters cooler, and there is more daily temperature shift, as well as less fog and drizzle.

Pluses: Mild, yet sunnier and warmer than coastal locations; ideal retirement climate.

Minuses: Some hot weather.

Places Rated Score: 732

Places Rated Rank: 19

Elevation: 167 feet

Relative Humidity: 70%
Wind Speed: 7 mph

Seasonal Change

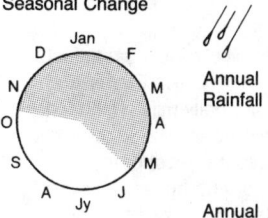

Annual Rainfall 30 in

Annual Snowfall 0 in

Clear 176 days

Partly Cloudy 109 days

Cloudy 80 days

Precipitation Days: 47   Storm Days: 4

Average Temperatures			
	Daily High	Daily Low	Monthly Mean
January	57.1	35.7	46.4
February	62.3	37.9	50.1
March	66.6	39.5	53.1
April	70.1	40.1	55.1
May	75.0	44.6	59.8
June	80.2	49.2	64.1
July	83.6	48.8	66.4
August	83.4	48.8	66.1
September	83.3	47.7	65.5
October	77.7	44.3	61.0
November	67.7	39.2	53.5
December	58.4	37.0	47.7

Zero-Degree Days: 0
Freezing Days: 43
90-Degree Days: 33
Heating- and Cooling-Degree Days: 3,900

Savannah, GA

Terrain: Surrounded by flat land, low and marshy to the north and east, rising to several feet above sea level to the west and south. About half the land to the west and south is clear of trees; the other half is woods, much of which lie in swamp.

Climate: Temperate with a seasonal mean temperature of 51° F in winter, 64° F in spring, 80° F in summer, and 66° F in autumn. Summer temperatures are moderated by thundershowers almost every afternoon. Sunshine is adequate in all seasons; seldom are there more than two or three days in succession without it. The long growing season is accompanied by abundant rain.

Pluses: Mild winters, pleasant autumns.

Minuses: Low, marshy terrain; humid summers.

Places Rated Score: 542

Places Rated Rank: 166

Elevation: 51 feet

Relative Humidity: 74%
Wind Speed: 8.1 mph

Seasonal Change

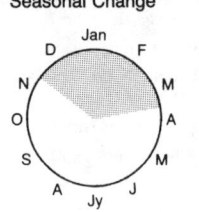

Annual Rainfall 51 in

Annual Snowfall .3 in

Clear 104 days | Partly Cloudy 113 days | Cloudy 148 days

Precipitation Days: 112 Storm Days: 64

Average Temperatures			
	Daily High	Daily Low	Monthly Mean
January	61.1	38.7	49.9
February	63.6	40.5	52.1
March	69.5	46.4	58.0
April	77.8	54.3	66.1
May	84.8	61.8	73.3
June	89.3	68.8	79.1
July	90.8	71.3	81.1
August	90.3	70.9	80.6
September	85.4	66.9	76.2
October	78.2	55.9	67.1
November	69.3	44.9	57.1
December	62.1	38.7	50.4

Zero-Degree Days: 0
Freezing Days: 35
90-Degree Days: 54
Heating- and Cooling-Degree Days: 4,269

★ Seattle, WA

Terrain: Located on Puget Sound on the northwest Pacific coast of Washington. The Cascade Range and the Olympic Mountains serve as barriers to easterly and northerly weather systems.

Climate: Midlatitude coast climate, characterized by moderate temperatures, a pronounced though not sharply defined rainy season, and considerable cloudiness, particularly during the winter. Occasionally, severe winter storms come in from the north. Summers are very pleasant, and winters are relatively mild, with prevailing temperatures in the 40s. Summer heat and winter cold are modified by the nearness of the ocean.

Pluses: Mild temperatures, especially pleasant summers and autumns.

Minuses: Wet winters, ground fogs, lots of drizzle.

Places Rated Score: 808

Places Rated Rank: 12

Elevation: 450 feet

Relative Humidity: 74%
Wind Speed: 9.3 mph

Seasonal Change

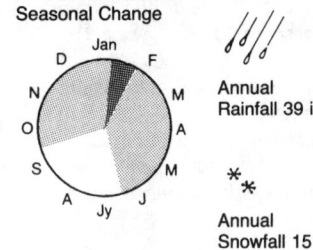

Annual Rainfall 39 in

Annual Snowfall 15 in

Clear 57 days | Partly Cloudy 79 days | Cloudy 229 days

Precipitation Days: 160 Storm Days: 7

Average Temperatures			
	Daily High	Daily Low	Monthly Mean
January	43.4	33.0	38.2
February	48.5	36.0	42.3
March	51.5	36.6	44.1
April	57.0	40.3	48.7
May	64.1	45.6	54.9
June	69.0	50.6	59.8
July	75.1	53.8	64.5
August	73.8	53.7	63.8
September	68.7	50.4	59.6
October	59.4	44.9	52.2
November	50.4	38.8	44.6
December	45.4	35.5	40.5

Zero-Degree Days: 0
Freezing Days: 32
90-Degree Days: 3
Heating- and Cooling-Degree Days: 5,314

Shreveport, LA

Terrain: Located on the west bank of the Red River opposite Bossier City, in the northwestern section of the state, some 30 miles south of Arkansas and 15 miles east of the Texas state line. Part of the city is situated in the Red River bottomlands and the remainder in the gently rolling hills that begin a mile west of the river.

Climate: Transitional between the humid subtropical climate prevalent to the south and the continental climates of the Great Plains and Middle West to the north. Winter months are normally mild, with cold spells generally of short duration. The typical pattern is a drop in temperature the first day, minimum temperatures the second day, and gradual warming on the third. Summers are hot and humid, relieved only by the thunderstorms that come about eight times per month during that season. April and May are pleasant. Fall, which lasts from late September until December, is delightful for outdoor activities.

Pluses: Mild winters, long falls.

Minuses: Hot, steamy summers; occasional flooding.

Places Rated Score: 508

Places Rated Rank: 221

Elevation: 259 feet

Relative Humidity: 71%
Wind Speed: 8.8 mph

Seasonal Change

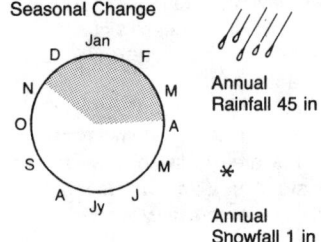

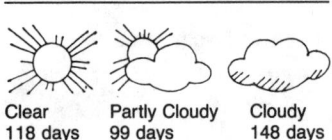

Annual Rainfall 45 in

Annual Snowfall 1 in

Clear 118 days | Partly Cloudy 99 days | Cloudy 148 days

Precipitation Days: 97 Storm Days: 54

Average Temperatures			
	Daily High	Daily Low	Monthly Mean
January	56.6	37.8	47.2
February	60.4	40.6	50.5
March	67.3	46.2	56.8
April	76.9	55.9	66.4
May	83.6	63.1	73.4
June	90.1	70.2	80.2
July	93.5	72.8	83.2
August	93.8	72.5	83.2
September	87.9	66.8	77.4
October	79.3	55.7	67.5
November	67.2	45.2	56.2
December	58.9	39.4	49.2

Zero-Degree Days: 0
Freezing Days: 1
90-Degree Days: 87
Heating- and Cooling-Degree Days: 4,705

Sioux City, IA–NE

Terrain: Sioux City is located along the Missouri River at a point where Iowa touches both Nebraska and South Dakota. The terrain is rolling, except for the river valleys and bottomlands. The Sioux City business district lies in the river valley, and the residential sections, for the most part, are spread over the hills, which range from 100 feet to 200 feet higher. Corn, small grains, and grazing grasses are products of abundant rainfall here.

Climate: Typically continental and largely determined by the movement and interaction of the large-scale weather systems. Under normal conditions, winters are cold and summers warm, with most rain falling between April and September. Except for an occasional dry year, rain is plentiful. There is considerable fluctuation in temperature and precipitation from season to season and year to year, as elsewhere in the northern Plains. Average growing season: 160 days. The first freeze is in early October and the last in late April.

Pluses: Variable.

Minuses: Rugged continental.

Places Rated Score: 385   **Places Rated Rank: 306**

Elevation: 1,103 feet

Relative Humidity: 69%
Wind Speed: 10.9 mph

Seasonal Change

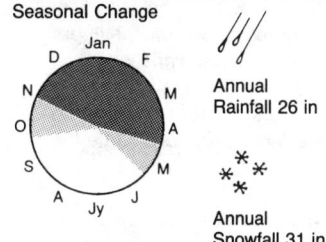

Annual Rainfall 26 in

Annual Snowfall 31 in

Clear 107 days | Partly Cloudy 103 days | Cloudy 155 days

Precipitation Days: 98   Storm Days: 45

	Daily High	Daily Low	Monthly Mean
Average Temperatures			
January	28.2	7.7	18.0
February	33.3	13.4	23.4
March	42.9	23.4	33.2
April	61.3	37.4	49.4
May	72.5	49.3	60.9
June	81.3	59.3	70.3
July	86.7	63.9	75.3
August	84.8	62.1	73.5
September	75.3	51.4	63.4
October	65.8	40.4	53.1
November	47.0	25.6	36.3
December	33.3	13.6	23.5

Zero-Degree Days: 22
Freezing Days: 150
90-Degree Days: 24
Heating- and Cooling-Degree Days: 7,885

Sioux Falls, SD

Terrain: Located in the Big Sioux River valley in the southeastern portion of South Dakota. Surrounding terrain is gently rolling. Within a 100-mile radius of the city, the land slopes upward 300 feet to 400 feet in the north and northwest and downward in the southeast. There is little change in elevation in the other directions.

Climate: Invigorating continental. Cold air masses from the north often move in very rapidly, causing strong, gusty winds for several hours. During late fall and winter, these cold fronts sometimes bring temperature drops of 20 degrees to 30 degrees in a day. Severe cold spells rarely last more than a few days. During a cold winter, frost may penetrate the ground to a depth of 3 feet to 4 feet unless there is heavy snow cover to protect the ground. There are usually one to two very heavy snowstorms each winter. Summer temperatures may climb over 100° F once or twice a year. Thunderstorms are frequent, especially during June and July. Occasional tornadoes and floods.

Pluses: Vigorous four-season climate.

Minuses: Extremes in temperature, snowy.

Places Rated Score: 276   **Places Rated Rank: 325**

Elevation: 1,427 feet

Relative Humidity: 69%
Wind Speed: 11.2 mph

Seasonal Change

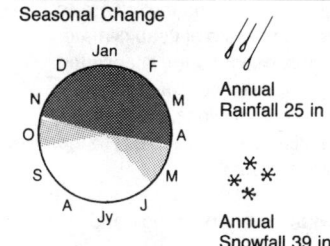

Annual Rainfall 25 in

Annual Snowfall 39 in

Clear 105 days | Partly Cloudy 105 days | Cloudy 155 days

Precipitation Days: 93   Storm Days: 43

	Daily High	Daily Low	Monthly Mean
Average Temperatures			
January	24.6	3.7	14.2
February	29.7	9.0	19.4
March	39.7	20.2	30.0
April	57.8	34.4	46.1
May	69.7	45.7	57.7
June	78.9	56.3	67.6
July	85.1	61.5	73.3
August	83.8	59.8	71.8
September	73.0	48.7	60.9
October	62.7	37.6	50.2
November	43.5	22.7	33.1
December	29.6	10.4	20.0

Zero-Degree Days: 33
Freezing Days: 171
90-Degree Days: 28
Heating- and Cooling-Degree Days: 8,557

Spokane, WA

Terrain: Spokane lies on the eastern edge of the broad Columbia Basin area of Washington, which is bounded by the Cascade Range on the west and the Rocky Mountains to the east. The elevations in eastern Washington vary from less than 400 feet above sea level near Pasco to 5,000 feet in the extreme eastern edge of the state. Spokane is in the upper plateau area, where the long, gradual slope from the Columbia River meets the sharp rise of the Rockies.

Climate: Combines some of the characteristics of the damp coastal climate with the arid interior climate. Most air masses are brought from the west or southwest and lose most of their moisture passing over the Coast and Cascade ranges. Sometimes dry, continental air masses from the east invade the area, bringing high temperatures with low humidity in the summer and subzero temperatures in the winter. Generally, Spokane has a mild, arid climate during summer and a cold, coastal climate during winter.

Pluses: Mild, dry summers.

Minuses: Damp winters.

Places Rated Score: 574   **Places Rated Rank: 113**

Elevation: 2,365 feet

Relative Humidity: 63%
Wind Speed: 8.7 mph

Seasonal Change

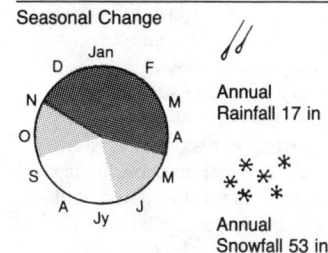

Annual Rainfall 17 in

Annual Snowfall 53 in

Clear 89 days | Partly Cloudy 87 days | Cloudy 189 days

Precipitation Days: 114   Storm Days: 11

	Daily High	Daily Low	Monthly Mean
Average Temperatures			
January	31.9	19.6	25.4
February	39.0	25.3	32.2
March	46.2	28.8	37.5
April	57.0	35.2	46.1
May	66.5	42.8	54.7
June	73.6	49.4	61.5
July	84.3	55.1	69.7
August	81.9	54.0	68.0
September	72.5	46.7	59.6
October	58.1	37.5	47.8
November	41.8	29.2	35.5
December	33.9	24.0	29.0

Zero-Degree Days: 5
Freezing Days: 141
90-Degree Days: 21
Heating- and Cooling-Degree Days: 7,225

Springfield, IL

Terrain: Surrounding country is nearly level. There are no large hills in the area, but rolling terrain is found near the Sangamon River and Spring Creek.

Climate: Typically continental in character, with warm to hot summers and cold winters. Monthly average temperatures range from the upper 20s in January to the upper 70s in July. Considerable variation takes place frequently within each season. Although summer weather is often uncomfortably warm and humid, winters are less severe than those farther to the north, although prairie winds may accentuate the cold. Summers are sunny.

Pluses: Changeable climate.

Minuses: Hot summers, rather cold winters.

Elevation: 613 feet

Relative Humidity: 71%
Wind Speed: 11.4 mph

Seasonal Change

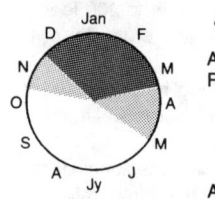

Annual Rainfall 35 in

Annual Snowfall 22 in

Clear 108 days   Partly Cloudy 92 days   Cloudy 165 days

Precipitation Days: 112   Storm Days: 50

Average Temperatures			
	Daily High	Daily Low	Monthly Mean
January	34.8	18.6	26.7
February	38.9	21.8	30.4
March	48.7	30.1	39.4
April	63.6	42.6	53.1
May	74.1	52.6	63.4
June	83.3	62.5	72.9
July	86.6	65.6	76.1
August	85.0	63.7	74.4
September	78.7	55.6	67.2
October	68.1	45.0	56.6
November	51.0	32.7	41.9
December	38.2	22.7	30.5

Zero-Degree Days: 8
Freezing Days: 119
90-Degree Days: 28
Heating- and Cooling-Degree Days: 6,674

Places Rated Score: 524   **Places Rated Rank: 196**

Springfield, MO

Terrain: Located on very gently rolling tableland, almost atop the crest of the Missouri Ozark Plateau. The average elevation of the city proper is just over 1,300 feet above sea level.

Climate: As a result of this advantageous position, the city and surrounding countryside enjoy what is described as a plateau climate. The area possesses the mild and changeable climate often associated with high places in southerly latitudes, with warmer winters and cooler summers than other parts of the state at lower elevations. The city sits astride two major drainage systems: the Missouri River system to the north and the White-Mississippi system to the south.

Pluses: Mild, changeable.

Minuses: Short springs and falls.

Elevation: 1,270 feet

Relative Humidity: 70%
Wind Speed: 11.2 mph

Seasonal Change

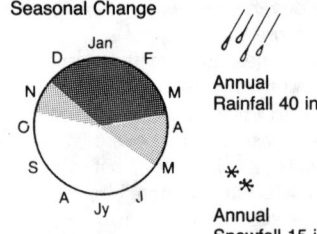

Annual Rainfall 40 in

Annual Snowfall 15 in

Clear 117 days   Partly Cloudy 99 days   Cloudy 149 days

Precipitation Days: 107   Storm Days: 58

Average Temperatures			
	Daily High	Daily Low	Monthly Mean
January	43.2	22.6	32.9
February	47.5	26.5	37.0
March	55.1	32.8	44.0
April	68.0	45.0	56.5
May	76.1	54.0	65.1
June	84.2	62.9	73.6
July	89.0	66.5	77.8
August	88.9	65.2	77.1
September	81.2	57.3	69.3
October	71.1	46.8	59.0
November	56.4	34.5	45.5
December	45.7	26.3	36.0

Zero-Degree Days: 3
Freezing Days: 105
90-Degree Days: 40
Heating- and Cooling-Degree Days: 5,952

Places Rated Score: 544   **Places Rated Rank: 161**

State College, PA

Terrain: Located in Centre County, the geographic center of Pennsylvania. The orientation of the ridges and valleys of the Appalachian Mountains is northeast to southwest. Elevations within Centre County vary from 977 feet to 2,400 feet. The largest valley in the area is Nittany Valley, much of which is under cultivation. The surrounding higher elevations are covered with second-growth forests.

Climate: A composite of the relatively dry midwestern continental climate and the more humid climate characteristic of the eastern seaboard. Prevailing westerly winds carry weather disturbances from the interior of the country into the area. Coastal storms occasionally affect the local weather as they move toward the northeast, but generally the Atlantic is too distant to have a noticeable effect on the climate. Winters are cold and relatively dry, with thick cloud cover. Summer and fall are the most pleasant seasons of the year.

Pluses: Nice falls and summers.

Minuses: Humid, lots of cloudy days.

Elevation: 1,200 feet

Relative Humidity: 67%
Wind Speed: 7.8 mph

Seasonal Change

Annual Rainfall 37 in

Annual Snowfall 48 in

Clear 66 days   Partly Cloudy 114 days   Cloudy 185 days

Precipitation Days: 122   Storm Days: 35

Average Temperatures			
	Daily High	Daily Low	Monthly Mean
January	34.2	19.8	27.0
February	36.1	20.2	28.2
March	45.4	27.7	36.5
April	59.2	38.9	49.1
May	70.2	48.8	59.3
June	78.7	57.3	68.0
July	82.6	61.1	71.9
August	80.7	59.1	69.9
September	73.5	52.0	62.8
October	62.9	42.5	52.7
November	48.7	33.2	41.0
December	36.3	22.9	29.6

Zero-Degree Days: 4
Freezing Days: 132
90-Degree Days: 8
Heating- and Cooling-Degree Days: 6,797

Places Rated Score: 575   **Places Rated Rank: 108**

Syracuse, NY

Terrain: Located at approximately the geographic center of New York State. Gently rolling terrain stretches northward for about 30 miles to the eastern end of Lake Ontario. Oneida Lake lies about 8 miles northeast of the city. Five miles to the south, hills rise to about 1,500 feet. Immediately to the west, terrain is gently rolling, with elevations 500 feet to 800 feet above sea level.

Climate: Continental and comparatively humid. Nearly all cyclonic systems moving from the interior of the country and passing through the St. Lawrence Valley will affect Syracuse. Seasonal and daily changes are marked and produce an invigorating climate. Winters can be cold and severe; daytime temperatures average 35° F, nighttime lows around 18° F. Autumn, winter, and spring show great changeability. Summer nights generally are cool, but days can be uncomfortable because of the humidity. The area is overcast, and the cloudiest months are December, January, and February.

Pluses: Changeable weather.

Minuses: Snowy, cloudy, rigorous.

Places Rated Score: 548

Places Rated Rank: 153

Elevation: 408 feet

Relative Humidity: 73%
Wind Speed: 9.8 mph

Seasonal Change

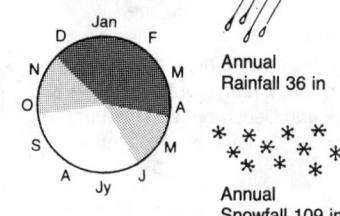

Annual Rainfall 36 in

Annual Snowfall 109 in

Clear 64 days | Partly Cloudy 100 days | Cloudy 201 days

Precipitation Days: 168 Storm Days: 29

Average Temperatures			
	Daily High	Daily Low	Monthly Mean
January	31.4	15.8	23.6
February	32.7	16.5	24.6
March	41.5	24.8	33.2
April	56.5	36.4	46.5
May	67.6	46.0	56.8
June	77.7	56.1	66.9
July	82.0	61.0	71.5
August	80.2	59.2	69.7
September	73.3	52.3	62.8
October	62.4	42.5	52.5
November	48.3	33.6	41.0
December	35.0	21.2	28.1

Zero-Degree Days: 9
Freezing Days: 138
90-Degree Days: 6
Heating- and Cooling-Degree Days: 7,229

Tallahassee, FL

Terrain: Located in flat topography in northwest Florida about 20 miles from the Gulf of Mexico.

Climate: Average year-round temperatures compare with those of southern portions of California, Brazil, China, and Australia. The yearly average of 68° F has varied from 64° F to 71° F. In contrast to the southern part of Florida, there is a more definite march of the four seasons here, with considerable winter rainfall and much less winter sunshine. Summer is the least pleasant time of the year; thunderstorms occur on the average of every other day. High humidities and high temperatures cause discomfort. Maxima of 90° F or higher occur on an average of almost 90 days per year, with readings as high as 95° F on 22 of those days.

Pluses: Warm winters, sufficient rainfall.

Minuses: Long, humid summers; few clear days relative to the rest of the state.

Places Rated Score: 404

Places Rated Rank: 298

Elevation: 68 feet

Relative Humidity: 76%
Wind Speed: 7.0 mph

Seasonal Change

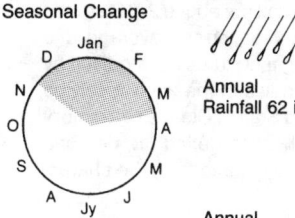

Annual Rainfall 62 in

Annual Snowfall 0 in

Clear 95 days | Partly Cloudy 138 days | Cloudy 132 days

Precipitation Days: 119 Storm Days: 86

Average Temperatures			
	Daily High	Daily Low	Monthly Mean
January	64.2	41.0	52.6
February	66.5	43.0	54.8
March	72.1	48.4	60.3
April	80.1	55.7	67.9
May	86.7	62.8	74.8
June	90.4	69.6	80.0
July	90.6	71.6	81.1
August	90.5	71.7	81.1
September	87.4	68.7	78.1
October	80.6	57.9	69.3
November	71.4	46.4	58.9
December	65.1	41.3	53.2

Zero-Degree Days: 0
Freezing Days: 36
90-Degree Days: 87
Heating- and Cooling-Degree Days: 4,126

Tampa–St. Petersburg–Clearwater, FL

Terrain: Located in flat topography on the Gulf coast of Florida.

Climate: An outstanding feature is the summer thunderstorm season. On the average, there are 88 days of thundershowers per year, occurring mostly in the afternoons in July, August, and September. The resulting temperature drop from 90° F to 70° F produces an agreeable physiologic reaction. Temperature throughout the year is modified by the waters of the Gulf of Mexico and surrounding bays. Snowfall is negligible, and freezing temperatures are rare; during the cooling season, however, night ground fogs occur frequently because of the flat terrain.

Pluses: Mild Gulf climate.

Minuses: Gulf hurricanes, regular summer thundershowers.

Places Rated Score: 440

Places Rated Rank: 279

Elevation: 11 feet

Relative Humidity: 74%
Wind Speed: 8.8 mph

Seasonal Change

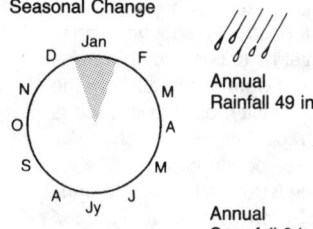

Annual Rainfall 49 in

Annual Snowfall 0 in

Clear 98 days | Partly Cloudy 140 days | Cloudy 127 days

Precipitation Days: 107 Storm Days: 88

Average Temperatures			
	Daily High	Daily Low	Monthly Mean
January	70.6	50.1	60.4
February	71.9	51.7	61.8
March	76.1	55.9	66.0
April	82.4	61.6	72.0
May	87.5	66.9	77.2
June	89.9	72.0	81.0
July	90.1	73.7	81.9
August	90.4	74.0	82.2
September	89.0	72.6	80.8
October	83.9	65.5	74.7
November	77.1	56.4	66.8
December	72.0	51.2	61.6

Zero-Degree Days: 0
Freezing Days: 4
90-Degree Days: 81
Heating- and Cooling-Degree Days: 4,084

Toledo, OH

Terrain: Located on the western end of Lake Erie at the mouth of the Maumee River, on flat ground. The city has excellent harbor facilities, making it a large transportation center for rail, water, and motor freight. Generally rich agricultural land is found in the surrounding area, especially up the Maumee River toward the Indiana state line.

Climate: Nearness to Lake Erie has a moderating effect on temperature, and extremes are seldom recorded. Humidity is high, and there is an excessive amount of cloudiness. In the winter months, the sun shines during only 30% of the daylight hours; December and January, the cloudiest months, sometimes receive as little as 16% of the possible amount of sunshine.

Pluses: Lakefront location moderates extreme temperatures.

Minuses: Humid, cloudy.

Places Rated Score: 518

Places Rated Rank: 204

Elevation: 692 feet

Relative Humidity: 72%
Wind Speed: 9.5 mph

Seasonal Change

Annual Rainfall 32 in

Annual Snowfall 37 in

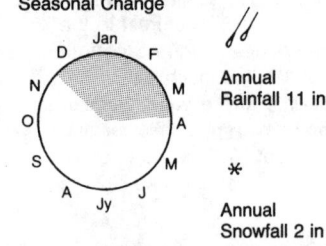

Clear 71 days — Partly Cloudy 110 days — Cloudy 184 days

Precipitation Days: 136 Storm Days: 40

Average Temperatures			
	Daily High	Daily Low	Monthly Mean
January	32.4	17.2	24.8
February	35.2	18.9	27.1
March	45.0	26.6	35.8
April	59.5	37.2	48.4
May	70.5	47.1	58.8
June	80.5	57.2	68.9
July	83.8	60.8	72.3
August	82.4	59.1	70.8
September	75.7	51.8	63.8
October	64.8	41.2	53.0
November	48.0	31.1	39.6
December	35.4	20.5	28.0

Zero-Degree Days: 8
Freezing Days: 145
90-Degree Days: 13
Heating- and Cooling-Degree Days: 7,066

Tucson, AZ

Terrain: Lies at the foot of the Catalina Mountains in a flat to gently rolling valley floor in southern Arizona.

Climate: Desert, characterized by a long, hot season beginning in April and ending in October. Temperature maxima above 90° F are the rule during this period; on 41 days each year, on the average, the temperature reaches 100° F. These high temperatures are modified by low humidity, reducing discomfort. Tucson lies in the zone receiving more sunshine than any other in the United States. Clear skies or very thin, high clouds permit intense surface heating during the day and active radiational cooling at night, a process enhanced by the characteristic atmospheric dryness.

Pluses: Clear, warm, dry.

Minuses: Intense summer heat.

Places Rated Score: 589

Places Rated Rank: 89

Elevation: 2,555 feet

Relative Humidity: 38%
Wind Speed: 8.2 mph

Seasonal Change

Annual Rainfall 11 in

Annual Snowfall 2 in

Clear 198 days — Partly Cloudy 89 days — Cloudy 78 days

Precipitation Days: 50 Storm Days: 40

Average Temperatures			
	Daily High	Daily Low	Monthly Mean
January	63.5	38.2	50.9
February	67.0	39.9	53.5
March	71.5	43.6	57.6
April	80.7	50.3	65.5
May	89.6	57.5	73.6
June	97.9	66.2	82.1
July	98.3	74.2	86.3
August	95.3	72.3	83.8
September	93.1	67.1	80.1
October	83.8	56.4	70.1
November	72.2	44.8	58.5
December	64.8	39.1	52.0

Zero-Degree Days: 0
Freezing Days: 21
90-Degree Days: 139
Heating- and Cooling-Degree Days: 4,566

Tulsa, OK

Terrain: Lies along the Arkansas River at an elevation of almost 700 feet above sea level. The surrounding terrain is gently rolling. There are no natural formations—such as mountains or large water surfaces—that influence its climate.

Climate: At a latitude of 30 degrees north, Tulsa is far enough north to escape long periods of heat in summer, yet far enough south to miss the extreme cold of winter. The influence of warm moist air from the Gulf of Mexico is often felt in the high humidity, but the climate is essentially continental, characterized by rapid temperature changes. Generally, the winter months are mild. Temperatures of 100° F or higher are frequently experienced from the latter part of July to early September but are usually accompanied by low humidity and a good southerly breeze. Fall is long, with a great number of pleasant, sunny days and cool, bracing nights.

Pluses: Four-season climate with long summers and pleasant falls.

Minuses: Hot periods during summer months, tornadoes.

Places Rated Score: 530

Places Rated Rank: 185

Elevation: 676 feet

Relative Humidity: 67%
Wind Speed: 10.6 mph

Seasonal Change

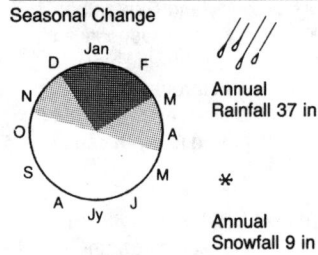

Annual Rainfall 37 in

Annual Snowfall 9 in

Clear 127 days — Partly Cloudy 101 days — Cloudy 137 days

Precipitation Days: 90 Storm Days: 52

Average Temperatures			
	Daily High	Daily Low	Monthly Mean
January	47.0	26.1	36.6
February	52.2	30.2	41.2
March	59.7	36.9	48.3
April	71.8	49.7	60.8
May	79.2	58.4	68.8
June	87.3	67.3	77.3
July	92.8	71.4	82.1
August	92.7	70.0	81.4
September	84.8	61.7	73.3
October	75.0	50.8	62.9
November	60.8	38.0	49.4
December	50.1	29.5	39.8

Zero-Degree Days: 1
Freezing Days: 85
90-Degree Days: 70
Heating- and Cooling-Degree Days: 5,629

Washington, DC–MD–VA

Terrain: Situated at the western edge of the Middle Atlantic Coastal Plain, 50 miles east of the Blue Ridge Mountains and 35 miles west of Chesapeake Bay at the junction of the Potomac and Anacostia rivers. **Climate:** Summers are warm and humid, winters mild; generally pleasant weather prevails in the spring and autumn. The coldest weather occurs in late January and early February, and the warmest month is July. There are no pronounced wet and dry seasons. Thunderstorms, during the summer, often bring sudden and heavy showers and damaging winds, hail, or lightning. In winter, snow accumulations of more than 10 inches are rare.

Pluses: Pleasant springs and autumns, relatively mild winters.

Minuses: Humid summers, heavy thunderstorms.

Places Rated Score: 631

Places Rated Rank: 51

Elevation: 65 feet

Relative Humidity: 64%
Wind Speed: 9.3 mph

Seasonal Change

Annual Rainfall 39 in

Annual Snowfall 16 in

Clear 101 days   Partly Cloudy 106 days   Cloudy 158 days

Precipitation Days: 111   Storm Days: 29

Average Temperatures			
	Daily High	Daily Low	Monthly Mean
January	43.5	27.7	35.6
February	46.0	28.6	37.3
March	55.0	35.2	45.1
April	67.1	45.7	56.4
May	76.6	55.7	66.2
June	84.6	64.6	74.6
July	88.2	69.1	78.7
August	86.6	67.6	77.1
September	80.2	61.0	70.6
October	69.8	49.7	59.8
November	57.2	38.8	48.0
December	45.2	29.5	37.4

Zero-Degree Days: 0
Freezing Days: 75
90-Degree Days: 37
Heating- and Cooling-Degree Days: 5,626

Waterloo–Cedar Falls, IA

Terrain: Situated on the banks of the Cedar River in northeast Iowa, this area is far removed from the moderating influences of any large body of water. The terrain is level to very gently rolling and is ideally suited to agriculture. The flat, open topography has no influence on climate other than the fact that it offers little resistance to winds, which in the winter can greatly enhance the windchill factor. **Climate:** Definitely continental in character, with hot summers, cold winters, and short springs and falls. The average annual rainfall is 34 inches, with 71% of this total falling in the April-to-September crop season. As befits its landlocked, northerly location, the temperature range in Waterloo–Cedar Falls is large: January's mean temperature is 16° F, July's 73° F. The lowest and highest temperatures ever recorded here are –34° F and 112° F. Bitterly cold days of zero or below average 31 in number. The mercury hits 90° F or above on an average of 15 days a year, including two 100-degree days.

Pluses: Sunny falls.

Minuses: Hot summers, cold winters.

Places Rated Score: 347

Places Rated Rank: 316

Elevation: 868 feet

Relative Humidity: 72%
Wind Speed: 10.7 mph

Seasonal Change

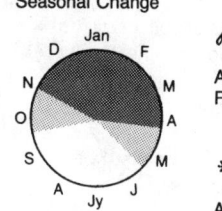

Annual Rainfall 34 in

Annual Snowfall 31 in

Clear 92 days   Partly Cloudy 102 days   Cloudy 171 days

Precipitation Days: 99   Storm Days: 43

Average Temperatures			
	Daily High	Daily Low	Monthly Mean
January	25.7	6.9	16.3
February	30.2	11.3	20.8
March	40.6	22.3	31.5
April	58.5	36.3	47.4
May	70.0	47.5	58.8
June	79.4	57.6	68.5
July	83.6	61.5	72.6
August	82.1	59.5	70.8
September	73.3	49.8	61.6
October	63.5	39.7	51.6
November	44.6	25.6	35.1
December	30.6	12.9	21.8

Zero-Degree Days: 31
Freezing Days: 159
90-Degree Days: 15
Heating- and Cooling-Degree Days: 8,090

Wichita, KS

Terrain: Located in gentle sloping topography. There are no large bodies of water nearby to affect the city's climate. **Climate:** Because it lies in the path of alternate masses of warm, moist air moving northward from the Gulf of Mexico and cold, dry air from the polar regions, the city is subject to frequent and often abrupt weather changes. Summers are usually warm and occasionally hot (there are more than 60 days over 90° F during that time). Winters are mild, and snowfalls are light, averaging 16 inches a year.

Pluses: Four-season Great Plains climate with mild winters.

Minuses: Tornadoes, long summers that can be hot.

Places Rated Score: 494

Places Rated Rank: 232

Elevation: 1,340 feet

Relative Humidity: 66%
Wind Speed: 12.6 mph

Seasonal Change

Annual Rainfall 31 in

Annual Snowfall 16 in

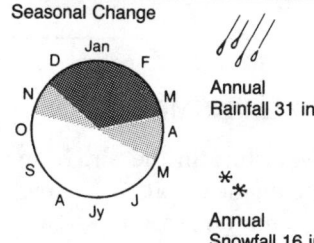

Clear 127 days   Partly Cloudy 97 days   Cloudy 141 days

Precipitation Days: 84   Storm Days: 55

Average Temperatures			
	Daily High	Daily Low	Monthly Mean
January	41.4	21.2	31.3
February	47.1	25.4	36.3
March	55.0	32.1	43.6
April	68.1	45.1	56.6
May	77.1	55.0	66.1
June	86.5	65.0	75.8
July	91.7	69.6	80.7
August	91.0	68.3	79.7
September	81.9	59.2	70.6
October	71.3	47.9	59.6
November	55.8	33.8	44.8
December	44.3	24.6	34.5

Zero-Degree Days: 2
Freezing Days: 114
90-Degree Days: 62
Heating- and Cooling-Degree Days: 6,360

Wilmington, NC

Terrain: Located in the Tidewater section of southeastern North Carolina, near the Atlantic Ocean. The city proper is built adjacent to the east bank of the Cape Fear River. The surrounding terrain, typical of the state's Coastal Plain, is low-lying (the average elevation is less than 40 feet) and level. There are many rivers, creeks, and lakes nearby, most with considerable swampy growth surrounding them. Large tracts of woods alternate with cultivated fields.

Climate: Wilmington's climate shows a strong maritime influence. Summers are quite warm and humid, but excessive heat is rare. During the colder part of the year, polar air masses reach the coastal areas, causing sharp drops in temperature. However, much of the coldness of these air masses has diminished by the time they reach the Wilmington area. Rainfall is ample and well distributed, with most occurring in summer in the form of thundershowers. In winter, rain may fall steadily for several days. Snowfall is very slight.

Pluses: Warm, moist, mild.

Minuses: Hot and muggy in summertime.

Places Rated Score: 564

Places Rated Rank: 124

Elevation: 30 feet

Relative Humidity: 75%
Wind Speed: 8.9 mph

Seasonal Change

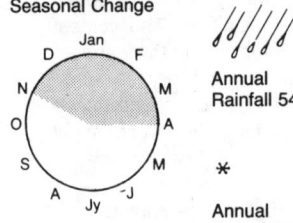

Annual Rainfall 54 in

Annual Snowfall 1.8 in

Clear 113 days   Partly Cloudy 106 days   Cloudy 146 days

Precipitation Days: 117   Storm Days: 46

Average Temperatures			
	Daily High	Daily Low	Monthly Mean
January	56.6	36.2	46.4
February	58.7	37.5	48.1
March	64.9	43.7	54.3
April	74.3	52.2	63.3
May	81.4	60.9	71.2
June	86.8	68.2	77.5
July	88.8	72.0	80.4
August	88.0	71.0	79.5
September	83.5	65.9	74.7
October	75.4	55.1	65.3
November	66.8	44.3	55.6
December	58.2	36.7	47.5

Zero-Degree Days: 0
Freezing Days: 45
90-Degree Days: 45
Heating- and Cooling-Degree Days: 4,397

Yakima, WA

Terrain: Located in a small east-west valley in the upper part of the irrigated Yakima Valley in Washington. The local topography is complex, with a number of minor valleys and ridges giving a local elevation as high as 500 feet.

Climate: Relatively mild and dry, with characteristics of both maritime and continental climates, modified by the Cascade and the Rocky Mountain ranges. Summers are dry and hot. Winters are cool with only light snowfall, usually 20 inches to 25 inches per year.

Pluses: Combination of marine and continental climatic features.

Minuses: Cloudy winters, hot summers.

Places Rated Score: 535

Places Rated Rank: 182

Elevation: 1,066 feet

Relative Humidity: 60%
Wind Speed: 7.2 mph

Seasonal Change

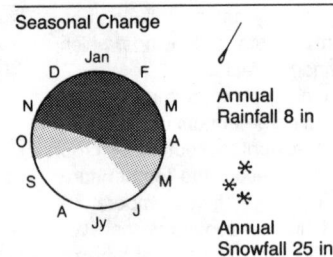

Annual Rainfall 8 in

Annual Snowfall 25 in

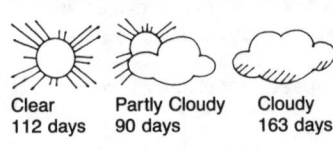

Clear 112 days   Partly Cloudy 90 days   Cloudy 163 days

Precipitation Days: 67   Storm Days: 7

Average Temperatures			
	Daily High	Daily Low	Monthly Mean
January	36.4	18.6	27.5
February	46.1	25.2	35.7
March	54.8	28.8	41.8
April	64.1	34.8	49.5
May	73.1	42.6	57.9
June	79.7	49.3	64.5
July	88.1	53.3	70.7
August	85.9	51.2	68.6
September	78.3	44.3	61.3
October	64.7	35.4	50.1
November	48.5	28.3	36.4
December	39.1	23.5	31.3

Zero-Degree Days: 4
Freezing Days: 150
90-Degree Days: 33
Heating- and Cooling-Degree Days: 6,488

Et Cetera

IT'S NOT THE HEAT, IT'S THE HUMIDITY

Humidity, or the amount of moisture in the air, is an extremely important factor in climatic comfort. As anyone who has experienced a hot, humid summer knows, humidity intensifies heat. A hot day that is also humid is uncomfortable because the body's natural cooling process of evaporation is retarded.

But there is another reason damp air increases felt heat in the summertime. Just as warm air is able to hold more moisture, so damp air is able to hold heat better, and longer. Therefore, in hot, humid climates, heat is retained in the damp air even after the sun goes down, resulting in nights that are almost as hot as the days. In contrast, dry climates offer greater comfort not only during hot summer days but also during the nights, which can be cool and sometimes even chilly.

Excessive humidity can aggravate certain types of arthritis and rheumatism and, combined with low temperatures, can have a harmful effect on those suffering

July Noon Average Relative Humidity

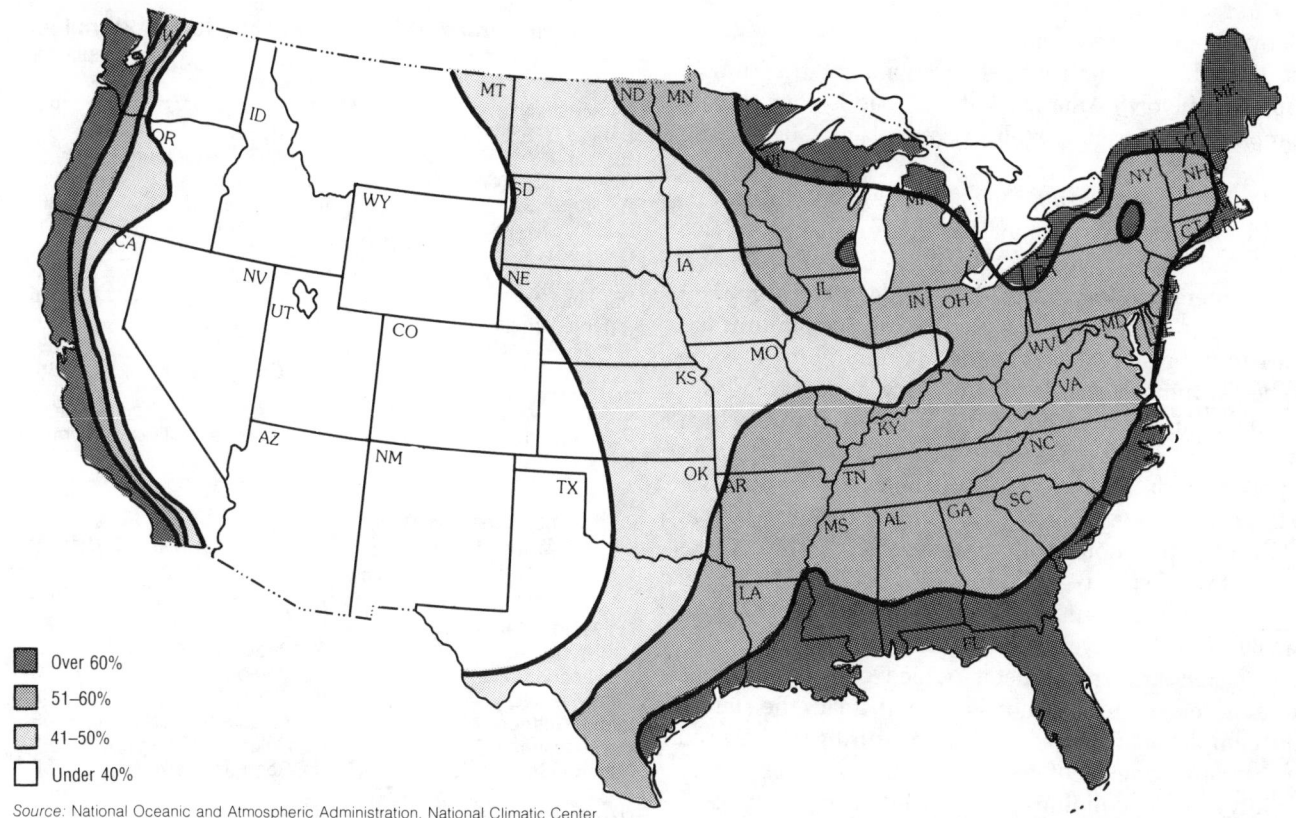

■ Over 60%

▨ 51–60%

░ 41–50%

☐ Under 40%

Source: National Oceanic and Atmospheric Administration, National Climatic Center.

from pulmonary diseases. Very moist air also encourages the growth of a wide variety of bacteria and molds, thus increasing the chances of infection.

Low humidity can also have undesirable consequences. When the humidity falls below 50 percent, most of us experience dry nasal passages and perhaps a dry, tickling throat. In some areas of the Southwest where the relative humidity can drop to 20 percent or below, many people suffer from nosebleeds, flaking skin, and a constant sore throat.

The table "Temperature, Humidity, and Apparent Temperature" examines the relationship between rela-

tive humidity and temperature. Relative humidity is the ratio of the amount of water vapor present in the air to the greatest possible amount of water vapor air can hold at that temperature. To find the apparent temperature, locate the air temperature at the left and the relative humidity along the bottom. The intersection of the horizontal row of figures opposite the temperature with the vertical row above the relative humidity is the apparent temperature. For example, an air temperature of 85 degrees Fahrenheit feels like 89 degrees at 55 percent relative humidity but like 102 when the humidity is 90 percent.

Temperature, Humidity, and Apparent Temperature

Apparent Temperature

Air Temperature (°F)	0	5	10	15	20	25	30	35	40	45	50	55	60	65	70	75	80	85	90	95	100
110	99	102	105	108	112	117	123	130	137	143	150										
105	95	97	100	102	105	109	113	118	123	129	135	142	149								
100	91	93	95	97	99	101	104	107	110	115	120	126	132	138	144						
95	87	88	90	91	93	94	96	98	101	104	107	110	114	119	124	130	136				
90	83	84	85	86	87	88	90	91	93	95	96	98	100	102	106	109	113	117	122		
85	78	79	80	81	82	83	84	85	86	87	88	89	90	91	93	95	97	99	102	105	108
80	73	74	75	76	77	77	78	79	79	80	81	81	82	83	85	86	86	87	88	89	91
75	69	69	70	71	72	72	73	73	74	74	75	75	76	76	77	77	78	78	79	79	80
70	64	64	65	65	66	66	67	67	68	68	69	69	70	70	70	70	71	71	71	71	72

Relative Humidity (%)

GOING TO EXTREMES

Many people gripe about local weather. True, extreme weather does occur routinely in some of the rugged climates of North America. But how bad is your climate compared with some really nasty places? Below are some extremes.

Mount Washington, New Hampshire. New England's highest peak, Mount Washington, claims to have the world's worst weather. Here, even in midsummer, the temperature may drop 50 or 60 degrees Fahrenheit in a matter of minutes. People visiting the summit are warned to bring parkas with them, even in July. Despite these warnings, deaths occur every year on Mount Washington. The weather station on the summit (which provides data for the NOAA's *Local Climatological Data*) reports winds in excess of 100 miles per hour with dismal regularity. On April 12, 1934, a gust traveling at 231 miles per hour was recorded here. This is the greatest wind speed—excluding those of tornado funnel clouds—ever measured on the earth's surface. In fact, the winds are so severe on Mount Washington's summit that a standard anemometer, which consists of three rotating metal cups, cannot survive. Instead, the station must employ a Pitot tube, a wind-measuring device used on aircraft. Fingers of ice, called rime ice, form very rapidly here on buildings and vehicles during icy weather and often measure up to two or three feet in length.

Meteorologically speaking, the summit of Mount Washington is an arctic island in an otherwise temperate zone. It is surrounded by clouds or fog on at least 300 days each year, the average annual snowfall is 242 inches, and the average year-round temperature is 27 degrees.

How would Mount Washington score according to the *Places Rated* formula? With, among other things, 66 zero-degree days, 243 freezing days, 13,878 heating-degree days, and many months during which the mean temperature is below 20 degrees, Mount Washington receives a climate mildness score of minus 19.

Greenland Ranch, Death Valley, California. So you think it gets hot where you live? Try Greenland Ranch, in California's Death Valley. America's all-time heat record of 134 degrees Fahrenheit was set here. This is only 2 degrees lower than the highest temperature ever recorded on the face of the earth, at Al Aziziyah, Libya, in 1922. The exact number of 90-degree days in Greenland Ranch is not recorded, but data show that during five months the mean daily temperature exceeds 80 degrees. In July, the mean daily temperature is above 100. The mean maximum temperatures for the months of May through September are as follows: 99.2, 109.2, 116.1, 113.6, and 105.5. Think about it the next time you complain about summer heat.

Barrow, Alaska. The settlement of Barrow is located on the northern coastline of Alaska, well above the Arctic Circle. The monthly mean temperatures are below zero during six months of the year. The average

The 10 Snowiest Metro Areas ... and the 11 Stormiest

	Inches per Year		Storm Days per Year
Syracuse, NY	109	Biloxi–Gulfport, MS	94
Bangor, ME	97	Fort Myers, FL	93
Buffalo, NY	90	Tampa–St. Petersburg–	
Binghamton, NY	86	Clearwater, FL	88
Burlington, VT	79	Tallahassee, FL	86
Duluth, MN–WI	78	Orlando, FL	81
Casper, WY	77	Mobile, AL	80
Grand Rapids, MI	77	Miami–Hialeah, FL	75
Portland, ME	74	Galveston–Texas City, TX	70
Albany–Schenec-		Alexandria, LA	69
tady–Troy, NY	71	Houston, TX	69
		New Orleans, LA	68

Listed above are those metro areas described in the Place Profiles that have more than 70 inches of snow per year or more than 65 storm days per year.

The 8 Dampest Metro Areas ... and the 7 Driest

	Relative Humidity		Relative Humidity
Galveston–Texas		Las Vegas, NV	29%
City, TX	78%	Phoenix, AZ	36
Alexandria, LA	77	Tucson, AZ	38
Asheville, NC	77	El Paso, TX	39
Biloxi–Gulfport, MS	77	Albuquerque, NM	43
Corpus Christi, TX	77	Colorado Springs, CO	49
Eugene–Springfield,		Reno, NV	50
OR	77		
Houston, TX	77		
New Orleans, LA	77		

Listed above are those metro areas described in the Place Profiles with an average relative humidity greater than 76 percent or lower than 51 percent.

daily maximum temperature in the hottest month, July, is only 44 degrees. Yet Barrow does record three 70-degree days thanks to its very long "summer" days. It has an average of 323 freezing days a year and 170 zero-degree days. It also has more than 20,000 heating-degree days.

ARE WE RUNNING OUT OF WATER?

Climate and terrain have an importance far more profound than simple considerations of pleasant weather and attractive surroundings. They also determine an area's access to one of America's most precious natural resources: the abundance of fresh water found in lakes, rivers, and streams, and in the underground aquifers that feed our wells. The Great Lakes, which the United States share with Canada, contain more than one-fifth of the world's supply of surface fresh water. By any reckoning, these giant inland seas of drinkable water are among the most valuable resources on the planet.

Yet we hear increasing cries of alarm concerning our supplies of fresh water. Some areas of the nation appear to be rapidly depleting both surface water and groundwater. In other areas, serious pollution threatens. Even in regions like New England, where water is plentiful, growing numbers of metro areas are faced with shortages due to antiquated water delivery systems and purification plants. The situation is further complicated by growing competition for water between farmers on the one hand and urban residents and industry on the other, and by the efforts of American Indians to recapture water rights taken from them more than a hundred years ago.

So is America really faced with a water shortage?

No. America has plenty of water. The national supply of renewable fresh water is about 1,400 billion gallons of water per day. Of this total, about 380 billion gallons per day are withdrawn for use by the nation's homes, farms, and industry. Of the 380 billion gallons withdrawn, about 280 billion gallons per day are returned to lakes and streams. Although a large percentage of the country's waste is carried by this return flow, much of the returned water is usable. Withdrawn water that is not returned to lakes or streams (either due to evaporation or ingestion by humans and livestock) is termed consumed water. On any given day, then, some 100 billion gallons of water are consumed, or only about one-fourteenth of the total amount of water available.

Yes. Although the total average supply is more than plentiful, the problem arises from the uneven distribution of that supply. Most places in America have adequate water supplies. Some have much more than they can ever use. And a few are already facing a water crisis. Predictably, the majority of areas that suffer most from lack of water are those that receive scant rainfall. The Great Basin area receives the least precipitation since it is located between two high mountain ranges, which block moisture-laden air. In Nevada, Arizona, and New Mexico, the southern part of this region, the water problem is greatest. Several other parts of the West and Southwest are also troubled by shortages.

Where Our Water Comes From

There are two main sources of water, those on the surface of the earth (rivers, lakes, and streams) and those below the surface. We're all familiar with the aboveground sources, and many people assume they represent all our water resources. Actually, 80 percent of U.S. water reserves are located below ground in aquifers. Aquifers are composed of water-permeable rock or gravel through which groundwater percolates from the earth's surface. Since the water flows through many layers of sand, gravel, and rock, it is usually cleaned by this natural filter as it flows. Therefore wells, which often tap aquifers, are known for the purity and high mineral content of their water. Unless otherwise polluted, well water is good water.

But as water is pumped out, the aquifer becomes depleted. It will refill with water if left alone for a while; its water level, or table, will rise again. The time required for the aquifer's water table to return to its normal level is called the recharge rate. If the rate of depletion exceeds the recharge rate, the aquifer will continue to be depleted, and its water table will continue to fall. This process is called groundwater mining.

Many aquifers are near big lakes or rivers that feed them. However, many of our biggest aquifers lie under dry ground, supplying water to what would otherwise be water-starved places.

One such formation is the huge High Plains aquifer, which lies deep below Texas, Oklahoma, New Mexico, Kansas, Colorado, Nebraska, South Dakota, and Wyoming, and covers 177,000 square miles. If it were on the surface instead of below ground, it would be the largest lake in the world (the largest is the Caspian Sea, at 152,084 square miles). For decades, this giant underground cistern has provided irrigation and drinking water for the eight states mentioned above. There are about 170,000 wells tapping the High Plains aquifer, watering 14.3 million acres of farmland that produce 15 percent of America's corn, wheat, sorghum, and cotton, and nourish 38 percent of its livestock. But the aquifer's water table is falling rapidly. Water is being pumped out of it eight times faster than it can recharge itself. If groundwater mining continues at the present rate, experts predict, the aquifer (which took at least 10,000 years to form) could begin to dry up around the year 2000.

Water-Resource Regions

The U.S. Geological Survey has divided the nation into 20 water-resource regions, based on their water systems and named accordingly. Thus there are the Great Lakes, the Missouri, and the Arkansas-Red-White regions, the last named for the system of rivers that feeds Oklahoma, northern Texas, and parts of New Mexico and Colorado.

The map "Water-Resource Regions" presents a vivid summary of water availability and rates of groundwater mining in America. The unshaded regions are in no danger of depleting their renewable supplies of water. The lightly shaded areas are at some risk of running short, but this probably will not happen in the immediate future unless there are several severe drought years in a row. The darker areas represent water-resource regions that are consuming more than 40 percent of their renewable water supplies. The region with the darkest shading, the Lower Colorado (so named for the Colorado River, whose lower section flows through Arizona and forms the boundary between Arizona and California), is using more than 100 percent of its supplies and is mining its groundwater reserves.

Metro Areas with Water Problems

Not only do areas of the country differ in the amount of water readily available to them; they also differ in the quality and purity of their water. The list on page 383 pinpoints the major water problems in 269 metro areas. Data are from the 1984 report from the U.S. Geological Survey entitled *Water-Supply Paper 2250*. Metro areas that do not appear on the list—a total of 60—have no significant water troubles.

**Water-Resource Regions, Showing Average Consumptive
Use As a Percentage of Renewable Water Supply**

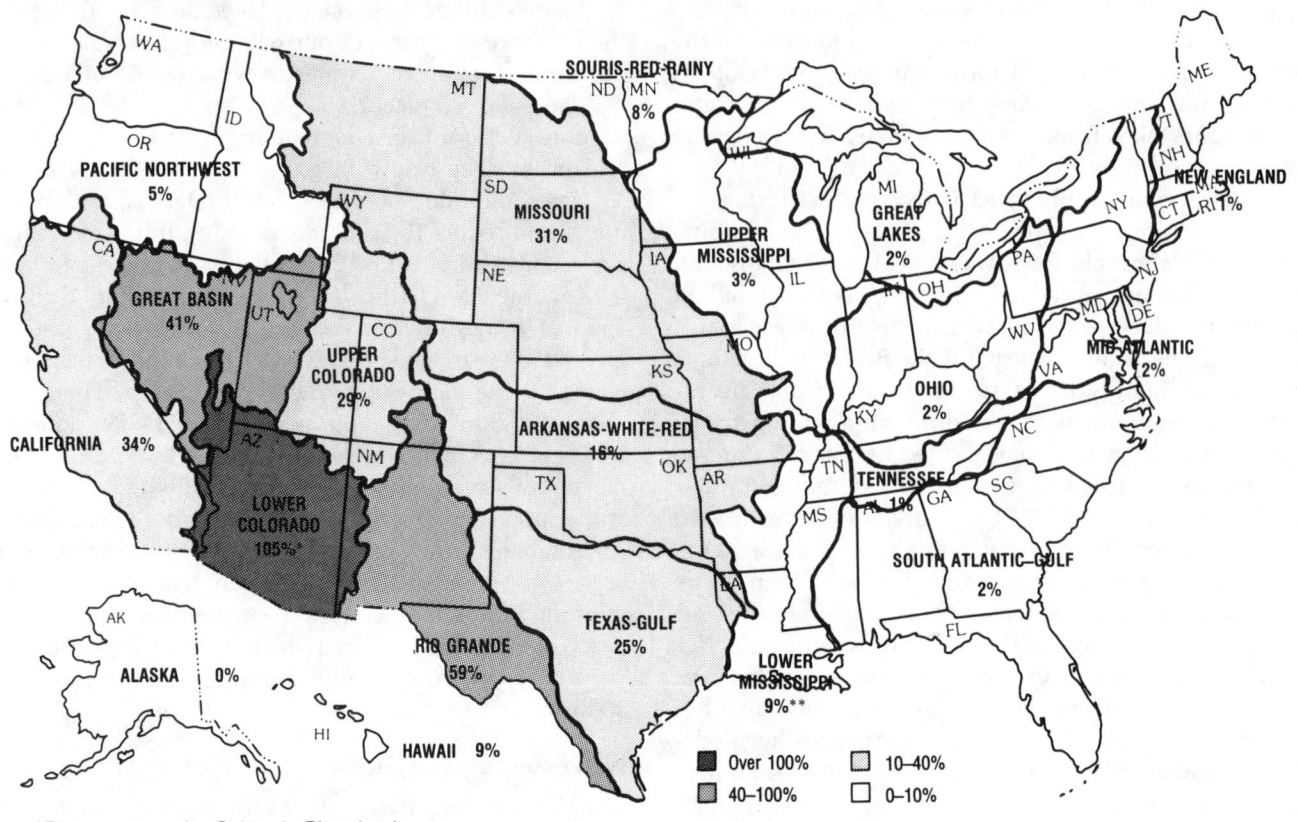

■ Over 100%	▨ 10–40%
▦ 40–100%	□ 0–10%

*Represents entire Colorado River basin
**Represents entire Mississippi River basin

Source: U.S. Geological Survey, *Water-Supply Paper 2250*, "National Water Summary 1983—Hydrologic Events and Issues."

The major problems delineated are: groundwater mining; insufficient surface water; decreased streamflow, or water in the stream channel, which reduces the water supply; hazardous wastes in groundwater; radioactive wastes in groundwater; pollution of groundwater and/or surface water; flooding; saline-water intrusion in aquifers; sedimentation, which can restrict shipping, increase the potential for flooding, and reduce the capacities of reservoirs; chemical-industrial wastes; wetlands depletion; rising groundwater tables; eutrophication of lakes (the process by which waters become enriched with plant nutrients from the addition of sewage, fertilizers, or wastes, thus upsetting the ecological balance, destroying plant and animal life, and rendering the water unusable for public consumption or recreation); and acid rain.

In some instances, problems arising from management of water resources are mentioned. For example, resource development, or the extracting of minerals from the earth, is considered hazardous by the U.S. Geological Survey because the water needed to mine and process minerals may reduce water supplies and because wastes that result from such mining can con-

taminate surface water and groundwater. In those metro areas where resource development is taking place, the kinds of mining under way are listed.

Metro areas that *Places Rated* deems especially prone to water problems, based on the U.S. Geological Survey paper, are preceded by one, two, or three triangles (▲), depending on the severity of the situation, with three triangles indicating the worst problems. Of the 269 metro areas described, 41 receive one triangle, 21 two triangles, and only 9 three triangles: Bakersfield, California; Fresno, California; Las Vegas, Nevada; Modesto, California; Norfolk–Virginia Beach–Newport News, Virginia; Phoenix, Arizona; Sacramento, California; Tucson, Arizona; and Visalia–Tulare–Porterville, California.

It should be noted that *Water-Supply Paper 2250* points out situations that may not now be causing damage but that will probably do so in the next few years. These problems should not discourage you from considering a move to a certain metro area. You should, however, make inquiries about the local water situation before reaching a final decision.

Metro Areas with Water Problems, by State

ALABAMA
Dothan: Groundwater mining.
Florence: Sinkholes.
Huntsville: Sinkholes.
Mobile: Pollution and increased sedimentation of Mobile River and Mobile Bay.
(See also Georgia, Columbus)

ALASKA
Anchorage: Current systems cannot meet projected demands, some septic pollution.

ARIZONA
▲▲▲ Phoenix: Groundwater pollution, hazardous wastes, severe groundwater mining.
▲▲▲ Tucson: Groundwater mining, hazardous wastes.

ARKANSAS
Fayetteville–Springdale: Surface-water pollution.
Fort Smith (AR–OK): Surface-water pollution.
Little Rock–North Little Rock: Surface-water pollution.
Pine Bluff: Groundwater mining.
(See also Tennessee, Memphis; Texas, Texarkana)

CALIFORNIA
▲ Anaheim–Santa Ana: Groundwater mining, saline-water intrusion.
▲▲▲ Bakersfield: Groundwater mining.
▲▲▲ Fresno: Groundwater mining, land subsidence.
▲ Los Angeles–Long Beach: Groundwater mining, saline-water intrusion.
▲▲▲ Modesto: Groundwater mining.
▲ Oakland: Decreased streamflow, some heavy-metal pollution.
▲ Oxnard–Ventura: Groundwater mining, saline-water intrusion.
Redding: Hazardous wastes.
Riverside–San Bernardino: Hazardous wastes.
▲▲▲ Sacramento: Groundwater mining, hazardous wastes.
▲ Salinas–Seaside–Monterey: Groundwater mining, saline-water intrusion.
▲ San Diego: Groundwater mining.
▲ San Francisco: Decreased streamflow, some heavy-metal pollution.
▲▲ San Jose: Groundwater mining, saline-water intrusion.
▲ Santa Cruz: Groundwater mining, saline-water intrusion.
Santa Rosa–Petaluma: Hazardous wastes.
▲▲ Stockton: Groundwater mining, decreased streamflow.
Vallejo–Fairfield–Napa: Decreased streamflow, hazardous wastes.
▲▲▲ Visalia–Tulare–Porterville: Groundwater mining, land subsidence.
Yuba City: Some groundwater mining.

COLORADO
Boulder–Longmont: Hazardous wastes.
▲ Denver: Hazardous wastes, eutrophication, pollution.

CONNECTICUT
Bridgeport–Milford: Groundwater mining.
Danbury: Groundwater mining.
Hartford: Surface-water pollution.
Middletown: Surface-water pollution.
New Haven–Meriden: Groundwater mining, surface-water pollution.
New London–Norwich (CT–RI): Groundwater mining, surface-water pollution.
Norwalk: Groundwater mining.
Stamford: Groundwater mining.

DELAWARE
▲ Wilmington (DE–NJ–MD): Groundwater mining, flooding, hazardous wastes.

FLORIDA
▲ Bradenton: Groundwater mining, saline-water intrusion.
Daytona Beach: Groundwater mining.
▲ Fort Lauderdale–Hollywood–Pompano Beach: Groundwater mining, hazardous wastes, saline-water intrusion.
Fort Myers: Groundwater mining.
Fort Pierce: Groundwater mining.
Fort Walton Beach: Groundwater mining.
▲ Jacksonville: Groundwater mining, hazardous wastes.
▲▲ Lakeland–Winter Haven: Groundwater mining, hazardous wastes, phosphate mining.
Melbourne–Titusville–Palm Bay: Groundwater mining.
▲▲ Miami–Hialeah: Groundwater mining, surface-water pollution, saline-water intrusion, hazardous wastes.
Ocala: Sinkholes.
Orlando: Groundwater mining.
▲ Pensacola: Groundwater mining, hazardous wastes.
Sarasota: Groundwater mining, saline-water intrusion.
Tallahassee: Some groundwater mining, sinkholes.
▲▲ Tampa–St. Petersburg–Clearwater: Groundwater mining, saline-water intrusion, hazardous wastes.
▲ West Palm Beach–Boca Raton–Delray Beach: Groundwater mining, saline-water intrusion, surface-water pollution.

GEORGIA
▲ Albany: Groundwater mining, pesticide pollution, sinkholes.
Athens: Surface-water shortages.
Atlanta: Surface-water pollution, some surface-water shortages.
Columbus (GA–AL): Groundwater mining.
Macon–Warner Robins: Surface-water pollution.
▲ Savannah: Groundwater mining, saline-water intrusion.
(See also Tennessee, Chattanooga)

HAWAII
▲▲ Honolulu: Groundwater mining, surface-water pollution, saline-water intrusion.

IDAHO
Boise City: Groundwater pollution, hazardous wastes.

ILLINOIS
Alton–Granite City: Rising groundwater tables.
Aurora–Elgin: Groundwater mining, flooding.
Champaign–Urbana–Rantoul: Surface-water pollution.
Chicago: Groundwater mining, flooding.
Decatur: Surface-water pollution.
East St. Louis–Belleville: Rising groundwater tables.
Joliet: Groundwater mining, flooding.
Kankakee: Surface-water pollution, hazardous wastes.
▲ Lake County: Groundwater mining, flooding, hazardous wastes.
Peoria: Surface-water pollution.
▲ Rockford: Surface-water pollution, hazardous wastes.
Springfield: Surface-water pollution.
(See also Iowa, Davenport–Rock Island–Moline; Missouri, St. Louis)

INDIANA
Anderson: Surface-water pollution.
Bloomington: Surface-water pollution, hazardous wastes in groundwater.
Elkhart–Goshen: Flooding, groundwater and surface-water pollution.
Fort Wayne: Hazardous wastes in groundwater.
▲▲ Gary–Hammond: Surface-water and groundwater pollution, hazardous wastes.
▲ Indianapolis: Extensive surface-water pollution.
Kokomo: Surface-water pollution.
Lafayette: Groundwater mining.
Muncie: Surface-water pollution.
▲ South Bend–Mishawaka: Flooding, surface-water and groundwater pollution, hazardous wastes.
Terre Haute: Surface-water pollution.
(See also Ohio, Cincinnati)

IOWA
Davenport–Rock Island–Moline (IA–IL): Surface-water pollution.
Des Moines: Surface-water and groundwater pollution, hazardous wastes.
Dubuque: Pollution in groundwater.
Sioux City (IA–NE): Surface-water scarcity.

KANSAS
Kansas City: Hazardous wastes in surface water and groundwater.
Topeka: Surface-water pollution.
▲ Wichita: Saline-water intrusion in surface water and groundwater, hazardous wastes.

KENTUCKY
Lexington–Fayette: Surface-water scarcity.
(See also Ohio, Cincinnati; Tennessee, Clarksville–Hopkinsville; West Virginia, Huntington–Ashland)

LOUISIANA
Alexandria: Hazardous wastes in groundwater.
Baton Rouge: Groundwater mining.
Houma–Thibodaux: Wetlands and estuaries threatened.
Lafayette: Groundwater mining.
Lake Charles: Groundwater mining.
Monroe: Groundwater mining.
▲ **New Orleans:** Wetlands and estuaries threatened, potential for radioactive wastes in groundwater.

MAINE
Lewiston–Auburn: Groundwater and surface-water shortages.
Portland: Hazardous wastes in surface water and groundwater.
(*See also* New Hampshire, Portsmouth–Dover–Rochester)

MARYLAND
▲▲ **Baltimore:** Hazardous wastes in groundwater, acid rain, Chesapeake Bay threatened by nutrient enrichment (the first step in eutrophication), hazardous wastes, and a decrease in important submerged aquatic vegetation.
Cumberland (MD–WV): Pollution from coal mining.
Hagerstown: Acid rain, hazardous wastes in groundwater.
(*See also* Delaware, Wilmington)

MASSACHUSETTS
Boston: Not enough fresh water for peak demand.
Fall River (MA–RI): Hazardous wastes in groundwater.
Fitchburg–Leominster: Hazardous wastes in surface water and groundwater.
Lawrence–Haverhill (MA–NH): Hazardous wastes in surface water and groundwater.
Lowell (MA–NH): Hazardous wastes and highway de-icing salts in groundwater.
Worcester: Highway de-icing salts in surface water and groundwater.
(*See also* Rhode Island, Pawtucket–Woonsocket–Attleboro)

MICHIGAN
Benton Harbor: Hazardous wastes in surface water.
Detroit: Hazardous wastes in surface water.
Flint: Hazardous wastes in surface water.
Kalamazoo: Hazardous wastes in surface water.
Lansing–East Lansing: Hazardous wastes in surface water.
Muskegon: Hazardous wastes in surface water (Lake Michigan).
Saginaw–Bay City–Midland: Hazardous wastes in surface water (Saginaw River and Saginaw Bay).

MINNESOTA
▲ **Duluth (MN–WI):** Natural salinity of groundwater, waste sites or landfills that contain hazardous materials, acid rain, erosion, and sedimentation.
▲ **Minneapolis–St. Paul (MN–WI):** Groundwater mining, eutrophication,

hazardous wastes.
Rochester: Nitrates in groundwater.
St. Cloud: Acid rain.
(*See also* North Dakota, Fargo–Moorhead)

MISSISSIPPI
Biloxi–Gulfport: Groundwater mining and surface-water depletion.
Jackson: Groundwater mining and surface-water depletion, flooding, saline-water intrusion.
Pascagoula: Groundwater mining and surface-water depletion.
(*See also* Tennessee, Memphis)

MISSOURI
Columbia: Some saline-water intrusion.
▲ **Joplin:** Dioxin in surface water and groundwater, resource development (lead and zinc mining).
Kansas City: Resource development (coal mining).
St. Joseph: Erosion and sedimentation, saline-water intrusion.
St. Louis (MO–IL): Dioxin in surface water and groundwater, possible depletion of river surface water.
▲ **Springfield:** Dioxin in surface water and groundwater, sinkholes, groundwater mining.

MONTANA
Great Falls: Erosion and sedimentation of surface water.

NEBRASKA
(*See* Iowa, Sioux City)

NEVADA
▲▲▲ **Las Vegas:** Surface-water depletion and groundwater mining, land subsidence, surface-water pollution, radioactive wastes, and chemicals in groundwater.
Reno: Surface-water depletion and pollution, some groundwater mining.

NEW HAMPSHIRE
Manchester: Surface-water and stream pollution.
Nashua: Hazardous wastes in surface water and groundwater.
Portsmouth–Dover–Rochester (NH–ME): Hazardous wastes in surface water and groundwater.
(*See also* Massachusetts, Lawrence–Haverhill and Lowell)

NEW JERSEY
▲ **Atlantic City:** Pollution of estuaries, flooding, saline-water intrusion, acid rain.
▲ **Bergen–Passaic:** Surface-water scarcity, surface-water pollution, flooding.
▲ **Jersey City:** Surface-water pollution and scarcity, pollution of estuaries, flooding.
▲ **Middlesex–Somerset–Hunterdon:** Surface-water pollution and scarcity, acid rain.
▲▲ **Monmouth–Ocean:** Surface-water scarcity, saline-water intrusion, pollution of estuaries, acid rain.
▲ **Newark:** Surface-water pollution and scarcity, flooding.
▲▲ **Trenton:** Surface-water pollution and scarcity, pollution of estuaries, flooding, acid rain.

▲ **Vineland–Millville–Bridgeton:** Saline-water intrusion, acid rain.
(*See also* Delaware, Wilmington; Pennsylvania, Allentown–Bethlehem and Philadelphia)

NEW MEXICO
▲▲ **Albuquerque:** Groundwater mining, nitrates and hazardous wastes in groundwater.

NEW YORK
Albany–Schenectady–Troy: Acid rain.
Glens Falls: Acid rain.
▲▲ **Nassau–Suffolk:** Bacteria in surface water, groundwater mining, saline-water intrusion, radioactive wastes in groundwater.
New York: Rising groundwater, some saline-water intrusion.
Niagara Falls: Rising groundwater levels.
Orange County: Some groundwater mining.
Rochester: Eutrophication.

NORTH CAROLINA
Asheville: Surface-water scarcity and pollution.
Burlington: Surface-water pollution.
Charlotte–Gastonia–Rock Hill (NC–SC): Surface-water pollution.
Greensboro–Winston-Salem–High Point: Surface-water pollution.
Hickory: Surface-water pollution.
Jacksonville: Groundwater mining.
Raleigh–Durham: Surface-water scarcity, surface-water pollution.

NORTH DAKOTA
▲ **Bismarck:** Resource development (lignite mining), wetlands drainage, eutrophication.
Fargo–Moorhead (ND–MN): Flooding, surface-water scarcity, and pollution.
Grand Forks: Flooding, surface-water pollution.

OHIO
Akron: Resource development (coal mining and oil and gas production), erosion, and sedimentation.
Canton: Resource development (coal mining and oil and gas production), erosion, and sedimentation.
Cincinnati (OH–KY–IN): Erosion and sedimentation, hazardous wastes in groundwater.
Cleveland: Erosion and sedimentation, resource development (oil and gas production).
Columbus: Erosion and sedimentation, resource development (oil and gas production).
Dayton–Springfield: Erosion and sedimentation.
Hamilton–Middletown: Erosion and sedimentation, hazardous wastes in groundwater.
Lima: Erosion and sedimentation.
Lorain–Elyria: Erosion and sedimentation.
Mansfield: Erosion and sedimentation, resource development (oil and gas production).
Steubenville–Weirton (OH–WV): Resource development (coal mining and oil

Water Wars

Although many small conflicts arising from water usage, pollution, and diversion exist throughout the nation, the biggest battles for water are being fought in the Southwest.

Arizona. Of all the states in the nation, this one is in the most danger of going dry. Arizonans now pump twice as much groundwater from their aquifers as is being replaced by natural recharge. Large, fast-growing metro areas like Phoenix and Tucson are headed for trouble. However, a U.S. Supreme Court decision has granted Arizona the right to tap the lower Colorado River, which it shares with California as a common boundary. Phoenix receives this river water through a series of aqueducts and canals, thus easing the strain on the underground aquifers; Tucson is slated to do the same in 1989. But this is not a total solution, since the water Arizona will get is now going to Southern California.

California. This state is hurting for water in two areas: the 20,000-square-mile Central Valley and the metro areas of Southern California. In the Central Valley, where almost half of America's fruits and vegetables are grown on land that is fertile, flat, and totally irrigated for year-round productivity, the groundwater supplies are being pumped dry at an alarming rate. Indeed, this valley is probably the most heavily pumped area in the nation, and not only groundwater mining but land subsidence, or sinking, is a direct result of this pumping. In the future, if alternative supplies are not developed, the amount of farming in the Central Valley will be drastically reduced. This could have serious implications for California's economy.

The giant metro areas of Los Angeles–Long Beach and San Diego have always been water-poor. As they have grown explosively over the last 30 years, the poverty has increased. Southern California depends on diverted water from the lower Colorado for half its water needs. Soon the Colorado water will also go to Phoenix and Tucson, thus aggravating the problem. The only viable solution is to pipe water from moisture-rich Northern California, which receives about 60 percent of the state's rainfall and has only 40 percent of the population. Plans for this massive undertaking are still in the preliminary stage.

The Southwest and High Plains. Eastern New Mexico, northwestern Texas, Oklahoma, and the states to the north of these make up the area known as the High Plains. This huge region is rife with dissent over water. New Mexico is bitter about the "piracy" of water by El Paso, Texas, from New Mexico's Elephant Butte Reservoir. The Land of Enchantment has also locked horns with Colorado over use of the Vermejo River, which rises in Colorado and flows through New Mexico.

Texas, a state emerging from an economic slump, now has grave water woes. Even in the Texas Gulf region, which receives plenty of rain, extensive groundwater mining has led to the intrusion of salt water in freshwater aquifers and to land subsidence. Those "mysterious" sinkholes you see on the evening news are actually easily explained: They're the result of water being sucked out of underlying rock strata. West Texas and North Texas continually face drought. When the High Plains aquifer begins to go dry, an alternative source will be as far away as the Mississippi River or the Great Lakes—and extremely costly.

The High Plains region, which has increased its agricultural yields dramatically in the past 20 years as a direct result of irrigation, faces long-term groundwater mining. The presence of the High Plains aquifer is critical. When that gigantic underground sea is drained, the entire region will be in considerable trouble.

---

and gas production).
Toledo: Erosion and sedimentation.
▲ **Youngstown–Warren:** Hazardous wastes in groundwater, resource development (coal mining and oil and gas production).
(*See also* West Virginia, Huntington–Ashland, Parkersburg–Marietta, and Wheeling)

OKLAHOMA
Oklahoma City: Surface-water pollution, hazardous wastes in groundwater.
Tulsa: Natural salinity of surface water.
(*See also* Arkansas, Fort Smith)

OREGON
Eugene–Springfield: Acid rain.
Medford: Acid rain, degradation of aquatic habitats in surface water.
Portland: Groundwater mining, hazardous wastes in groundwater.

Salem: Hazardous wastes in groundwater.

PENNSYLVANIA
Allentown–Bethlehem (PA–NJ): Hazardous wastes in groundwater, sinkholes, landslide-prone areas.
Erie: Hazardous wastes in groundwater.
Harrisburg–Lebanon–Carlisle: Sinkholes.
Lancaster: Agricultural runoff (fertilizers and organic or chemical wastes) in surface water and groundwater, sinkholes.
▲▲ **Philadelphia (PA–NJ):** Sinkholes, erosion and sedimentation, hazardous wastes and industrial wastes in groundwater.
▲ **Pittsburgh:** Hazardous wastes in groundwater, landslide-prone areas, inadequate river water.
Scranton–Wilkes-Barre: Hazardous wastes in groundwater.

State College: Sinkholes, hazardous wastes in groundwater.
York: Hazardous wastes in groundwater.

RHODE ISLAND
Pawtucket–Woonsocket–Attleboro (RI–MA): Groundwater insufficiency, hazardous wastes in groundwater.
Providence: Groundwater insufficiency, hazardous wastes in groundwater.
(*See also* Connecticut, New London–Norwich; Massachusetts, Fall River)

SOUTH CAROLINA
Anderson: Hazardous wastes in river water.
Charleston: Surface-water scarcity, excess fluoride and chloride in groundwater.
Columbia: Saline-water intrusion, excess fluoride and chloride in groundwater.
Florence: Excess fluoride and chloride in groundwater, saline-water intrusion.

Greenville–Spartanburg: Surface-water scarcity.
(See also North Carolina, Charlotte–Gastonia–Rock Hill)

SOUTH DAKOTA
Sioux Falls: Eutrophication, groundwater mining.

TENNESSEE
Chattanooga (TN–GA): Resource development (coal mining), sinkholes, surface-water pollution, hazardous wastes in groundwater.
Clarksville–Hopkinsville (TN–KY): Surface-water pollution, sinkholes.
Johnson City–Kingsport–Bristol (TN–VA): Sinkholes, surface-water pollution.
Knoxville: Sinkholes, radioactive wastes in groundwater.
Memphis (TN–AR–MS): Surface-water pollution, hazardous wastes in groundwater.
▲ Nashville: Surface-water scarcity, sinkholes, surface-water pollution.

TEXAS
Abilene: Groundwater pollution.
▲▲ Amarillo: Groundwater mining and pollution, eutrophication, natural salinity of surface water.
Austin: Groundwater and surface-water pollution.
▲ Beaumont–Port Arthur: Groundwater mining, surface-water pollution, hazardous wastes in groundwater.
▲▲ Brazoria: Groundwater mining, land subsidence, hazardous wastes in groundwater, surface-water pollution.
Brownsville–Harlingen: Pollution of groundwater and surface water.
Bryan–College Station: Pollution of groundwater, resource development (lignite mining).
Corpus Christi: Groundwater mining and pollution.
▲ Dallas: Groundwater mining, hazardous wastes in groundwater, groundwater pollution, eutrophication.
El Paso: Groundwater mining, surface-water pollution, water disputes with New Mexico and Mexico.
▲▲ Fort Worth–Arlington: Groundwater mining and pollution, hazardous wastes and eutrophication in groundwater, surface-water pollution.
▲▲ Galveston–Texas City: Groundwater mining, saline-water intrusion, land subsidence, hazardous wastes in groundwater, surface-water pollution.
▲▲ Houston: Groundwater mining, saline-water intrusion, land subsidence, hazardous wastes in groundwater, surface-water pollution.

Killeen–Temple: Groundwater mining, surface-water pollution.
Longview–Marshall: Groundwater pollution, resource development (lignite mining).
Lubbock: Groundwater mining.
McAllen–Edinburg–Mission: Surface-water and groundwater pollution.
Midland: Groundwater mining and pollution.
Odessa: Groundwater mining and pollution.
San Angelo: Groundwater pollution.
▲ San Antonio: Groundwater mining and pollution, surface-water pollution.
Sherman–Denison: Groundwater mining, eutrophication.
Texarkana, TX–Texarkana, AR: Resource development (lignite mining).
Tyler: Groundwater pollution, resource development (lignite mining).
Waco: Groundwater mining, eutrophication.
Wichita Falls: Groundwater pollution, natural salinity of surface water.

UTAH
▲▲ Provo–Orem: Surface-water and groundwater shortages, landslides, flooding.
▲▲ Salt Lake City–Ogden: Groundwater depletion, acid rain, surface-water pollution, flooding.

VERMONT
▲ Burlington: Flooding, eutrophication, hazardous wastes in surface water and groundwater.

VIRGINIA
Charlottesville: Radioactivity in groundwater, flooding.
Danville: Radioactivity in groundwater.
Lynchburg: Radioactivity in groundwater.
▲▲▲ Norfolk–Virginia Beach–Newport News: Eutrophication, surface-water depletion, groundwater mining, pollution of surface water and bottom sediments, hazardous wastes in surface water and groundwater, bacteria and chemical elements in groundwater.
Richmond–Petersburg: Bacteria and chemical elements in groundwater, radioactivity in groundwater.
Roanoke: Flooding, hazardous wastes in surface water and groundwater.
(See also Tennessee, Johnson City–Kingsport–Bristol)

WASHINGTON
Bellingham: Groundwater mining, saline-water intrusion, volcanic danger.

Bremerton: Saline-water intrusion, groundwater mining.
Olympia: Pollution of bottom sediments.
Richland–Kennewick–Pasco: Natural salinity of groundwater.
Seattle: Hazardous wastes in groundwater, volcanic danger.
Spokane: Nitrates in, and natural salinity of, groundwater.
Tacoma: Pollution of bottom sediments, volcanic danger.
Vancouver: Hazardous wastes in groundwater.
Yakima: Hazardous wastes in, and natural salinity of, groundwater.

WEST VIRGINIA
▲▲ Charleston: Resource development (coal mining), surface-water pollution, surface-water scarcity, possibility of unsafe dams.
Huntington–Ashland (WV–KY–OH): Resource development (coal mining), hazardous wastes in surface water and groundwater, surface-water scarcity.
Parkersburg–Marietta (WV–OH): Hazardous wastes in surface water and groundwater, surface-water scarcity.
Wheeling (WV–OH): Resource development (coal mining), surface-water scarcity, possibility of unsafe dams.
(See also Maryland, Cumberland; Ohio, Steubenville–Weirton)

WISCONSIN
Appleton–Oshkosh–Neenah: Groundwater mining, surface-water pollution.
Eau Claire: Acid rain.
Green Bay: Groundwater mining, surface-water pollution.
Janesville–Beloit: Surface-water pollution.
Kenosha: Groundwater mining, surface-water pollution.
La Crosse: Surface-water pollution.
Madison: Surface-water and groundwater pollution.
Milwaukee: Groundwater mining, surface-water pollution.
Racine: Groundwater mining, surface-water pollution.
Sheboygan: Groundwater mining, surface-water pollution.
Wausau: Acid rain, surface-water pollution.
(See also Minnesota, Duluth and Minneapolis–St. Paul)

WYOMING
Casper: Resource development (mining of coal, oil shale, and uranium, and oil and gas production), eutrophication, insufficient drainage.

NATURAL HAZARDS

Perhaps no sight in recent memory was more dramatic than the eruption of Mount St. Helens in 1980, an initial blast equivalent to 10 million tons of TNT, which blew off the topmost 1,300 feet of the mountain. Volcanic eruptions can wipe out lives and property in an instant. Fortunately, however, volcanoes usually give warning of impending activity. Even more fortunately, the places where volcanic activity is a potential hazard are very few. A number of violent natural events are much more common and widespread, and although they may be less cataclysmic than a full-blown volcanic eruption, they can cause great damage and threaten lives. Many of these natural hazards follow definite geographic patterns within the United States, and some metro areas are at much greater risk than others.

The Sun Belt Is Also a Storm Belt

Many if not most severe storms occur in the southern half of the nation. For this reason, you might say that the Sun Belt is also a storm belt.

Thunderstorms and Lightning. Thunderstorms are common and don't usually cause death. But lightning kills 200 Americans a year. It remains the most common and frequent natural danger. At any given moment there are about 2,000 thunderstorms in progress around the globe; in the time it takes you to read this paragraph, lightning will have struck the earth 700 times.

Florida, the Sunshine State, is actually the country's stormiest state, with three times as much thunder and lightning as any other. California, on the other hand, is one of the most storm-free states, along with Oregon and Washington. In a typical year, coastal California towns will average between two and five thunderstorm episodes. Most American towns average between 35 and 50. Fort Myers, Florida, averages 128. (A thunderstorm episode represents the presence of a single storm cell; a place like Fort Myers can register four or five episodes in a single day.)

The Place Profiles earlier in this chapter tell how many thunderstorm days each place can expect in an average year. The southeastern quadrant of the country generally receives more rain and thunderstorms than the rest, although the thunderstorms of the Great Plains are awesome spectacles.

Tornadoes. While they are not nearly as large or long-lived as hurricanes and release much less total force, tornadoes have more destructive and killing power concentrated in a small area than any other storm known. For absolute ferocity and wind speed, a tornado has no rival.

The hallmark of this vicious inland storm is the huge, snakelike funnel cloud that sweeps and bounces along the ground, destroying buildings, sweeping up cars, trains, livestock, and trees, and sucking them up hundreds of feet into the whirling vortex. Wind speeds close to 300 miles per hour have been recorded.

Although no one can tell for certain just where a particular tornado might touch down, their season, origin, and direction of travel are fairly predictable. Tornado season reaches its peak in late spring and early summer, and most storms originate in the central and southern Great Plains, in the states of Oklahoma, Texas, Arkansas, Kansas, and Missouri. After forming in the intense heat and rising air of the Plains, these storms proceed toward the northeast at speeds averaging 25 to 40 miles per hour. Most tornadoes do not last very long or travel very far. Half of all tornadoes reported travel less than five miles on the ground; a few have been tracked for more than 200 miles.

Metro areas in Oklahoma, eastern Texas, Arkansas, northern Louisiana and Mississippi, eastern Tennessee, Kansas, Missouri, and parts of Nebraska, Iowa, and Illinois have a high potential for tornado damage and danger. Nearly one third of all tornadoes ever reported in the United States have occurred within the boundaries of Kansas, Oklahoma, and Texas.

Hurricanes. Giant tropical cyclonic storms that originate at sea, hurricanes are unmatched for sheer power over a very large area. Hurricanes last for days, measure hundreds of miles across, and release tremendous energy in the form of high winds, torrential rains, lightning, and tidal surges. They usually occur from June through November and strike the Gulf states and southern segments of the Atlantic Coast primarily, though they will also strike locations farther north. Like thunderstorms, hurricanes are much less frequent and less severe on the Pacific Coast.

Hurricanes usually originate in the tropical waters of the Atlantic Ocean. Most of them occur toward summer's end because it takes that long for the water temperature and evaporation rate to rise sufficiently to begin the cyclonic, counterclockwise rotation of a wind system around a low-pressure system. When the wind velocities are less than 39 miles per hour, this cyclone is called a tropical depression; when wind velocities are between 39 and 74 miles per hour, the cyclone is called a tropical storm. And when the winds reach 74 miles per hour, the storm becomes a hurricane.

Often the greatest danger and destruction from hurricanes are due not to the winds but to the tidal surges that can sweep ashore with seas 15 or more feet higher than normal high tides. Although Florida and the southern coasts are most vulnerable to hurricanes, locations as far north as Cape Cod and the coast of Maine are by no means immune.

Earthquake Risks

The cause of an earthquake is the pressure building between two contiguous masses of rock—called plates—that are moving slowly but inexorably toward each other in slightly different directions. When the pressure becomes too great for the rock substance to hold, it shears suddenly. This shearing, along with the consequent shuddering, swaying, and even shifting of

Tornado and Hurricane Risk Areas

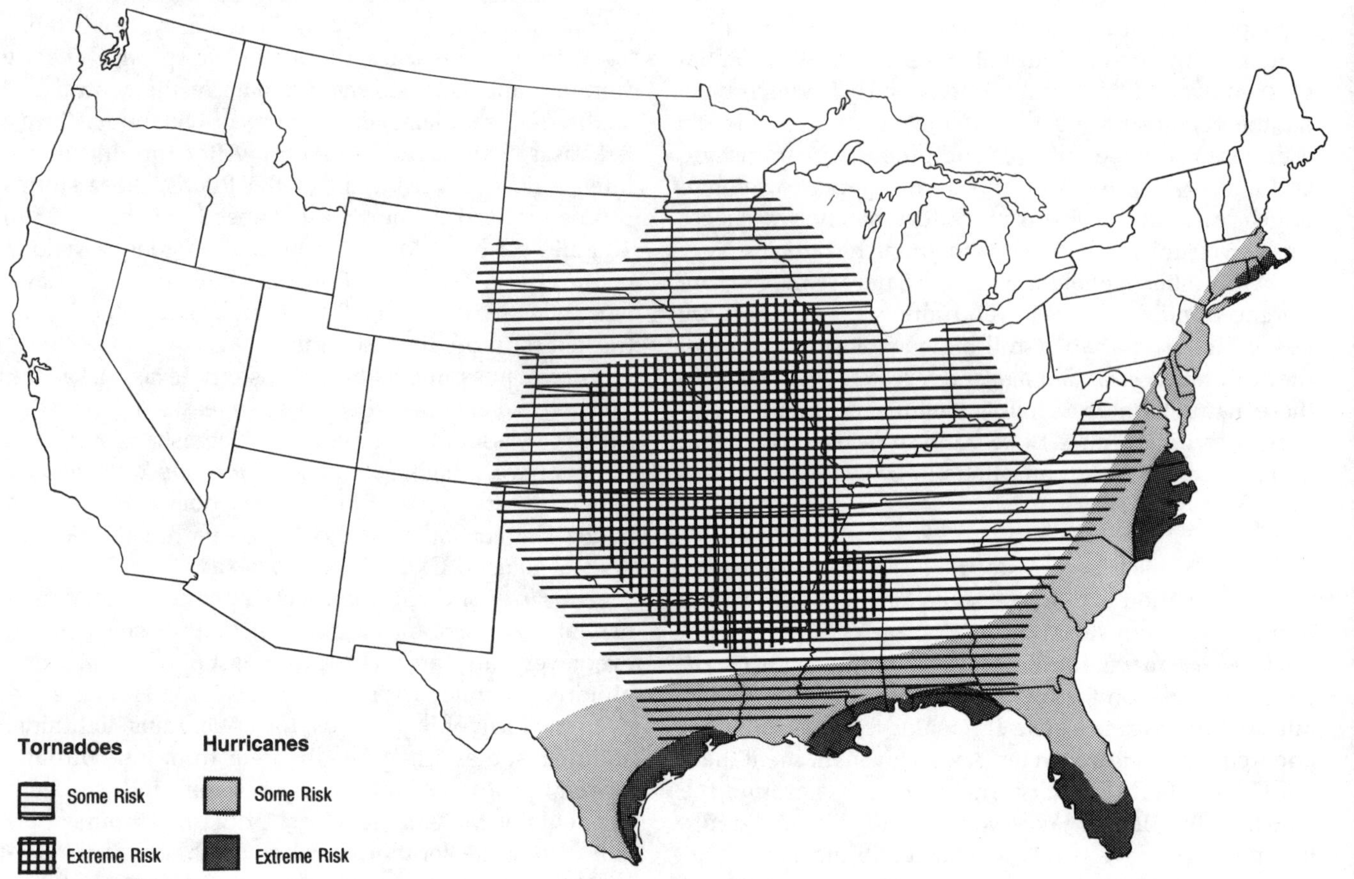

Tornadoes

▤ Some Risk

▦ Extreme Risk

Hurricanes

▨ Some Risk

◼ Extreme Risk

Earthquake Hazard Zones

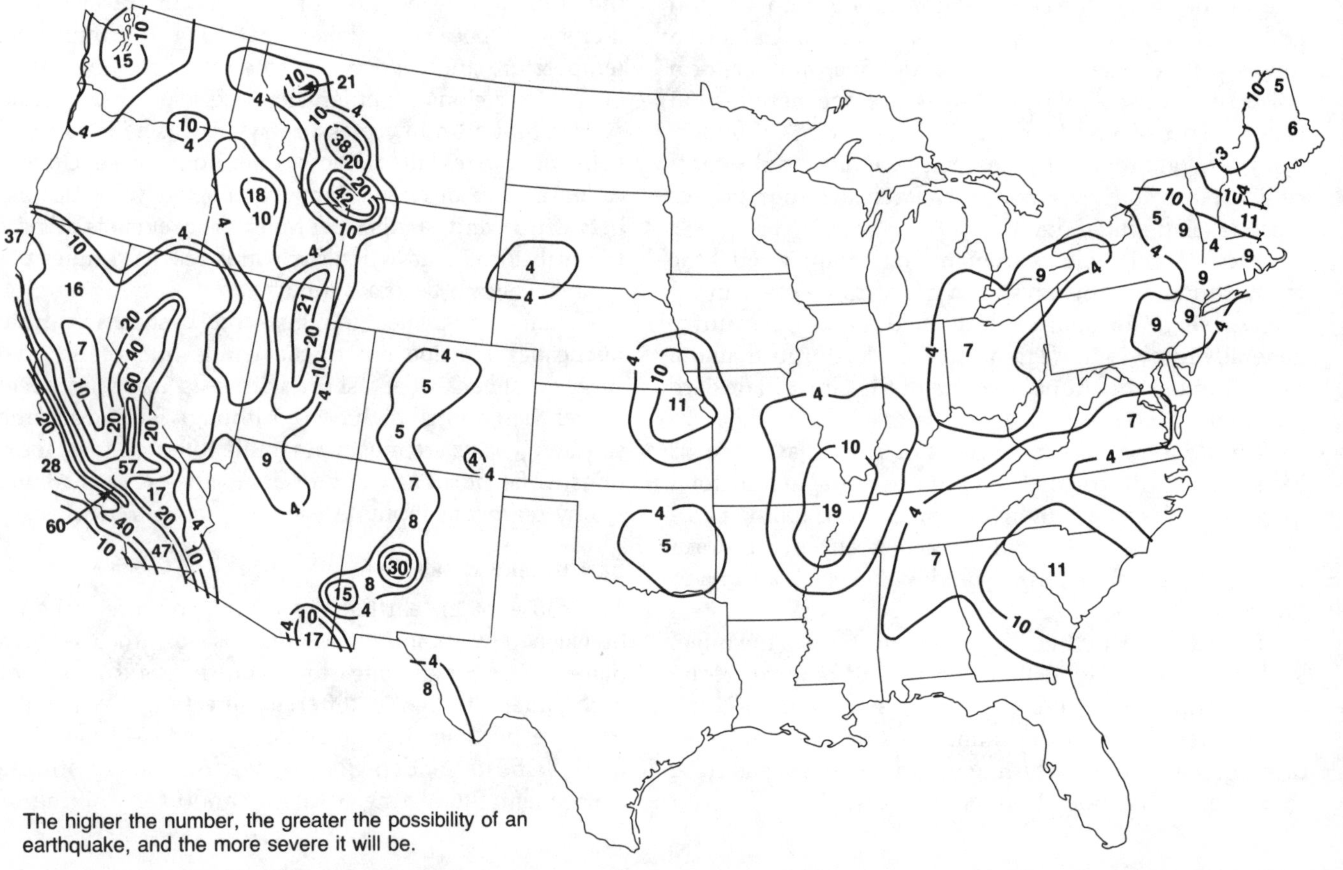

The higher the number, the greater the possibility of an earthquake, and the more severe it will be.

Source: U.S. Geological Survey Open-File Report 76-416, 1976.

immense masses of underground rock, is experienced on the earth's surface as an earthquake.

Those conditions necessary to cause an earthquake exist only in certain areas. The entire area ringing the Pacific Ocean is earthquake-prone, from western South America to Central America, North America's Pacific states, and Alaska, through the Aleutian chain across to Japan, down through China, and ending in New Zealand (which has more earthquakes than any other place in the world).

According to the map "Earthquake Hazard Zones," although huge stretches of America are free from the threat of earthquakes, some areas appear to be resting on powder kegs. (U.S. Geological Survey seismologists warn that the map is still experimental and that its predictions cannot be guaranteed.)

Northeast. There is a good deal of disagreement among geologists concerning earthquake risk in the Northeast. A number of theories about seismic trends have been advanced, and attempts have been made to relate these trends to various fault systems. The best known of these systems is the Boston-Ottawa trend, shown on the map as a continuous area from the Atlantic coast of Massachusetts to the St. Lawrence River valley, encompassing the two cities for which it is named. Most people are unaware that Boston suffered a severe earthquake in the 1700s and that it remains earthquake-prone today.

Southeast. One theory about earthquake risk is that possible earthquake epicenters (the points of origin of ground tremors) are not randomly distributed but occur in zones. In the Southeast, these zones run both parallel to and across the Appalachian Mountains. The greatest shock recorded east of the Mississippi occurred in Charleston, South Carolina, in 1886. The present hazard in South Carolina and eastern Georgia is as high as in the Boston-Ottawa trend.

Midwest and Rocky Mountains Regions. The zone of greatest hazard in the Mississippi Valley lies around the side of the cataclysmic series of quakes that occurred near New Madrid, Missouri. The biggest city in this zone is Memphis. The risk of seismic activity is greater in the Rocky Mountains region. The three biggest mountain cities—Denver, Albuquerque, and Salt Lake City—all lie within risk zones.

Pacific Northwest. The Puget Sound area near Seattle has experienced two major shocks within the past 30 years, both causing considerable damage. And in 1964, an earthquake in Anchorage registered 8.4 on the Richter scale (a nine-point span on a seismograph used to express the relative magnitude of an earthquake).

America's Other Earthquake Hazard

Most people know that California is the most earthquake-ridden state in America. Three major faults, or unstable cracks in the earth's surface, contribute to continual and severe seismic activity there. The most destructive earthquake in U.S. history in terms of property and casualties occurred in San Francisco in 1906, killing 452 people and destroying 28,000 buildings through tremors and resulting fire.

But what was probably the most powerful earthquake ever to strike in America took place in another danger zone, one less well-known than the quake-prone Golden State—the Mississippi Valley. This earthquake hit on February 7, 1812, in New Madrid, Missouri, and its tremors cracked pavement and rang church bells as far away as Washington, D.C., about 700 miles distant. Its force has been estimated at 8.6 on the Richter scale (the San Francisco earthquake has been estimated at 8.3). This was one of a series of severe quakes over the winter of 1811–12 that changed the course of the Mississippi River and created nearby Reelfoot Lake. Yet another major earthquake followed in 1895, striking the area with a Richter force of 6.5.

All these quakes have been attributed to the New Madrid Fault, which runs along the eastern border of Tennessee. According to a statement made by the Federal Emergency Management Agency in early 1984, scientists believe it is likely that increasing pressure on the fault will lead to a recurrence before the year 2000, one that could cause thousands of deaths and up to $60 billion in damage. Such a quake could register as high as 7.5, experts say, and affect 21 states, from Kansas east to Pennsylvania and from Illinois south to Louisiana.

California and Nevada. Much more seismic activity (and, therefore, more research and data) is present in California and Nevada than anywhere else in America. The greatest hazards in the United States are found in the San Andreas, Owens Valley, and Garlock fault systems, which are shown on the map as zones numbered as high as 60. All the metro areas in California are affected by these faults, particularly (in alphabetical order) Bakersfield, Los Angeles–Long Beach, Oakland, San Francisco, and San Jose. These places, most of which have mild climates and pleasant terrain, are in real danger.

Putting It All Together

Question: Where will you find a mild climate, low costs of living, extensive health-care facilities, a low crime rate, a wide range of transportation modes, excellent opportunities for higher education, a variety of recreational amenities, a generous helping of the arts, and a bright employment outlook?

Answer: The best place to live in America. But if you think of the odds of finding these qualities in one place, it all sounds too good to be true. Does such a place actually exist?

In order to meet all of the requirements, this ideal place would have San Francisco's year-round climate, where the weather is moderated by the warm Pacific Ocean and the temperature seldom varies much from a mild 65°. Its typical prices for housing, utilities, food, and other goods might resemble those of Pine Bluff, AR, where the costs of living are the lowest in metropolitan America.

This ideal place would also have to be large enough to match metropolitan New York's unrivaled variety of higher education options, its array of amenities related to the arts, and its public transit options in town and ease of travel to other parts of the country. It would also be large and affluent enough to equal Los Angeles's supply of physicians and health-care facilities.

Yet this place would also need to be small if it were to have a crime rate as low as Beaver County, PA. For quality and variety of man-made and natural recreation amenities, the standard set by Seattle would have to be met. And finally, our ideal location would have to present individuals with employment prospects as bright as those of Anaheim–Santa Ana, CA.

Obviously, this ideal spot is fictional. You can explore the geography long and hard, but you will never find the single metro area that combines all of the "bests" in each of *Places Rated Almanac*'s nine categories. Moreover, because one person's long-sought heaven can be another's purgatory, one can argue that there really is no such thing as *the* ideal metro area.

If you can move anywhere you wish, choosing your destination is still not easy. The best strategy is to focus on *your* own preferences and needs (the chapter "Decisions, Decisions" at the front of the book can help you identify what these preferences and needs might be). Having said as much, we can still try to discover which of America's 333 metro areas come closest to the ideal.

If You Read This Chapter First: Some Caveats

Readers who've skipped ahead to see how it all comes out may be surprised by many of the results shown in the cumulative table on pages 394–402. If you are curious how a metro area receives a rank in a particular category, consult the explanation of the scoring system in the appropriate chapter.

Aside from climate, *Places Rated*'s categories include five scored on facilities (health care, education, recreation, transportation, and the arts) and three scored on indicators (crime, costs of living, and jobs). Generally, smaller metro areas rank better on the indicators (these places typically have lower crime rates and lower costs of living), while larger places score higher on facilities. Because of *Places Rated*'s emphasis on facilities, the larger metro areas perhaps have an edge.

When you review the rankings in each of the chapters, be sure to note the close groupings of scores. With such close results, ranking metro areas from first to 333rd may give the impression of greater differences among them than actually exist.

Remember, too, that throughout this almanac the unit of comparison is not the incorporated city but the officially defined metropolitan area, typically made up of one or more counties.

FINDING THE BEST PLACES TO LIVE IN AMERICA

In 1970 the prestigious Urban Institute, located in Washington, DC, rated 18 large American cities for liveability according to such diverse factors as unemployment rates, crime rates, and per capita contributions to charity. Their method for determining the best all-around city (it was Minneapolis, by the way) was very simple: the ranks for each city for each of the factors were added together for a cumulative score.

Places Rated's method, in this edition and in previous ones, is the same as the Urban Institute's. Each metro area's ranks for the nine factors are totaled. Duluth, MN, for example, ranks 75th in costs of living, 311th in job outlook, 48th in safety from crime, 274th in the arts, 205th in transportation, 285th in education, 97th in health care, 177th in recreation, and 330th in climate mildness. The total of these ranks equals 1,177. Because the system is based on ranks, the lower the cumulative score, the better the metro area is judged to be all-around. (Duluth places 73rd overall among the metro areas.) The adjacent list highlights the metro areas that rise to the top as the best places to live in America.

In many respects, the list of the top 50 metro areas in this edition of *Places Rated Almanac* closely resembles that of the previous (1985) edition. Although their rankings have changed somewhat, 34 of the metro areas were in the top 50 before. Sixteen places have dropped from the list this time around, but only two—Asheville, NC, and Jacksonville, FL—dropped below 100th place.

America's Top 50 Metro Areas

Metro Area	Cumulative Score
1. Seattle, WA	666
2. San Francisco, CA*	676
3. Pittsburgh, PA	679
4. Washington, DC–MD–VA	702
5. San Diego, CA*	760
6. Boston, MA*	761
7. New York, NY*	786
8. Anaheim–Santa Ana, CA*	801
8. Louisville, KY–IN	801
10. Nassau–Suffolk, NY*	802
11. Atlanta, GA	812
12. Cleveland, OH	815
13. Philadelphia, PA–NJ	817
14. Cincinnati, OH–KY–IN	820
15. Los Angeles–Long Beach, CA*	833
16. *Salt Lake City–Ogden, UT*	834
17. Baltimore, MD*	839
18. Chicago, IL*	851
19. *Oakland, CA*	856
20. *Miami–Hialeah, FL*	860
21. Syracuse, NY	864
22. *Santa Barbara–Santa Maria–Lompoc, CA*	876
23. Raleigh–Durham, NC	881
24. *Portland, OR*	884
25. San Jose, CA	891
26. Richmond–Petersburg, VA	894
27. Nashville, TN	912
28. *Minneapolis–St. Paul, MN–WI*	920
29. St. Louis, MO–IL	922
30. *Indianapolis, IN*	941
31. Buffalo, NY	942
32. *Honolulu, HI*	950
33. Norfolk–Virginia Beach–Newport News, VA	973
34. Albuquerque, NM*	975
35. Knoxville, TN	984
36. *Scranton–Wilkes-Barre, PA*	988
37. *Phoenix, AZ*	992
38. *Eugene–Springfield, OR*	996
39. Denver, CO	1,006
40. Dallas, TX*	1,007
41. *Kansas City, MO–KS*	1,014
41. *Spokane, WA*	1,014
41. *Tucson, AZ*	1,014
44. Albany–Schenectady–Troy, NY	1,015
44. *Milwaukee, WI*	1,015
46. Rochester, NY	1,017
47. *Sacramento, CA*	1,036
48. Monmouth–Ocean, NJ*	1,048
49. Oklahoma City, OK	1,050
50. Bergen–Passaic, NJ*	1,057

* These places rank at the bottom—that is, 300th or lower—in one or more of *Places Rated Almanac*'s nine categories.

Metro areas in *italics* are newcomers to the top 50.

Consistency Counts

Many high-ranking metro areas have combinations of superior and dismal rankings in *Places Rated*'s nine categories. New York City is the classic example of an uneven performance. The Big Apple has no less than three first-place finishes: transportation, the arts, and options for higher education. Anyone who knows New York can appreciate these rankings, too. But what of its miserable showings in costs of living (#319) and crime (#332)? High costs of living and dangerous streets could, for many people, cancel out this super-city's finer points.

Places Rated decided to seek out those metro areas that show steady strength in *all* the categories, even though they might not have any dramatic first-place showings. We searched, in vain, for places with no rankings below 150th. Since we struck out with this stringent standard, we looked for those with no ranks lower than 200th. Even with this more liberal guideline, we came up with just a handful of metro areas that showed consistent strength in all nine of the *Places Rated* categories.

Interestingly, but for metropolitan Salt Lake City, all of these super-solid places are found in the same geographic area stretching from the Ohio Valley in the north to the Appalachian regions of the Mid-South.

Somewhat disappointed at the small number of extremely solid places, we went through the rankings again and selected those with only one rank below 200th. The list of runners-up (solid metro areas) follows.

Does this kind of consistency count? It certainly does: of these 33 solid and super-solid places, just 11 fail to make it into *Places Rated*'s list of the 50 best places to live in America.

Super-Solid Metro Areas

Metro Area (Overall Rank)	Highest Rank	Lowest Rank
Buffalo, NY (31)	Education (44)	Costs of Living (190)
Cleveland, OH (12)	The Arts (21)	Costs of Living (194)
Indianapolis, IN (30)	Transportation (41)	Crime (181)
Knoxville, TN (35)	Climate (26)	Transportation (178)
Lexington–Fayette, KY (66)	Health Care (8)	Recreation (173)
Louisville, KY–IN (8)	The Arts (36)	Jobs (151)
Pittsburgh, PA (3)	Education (21)	Costs of Living (157)
Salt Lake City–Ogden, UT (16)	Transportation (13)	Climate (120)
Scranton–Wilkes-Barre, PA (36)	Crime (6)	Transportation (183)

Solid Metro Areas

Metro Area (Overall Rank)	Highest Rank	Lowest Rank
Anaheim–Santa Ana, CA (8)	Jobs (1)	Costs of Living (329)
Champaign–Urbana–Rantoul, IL (88)	Transportation (11)	Crime (254)
Charleston, SC (84)	Recreation (11)	Crime (262)
Cincinnati, OH–KY–IN (14)	Education (34)	Costs of Living (214)
Columbia, MO (106)	Health Care (23)	Crime (213)
Erie, PA (64)	Crime (50)	Jobs (267)
Eugene–Springfield, OR (38)	Recreation (13)	Jobs (215)
Harrisburg–Lebanon–Carlisle, PA (65)	Transportation (43)	Health Care (214)
Honolulu, HI (32)	Transportation (16)	Costs of Living (330)
Kansas City, MO–KS (41)	Health Care (39)	Crime (298)
La Crosse, WI (95)	Health Care (30)	Climate (314)
Oklahoma City, OK (49)	Costs of Living (25)	Crime (282)
Omaha, NE–IA (63)	Health Care (61)	Climate (279)
Philadelphia, PA–NJ (13)	Health Care (4)	Costs of Living (277)
Portland, OR (24)	Climate (16)	Crime (322)
Providence, RI (68)	Transportation (46)	Costs of Living (287)
Richmond–Petersburg, VA (26)	Transportation (25)	Costs of Living (216)
Rochester, NY (46)	Recreation (23)	Costs of Living (251)
San Jose, CA (25)	Jobs (12)	Costs of Living (328)
Santa Barbara–Santa Maria–Lompoc, CA (22)	Climate (5)	Costs of Living (314)
Spokane, WA (41)	Transportation (38)	Jobs (236)
Springfield, MO (98)	Costs of Living (98)	Recreation (215)
Syracuse, NY (21)	Transportation (14)	Health Care (210)
Wilmington, DE–NJ–MD (89)	Education (59)	Costs of Living (239)

RANKINGS: Putting It All Together

The following table shows the rank of every metro area for each of *Places Rated*'s nine categories. The sum of these—the cumulative score—is also shown, as is the overall rank. Abilene's cumulative score of 1,787, for example, ranks it 245th overall among the 333 metro areas; Akron's cumulative score of 1,172 ranks it 72nd. As in golf, the lower the cumulative score, the better. The highest possible score would be 9, meaning a first-place rank in all nine categories.

Metro Area	Costs of Living	Jobs	Crime	Health Care & Environment	Transportation	Education	The Arts	Recreation	Climate	Cumulative Score	Overall Rank
Abilene, TX	85	258	155	131	165	218	287	288	200	1,787	245
Akron, OH	77	223	167	288	113	45	68	84	108	1,173	72
Albany, GA	40	241	231	260	283	293	191	323	259	2,121	324
Albany–Schenectady–Troy, NY	270	73	62	95	15	48	40	160	252	1,015	44
Albuquerque, NM	250	82	325	36	22	100	67	64	30	976	34
Alexandria, LA	44	305	146	100	216	312	193	250	203	1,769	240
Allentown–Bethlehem, PA–NJ	245	173	29	135	259	134	107	284	132	1,498	162
Altoona, PA	27	194	12	121	154	291	282	291	127	1,499	164
Amarillo, TX	35	207	216	64	150	210	279	303	69	1,533	176
Anaheim–Santa Ana, CA	329	1	184	10	197	7	19	49	5	801	8
Anchorage, AK	289	68	226	115	73	195	137	42	328	1,473	157
Anderson, IN	46	302	103	192	301	306	309	310	185	2,054	311
Anderson, SC	16	228	164	306	277	318	307	299	87	2,002	302
Ann Arbor, MI	271	97	274	19	109	28	58	170	157	1,183	75
Anniston, AL	9	288	236	188	209	225	329	297	130	1,911	282
Appleton–Oshkosh–Neenah, WI	90	203	27	248	184	160	205	121	304	1,542	178
Asheville, NC	193	247	81	45	133	250	194	213	25	1,381	123
Athens, GA	109	285	114	232	308	119	251	274	77	1,769	240
Atlanta, GA	227	2	285	106	4	23	14	127	24	812	11
Atlantic City, NJ	268	25	324	312	49	226	201	61	61	1,527	174
Augusta, GA–SC	106	107	131	136	278	205	172	289	184	1,608	199
Aurora–Elgin, IL	256	79	105	236	93	89	80	246	255	1,439	144
Austin, TX	233	24	259	243	168	26	100	264	284	1,601	196
Bakersfield, CA	288	159	300	282	204	187	189	205	130	1,944	293
Baltimore, MD	260	37	318	47	6	18	12	19	122	839	17
Bangor, ME	228	257	53	70	53	175	132	81	274	1,323	105
Baton Rouge, LA	108	98	329	310	219	77	169	226	288	1,824	256

Metro Area	Costs of Living	Jobs	Crime	Health Care & Environment	Transportation	Education	The Arts	Recreation	Climate	Cumulative Score	Overall Rank
Battle Creek, MI	104	311	251	216	142	266	216	212	189	1,907	280
Beaumont–Port Arthur, TX	141	221	199	203	284	180	237	142	292	1,899	277
Beaver County, PA	34	165	1	314	261	182	220	249	90	1,516	170
Bellingham, WA	204	226	102	211	177	202	187	24	15	1,348	112
Benton Harbor, MI	64	327	297	197	271	257	195	179	123	1,910	281
Bergen–Passaic, NJ	326	51	100	84	206	24	22	112	132	1,057	50
Billings, MT	161	311	113	146	27	264	198	240	273	1,733	231
Biloxi–Gulfport, MS	65	190	154	174	290	325	210	97	95	1,600	195
Binghamton, NY	220	196	7	277	111	156	128	190	149	1,434	143
Birmingham, AL	208	149	241	57	124	114	106	251	67	1,317	103
Bismarck, ND	124	242	25	25	158	302	227	245	331	1,679	215
Bloomington, IN	112	172	91	264	312	95	157	113	137	1,453	149
Bloomington–Normal, IL	199	279	82	159	33	122	228	223	241	1,566	184
Boise City, ID	235	145	123	226	23	197	132	181	85	1,347	111
Boston, MA	318	29	255	5	30	4	7	57	56	761	6
Boulder–Longmont, CO	246	126	174	154	17	108	121	20	267	1,233	86
Bradenton, FL	215	80	319	229	138	283	300	166	279	2,009	303
Brazoria, TX	84	216	57	300	306	166	244	229	292	1,894	274
Bremerton, WA	201	158	55	283	179	297	308	108	12	1,601	196
Bridgeport–Milford, CT	323	122	219	75	134	42	16	144	34	1,109	57
Bristol, CT	298	248	36	189	238	235	258	321	207	2,030	305
Brockton, MA	276	87	172	327	213	78	151	273	108	1,685	218
Brownsville–Harlingen, TX	15	119	260	319	286	253	270	39	279	1,840	258
Bryan–College Station, TX	110	59	222	317	304	82	230	247	307	1,878	268
Buffalo, NY	190	85	181	162	54	44	56	55	115	942	31
Burlington, NC	123	200	62	241	323	258	328	317	45	1,897	275
Burlington, VT	266	105	161	72	9	158	161	59	307	1,298	99
Canton, OH	3	224	87	303	125	239	141	237	108	1,467	152
Casper, WY	132	333	127	230	164	330	291	215	301	2,123	325
Cedar Rapids, IA	107	234	120	247	88	232	240	140	285	1,693	220
Champaign–Urbana–Rantoul, IL	174	156	254	55	11	64	156	176	195	1,241	88
Charleston, SC	166	74	262	139	162	153	145	11	118	1,230	84
Charleston, WV	160	224	66	119	67	213	243	187	53	1,332	108
Charlotte–Gastonia–Rock Hill, NC–SC	218	32	277	324	39	74	45	164	38	1,211	79
Charlottesville, VA	236	164	96	80	31	122	206	172	58	1,165	70
Chattanooga, TN–GA	92	264	159	149	217	171	159	254	106	1,571	186
Cheyenne, WY	177	298	77	92	131	310	276	274	217	1,852	263
Chicago, IL	269	18	321	3	7	3	3	16	211	851	18
Chico, CA	283	106	177	48	198	147	304	248	73	1,584	190
Cincinnati, OH–KY–IN	214	75	138	104	63	34	41	56	95	820	14

Metro Area	Costs of Living	Jobs	Crime	Health Care & Environment	Transportation	Education	The Arts	Recreation	Climate	Cumulative Score	Overall Rank
Clarksville–Hopkinsville, TN–KY	11	297	115	299	306	245	312	73	161	1,819	253
Cleveland, OH	194	191	169	22	26	36	21	52	104	815	12
Colorado Springs, CO	95	91	216	275	229	159	110	78	191	1,444	146
Columbia, MO	153	213	152	23	144	117	164	190	170	1,326	106
Columbia, SC	183	56	289	163	42	106	126	203	191	1,359	115
Columbus, GA–AL	19	260	139	272	262	230	213	296	206	1,897	275
Columbus, OH	202	45	214	225	127	27	50	106	137	1,133	61
Corpus Christi, TX	187	217	224	112	260	214	151	149	313	1,827	257
Cumberland, MD–WV	62	195	5	76	182	253	325	283	87	1,468	153
Dallas, TX	258	7	326	93	2	22	39	99	161	1,007	40
Danbury, CT	327	95	21	62	281	58	26	230	118	1,218	80
Danville, VA	4	325	4	330	240	309	288	328	159	1,987	300
Davenport–Rock Island– Moline, IA–IL	71	187	130	234	121	178	135	135	279	1,470	155
Dayton–Springfield, OH	120	154	201	209	83	54	53	269	161	1,304	102
Daytona Beach, FL	69	112	280	208	212	135	230	27	127	1,400	129
Decatur, AL	43	302	38	239	327	281	288	220	80	1,818	252
Decatur, IL	36	311	146	279	97	280	253	284	248	1,934	289
Denver, CO	224	33	276	85	5	47	35	101	200	1,006	39
Des Moines, IA	134	135	247	183	75	163	162	133	276	1,508	167
Detroit, MI	226	70	323	77	126	9	32	34	176	1,073	53
Dothan, AL	12	137	150	138	293	277	315	329	318	1,969	299
Dubuque, IA	75	311	48	97	205	285	274	177	294	1,766	239
Duluth, MN–WI	111	245	31	64	91	151	104	50	330	1,177	73
Eau Claire, WI	149	210	22	78	232	179	208	227	326	1,631	204
El Paso, TX	122	81	294	285	211	130	215	276	85	1,699	222
Elkhart–Goshen, IN	144	150	60	302	175	328	171	270	200	1,800	249
Elmira, NY	63	255	61	128	176	306	250	161	260	1,660	212
Enid, OK	24	311	157	94	316	328	271	294	265	2,060	313
Erie, PA	76	267	50	193	58	161	158	110	71	1,144	64
Eugene–Springfield, OR	98	215	141	169	82	128	132	13	18	996	38
Evansville, IN–KY	156	296	107	175	228	208	149	168	149	1,636	207
Fall River, MA–RI	286	157	197	308	47	227	283	138	40	1,683	216
Fargo–Moorhead, ND–MN	152	236	31	17	32	132	147	289	332	1,368	118
Fayetteville, NC	137	211	272	314	173	223	268	307	127	2,032	306
Fayetteville–Springdale, AR	31	291	47	70	242	165	234	169	151	1,400	129
Fitchburg–Leominster, MA	285	175	54	165	291	236	260	278	222	1,966	298
Flint, MI	154	311	331	295	120	139	85	235	172	1,842	259
Florence, AL	7	311	34	261	331	246	264	279	157	1,890	271
Florence, SC	47	229	269	96	98	259	248	332	147	1,725	227
Fort Collins–Loveland, CO	179	140	141	221	295	140	276	7	235	1,634	205
Fort Lauderdale–Hollywood– Pompano Beach, FL	252	10	307	124	172	125	81	174	114	1,359	115

Metro Area	Costs of Living	Jobs	Crime	Health Care & Environment	Transportation	Education	The Arts	Recreation	Climate	Cumulative Score	Overall Rank
Fort Myers–Cape Coral, FL	253	28	110	237	156	279	112	22	317	1,514	168
Fort Pierce, FL	240	30	305	290	300	248	280	33	76	1,802	250
Fort Smith, AR–OK	5	141	75	177	258	312	312	126	246	1,652	210
Fort Walton Beach, FL	151	61	64	249	276	315	331	150	176	1,773	243
Fort Wayne, IN	135	222	83	186	64	173	138	171	217	1,389	125
Fort Worth–Arlington, TX	231	35	316	274	117	39	74	139	188	1,413	137
Fresno, CA	290	148	309	167	132	109	178	36	132	1,501	166
Gadsden, AL	33	311	128	234	311	315	285	333	191	2,141	326
Gainesville, FL	198	92	316	27	201	73	118	199	300	1,524	172
Galveston–Texas City, TX	168	307	268	31	252	157	232	87	20	1,522	171
Gary–Hammond, IN	136	181	175	244	56	61	94	162	242	1,351	113
Glens Falls, NY	133	230	44	178	299	323	160	125	252	1,744	232
Grand Forks, ND	126	298	24	14	37	199	197	260	333	1,488	159
Grand Rapids, MI	146	72	158	296	215	104	122	124	214	1,451	148
Great Falls, MT	118	289	103	42	45	327	267	93	297	1,581	188
Greeley, CO	38	283	224	320	324	167	263	314	235	2,168	327
Green Bay, WI	213	138	59	238	137	207	240	99	311	1,642	208
Greensboro–Winston-Salem–High Point, NC	219	47	168	224	155	81	72	114	54	1,134	62
Greenville–Spartanburg, SC	94	55	227	245	192	102	87	189	32	1,223	81
Hagerstown, MD	175	276	41	324	191	325	190	201	121	1,844	261
Hamilton–Middletown, OH	91	246	145	309	226	121	163	219	166	1,686	219
Harrisburg–Lebanon–Carlisle, PA	185	131	56	214	43	140	116	122	143	1,150	65
Hartford, CT	308	89	211	130	10	56	55	143	207	1,209	78
Hickory, NC	142	117	92	218	275	268	288	301	56	1,757	236
Honolulu, HI	330	110	118	181	16	79	62	32	22	950	32
Houma–Thibodaux, LA	86	325	78	286	333	229	319	77	288	2,021	304
Houston, TX	206	39	286	40	115	16	31	129	290	1,152	66
Huntington–Ashland, WV–KY–OH	98	284	71	178	210	176	167	280	46	1,510	168
Huntsville, AL	162	143	178	281	250	189	95	180	80	1,558	180
Indianapolis, IN	178	66	181	116	41	87	49	82	141	941	30
Iowa City, IA	217	209	133	6	233	101	176	204	285	1,564	182
Jackson, MI	67	327	260	326	160	260	295	91	204	1,990	301
Jackson, MS	101	198	189	12	129	146	96	243	295	1,409	133
Jackson, TN	57	239	299	89	256	273	333	326	238	2,110	322
Jacksonville, FL	167	54	327	142	100	136	88	37	268	1,319	104
Jacksonville, NC	97	226	166	316	318	318	291	239	124	2,095	321
Janesville–Beloit, WI	148	254	131	291	169	196	244	194	262	1,889	271
Jersey City, NJ	280	166	301	187	96	33	25	91	77	1,256	91
Johnson City–Kingsport–Bristol, TN–VA	114	201	27	154	285	169	98	130	29	1,207	77
Johnstown, PA	56	281	3	193	157	255	301	243	156	1,645	209

Metro Area	Costs of Living	Jobs	Crime	Health Care & Environment	Transportation	Education	The Arts	Recreation	Climate	Cumulative Score	Overall Rank
Joliet, IL	223	103	119	323	57	60	102	174	250	1,411	135
Joplin, MO	51	197	65	206	287	242	165	309	101	1,623	201
Kalamazoo, MI	192	238	311	103	86	112	168	298	189	1,697	221
Kankakee, IL	119	204	210	202	231	278	312	271	242	2,069	315
Kansas City, MO–KS	180	90	298	39	51	63	54	88	151	1,014	41
Kenosha, WI	237	233	134	142	143	76	93	109	230	1,397	126
Killeen–Temple, TX	49	134	90	184	297	240	275	312	312	1,893	273
Knoxville, TN	150	128	73	134	178	105	135	54	26	983	35
Kokomo, IN	80	305	14	144	325	274	255	293	216	1,906	279
La Crosse, WI	131	193	51	30	59	187	185	119	314	1,269	95
Lafayette, LA	184	211	238	211	81	154	204	136	287	1,706	226
Lafayette–West Lafayette, IN	186	256	30	123	112	90	188	159	232	1,376	121
Lake Charles, LA	146	332	232	173	246	224	258	210	257	2,078	317
Lake County, IL	291	49	101	117	245	83	74	75	211	1,246	90
Lakeland–Winter Haven, FL	138	136	310	291	220	230	310	79	323	2,037	308
Lancaster, PA	249	114	16	287	171	182	246	304	132	1,701	224
Lansing–East Lansing, MI	248	166	180	280	61	41	89	223	248	1,536	177
Laredo, TX	2	188	258	328	230	285	311	325	290	2,217	331
Las Cruces, NM	128	101	238	329	272	169	207	137	147	1,728	228
Las Vegas, NV	255	20	303	291	69	144	144	30	143	1,399	128
Lawrence, KS	127	242	207	322	313	115	236	152	214	1,928	285
Lawrence–Haverhill, MA–NH	305	53	76	151	237	98	113	145	153	1,331	107
Lawton, OK	8	282	186	216	227	247	327	207	250	1,950	295
Lewiston–Auburn, ME	205	274	85	100	294	315	219	146	235	1,873	267
Lexington–Fayette, KY	191	184	173	8	128	118	129	173	48	1,152	66
Lima, OH	26	300	122	168	186	295	196	252	199	1,744	232
Lincoln, NE	165	278	156	151	48	110	119	167	302	1,496	161
Little Rock–North Little Rock, AR	116	124	279	34	174	133	131	178	228	1,397	126
Longview–Marshall, TX	23	271	140	199	303	271	315	324	224	2,070	316
Lorain–Elyria, OH	143	286	35	270	223	191	148	228	104	1,628	203
Los Angeles–Long Beach, CA	324	6	330	1	159	2	2	4	5	833	15
Louisville, KY–IN	89	151	137	91	60	88	36	89	60	801	8
Lowell, MA–NH	301	62	79	250	208	79	109	305	191	1,584	190
Lubbock, TX	59	162	314	14	189	120	181	260	72	1,371	120
Lynchburg, VA	41	263	70	233	80	194	256	188	42	1,367	117
Macon–Warner Robins, GA	78	265	125	164	239	212	172	256	275	1,786	244
Madison, WI	232	127	94	46	35	43	100	90	309	1,076	54
Manchester, NH	303	84	87	139	114	220	217	267	298	1,729	229
Mansfield, OH	52	259	229	259	309	306	251	242	137	2,044	309
McAllen–Edinburg–Mission, TX	6	93	149	321	330	211	317	313	327	2,067	314

Metro Area	Costs of Living	Jobs	Crime	Health Care & Environment	Transportation	Education	The Arts	Recreation	Climate	Cumulative Score	Overall Rank
Medford, OR	72	199	95	54	52	260	77	302	68	1,179	74
Melbourne–Titusville–Palm Bay, FL	125	154	266	276	288	185	229	29	100	1,652	210
Memphis, TN–AR–MS	197	120	320	132	29	94	84	146	211	1,333	109
Merced, CA	263	133	148	256	141	281	297	308	101	1,928	285
Miami–Hialeah, FL	247	21	333	21	102	37	44	6	49	860	20
Middlesex–Somerset–Hunterdon, NJ	311	13	52	213	147	19	15	263	132	1,165	70
Middletown, CT	313	123	68	153	222	199	166	262	84	1,590	193
Midland, TX	182	270	194	304	148	312	286	319	73	2,088	319
Milwaukee, WI	230	108	161	38	110	35	23	44	266	1,015	44
Minneapolis–St. Paul, MN–WI	243	34	153	58	44	13	8	43	324	920	28
Mobile, AL	87	218	295	242	224	164	222	128	277	1,857	265
Modesto, CA	257	152	263	150	320	206	233	315	43	1,939	290
Monmouth–Ocean, NJ	309	27	89	196	266	32	30	38	61	1,048	48
Monroe, LA	102	291	218	126	218	204	261	241	271	1,932	287
Montgomery, AL	140	220	92	191	195	171	153	272	242	1,676	214
Muncie, IN	21	280	86	307	152	137	183	211	185	1,562	181
Muskegon, MI	48	301	308	262	269	285	248	58	101	1,880	269
Naples, FL	262	59	211	269	321	332	323	24	315	2,116	323
Nashua, NH	307	64	8	141	268	115	110	282	174	1,469	154
Nashville, TN	203	42	204	28	72	72	115	96	80	912	27
Nassau–Suffolk, NY	306	11	58	41	329	8	9	9	31	802	10
New Bedford, MA	272	183	215	313	99	217	261	198	40	1,798	247
New Britain, CT	302	244	144	108	78	144	265	256	207	1,748	234
New Haven–Meriden, CT	312	142	206	107	68	91	45	193	98	1,262	92
New London–Norwich, CT–RI	297	180	49	257	118	255	143	221	98	1,618	200
New Orleans, LA	145	53	315	37	139	57	82	7	227	1,062	51
New York, NY	319	71	332	2	1	1	1	15	44	786	7
Newark, NJ	322	40	291	18	92	10	10	231	77	1,091	55
Niagara Falls, NY	82	202	107	255	77	201	212	76	145	1,357	114
Norfolk–Virginia Beach–Newport News, VA	222	44	179	121	246	49	48	14	50	973	33
Norwalk, CT	332	179	112	24	235	67	24	154	34	1,161	68
Oakland, CA	325	16	306	29	40	12	20	107	1	856	19
Ocala, FL	55	50	283	331	236	320	268	48	320	1,911	282
Odessa, TX	105	311	265	333	319	267	273	320	73	2,266	332
Oklahoma City, OK	25	132	282	99	140	38	73	116	145	1,050	49
Olympia, WA	195	113	74	246	101	244	247	218	21	1,459	151
Omaha, NE–IA	117	178	190	61	84	98	64	66	279	1,137	63
Orange County, NY	293	96	117	147	257	53	27	195	217	1,402	132
Orlando, FL	211	5	312	222	61	102	65	41	268	1,287	97

Metro Area	Costs of Living	Jobs	Crime	Health Care & Environment	Transportation	Education	The Arts	Recreation	Climate	Cumulative Score	Overall Rank
Owensboro, KY	60	311	42	200	296	322	221	300	196	1,948	294
Oxnard–Ventura, CA	315	23	98	147	314	50	86	35	4	1,072	52
Panama City, FL	158	111	223	252	265	300	293	72	176	1,850	262
Parkersburg–Marietta, WV–OH	61	287	14	222	167	274	239	266	59	1,589	192
Pascagoula, MS	10	219	125	318	328	332	326	118	95	1,871	266
Pawtucket–Woonsocket–Attleboro, RI–MA	278	192	46	157	203	203	276	182	90	1,627	202
Pensacola, FL	196	115	292	178	267	186	125	67	176	1,602	198
Peoria, IL	30	182	129	205	202	192	124	111	234	1,409	133
Philadelphia, PA–NJ	277	26	191	4	71	5	6	185	52	817	13
Phoenix, AZ	234	8	275	83	103	25	43	45	176	992	37
Pine Bluff, AR	1	311	203	301	305	288	293	327	264	2,293	333
Pittsburgh, PA	157	76	72	35	78	21	33	117	90	679	3
Pittsfield, MA	264	250	42	69	181	321	130	132	246	1,635	206
Portland, ME	292	109	165	26	108	184	97	40	242	1,263	93
Portland, OR	188	100	322	51	34	55	59	59	16	884	24
Portsmouth–Dover–Rochester, NH–ME	295	48	39	294	310	154	105	68	257	1,570	185
Poughkeepsie, NY	282	101	67	240	163	189	180	206	238	1,666	213
Providence, RI	287	116	183	189	46	69	83	98	90	1,161	68
Provo–Orem, UT	70	99	40	305	221	92	155	24	224	1,230	84
Pueblo, CO	21	208	278	170	255	260	214	186	228	1,820	254
Racine, WI	169	273	211	263	76	237	186	197	230	1,842	259
Raleigh–Durham, NC	267	19	169	67	36	29	37	221	37	882	23
Rapid City, SD	121	272	163	42	161	305	200	21	310	1,595	194
Reading, PA	242	266	45	283	241	192	272	208	66	1,815	251
Redding, CA	254	144	197	114	50	268	254	62	27	1,370	119
Reno, NV	274	171	247	56	20	173	203	86	182	1,412	136
Richland–Kennewick–Pasco, WA	74	185	121	207	24	291	284	258	27	1,471	156
Richmond–Petersburg, VA	216	57	191	63	25	75	42	131	94	894	26
Riverside–San Bernardino, CA	281	14	304	136	280	17	38	104	61	1,235	87
Roanoke, VA	173	231	98	66	149	240	178	105	33	1,273	96
Rochester, MN	243	104	19	20	146	297	210	196	321	1,556	179
Rochester, NY	251	69	135	170	95	51	47	23	176	1,017	46
Rockford, IL	225	206	240	158	234	248	184	157	262	1,914	284
Sacramento, CA	275	22	281	111	105	31	52	53	106	1,036	47
Saginaw–Bay City–Midland, MI	95	308	220	271	244	181	140	102	210	1,771	242
St. Cloud, MN	210	86	10	204	136	148	225	234	329	1,582	189
St. Joseph, MO	44	331	151	219	288	271	306	331	254	2,195	329
St. Louis, MO–IL	212	77	237	60	18	20	29	94	175	922	29

Metro Area	Costs of Living	Jobs	Crime	Health Care & Environment	Transportation	Education	The Arts	Recreation	Climate	Cumulative Score	Overall Rank
Salem, OR	14	276	188	289	153	209	257	115	23	1,524	172
Salem–Gloucester, MA	316	161	20	86	263	85	69	83	38	1,121	60
Salinas–Seaside–Monterey, CA	320	65	243	278	187	227	90	12	9	1,431	140
Salt Lake City–Ogden, UT	159	41	175	156	13	68	34	18	170	834	16
San Angelo, TX	78	262	201	90	249	242	305	277	238	1,942	291
San Antonio, TX	130	31	284	172	70	71	60	183	302	1,303	100
San Diego, CA	310	15	253	59	89	11	17	3	3	760	5
San Francisco, CA	331	17	290	7	8	15	5	2	1	676	2
San Jose, CA	328	12	160	110	85	14	18	156	8	891	25
Santa Barbara–Santa Maria–Lompoc, CA	314	46	143	44	74	107	126	17	5	876	22
Santa Cruz, CA	321	60	235	182	90	96	71	199	9	1,263	93
Santa Fe, NM	273	88	195	50	315	276	103	65	61	1,426	138
Santa Rosa–Petaluma, CA	317	38	136	120	274	86	92	146	19	1,228	83
Sarasota, FL	259	63	229	125	188	331	120	63	305	1,683	216
Savannah, GA	163	240	271	160	28	251	170	51	166	1,500	165
Scranton–Wilkes-Barre, PA	93	130	6	105	183	92	108	163	108	988	36
Seattle, WA	261	36	270	33	12	30	11	1	12	666	1
Sharon, PA	32	251	10	195	317	265	330	233	116	1,749	235
Sheboygan, WI	172	308	23	176	150	324	235	134	277	1,799	248
Sherman–Denison, TX	13	290	245	98	322	289	319	316	196	2,088	319
Shreveport, LA	113	268	296	31	170	234	138	232	221	1,703	225
Sioux City, IA–NE	28	311	185	161	166	301	192	236	306	1,886	270
Sioux Falls, SD	115	169	37	9	55	295	238	287	325	1,530	175
South Bend–Mishawaka, IN	73	253	204	185	66	142	142	120	159	1,344	110
Spokane, WA	39	236	169	79	38	128	117	95	113	1,014	41
Springfield, IL	189	186	221	129	19	222	174	152	196	1,488	159
Springfield, MA	284	118	196	228	21	46	76	141	272	1,382	124
Springfield, MO	98	129	105	113	190	127	150	215	161	1,288	98
Stamford, CT	333	176	115	11	144	70	13	213	34	1,109	57
State College, PA	229	214	26	268	253	84	199	192	108	1,573	187
Steubenville–Weirton, OH–WV	18	249	18	258	332	299	296	265	166	1,901	278
Stockton, CA	279	146	287	254	119	177	222	252	55	1,791	246
Syracuse, NY	181	83	69	210	14	66	57	31	153	864	21
Tacoma, WA	241	163	273	273	65	126	66	5	12	1,224	82
Tallahassee, FL	164	78	288	226	116	97	176	122	298	1,565	183
Tampa–St. Petersburg–Clearwater, FL	199	3	313	109	105	40	28	28	279	1,104	56
Terre Haute, IN	68	330	83	253	199	168	242	215	141	1,699	222
Texarkana, TX–Texarkana, AR	57	294	187	74	270	289	302	321	260	2,054	311
Toledo, OH	139	205	209	52	94	62	79	69	204	1,113	59

Metro Area	Costs of Living	Jobs	Crime	Health Care & Environment	Transportation	Education	The Arts	Recreation	Climate	Cumulative Score	Overall Rank
Topeka, KS	170	295	207	127	87	233	209	208	223	1,759	237
Trenton, NJ	299	170	256	52	122	52	51	255	46	1,303	100
Tucson, AZ	209	67	292	86	135	65	61	10	89	1,014	41
Tulsa, OK	81	153	232	219	214	149	63	151	185	1,447	147
Tuscaloosa, AL	53	327	244	201	130	143	297	242	256	1,943	292
Tyler, TX	129	168	228	68	282	219	324	311	224	1,953	296
Utica–Rome, NY	54	232	9	266	105	198	98	71	153	1,186	76
Vallejo–Fairfield–Napa, CA	304	43	256	215	243	111	91	165	11	1,439	144
Vancouver, WA	83	125	97	332	104	215	202	281	16	1,455	150
Victoria, TX	50	302	234	14	326	303	317	330	318	2,194	328
Vineland–Millville–Bridgeton, NJ	155	308	242	145	254	124	145	295	61	1,729	229
Visalia–Tulare–Porterville, CA	238	235	252	265	248	252	332	47	165	2,034	307
Waco, TX	20	252	267	251	184	150	299	103	295	1,821	255
Washington, DC–MD–VA	296	4	245	13	3	6	4	80	51	702	4
Waterbury, CT	300	189	110	166	292	283	280	306	118	2,044	309
Waterloo–Cedar Falls, IA	17	311	80	102	264	161	153	74	316	1,478	158
Wausau, WI	176	274	33	297	207	310	222	238	321	2,078	317
West Palm Beach–Boca Raton–Delray Beach, FL	265	9	329	118	180	138	78	46	217	1,380	122
Wheeling, WV–OH	37	177	2	88	298	237	226	202	166	1,433	141
Wichita, KS	88	260	200	81	225	130	114	225	232	1,400	129
Wichita Falls, TX	66	147	264	82	273	263	266	70	270	1,856	264
Williamsport, PA	42	311	17	73	279	293	322	286	137	1,760	238
Wilmington, DE–NJ–MD	239	121	193	197	123	59	70	158	83	1,243	89
Wilmington, NC	171	139	250	133	194	220	182	85	124	1,498	162
Worcester, MA	294	93	124	48	196	113	175	258	126	1,427	139
Yakima, WA	103	293	249	231	200	303	217	155	182	1,933	288
York, PA	221	160	12	310	302	215	303	268	172	1,963	297
Youngstown–Warren, OH	29	174	107	298	251	151	123	184	116	1,433	141
Yuba City, CA	207	269	302	267	193	270	319	318	70	2,215	330

Appendix

Consolidated Metropolitan Statistical Areas (CMSAs)
& Their Primary Metropolitan Statistical Area (PMSA) Components

**Boston–Lawrence–
Salem, MA–NH**
Boston, MA
Brockton, MA
Lawrence–Haverhill, MA–NH
Lowell, MA–NH
Nashua, NH
Salem–Gloucester, MA

Buffalo–Niagara Falls, NY
Buffalo, NY
Niagara Falls, NY

**Chicago–Gary–Lake County,
IL–IN–WI**
Aurora–Elgin, IL
Chicago, IL
Gary–Hammond, IN
Joliet, IL
Kenosha, WI
Lake County, IL

Cincinnati–Hamilton, OH–KY–IN
Cincinnati, OH–KY–IN
Hamilton–Middletown, OH

Cleveland–Akron–Lorain, OH
Akron, OH
Cleveland, OH
Lorain–Elyria, OH

Dallas–Fort Worth, TX
Dallas, TX
Fort Worth–Arlington, TX

Denver–Boulder, CO
Boulder–Longmont, CO
Denver, CO

Detroit–Ann Arbor, MI
Ann Arbor, MI
Detroit, MI

**Hartford–New Britain–
Middletown, CT**
Bristol, CT
Hartford, CT
Middletown, CT
New Britain, CT

Houston–Galveston–Brazoria, TX
Brazoria, TX
Galveston–Texas City, TX
Houston, TX

**Los Angeles–Anaheim–
Riverside, CA**
Anaheim–Santa Ana, CA
Los Angeles–Long Beach, CA
Oxnard–Ventura, CA
Riverside–San Bernardino, CA

Miami–Fort Lauderdale, FL
Fort Lauderdale–Hollywood–Pompano
    Beach, FL
Miami–Hialeah, FL

Milwaukee–Racine, WI
Milwaukee, WI
Racine, WI

**New York–Northern New Jersey–
Long Island, NY–NJ–CT**
Bergen–Passaic, NJ
Bridgeport–Milford, CT
Danbury, CT
Jersey City, NJ
Middlesex–Somerset–Hunterdon, NJ
Monmouth–Ocean, NJ
Nassau–Suffolk, NY
New York, NY
Newark, NJ

Norwalk, CT
Orange County, NY
Stamford, CT

**Philadelphia–Wilmington–Trenton,
PA–NJ–DE–MD**
Philadelphia, PA–NJ
Trenton, NJ
Vineland–Millville–Bridgeton, NJ
Wilmington, DE–NJ–MD

Pittsburgh–Beaver Valley, PA
Beaver County, PA
Pittsburgh, PA

Portland–Vancouver, OR–WA
Portland, OR
Vancouver, WA

**Providence–Pawtucket–Fall River,
RI–MA**
Fall River, MA–RI
Pawtucket–Woonsocket–
    Attleboro, RI–MA
Providence, RI

**San Francisco–Oakland–
San Jose, CA**
Oakland, CA
San Francisco, CA
San Jose, CA
Santa Cruz, CA
Santa Rosa–Petaluma, CA
Vallejo–Fairfield–Napa, CA

Seattle–Tacoma, WA
Seattle, WA
Tacoma, WA

Metro Areas by State*

Alabama
Anniston
Birmingham
Columbus (GA–AL)
Decatur
Dothan
Florence
Gadsden
Huntsville
Mobile
Montgomery
Tuscaloosa

Alaska
Anchorage

Arizona
Phoenix
Tucson

Arkansas
Fayetteville–Springdale
Fort Smith (AR–OK)
Little Rock–North Little Rock
Memphis (TN–AR–MS)
Pine Bluff
Texarkana (TX)–Texarkana
(AR)

California
Anaheim–Santa Ana
Bakersfield
Chico
Fresno
Los Angeles–Long Beach
Merced
Modesto
Oakland
Oxnard–Ventura
Redding
Riverside–San Bernardino
Sacramento
Salinas–Seaside–Monterey
San Diego
San Francisco
San Jose
Santa Barbara–Santa
Maria–Lompoc
Santa Cruz
Santa Rosa–Petaluma
Stockton
Vallejo–Fairfield–Napa
Visalia–Tulare–Porterville
Yuba City

Colorado
Boulder–Longmont
Colorado Springs
Denver
Fort Collins–Loveland
Greeley
Pueblo

Connecticut
Bridgeport–Milford
Bristol
Danbury
Hartford
Middletown
New Britain
New Haven–Meriden
New London–Norwich (CT–RI)

Norwalk
Stamford
Waterbury

Delaware
Wilmington (DE–NJ–MD)

District of Columbia
Washington (DC–MD–VA)

Florida
Bradenton
Daytona Beach
Fort Lauderdale–Hollywood–
Pompano Beach
Fort Myers–Cape Coral
Fort Pierce
Fort Walton Beach
Gainesville
Jacksonville
Lakeland–Winter Haven
Melbourne–Titusville–Palm
Bay
Miami–Hialeah
Naples
Ocala
Orlando
Panama City
Pensacola
Sarasota
Tallahassee
Tampa–St. Petersburg–
Clearwater
West Palm Beach–Boca
Raton–Delray Beach

Georgia
Albany
Athens
Atlanta
Augusta (GA–SC)
Chattanooga (TN–GA)
Columbus (GA–AL)
Macon–Warner Robins
Savannah

Hawaii
Honolulu

Idaho
Boise City

Illinois
Aurora–Elgin
Bloomington–Normal
Champaign–Urbana–Rantoul
Chicago
Davenport–Rock
Island–Moline (IA–IL)
Decatur
Joliet
Kankakee
Lake County
Peoria
Rockford
St. Louis (MO–IL)
Springfield

Indiana
Anderson
Bloomington
Cincinnati (OH–KY–IN)
Elkhart–Goshen

Evansville (IN–KY)
Fort Wayne
Gary–Hammond
Indianapolis
Kokomo
Lafayette–West Lafayette
Louisville (KY–IN)
Muncie
South Bend–Mishawaka
Terre Haute

Iowa
Cedar Rapids
Davenport–Rock
Island–Moline (IA–IL)
Des Moines
Dubuque
Iowa City
Omaha (NE–IA)
Sioux City (IA–NE)
Waterloo–Cedar Falls

Kansas
Lawrence
Topeka
Wichita

Kentucky
Cincinnati (OH–KY–IN)
Clarksville–Hopkinsville
(TN–KY)
Evansville (IN–KY)
Huntington–Ashland
(WV–KY–OH)
Lexington–Fayette
Louisville (KY–IN)
Owensboro

Louisiana
Alexandria
Baton Rouge
Houma–Thibodaux
Lafayette
Lake Charles
Monroe
New Orleans
Shreveport

Maine
Bangor
Lewiston–Auburn
Portland
Portsmouth–Dover–Rochester
(NH–ME)

Maryland
Baltimore
Cumberland (MD–WV)
Hagerstown
Washington (DC–MD–VA)
Wilmington (DE–NJ–MD)

Massachusetts
Boston
Brockton
Fall River (MA–RI)
Fitchburg–Leominster
Lawrence–Haverhill (MA–NH)
Lowell (MA–NH)
New Bedford
Pawtucket–Woonsocket–
Attleboro (RI–MA)
Pittsfield

Salem–Gloucester
Springfield
Worcester

Michigan
Ann Arbor
Battle Creek
Benton Harbor
Detroit
Flint
Grand Rapids
Jackson
Kalamazoo
Lansing–East Lansing
Muskegon
Saginaw–Bay City–Midland

Minnesota
Duluth (MN–WI)
Fargo–Moorhead (ND–MN)
Minneapolis–St. Paul
(MN–WI)
Rochester
St. Cloud

Mississippi
Biloxi–Gulfport
Jackson
Memphis (TN–AR–MS)
Pascagoula

Missouri
Columbia
Joplin
Kansas City
St. Joseph
St. Louis (MO–IL)
Springfield

Montana
Billings
Great Falls

Nebraska
Lincoln
Omaha (NE–IA)
Sioux City (IA–NE)

Nevada
Las Vegas
Reno

New Hampshire
Lawrence–Haverhill (MA–NH)
Lowell (MA–NH)
Manchester
Nashua
Portsmouth–Dover–Rochester
(NH–ME)

New Jersey
Allentown–Bethlehem (PA–NJ)
Atlantic City
Bergen–Passaic
Jersey City
Middlesex–Somerset–
Hunterdon
Monmouth–Ocean
Newark
Philadelphia (PA–NJ)
Trenton
Vineland–Millville–Bridgeton
Wilmington (DE–NJ–MD)

---

*Many metro areas include parts of two or more states; these are listed under every state in which they have a component county.

New Mexico
Albuquerque
Las Cruces
Santa Fe

New York
Albany–Schenectady–Troy
Binghamton
Buffalo
Elmira
Glens Falls
Nassau–Suffolk
New York
Niagara Falls
Orange County
Poughkeepsie
Rochester
Syracuse
Utica–Rome

North Carolina
Asheville
Burlington
Charlotte–Gastonia–Rock Hill
(NC–SC)
Fayetteville
Greensboro–Winston-Salem–
High Point
Hickory
Jacksonville
Raleigh–Durham
Wilmington

North Dakota
Bismarck
Fargo–Moorhead (ND–MN)
Grand Forks

Ohio
Akron
Canton
Cincinnati (OH–KY–IN)
Cleveland
Columbus
Dayton–Springfield
Hamilton–Middletown
Huntington–Ashland
(WV–KY–OH)
Lima
Lorain–Elyria
Mansfield
Parkersburg–Marietta
(WV–OH)
Steubenville–Weirton (OH–WV)

Toledo
Wheeling (WV–OH)
Youngstown–Warren

Oklahoma
Enid
Fort Smith (AR–OK)
Lawton
Oklahoma City
Tulsa

Oregon
Eugene–Springfield
Medford
Portland
Salem

Pennsylvania
Allentown–Bethlehem (PA–NJ)
Altoona
Beaver County
Erie
Harrisburg–Lebanon–Carlisle
Johnstown
Lancaster
Philadelphia (PA–NJ)
Pittsburgh
Reading
Scranton–Wilkes-Barre
Sharon
State College
Williamsport
York

Rhode Island
Fall River (MA–RI)
New London–Norwich (CT–RI)
Pawtucket–Woonsocket–
Attleboro (RI–MA)
Providence

South Carolina
Anderson
Augusta (GA–SC)
Charleston
Charlotte–Gastonia–Rock Hill
(NC–SC)
Columbia
Florence
Greenville–Spartanburg

South Dakota
Rapid City
Sioux Falls

Tennessee
Chattanooga (TN–GA)
Clarksville–Hopkinsville (TN–KY)
Jackson
Johnson City–Kingsport–
Bristol (TN–VA)
Knoxville
Memphis (TN–AR–MS)
Nashville

Texas
Abilene
Amarillo
Austin
Beaumont–Port Arthur
Brazoria
Brownsville–Harlingen
Bryan–College Station
Corpus Christi
Dallas
El Paso
Fort Worth–Arlington
Galveston–Texas City
Houston
Killeen–Temple
Laredo
Longview–Marshall
Lubbock
McAllen–Edinburg–Mission
Midland
Odessa
San Angelo
San Antonio
Sherman–Denison
Texarkana (TX)–Texarkana
(AR)
Tyler
Victoria
Waco
Wichita Falls

Utah
Provo–Orem
Salt Lake City–Ogden

Vermont
Burlington

Virginia
Charlottesville
Danville
Johnson City–Kingsport–
Bristol (TN–VA)
Lynchburg

Norfolk–Virginia Beach–
Newport News
Richmond–Petersburg
Roanoke
Washington (DC–MD–VA)

Washington
Bellingham
Bremerton
Olympia
Richland–Kennewick–Pasco
Seattle
Spokane
Tacoma
Vancouver
Yakima

West Virginia
Charleston
Cumberland (MD–WV)
Huntington–Ashland
(WV–KY–OH)
Parkersburg–Marietta
(WV–OH)
Steubenville–Weirton (OH–WV)
Wheeling (WV–OH)

Wisconsin
Appleton–Oshkosh–Neenah
Duluth (MN–WI)
Eau Claire
Green Bay
Janesville–Beloit
Kenosha
La Crosse
Madison
Milwaukee
Minneapolis–St. Paul (MN–WI)
Racine
Sheboygan
Wausau

Wyoming
Casper
Cheyenne

Metropolitan Place Finder

The following listing includes 2,435 cities, towns, and unincorporated areas with populations over 10,000 within metro area boundaries. Whenever these boundaries cross state lines, the state abbreviation for each place is also included.

Abilene, TX
Abilene, 112,430

Akron, OH
Akron, 222,060
Barberton, 27,790
Cuyahoga Falls, 41,820
Kent, 27,950
Norton, 11,980
Portage Lakes, 11,310
Ravenna, 11,610
Stow, 25,770
Tallmadge, 14,420

Albany, GA
Albany, 84,950

Albany–Schenectady–Troy, NY
Albany, 97,020
Amsterdam, 20,760
Cohoes, 17,120
Latham, 11,182
Loudonville, 11,480
Roessleville, 11,685
Rotterdam, 22,933
Saratoga Springs, 24,360
Schenectady, 67,210
Troy, 53,960
Watervliet, 11,390

Albuquerque, NM
Albuquerque, 366,750
North Valley, 13,006
South Valley, 38,916

Alexandria, LA
Alexandria, 51,440
Pineville, 14,380

Allentown–Bethlehem, PA–NJ
Allentown, PA, 104,360
Bethlehem, PA, 70,340
Easton, PA, 26,540
Emmaus, PA, 11,110
Phillipsburg, NJ, 16,060

Altoona, PA
Altoona, 53,160

Amarillo, TX
Amarillo, 165,850
Canyon, 11,250

Anaheim–Santa Ana, CA
Anaheim, 240,730
Brea, 32,700
Buena Park, 66,170

Costa Mesa, 88,270
Cypress, 43,210
Fountain Valley, 55,390
Fullerton, 108,750
Garden Grove, 134,850
Huntington Beach, 183,620
Irvine, 88,440
La Habra, 48,160
La Palma, 15,870
Laguna Beach, 18,660
Laguna Hills, 33,600
Los Alamitos, 11,880
Mission Viejo, 50,666
Newport Beach, 66,740
Orange, 100,740
Placentia, 38,250
Rossmoor, 10,457
San Clemente, 33,200
San Juan Capistrano, 23,000
Santa Ana, 236,780
Seal Beach, 26,870
Stanton, 27,880
Tustin, 41,970
Westminster, 73,230
Yorba Linda, 39,810

Anchorage, AK
Anchorage, 235,000

Anderson, IN
Anderson, 61,020
Elwood, 10,030

Anderson, SC
Anderson, 28,680

Ann Arbor, MI
Ann Arbor, 107,810
Ypsilanti, 23,130

Anniston, AL
Anniston, 29,370
Saks, 11,118

Appleton–Oshkosh–Neenah, WI
Appleton, 64,190
Kaukauna, 12,260
Menasha, 14,750
Neenah, 23,410
Oshkosh, 51,190

Asheville, NC
Asheville, 60,290

Athens, GA
Athens, 43,100

Atlanta, GA
Atlanta, 421,910

Belvedere Park, 17,766
Candler–McAfee, 27,306
College Park, 27,480
Covington, 12,670
Decatur, 18,470
Druid Hills, 12,700
Dunwoody, 17,768
East Point, 37,590
Forest Park, 18,260
Griffin, 22,810
Lawrenceville, 15,360
Mableton, 25,111
Marietta, 42,810
Newnan, 15,150
North Atlanta, 30,521
North Decatur, 11,830
North Druid Hills, 12,438
Panthersville, 11,366
Peachtree City, 12,180
Roswell, 40,390
Sandy Springs, 46,877
Smyrna, 23,630
Snellville, 12,520
Tucker, 25,399

Atlantic City, NJ
Atlantic City, 35,980
Hammonton, 12,300
Ocean City, 15,430
Pleasantville, 14,270
Somers Point, 10,600
Ventnor City, 11,670

Augusta, GA–SC
Aiken, SC 18,290
Augusta, GA 45,440
Martinez, GA 16,472
North Augusta, GA 16,290
South Augusta, GA 51,072
West Augusta, GA 24,242

Aurora–Elgin, IL
Aurora, 85,350
Batavia, 13,840
Carpentersville, 24,960
Elgin, 72,110
Geneva, 10,890
St. Charles, 18,420

Austin, TX
Austin, 466,550
Cedar Hill, 12,470
Georgetown, 15,230
Round Rock, 21,940
San Marcos, 28,690
Taylor, 11,640

Bakersfield, CA
Bakersfield, 150,400

Delano, 20,070
Oildale, 23,382
Ridgecrest, 24,970
Wasco, 11,630

Baltimore, MD
Aberdeen, 11,940
Annapolis, 33,360
Arnold, 12,285
Baltimore, 752,800
Brooklyn Park, 11,508
Carney, 21,488
Catonsville, 33,208
Cockeysville, 17,013
Columbia, 52,518
Crofton, 12,009
Dundalk, 71,293
East Riverdale, 14,117
Edgewood, 19,455
Ellicott City, 21,784
Essex, 39,614
Ferndale, 14,314
Glen Burnie, 37,263
Hillcrest Heights, 17,021
Joppa, 11,348
Lake Shore, 10,181
Lansdowne, 16,759
Lochearn, 26,908
Lutherville–Timonium, 17,854
Middle River, 26,756
Milford Mill, 20,354
Odenton, 13,270
Overlea, 12,965
Parkville, 35,159
Perry Hall, 13,455
Pikesville, 22,555
Randallstown, 25,927
Reisterstown, 19,385
Rosedale, 19,956
Security, 29,453
Severn, 21,147
Severna Park, 21,253
South Gate, 24,185
Towson, 51,083
Westminster, 10,230

Bangor, ME
Bangor, 30,160

Baton Rouge, LA
Baker, 13,900
Baton Rouge, 369,250
Denham Springs, 10,900
Scotlandville, 15,113

Battle Creek, MI
Albion, 10,340
Battle Creek, 54,080
Lakeview, 13,345

Beaumont–Port Arthur, TX
Beaumont, 119,900
Groves, 16,440
Nederland, 16,730
Orange, 24,200
Port Arthur, 62,360
Port Neches, 13,990
Vidor, 12,250

Beaver County, PA
Aliquippa, 15,750
Beaver Falls, 11,110

Bellingham, WA
Bellingham, 44,960

Benton Harbor, MI
Benton Harbor, 14,160
Niles, 12,500
St. Joseph, 10,000

Bergen–Passaic, NJ
Bergenfield, 25,160
Cliffside Park, 20,690
Clifton, 76,430
Dumont, 17,940
Elmwood Park, 18,020
Englewood, 23,410
Fair Lawn, 31,280
Fairview, 10,310
Fort Lee, 32,550
Garfield, 26,350
Glen Rock, 11,010
Hackensack, 35,820
Hasbrouck Heights, 11,720
Hawthorne, 18,620
Hillsdale, 10,350
Lodi, 22,910
New Milford, 16,320
North Arlington, 15,980
Oakland, 12,960
Palisades Park, 13,490
Paramus, 25,840
Passaic, 53,870
Paterson, 139,130
Pompton Lakes, 10,990
Ramsey, 13,150
Ridgefield, 10,000
Ridgefield Park, 12,220
Ridgewood, 24,850
Ringwood, 13,270
River Edge, 10,620
Rutherford, 18,470
Tenafly, 13,300
Totowa, 11,230
Waldwick, 10,450
Wallington, 10,450
Wanaque, 10,590
West Paterson, 11,400
Westwood, 10,910

Billings, MT
Billings, 80,310

Biloxi–Gulfport, MS
Bay St. Louis, 10,260
Biloxi, 47,750
D'Iberville, 13,369
Gulfport, 43,410
Long Beach, 16,850
Orange Grove, 13,476

Binghamton, NY
Binghamton, 52,910
Endicott, 14,110
Endwell, 13,745
Johnson City, 16,460

Birmingham, AL
Alabaster, 12,890
Bessemer, 32,030
Birmingham, 277,510
Center Point, 23,317
Fairfield, 12,880
Forestdale, 10,814
Homewood, 22,000
Hoover, 30,150
Hueytown, 16,560
Jasper, 12,470
Leeds, 10,670
Mountain Brook, 20,260
Vestavia Hills, 17,300

Bismarck, ND
Bismarck, 48,040
Mandan, 15,770

Bloomington, IN
Bloomington, 52,500

Bloomington–Normal, IL
Bloomington, 46,250
Normal, 36,790

Boise City, ID
Boise, 108,390

Boston, MA
Acton, 17,350
Arlington, 44,350
Ashland, 10,870
Bedford, 12,490
Bellingham, 14,230
Belmont, 25,020
Boston, 573,600
Braintree, 34,690
Brookline, 52,360
Burlington, 22,750
Cambridge, 91,260
Canton, 18,340
Carver, 10,470
Chelsea, 25,640
Concord, 16,470
Dedham, 23,810
Duxbury, 13,820
Everett, 36,330
Foxborough, 14,550
Framingham, 63,890
Franklin, 19,620
Hanover, 11,560
Harvard, 13,140
Hingham, 19,670
Holbrook, 10,880
Holliston, 12,980
Hudson, 17,550
Lexington, 28,610
Lynn, 78,560
Lynnfield, 11,350
Malden, 53,490
Mansfield, 14,920
Marlborough, 31,180
Marshfield, 22,180
Medfield, 10,610
Medford, 56,830
Melrose, 28,790
Middleborough, 17,410
Milford, 24,230
Milton, 25,500
Natick, 30,270
Needham, 27,240
Newton, 82,140
North Reading, 11,880
Norton, 13,710
Norwood, 28,220
Pembroke, 14,540
Plymouth, 40,290

Quincy, 82,630
Randolph, 28,580
Reading, 22,550
Revere, 43,510
Rockland, 15,340
Saugus, 25,860
Scituate, 16,960
Sharon, 14,660
Somerville, 72,280
Stoneham, 22,550
Stoughton, 27,190
Sudbury, 14,140
Wakefield, 25,170
Walpole, 19,720
Waltham, 57,090
Watertown, 32,890
Wayland, 12,190
Wellesley, 26,550
Weston, 10,700
Westwood, 12,580
Weymouth, 54,480
Wilmington, 17,530
Winchester, 20,120
Winthrop, 18,640
Woburn, 37,380

Boulder–Longmont, CO
Boulder, 76,480
Broomfield, 24,420
Lafayette, 13,840
Longmont, 50,660

Bradenton, FL
Bayshore Gardens, 14,945
Bradenton, 37,450
South Bradenton, 14,297

Brazoria, TX
Alvin, 19,400
Angleton, 15,700
Freeport, 12,310
Lake Jackson, 20,740
Pearland, 17,020

Bremerton, WA
Bremerton, 34,100

Bridgeport–Milford, CT
Ansonia, 18,980
Bridgeport, 141,860
Derby, 12,040
Fairfield, 52,670
Milford, 49,250
Monroe, 16,120
Seymour, 13,580
Shelton, 34,840
Stratford, 50,370
Trumbull, 33,180

Bristol, CT
Bristol, 58,940
Plymouth, 11,090

Brockton, MA
Abington, 13,630
Bridgewater, 18,420
Brockton, 93,870
East Bridgewater, 10,080
Easton, 19,090
Whitman, 13,350

Brownsville–Harlingen, TX
Brownsville, 102,110
Harlingen, 54,980
San Benito, 21,670

Bryan–College Station, TX
Bryan, 62,220
College Station, 45,910

Buffalo, NY
Buffalo, 324,820
Cheektowaga, 92,145
Depew, 19,340
Hamburg, 10,580
Kenmore, 17,290
Lackawanna, 21,380
Lancaster, 13,410
Tonawanda, 18,240

Burlington, NC
Burlington, 36,830

Burlington, VT
Burlington, 38,310
Colchester, 14,590
Essex, 15,420
South Burlington, 11,420

Canton, OH
Alliance, 23,320
Canton, 87,110
Massillon, 31,880
North Canton, 14,500

Casper, WY
Casper, 47,310

Cedar Rapids, IA
Cedar Rapids, 108,370
Marion, 20,570

Champaign–Urbana–Rantoul, IL
Champaign, 59,180
Rantoul, 20,690
Urbana, 35,770

Charleston, SC
Charleston, 68,900
Goose Creek, 25,020
Hanahan, 13,710
James Island, 24,124
Ladson, 13,246
Mount Pleasant, 22,070
North Charleston, 61,430
Summerville, 17,170

Charleston, WV
Charleston, 57,920
St. Albans, 12,010
South Charleston, 14,990

Charlotte–Gastonia–Rock Hill, NC–SC
Charlotte, NC, 352,070
Concord, NC, 20,100
Gastonia, NC, 52,850
Kannapolis, NC, 34,564
Mint Hill, NC, 13,460
Monroe, NC, 17,900
North Belmont, NC, 10,762
Rock Hill, SC, 41,930
Salisbury, NC, 24,220

Charlottesville, VA
Charlottesville, 41,100

Chattanooga, TN–GA
Chattanooga, TN, 162,170
East Ridge, TN, 20,810
Middle Valley, TN, 11,420
Red Bank, TN, 12,910

Cheyenne, WY
Cheyenne, 53,960

Chicago, IL
Addison, 30,700

Alsip, 18,210
Arlington Heights, 70,180
Bartlett, 15,900
Bellwood, 21,730
Bensenville, 15,950
Berwyn, 45,010
Bloomingdale, 13,600
Blue Island, 22,740
Bridgeview, 14,570
Brookfield, 19,020
Buffalo Grove, 27,060
Burbank, 28,530
Calumet City, 39,820
Carol Stream, 22,030
Chicago, 3,009,530
Chicago Heights, 35,540
Chicago Ridge, 14,200
Cicero, 61,600
Country Club Hills, 15,440
Crestwood, 11,830
Crystal Lake, 20,460
Darien, 16,390
Des Plaines, 56,170
Dolton, 23,910
Downers Grove, 42,400
Elk Grove, 32,220
Elmhurst, 42,410
Elmwood Park, 23,220
Evanston, 71,570
Evergreen Park, 21,010
Forest Park, 15,290
Franklin Park, 18,140
Glen Ellyn, 24,750
Glendale Heights, 24,890
Glenview, 34,500
Glenwood, 10,400
Hanover Park, 31,290
Harvey, 35,370
Hazel Crest, 13,780
Hickory Hills, 14,260
Hinsdale, 16,060
Hoffman Estates, 41,490
Homewood, 18,970
Justice, 10,870
La Grange, 15,270
La Grange Park, 12,740
Lansing, 28,910
Lincolnwood, 11,950
Lisle, 16,070
Lombard, 37,890
Markham, 15,300
Matteson, 11,980
Maywood, 27,270
McHenry, 13,550
Melrose Park, 20,920
Midlothian, 14,440
Morton Grove, 23,650
Mount Prospect, 54,630
Naperville, 66,930
Niles, 29,480
Norridge, 15,620
Northbrook, 31,920
Northlake, 12,290
Oak Forest, 25,020
Oak Lawn, 58,240
Oak Park, 54,320
Orland Park, 29,250
Palatine, 34,080
Palos Heights, 10,600
Palos Hills, 16,970
Park Forest, 25,880
Park Ridge, 37,420
Prospect Heights, 13,500
Richton Park, 10,260
River Forest, 11,700
River Grove, 10,180
Riverdale, 12,510

Rolling Meadows, 21,830
Roselle, 19,670
Sauk Village, 10,860
Schaumburg, 60,120
Schiller Park, 11,330
Skokie, 59,430
South Holland, 23,480
Streamwood, 24,420
Summit, 10,330
Tinley Park, 28,400
Villa Park, 21,810
West Chicago, 14,230
Westchester, 17,280
Western Springs, 12,480
Westmont, 20,450
Wheaton, 47,610
Wheeling, 26,420
Wilmette, 26,900
Winnetka, 12,370
Wood Dale, 11,320
Woodridge, 25,190
Woodstock, 12,500
Worth, 11,830

Chico, CA

Chico, 32,680
Chico North, 11,733
Paradise, 25,130

Cincinnati, OH–KY–IN

Blue Ash, OH, 10,360
Bridgetown, OH, 11,460
Cincinnati, OH, 369,750
Covington, KY, 45,670
Delhi Hills, OH, 27,647
Erlanger, KY, 14,540
Florence, KY, 17,750
Forest Park, OH, 18,330
Fort Thomas, KY, 15,670
Franklin, OH, 10,640
Mason, OH, 11,050
Montgomery, OH, 11,110
Newport, KY, 19,780
North College Hill, OH, 10,490
Norwood, OH, 24,980
Reading, OH, 11,960
Sharonville, OH, 11,200
Springdale, OH, 12,220

Clarksville–Hopkinsville, TN–KY

Clarksville, TN 60,730
Hopkinsville, KY 29,100

Cleveland, OH

Bay Village, 17,480
Bedford, 14,620
Bedford Heights, 12,350
Berea, 18,770
Brecksville, 11,160
Broadview Heights, 10,710
Brook Park, 24,790
Brooklyn, 12,020
Brunswick, 28,590
Cleveland, 535,830
Cleveland Heights, 54,720
East Cleveland, 36,330
Eastlake, 21,740
Euclid, 57,390
Fairview Park, 18,290
Garfield Heights, 33,360
Lakewood, 59,540
Lyndhurst, 16,430
Maple Heights, 28,350
Mayfield Heights, 19,820
Medina, 16,530
Mentor, 43,190
Middleburg Heights, 14,990

North Olmsted, 35,880
North Royalton, 19,580
Painesville, 16,350
Parma, 89,460
Parma Heights, 21,970
Rocky River, 20,280
Seven Hills, 13,070
Shaker Heights, 30,850
Solon, 16,760
South Euclid, 24,950
Strongsville, 32,690
University Heights, 15,240
Wadsworth, 15,210
Warrensville Heights, 16,070
Westlake, 23,160
Wickliffe, 15,260
Willoughby, 19,370
Willowick, 16,080

Colorado Springs, CO

Colorado Springs, 272,660
Fountain, 10,710
Security–Widefield, 18,768

Columbia, MO

Columbia, 63,140

Columbia, SC

Cayce, 11,020
Columbia, 93,020
Dentsville, 13,579
North Trenholm, 10,962
Seven Oaks, 16,604
St. Andrews, 22,456
West Columbia, 11,240

Columbus, GA–AL

Columbus, GA 180,180
Phenix City, AL 27,240

Columbus, OH

Bexley, 13,540
Blacklick Estates, 11,223
Circleville, 11,980
Columbus, 566,030
Delaware, 19,380
Gahanna, 21,470
Grove City, 18,390
Lancaster, 34,670
Lincoln Village, 10,548
Newark, 41,200
Reynoldsburg, 22,850
Upper Arlington, 36,620
Westerville, 26,870
Whitehall, 22,640
Worthington, 21,020

Corpus Christi, TX

Corpus Christi, 263,900
Portland, 12,450
Robstown, 13,220

Cumberland, MD–WV

Cumberland, MD, 23,230

Dallas, TX

Allen, 15,340
Balch Springs, 19,440
Carrollton, 61,960
Dallas, 1,003,520
Denton, 55,160
De Soto, 25,440
Duncanville, 35,080
Ennis, 13,460
Farmers Branch, 29,410
Garland, 176,510
Grand Prairie, 95,880
Irving, 128,530
Lancaster, 20,430

Lewisville, 27,630
McKinney, 20,570
Mesquite, 88,700
Plano, 111,030
Richardson, 78,040
Rockwall, 10,630
Rowlett, 12,100
Terrell, 14,470
The Colony, 27,480
University Park, 24,690
Waxahachie, 18,230

Danbury, CT

Bethel, 17,430
Brookfield, 14,320
Danbury, 64,530
New Fairfield, 13,810
New Milford, 21,720
Newtown, 21,280
Ridgefield, 21,660

Danville, VA

Danville, 44,700

Davenport–Rock Island–Moline, IA–IL

Bettendorf, IA, 27,930
Davenport, IA, 98,750
East Moline, IL, 20,760
Kewanee, IL, 13,150
Moline, IL, 44,500
Rock Island, IL, 43,720

Dayton–Springfield, OH

Beavercreek, 34,400
Centerville, 20,050
Dayton, 178,920
Englewood, 11,300
Fairborn, 28,060
Huber Heights, 45,530
Kettering, 59,810
Miamisburg, 16,980
Overlook–Page Manor, 14,825
Piqua, 20,320
Shiloh, 11,735
Springfield, 69,500
Troy, 19,620
Vandalia, 12,440
West Carrollton, 13,430
Xenia, 23,740

Daytona Beach, FL

Daytona Beach, 58,050
De Land, 18,440
Deltona, 15,710
Edgewater, 11,630
Holly Hill, 11,030
New Smyrna Beach, 15,010
Ormond Beach, 28,240
Port Orange, 29,600
South Daytona, 12,000

Decatur, AL

Decatur, 45,000

Decatur, IL

Decatur, 90,360

Denver, CO

Applewood, 12,040
Arvada, 91,310
Aurora, 217,990
Brighton, 14,540
Castlewood, 16,413
Columbine, 23,523
Commerce City, 17,130
Denver, 505,000
Englewood, 30,490
Golden, 14,630
Ken Caryl, 10,661

Lakewood, 122,140
Littleton, 32,270
Northglenn, 29,480
Sherrelwood, 17,629
Southglenn, 37,787
Thornton, 50,000
Westminster, 66,800
Wheat Ridge, 30,050

Des Moines, IA
Ankeny, 16,730
Des Moines, 192,060
Indianola, 11,670
Urbandale, 19,760
West Des Moines, 23,790

Detroit, MI
Allen Park, 31,130
Auburn Hills, 16,000
Berkley, 17,470
Beverly Hills, 10,880
Birmingham, 20,540
Bloomfield Township, 42,876
Clawson, 14,100
Dearborn, 86,420
Dearborn Heights, 61,850
Detroit, 1,086,220
East Detroit, 35,120
Ecorse, 13,050
Farmington, 10,120
Farmington Hills, 65,340
Ferndale, 25,070
Fraser, 13,830
Garden City, 32,530
Grosse Pointe Farms, 10,551
Grosse Pointe Park, 14,230
Grosse Pointe Woods, 16,440
Hamtramck, 18,690
Harper Woods, 14,710
Hazel Park, 20,200
Highland Park, 25,620
Inkster, 31,900
Lincoln Park, 42,850
Livonia, 100,540
Madison Heights, 33,540
Melvindale, 11,150
Monroe, 21,830
Mount Clemens, 19,300
Novi, 27,990
Oak Park, 31,120
Pontiac, 71,030
Port Huron, 33,770
River Rouge, 11,350
Riverview, 14,000
Rochester Hills, 49,670
Romulus, 24,100
Roseville, 51,790
Royal Oak, 66,190
St. Clair Shores, 72,100
Southfield, 72,910
Southgate, 30,390
Sterling Heights, 111,960
Taylor, 72,440
Trenton, 21,170
Troy, 67,270
Warren, 149,800
Wayne, 21,000
Westland, 81,190
Woodhaven, 11,170
Wyandotte, 31,350

Dothan, AL
Dothan, 53,310
Ozark, 14,910

Dubuque, IA
Dubuque, 59,700

Duluth, MN–WI
Duluth, MN 82,380
Hibbing, MN 19,030
Superior, WI 26,950

Eau Claire, WI
Chippewa Falls, 12,840
Eau Claire, 54,580

El Paso, TX
El Paso, 491,800

Elkhart–Goshen, IN
Elkhart, 44,180
Goshen, 21,370

Elmira, NY
Elmira, 32,450

Enid, OK
Enid, 50,350

Erie, PA
Erie, 115,270

Eugene–Springfield, OR
Eugene, 105,410
River Road, 10,370
Santa Clara, 14,288
Springfield, 38,400

Evansville, IN–KY
Evansville, IN, 129,480
Henderson, KY, 25,560

Fall River, MA–RI
Fall River, MA, 90,420
Somerset, MA, 18,230
Swansea, MA, 15,790
Tiverton, RI, 14,240
Westport, MA, 14,010

Fargo–Moorhead, ND–MN
Fargo, ND, 68,020
Moorhead, MN, 28,360
West Fargo, ND, 11,260

Fayetteville, NC
Fayetteville, 75,770

Fayetteville–Springdale, AR
Fayetteville, 40,110
Springdale, 26,170

Fitchburg–Leominster, MA
Fitchburg, 39,040
Leominster, 35,060

Flint, MI
Beecher, 17,178
Burton, 29,420
Flint, 145,590

Florence, AL
Florence, 36,100
Sheffield, 10,910

Florence, SC
Florence, 31,670

Fort Collins–Loveland, CO
Fort Collins, 74,140
Loveland, 35,510

**Fort Lauderdale–
Hollywood–Pompano
Beach, FL**
Coconut Creek, 20,510
Cooper City, 15,820
Coral Springs, 60,460
Dania, 12,370

Davie, 37,350
Deerfield Beach, 44,010
Fort Lauderdale, 148,620
Hallandale, 36,760
Hollywood, 120,910
Lauderdale Lakes, 27,440
Lauderhill, 42,500
Lighthouse Point, 11,270
Margate, 39,610
Miramar, 36,950
North Lauderdale, 23,070
Oakland Park, 25,120
Pembroke Pines, 49,160
Plantation, 55,880
Pompano Beach, 66,740
Pompano Beach Highlands, 16,154
Sunrise, 52,740
Tamarac, 34,590
Wilton Manors, 12,350

Fort Myers–Cape Coral, FL
Cape Coral, 50,210
Fort Myers, 39,530
North Fort Myers, 22,808

Fort Pierce, FL
Fort Pierce, 36,890
Port St. Lucie, 35,300
Stuart, 10,790

Fort Smith, AR–OK
Fort Smith, AR, 74,320
Van Buren, AR, 12,720

Fort Walton Beach, FL
Fort Walton Beach, 22,890
Niceville, 11,370
Wright, 13,011

Fort Wayne, IN
Fort Wayne, 172,900

Fort Worth–Arlington, TX
Arlington, 249,770
Bedford, 33,390
Benbrook, 19,160
Burleson, 17,030
Cleburne, 22,990
Euless, 29,170
Forest Hill, 14,720
Fort Worth, 429,550
Grapevine, 20,990
Haltom City, 33,440
Hurst, 35,150
Mansfield, 12,650
North Richland Hills, 43,960
Watauga, 20,210
Weatherford, 17,240
White Settlement, 17,890

Fresno, CA
Clovis, 41,090
Fresno, 284,660
Reedley, 13,520
Sanger, 14,270
Selma, 13,360

Gadsden, AL
Gadsden, 45,180

Gainesville, FL
Gainesville, 85,170

Galveston–Texas City, TX
Friendswood, 23,550
Galveston, 60,210
La Marque, 15,600
League City, 25,090
Texas City, 42,250

Gary–Hammond, IN
Crown Point, 16,490
East Chicago, 36,950
Gary, 136,790
Griffith, 16,110
Hammond, 86,380
Highland, 24,160
Hobart, 22,140
Lake Station, 14,170
Merrillville, 26,530
Munster, 20,010
Portage, 28,420
Schererville, 14,310
Valparaiso, 22,280

Glens Falls, NY
Glens Falls, 16,080

Grand Forks, ND
Grand Forks, 45,090

Grand Rapids, MI
East Grand Rapids, 11,770
Grand Haven, 12,350
Grand Rapids, 186,530
Grandville, 14,020
Holland, 28,940
Jenison, 16,330
Kentwood, 35,750
Northview, 11,662
Walker, 16,220
Wyoming, 62,420

Great Falls, MT
Great Falls, 57,310

Greeley, CO
Greeley, 56,920

Green Bay, WI
Allouez, 14,882
Ashwaubenon, 15,340
De Pere, 16,070
Green Bay, 93,470

**Greensboro–Winston-Salem–
High Point, NC**
Asheboro, 15,780
Greensboro, 176,650
High Point, 66,560
Lexington, 15,460
Thomasville, 15,490
Winston-Salem, 148,080

Greenville–Spartanburg, SC
Berea, 13,164
Easley, 17,080
Gantt, 13,719
Greenville, 58,370
Greer, 13,040
Simpsonville, 12,640
Spartanburg, 44,210
Taylors, 15,801
Wade Hampton, 20,180

Hagerstown, MD
Hagerstown, 33,670

Hamilton–Middletown, OH
Fairfield, 34,150
Hamilton, 65,050
Middletown, 46,090
Oxford, 16,590
Pisgah, 15,660

**Harrisburg–Lebanon–
Carlisle, PA**
Carlisle, 19,980
Harrisburg, 51,530

Hershey, 13,249
Lebanon, 26,390
Middletown, 10,330

Hartford, CT
Avon, 13,480
Bloomfield, 19,640
East Hartford, 48,520
Ellington, 10,790
Enfield, 42,880
Farmington, 17,830
Glastonbury, 26,380
Hartford, 137,980
Manchester, 49,710
Newington, 29,070
Rocky Hill, 15,820
Simsbury, 22,190
South Windsor, 20,410
Suffield, 10,830
Tolland, 10,720
Vernon, 28,620
West Hartford, 57,650
Wethersfield, 25,910
Windsor, 26,440
Windsor Locks, 11,870

Hickory, NC
Hickory, 25,750
Morganton, 15,420
St. Stephens, 10,797

Honolulu, HI
Aiea, 32,879
Ewa Beach, 14,369
Honolulu, 365,048
Kailua, 35,812
Kaneohe, 29,919
Mililani, 21,365
Mokapu, 11,615
Pearl City, 42,575
Wahiawa, 16,911
Waipahu, 29,139

Houma–Thibodaux, LA
Bayou Cane, 15,723
Houma, 101,600
Thibodaux, 16,700

Houston, TX
Aldine, 12,623
Baytown, 62,770
Bellaire, 14,500
Champions, 14,692
Channelview, 17,471
Cloverleaf, 17,317
Conroe, 20,800
Deer Park, 25,380
Galena Park, 10,040
Houston, 1,728,910
Humble, 12,220
Jacinto City, 11,130
Katy, 10,610
Kingwood, 16,261
La Porte, 25,030
Missouri City, 32,020
Pasadena, 118,050
Richmond, 16,770
Rosenberg, 22,290
South Houston, 14,450
Sugar Land, 21,840
West University Place, 13,340

Huntington–Ashland, WV–KY–OH
Ashland, KY, 26,060
Huntington, WV, 59,310
Ironton, OH, 13,110

Huntsville, AL
Huntsville, 163,420

Indianapolis, IN
Beech Grove, 13,210
Carmel, 20,820
Franklin, 12,110
Greenfield, 11,680
Greenwood, 22,880
Indianapolis, 719,820
Lawrence, 26,480
Lebanon, 11,810
Martinsville, 11,920
Noblesville, 15,160
Plainfield, 10,350
Shelbyville, 14,390
Speedway, 12,510

Iowa City, IA
Iowa City, 50,490

Jackson, MI
Jackson, 39,739

Jackson, MS
Brandon, 14,270
Canton, 11,190
Clinton, 18,590
Jackson, 208,420
Pearl, 21,530
Ridgeland, 10,900

Jackson, TN
Jackson, 52,810

Jacksonville, FL
Jacksonville, 609,860
Jacksonville Beach, 18,720
Lakeside, 10,534
Orange Park, 10,410
St. Augustine, 12,260

Jacksonville, NC
Jacksonville, 28,780

Janesville–Beloit, WI
Beloit, 33,760
Janesville, 51,790

Jersey City, NJ
Bayonne, 62,900
Harrison, 12,470
Hoboken, 41,650
Jersey City, 219,480
Kearny, 34,930
Secaucus, 15,260
Union City, 55,790
West New York, 40,770

Johnson City–Kingsport–Bristol, TN–VA
Bristol, TN, 23,460
Bristol, VA, 18,000
Elizabethton, TN, 12,300
Johnson City, TN, 44,700
Kingsport, TN, 31,470

Johnstown, PA
Johnstown, 31,840

Joliet, IL
Joliet, 76,010
Lockport, 10,160
Romeoville, 15,180

Joplin, MO
Carthage, 11,240
Joplin, 40,220

Kalamazoo, MI
Kalamazoo, 77,230
Portage, 40,430

Kankakee, IL
Bourbonnais, 13,420
Bradley, 10,980
Kankakee, 27,220

Kansas City, MO–KS
Belton, MO, 14,830
Blue Springs, MO, 33,230
Excelsior Springs, MO, 10,880
Gladstone, MO, 27,620
Grandview, MO, 25,050
Independence, MO, 112,950
Kansas City, KS, 162,070
Kansas City, MO, 441,170
Leavenworth, KS, 36,230
Leawood, KS, 16,070
Lees Summit, MO, 36,070
Lenexa, KS, 27,380
Liberty, MO, 18,490
Merriam, KS, 12,020
Olathe, KS, 52,180
Overland Park, KS, 96,510
Prairie Village, KS, 23,820
Raytown, MO, 30,850
Shawnee, KS, 30,240

Kenosha, WI
Kenosha, 74,960

Killeen–Temple, TX
Belton, 12,860
Copperas Cove, 20,960
Killeen, 59,560
Temple, 46,580

Knoxville, TN
Cedar Bluff, 10,654
Halls, 10,363
Knoxville, 173,210
Maryville, 18,060
Oak Ridge, 26,920

Kokomo, IN
Kokomo, 45,610

La Crosse, WI
La Crosse, 47,650
Onalaska, 10,970

Lafayette, LA
Lafayette, 89,830

Lafayette–West Lafayette, IN
Lafayette, 44,240
West Lafayette, 21,110

Lake Charles, LA
Lake Charles, 73,400
Sulphur, 21,450

Lake County, IL
Barrington, 10,220
Deerfield, 17,020
Highland Park, 30,580
Lake Forest, 16,200
Lake Zurich, 10,480
Libertyville, 17,400
Mundelein, 17,910
North Chicago, 43,190
Round Lake Beach, 13,910
Vernon Hills, 12,500
Waukegan, 74,480
Zion, 19,110

Lakeland–Winter Haven, FL
Bartow, 16,080
Haines City, 12,880
Lakeland, 61,890
Lakeland Highlands, 10,426
Winter Haven, 23,790

Lancaster, PA
Columbia, 11,230
Ephrata, 12,270
Lancaster, 57,200

Lansing–East Lansing, MI
Holt, 10,097
Lansing, 128,980

Laredo, TX
Laredo, 117,060

Las Cruces, NM
Las Cruces, 54,090

Las Vegas, NV
Boulder City, 11,280
Henderson, 46,950
Las Vegas, 191,510
North Las Vegas, 50,290
Paradise, 84,818
Sunrise Manor, 44,155
Winchester, 19,728

Lawrence, KS
Lawrence, 56,490

Lawrence–Haverhill, MA–NH
Amesbury, MA, 14,780
Andover, MA, 27,230
Derry, NH, 24,330
Haverhill, MA, 48,620
Lawrence, MA, 63,420
Methuen, MA, 39,470
Newburyport, MA, 16,890
North Andover, MA, 22,390
Salem, NH, 25,210

Lawton, OK
Lawton, 82,830

Lewiston–Auburn, ME
Auburn, 22,870
Lewiston, 38,980

Lexington–Fayette, KY
Georgetown, 12,360
Lexington, 212,900
Nicholasville, 14,010
Winchester, 16,120

Lima, OH
Lima, 45,990

Lincoln, NE
Lincoln, 183,050

Little Rock–North Little Rock, AR
Benton, 18,220
Conway, 23,450
Jacksonville, 29,650
Little Rock, 181,030
North Little Rock, 63,540
Sherwood, 15,450

Longview–Marshall, TX
Kilgore, 12,200
Longview, 73,870
Marshall, 24,210

Lorain–Elyria, OH
Amherst, 10,430

Avon Lake, 13,400
Elyria, 57,270
Lorain, 72,210
North Ridgeville, 21,960
Sheffield Lake, 10,380

Los Angeles–Long Beach, CA

Agoura Hills, 17,040
Alhambra, 71,690
Alondra, 12,096
Altadena, 40,983
Arcadia, 47,740
Artesia, 14,940
Avocado Heights, 11,721
Azusa, 35,750
Baldwin Park, 63,040
Bell, 29,240
Bell Gardens, 36,930
Bellflower, 58,530
Beverly Hills, 33,690
Burbank, 89,120
Canyon Country, 15,728
Carson, 87,840
Cerritos, 57,180
Citrus, 12,450
Claremont, 34,650
Commerce, 11,220
Compton, 93,530
Covina, 40,870
Cudahy, 20,930
Culver City, 39,680
Diamond Bar, 28,045
Downey, 85,370
Duarte, 20,760
East Los Angeles, 110,017
El Monte, 96,620
El Segundo, 15,130
Florence–Graham, 48,662
Gardena, 49,270
Glendale, 153,660
Glendora, 41,190
Hacienda Heights, 49,422
Hawaiian Gardens, 12,480
Hawthorne, 60,810
Hermosa Beach, 18,620
Huntington Park, 55,010
Inglewood, 102,550
La Canada Flintridge, 20,290
La Crescenta–Montrose, 16,531
La Mirada, 41,660
La Puente, 33,970
La Verne, 28,030
Lakewood, 75,840
Lancaster, 63,530
Lawndale, 26,450
Lennox, 18,445
Lomita, 19,960
Long Beach, 396,280
Los Angeles, 3,259,340
Lynwood, 55,890
Manhattan Beach, 34,580
Maywood, 25,970
Monrovia, 33,120
Montebello, 54,750
Monterey Park, 60,850
Newhall, 12,029
Norwalk, 90,050
Palmdale, 27,340
Palos Verdes Estates, 14,590
Paramount, 42,750
Pasadena, 129,900
Pico Rivera, 54,340
Pomona, 115,540
Rancho Palos Verdes, 46,540
Redondo Beach, 63,830
Rosemead, 47,520

San Dimas, 28,840
San Fernando, 20,280
San Gabriel, 33,050
San Marino, 13,780
Santa Fe Springs, 15,340
Santa Monica, 93,170
Saugus, 16,283
Sierra Madre, 10,990
South El Monte, 17,960
South Gate, 80,580
South Oasadena, 23,660
South San Jose Hills, 16,049
South Whittier, 43,815
Temple City, 31,080
Torrance, 135,570
Valencia, 12,163
Valinda, 18,700
Walnut, 20,780
Walnut Park, 11,811
West Carson, 17,997
West Covina, 96,890
West Hollywood, 35,703
West Puente Valley, 20,445
West Whittier–Los Nietos, 21,001
Whittier, 72,660
Willow Brook, 30,845

Louisville, KY–IN

Clarksville, IN, 14,480
Fern Creek, KY, 16,866
Highview, KY, 13,286
Jeffersontown, KY, 19,700
Jeffersonville, IN, 21,330
Louisville, KY, 286,470
New Albany, IN, 37,260
Newburg, KY, 24,612
Okolona, KY, 20,039
Pleasure Ridge Park, KY, 27,332
St. Matthews, KY, 13,920
Shively, KY, 14,790
Valley Station, KY, 24,474

Lowell, MA–NH

Billerica, MA, 38,230
Chelmsford, MA, 31,810
Dracut, MA, 24,040
Lowell, MA, 92,880
Tewksbury, MA, 25,660
Westford, MA, 15,210

Lubbock, TX

Lubbock, 186,400

Lynchburg, VA

Lynchburg, 68,000
Madison Heights, 14,146

Macon–Warner Robins, GA

Macon, 118,420
Perry, 10,880
Warner Robins, 45,620

Madison, WI

Fitchburg, 14,270
Madison, 175,830
Middleton, 13,410
Sun Prairie, 14,250

Manchester, NH

Bedford, 11,590
Goffstown, 13,520
Manchester, 97,280

Mansfield, OH

Mansfield, 51,340
Shelby, 10,150

McAllen–Edinburg–Mission, TX

Donna, 12,380

Edinburg, 31,560
McAllen, 83,300
Mercedes, 13,910
Mission, 31,230
Pharr, 25,920
San Juan, 11,100
Weslaco, 24,410

Medford, OR

Ashland, 15,680
Medford, 43,580

Melbourne–Titusville–Palm Bay, FL

Cocoa, 19,120
Cocoa Beach, 12,420
Melbourne, 56,740
Merritt Island, 30,708
Palm Bay, 45,660
Rockledge, 14,190
Titusville, 41,950

Memphis, TN–AR–MS

Bartlett, TN, 22,910
Germantown, TN, 29,240
Memphis, TN, 652,640
Millington, TN, 18,200
Southhaven, MS, 17,650
West Memphis, AR, 27,810

Merced, CA

Atwater, 19,920
Los Banos, 13,240
Merced, 47,020

Miami–Hialeah, FL

Brownsville, 18,058
Carol City, 47,349
Coral Gables, 41,850
Coral Terrace, 20,702
Cutler, 15,593
Cutler Ridge, 20,886
Gladeview, 18,919
Glenvar Heights, 13,216
Golden Glades, 23,154
Hialeah, 161,760
Homestead, 22,280
Ives Estates, 12,623
Kendale Lakes, 32,769
Kendall, 73,758
Leisure City, 17,905
Lindgren Acres, 11,986
Miami, 373,940
Miami Beach, 95,000
Miami Springs, 11,930
Naranja–Princeton, 10,381
Norland, 19,471
North Miami, 42,650
North Miami Beach, 35,850
Olympis Heights, 33,112
Opa-locka, 14,550
Palmetto Estates, 11,116
Perrine, 16,129
Pinewood, 16,252
South Miami, 10,944
South Miami Heights, 23,599
Sunny Isles, 12,564
Sunset, 13,531
Tamiami, 17,607
West Little River, 32,492
Westchester, 29,272
Westwood Lakes, 11,478

Middlesex–Somerset–Hunterdon, NJ

Carteret, 19,530
Highland Park, 13,090
Manville, 10,880

Metuchen, 13,120
Middlesex, 13,290
New Brunswick, 40,230
North Plainfield, 17,910
Old Bridge, 21,815
Perth Amboy, 37,530
Sayreville, 34,310
Somerset, 21,731
Somervillle, 11,540
South Plainfield, 20,330
South River, 13,470

Middletown, CT

Cromwell, 11,210
Middletown, 38,850

Midland, TX

Midland, 98,060

Milwaukee, WI

Brookfield, 33,390
Brown Deer, 12,470
Cudahy, 18,970
Franklin, 19,640
Germantown, 11,980
Glendale, 13,900
Greendale, 16,290
Greenfield, 31,890
Menomonee Falls, 26,720
Mequon, 16,670
Milwaukee, 605,090
Muskego, 15,970
New Berlin, 30,900
Oak Creek, 18,020
Oconomowoc, 10,180
Shorewood, 14,330
South Milwaukee, 20,290
Waukesha, 52,770
Wauwatosa, 49,640
West Allis, 63,940
West Bend, 22,690
Whitefish Bay, 14,270

Minneapolis–St. Paul, MN–WI

Andover, MN, 10,650
Anoka, MN, 15,380
Apple Valley, MN, 28,200
Blaine, MN, 34,430
Bloomington, MN, 85,740
Brooklyn Center, MN, 31,840
Brooklyn Park, MN, 53,550
Burnsville, MN, 40,570
Champlin, MN, 12,400
Columbia Heights, MN, 19,250
Coon Rapids, MN, 43,210
Cottage Grove, MN, 20,900
Crystal, MN, 24,650
Eagan, MN, 32,120
Eden Prairie, MN, 25,840
Edina, MN, 46,330
Fridley, MN, 29,370
Golden Valley, MN, 22,880
Hastings, MN, 14,160
Hopkins, MN, 14,450
Inver Grove Heights, MN, 19,030
Lakeville, MN, 18,870
Maple Grove, MN, 30,150
Maplewood, MN, 32,000
Minneapolis, MN, 356,840
Minnetonka, MN, 44,330
Mounds View, MN, 14,060
New Brighton, MN, 21,850
New Hope, MN, 22,810
North St. Paul, MN, 10,990
Oakdale, MN, 15,370
Plymouth, MN, 46,590
Ramsey, MN, 12,100

Richfield, MN, 36,020
Robbinsdale, MN, 13,910
Roseville, MN, 33,910
St. Louis Park, MN, 43,630
St. Paul, MN, 263,680
Shakopee, MN, 10,790
Shoreview, MN, 24,190
South St. Paul, MN, 20,570
Stillwater, MN, 12,780
Vadnais Heights, MN, 10,150
West St. Paul, MN, 18,620
White Bear Lake, MN, 23,790
Woodbury, MN, 14,760

Mobile, AL

Mobile, 203,260
Prichard, 38,820
Saraland, 10,220
Tillmans Corner, 15,941

Modesto, CA

Ceres, 17,510
Modesto, 132,940
South Modesto, 12,492
Turlock, 33,960

Monmouth–Ocean, NJ

Asbury Park, 16,230
Eatontown, 13,460
Freehold, 10,120
Keansburg, 10,560
Lakewood, 22,863
Long Branch, 29,500
Middletown, 61,615
Point Pleasant, 18,390
Red Bank, 11,710

Monroe, LA

Monroe, 56,210
West Monroe, 16,540

Montgomery, AL

Montgomery, 194,290
Oxford, 10,990
Prattville, 21,120

Muncie, IN

Muncie, 72,600

Muskegon, MI

Muskegon, 39,810
Muskegon Heights, 14,610
Norton Shores, 21,710

Naples, FL

East Naples, 12,127
Immokalee, 11,038
Naples, 19,490

Nashua, NH

Hudson, 17,190
Londonderry, 16,630
Merrimack, 19,220
Milford, 10,270
Nashua, 76,510

Nashville, TN

Brentwood, 12,610
Franklin, 18,500
Gallatin, 19,350
Hendersonville, 30,170
Lebanon, 13,950
Murfreesboro, 40,960
Nashville–Davidson, 473,670
Smyrna, 13,610
Springfield, 10,790

Nassau–Suffolk, NY

Babylon, 12,470
Baldwin, 35,100

Bay Shore, 10,784
Bellmore, 18,106
Bethpage, 16,840
Brentwood, 44,321
Centereach, 30,136
Central Islip, 19,734
Commack, 34,719
Copiague, 20,132
Coram, 24,752
Deer Park, 30,394
Dix Hills, 26,693
East Meadow, 39,317
East Northport, 21,087
East Patchogue, 18,139
East Rockaway, 10,640
East Islip, 13,852
Elmont, 27,592
Elwood, 11,847
Farmingville, 13,398
Floral Park, 16,970
Franklin Square, 29,051
Freeport, 40,320
Garden City, 22,110
Glen Cove, 24,050
Greenlawn, 13,869
Hauppauge, 20,960
Hempstead, 42,730
Hicksville, 43,245
Holbrook, 24,382
Holtsville, 13,515
Huntington, 21,727
Huntington Station, 28,769
Islip, 13,438
Jericho, 12,739
Kings Park, 16,131
Lake Ronkonkoma, 38,336
Levittown, 57,045
Lindenhurst, 26,590
Long Beach, 32,890
Lynbrook, 19,750
Massapequa, 24,454
Massapequa Park, 18,830
Mastic, 10,413
Medford, 20,418
Merrick, 24,478
Mineola, 20,180
Nesconset, 10,706
North Amityville, 13,140
North Babylon, 19,019
North Bayshore, 35,020
North Bellmore, 20,630
North Great River, 11,416
North Lindenhurst, 11,511
North Massapequa, 21,385
North Merrick, 12,848
North New Hyde Park, 15,114
North Valley Stream, 14,530
North Wantagh, 12,677
Oceanside, 33,639
Patchogue, 11,720
Plainview, 28,037
Port Jefferson Station, 17,009
Port Washington, 14,521
Rockville Centre, 25,450
Roosevelt, 14,109
St. James, 12,122
Sayville, 12,013
Seaford, 16,117
Selden, 17,259
Setauket–East Setauket, 10,176
Shirely, 18,072
Smithtown, 30,906
South Farmingdale, 16,439
South Huntington, 14,854
Stony Brook, 16,155
Uniondale, 20,016
Valley Stream, 34,740

Wantagh, 19,817
West Babylon, 41,699
West Hempstead, 18,536
West Islip, 29,533
Westbury, 13,640
Woodmere, 17,205

New Bedford, MA

Dartmouth, 25,610
Fairhaven, 15,690
New Bedford, 96,450

New Britain, CT

Berlin, 16,100
New Britain, 72,040
Plainville, 17,390
Southington, 39,050

New Haven–Meriden, CT

Branford, 25,250
Cheshire, 24,130
East Haven, 25,310
Guilford, 19,160
Hamden, 51,690
Madison, 15,690
Meriden, 58,320
New Haven, 123,450
North Branford, 12,590
North Haven, 22,260
Orange, 13,030
Wallingford, 39,210
West Haven, 53,280

New London–Norwich, CT–RI

East Lyme, CT, 14,400
Groton, CT, 39,730
Ledyard, CT, 14,520
Montville, CT, 17,020
New London, CT, 28,600
Norwich, CT, 38,010
Stonington, CT, 16,660
Waterford, CT, 17,780
Westerly, RI, 19,600

New Orleans, LA

Arabie, 10,248
Chalmette, 33,847
Covington, 10,060
Estelle, 12,724
Gretna, 20,540
Harahan, 11,230
Harvey, 22,709
Jefferson, 15,550
Kenner, 75,710
La Place, 16,112
Marrero, 36,548
Metairie, 164,160
New Orleans, 554,500
River Ridge, 17,146
Slidell, 35,780
Terrytown, 23,548
Timberlane, 11,579
Violet, 11,678
Westwego, 12,010

New York, NY

Eastchester, 20,305
Harrison, 22,920
Hartsdale, 10,216
Jefferson Valley–Yorktown, 13,380
Mamaroneck, 17,040
Monsey, 12,380
Mount Vernon, 68,400
Nanuet, 12,578
New City, 35,859
New Rochelle, 69,170
New York, 7,262,750

Ossining, 21,270
Pearl River, 15,893
Peekskill, 19,420
Port Chester, 22,860
Rye, 14,970
Scarsdale, 17,660
Spring Valley, 21,690
Suffern, 11,000
Tarrytown, 10,750
White Plains, 45,340
Yonkers, 186,080

Newark, NJ

Dover, 14,400
East Orange, 77,420
Elizabeth, 106,540
Florham Park, 10,490
Hopatcong, 15,210
Linden, 37,700
Madison, 15,340
Morristown, 16,760
New Providence, 12,200
Newark, 316,240
Plainfield, 45,980
Rahway, 26,670
Roselle, 20,490
Roselle Park, 13,070
Succasunna–Kenvil, 10,931
Summit, 20,990
Westfield, 30,300

Niagara Falls, NY

Lewiston, 15,360
Lockport, 24,640
Niagara Falls, 64,550
North Tonawanda, 34,540

Norfolk–Virginia Beach–Newport News, VA

Chesapeake, 134,400
Hampton, 126,000
Newport News, 161,700
Norfolk, 274,800
Poquoson, 10,100
Portsmouth, 111,000
Suffolk, 51,300
Virginia Beach, 333,400
Williamsburg, 11,400

Norwalk, CT

Norwalk, 77,220
Westport, 25,080
Wilton, 15,970

Oakland, CA

Alameda, 72,630
Albany, 15,340
Antioch, 50,090
Ashland, 14,810
Berkeley, 104,110
Castro Valley, 44,011
Concord, 105,980
Danville, 28,000
Dublin, 19,110
El Cerrito, 22,940
El Sobrante, 10,535
Fremont, 153,580
Hayward, 101,520
Hercules, 10,580
Lafayette, 22,520
Livermore, 53,790
Martinez, 27,450
Moraga, 15,130
Newark, 37,420
Oakland, 356,960
Orinda, 17,270
Piedmont, 10,420
Pinole, 14,910

Pittsburg, 41,240
Pleasant Hill, 28,480
Pleasanton, 44,350
Richmond, 77,860
San Leandro, 65,800
San Lorenzo, 20,545
San Pablo, 21,560
San Ramon, 26,130
Union City, 50,730
Walnut Creek, 58,650

Ocala, FL

Ocala, 45,120

Odessa, TX

Odessa, 101,210

Oklahoma City, OK

Bethany, 21,920
Choctaw, 10,100
Del City, 26,120
Edmond, 50,980
El Reno, 16,770
Guthrie, 12,250
Midwest City, 53,470
Moore, 41,860
Mustang, 10,980
Norman, 78,390
Oklahoma City, 446,120
Shawnee, 27,570
The Village, 12,290
Warr Acres, 10,640
Yukon, 25,030

Olympia, WA

Lacey, 15,630
Olympia, 29,710

Omaha, NE–IA

Bellevue, NE, 32,200
Council Bluffs, IA, 56,900
La Vista, NE, 10,960
Omaha, NE, 349,270
Papillion, NE, 11,100

Orange County, NY

Middletown, 22,160
Newburgh, 24,370

Orlando, FL

Altamonte Springs, 29,000
Casselberry, 19,360
Conway, 24,027
Fairview Shores, 10,174
Goldenrod, 13,682
Holden Heights, 13,864
Kissimmee, 25,850
Lockhart, 10,569
Longwood, 12,590
Oak Ridge, 15,477
Ocoee, 11,660
Orlando, 145,900
Pine Hills, 35,771
St. Cloud, 11,110
Sanford, 29,580
Union Park, 19,175
Winter Park, 23,340
Winter Springs, 18,680

Owensboro, KY

Owensboro, 56,280

Oxnard–Ventura, CA

Camarillo, 44,560
Fillmore, 10,900
Moorpark, 15,750
Oxnard, 126,980
Port Hueneme, 20,090
Santa Paula, 23,040

Simi Valley, 90,030
Thousand Oaks, 96,280
Ventura, 85,690

Panama City, FL

Callaway, 11,090
Panama City, 35,630

Parkersburg–Marietta, WV–OH

Marietta, OH, 16,140
Parkersburg, WV, 38,540
Vienna, WV, 11,370

Pascagoula, MS

Gautier, 11,580
Moss Point, 19,290
Ocean Springs, 17,600
Pascagoula, 30,860

Pawtucket–Woonsocket–Attleboro, RI–MA

Attleboro, MA, 34,910
Burrillville, RI, 15,650
Central Falls, RI, 17,030
Cumberland, RI, 26,930
Lincoln, RI, 17,520
North Attleborough, MA, 23,460
North Smithfield, RI, 10,600
Pawtucket, RI, 72,640
Seekonk, MA, 12,710
Smithfield, RI, 17,950
Woonsocket, RI, 44,970

Pensacola, FL

Myrtle Grove, 14,238
Pensacola, 63,820
Warrington, 15,792
West Pensacola, 24,371

Peoria, IL

East Peoria, 21,300
Morton, 13,430
Pekin, 31,280
Peoria, 110,290

Philadelphia, PA–NJ

Bellmawr, NJ, 13,600
Browns Mills, NJ, 10,568
Bristol, PA, 10,540
Burlington, NJ, 10,390
Camden, NJ, 82,810
Cheltenham, PA, 35,509
Chester, PA, 43,680
Coatesville, PA, 11,400
Collingswood, NJ, 15,440
Darby, PA, 11,020
East Norriton, PA, 12,711
Glassboro, NJ, 14,420
Gloucester City, NJ, 13,250
Haddonfield, NJ, 12,200
Lansdale, PA, 18,090
Lansdowne, PA, 11,670
Lindenwold, NJ, 18,440
Lower Merion, PA, 59,651
Lower Moreland, PA, 12,472
Morrisville, PA, 10,230
Norristown, PA, 33,780
Philadelphia, PA, 1,642,900
Phoenixville, PA, 13,990
Pottstown, PA, 23,650
Springfield, PA, 20,344
Upper Merion, PA, 26,138
Upper Moreland, PA, 25,874
West Chester, PA, 18,740
West Noriton, PA, 14,034
Whitemarsh, PA, 15,101
Woodbury, NJ, 10,410
Yeadon, PA, 12,310

Phoenix, AZ

Chandler, 68,220
Gilbert, 12,970
Glendale, 125,820
Mesa, 251,430
Paradise Valley, 11,480
Peoria, 29,690
Phoenix, 894,070
Scottsdale, 111,140
Sun City, 40,505
Tempe, 136,480

Pine Bluff, AR

Pine Bluff, 61,320

Pittsburgh, PA

Baldwin, 23,640
Bethel Park, 33,990
Brentwood, 11,220
Carnot–Moon, 11,102
Clairton, 11,860
Dormont, 10,770
Greensburg, 16,840
Jeannette, 12,270
Lower Burrell, 12,690
McKeesport, 27,180
Monessen, 10,430
Monroeville, 29,640
Munhall, 13,660
Murrysville, 16,200
New Kensington, 17,580
Pittsburgh, 387,490
Plum, 25,150
Swissvale, 11,160
Uniontown, 13,030
Washington, 17,730
West Mifflin, 24,610
Whitehall, 14,000
Wilkinsburg, 21,940

Pittsfield, MA

Pittsfield, 49,580

Portland, ME

Gorham, 11,040
Portland, 62,670
Scarborough, 12,330
South Portland, 21,620
Westbrook, 15,310
Windham, 13,020

Portland, OR

Aloha, 28,353
Beaverton, 34,320
Centennial, 22,118
Cully, 10,569
Errol Heights, 10,487
Forest Grove, 11,810
Gresham, 38,850
Hazelwood, 25,541
Hillsboro, 30,930
Lake Oswego, 26,070
McMinnville, 15,130
Milwaukie, 17,960
Newberg, 11,310
Oak Grove, 11,640
Oregon City, 14,810
Parkrose, 21,108
Portland, 387,870
Powellhurst, 20,132
Tigard, 19,330
Tualatin, 11,040
West Linn, 13,300
Wilkes–Rockwood, 23,216

Portsmouth–Dover–Rochester, NH–ME

Dover, NH, 23,770

Durham, NH, 12,440
Exeter, NH, 12,260
Hampton, NH, 11,760
Portsmouth, NH, 25,970
Rochester, NH, 23,370
Somersworth, NH, 10,790
York, ME, 10,310

Poughkeepsie, NY

Arlington, 11,305
Beacon, 13,700
Poughkeepsie, 29,990

Providence, RI

Barrington, 16,110
Bristol, 20,280
Coventry, 30,170
Cranston, 73,760
East Greenwich, 10,550
East Providence, 50,440
Johnston, 25,890
Narragansett, 13,210
North Kingstown, 24,080
North Providence, 29,030
Providence, 157,200
South Kingstown, 21,220
Warren, 11,280
Warwick, 86,960
West Warwick, 28,570

Provo–Orem, UT

American Fork, 15,270
Orem, 61,590
Pleasant Grove, 13,200
Provo, 77,480
Spanish Fork, 10,910
Springville, 13,300

Pueblo, CO

Pueblo, 101,240

Racine, WI

Racine, 82,440

Raleigh–Durham, NC

Cary, 31,370
Chapel Hill, 34,000
Durham, 113,890
Garner, 12,750
Raleigh, 180,430

Rapid City, SD

Rapid City, 52,480

Reading, PA

Reading, 77,620

Redding, CA

Redding, 51,490

Reno, NV

Reno, 110,430
Sparks, 51,980

Richland–Kennewick–Pasco, WA

Kennewick, 39,450
Pasco, 19,150
Richland, 32,580

Richmond–Petersburg, VA

Bon Air, 16,224
Chester, 11,728
Colonial Heights, 16,700
East Highland Park, 11,797
Highland Springs, 12,146
Hopewell, 24,100
Lakeside, 12,289
Laurel, 10,569
Petersburg, 39,800

Richmond, 217,700
Tukahoe, 39,868

Riverside–San Bernardino, CA

Apple Valley, 14,305
Banning, 16,940
Barstow, 20,250
Bloomington, 12,781
Cathedral City, 20,300
Chino, 50,830
Coachella, 13,040
Colton, 29,390
Corona, 46,480
East Hemet, 14,712
Fontana, 55,410
Grand Terrace, 10,240
Hemet, 26,680
Highland, 10,908
Indio, 29,220
Lake Elsinore, 11,950
Loma Linda, 12,140
Montclair, 25,530
Moreno Valley, 68,020
Norco, 22,940
Ontario, 114,320
Palm Desert, 16,900
Palm Springs, 31,010
Perris, 10,160
Rancho Cucamonga, 75,760
Redlands, 52,900
Rialto, 53,790
Riverside, 196,750
Rubidoux, 16,763
San Bernardino, 138,620
San Jacinto, 11,300
Upland, 57,160
Victorville, 22,890
Yucaipa, 23,345

Roanoke, VA

Cave Spring, 21,682
Hollins, 12,295
Roanoke, 101,900
Salem, 23,700

Rochester, MN

Rochester, 58,130

Rochester, NY

Canandaigua, 12,190
Gates, 15,244
Geneva, 15,520
Greece, 16,177
Rochester, 235,970

Rockford, IL

Belvidere, 15,550
Loves Park, 14,250
Machesney Park, 20,870
North Park, 15,806
Rockford, 135,760

Sacramento, CA

Arcade, 41,200
Arden, 54,000
Broderick, 10,194
Carmichael, 43,108
Citrus Heights, 85,911
Davis, 41,230
Fair Oaks, 22,602
Folsom, 18,210
Foothill Farms, 13,700
North Highlands, 37,825
Orangevale, 20,585
Parkway, 12,000
Rancho Cordova, 42,881
Rocklin, 10,150

Roseville, 29,570
Sacramento, 323,550
Sacramento South, 16,400
South Lake Tahoe, 21,290
West Sacramento, 26,250
Woodland, 34,390

Saginaw–Bay City–Midland, MI

Bay City, 39,700
Midland, 35,890
Saginaw, 72,470

St. Cloud, MN

St. Cloud, 42,850

St. Joseph, MO

St. Joseph, 74,070

St. Louis, MO–IL

Affton, MO, 23,181
Alton, IL, 32,960
Arnold, MO, 20,250
Ballwin, MO, 13,750
Bellefontaine Neighbors, MO, 11,610
Belleville, IL, 42,840
Berkeley, MO, 16,900
Bridgeton, MO, 18,410
Cahokia, IL, 18,280
Centreville, IL, 10,130
Clayton, MO, 13,660
Collinsville, IL, 20,650
Concord, MO, 20,896
Crestwood, MO, 12,090
East St. Louis, IL, 49,470
Edwardsville, IL, 13,100
Fairview Heights, IL, 11,880
Ferguson, MO, 23,910
Florissant, MO, 59,040
Granite City, IL, 35,150
Hazelwood, MO, 16,470
Jennings, MO, 17,290
Kirkwood, MO, 27,430
Lemay, MO, 35,424
Maryland Heights, MO, 27,660
O'Fallon, IL, 12,090
O'Fallon, MO, 14,670
Overland, MO, 18,730
Richmond Heights, MO, 10,800
St. Ann, MO, 14,960
St. Charles, MO, 41,990
St. Louis, MO, 426,300
St. Peters, MO, 27,280
Sappington, MO, 11,388
Spanish Lake, MO, 20,632
University City, MO, 42,270
Washington, MO, 10,210
Webster Groves, MO, 23,130
Wood River, IL, 12,050

Salem, OR

Four Corners, 11,331
Keizer, 20,130
Salem, 93,920
Woodburn, 11,730

Salem–Gloucester, MA

Beverly, 36,980
Danvers, 24,150
Gloucester, 28,230
Ipswich, 11,750
Marblehead, 19,580
Peabody, 46,300
Salem, 38,050
Swampscott, 13,330

Salinas–Seaside–Monterey, CA

Marina, 27,130

Monterey, 30,040
Pacific Grove, 16,430
Salinas, 96,960
Seaside, 37,050

Salt Lake City–Ogden, UT

Bountiful, 34,510
Centerville, 10,740
Clearfield, 22,670
Cottonwood, 11,554
Cottonwood Heights, 22,665
East Millcreek, 24,150
Holladay, 22,189
Kaysville, 12,370
Kearns, 21,353
Layton, 35,280
Magna, 13,138
Midvale, 11,390
Murray, 23,730
North Ogden, 10,660
Ogden, 67,490
Roy, 23,500
Salt Lake City, 158,440
Sandy, 67,430
South Cottonwood, 11,117
South Jordan, 11,030
South Ogden, 12,240
South Salt Lake, 12,340
Taylorsville, 17,448
West Jordan, 44,440
West Valley, 90,770

San Angelo, TX

San Angelo, 86,260

San Antonio, TX

Leon Valley, 11,910
New Braunfels, 27,960
San Antonio, 914,350
Seguin, 20,460
Universal City, 12,660

San Diego, CA

Cardiff-By-The-Sea, 10,054
Carlsbad, 50,800
Casa De Oro–Mount Helix, 19,651
Castle Park–Otay, 21,049
Chula Vista, 118,840
Coronado, 20,840
El Cajon, 84,460
Encinitas, 10,796
Escondido, 83,550
Fallbrook, 14,041
Imperial Beach, 25,180
La Mesa, 51,840
Lakeside, 23,921
Lemon Grove, 22,480
National City, 57,390
Oceanside, 99,140
Poway, 38,450
San Diego, 1,015,190
San Marcos, 21,540
Santee, 51,210
Solana Beach, 14,900
Spring Valley, 40,191
Vista, 48,000

San Francisco, CA

Belmont, 24,590
Burlingame, 26,260
Daly City, 83,000
East Palo Alto, 18,630
Foster City, 26,030
Hillsborough, 10,830
Larkspur, 11,120
Menlo Park, 27,280
Mill Valley, 12,890
Millbrae, 20,210

Novato, 45,720
Pacifica, 36,960
Redwood City, 57,340
San Anselmo, 11,980
San Bruno, 35,190
San Carlos, 25,650
San Francisco, 749,000
San Mateo, 81,020
San Rafael, 44,730
South San Francisco, 51,550

San Jose, CA

Alum Rock, 18,355
Campbell, 34,150
Cupertino, 38,130
Gilroy, 27,530
Los Altos, 27,690
Los Gatos, 27,770
Milpitas, 44,120
Morgan Hill, 21,170
Mountain View, 60,990
Palo Alto, 55,950
San Jose, 712,080
Santa Clara, 88,560
Saratoga, 29,520
Sunnyvale, 112,130

Santa Barbara–Santa Maria–Lompoc, CA

Carpinteria, 11,920
Lompoc, 31,120
Santa Barbara, 79,290
Santa Maria, 51,270

Santa Cruz, CA

Live Oak, 11,482
Santa Cruz, 45,890
Watsonville, 28,210

Santa Fe, NM

Los Alamos, 11,039
Santa Fe, 55,980

Santa Rosa–Petaluma, CA

Petaluma, 38,560
Rohnert Park, 30,970
Santa Rosa, 97,600

Sarasota, FL

Englewood, 10,229
Sarasota, 51,500
Sarasota Springs, 13,860
Venice, 15,050

Savannah, GA

Savannah, 146,800

Scranton–Wilkes-Barre, PA

Berwick, 10,980
Bloomsburg, 11,550
Carbondale, 10,880
Dunmore, 16,180
Hazleton, 25,270
Kingston, 15,110
Nanticoke, 12,190
Scranton, 82,260
Wilkes-Barre, 47,890

Seattle, WA

Alderwood Manor, 16,524
Auburn, 29,860
Bellevue, 80,940
Bryn Mahr–Skyway, 11,754
Burien, 23,189
Cascade–Fairwood, 16,939
Des Moines, 13,690
East Renton Highlands, 12,033
Edmonds, 28,440
Esperance, 11,120

Everett, 60,380
Inglewood, 12,467
Juanita, 17,232
Kent, 28,920
Kingsgate, 12,652
Kirkland, 19,340
Lakeland North, 11,451
Lynnwood, 24,400
Mercer Island, 20,610
Mountlake Terrace, 15,730
Newport Hills, 12,245
North City–Ridgecrest, 13,551
North Hill, 10,170
North Marysville, 15,159
Redmond, 28,930
Renton, 34,410
Richmond Highlands, 24,463
Riverton, 14,182
Seattle, 486,200
Silver Lake–Fircrest, 10,299
Twin Lakes, 14,535
Valley Ridge, 17,961
West Federal Way, 16,872
White Center–Shorewood, 19,362

Sharon, PA
Hermitage, 16,690
Sharon, 16,150

Sheboygan, WI
Sheboygan, 47,410

Sherman–Denison, TX
Denison, 24,640
Sherman, 31,530

Shreveport, LA
Bossier City, 57,060
Shreveport, 220,380

Sioux City, IA–NE
Sioux City, IA, 79,590

Sioux Falls, SD
Sioux Falls, 97,550

South Bend–Mishawaka, IN
Mishawaka, 41,400
South Bend, 107,190

Spokane, WA
Spokane, 172,890

Springfield, IL
Springfield, 100,290

Springfield, MO
Springfield, 139,360

Springfield, MA
Agawam, 27,130
Chicopee, 57,100
East Longmeadow, 12,910
Easthampton, 16,330
Holyoke, 42,000
Longmeadow, 16,380
Ludlow, 18,740
Northampton, 28,360
Palmer, 11,800
South Hadley, 16,230
Springfield, 149,410
West Springfield, 26,800
Westfield, 37,710
Wilbraham, 12,420

Stamford, CT
Darien, 18,070
Greenwich, 58,270
New Canaan, 17,660
Stamford, 101,080

State College, PA
State College, 34,330

Steubenville–Weirton, OH–WV
Steubenville, OH, 23,580
Weirton, WV, 23,640

Stockton, CA
Lodi, 44,070
Manteca, 36,180
Stockton, 183,430
Tracy, 26,270

Syracuse, NY
Bayberry–Lynelle Meadows, 14,813
Fairmount, 13,415
Fulton, 13,560
Oneida, 10,450
Oswego, 18,910
Syracuse, 160,750

Tacoma, WA
Harkland, 23,355
Lakes District, 54,533
Puyallup, 19,460
Tacoma, 158,950
University Place, 20,381

Tallahassee, FL
Tallahassee, 119,450

Tampa–St. Petersburg–Clearwater, FL
Bayonet Point, 16,455
Brandon, 41,826
Clearwater, 97,520
Dunedin, 32,030
Egypt Lake, 11,932
Elfers, 11,396
Gulfport, 11,520
Holiday, 18,392
Jasmine Estates, 11,995
Lake Carroll, 13,012
Largo, 62,420
Lealman, 19,875
New Port Richey, 13,610
Palm River–Clair Mell, 14,447
Pinellas Park, 40,670
Plant City, 19,040
Safety Harbor, 12,540
St. Petersburg, 239,410
Tampa, 277,580
Tarpon Springs, 15,950
Temple Terrace, 12,440
Town N' Country, 37,834
University, 24,514

Terre Haute, IN
Terre Haute, 57,920

Texarkana, TX–Texarkana, AR
Texarkana, AR, 22,240
Texarkana, TX, 33,130

Toledo, OH
Bowling Green, 25,100
Maumee, 16,740
Oregon, 18,460
Perrysburg, 11,080
Sylvania, 16,140
Toledo, 340,680

Topeka, KS
Topeka, 118,580

Trenton, NJ
Mercerville–Hamilton Square, 25,446
Princeton, 12,270

Trenton, 91,160
White Horse, 10,098

Tucson, AZ
Tucson, 358,850

Tulsa, OK
Broken Arrow, 51,470
Claremore, 16,290
Sand Springs, 15,120
Sapulpa, 20,200
Tulsa, 373,750

Tuscaloosa, AL
Northport, 15,720
Tuscaloosa, 73,830

Tyler, TX
Tyler, 75,440

Utica–Rome, NY
Rome, 42,030
Utica, 69,440

Vallejo–Fairfield–Napa, CA
Benicia, 21,930
Dixon, 10,390
Fairfield, 68,750
Napa, 56,760
Suisun City, 16,920
Vacaville, 54,910
Vallejo, 93,260

Vancouver, WA
Vancouver, 43,930

Victoria, TX
Victoria, 56,640

Vineland–Millville–Bridgeton, NJ
Bridgeton, 18,620
Millville, 25,330
Vineland, 53,640

Visalia–Tulare–Porterville, CA
Dinuba, 11,290
Porterville, 24,470
Tulare, 26,820
Visalia, 61,550

Waco, TX
Waco, 105,220

Washington, DC–MD–VA
Adelphi, MD, 12,530
Alexandria, VA, 107,800
Annandale, VA, 49,524
Arlington, VA, 152,599
Aspen Hill, MD, 47,455
Baileys Crossroads, VA, 12,564
Beltsville, MD, 12,760
Bethesda, MD, 62,736
Bowie, MD, 35,740
Burke, VA, 33,835
Chantilly, VA, 12,259
Chevy Chase, MD, 12,323
Chillum, MD, 32,775
Clinton, MD, 16,438
Colesville, MD, 14,359
College Park, MD, 21,810
Coral Hills, MD, 11,602
Dale City, VA, 33,127
Fairfax, VA, 19,900
Forestville, MD, 16,401
Frederick, MD, 33,800
Gaithersburg, MD, 32,350
Greenbelt, MD, 16,100
Groveton, VA, 18,860
Herndon, VA, 16,780

Hyattsville, MD, 11,470
Hybla Valley, VA, 15,533
Idlewood, VA, 11,982
Jefferson, VA, 24,342
Lake Ridge, VA, 11,072
Langley Park, MD, 14,038
Lanham–Seabrook, MD, 15,814
Laurel, MD, 12,190
Leesburg, VA, 10,810
Lincolnia, VA, 10,350
Manassas, VA, 20,100
McLean, VA, 35,664
Montgomery Village, MD, 18,725
Mount Vernon, VA, 24,058
New Carrollton, MD, 12,180
North Bethesda, MD, 22,671
Oakton, VA, 19,150
Olney, MD, 13,026
Oxon Hill, MD, 36,267
Potomac, MD, 40,402
Redland, MD, 10,759
Reston, VA, 36,407
Rockville, MD, 46,900
Rosehill, VA, 11,926
St. Charles, MD, 13,921
Silver Spring, MD, 72,893
South Laurel, MD, 18,034
Springfield, VA, 21,435
Sterling Park, VA, 16,080
Suitland, MD, 32,164
Takoma Park, MD, 14,360
Tysons Corner, VA, 10,065
Vienna, VA, 17,160
Walker Mill, MD, 10,651
Washington, DC, 626,000
West Springfield, VA, 25,012
Wheaton, MD, 48,598
White Oak, MD, 13,702
Woodbridge, VA, 24,004

Waterbury, CT
Naugatuck, 30,510
Southbury, 15,500
Waterbury, 102,300
Watertown, 19,650
Wolcott, 12,860

Waterloo–Cedar Falls, IA
Cedar Falls, 33,200
Waterloo, 70,010

Wausau, WI
Wausau, 32,240

West Palm Beach–Boca Raton–Delray Beach, FL
Belle Glade, 17,000
Boca Raton, 58,510
Boynton Beach, 42,930
Century Village, 10,619
Delray Beach, 44,350
Greenacres City, 23,710
Jupiter, 21,990
Lake Worth, 27,380
North Palm Beach, 12,230
Palm Beach, 11,160
Palm Beach Gardens, 21,920
Riviera Beach, 27,780
West Palm Beach, 68,570

Wheeling, WV–OH
Moundsville, WV, 11,590
Wheeling, WV, 39,980

Wichita, KS
Derby, 12,940
El Dorado, 10,990
Newton, 16,380
Wichita, 288,870

Wichita Falls, TX
Burkburnett, 10,900
Wichita Falls, 99,940

Williamsport, PA
Williamsport, 31,710

Wilmington, DE–NJ–MD
Brookside, DE, 15,255
Claymont, DE, 10,022
Newark, DE, 24,180
Pennsville, NJ, 12,467

Wilmington, DE, 69,690

Wilmington, NC
Wilmington, 54,430

Worcester, MA
Auburn, 14,580
Clinton, 12,440
Grafton, 11,840
Holden, 13,750
Millbury, 11,840
Northborough, 11,320

Northbridge, 12,440
Shrewsbury, 22,560
Spencer, 11,540
Webster, 15,090
Westborough, 13,210
Worcester, 157,770

Yakima, WA
Yakima, 49,370

York, PA
Hanover, 15,400
York, 44,430

Youngstown–Warren, OH
Austintown, 33,636
Boardman, 39,161
Campbell, 10,770
Girard, 12,530
Niles, 22,030
Struthers, 12,650
Warren, 52,900
Youngstown, 104,690

Yuba City, CA
Marysville, 10,940
Yuba City, 21,560

Source: Places Rated Partnership estimates, 1989. Population figures for unincorporated areas are from the 1980 Census.

List of Tables, Maps, & Diagrams

ABOUT THE AUTHORS

Since the first appearance of *Places Rated Almanac* in 1981, authors Richard Boyer and David Savageau have been featured on the CBS Evening News, Today, and Good Morning America, as well as numerous local television and radio programs. In 1987 they collaborated on the highly successful *Retirement Places Rated,* which rates and ranks 131 places, many of them non-metropolitan areas, for retirement living.

Richard Boyer is writer-in-residence at Western Carolina University. In addition to co-authoring *Places Rated Almanac* and *Retirement Places Rated,* he is author of six novels, including *Billingsgate Shoal* (winner of the Mystery Writers of America's Edgar award for Best Mystery Novel of 1982). Formerly of Chicago and Boston, Mr. Boyer, upon completion of the first edition of *Places Rated Almanac,* followed the book's advice for selecting good places to live and now resides in Asheville, North Carolina.

David Savageau, since the first publication of *Places Rated Almanac,* has made public appearances throughout the country discussing the inexhaustible topic of quality of life. Mr. Savageau is principal-in-charge of Pre-LOCATION, a personal relocation consulting firm. Over the previous 15 years, he and his wife, Karyl, have lived successively in Denver, St. Louis, Indianapolis, and Boston. They now make their home in Gloucester, Massachusetts.